Davis Chapman

Jeff Heaton

SAMS

Teach Yourself

Visual C++® 6

in 21 Days

**Professional
Reference Edition**

SAMS

A Division of Macmillan Computer Publishing
201 West 103rd St., Indianapolis, Indiana, 46290 USA

Sams Teach Yourself Visual C++® 6 in 21 Days, Professional Reference Edition

Copyright © 1999 by Sams Publishing

International Standard Book Number: 0-672-31404-5

Library of Congress Catalog Card Number: 98-86199

Printed in the United States of America

First Printing: December, 1998

01   00   99   98   4   3   2   1

Trademarks

Warning and Disclaimer

EXECUTIVE EDITOR
Brad Jones

ACQUISITIONS EDITORS
Ron Gallagher
Kelly Marshall

DEVELOPMENT EDITOR
Matt Purcell

MANAGING EDITOR
Jodi Jensen

PROJECT EDITORS
Dana Rhodes Lesh
Heather Talbot

COPY EDITORS
Mike Henry
Linda Morris
Kris Simmons

INDEXER
Erika Millen

PROOFREADERS
Mona Brown
Jennifer Earhart
Cynthia Fields

TECHNICAL EDITORS
Matt Butler
Larry Richardson

SOFTWARE SPECIALIST
Dan Scherf

TEAM COORDINATOR
Carol Ackerman

INTERIOR DESIGN
Gary Adair

COVER DESIGN
Aren Howell

LAYOUT TECHNICIANS
Michael Dietsch
Susan Geiselman
Staci Somers

Overview

Contents

About the Authors

DAVIS CHAPMAN first began programming computers while working on his master's degree in music composition. Writing applications for computer music, he discovered that he enjoyed designing and developing computer software. It wasn't long before he came to the realization that he stood a much better chance of eating if he stuck with his new-found skill and demoted his hard-earned status as a "starving artist" to a part-time hobby. Since that time, Davis has focused on the art of software design and development, with a strong emphasis on the practical application of client/server technology. Davis is the lead author of *Web Development with Visual Basic 5* and *Building Internet Applications with Delphi 2*. Davis is also a contributing author of *Special Edition Using Active Server Pages* and *Running a Perfect Web Site, Second Edition*. He has been a consultant working and living in Dallas, Texas, for the past eight years, and he can be reached at davischa@onramp.net.

JEFF HEATON is a consultant, author, and instructor, and has been programming for ten years. As an instructor at St. Louis Community College at Meramec, Jeff teaches Visual C++ and Java programming. He is currently working as a consultant for the Internet development group at Navisys in St. Louis, Missouri. Jeff can be reached through his web site at http://www.heat-on.com.

Contributing Author

JON BATES has worked on a whole range of commercial, industrial, and military software development projects worldwide over the past fifteen years. He is currently working as a self-employed software design consultant and contract software developer, specializing in Visual C++ application development for Windows NT/95/98.

Jon began his career writing computer games for popular microcomputers and has since worked with a number of operating systems, such as CPM, DOS, TRIPOS, UNIX, and Windows, and a number of Assembly, third-generation, and object-oriented languages.

He has written system and application software as diverse as device drivers, email, production modeling, motion video, image analysis, network and telecommunications, data capture, control systems, estimating and costing, and visualization software. He has also written a number of technical articles for computing journals on a range of topics.

Jon lives with his wife, Ruth, and dog, Chaos, in the middle of cool Britannia. When not playing with computers, he likes to sleep and dream of fractals.

You can reach Jon at jon@chaos1.demon.co.uk and visit his Web site at www.chaos1.demon.co.uk.

Dedication

To Dore, and the rest of my family, for being very patient with me while I was busy writing yet another book.

—Davis Chapman

For always being there for me, I would like to dedicate this book to my parents, Mary and William, and my sister Carrie.

—Jeff Heaton

Acknowledgments

There are numerous people without whom this book might never have been written. Among those who deserve credit is Kelly Marshall, for enabling me to take on this project and for sticking with me even though I know I made her life stressful at times. Credit needs to go to the entire editing team at Macmillan. I've seen what some of the material you have to work with looks like when it comes in from the authors, and I don't want to trade jobs with any of you. I'd also like to thank my family for continuing to allow me to put in the work required to produce this book—and for not disowning me in the process.

—Davis Chapman

This book would not have been possible without some people to whom I owe the deepest thanks. I would like to thank Ron Gallagher, Matt Purcell, Brad Jones, and everyone else at Macmillan Publishing. I would also like to thank Jack Bader for introducing me to the world of computer consulting; and Vince Arter and everyone at Navisys for not overloading me with project work while I was working on this book. Additionally, I would like to thank Christine Guenette, my friend and fellow programmer, for our many hours learning the newest features of Internet programming together.

—Jeff Heaton

Tell Us What You Think!

As the reader of this book, *you* are our most important critic and commentator. We value your opinion and want to know what we're doing right, what we could do better, what areas you'd like to see us publish in, and any other words of wisdom you're willing to pass our way.

As the executive editor for the Programming team at Macmillan Computer Publishing, I welcome your comments. You can fax, email, or write me directly to let me know what you did or didn't like about this book—as well as what we can do to make our books stronger.

Please note that I cannot help you with technical problems related to the topic of this book, and that due to the high volume of mail I receive, I might not be able to reply to every message.

When you write, please be sure to include this book's title and author as well as your name and phone or fax number. I will carefully review your comments and share them with the author and editors who worked on the book.

Fax: 317-817-7070

Email: adv_prog@mcp.com

Mail: Brad Jones, Executive Editor
          Programming Team
          Macmillan Computer Publishing
          201 West 103rd Street
          Indianapolis, IN 46290 USA

Introduction

Welcome to Visual C++. Over the next 21 days, you will learn how to use the features that Microsoft has built into its C++ development environment to enable you to create very advanced applications for the Windows and NT platforms. When Microsoft's developers first came up with the idea behind Visual C++, they decided to take their world-class C++ compiler and create a development environment and set of tools that would enable developers to create Windows applications with a level of ease and speed that was unheard of among C++ development environments. Since that first version, Microsoft has continued to improve the tools that are a part of Visual C++ to make it even easier to create Windows applications. As Microsoft has introduced new technologies into the Windows platforms, it has also introduced tools into the Visual C++ suite to make it easy to integrate these new technologies into your applications.

If you are new to C++, don't worry. I've tried to make it easy for you to learn the C++ programming language while also learning how to build applications using the Visual C++ tools. Just in case you find yourself having trouble understanding some aspect of C++, I've included a brief overview of the programming language in Appendix A, "C++ Review."

If you've looked at previous versions of this book, you might notice that I've completely rewritten the entire book. Our goal with this new version is not just to introduce you to and guide you through the various tools and resources that you will use to build applications with Visual C++; I've also tried to include a great deal more detail about the various options that are available to you with each of the features that are covered. This way, you'll be able to get a lot of use out of this book long after the initial 21 days.

How This Book Is Organized

This book is organized in weeks, with each set of seven days set off into a part unto itself. However, even though the book is organized in weeks, the topics are not neces-sarily organized that way.

For the first week, you'll be covering the basics of building applications with Visual C++. You'll learn how to use designers to design your application windows. You'll learn how to use various controls available to you as a Windows application developer. You'll also learn a lot about the Visual C++ development environment and the tools that it makes available to you.

By the time you begin the second week, you'll be doing more and more programming, as the topics become more involved. You'll still be using the Visual C++ tools to construct your applications, but the programming code will be getting a little more involved. You'll also start learning about more advanced topics, such as displaying graphics and creating SDI and MDI applications. Toward the end of the second week, you'll begin to work with databases. This topic spills over into the third and final week.

In the third week, you'll learn how to create your own modules, DLLs, and ActiveX controls. You'll also learn how to build multitasking applications, which perform multiple tasks at a time. Finally, you'll learn how to integrate Microsoft Internet Explorer, and the ActiveX controls it provides, into your applications so that you can extend your applications over the Internet.

After you finish the third week, you'll be ready to tackle the world of Windows programming with Visual C++. You'll have the skills and know-how required to build most Windows applications available today. To assist you even more in creating your applications, we have provided some valuable quick references. These references are:

Appendix A, "C++ Overview," provides you with an overview of the various aspects of programming C++ and its syntax.

Appendix B, "Answers," gives you the answers to the quizzes and exercises from each chapter.

Appendix C, "MFC Class Reference," provides an alphabetical listing of the major MFC classes used for application development. This section lists common classes that are used to create standard document/view applications, as well as database access.

Appendix D, "Standard and Common Control Reference," is an alphabetical listing of the standard and common controls included with MFC. This section lists the controls that can be added to MFC windows and dialogs.

Appendix E, "Microsoft Developer Studio for Visual C++" explains how to use Microsoft Developer Studio for Visual C++. This section presents the most common parts of Developer Studio used for Visual C++ development.

Appendix F, "Structures and Global Functions," contains an alphabetical list of structures and global functions. This section lists the most common structures used to communicate with MFC. The most frequently used MFC global functions are also listed.

Appendix G, "ANSI/ASCII/Unicode Charts," contains Unicode, ANSI, and ASCII charts—the character sets that can be used with Windows.

Appendix H, "Windows Types," lists Windows and C++ types. This section presents the data types provided by both C++ and MFC.

Appendix I, "MFC Messages," is a table of MFC messages. This section presents the most common messages that MFC will send to a window.

Appendix J, "What's on the CD-ROM," lists the software included on the CD-ROM. The CD-ROM included with this book contains many helpful controls and tools for Visual C++ programmers.

Conventions Used in This Book

While you are reading this book, you will probably notice a couple conventions that have been used to make it easier for you to learn the topic being discussed.

All the source code in this book is provided in a `monospaced` font, as shown in Listing 0.1. This includes all the source code from the applications that you will be building and illustrations of how various functions can be used. Whenever you are adding new code, or changing code in a function with other code already there, the line numbers of the code that you add or change will be pointed out in the text.

LISTING 0.1. SOME SAMPLE CODE.

```
1: void main()
2: {
3:     // if you are adding or changing code in an existing
4:     // code snippet, I will point out the line numbers in the text.
5: }
```

If a topic needs special attention, it will be set apart from the rest of the text by one of several special markers:

- Notes
- Tips
- Cautions

Note Notes offer a deeper explanation of a topic or explain interesting or important points.

Tip Tips are pieces of information that can make things easier.

Caution | Cautions warn you about traps that you will want to avoid.

At the end of each day, you'll find a short quiz and one or two exercises to help make sure that you learned the topic you were studying. Don't worry—just in case you need the answers to the quizzes and some guidance when building the exercises, the solutions are provided in Appendix B, "Answers."

Enough said! You didn't buy this book to read about this book. You bought this book to learn how to use Visual C++ to build Windows applications. So go ahead and flip the page and get started programming...

WEEK 1

At a Glance

Welcome to the world of Visual C++. Over the next three weeks, you'll learn how to build a wide variety of applications using this extremely flexible and complete programming tool. Each day you'll learn about a different area of functionality and how you can use it in your applications. What's more—every one of the areas of functionality will be accompanied with a hands-on sample application that you will build yourself. There's not a more effective way of learning new technologies than to work with them yourself. Learning by doing…that's what you'll do as you make your way through this book.

Over the course of the first week, you'll learn about several of the basics that are involved in building applications with Visual C++. This starts on the first day as you learn about and become familiar with the Visual C++ development environment by building a simple application.

On Day 2, you'll begin learning more about the specifics of building applications in Visual C++. You'll learn about the standard controls that are used in Windows applications, how you can place and configure these on an application window, and how you can interact with them.

On Day 3, you'll learn how you can capture mouse and keyboard events and react to them in your applications. You'll see how you can determine where the mouse is in your application space. You'll also learn how to determine what keys the user is pressing on the keyboard and how you can react to these user actions.

1

2

3

4

5

6

7

On Day 4, you'll learn how to work with timers in a Visual C++ application. You'll learn how to have two or more timers running at the same time and how you can tell them apart.

On Day 5, you'll see how you can add additional windows to your application and how you can use them to get information from the user. You'll see how you can use built-in dialogs to ask the user simple questions and how you can build your own custom dialogs to get more detailed information.

On Day 6, you'll learn how to create menus to add to your application. You'll see how you can call functions in your application from menus that you have added to your application.

On Day 7, you'll learn about the font infrastructure in Windows and how you can access it in your Visual C++ applications. You'll see how you can build a list of available fonts and how you can display text in any of these fonts.

That will end the first week of this book. At that time, you can look back over what you have learned during the week and think about all that you can do with what you have learned when you build applications. So, without further ado, go ahead and jump in and get started.

DAY 1

The Visual C++ Development Environment—Building Your First Visual C++ Application

Welcome to *Sams Teach Yourself Visual C++ 6 in 21 Days*. Over the next three weeks, you will learn how to build a wide variety of applications with Microsoft's Visual C++. What's even better is that you will learn how to create these types of applications by actually building them yourself. As you read this book, you will be gaining actual programming experience using Visual C++. So let's get started!

Today, your focus will be on learning about the Visual C++ development environment and some of the tools that it provides for building applications. Although Visual C++ provides more tools than you would probably use in any one application development effort—even more than you could possibly learn to use in a single day—I limit the focus to the primary tools that you will use throughout this book, as well as in just about every application you build with Visual C++. Today, you'll learn about the following:

- The primary areas of the Visual C++ development environment
- The Application Wizard—how you can use it to build the basic infrastructure for your applications
- The Dialog Painter—how you can use it to paint dialog windows, much in the same way that you can build windows with Visual Basic, PowerBuilder, or Delphi
- The Class Wizard—how you can use it to attach functionality to your application windows

The Visual C++ Development Environment

Before you begin your quick tour around the Visual C++ development environment, you should start Visual C++ on your computer so that you can see firsthand how each of the areas are arranged and how you can change and alter that arrangement yourself.

After Developer Studio (the Microsoft Visual development environment) starts, you see a window that looks like Figure 1.1. Each of the areas has a specific purpose in the Developer Studio environment. You can rearrange these areas to customize the Developer Studio environment so that it suits your particular development needs.

The Workspace

When you start Visual C++ for the first time, an area on the left side of Developer Studio looks like it is taking up a lot of real estate and providing little to show for it. This area is known as the workspace, and it is your key to navigating the various pieces and parts of your development projects. The workspace allows you to view the parts of your application in three different ways:

- Class View allows you to navigate and manipulate your source code on a C++ class level.
- Resource View allows you to find and edit each of the various resources in your application, including dialog window designs, icons, and menus.
- File View allows you to view and navigate all the files that make up your application.

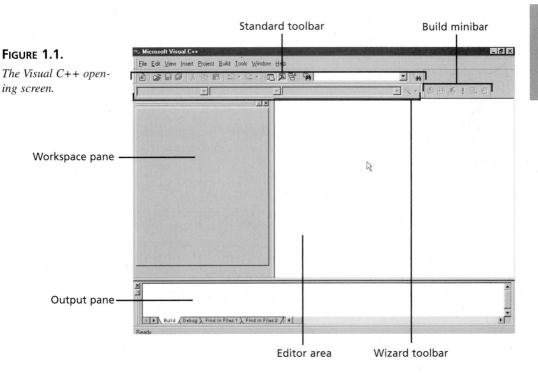

FIGURE 1.1.

The Visual C++ opening screen.

Standard toolbar

Build minibar

Workspace pane

Output pane

Editor area

Wizard toolbar

The Output Pane

The Output pane might not be visible when you start Visual C++ for the first time. After you compile your first application, it appears at the bottom of the Developer Studio environment and remains open until you choose to close it. The Output pane is where Developer Studio provides any information that it needs to give you; where you see all the compiler progress statements, warnings, and error messages; and where the Visual C++ debugger displays all the variables with their current values as you step through your code. After you close the Output pane, it reopens itself when Visual C++ has any message that it needs to display for you.

The Editor Area

The area on the right side of the Developer Studio environment is the editor area. This is the area where you perform all your editing when using Visual C++, where the code editor windows display when you edit C++ source code, and where the window painter displays when you design a dialog box. The editor area is even where the icon painter displays when you design the icons for use in your applications. The editor area is basically the entire Developer Studio area that is not otherwise occupied by panes, menus, or toolbars.

Menu Bars

The first time you run Visual C++, three toolbars display just below the menu bar. Many other toolbars are available in Visual C++, and you can customize and create your own toolbars to accommodate how you best work. The three toolbars that are initially open are the following:

- The Standard toolbar contains most of the standard tools for opening and saving files, cutting, copying, pasting, and a variety of other commands that you are likely to find useful.
- The WizardBar toolbar enables you to perform a number of Class Wizard actions without opening the Class Wizard.
- The Build minibar provides you with the build and run commands that you are most likely to use as you develop and test your applications. The full Build toolbar also lets you switch between multiple build configurations (such as between the Debug and Release build configurations).

Rearranging the Developer Studio Environment

The Developer Studio provides two easy ways to rearrange your development environment. The first is by right-clicking your mouse over the toolbar area. This action opens the pop-up menu shown in Figure 1.2, allowing you to turn on and off various toolbars and panes.

FIGURE 1.2.

Toolbar on and off menu.

Another way that you can easily rearrange your development environment is to grab the double bars at the left end of any of the toolbars or panes with the mouse. You can drag the toolbars away from where they are currently docked, making them floating toolbars, as in Figure 1.3. You can drag these toolbars (and panes) to any other edge of the Developer Studio to dock them in a new spot. Even when the toolbars are docked, you can use the double bars to drag the toolbar left and right to place the toolbar where you want it to be located.

FIGURE 1.3.

Example of a floating toolbar.

> **Note**
>
> On the workspace and Output panes, the double bars that you can use to drag the pane around the Developer Studio environment might appear on the top of the pane or on the left side, depending on how and where the pane is docked.

Starting Your First Project

For your first Visual C++ application, you are going to create a simple application that presents the user with two buttons, as in Figure 1.4. The first button will present the user with a simple greeting message, shown in Figure 1.5, and the second button will close the application. In building this application, you will need to do the following things:

1. Create a new project workspace.
2. Use the Application Wizard to create the application framework.
3. Rearrange the dialog that is automatically created by the Application Wizard to resemble how you want the application to look.
4. Add the C++ code to show the greeting to the user.
5. Create a new icon for the application.

FIGURE 1.4.

Your first Visual C++ application.

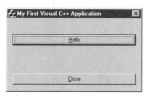

FIGURE 1.5.

If the user clicks the first button, a simple greeting is shown.

Creating the Project Workspace

Every application development project needs its own project workspace in Visual C++. The workspace includes the directories where the application source code is kept, as well as the directories where the various build configuration files are located. You can create a new project workspace by following these steps:

1. Select File | New. This opens the New Wizard shown in Figure 1.6.

FIGURE 1.6.

The New Wizard.

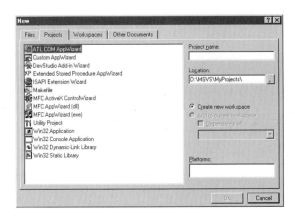

2. On the Projects tab, select MFC AppWizard (exe).

3. Type a name for your project, such as Hello, in the Project Name field.

4. Click OK. This causes the New Wizard to do two things: create a project directory (specified in the Location field) and then start the AppWizard.

Using the Application Wizard to Create the Application Shell

The AppWizard asks you a series of questions about what type of application you are building and what features and functionality you need. It uses this information to create a shell of an application that you can immediately compile and run. This shell provides you with the basic infrastructure that you need to build your application around. You will see how this works as you follow these steps:

1. In Step 1 of the AppWizard, specify that you want to create a Dialog-based application. Click Next at the bottom of the wizard.

2. In Step 2 of the AppWizard, the wizard asks you about a number of features that you can include in your application. You can uncheck the option for including support for ActiveX controls if you will not be using any ActiveX controls in your application. Because you won't be using any ActiveX controls in today's application, go ahead and uncheck this box.

3. In the field near the bottom of the wizard, delete the project name (Hello) and type in the title that you want to appear in the title bar of the main application window,

1

such as **My First Visual C++ Application**. Click Next at the bottom of the wizard.

4. In Step 3 of the AppWizard, leave the defaults for including source file comments and using the MFC library as a DLL. Click Next at the bottom of the wizard to proceed to the final AppWizard step.

5. The final step of the AppWizard shows you the C++ classes that the AppWizard will create for your application. Click Finish to let AppWizard generate your application shell.

6. Before AppWizard creates your application shell, it presents you with a list of what it is going to put into the application shell, as shown in Figure 1.7, based on the options you selected when going through the AppWizard. Click OK and AppWizard generates your application.

FIGURE **1.7.**

*The New Project
Information screen.*

7. After the AppWizard generates your application shell, you are returned to the Developer Studio environment. You will notice that the workspace pane now presents you with a tree view of the classes in your application shell, as in Figure 1.8. You might also be presented with the main dialog window in the editor area of the Developer Studio area.

8. Select Build | Build Hello.exe to compile your application.

9. As the Visual C++ compiler builds your application, you see progress and other compiler messages scroll by in the Output pane. After your application is built, the Output pane should display a message telling you that there were no errors or warnings, as in Figure 1.9.

FIGURE 1.8.

Your workspace with a tree view of the project's classes.

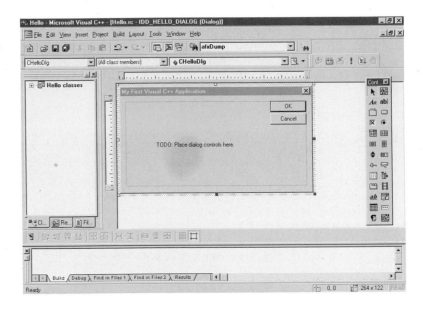

FIGURE 1.9.

The Output pane displays any compiler errors.

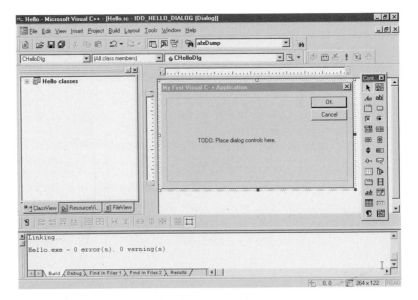

10. Select Build | Execute Hello.exe to run your application.

11. Your application presents a dialog with a TODO message and OK and Cancel buttons, as shown in Figure 1.10. You can click either button to close the application.

FIGURE 1.10.

The unmodified application shell.

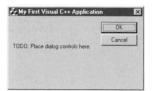

Designing Your Application Window

Now that you have a running application shell, you need to turn your focus to the window layout of your application. Even though the main dialog window may already be available for painting in the editor area, you should still navigate to find the dialog window in the workspace so that you can easily find the window in subsequent development efforts. To redesign the layout of your application dialog, follow these steps:

1. Select the Resource View tab in the workspace pane, as in Figure 1.11.

FIGURE 1.11.

The Resource View tab in the workspace pane.

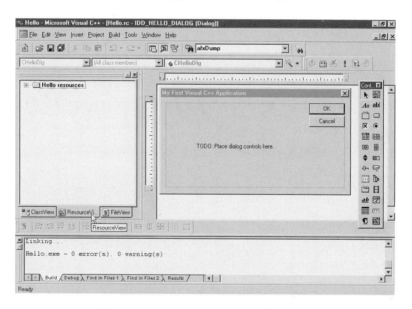

2. Expand the resources tree to display the available dialogs. At this point, you can double-click the IDD_DAY1_DIALOG dialog to open the window in the Developer Studio editor area.

3. Select the text displayed in the dialog and delete it using the Delete key.

4. Select the Cancel button, drag it down to the bottom of the dialog, and resize it so that it is the full width of the layout area of the window, as in Figure 1.12.

FIGURE 1.12.

Positioning the Cancel button.

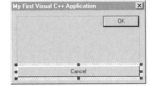

5. Right-click the mouse over the Cancel button, opening the pop-up menu in Figure 1.13. Select Properties from the menu, and the properties dialog in Figure 1.14 opens.

FIGURE 1.13.

Right-clicking the mouse to open a pop-up menu.

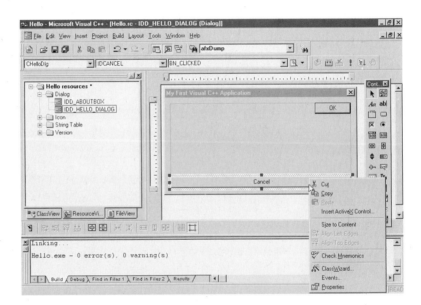

FIGURE 1.14.

The Cancel button properties dialog.

6. Change the value in the Caption field to &Close. Close the properties dialog by clicking the Close icon in the upper-right corner of the dialog.

7. Move and resize the OK button to around the middle of the window, as in Figure 1.15.

FIGURE 1.15.

Positioning the OK button.

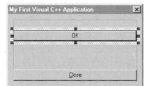

8. On the OK button properties dialog, change the ID value to IDHELLO and the caption to &Hello.

9. Now when you compile and run your application, it will look like what you've just designed, as shown in Figure 1.16.

FIGURE 1.16.

Running your redesigned application.

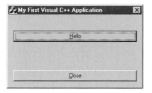

Note

If you play with your application, you will notice that the Close button still closes the application. However, the Hello button no longer does anything because you changed the ID of the button. MFC applications contain a series of macros in the source code that determine which functions to call based on the ID and event message of each control in the application. Because you changed the ID of the Hello button, these macros no longer know which function to call when the button is clicked.

Adding Code to Your Application

You can attach code to your dialog through the Visual C++ Class Wizard. You can use the Class Wizard to build the table of Windows messages that the application might receive, including the functions they should be passed to for processing, that the MFC macros use for attaching functionality to window controls. You can attach the functionality for this first application by following these steps:

1. To attach some functionality to the Hello button, right-click over the button and select Class Wizard from the pop-up menu.

2. If you had the Hello button selected when you opened the Class Wizard, it is already selected in the list of available Object IDs, as in Figure 1.17.

FIGURE 1.17.

The Class Wizard.

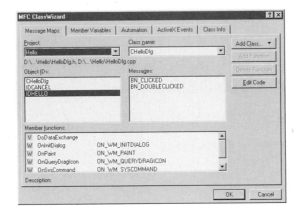

3. With IDHELLO selected in the Object ID list, select BN_CLICKED in the list of messages and click Add Function. This opens the Add Member Function dialog shown in Figure 1.18. This dialog contains a suggestion for the function name. Click OK to create the function and add it to the message map.

FIGURE 1.18.

The Class Wizard Add Member Function dialog.

4. After the function is added for the click message on the Hello button, select the OnHello function in the list of available functions, as in Figure 1.19. Click the Edit Code button so that your cursor is positioned in the source code for the function, right at the position where you should add your functionality.

FIGURE 1.19.

The list of available functions in the Class Wizard.

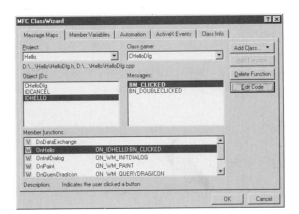

5. Add the code in Listing 1.1 just below the TODO comment line, as shown in Figure 1.20.

FIGURE 1.20.

Source code view where you insert Listing 1.1.

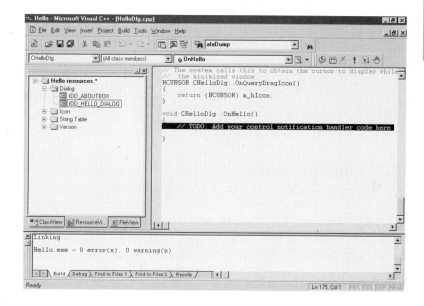

LISTING 1.1. HELLODLG.CPP—THE OnHello FUNCTION.

```
 1: void CHelloDlg::OnHello()
 2: {
 3:     // TODO: Add your control notification handler code here
 4:
 5:     /////////////////////////
 6:     // MY CODE STARTS HERE
 7:     /////////////////////////
 8:
 9:     // Say hello to the user
10:     MessageBox("Hello. This is my first Visual C++ Application!");
11:
12:     /////////////////////////
13:     // MY CODE ENDS HERE
14:     /////////////////////////
15: }
```

6. When you compile and run your application, the Hello button should display the message shown in Figure 1.21.

Figure 1.21.

Now your application will say hello to you.

Figure 1.21.

Now your application will say hello to you.

Finishing Touches

Now that your application is functionally complete, you can still add a few details to finish off the project. Those finishing touches include

- Creating the dialog box icon
- Adding maximize and minimize buttons

Creating the Dialog Box Icon

If you noticed the icon in the top-left corner of your application window, you saw three blocks with the letters M, F, and C. What does MFC have to do with your application? MFC stands for Microsoft Foundation Classes. Technically, it's the C++ class library that your application is built with, but do you want to broadcast that to every user who sees your application? Most likely not. You need to edit the application icon to display an image that you do want to represent your application. Let's get busy!

1. In the tree view of your application resources in the workspace pane, expand the icon branch and select the IDR_MAINFRAME icon, as in Figure 1.22. This brings the application icon into the editor area of the Developer Studio.

Figure 1.22.

The standard MFC icon.

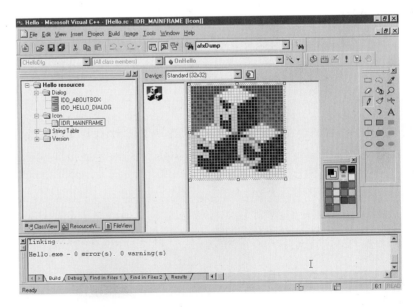

2. Using the painting tools provided, repaint the icon to display an image that you want to use to represent your application, as in Figure 1.23.

FIGURE 1.23.

Your own custom icon for your application.

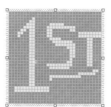

3. When you compile and run your application, you will notice your custom icon in the top-left corner of your application window. Click the icon and select About Hello from the drop-down menu.

4. On the About dialog that Visual C++ created for you, you can see a large version of your custom icon in all its glory, as shown in Figure 1.24.

FIGURE 1.24.

Your application's About window.

Note

When you open an application icon in the icon designer, the icon is sized by default at 32×32. You can also select a 16×16 size icon from the drop-down list box just above where you are drawing the icon. You should draw both of these icons because there are some instances in which the large icon will be displayed and some instance in which the small icon will be shown. You will want both icons to show the same image to represent your application.

Adding Maximize and Minimize Buttons

In the dialog editor, where you design your application window, you can add the minimize and maximize buttons to the title bar of your application window by following these steps:

1. Select the dialog window itself as if you were going to resize the window.

2. Using the pop-up menu (from right-clicking the mouse), select the dialog properties.

3. Select the Styles tab, as shown in Figure 1.25.

FIGURE 1.25.

*Turning the minimize
and maximize buttons
on and off.*

4. After you turn on the minimize and maximize boxes, you can compile and run
   your application. The minimize and maximize buttons appear on the title bar, as in
   Figure 1.26.

FIGURE 1.26.

*The application win-
dow with the minimize
and maximize buttons.*

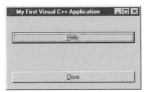

Summary

Today you got your first taste of building applications using Visual C++. You learned
about the different areas of the Visual C++ Developer Studio and what function each of
these areas serves. You also learned how you can rearrange the Developer Studio environment to suit the way you work. You also learned how you can use the Visual C++
wizards to create an application shell and then attach functionality to the visual components that you place on your application windows.

Q&A

**Q How can I change the title on the message box, instead of using the applica-
tion name?**

A By default, the message box window uses the application name as the window
title. You can change this by adding a second text string to the MessageBox function call. The first string is always the message to be displayed, and the second
string is used as the window title. For example, the OnHello function would look
like

```
// Say hello to the user
MessageBox("Hello. This is my first Visual C++ Application!",
          "My First Application");
```

Q **Can I change the text on the About window to give my company name and more detailed copyright information?**

A Yes, the About window is in the Dialogs folder in the Resources View tab of the workspace pane. If you double-click the `IDD_ABOUTBOX` dialog, the About box will be opened in the dialog designer, where you can redesign it however you want.

Workshop

The Workshop provides quiz questions to help solidify your understanding of the material covered and exercises to provide you with experience in using what you've learned. The answers to the quiz questions and exercises are provided in Appendix B, "Answers."

Quiz

1. How do you change the caption on a button?
2. What can you do with the Visual C++ AppWizard?
3. How do you attach functionality to the click of a button?

Exercise

Add a second button to the About window in your application. Have the button display a different message from the one on the first window.

DAY 2

Using Controls in Your Application

Some of the things that you will find in just about every Windows application are buttons, check boxes, text fields, and drop-down list boxes. These are known as controls, and many of these controls are built into the operating system itself. With Visual C++, using these common controls is as easy as placing them on a dialog window with a drag-and-drop window design method. Today you are going to learn

- What the basic controls in Visual C++ are
- How to declare and attach variables to a controls
- How to synchronize the values between a control and a variable
- How to specify the order users navigate around your application windows
- How to trigger actions with controls
- How to manipulate and alter the appearance of controls (while your application is running)

The Basic Windows Controls

Several standard controls are built into the Windows operating system, including such things as sliders, tree and list controls, progress bars, and so on. However, today you will work with a half dozen controls that appear in just about every Windows application:

- Static text
- Edit box
- Command button
- Check box
- Radio button
- Drop-down list box (also known as a combo box)

These and other controls are readily available for use in Visual C++ applications. They can be found on the controls palette in the Dialog Painter editor in the Developer Studio, as shown in Figure 2.1.

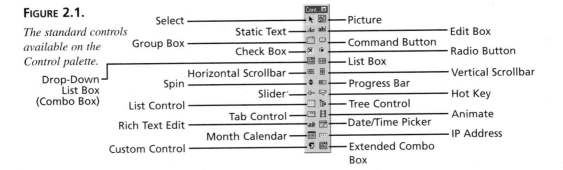

FIGURE 2.1.

The standard controls available on the Control palette.

The Static Text Control

You use the static text control to present text to the user. The user will not be able to change the text or otherwise interact with the control. Static text is intended as a read-only control. However, you can easily change the text displayed by the control as your application is running through the code you create for your application.

The Edit Box Control

An edit box allows the user to enter or change text. The edit box is one of the primary tools for allowing the user to enter specific information that your application needs. It is a control that allows the user to type a specific amount of text, which you can capture and use for any needed purpose. The edit box accepts plain text only; no formatting is available to the user.

The Command Button Control

A command button is a button that the user can press to trigger some action. Command buttons have a textual label that can give users some idea of what will happen when they click that button. Buttons can also have images as part of the button, allowing you to place an image on the button—alone or along with a textual description—to convey what the button does.

The Check Box Control

A check box is a square that the user can click to check ($\times$) or uncheck. The check box control is used to turn a particular value on and off. They are basically on/off switches with an occasional third, in-between state. You normally use check boxes to control discrete, on/off-type variables.

The Radio Button Control

A radio button is a circle that the user can click to fill with a black spot. The radio button is similar to the check box control, but it is used in a group of two or more where only one of the values can be in the on state at a time. You normally use radio buttons in groups of at least three, surrounded by a group box. The group box allows each group of radio buttons to be independent so that only one radio button in each group can be in the on state at any time.

The Drop-Down List Box Control

A drop-down list box, or combo control, is an edit box with a list of available values attached. You use the drop-down list box to provide a list of choices, from which the user may select one value from the list. Sometimes, the user is given the option of typing in his own value when a suitable one isn't provided in the list.

Adding Controls to Your Window

The application you are going to build today will have a number of controls on a single dialog window, as shown in Figure 2.2. These controls have a number of different functions. At the top of the window is an edit field where the user can enter a message that displays in a message box when he or she clicks the button beside the field. Below this edit field are two buttons that either populate the edit field with a default message or clear the edit field. Below these buttons is a drop-down list box that contains a list of standard Windows applications. When the user selects one of these programs and then clicks the button beside the drop-down list, the selected program will run. Next are two groups of check boxes that affect the controls you add to the top half of the dialog: the controls for displaying a user message and the controls for running another program. The left set of check boxes will enable and disable each group of controls you provide. The right set of check boxes will show and hide each group of controls. At the bottom of the dialog box is a button that can be clicked to close the application.

FIGURE 2.2.

Today's application will use a number of standard controls.

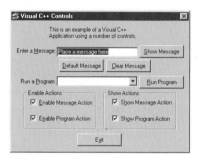

Creating the Application Shell and Dialog Layout

Using what you learned yesterday, create a new application shell and design the application dialog layout as follows:

1. Create a new AppWizard workspace project, calling the project **Day2**.

2. Use the same settings in the AppWizard as you used yesterday; specify the dialog title **Visual C++ Controls**.

3. After you create the application shell, lay out the main dialog as shown earlier in Figure 2.2.

4. Configure the control properties as specified in Table 2.1.

TABLE 2.1. PROPERTY SETTINGS FOR THE CONTROLS ON THE APPLICATION DIALOG.

Object	Property	Setting
Static Text	ID	IDC_STATIC
	Caption	This is an example of a Visual C++ Application using a number of controls.
Static Text	ID	IDC_STATICMSG
	Caption	Enter a &Message:
Static Text	ID	IDC_STATICPGM
	Caption	Run a &Program:

Object	Property	Setting
Edit Box	ID	IDC_MSG
Button	ID	IDC_SHWMSG
	Caption	&Show Message
Button	ID	IDC_DFLTMSG
	Caption	&Default Message
Button	ID	IDC_CLRMSG
	Caption	&Clear Message
Button	ID	IDC_RUNPGM
	Caption	&Run Program
Button	ID	IDC_EXIT
	Caption	E&xit
Combo Box	ID	IDC_PROGTORUN
Group Box	ID	IDC_STATIC
	Caption	Enable Actions
Group Box	ID	IDC_STATIC
	Caption	Show Actions
Check Box	ID	IDC_CKENBLMSG
	Caption	&Enable Message Action
Check Box	ID	IDC_CKENBLPGM
	Caption	E&nable Program Action
Check Box	ID	IDC_CKSHWMSG
	Caption	S&how Message Action
Check Box	ID	IDC_CKSHWPGM
	Caption	Sh&ow Program Action

Tip

When adding a combo box control to the window, it is important that you click and drag the area for the control as large as you want the drop-down list to be. After you draw the control on the window, you can resize the width of the control as you would normally expect to do. To resize how far the list drops down, you need to click the arrow, as if you were trying to trigger the drop-down list while the application was running.

5. After you place all these controls on the dialog window and configure all their properties, reopen the properties dialog for the combo box that you placed on the window. On the Data tab of the properties dialog, enter the following values, using a Control+Enter key combination to add the second and third items, as shown in Figure 2.3.

- Notepad
- Paint
- Solitaire

FIGURE 2.3.

Use the properties dialog to add entries in the combo box's dropdown list.

Specifying the Control Tab Order

Now that you have all the controls laid out on the window, you need to make sure that the user navigates in the order you want if he or she uses the Tab key to move around the window. You can specify the tab order by following these steps:

1. Select either the dialog window or one of the controls on the window in the editing area of the Developer Studio.

2. Choose Layout | Tab Order from the menu. By turning on the Tab Order, you see a number beside each of the controls on the window. The numbers indicate the order in which the dialog will be navigated, as shown in Figure 2.4.

FIGURE 2.4.

Turning on Tab Order shows the order in which the dialog will be navigated.

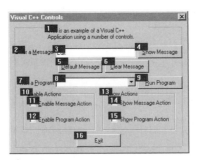

3. Using the mouse, click each of the number boxes in the order that you want the user to navigate the window. The controls will renumber themselves to match the order in which you selected them.

4. Once you specify the tab order, select Layout | Tab Order once again to return to the layout editor.

 Note

> Any static text that has a mnemonic should appear just before the control that accompanies the text in the tab order. Because the user cannot interact with the static text, when the user chooses the mnemonic, the focus will go directly to the next control in the tab order.

2

A mnemonic is the underlined character in the caption on a button, check box, menu, or other control label. The user can press this underlined character and the Alt key at the same time to go directly to that control or to trigger the clicked event on the control. You specify a mnemonic by placing an ampersand (&) in front of the character to be used as the mnemonic when you type the Caption value. It is important to make certain that you do not use the same mnemonic more than once on the same window, or set of menus, because the user can get confused when choosing a mnemonic doesn't result in the action that he or she expects.

One last thing that you want to do before getting into the details of the application code is check your mnemonics to make certain that there are no conflicts in your controls. Follow these steps:

1. Select the dialog window or one of the controls in the layout editor. Right-click the mouse and select Check Mnemonics.

2. If there are no conflicts in your mnemonics, Visual C++ returns a message box dialog, letting you know that there are no conflicts (see Figure 2.5).

FIGURE 2.5.

The mnemonic checker tells you whether there are conflicts.

3. If any conflicts exist, the dialog indicates the conflicting letter and gives you the option of automatically selecting the controls containing the conflicting mnemonics, as in Figure 2.6.

FIGURE 2.6.

Duplicate mnemonics can be automatically selected.

Attaching Variables to Your Controls

At this point, if you've programmed using Visual Basic or PowerBuilder, you probably figure that you're ready to start slinging some code. Well, with Visual C++, it's not quite the same process. Before you can begin coding, you have to assign variables to each of the controls that will have a value attached—everything except the static text and the command buttons. You will interact with these variables when you write the code for your application. The values that the user enters into the screen controls are placed into these variables for use in the application code. Likewise, any values that your application code places into these variables are updated in the controls on the window for the user to see.

How do you declare these variables and associate them with the controls that you placed on the window? Follow these steps:

1. Open the Class Wizard, as you learned yesterday.

2. Select the Member Variables tab, as shown in Figure 2.7.

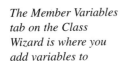

FIGURE 2.7.

The Member Variables tab on the Class Wizard is where you add variables to controls.

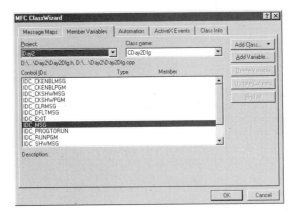

3. Select the ID of one of the controls that you need to attach a variable to, such as `IDC_MSG`.

4. Click the Add Variable button.

5. In the Add Member Variable dialog, enter the variable name, specifying the category and variable type, as shown in Figure 2.8. Click OK.

6. Repeat steps 3 through 5 for all the other controls for which you need to add variables. You should add the variables for your application as listed in Table 2.2.

FIGURE 2.8.

Adding a variable to a control.

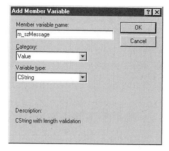

TABLE 2.2. VARIABLES FOR APPLICATION CONTROLS.

Control	Variable Name	Category	Type
IDC_MSG	m_strMessage	Value	CString
IDC_PROGTORUN	m_strProgToRun	Value	CString
IDC_CKENBLMSG	m_bEnableMsg	Value	BOOL
IDC_CKENBLPGM	m_bEnablePgm	Value	BOOL
IDC_CKSHWMSG	m_bShowMsg	Value	BOOL
IDC_CKSHWPGM	m_bShowPgm	Value	BOOL

Tip

All these variables are prefixed with m_ because they are class member variables. This is an MFC naming convention. After the m_, a form of Hungarian notation is used, in which the next few letters describe the variable type. In this case, b means boolean, and str indicates that the variable is a string. You'll see this naming convention in use in this book and other books about programming with Visual C++ and MFC. Following this naming convention will make your code more readable for other programmers; knowing the convention will make it easier for you to read other programmer's code as well.

7. After you add all the necessary variables, click the OK button to close the Class Wizard.

Attaching Functionality to the Controls

Before you begin adding code to all the controls on your application window, you need to add a little bit of code to initialize the variables, setting starting values for most of them. Do this by following these steps:

1. Using the Class Wizard, on the Message Maps tab, select the OnInitDialog function in the list of member functions. You can do this by finding the function in the Member Functions list, or by selecting the CDay2Dlg object in the list of object IDs and then selecting the WM_INITDIALOG message in the messages list, as shown in Figure 2.9.

Figure 2.9.

You can use the Class Wizard to locate existing functions.

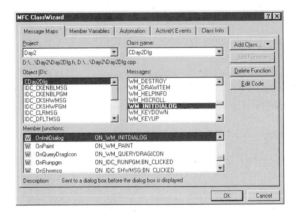

2. Click Edit Code to be taken to the source code for the OnInitDialog function.

3. Find the TODO marker, which indicates where to begin adding your code, and add the code in Listing 2.1.

Listing 2.1. DAY2DLG.CPP—THE OnInitDialog FUNCTION IS WHERE YOU NEED TO ADD INITIALIZATION CODE.

```
 1: BOOL CDay2Dlg::OnInitDialog()
 2: {
 3:     CDialog::OnInitDialog();
 4:
 5: .
 6: .
 7: .
 8:
 9:     // TODO: Add extra initialization here
10:
11:     ////////////////////////
12:     // MY CODE STARTS HERE
13:     ////////////////////////
14:
15:     // Put a default message in the message edit
16:     m_strMessage = "Place a message here";
17:
18:     // Set all of the check boxes to checked
```

```
19:        m_bShowMsg = TRUE;
20:        m_bShowPgm = TRUE;
21:        m_bEnableMsg = TRUE;
22:        m_bEnablePgm = TRUE;
23:
24:        // Update the dialog with the values
25:        UpdateData(FALSE);
26:
27:        /////////////////////////
28:        // MY CODE ENDS HERE
29:        /////////////////////////
30:
31:        return TRUE;  // return TRUE  unless you set the focus to a
    ➥control
32: }
```

Note

There is more code in the OnInitDialog function than has been included in Listing 2.1. I won't include all the code for every function in the code listings throughout this book as a means of focusing on the code that you need to add or modify (and as a means of keeping this book down to a reasonable size). You are welcome to look at the code that has been left out, to learn what it is and what it does, as you build your understanding of MFC and Visual C++.

Note

If you've programmed in C or C++ before, you've noticed that you are set-ting the value of the m_strMessage variable in a very un–C-like manner. It looks more like how you would expect to set a string variable in Visual Basic or PowerBuilder. That's because this variable is a CString type variable. The CString class enables you to work with strings in a Visual C++ application in much the same way that you would work with strings in one of these other programming languages. However, because this is the C++ programming language, you still need to add a semicolon at the end of each command.

This initialization code is simple. You are setting an initial message in the edit box that you will use to display messages for the user. Next, you are setting all the check boxes to the checked state. It's the last line of the code you added to this function that you really need to notice.

The UpdateData function is the key to working with control variables in Visual C++. This function takes the data in the variables and updates the controls on the screen with the variable values. It also takes the data from the controls and populates the attached variables with any values changed by the user. This process is controlled by the argument passed into the UpdateData function. If the argument is FALSE, the values in the variables are passed to the controls on the window. If the argument is TRUE, the variables are updated with whatever appears in the controls on the window. As a result, which value you pass this function depends on which direction you need to update. After you update one or more variables in your code, then you need to call UpdateData, passing it FALSE as its argument. If you need to read the variables to get their current value, then you need to call UpdateData with a TRUE value before you read any of the variables. You'll get the hang of this as you add more code to your application.

Closing the Application

The first thing that you want to take care of is making sure that the user can close your application. Because you deleted the OK and Cancel buttons and added a new button for closing the application window, you need to place code into the function called by the Exit button to close the window. To do this, follow these steps:

1. Using the Class Wizard, add a function for the IDC_EXIT object on the BN_CLICKED message, as you learned to do yesterday.

2. Click the Edit Code button to take you to the new function that you just added.

3. Enter the code in Listing 2.2.

LISTING 2.2. DAY2DLG.CPP—THE OnExit FUNCTION.

```
 1: void CDay2Dlg::OnExit()
 2: {
 3:     // TODO: Add your control notification handler code here
 4:
 5:     ///////////////////////
 6:     // MY CODE STARTS HERE
 7:     ///////////////////////
 8:
 9:     // Exit the program
10:     OnOK();
11:
12:     ///////////////////////
13:     // MY CODE ENDS HERE
14:     ///////////////////////
15: }
```

A single function call within the OnExit function closes the Window and exits the application. Where did this OnOK function come from, and why didn't you have to call it in yesterday's application? Two functions, OnOK and OnCancel, are built into the ancestor

CDialog class from which your CDay2Dlg class is inherited. In the CDialog class, the message map already has the object IDs of the OK and Cancel buttons attached to the OnOK and OnCancel functions so that buttons with these IDs automatically call these functions. If you had specified the Exit button's object ID as IDOK, you would not have needed to add any code to the button unless you wanted to override the base OnOK functionality.

Showing the User's Message

Showing the message that the user typed into the edit box should be easy because it's similar to what you did in yesterday's application. You can add a function to the Show Message button and call the MessageBox function, as in Listing 2.3.

LISTING 2.3. DAY2DLG.CPP—THE OnShwmsg FUNCTION DISPLAYS THE USER MESSAGE.

```
 1: void CDay2Dlg::OnShwmsg()
 2: {
 3:     // TODO: Add your control notification handler code here
 4:
 5:     /////////////////////////
 6:     // MY CODE STARTS HERE
 7:     /////////////////////////
 8:
 9:     // Display the message for the user
10:     MessageBox(m_strMessage);
11:
12:     /////////////////////////
13:     // MY CODE ENDS HERE
14:     /////////////////////////
15: }
```

If you compile and run the application at this point, you'll see one problem with this code. It displays the string that you initialized the m_strMessage variable within the OnInitDialog function. It doesn't display what you type into the edit box. This happens because the variable hasn't been updated with the contents of the control on the window yet. You need to call UpdateData, passing it a TRUE value, to take the values of the controls and update the variables before calling the MessageBox function. Alter the OnShwmsg function as in Listing 2.4.

LISTING 2.4. DAY2DLG.CPP—UPDATED OnShwmsg FUNCTION.

```
 1: void CDay2Dlg::OnShwmsg()
 2: {
```

continues

LISTING 2.4. CONTINUED

```
 3:      // TODO: Add your control notification handler code here
 4:
 5:      ////////////////////////
 6:      // MY CODE STARTS HERE
 7:      ////////////////////////
 8:
 9:      // Update the message variable with what the user entered
10:      UpdateData(TRUE);
11:
12:      // Display the message for the user
13:      MessageBox(m_strMessage);
14:
15:      ////////////////////////
16:      // MY CODE ENDS HERE
17:      ////////////////////////
18: }
```

Now if you compile and run your application, you should be able to display the message you type into the edit box, as shown in Figure 2.10.

FIGURE 2.10.

The message entered in the edit box is displayed to the user.

Clearing the User's Message

If the user prefers the edit box to be cleared before he or she types a message, you can attach a function to the Clear Message button to clear the contents. You can add this function through the Class Wizard in the usual way. The functionality is a simple matter of setting the m_strMessage variable to an empty string and then updating the controls on the window to reflect this. The code to do this is in Listing 2.5.

LISTING 2.5. DAY2DLG.CPP—THE OnClrmsg FUNCTION.

```
 1: void CDay2Dlg::OnClrmsg()
 2: {
 3:      // TODO: Add your control notification handler code here
 4:
 5:      ////////////////////////
 6:      // MY CODE STARTS HERE
 7:      ////////////////////////
 8:
 9:      // Clear the message
```

```
10:     m_strMessage = "";
11:
12:     // Update the screen
13:     UpdateData(FALSE);
14:
15:     ///////////////////////
16:     // MY CODE ENDS HERE
17:     ///////////////////////
18: }
```

Disabling and Hiding the Message Controls

The last thing that you want to do with the message controls is add functionality to the Enable Message Action and Show Message Action check boxes. The first of these check boxes enables or disables the controls dealing with displaying the user message. When the check box is in a checked state, the controls are all enabled. When the check box is in an unchecked state, all those same controls are disabled. In a likewise fashion, the second check box shows and hides this same set of controls. The code for these two functions is in Listing 2.6.

LISTING 2.6. DAY2DLG.CPP—THE FUNCTIONS FOR THE ENABLE AND SHOW MESSAGE ACTIONS CHECK BOXES.

```
 1: void CDay2Dlg::OnCkenblmsg()
 2: {
 3:     // TODO: Add your control notification handler code here
 4:
 5:     ///////////////////////
 6:     // MY CODE STARTS HERE
 7:     ///////////////////////
 8:
 9:     // Get the current values from the screen
10:     UpdateData(TRUE);
11:
12:     // Is the Enable Message Action check box checked?
13:     if (m_bEnableMsg == TRUE)
14:     {
15:         // Yes, so enable all controls that have anything
16:         // to do with showing the user message
17:         GetDlgItem(IDC_MSG)->EnableWindow(TRUE);
18:         GetDlgItem(IDC_SHWMSG)->EnableWindow(TRUE);
19:         GetDlgItem(IDC_DFLTMSG)->EnableWindow(TRUE);
20:         GetDlgItem(IDC_CLRMSG)->EnableWindow(TRUE);
21:         GetDlgItem(IDC_STATICMSG)->EnableWindow(TRUE);
22:     }
```

continues

LISTING 2.6. CONTINUED

```
23:     else
24:     {
25:         // No, so disable all controls that have anything
26:         // to do with showing the user message
27:         GetDlgItem(IDC_MSG)->EnableWindow(FALSE);
28:         GetDlgItem(IDC_SHWMSG)->EnableWindow(FALSE);
29:         GetDlgItem(IDC_DFLTMSG)->EnableWindow(FALSE);
30:         GetDlgItem(IDC_CLRMSG)->EnableWindow(FALSE);
31:         GetDlgItem(IDC_STATICMSG)->EnableWindow(FALSE);
32:     }
33:
34:     /////////////////////////
35:     // MY CODE ENDS HERE
36:     /////////////////////////
37: }
38:
39: void CDay2Dlg::OnCkshwmsg()
40: {
41:     // TODO: Add your control notification handler code here
42:
43:     /////////////////////////
44:     // MY CODE STARTS HERE
45:     /////////////////////////
46:
47:     // Get the current values from the screen
48:     UpdateData(TRUE);
49:
50:     // Is the Show Message Action check box checked?
51:     if (m_bShowMsg == TRUE)
52:     {
53:         // Yes, so show all controls that have anything
54:         // to do with showing the user message
55:         GetDlgItem(IDC_MSG)->ShowWindow(TRUE);
56:         GetDlgItem(IDC_SHWMSG)->ShowWindow(TRUE);
57:         GetDlgItem(IDC_DFLTMSG)->ShowWindow(TRUE);
58:         GetDlgItem(IDC_CLRMSG)->ShowWindow(TRUE);
59:         GetDlgItem(IDC_STATICMSG)->ShowWindow(TRUE);
60:     }
61:     else
62:     {
63:         // No, so hide all controls that have anything
64:         // to do with showing the user message
65:         GetDlgItem(IDC_MSG)->ShowWindow(FALSE);
66:         GetDlgItem(IDC_SHWMSG)->ShowWindow(FALSE);
67:         GetDlgItem(IDC_DFLTMSG)->ShowWindow(FALSE);
68:         GetDlgItem(IDC_CLRMSG)->ShowWindow(FALSE);
69:         GetDlgItem(IDC_STATICMSG)->ShowWindow(FALSE);
70:     }
71:
```

```
72:      ///////////////////////
73:      // MY CODE ENDS HERE
74:      ///////////////////////
75: }
```

By now, you should understand the first part of these functions. First, you update the variables with the current values of the controls on the window. Next, you check the value of the boolean variable attached to the appropriate check box. If the variable is TRUE, you want to enable or show the control. If the variable if FALSE, you want to disable or hide the control.

At this point, the code begins to be harder to understand. The first function, GetDlgItem, is passed the ID of the control that you want to change. This function returns the object for that control. You can call this function to retrieve the object for any of the controls on the window while your application is running. The next part of each command is where a member function of the control object is called. The second function is a member function of the object returned by the first function. If you are not clear on how this works, then you might want to check out Appendix A, "C++ Review," to brush up on your C++.

The second functions in these calls, EnableWindow and ShowWindow, look like they should be used on windows, not controls. Well, yes, they should be used on windows; they happen to be members of the CWnd class, which is an ancestor of the CDialog class from which your CDay2Dlg class is inherited. It just so happens that, in Windows, all controls are themselves windows, completely separate from the window on which they are placed. This allows you to treat controls as windows and to call windows functions on them. In fact, all the control classes are inherited from the CWnd class, revealing their true nature as windows.

If you compile and run your application now, you can try the Enable and Show Message Action check boxes. They should work just fine, as shown in Figure 2.11.

FIGURE 2.11.

The user message controls can now be disabled.

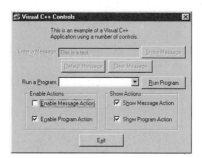

Running Another Application

The last major piece of functionality to be implemented in your application is for the set of controls for running another program. If you remember, you added the names of three Windows applications into the combo box, and when you run your application, you can see these application names in the drop-down list. You can select any one of them, and the value area on the combo box is updated with that application name. With that part working as it should, you only need to add code to the Run Program button to actually get the value for the combo box and run the appropriate program. Once you create the function for the Run Program button using the Class Wizard, add the code in Listing 2.7 to the function.

LISTING 2.7. DAY2DLG.CPP—THE OnRunpgm FUNCTION STARTS OTHER WINDOWS APPLICATIONS.

```
 1: void CDay2Dlg::OnRunpgm()
 2: {
 3:     // TODO: Add your control notification handler code here
 4:
 5:     ///////////////////////
 6:     // MY CODE STARTS HERE
 7:     ///////////////////////
 8:
 9:     // Get the current values from the screen
10:     UpdateData(TRUE);
11:
12:     // Declare a local variable for holding the program name
13:     CString strPgmName;
14:
15:     // Copy the program name to the local variable
16:     strPgmName = m_strProgToRun;
17:
18:     // Make the program name all uppercase
19:     strPgmName.MakeUpper();
20:
21:     // Did the user select to run the Paint program?
22:     if (strPgmName == "PAINT")
23:         // Yes, run the Paint program
24:         WinExec("pbrush.exe", SW_SHOW);
25:
26:     // Did the user select to run the Notepad program?
27:     if (strPgmName == "NOTEPAD")
28:         // Yes, run the Notepad program
29:         WinExec("notepad.exe", SW_SHOW);
30:
31:     // Did the user select to run the Solitaire program?
32:     if (strPgmName == "SOLITAIRE")
33:         // Yes, run the Solitaire program
34:         WinExec("sol.exe", SW_SHOW);
```

```
35:
36:       ////////////////////////
37:       // MY CODE ENDS HERE
38:       ////////////////////////
39: }
```

As you expect, the first thing that you do in this function is call UpdateData to populate the variables with the values of the controls on the window. The next thing that you do, however, might seem a little pointless. You declare a new CString variable and copy the value of the combo box to it. Is this really necessary when the value is already in a CString variable? Well, it depends on how you want your application to behave. The next line in the code is a call to the CString function MakeUpper, which converts the string to all uppercase. If you use the CString variable that is attached to the combo box, the next time that UpdateData is called with FALSE as the argument, the value in the combo box is converted to uppercase. Considering that this is likely to happen at an odd time, this is probably not desirable behavior. That's why you use an additional CString in this function.

Once you convert the string to all uppercase, you have a series of if statements that compare the string to the names of the various programs. When a match is found, the WinExec function is called to run the application. Now, if you compile and run your application, you can select one of the applications in the drop-down list and run it by clicking the Run Program button.

Caution

It is important to understand the difference in C and C++ between using a single equal sign (=) and a double equal sign (==). The single equal sign performs an assignment of the value on the right side of the equal sign to the variable on the left side of the equal sign. If a constant is on the left side of the equal sign, your program will not compile, and you'll get a nice error message telling you that you cannot assign the value on the right to the constant on the left. The double equal sign (==) is used for comparison. It is important to make certain that you use the double equal sign when you want to compare two values because if you use a single equal sign, you alter the value of the variable on the left. This confusion is one of the biggest sources of logic bugs in C/C++ programs.

> **Note**
>
> The `WinExec` function is an obsolete Windows function. You really should use the `CreateProcess` function instead. However, the `CreateProcess` function has a number of arguments that are difficult to understand this early in programming using Visual C++. The `WinExec` function is still available and is implemented as a macro that calls the `CreateProcess` function. This allows you to use the much simpler `WinExec` function to run another application while still using the function that Windows wants you to use.
>
> Another API function that can be used to run another application is the `ShellExecute` function. This function was originally intended for opening or printing files, but can also be used to run other programs.

Summary

Today, you learned how you can use standard windows controls in a Visual C++ application. You learned how to declare and attach variables to each of these controls and how to synchronize the values between the controls and the variables. You also learned how you can manipulate the controls by retrieving the control objects using their object ID and how you can manipulate the control by treating it as a window. You also learned how to specify the tab order of the controls on your application windows, thus enabling you to control how users navigate your application windows. Finally, you learned how to attach application functionality to the controls on your application window, triggering various actions when the user interacts with various controls. As an added bonus, you learned how you can run other Windows applications from your own application.

Q&A

Q When I specified the object IDs of the controls on the window, three controls had the same ID, `IDC_STATIC`. These controls were the text at the top of the window and the two group boxes. The other two static text controls started out with this same ID until I changed them. How can these controls have the same ID, and why did I have to change the ID on the two static texts where I did change them?

A All controls that don't normally have any user interaction, such as static text and group boxes, are by default given the same object ID. This works fine as long as your application doesn't need to perform any actions on any of these controls. If you do need to interact with one of these controls, as you did with the static text prompts for the edit box and combo box, then you need to give that control a unique ID. In this case, you needed the unique ID to be able to retrieve the control object so that you could enable or disable and show or hide the control. You also need to assign it a unique ID if you want to attach a variable to the control so that you could dynamically alter the text on the control.

The application behaves in a somewhat unpredictable way if you try to alter any of the static controls that share the same ID. As a general rule of thumb, you can allow static controls to share the same object ID if you are not going to alter the controls at all. If you might need to perform any interaction with the controls, then you need to assign each one a unique object ID.

Q Is there any other way to manipulate the controls, other than retrieving the control objects using their object IDs?

A You can declare variables in the Control category. This basically gives you an object that is the control's MFC class, providing you with a direct way of altering and interacting with the control. You can then call all of the CWnd class functions on the control, as you did to enable or disable and show or hide the controls in your application, or you can call the control class methods, enabling you to do things in the code that are specific to that type of control. For instance, if you add another variable to the combo box control and specify that it is a Control category variable, you can use it to add items to the drop-down list on the control.

Workshop

The Workshop provides quiz questions to help you solidify your understanding of the material covered and exercises to provide you with experience in using what you've learned. The answers to the quiz questions and exercises appear in Appendix B, "Answers."

Quiz

1. Why do you need to specify the tab order of the controls on your application windows?

2. How can you include a mnemonic in a static text field that will take the user to the edit box or combo box beside the text control?

3. Why do you need to give unique object IDs to the static text fields in front of the edit box and combo boxes?

4. Why do you need to call the UpdateData function before checking the value of one of the controls?

Exercises

1. Add code to the Default Message button to reset the edit box to say Enter a message here.

2. Add code to enable or disable and show or hide the controls used to select and run another application.

3. Extend the code in the OnRunpgm function to allow the user to enter his own program name to be run.

DAY 3

Allowing User Interaction—Integrating the Mouse and Keyboard in Your Application

Depending on the type of application you are creating, you might need to notice what the user is doing with the mouse. You need to know when and where the mouse was clicked, which button was clicked, and when the button was released. You also need to know what the user did while the mouse button was being held down.

Another thing that you might need to do is read the keyboard events. As with the mouse, you might need to know when a key was pressed, how long it was held down, and when it was released.

Today you are going to learn

- What mouse events are available for use and how to determine which one is appropriate for your application's needs.
- How you can listen to mouse events and how to react to them in your Visual C++ application.
- What keyboard events are available for use and what actions will trigger each of these events.
- How to capture keyboard events and take action based on what the user pressed.

Understanding Mouse Events

As you learned yesterday, when you are working with most controls, you are limited to a select number of events that are available in the Class Wizard. When it comes to mouse events, you are limited for the most part to click and double-click events. Just looking at your mouse tells you that there must be more to capturing mouse events than recognizing these two. What about the right mouse button? How can you tell if it has been pressed? And what about drawing programs? How can they follow where you drag the mouse?

If you open the Class Wizard in one of your projects, select the dialog in the list of object IDs, and then scroll through the list of messages that are available, you will find a number of mouse-related events, which are also listed in Table 3.1. These event messages enable you to perform any task that might be required by your application.

TABLE 3.1. MOUSE EVENT MESSAGES.

Message	Description
WM_LBUTTONDOWN	The left mouse button has been pressed.
WM_LBUTTONUP	The left mouse button has been released.
WM_LBUTTONDBLCLK	The left mouse button has been double-clicked.
WM_RBUTTONDOWN	The right mouse button has been pressed.
WM_RBUTTONUP	The right mouse button has been released.
WM_RBUTTONDBLCLK	The right mouse button has been double-clicked.
WM_MOUSEMOVE	The mouse is being moved across the application window space.
WM_MOUSEWHEEL	The mouse wheel is being moved.

Drawing with the Mouse

Today you are going to build a simple drawing program that uses some of the available mouse events to let the user draw simple figures on a dialog window. This application depends mostly on the WM_MOUSEMOVE event message, which signals that the mouse is being moved. You will look at how you can tell within this event function whether the left mouse button is down or up. You will also learn how you can tell where the mouse is on the window. Sound's fairly straight ahead, so let's get going by following these steps:

1. Create a new MFC AppWizard workspace project, calling the project **Mouse**.

2. Specify that this project will be a dialog-based application in the first AppWizard step.

3. Use the default settings in the AppWizard. In the second step, specify a suitable dialog title, such as **Mouse and Keyboard**.

4. After the application shell is created, remove all controls from the dialog window. This provides the entire dialog window surface for drawing. This step is also necessary for your application to capture any keyboard events.

Note

> If there are any controls on a dialog, all keyboard events are directed to the control that currently has input focus—the control that is highlighted or has the cursor visible in it. To capture any keyboard events in a dialog, you have to remove all controls from the dialog.

5. Open the Class Wizard. Select WM_MOUSEMOVE from the list of messages, and add a function by clicking the Add Function button. Click the OK button to accept the suggested function name.

6. Click the Edit Code button to edit the OnMouseMove function you just created, adding the code in Listing 3.1.

LISTING 3.1. THE OnMouseMove FUNCTION.

```
1: void CMouseDlg::OnMouseMove(UINT nFlags, CPoint point)
2: {
3:     // TODO: Add your message handler code here and/or call default
4:
5:     ////////////////////////
6:     // MY CODE STARTS HERE
7:     ////////////////////////
8:
```

continues

LISTING 3.1. CONTINUED

```
 9:     // Check to see if the left mouse button is down
10:     if ((nFlags & MK_LBUTTON) == MK_LBUTTON)
11:     {
12:         // Get the Device Context
13:         CClientDC dc(this);
14:
15:         // Draw the pixel
16:         dc.SetPixel(point.x, point.y, RGB(0, 0, 0));
17:     }
18:
19:     /////////////////////////
20:     // MY CODE ENDS HERE
21:     /////////////////////////
22:
23:     CDialog::OnMouseMove(nFlags, point);
24: }
```

Look at the function definition at the top of the listing. You will notice that two arguments are passed into this function. The first of these arguments is a set of flags that can be used to determine whether a mouse button is depressed (and which one). This determination is made in the first line of your code with the `if` statement:

```
if ((nFlags & MK_LBUTTON) == MK_LBUTTON)
```

In the first half of the condition being evaluated, the flags are filtered down to the one that indicates that the left mouse button is down. In the second half, the filtered flags are compared to the flag that indicates that the left mouse button is down. If the two match, then the left mouse button is down.

The second argument to this function is the location of the mouse. This argument gives you the coordinates on the screen where the mouse currently is. You can use this information to draw a spot on the dialog window.

Before you can draw any spots on the dialog window, you need to get the device context for the dialog window. This is done by declaring a new instance of the CClientDC class. This class encapsulates the device context and most of the operations that can be performed on it, including all the screen drawing operations. In a sense, the device context is the canvas upon which you can draw with your application. Until you have a canvas, you cannot do any drawing or painting. After the device context object is created, you can call its SetPixel function, which colors the pixel at the location specified in the first two arguments with the color specified in the third argument. If you compile and run your program, you can see how it allows you to draw on the window surface with the mouse, as shown in Figure 3.1.

FIGURE 3.1.

Drawing on the window with the mouse.

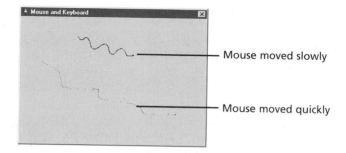

Mouse moved slowly

Mouse moved quickly

Note

In Windows, colors are specified as a single number that is a combination of three numbers. The three numbers are the brightness levels for the red, green, and blue pixels in your computer display. The RGB function in your code is a macro that combines these three separate values into the single number that must be passed to the SetPixel function or to any other function that requires a color value. These three numbers can be any value between and including 0 and 255.

Using the AND and OR Binaries

If you are new to C++, you need to understand how the different types of AND and OR work. The two categories of ANDs and ORs are logical and binary. The logical ANDs and ORs are used in logical or conditional statements, such as an if or while statement that is controlling the logic flow. The binary ANDs and ORs are used to combine two values on a binary level.

The ampersand character (&) is used to denote AND. A single ampersand (&) is a binary AND, and a double ampersand (&&) is a logical AND. A logical AND works much like the word AND in Visual Basic or PowerBuilder. It can be used in an if statement to say "if this condition AND this other condition..." where both conditions must be true before the entire statement is true. A binary AND is used to set or unset bits. When two values are binary ANDed, only the bits that are set to 1 in both values remain as 1; all the rest of the bits are set to 0. To understand how this works, start with two 8-bit values such as the following:

Value 1	01011001
Value 2	00101001

If you binary AND these two values together, you wind up with the following value:

ANDed Value	00001001

All the bits that had 1 in one of the values, but not in the other value, were set to 0. All the bits that were 1 in both values remained set to 1. All the bits that were 0 in both values remained 0.

OR is represented by the pipe character (¦), and as with AND, a single pipe (¦) is a binary OR, whereas a double pipe (¦¦) is a logical OR. As with AND, a logical OR can be used in conditional statements such as if or while statements to control the logical flow, much like the word OR in Visual Basic and PowerBuilder. It can be used in an if statement to say "if this condition OR this other condition…" and if either condition is true, the entire statement is true. You can use a binary OR to combine values on a binary level. With OR, if a bit is set to 1 in either value, the resulting bit is set to 1. With a binary OR, the only way that a bit is set to 0 in the resulting value is if the bit was already 0 in both values. Take the same two values that were used to illustrate the binary AND:

| Value 1 | 01011001 |
| Value 2 | 00101001 |

If you binary OR these two values together, you get the following value:

| ORed Value | 01111001 |

In this case, every bit that was set to 1 in either value was set to 1 in the resulting value. Only those bits that were 0 in both values were 0 in the resulting value.

Binary Attribute Flags

Binary ANDs and ORs are used in C++ for setting and reading attribute flags. Attribute flags are values where each bit in the value specifies whether a specific option is turned on or off. This enables programmers to use defined flags. A defined flag is a value with only one bit set to 1 or a combination of other values in which a specific combination of bits is set to 1 so that multiple options are set with a single value. The flags controlling various options are ORed together, making a composite flag specifying which options should be on and which should be off.

If two flags that specify certain conditions are specified as two different bits in a byte, those two flags can often be ORed together as follows:

Flag 1	00001000
Flag 2	00100000
Combination	**00101000**

This is how flags are combined to specify a number of settings in a limited amount of memory space. In fact, this is what is done with most of the check box settings on the window and control properties dialogs. These on/off settings are ORed together to form one or two sets of flags that are examined by the Windows operating system to determine how to display the window or control and how it should behave.

On the flip side of this process, when you need to determine if a specific flag is included in the combination, you can AND the combination flag with the specific flag that you are looking for as follows:

Combination	00101000
Flag 1	00001000
Result	**00001000**

The result of this operation can be compared to the flag that you used to filter the combined flag. If the result is the same, the flag was included. Another common approach is to check whether the filtered combination flag is nonzero. If the flag being used for filtering the combination had not been included, the resulting flag would be zero. As a result, you could have left the comparison out of the if statement in the preceding code, leaving you with an if statement that looks like the following:

```
if (nFlags & MK_LBUTTON)
```

You can modify this approach to check whether a flag is not in the combination as follows:

```
if (!(nFlags & MK_LBUTTON))
```

You might find one of these ways of checking for a flag easier to understand than the others. You'll probably find all of them in use.

Improving the Drawing Program

If you ran your program, you probably noticed a small problem. To draw a solid line, you need to move the mouse very slowly. How do other painting programs solve this problem? Simple, they draw a line between two points drawn by the mouse. Although this seems a little like cheating, it's the way that computer drawing programs work.

As you move the mouse across the screen, your computer is checking the location of the mouse every few clock ticks. Because your computer doesn't have a constant trail of where your mouse has gone, it has to make some assumptions. The way your computer makes these assumptions is by taking the points that the computer does know about and drawing lines between them. When you draw lines with the freehand tool in Paint, your computer is playing connect the dots.

Because all the major drawing programs draw lines between each pair of points, what do you need to do to adapt your application so that it also uses this technique? First, you need to keep track of the previous position of the mouse. This means you need to add two variables to the dialog window to maintain the previous X and Y coordinates. You can do this by following these steps:

1. In the workspace pane, select the Class View tab.

2. Select the dialog class—in this case, the CMouseDlg class.

3. Right-click the mouse and select Add Member Variable from the pop-up menu.

4. Enter **int** as the Variable Type and **m_iPrevY** as the Variable Name and specify Private for the access in the Add Member Variable dialog, as shown in Figure 3.2.

FIGURE 3.2.

*The Add Member
Variable dialog.*

5. Click OK to add the variable.

6. Repeat steps 3 through 5, specifying the Variable Name as **m_iPrevX** to add the second variable.

After you add the variables needed to keep track of the previous mouse position, you can make the necessary modifications to the OnMouseMove function, as shown in Listing 3.2.

LISTING 3.2. THE REVISED OnMouseMove FUNCTION.

```
 1: void CMouseDlg::OnMouseMove(UINT nFlags, CPoint point)
 2: {
 3:     // TODO: Add your message handler code here and/or call default
 4:
 5:     /////////////////////////
 6:     // MY CODE STARTS HERE
 7:     /////////////////////////
 8:
 9:     // Check to see if the left mouse button is down
10:     if ((nFlags & MK_LBUTTON) == MK_LBUTTON)
11:     {
12:         // Get the Device Context
13:         CClientDC dc(this);
14:
15:         // Draw a line from the previous point to the current point
16:         dc.MoveTo(m_iPrevX, m_iPrevY);
```

```
17:          dc.LineTo(point.x, point.y);
18:
19:          // Save the current point as the previous point
20:          m_iPrevX = point.x;
21:          m_iPrevY = point.y;
22:     }
23:
24:     ////////////////////////
25:     // MY CODE ENDS HERE
26:     ////////////////////////
27:
28:     CDialog::OnMouseMove(nFlags, point);
29: }
```

Look at the code that draws the line from the previous point to the current point:

```
dc.MoveTo(m_iPrevX, m_iPrevY);
dc.LineTo(point.x, point.y);
```

You see that you need to move to the first position and then draw a line to the second point. The first step is important because without it, there is no telling where Windows might think the starting position is. If you compile and run your application, it draws a bit better. However, it now has a peculiar behavior. Every time you press the left mouse button to begin drawing some more, your application draws a line from where you ended the last line you drew, as shown in Figure 3.3.

FIGURE 3.3.

The drawing program with a peculiar behavior.

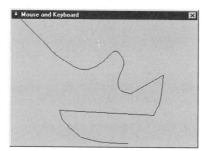

Adding the Finishing Touches

Your application is doing all its drawing on the mouse move event when the left button is held down. Initializing the previous position variables with the position of the mouse when the left button is pressed should correct this application behavior. Let's try this approach by following these steps:

1. Using the Class Wizard, add a function for the WM_LBUTTONDOWN message on the dialog object.

2. Edit the OnLButtonDown function that you just created, adding the code in Listing 3.3.

LISTING 3.3. THE OnLButtonDown FUNCTION.

```
 1: void CMouseDlg::OnLButtonDown(UINT nFlags, CPoint point)
 2: {
 3:     // TODO: Add your message handler code here and/or call default
 4:
 5:     //////////////////////////
 6:     // MY CODE STARTS HERE
 7:     //////////////////////////
 8:
 9:     // Set the current point as the starting point
10:     m_iPrevX = point.x;
11:     m_iPrevY = point.y;
12:
13:     //////////////////////////
14:     // MY CODE ENDS HERE
15:     //////////////////////////
16:
17:     CDialog::OnLButtonDown(nFlags, point);
18: }
```

When you compile and run your application, you should find that you can draw much like you would expect with a drawing program, as shown in Figure 3.4.

FIGURE 3.4.

The finished drawing program.

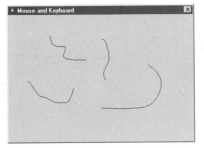

Capturing Keyboard Events

Reading keyboard events is similar to reading mouse events. As with the mouse, there are event messages for when a key is pressed and when it is released. These events are listed in Table 3.2.

TABLE 3.2. KEYBOARD EVENT MESSAGES.

Message	Description
WM_KEYDOWN	A key has been pressed down.
WM_KEYUP	A key has been released.

The keyboard obviously has fewer messages than the mouse does. Then again, there are only so many things that you can do with the keyboard. These event messages are available on the dialog window object and are triggered only if there are no enabled controls on the window. Any enabled controls on the window have input focus, so all keyboard events go to them. That's why you remove all controls from the main dialog for your drawing application.

Changing the Drawing Cursor

To get a good idea of how you can use keyboard-related event messages, why don't you use certain keys to change the mouse cursor in your drawing application? Make the A key change the cursor to the default arrow cursor, which your application starts with. Then you can make B change the cursor to the I-beam and C change the cursor to the hourglass. To get started adding this functionality, follow these steps:

1. Using the Class Wizard, add a function for the WM_KEYDOWN message on the dialog object.

2. Edit the OnKeyDown function that you just created, adding the code in Listing 3.4.

LISTING 3.4. THE OnKeyDown FUNCTION.

```
 1: void CMouseDlg::OnKeyDown(UINT nChar, UINT nRepCnt, UINT nFlags)
 2: {
 3:     // TODO: Add your message handler code here and/or call default
 4:
 5:     ///////////////////////
 6:     // MY CODE STARTS HERE
 7:     ///////////////////////
 8:
 9:     char lsChar;        // The current character being pressed
10:     HCURSOR lhCursor;   // The handle to the cursor to be displayed
11:
12:     // Convert the key pressed to a character
13:     lsChar = char(nChar);
14:
15:     // Is the character "A"
16:     if (lsChar == 'A')
```

continues

LISTING 3.4. CONTINUED

```
17:      {
18:          // Load the arrow cursor
19:          lhCursor = AfxGetApp()->LoadStandardCursor(IDC_ARROW);
20:          // Set the screen cursor
21:          SetCursor(lhCursor);
22:      }
23:
24:      // Is the character "B"
25:      if (lsChar == 'B')
26:      {
27:          // Load the I beam cursor
28:          lhCursor = AfxGetApp()->LoadStandardCursor(IDC_IBEAM);
29:          // Set the screen cursor
30:          SetCursor(lhCursor);
31:      }
32:
33:      // Is the character "C"
34:      if (lsChar == 'C')
35:      {
36:          // Load the hourglass cursor
37:          lhCursor = AfxGetApp()->LoadStandardCursor(IDC_WAIT);
38:          // Set the screen cursor
39:          SetCursor(lhCursor);
40:      }
41:
42:      // Is the character "X"
43:      if (lsChar == 'X')
44:      {
45:          // Load the arrow cursor
46:          lhCursor = AfxGetApp()->LoadStandardCursor(IDC_ARROW);
47:          // Set the screen cursor
48:          SetCursor(lhCursor);
49:          // Exit the application
50:          OnOK();
51:      }
52:
53:      /////////////////////////
54:      // MY CODE ENDS HERE
55:      /////////////////////////
56:
57:      CDialog::OnKeyDown(nChar, nRepCnt, nFlags);
58: }
```

In the function definition, you see three arguments to the OnKeyDown function. The first is the key that was pressed. This argument is the character code of the character, which needs to be converted into a character in the first line of your code. After you convert the character, you can perform straight-ahead comparisons to determine which key was pressed:

```
void CMouseDlg::OnKeyDown(UINT nChar, UINT nRepCnt, UINT nFlags)
```

The second argument to the OnKeyDown function is the number of times that the key is pressed. Normally, if the key is pressed and then released, this value is 1. If the key is pressed and held down, however, the repeat count rises for this key. In the end, this value tells you how many times that Windows thinks the key has been pressed.

The third argument to the OnKeyDown function is a combination flag that can be examined to determine whether the Alt key was pressed at the same time as the key or whether the key being pressed is an extended key. This argument does not tell you whether the shift or control keys were pressed.

When you determine that a specific key was pressed, then it's time to change the cursor to whichever cursor is associated with that key. There are two steps to this process. The first step is to load the cursor into memory. You accomplish this step with the LoadStandardCursor function, which loads one of the standard Windows cursors and returns a handle to the cursor.

Note

> A sister function, LoadCursor, can be passed the file or resource name of a custom cursor so that you can create and load your own cursors. If you design your own cursor in the resource editor in Visual C++, you can pass the cursor name as the only argument to the LoadCursor function. For example, if you create your own cursor and name it IDC_MYCURSOR, you can load it with the following line of code:
>
> ```
> lhCursor = AfxGetApp()->LoadCursor(IDC_MYCURSOR);
> ```
>
> After you load your own cursor, you can set the mouse pointer to your cursor using the SetCursor function, as with a standard cursor.

After the cursor is loaded into memory, the handle to that cursor is passed to the SetCursor function, which switches the cursor to the one the handle points to. If you compile and run your application, you should be able to press one of these keys and get the cursor to change, as in Figure 3.5. However, the moment you move the mouse to do any drawing, the cursor switches back to the default arrow cursor. The following section describes how to make your change stick.

FIGURE 3.5.

*Changing the cursor
with specific keys.*

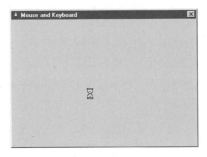

Making the Change Stick

The problem with your drawing program is that the cursor is redrawn every time you
move the mouse. There must be some way of turning off this behavior.

Each time the cursor needs to be redrawn—because the mouse has moved, because
another window that was in front of your application has gone away, or because of whatever other reason—a WM_SETCURSOR event message is sent to your application. If you
override the native behavior of your application on this event, the cursor you set remains
unchanged until you change it again. To do this, follow these steps:

1. Add a new variable to the CMouseDlg class, as you did for the previous position
   variables. This time, declare the type as BOOL and name the variable **m_bCursor**, as
   shown in Figure 3.6.

FIGURE 3.6.

*Defining a class mem-
ber variable.*

2. Initialize the m_bCursor variable in the OnInitDialog with the code in Listing 3.5.

LISTING 3.5. THE OnInitDialog FUNCTION.

```
1: BOOL CMouseDlg::OnInitDialog()
2: {
3:     CDialog::OnInitDialog();
4:
5: .
6: .
7: .
8:     // Set the icon for this dialog.  The framework does this
    ➥automatically
```

```
 9:       //  when the application's main window is not a dialog
10:       SetIcon(m_hIcon, TRUE);              // Set big icon
11:       SetIcon(m_hIcon, FALSE);             // Set small icon
12:
13:       // TODO: Add extra initialization here
14:
15:       ///////////////////////
16:       // MY CODE STARTS HERE
17:       ///////////////////////
18:
19:       // Initialize the cursor to the arrow
20:       m_bCursor = FALSE;
21:
22:       ///////////////////////
23:       // MY CODE ENDS HERE
24:       ///////////////////////
25:
26:       return TRUE;  // return TRUE  unless you set the focus to a
          ➥control
27: }
```

3. Alter the OnKeyDown function to set the m_bCursor flag to TRUE when you change the cursor, as in Listing 3.6.

LISTING 3.6. THE OnKeyDown FUNCTION.

```
1: void CMouseDlg::OnKeyDown(UINT nChar, UINT nRepCnt, UINT nFlags)
2: {
3:       // TODO: Add your message handler code here and/or call default
4:
5:       ///////////////////////
6:       // MY CODE STARTS HERE
7:       ///////////////////////
8:
9:       char lsChar;        // The current character being pressed
10:      HCURSOR lhCursor;    // The handle to the cursor to be displayed
11:
12:      // Convert the key pressed to a character
13:      lsChar = char(nChar);
14:
15:      // Is the character "A"
16:      if (lsChar == 'A')
17:          // Load the arrow cursor
18:          lhCursor = AfxGetApp()->LoadStandardCursor(IDC_ARROW);
19:
20:      // Is the character "B"
21:      if (lsChar == 'B')
```

continues

LISTING 3.6. CONTINUED

```
22:          // Load the I beam cursor
23:          lhCursor = AfxGetApp()->LoadStandardCursor(IDC_IBEAM);
24:
25:      // Is the character "C"
26:      if (lsChar == 'C')
27:          // Load the hourglass cursor
28:          lhCursor = AfxGetApp()->LoadStandardCursor(IDC_WAIT);
29:
30:      // Is the character "X"
31:      if (lsChar == 'X')
32:      {
33:          // Load the arrow cursor
34:          lhCursor = AfxGetApp()->LoadStandardCursor(IDC_ARROW);
35:          // Set the cursor flag
36:          m_bCursor = TRUE;
37:          // Set the screen cursor
38:          SetCursor(lhCursor);
39:          // Exit the application
40:          OnOK();
41:      }
42:      else
43:      {
44:          // Set the cursor flag
45:          m_bCursor = TRUE;
46:          // Set the screen cursor
47:          SetCursor(lhCursor);
48:      }
49:
50:      ///////////////////////
51:      // MY CODE ENDS HERE
52:      ///////////////////////
53:
54:      CDialog::OnKeyDown(nChar, nRepCnt, nFlags);
55: }
```

4. Using the Class Wizard, add a function for the WM_SETCURSOR message on the dialog object.

5. Edit the OnSetCursor function that you just created, adding the code in Listing 3.7.

LISTING 3.7. THE OnSetCursor FUNCTION.

```
1: BOOL CMouseDlg::OnSetCursor(CWnd* pWnd, UINT nHitTest, UINT message)
2: {
3:      // TODO: Add your message handler code here and/or call default
4:
```

```
 5:      ////////////////////////
 6:      // MY CODE STARTS HERE
 7:      ////////////////////////
 8:
 9:      // If the cursor has been set, then return TRUE
10:      if (m_bCursor)
11:          return TRUE;
12:      else
13:
14:      ////////////////////////
15:      // MY CODE ENDS HERE
16:      ////////////////////////
17:
18:      return CDialog::OnSetCursor(pWnd, nHitTest, message);
19: }
```

3

The OnSetCursor function needs to always return TRUE or else call the ancestor function. The ancestor function resets the cursor and does need to be called when the application first starts. Because of this, you need to initialize your variable to FALSE so that until the user presses a key to change the cursor, the default OnSetCursor processing is executed. When the user changes the cursor, you want to bypass the default processing and return TRUE instead. This allows the user to draw with whichever cursor has been selected, including the hourglass, as shown in Figure 3.7.

FIGURE 3.7.

Drawing with the hourglass cursor.

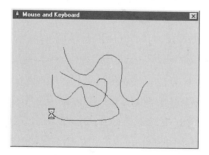

Note

The most common cursor change that you are likely to use in your programs is setting the cursor to the hourglass while your program is working on something that might take a while. There are actually two functions available in MFC that you can use to handle this task. The first is BeginWaitCursor, which displays the hourglass cursor for the user. The second function is EndWaitCursor, which restores the cursor to the default cursor. Both of these functions are members of the CCmdTarget class, from which all of the MFC window and control classes are derived.

> If you have a single function controlling all the processing during which you need to display the hourglass and you don't need to display the hourglass after the function has finished, an easier way to show the hourglass cursor is to declare a variable of the CWaitCursor class at the beginning of the function. This automatically displays the hourglass cursor for the user. As soon as the program exits the function, the cursor will be restored to the previous cursor.

Summary

In this chapter, you learned about how you can capture mouse event messages and perform some simple processing based upon these events. You used the mouse events to build a simple drawing program that you could use to draw freehand figures on a dialog window.

You also learned how to grab keyboard events and determine which key is being pressed. You used this information to determine which cursor to display for drawing. For this to work, you had to learn about the default cursor drawing in MFC applications and how you could integrate your code with this behavior to make your application behave the way you want it to.

From here, you will learn how to use the Windows timer to trigger events at regular intervals. You will also learn how to use additional dialog windows to get feedback from the user so that you can integrate that feedback into how your application behaves. After that, you will learn how to create menus for your applications.

Q&A

Q How can I change the type of line that I am drawing? I would like to draw a larger line with a different color.

A When you use any of the standard device context commands to draw on the screen, you are drawing with what is known as a pen, much like the pen you use to draw on a piece of paper. To draw bigger lines, or different color lines, you need to select a new pen. You can do this by adapting the code in the OnMouseMove function, starting where you get the device context. The following code enables you to draw with a big red pen:

```
// Get the Device Context
CClientDC dc(this);

// Create a new pen
CPen lpen(PS_SOLID, 16, RGB(255, 0, 0));
```

```
// Use the new pen
dc.SelectObject(&lpen);

// Draw a line from the previous point to the current point
dc.MoveTo(m_iPrevX, m_iPrevY);
dc.LineTo(point.x, point.y);
```

Q How can you tell whether the Shift or Ctrl keys are being held down when you receive the WM_KEYDOWN message?

A You can call another function, ::GetKeyState, with a specific key code to determine whether that key is being held down. If the return value of the ::GetKeyState function is negative, the key is being held down. If the return value is nonnegative, the key is not being held down. For instance, if you want to determine whether the Shift key is being held down, you can use this code:

```
if (::GetKeyState(VK_SHIFT) < 0)
    MessageBox("Shift key is down!");
```

A number of virtual key codes are defined in Windows for all the special keys. These codes let you look for special keys without worrying about OEM scan codes or other key sequences. You can use these virtual key codes in the ::GetKeyState function and pass them to the OnKeyDown function as the nChar argument. Refer to the Visual C++ documentation for a list of the virtual key codes.

Workshop

The Workshop provides quiz questions to help you solidify your understanding of the material covered and exercises to provide you with experience in using what you've learned. The answers to the quiz questions and exercises are provided in Appendix B, "Answers."

Quiz

1. What are the possible mouse messages that you can add functions for?
2. How can you tell if the left mouse button is down on the WM_MOUSEMOVE event message?
3. How can you prevent the cursor from changing back to the default cursor after you set it to a different one?

Exercises

1. Modify your drawing program so that the left mouse button can draw in red and the right mouse button can draw in blue.

2. Extend the `OnKeyDown` function to add some of the following standard cursors:

- `IDC_CROSS`
- `IDC_UPARROW`
- `IDC_SIZEALL`
- `IDC_SIZENWSE`
- `IDC_SIZENESW`
- `IDC_SIZEWE`
- `IDC_SIZENS`
- `IDC_NO`
- `IDC_APPSTARTING`
- `IDC_HELP`

DAY 4

Working with Timers

You may often find yourself building an application that needs to perform a specific action on a regular basis. The task can be something simple such as displaying the current time in the status bar every second or writing a recovery file every five minutes. Both of these actions are regularly performed by several applications that you probably use on a daily basis. Other actions that you might need to perform include checking specific resources on a regular basis, as a resource monitor or performance monitor does. These examples are just a few of the situations where you want to take advantage of the availability of timers in the Windows operating system.

Today you are going to learn

- How to control and use timers in your Visual C++ applications.
- How to set multiple timers, each with a different recurrence interval.
- How to know which timer has triggered.
- How you can incorporate this important resource into all your Visual C++ applications.

Understanding Windows Timers

Windows timers are mechanisms that let you set one or more timers to be triggered at a specific number of milliseconds. If you set a timer to be triggered at a 1,000 millisecond interval, it triggers every second. When a timer triggers, it sends a WM_TIMER message to your application. You can use the Class Wizard to add a function to your application to handle this timer message.

Timer events are placed only in the application event queue if that queue is empty and the application is idle. Windows does not place timer event messages in the application event queue if the application is already busy. If your application has been busy and has missed several timer event messages, Windows places only a single timer message in the event queue. Windows does not send your application all the timer event messages that occurred while your application was busy. It doesn't matter how many timer messages your application may have missed; Windows still places only a single timer message in your queue.

When you start or stop a timer, you specify a timer ID, which can be any integer value. Your application uses this timer ID to determine which timer event has triggered, as well as to start and stop timers. You'll get a better idea of how this process works as you build your application for today.

Placing a Clock on Your Application

In the application that you will build today, you will use two timers. The first timer maintains a clock on the window. This timer is always running while the application is running. The second timer is configurable to trigger at whatever interval the user specifies in the dialog. The user can start and stop this timer at will. Let's get started.

Creating the Project and Application

You will build today's sample application in three phases. In the first phase, you will add all the controls necessary for the entire application. In the second phase, you will add the first of the two timers. This first timer will control the clock on the application dialog. In the third phase, you will add the second timer, which the user can tune, start, and stop as desired.

To create today's application, follow these steps:

1. Create a new project, named **Timers**, using the same AppWizard settings that you've used for the past three days. Specify the application title as **Timers**.

2. Lay out the dialog window as shown in Figure 4.1, using the control properties in Table 4.1. Remember that when you place a control on the window, you can right-click the mouse to open the control's properties from the pop-up menu.

FIGURE 4.1.

The Timers application dialog layout.

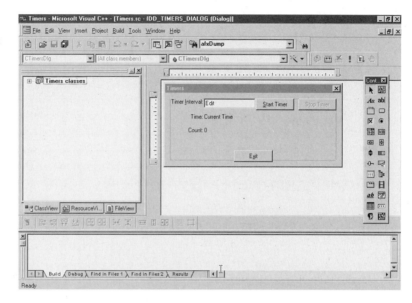

4

TABLE 4.1. CONTROL PROPERTY SETTINGS.

Object	Property	Setting
Static Text	ID	IDC_STATIC
	Caption	Timer &Interval:
Edit Box	ID	IDC_INTERVAL
Button	ID	IDC_STARTTIME
	Caption	&Start Timer
Button	ID	IDC_STOPTIMER
	Caption	S&top Timer
	Disabled	Checked
Static Text	ID	IDC_STATIC
	Caption	Time:
Static Text	ID	IDC_STATICTIME
	Caption	Current Time

continues

TABLE 4.1. CONTINUED

Object	Property	Setting
Static Text	ID	`IDC_STATIC`
	Caption	`Count:`
Static Text	ID	`IDC_STATICCOUNT`
	Caption	`0`
Button	ID	`IDC_EXIT`
	Caption	`E&xit`

3. Set the tab order as you learned on Day 2, "Using Controls in Your Application."

4. Add code to the Exit button to close the application, as you did on Day 2.

Adding the Timer IDs

Because you will be using two timers in this application, you should add two IDs to your application to represent the two timer IDs. This can be done by following these steps:

1. On the Resource View tab in the workspace pane, right-click the mouse over the Timers resources folder at the top of the resource tree. Select Resource Symbols from the pop-up menu, as in Figure 4.2.

FIGURE 4.2.

The Resource pop-up menu.

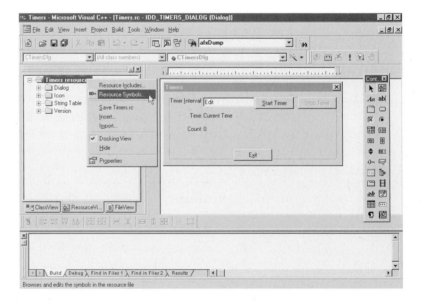

2. On the Resource Symbols dialog, click the New button.

3. On the New Symbol dialog, enter **ID_CLOCK_TIMER** as the symbol name and **1** as the value, as shown in Figure 4.3.

FIGURE 4.3.

Adding a new resource symbol.

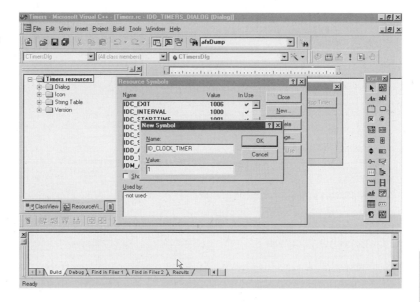

4. Repeat steps 2 and 3, specifying **ID_COUNT_TIMER** as the symbol name and **2** as the value.

5. Click the Close button to close the Resource Symbols dialog. The two timer IDs are now in your application and ready for use.

Starting the Clock Timer

To start the clock timer, you need to edit the OnInitDialog function, as you did in the previous two days. Add the new code in Listing 4.1.

LISTING 4.1. THE OnInitDialog FUNCTION.

```
1: BOOL CTimersDlg::OnInitDialog()
2: {
3:     CDialog::OnInitDialog();
4: .
5: .
6: .
7:     // TODO: Add extra initialization here
8:
9:     /////////////////////////
```

continues

LISTING 4.1. CONTINUED

```
10:     // MY CODE STARTS HERE
11:     ////////////////////////
12:
13:     // Start the clock timer
14:     SetTimer(ID_CLOCK_TIMER, 1000, NULL);
15:
16:     ////////////////////////
17:     // MY CODE ENDS HERE
18:     ////////////////////////
19:
20:     return TRUE;  // return TRUE  unless you set the focus to a
                         ➥control
21: }
```

In this listing, you started the clock timer with the SetTimer function. The first argument that you passed to the SetTimer function is the ID for the clock timer. The second argument is how often you want to trigger the event. In this case, the clock timer event is triggered every 1,000 milliseconds, or about every second. The third argument is the address of an optional callback function that you can specify to bypass the WM_TIMER event. If you pass NULL for this argument, the WM_TIMER event is placed in the application message queue.

> **Note**
>
> A callback function is a function you create that is called directly by the Windows operating system. Callback functions have specific argument definitions, depending on which subsystem calls the function and why. After you get past the function definition, however, you can do whatever you want or need to do in the function.
>
> A callback function works by passing the address of the function as an argument to a Windows function that accepts callback functions as arguments. When you pass the function address to Windows, your function is called directly every time the circumstances occur that require Windows to call the callback function.

Handling the Clock Timer Event

Now that you've started a timer, you need to add the code to handle the timer event message. You can do this by following these steps:

1. Using the Class Wizard, add a variable to the IDC_STATICTIME control of type CString named m_sTime.

2. Using the Class Wizard, add a function to handle the WM_TIMER message for the CTimersDlg object.

3. Edit the OnTimer function, adding the code in Listing 4.2.

LISTING 4.2. THE OnTimer FUNCTION.

```
 1: void CTimersDlg::OnTimer(UINT nIDEvent)
 2: {
 3:     // TODO: Add your message handler code here and/or call default
 4:
 5:     ////////////////////////
 6:     // MY CODE STARTS HERE
 7:     ////////////////////////
 8:
 9:     // Get the current time
10:     CTime curTime = CTime::GetCurrentTime();
11:
12:     // Display the current time
13:     m_sTime.Format("%d:%d:%d", curTime.GetHour(),
14:         curTime.GetMinute(),
15:         curTime.GetSecond());
16:
17:     // Update the dialog
18:     UpdateData(FALSE);
19:
20:     ////////////////////////
21:     // MY CODE ENDS HERE
22:     ////////////////////////
23:
24:     CDialog::OnTimer(nIDEvent);
25: }
```

In this listing, you declare an instance of the CTime class, initializing it to the current system time. The next thing that you do is set the m_sTime string to the current time, using the Format method to format the time in the familiar HH:MM:SS format. Finally, you update the dialog window with the current time. If you compile and run your application now, you should see a clock running in the middle of your dialog window, as in Figure 4.4.

FIGURE 4.4.

A running clock on your application dialog.

Adding a Second Timer to Your Application

As you have seen, adding a single timer to an application is a pretty simple task. All it takes is calling the SetTimer function and then placing the timer code in the OnTimer function. However, sometimes you need more than one timer running simultaneously in the same application. Then things get a little bit more involved.

Adding the Application Variables

Before you add the second timer to your application, you need to add a few variables to the controls. With the clock timer, you needed only a single variable for updating the clock display. Now you need to add a few other variables for the other controls, as listed in Table 4.2.

TABLE 4.2. CONTROL VARIABLES.

Object	Name	Category	Type
IDC_STATICCOUNT	m_sCount	Value	CString
IDC_INTERVAL	m_iInterval	Value	int
IDC_STARTTIME	m_cStartTime	Control	CButton
IDC_STOPTIMER	m_cStopTime	Control	CButton

After you add all the variables using the Class Wizard, follow these steps:

1. Using the Class Wizard, select the m_iInterval variable and specify a Minimum Value of 1 and a Maximum Value of 100000 in the two edit boxes below the list of variables, as shown in Figure 4.5.

FIGURE 4.5.

Specifying a range for a variable.

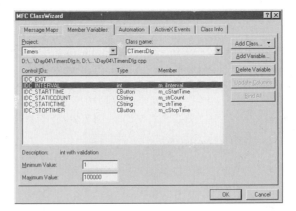

2. On the Class View tab in the workspace pane, add a member variable to the CTimersDlg class as you learned yesterday. Specify the variable type as int, the variable name as m_iCount, and the access as Private.

3. Using the Class Wizard, add a function on the EN_CHANGE event message for the IDC_INTERVAL control ID (the edit box). Edit the function and add the code in Listing 4.3.

LISTING 4.3. THE OnChangeInterval FUNCTION.

```
 1: void CTimersDlg::OnChangeInterval()
 2: {
 3:     // TODO: If this is a RICHEDIT control, the control will not
 4:     // send this notification unless you override the
        ➥CDialog::OnInitialUpdate()
 5:     // function and call CRichEditCrtl().SetEventMask()
 6:     // with the EN_CHANGE flag ORed into the mask.
 7:
 8:     // TODO: Add your control notification handler code here
 9:
10:     ///////////////////////////
11:     // MY CODE STARTS HERE
12:     ///////////////////////////
13:
14:     // Update the variables
15:     UpdateData(TRUE);
16:
17:     ///////////////////////////
18:     // MY CODE ENDS HERE
19:     ///////////////////////////
20: }
```

When you specify a value range for the timer interval variable, Visual C++ automatically prompts the user, stating the available value range if the user enters a value outside of the specified range. This prompt is triggered by the UpdateData function call in the OnChangeInterval function. The last variable that was added through the workspace pane is used as the actual counter, which is incremented with each timer event.

Starting and Stopping the Counting Timer

To make your second timer operational, you need to

- Initialize the m_iInterval variable.
- Start the timer when the IDC_STARTTIME button is clicked.
- Increment the m_iCount variable and update the dialog on each timer event.
- Stop the timer when the IDC_STOPTIMER button is clicked.

To implement this additional functionality, perform the following steps:

1. Edit the OnInitDialog function, updating the code as in Listing 4.4.

LISTING 4.4. THE UPDATED OnInitDialog FUNCTION.

```
1: BOOL CTimersDlg::OnInitDialog()
2: {
3:      CDialog::OnInitDialog();
4: .
5: .
6: .
7:      // TODO: Add extra initialization here
8:
9:      /////////////////////////
10:     // MY CODE STARTS HERE
11:     /////////////////////////
12:
13:     // Initialize the counter interval
14:     m_iInterval = 100;
15:
16:     // Update the dialog
17:     UpdateData(FALSE);
18:
19:     // Start the clock timer
20:     SetTimer(ID_CLOCK_TIMER, 1000, NULL);
21:
22:     /////////////////////////
23:     // MY CODE ENDS HERE
24:     /////////////////////////
25:
26:     return TRUE;  // return TRUE  unless you set the focus to a
                          ➥control
27: }
```

2. Using the Class Wizard, add a function to the BN_CLICKED message on the
    IDC_STARTTIME button. Edit the OnStarttime function as in Listing 4.5.

LISTING 4.5. THE OnStarttime FUNCTION.

```
1: void CTimersDlg::OnStarttime()
2: {
3:      // TODO: Add your control notification handler code here
4:
5:      /////////////////////////
6:      // MY CODE STARTS HERE
7:      /////////////////////////
8:
9:      // Update the variables
```

```
10:        UpdateData(TRUE);
11:
12:        // Initialize the count
13:        m_iCount = 0;
14:        // Format the count for displaying
15:        m_sCount.Format("%d", m_iCount);
16:
17:        // Update the dialog
18:        UpdateData(FALSE);
19:        // Start the timer
20:        SetTimer(ID_COUNT_TIMER, m_iInterval, NULL);
21:
22:        /////////////////////////
23:        // MY CODE ENDS HERE
24:        /////////////////////////
25: }
```

3. Using the Class Wizard, add a function to the BN_CLICKED message on the IDC_STOPTIMER button. Edit the OnStoptimer function as in Listing 4.6.

LISTING 4.6. THE OnStoptimer FUNCTION.

```
1: void CTimersDlg::OnStoptimer()
2: {
3:        // TODO: Add your control notification handler code here
4:
5:        /////////////////////////
6:        // MY CODE STARTS HERE
7:        /////////////////////////
8:
9:        // Stop the timer
10:        KillTimer(ID_COUNT_TIMER);
11:
12:        /////////////////////////
13:        // MY CODE ENDS HERE
14:        /////////////////////////
15: }
```

4. Edit the OnTimer function, updating the code as in Listing 4.7.

LISTING 4.7. THE UPDATED OnTimer FUNCTION.

```
1: void CTimersDlg::OnTimer(UINT nIDEvent)
2: {
3:        // TODO: Add your message handler code here and/or call default
4:
```

continues

LISTING 4.7. CONTINUED

```
 5:      ///////////////////////
 6:      // MY CODE STARTS HERE
 7:      ///////////////////////
 8:
 9:      // Get the current time
10:      CTime curTime = CTime::GetCurrentTime();
11:
12:      // Which timer triggered this event?
13:      switch (nIDEvent)
14:      {
15:          // The clock timer?
16:      case ID_CLOCK_TIMER:
17:          // Display the current time
18:          m_sTime.Format("%d:%d:%d", curTime.GetHour(),
19:              curTime.GetMinute(),
20:              curTime.GetSecond());
21:          break;
22:          // The count timer?
23:      case ID_COUNT_TIMER:
24:          // Increment the count
25:          m_iCount++;
26:          // Format and display the count
27:          m_sCount.Format("%d", m_iCount);
28:          break;
29:      }
30:
31:      // Update the dialog
32:      UpdateData(FALSE);
33:
34:      ///////////////////////
35:      // MY CODE ENDS HERE
36:      ///////////////////////
37:
38:      CDialog::OnTimer(nIDEvent);
39: }
```

In the OnInitDialog function, you added the initialization of the m_iInterval variable, starting it at 100. This initialization is reflected on the dialog window by calling the UpdateData function.

In the OnStarttime function, you first synchronize the variables with the control values, allowing you to get the current setting of the m_iInterval variable. Next, you initialize the m_iCount variable, setting it to 0, and then format the value in the m_sCount CString variable, which is updated in the dialog window. The last thing that you do is to start the timer, specifying the ID_COUNT_TIMER ID and using the interval from the m_iInterval variable.

In the OnStoptimer function, all you really need to do is stop the timer. You do this by calling the KillTimer function, passing the timer ID as the only argument.

It is in the OnTimer function that things begin to get interesting. Here, you still see the code for handling the clock timer event. To add the functionality for the counter timer, you need to determine which timer has triggered this function. The only argument to the OnTimer function just happens to be the timer ID. You can use this ID in a switch statement to determine which timer has called this function and to control which set of code is executed. The clock timer code is still the same as it was in Listing 4.2. The counter timer code is placed into its spot in the switch statement, incrementing the counter and then updating the m_sCount variable with the new value. You can compile and run your application at this point, and you can specify a timer interval and start the timer running, as in Figure 4.6.

FIGURE 4.6.

A running counter on your application dialog.

Enabling the Stop Button

If you run your application, you'll find that it works well except for one small problem. When you start your second timer, you can't stop it. When you were specifying all the properties of the controls, you disabled the Stop Timer button. Before you can stop the timer, you need to enable this button.

What makes the most sense is enabling the stop button and disabling the start button once the timer starts. Then you reverse the situation when the timer stops again. You can do this in the same way you enabled and disabled controls on Day 2, or you can modify your approach just a little.

Remember that when you added variables to the controls, you added variables to the start and stop buttons. These were not normal variables, but control variables. Instead of getting a pointer to these controls using their IDs, you can work directly with the control variables. Try that now by updating the OnStarttime and OnStoptimer functions as in Listing 4.8.

LISTING 4.8. THE REVISED OnStarttime AND OnStoptimer FUNCTIONS.

```
 1: void CTimersDlg::OnStarttime()
 2: {
 3:     // TODO: Add your control notification handler code here
 4:
 5:     //////////////////////////
 6:     // MY CODE STARTS HERE
 7:     //////////////////////////
 8:
 9:     // Update the variables
10:     UpdateData(TRUE);
11:
12:     // Initialize the count
13:     m_iCount = 0;
14:     // Format the count for displaying
15:     m_sCount.Format("%d", m_iCount);
16:
17:     // Update the dialog
18:     UpdateData(FALSE);
19:     // Start the timer
20:     SetTimer(ID_COUNT_TIMER, m_iInterval, NULL);
21:
22:     // Enable the Stop Timer button
23:     m_cStopTime.EnableWindow(TRUE);
24:     // Disable the Start Timer button
25:     m_cStartTime.EnableWindow(FALSE);
26:
27:     //////////////////////////
28:     // MY CODE ENDS HERE
29:     //////////////////////////
30: }
31:
32: void CTimersDlg::OnStoptimer()
33: {
34:     // TODO: Add your control notification handler code here
35:
36:     //////////////////////////
37:     // MY CODE STARTS HERE
38:     //////////////////////////
39:
40:     // Stop the timer
41:     KillTimer(ID_COUNT_TIMER);
42:
43:     // Disable the Stop Timer button
44:     m_cStopTime.EnableWindow(FALSE);
45:     // Enable the Start Timer button
46:     m_cStartTime.EnableWindow(TRUE);
47:
48:     //////////////////////////
49:     // MY CODE ENDS HERE
```

```
50:        ////////////////////////
51: }
```

Now when you compile and run your application, it looks more like Figure 4.7, where you can start and stop the counter timer. This enables you to play with the timer interval, putting in a variety of time intervals and observing the difference, with the clock ticking above the counter for reference.

FIGURE 4.7.

The finished application.

Summary

Today you learned how to use the timers built into the Windows operating system to trigger your application at various time intervals that you can control. You learned how to use multiple timers in the same application, running them simultaneously and triggering different actions.

In the coming days, you'll learn how to use additional dialog windows to get feedback from the user so that you can integrate that feedback into how your application behaves. After that, you will learn how to a create menus for your applications. Then you will learn how you can work with text and fonts in your applications.

Q&A

Q What is the interval range that I can set for timers in my applications?

A The available range that you can set for timers in your applications is around 55 milliseconds on the short end to $2^{32} - 1$ milliseconds, or around 49 1/2 days, on the long end.

Q How many timers can I have running at the same time in my application?

A That depends. There are a limited number of timers available to all applications in the Windows operating system. Although the number that is available should be more than sufficient for all running applications using no more than a handful of timers, if an application goes overboard and begins hogging the timers, the operating system may run out. It could be your application that is denied the use of some timers, or it could be other applications that don't have any to use. As a general

rule, if you use more than two or three timers at the same time, you might want to reconsider your application design and determine if there is another way to design and build your application so that it can work with fewer timers.

Q Is there any way to trigger my application to perform some work when it is idle, instead of using a timer to trigger the work when I think my app might be idle?

A Yes, there is. All Windows applications have an OnIdle function that can be used to trigger idle processing. OnIdle is discussed later on Day 18, "Doing Multiple Tasks at One Time—Multitasking."

Workshop

The Workshop provides quiz questions to help you solidify your understanding of the material covered and exercises to provide you with experience in using what you've learned. The answers to the quiz questions and exercises are provided in Appendix B, "Answers."

Quiz

1. What did you accomplish by adding the two timer IDs to the resource symbols?

2. What is another way to add these two IDs to the application?

3. How can you tell two timers apart in the OnTimer function?

4. How many timer events does your application receive if the timer is set for one second and your application has been busy for one minute, preventing it from receiving any timer event messages?

Exercise

Update your application so that when the counter timer is started, the clock timer is reset to run at the same interval as the counter timer. When the counter timer is stopped, return the clock timer to a one-second interval.

DAY 5

Getting User Feedback— Adding Dialog Boxes to Your Application

With most applications that you might use, there are numerous situations where the application asks you for information—how you want the application configured or whether you want to save your work before exiting, for example. In most of these situations, the application opens a new window to ask these questions. These windows are called dialog windows.

Dialog windows typically have one or more controls and some text explaining what information the program needs from you. Dialog windows typically do not have a large blank work area, as you find in the main windows of a word processor or a programming editor. All the applications that you have built in the preceding days have been dialog windows, and your projects will continue to be dialog windows for the next few days.

All the dialogs that you have created up to now have been single window dialog applications. Today you are going to learn

- How to use dialog windows in a more flexible way.
- How to call other dialog windows and take the information entered by the user on these windows back to the main application window for use in the application.
- How to use both standard dialogs, such as the message boxes you used in previous days and custom dialogs that you have created.

Using Pre-existing (or System) Dialog Windows

The Windows operating system provides a number of pre-existing dialog windows. Simple dialog windows, also known as message boxes, present the user with a message and provide one to three buttons to click. More complex dialogs, such as the File Open, Save, or Print dialogs, are also provided with Windows. These system (or common) dialogs are created and used with a combination of a variable declaration of a C++ class and a series of interactions with the class instance.

Using Message Boxes

As you learned in the previous days, using message boxes is as simple as making a single function call, passing the message text as the only argument. This results in a message box that displays the message to the user with an icon and gives the user one button to click to acknowledge the message. As you probably know from using other Windows software, you have a whole range of other message box possibilities with various button combinations and various icons that can be displayed.

The MessageBox Function

As you have seen in previous days, the MessageBox function can be passed one or two arguments. The first argument is the message to be displayed to the user. The second argument, which is completely optional, is displayed in the title bar on the message box. You can use a third argument, which is also optional, to specify the buttons to be presented to the user and the icon to be displayed beside the message. In addition to this third argument, the MessageBox function returns a result value that indicates which button was clicked by the user. Through the combination of the third argument and the return value, the MessageBox function can provide a whole range of functionality in your Visual C++ applications.

Note

If you use the third argument to the MessageBox function to specify the buttons or the icon to be presented to the user, the second argument (the message box title) is no longer optional. You must provide a value for the title bar of the message box.

The button combinations that you can use in the MessageBox function are limited. You do not have the freedom to make up your own button combination. If you get to the point where you need to make up your own, you have to create a custom dialog window that looks like a message box. The button combinations that you can use are listed in Table 5.1.

TABLE 5.1. MessageBox button combination IDs.

ID	Buttons
MB_ABORTRETRYIGNORE	Abort, Retry, Ignore
MB_OK	OK
MB_OKCANCEL	OK, Cancel
MB_RETRYCANCEL	Retry, Cancel
MB_YESNO	Yes, No
MB_YESNOCANCEL	Yes, No, Cancel

To specify the icon to be displayed, you can add the icon ID to the button combination ID. The icons that are available are listed in Table 5.2. If you want to specify either the icon or the button combination, and you want to use the default for the other, you can just specify the one ID that you want to use.

TABLE 5.2. MessageBox icon IDs.

ID	Icon
MB_ICONINFORMATION	Informational icon
MB_ICONQUESTION	Question mark icon
MB_ICONSTOP	Stop sign icon
MB_ICONEXCLAMATION	Exclamation mark icon

When you do specify a button combination, you want to capture the return value so that you can determine which button the user clicked. The return value is defined as an integer data type; the return value IDs are listed in Table 5.3.

5

TABLE 5.3. MessageBox return value IDs.

ID	Button Clicked
IDABORT	Abort
IDRETRY	Retry
IDIGNORE	Ignore
IDYES	Yes
IDNO	No
IDOK	OK
IDCANCEL	Cancel

Creating a Dialog Application

To get a good understanding of how you can use the MessageBox function in your applications to get information from the user, you will build a simple application that uses the MessageBox function in a couple of different ways. Your application will have two separate buttons that call two different versions of the MessageBox function so that you can see the differences and similarities between the various options of the function. Later in the day, you will add a standard File Open dialog so that you can see how the standard dialogs can be used to allow the user to specify a filename or perform other standard functions. Finally, you will create a custom dialog that allows the user to enter a few different types of values, and you will see how you can read these values from the main application dialog after the user has closed the custom dialog.

To start this application, follow these steps:

1. Create a new MFC AppWizard workspace project, naming it **Dialogs**.
2. Choose the same settings as for the previous days' applications, giving the application a title of **Dialogs**.
3. Lay out the main application dialog as shown in Figure 5.1 using the properties in Table 5.4.

TABLE 5.4. Control property settings.

Object	Property	Setting
Command Button	ID	IDC_YESNOCANCEL
	Caption	&Yes, No, Cancel
Command Button	ID	IDC_ABORTRETRYIGNORE
	Caption	&Abort, Retry, Ignore

Object	Property	Setting
Command Button	ID	IDC_FILEOPEN
	Caption	&File Open
Command Button	ID	IDC_BCUSTOMDIALOG
	Caption	&Custom Dialog
Command Button	ID	IDC_BWHICHOPTION
	Caption	&Which Option?
	Disabled	Checked
Command Button	ID	IDC_EXIT
	Caption	E&xit
Static Text	ID	IDC_STATIC
	Caption	Dialog Results:
Edit Box	ID	IDC_RESULTS
	Multiline	Checked
	Auto Vscroll	Checked

FIGURE 5.1.

The application main dialog layout.

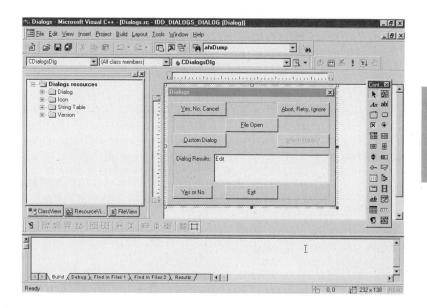

4. Using the Class Wizard, attach variables to the controls as listed in Table 5.5.

TABLE 5.5. CONTROL VARIABLES.

Object	Name	Category	Type
IDC_RESULTS	m_sResults	Value	CString
IDC_BWHICHOPTION	m_cWhichOption	Control	CButton

5. Using the Class Wizard, attach code to the Exit button to close the application, as on previous days.

Coding the Message Box Dialogs

For the first command button (the Yes, No, Cancel button), create a function on the clicked event using the Class Wizard, just as you did on previous days. Edit the function on this button, adding the code in Listing 5.1.

LISTING 5.1. THE OnYesnocancel FUNCTIONS.

```
 1: void CDialogsDlg::OnYesnocancel()
 2: {
 3:     // TODO: Add your control notification handler code here
 4:
 5:     ///////////////////////
 6:     // MY CODE STARTS HERE
 7:     ///////////////////////
 8:
 9:     int iResults; // This variable will capture the button selection
10:
11:     // Ask the user
12:     iResults = MessageBox("Press the Yes, No, or Cancel button",
13:                 "Yes, No, Cancel Dialog",
14:                 MB_YESNOCANCEL | MB_ICONINFORMATION);
15:
16:     // Determine which button the user clicked
17:     // Give the user a message showing which button was clicked
18:     switch (iResults)
19:     {
20:     case IDYES:     // The Yes button?
21:         m_sResults = "Yes! Yes! Yes!";
22:         break;
23:     case IDNO:      // The No button?
24:         m_sResults = "No, no, no, no, no.";
25:         break;
26:     case IDCANCEL:      // The Cancel button?
27:         m_sResults = "Sorry, canceled.";
28:         break;
29:     }
30:
31:     // Update the dialog
```

```
32:     UpdateData(FALSE);
33:
34:     //////////////////////
35:     // MY CODE ENDS HERE
36:     //////////////////////
37: }
```

If you compile and run your application, you can see how selecting the different buttons on the message box can determine the next course of action in your application. If you add a function to the clicked event of the Abort, Retry, Ignore button using the Class Wizard and enter the same code as in Listing 5.1, substituting the MB_ABORTRETRYIGNORE and MB_ICONQUESTION values and changing the prompts and messages, you can see how this other button combination can be used in the same way.

Both of these control event functions are virtually the same. In each function, there is an integer variable declared to capture the return value from the MessageBox function. Next, the MessageBox function is called with a message to be displayed to the user, a title for the message box, and a combination of a button combination ID and an icon ID.

When the return value is captured from the MessageBox function, that value is passed through a switch statement to determine which value was returned. A message is displayed to the user to indicate which button was clicked on the message box. You can just as easily use one or two if statements to control the program execution based on the user's selection, but the return value being an integer lends itself to using a switch statement.

If you compile and run your application at this point, you can click either of the top two buttons and see a message box, as in Figure 5.2. When you click one of the message box buttons, you see a message in the edit box on the main dialog, indicating which button you selected, as in Figure 5.3.

FIGURE 5.2.

The MessageBox *with three choices.*

FIGURE 5.3.

A message is displayed based on which button was clicked.

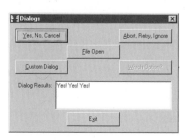

Using Common Dialogs

Using common dialogs is not quite as simple and easy as using the MessageBox function, but it's still quite easy. The Microsoft Foundation Classes (MFC) provides several C++ classes for common Windows dialogs. These classes are listed in Table 5.6.

TABLE 5.6. COMMON DIALOG CLASSES.

Class	Dialog Type
CFileDialog	File selection
CFontDialog	Font selection
CColorDialog	Color selection
CPageSetupDialog	Page setup for printing
CPrintDialog	Printing
CFindReplaceDialog	Find and Replace

The common dialogs encapsulated in these classes are the standard dialogs that you use every day in most Windows applications to open and save files, configure printing options, print, perform find and replace on documents, and so on. In addition to these choices, a series of OLE common dialog classes provide several common functions to OLE or ActiveX components and applications.

All these dialogs are used in the same manner, although the individual properties and class functions vary according to the dialog functionality. To use one of these dialogs, you must follow these steps:

1. Declare a variable of the class type.
2. Set any properties that need to be configured before displaying the dialog to the user.
3. Call the DoModal method of the class to display the dialog to the user.
4. Capture the return value of the DoModal method to determine whether the user clicked the OK or Cancel button.
5. If the user clicks the OK button, read any properties that the user may have set when using the dialog.

To better understand how this works, you'll add the CFileDialog class to your application. To do this, add a function to the clicked message on the File Open button using the Class Wizard. Edit this function, adding the code in Listing 5.2.

LISTING 5.2. THE OnFileopen FUNCTION.

```
 1: void CDialogsDlg::OnFileopen()
 2: {
 3:     // TODO: Add your control notification handler code here
 4:
 5:     ////////////////////////
 6:     // MY CODE STARTS HERE
 7:     ////////////////////////
 8:
 9:     CFileDialog m_ldFile(TRUE);
10:
11:     // Show the File open dialog and capture the result
12:     if (m_ldFile.DoModal() == IDOK)
13:     {
14:         // Get the filename selected
15:         m_sResults = m_ldFile.GetFileName();
16:         // Update the dialog
17:         UpdateData(FALSE);
18:     }
19:
20:     ////////////////////////
21:     // MY CODE ENDS HERE
22:     ////////////////////////
23: }
```

In this code, the first thing that you do is declare an instance of the CFileDialog class. This instance is passed TRUE as an argument to the class constructor. This tells the class that it is a File Open dialog. If you pass it FALSE, it displays as a File Save dialog. There's no real functional difference between these two, only a visual difference. You can pass many more arguments to the constructor, specifying the file extensions to show, the default starting file and location, and filters to use when displaying the files. All the rest of these constructor arguments have default values, so you don't have to supply any of them.

After creating the instance of the File Open dialog, you call its DoModal function. This is a member function of the CDialog ancestor class, and it is available in all dialog windows. The DoModal function displays the File Open dialog to the user, as shown in Figure 5.4. The return value of the DoModal function is examined to determine which button the user clicked. If the user clicks the Open button, the IDOK value is returned, as with the MessageBox function. This is how you can determine whether your application needs to take any action on what the user selected with the dialog window.

5

FIGURE 5.4.

The File Open dialog.

> **Note**
>
> There are two modes in which a dialog window can be displayed to the user. The first is as a modal window. A modal window halts all other user interaction while it is displayed. The user cannot do anything else in the application until the dialog is closed. A good example of a modal dialog window is a message box where the user cannot continue working with the application until she clicks one of the buttons on the message box.
>
> The second mode in which a dialog window can be displayed to the user is as a modeless window. A modeless window can be open while the user is doing something else in the application, and it doesn't prevent the user from performing other tasks while the dialog is visible. Good examples of a modeless dialog window are the Find and Find and Replace dialogs in Microsoft Word. These dialog windows can be open and displayed on the screen while you are still editing the document that you are searching.

To display the name of the file selected, you set the m_sResults variable to the return value from the GetFileName method of the CFileDialog class. This method returns only the filename without the directory path or drive name, as shown in Figure 5.5. You can use other class methods for getting the directory path (GetPathName) or file extension (GetFileExt).

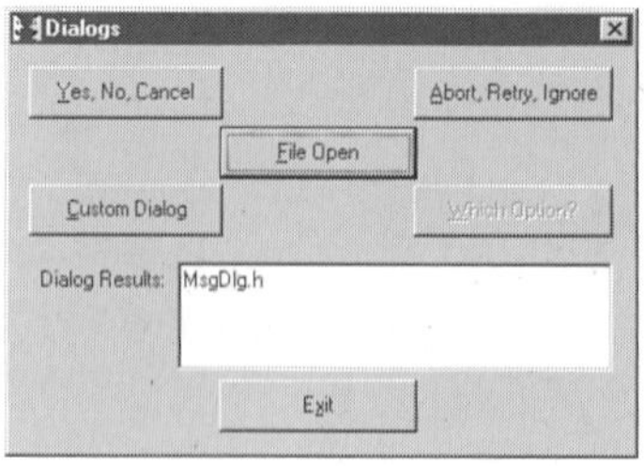

FIGURE 5.5.

Displaying the selected filename.

Creating Your Own Dialog Windows

Now you have an understanding of using standard dialogs. What if you need to create a custom dialog for your application? This task is fairly simple to do because it is mostly a combination of the process that you have already used to create and use the main dialog windows in all your applications and the methods you employed to use the common dialogs. You have to work through a few additional steps, but they are few and you should be comfortable with them soon.

Creating the Dialog Window

For the custom dialog that you will add to your application, you will provide the user with a edit box in which to enter some text and a group of radio buttons from which the user can select one. When the user clicks the OK button, your application will display the text entered by the user in the display area of the main application dialog window. There is another button that the user can click to display which one of the radio buttons was selected. This exercise enables you to see how you can use custom dialog windows to gather information from the user and how you can read the user's selections after the dialog window is closed.

To create a custom dialog for your application, you need to

- Add another dialog to your application resources.
- Design the dialog window layout.
- Declare the base class from which the dialog will be inherited.
- Attach variables to the controls on the dialog.

After doing these things, your custom dialog will be ready for your application. To accomplish these tasks, follow these steps:

1. Select the Resource View tab in the project workspace pane.
2. Right-click the Dialogs folder, and select Insert Dialog from the pop-up menu.
3. Right-click the new dialog in the resource tree view, and select Properties from the pop-up menu.
4. Change the object ID for the new dialog to IDD_MESSAGEDLG.
5. When editing the new dialog window, do not delete the OK and Cancel buttons. Move them to the location shown in Figure 5.6.

5

FIGURE 5.6.

The custom dialog window layout.

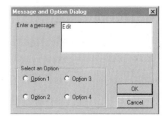

6. Design the rest of the window using the object properties in Table 5.7.

TABLE 5.7. THE CUSTOM DIALOG CONTROL PROPERTY SETTINGS.

Object	Property	Setting
Static Text	ID	IDC_STATIC
	Caption	Enter a &message:
Edit Box	ID	IDC_MESSAGE
	Multiline	Checked
	Auto Vscroll	Checked
Group Box	ID	IDC_STATIC
	Caption	Select an Option
Radio Button	ID	IDC_OPTION1
	Caption	&Option 1
	Group	Checked
Radio Button	ID	IDC_OPTION2
	Caption	O&ption 2
Radio Button	ID	IDC_OPTION3
	Caption	Op&tion 3
Radio Button	ID	IDC_OPTION4
	Caption	Opt&ion 4

7. After you design the dialog, open the Class Wizard. You see the dialog in Figure 5.7.

FIGURE 5.7.

The Adding a Class dialog.

8. Leave the selection on this dialog at the default setting of Create a New Class and click OK. Another dialog appears to allow you to specify the name for the new class and the base class from which it is inherited.

9. Enter the class name **CMsgDlg** into the Name field, and make sure that the Base Class is set to CDialog, as shown in Figure 5.8.

FIGURE 5.8.

The New Class dialog.

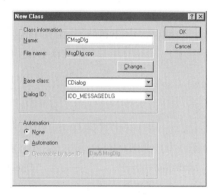

10. Click OK, leaving the other settings on this dialog at their defaults.

11. Once the Class Wizard opens, attach the variables to the controls on the new dialog as specified in Table 5.8.

TABLE 5.8. CONTROL VARIABLES.

Object	Name	Category	Type
IDC_MESSAGE	m_sMessage	Value	CString
IDC_OPTION1	m_iOption	Value	int

You should notice two things in the way that you configured the control properties and variables in the custom dialog. First, you should have selected the Group property on only the first of the radio buttons. This designates that all the radio buttons following that one belong to a single group, where only one of the radio buttons may be selected at a time. If you select the Group property on all the radio buttons, they are all independent of each other, allowing you to select all the buttons simultaneously. This property makes them behave somewhat like check boxes, but the primary difference is that the user would find it difficult to uncheck one of these controls due to the default behavior where one radio button in each group is always checked. The other difference is in their appearance; the radio buttons have round selection areas instead of the square areas of check boxes.

5

The other thing to notice is that you declared a single integer variable for the one radio button with the Group property checked. This variable value is controlled by which radio button is selected. The first radio button causes this variable to have a value of 0, the second sets this variable to 1, and so on. Likewise, if you want to automatically select a particular radio button, you can set this variable to one less than the sequence number of the radio button in the group of radio buttons.

Note
> Because this is the C++ programming language, all numbering begins with 0, not 1. Therefore, the first position in an array or a set of controls is position 0. The second position is position 1. The third position is number 2, and so on.

You have now finished all that you need to do to the second dialog window to make it ready for use. You would expect to need an `UpdateData` or two in the code behind the dialog, but because you didn't remove the OK and Cancel buttons from the dialog, the `UpdateData` call is already performed when the user clicks the OK button. As a result, you don't have to touch any code in this second dialog, only in the first dialog.

Using the Dialog in Your Application

Now that your custom dialog is ready for your application, using it is similar to the way that you use the common dialogs that are built into Windows. First, you have to declare an instance of the custom dialog class, which calls the class constructor and creates an instance of the class. Next, you call the dialog's `DoModal` method and capture the return value of that function. Finally, you read the values of the variables that you associated with the controls on the dialog.

Creating the Dialog Instance

Before you can use your custom dialog in your application, you have to make your main dialog window aware of the custom dialog, its variables, and methods and how your main dialog can interact with your custom dialog. You accomplish this by including the header file for your custom dialog in the main source file for your main application dialog. Follow these steps:

1. Select the File View tab on the workspace pane.

2. Expand the Dialog Files and Source Files folders.

3. Double-click the `DialogsDlg.cpp` file. This opens the source code file for the main application dialog in the editing area of Developer Studio.

4. Scroll to the top of the source code file where the #include statements are located, and add an include for the MsgDlg.h file before the DialogsDlg.h file, as in Listing 5.3.

LISTING 5.3. THE HEADER FILE INCLUDES.

```
 1: // DialogsDlg.cpp : implementation file
 2: //
 3:
 4: #include "stdafx.h"
 5: #include "Dialogs.h"
 6: #include "MsgDlg.h"
 7: #include "DialogsDlg.h"
 8:
 9: #ifdef _DEBUG
10: #define new DEBUG_NEW
11: #undef THIS_FILE
12: static char THIS_FILE[] = __FILE__;
13: #endif
14:
15://////////////////////////////////////////////////////////////////////
16: // CAboutDlg dialog used for App About
```

It is important that you place the #include statement for the MsgDlg.h file before the #include statement for the DialogsDlg.h file. The reason is that you will be adding a variable declaration for your custom dialog to the main dialog class in the main dialog's header file. If the MsgDlg.h header file is included after the header file for the main dialog, the compiler will complain loudly and will refuse to compile your application until you move the #include of the MsgDlg.h file above the #include of the DialogsDlg.h file.

5

Note

The #include statement is what is known as a compiler directive in the C and C++ programming languages. What it tells the compiler to do is read the contents of the file named into the source code that is being compiled. It is used to separate class, structure, and function declarations into a file that can be included in any source code that needs to be aware of the information in the header file. For more information on how the #include statements work, and why you use them, see Appendix A, "C++ Review."

Now that you have made your main application dialog aware of the custom dialog that you created, you need to declare a variable of your custom dialog. Follow these steps:

1. Select the Class View tab in the workspace pane.
2. Right-click the CDialogsDlg class to bring up the pop-up menu.
3. Select Add Member Variable from the pop-up menu.
4. Specify the Variable Type as **CMsgDlg**, the Variable Name as **m_dMsgDlg**, and the Access as Private. Click OK to add the variable to your main dialog.

If you expand the CDialogsDlg class in the tree view, you should see the instance of your custom dialog as a member of the main application dialog class. This means that you are ready to begin using the custom dialog in your application.

Calling the Dialog and Reading the Variables

Now that you have added your custom dialog to the main application dialog as a variable that is always available, not just as a local variable available only within a single function (as with the CFileDialog variable), you can add code to use the dialog. To do this, follow these steps:

1. Open the Class Wizard and add a function to the clicked event message of the IDC_BCUSTOMDIALOG button.
2. Add a function for the clicked event message (BN_CLICKED) for the IDC_BWHICHOPTION button.
3. Edit the OnBcustomdialog function, adding the code in Listing 5.4.

LISTING 5.4. THE OnBcustomdialog FUNCTION.

```
 1: void CDialogsDlg::OnBcustomdialog()
 2: {
 3:     // TODO: Add your control notification handler code here
 4:
 5:     ////////////////////////
 6:     // MY CODE STARTS HERE
 7:     ////////////////////////
 8:
 9:     // Show the message dialog and capture the result
10:     if (m_dMsgDlg.DoModal () == IDOK)
11:     {
12:         // The user checked OK, display the message the
13:         // user typed in on the message dialog
14:         m_sResults = m_dMsgDlg.m_sMessage;
15:         // Update the dialog
16:         UpdateData(FALSE);
17:         // Enable the Which Option button
```

```
18:            m_cWhichOption.EnableWindow(TRUE);
19:        }
20:
21:        /////////////////////////
22:        // MY CODE ENDS HERE
23:        /////////////////////////
24: }
```

4. Edit the OnBwhichoption function, adding the code in Listing 5.5.

LISTING 5.5. THE OnBwhichoption FUNCTION.

```
1: void CDialogsDlg::OnBwhichoption()
2: {
3:     // TODO: Add your control notification handler code here
4:
5:     /////////////////////////
6:     // MY CODE STARTS HERE
7:     /////////////////////////
8:
9:     // Determine which radio button was selected, and display
10:     // a message for the user to show which one was selected.
11:     switch(m_dMsgDlg.m_iOption)
12:     {
13:     case 0:    // Was it the first radio button?
14:         m_sResults = "The first option was selected.";
15:         break;
16:     case 1:    // Was it the second radio button?
17:         m_sResults = "The second option was selected.";
18:         break;
19:     case 2:    // Was it the third radio button?
20:         m_sResults = "The third option was selected.";
21:         break;
22:     case 3:    // Was it the fourth radio button?
23:         m_sResults = "The fourth option was selected.";
24:         break;
25:     default:    // Were none of the radio buttons selected?
26:         m_sResults = "No option was selected.";
27:         break;
28:     }
29:
30:     // Update the dialog
31:     UpdateData(FALSE);
32:
33:     /////////////////////////
34:     // MY CODE ENDS HERE
35:     /////////////////////////
36:
```

5

In the first listing, you called the DoModal method of the custom dialog, which displayed the dialog for the user, waiting for the user to click one of the two buttons on the dialog, as in Figure 5.9. If the user clicks the OK button, you copy the message the user typed in the custom dialog into the edit box variable to be displayed to the user. After updating the dialog display with the new variable values, you enable the Which Option button, as shown in Figure 5.10. If the user clicks the Cancel button, none of this is done. The dialog display is not changed.

FIGURE 5.9.

The custom dialog allows the user to enter a message.

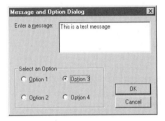

FIGURE 5.10.

The message entered on the custom dialog is displayed for the user.

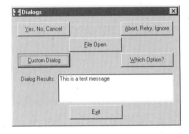

When the user clicks the Which Option button, you pass the radio button variable on the custom dialog to a switch statement, selecting a message that tells the user which radio button was selected, as shown in Figure 5.11. Notice that in both of these functions, you can access the control variables on the custom dialog directly from the main dialog. That is because the Class Wizard automatically declares the variables associated with controls as public, making them completely accessible outside the dialog class. You can change this by placing a private: access specifier where the public: access specifier is. You don't want to place anything after the //{{AFX_DATA line, where the variables are declared, because the variables are declared within an MFC Class Wizard macro, which enables the Developer Studio wizards to locate and manipulate the variables as needed without interfering with the Visual C++ compiler when you compile your application.

FIGURE 5.11.

The option selected on the custom dialog is displayed for the user.

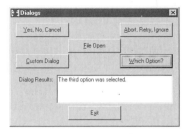

Summary

Today you learned how you can use additional dialog windows in your application to provide interactive experience for your users. You learned about the options available to you with the simple MessageBox function, how you can provide your users a variety of button combinations, and how you can determine which button the user selects. You saw how you can use this information to determine which path to take in your application logic.

You also learned about some of the common dialogs that are built into the Windows operating systems and how they have been encapsulated into C++ classes in the MFC class library. You learned how you can use the File Open dialog to present the user with the standard file selection dialog and how you can determine which file the user selected.

Finally, you learned how you can design your own additional dialogs that you can add to your applications to get information from the user and how you can capture that information and use it in your application.

Q&A

Q **There was no code added to the custom dialog. Do I have to design my custom dialogs this way, or can I add code to them?**

A The custom dialog windows are no different from the main dialog windows that you have been using in all your applications so far. If you need to control the behavior of the dialog on an interactive basis, you can put as much code into the dialog as you need. You didn't add any code to the custom dialog today because there wasn't any need to add any code. The only functionality that the dialog needed to perform was calling the UpdateData function before closing, which is automatically done by the OnOK function. Because you did not delete the OK and Cancel buttons, you already had this functionality built in.

Q What happens if I specify two or more button combinations in the same MessageBox function call?

A Nothing happens. Your application compiles just fine, but when the MessageBox function is called, nothing happens. The message box does not open, and the user does not get to answer the question you are presenting.

Q How can I integrate the File Open dialog into my application where it opens in a specific directory that I specify?

A The CFileDialog class has a public property called m_ofn. This property is a structure that contains numerous attributes of the File Open dialog, including the initial directory. This structure is defined as the OPENFILENAME structure in Listing 5.6.

LISTING 5.6. THE OPENFILENAME STRUCTURE.

```
 1: typedef struct tagOFN { // ofn
 2:      DWORD           lStructSize;
 3:      HWND            hwndOwner;
 4:      HINSTANCE       hInstance;
 5:      LPCTSTR         lpstrFilter;
 6:      LPTSTR          lpstrCustomFilter;
 7:      DWORD           nMaxCustFilter;
 8:      DWORD           nFilterIndex;
 9:      LPTSTR          lpstrFile;
10:      DWORD           nMaxFile;
11:      LPTSTR          lpstrFileTitle;
12:      DWORD           nMaxFileTitle;
13:      LPCTSTR         lpstrInitialDir;
14:      LPCTSTR         lpstrTitle;
15:      DWORD           Flags;
16:      WORD            nFileOffset;
17:      WORD            nFileExtension;
18:      LPCTSTR         lpstrDefExt;
19:      DWORD           lCustData;
20:      LPOFNHOOKPROC   lpfnHook;
21:      LPCTSTR         lpTemplateName;
22: } OPENFILENAME;
```

You can set any of these attributes before calling the DoModal class method to control the behavior of the File Open dialog. For instance, if you set the starting directory to C:\Temp before calling the DoModal method, as in Listing 5.7, the File Open dialog opens in that directory.

LISTING 5.7. THE REVISED OnFileopen FUNCTION.

```
 1: void CDialogsDlg::OnFileopen()
 2: {
 3:     // TODO: Add your control notification handler code here
 4:
 5:     //////////////////////////
 6:     // MY CODE STARTS HERE
 7:     //////////////////////////
 8:
 9:     CFileDialog m_ldFile(TRUE);
10:
11:     // Initialize the starting directory
12:     m_ldFile.m_ofn.lpstrInitialDir = "C:\\Temp\\";
13:
14:     // Show the File open dialog and capture the result
15:     if (m_ldFile.DoModal() == IDOK)
16:     {
17:         // Get the filename selected
18:         m_sResults = m_ldFile.GetFileName();
19:         // Update the dialog
20:         UpdateData(FALSE);
21:     }
22:
23:     //////////////////////////
24:     // MY CODE ENDS HERE
25:     //////////////////////////
26: }
```

5

Workshop

The Workshop provides quiz questions to help you solidify your understanding of the material covered and exercises to provide you with experience in using what you've learned. The answers to the quiz questions and exercises are provided in Appendix B, "Answers."

Quiz

1. What are the possible return codes that your application might receive from the MessageBox function call when you specify the MB_RETRYCANCEL button combination?

2. What are the common dialogs that are built into the Windows operating systems that are defined as MFC classes?

3. What is the difference between a modal dialog and a modeless dialog?

4. How can you display a File Save dialog for the user instead of the File Open dialog that you did have in your application?

5. Why did you not need to create any functions and add any code to your custom dialog?

Exercises

1. Modify your application so that it includes the directory with the filename in the application. (Hint: The GetPathName function returns the path and filename that was selected in the File Open dialog.)

2. Add a button on the custom dialog that calls the MessageBox function with a Yes or No selection. Pass the result back to the main application dialog.

DAY 6

Creating Menus for Your Application

Most Windows applications use pull-down menus to provide the user a number of functions without having to provide buttons on the window. This enables you to provide your users a large amount of functionality while preserving most of your valuable screen real estate for other stuff.

Today you will learn

- How to create menus for your Visual C++ application
- How to attach a menu to your application's main dialog window
- How to call application functions from a menu
- How to create a pop-up menu that can be triggered with the right mouse button
- How to set up accelerator keys for keyboard shortcuts to menus

Menus

Back when the first computer terminals were introduced and users began using computer software, even on large mainframe systems software developers found the need to provide the users with some sort of menu of the functions that the computer could perform. These early menus were crude by today's standards and were difficult to use and navigate. Menus have progressed since then; they've become standardized in how they are used and easy to learn.

The software designers that first came up with the idea of a graphical user interface (GUI) planned to make computer systems and applications easier to learn by making everything behave in a consistent manner. Menus used for selecting application functionality were one part of the GUI design that could be more easily learned if they all worked the same. As a result, a number of standard menu styles were developed.

Menu Styles

The first menu styles that were standardized are the pull-down and cascading menus. These are the menus with the categories all listed in a row across the top of the application window. If you select one of the categories, a menu drops down below the category, with a number of menu entries that can be selected to trigger various functions in the application.

A variation on this menu style is the *cascading menu*, which has another submenu that opens to the right of a menu entry. This submenu is similar to the pull-down menu, with a number of entries that trigger application functions. The menu designers placed no limit on how many cascading menus can be strung together, but it quickly became clear to most developers that more than two cascading levels is a little unwieldy.

Eventually, a third style of menu was developed, called a *pop-up* or *context menu*—a menu that pops up in the middle of the application area, floating freely above the application work area. This is also called a context menu because the specific menu that pops up is dependent on the selected object or workspace area where the cursor or mouse pointer is.

Keyboard Shortcut–Enabling Menus

When users began working with keyboard-intensive applications, such as word processors, it was discovered that taking your hands off the keyboard to use the mouse to make menu selections dramatically reduced productivity. Software designers decided that they needed to add keyboard shortcuts for the various menu entries (especially the most frequently used menu options). For this reason, keyboard shortcuts (accelerators) and hotkeys were added.

Hotkeys are letters that are underlined in each menu entry. If you press the Alt key with the underlined letter, you can select the menu entry that contains the underlined letter. This is a means of navigating application menus without taking your hands off the keyboard.

For more advanced users, application designers added *keyboard shortcuts*, or *accelerators*. An accelerator is a single key combination that you can press to trigger an application function instead of having to navigate through the application menus. This allows advanced users to avoid the overhead of using menus for the most common application functions. To enable users to learn what accelerators are available in an application, the key combination is placed on the menu entry that it can be used to replace, positioned at the right edge of the menu window.

Menu Standards and Conventions

Although there are no standards in how menus are designed, there are a number of conventions for how they are designed and organized. All these conventions are available in *Windows Interface Guidelines for Software Design*, published by Microsoft for use by Windows software developers. The purpose of this publication is to facilitate the development of consistent application behaviors, which will help accomplish one of the primary goals behind the development of GUI systems. The conventions are as follows:

- Use single-word menu categories across the top menu bar. A two-word category can easily be mistaken for two one-word categories.
- The File menu is located as the first menu on the left. It contains all file-oriented functions (such as New, Open, Save, Print, and so on), as well as the Exit function. The Exit option is located at the bottom of the menu, separated from the rest of the menu entries by a border.
- The Edit menu is next to the File menu. The Edit menu contains all editing functions such as Copy, Cut, Paste, Undo, Redo, and so on.
- The View menu contains menu entries that control and affect the appearance of the application work area.
- The Window menu is used in Multiple Document Interface (MDI) style applications. This has functions for controlling the child windows, selecting the current window, and altering the layout. This menu is the next-to-last menu from the right end of the menu bar.
- The Help menu is the final menu on the right end of the menu bar. It contains menu entries that provide instruction or documentation on the application. If the application has any copyrighted or corporate information that needs to be available for viewing, this should be located as the final entry on this menu, labeled About *<application name>*.

6

Designing Menus

Menus are defined as a resource in Visual C++ applications. Because they are a resource, you can design menus in the Visual C++ editor through the Resource View tab on the workspace pane. When you first create a dialog-style application, there won't be a menu folder in the resource tree, but you can change that.

> **Note**
>
> Various aspects of Windows applications are considered to be resources, including window layouts, menus, toolbars, images, text strings, accelerators, and so on. All these features are organized in what is known as a *resource file*, which is used by the Visual C++ compiler to create these objects from their definitions. The resource file is a text file with an .rc filename extension and contains a textual description of all the various objects, including IDs, captions, dimensions, and so on.
>
> Some resources, such as images and sounds, cannot be described in text, but have to be stored in a binary format. These resources are stored in individual files, with the filenames and locations included in the resource file.

Creating a Menu

Creating a menu is not difficult. You will follow several steps:

1. Create the application that will house the menu.
2. Add a menu resource to your project.
3. Customize the menu resource to include the menu items for your application.
4. Add functionality to your menu by connecting routines to your menu items.

Creating the Application

For the example in this chapter, you will create a simple dialog-style application that contains a single button and a menu. To create your application, do the following:

1. Create a new MFC AppWizard application, naming the project **Menus**.
2. Select the default AppWizard settings on all screens. For the dialog title, enter **Menus**.
3. When the AppWizard has generated your application shell, delete all the controls from the dialog.
4. Add a single button to the dialog. Name the button IDC_EXIT, and specify the caption as E&xit.

5. Add a function to the button using the Class Wizard. Change the code in this function to call OnOK. Remember, the OnOK function causes the application to close.

Note

> If you don't remember how to add the OnOK function, review the section "Closing the Application" on Day 2, "Using Controls in Your Application," for an example.

Adding and Customizing a Menu

Now that you have the basic application built, it's time to start creating a menu for the application. To create a menu, you will first add a menu resource to your project. When you add the resource, Visual C++ automatically invokes the Menu Designer, which allows you to customize the menu. The following steps show you how to add and customize a menu:

1. Select the Resource View tab in the workspace pane.

2. Select the project resources folder at the top of the tree; in your example, this is Menus.

3. Right-click the mouse to bring up a pop-up menu.

4. Select Insert from the pop-up menu.

5. In the Insert Resource dialog that opens, select Menu from the list of available resources, as in Figure 6.1. Click the New button.

FIGURE 6.1.

The Insert Resource dialog.

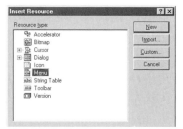

6

6. The Menu Designer opens in the editing area of Developer Studio. The first menu spot is highlighted, as shown in Figure 6.2.

FIGURE 6.2.

An empty menu.

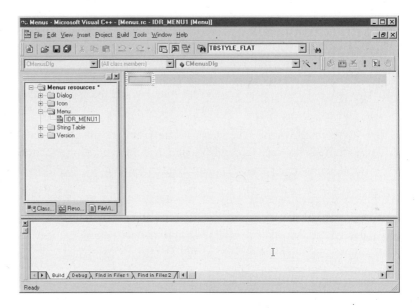

At this point, you have created the menu resource and you are ready to customize it by adding menu items. To add a menu item, follow these steps:

1. Right-click the mouse on the highlighted area and select Properties from the pop-up menu.

2. Enter the menu item's Caption. For this example, enter **&File** and close the Properties dialog.

Note

> You are in the menu Properties dialog to specify the text that the user will see on the menu bar while the application is running. Because the Pop-up check box is checked (by default on any menu items on the top-level menu bar), this menu element doesn't trigger any application functionality and thus doesn't need to have an object ID assigned to it.

3. The first drop-down menu location is highlighted. To add this menu item, right-click the mouse again on the highlighted area and select Properties from the pop-up menu.

4. Enter an ID and caption for the menu item. For this example, enter **IDM_FILE_HELLO** for the ID and **&Hello** for the Caption. Close the dialog.

Note

This time in the menu Properties dialog, you not only specify the text that the user will see when the menu is opened from the menu bar, but you also specify the object ID that will be used in the event message handler to determine what function receives each of the menu events.

At this point you have created a menu with a single menu item. You can continue to add menu items by repeating steps 3 and 4 of the preceding list for each of the highlighted areas. You can also add separators onto the menu. A *separator* is a dividing line that runs across the menu to separate two functional areas of menu selections. To add a separator, perform the following steps:

FIGURE 6.3.

Specifying a menu separator.

1. Select the highlighted area where you want the separator to be placed. In the example you created, the second drop-down menu location should be highlighted. Open the properties dialog as you did in step 3 in the preceding list. To add a separator, simply select the Separator option, as shown in Figure 6.3, and close the dialog.

To complete your sample program, follow the same steps I just described to add an Exit item to your File menu and a second menu called Help with one menu item called About. The following steps, which resemble the preceding list of steps, walk you through adding these additional items:

1. Open the properties dialog for the third drop-down location and specify the ID as IDM_FILE_EXIT and the caption as E&xit. Close the dialog.

2. Select the second top-level menu location and open the properties dialog. Specify the caption as &Help and close the dialog.

3. Open the properties dialog for the first drop-down location on the second top-level menu. Specify the ID as ID_HELP_ABOUT and the caption as &About. Close the dialog.

At this point, your menu is created; however, it is not attached to your application.

6

Attaching the Menu to Your Dialog Window

You now have a menu that you can use in your application. If you compile and run your application at this point, however, the menu doesn't appear. You still need to attach the menu to your dialog window. You can attach a menu by following these steps:

1. Open the dialog painter by double-clicking the primary application dialog in the Dialog folder in the Workspace pane. For this example, double-click on IDD_MENUS_DIALOG.

2. Select the entire dialog window, making sure that no controls are selected, and open the dialog's properties dialog. (What you are doing is opening the properties for the dialog window itself, not for any of the controls that might be on the window.)

3. Select the menu you have designed from the Menu drop-down list box, as shown in Figure 6.4.

FIGURE 6.4.

Attaching the menu to the dialog window.

If you compile and run your application, you find that the menu is attached to the application dialog, as shown in Figure 6.5. You can select menu entries as you do with any other Windows application—with one small difference. At this point, when you select one of the menu entries, nothing happens. You still need to attach functionality to your menu.

FIGURE 6.5.

The menu is now part of the application dialog.

Attaching Functionality to Menu Entries

Now that you have a menu as part of your application, it sure would be nice if it actually did something. Well, before your menu can do anything, you have to tell it what to do, just like everything else in your Visual C++ applications. To attach some functionality to your menu, follow these steps:

FIGURE 6.6.

The menu is now part of the application.

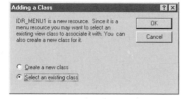

1. Open the Menu Designer to your menu.

2. Open the Class Wizard from the View menu.

3. The Adding a Class dialog is displayed for you, just as it was yesterday when you added a second dialog. Leave the dialog selection on Select an Existing Class and click OK (see Figure 6.6).

   Yesterday, when you were adding a second dialog window to your application, you needed to create a new C++ class for that window. For today's menu, you want to attach it to the existing C++ class for the dialog window to which the menu is attached.

4. Choose the C++ class of the primary dialog window from the list of available classes in the Select Class dialog. For this example, select CMenusDlg, as shown in Figure 6.7. This tells Visual C++ that all the functionality that you will call from the various menu entries is part of the same dialog class of the window that it's attached to.

FIGURE 6.7.

The Select Class dialog.

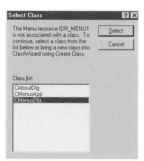

For the menu elements that you want to use to trigger new functions in your application, you can add event-handler functions through the Class Wizard, just as you can with controls that you place on the dialog window.

For this example, add a function for the IDM_FILE_HELLO object (the Hello menu) on the COMMAND event message. Name the function OnHello and add the code in Listing 6.1 to the function.

LISTING 6.1. THE ONHELLO FUNCTION.

```
 1: void CMenusDlg::OnHello()
 2: {
 3:      // TODO: Add your command handler code here
 4:
 5:      ///////////////////////
 6:      // MY CODE STARTS HERE
 7:      ///////////////////////
 8:
 9:      // Display a message for the user
10:      MessageBox("Hello there", "Hello");
11:
12:      ///////////////////////
13:      // MY CODE ENDS HERE
14:      ///////////////////////
15: }
```

Note The COMMAND event message is the message that is passed to the application window when a menu entry is selected. Placing a function on this event message has the same effect as placing a function on the menu entry selection.

You can call existing event handlers from menu elements by adding the existing function to the menu COMMAND event. You can do this by adding a function to the menu object ID and then specifying the existing function name instead of accepting the suggested function name.

To reuse the OnExit function for the Exit menu element, reopen the Menu Designer and then reopen the Class Wizard. When the Class Wizard is displayed, add a function for the IDM_FILE_EXIT object on the COMMAND event message. Do not accept the default function name presented to you by the Class Wizard. Enter the function name **OnExit**. This automatically attaches the existing OnExit function that you created with your Exit button earlier.

To round out your example's functionality, add a function to the ID_HELP_ABOUT object on the COMMAND event message. Edit the function as in Listing 6.2.

LISTING 6.2. THE ONHELPABOUT FUNCTION.

```
 1: void CMenusDlg::OnHelpAbout()
 2: {
 3:      // TODO: Add your command handler code here
 4:
```

```
 5:        /////////////////////////
 6:        // MY CODE STARTS HERE
 7:        /////////////////////////
 8:
 9:        // Declare an instance of the About window
10:        CAboutDlg dlgAbout;
11:
12:        // Show the About window
13:        dlgAbout.DoModal();
14:
15:        /////////////////////////
16:        // MY CODE ENDS HERE
17:        /////////////////////////
18: }
```

You attached the File | Exit menu entry to an existing function that closes the application. On the File | Hello, you added a new function that called the `MessageBox` function to display a simple message to the user. With Help | About, you added another function that declared an instance of the About dialog window and called its `DoModal` method.

If you compile and run your application, you find that all the menu entries are working. If you select Help | About, as shown in Figure 6.8, you see the application About dialog (see Figure 6.9). If you select File | Hello, you see a `Hello there` message box, as shown in Figure 6.10. And if you select File | Exit, your application closes.

FIGURE 6.8.

The Help | About menu entry.

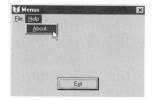

FIGURE 6.9.

The About dialog.

FIGURE 6.10.

The Hello there message box.

6

Creating Pop-Up Menus

Most Windows applications have what are called either pop-up or context menus, which are triggered by the user right-clicking an object. These are called *pop-up menus* because they pop up in the middle of the application area, not attached to a menu bar, the window frame, or anything else on the computer screen (not counting the mouse pointer). These menus are often referred to as *context menus* because the contents of a menu depend on the context in which it is opened; the elements available on the menu depend on what objects are currently selected in the application or what the mouse pointer is positioned over.

To provide a pop-up menu in your application, you have two approaches available. You can either design a menu specifically for use as a pop-up menu, or you can use one of the pull-down menus from the primary menu that you have already designed. If you design a menu specifically for use as a pop-up menu, you will need to skip the top-level, menu bar element by placing a space or some other text in the caption, knowing that it will not be seen. You will see how this works when you build a custom menu specifically for use as a pop-up menu on Day 11, "Creating Multiple Document Interface Applications," in the section "Adding a Context Menu."

Every drop-down portion of a menu can also be used as a pop-up menu. To use it in this way, you must get a handle to the submenu (the drop-down menu) and then call the TrackPopupMenu function on the submenu. The rest of the pop-up menu functionality is already covered in the other menu building and coding that you have already done. To add a pop-up menu to your application, follow these steps:

1. Using the Class Wizard, add a function for the WM_CONTEXTMENU event message in your dialog window.

> **Note**
>
> There are two dialog event messages that you can use to trigger your context menu. The event that you'd expect to use is the WM_RBUTTONDOWN event, which is triggered by the user right-clicking. The other event that can (and should) be used is the WM_CONTEXTMENU event, which is intended for use specifically to trigger a context menu. This event is triggered by a couple user actions: One of these is the release of the right mouse button, and another is the pressing of the context menu button on one of the newer Windows-enabled keyboards.

2. Edit the function, adding the code in Listing 6.3.

LISTING 6.3. THE *ONCONTEXTMENU* FUNCTION.

```
 1: void CMenusDlg:: OnContextMenu(CWnd* pWnd, CPoint point)
 2: {
 3:     // TODO: Add your message handler code here
 4:
 5:     ///////////////////////
 6:     // MY CODE STARTS HERE
 7:     ///////////////////////
 8:
 9:     // Declare local variables
10:     CMenu *m_lMenu;       // A pointer to the menu
11:     CPoint m_pPoint;      // A copy of the mouse position
12:
13:     // Copy the mouse position to a local variable
14:     m_pPoint = point;
15:     // Convert the position to a screen position
16:     ClientToScreen(&m_pPoint);
17:     // Get a pointer to the window menu
18:     m_lMenu = GetMenu();
19:     // Get a pointer to the first submenu
20:     m_lMenu = m_lMenu->GetSubMenu(0);
21:     // Show the Popup Menu
22:     m_lMenu->TrackPopupMenu(TPM_CENTERALIGN + TPM_LEFTBUTTON,
23:         m_pPoint.x, m_pPoint.y, this, NULL);
24:
25:     ///////////////////////
26:     // MY CODE ENDS HERE
27:     ///////////////////////
28: }
```

In Listing 6.3, the first thing that you did was make a copy of the mouse position. This mouse position is a relative position within the window area. It must be converted to an absolute position on the entire screen area for displaying the pop-up menu. If you don't convert the position coordinates, you can't predict where your pop-up menu will appear.

After you convert the position to an absolute position, you get a pointer to the window menu. This pointer should always be a local pointer within the function where you are going to use it because the location of the menu might change as the application runs. From the menu pointer, you next get a pointer to the first drop-down menu (submenu numbering begins with 0, like just about everything else in C/C++). After you have a pointer to the submenu, you can treat it as a regular CMenu class instance.

The final piece in this puzzle is the call to the CMenu member function TrackPopupMenu. This function takes five arguments and uses them to determine where and how to show

6

the pop-up menu. The first argument is a combination of two flags. The first flag, TPM_CENTERALIGN, centers the pop-up menu on the mouse point. You can also use TPM_LEFTALIGN or TPM_RIGHTALIGN instead. These flags line up the left or right edge of the pop-up menu with the mouse position. The second part of this flag combination is TPM_LEFTBUTTON, which makes the pop-up menu trigger from the left mouse button. You can also use TPM_RIGHTBUTTON to make the menu trigger from the right mouse button.

The second and third arguments to the TrackPopupMenu function specify the screen position for the pop-up menu. This is the absolute position on the screen, not a relative position within the window area. The fourth argument is a pointer to the window that receives the menu command messages. The final argument is a rectangle that the user can click without closing the pop-up menu. By passing NULL, you specify that if the user clicks outside the pop-up menu, the menu closes. This code enables you to include a pop-up menu in your application, as shown in Figure 6.11.

FIGURE 6.11.

The pop-up menu in action.

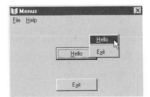

Creating a Menu with Accelerators

One of the original keyboard shortcuts for selecting menu entries were accelerator keys. As mentioned earlier in the chapter, accelerator keys are specific key combinations, usually the Ctrl key combined with another key, or function keys, that are unique within the entire application. Each of these key combinations triggers one menu event function.

The way that accelerator keys work is similar to the way menus work. They are also an application resource that is defined in a table in the resource tab of the workspace pane. Each table entry has an object ID and a key code combination. After you define the accelerators, you can attach functionality to the object IDs. You can also assign accelerator entries the same object ID as the corresponding menu entry so that you have to define only a single entry in the application message map.

After you define all your accelerator keys, you can add the key combination to the menu entry so that the user will know about the accelerator key combination. Add \t to the end of the menu entry caption, followed by the key combination. The \t is replaced in the menu display by a tab, which separates the menu caption from the accelerator key combination.

Unfortunately, accelerator keys don't work in dialog-style windows, so you cannot add them to today's application. You will learn how to attach accelerator keys to menus in a few days when you learn about single and multi-document interface style applications.

Summary

Today you learned about menus in Visual C++ applications. You learned how to use the tools in Visual C++ to create a menu for use in your application and then how to attach the menu to a window in your application. After you had the menu attached to your window, you learned how to attach functionality to the various menu entries. Later in the day, you learned how you can use a portion of your menu as a pop-up, or context, menu. Finally, you learned how accelerator keys are added to most applications.

Q&A

Q Do I have to name my menu items the same names everyone else uses? For example, a lot of applications use File and Help. Can I name my menus something else?

A You can name your top-level menus anything you want. However, there are accepted menu name conventions that place all file-oriented functionality under a menu labeled File and all help-related functionality under a menu labeled Help. If you have a menu with entries such as Broccoli, Corn, and Carrots, you will probably want to call the menu Vegetables, although an equally valid label would be Food or Plants. In general, if you want to make your application easy for your users to learn, you will want to use menu labels that make sense for the entries on the pull-down portion of the menu.

Q Why can't I specify a single character as an accelerator key?

A The single character would trigger the WM_KEY messages, not the menu messages. When the designers of Windows were deciding how accelerator keys would work, they decided that single-character keys would most likely be input to the active application. If they had allowed single-character accelerators, Windows wouldn't be able to determine whether the character was input or a shortcut. By requiring a key combination (with the exception of function keys), the designers ensured that Windows won't have to make this determination.

6

Workshop

The Workshop provides quiz questions to help you solidify your understanding of the material covered and exercises to provide you with experience in using what you've learned. The answers to the quiz questions are provided in Appendix B, "Answers."

Quiz

1. What event message does a menu selection send to the window message queue?
2. How do you attach a menu to a dialog window?
3. Which existing class do you specify for handling event messages for the menu?
4. What event message should a pop-up menu be triggered by?

Exercises

1. Add a button to the main window and have it call the same function as the Hello menu entry.
2. Add a pop-up menu to your application that uses the Help drop-down menu as the pop-up menu.

DAY 7

Working with Text and Fonts

In most Windows applications, you don't need to worry about specifying fonts, much less their weight, height, and so on. If you don't specify the font to be used, Windows supplies a default font for your application. If you do need to use a particular font, you can specify a font to use for a particular dialog window through the dialog properties. Sometimes, however, you want or need to control the font used in your application. You might need to change the font being used or allow the user to select a font to use in a particular instance. It is for those circumstances that you will learn how to change and list fonts today. Among the things that you will learn are

- How to build a list of available fonts.
- How to specify a font for use.
- How to change fonts dynamically.

Finding and Using Fonts

One of the first things that you need to know when working with fonts is that not every system that your applications run on will have the same fonts installed. Fonts are specified in files that can be installed and removed from Windows systems with relative ease. Every computer user can customize his system with whatever combination of fonts he wants. If you specify a font that doesn't exist on the system, Windows will choose either the system default font or what the operating system considers to be a reasonably close alternative font.

What you can do instead is ask the operating system what fonts are available. This method allows you to make your own decisions on which font to use or let the user make the decision. When you ask what fonts are available, you can limit the types of fonts that are listed, or you can choose to list them all and select various fonts based on various attributes.

Listing the Available Fonts

To get a list of all available fonts on a computer, you call a Windows API (Application Programming Interface) function called EnumFontFamiliesEx. This function tells Windows that you want a list of the fonts on the system. Before you start using this function and expecting it to pass you a big list of available fonts, you need to understand how it gives you the list.

Callback Functions

One of the key arguments to the EnumFontFamiliesEx function is the address of another function. This second function is what is known as a callback function, which is called by the operating system. For almost every enumeration function in the Windows operating system, you pass the address of a callback function as an argument because the callback function is called once for each of the elements in the enumerated list. In other words, you have to include a function in your application to receive each individual font that is on the system and then build the list of fonts yourself.

When you create this function to receive each font and build your list, you cannot define your callback function in any way you want. All callback functions are already defined in the Windows API. You have to use a specific type of callback function to receive the list of fonts. For getting a list of fonts, the function type is EnumFontFamProc. This function type specifies how your function must be defined, what its arguments must be, and what type of return value it must return. It does not specify what your function should be named or how it needs to work internally. These aspects are left completely up to you.

The `EnumFontFamiliesEx` Function

The `EnumFontFamiliesEx` function, which you call to request the list of available fonts, takes five arguments. A typical use of this function follows:

```
// Create a device context variable
CClientDC dc (this);
// Declare a LOGFONT structure
LOGFONT lLogFont;

// Specify the character set
lLogFont.lfCharSet = DEFAULT_CHARSET;
// Specify all fonts
lLogFont.lfFaceName[0] = NULL;
// Must be zero unless Hebrew or Arabic
lLogFont.lfPitchAndFamily = 0;
// Enumerate the font families
::EnumFontFamiliesEx((HDC) dc, &lLogFont,
(FONTENUMPROC) EnumFontFamProc, (LPARAM) this, 0);
```

The first argument is a device context, which can be an instance of the `CClientDC` class. Every application running within the Windows operating system has a device context. The device context provides a lot of necessary information to the operating system about what is available to the application and what is not.

The second argument is a pointer to a `LOGFONT` structure. This structure contains information about the fonts that you want listed. You can specify in this structure which character set you want to list or whether you want all the fonts in a particular font family. If you want all the fonts on the system, you pass `NULL` in the place of this argument.

The third argument is the address of the callback function that will be used to build your list of fonts. Passing the address of your callback function is a simple matter of using the function name as the argument. The Visual C++ compiler takes care of replacing the function name with the function address. However, you do need to cast the function as the type of callback function that the function requires.

The fourth argument is a `LPARAM` value that will be passed to the callback function. This parameter is not used by Windows but provides your callback function with a context in which to build the font list. In the example, the value being passed is a pointer to the window in which the code is being run. This way, the callback function can use this pointer to access any structures it needs to build the list of fonts. This pointer can also be the first node in a linked list of fonts or other such structure.

The fifth and final argument is always `0`. This reserved argument may be used in future versions of Windows, but for now, it must be `0` so that your application passes a value that won't cause the function to misbehave.

7

The `EnumFontFamProc` Function Type

When you create your callback function, it must be defined as an independent function, not as a member of any C++ class. A typical `EnumFontFamProc` function declaration follows:

```
int CALLBACK EnumFontFamProc(
LPENUMLOGFONT lpelf,
LPNEWTEXTMETRIC lpntm,
DWORD nFontType,
long lParam)
{
    // Create a pointer to the dialog window
    CMyDlg* pWnd = (CMyDlg*) lParam;

    // Add the font name to the list box
    pWnd->m_ctlFontList.AddString(lpelf->elfLogFont.lfFaceName);
    // Return 1 to continue font enumeration
    return 1;
}
```

The first argument to this function is a pointer to an `ENUMLOGFONTEX` structure. This structure contains information about the logical attributes of the font, including the font name, style, and script. You may have numerous fonts listed with the same name but different styles. You can have one for normal, one for bold, one for italic, and one for bold italic.

The second argument is a pointer to a `NEWTEXTMETRICEX` structure. This structure contains information about the physical attributes of the font, such as height, width, and space around the font. These values are all relative in nature because they need to scale as the font is made larger or smaller.

The third argument is a flag that specifies the type of font. This value may contain a combination of the following values:

- `DEVICE_FONTYPE`
- `RASTER_FONTYPE`
- `TRUETYPE_FONTYPE`

Finally, the fourth argument is the value that was passed into the `EnumFontFamiliesEx` function. In the example, it was a pointer to the dialog on which the list of fonts is being built. If you cast this value as a pointer to the dialog, the function can access a list box control to add the font names.

The return value from this function determines whether the listing of fonts continues. If `0` is returned from this function, the operating system quits listing the available fonts. If `1` is returned, the operating system continues to list the available fonts.

Using a Font

To use a particular font in an application, you call an instance of the CFont class. By calling the CreateFont method, you can specify the font to be used, along with the size, style, and orientation. Once you've created a font, you can tell a control or window to use the font by calling the object's SetFont method. An example of this process follows:

```
CFont m_fFont;    // The font to be used

// Create the font to be used
m_fFont.CreateFont(12, 0, 0, 0, FW_NORMAL,
        0, 0, 0, DEFAULT_CHARSET, OUT_CHARACTER_PRECIS,
        CLIP_CHARACTER_PRECIS, DEFAULT_QUALITY, DEFAULT_PITCH |
        FF_DONTCARE, m_sFontName);

// Set the font for the display area
m_ctlDisplayText.SetFont(&m_fFont);
```

Tip

> The CFont variable used in the previous code should be declared as a member variable of the class in which this code is placed. In the sample code, it is declared above where it is used to show how it is declared. This variable should not be declared or used as a local variable in a function.

Seems simple enough—just two function calls—but that CreateFont function needs an awful lot of arguments passed to it. It is these arguments that make the CreateFont method a flexible function with a large amount of functionality. Once you create the font, using it is a simple matter of passing the font to the SetFont method, which is a member of the CWnd class and thus available to all window and control classes in Visual C++. This means that you can use this technique on any visible object within a Visual C++ application.

To understand how the CreateFont function works, let's look at the individual arguments that you have to pass to it. The function is defined as

```
BOOL CreateFont(
int nHeight,
    int nWidth,
    int nEscapement,
    int nOrientation,
    int nWeight,
    BYTE bItalic,
    BYTE bUnderline,
    BYTE cStrikeOut,
    BYTE nCharSet,
```

7

```
BYTE nOutPrecision,
BYTE nClipPrecision,
BYTE nQuality,
BYTE nPitchAndFamily,
LPCTSTR lpszFaceName);
```

The first of these arguments, `nHeight`, specifies the height of the font to be used. This logical value is translated into a physical value. If the value is `0`, a reasonable default value is used. If the value is greater or less than `0`, the absolute height is converted into device units. It is key to understand that height values of `10` and `-10` are basically the same.

The second argument, `nWidth`, specifies the average width of the characters in the font. This logical value is translated into a physical value in much the same way as the height is.

The third argument, `nEscapement`, determines the angle at which the text will be printed. This value is specified in 0.1-degree units in a counterclockwise pattern. If you want to print vertical text that reads from bottom to top, you supply `900` as the value for this argument. For printing normal horizontal text that flows from left to right, supply `0` as this value.

The fourth argument, `nOrientation`, determines the angle of each individual character in the font. This works on the same basis as the previous argument, but it controls the output on a character basis, not a line-of-text basis. To print upside-down characters, set this value to `1800`. To print characters on their backs, set this value to `900`.

The fifth argument, `nWeight`, specifies the weight, or boldness, of the font. This can be any value from `0` to `1000`, with `1000` being heavily bolded. You can use constants defined for this argument to control this value with ease and consistency. These constants are listed in Table 7.1.

TABLE 7.1. FONT WEIGHT CONSTANTS.

Constant	Value
FW_DONTCARE	0
FW_THIN	100
FW_EXTRALIGHT	200
FW_ULTRALIGHT	200
FW_LIGHT	300
FW_NORMAL	400
FW_REGULAR	400
FW_MEDIUM	500

Constant	Value
FW_SEMIBOLD	600
FW_DEMIBOLD	600
FW_BOLD	700
FW_EXTRABOLD	800
FW_ULTRABOLD	800
FW_BLACK	900
FW_HEAVY	900

The actual interpretation and availability of these weights depend on the font. Some fonts only have FW_NORMAL, FW_REGULAR, and FW_BOLD weights. If you specify FW_DONTCARE, a default weight is used, just as with most of the rest of the arguments.

The sixth argument, bItalic, specifies whether the font is to be italicized. This is a boolean value; 0 indicates that the font is not italicized, and any other value indicates that the font is italicized.

The seventh argument, bUnderline, specifies whether the font is to be underlined. This is also a boolean value; 0 indicates that the font is not underlined, and any other value indicates that the font is underlined.

The eighth argument, cStrikeOut, specifies whether the characters in the font are displayed with a line through the character. This is another boolean value using a non-zero value as TRUE and 0 as FALSE.

The ninth argument, nCharSet, specifies the font's character set. The available constants for this value are listed in Table 7.2.

TABLE 7.2. FONT CHARACTER SET CONSTANTS.

Constant	Value
ANSI_CHARSET	0
DEFAULT_CHARSET	1
SYMBOL_CHARSET	2
SHIFTJIS_CHARSET	128
OEM_CHARSET	255

The system on which your application is running might have other character sets, and the OEM character set is system dependent, making it different for systems from different

7

manufacturers. If you are using one of these character sets, it is risky to try to manipulate the strings to be output, so it's best to just pass along the string to be displayed.

The tenth argument, nOutPrecision, specifies how closely the output must match the requested font's height, width, character orientation, escapement, and pitch. The available values for this argument are

- OUT_CHARACTER_PRECIS
- OUT_DEFAULT_PRECIS
- OUT_DEVICE_PRECIS
- OUT_RASTER_PRECIS
- OUT_STRING_PRECIS
- OUT_STROKE_PRECIS
- OUT_TT_PRECIS

The OUT_DEVICE_PRECIS, OUT_RASTER_PRECIS, and OUT_TT_PRECIS values control which font is chosen if there are multiple fonts with the same name. For instance, if you use the OUT_TT_PRECIS value and specify a font with both a TrueType and raster version, then the TrueType version is used. In fact, the OUT_TT_PRECIS value forces the system to use a TrueType font, even when the specified font does not have a TrueType version.

The eleventh argument, nClipPrecision, specifies how to clip characters that are partially outside of the display area. The values for this argument are

- CLIP_CHARACTER_PRECIS
- CLIP_DEFAULT_PRECIS
- CLIP_ENCAPSULATE
- CLIP_LH_ANGLES
- CLIP_MASK
- CLIP_STROKE_PRECIS
- CLIP_TT_ALWAYS

These values can be ORed together to specify a combination of clipping techniques.

The twelfth argument, nQuality, specifies the output quality and how carefully the GDI (Graphics Device Interface) must attempt to match the logical font attributes to the physical font output. The available values for this argument are

- DEFAULT_QUALITY
- DRAFT_QUALITY
- PROOF_QUALITY

The thirteenth argument, `nPitchAndFamily`, specifies the pitch and family of the font. This value consists of two values that are ORed together to create a combination value. The first set of available values is

- `DEFAULT_PITCH`
- `VARIABLE_PITCH`
- `FIXED_PITCH`

This value specifies the pitch to be used with the font. The second set of available values specifies the family of fonts to be used. The available values for this portion of the argument are

- `FF_DECORATIVE`
- `FF_DONTCARE`
- `FF_MODERN`
- `FF_ROMAN`
- `FF_SCRIPT`
- `FF_SWISS`

The font family describes in a general way the appearance of a font. You can use the font family value to choose an alternative font when a specific font does not exist on a system. The final argument, `lpszFacename`, is a standard C-style string that contains the name of the font to be used. This font name comes from the font information received by the `EnumFontFamProc` callback function.

Using Fonts

Today you will build an application that allows the user to select from a list of available fonts to be displayed. The user will be able to enter some text to be displayed in the selected font, allowing the user to see what the font looks like.

Creating the Application Shell

To begin today's application, follow these steps:

1. Create a new project workspace using the MFC AppWizard. Name the project **Day7**.
2. Use the same defaults that you used for the previous day's projects, giving the application a title of **Fonts**.
3. Design the main dialog as in Figure 7.1, using the properties in Table 7.3.

7

FIGURE 7.1.

*The main dialog
layout.*

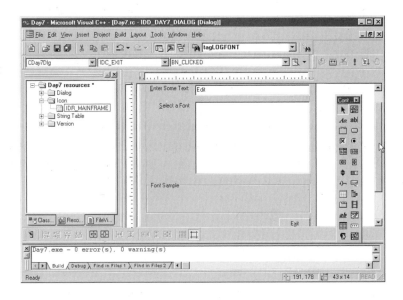

TABLE 7.3. CONTROL PROPERTY SETTINGS.

Object	Property	Setting
Static Text	ID	IDC_STATIC
	Caption	&Enter Some Text:
Edit Box	ID	IDC_ESAMPTEXT
Static Text	ID	IDC_STATIC
	Caption	&Select a Font
List Box	ID	IDC_LFONTS
Group Box	ID	IDC_STATIC
	Caption	Font Sample
Static Text	ID	IDC_DISPLAYTEXT
(inside group box; size to	Caption	Empty string
fill the group box)		
Command Button	ID	IDC_EXIT
	Caption	E&xit

4. Using the Class Wizard, add the variables in Table 7.4 to the controls on the dialog.

TABLE 7.4. CONTROL VARIABLES.

Object	Name	Category	Type
IDC_DISPLAYTEXT	m_ctlDisplayText	Control	CStatic
	m_strDisplayText	Value	CString
IDC_LFONTS	m_ctlFontList	Control	CListBox
	m_strFontName	Value	CString
IDC_ESAMPTEXT	m_strSampText	Value	CString

5. Attach a function to the IDC_EXIT button to close the application, as in the previous day's applications.

Building a List of Fonts

To be able to create your list of fonts, you need to add your callback function to get each font list and add it to the list box that you placed on the dialog window. To do this, edit the Day7Dlg.h header file and add the function declaration in Listing 7.1 near the top of the file. This function cannot be added through any of the tools available in Visual C++. You need to open the file and add it yourself.

LISTING 7.1. THE CALLBACK FUNCTION DECLARATION IN THE Day7Dlg.h HEADER FILE.

```
1: #if _MSC_VER > 1000
2: #pragma once
3: #endif // _MSC_VER > 1000
4:
5: int CALLBACK EnumFontFamProc(LPENUMLOGFONT lpelf,
6: LPNEWTEXTMETRIC lpntm, DWORD nFontType, long lParam);
7:
8: //////////////////////////////////////////////////////////////////
9: // CDay7Dlg dialog
10:
11: class CDay7Dlg : public CDialog
12: .
13: .
14: .
```

Once you add the function declaration to the header file, open the Day7Dlg.cpp source-code file, scroll to the bottom of the file, and add the function definition in Listing 7.2.

7

LISTING 7.2. THE CALLBACK FUNCTION DEFINITION IN THE `Day7Dlg.cpp` SOURCE FILE.

```
 1: int CALLBACK EnumFontFamProc(LPENUMLOGFONT lpelf,
 2: LPNEWTEXTMETRIC lpntm, DWORD nFontType, long lParam)
 3: {
 4:     // Create a pointer to the dialog window
 5:     CDay7Dlg* pWnd = (CDay7Dlg*) lParam;
 6:
 7:     // Add the font name to the list box
 8:     pWnd->m_ctlFontList.AddString(lpelf->elfLogFont.lfFaceName);
 9:     // Return 1 to continue font enumeration
10:     return 1;
11: }
```

Now that you have the callback function defined, you need to add a function to request the list of fonts from the operating system. To add this function, follow these steps:

1. Select the Class View tab on the project workspace pane.

2. Select the CDay7Dlg class, right-click the mouse, and select Add Member Function from the pop-up menu.

3. Specify the function type as void, the function declaration as FillFontList, and the access as Private. Click the OK button to close the dialog and add the function.

4. Edit the function definition as in Listing 7.3.

LISTING 7.3. THE `FillFontList` FUNCTION.

```
 1: void CDay7Dlg::FillFontList()
 2: {
 3:     LOGFONT lf;
 4:
 5:     // Initialize the LOGFONT structure
 6:     lf.lfCharSet = DEFAULT_CHARSET;
 7:     strcpy(lf.lfFaceName, "");
 8:     // Clear the list box
 9:     m_ctlFontList.ResetContent();
10:     // Create a device context variable
11:     CClientDC dc (this);
12:     // Enumerate the font families
13:     ::EnumFontFamiliesEx((HDC) dc, &lf,
14: (FONTENUMPROC) EnumFontFamProc, (LPARAM) this, 0);
15: }
```

5. Edit the OnInitDialog function to call the FillFontList function, as in Listing 7.4.

LISTING 7.4. THE EDITED `OnInitDialog` FUNCTION.

```
 1: BOOL CDay7Dlg::OnInitDialog()
 2: {
 3:     CDialog::OnInitDialog();
 4: .
 5: .
 6: .
 7:     // TODO: Add extra initialization here
 8:
 9:     /////////////////////////
10:     // MY CODE STARTS HERE
11:     /////////////////////////
12:
13:     // Fill the font list box
14:     FillFontList();
15:
16:     /////////////////////////
17:     // MY CODE ENDS HERE
18:     /////////////////////////
19:
20:     return TRUE;  // return TRUE  unless you set the focus to a control
21: }
```

If you compile and run your application now, you should find that your list box is filled with the names of all the fonts available on the system. However, there's one aspect of this list that you probably don't want in your application. Figure 7.2 shows many duplicate entries in the list of fonts in the list box. It would be nice if you could eliminate these duplicates and have only one line per font.

FIGURE 7.2.

Listing all the fonts in the system.

It turns out that the `EnumFontFamiliesEx` function call is synchronous in nature. This means that it doesn't return until all the fonts in the system are listed in calls to your

7

callback function. You can place code in the FillFontList function to remove all the duplicate entries once the list box is filled. To do this, modify the FillFontList function as in Listing 7.5.

LISTING 7.5. THE MODIFIED FillFontList FUNCTION.

```
 1: void CDay7Dlg::FillFontList()
 2: {
 3:     int iCount;              // The number of fonts
 4:     int iCurCount;           // The current font
 5:     CString strCurFont;         // The current font name
 6:     CString strPrevFont = "";    // The previous font name
 7:     LOGFONT lf;
 8:
 9:     // Initialize the LOGFONT structure
10:     lf.lfCharSet = DEFAULT_CHARSET;
11:     strcpy(lf.lfFaceName, "");
12:     // Clear the list box
13:     m_ctlFontList.ResetContent();
14:     // Create a device context variable
15:     CClientDC dc (this);
16:     // Enumerate the font families
17:     ::EnumFontFamiliesEx((HDC) dc, &lf,
18: (FONTENUMPROC) EnumFontFamProc, (LPARAM) this, 0);
19:     // Get the number of fonts in the list box
20:     iCount = m_ctlFontList.GetCount();
21:     // Loop from the last entry in the list box to the first,
22:     // searching for and deleting the duplicate entries
23:     for (iCurCount = iCount; iCurCount > 0; iCurCount--)
24:     {
25:         // Get the current font name
26:         m_ctlFontList.GetText((iCurCount - 1), strCurFont);
27:         // Is it the same as the previous font name?
28:         if (strCurFont == strPrevFont)
29:         {
30:             // If yes, then delete it
31:             m_ctlFontList.DeleteString((iCurCount - 1));
32:         }
33:         // Set the previous font name to the current font name
34:         strPrevFont = strCurFont;
35:     }
36: }
```

Notice that the for loop started at the end of the list and worked backward. This allowed you to delete the current entry without worrying about manipulating the loop counter to prevent skipping lines in the list box. If you compile and run your application, there shouldn't be any duplicate entries in the list of available fonts.

Setting the Font Sample Text

Before you can display the font for the user, you need to place some text into the display area. The edit box near the top of the dialog is where the user enters text to be displayed in the font selected. To add the functionality, do the following:

1. Edit the `OnInitDialog` function to add code to initialize the edit box and display text, as in Listing 7.6.

LISTING 7.6. THE MODIFIED `OnInitDialog` FUNCTION.

```
 1: BOOL CDay7Dlg::OnInitDialog()
 2: {
 3:     CDialog::OnInitDialog();
 4: .
 5: .
 6: .
 7:     // TODO: Add extra initialization here
 8:
 9:     ///////////////////////
10:     // MY CODE STARTS HERE
11:     ///////////////////////
12:
13:     // Fill the font list box
14:     FillFontList();
15:
16:     // Initialize the text to be entered
17:     m_strSampText = "Testing";
18:     // Copy the text to the font sample area
19:     m_strDisplayText = m_strSampText;
20:     // Update the dialog
21:     UpdateData(FALSE);
22:
23:     ///////////////////////
24:     // MY CODE ENDS HERE
25:     ///////////////////////
26:
27:     return TRUE;  // return TRUE  unless you set the focus to a control
28: }
```

2. Using the Class Wizard, add a function on the EN_CHANGE event message for the IDC_ESAMPTEXT edit box control.

3. Edit the function you just added, adding the code in Listing 7.7.

7

LISTING 7.7. THE `OnChangeEsamptext` FUNCTION.

```
 1: void CDay7Dlg::OnChangeEsamptext()
 2: {
 3:     // TODO: If this is a RICHEDIT control, the control will not
 4:     // send this notification unless you override the
          ➥CDialog::OnInitialUpdate()
 5:     // function and call CRichEditCrtl().SetEventMask()
 6:     // with the EN_CHANGE flag ORed into the mask.
 7:
 8:     // TODO: Add your control notification handler code here
 9:
10:     ///////////////////////
11:     // MY CODE STARTS HERE
12:     ///////////////////////
13:
14:     // Update the variables with the dialog controls
15:     UpdateData(TRUE);
16:
17:     // Copy the current text to the font sample
18:     m_strDisplayText = m_strSampText;
19:
20:     // Update the dialog with the variables
21:     UpdateData(FALSE);
22:
23:     ///////////////////////
24:     // MY CODE ENDS HERE
25:     ///////////////////////
26: }
```

If you compile and run your application, you should be able to type text into the edit box and see it change in the font display area in the group box below.

Selecting a Font to Display

Before you can start changing the font for the display area, you'll need to have a CFont member variable of the dialog class that you can use to set and change the display font. To add this variable, follow these steps:

1. In the Class View of the workspace pane, right-click the mouse on the CDay7Dlg class. Select Add Member Variable from the pop-up menu.

2. Specify the variable type as CFont, the variable name as m_fSampFont, and the access as Private. Click the OK button to close the dialog box and add the variable.

When adding the code to use the selected font, you'll add it as a separate function that is not attached to a control. Why you do this will become clear as you proceed further through building and running today's application. To add the function to display and use the selected font, follow these steps:

1. In the Class View of the workspace pane, right-click the mouse on the CDay7Dlg class. Select Add Member Function from the pop-up menu.

2. Specify the function type as void, the function declaration as SetMyFont, and the access as Private. Click the OK button to close the dialog and add the function.

3. Edit the function, adding the code in Listing 7.8.

LISTING 7.8. THE SetMyFont FUNCTION.

```
 1: void CDay7Dlg::SetMyFont()
 2: {
 3:     CRect rRect;        // The rectangle of the display area
 4:     int iHeight;    // The height of the display area
 5:
 6:     // Has a font been selected?
 7:     if (m_strFontName != "")
 8:     {
 9:         // Get the dimensions of the font sample display area
10:         m_ctlDisplayText.GetWindowRect(&rRect);
11:         // Calculate the area height
12:         iHeight = rRect.top - rRect.bottom;
13:         // Make sure the height is positive
14:         if (iHeight < 0)
15:             iHeight = 0 - iHeight;
16:         // Release the current font
17:         m_fSampFont.Detach();
18:         // Create the font to be used
19:         m_fSampFont.CreateFont((iHeight - 5), 0, 0, 0, FW_NORMAL,
20:                 0, 0, 0, DEFAULT_CHARSET, OUT_CHARACTER_PRECIS,
21:                 CLIP_CHARACTER_PRECIS, DEFAULT_QUALITY, DEFAULT_PITCH |
22:                 FF_DONTCARE, m_strFontName);
23:
24:         // Set the font for the sample display area
25:         m_ctlDisplayText.SetFont(&m_fSampFont);
26:     }
27: }
```

4. Using the Class Wizard, add a function to the LBN_SELCHANGE event message for the IDC_LFONTS list box. Edit the function, adding the code in Listing 7.9.

7

LISTING 7.9. THE `OnSelchangeLfonts` FUNCTION.

```
 1: void CDay7Dlg::OnSelchangeLfonts()
 2: {
 3:     // TODO: Add your control notification handler code here
 4:
 5:     ///////////////////////
 6:     // MY CODE STARTS HERE
 7:     ///////////////////////
 8:
 9:     // Update the variables with the dialog controls
10:     UpdateData(TRUE);
11:
12:     // Set the font for the sample
13:     SetMyFont();
14:
15:     ///////////////////////
16:     // MY CODE ENDS HERE
17:     ///////////////////////
18: }
```

In the `SetMyFont` function, you first checked to make sure that a font had been selected. Next, you retrieved the area of the static text control that will be used to display the font. This enables you to specify a font height just slightly smaller than the height of the area you have available to display the font in. After you calculated the height of the static text control and made sure that it is a positive value, you created the selected font and told the static text control to use the newly created font.

In the `OnSelchangeLfonts` function, you copy the control values to the attached variables and then call the `SetMyFont` function to use the selected font. If you compile and run your application, you should be able to select a font and see it displayed in the sample static text control, as in Figure 7.3.

FIGURE 7.3.

Displaying the selected font.

Summary

Today you learned how to use fonts in Visual C++ applications. You learned how to get a list of the available fonts that are loaded on the system and then how to create a font for use on a display object. You learned how you can create and use callback functions to get a list of resources from the Windows operating system. You also learned how you can access controls from the callback function using a window pointer that you passed to the function requesting the resource list.

Q&A

Q **The `CreateFont` function has a lot of arguments to specify and pass. Is there any other alternative to using this function?**

A Yes, there is, although you still specify all of the same information. A structure called LOGFONT contains all the same attributes that are passed to the `CreateFont` function. You can declare an instance of this structure, initializing the attributes to default values, and then pass this structure to the `CreateFontIndirect` function. If you make numerous font changes, this approach is preferable because you could use the same instance of the structure, modifying those attributes that are changing from the current settings and using it to create the various fonts.

The way that you use this alternative way of creating the font is to declare an instance of the LOGFONT structure as a member of the dialog class and then initialize all the attributes before calling the SetMyFont function. In the SetMyFont function, you modify it as shown in Listing 7.10.

LISTING 7.10. THE MODIFIED SetMyFont FUNCTION.

```
1: void CDay7Dlg::SetMyFont()
2: {
3:
4:     // Has a font been selected?
5:     if (m_strFontName != "")
6:     {
7:         // Assume that the font size has already been initialized in the
8:         // m_lLogFont structure. This allows you to only have to specify
9:         // the font name.
10:        tcscpy(m_lLogFont.lfFaceName, m_strFontName);
11:        // Create the font to be used
12:        m_fSampFont.CreateFontIndirect(&m_lLogFont);
13:
14:        // Set the font for the sample display area
15:        m_ctlDisplayText.SetFont(&m_fSampFont);
16:    }
17: }
```

7

Q How can I limit the fonts in my list to just the TrueType fonts?

A You can check the nFontType argument to your callback function to determine the font type. For instance, if you want to include only TrueType fonts in your list of fonts, you modify your callback function to mask the nFontType argument with the TRUETYPE_FONTTYPE constant and check to see if the resulting value equals the TRUETYPE_FONTTYPE value, as in the following:

```
int CALLBACK EnumFontFamProc(LPENUMLOGFONT lpelf,
LPNEWTEXTMETRIC lpntm, DWORD nFontType, long lParam)
{
    // Create a pointer to the dialog window
    CDay7Dlg* pWnd = (CDay7Dlg*) lParam;

    // Limit the list to TrueType fonts
    if ((nFontType & TRUETYPE_FONTTYPE) == TRUETYPE_FONTTYPE)
    {
        // Add the font name to the list box
        pWnd->m_ctlFontList.AddString(
                        lpelf->elfLogFont.lfFaceName);
    }
    // Return 1 to continue font enumeration
    return 1;
}
```

Workshop

The Workshop provides quiz questions to help you solidify your understanding of the material covered and exercises to provide you with experience in using what you've learned. The answers to the quiz questions and exercises are provided in Appendix B, "Answers."

Quiz

1. How can you specify that the text is to be underlined?
2. How can you print your text upside down?
3. How many times is the EnumFontFamProc callback function called by the operating system?

Exercises

1. Add a check box to switch between using the entered text to display the font and using the font name to display the font, as in Figure 7.4.

FIGURE 7.4.

Displaying the selected font with the font name.

2. Add a check box to display the font sample in italics, as in Figure 7.5.

FIGURE 7.5.

Displaying the selected font in italics.

7

WEEK 1

In Review

Well, you've made it through the first week. By this point, you've gotten a good taste for what's possible when building applications with Visual C++. Now it's time to look back over what's been covered and what you should have learned up to this point.

What you might want to do at this point, to cement your understanding of how you can use these elements in your own applications, is to try designing and building a couple of simple applications of your own. You can use a variety of controls and add some additional dialogs, just so you can make sure that you do understand and are comfortable with these topics. In fact, you might want to try out all the topics that I've covered up to this point in small applications of your own design. That's the true test of your understanding of how the concepts work. You might also want to dive into the MFC documentation to learn a little about some of the more advanced functionality that I haven't covered to see if you can figure out how you can use and incorporate it into your applications.

One of the most important things that you should understand at this point is how you can use controls and dialog windows in your applications to get and display information to the user. This is an important part of any Windows application because just about every application interacts with the user in some way. You should be able to place any of the standard controls on a dialog in your application and be able to incorporate them into your application without any problem. Likewise, you should be comfortable with using the standard message box and dialog windows provided to your application by the Windows operating system. You should also be able to create and incorporate your own custom dialog windows into any application you might want to build. If you don't feel comfortable with any of these topics, you might want to go back and review Day 2 to get a better understanding of how you can use controls and Day 5 to understand how you can incorporate standard and custom dialog windows into your applications.

Another key skill that you will be using in the majority of your applications is the ability to build and incorporate menus into your applications. You need to have a firm understanding of how to design a good menu, how to make sure that there are no conflicting mnemonics, and how you can attach application functionality to the menu selections. At this point, you should be able to create your own customized menus, with entries for each of the various functions that your application performs, and integrate it with your application with no problems. If you aren't 100% comfortable with this topic, you might want to go back and study Day 6 a little more.

You will find that there are various situations in which you need to have some means of triggering actions on a regular basis or in which you need to keep track of how long some process has been running. For both of these situations, as well as numerous others, you'll often find yourself turning to the use of timers in your application. If you are even slightly foggy on how you can integrate timers into your applications, you will definitely want to go back and review Day 4.

Understanding how you can use text and fonts in your applications will allow you to build more flexibility into the appearance of your applications—to give your users the ability to customize the appearance as they want. You will be able to examine the available fonts on the computer on which your application is running and, if a font that you want to use in your application isn't available, choose another font that is close to use instead. If you still have any questions on how the font infrastructure in Windows works and how you can use it in your applications, you'll want to go back and review Day 7 once more.

Depending on the nature of your application, being able to capture and track mouse and keyboard actions by the user can be very important. If you are building a drawing application, this is crucial information. If you are building an application that needs to include drag-and-drop capabilities, this is important once again. There are any number of situations in which you'll want to include this functionality into your applications. By this point, you should understand how you can capture the various mouse events and determine which mouse buttons are involved in the event. You should also be able to capture keyboard events in situations where the keyboard input isn't captured by any controls that are on the window. If you don't feel like you have a complete grasp of this, you should take another look at Day 3.

Finally, you should be familiar with the Visual C++ development environment, the Developer Studio. You should have a good understanding of what each area of the environment is for and how you can use the various tools and utilities in building your applications. You should be comfortable with using the workspace pane to navigate around your application project, locating and bringing into the various editors and designers any part of your application. You should be comfortable with locating and redesigning the icon that will be displayed to represent your application and with finding any member functions or variables in any of your application's classes.

By now you should be getting fairly comfortable working with Visual C++. If you feel like you understand all the topics that I've covered so far, you are ready to continue forward, learning more about the various things that you can do, and functionality that you can build, using Visual C++ as your programming tool. With that said, it's on to the second week…

WEEK 2

At a Glance

In the second week, you'll dive into several more involved
topics. These topics are still very much core to building
Windows applications. You'll find yourself using what you
learn in this week, along with what you learned during the
first week, in just about all the applications that you build
with Visual C++.

To start the week, on Day 8, you'll learn how to draw
graphics in a Windows application. You'll learn how to
draw simple lines, rectangles, and ellipses. What's more
important—you'll learn about the device context and how you
can use it to draw your graphics without worrying
about the graphics hardware your users might or might not
have in their computers.

On Day 9, you'll learn how easy it is to incorporate ActiveX
controls into your applications. You'll see how Visual C++
builds custom C++ classes around the controls that you add
to your project, enabling you to interact with an added control
just as if it were another C++ object.

On Day 10, you'll learn how to build a basic Single
Document Interface (SDI) application. You'll learn about the
Document/View architecture that is used with Visual C++ for
building this style of application, and you'll learn how you
can use it to build your own applications.

On Day 11, you'll learn how you can apply what you learned
about building SDI applications to building Multiple
Document Interface (MDI) applications. You'll see how you
can use the same Document/View architecture to create MDI
applications, some of the most common style of Windows
applications available today.

8

9

10

11

12

13

14

On Day 12, you'll learn how you can create and modify your own toolbars and status bars. You'll learn how you can attach toolbar buttons to menus in your application and how you can add additional toolbars. You'll also learn how you can place your own informational elements on the status bar at the bottom of most Windows applications and how you can keep the status bar updated with the status of your application.

On Day 13, you'll see how you can use the structure provided for you by the Document/View architecture to save and restore the data created in your application. You'll learn how flexible this facility is and how you can store different data types in the same file, restoring them to your application just as they were when you first saved them.

Finally, rounding out the week on Day 14, you'll learn how easy it is to build a database application with an ODBC database. You'll learn how to query a set of records from the database and how to allow the user to edit and modify them, saving the changes back to the database.

When you finish this week, you'll be well prepared for tackling most basic application development tasks with Visual C++. You might want to take a short break at that point to experiment a bit—trying to build various types of applications, pushing your skills, and learning what your limits are (and aren't)—before jumping into the final week of more advanced topics.

DAY 8

Adding Flash— Incorporating Graphics, Drawing, and Bitmaps

You've probably noticed that a large number of applications use graphics and display images. This adds a certain level of flash and polish to the application. With some applications, graphics are an integral part of their functionality. Having a good understanding of what's involved in adding these capabilities to your applications is a key part of programming for the Windows platform. You've already learned how you can draw lines and how you can string a series of these lines together to make a continuous drawing. Today, you're going to go beyond that capacity and learn how you can add more advanced graphics capabilities to your applications. Today, you will learn

- How Windows uses a device context to translate drawing instructions into graphics output.

- How you can determine the level of control you have over the graphics output through different mapping modes.

- How Windows uses pens and brushes to draw different portions of the graphics image.
- How you can load and display bitmaps dynamically.

Understanding the Graphics Device Interface

The Windows operating system provides you with a couple of levels of abstraction for creating and using graphics in your applications. During the days of DOS programming, you needed to exercise a great deal of control over the graphics hardware to draw any kind of images in an application. This control required an extensive knowledge and understanding of the various types of graphics cards that users might have in their computers, along with their options for monitors and resolutions. There were a few graphics libraries that you could buy for your applications, but overall, it was fairly strenuous programming to add this capability to your applications.

With Windows, Microsoft has made the job much easier. First, Microsoft provides you with a virtual graphics device for all of your Windows applications. This virtual device doesn't change with the hardware but remains the same for all possible graphics hardware that the user might have. This consistency provides you with the ability to create whatever kind of graphics you want in your applications because you know that the task of converting them to something that the hardware understands isn't your problem.

Device Contexts

Before you can create any graphics, you must have the device context in which the graphics will be displayed. The device context contains information about the system, the application, and the window in which you are drawing any graphics. The operating system uses the device context to learn in which context a graphic is being drawn, how much of the area is visible, and where on the screen it is currently located.

When you draw graphics, you always draw them in the context of an application window. At any time, this window may be full view, minimized, partly hidden, or completely hidden. This status is not your concern because you draw your graphics on the window using its device context. Windows keeps track of each device context and uses it to determine how much and what part of the graphics you draw to actually display for the user. In essence, the device context you use to display your graphics is the visual context of the window in which you draw them.

The device context uses two resources to perform most of its drawing and graphics functions. These two resources are pens and brushes. Much like their real-world counterparts, pens and brushes perform similar yet different tasks. The device context uses pens to

8

draw lines and shapes, whereas brushes paint areas of the screen. It's the same idea as working on paper when you use a pen to draw an outline of an image and then pick up a paintbrush to fill in the color between the lines.

The Device Context Class

In Visual C++, the MFC device context class (CDC) provides numerous drawing functions for drawing circles, squares, lines, curves, and so on. All these functions are part of the device context class because they all use the device context information to draw on your application windows.

You create a device context class instance with a pointer to the window class that you want to associate with the device context. This allows the device context class to place all of the code associated with allocating and freeing a device context in the class constructor and destructors.

Note

Device context objects, as well as all of the various drawing objects, are classified as resources in the Windows operating system. The operating system has only a limited amount of these resources. Although the total number of resources is large in recent versions of Windows, it is still possible to run out of resources if an application allocates them and doesn't free them correctly. This loss is known as a resource leak, and much like a memory leak, it can eventually lock up a user's system. As a result, it's advisable to create these resources in the functions where they will be used and then delete them as soon as you are finished with them.

Following this advised approach to using device contexts and their drawing resources, you use them almost exclusively as local variables within a single function. The only real exception is when the device context object is created by Windows and passed into the event-processing function as an argument.

The Pen Class

You have already seen how you can use the pen class, CPen, to specify the color and width for drawing lines onscreen. CPen is the primary resource tool for drawing any kind of line onscreen. When you create an instance of the CPen class, you can specify the line type, color, and thickness. After you create a pen, you can select it as the current drawing tool for the device context so that it is used for all of your drawing commands to the device context. To create a new pen, and then select it as the current drawing pen, you use the following code:

```
// Create the device context
CDC dc(this);
// Create the pen
CPen lPen(PS_SOLID, 1, RGB(0, 0, 0));
// Select the pen as the current drawing pen
dc.SelectObject(&lPen);
```

You can use a number of different pen styles. These pen styles all draw different patterns when drawing lines. Figure 8.1 shows the basic styles that can be used in your applications with any color.

FIGURE 8.1.

Windows pen styles.

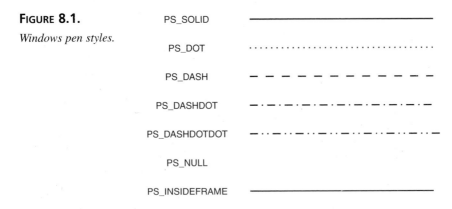

PS_SOLID	————————————
PS_DOT	··························
PS_DASH	— — — — — — — — — — —
PS_DASHDOT	— · — · — · — · — · — · — · —
PS_DASHDOTDOT	— · · — · · — · · — · · — · · —
PS_NULL	
PS_INSIDEFRAME	————————————

Note

When you use any of these line styles with a pen thickness greater than 1, all of the lines appear as solid lines. If you want to use any line style other than PS_SOLID, you need to use a pen width of 1.

Along with the line style that the pen should draw, you also have to specify the pen's width and color. The combination of these three variables specifies the appearance of the resulting lines. The line width can range from 1 on up, although when you reach a width of 32, it's difficult to exercise any level of precision in your drawing efforts.

You specify the color as a RGB value, which has three separate values for the brightness of the red, green, and blue color components of the pixels on the computer screen. These three separate values can range from 0 to 255, and the RGB function combines them into a single value in the format needed by Windows. Some of the more common colors are listed in Table 8.1.

TABLE 8.1. COMMON WINDOWS COLORS.

Color	Red	Green	Blue
Black	0	0	0
Blue	0	0	255
Dark blue	0	0	128
Green	0	255	0
Dark green	0	128	0
Cyan	0	255	255
Dark cyan	0	128	128
Red	255	0	0
Dark red	128	0	0
Magenta	255	0	255
Dark magenta	128	0	128
Yellow	255	255	0
Dark yellow	128	128	0
Dark gray	128	128	128
Light gray	192	192	192
White	255	255	255

The Brush Class

The brush class, CBrush, allows you to create brushes that define how areas will be filled in. When you draw shapes that enclose an area and fill in the enclosed area, the outline is drawn with the current pen, and the interior of the area is filled by the current brush. Brushes can be solid colors (specified using the same RGB values as with the pens), a pattern of lines, or even a repeated pattern created from a small bitmap. If you want to create a solid-color brush, you need to specify the color to use:

```
CBrush lSolidBrush(RGB(255, 0, 0));
```

To create a pattern brush, you need to specify not only the color but also the pattern to use:

```
CBrush lPatternBrush(HS_BDIAGONAL, RGB(0, 0, 255));
```

After you create a brush, you can select it with the device context object, just like you do with pens. When you select a brush, it is used as the current brush whenever you draw something that uses a brush.

As with pens, you can select a number of standard patterns when creating a brush, as shown in Figure 8.2. In addition to these patterns, an additional style of brush, HS_BITMAP, uses a bitmap as the pattern for filling the specified area. This bitmap is limited in size to 8 pixels by 8 pixels, which is a smaller bitmap than normally used for toolbars and other small images. If you supply it with a larger bitmap, it takes only the upper-left corner, limiting it to an 8-by-8 square. You can create a bitmap brush by creating a bitmap resource for your application and assigning it an object ID. After you do this, you can create a brush with it by using the following code:

```
CBitmap m_bmpBitmap;

// Load the image
m_bmpBitmap.LoadBitmap(IDB_MYBITMAP);
// Create the brush
CBrush lBitmapBrush(&m_bmpBitmap);
```

FIGURE 8.2.

Standard brush patterns.

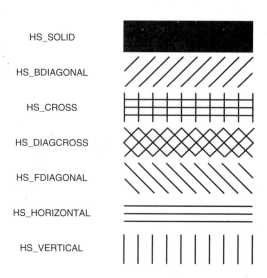

HS_SOLID	
HS_BDIAGONAL	
HS_CROSS	
HS_DIAGCROSS	
HS_FDIAGONAL	
HS_HORIZONTAL	
HS_VERTICAL	

> **Tip**
>
> If you want to create your own custom pattern for use as a brush, you can create the pattern as an 8-by-8 bitmap and use the bitmap brush. This allows you to extend the number of brush patterns far beyond the limited number of standard patterns.

The Bitmap Class

When you want to display images in your applications, you have a couple of options. You can add fixed bitmaps to your application, as resources with object IDs assigned to them and use static picture controls or an ActiveX control that displays images. You can also use the bitmap class, CBitmap, to exercise complete control over the image display. If you use the bitmap class, you can dynamically load bitmap images from files on the system disk, resizing the images as necessary to make them fit in the space you've allotted.

If you add the bitmap as a resource, you can create an instance of the CBitmap class using the resource ID of the bitmap as the image to be loaded. If you want to load a bitmap from a file, you can use the LoadImage API call to load the bitmap from the file. After you load the bitmap, you can use the handle for the image to attach the image to the CBitmap class, as follows:

```
// Load the bitmap file
HBITMAP hBitmap = (HBITMAP)::LoadImage(AfxGetInstanceHandle(),
                   m_sFileName, IMAGE_BITMAP, 0, 0,
                   LR_LOADFROMFILE | LR_CREATEDIBSECTION);
// Attach the loaded image to the CBitmap object.
m_bmpBitmap.Attach(hBitmap);
```

After you load the bitmap into the CBitmap object, you can create a second device context and select the bitmap into it. When you've created the second device context, you need to make it compatible with the primary device context before the bitmap is selected into it. Because device contexts are created by the operating system for a specific output device (screen, printer, and so on), you have to make sure that the second device context is also attached to the same output device as the first.

```
// Create a device context
CDC dcMem;
// Make the new device context compatible with the real DC
dcMem.CreateCompatibleDC(dc);
// Select the bitmap into the new DC
dcMem.SelectObject(&m_bmpBitmap);
```

When you select the bitmap into a compatible device context, you can copy the bitmap into the regular display device context using the BitBlt function:

```
// Copy the bitmap to the display DC
dc->BitBlt(10, 10, bm.bmWidth,
             bm.bmHeight, &dcMem, 0, 0,
             SRCCOPY);
```

You can also copy and resize the image using the StretchBlt function:

```
// Resize the bitmap while copying it to the display DC
dc->StretchBlt(10, 10, (lRect.Width() - 20),
               (lRect.Height() - 20), &dcMem, 0, 0,
               bm.bmWidth, bm.bmHeight, SRCCOPY);
```

By using the StretchBlt function, you can resize the bitmap so that it will fit in any area on the screen.

Mapping Modes and Coordinate Systems

When you are preparing to draw some graphics on a window, you can exercise a lot of control over the scale you are using and the area in which you can draw. You can control these factors by specifying the mapping mode and the drawing area.

By specifying the mapping mode, you can control how the coordinates that you specify are translated into locations on the screen. The different mapping modes translate each point into a different distance. You can set the mapping mode by using the SetMapMode device context function:

```
dc->SetMapMode(MM_ANISOTROPIC);
```

The available mapping modes are listed in Table 8.2.

TABLE 8.2. MAPPING MODES.

Mode	Description
MM_ANISOTROPIC	Logical units are converted into arbitrary units with arbitrary axes.
MM_HIENGLISH	Each logical unit is converted into 0.001 inch. Positive x is to the right, and positive y is up.
MM_HIMETRIC	Each logical unit is converted into 0.01 millimeter. Positive x is to the right, and positive y is up.
MM_ISOTROPIC	Logical units are converted into arbitrary units with equally scaled axes.
MM_LOENGLISH	Each logical unit is converted into 0.01 inch. Positive x is to the right, and positive y is up.
MM_LOMETRIC	Each logical unit is converted into 0.1 millimeter. Positive x is to the right, and positive y is up.
MM_TEXT	Each logical unit is converted into 1 pixel. Positive x is to the right, and positive y is down.
MM_TWIPS	Each logical unit is converted into 1/20 of a point (approximately 1/1440 inch). Positive x is to the right, and positive y is up.

If you use either the MM_ANISOTROPIC or MM_ISOTROPIC mapping modes, you can use either the SetWindowExt or SetViewportExt functions to specify the drawing area where your graphics should appear.

Creating a Graphics Application

To get a good understanding of how you can put all of this information to use, you'll build an application that incorporates a lot of what I've covered so far today. This application will have two independent windows, one with a number of options to choose for the shape, tool, and color to be displayed. The other window will act as a canvas, where all of the selected options will be drawn. The user can select whether to display lines, squares, circles, or a bitmap on the second window. The user can also specify the color and choose whether to display the pen or brush for the circles and squares.

Generating the Application Shell

As you have learned by now, the first step in building an application is generating the initial application shell. This shell provides the basic application functionality, displaying your first application dialog, along with all startup and shutdown functionality.

For the application that you will build today, you need to start with a standard dialog-style application shell. You can create this for your application by starting a new AppWizard project, providing a suitable project name, such as Graphics. After you are in the AppWizard, specify that you are creating a dialog-style application. At this point, you can accept all of the default settings, although you won't need ActiveX support, and you can specify a more descriptive window title if you want.

Designing the Main Dialog

After you make your way through the AppWizard, you're ready to start designing your primary dialog. This window will contain three groups of radio buttons: one group for specifying the drawing tool, the next to specify the drawing shape, and the third to specify the color. Along with these groups of radio buttons, you'll have two buttons on the window: one to open a File Open dialog, for selecting a bitmap to be displayed, and the other to close the application.

To add all these controls to your dialog, lay them out as shown in Figure 8.3 and specify the control properties listed in Table 8.3.

FIGURE 8.3.

The main dialog layout.

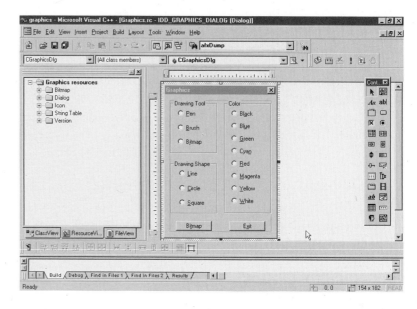

TABLE 8.3. CONTROL PROPERTY SETTINGS.

Object	Property	Setting
Group Box	ID	IDC_STATIC
	Caption	Drawing Tool
Radio Button	ID	IDC_RTPEN
	Caption	&Pen
	Group	Checked
Radio Button	ID	IDC_RTBRUSH
	Caption	&Brush
Radio Button	ID	IDC_RTBITMAP
	Caption	B&itmap
Group Box	ID	IDC_STATIC
	Caption	Drawing Shape
Radio Button	ID	IDC_RSLINE
	Caption	&Line
	Group	Checked
Radio Button	ID	IDC_RSCIRCLE
	Caption	&Circle

Object	Property	Setting
Radio Button	ID	IDC_RSSQUARE
	Caption	&Square
Group Box	ID	IDC_STATIC
	Caption	Color
Radio Button	ID	IDC_RCBLACK
	Caption	Bl&ack
	Group	Checked
Radio Button	ID	IDC_RCBLUE
	Caption	Bl&ue
Radio Button	ID	IDC_RCGREEN
	Caption	&Green
Radio Button	ID	IDC_RCCYAN
	Caption	Cya&n
Radio Button	ID	IDC_RCRED
	Caption	&Red
Radio Button	ID	IDC_RCMAGENTA
	Caption	&Magenta
Radio Button	ID	IDC_RCYELLOW
	Caption	&Yellow
Radio Button	ID	IDC_RCWHITE
	Caption	&White
Command Button	ID	IDC_BBITMAP
	Caption	Bi&tmap
Command Button	ID	IDC_BEXIT
	Caption	E&xit

When you finish designing your main dialog, you need to assign one variable to each of the groups of radio buttons. To do this, open the Class Wizard and assign one integer variable to each of the three radio button object IDs there. Remember that only the object IDs for the radio buttons with the Group option checked will appear in the Class Wizard. All of the radio buttons that follow will be assigned to the same variable, with sequential values, in the order of the object ID values. For this reason, it is important to create all of the radio buttons in each group in the order that you want their values to be sequenced.

To assign the necessary variables to the radio button groups in your application, open the Class Wizard and add the variables in Table 8.4 to the objects in your dialog.

TABLE 8.4. CONTROL VARIABLES.

Object	Name	Category	Type
IDC_RTPEN	m_iTool	Value	int
IDC_RSLINE	m_iShape	Value	int
IDC_RCBLACK	m_iColor	Value	int

While you have the Class Wizard open, you might want to switch back to the first tab and add an event-handler function to the Exit button, calling the OnOK function in the code for this button. You can compile and run your application now, making sure that you have all of the radio button groups defined correctly, that you can't select two or more buttons in any one group, and that you can select one button in each group without affecting either of the other two groups.

Adding the Second Dialog

When you design the main dialog, you'll add the second window that you'll use as a canvas to paint your graphics on. This dialog will be a modeless dialog, which will remain open the entire time the application is running. You will put no controls on the dialog, providing a clean canvas for drawing.

To create this second dialog, go to the Resources tab in the workspace pane. Right-click the Dialogs folder in the resource tree. Select Insert Dialog from the pop-up menu. When the new dialog is open in the window designer, remove all of the controls from the window. After you remove all of the controls, open the properties dialog for the window and uncheck the System Menu option on the second tab of properties. This will prevent the user from closing this dialog without exiting the application. You'll also want to give this dialog window an object ID that will describe its function, such as IDD_PAINT_DLG.

After you finish designing the second dialog, create a new class for this window by opening the Class Wizard. When you try to open the Class Wizard, you'll be asked if you want to create a new class for the second dialog window. Leave this option at its default setting and click the OK button. When asked to specify the name of the new class on the next dialog, give the class a suitable name, such as CPaintDlg, and be sure that the base class is set to CDialog. After you click OK on this dialog and create the new class, you can close the Class Wizard.

Note You need to make sure that the new dialog is selected when you try to open the Class Wizard. If the dialog is not selected, and you've switched to another object, or even some code in your application, the Class Wizard will not know that you need a class for the second dialog in your application.

Now that you have the second dialog defined, you need to add the code in the first dialog window to open the second dialog. You can accomplish this by adding two lines of code to the `OnInitDialog` function in the first window's class. First, create the dialog using the `Create` method of the `CDialog` class. This function takes two arguments: the object ID of the dialog and a pointer to the parent window, which will be the main dialog. The second function will be the `ShowWindow` function, passing the value `SW_SHOW` as the only argument. This function displays the second dialog next to the first dialog. Add a couple of lines of variable initialization to make your `OnInitDialog` function resemble Listing 8.1.

LISTING 8.1. THE `OnInitDialog` FUNCTION.

```
1:   BOOL CGraphicsDlg::OnInitDialog()
2:   {
3:       CDialog::OnInitDialog();
4:
.
.
.
27:
28:      // TODO: Add extra initialization here
29:
30:      /////////////////////////
31:      // MY CODE STARTS HERE
32:      /////////////////////////
33:
34:      // Initialize the variables and update the dialog window
35:      m_iColor = 0;
36:      m_iShape = 0;
37:      m_iTool = 0;
38:      UpdateData(FALSE);
39:
40:      // Create the second dialog window
41:      m_dlgPaint.Create(IDD_PAINT_DLG, this);
42:      // Show the second dialog window
43:      m_dlgPaint.ShowWindow(SW_SHOW);
```

continues

LISTING 8.1. CONTINUED

```
44:
45:        //////////////////////
46:        // MY CODE ENDS HERE
47:        //////////////////////
48:
49:        return TRUE;  // return TRUE  unless you set the focus to a control
50: }
```

Before you can compile and run your application, you'll need to include the header for
the second dialog class in the source code for the first dialog. You'll also need to add the
second dialog class as a variable to the first—which is a simple matter of adding a member variable to the first dialog class, specifying the variable type as the class type, in this
case CPaintDlg, giving the variable the name that you used in Listing 8.1, m_dlgPaint,
and specifying the variable access as private. To include the header file in the first dialog,
scroll to the top of the source code for the first dialog and add an include statement, as in
Listing 8.2.

LISTING 8.2. THE INCLUDE STATEMENT OF THE MAIN DIALOG.

```
1: // GraphicsDlg.cpp : implementation file
2: //
3:
4: #include "stdafx.h"
5: #include "Graphics.h"
6: #include "PaintDlg.h"
7: #include "GraphicsDlg.h"
8:
```

Conversely, you'll need to include the header file for the main dialog in the source code
for the second dialog. You can edit this file, PaintDlg.cpp, making the include statements
match those in Listing 8.2.

If you compile and run your application, you should see your second dialog window
open along with the first window. What you'll also noticed is that when you close the
first dialog, and thus close the application, the second dialog window also closes, even
though you didn't add any code to make this happen. The second dialog is a child window to the first dialog. When you created the second dialog, on line 41 of the code listing, you passed a pointer to the first dialog window as the parent window for the second
window. This set up a parent-child relationship between these two windows. When the

parent closes, so does the child. This is the same relationship the first dialog window has with all of the controls you placed on it. Each of those controls is a child window of the dialog. In a sense, what you've done is make the second dialog just another control on the first dialog.

Adding the Graphics Capabilities

Because all of the radio button variables are declared as public, the second dialog will be able to see and reference them as it needs to. You can place all of the graphic drawing functionality into the second dialog class. However, you do need to place some functionality into the first dialog to keep the variables synchronized and to tell the second dialog to draw its graphics. Accomplishing this is simpler than you might think.

Whenever a window needs to be redrawn (it may have been hidden behind another window and come to the front or minimized or off the visible screen and now in view), the operating system triggers the dialog's OnPaint function. You can place all the functionality for drawing your graphics in this function and make persistent the graphics you display.

Now that you know where to place your code to display the graphics, how can you cause the second dialog to call its OnPaint function whenever the user changes one of the selections on the first dialog? Well, you could hide and then show the second dialog, but that might look a little peculiar to the user. Actually, a single function will convince the second window that it needs to redraw its entire dialog. This function, Invalidate, requires no arguments and is a member function of the CWnd class, so it can be used on any window or control. The Invalidate function tells the window, and the operating system, that the display area of the window is no longer valid and that it needs to be redrawn. You can trigger the OnPaint function in the second dialog at will, without resorting to any awkward tricks or hacks.

At this point, we have determined that all of the radio buttons can use the same functionality on their clicked events. You can set up a single event-handler function for the clicked event on all of the radio button controls. In this event function, you'll need to synchronize the class variables with the dialog controls by calling the UpdateData function and then tell the second dialog to redraw itself by calling its Invalidate function. You can write a single event handler that does these two things with the code in Listing 8.3.

LISTING 8.3. THE OnRSelection FUNCTION.

```
1: void CGraphicsDlg::OnRSelection()
2: {
3:     // TODO: Add your control notification handler code here
4:
5:     // Synchronize the data
6:     UpdateData(TRUE);
7:     // Repaint the second dialog
8:     m_dlgPaint.Invalidate();
9: }
```

Drawing Lines

You can compile and run your application at this point, and the second dialog redraws itself whenever you choose a different radio button on the main dialog, but you wouldn't notice anything happening. At this point, you are triggering the redraws, but you haven't told the second dialog what to draw, which is the next step in building this application.

The easiest graphics to draw on the second dialog will be different styles of lines because you already have some experience drawing them. What you'll want to do is create one pen for each of the different pen styles, using the currently selected color. After you have created all of the pens, you'll loop through the different pens, selecting each one in turn and drawing a line across the dialog with each one. Before you start this loop, you need to perform a few calculations to determine where each of the lines should be on the dialog, with their starting and stopping points.

To begin adding this functionality to your application, you first add a color table, with one entry for each of the colors in the group of available colors on the first dialog. To create this color table, add a new member variable to the second dialog class, CPaintDlg, and specify the variable type as static const COLORREF, the name as m_crColors[8], and the access as public. Open the source code file for the second dialog class, and add the color table in Listing 8.4 near the top of the file before the class constructor and destructor.

LISTING 8.4. THE COLOR TABLE.

```
1:  const COLORREF CPaintDlg::m_crColors[8] = {
2:      RGB(   0,   0,   0),    // Black
3:      RGB(   0,   0, 255),    // Blue
4:      RGB(   0, 255,   0),    // Green
5:      RGB(   0, 255, 255),    // Cyan
6:      RGB( 255,   0,   0),    // Red
7:      RGB( 255,   0, 255),    // Magenta
```

```
8:      RGB( 255, 255,   0),    // Yellow
9:      RGB( 255, 255, 255)     // White
10: };
11: //////////////////////////////////////////////////////////////
12: // CPaintDlg dialog
 .
 .
 .
```

With the color table in place, you can add a new function for drawing the lines. To keep the OnPaint function from getting too cluttered and difficult to understand, it makes more sense to place a limited amount of code in it to determine what should be drawn on the second dialog and then call other more specialized functions to draw the various shapes. With this in mind, you need to create a new member function for the second dialog class for drawing the lines. Declare this as a void function, and specify its declaration as DrawLine(CPaintDC *pdc, int iColor) and its access as private. You can edit this function, adding the code in Listing 8.5.

LISTING 8.5. THE DrawLine FUNCTION.

```
1:  void CPaintDlg::DrawLine(CPaintDC *pdc, int iColor)
2:  {
3:      // Declare and create the pens
4:      CPen lSolidPen (PS_SOLID, 1, m_crColors[iColor]);
5:      CPen lDotPen (PS_DOT, 1, m_crColors[iColor]);
6:      CPen lDashPen (PS_DASH, 1, m_crColors[iColor]);
7:      CPen lDashDotPen (PS_DASHDOT, 1, m_crColors[iColor]);
8:      CPen lDashDotDotPen (PS_DASHDOTDOT, 1, m_crColors[iColor]);
9:      CPen lNullPen (PS_NULL, 1, m_crColors[iColor]);
10:     CPen lInsidePen (PS_INSIDEFRAME, 1, m_crColors[iColor]);
11:
12:     // Get the drawing area
13:     CRect lRect;
14:     GetClientRect(lRect);
15:     lRect.NormalizeRect();
16:
17:     // Calculate the distance between each of the lines
18:     CPoint pStart;
19:     CPoint pEnd;
20:     int liDist = lRect.Height() / 8;
21:     CPen *lOldPen;
22:     // Specify the starting points
23:     pStart.y = lRect.top;
24:     pStart.x = lRect.left;
```

continues

LISTING 8.5. CONTINUED

```
25:        pEnd.y = pStart.y;
26:        pEnd.x = lRect.right;
27:        int i;
28:        // Loop through the different pens
29:        for (i = 0; i < 7; i++)
30:        {
31:            // Which pen are we on?
32:            switch (i)
33:            {
34:            case 0:    // Solid
35:                lOldPen = pdc->SelectObject(&lSolidPen);
36:                break;
37:            case 1:    // Dot
38:                pdc->SelectObject(&lDotPen);
39:                break;
40:            case 2:    // Dash
41:                pdc->SelectObject(&lDashPen);
42:                break;
43:            case 3:    // Dash Dot
44:                pdc->SelectObject(&lDashDotPen);
45:                break;
46:            case 4:    // Dash Dot Dot
47:                pdc->SelectObject(&lDashDotDotPen);
48:                break;
49:            case 5:    // Null
50:                pdc->SelectObject(&lNullPen);
51:                break;
52:            case 6:    // Inside
53:                pdc->SelectObject(&lInsidePen);
54:                break;
55:            }
56:            // Move down to the next position
57:            pStart.y = pStart.y + liDist;
58:            pEnd.y = pStart.y;
59:            // Draw the line
60:            pdc->MoveTo(pStart);
61:            pdc->LineTo(pEnd);
62:        }
63:        // Select the original pen
64:        pdc->SelectObject(lOldPen);
65: }
```

Now you need to edit the OnPaint function so that the DrawLine function is called when it needs to be called. Add this function through the Class Wizard as an event-handler function for the WM_PAINT message. You'll notice that the generated code for this function creates a CPaintDC variable instead of the normal CDC class. The CPaintDC class is a descendent of the CDC device context class. It automatically calls the BeginPaint and EndPaint API functions that all Windows applications must call before drawing any graphics during the WM_PAINT event message processing. It can be treated just like a regular device context object, calling all of the same functions.

When you are in the OnPaint function, you need to get a pointer to the parent window so that you can check the values of the variables tied to the groups of radio buttons to determine the color, tools, and shape to be drawn on the second dialog. This information tells you whether to call the DrawLine function or another function that you haven't written yet.

To add this functionality to your application, add an event handler for the WM_PAINT message on the second dialog class, adding the code in Listing 8.6 to the function created in your class.

LISTING 8.6. THE OnPaint FUNCTION.

```
1:   void CPaintDlg::OnPaint()
2:   {
3:       CPaintDC dc(this); // device context for painting
4:
5:       // TODO: Add your message handler code here
6:
7:       // Get a pointer to the parent window
8:       CGraphicsDlg *pWnd = (CGraphicsDlg*)GetParent();
9:       // Do we have a valid pointer?
10:      if (pWnd)
11:      {
12:          // Is the tool a bitmap?
13:          if (pWnd->m_iTool == 2)
14:          {
15:          }
16:          else    // No, we're drawing a shape
17:          {
18:              // Are we drawing a line?
19:              if (pWnd->m_iShape == 0)
20:                  DrawLine(&dc, pWnd->m_iColor);
21:          }
22:      }
23:      // Do not call CDialog::OnPaint() for painting messages
24:}
```

At this point, if you compile and run your application, you should be able to draw lines across the second dialog, as shown in Figure 8.4.

FIGURE 8.4.

Drawing lines on the second dialog.

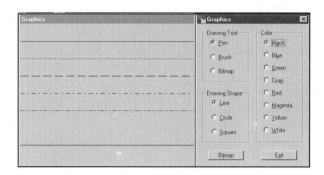

Drawing Circles and Squares

Now that you have the basic structure in place, and you can see how you can change what is drawn on the second dialog at will, you are ready to add code to the second dialog to draw the circles and squares. To draw these figures, you use the `Ellipse` and `Rectangle` device context functions. These functions will use the currently selected pen and brush to draw these figures at the specified location. With both functions, you pass a `CRect` object to specify the rectangle in which to draw the specified figure. The `Rectangle` function fills the entire space specified, and the `Ellipse` function draws a circle or ellipse where the middle of each side of the rectangle touches the edge of the ellipse. Because these functions use both the pen and brush, you'll need to create and select an invisible pen and invisible brush to allow the user to choose either the pen or the brush. For the pen, you can use the null pen for this purpose, but for the brush, you'll need to create a solid brush the color of the window background (light gray).

When you calculate the position for each of these figures, you need to take a different approach from what you used with the lines. With the lines, you were able to get the height of the window, divide it by 8, and then draw a line at each of the divisions from the left edge to the right edge. With the ellipses and rectangles, you'll need to divide the dialog window into eight even rectangles. The easiest way to do this is to create two rows of figures with four figures in each row. Leave a little space between each figure so that the user can see the different pens used to outline each figure.

To add this functionality to your application, add a new function to the second dialog class. Specify the function type as void, the declaration as `DrawRegion(CPaintDC *pdc, int iColor, int iTool, int iShape)`, and the access as private. Edit the code in this function, adding the code in Listing 8.7.

LISTING 8.7. THE DrawRegion FUNCTION.

```
 1:  void CPaintDlg::DrawRegion(CPaintDC *pdc, int iColor, int iTool, int
     ➥iShape)
 2:  {
 3:      // Declare and create the pens
 4:      CPen lSolidPen (PS_SOLID, 1, m_crColors[iColor]);
 5:      CPen lDotPen (PS_DOT, 1, m_crColors[iColor]);
 6:      CPen lDashPen (PS_DASH, 1, m_crColors[iColor]);
 7:      CPen lDashDotPen (PS_DASHDOT, 1, m_crColors[iColor]);
 8:      CPen lDashDotDotPen (PS_DASHDOTDOT, 1, m_crColors[iColor]);
 9:      CPen lNullPen (PS_NULL, 1, m_crColors[iColor]);
10:      CPen lInsidePen (PS_INSIDEFRAME, 1, m_crColors[iColor]);
11:
12:      // Declare and create the brushes
13:      CBrush lSolidBrush(m_crColors[iColor]);
14:      CBrush lBDiagBrush(HS_BDIAGONAL, m_crColors[iColor]);
15:      CBrush lCrossBrush(HS_CROSS, m_crColors[iColor]);
16:      CBrush lDiagCrossBrush(HS_DIAGCROSS, m_crColors[iColor]);
17:      CBrush lFDiagBrush(HS_FDIAGONAL, m_crColors[iColor]);
18:      CBrush lHorizBrush(HS_HORIZONTAL, m_crColors[iColor]);
19:      CBrush lVertBrush(HS_VERTICAL, m_crColors[iColor]);
20:      CBrush lNullBrush(RGB(192, 192, 192));
21:
22:      // Calculate the size of the drawing regions
23:      CRect lRect;
24:      GetClientRect(lRect);
25:      lRect.NormalizeRect();
26:      int liVert = lRect.Height() / 2;
27:      int liHeight = liVert - 10;
28:      int liHorz = lRect.Width() / 4;
29:      int liWidth = liHorz - 10;
30:      CRect lDrawRect;
31:      CPen *lOldPen;
32:      CBrush *lOldBrush;
33:      int i;
34:      // Loop through all of the brushes and pens
35:      for (i = 0; i < 7; i++)
36:      {
37:          switch (i)
38:          {
39:          case 0:    // Solid
40:              // Determine the location for this figure.
41:              // Start the first row
42:              lDrawRect.top = lRect.top + 5;
43:              lDrawRect.left = lRect.left + 5;
44:              lDrawRect.bottom = lDrawRect.top + liHeight;
45:              lDrawRect.right = lDrawRect.left + liWidth;
46:              // Select the appropriate pen and brush
```

continues

LISTING 8.7. CONTINUED

```
47:                lOldPen = pdc->SelectObject(&lSolidPen);
48:                lOldBrush = pdc->SelectObject(&lSolidBrush);
49:                break;
50:        case 1:     // Dot - Back Diagonal
51:                // Determine the location for this figure.
52:                lDrawRect.left = lDrawRect.left + liHorz;
53:                lDrawRect.right = lDrawRect.left + liWidth;
54:                // Select the appropriate pen and brush
55:                pdc->SelectObject(&lDotPen);
56:                pdc->SelectObject(&lBDiagBrush);
57:                break;
58:        case 2:     // Dash - Cross Brush
59:                // Determine the location for this figure.
60:                lDrawRect.left = lDrawRect.left + liHorz;
61:                lDrawRect.right = lDrawRect.left + liWidth;
62:                // Select the appropriate pen and brush
63:                pdc->SelectObject(&lDashPen);
64:                pdc->SelectObject(&lCrossBrush);
65:                break;
66:        case 3:     // Dash Dot - Diagonal Cross
67:                // Determine the location for this figure.
68:                lDrawRect.left = lDrawRect.left + liHorz;
69:                lDrawRect.right = lDrawRect.left + liWidth;
70:                // Select the appropriate pen and brush
71:                pdc->SelectObject(&lDashDotPen);
72:                pdc->SelectObject(&lDiagCrossBrush);
73:                break;
74:        case 4:     // Dash Dot Dot - Forward Diagonal
75:                // Determine the location for this figure.
76:                // Start the second row
77:                lDrawRect.top = lDrawRect.top + liVert;
78:                lDrawRect.left = lRect.left + 5;
79:                lDrawRect.bottom = lDrawRect.top + liHeight;
80:                lDrawRect.right = lDrawRect.left + liWidth;
81:                // Select the appropriate pen and brush
82:                pdc->SelectObject(&lDashDotDotPen);
83:                pdc->SelectObject(&lFDiagBrush);
84:                break;
85:        case 5:     // Null - Horizontal
86:                // Determine the location for this figure.
87:                lDrawRect.left = lDrawRect.left + liHorz;
88:                lDrawRect.right = lDrawRect.left + liWidth;
89:                // Select the appropriate pen and brush
90:                pdc->SelectObject(&lNullPen);
91:                pdc->SelectObject(&lHorizBrush);
92:                break;
93:        case 6:     // Inside - Vertical
94:                // Determine the location for this figure.
```

```
95:                    lDrawRect.left = lDrawRect.left + liHorz;
96:                    lDrawRect.right = lDrawRect.left + liWidth;
97:                    // Select the appropriate pen and brush
98:                    pdc->SelectObject(&lInsidePen);
99:                    pdc->SelectObject(&lVertBrush);
100:                   break;
101:           }
102:           // Which tool are we using?
103:           if (iTool == 0)
104:                   pdc->SelectObject(lNullBrush);
105:           else
106:                   pdc->SelectObject(lNullPen);
107:           // Which shape are we drawing?
108:           if (iShape == 1)
109:                   pdc->Ellipse(lDrawRect);
110:           else
111:                   pdc->Rectangle(lDrawRect);
112:       }
113:       // Reset the original brush and pen
114:       pdc->SelectObject(lOldBrush);
115:       pdc->SelectObject(lOldPen);
116:}
```

Now that you have the capability to draw the circles and squares in the second dialog, you'll need to call this function when the user has selected either of these two figures with either a pen or a brush. To do this, add the two lines starting at line 21 in Listing 8.8 to the OnPaint function.

LISTING 8.8. THE MODIFIED OnPaint FUNCTION.

```
1:   void CPaintDlg::OnPaint()
2:   {
3:       CPaintDC dc(this); // device context for painting
4:
5:       // TODO: Add your message handler code here
6:
7:       // Get a pointer to the parent window
8:       CGraphicsDlg *pWnd = (CGraphicsDlg*)GetParent();
9:       // Do we have a valid pointer?
10:      if (pWnd)
11:      {
12:          // Is the tool a bitmap?
13:          if (pWnd->m_iTool == 2)
14:          {
15:          }
16:          else    // No, we're drawing a shape
```

continues

LISTING 8.8. CONTINUED

```
17:        {
18:            // Are we drawing a line?
19:            if (m_iShape == 0)
20:                DrawLine(&dc, pWnd->m_iColor);
21:            else    // We're drawing a ellipse or rectangle
22:                DrawRegion(&dc, pWnd->m_iColor, pWnd->m_iTool,
    ➥pWnd->m_iShape);
23:        }
24:    }
25:    // Do not call CDialog::OnPaint() for painting messages
26:}
```

Now you should be able to compile and run your application and display not only lines, but also squares and circles, switching between displaying the outlines and the filled-in figure without any outline, as shown in Figure 8.5.

FIGURE 8.5.

Drawing rectangles on the second dialog.

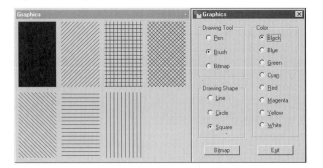

Loading Bitmaps

Now that you can draw various graphic images on the second dialog window, all that's left is to add the functionality to load and display bitmaps. You could easily add the bitmaps to the resources in the application, give them their own object IDs, and then use the LoadBitmap and MAKEINTRESOURCE functions to load the bitmap into a CBitmap class object, but that isn't extremely useful when you start building your own applications. What would be really useful is the ability to load bitmaps from files on the computer disk. To provide this functionality, you use the LoadImage API function to load the bitmap images into memory and then attach the loaded image to the CBitmap object.

To do this in your application, you can attach a function to the bitmap button on the first dialog that displays the File Open dialog to the user, allowing the user to select a bitmap to be displayed. You'll want to build a filter for the dialog, limiting the available files to bitmaps that can be displayed in the second dialog. After the user selects a bitmap, you'll get the file and path name from the dialog and load the bitmap using the LoadImage function. When you have a valid handle to the bitmap that was loaded into memory, you'll delete the current bitmap image from the CBitmap object. If there was a bitmap loaded into the CBitmap object, you'll detach the CBitmap object from the now deleted image. After you make sure that there isn't already an image loaded in the CBitmap object, you attach the image you just loaded into memory, using the Attach function. At this point, you want to invalidate the second dialog so that if it's displaying a bitmap, it displays the newly loaded bitmap.

To support this functionality, you need to add a string variable to hold the bitmap name, and a CBitmap variable to hold the bitmap image, to the first dialog class. Add these two variables as listed in Table 8.5.

TABLE 8.5. Bitmap variables.

Name	Type	Access
m_sBitmap	CString	Public
m_bmpBitmap	CBitmap	Public

After you add the variables to the first dialog class, add an event-handler function to the clicked event of the Bitmap button using the Class Wizard. After you add this function, edit it, adding the code in Listing 8.9.

LISTING 8.9. THE OnBbitmap FUNCTION.

```
1:  void CGraphicsDlg::OnBbitmap()
2:  {
3:      // TODO: Add your control notification handler code here
4:
5:      // Build a filter for use in the File Open dialog
6:      static char BASED_CODE szFilter[] = "Bitmap Files (*.bmp)|*.bmp||";
7:      // Create the File Open dialog
8:      CFileDialog m_ldFile(TRUE, ".bmp", m_sBitmap,
9:          OFN_HIDEREADONLY | OFN_OVERWRITEPROMPT, szFilter);
10:
11:     // Show the File Open dialog and capture the result
12:     if (m_ldFile.DoModal() == IDOK)
13:     {
14:         // Get the filename selected
15:         m_sBitmap = m_ldFile.GetPathName();
16:         // Load the selected bitmap file
```

continues

LISTING 8.9. CONTINUED

```
17:          HBITMAP hBitmap = (HBITMAP) ::LoadImage(AfxGetInstanceHandle(),
18:              m_sBitmap, IMAGE_BITMAP, 0, 0,
19:              LR_LOADFROMFILE | LR_CREATEDIBSECTION);
20:
21:          // Do we have a valid handle for the loaded image?
22:          if (hBitmap)
23:          {
24:              // Delete the current bitmap
25:              if (m_bmpBitmap.DeleteObject())
26:                  // If there was a bitmap, detach it
27:                  m_bmpBitmap.Detach();
28:              // Attach the currently loaded bitmap to the bitmap object
29:              m_bmpBitmap.Attach(hBitmap);
30:          }
31:          // Invalidate the second dialog window
32:          m_dlgPaint.Invalidate();
33:      }
34: }
```

Displaying Bitmaps

Now that you can load bitmaps into memory, you need to display them for the user. You need to copy the bitmap from the CBitmap object to a BITMAP structure, using the GetBitmap function, which will get the width and height of the bitmap image. Next, you'll create a new device context that is compatible with the screen device context. You'll select the bitmap into the new device context and then copy it from this second device context to the original device context, resizing it as it's copied, using the StretchBlt function.

To add this functionality to your application, add a new member function to the second dialog class. Specify the function type as void, the function declaration as ShowBitmap(CPaintDC *pdc, CWnd *pWnd), and the function access as private. Edit the function, adding the code in Listing 8.10.

 Note

Notice that you have declared the window pointer being passed in as a pointer to a CWnd object, instead of the class type of your main dialog. To declare it as a pointer to the class type of the first dialog, you'd need to declare the class for the first dialog before the class declaration for the second dialog. Meanwhile, the first dialog requires that the second dialog class be declared first. This affects the order in which the include files are added to the source code at the top of each file. You cannot have both classes declared before the other; one has to be first. Although there are ways to get around this problem, by declaring a place holder for the second class before the declaration of the first class, it's easier to cast the pointer as a pointer to the first dialog class in the function in this instance. To learn how to declare a place holder for the second class, see Appendix A, "C++ Review."

LISTING 8.10. THE ShowBitmap FUNCTION.

```
 1:  void CPaintDlg::ShowBitmap(CPaintDC *pdc, CWnd *pWnd)
 2:  {
 3:      // Convert the pointer to a pointer to the main dialog class
 4:      CGraphicsDlg *lpWnd = (CGraphicsDlg*)pWnd;
 5:      BITMAP bm;
 6:      // Get the loaded bitmap
 7:      lpWnd->m_bmpBitmap.GetBitmap(&bm);
 8:      CDC dcMem;
 9:      // Create a device context to load the bitmap into
10:      dcMem.CreateCompatibleDC(pdc);
11:      // Select the bitmap into the compatible device context
12:      CBitmap* pOldBitmap = (CBitmap*)dcMem.SelectObject
            ➥(lpWnd->m_bmpBitmap);
13:      CRect lRect;
14:      // Get the display area available
15:      GetClientRect(lRect);
16:      lRect.NormalizeRect();
17:      // Copy and resize the bitmap to the dialog window
18:      pdc->StretchBlt(10, 10, (lRect.Width() - 20),
19:              (lRect.Height() - 20), &dcMem, 0, 0,
20:              bm.bmWidth, bm.bmHeight, SRCCOPY);
21:  }
```

Now that you have the ability to display the currently selected bitmap on the dialog, you'll need to add the functionality to call this function to the OnPaint function in the second dialog. You can determine whether a bitmap has been specified by checking the value of the m_sBitmap variable on the first dialog. If this string is empty, there is no bitmap to be displayed. If the string is not empty, you can call the ShowBitmap function. To add this last bit of functionality to this application, edit the OnPaint function, adding lines 15 through 18 from Listing 8.11.

LISTING 8.11. THE MODIFIED `OnPaint` FUNCTION.

```
 1:  void CPaintDlg::OnPaint()
 2:  {
 3:      CPaintDC dc(this); // device context for painting
 4:
 5:      // TODO: Add your message handler code here
 6:
 7:      // Get a pointer to the parent window
 8:      CGraphicsDlg *pWnd = (CGraphicsDlg*)GetParent();
 9:      // Do we have a valid pointer?
10:      if (pWnd)
11:      {
12:          // Is the tool a bitmap?
13:          if (pWnd->m_iTool == 2)
14:          {
15:              // Is there a bitmap selected and loaded?
16:              if (pWnd->m_sBitmap != "")
17:                  // Display it
18:                  ShowBitmap(&dc, pWnd);
19:          }
20:          else    // No, we're drawing a shape
21:          {
22:              // Are we drawing a line?
23:              if (m_iShape == 0)
24:                  DrawLine(&dc, pWnd->m_iColor);
25:              else    // We're drawing a ellipse or rectangle
26:                  DrawRegion(&dc, pWnd->m_iColor, pWnd->m_iTool,
27:                                  pWnd->m_iShape);
28:          }
29:      }
30:      // Do not call CDialog::OnPaint() for painting messages
31: }
```

At this point, you should be able to select a bitmap from your system and display it in the second dialog, as shown in Figure 8.6.

FIGURE 8.6.

Showing a bitmap in the second dialog.

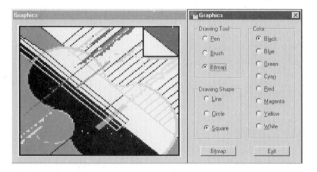

Summary

What a way to start the week! You learned a lot today. You learned how Windows uses device context objects to allow you to draw graphics in the same way every time, without having to worry about what hardware users might have in their computers. You learned about some of the basic GDI objects, such as pens and brushes, and how they are used to draw figures on windows and dialogs. You also learned how you can load bitmaps from the system disk and display them onscreen for the user to see. You learned about the different pen and brush styles and how you can use these to draw the type of figure you want to draw. You also learned how you can specify colors for use with pens and brushes so that you can control how images appear to the user.

Q&A

Q Why do I need to specify both a pen and a brush if I just want to display one or the other?

A You are always drawing with both when you draw any object that is filled in. The pen draws the outline, and the brush fills in the interior. You cannot choose to use one or the other; you have to use both. If you only want to display one or the other, you need to take special steps.

Q Why do all of the pen styles become solid when I increase the pen width above 1?

A When you increase the pen width, you are increasing the size of the dot that is used to draw with. If you remember Day 3, "Allowing User Interaction—Integrating the Mouse and Keyboard in Your Application," when you first tried to draw by capturing each spot the mouse covered, all you drew were a bunch of dots. Well, when you increase the size of the dots that you are drawing the line with, the gaps between the dots are filled in from both sides, providing an unbroken line.

Workshop

The Workshop provides quiz questions to help you solidify your understanding of the material covered and exercises to provide you with experience in using what you've learned. The answers to the quiz questions and exercises are provided in Appendix B, "Answers."

Quiz

1. What are the three values that are combined to specify a color?
2. What do you use to draw on windows without needing to know what graphics card the user has?
3. What size bitmap can you use to make a brush from it?
4. What event message is sent to a window to tell it to redraw itself?
5. How can you cause a window to repaint itself?

Exercises

1. Make the second dialog window resizable, and make it adjust the figures drawn on it whenever it's resized.
2. Add a bitmap brush to the set of brushes used to create the rectangles and ellipses.

DAY 9

Adding ActiveX Controls to Your Application

In today's application develop market, there are thousands of prebuilt components that you can plug into your applications, extending the functionality of your applications instantaneously. Originally the domain of Visual Basic programmers, now you can use readily available ActiveX controls with just about any Windows programming language, including Visual C++. Today you will learn how you can add ActiveX controls to your Visual C++ applications, taking advantage of their existing functionality. Some of the topics that you will cover today are

- What ActiveX controls are and how they work.
- How you can add ActiveX controls to your project workspace.
- How you can use the ActiveX control in your Visual C++ application.
- How to call the various methods associated with the ActiveX control.
- How to handle events that are triggered by the ActiveX control.

What Is an ActiveX Control?

An ActiveX control is a software component that can be plugged into many different programs and used as if it were a native part of the program. It's similar to the concept of separate stereo components. If you buy a new tape deck, you can just plug it into the rest of your stereo and it works with everything else you already have. ActiveX controls bring this same type of interoperability to software applications.

ActiveX used to be called OLE 2.0. OLE 2.0 was Microsoft's technology for combining two or more applications to make them work as one (or at least to switch between the various applications within the same application shell). This idea was an expansion from the original OLE (Object Linking and Embedding) technology, which only enabled you to combine documents created with different applications into a single document. When revamping OLE technologies to work in a distributed environment (such as on the Internet), Microsoft decided to also revamp the name. Thus, ActiveX was born.

ActiveX and the IDispatch Interface

The ActiveX technology is built on top of Microsoft's COM (Component Object Model) technology, utilizing its interface and interaction model for making ActiveX control integration fairly seamless. The COM technology defines how ActiveX objects are constructed and how their interfaces are designed. The ActiveX technology defines a layer that is built on top of COM, what interfaces various objects should support, and how different types of objects should interact.

Note

> Microsoft's COM technology defines how applications and components can interact through the use of interfaces. An interface is like a function call into an ActiveX component. However, COM specifies how that function call must be built and called, and what supporting functionality must accompany the function call.
>
> There are interfaces, like the IUnknown interface, that are required in every COM object, and which are used to query the component to find out what other interfaces are supported by the component. Each interface supports a specific set of functionality; you might have one interface to handle the visual appearance of the control, another to control how the control appearance interacts with the surrounding application, another that triggers events in the surrounding application, and so on.

One of the key technologies in ActiveX controls is *automation*. Automation enables an application embedded within another application to activate itself and control its part of the user interface or document, making its changes and then shutting itself down when the user moves on to another part of the application that isn't controlled by the embedded application.

This process is what happens when you have an Excel spreadsheet embedded within a Word document. If you click the spreadsheet, Excel becomes active and you can edit the spreadsheet using Excel, even though you're still working in Word. Then, once you finish making your changes to the spreadsheet, Excel closes itself down and you can continue working in Word.

One of the keys to making automation work is a special interface called the IDispatch (also known as the dispinterface) interface. The IDispatch interface consists of a pointer to a table of available methods that can be run in the ActiveX control or embedded application. These methods have ID numbers, called DISPIDs, which are also loaded into a table that can be used to look up the ID for a specific method. Once you know the DISPID for a specific method, you can call that method by calling the Invoke method of the IDispatch interface, passing the DISPID to identify the method to be run. Figure 9.1 shows how the IDispatch interface uses the Invoke method to run methods in the ActiveX object.

FIGURE 9.1.

The IDispatch ActiveX interface.

IDispatch::Invoke(DISPID)

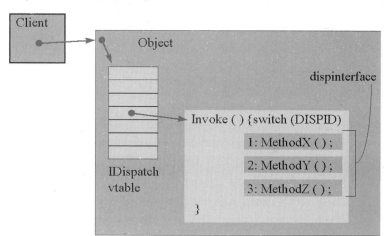

ActiveX Containers and Servers

To embed one ActiveX object within another ActiveX object, you have to implement the embedded object as an ActiveX *server*, and the object containing the first object must be an ActiveX *container*. Any ActiveX object that can be embedded within another is an ActiveX server, whether it is an entire application or just a small ActiveX control. Any ActiveX object that can have other ActiveX objects embedded within it is an ActiveX container.

 Note

> Don't confuse the use of the terms *container* and *server* with the term *client* in the previous figure. The client is the object calling the other object's IDispatch interface. As you'll learn in a page or so, both the container and server call the other's IDispatch interfaces, making each one the client of the other.

These two types of ActiveX objects are not mutually exclusive. An ActiveX server can also be an ActiveX container. A good example of this concept is Microsoft's Internet Explorer Web browser. Internet Explorer is implemented as an ActiveX server that runs within an ActiveX container shell (that can also house Word, Excel, PowerPoint, or any other ActiveX server application). At the same time that Internet Explorer is an ActiveX server running within the browser shell, it can contain other ActiveX controls.

ActiveX controls are a special instance of an ActiveX server. Some ActiveX servers are also applications that can run on their own. ActiveX controls cannot run on their own and must be embedded within an ActiveX container. By using ActiveX components in your Visual C++ application, you automatically make your application an ActiveX container.

Most of the interaction between the ActiveX container and an ActiveX control takes place through three IDispatch interfaces. One of these IDispatch interfaces is on the control, and it is used by the container to make calls to the various methods that the ActiveX control makes available to the container.

The container provides two IDispatch interfaces to the control. The first of these IDispatch interfaces is used by the control to trigger events in the container application. The second interface is used to set properties of the control, as shown in Figure 9.2. Most properties of an ActiveX control are actually provided by the container but are maintained by the control. When you set a property for the control, the container calls a method in the control to tell the control to read the properties from the container. Most of this activity is transparent to you because Visual C++ builds a series of C++ classes around the ActiveX control's interfaces. You will interact with the methods exposed by the C++ classes, not directly calling the control's IDispatch interface.

FIGURE 9.2.

An ActiveX container and control interact primarily through a few IDispatch interfaces.

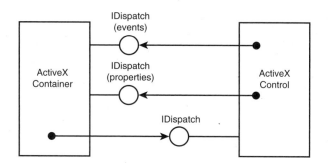

Adding an ActiveX Control to Your Project

Looking into how ActiveX controls work can be deceptive because of how easy it really is to use them in your applications. Visual C++ makes it easy to add ActiveX controls to your applications and even easier to use them. Before you begin adding the ActiveX control to your application, let's create an application shell into which you will add an ActiveX control:

1. Create a new MFC AppWizard project named ActiveX.

2. Use the same defaults on the AppWizard as in previous days, but leave the check box for ActiveX Controls checked on the second AppWizard step. Give your application the title ActiveX Controls.

3. Once you generate an application shell, remove all the controls and add a single command button.

4. Set the button's ID to IDC_EXIT and its caption to E&xit.

5. Using the Class Wizard, add a function to your command button on the BN_CLICKED event message.

6. Edit the function you just created, calling the OnOK function, as on earlier days.

Registering the Control

Before you add an ActiveX control to your dialog window, you need to register the control, both with Windows and with Visual C++. There are two possible ways to register the ActiveX control with Windows. The first way is to run any installation routine that came with the ActiveX control. If you do not have an installation routine, you need to register the control manually. To register the control manually, follow these steps:

1. Open a DOS shell.

2. Change directory to where the ActiveX control is on your system.

3. Run the regsvr32 command, specifying the name of the ActiveX control as the

only command-line argument. For instance, if you were registering a control named MYCTL.OCX and it was located in your WINDOWS\SYSTEM directory, you would perform the following:

```
C:\WINDOWS> CD system
C:\WINDOWS\SYSTEM> regsvr32 MYCTL.OCX
```

Caution

It is preferable to run any installation routine that comes with the control because registering the control manually might not enable the control for development usage. Controls can be licensed for development or deployment. If a control is licensed for deployment, you will not be able to use it in your Visual C++ applications. This is a mechanism that protects control developers by requiring that developers purchase a development license for controls; they can't just use the controls they may have installed on their system with another application.

Note

COM and ActiveX objects store a lot of information in the Windows Registry database. Whenever an application uses an ActiveX object, the operating system refers to the information in the Windows Registry to find the object and to determine whether the application can use the object in the way that it requested. Using the regsvr32.exe utility to register an ActiveX control places most of the required information about the control into the system Registry. However, there may be additional information about the control that needs to be in the Registry for the control to function properly.

Now that the ActiveX control that you want to use is registered with the operating system, you need to register it with Visual C++ and add it to your project. To do this, follow these steps:

1. Select Project | Add To Project | Components and Controls from the Visual C++ menu.

2. In the Components and Controls Gallery dialog, navigate to the Registered ActiveX Controls folder, as in Figure 9.3.

FIGURE 9.3.

The ActiveX controls that can be added to your project.

3. Select the control you want to register, such as the Microsoft FlexGrid control, and click the Insert button.

4. Click OK on the message box asking whether you want to insert this component in your project.

5. On the Confirm Classes dialog, click the OK button to add the C++ classes specified, as in Figure 9.4.

FIGURE 9.4.

Visual C++ tells you what classes will be added to your project.

6. Click the Close button on the Components and Controls Gallery dialog to finish adding controls to your project.

7. The FlexGrid control should have been added to the Control Palette for your dialog window, as in Figure 9.5.

FIGURE 9.5.

*The ActiveX control
FlexGrid is added to
the Control Palette for
use on your dialog
windows.*

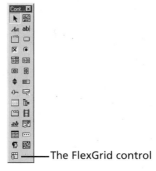
———The FlexGrid control

If you examine the Class View area of the workspace pane, you see the four classes that
Visual C++ added to your project. Expand the class trees and you see numerous methods
for these classes. Visual C++ created these classes and methods by examining the
ActiveX control that you just added and created class methods to call each of the methods
in the control's IDispatch interface.

Note

If you use older ActiveX controls in your Visual C++ applications, Visual C++
might not be able to generate the classes and methods to encapsulate the
control's functionality. The information in the control that provided Visual
C++ with the information necessary to build these classes and methods is a
more recent addition to the ActiveX specification. As a result, older controls
might not provide this information, making them more difficult to use with
Visual C++.

Adding the Control to Your Dialog

Now that you have added the FlexGrid control to your project, you can add it to your dialog window just as you would any other control. Set the control properties as in Table 9.1.

TABLE 9.1. CONTROL PROPERTY SETTINGS.

Object	Property	Setting
FlexGrid control	ID	IDC_MSFGRID
	Rows	20
	Cols	4
	MergeCells	2 - Restrict Rows
	Format (FormatString)	< Region ¦< Product ¦< Employee ¦>Sales

Once you add the control to your dialog window, you will notice that there is an additional tab on the properties dialog with all the control properties, as in Figure 9.6. You can choose to use this tab to set all the properties on the control, or you can go through the other tabs to set the properties, just as you would with the standard controls.

FIGURE 9.6.

ActiveX controls have a property tab that contains all control properties.

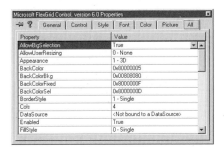

Once you have finished setting all the properties for the control, you'll need to add a variable for the control so that you can interact with the control in your code. To add this variable, open the Member Variables tab on the Class Wizard and add a variable for the control. Because you are adding a variable for an ActiveX control, you can only add a control variable, so the only thing available for you to specify is the variable name. For this example application, name the variable `m_ctlFGrid`.

Using an ActiveX Control in Your Application

Once Visual C++ has generated all the classes to encapsulate the ActiveX control, working with the control is a simple matter of calling the various methods and responding to control events just like the standard controls. You'll start with using the control methods to get information about the control and to modify data within the control. Then you'll learn how to respond to control events with Visual C++.

Interacting with the Control

The application that you are building today will generate a number of product sales over five sales regions with four salespeople. You will be able to scroll through the data, which will be sorted by region and product, to compare how each salesperson did for each product.

To make this project, you will build an array of values that will be loaded into cells in the grid. The grid will then be sorted in ascending order, using the FlexGrid control's internal sorting capabilities.

Loading Data into the Control

The first thing you will do is create a function to load data into the FlexGrid control. Add
a new function to the CActiveXDlg class by right-clicking the Class View of the workspace and choosing Add Member Function. Specify the Function Type as void, the
Function Declaration as LoadData, and the access as Private. Click the OK button and
edit the function, adding the code in Listing 9.1.

LISTING 9.1. THE LoadData FUNCTION.

```
 1: void CActiveXDlg::LoadData()
 2: {
 3:     int liCount;          // The grid row count
 4:     CString lsAmount;     // The sales amount
 5:
 6:     // Initialize the random number generator
 7:     srand((unsigned)time(NULL));
 8:     // Create Array in the control
 9:     for (liCount = m_ctlFGrid.GetFixedRows();
10:         liCount < m_ctlFGrid.GetRows(); liCount++)
11:     {
12:         // Generate the first column (region) values
13:         m_ctlFGrid.SetTextArray(GenID(liCount, 0), RandomStringValue(0));
14:         // Generate the second column (product) values
15:         m_ctlFGrid.SetTextArray(GenID(liCount, 1), RandomStringValue(1));
16:         // Generate the third column (employee) values
17:         m_ctlFGrid.SetTextArray(GenID(liCount, 2), RandomStringValue(2));
18:         // Generate the sales amount values
19:         lsAmount.Format("%5d.00", rand());
20:         // Populate the fourth column
21:         m_ctlFGrid.SetTextArray(GenID(liCount, 3), lsAmount);
22:     }
23:
24:     // Merge the common subsequent rows in these columns
25:     m_ctlFGrid.SetMergeCol(0, TRUE);
26:     m_ctlFGrid.SetMergeCol(1, TRUE);
27:     m_ctlFGrid.SetMergeCol(2, TRUE);
28:
29:     // Sort the grid
30:     DoSort();
31: }
```

In this function, the first thing that you do is initialize the random number generator.
Next, you loop through all of the rows in the control, placing data in each of the cells.
You get the total number of rows in the control by calling the GetRows method and the
number of the header row by calling the GetFixedRows method. You are able to add data

to the control cells by calling the SetTextArray method, which has the cell ID as the first argument and the cell contents as the second argument, both of which are generated by functions you'll be creating in a few moments.

Once you have data in the grid cells, you call SetMergeCol, which tells the control that it can merge cells in the first three columns if adjacent rows contain the same value. Finally, you sort the control, using another function you have yet to create.

Calculating the Cell ID

The cells in the FlexGrid control are numbered sequentially from left to right, top to bottom. With your control, the first row, which contains the headers (and is already populated), has cells 0 through 3, the second row cells 4 through 7, and so on. Therefore, you can calculate the ID of a cell by adding its column number to the total number of columns in the control, multiplied by the current row number. For instance, if your control has four columns, and you are in the third column and fourth row, you can calculate your cell ID as 2 + (4 * 3) = 14. (Remember that the column and row numbers start with 0, so the third column is 2 and the fourth row is number 3.)

Now that you understand how you can calculate the cell ID, you need to implement that formula in a function. Add a new function to the CActiveXDlg class using the same method as for the LoadData function. The type of this function should be int and the description should be GenID(int m_iRow, int m_iCol). Once you add the function, edit it with the code in Listing 9.2.

LISTING 9.2. THE GenID FUNCTION.

```
1: int CActiveXDlg::GenID(int m_iRow, int m_iCol)
2: {
3:     // Get the number of columns
4:     int liCols = m_ctlFGrid.GetCols();
5:
6:     // Generate an ID based on the number of columns,
7:     // the current column, and the current row
8:     return (m_iCol + liCols * m_iRow);
9: }
```

Generating Random Data

To populate the first three columns in the grid, you want to randomly generate data. In the first column, you want to put region names. In the second column, you want to put product names. And in the third column, you want to put salesperson names. By using a switch statement to determine which column you are generating data for and then using a modulus division on a randomly generated number in another switch statement, you can randomly select between a limited set of data strings.

To implement this functionality, add another function to the CActiveXDlg class with a type of CString and a description of RandomStringValue(int m_iColumn). Edit the resulting function, adding the code in Listing 9.3.

LISTING 9.3. THE RandomStringValue FUNCTION.

```
 1: CString CActiveXDlg::RandomStringValue(int m_iColumn)
 2: {
 3:     CString lsStr;      // The return string
 4:     int liCase;         // A random value ID
 5:
 6:     // Which column are we generating for?
 7:     switch (m_iColumn)
 8:     {
 9:     case 0:     // The first column (region)
10:         // Generate a random value between 0 and 4
11:         liCase = (rand() % 5);
12:         // What value was generated?
13:         switch (liCase)
14:         {
15:         case 0:
16:             // 0 - Northwest region
17:             lsStr = "Northwest";
18:             break;
19:         case 1:
20:             // 1 - Southwest region
21:             lsStr = "Southwest";
22:             break;
23:         case 2:
24:             // 2 - Midwest region
25:             lsStr = "Midwest";
26:             break;
27:         case 3:
28:             // 3 - Northeast region
29:             lsStr = "Northeast";
30:             break;
31:         default:
32:             // 4 - Southeast region
33:             lsStr = "Southeast";
34:             break;
35:         }
36:         break;
37:     case 1:     // The second column (product)
38:         // Generate a random value between 0 and 4
39:         liCase = (rand() % 5);
40:         // What value was generated?
41:         switch (liCase)
```

```
42:            {
43:            case 0:
44:                // 0 - Dodads
45:                lsStr = "Dodads";
46:                break;
47:            case 1:
48:                // 1 - Thingamajigs
49:                lsStr = "Thingamajigs";
50:                break;
51:            case 2:
52:                // 2 - Whatchamacallits
53:                lsStr = "Whatchamacallits";
54:                break;
55:            case 3:
56:                // 3 - Round Tuits
57:                lsStr = "Round Tuits";
58:                break;
59:            default:
60:                // 4 - Widgets
61:                lsStr = "Widgets";
62:                break;
63:            }
64:            break;
65:        case 2:      // The third column (employee)
66:            // Generate a random value between 0 and 3
67:            liCase = (rand() % 4);
68:            // What value was generated?
69:            switch (liCase)
70:            {
71:            case 0:
72:                // 0 - Dore
73:                lsStr = "Dore";
74:                break;
75:            case 1:
76:                // 1 - Harvey
77:                lsStr = "Harvey";
78:                break;
79:            case 2:
80:                // 2 - Pogo
81:                lsStr = "Pogo";
82:                break;
83:            default:
84:                // 3 - Nyra
85:                lsStr = "Nyra";
86:                break;
87:            }
88:            break;
89:        }
90:    // Return the generated string
91:    return lsStr;
92: }
```

Sorting the Control

To sort the Grid control, you need to select all the columns and then set the sort to ascending. To implement this functionality, add one more function to the CActiveXDlg class with a type of void and a definition of DoSort. Edit the function as in Listing 9.4.

LISTING 9.4. THE DoSort FUNCTION.

```
1: void CActiveXDlg::DoSort()
2: {
3:     // Set the current column to column 0
4:     m_ctlFGrid.SetCol(0);
5:     // Set the column selection to all columns
6:     m_ctlFGrid.SetColSel((m_ctlFGrid.GetCols() - 1));
7:     // Generic Ascending Sort
8:     m_ctlFGrid.SetSort(1);
9: }
```

In the DoSort function, you set the current column to the first column using the SetCol method. Next you select from the current column to the last column using the SetColSel method, effectively selecting all columns in the control. Finally, you tell the control to sort the columns in ascending order by using the SetSort method, passing 1 as the flag for the sort order.

Now that you have all the functionality necessary to load the control with data, you need to call the LoadData function in the OnInitDialog function to load the data before the control is visible to the user. Edit the OnInitDialog function as in Listing 9.5 to load the data.

LISTING 9.5. THE OnInitDialog FUNCTION.

```
 1: BOOL CActiveXDlg::OnInitDialog()
 2: {
 3:     CDialog::OnInitDialog();
 4: .
 5: .
 6: .
 7:     // TODO: Add extra initialization here
 8:
 9:     //////////////////////////
10:     // MY CODE STARTS HERE
11:     //////////////////////////
12:
13:     // Load data into the Grid control
14:     LoadData();
```

```
15:
16:      //////////////////////////
17:      // MY CODE ENDS HERE
18:      //////////////////////////
19:
20:      return TRUE;  // return TRUE  unless you set the focus to a control
21: }
```

If you compile and run your application at this point, you find that it is loading the data and sorting it, as in Figure 9.7.

9

FIGURE 9.7.

The FlexGrid populated with data.

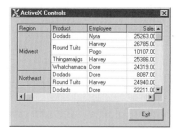

Responding to Control Events

If you play with your application at this point, you know that the Grid control does not respond to any input that you might try to give it. If you click one of the cells and try to change the value, it doesn't respond. What you need to do is add a control event to handle the input. ActiveX controls make several events available for use in Visual C++ applications. You can use the Class Wizard to browse through the available events and determine which events you need to give functionality and which to ignore. Most ActiveX controls don't have any default functionality attached to the available events but instead expect you to tell the control what to do on each event.

You are going to add two control events to capture the mouse clicks and movements. You will add functionality to allow the user to click a column header and drag it to another position, thus rearranging the column order. To implement this functionality, you have to capture two control events, when the mouse button is pressed down and when it is released. On the first event, you need to check whether the user clicked a header, and if so, you capture the column selected. On the second event, you need to move the selected column to the column on which the mouse button was released.

To accomplish this functionality, you need to create a new class variable to maintain the clicked column number between the two events. Add a new variable to the CActiveXDlg class, just like you added the functions earlier, specifying the type as int, the variable name as m_iMouseCol, and the access as Private.

Capturing the Column Selected

To capture the mouse click event for the control, follow these steps:

1. Using the Class Wizard, add a function for the MouseDown event message for the IDC_MSFGRID object.

2. Edit the function using the code in Listing 9.6.

LISTING 9.6. THE OnMouseDownMsfgrid FUNCTION.

```
 1: void CActiveXDlg::OnMouseDownMsfgrid(short Button, short Shift, long
     ➥x, long y)
 2: {
 3:     // TODO: Add your control notification handler code here
 4:
 5:     /////////////////////////
 6:     // MY CODE STARTS HERE
 7:     /////////////////////////
 8:
 9:     // Did the user click on a data row and not the
10:     // header row?
11:     if (m_ctlFGrid.GetMouseRow() != 0)
12:     {
13:         // If so, then zero out the column variable
14:         // and exit
15:         m_iMouseCol = 0;
16:         return;
17:     }
18:     // Save the column clicked on
19:     m_iMouseCol = m_ctlFGrid.GetMouseCol();
20:
21:     /////////////////////////
22:     // MY CODE ENDS HERE
23:     /////////////////////////
24: }
```

In this function, you checked the row clicked by calling the GetMouseRow method. If the row is not the first row, then zero out the column-holding variable and exit the function. Otherwise, you need to get the column clicked by calling the GetMouseCol method. You can store the returned column number in the m_iMouseCol variable that you just added to the class.

Moving the Column Where Released

Now that you are capturing the selected column number, you need to capture the column on which the mouse is released. To capture the mouse release event for the control, follow these steps:

1. Using the Class Wizard, add a function for the MouseUp event message for the IDC_MSFGRID object.

2. Edit the function using the code in Listing 9.7.

LISTING 9.7. THE OnMouseUpMsfgrid FUNCTION.

```
 1: void CActiveXDlg::OnMouseUpMsfgrid(short Button, short Shift, long x,
    ➥long y)
 2: {
 3:     // TODO: Add your control notification handler code here
 4:
 5:     ///////////////////////
 6:     // MY CODE STARTS HERE
 7:     ///////////////////////
 8:
 9:     // If the selected column was the first column,
10:     // there's nothing to do
11:     if (m_iMouseCol == 0)
12:         return;
13:     // Turn the control redraw off
14:     m_ctlFGrid.SetRedraw(FALSE);
15:     // Change the selected column position
16:     m_ctlFGrid.SetColPosition(m_iMouseCol, m_ctlFGrid.GetMouseCol());
17:     // Resort the grid
18:     DoSort();
19:     // Turn redraw back on
20:     m_ctlFGrid.SetRedraw(TRUE);
21:
22:     ///////////////////////
23:     // MY CODE ENDS HERE
24:     ///////////////////////
25: }
```

In this function, you first check to see if there is a selected column to be moved. If not, you exit the function with nothing to do. If there is a column selected, you turn off the redraw on the control using the SetRedraw method so that none of the movement is seen by the user. Next, you move the selected column to the release column using the SetColPosition method. Once you move the column, you resort the grid by calling the DoSort function. Finally, you turn the control's redraw back on so that the control is refreshed to show the user the moved column. If you compile and link your application, you should now be able to grab column headers and move the columns about, as in Figure 9.8.

FIGURE 9.8.

The FlexGrid with reordered columns.

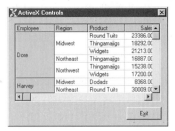

Summary

Today you learned how you can use ActiveX controls in your Visual C++ applications to easily extend your application's functionality. You learned the basics of how ActiveX controls work and how they interact with the containing application. You also learned how you can add an ActiveX control to your development project so that you can use it in your application. You saw how Visual C++ creates C++ classes to encapsulate the ActiveX controls that you add and how you can interact with the control through the exposed methods of these generated C++ classes. You also saw how you can capture events that are generated by the ActiveX control so that you can program your application to react to the events.

Q&A

Q How can I determine what methods are available to me when working with an ActiveX control?

A By examining the C++ classes that Visual C++ builds to encapsulate the control, you can get a good idea of what functionality is available to you. If you have documentation for the control, you can compare it to the C++ class to determine which class method calls which control method. You can examine the events listed for the control in the Class Wizard to determine which events are also available.

Q How can I use the ActiveX controls that were installed on my machine with another application in my Visual C++ applications?

A It depends on how the controls are licensed and what application installed the controls. If the controls were installed by another application development tool, chances are that you have a development license for the control, in which case you should be able to use them in your Visual C++ applications. If the controls were installed by an end-user application, such as Word or Quicken, then odds are that you have only a runtime license for the control. If you want to use these controls in your own applications, you need to contact the control developer to acquire a development license for the controls.

Q Because the FlexGrid control does not allow me to enter data directly into the control, how can I let my users enter data into the grid as if they were using a spreadsheet?

A To implement this functionality for the FlexGrid control, you need to add a floating Edit Box control to your window. Your code needs to determine which cell the user wants to edit and float the edit box in front of that cell. This arrangement allows the user to feel as if he is entering data directly into the cell. Another approach is to have a data-entry field outside the grid, much like is used in Excel, into which the user enters the data. You can highlight the cells as the user maneuvers around the Grid control to give the user visceral feedback for her actions.

9

Workshop

The Workshop provides quiz questions to help you solidify your understanding of the material covered and exercises to provide you with experience in using what you've learned. The answers to the quiz questions and exercises are provided in Appendix B, "Answers."

Quiz

1. How does an ActiveX container call methods in an ActiveX control?

2. How does an ActiveX control trigger events in the container application?

3. What AppWizard option must be selected for ActiveX controls to work properly in a Visual C++ application?

4. How does Visual C++ make it easy to work with ActiveX controls?

5. Why might it be difficult to work with older controls in Visual C++?

Exercise

Modify the application so that the user can double-click a column header and make it the first column in the grid.

DAY 10

Creating Single Document Interface Applications

Today you will learn a different way of approaching application development with Visual C++ than you have used with the previous days' lessons. Today you will learn how to create Single Document Interface (SDI) applications. An SDI application is a document-centric application that can only work with one document at a time, and can only work with one type of document.

Some good examples of SDI applications are Notepad, WordPad, and Paint. All of these applications can do only one type of task and can only work on one task at a time. WordPad is almost like an SDI version of Word. It's able to perform a large number of the tasks that Word does, but although Word allows you to work on numerous documents at the same time, WordPad limits you to only one document.

Some of the things that you will learn today are

- The Document/View architecture that Visual C++ uses for creating SDI applications.

- How to create an SDI application shell.
- How to separate your data from the visual representation of the data.
- How to encapsulate your data in its own C++ class.
- How to create interaction between the data and the menus.

The Document/View Architecture

When you create an SDI application, more classes are created for an SDI application than for a dialog-style application. Each of these classes serves a specific purpose in how SDI applications operate. Ignoring the About window dialog class, four specific classes make up an SDI application:

- The CWinApp-derived class
- The CFrameView-derived class
- The CDocument-derived class
- The CView-derived class

The CWinApp class creates all the other components in the application. It is the class that receives all the event messages and then passes the messages to the CFrameView and CView classes.

The CFrameView class is the window frame. It holds the menu, toolbar, scrollbars, and any other visible objects attached to the frame. This class determines how much of the document is visible at any time. Very little (if any) of your programming efforts on SDI applications will require making any modifications or additions to either of these first two classes.

The CDocument class houses your document. This class is where you will build the data structures necessary to house and manipulate the data that makes up your document. This class receives input from the CView class and passes display information to the CView class. This class is also responsible for saving and retrieving the document data from files.

The CView class is the class that displays the visual representation of your document for the user. This class passes input information to the CDocument class and receives display information from the CDocument class. Most of the coding that you will do for this class consists of drawing the document for the user and handling the input from the user. The CView class has several descendent classes that can be used as the ancestor for the view class. These descendent classes are listed in Table 10.1.

TABLE 10.1. THE `CView` DESCENDENT CLASSES.

Class	Description
CEditView	Provides the functionality of a edit box control. Can be used to implement simple text-editor functionality.
CFormView	The base class for views containing controls. Can be used to provide form-based documents in applications.
CHtmlView	Provides the functionality of a Web browser. This view directly handles the URL navigation, hyperlinking, and so on. Maintains a history list for browsing forward and back.
CListView	Provides list-control functionality in the Document/View architecture.
CRichEditView	Provides character and paragraph formatting functionality. Can be used to implement a word-processor application.
CScrollView	Provides scrolling capabilities to a CView class.
CTreeView	Provides tree-control functionality in the Document/View architecture.

All four of these classes work together to make up the full functionality of an SDI application, as shown in Figure 10.1. By taking advantage of this architecture, you can build powerful document-centric applications with relative ease.

FIGURE 10.1.

The Document/View architecture.

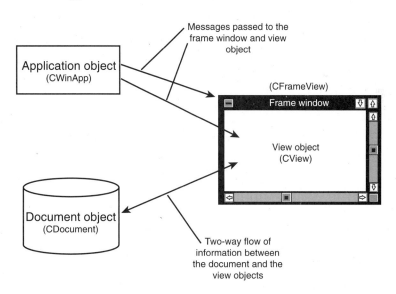

Note

Don't let the term document mislead you. This doesn't mean that you can only create applications such as word processors and spreadsheets. In this situation, the term document refers to the data that is processed by your application, whereas view refers to the visual representation of that data. For instance, the Solitaire application could be implemented as a Document/View application, with the document being the cards and their position in the playing area. In this case, the view is the display of the cards, drawing each card where the document specifies it should be.

Creating an SDI Application

To get a good idea of how the Document/View architecture works, and of how you can use it to build applications, you will build a new version of the drawing application you created on Day 3, "Allowing User Interaction—Integrating the Mouse and Keyboard in Your Application." In this version, the user's drawing will be persistent, which means it is not erased each time another window is placed in front of the application. This version will also be able to save and restore drawings.

Building the Application Shell

To create the application shell for today's application, follow these steps:

1. Create a new AppWizard project. Name the project **Day10**.

2. On the first step of the AppWizard, select Single Document.

3. Use the default values on the second step of the AppWizard.

4. On the third step of the AppWizard, uncheck the support for ActiveX Controls.

5. On the fourth step of the AppWizard, leave all the default values. Click the Advanced button.

6. In the Advanced Options dialog, enter a three-letter file extension for the files that your application will generate (for example, dhc or dvp). Click the Close button to close the dialog and then click Next to move to the next step of the AppWizard.

7. Use the default settings on the fifth step of the AppWizard.

8. On the sixth and final AppWizard step, you can choose the base class on which your view class will be based. Leave the base class as CView and click Finish. The AppWizard will generate the application shell.

Creating a Line Class

One of the first issues that you will need to tackle is how to represent your data in the document class. For the drawing application, you have a series of lines. Each line consists of a starting point and ending point. You might think that you can use a series of points for the data representation. If you do this, you also have to make special accommodations for where one series of lines between points ends and the next begins. It makes much more sense to represent the drawing as a series of lines. This allows you to store each individual line that is drawn on the window without having to worry where one set of contiguous lines ends and where the next begins.

Unfortunately, the Microsoft Foundation Classes (MFC) does not have a line object class, although it does have a point object class (CPoint). I guess you'll just have to create your own line class by following these steps:

1. In the Class View tab of the workspace pane, select the top-level object in the tree (Day10 classes). Right-click the mouse and select New Class from the pop-up menu.

2. In the New Class dialog, select Generic Class for the class type. Enter CLine for the class name and click in the first line in the Base Class list box. Enter CObject as the base class, leaving the class access as public, as in Figure 10.2.

FIGURE 10.2.

The New Class Wizard.

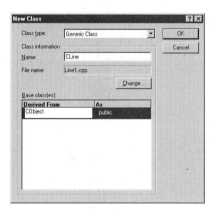

3. When you click the OK button to add the CLine class, you may be told that the Class Wizard cannot find the appropriate header file for inheriting the CLine class from the CObject class, as in Figure 10.3. Click on the OK button on this message box.

FIGURE 10.3.

Warning about including the base class definition.

>
>
> **Note**
>
> The appropriate header class is already included in the `CLine` class files. Until your compiler complains because it can't find the definition for the `CObject` class, don't worry about this message. However, if you are using a base class that's a bit further down the MFC class hierarchy, you might need to heed this message and add the appropriate header file to the include statements in the class source code file.

Constructing the `CLine` Class

At this time, your `CLine` class needs to hold only two data elements, the two end points of the line that it represents. You want to add those two data elements and add a class constructor that sets both values when creating the class instance. To do this, follow these steps:

1. In the Class View tab of the workspace pane, select the `CLine` class.

2. Right-click the `CLine` class and choose Add Member Variable from the pop-up menu.

3. Enter `CPoint` as the variable type and `m_ptFrom` as the variable name, and mark the access as Private. Click OK to add the variable.

4. Repeat steps 2 and 3, naming this variable `m_ptTo`.

5. Right-click the `CLine` class and choose Add Member Function from the pop-up menu.

6. Leave the function type blank, and enter `CLine(CPoint ptFrom, CPoint ptTo)` for the function declaration. Click OK to add the function.

7. Edit the new function, adding the code in Listing 10.1.

LISTING 10.1. THE `CLine` CONSTRUCTOR.

```
1: CLine::CLine(CPoint ptFrom, CPoint ptTo)
2: {
3:     //Initialize the from and to points
4:     m_ptFrom = ptFrom;
5:     m_ptTo = ptTo;
6: }
```

In this object constructor, you are initializing the from and to points with the points that were passed in to the constructor.

Drawing the CLine Class

To follow correct object-oriented design, your CLine class should be able to draw itself so that when the view class needs to render the line for the user, it can just pass a message to the line object, telling it to draw itself. To add this functionality, follow these steps:

1. Add a new function to the CLine class by selecting Add Member Function from the pop-up menu.

2. Specify the function type as void and the function declaration as Draw(CDC *pDC).

3. Add the code in Listing 10.2 to the Draw function you just added.

10

LISTING 10.2. THE CLine Draw FUNCTION.

```
1: void CLine::Draw(CDC * pDC)
2: {
3:     // Draw the line
4:     pDC->MoveTo(m_ptFrom);
5:     pDC->LineTo(m_ptTo);
6: }
```

This function is taken almost directly from the application you built a week ago. It's a simple function that moves to the first point on the device context and then draws a line to the second point on the device context.

Implementing the Document Functionality

Now that you have an object to use for representing the drawings made by the user, you can store these CLine objects on the document object in a simple dynamic array. To hold this array, you can add a CObArray member variable to the document class.

The CObArray class is an object array class that dynamically sizes itself to accommodate the number of items placed in it. It can hold any objects that are descended from the CObject class, and it is limited in size only by the amount of memory in the system. Other dynamic array classes in MFC include CStringArray, CByteArray, CWordArray, CDWordArray, and CPtrArray. These classes differ by the type of objects they can hold.

Add the CObArray to CDay10Doc, using the Add Member Variable Wizard and giving it a name of m_oaLines.

Adding Lines

The first functionality that you need to add to the document class is the ability to add new lines. This should be a simple process of getting the from and to points, creating a new line object, and then adding it to the object array. To implement this function, add a new member function to the CDay10Doc class, specifying the type as CLine* and the declaration as AddLine(CPoint ptFrom, CPoint ptTo) with public access. Edit the function, adding the code in Listing 10.3.

LISTING 10.3. THE CDay10Doc AddLine FUNCTION.

```
 1: CLine * CDay10Doc::AddLine(CPoint ptFrom, CPoint ptTo)
 2: {
 3:     // Create a new CLine object
 4:     CLine *pLine = new CLine(ptFrom, ptTo);
 5:     try
 6:     {
 7:         // Add the new line to the object array
 8:         m_oaLines.Add(pLine);
 9:         // Mark the document as dirty
10:         SetModifiedFlag();
11:     }
12:     // Did we run into a memory exception?
13:     catch (CMemoryException* perr)
14:     {
15:         // Display a message for the user, giving him or her the
16:         // bad news
17:         AfxMessageBox("Out of memory", MB_ICONSTOP | MB_OK);
18:         // Did we create a line object?
19:         if (pLine)
20:         {
21:             // Delete it
22:             delete pLine;
23:             pLine = NULL;
24:         }
25:         // Delete the exception object
26:         perr->Delete();
27:     }
28:     return pLine;
29: }
```

At first, this function is understandable. You create a new CLine instance, passing the from and to points as constructor arguments. Right after that, however, you have something interesting, the following flow control construct:

```
try
{
    .
```

```
 .
 .
 .
}
catch (...)
{
 .
 .
 .
}
```

What is this? This construct is an example of structured exception handling. Some code could fail because of a factor beyond your control, such as running out of memory or disk space, you can place a try section around the code that might have a problem. The try section should always be followed by one or more catch sections. If a problem occurs during the code in the try section, the program immediately jumps to the catch sections. Each catch section specifies what type of exception it handles (in the case of the AddLine function, it specifically handles memory exceptions only), and if there is a matching catch section for the type of problem that did occur, that section of code is executed to give the application a chance to recover from the problem. If there is no catch section for the type of problem that did occur, your program jumps to a default exception handler, which will most likely shut down your application. For more information on structured exception handling, see Appendix A, "C++ Review."

Within the try section, you add the new CLine instance to the array of line objects. Next, you call the SetModifiedFlag function, which marks the document as "dirty" (unsaved) so that if you close the application or open another file without saving the current drawing first, the application prompts you to save the current drawing (with the familiar Yes, No, Cancel message box).

In the catch section, you inform the user that the system is out of memory and then clean up by deleting the CLine object and the exception object.

Finally, at the end of the function, you return the CLine object to the calling routine. This enables the view object to let the line object draw itself.

Getting the Line Count

The next item you will add to the document class is a function to return the number of lines in the document. This functionality is necessary because the view object needs to loop through the array of lines, asking each line object to draw itself. The view object will need to be able to determine the total number of lines in the document and retrieve any specific line from the document.

Returning the number of lines in the document is a simple matter of returning the number of lines in the object array, so you can just return the return value from the GetSize method of the CObArray class. To implement this function, add a new member function to the CDay10Doc class, specifying the type as int and the declaration as GetLineCount with public access. Edit the function, adding the code in Listing 10.4.

LISTING 10.4. THE CDay10Doc GetLineCount FUNCTION.

```
1: int CDay10Doc::GetLineCount()
2: {
3:     // Return the array count
4:     return m_oaLines.GetSize();
5: }
```

Retrieving a Specific Line

Finally, you need to add a function to return a specific line from the document. This is a simple matter of returning the object at the specified position in the object array. To implement this function, add a new member function to the CDay10Doc class, specifying the type as CLine* and the declaration as GetLine(int nIndex) with public access. Edit the function, adding the code in Listing 10.5.

LISTING 10.5. THE CDay10Doc GetLine FUNCTION.

```
1: CLine * CDay10Doc::GetLine(int nIndex)
2: {
3:     // Return a pointer to the line object
4:     // at the specified point in the object array
5:     return (CLine*)m_oaLines[nIndex];
6: }
```

 Note   Notice that the object being returned had to be cast as a pointer to a CLine object. Because the CObArray class is an array of CObjects, every element that is returned by the array is a CObject instance, not a CLine object instance.

Showing the User

Now that you have built the capability into the document class to hold the drawing, you need to add the functionality to the view object to read the user's drawing input and to draw the image. The mouse events to capture the user input are almost identical to those you created a week ago. The second part of the functionality that you need to implement is drawing the image. You will make an addition to a function that already exists in the view object class.

Before adding these functions, you need to add a member variable to the CDay10View class to maintain the previous mouse point, just as you did a week ago. Add a member variable to the CDay10View class through the workspace pane, specifying the type as CPoint, the name as m_ptPrevPos, and the access as private.

Adding the Mouse Events

To add the mouse events to capture the user's drawing efforts, open the Class Wizard and add functions to the CDay10View class for the WM_LBUTTONDOWN, WM_LBUTTONUP, and WM_MOUSEMOVE event messages. Edit the functions as in Listing 10.6.

LISTING 10.6. THE CDay10View MOUSE FUNCTIONS.

```
 1: void CDay10View::OnLButtonDown(UINT nFlags, CPoint point)
 2: {
 3:     // TODO: Add your message handler code here and/or call default
 4:
 5:     /////////////////////////
 6:     // MY CODE STARTS HERE
 7:     /////////////////////////
 8:
 9:     // Capture the mouse, so no other application can
10:     // grab it if the mouse leaves the window area
11:     SetCapture();
12:     // Save the point
13:     m_ptPrevPos = point;
14:
15:     /////////////////////////
16:     // MY CODE ENDS HERE
17:     /////////////////////////
18:
19:     CView::OnLButtonDown(nFlags, point);
20: }
21:
22: void CDay10View::OnLButtonUp(UINT nFlags, CPoint point)
23: {
24:     // TODO: Add your message handler code here and/or call default
25:
26:     /////////////////////////
27:     // MY CODE STARTS HERE
28:     /////////////////////////
29:
30:     // Have we captured the mouse?
```

continues

LISTING 10.6. CONTINUED

```
31:     if (GetCapture() == this)
32:         // If so, release it so other applications can
33:         // have it
34:         ReleaseCapture();
35:
36:     ///////////////////////
37:     // MY CODE ENDS HERE
38:     ///////////////////////
39:
40:     CView::OnLButtonUp(nFlags, point);
41: }
42:
43: void CDay10View::OnMouseMove(UINT nFlags, CPoint point)
44: {
45:     // TODO: Add your message handler code here and/or call default
46:
47:     ///////////////////////
48:     // MY CODE STARTS HERE
49:     ///////////////////////
50:
51:     // Check to see if the left mouse button is down
52:     if ((nFlags & MK_LBUTTON) == MK_LBUTTON)
53:     {
54:         // Have we captured the mouse?
55:         if (GetCapture() == this)
56:         {
57:             // Get the Device Context
58:             CClientDC dc(this);
59:
60:             // Add the line to the document
61:             CLine *pLine = GetDocument()->AddLine(m_ptPrevPos, point);
62:
63:             // Draw the current stretch of line
64:             pLine->Draw(&dc);
65:
66:             // Save the current point as the previous point
67:             m_ptPrevPos = point;
68:         }
69:     }
70:
71:     ///////////////////////
72:     // MY CODE ENDS HERE
73:     ///////////////////////
74:
75:     CView::OnMouseMove(nFlags, point);
76: }
```

In the `OnLButtonDown` function, the first thing you do is call the `SetCapture` function. This function "captures" the mouse, preventing any other applications from receiving any mouse events, even if the mouse leaves the window space of this application. This enables the user to drag the mouse outside the application window while drawing and then drag the mouse back into the application window, without stopping the drawing. All mouse messages are delivered to this application until the mouse is released in the `OnLButtonUp` function, using the `ReleaseCapture` function. In the meantime, by placing the `GetCapture` function in an `if` statement and comparing its return value to `this`, you can determine whether your application has captured the mouse. If you capture the mouse, you want to execute the rest of the code in those functions; otherwise, you don't.

In the `OnMouseMove` function, after you create your device context, you do several things in a single line of code. The line

```
CLine *pLine = GetDocument()->AddLine(m_ptPrevPos, point);
```

creates a new pointer to a `CLine` class instance. Next, it calls the `GetDocument` function, which returns a pointer to the document object. This pointer is used to call the document class's `AddLine` function, passing the previous and current points as arguments. The return value from the `AddLine` function is used to initialize the `CLine` object pointer. The `CLine` pointer can now be used to call the line object's `Draw` function.

Note

A pointer is the address of an object. It is used to pass an object more efficiently around a program. Passing a pointer to an object, instead of the object itself, is like telling someone that the remote control is "on the couch between the second and third cushion, beside the loose pocket change" instead of handing the remote to the person. Actually, in programming terms, handing the remote to the person requires making an exact copy of the remote and handing the copy to the other person. It is obviously more efficient to tell the person where to find the remote than to manufacture an exact copy of the remote.

The notation `->` denotes that the object's functions or properties are accessed through a pointer, as opposed to directly through the object itself with the period (.) notation.

Drawing the Painting

In the view class, the function `OnDraw` is called whenever the image presented to the user needs to be redrawn. Maybe another window was in front of the application window, the window was just restored from being minimized, or a new document was just loaded from a file. Why the view needs to be redrawn doesn't matter. All you need to worry about as the application developer is adding the code to the OnDraw function to render the document that your application is designed to create.

Locate the OnDraw function in the CDay10View class and add the code in Listing 10.7.

LISTING **10.7.** THE CDay10View OnDraw FUNCTION.

```
 1: void CDay10View::OnDraw(CDC* pDC)
 2: {
 3:     CDay10Doc* pDoc = GetDocument();
 4:     ASSERT_VALID(pDoc);
 5:
 6:     // TODO: add draw code for native data here
 7:
 8:     /////////////////////////
 9:     // MY CODE STARTS HERE
10:     /////////////////////////
11:
12:     // Get the number of lines in the document
13:     int liCount = pDoc->GetLineCount();
14:
15:     // Are there any lines in the document?
16:     if (liCount)
17:     {
18:         int liPos;
19:         CLine *lptLine;
20:
21:         // Loop through the lines in the document
22:         for (liPos = 0; liPos < liCount; liPos++)
23:         {
24:             // Get the from and to point for each line
25:             lptLine = pDoc->GetLine(liPos);
26:             // Draw the line
27:             lptLine->Draw(pDC);
28:         }
29:     }
30:
31:     /////////////////////////
32:     // MY CODE ENDS HERE
33:     /////////////////////////
34: }
```

In this function, the first thing you did was find out how many lines are in the document to be drawn. If there aren't any lines, then there is nothing to do. If there are lines in the document, you loop through the lines using a for loop, getting each line object from the document and then calling the line object's Draw function.

Before you can compile and run your application, you'll need to include the header file for the Cline class in the source code file for the document and view classes. To add this to your application, edit these files (Day10Doc.cpp, Day10View.cpp, Day10.cpp, and MainFrm.cpp), adding the Line.h file to the includes, as shown in Listing 10.8.

LISTING 10.8. THE CDay10Doc includes.

```
1: #include "stdafx.h"
2: #include "Day10.h"
3: #include "MainFrm.h"
4: #include "Line.h"
5: #include "Day10Doc.h"
```

At this point, you should be able to compile and run your application, drawing figures in it as shown in Figure 10.4. If you minimize the window and then restore it, or if you place another application window in front of your application window, your drawing should still be there when your application window is visible again (unlike the application you built a week ago).

FIGURE 10.4.

Drawing with your application.

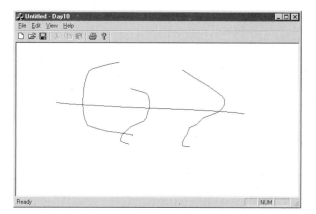

Saving and Loading the Drawing

Now that you can create drawings that don't disappear the moment you look away, it'd be nice if you could make them even more persistent. If you play with the menus on your application, it appears that the Open, Save, and Save As menu entries on the File menu activate, but they don't seem to do anything. The printing menu entries all work, but the entries for saving and loading a drawing don't. Not even the New menu entry works! Well, you can do something to fix this situation.

Deleting the Current Drawing

If you examine the CDay10Doc class, you'll see the OnNewDocument function that you can edit to clear out the current drawing. Wrong! This function is intended for initializing any class settings for starting work on a new drawing and not for clearing out an existing drawing. Instead, you need to open the Class Wizard and add a function on the DeleteContents event message. This event message is intended for clearing the current contents of the document class. Edit this new function, adding the code in Listing 10.9.

LISTING 10.9. THE CDay10Doc DeleteContents FUNCTION.

```
 1: void CDay10Doc::DeleteContents()
 2: {
 3:     // TODO: Add your specialized code here and/or call the base class
 4:
 5:     ////////////////////////
 6:     // MY CODE STARTS HERE
 7:     ////////////////////////
 8:
 9:     // Get the number of lines in the object array
10:     int liCount = m_oaLines.GetSize();
11:     int liPos;
12:
13:     // Are there any objects in the array?
14:     if (liCount)
15:     {
16:         // Loop through the array, deleting each object
17:         for (liPos = 0; liPos < liCount; liPos++)
18:             delete m_oaLines[liPos];
19:         // Reset the array
20:         m_oaLines.RemoveAll();
21:     }
22:
23:     ////////////////////////
24:     // MY CODE ENDS HERE
25:     ////////////////////////
26:
27:     CDocument::DeleteContents();
28: }
```

This function loops through the object array, deleting each line object in the array. Once all the lines are deleted, the array is reset by calling its RemoveAll method. If you compile and run your application, you'll find that you can select File | New, and if you decide not to save your current drawing, your window is wiped clean.

Saving and Restoring the Drawing

Adding the functionality to save and restore your drawings is pretty easy to implement, but it might not be so easy to understand. That's okay; you'll spend an entire day on understanding saving and restoring files, also known as serialization, in three days. In the meantime, find the Serialize function in the CDay10Doc class. The function should look something like

```
 1: void CDay10Doc::Serialize(CArchive& ar)
 2: {
 3:     if (ar.IsStoring())
 4:     {
 5:         // TODO: add storing code here
 6:     }
 7:     else
 8:     {
 9:         // TODO: add loading code here
10:     }
11: }
```

Remove all the contents of this function, and edit the function so that it looks like Listing 10.10.

LISTING **10.10.** THE CDay10Doc Serialize FUNCTION.

```
 1: void CDay10Doc::Serialize(CArchive& ar)
 2: {
 3:     //////////////////////
 4:     // MY CODE STARTS HERE
 5:     //////////////////////
 6:
 7:     // Pass the serialization on to the object array
 8:     m_oaLines.Serialize(ar);
 9:
10:     //////////////////////
11:     // MY CODE ENDS HERE
12:     //////////////////////
13: }
```

This function takes advantage of the functionality of the CObArray class. This object array will pass down its array of objects, calling the Serialize function on each of the objects. This means that you need to add a Serialize function to the CLine class. Specify it as a void function type with the declaration of Serialize(CArchive& ar). Edit the function, adding the code in Listing 10.11.

LISTING 10.11. THE `CLine` `Serialize` FUNCTION.

```
1: void CLine::Serialize(CArchive &ar)
2: {
3:      CObject::Serialize(ar);
4:
5:      if (ar.IsStoring())
6:          ar << m_ptFrom << m_ptTo;
7:      else
8:          ar >> m_ptFrom >> m_ptTo;
9: }
```

This function follows basically the same flow that the original `Serialize` function would have followed in the `CDay10Doc` class. It uses the I/O stream functionality of C++ to save and restore its contents.

At this point, if you compile and run your application, you expect the save and open functions to work. Unfortunately, they don't (yet). If you run your application and try to save a drawing, a message box will tell you that the application was unable to save the file, as in Figure 10.5.

FIGURE 10.5.

Unable to save drawings.

The reason that you are unable to save your drawing is that Visual C++ must be told that a class should be serializable. To do this, you add one line to the `CLine` class header file and one line to the `CLine` source code file. Open the `CLine` header file (`Line.h`), and add the `DECLARE_SERIAL` line in Listing 10.12 just after the first line of the class definition.

LISTING 10.12. THE `Line.h` EDIT FOR SERIALIZATION.

```
1: class CLine : public CObject
2: {
3:      DECLARE_SERIAL (CLine)
4: public:
5:      CLine(CPoint ptFrom, CPoint ptTo, UINT nWidth, COLORREF crColor);
```

Next, open the `CLine` source code file, and add the `IMPLEMENT_SERIAL` line in Listing 10.13 just before the class constructor functions.

LISTING 10.13. THE Line.cpp EDIT FOR SERIALIZATION.

```
 1: // Line.cpp: implementation of the CLine class.
 2: //
 3: //////////////////////////////////////////////////////////////////////
 4:
 5: #include "stdafx.h"
 6: #include "Day10.h"
 7: #include "Line.h"
 8:
 9: #ifdef _DEBUG
10: #undef THIS_FILE
11: static char THIS_FILE[]=__FILE__;
12: #define new DEBUG_NEW
13: #endif
14:
15: IMPLEMENT_SERIAL (CLine, CObject, 1)
16: //////////////////////////////////////////////////////////////////////
17: // Construction/Destruction
18: //////////////////////////////////////////////////////////////////////
19:
20: CLine::CLine()
21: {
22:
23: }
```

Now if you compile and run your application, you should be able to draw your own self-portrait and save it for posterity, as shown in Figure 10.6.

FIGURE 10.6.

My self-portrait.

Interacting with the Menu

Now that you have a working drawing program, it would be nice if the user could choose the color with which she wants to draw. Adding this functionality requires making changes in the CLine class to associate the color with the line and to CDay10Doc to maintain the currently selected color. Finally, you need to add a pull-down menu to select the desired color.

Adding Color to the CLine Class

The changes to the CLine class are fairly straightforward. The first thing that you need to do is to add another member variable to the CLine class to hold the color of each line. Next, you need to modify the class constructor to add color to the list of attributes to be passed in. Third, you need to modify the Draw function to use the specified color. Finally, you need to modify the Serialize function to save and restore the color information along with the point information. To do all these things, follow these steps:

1. Select the CLine class in the Class View tab of the workspace pane. Right-click the mouse and select Add Member Variable from the pop-up menu.

2. Specify the variable type as COLORREF, the name as m_crColor, and the access as private. Click OK to add the variable.

3. Right-click the CLine constructor in the Class View tree. Select Go to Declaration from the pop-up menu.

4. Add COLORREF crColor as a third argument to the constructor declaration.

5. Right-click the CLine constructor in the Class View tree. Select Go to Definition from the pop-up menu.

6. Modify the constructor to add the third argument and to set the m_crColor member to the new argument, as in Listing 10.14.

LISTING 10.14. THE MODIFIED CLine CONSTRUCTOR.

```
1: CLine::CLine(CPoint ptFrom, CPoint ptTo, COLORREF crColor)
2: {
3:      //Initialize the from and to points
4:      m_ptFrom = ptFrom;
5:      m_ptTo = ptTo;
6:      m_crColor = crColor;
7: }
```

7. Scroll down to the Draw function and modify it as in Listing 10.15.

LISTING 10.15. THE MODIFIED Draw FUNCTION.

```
 1: void CLine::Draw(CDC * pDC)
 2: {
 3:     // Create a pen
 4:     CPen lpen (PS_SOLID, 1, m_crColor);
 5:
 6:     // Set the new pen as the drawing object
 7:     CPen* pOldPen = pDC->SelectObject(&lpen);
 8:     // Draw the line
 9:     pDC->MoveTo(m_ptFrom);
10:     pDC->LineTo(m_ptTo);
11:     // Reset the previous pen
12:     pDC->SelectObject(pOldPen);
13: }
```

8. Scroll down to the Serialize function and modify it as in Listing 10.16.

LISTING 10.16. THE MODIFIED Serialize FUNCTION.

```
 1: void CLine::Serialize(CArchive &ar)
 2: {
 3:     CObject::Serialize(ar);
 4:
 5:     if (ar.IsStoring())
 6:         ar << m_ptFrom << m_ptTo << (DWORD) m_crColor;
 7:     else
 8:         ar >> m_ptFrom >> m_ptTo >> (DWORD) m_crColor;
 9: }
```

The only part of any of these steps that should be a surprise is that you are capturing the return value from the SelectObject function when you are specifying the pen to use in drawing the lines. You didn't do this last week. The return value from the SelectObject function is the pen that was in use before you changed it. This way, you can use the previous pen to restore it to the device context when you are done drawing.

Adding Color to the Document

The changes that you need to make to the CDay10Doc class are just slightly more extensive than those made to the CLine class. You need to add a member variable to hold the current color and a color table to convert color IDs into RGB values. You need to initialize the current color variable in the OnNewDocument function. Then, you need to modify the AddLine function to add the current color to the CLine constructor. Finally, you add a function to return the current color. That's all that you need to do for now until you start adding menu message handlers for setting the current color. To do these things, follow these steps:

1. Select the CDay10Doc class in the Class View tab on the workspace pane. Right-click the mouse and choose Add Member Variable from the pop-up menu.

2. Specify the variable type as UINT, the name as m_nColor, and the access as private. Click OK to add the variable.

3. Repeat step 1.

4. Specify the variable type as "static const COLORREF," the name as m_crColors[8], and the access as public.

5. Open the CDay10Doc source code (Day10Doc.cpp) and add the population of the m_crColors color table as in Listing 10.17.

LISTING 10.17. THE COLOR TABLE SPECIFICATION.

```
 1:     //}}AFX_MSG_MAP
 2: END_MESSAGE_MAP()
 3:
 4: const COLORREF CDay10Doc::m_crColors[8] = {
 5:     RGB(   0,   0,   0),    // Black
 6:     RGB(   0,   0, 255),    // Blue
 7:     RGB(   0, 255,   0),    // Green
 8:     RGB(   0, 255, 255),    // Cyan
 9:     RGB( 255,   0,   0),    // Red
10:     RGB( 255,   0, 255),    // Magenta
11:     RGB( 255, 255,   0),    // Yellow
12:     RGB( 255, 255, 255)     // White
13: };
14:
15: ///////////////////////////////////////////////////////////////////////
16: // CDay10Doc construction/destruction
17:
18: CDay10Doc::CDay10Doc()
19: .
20: .
21: .
22: }
```

6. Scroll down to the OnNewDocument function and edit it as in Listing 10.18.

LISTING 10.18. THE MODIFIED OnNewDocument FUNCTION.

```
 1: BOOL CDay10Doc::OnNewDocument()
 2: {
 3:     if (!CDocument::OnNewDocument())
 4:         return FALSE;
 5:
 6:     // TODO: add reinitialization code here
 7:     // (SDI documents will reuse this document)
 8:
 9:     ///////////////////////
10:     // MY CODE STARTS HERE
11:     ///////////////////////
12:
13:     // Initialize the color to black
14:     m_nColor = ID_COLOR_BLACK - ID_COLOR_BLACK;
15:
16:     ///////////////////////
17:     // MY CODE ENDS HERE
18:     ///////////////////////
19:
20:     return TRUE;
21: }
```

7. Scroll down to the AddLine function, and modify it as in Listing 10.19.

LISTING 10.19. THE MODIFIED AddLine FUNCTION.

```
 1: CLine * CDay10Doc::AddLine(CPoint ptFrom, CPoint ptTo)
 2: {
 3:     // Create a new CLine object
 4:     CLine *pLine = new CLine(ptFrom, ptTo, m_crColors[m_nColor]);
 5:     try
 6:     {
 7:         // Add the new line to the object array
 8:         m_oaLines.Add(pLine);
 9:         // Mark the document as dirty
10:         SetModifiedFlag();
11:     }
12:     // Did we run into a memory exception?
13:     catch (CMemoryException* perr)
14:     {
15:         // Display a message for the user, giving him or her the
16:         // bad news
17:         AfxMessageBox("Out of memory", MB_ICONSTOP | MB_OK);
18:         // Did we create a line object?
19:         if (pLine)
```

continues

LISTING 10.19. CONTINUED

```
20:            {
21:                // Delete it
22:                delete pLine;
23:                pLine = NULL;
24:            }
25:            // Delete the exception object
26:            perr->Delete();
27:        }
28:        return pLine;
29: }
```

8. Add a new member function to the CDay10Doc class. Specify the function type as UINT, the declaration as GetColor, and the access as public.

9. Edit the GetColor function, adding the code in Listing 10.20.

LISTING 10.20. THE GetColor FUNCTION.

```
1: UINT CDay10Doc::GetColor()
2: {
3:     // Return the current color
4:     return ID_COLOR_BLACK + m_nColor;
5: }
```

In the OnNewDocument and the GetColor functions, the color is added and subtracted from ID_COLOR_BLACK. This is the lowest numbered color menu ID when you add the menu entries. These calculations maintain the variable as a number between 0 and 7, but when working with the menus, they allow comparison with the actual menu IDs.

Modifying the Menu

Now comes the fun part. You need to add a new pull-down menu to the main menu. You need to add menu entries for all the colors in the color table. You need to add message handlers for all the color menu entries. Finally, you need to add event handlers to check the menu entry that is the current color. To do all of this, follow these steps:

1. Select the Resource View tab in the workspace pane. Expand the tree so that you can see the contents of the Menu folder. Double-click the menu resource.

2. Grab the blank top-level menu (at the right end of the menu bar) and drag it to the left, dropping it in front of the View menu entry.

3. Open the properties for the blank menu entry. Specify the caption as &Color. Close the properties dialog.

4. Add submenu entries below the Color top-level menu. Specify the submenus in order, setting their properties as specified in Table 10.2. You should wind up with a menu looking like Figure 10.7.

FIGURE 10.7.

The Color menu as designed.

TABLE 10.2. MENU PROPERTY SETTINGS.

Object	Property	Setting
Menu Entry	ID	ID_COLOR_BLACK
	Caption	&Black
Menu Entry	ID	ID_COLOR_BLUE
	Caption	B&lue
Menu Entry	ID	ID_COLOR_GREEN
	Caption	&Green
Menu Entry	ID	ID_COLOR_CYAN
	Caption	&Cyan
Menu Entry	ID	ID_COLOR_RED
	Caption	&Red
Menu Entry	ID	ID_COLOR_MAGENTA
	Caption	&Magenta
Menu Entry	ID	ID_COLOR_YELLOW
	Caption	&Yellow
Menu Entry	ID	ID_COLOR_WHITE
	Caption	&White

5. Open the Class Wizard. Select the CDay10Doc in the Class Name combo box.

6. Add functions for both the COMMAND and UPDATE_COMMAND_UI event messages for all the color menu entries.

7. After the final menu entry function has been added, click Edit Code.

8. Edit the Black menu functions as in Listing 10.21.

LISTING 10.21. THE BLACK MENU FUNCTIONS.

```
 1: void CDay10Doc::OnColorBlack()
 2: {
 3:     // TODO: Add your command handler code here
 4:
 5:     ///////////////////////
 6:     // MY CODE STARTS HERE
 7:     ///////////////////////
 8:
 9:     // Set the current color to black
10:     m_nColor = ID_COLOR_BLACK - ID_COLOR_BLACK;
11:
12:     ///////////////////////
13:     // MY CODE ENDS HERE
14:     ///////////////////////
15: }
16:
17: void CDay10Doc::OnUpdateColorBlack(CCmdUI* pCmdUI)
18: {
19:     // TODO: Add your command update UI handler code here
20:
21:     ///////////////////////
22:     // MY CODE STARTS HERE
23:     ///////////////////////
24:
25:     // Determine if the Black menu entry should be checked
26:     pCmdUI->SetCheck(GetColor() == ID_COLOR_BLACK ? 1 : 0);
27:
28:     ///////////////////////
29:     // MY CODE ENDS HERE
30:     ///////////////////////
31: }
```

9. Edit the Blue menu functions as in Listing 10.22. Edit the remaining menu functions in the same way, substituting their menu IDs for ID_COLOR_BLUE.

LISTING 10.22. THE BLUE MENU FUNCTIONS.

```
 1: void CDay10Doc::OnColorBlue()
 2: {
 3:     // TODO: Add your command handler code here
 4:
 5:     ///////////////////////
 6:     // MY CODE STARTS HERE
 7:     ///////////////////////
 8:
 9:     // Set the current color to blue
```

```
10:        m_nColor = ID_COLOR_BLUE - ID_COLOR_BLACK;
11:
12:        /////////////////////////
13:        // MY CODE ENDS HERE
14:        /////////////////////////
15: }
16:
17: void CDay10Doc::OnUpdateColorBlue(CCmdUI* pCmdUI)
18: {
19:        // TODO: Add your command update UI handler code here
20:
21:        /////////////////////////
22:        // MY CODE STARTS HERE
23:        /////////////////////////
24:
25:        // Determine if the Blue menu entry should be checked
26:        pCmdUI->SetCheck(GetColor() == ID_COLOR_BLUE ? 1 : 0);
27:
28:        /////////////////////////
29:        // MY CODE ENDS HERE
30:        /////////////////////////
31: }
```

In the first of the two menu functions, the COMMAND function, the current color variable is set to the new color. If you add the menu entries in the correct order, their ID numbers are sequential, starting with ID_COLOR_BLACK. Subtracting ID_COLOR_BLACK from the menu ID should always result in the correct position in the color table for the selected color. For example, the Black color is position 0 in the color table. ID_COLOR_BLACK – ID_COLOR_BLACK = 0. Blue is position 1 in the color table. Because ID_COLOR_BLUE should be one greater than ID_COLOR_BLACK, ID_COLOR_BLUE – ID_COLOR_BLACK = 1.

The second function, the UPDATE_COMMAND_UI function, may need a little explaining. The UPDATE_COMMAND_UI event is called for each menu entry just before it is displayed. You can use this event message function to check or uncheck the menu entry, based on whether it is the current color. You can also use this event to enable or disable menu entries or make other modifications as necessary. The code in this function

```
pCmdUI->SetCheck(GetColor() == ID_COLOR_BLUE ? 1 : 0);
```

does several things. First, the pCmdUI object that is passed in as the only argument is a pointer to a menu object. The SetCheck function can check or uncheck the menu entry, depending on whether the argument passed is 1 or 0 (1 checks, 0 unchecks). The argument portion for the SetCheck function is a flow-control construct that can be somewhat confusing if you haven't spent a large amount of time programming in C/C++. The first half

```
GetColor() == ID_COLOR_BLUE
```

is a simple boolean conditional statement. It results in a true or false result. The portion following this conditional statement

```
? 1 : 0
```

is basically an `if...else` statement in shorthand. If the conditional statement is `true`, then the value is `1`, and if the statement is `false`, the value is `0`. This is a fancy way of placing an `if..else` flow control within the argument to another function.

If you compile and run your application, you should be able to change the color that you are drawing with. When you pull down the color menu, you should see the current drawing color checked on the menu, as in Figure 10.8.

FIGURE 10.8.

Specifying the current color on the menu.

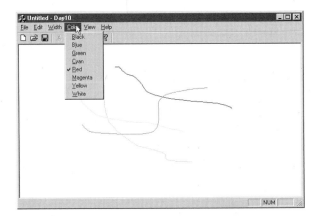

Summary

Whew! What a day! You learned quite a bit today because this was a packed chapter. You initially learned about the SDI style application and about a couple of standard applications that you have probably used that are SDI applications. You next learned about the Document/View architecture that Visual C++ uses for SDI applications. You learned to create a simple class of your own for use in your drawing application. You created a drawing application that can maintain the images drawn using it. You learned how you can save and restore documents in the Document/View architecture. You also learned about the CObArray object array class and how you can use it to create a dynamic object array for storing various classes. Finally, you learned how you can check and uncheck menu entries in MFC applications.

Q&A

Q **Is there any way that you can reduce the number of COMMAND and UPDATE_ COMMAND_UI functions for the menus?**

A Yes, you can send all the color COMMAND events to the same function. From there, you can examine the nID value (which is passed as an argument) and compare it to the menu IDs to determine which menu is calling the function. As a result, you can write the COMMAND function for the color menus as follows:

```
void CDay10Doc::OnColorCommand(UINT nID)
{
    // TODO: Add your command handler code here

    /////////////////////////
    // MY CODE STARTS HERE
    /////////////////////////

    // Set the current color
    m_nColor = nID - ID_COLOR_BLACK;

    /////////////////////////
    // MY CODE ENDS HERE
    /////////////////////////
}
```

For the UPDATE_COMMAND_UI functions, you can do the same thing, only slightly differently. In this case, you can examine the pCmdUI->m_nID value to determine which menu the function is being called for. This makes the UPDATE_COMMAND_UI function look like the following:

```
void CDay10Doc::OnUpdateColor(CCmdUI* pCmdUI)
{
    // TODO: Add your command update UI handler code here

    /////////////////////////
    // MY CODE STARTS HERE
    /////////////////////////

    // Determine menu entry should be checked
    pCmdUI->SetCheck(GetColor() == pCmdUI->m_nID ? 1 : 0);

    /////////////////////////
    // MY CODE ENDS HERE
    /////////////////////////
}
```

10

Q What's the difference between SDI and MDI applications?

**A Although SDI applications can perform only one task, MDI (Multiple Document
Interface) applications can have multiple documents open at the same time. Plus, in
an MDI application, not all document types need be the same. You'll learn more
about MDI applications tomorrow.**

Workshop

The Workshop provides quiz questions to help you solidify your understanding of the
material covered and exercises to provide you with experience in using what you've
learned. The answers to the quiz questions and exercises are provided in Appendix B,
"Answers."

Quiz

1. What does SDI stand for?
2. What functionality is in the view class?
3. What function is called to redraw the document if the window has been hidden
   behind another window?
4. Where do you place code to clear out the current document before starting a new
   document?
5. What is the purpose of the document class?

Exercise

Add another pull-down menu to control the width of the pen used for drawing. Give it
the following settings:

Menu Entry	Width Setting
Very Thin	1
Thin	8
Medium	16
Thick	24
Very Thick	32

Tip

In the pen constructor, the second argument is the width.

DAY **11**

Creating Multiple Document Interface Applications

Today, you will learn how to build Multiple Document Interface (MDI) applications using Visual C++. You will be able to build applications that allow users to work on multiple documents at one time, switching between the windows of the application to do their work. In this chapter, you will learn

- The difference between SDI and MDI applications.
- How to create an MDI application.
- How to send multiple menu entries to a single event-handling function.
- How to add a context menu to a Document/View style application.

What Is an MDI Application?

As far as coding an MDI application with Visual C++, there's little difference between creating an SDI and an MDI application. However, when you get deeper into the two application styles, you'll find quite a few differences. Although an SDI application allows the user to work on only one document at a time, it also normally limits the user to working on a specific type of document. MDI applications not only enable the user to work on multiple documents at the same time, but also MDI applications can allow the user to work on multiple types of documents.

An MDI application uses a window-in-a-window style, where there is a frame window around one or more child windows. This is a common application style with many popular software packages, including Word and Excel.

Architecturally, an MDI application is similar to an SDI application. In fact, with a simple MDI application, the only difference is the addition of a second frame class to the other classes that the AppWizard creates, as shown in Figure 11.1. As you can see, the Document/View architecture is still very much the approach you use for developing MDI applications as well as SDI applications.

FIGURE 11.1.

The MDI Document/View architecture.

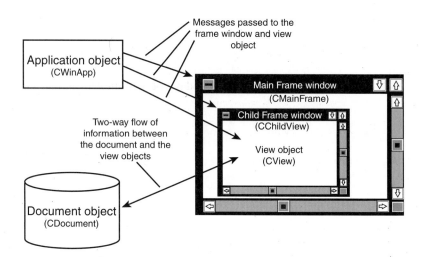

When you create an MDI application, you will create just one more class than you created with an SDI application. The classes are

- The CWinApp derived class
- The CMDIFrameWnd derived class
- The CMDIChildWnd derived class
- The CDocument derived class
- The CView derived class

The two MDI derived classes, CMDIFrameWnd (the CMainFrame class in your project) and CMDIChildWnd (the CChildFrame class in your project), are the only two classes that are different from the SDI application that you created.

The first of these two classes, the CMDIFrameWnd-derived CMainFrame, is the main frame of the application. It provides an enclosed space on the desktop within which all application interaction takes place. This frame window is the frame to which the menu and toolbars are attached.

The second of these two classes, the CMDIChildWnd-derived CChildFrame class, is the frame that holds the CView class. It is the frame that passes messages and events to the view class for processing or display.

In a sense, the functionality of the frame class in the SDI application has been split into these two classes in an MDI application. There is additional support for running multiple child frames with their own document/view class instances at the same time.

Creating an MDI Drawing Program

To get a good understanding of just how alike the Document/View architectures are for the SDI and MDI applications, today you will implement that same drawing application that you created yesterday, only this time as an MDI application.

Building the Application Shell

To create the application shell for today's application, follow these steps:

1. Create a new AppWizard project. Name the project **Day11**.

2. On the first step of the AppWizard, select Multiple Documents, as shown in Figure 11.2.

FIGURE 11.2.

Specifying an MDI application.

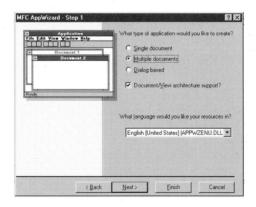

3. Use the default values on the second step of the AppWizard.

4. On the third step of the AppWizard, uncheck the support for ActiveX Controls.

5. On the fourth step of the AppWizard, leave all the default values. Click the Advanced button.

6. In the Advanced Options dialog, enter a three-letter file extension for the files that your application will generate (for example, dhc or dvp). Click the Close button to close the dialog and then click Next to move to the next step of the AppWizard.

7. Use the default settings on the fifth step of the AppWizard.

8. On the sixth and final AppWizard step, leave the base class as CView and click Finish. The AppWizard generates the application shell.

Building the Drawing Functionality

Because you are creating the same application that you created yesterday, only as an MDI application this time, you need to add the same functionality to the application that you added yesterday. To save time, and to reemphasize how alike these two application architectures are, perform the same steps you did yesterday to create the CLine class and add the functionality to the CDay11Doc and CDay11View classes. Add the support into the CDay11Doc and CLine classes for selecting colors and widths, but do not add any menu event message handlers or create the color menu. When you finish adding all that functionality, you should have an application in which you can open multiple drawings, all drawing with only the color black.

Caution

> Because you haven't created the menus yet, and the color initialization uses the color menu IDs, you will probably have to hard-code the initialization of the color to 0 to get your application to compile. Once you add the color menu, the menu IDs should have been added, so you will be able to return to using the IDs in your code. For the time being, change the line of code in the OnNewDocument function in the CDay11Doc class from
>
> ```
> m_nColor = ID_COLOR_BLACK - ID_COLOR_BLACK;
> ```
>
> to
>
> ```
> m_nColor = 0;
> ```
>
> You will also need to make the same sort of change to the GetColor function because it uses one of the color menu IDs also.

Adding Menu Handling Functionality

Now that you've got all the functionality in your application, you would probably like to add the color menu so you can use all those available colors in your drawings. When you expand the Resource View tree and look in the Menu folder, you'll find not one, but two menus defined. Which one do you add the color menu to?

The IDR_MAINFRAME menu is the menu that is available when no child windows are open. If you run your application and close all child windows, you'll see the menu change, removing all the menus that apply to child windows. Once you open another document, either by creating a new document or by opening an existing document, the menu changes back, returning all the menus that apply to the documents.

The IDR_DAY11TYPE menu is the menu that appears when a child window is open. This menu contains all the functions that apply to documents. Therefore, this is the menu that you need to add the color menu to. Add the color menu by following the same directions as yesterday, using the same menu properties.

Once you add all the menus, you need to add the menu event handlers. Today, you are going to take a different approach to implementing the menu event handlers than you did yesterday. The Q&A section at the end of yesterday's chapter had a discussion of using a single event-handler function for all the color menus. That is what you are going to implement today. Unfortunately, the Class Wizard doesn't understand how to route multiple menu event messages to the same function correctly, so you're going to implement this yourself by following these steps:

1. Open the Day11Doc.h header file.

2. Scroll down toward the bottom of the header file until you find the protected section where the AFX_MSG message map is declared (search for //{{AFX_MSG(CDay11Doc)).

3. Add the function declarations in Listing 11.1 before the line that you searched for. (The string that you searched for is the beginning marker for the Class Wizard maintained message map. Anything you place between it and the end marker, //}}AFX_MSG, is likely to be removed or corrupted by the Class Wizard.)

LISTING 11.1. THE EVENT-HANDLER DECLARATIONS IN Day11Doc.h.

```
    .
    .
    .
1: #ifdef _DEBUG
2:     virtual void AssertValid() const;
```

continues

LISTING 11.1. CONTINUED

```
 3:      virtual void Dump(CDumpContext& dc) const;
 4: #endif
 5:
 6: protected:
 7:
 8: // Generated message map functions
 9: protected:
10:      afx_msg void OnColorCommand(UINT nID);
11:      afx_msg void OnUpdateColorUI(CCmdUI* pCmdUI);
12:      //{{AFX_MSG(CDay11Doc)
13:          // NOTE - the ClassWizard will add and remove member functions
➥here.
14:          //    DO NOT EDIT what you see in these blocks of generated
➥code !
15:      //}}AFX_MSG
16:      DECLARE_MESSAGE_MAP()
17: private:
18:      UINT m_nColor;
19:      CObArray m_oaLines;
20: };
```

4. Open the Day11Doc.cpp source-code file.

5. Search for the line BEGIN_MESSAGE_MAP and add the lines in Listing 11.2 just after it. It's important that this code be between the BEGIN_MESSAGE_MAP line and the //{{AFX_MSG_MAP line. If these commands are between the //{{AFX_MSG_MAP and //}}AFX_MSG_MAP lines, then the Class Wizard will remove or corrupt them.

LISTING 11.2. THE EVENT-HANDLER MESSAGE MAP ENTRIES IN Day11Doc.cpp.

```
 1: ///////////////////////////////////////////////////////////////////////
 2: // CDay11Doc
 3:
 4: IMPLEMENT_DYNCREATE(CDay11Doc, CDocument)
 5:
 6: BEGIN_MESSAGE_MAP(CDay11Doc, CDocument)
 7:      ON_COMMAND_RANGE(ID_COLOR_BLACK, ID_COLOR_WHITE, OnColorCommand)
 8:      ON_UPDATE_COMMAND_UI_RANGE(ID_COLOR_BLACK, ID_COLOR_WHITE,
➥OnUpdateColorUI)
 9:      //{{AFX_MSG_MAP(CDay11Doc)
10:          // NOTE - the ClassWizard will add and remove mapping macros
➥here.
```

```
11:            //    DO NOT EDIT what you see in these blocks of generated
➥code!
12:      //}}AFX_MSG_MAP
13: END_MESSAGE_MAP()
14:
15: const COLORREF CDay11Doc::m_crColors[8] = {
16:     RGB(  0,   0,   0),   // Black
17:     RGB(  0,   0, 255),   // Blue
18: .
19: .
20: .
```

6. Scroll to the bottom of the file and add the two event message handler functions in Listing 11.3.

LISTING 11.3. THE COLOR MENU EVENT-HANDLER FUNCTIONS.

```
 1: void CDay11Doc::OnColorCommand(UINT nID)
 2: {
 3:     // Set the current color
 4:     m_nColor = nID - ID_COLOR_BLACK;
 5: }
 6:
 7: void CDay11Doc::OnUpdateColorUI(CCmdUI* pCmdUI)
 8: {
 9:     // Determine if the menu entry should be checked
10:     pCmdUI->SetCheck(GetColor() == pCmdUI->m_nID ? 1 : 0);
11: }
```

In Listing 11.1, the two function declarations that you added are specified as event message handlers by the afx_msg function type declarations. These type of function declarations need to have protected access. Otherwise, they are virtually identical to any other class member function declaration.

In Listing 11.2, the two message map entries, ON_COMMAND_RANGE and ON_UPDATE_COMMAND_UI_RANGE, are standard message map entries, but the Class Wizard does not support or understand them. If you examine the message map entries from the previous day's applications, you will notice that there are ON_COMMAND and ON_UPDATE_COMMAND_UI message map entries. These macros have two arguments, the message ID and the event-handler function name that should be called for the event message. These new message map entries function in the same way, but they have two event ID arguments instead of one. The two event ID arguments mark the two ends of a range of event IDs that should be passed to the function specified. These two event IDs should be the first and last menu entries you created when building the color menu.

Note

> The message map is a mechanism used by Visual C++ and MFC to easily specify event messages and the functions that should be called to handle the event. These message-map commands are converted by the Visual C++ compiler into a fast and efficient map for calling the appropriate event functions when a message is received by the application. Whenever you add a function through the Class Wizard, you are not only adding the function to the code, but you are also adding an entry into the message map for that class.

When you use the ON_COMMAND_RANGE message-map entry, the event message ID is automatically passed as an argument to the event-handler function. This allows you to create the function in Listing 11.3 to handle the color selection event messages. If you compile and run your application at this point, you should find that the color selection functionality is all working just as it did yesterday, as shown in Figure 11.3.

FIGURE 11.3.

Running the MDI application.

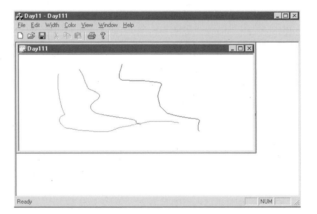

Adding a Context Menu

In most Windows applications, you can right-click the mouse and what is known as a context menu, or pop-up menu, appears. Back on Day 6, "Creating Menus for Your Application," you implemented a simple pop-up menu. However, there is a mechanism for creating and using these context menus when Windows thinks that the menu should be opened. This process allows you to add context menus that behave more consistently with other Windows applications (and if Microsoft changes how the context menus are triggered with a new version of Windows, yours will still behave according to the Windows standard).

An event message WM_CONTEXTMENU is passed to the event queue when the right mouse button is released or when the context menu button is pressed (if you have a newer Windows-enabled keyboard with the context menu button). If you place an event-handler function on the WM_CONTEXTMENU event message, you can display a pop-up menu with confidence that you are showing it at the appropriate time.

To add the context menu to your application, you create a new menu for use as the context menu. To do this, follow these steps:

1. In the Resource View tab on the workspace pane, right-click the Menu folder.

2. Select Insert Menu from the pop-up menu (or should I say context menu).

3. Select the new menu (still in the workspace pane), open its properties dialog, and name the menu IDR_CONTEXTMENU.

4. In the Menu Designer, specify the top-level menu caption as a single space. This causes Visual C++ to add the first entry in the drop-down portion of the menu.

5. In the first drop-down menu entry, specify the caption as &Width and check the Pop-up check box. (This causes the ID combo box to be disabled and an arrow to display beside the caption, along with another menu entry to the right of the menu entry you are modifying.)

6. Do not add any menu entries into the Width cascading menu at this time (that is left for an exercise at the end of the chapter). Instead, select the menu entry below the Width entry and open its properties dialog. Specify the caption as &Colors and check the Pop-up check box.

7. In the colors cascading menu, add the color menu entries as you did for the IDR_DAY11TYPE menu, using the same property settings. You can select the ID from the drop-down list of IDs, if you would rather search for them instead of type. When you finish, your menu should look like the one in Figure 11.4.

8. Select the Class View tab in the workspace pane.

9. Select the CDay11View class. Open the Class Wizard by selecting View | ClassWizard from the menu.

11

FIGURE 11.4.

The context menu design.

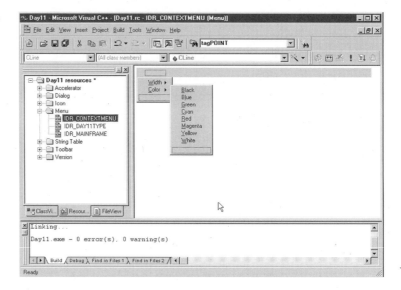

10. Add a function for the WM_CONTEXTMENU event message on the CDay11View class.

11. Edit the function, adding the code in Listing 11.4.

LISTING 11.4. THE CDay11View OnContextMenu FUNCTION.

```
1: void CDay11View::OnContextMenu(CWnd* pWnd, CPoint point)
2: {
3:      // TODO: Add your message handler code here
4:
5:      /////////////////////////
6:      // MY CODE STARTS HERE
7:      /////////////////////////
8:
9:      CMenu menu;
10:
11:     // Load the context menu
12:     menu.LoadMenu(IDR_CONTEXTMENU);
13:     // Get the first sub menu (the real menu)
14:     CMenu *pContextMenu = menu.GetSubMenu(0);
15:
16:     // Display the context menu for the user
17:     pContextMenu->TrackPopupMenu(TPM_LEFTALIGN |
18:         TPM_LEFTBUTTON | TPM_RIGHTBUTTON,
19:         point.x, point.y, AfxGetMainWnd());
20:
21:     /////////////////////////
```

```
22:      // MY CODE ENDS HERE
23:      /////////////////////////
24: }
```

This code should all look familiar to you from what you learned on Day 6. If you compile and run your application now, you should be able to click your right mouse button on the child window and change your drawing color from the context menu that opened, as shown in Figure 11.5.

FIGURE 11.5.

Using the context menu to change drawing colors.

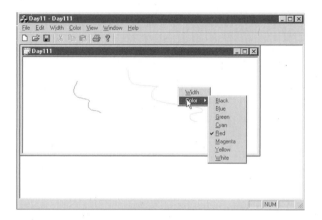

Summary

That wasn't too bad; was it? After yesterday, you probably needed the easy day today, along with all the review of what you did yesterday to help it all sink in. But you did get to learn some new things today. You learned about MDI applications, what they are, and how they differ from SDI applications. You learned how you could take a series of menus and use a single event-handler function for all of them. You also learned how you can create a menu specifically for use as a pop-up context menu and how you can integrate it into an MDI application.

Q&A

Q Because it's basically the same code to create an MDI or SDI application, why would I want to create an SDI application? Why wouldn't I want to make all my applications MDI applications?

A It depends on the application and how it's going to be used. You probably use both types of applications on a daily basis. If you are writing a memo or working on a spreadsheet, you are probably using an MDI application. If you are browsing the World Wide Web, your Web browser is most likely an SDI application. A simple text editor such as Notepad would probably be more difficult for the user as an MDI style application, but as an SDI application, it's just about right (for the task it handles). Certain applications make more sense implemented as an SDI application than as an MDI application. You need to think through how your application is going to be used and determine which model it's more suited for.

Q **Some entries on my color menu are changing to the wrong color. How can I determine the problem?**

A The problem is that the color menu IDs are probably not in sequential order or are out of order. You can check them by right-clicking on the Day11 resources in the Resource View tab of the workspace pane. Select Resource Symbols from the pop-up menu to display a list of the IDs and the numbers assigned to them in alphabetical order. Start with the Black ID and make sure that the numbers increase by 1 without skipping any numbers. Be sure to check these IDs in the order that the colors appear on the menu (and in the color table in the `Day11Doc.cpp` file), not in the alphabetical order in which they are displayed in this list. If you find some errors, you have to close Visual C++ and open the `Resource.h` file in a text editor to renumber the IDs correctly. Once you make the corrections (be sure to delete any duplicates), save your corrections, restart Visual C++, and recompile your application. The color menu should work correctly.

Workshop

The Workshop provides quiz questions to help you solidify your understanding of the material covered and exercises to provide you with experience in using what you've learned. The answers to the quiz questions and exercises are provided in Appendix B, "Answers."

Quiz

1. What are the five base classes that are used in MDI applications?

2. Why do you have to place the `ON_COMMAND_RANGE` message map entry outside the section maintained by the Class Wizard?

3. What argument does `ON_COMMAND_RANGE` pass to the event function?

4. What event message should you use to display a pop-up menu?

Exercise

Add the pull-down and context menus for the width, using the same pen widths as yesterday.

11

DAY **12**

Adding Toolbars and Status Bars

When you created your SDI and MDI applications, they not only came with default menus already attached, but also they came with simple toolbars to go with the menus. These simple toolbars had the standard set of functions (New, Open, Save, Print, Cut, Copy, and Paste) that are on the toolbars of most Windows applications. Most applications don't limit their toolbars to just this standard selection of functions but have customized toolbars that reflect the specific functionality of the application.

In addition to the toolbars, the SDI and MDI applications have a status bar at the bottom of the frame that provides textual descriptions of the toolbar buttons and menu entries. The status bar also has default areas that display whether the Caps, Num, and Scroll Lock keys are on.

Today, you will learn

- How to design your own toolbar.
- How to attach your toolbar to the application frame.

- How to show and hide your toolbar with a menu entry.
- How to place a combo box on your toolbar.
- How to display descriptions of your toolbar entries in the status bar.
- How to add your own status bar elements.

Toolbars, Status Bars, and Menus

One of the driving intentions behind the development of Graphical User Interfaces (GUI) such as Windows was the goal of making computers easier to use and learn. In the effort to accomplish this goal, GUI designers stated that all applications should use a standard set of menus and that the menus should be organized in a standardized manner. When Microsoft designed the Windows operating system, it followed this same philosophy, using a standard set of menus organized in a standard order on most of its applications.

A funny thing happened once Windows became widely used. The application designers found that new users still had a difficult time learning new applications and that advanced users found the menus cumbersome. As a result, the application designers invented toolbars as one solution to both problems.

A toolbar is a small band attached to the window frame or a dialog window that is floating independent of the application frame. This band (or dialog) has a number of small buttons containing graphic images that can be used in place of the menus. The application designers place the most commonly used functions for their applications on these toolbars and do their best to design graphical images that illustrate the functions the buttons serve.

Once advanced users learned what each of the toolbar buttons do, the toolbars were a hit. However, novice users still had problems learning what the toolbar does. As a result, the application designers went back to the drawing board to come up with ways to help the new user learn how use the toolbar buttons.

One of the solutions was to use the information bar that many of them had begun placing at the bottom of application windows to provide detailed descriptions of both menu entries and toolbar buttons. One of the other solutions was to provide a little pop-up window with a short description of the button that appears whenever the mouse is positioned over the button for more than a couple of seconds. The first of these solutions became known as the status bar, and the second became known as tooltips. Both solutions are in common practice with most Windows applications today.

If you want to design and use your own toolbars and status bars in your applications, you might think that Visual C++ provides plenty of support for your efforts and even makes it easy to implement. After all, Microsoft's own application developers have been in the forefront of developing these elements, and most, if not all, of Microsoft's Windows applications are developed using its own Visual C++. Well, you are correct in making that assumption, and today, you'll learn how to create your own custom toolbars and status bars for your applications.

Designing a Toolbar

For learning how to create your own toolbar, you will modify the application that you created on Day 10, "Creating Single Document Interface Applications," the SDI drawing application, to add a toolbar for selecting the color to use in drawing.

> **Note**
>
> Although the sample application you are working with today is an extension to the application you built on Day 10, all file and class names have been changed from Day10 to Toolbar. If you are making the changes in the Day 10 project, then when the following text specifies that you make changes to the CToolbarDoc class, you should make the changes to the CDay10Doc class. Likewise, when you are asked to edit the Toolbar.rc file, you can edit the Day10.rc file.

If all you want to do is add a few additional toolbar buttons to the default toolbar that the AppWizard creates when you start a new SDI or MDI application, you can pull up the toolbar in the Visual C++ designer through the Resource View in the workspace pane and begin adding new buttons. Just as in the Menu Designer, the end of the toolbar always has a blank entry, waiting for you to turn it into another toolbar button, as shown in Figure 12.1. All you have to do is select this blank button, drag it to the right if you want a separator between it and the button beside it, or drag it to a different position if you want it moved. After you have the button in the desired location, you paint an icon on the button that illustrates the function that the button will trigger. Finally, double-click the button in the toolbar view to open the button's properties dialog and give the button the same ID as the menu that it will trigger. The moment that you compile and run your application, you will have a new toolbar button that performs a menu selection that you chose. If you want to get rid of a toolbar button, just grab it on the toolbar view, and drag it off the toolbar.

12

FIGURE 12.1.

The toolbar designer.

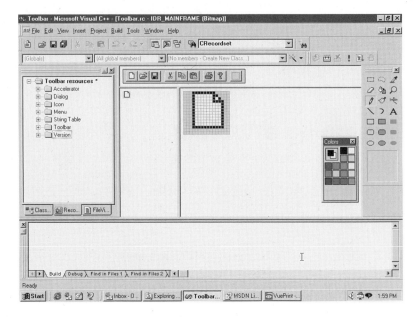

Creating a New Toolbar

To insert a new toolbar, right-click on the Toolbar folder and select Insert Toolbar from the pop-up menu. This creates an empty toolbar with a single blank button. As you start drawing an icon on each of the blank buttons in the toolbar, another blank button is added on the end.

For use in your drawing application, fill eight buttons with the eight colors available in the drawing application.

Once you draw icons on each of the buttons in your toolbar, double-click on the first button in the toolbar view. This should open the toolbar button properties dialog. In the ID field, enter (or select from the drop-down list) the ID of the menu that this toolbar button should trigger. In the Prompt field, enter the description that should appear in the status bar for this toolbar button. (If you entered a prompt for the menu, then this field is automatically populated with the menu description.) At the end of the status bar description, add \n and a short description to appear in the tooltips for the toolbar button.

Note

In C/C++, the \n string is a shorthand notation for "begin a new line." In the prompt for toolbar buttons and menu entries, this string is used to separate the status bar descriptions of the menu entries and the tooltips pop-up prompt that appears when the mouse is held over a toolbar button for a few seconds. The first line of the prompt is used for the status bar description, and the second line is used for the tooltips description. The tooltips description is only used with the toolbars, so there's no reason to add this for menu entries that will have no toolbar equivalents.

For example, for the black button on the toolbar that you are creating for your drawing application, enter an ID of **ID_COLOR_BLACK** and a prompt of **Black drawing color\nBlack**, as shown in Figure 12.2.

FIGURE 12.2.

The toolbar button properties dialog.

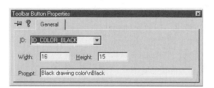

Once you finish designing your toolbar and have icons on all of your buttons with the properties set for each button, you will change the toolbar ID. In the workspace pane, right-click the new toolbar that you just added and open its properties dialog. Change the toolbar ID to a descriptive name.

As an example, for the color toolbar that you created for your drawing application, change the toolbar ID to IDR_TBCOLOR.

Attaching the Toolbar to the Application Frame

In the previous SDI and MDI applications, you didn't add any functionality that required you to touch the frame window. Well, because the toolbar is attached to the frame, you'll have to begin adding and modifying code in that module. If you open the CMainFrame class to the OnCreate function, you'll see where it's creating the existing toolbar and then later in this function where the toolbar is being attached to the frame.

Before you can add your toolbar to the application frame, you need to add a variable to the CMainFrame class to hold the new toolbar. This variable of type CToolBar should be protected in accessibility.

12

To add your color toolbar to your draw application, right-click the CMainFrame class in the Class View tab of the workspace pane. Select Add Member Variable from the pop-up menu, and specify the variable type as CToolBar, the name as m_wndColorBar, and the access as protected.

After you add a variable for your toolbar, you need to add some code in the OnCreate function in the CMainFrame class to add the toolbar and attach it to the frame. Make the modifications in Listing 12.1 to add the color toolbar to your drawing application.

LISTING 12.1. THE MODIFIED CMainFrame.OnCreate FUNCTION.

```
 1:   int CMainFrame::OnCreate(LPCREATESTRUCT lpCreateStruct)
 2:   {
 3:       if (CFrameWnd::OnCreate(lpCreateStruct) == -1)
 4:           return -1;
 5:
 6:       if (!m_wndToolBar.CreateEx(this, TBSTYLE_FLAT,
         ➥WS_CHILD | WS_VISIBLE | CBRS_TOP
 7:           | CBRS_GRIPPER | CBRS_TOOLTIPS | CBRS_FLYBY |
         ➥CBRS_SIZE_DYNAMIC) ||
 8:           !m_wndToolBar.LoadToolBar(IDR_MAINFRAME))
 9:       {
10:           TRACE0("Failed to create toolbar\n");
11:           return -1;        // fail to create
12:       }
13:
14:       ///////////////////////
15:       // MY CODE STARTS HERE
16:       ///////////////////////
17:
18:       // Add the color toolbar
19:       int iTBCtlID;
20:       int i;
21:
22:       // Create the Color Toolbar
23:       if (!m_wndColorBar.CreateEx(this, TBSTYLE_FLAT, WS_CHILD |
24:           WS_VISIBLE | CBRS_TOP | CBRS_GRIPPER | CBRS_TOOLTIPS |
25:           CBRS_FLYBY | CBRS_SIZE_DYNAMIC) ||
26:           !m_wndColorBar.LoadToolBar(IDR_TBCOLOR))
27:       {
28:           TRACE0("Failed to create toolbar\n");
29:           return -1;        // fail to create
30:       }
31:       // Find the Black button on the toolbar
32:       iTBCtlID = m_wndColorBar.CommandToIndex(ID_COLOR_BLACK);
33:       if (iTBCtlID >= 0)
34:       {
```

```
35:           // Loop through the buttons, setting them to act as radio
                 ➡buttons
36:           for (i= iTBCtlID; i < (iTBCtlID + 8); i++)
37:               m_wndColorBar.SetButtonStyle(i, TBBS_CHECKGROUP);
38:       }
39:
40:       /////////////////////////
41:       // MY CODE ENDS HERE
42:       /////////////////////////
43:
44:       if (!m_wndStatusBar.Create(this) ¦¦
45:           !m_wndStatusBar.SetIndicators(indicators,
46:             sizeof(indicators)/sizeof(UINT)))
47:       {
48:           TRACE0("Failed to create status bar\n");
49:           return -1;      // fail to create
50:       }
51:
52:       // TODO: Delete these three lines if you don't want the toolbar to
53:       //   be dockable
54:       m_wndToolBar.EnableDocking(CBRS_ALIGN_ANY);
55:
56:       /////////////////////////
57:       // MY CODE STARTS HERE
58:       /////////////////////////
59:
60:       // Enable docking for the Color Toolbar
61:       m_wndColorBar.EnableDocking(CBRS_ALIGN_ANY);
62:
63:       /////////////////////////
64:       // MY CODE ENDS HERE
65:       /////////////////////////
66:
67:       EnableDocking(CBRS_ALIGN_ANY);
68:       DockControlBar(&m_wndToolBar);
69:
70:       /////////////////////////
71:       // MY CODE STARTS HERE
72:       /////////////////////////
73:
74:       // Dock the Color Toolbar
75:       DockControlBar(&m_wndColorBar);
76:
77:       /////////////////////////
78:       // MY CODE ENDS HERE
79:       /////////////////////////
80:
81:       return 0;
82: }
```

12

Creating the Toolbar

The first part of the code you added,

```
if (!m_wndColorBar.CreateEx(this, TBSTYLE_FLAT, WS_CHILD |
    WS_VISIBLE | CBRS_TOP | CBRS_GRIPPER | CBRS_TOOLTIPS |
    CBRS_FLYBY | CBRS_SIZE_DYNAMIC) ||
    !m_wndColorBar.LoadToolBar(IDR_TBCOLOR))
```

contains two separate functions that are necessary in creating a toolbar. The first function, CreateEx, creates the toolbar itself, whereas the second, LoadToolBar, loads the toolbar that you designed in the toolbar designer. The second function, LoadToolBar, requires a single argument, the ID for the toolbar that you want to create.

The CreateEx function has several arguments that you can pass with the function. The first argument, and the only required argument, is a pointer to the parent window. In this case (which is normally the case), this argument is a pointer to the frame window to which the toolbar will be attached.

The second argument is the style of controls on the toolbar that is to be created. Several toolbar control styles are available for use, some of which have been introduced with the last two versions of Internet Explorer. Table 12.1 lists the available styles.

TABLE 12.1. TOOLBAR CONTROL STYLES.

Style	Description
TBSTYLE_ALTDRAG	Allows the user to move the toolbar by dragging it while holding down the Alt key.
TBSTYLE_CUSTOMERASE	Generates a NM_CUSTOMDRAW message when erasing the toolbar and button background, allowing the programmer to choose when and whether to control the background erasing process.
TBSTYLE_FLAT	Creates a flat toolbar. Button text appears under the bitmap image.
TBSTYLE_LIST	Button text appears to the right of the bitmap image.
TBSTYLE_REGISTERDROP	For use in dragging and dropping objects onto toolbar buttons.
TBSTYLE_TOOLTIPS	Creates a tooltip control that can be used to display descriptive text for the buttons.
TBSTYLE_TRANSPARENT	Creates a transparent toolbar.
TBSTYLE_WRAPABLE	Creates a toolbar that can have multiple rows of buttons.

The third argument is the style of the toolbar itself. This argument is normally a combination of window and control bar styles. Normally, only two or three window styles are used, and the rest of the toolbar styles are control bar styles. The list of the normally used toolbar styles appears in Table 12.2.

TABLE 12.2. TOOLBAR STYLES.

Style	Description
WS_CHILD	The toolbar is created as a child window.
WS_VISIBLE	The toolbar will be visible when created.
CBRS_ALIGN_TOP	Allows the toolbar to be docked to the top of the view area of the frame window.
CBRS_ALIGN_BOTTOM	Allows the toolbar to be docked to the bottom of the view area of the frame window.
CBRS_ALIGN_LEFT	Allows the toolbar to be docked to the left side of the view area of the frame window.
CBRS_ALIGN_RIGHT	Allows the toolbar to be docked to the right side of the view area of the frame window.
CBRS_ALIGN_ANY	Allows the toolbar to be docked to any side of the view area of the frame window.
CBRS_BORDER_TOP	Places a border on the top edge of the toolbar when the top of the toolbar is not docked.
CBRS_BORDER_BOTTOM	Places a border on the bottom edge of the toolbar when the top of the toolbar is not docked.
CBRS_BORDER_LEFT	Places a border on the left edge of the toolbar when the top of the toolbar is not docked.
CBRS_BORDER_RIGHT	Places a border on the right edge of the toolbar when the top of the toolbar is not docked.
CBRS_FLOAT_MULTI	Allows multiple toolbars to be floated in a single miniframe window.
CBRS_TOOLTIPS	Causes tooltips to be displayed for the toolbar buttons.
CBRS_FLYBY	Causes status bar message text to be updated for the toolbar buttons at the same time as the tooltips.
CBRS_GRIPPER	Causes a gripper to be drawn on the toolbar.

The fourth argument, which you did not provide in your code, is the size of the toolbar borders. This argument is passed as a standard CRect rectangle class to provide the length and height desired for the toolbar. The default value is 0 for all of the rectangle dimensions, thus resulting in a toolbar with no borders.

The fifth and final argument, which you also did not provide in your code, is the toolbar's child window ID. This defaults to AFX_IDW_TOOLBAR, but you can specify any defined ID that you need or want to use for the toolbar.

12

Setting the Button Styles

After you create the toolbar, there is a curious bit of code:

```
// Find the Black button on the toolbar
iTBCtlID = m_wndColorBar.CommandToIndex(ID_COLOR_BLACK);
if (iTBCtlID >= 0)
{
    // Loop through the buttons, setting them to act as radio buttons
    for (i= iTBCtlID; i < (iTBCtlID + 8); i++)
        m_wndColorBar.SetButtonStyle(i, TBBS_CHECKGROUP);
}
```

The first line in this code snippet uses the CommandToIndex toolbar function to locate the control number of the ID_COLOR_BLACK button. If you design your toolbar in the order of colors that you used on the menu, this should be the first control, with a index of 0. It's best to use the CommandToIndex function to locate the index of any toolbar button that you need to alter, just in case it's not where you expect it to be. This function returns the index of the toolbar control specified, and you use this as a starting point to specify the button style of each of the color buttons.

In the loop, where you are looping through each of the eight color buttons on the toolbar, you use the SetButtonStyle function to control the behavior of the toolbar buttons. The first argument to this function is the index of the button that you are changing. The second argument is the style of button that you want for the toolbar button specified. In this case, you are specifying that each of the buttons be TBBS_CHECKGROUP buttons, which makes them behave like radio buttons, where only one of the buttons in the group can be selected at any time. The list of the available button styles is in Table 12.3.

TABLE 12.3. TOOLBAR BUTTON STYLES.

Style	Description
TBSTYLE_AUTOSIZE	The button's width will be calculated based on the text on the button.
TBSTYLE_BUTTON	Creates a standard push button.
TBSTYLE_CHECK	Creates a button that acts like a check box, toggling between the pressed and unpressed state.
TBSTYLE_CHECKGROUP	Creates a button that acts like a radio button, remaining in the pressed state until another button in the group is pressed. This is actually the combination of the TBSTYLE_CHECK and TBSTYLE_GROUP button styles.
TBSTYLE_DROPDOWN	Creates a drop-down list button.
TBSTYLE_GROUP	Creates a button that remains pressed until another button in the group is pressed.

Style	Description
TBSTYLE_NOPREFIX	The button text will not have an accelerator prefix associated with it.
TBSTYLE_SEP	Creates a separator, making a small gap between the buttons on either side.

Docking the Toolbar

The last thing that you do in the code that you add to the OnCreate function in the CMainFrame class is the following:

```
// Enable docking for the Color Toolbar
m_wndColorBar.EnableDocking(CBRS_ALIGN_ANY);

EnableDocking(CBRS_ALIGN_ANY);   // (AppWizard generated line)

// Dock the Color Toolbar
DockControlBar(&m_wndColorBar);
```

In the first of these lines, you called the EnableDocking toolbar function. This function enables the toolbar for docking with the frame window. The value passed to this toolbar function must match the value passed in the following EnableDocking function that is called for the frame window. The available values for these functions are listed in Table 12.4. These functions enable the borders of the toolbar, and the frame window, for docking. If these functions are not called, then you will not be able to dock the toolbar with the frame window. If a specific side is specified in these functions for use in docking, and the sides do not match, you will not be able to dock the toolbar with the frame.

TABLE 12.4. TOOLBAR DOCKING SIDES.

Style	Description
CBRS_ALIGN_TOP	Allows the toolbar to be docked to the top of the view area of the frame window.
CBRS_ALIGN_BOTTOM	Allows the toolbar to be docked to the bottom of the view area of the frame window.
CBRS_ALIGN_LEFT	Allows the toolbar to be docked to the left side of the view area of the frame window.
CBRS_ALIGN_RIGHT	Allows the toolbar to be docked to the right side of the view area of the frame window.
CBRS_ALIGN_ANY	Allows the toolbar to be docked to any side of the view area of the frame window.
CBRS_FLOAT_MULTI	Allows multiple toolbars to be floated in a single miniframe window.
0	The toolbar will not be able to dock with the frame.

12

The final function that you added was a frame window function, `DockControlBar`, which is passed the address of the toolbar variable. This function physically docks the toolbar to the frame window. Because all of this code appears in the `OnCreate` function for the frame window, the toolbar is docked before the user sees either the window or the toolbar.

Now, after adding all of this code to the `OnCreate` function of the `CMainFrame` class, if you compile and run your application, you'll find a working color toolbar that you can use to select the drawing color, as shown in Figure 12.3.

FIGURE 12.3.

The color toolbar on the drawing program.

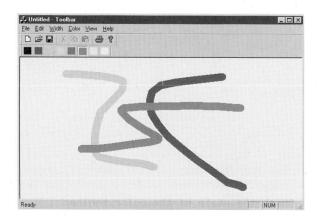

Controlling the Toolbar Visibility

Now that you have your color toolbar on the frame of your drawing application, it would be nice to be able to show and hide it just as you can the default toolbar and status bar through the View menu. This is simple enough functionality to add, but it doesn't necessarily work the way you might expect it to.

The first thing you need to do is add a menu entry to toggle the visibility of the color bar. Do this through the Menu Designer, adding a new menu entry on the View menu. Specify the menu properties as shown in Table 12.5.

TABLE 12.5. COLOR BAR MENU PROPERTIES.

Property	Setting
ID	ID_VIEW_COLORBAR
Caption	&Color Bar
Prompt	Show or hide the colorbar\nToggle ColorBar

Updating the Menu

To determine whether the toolbar is visible or hidden, you can get the current style of the toolbar and mask out for the WS_VISIBLE style flag. If the flag is in the current toolbar style, then the toolbar is visible. By placing this evaluation into the SetCheck function in the UPDATE_COMMAND_UI event message handler, you can check and uncheck the color bar menu entry as needed.

To add this functionality to your drawing program, add an event handler for the UPDATE_COMMAND_UI event message on the ID_VIEW_COLORBAR menu. Be sure to add this event-handler function into the CMainFrame class. (You're still making all of your coding changes so far in the frame class.) Edit the event-handler function, adding the code in Listing 12.2.

LISTING 12.2. THE MODIFIED CMainFrame.OnUpdateViewColorbar FUNCTION.

```
 1: void CMainFrame::OnUpdateViewColorbar(CCmdUI* pCmdUI)
 2: {
 3:     // TODO: Add your command update UI handler code here
 4:     ///////////////////////
 5:     // MY CODE STARTS HERE
 6:     ///////////////////////
 7:
 8:     // Check the state of the color toolbar
 9:     pCmdUI->SetCheck(((m_wndColorBar.GetStyle() & WS_VISIBLE) != 0));
10:
11:     ///////////////////////
12:     // MY CODE ENDS HERE
13:     ///////////////////////
14: }
```

Toggling the Toolbar Visibility

Because the CToolBar class is derived from the CWnd class (via the CControlBar class), you might think that you could call the ShowWindow function on the toolbar itself to show and hide the toolbar. Well, you can, but the background for the toolbar will not be hidden along with the toolbar. All the user would notice is the toolbar buttons appearing and disappearing. (Of course, this might be the effect you are after, but your users might not like it.)

Instead, you use a frame window function, ShowControlBar, to show and hide the toolbar. This function takes three arguments. The first argument is the address for the toolbar variable. The second argument is a boolean, specifying whether to show the toolbar.

12

(TRUE shows the toolbar; FALSE hides the toolbar.) Finally, the third argument specifies whether to delay showing the toolbar. (TRUE delays showing the toolbar; FALSE shows the toolbar immediately.)

Once a toolbar is toggled on or off, you need to call another frame window function, RecalcLayout. This function causes the frame to reposition all of the toolbars, status bars, and anything else that is within the frame area. This is the function that causes the color toolbar to move up and down if you toggle the default toolbar on and off.

To add this functionality to your drawing program, add an event handler for the COMMAND event message on the ID_VIEW_COLORBAR menu. Be sure to add this event-handler function into the CMainFrame class. (You're still making all of your coding changes so far in the frame class.) Edit the event-handler function, adding the code in Listing 12.3.

LISTING 12.3. THE MODIFIED CMainFrame.OnViewColorbar FUNCTION.

```
 1: void CMainFrame::OnViewColorbar()
 2: {
 3:     // TODO: Add your command handler code here
 4:
 5:     /////////////////////////
 6:     // MY CODE STARTS HERE
 7:     /////////////////////////
 8:     BOOL bVisible;
 9:
10:     // Check the state of the color toolbar
11:     bVisible = ((m_wndColorBar.GetStyle() & WS_VISIBLE) != 0);
12:
13:     // Toggle the color bar
14:     ShowControlBar(&m_wndColorBar, !bVisible, FALSE);
15:     // Reshuffle the frame layout
16:     RecalcLayout();
17:
18:     /////////////////////////
19:     // MY CODE ENDS HERE
20:     /////////////////////////
21: }
```

At this point, after compiling and running your application, you should be able to toggle your color toolbar on and off using the View menu.

Adding a Combo Box to a Toolbar

It's commonplace now to use applications that have more than just buttons on toolbars. Look at the Visual C++ Developer Studio, for example. You've got combo boxes that enable you to navigate through your code by selecting the class, ID, and function to edit right on the toolbar. So how do you add a combo box to a toolbar? It's not available in the toolbar designer; all you have there are buttons that you can paint icons on. You can't add a combo box to any toolbar by using any of the Visual C++ wizards. You have to write a little C++ code to do it.

To learn how to add a combo box to a toolbar, you'll add a combo box to the color tool-bar you just created. The combo box will be used to select the width of the pen the user will use to draw images. (If you haven't added the support for different drawing widths from the exercise at the end of Day 10, you might want to go back and add that now.)

Editing the Project Resources

To add a combo box to your toolbar, the first thing that you need to do is what Visual C++ was designed to prevent you from having to do. You need to edit the resource file yourself. You cannot do this through the Visual C++ Developer Studio. If you try to open the resource file in the Developer Studio, you will be popped into the Resource View tab of the workspace pane, editing the resource file through the various resource editors and designers. No, you'll have to edit this file in another editor, such as Notepad.

Close Visual C++, the only way to guarantee that you don't write over your changes. Open Notepad and navigate to your project directory. Open the resource file, which is named after the project with a .rc filename extension. Once you open this file in Notepad, scroll down until you find the toolbar definitions. (You can search for the word "toolbar.") Once you've found the toolbar definitions, go to the end of the Color toolbar definition and add two separator lines at the bottom of the toolbar definition.

For instance, to make these changes to your drawing application, you need to navigate to the Toolbar project directory and then open the Toolbar.rc file. (If you are adding these toolbars to the MDI drawing application, you need to look for the Day11.rc file.) Search for the toolbar section, and then add two SEPARATOR lines just before the end of the IDR_TBCOLOR section, as shown in Listing 12.4. Once you add these two lines, save the file, exit Notepad, and restart Visual C++, reloading the project.

12

LISTING 12.4. THE MODIFIED PROJECT RESOURCE FILE (Toolbar.rc).

```
 1: /////////////////////////////////////////////////////////////////////
 2: //
 3: // Toolbar
 4: //
 5:
 6: IDR_MAINFRAME TOOLBAR DISCARDABLE  16, 15
 7: BEGIN
 8:        BUTTON        ID_FILE_NEW
 9:        BUTTON        ID_FILE_OPEN
10:        BUTTON        ID_FILE_SAVE
11:        SEPARATOR
12:        BUTTON        ID_EDIT_CUT
13:        BUTTON        ID_EDIT_COPY
14:        BUTTON        ID_EDIT_PASTE
15:        SEPARATOR
16:        BUTTON        ID_FILE_PRINT
17:        BUTTON        ID_APP_ABOUT
18: END
19:
20: IDR_TBCOLOR TOOLBAR DISCARDABLE  16, 15
21: BEGIN
22:        BUTTON        ID_COLOR_BLACK
23:        BUTTON        ID_COLOR_BLUE
24:        BUTTON        ID_COLOR_GREEN
25:        BUTTON        ID_COLOR_CYAN
26:        BUTTON        ID_COLOR_RED
27:        BUTTON        ID_COLOR_MAGENTA
28:        BUTTON        ID_COLOR_YELLOW
29:        BUTTON        ID_COLOR_WHITE
30:        SEPARATOR
31:        SEPARATOR
32: END
```

You added these two SEPARATOR lines in the toolbar definition so that the second separator can act as a place holder for the combo box that you are going to add to the toolbar.
There are two reasons that you had to make this edit by hand and not use the Visual C++
toolbar designer. The first reason is that the toolbar designer would not allow you to add
more than one separator to the end of the toolbar. The second reason is that, if you don't
add anything else on the end of your toolbar after the separator, the toolbar designer
decides that the separator is a mistake and removes it for you. In other words, the Visual
C++ toolbar designer does not allow you to add the place holder for the combo box to
your toolbar.

Next, you need to add the text strings that you will load into your combo box. To add these strings, you need to open the string table in the Resource View of the workspace pane. Here you find all of the strings that you entered as prompts in various properties dialogs. This table has a number of IDs, the values of those IDs, and textual strings that are associated with those IDs, as shown in Figure 12.4. You'll need to add the strings to be placed into your toolbar combo box in the string table; each line in the drop-down list must have a unique ID and entry in the strings table.

FIGURE 12.4.

The string table editor.

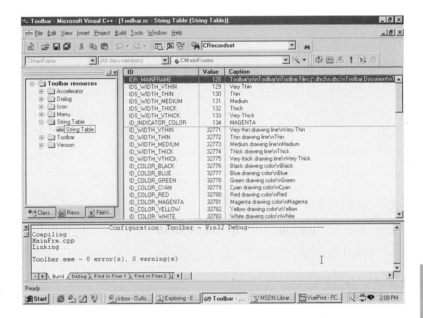

For instance, to add the strings for the combo box that you will be adding to the color toolbar, insert a new string, either by selecting Insert|New String from the menu or by right-clicking the string table and selecting New String from the pop-up menu.

In the String properties dialog, specify a string ID for the string and then enter the string to appear in the drop-down list. Close the properties dialog to add the string. For the strings in the Width combo box that you are going to add to the color toolbar, add the strings in Table 12.6.

TABLE 12.6. WIDTH TOOLBAR COMBO BOX STRINGS.

ID	Caption
IDS_WIDTH_VTHIN	Very Thin
IDS_WIDTH_THIN	Thin
IDS_WIDTH_MEDIUM	Medium
IDS_WIDTH_THICK	Thick
IDS_WIDTH_VTHICK	Very Thick

Creating the Toolbar Combo Box

Before you can add the combo box to the color toolbar, you need to create a combo box variable that you can use for the combo box. Because you are not able to add this combo box through any of the designers, you need to add it as a variable to the CMainFrame class.

To add the combo box variable to the main frame class for the color toolbar, select the Class View tab in the workspace pane. Right-click the CMainFrame class and select Add Member Variable from the pop-up menu. Specify the variable type as CComboBox, the name as m_ctlWidth, and the access as protected.

Once you add the combo box variable to the main frame class, you need to perform a series of actions, all once the toolbar has been created:

1. Set the width and the ID of the combo box place holder on the toolbar to the width and ID of the combo box.
2. Get the position of the toolbar placeholder and use it to size and position the combo box.
3. Create the combo box, specifying the toolbar as the parent window of the combo box.
4. Load the strings into the drop-down list on the combo box.

To organize this so that it doesn't get too messy, it might be advisable to move the creation of the color toolbar to its own function that can be called from the OnCreate function of the main frame class. To create this function, right-click the CMainFrame class in the workspace pane and select Add Member Function from the pop-up menu. Specify the function type as BOOL, the function description as CreateColorBar, and the access as public. Edit the new function, adding the code in Listing 12.5.

LISTING 12.5. THE `CMainFrame CreateColorBar` FUNCTION.

```
 1: BOOL CMainFrame::CreateColorBar()
 2: {
 3:     int iTBCtlID;
 4:     int i;
 5:
 6:     if (!m_wndColorBar.CreateEx(this, TBSTYLE_FLAT,
        ➥WS_CHILD ¦ WS_VISIBLE ¦ CBRS_TOP
 7:            ¦ CBRS_GRIPPER ¦ CBRS_TOOLTIPS ¦ CBRS_FLYBY ¦
        ➥CBRS_SIZE_DYNAMIC) ¦¦
 8:            !m_wndColorBar.LoadToolBar(IDR_TBCOLOR))
 9:     {
10:         TRACE0("Failed to create toolbar\n");
11:         return FALSE;        // fail to create
12:     }
13:     iTBCtlID = m_wndColorBar.CommandToIndex(ID_COLOR_BLACK);
14:     if (iTBCtlID >= 0)
15:     {
16:         for (i= iTBCtlID; i < (iTBCtlID + 8); i++)
17:             m_wndColorBar.SetButtonStyle(i, TBBS_CHECKGROUP);
18:     }
19:     // Add the Combo
20:     int nWidth = 100;
21:     int nHeight = 125;
22:
23:     // Configure the combo place holder
24:     m_wndColorBar.SetButtonInfo(9, IDC_CBWIDTH, TBBS_SEPARATOR,
        ➥nWidth);
25:
26:     // Get the colorbar height
27:     CRect rect;
28:     m_wndColorBar.GetItemRect(9, &rect);
29:     rect.bottom = rect.top + nHeight;
30:
31:     // Create the combo box
32:     m_ctlWidth.Create(WS_CHILD ¦ WS_VISIBLE ¦ WS_VSCROLL ¦
33:         CBS_DROPDOWNLIST, rect, &m_wndColorBar, IDC_CBWIDTH);
34:
35:     //  Fill the combo box
36:     CString szStyle;
37:     if (szStyle.LoadString(IDS_WIDTH_VTHIN))
38:         m_ctlWidth.AddString((LPCTSTR)szStyle);
39:     if (szStyle.LoadString(IDS_WIDTH_THIN))
40:         m_ctlWidth.AddString((LPCTSTR)szStyle);
41:     if (szStyle.LoadString(IDS_WIDTH_MEDIUM))
42:         m_ctlWidth.AddString((LPCTSTR)szStyle);
43:     if (szStyle.LoadString(IDS_WIDTH_THICK))
```

12

continues

LISTING 12.5. CONTINUED

```
44:         m_ctlWidth.AddString((LPCTSTR)szStyle);
45:     if (szStyle.LoadString(IDS_WIDTH_VTHICK))
46:         m_ctlWidth.AddString((LPCTSTR)szStyle);
47:
48:     return TRUE;
49: }
```

On line 24 in Listing 12.5, you specify that the combo box should be created using the object ID IDC_CBWIDTH. This object ID is used to identify the combo box when the combo box sends an event message to the application or when you need to specify what list entry is displayed in the edit field. However, this object ID doesn't exist in your application. Before you can compile the application, you'll need to add this ID to the project resource IDs, just as you did on Day 4, "Working with Timers." To add this ID to your project, select the Resource view in the workspace pane. Select the top of the resource tree and right-click the mouse to trigger the context menu. Select Resource Symbols from the pop-up menu and add the object ID IDC_CBWIDTH. Make sure that you add the new object ID with a unique numerical value so that it won't conflict with any other objects in use in your application.

Configuring the Placeholder

After creating the toolbar and configuring all of the toolbar buttons, the first thing you need to do is to configure the separator that is acting as the place holder for the combo box you are about to create. You do this with the SetButtonInfo toolbar function, as follows:

```
m_wndColorBar.SetButtonInfo(9, IDC_CBWIDTH, TBBS_SEPARATOR, nWidth);
```

This function takes four arguments. The first argument is the current index of the control in the toolbar—in this case, the tenth control in the toolbar (eight color buttons and two separators). The second argument is the new ID of the toolbar control. This is the ID that will be placed in the event message queue when a control event occurs. The third argument is the type of toolbar control this control should be. The fourth and final argument is somewhat deceptive. If you look at the function documentation, the fourth argument is the new index of the control in the toolbar. This is the position to which the control will be moved. However, if the control is a separator, this argument specifies the width of the control and doesn't move it anywhere. Because this toolbar control is a separator, this argument has the effect of setting it to be as wide as the combo box that you are going to create.

Getting the Toolbar Combo Box Position

Now that you have configured the toolbar separator as the place holder for the combo box, you need to get the position of the combo box place holder on the toolbar so that you can use it to set the position of the combo box:

```
m_wndColorBar.GetItemRect(9, &rect);
rect.bottom = rect.top + nHeight;
```

In the first line, you called the toolbar function `GetItemRect` to get the position and size of the placeholder for the combo box. In the next line, you added the height of the drop-down list to the height that the combo box will eventually be.

Creating the Combo Box

Now that you've got a place holder sized correctly, and you have the position and size for the combo box, it's time to create the combo box. You do this with the `Create` combo box function, as follows:

```
m_ctlWidth.Create(WS_CHILD | WS_VISIBLE | WS_VSCROLL |
    CBS_DROPDOWNLIST, rect, &m_wndColorBar, IDC_CBWIDTH);
```

The first argument to the combo box `Create` function is the combo box style. Normally, several style flags are combined to create a combination style value. Table 12.7 lists the flags that you can use in this value.

TABLE 12.7. COMBO BOX STYLES.

Style	Description
WS_CHILD	Designates this as a child window (required).
WS_VISIBLE	Makes the combo box visible.
WS_DISABLED	Disables the combo box.
WS_VSCROLL	Adds vertical scrolling to the drop-down list.
WS_HSCROLL	Adds horizontal scrolling to the drop-down list.
WS_GROUP	Groups controls.
WS_TABSTOP	Includes the combo box in the tabbing order.
CBS_AUTOHSCROLL	Automatically scrolls the text in the edit control to the right when the user types a character at the end of the line. This allows the user to enter text wider than the edit control into the combo box.
CBS_DROPDOWN	Similar to CBS_SIMPLE, but the list is not displayed unless the user selects the icon next to the edit control.

continues

12

TABLE 12.7. CONTINUED

Style	Description
CBS_DROPDOWNLIST	Similar to CBS_DROPDOWN, but the edit control is replaced with a static-text item displaying the currently selected item in the list.
CBS_HASSTRINGS	The owner of the list box is responsible for drawing the list box contents. The list box items consist of strings.
CBS_OEMCONVERT	Text entered in the edit control is converted from ANSI to the OEM character set and then back to ANSI.
CBS_OWNERDRAWFIXED	The owner of the list box is responsible for drawing the list box contents. The contents of the list are fixed in height.
CBS_OWNERDRAWVARIABLE	The owner of the list box is responsible for drawing the list box contents. The contents of the list are variable in height.
CBS_SIMPLE	The list box is displayed at all times.
CBS_SORT	Automatically sorts the strings in the list box.
CBS_DISABLENOSCROLL	List shows a disabled scrollbar when there are not enough items in the list to require scrolling.
CBS_NOINTEGRALHEIGHT	Specifies that the combo box is exactly the size specified.

The second argument is the rectangle that the combo box is to occupy. This argument is the position within the parent window—in this case, the toolbar—that the combo box will stay in. It will move with the parent window (the toolbar), staying in this position the entire time.

The third argument is a pointer to the parent window. This is the address of the color toolbar variable.

The fourth argument is the object ID for the combo box.

Populating the Combo Box

The final action that you have to do in creating the combo box on the color toolbar is populate the drop-down list with the available items that the user can select from. You do this with the combination of two functions:

```
if (szStyle.LoadString(IDS_WIDTH_VTHIN))
    m_ctlWidth.AddString((LPCTSTR)szStyle);
```

The first function is a CString function, LoadString. This function takes a string ID and loads the string matching the ID from the string table. The second function is a combo box function, AddString, which adds the string passed in as an argument to the drop-down list. By calling this function combination for each of the elements that should be in the drop-down list, you can populate the combo box from the application string table.

Updating the `OnCreate` Function

After moving all of the code to create the color toolbar to a separate function, you can update the `OnCreate` function so that it calls the `CreateColorBar` function where it used to create the color toolbar, as in Listing 12.6.

LISTING 12.6. THE MODIFIED `CMainFrame.OnCreate` FUNCTION.

```
 1:  int CMainFrame::OnCreate(LPCREATESTRUCT lpCreateStruct)
 2:  {
 3:      if (CFrameWnd::OnCreate(lpCreateStruct) == -1)
 4:          return -1;
 5:
 6:      if (!m_wndToolBar.CreateEx(this, TBSTYLE_FLAT,
         ➡WS_CHILD | WS_VISIBLE | CBRS_TOP
 7:          | CBRS_GRIPPER | CBRS_TOOLTIPS | CBRS_FLYBY |
         ➡CBRS_SIZE_DYNAMIC) ||
 8:          !m_wndToolBar.LoadToolBar(IDR_MAINFRAME))
 9:      {
10:          TRACE0("Failed to create toolbar\n");
11:          return -1;      // fail to create
12:      }
13:
14:      /////////////////////////
15:      // MY CODE STARTS HERE
16:      /////////////////////////
17:
18:      // Add the color toolbar
19:      if (!CreateColorBar())
20:      {
21:          TRACE0("Failed to create color toolbar\n");
22:          return -1;      // fail to create
23:      }
24:
25:      /////////////////////////
26:      // MY CODE ENDS HERE
27:      /////////////////////////
28:
29:      if (!m_wndStatusBar.Create(this) ||
30:          !m_wndStatusBar.SetIndicators(indicators,
31:            sizeof(indicators)/sizeof(UINT)))
32:      {
33:          TRACE0("Failed to create status bar\n");
34:          return -1;      // fail to create
35:      }
36:
37:      // TODO: Delete these three lines if you don't want the toolbar to
38:      //  be dockable
39:      m_wndToolBar.EnableDocking(CBRS_ALIGN_ANY);
```

continues

12

LISTING 12.6. CONTINUED

```
40:
41:        /////////////////////////
42:        // MY CODE STARTS HERE
43:        /////////////////////////
44:
45:        // Enable docking for the Color Toolbar
46:        m_wndColorBar.EnableDocking(CBRS_ALIGN_ANY);
47:
48:        /////////////////////////
49:        // MY CODE ENDS HERE
50:        /////////////////////////
51:
52:        EnableDocking(CBRS_ALIGN_ANY);
53:        DockControlBar(&m_wndToolBar);
54:
55:        /////////////////////////
56:        // MY CODE STARTS HERE
57:        /////////////////////////
58:
59:        // Dock the Color Toolbar
60:        DockControlBar(&m_wndColorBar);
61:
62:        /////////////////////////
63:        // MY CODE ENDS HERE
64:        /////////////////////////
65:
66:        return 0;
67: }
```

Now when you compile and run your application, you should have a combo box on the end of your color toolbar, as in Figure 12.5. However, the combo box doesn't do anything yet.

FIGURE 12.5.

The color toolbar with a width combo box.

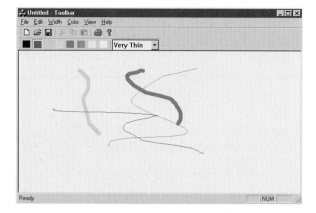

Handling the Toolbar Combo Box Events

Adding an event handler for the combo box is fairly simple, although it does have to be done by hand (because the Class Wizard doesn't even know that the combo box exists). You have to add an ON_CBN_SELCHANGE entry into the message map and then add the actual message-handler function into the CMainFrame class.

To start with, add the message-handler function by selecting the CMainFrame class in the workspace pane and selecting Add Member Function from the pop-up menu. Enter the function type as afx_msg void, the function definition as OnSelChangeWidth, and the access as protected. Edit the new function as in Listing 12.7.

LISTING 12.7. THE OnSelChangeWidth FUNCTION.

```
 1: void CMainFrame::OnSelChangeWidth()
 2: {
 3:      // Get the new combo selection
 4:      int nIndex = m_ctlWidth.GetCurSel();
 5:      if (nIndex == CB_ERR)
 6:          return;
 7:
 8:      // Get the active document
 9:      CToolbarDoc* pDoc = (CToolbarDoc*)GetActiveDocument();
10:      // Do we have a valid document?
11:      if (pDoc)
12:          // Set the new drawing width
13:          pDoc->SetWidth(nIndex);
14:
15: }
```

In this function, you first get the current selection from the combo box. Remember that the entries were added in order, and the CBS_SORT flag was not specified in the combo box creation, so the selection index numbers should correspond to the widths in the document. As a result, you can get a pointer to the current document instance, using the GetActiveDocument function, and then pass the new width to the document using its SetWidth function.

For the combo box selection changes to call this message-handler function, you need to add the appropriate entry to the CMainFrame message map. Scroll to the top of the CMainFrame source code until you find the message map section. Add line 12 in Listing 12.8 to the message map.

LISTING 12.8. THE MODIFIED `CMainFrame` MESSAGE MAP.

```
 1: //////////////////////////////////////////////////////////////////
 2: // CMainFrame
 3:
 4: IMPLEMENT_DYNCREATE(CMainFrame, CFrameWnd)
 5:
 6: BEGIN_MESSAGE_MAP(CMainFrame, CFrameWnd)
 7:     //{{AFX_MSG_MAP(CMainFrame)
 8:     ON_WM_CREATE()
 9:     ON_COMMAND(ID_VIEW_COLORBAR, OnViewColorbar)
10:     ON_UPDATE_COMMAND_UI(ID_VIEW_COLORBAR, OnUpdateViewColorbar)
11:     //}}AFX_MSG_MAP
12:     ON_CBN_SELCHANGE(IDC_CBWIDTH, OnSelChangeWidth)
13: END_MESSAGE_MAP()
```

This message map entry

```
ON_CBN_SELCHANGE(IDC_CBWIDTH, OnSelChangeWidth)
```

specifies that on combo box selection change events with the object ID of the color tool-bar combo box, the `OnSelChangeWidth` function should be called. Now if you compile and run your application, you should be able to change the drawing width with the combo box on the color toolbar.

Updating the Toolbar Combo Box

The one remaining problem with the combo box is that it needs to be updated if the user selects a new value from the menu instead of the combo box. One of the most efficient methods of doing this is to set the current selection in the combo box when any of the menu selections are triggered. This requires a function in the main frame class that can be called from the document class to accomplish this action. All the function in the main frame needs to do is to set the current selection in the combo box.

To implement this function in the main frame, add a new member function to the `CMainFrame` class, specifying the function type as void, the definition as `UpdateWidthCB(int nIndex)`, and the access as public. Once you add this function, edit the function as in Listing 12.9.

LISTING 12.9. THE `CMainFrame.UpdateWidthCB` FUNCTION.

```
1: void CMainFrame::UpdateWidthCB(int nIndex)
2: {
3:     // Set the new selection in the combo box
4:     m_wndColorBar.m_ctlWidth.SetCurSel(nIndex);
5: }
```

This function uses a single combo box function, `SetCurSel`, which sets the current selection in the combo box drop-down list to the entry specified with the index number. The edit control of the combo box is updated with the new selected list entry. If an index number that doesn't exist in the drop-down list is supplied to the combo box, then the function returns an error.

On the document side, you need to call this function in the main frame whenever the appropriate menu event-handling functions are called. Because this could occur in several functions, it makes the most sense to enclose the necessary functionality in a single function. This function needs to get a pointer to the view associated with the document and then, through the view, get a pointer to the frame, which can then be used to call the `UpdateWidthCB` function that you just added to the main frame class.

To add this function to your application, select the `CToolbarDoc` class in the workspace pane, and select Add Member Function from the pop-up menu. Specify void as the function type, `UpdateColorbar(int nIndex)` as the function definition, and private as the function access. Edit the function as in Listing 12.10.

LISTING 12.10. THE `CToolbarDoc.UpdateColorbar` FUNCTION.

```
1: void CToolbarDoc::UpdateColorbar(int nIndex)
2: {
3:     // Get the position of the first view
4:     POSITION pos = GetFirstViewPosition();
5:     // Did we get a valid position?
6:     if (pos != NULL)
7:     {
8:         // Get a pointer to the view in that position
9:         CView* pView = GetNextView(pos);
10:        // Do we have a valid pointer to the view?
11:        if (pView)
12:        {
13:            // Get a pointer to the frame through the view
```

12

continues

LISTING **12.10.** CONTINUED

```
14:                CMainFrame* pFrame = (CMainFrame*)pView-
➥GetTopLevelFrame();
15:             // Did we get a pointer to the frame?
16:             if (pFrame)
17:                 // Update the combo box on the color toolbar
18:                 // through the frame
19:                 pFrame->UpdateWidthCB(nIndex);
20:         }
21:     }
22: }
```

This function traces through the path that you have to follow to get to the application frame from the document class. The first thing that you did was get the position of the first view associated with the document, using the GetFirstViewPosition function. A document may have multiple views open at the same time, and this function returns the position of the first of those views.

The next function, GetNextView, returns a pointer to the view specified by the position. This function also updates the position variable to point to the next view in the list of views associated with the current document.

Once you have a pointer to the view, you can call the window function, GetTopLevelFrame, which returns a pointer to the application frame window. You have to call this function through the view because the document is not descended from the CWnd class, although the view is.

Once you have a pointer to the frame window, you can use this pointer to call the function you created earlier to update the combo box on the toolbar. Now if you call this new function from the Width menu command event handlers, as in Listing 12.11, the combo box that you placed on the color toolbar is automatically updated to reflect the currently selected drawing width, regardless of whether the width was selected from the combo box or the pull-down menu.

LISTING **12.11.** AN UPDATED WIDTH MENU COMMAND EVENT HANDLER.

```
1: void CToolbarDoc::OnWidthVthin()
2: {
3:     // TODO: Add your command handler code here
4:     // Set the new width
5:     m_nWidth = 0;
6:     // Update the combo box on the color toolbar
7:     UpdateColorbar(0);
8: }
```

Adding a New Status Bar Element

Earlier today, you learned how to specify status bar messages and tooltips for both tool-bar buttons and menus. What if you want to use the status bar to provide the user with more substantial information? What if, as in the Visual C++ Developer Studio, you want to provide information about what the user is doing, where he is in the document he is editing, or the mode that the application is in? This information goes beyond the Caps, Num, and Scroll lock keys that Visual C++ automatically reports on the status bar.

It's actually easy to add additional panes to the status bar, as well as take away the panes that are already there. To learn just how easy a change this is, you will add a new pane to the status bar in your drawing application that will display the color currently in use.

Adding a New Status Bar Pane

Before you add a new status bar pane, you need to add a new entry to the application string table for use in the status bar pane. This string table entry will perform two func-tions for the status bar pane. The first thing it will do is provide the object ID for the sta-tus bar pane. You will use this ID for updating the pane as you need to update the text in the pane. The second function this string table entry will perform is size the pane. To size the pane correctly, you need to provide a caption for the string table entry that is at least as wide as the widest string that you will place in the status bar pane.

Add a new string to your application string table, using the same steps you used earlier when adding the text for the combo box you placed on the color toolbar. Specify the string ID as ID_INDICATOR_COLOR and the caption as MAGENTA (the widest string that you will put into the status bar pane).

A small section in the first part of the main frame source code defines the status bar lay-out. This small table contains the object IDs of the status bar panes as table elements, in the order in which they are to appear from left to right on the status bar.

To add the color pane to the status bar, add the ID of the color pane to the status bar indi-cator table definition, just after the message map in the source-code file for the main frame. Place the color pane ID in the table definition in the position that you want it to be on the status bar, as in line 18 of Listing 12.12.

12

LISTING **12.12.** A MODIFIED STATUS BAR INDICATOR TABLE DEFINITION.

```
 1://////////////////////////////////////////////////////////////////
 2: // CMainFrame
 3:
 4: IMPLEMENT_DYNCREATE(CMainFrame, CFrameWnd)
 5:
 6: BEGIN_MESSAGE_MAP(CMainFrame, CFrameWnd)
 7:     //{{AFX_MSG_MAP(CMainFrame)
 8:     ON_WM_CREATE()
 9:     ON_COMMAND(ID_VIEW_COLORBAR, OnViewColorbar)
10:     ON_UPDATE_COMMAND_UI(ID_VIEW_COLORBAR, OnUpdateViewColorbar)
11:     //}}AFX_MSG_MAP
12:     ON_CBN_SELCHANGE(IDC_CBWIDTH, OnSelChangeWidth)
13: END_MESSAGE_MAP()
14:
15: static UINT indicators[] =
16: {
17:     ID_SEPARATOR,              // status line indicator
18:     ID_INDICATOR_COLOR,
19:     ID_INDICATOR_CAPS,
20:     ID_INDICATOR_NUM,
21:     ID_INDICATOR_SCRL,
22: };
23:
24://////////////////////////////////////////////////////////////////
25: // CMainFrame construction/destruction
```

If you want to drop any of the lock key indicators from the status bar, just remove them from the indicators table definition. If you examine the OnCreate function, where the status bar is created (just after the toolbars are created), you'll see where this table is used to create the status bar with the following code:

```
if (!m_wndStatusBar.Create(this) ||
    !m_wndStatusBar.SetIndicators(indicators,
        sizeof(indicators)/sizeof(UINT)))
```

Once the status bar is created, the SetIndicators function is called on the status bar to add the panes as they are defined in the indicators table. The strings associated with the IDs in the indicators table are used to initialize the panes and set their size. If you compile and run your application at this point, you see the new color pane on the status bar with the caption from the string table displayed within.

Setting a Status Bar Pane Text

Once you've added the pane to the status bar, you can let the UPDATE_COMMAND_UI event do all the updating of the pane. All you need to do is add an event handler for this event on the object ID of the pane and use this event to set the pane text. Because the status bar is always visible, the UPDATE_COMMAND_UI event for the panes on the status bar is triggered every time that the application is idle. This means that it is triggered after the application is finished processing just about every keystroke and mouse movement. In almost a week, on Day 18, "Doing Multiple Tasks at One Time—Multitasking," you will learn more about how often and when any tasks that are performed when the application is idle are triggered.

In the event handler, you need to create a string containing the name of the current color (or whatever other text you want to display in the status bar pane). Next, you have to make sure that the pane is enabled. Finally, you need to set the text of the pane to the string that you have created.

To implement this in your application, you need to create an UPDATE_COMMAND_UI event handler. Once again, the Class Wizard does not know about the status bar pane, so you have to create the message handler and add it to the message map yourself. To create the message handler, add a new member function to the document class (CToolbarDoc) with a type of afx_msg void, a definition of OnUpdateIndicatorColor (CCmdUI *pCmdUI), and an access of protected. Edit the newly created function, adding the code in Listing 12.13.

LISTING **12.13.** THE `OnUpdateIndicatorColor` FUNCTION.

```
1: void CToolbarDoc::OnUpdateIndicatorColor(CCmdUI *pCmdUI)
2: {
3:     CString strColor;
4:
5:     // What is the current color?
6:     switch (m_nColor)
7:     {
8:     case 0:    // Black
9:         strColor = "BLACK";
10:        break;
11:    case 1:    // Blue
12:        strColor = "BLUE";
13:        break;
14:    case 2:    // Green
```

12

continues

LISTING 12.13. CONTINUED

```
15:           strColor = "GREEN";
16:           break;
17:     case 3:      // Cyan
18:           strColor = "CYAN";
19:           break;
20:     case 4:      // Red
21:           strColor = "RED";
22:           break;
23:     case 5:      // Magenta
24:           strColor = "MAGENTA";
25:           break;
26:     case 6:      // Yellow
27:           strColor = "YELLOW";
28:           break;
29:     case 7:      // White
30:           strColor = "WHITE";
31:           break;
32:     }
33:     // Enable the status bar pane
34:     pCmdUI->Enable(TRUE);
35:     // Set the text of the status bar pane
36:     // to the current color
37:     pCmdUI->SetText(strColor);
38: }
```

In this function, you followed three steps exactly: You created a string with the current color name, made sure that the pane was enabled, and set the pane text to the string that you had created.

Now, to make sure that your new message handler is called when it is supposed to be, you need to add an ON_UPDATE_COMMAND_UI entry to the message map at the top of the document source code file, as specified in Listing 12.14.

LISTING 12.14. THE MODIFIED CToolbarDoc MESSAGE MAP.

```
1://////////////////////////////////////////////////////////////////////////
2: // CToolbarDoc
3:
4: IMPLEMENT_DYNCREATE(CToolbarDoc, CDocument)
5:
6: BEGIN_MESSAGE_MAP(CToolbarDoc, CDocument)
7:     ON_UPDATE_COMMAND_UI(ID_INDICATOR_COLOR, OnUpdateIndicatorColor)
8:     //{{AFX_MSG_MAP(CToolbarDoc)
9:     ON_UPDATE_COMMAND_UI(ID_WIDTH_VTHIN, OnUpdateWidthVthin)
10: .
```

```
11: .
12:     ON_COMMAND(ID_WIDTH_VTHIN, OnWidthVthin)
13:     //}}AFX_MSG_MAP
14: END_MESSAGE_MAP()
```

After adding the message handler and message map entry, you should now be able to compile and run your application and see the color status bar pane automatically updated to reflect the current drawing color, as shown in Figure 12.6.

FIGURE 12.6.

The drawing application with the current color displayed in the status bar.

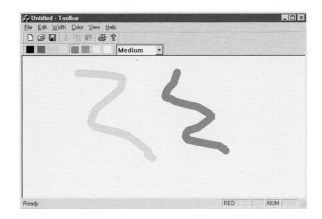

Summary

You learned quite a bit today. (Is this becoming a trend?) You learned how to design and create your own toolbars. Along with learning how to design toolbars, you learned how to specify status bar prompts for the toolbar buttons and menus, along with tooltips text that will display after holding the mouse over toolbar buttons for a couple of seconds. You learned how to create these toolbars and how to attach them to the application frame. You also learned how you can control whether the toolbar is visible from a menu entry.

Next you learned how to place a combo box on a toolbar so that you can provide your application users with the same level of convenience that you have when using many popular software packages. In learning how to add this combo box to the toolbar, you learned how to create a combo box in code, without having to depend on the dialog designers to create combo boxes, and how to populate the combo box drop-down list with text entries. Then, you learned how to tie the combo box into your application by

12

adding event handlers for the combo box events and how to update the combo box to reflect changes made through the application menus.

Finally, you learned how to add your own panes to the status bar and how you can update the pane to reflect the current status of the application.

Q&A

Q In some applications, toolbars have the option of showing text, as in Internet Explorer. How can I add text to my toolbar buttons?

A Unfortunately, the toolbar designer provides no way to add text to the toolbar buttons. This means that you have to add the text to the buttons in your application code, much in the same way that you had to specify for all of the color toolbar buttons to behave as radio buttons. You use the `SetButtonText` function to set the text on each toolbar button individually. This function takes two arguments: The first is the index number of the button, and the second is the text for the button. If you really want to place text on the toolbar buttons, you also have to resize the toolbar to allow the room for the text to be displayed.

Q I made some changes to the color toolbar in the toolbar designer, and now I get an assertion error every time I try to run my application. What happened?

A The problem is that the toolbar designer found the separators you added to the resource file as place holders for the combo box. The toolbar designer assumed that these were mistakes and removed them for you. The error that you are getting occurs because you are trying to work with a control in the color toolbar that doesn't exist. To fix this problem, reopen the resource file in Notepad and again add the two separators at the end of the color toolbar definition. Then, reload the project into Visual C++ and recompile the application.

Q The combo box on my toolbars looks too big. How can I get it to fit within the toolbar a little better?

A To make the combo box fit within the toolbar like the combo boxes in the Visual C++ Developer Studio, you need to do a couple of things. First, lower the top of the combo box by 3; this places a small border between the top of the combo box and the edge of the toolbar. Next, set the font in the combo box to a smaller font that will fit within the toolbar better. You can experiment with fonts and pitches until you have a font that you like for the combo box in the toolbar.

Q How can I set the text in the first section of the status bar other than by using menu and toolbar prompts?

A You can use `SetWindowText` to set the text in the first pane of the status bar. As a default setting, the first pane in the status bar is a separator that automatically expands to fill the width of the status bar with the other panes right-justified on the bar. The `SetWindowText` function, called on the status bar variable, sets the text in the first pane only. If you want to set the text in any other pane, at any other time than in the `ON_UPDATE_COMMAND_UI` event handler, you can use the `SetPaneText` function. There are two ways that you can set the text in the main part of the status bar. The first is like this:

```
CString myString = "This is my string"
m_wndStatusBar.SetWindowText(myString);
```

The other method is

```
CString myString = "This is my string"
m_wndStatusBar.SetPaneText(0, myString);
```

Workshop

The Workshop provides quiz questions to help you solidify your understanding of the material covered and exercises to provide you with experience in using what you've learned. The answers to the quiz questions and exercises are provided in Appendix B, "Answers."

Quiz

1. How do you tie a toolbar button to a menu entry that triggers that same function?
2. How do you make sure that a toolbar can be docked with the frame window?
3. How can you remove the Num Lock status indicator from the status bar?
4. Why do you have to edit the resource file to add a combo box to a toolbar?

Exercises

1. Add another pane to the status bar to display the current width selected.
2. Add a button to the main toolbar that can be used to toggle the color toolbar on and off, as in Figure 12.7.

12

FIGURE 12.7.

The color toolbar on/off button.

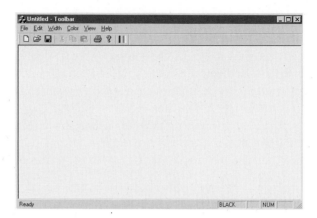

DAY 13

Saving and Restoring Work—File Access

Most applications provide the user the option of saving what has been created. The creation can be a word-processing document, a spreadsheet, a drawing, or a set of data records. Today, you will explore how Visual C++ provides you with the means to implement this functionality easily. Today, you will learn

- How Visual C++ uses C++ streams to save information about your application
- How to store your application data in binary files
- How to make your application objects serializable
- How you can store variables of differing data types into a single file

Serialization

There are two parts of serialization. When application data is stored on the system drive in the form of a file, it is called serialization. When the application state is restored from the file, it is called deserialization. The combination of these two parts makes up the serialization of application objects in Visual C++.

The CArchive and CFile Classes

Serialization in Visual C++ applications is accomplished through the CArchive class. The CArchive class is designed to act as an input/output (I/O) stream for a CFile object, as shown in Figure 13.1. It uses C++ streams to enable efficient data flow to and from the file that is the storage of the application data. The CArchive class cannot exist without a CFile class object to which it is attached.

FIGURE 13.1.

The CArchive class stores application data in a CFile object.

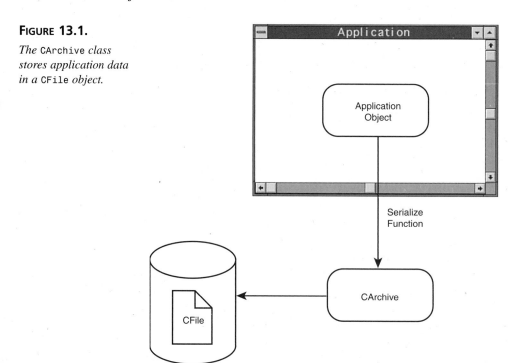

The CArchive class can store data in a number of types of files, all of which are descendants of the CFile class. By default, the AppWizard includes all the functionality to create and open regular CFile objects for use with CArchive. If you want or need to work with one of these other file types, you might need to add additional code to your application to enable the use of these different file types.

The Serialize Function

The CArchive class is used in the Serialize function on the document and data objects in Visual C++ applications. When an application is reading or writing a file, the document object's Serialize function is called, passing the CArchive object that is used to write to or read from the file. In the Serialize function, the typical logic to follow is to determine whether the archive is being written to or read from by calling the CArchive IsStoring or IsLoading functions. The return value from either of these two functions determines if your application needs to be writing to or reading from the CArchive class's I/O stream. A typical Serialize function in the view class looks like Listing 13.1.

LISTING 13.1. A TYPICAL Serialize FUNCTION.

```
 1: void CAppDoc::Serialize(CArchive& ar)
 2: {
 3:     // Is the archive being written to?
 4:     if (ar.IsStoring())
 5:     {
 6:         // Yes, write my variable
 7:         ar << m_MyVar;
 8:     }
 9:     else
10:     {
11:         // No, read my variable
12:         ar >> m_MyVar;
13:     }
14: }
```

You can place a Serialize function in any classes you create so that you can call their Serialize function from the document Serialize function. If you place your custom objects into an object array, such as the CObArray that you used in your drawing application for the past three days, you can call the array's Serialize function from the document's Serialize function. The object array will, in turn, call the Serialize function of any objects that have been stored in the array.

Making Objects Serializable

When you created the CLine class on Day 10, "Creating Single Document Interface Applications," you had to add two macros before you could save and restore your drawings. These two macros, DECLARE_SERIAL and IMPLEMENT_SERIAL, include functionality in your classes that are necessary for the Serialize function to work correctly.

13

Including the DECLARE_SERIAL Macro

You must include the DECLARE_SERIAL macro in your class declaration, as shown in Listing 13.2. The DECLARE_SERIAL macro takes a single argument, the class name. This macro automatically adds to your class some standard function and operator declarations that are necessary for serialization to work correctly.

LISTING 13.2. INCLUDING THE DECLARE_SERIAL MACRO IN THE CLASS DECLARATION.

```
1: class CMyClass : public CObject
2: {
3:     DECLARE_SERIAL (CMyClass)
4: public:
5:     virtual void Serialize(CArchive &ar);
6:     CMyClass();
7:     virtual ~CMyClass();
8: };
```

Including the IMPLEMENT_SERIAL Macro

You need to add the IMPLEMENT_SERIAL macro to the implementation of your class. This macro needs to appear outside any other class functions because it adds the code for the class functions that were declared with the DECLARE_SERIAL macro.

The IMPLEMENT_SERIAL macro takes three arguments. The first argument is the class name, as in the DECLARE_SERIAL macro. The second argument is the name of the base class, from which your class is inherited. The third argument is a version number that can be used to determine whether a file is the correct version for reading into your application. The version number, which must be a positive number, should be incremented each time the serialization method of the class is changed in any way that alters the data being written to or read from a file. A typical usage of the IMPLEMENT_SERIAL macro is provided in Listing 13.3.

LISTING 13.3. INCLUDING THE IMPLEMENT_SERIAL MACRO IN THE CLASS IMPLEMENTATION.

```
1: // MyClass.cpp: implementation of the CMyClass class.
2: //
3: //////////////////////////////////////////////////////////////////////
4:
5: #include "stdafx.h"
6: #include "MyClass.h"
7:
8: #ifdef _DEBUG
9: #undef THIS_FILE
10: static char THIS_FILE[]=__FILE__;
```

```
11: #define new DEBUG_NEW
12: #endif
13:
14: IMPLEMENT_SERIAL (CMyClass, CObject, 1)
15: /////////////////////////////////////////////////////////////////
16: // Construction/Destruction
17: /////////////////////////////////////////////////////////////////
18:
19: CMyClass::CMyClass()
20: {
21: }
22:
23: CMyClass::~CMyClass()
24: {
25: }
```

Defining the `Serialize` Function

Along with the two macros, you need to include a `Serialize` function in your class. This function should be declared as a `void` function with a single argument (`CArchive &ar`), public access, and the virtual check box selected—producing the function declaration in Listing 13.2. When you implement the `Serialize` function for your class, you typically use the same approach as that used in the document class, shown in Listing 13.1, where you check to determine whether the file is being written to or read from.

Implementing a Serializable Class

When you begin designing a new application, one of the first things you need to design is how to store the data in the document class that your application will create and operate on. If you are creating a data-oriented application that collects sets of data from the user, much like a contact database application, how are you going to hold that data in the application memory? What if you are building a word processor application—how are you going to hold the document being written in the application memory? Or a spreadsheet? Or a painting program? Or...you get the idea.

Once you determine how you are going to design the data structures on which your application will operate, then you can determine how best to serialize your application and classes. If you are going to hold all data directly in the document class, all you need to worry about is writing the data to and reading the data from the `CArchive` object in the document's `Serialize` function. If you are going to create your own class to hold your application data, you need to add the serialization functionality to your data classes so that they can save and restore themselves.

In the application that you are going to build today, you will create a simple, flat-file database application that illustrates how you can combine a mixture of data types into a single data stream in the application serialization. Your application will display a few fields of data, some of which are variable-length strings, and others that are integer or boolean, and will save and restore them in a single data stream to and from the CArchive object.

Creating a Serialized Application

You can create your own classes, which can also be serialized, for use in an SDI or MDI application. In short, any application that works with any sort of data, whether a database or a document, can be serialized. Now you will create a simple, flat-file database application that you will serialize.

 Note

A flat-file database is one of the original types of databases. It is a simple file-based database, with the records sequentially appended to the end of the previous record. It has none of the fancy relational functionality that is standard in most databases today. The database that you will build today is closer to an old dBASE or Paradox database, without any indexes, than to databases such as Access or SQL Server.

Creating the Application Shell

To get your application started, create a new AppWizard application. Give your application a name, such as Serialize, and click OK to start the AppWizard.

In the AppWizard, select to create a single document style application using the Document/View architecture. You can choose to include support for ActiveX controls in the third AppWizard step, although it's not really necessary for the example that you will build.

In the fourth step, be sure to specify the file extension for the files that your application will create and read. An example of a file extension that you might want to use is ser for serialize or fdb for flat-file database.

In the sixth AppWizard step, you need to specify which base class to use for the application view class. For the sample application you are building, because it will be a database application, you'll find it easiest to use CFormView as the base class from which your view class will be inherited. This enables you to use the dialog designer for your application view.

Once you finish making your way through the AppWizard and let the AppWizard create your application shell, you will see a large window canvas in the dialog designer as if you had created a dialog-style application, only without the OK and Cancel buttons, as shown in Figure 13.2.

FIGURE 13.2.

The window designer for an SDI application.

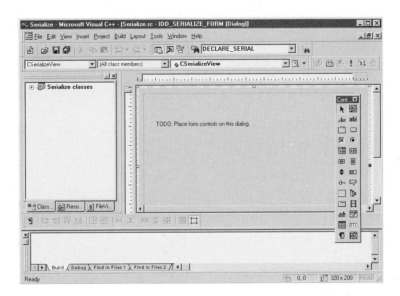

Designing Your Application Window

After you create an SDI or MDI application where the view class is based on the CFormView class, you need to design your application view. Designing the view is much like designing the window layout for a dialog window, but you don't need to worry about including any buttons to close the window while either saving or canceling the work done by the user. With an SDI or MDI application, the functionality to save and exit the window is traditionally located on the application menus or on the toolbar. As a result, you need to include only the controls for the function that your application window will perform.

13

Note

If you are building dialog-style applications, the AppWizard doesn't provide any serialization code in your application shell. If you need to serialize a dialog-style application, you'll need to add all this code yourself.

For the sample application that you are building today, lay out controls on the window canvas as shown in Figure 13.3 using the control properties listed in Table 13.1.

FIGURE 13.3.

The sample application window layout.

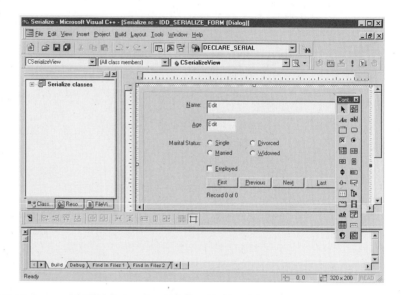

TABLE 13.1. CONTROL PROPERTY SETTINGS.

Object	Property	Setting
Static Text	ID	IDC_STATIC
	Caption	&Name:
Edit Box	ID	IDC_ENAME
Static Text	ID	IDC_STATIC
	Caption	&Age
Edit Box	ID	IDC_EAGE
Static Text	ID	IDC_STATIC
	Caption	Marital Status:
Radio Button	ID	IDC_RSINGLE
	Caption	&Single
	Group	Checked
Radio Button	ID	IDC_RMARRIED
	Caption	&Married
Radio Button	ID	IDC_RDIVORCED
	Caption	&Divorced

Object	Property	Setting
Radio Button	ID	IDC_RWIDOW
	Caption	&Widowed
Check Box	ID	IDC_CBEMPLOYED
	Caption	&Employed
Button	ID	IDC_BFIRST
	Caption	&First
Button	ID	IDC_BPREV
	Caption	&Previous
Button	ID	IDC_BNEXT
	Caption	Nex&t
Button	ID	IDC_BLAST
	Caption	&Last
Static Text	ID	IDC_SPOSITION
	Caption	Record 0 of 0

When you were developing dialog-style applications or windows, you attached variables to the controls on the window in the dialog class. However, with an SDI or MDI application, which class do you create the variables in? Because the UpdateData function is a member of the CWnd class, and the view class is descended from the CWnd class, although the document is not, then the view class is the most logical place to add the variables that you will attach to the controls you placed on the window.

To attach variables to the controls in your sample application, open the Class Wizard and add variables to the controls, specifying that the place to add them is the view class (in this case, CSerializeView). For the sample application, add the variables in Table 13.2 to the controls specified.

TABLE 13.2. CONTROL VARIABLES.

Object	Name	Category	Type
IDC_CBEMPLOYED	m_bEmployed	Value	BOOL
IDC_EAGE	m_iAge	Value	int
IDC_ENAME	m_sName	Value	CString
IDC_RSINGLE	m_iMaritalStatus	Value	int
IDC_SPOSITION	m_sPosition	Value	CString

13

If you examine the source code for the view class, you will notice that there is no `OnDraw` function. If you are using the `CFormView` ancestor class for your SDI or MDI application, you don't need to worry about the `OnDraw` function. Instead, you treat the view class very much as you would the dialog class in a dialog window or dialog-style application. The primary difference is that the data that you need to use to populate the controls on the window are not in the view class, but in the document class. As a result, you need to build the interaction between these two classes to pass the data for the controls back and forth.

Creating a Serializable Class

When you create a form-based application, it is assumed that your application will hold multiple records in the form and that the user will be able to scroll through the records to make changes. The user will be able to add additional records or even remove records from the record set. The challenge at this point in building this application is how you represent this set of records, supporting all the necessary functionality.

One approach is to create a class that would encapsulate each record, and then hold these records in an array, much as you did with the drawing application that you created and enhanced over the past few days. This class would need to descend from the `CObject` class and would need to contain variables for all the control variables that you added to the view class, along with methods to read and write all of these variables. Along with adding the methods to set and read all of the variables, you need to make the class serializable by adding the `Serialize` function to the class, as well as the two macros that complete the serialization of the class.

Creating the Basic Class

As you may remember from Day 10, when you want to create a new class, you can select the project in the Class View tab of the workspace pane, right-click the mouse button, and select New Class from the context menu. This opens the New Class dialog.

In the New Class dialog, you specify the type of class, whether it's an MFC class, a generic class, or a form class. To create a class that can contain one record's data, you most likely want to create a generic class. You'll learn more about how to determine which of these types of classes to create on Day 16, "Creating Your Own Classes and Modules." The other things that you need to do are give your class a name and specify the base class from which it will be inherited.

For your sample application, because the form that you created has information about a person, you might want to call your class something like `CPerson`. To be able to hold your class in the object array, you need to give it `CObject` as the base class. Just like on

Day 10, the New Class dialog will claim that it cannot find the header with the base class in it and that you need to add this. Well, it's already included, so you can ignore this message. (On Day 16, you'll learn when you need to pay attention to this message.)

Once you create your new class, you'll need to add the variables for holding the data elements that will be displayed on the screen for the user. Following good object-oriented design, these variables will all be declared as private variables, where they cannot be directly manipulated by other classes. The variable types should match the variable types of the variables that are attached to the window controls in the view class.

With the sample application you are creating, you need to add the variables in Table 13.3.

TABLE 13.3. CLASS VARIABLES FOR THE CPerson CLASS.

Name	Type
m_bEmployed	BOOL
m_iAge	int
m_sName	CString
m_iMaritalStatus	int

Adding Methods for Reading and Writing Variables

Once you create your class, you need to provide a means for reading and writing to the variables in the class. One of the easiest ways to provide this functionality is to add inline functions to the class definition. You create a set of inline functions to set each of the variables and then make another set for retrieving the current value of each variable.

> **Note**
>
> An inline function is a short C++ function in which, when the application is being compiled, the function body is copied in place of the function call. As a result, when the compiled application is running, the function code is executed without having to make a context jump to the function and then jump back once the function has completed. This reduces the overhead in the running application, increasing the execution speed slightly, but also makes the resulting executable application slightly larger. The more places the inline function is called, the larger the application will eventually get. For more information on inline functions, consult Appendix A, "C++ Review."

13

If you want to implement the Get and Set variable functions for your CPerson class in the sample application that you are building, edit the Person.h header file, adding the lines in Listing 13.4.

LISTING **13.4.** THE Get AND Set INLINE FUNCTION DECLARATIONS.

```
 1: class CPerson : public CObject
 2: {
 3: public:
 4:     // Functions for setting the variables
 5:     void SetEmployed(BOOL bEmployed) { m_bEmployed = bEmployed;}
 6:     void SetMaritalStat(int iStat) { m_iMaritalStatus = iStat;}
 7:     void SetAge(int iAge) { m_iAge = iAge;}
 8:     void SetName(CString sName) { m_sName = sName;}
 9:     // Functions for getting the current settings of the variables
10:     BOOL GetEmployed() { return m_bEmployed;}
11:     int GetMaritalStatus() { return m_iMaritalStatus;}
12:     int GetAge() {return m_iAge;}
13:     CString GetName() {return m_sName;}
14:     CPerson();
15:     virtual ~CPerson();
16:
17: private:
18:     BOOL m_bEmployed;
19:     int m_iMaritalStatus;
20:     int m_iAge;
21:     CString m_sName;
22: };
```

After you have the methods for setting and retrieving the values of the variables in your custom class, you'll probably want to make sure that the variables are initialized when the class is first created. You can do this in the class constructor by setting each of the variables to a default value. For instance, in your sample application, you add the code in Listing 13.5 to the constructor of the CPerson class.

LISTING **13.5.** THE CPerson CONSTRUCTOR.

```
1: CPerson::CPerson()
2: {
3:     // Initialize the class variables
4:     m_iMaritalStatus = 0;
5:     m_iAge = 0;
6:     m_bEmployed = FALSE;
7:     m_sName = "";
8: }
```

Serializing the Class

After you have your custom class with all variables defined and initialized, you need to make the class serializable. Making your class serializable involves three steps. The first step is adding the Serialize function to the class. This function writes the variable values to, and reads them back from, the CArchive object using C++ streams. The other two steps consist of adding the DECLARE_SERIAL and IMPLEMENT_SERIAL macros. Once you add these elements, your custom class will be serializable and ready for your application.

To add the Serialize function to your custom class, add a member function through the Class View tab in the workspace pane. Specify the function type as void, the function declaration as Serialize(CArchive &ar), and the access as public and check the Virtual check box. This should add the Serialize function and place you in the editor, ready to flesh out the function code.

In the Serialize function, the first thing you want to do is to call the ancestor's Serialize function. When you call the ancestor's function first, any foundation information that has been saved is restored first, providing the necessary support for your class before the variables in your class are restored. Once you call the ancestor function, you need to determine whether you need to read or write the class variables. You can do this by calling CArchive's IsStoring method. This function returns TRUE if the archive is being written to and FALSE if it's being read from. If the IsStoring function returns TRUE, you can use C++ I/O streams to write all your class variables to the archive. If the function returns FALSE, you can use C++ streams to read from the archive. In both cases, you must be certain to order the variables in the same order for both reading and writing. If you need more information about C++ streams, see Appendix A.

An example of a typical Serialize function for your sample custom class is shown in Listing 13.6. Notice that the CPerson variables are in the same order when writing to and reading from the archive.

LISTING 13.6. THE CPerson.Serialize FUNCTION.

```
1: void CPerson::Serialize(CArchive &ar)
2: {
3:     // Call the ancestor function
4:     CObject::Serialize(ar);
5:
6:     // Are we writing?
7:     if (ar.IsStoring())
8:         // Write all of the variables, in order
9:         ar << m_sName << m_iAge << m_iMaritalStatus << m_bEmployed;
10:    else
11:        // Read all of the variables, in order
12:        ar >> m_sName >> m_iAge >> m_iMaritalStatus >> m_bEmployed;
13: }
```

13

Once you have the Serialize function in place, you need to add the macros to your custom class. The first macro, DECLARE_SERIAL, needs to go in the class header and is passed the class name as its only argument.

For example, to add the DECLARE_SERIAL macro to the custom CPerson class in your sample application, you add the macro just below the start of the class declaration, where it will receive the default access for the class. You specify the class name, CPerson, as the only argument to the macro, as in Listing 13.7.

LISTING **13.7.** THE SERIALIZED CPerson CLASS DECLARATION.

```
 1: class CPerson : public CObject
 2: {
 3:     DECLARE_SERIAL (CPerson)
 4: public:
 5:     // Functions for setting the variables
 6:     void SetEmployed(BOOL bEmployed) { m_bEmployed = bEmployed;}
 7:     void SetMaritalStat(int iStat) { m_iMaritalStatus = iStat;}
 8:     void SetAge(int iAge) { m_iAge = iAge;}
 9:     void SetName(CString sName) { m_sName = sName;}
10:     // Functions for getting the current settings of the variables
11:     BOOL GetEmployed() { return m_bEmployed;}
12:     int GetMaritalStatus() { return m_iMaritalStatus;}
13:     int GetAge() {return m_iAge;}
14:     CString GetName() {return m_sName;}
15:     CPerson();
16:     virtual ~CPerson();
17:
18: private:
19:     BOOL m_bEmployed;
20:     int m_iMaritalStatus;
21:     int m_iAge;
22:     CString m_sName;
23: };
```

Note
The default access permission for functions and variables in C++ classes is public. All functions and variables that are declared before the first access declaration are public by default. You could easily add all of the public class functions and variables in this area of the class declaration, but explicitly declaring the access permission for all functions and variables is better practice—because that way, there is little to no confusion about the visibility of any of the class functions or variables.

Note

> Most C++ functions need a semicolon at the end of the line of code. The two serialization macros do not, due to the C preprocessor, which replaces each of the macros with all of the code before compiling the application. It doesn't hurt to place the semicolons there; they are simply ignored.

To complete the serialization of your custom class, you need to add the IMPLEMENT_SERIAL macro to the class definition. The best place to add this macro is before the constructor definition in the CPP file containing the class source code. This macro takes three arguments: the custom class name, the base class name, and the version number. If you make any changes to the Serialize function, you should increment the version number argument to the IMPLEMENT_SERIAL macro. This version number indicates when a file was written using a previous version of the Serialize function and thus may not be readable by the current version of the application.

Note

> In practice, if you read a file that was written using a previous version of the Serialize function in your class, your application will raise an exception, which you can then catch using standard C++ exception-handling techniques. This allows you to add code to your application to recognize and convert files created with earlier versions of your application. For information on C++ exception handling, see Appendix A.

To add the IMPLEMENT_SERIAL macro to your sample application, add it into the Person.cpp file just before the CPerson class constructor. Pass CPerson as the first argument (the class name), CObject as the second argument (the base class), and 1 as the version number, as in Listing 13.8.

LISTING 13.8. THE IMPLEMENT_SERIAL MACRO IN THE CPerson CODE.

13

```
1: // Person.cpp: implementation of the CPerson class.
2: //
3: //////////////////////////////////////////////////////////////////
4:
5: #include "stdafx.h"
6: #include "Serialize.h"
7: #include "Person.h"
8:
9: #ifdef _DEBUG
10: #undef THIS_FILE
```

continues

LISTING 13.8. CONTINUED

```
11: static char THIS_FILE[]=__FILE__;
12: #define new DEBUG_NEW
13: #endif
14:
15: IMPLEMENT_SERIAL (CPerson, CObject, 1)
16: /////////////////////////////////////////////////////////////////////
17: // Construction/Destruction
18: /////////////////////////////////////////////////////////////////////
19:
20: CPerson::CPerson()
21: {
22:     // Initialize the class variables
23:     m_iMaritalStatus = 0;
24:     m_iAge = 0;
25:     m_bEmployed = FALSE;
26:     m_sName = "";
27: }
```

Building Support in the Document Class

When you build a form-based application, where the form on the window is the primary place for the user to interact with the application, there is an unstated assumption that your application will allow the user to work with a number of records. This means that you need to include support for holding and navigating these records. The support for holding the records can be as simple as adding an object array as a variable to the document class, as you did back on Day 10. This allows you to add additional record objects as needed. The navigation could be a number of functions for retrieving the first, last, next, or previous record objects. Finally, you need informational functionality so that you can determine what record in the set the user is currently editing.

To hold and support this functionality, the document class will probably need two variables, the object array and the current record number in the array. These two variables will provide the necessary support for holding and navigating the record set.

For your example, add the two variables for supporting the record set of CPerson objects as listed in Table 13.4. Specify private access for both variables.

TABLE 13.4. DOCUMENT CLASS VARIABLES.

Name	Type
m_iCurPosition	int
m_oaPeople	CObArray

The other thing that you need to do to the document class to provide support for the record objects is make sure that the document knows about and understands the record object that it will be holding. You do this by including the custom class header file before the header file for the document class is included in the document class source code file. Because the document class needs to trigger actions in the view class, it's a good idea to also include the header file for the view class in the document class.

To include these header files in your sample application, open the source-code file for the document class and add the two #include statements as shown in Listing 13.9.

LISTING 13.9. INCLUDING THE CUSTOM AND VIEW CLASSES IN THE DOCUMENT CLASS IMPLEMENTATION.

```
 1: // SerializeDoc.cpp : implementation of the CSerializeDoc class
 2: //
 3:
 4: #include "stdafx.h"
 5: #include "Serialize.h"
 6:
 7: #include "Person.h"
 8: #include "SerializeDoc.h"
 9: #include "SerializeView.h"
10:
11: #ifdef _DEBUG
12: #define new DEBUG_NEW
13: #undef THIS_FILE
14: static char THIS_FILE[] = __FILE__;
15: #endif
16:
17: ///////////////////////////////////////////////////////////////////////
18: // CSerializeDoc
```

Adding New Records

Before you can navigate the record set, you need to be able to add new records to the object array. If you add a private function for adding new records, you can add new records to the set dynamically as new records are needed. Because new records should be presenting the user with blank or empty data fields, you don't need to set any of the record variables when adding a new record to the object array, so you can use the default constructor.

Following the same logic that you used to add new line records on Day 10, you should add a new person record to the object array in your document class in today's sample

13

application. Once you add a new record, you can return a pointer to the new record so that the view class can directly update the variables in the record object.

Once the new record is added, you will want to set the current record position marker to the new record in the array. This way, the current record number can easily be determined by checking the position counter.

If there are any problems in creating the new person record object, let the user know that the application has run out of available memory and delete the allocated object, just as you did on Day 10.

To add this functionality to your sample application, add a new member function to the document class. Specify the type as a pointer to your custom class. If you named your custom class CPerson, the function type is CPerson*. This function needs no arguments. Give the function a name that reflects what it does, such as AddNewRecord. Specify the access for this function as private because it will only be accessed from other functions within the document class. You can edit the resulting function, adding the code in Listing 13.10.

LISTING 13.10. THE CSerializeDoc.AddNewRecord FUNCTION.

```
 1: CPerson * CSerializeDoc::AddNewRecord()
 2: {
 3:     // Create a new CPerson object
 4:     CPerson *pPerson = new CPerson();
 5:     try
 6:     {
 7:         // Add the new person to the object array
 8:         m_oaPeople.Add(pPerson);
 9:         // Mark the document as dirty
10:         SetModifiedFlag();
11:         // Set the new position mark
12:         m_iCurPosition = (m_oaPeople.GetSize() - 1);
13:     }
14:     // Did we run into a memory exception?
15:     catch (CMemoryException* perr)
16:     {
17:         // Display a message for the user, giving them the
18:         // bad news
19:         AfxMessageBox("Out of memory", MB_ICONSTOP | MB_OK);
20:         // Did we create a person object?
21:         if (pPerson)
22:         {
23:             // Delete it
24:             delete pPerson;
```

```
25:              pPerson = NULL;
26:          }
27:          // Delete the exception object
28:          perr->Delete();
29:      }
30:      return pPerson;
31: }
```

Getting the Current Position

To aid the user in navigating the record set, it's always helpful to provide a guide about where the user is in the record set. To provide this information, you need to be able to get the current record number and the total number of records from the document to display for the user.

The functions to provide this information are both fairly simple. For the total number of records in the object array, all you need to do is get the size of the array and return that to the caller.

For your sample application, add a new member function to the document class. Specify the function type as int, the function name as GetTotalRecords, and the access as public. Once you add the function, edit it using the code in Listing 13.11.

LISTING 13.11. THE `CSerializeDoc.GetTotalRecords` FUNCTION.

```
1: int CSerializeDoc::GetTotalRecords()
2: {
3:     // Return the array count
4:     return m_oaPeople.GetSize();
5: }
```

Getting the current record number is almost just as simple. If you are maintaining a position counter in the document class, this variable contains the record number that the user is currently editing. As a result, all you need to do is return the value of this variable to the calling routine. Because the object array begins with position 0, you probably need to add 1 to the current position before returning to display for the user.

To add this function to your sample application, add another new member function to the document class. Specify the type as int, the function name as GetCurRecordNbr, and the access as public. Edit the function using the code in Listing 13.12.

13

```
1: int CSerializeDoc::GetCurRecordNbr()
2: {
3:     // Return the current position
4:     return (m_iCurPosition + 1);
5: }
```

Navigating the Record Set

To make your application really useful, you will need to provide the user with some way of navigating the record set. A base set of functionality for performing this navigation is a set of functions in the document class to get pointers to specific records in the record set. First is a function to get a pointer to the current record. Next are functions to get pointers to the first and last records in the set. Finally, you need functions to get the previous record in the set and the next record in the set. If the user is already editing the last record in the set and attempts to move to the next record, you can automatically add a new record to the set and provide the user with this new, blank record.

To add all this functionality, start with the function to return the current record. This function needs to check the value in the position marker to make sure that the current record is a valid array position. Once it has made sure that the current position is valid, the function can return a pointer to the current record in the array.

To add this function to your sample application, add a new member function to the document class. Specify the function type as CPerson* (a pointer to the custom class), the function name as GetCurRecord, and the access as public. Edit the function, adding the code in Listing 13.13.

LISTING 13.13. THE CSerializeDoc.GetCurRecord FUNCTION.

```
1: CPerson* CSerializeDoc::GetCurRecord()
2: {
3:     // Are we editing a valid record number?
4:     if (m_iCurPosition >= 0)
5:         // Yes, return the current record
6:         return (CPerson*)m_oaPeople[m_iCurPosition];
7:     else
8:         // No, return NULL
9:         return NULL;
10: }
```

The next function you might want to tackle is the function to return the first record in the array. In this function, you need to first check to make sure that the array has records. If there are records in the array, set the current position marker to 0 and return a pointer to the first record in the array.

To add this function to your sample application, add a new member function to the document class. Specify the function type as CPerson* (a pointer to the custom class), the function name as GetFirstRecord, and the access as public. Edit the function, adding the code in Listing 13.14.

LISTING 13.14. THE CSerializeDoc.GetFirstRecord FUNCTION.

```
 1: CPerson* CSerializeDoc::GetFirstRecord()
 2: {
 3:     // Are there any records in the array?
 4:     if (m_oaPeople.GetSize() > 0)
 5:     {
 6:         // Yes, move to position 0
 7:         m_iCurPosition = 0;
 8:         // Return the record in position 0
 9:         return (CPerson*)m_oaPeople[0];
10:     }
11:     else
12:         // No records, return NULL
13:         return NULL;
14: }
```

For the function to navigate to the next record in the set, you need to increment the current position marker and then check to see if you are past the end of the array. If you are not past the end of the array, you need to return a pointer to the current record in the array. If you are past the end of the array, you need to add a new record to the end of the array.

To add this function to your sample application, add a new member function to the document class. Specify the function type as CPerson* (a pointer to the custom class), the function name as GetNextRecord, and the access as public. Edit the function, adding the code in Listing 13.15.

LISTING 13.15. THE CSerializeDoc.GetNextRecord FUNCTION.

```
 1: CPerson * CSerializeDoc::GetNextRecord()
 2: {
 3:     // After incrementing the position marker, are we
 4:     // past the end of the array?
 5:     if (++m_iCurPosition < m_oaPeople.GetSize())
 6:         // No, return the record at the new current position
```

continues

13

LISTING 13.15. CONTINUED

```
 7:            return (CPerson*)m_oaPeople[m_iCurPosition];
 8:        else
 9:            // Yes, add a new record
10:            return AddNewRecord();
11: }
```

For the function to navigate to the previous record in the array, you need to make several checks. First, you need to verify that the array has records. If there are records in the array, you need to decrement the current position marker. If the marker is less than zero, you need to set the current position marker to equal zero, pointing at the first record in the array. Once you've made it through all of this, you can return a pointer to the current record in the array.

To add this function to your sample application, add a new member function to the document class. Specify the function type as CPerson* (a pointer to the custom class), the function name as GetPrevRecord, and the access as public. Edit the function, adding the code in Listing 13.16.

LISTING 13.16. THE CSerializeDoc.GetPrevRecord FUNCTION.

```
 1: CPerson * CSerializeDoc::GetPrevRecord()
 2: {
 3:     // Are there any records in the array?
 4:     if (m_oaPeople.GetSize() > 0)
 5:     {
 6:         // Once we decrement the current position,
 7:         // are we below position 0?
 8:         if (--m_iCurPosition < 0)
 9:             // If so, set the record to position 0
10:             m_iCurPosition = 0;
11:         // Return the record at the new current position
12:         return (CPerson*)m_oaPeople[m_iCurPosition];
13:     }
14:     else
15:         // No records, return NULL
16:         return NULL;
17: }
```

For the function that navigates to the last record in the array, you still need to check to make sure that there are records in the array. If the array does have records, you can get the current size of the array and set the current position marker to one less than the number of records in the array. This is actually the last record in the array because the first record in the array is record 0. Once you set the current position marker, you can return a pointer to the last record in the array.

To add this function to your sample application, add a new member function to the document class. Specify the function type as `CPerson*` (a pointer to the custom class), the function name as `GetLastRecord`, and the access as public. Edit the function, adding the code in Listing 13.17.

LISTING 13.17. THE `CSerializeDoc.GetLastRecord` FUNCTION.

```
 1: CPerson * CSerializeDoc::GetLastRecord()
 2: {
 3:     // Are there any records in the array?
 4:     if (m_oaPeople.GetSize() > 0)
 5:     {
 6:         // Move to the last position in the array
 7:         m_iCurPosition = (m_oaPeople.GetSize() - 1);
 8:         // Return the record in this position
 9:         return (CPerson*)m_oaPeople[m_iCurPosition];
10:     }
11:     else
12:         // No records, return NULL
13:         return NULL;
14: }
```

Serializing the Record Set

When filling in the `Serialize` functionality in the document class, there's little to do other than pass the `CArchive` object to the object array's `Serialize` function, just as you did on Day 10.

When reading data from the archive, the object array will query the `CArchive` object to determine what object type it needs to create and how many it needs to create. The object array will then create each object in the array and call its `Serialize` function, passing the `CArchive` object to each in turn. This enables the objects in the object array to read their own variable values from the `CArchive` object in the same order that they were written.

When writing data to the file archive, the object array will call each object's `Serialize` function in order, passing the `CArchive` object (just as when reading from the archive). This allows each object in the array to write its own variables into the archive as necessary.

For the sample application, edit the document class's `Serialize` function to pass the `CArchive` object to the object array's `Serialize` function, as in Listing 13.18.

13

LISTING 13.18. THE `CSerializeDoc.Serialize` FUNCTION.

```
1: void CSerializeDoc::Serialize(CArchive& ar)
2: {
3:     // Pass the serialization on to the object array
4:     m_oaPeople.Serialize(ar);
5: }
```

Cleaning Up

Now you need to add the code to clean up the document once the document is closed or a new document is opened. This consists of looping through all objects in the object array and deleting each and every one. Once all the objects are deleted, the object array can be reset when you call its `RemoveAll` function.

To implement this functionality in your sample application, add an event-handler function to the document class on the `DeleteContents` event message using the Class Wizard. When editing the function, add the code in Listing 13.19.

LISTING 13.19. THE `CSerializeDoc.DeleteContents` FUNCTION.

```
 1: void CSerializeDoc::DeleteContents()
 2: {
 3:     // TODO: Add your specialized code here and/or call the base class
 4:
 5:     /////////////////////////
 6:     // MY CODE STARTS HERE
 7:     /////////////////////////
 8:
 9:     // Get the number of persons in the object array
10:     int liCount = m_oaPeople.GetSize();
11:     int liPos;
12:
13:     // Are there any objects in the array?
14:     if (liCount)
15:     {
16:         // Loop through the array, deleting each object
17:         for (liPos = 0; liPos < liCount; liPos++)
18:             delete m_oaPeople[liPos];
19:         // Reset the array
20:         m_oaPeople.RemoveAll();
21:     }
22:
23:     /////////////////////////
24:     // MY CODE ENDS HERE
25:     /////////////////////////
26:
27:     CDocument::DeleteContents();
28: }
```

Opening a New Document

When a new document is started, you need to present the user with an empty form, ready for new information. To make that empty record ready to accept new information, you need to add a new record into the object array, which is otherwise empty. This results in only one record in the object array. Once the new record is added to the array, you must modify the view to show that a new record exists; otherwise, the view will continue to display the last record edited from the previous record set (and the user will probably wonder why your application didn't start a new record set).

To implement this functionality, you will need to edit the OnNewDocument function in your document class. This function is already in the document class, so you do not need to add it through the Class Wizard. The first thing that you do in this function is add a new record to the object array. Once the new record is added, you need to get a pointer to the view object. You use the GetFirstViewPosition function to get the position of the view object. Using the position returned for the view object, you can use the GetNextView function to retrieve a pointer to the view object. Once you have a valid pointer, you can use it to call a function that you will create in the view class to tell the view to refresh the current record information being displayed in the form.

Note

> One thing to keep in mind when writing this code is that you need to cast the pointer to the view as a pointer of the class of your view object. The GetNextView function returns a pointer of type CView, so you will not be able to call any of your additions to the view class until you cast the pointer to your view class. Casting the pointer tells the compiler that the pointer is really a pointer to your view object class and thus does contain all the functions that you have added. If you don't cast the pointer, the compiler will assume that the view object does not contain any of the functions that you have added and will not allow you to compile your application.

Locate the OnNewDocument function in the document class source code, and add the code in Listing 13.20. Before you will be able to compile your application, you will need to add the NewDataSet function to the view class.

LISTING 13.20. THE CSerializeDoc.OnNewDocument FUNCTION.

```
1: BOOL CSerializeDoc::OnNewDocument()
2: {
3:     if (!CDocument::OnNewDocument())
4:         return FALSE;
5:
```

continues

13

LISTING **13.20.** CONTINUED

```
 6:      // TODO: add reinitialization code here
 7:      // (SDI documents will reuse this document)
 8:
 9:      /////////////////////////
10:      // MY CODE STARTS HERE
11:      /////////////////////////
12:
13:      // If unable to add a new record, return FALSE
14:      if (!AddNewRecord())
15:          return FALSE;
16:
17:      // Get a pointer to the view
18:      POSITION pos = GetFirstViewPosition();
19:      CSerializeView* pView = (CSerializeView*)GetNextView(pos);
20:      // Tell the view that it's got a new data set
21:      if (pView)
22:          pView->NewDataSet();
23:
24:      /////////////////////////
25:      // MY CODE ENDS HERE
26:      /////////////////////////
27:
28:      return TRUE;
29: }
```

When opening an existing data set, you don't need to add any new records, but you still need to let the view object know that it needs to refresh the record being displayed for the user. As a result, you can add the same code to the OnOpenDocument function as you added to the OnNewDocument, only leaving out the first part where you added a new record to the object array.

Add an event-handler function to the document class for the OnOpenDocument event using the Class Wizard. Once you add the function, edit it adding the code in Listing 13.21.

LISTING **13.21.** THE CSerializeDoc.OnOpenDocument FUNCTION.

```
1: BOOL CSerializeDoc::OnOpenDocument(LPCTSTR lpszPathName)
2: {
3:     if (!CDocument::OnOpenDocument(lpszPathName))
4:         return FALSE;
5:
6:     // TODO: Add your specialized creation code here
7:
8:     /////////////////////////
```

```
 9:        // MY CODE STARTS HERE
10:        /////////////////////////
11:
12:        // Get a pointer to the view
13:        POSITION pos = GetFirstViewPosition();
14:        CSerializeView* pView = (CSerializeView*)GetNextView(pos);
15:        // Tell the view that it's got a new data set
16:        if (pView)
17:            pView->NewDataSet();
18:
19:        /////////////////////////
20:        // MY CODE ENDS HERE
21:        /////////////////////////
22:
23:        return TRUE;
24: }
```

Adding Navigating and Editing Support in the View Class

Now that you've added support for the record set to your document class, you need to add the functionality into the view class to navigate, display, and update the records. When you first designed your view class, you placed a number of controls on the window for viewing and editing the various data elements in each record. You also included controls for navigating the record set. Now you need to attach functionality to those controls to perform the record navigation and to update the record with any data changes the user makes.

Because of the amount of direct interaction that the form will have with the record object—reading variable values from the record and writing new values to the record—it makes sense that you want to add a record pointer to the view class as a private variable. For your example, add a new member variable to the view class, specify the type as CPerson*, give it a name such as m_pCurPerson, and specify the access as private. Next, edit the view source code file and include the header file for the person class, as in Listing 13.22.

LISTING 13.22. INCLUDING THE CUSTOM OBJECT HEADER IN THE VIEW CLASS SOURCE CODE.

```
1: // SerializeView.cpp : implementation of the CSerializeView class
2: //
3:
4: #include "stdafx.h"
5: #include "Serialize.h"
6:
```

13

continues

LISTING **13.22.** CONTINUED

```
 7: #include "Person.h"
 8: #include "SerializeDoc.h"
 9: #include "SerializeView.h"
10:
11: #ifdef _DEBUG
12: .
13: .
14: .
```

Displaying the Current Record

The first functionality that you will want to add to the view class is the functionality to display the current record. Because this functionality will be used in several different places within the view class, it makes the most sense to create a separate function to perform this duty. In this function, you get the current values of all the variables in the record object and place those values in the view class variables that are attached to the controls on the window. The other thing that you want to do is get the current record number and the total number of records in the set and display those for the user so that the user knows his or her relative position within the record set.

In your sample application, add a new member function, specify the function type as void, give the function a name that makes sense, such as PopulateView, and specify the access as private. In the function, get a pointer to the document object. Once you have a valid pointer to the document, format the position text display with the current record number and the total number of records in the set, using the GetCurRecordNbr and GetTotalRecords functions that you added to the document class earlier. Next, if you have a valid pointer to a record object, set all the view variables to the values of their respective fields in the record object. Once you set the values of all of the view class variables, update the window with the variable values, as shown in Listing 13.23.

LISTING **13.23.** THE CSerializeView.PopulateView FUNCTION.

```
 1: void CSerializeView::PopulateView()
 2: {
 3:      // Get a pointer to the current document
 4:      CSerializeDoc* pDoc = GetDocument();
 5:      if (pDoc)
 6:      {
 7:          // Display the current record position in the set
 8:          m_sPosition.Format("Record %d of %d", pDoc->GetCurRecordNbr(),
 9:                  pDoc->GetTotalRecords());
10:      }
```

```
11:      // Do we have a valid record object?
12:      if (m_pCurPerson)
13:      {
14:          // Yes, get all of the record values
15:          m_bEmployed = m_pCurPerson->GetEmployed();
16:          m_iAge = m_pCurPerson->GetAge();
17:          m_sName = m_pCurPerson->GetName();
18:          m_iMaritalStatus = m_pCurPerson->GetMaritalStatus();
19:      }
20:      // Update the display
21:      UpdateData(FALSE);
22: }
```

Navigating the Record Set

If you added navigation buttons to your window when you were designing the form, then adding navigation functionality is a simple matter of adding event-handler functions for each of these navigation buttons and calling the appropriate navigation function in the document. Once the document navigates to the appropriate record in the set, you need to call the function you just created to display the current record. If the document navigation functions are returning pointers to the new current record object, you should capture that pointer before calling the function to display the current record.

To add this functionality to your sample application, add an event handler to the clicked event for the First button using the Class Wizard. In the function, get a pointer to the document object. Once you have a valid pointer to the document, call the document object's GetFirstRecord function, capturing the returned object pointer in the view CPerson pointer variable. If you receive a valid pointer, call the PopulateView function to display the record data, as in Listing 13.24.

LISTING 13.24. THE CSerializeView.OnBfirst FUNCTION.

```
1: void CSerializeView::OnBfirst()
2: {
3:      // TODO: Add your control notification handler code here
4:
5:      // Get a pointer to the current document
6:      CSerializeDoc * pDoc = GetDocument();
7:      if (pDoc)
8:      {
9:          // Get the first record from the document
10:         m_pCurPerson = pDoc->GetFirstRecord();
11:         if (m_pCurPerson)
12:         {
```

13

continues

LISTING 13.24. CONTINUED

```
13:                    // Display the current record
14:                    PopulateView();
15:            }
16:        }
17: }
```

For the Last button, perform the same steps as for the First button, but call the document object's `GetLastRecord` function, as in Listing 13.25.

LISTING 13.25. THE `CSerializeView.OnBlast` FUNCTION.

```
 1: void CSerializeView::OnBlast()
 2: {
 3:     // TODO: Add your control notification handler code here
 4:
 5:     // Get a pointer to the current document
 6:     CSerializeDoc * pDoc = GetDocument();
 7:     if (pDoc)
 8:     {
 9:         // Get the last record from the document
10:         m_pCurPerson = pDoc->GetLastRecord();
11:         if (m_pCurPerson)
12:         {
13:             // Display the current record
14:             PopulateView();
15:         }
16:     }
17: }
```

For the Previous and Next buttons, repeat the same steps again, but call the document object's `GetPrevRecord` and `GetNextRecord` functions. This final step provides your application with all the navigation functionality necessary to move through the record set. Also, because calling the document's `GetNextRecord` on the last record in the set automatically adds a new record to the set, you also have the ability to add new records to the set as needed.

Saving Edits and Changes

When the user enters changes to the data in the controls on the screen, these changes somehow need to make their way into the current record in the document. If you are maintaining a pointer in the view object to the current record object, you can call the record object's various set value functions, passing in the new value, to set the value in the record object.

To implement this in your sample application, add an event handler to the BN_CLICKED event for the Employed check box using the Class Wizard. In the function that you created, first call the UpdateData to copy the values from the form to the view variables. Check to make sure that you have a valid pointer to the current record object, and then call the appropriate Set function on the record object (in this case, the SetEmployed function as in Listing 13.26).

LISTING 13.26. THE CSerializeView.OnCbemployed FUNCTION.

```
 1: void CSerializeView::OnCbemployed()
 2: {
 3:     // TODO: Add your control notification handler code here
 4:
 5:     // Sync the data in the form with the variables
 6:     UpdateData(TRUE);
 7:     // If we have a valid person object, pass the data changes to it
 8:     if (m_pCurPerson)
 9:         m_pCurPerson->SetEmployed(m_bEmployed);
10: }
```

Repeat these same steps for the other controls, calling the appropriate record object functions. For the Name and Age edit boxes, you add an event handler on the EN_CHANGE event and call the SetName and SetAge functions. For the marital status radio buttons, add an event handler for the BN_CLICKED event and call the same event-handler function for all four radio buttons. In this function, you call the SetMaritalStat function in the record object.

Displaying a New Record Set

The last functionality that you need to add is the function to reset the view whenever a new record set is started or opened so that the user doesn't continue to see the old record set. You will call the event handler for the First button, forcing the view to display the first record in the new set of records.

To implement this functionality in your sample application, add a new member function to the view class. Specify the function type as void, give the function the name that you were calling from the document object (NewDataSet), and specify the access as public (so that it can be called from the document class). In the function, call the First button event handler, as in Listing 13.27.

13

LISTING **13.27.** THE `CSerializeView.NewDataSet` FUNCTION.

```
1: void CSerializeView::NewDataSet()
2: {
3:      // Display the first record in the set
4:      OnBfirst();
5: }
```

Wrapping Up the Project

Before you can compile and run your application, you need to include the header file for your custom class in the main application source-code file. This file is named the same as your project with the CPP extension. Your custom class header file should be included before the header files for either the document or view classes. For your sample application, you edit the `Serialize.cpp` file, adding line 8 in Listing 13.28.

LISTING **13.28.** INCLUDING THE RECORD CLASS HEADER IN THE MAIN SOURCE FILE.

```
 1: // Serialize.cpp : Defines the class behaviors for the application.
 2: //
 3:
 4: #include "stdafx.h"
 5: #include "Serialize.h"
 6:
 7: #include "MainFrm.h"
 8: #include "Person.h"
 9: #include "SerializeDoc.h"
10: #include "SerializeView.h"
11:
12: #ifdef _DEBUG
13: .
14: .
15: .
```

At this point, you can add, edit, save, and restore sets of records with your application. If you compile and run your application, you can create records of yourself and all your family members, your friends, and anyone else you want to include in this application. If you save the record set you create and then reopen the record set the next time that you run your sample application, you should find that the records are restored back to the state that you originally entered them, as in Figure 13.4.

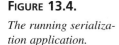

Figure 13.4.

The running serialization application.

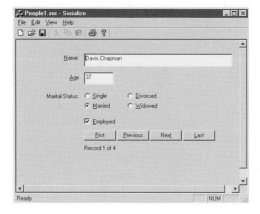

Summary

Today, you learned quite a bit. You learned how serialization works and what it does. You learned how to make a custom class serializable and why and how to use the two macros that are necessary to serialize a class. You also learned how to design and build a form-based SDI application, maintaining a set of records in a flat-file database for use in the application. You learned how to use serialization to create and maintain the flat-file database and how to construct the functionality in the document and view classes to provide navigating and editing capabilities on these record sets.

Q&A

Q **If I make any changes to one of the records in my record set after I save the record set and then I close the application, or open a different set of records, my application doesn't ask if I want to save my changes. How do I get it to ask me? How do I get my application to prompt for saving when data has been changed?**

A One function call in the `AddNewRecord` function in the document object is the key to this problem. After adding a new record to the object array, you call the `SetModifiedFlag` function. This function marks the document as "dirty." When you save the record set, the document is automatically set to a "clean" state (unless the application is unable to save the record set for any reason). What you need to do when saving the edits is set the document to the "dirty" state so that the application knows that the document has unsaved changes.

13

You can fix this by adding some code to each of your data control event handlers. Once you save the new value to the current record, get a pointer to the document object and call the document's SetModifiedFlag function, as in Listing 13.29. If you make this same addition to all the data change event handlers, your application will ask you whether to save the changes you made since the last time the record set was saved.

LISTING 13.29. THE MODIFIED CSerializeView.OnCbemployed FUNCTION.

```
 1: void CSerializeView::OnCbemployed()
 2: {
 3:     // TODO: Add your control notification handler code here
 4:
 5:     // Sync the data in the form with the variables
 6:     UpdateData(TRUE);
 7:     // If we have a valid person object, pass the data changes to it
 8:     if (m_pCurPerson)
 9:         m_pCurPerson->SetEmployed(m_bEmployed);
10:     // Get a pointer to the document
11:     CSerializeDoc * pDoc = GetDocument();
12:     if (pDoc)
13:         // Set the modified flag in the document
14:         pDoc->SetModifiedFlag();
15: }
```

Q Why do I need to change the version number in the IMPLEMENT_SERIAL macro if I change the Serialize function in the record custom class?

A Whether you need to increment the version number depends on the type of change you make. For instance, if you add a calculated field in the record class and you add the code to calculate this new variable from the values you read in the variables from the CArchive object, then you don't really need to increment the version number because the variables and order of the variables that you are writing to and reading from the archive did not change. However, if you add a new field to the record class and add the new field into the I/O stream being written to and read from the CArchive object, then what you are writing to and reading from the archive will have changed, and you do need to increment the version number. If you don't increment the version number, reading files created using the previous version of your application will result in an "Unexpected file format" message instead of the file being read. Once you increment the version number and you read a file written with the old version number, you get the same message, but you have the option of writing your own code to handle the exception and redirecting the archive to a conversion routine to convert the file to the new file format.

Workshop

The Workshop provides quiz questions to help you solidify your understanding of the material covered and exercises to provide you with experience in using what you've learned. The answers to the quiz questions and exercises are provided in Appendix B, "Answers."

Quiz

1. What two macros do you have to add to a class to make it serializable?
2. How can you determine whether the CArchive object is reading from or writing to the archive file?
3. What arguments do you need to pass to the IMPLEMENT_SERIAL macro?
4. What class do you need to inherit the view class from to be able to use the dialog designer to create a form for the main window in an SDI or MDI application?
5. What type of file does the CArchive write to by default?

Exercise

Add a couple of radio buttons to the form to specify the person's sex, as shown in Figure 13.5. Incorporate this change into the CPerson class to make the field persistent.

FIGURE 13.5.

The running serialization application with the person's sex.

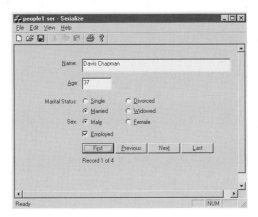

13

DAY 14

Retrieving Data from an ODBC Database

A large number of applications use a database. Everything from a personal organizer to a large, corporate personnel system uses a database to store and maintain all the records that the applications use and manipulate. Visual C++ provides you with four different technologies for using and accessing databases in your applications, Data Access Objects (DAO), ODBC, OLE DB, and ActiveX Data Objects (ADO). Today and tomorrow, you'll learn about two of these technologies, how they differ, and how you can use them in your own applications. Today, you will learn

- How the ODBC interface allows you to use a consistent way to access a database.

- How Visual C++ uses the CRecordset class to provide access to an ODBC data source.

- How you can create a simple database application using the Wizards in Visual C++.

- How you can add and delete records from an ODBC database in Visual C++.

Database Access and ODBC

Most business applications work with data. They maintain, manipulate, and access records of data that are stored in databases. If you build business applications, odds are that you will need to be able to access a database with your applications. The question is, which database?

There are a number of databases on the market. If you need to create a single-user application that is self-contained on a single computer, you can use any one of numerous PC-based databases, such as Microsoft's Access, FoxPro, or Borland's Paradox. If you are building applications that need to access large, shared databases, you are probably using an SQL-based (Structured Query Language) database such as SQL Server or Oracle. All of these databases provide the same basic functionality, maintaining records of data. Each will allow you to retrieve several records or a single record, depending on your needs. They'll all let you add, update, or delete records as needed. Any of these databases will be able to serve your application's needs, so you should be able to use any database for one application and then switch to another for the next application, based on the needs of the application and which database is most suited for the specific application needs (or your employer's whim).

Note

> To be completely honest, there are numerous differences between the various databases that are available today. Each of these databases has specific strengths and weaknesses, making one more suitable for a specific situation than another. However, a discussion of the differences between any of these databases is beyond the scope of this book. For the discussions of databases today and tomorrow, you can assume that all of these databases are functionally equal and interchangeable.

The problem that you will encounter when you switch from one database to another is that each database requires you to use a different interface for accessing the database. Therefore, you have to learn and use a whole new set of programming techniques and functions for each database that you need to work with. This is the problem that the ODBC interface was designed to correct.

The Open Database Connector (ODBC) Interface

Microsoft saw the incompatibility between database interfaces as a problem. Each database had its own application development language that was well integrated with the database but didn't work with any other database. This presented a problem to any developer who needed to use one database for an application and then a different database for the next application. The developer had to learn the specific development language for each of the databases and couldn't use any languages that she already knew. For programmers to work with any database with the programming language of the developer's choice, they needed a standardized interface that works with every database.

The Open Database Connector (ODBC) interface is implemented as a standard, SQL-based interface that is an integral part of the Windows operating system. Behind this interface are plug-ins for each database that take the ODBC function calls and convert them into calls to the specific interface for that database. The ODBC interface also uses a central set of database connection configurations, with a standardized way of specifying and maintaining them. This setup allows programmers to learn and use a single database interface for all databases. This also allowed programming language vendors to add ODBC support into their languages and development tools to make database access all but transparent.

The CRecordset Class

In the Visual C++ development environment, most of the ODBC functionality has been encapsulated into two classes, CRecordset and CDatabase. The CDatabase class contains the database connection information and can be shared across an entire application. The CRecordset class encapsulates a set of records from the database. The CRecordset class allows you to specify a SQL query to be run, and the CRecordset class will run the query and maintain the set of records that are returned by the database. You can modify and update the records in the record set, and your changes will be passed back to the database. You can add or delete records from the record set, and those same actions can be passed back to the database.

Connecting to the Database

Before the CRecordset class can perform any other functions, it has to be connected to a database. This is accomplished through the use of the CDatabase class. You don't need to create or set the CDatabase instance; the first instance of the CRecordset class does this for you. When you create an application using the AppWizard and choose to include ODBC database support, the AppWizard includes the database connection information in the first CRecordset-derived class that it creates. When this CRecordset class is created without being passed a CDatabase object, it uses the default connection information, which was added by the AppWizard, to create its own database connection.

Opening and Closing the Record Set

Once the CRecordset object is created and connected to the database, you need to open the record set to retrieve the set of records from the database. Do this by calling the Open member function of the CRecordset object. You can call this function without any

14

arguments if you want to take the default values for everything, including the SQL statement to be executed.

The first argument to the Open function is the record set type. The default value for this, AFX_DB_USE_DEFAULT_TYPE, is to open the record set as a snapshot set of records. Table 14.1 lists the four types of record set types. Only two of these record set types are available in the AppWizard when you are specifying the data source.

TABLE 14.1. RECORD SET TYPES.

Type	Description
CRecordset::dynaset	A set of records that can be refreshed by calling the Fetch function so that changes made to the record set by other users can be seen.
CRecordset::snapshot	A set of records that cannot be refreshed without closing and then reopening the record set.
CRecordset::dynamic	Very similar to the CRecordset::dynaset type, but it is not available in many ODBC drivers.
CRecordset::forwardOnly	A read-only set of records that can only be scrolled from the first to the last record.

The second argument to the Open function is the SQL statement that is to be executed to populate the record set. If a NULL is passed for this argument, the default SQL statement that was created by the AppWizard is executed.

The third argument is a set of flags that you can use to specify how the set of records is to be retrieved into the record set. Most of these flags require an in-depth understanding of the ODBC interface so you understand how the flags can and should be used in your applications. Because of this, I'll discuss only a few of these flags in Table 14.2.

TABLE 14.2. RECORD SET OPEN FLAGS.

Flag	Description
CRecordset::none	The default value for this argument; specifies that no options affect how the record set is opened and used.
CRecordset::appendOnly	This flag prevents the user from being able to edit or delete any of the existing records in the record set. The user will only be able to add new records to the set of records. You cannot use this option with the CRecordset::readOnly flag.
CRecordset::readOnly	This flag specifies that the record set is read-only and no changes can be made by the user. You cannot use this option with the CRecordset::appendOnly flag.

Once the user finishes working with the record set, you can call the Close function to close the record set and free any resources used by the record set. The Close function doesn't take any arguments.

Navigating the Record Set

Once you have a set of records retrieved from the database, you need to be able to navigate the set of records (unless the set has only one record). The CRecordset class provides several functions for navigating the record set, allowing you to move the user to any record. Table 14.3 lists the functions that you use to navigate the record set.

TABLE 14.3. RECORD SET NAVIGATION FUNCTIONS.

Function	Description
MoveFirst	Moves to the first record in the set.
MoveLast	Moves to the last record in the set.
MoveNext	Moves to the next record in the set.
MovePrev	Moves to the previous record in the set.
Move	Can be used to move a specific number of records from the current record or from the first record in the set.
SetAbsolutePosition	Moves to the specified record in the set.
IsBOF	Returns TRUE if the current record is the first record in the set.
IsEOF	Returns TRUE if the current record is the last record in the set.
GetRecordCount	Returns the number of records in the set.

Of all of these navigation and informational functions, only two, Move and SetAbsolutePosition, take any arguments. The SetAbsolutePosition function takes a single numeric argument to specify the row number of the record toward which to navigate. If you pass 0, it navigates to the beginning-of-file (BOF) position, whereas 1 takes you to the first record in the set. You can pass negative numbers to this function to cause it to count backward from the last record in the set. (For example, -1 takes you to the last record in the set, -2 to the next-to-last record, and so on.)

The Move function takes two arguments. The first argument is the number of rows to move. This can be a positive or negative number; a negative number indicates a backward navigation through the record set. The second argument specifies how you will move through the set of rows. The possible values for the second argument are listed in Table 14.4 with descriptions of how they affect the navigation.

14

TABLE 14.4. MOVE NAVIGATION TYPES.

Type	Description
SQL_FETCH_RELATIVE	Moves the specified number of rows from the current row.
SQL_FETCH_NEXT	Moves to the next row, ignoring the number of rows specified. The same as calling the MoveNext function.
SQL_FETCH_PRIOR	Moves to the previous row, ignoring the number of rows specified. The same as calling the MovePrev function.
SQL_FETCH_FIRST	Moves to the first row, ignoring the number of rows specified. The same as calling the MoveFirst function.
SQL_FETCH_LAST	Moves to the last row, ignoring the number of rows specified. The same as calling the MoveLast function.
SQL_FETCH_ABSOLUTE	Moves the specified number of rows from the start of the set of rows. The same as calling the SetAbsolutePosition function.

Adding, Deleting, and Updating Records

Navigating a set of records from a database is only part of what you need to be able to do. You also need to be able to add new records to the record set, edit and update existing records, and delete records. These actions are all possible through the various functions that the CRecordset class provides. The functions that you will use to provide this functionality to the user are listed in Table 14.5.

TABLE 14.5. RECORD SET EDITING FUNCTIONS.

Function	Description
AddNew	Adds a new record to the record set.
Delete	Deletes the current record from the record set.
Edit	Allows the current record to be edited.
Update	Saves the current changes to the database.
Requery	Reruns the current SQL query to refresh the record set.

None of these functions takes any arguments. However, some of them require following a few specific steps to get them to work correctly.

To add a new record to the database, you can call the AddNew function. The next thing that you need to do is set default values in any of the fields that require values, such as the key fields. Next, you must call the Update function to add the new record to the database. If you try to navigate to another record before calling the Update function, the new record will be lost. Once you save the new record, you need to call the `Requery` function to refresh the record set so that you can navigate to the new record and let the user edit it. This sequence of function calls typically looks like the following:

```
// Add a new record to the record set
m_pSet.AddNew();
// Set the key field on the new record
m_pSet.m_AddressID = m_lNewID;
// Save the new record to the database
m_pSet.Update();
// Refresh the record set
m_pSet.Requery();
// Move to the new record
m_pSet.MoveLast();
```

When you need to delete the current record, you can simply call the `Delete` function. Once you delete the current record, you need to navigate to another record so the user isn't still looking at the record that was just deleted. Once you delete the current record, there is no current record until you navigate to another one. You do not need to explicitly call the `Update` function because the navigation functions call it for you. This allows you to write the following code to delete the current record:

```
// Delete the current record
m_pSet.Delete();
// Move to the previous record
m_pSet.MovePrev();
```

Finally, to allow the user to edit the current record, you need to call the `Edit` function. This allows you to update the fields in the record with the new values entered by the user or calculated by your application. Once all changes are made to the current record, you need to call the `Update` function to save the changes:

```
// Allow the user to edit the current record
m_pSet.Edit();
// Perform all data exchange, updating the fields in the recordset
  .
  .
  .
// Save the user's changes to the current record
m_pSet.Update();
```

You might be wondering how you get to the fields in the records to update them. When the AppWizard creates the `CRecordset`-derived class for your application, it adds all the fields in the records that will be in the record set as member variables in order of the record set class. As a result, you can access the member variables in order to access and manipulate the data elements in the database records that are members of the record set.

14

Creating a Database Application Using ODBC

For the sample application that you will build today, you'll create an SDI application with ODBC database support. The application will retrieve records from an ODBC database, allowing the user to edit and update any of the records. You'll also add functionality to enable the user to add new records to the database and to delete records from the database.

Preparing the Database

Before you can begin building an application that uses a database, you need a database to use with your application. Almost every database that you can purchase for your applications comes with tools for creating a new database. You'll need to use these tools to create your database and then use the ODBC administrator to configure an ODBC data source for your new database.

For the sample application in this chapter, I used Access 95 to create a new database. I used the Access Database Wizard to create the database, choosing the Address Book database template as the database to be created. When the Database Wizard started, I selected the default set of fields for including in the database and selected the option to include sample data, as shown in Figure 14.1. I then accepted the rest of the default settings offered in the Database Wizard.

FIGURE 14.1.

*Including sample data
in the database.*

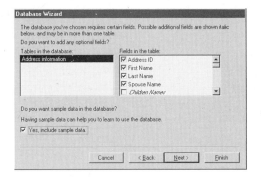

Once you create the database, you need to configure an ODBC data source to point to the database you just created. To do this, run the ODBC Administrator, which is in the Control Panel on your computer.

Once in the ODBC Administrator, you'll add a new data source. You can do this by clicking the Add button, as shown in Figure 14.2. This opens another dialog, which allows you to select the database driver for the new data source, as shown in Figure 14.3.

For the sample application that you will build today, because the database was created using Access, select the Microsoft Access Driver and click the Finish button.

FIGURE 14.2.

The ODBC Data Source Administrator.

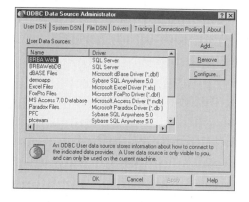

FIGURE 14.3.

The Create New Data Source dialog.

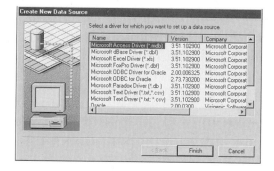

In the ODBC Microsoft Access Setup dialog, shown in Figure 14.4, you'll provide a short, simple name for the data source. Your application will use this name to specify the ODBC data source configuration to use for the database connection, so it should reflect the function that the database will be serving, or it should be similar to the name of the application that will be using this database. For the purposes of the sample application database, name your data source **TYVCDB** (for Teach Yourself Visual C++ Database) and enter a description for the database in the next field.

Once you enter a name and description for the data source, you need to specify where the database is. Click the Select button and then specify the Access database that you created. Once you finish configuring the ODBC data source for your database, click the OK button to add the new data source to the ODBC Administrator. You can click the OK button to finish the task and close the ODBC Administrator because you are now ready to turn your attention to building your application.

14

FIGURE 14.4.

The ODBC Microsoft Access 97 Setup dialog.

Creating the Application Shell

For the sample application that you will build today, you'll create a standard SDI-style application with database support. First, start a new project, selecting the AppWizard, and give your application a suitable name, such as DbOdbc.

On the first AppWizard form, specify that you want to build an SDI application. On the second AppWizard form, specify that you want to include Database view with file support. Click the Data Source button to specify which data source you will use in your application. In the Database Options dialog, specify that you are using an ODBC data source, and select the ODBC configuration from the list that you configured for your Access database, as shown in Figure 14.5. You can set the record set type to either Snapshot or Dynaset.

FIGURE 14.5.

The Database Options dialog.

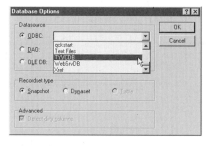

Once you click the OK button, another dialog opens, presenting you with the available tables in the database you selected. Select the Addresses table, as shown in Figure 14.6, and click the OK button to close this dialog and return to the AppWizard.

You can continue through the rest of the AppWizard, accepting all of the default settings. When you reach the final AppWizard step, you'll notice that the AppWizard is going to create an extra class. If you select this class, you'll see that it is derived from the CRecordset class, and it is the record set class for your application. You'll also notice that the view class is derived from the CRecordView class, which is a descendent of the CFormView class, with some added support for database functionality.

FIGURE **14.6.**

*The Select Database
Tables dialog.*

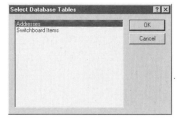

Designing the Main Form

Once you create the application shell, you need to design the main form that will be used for viewing and editing the database records. You can design this form using the standard controls that are part of Visual C++, without adding any special ActiveX controls. For designing the main form in your sample application, lay out the main form as shown in Figure 14.7, and configure the controls with the properties specified in Table 14.6.

Tip

If you want to save a little time when building the example, you can leave out most of the controls and database fields from the application. The key fields that you'll need to include are ID, First and Last Names, Birthdate, and Send Card. If you want to leave out the other fields from the application, that's fine.

TABLE 14.6. CONTROL PROPERTY SETTINGS.

Object	Property	Setting
Static Text	ID	IDC_STATIC
	Caption	ID:
Edit Box	ID	IDC_EID
Static Text	ID	IDC_STATIC
	Caption	First Name:
Edit Box	ID	IDC_EFNAME
Static Text	ID	IDC_STATIC
	Caption	Last Name:
Edit Box	ID	IDC_ELNAME

continues

14

TABLE 14.6. CONTINUED

Object	Property	Setting
Static Text	ID	IDC_STATIC
	Caption	Spouse Name:
Edit Box	ID	IDC_ESNAME
Static Text	ID	IDC_STATIC
	Caption	Address:
Edit Box	ID	IDC_EADDR
	Multiline	Checked
Static Text	ID	IDC_STATIC
	Caption	City:
Edit Box	ID	IDC_ECITY
Static Text	ID	IDC_STATIC
	Caption	State:
Edit Box	ID	IDC_ESTATE
Static Text	ID	IDC_STATIC
	Caption	Zip:
Edit Box	ID	IDC_EZIP
Static Text	ID	IDC_STATIC
	Caption	Country:
Edit Box	ID	IDC_ECOUNTRY
Static Text	ID	IDC_STATIC
	Caption	E-Mail:
Edit Box	ID	IDC_EEMAIL
Static Text	ID	IDC_STATIC
	Caption	Home Phone:
Edit Box	ID	IDC_EHPHONE
Static Text	ID	IDC_STATIC
	Caption	Work Phone:
Edit Box	ID	IDC_EWPHONE
Static Text	ID	IDC_STATIC
	Caption	Extension:
Edit Box	ID	IDC_EWEXT
Static Text	ID	IDC_STATIC
	Caption	Fax:

Object	Property	Setting
Edit Box	ID	IDC_EFAX
Static Text	ID	IDC_STATIC
	Caption	Birthdate:
Edit Box	ID	IDC_EDOB
Check Box	ID	IDC_CBCARD
	Caption	Send Card
Static Text	ID	IDC_STATIC
	Caption	Notes:
Edit Box	ID	IDC_ENOTES
	Multiline	Checked

FIGURE 14.7.

The main form design.

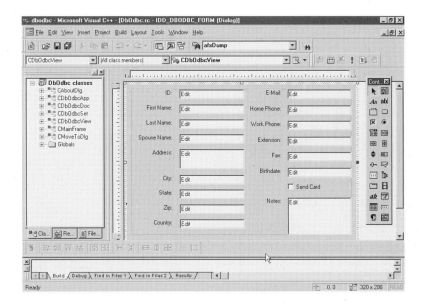

Once you have added and configured all the controls on the main form for your application, you're ready to begin associating the controls with database fields. When you click the Member Variables tab of the Class Wizard and select a control to add a variable for, you'll notice that the Add Member Variable dialog has a drop-down combo box where you enter the variable name. If you click the arrow to drop down the list, you'll find that it's filled with the fields in the record set, as shown in Figure 14.8. This enables you to attach the database fields directly to the controls on the form. To attach the database fields to the controls on your application form, add the variables specified in Table 14.7.

14

FIGURE 14.8.

The Add Member
Variable dialog with
record set fields.

TABLE 14.7. CONTROL VARIABLES.

Object	Name
IDC_CBCARD	m_pSet->m_SendCard
IDC_EADDR	m_pSet->m_Address
IDC_ECITY	m_pSet->m_City
IDC_ECOUNTRY	m_pSet->m_Country
IDC_EEMAIL	m_pSet->m_EmailAddress
IDC_EFAX	m_pSet->m_FaxNumber
IDC_EFNAME	m_pSet->m_FirstName
IDC_EHPHONE	m_pSet->m_HomePhone
IDC_EID	m_pSet->m_AddressID
IDC_ELNAME	m_pSet->m_LastName
IDC_ENOTES	m_pSet->m_Notes
IDC_ESNAME	m_pSet->m_SpouseName
IDC_ESTATE	m_pSet->m_StateOrProvince
IDC_EWEXT	m_pSet->m_WorkExtension
IDC_EWPHONE	m_pSet->m_WorkPhone
IDC_EZIP	m_pSet->m_PostalCode

You probably noticed when it was time to attach a database field to the birthdate control
that the birthday field is missing from the list of database fields. If you look at the record
set class in the class view and expand its tree, you'll notice that the birthdate field is
included as one of the database fields, but it's not available in the list of available
columns for use with the controls. Double-click on the birthdate field in the record set
class to view its definition. You'll notice that the m_Birthdate variable is declared as a
CTime variable. This is the reason that it's not available in the list of database fields that
can be attached to controls. There isn't a macro or function you can call for exchanging

data between a control and a CTime variable. This is also a problem because the CTime variable type cannot handle dates before December 31, 1969. To use this database field, you'll need to change its definition from a CTime to a COleDateTime variable type, as in line 17 in Listing 14.1. Once you change the variable type of this database field, you will be able to attach it to the IDC_EDOB control.

LISTING **14.1.** THE DATABASE FIELD VARIABLE DECLARATIONS.

```
 1:   // Field/Param Data
 2:       //{{AFX_FIELD(CTestdb5Set, CRecordset)
 3:       long    m_AddressID;
 4:       CString    m_FirstName;
 5:       CString    m_LastName;
 6:       CString    m_SpouseName;
 7:       CString    m_Address;
 8:       CString    m_City;
 9:       CString    m_StateOrProvince;
10:       CString    m_PostalCode;
11:       CString    m_Country;
12:       CString    m_EmailAddress;
13:       CString    m_HomePhone;
14:       CString    m_WorkPhone;
15:       CString    m_WorkExtension;
16:       CString    m_FaxNumber;
17:       COleDateTime    m_Birthdate;
18:       BOOL    m_SendCard;
19:       CString    m_Notes;
20:       //}}AFX_FIELD
```

> **Note**
>
> Normally, you do not want to edit the portions of code in your applications that are created and maintained by the various wizards. The change I outline here is one of the few exceptions to this rule. This obstacle could possibly be considered a bug in the Visual C++ AppWizard, although it's technically not a bug. You can convert the date/time database field to several variable types when creating a class variable to represent that field. CTime is one of these variable types; COleDateTime is another. Because these are both equally valid choices, and the functions that populate this variable can work with either, making this change is possible without dire consequences.

Once you make the change to the variable type for the m_Birthdate variable in the record set class (CDbOdbcSet), and attach this database field to the Birthdate control on the form, you might think that you are ready to compile and run your application. Unfortunately, your application will not compile. You'll get a compiler error stating that

14

the DDX_FieldText cannot convert the COleDateTime variable type. What you need to do is add the code to perform this conversion yourself. Return to the Class Wizard and delete the variable that you added to the IDC_EDOB control. Add a new variable to this control. Specify that the variable is type COleDateTime, and give the variable a name such as m_oledtDOB. Pull up the DoDataExchange function in the view class, CDbOdbcView, into the editor, and add lines 4 through 6 and lines 26 through 28 to the function, as shown in Listing 14.2.

LISTING 14.2. THE CDbOdbcView DoDataExchange FUNCTION.

```
1:   void CDbOdbcView::DoDataExchange(CDataExchange* pDX)
2:   {
3:       CRecordView::DoDataExchange(pDX);
4:       // Copy the DOB from the record set to the view variable
5:       if (pDX->m_bSaveAndValidate == FALSE)
6:           m_oledtDOB = m_pSet->m_Birthdate;
7:       //{{AFX_DATA_MAP(CDbOdbcView)
8:       DDX_FieldText(pDX, IDC_EID, m_pSet->m_AddressID, m_pSet);
9:       DDX_FieldText(pDX, IDC_EFNAME, m_pSet->m_FirstName, m_pSet);
10:      DDX_FieldText(pDX, IDC_ELNAME, m_pSet->m_LastName, m_pSet);
11:      DDX_FieldText(pDX, IDC_ESNAME, m_pSet->m_SpouseName, m_pSet);
12:      DDX_FieldText(pDX, IDC_ESTATE, m_pSet->m_StateOrProvince, m_pSet);
13:      DDX_FieldText(pDX, IDC_ECITY, m_pSet->m_City, m_pSet);
14:      DDX_FieldText(pDX, IDC_EADDR, m_pSet->m_Address, m_pSet);
15:      DDX_FieldCheck(pDX, IDC_CBCARD, m_pSet->m_SendCard, m_pSet);
16:      DDX_FieldText(pDX, IDC_ECOUNTRY, m_pSet->m_Country, m_pSet);
17:      DDX_FieldText(pDX, IDC_EEMAIL, m_pSet->m_EmailAddress, m_pSet);
18:      DDX_FieldText(pDX, IDC_EFAX, m_pSet->m_FaxNumber, m_pSet);
19:      DDX_FieldText(pDX, IDC_EHPHONE, m_pSet->m_HomePhone, m_pSet);
20:      DDX_FieldText(pDX, IDC_ENOTES, m_pSet->m_Notes, m_pSet);
21:      DDX_FieldText(pDX, IDC_EWEXT, m_pSet->m_WorkExtension, m_pSet);
22:      DDX_FieldText(pDX, IDC_EWPHONE, m_pSet->m_WorkPhone, m_pSet);
23:      DDX_FieldText(pDX, IDC_EZIP, m_pSet->m_PostalCode, m_pSet);
24:      DDX_Text(pDX, IDC_EDOB, m_oledtDOB);
25:      //}}AFX_DATA_MAP
26:      // Copy the DOB variable back from the view variable to the record
         ➥set
27:      if (pDX->m_bSaveAndValidate == TRUE)
28:          m_pSet->m_Birthdate = m_oledtDOB;
29:  }
```

In addition to the above change, you have to remove the initialization of the m_Birthdate variable in the set class. This is also code that was added by the AppWizard, and once again you have to break the rules by modifying the code that you are never supposed to touch. To make this change, you can take the simple approach by commenting out the initialization of this variable in the set class constructor, in line 19 of Listing 14.3.

LISTING 14.3. THE `CDbOdbcSet` CONSTRUCTOR.

```
 1: CDbOdbcSet::CDbOdbcSet(CDatabase* pdb)
 2:     : CRecordset(pdb)
 3: {
 4:     //{{AFX_FIELD_INIT(CTestdb5Set)
 5:     m_AddressID = 0;
 6:     m_FirstName = _T("");
 7:     m_LastName = _T("");
 8:     m_SpouseName = _T("");
 9:     m_Address = _T("");
10:     m_City = _T("");
11:     m_StateOrProvince = _T("");
12:     m_PostalCode = _T("");
13:     m_Country = _T("");
14:     m_EmailAddress = _T("");
15:     m_HomePhone = _T("");
16:     m_WorkPhone = _T("");
17:     m_WorkExtension = _T("");
18:     m_FaxNumber = _T("");
19:     //m_Birthdate = 0;
20:     m_SendCard = FALSE;
21:     m_Notes = _T("");
22:     m_nFields = 17;
23:     //}}AFX_FIELD_INIT
24:     m_nDefaultType = dynaset;
25: }
```

Now compile and run your application once again. You'll find that you have a fully functioning database application that retrieves a set of records from the database and allows you to scroll through them and make changes to the data, as shown in Figure 14.9.

Adding New Records

You've already created a fully functioning database application without writing a single line of code. However, a few functions are missing. Most database applications let the user add new records to the database. To add a new record to the database, you'll want to figure out what the next ID number should be, so you'll scroll to the last record in the set to get the ID and then increment it by one. Next, you'll call the AddNew function to add a new record, set the ID field to the new ID you calculated, and then call the Update function to save the new record. Finally, you'll call the Requery function to refresh the set of records and then scroll to the last record in the set to let the user enter data into the new record.

14

FIGURE **14.9.**

*The running appli-
cation.*

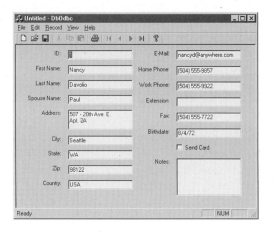

> **Tip**
>
> Because the ID field in the database in defined as an AutoIncrement field, you do not normally specify your own ID for the field. However, because the record set is creating a new record with the ID field, you need to assign a valid ID to the record or you won't be able to add it to the database. The method used in this application will not work with any multiuser database because each person would generate the same IDs for new records. In this situation, a centralized method for generating new IDs, such as a counter field in the database, is a better solution. The other option is to create a SQL statement to insert a new record into the database that was missing the ID field. This allows the auto-increment functionality to work correctly.

To add this functionality to your application, start by adding a function to your record set class to determine the next ID number to be used. Add a member function to the record set class, CDbOdbcSet. Specify the function type as long, the function declaration as GetMaxID, and the access as public. Edit the function, adding the code in Listing 14.4.

LISTING 14.4. THE CDbOdbcSet GetMaxID FUNCTION.

```
1: long CDbOdbcSet::GetMaxID()
2: {
3:     // Move to the last record
4:     MoveLast();
5:     // return the ID of this record
6:     return m_AddressID;
7: }
```

Next, you'll need a menu entry that the user can select to add a new record to the database. Add a new menu entry to the Record menu. Configure the new menu entry with the properties in Table 14.8.

TABLE 14.8. MENU PROPERTY SETTINGS.

Object	Property	Setting
Menu Entry	ID	IDM_RECORD_NEW
	Caption	N&ew Record
	Prompt	Add a new record\nNew Record

Using the Class Wizard, add an event-handler function for the COMMAND event message for this menu to the view class, CDbOdbcView. Edit this function, adding the code in Listing 14.5.

LISTING 14.5. THE CDbOdbcView OnRecordNew FUNCTION.

```
 1:  void CDbOdbcView::OnRecordNew()
 2:  {
 3:      // TODO: Add your command handler code here
 4:      // Get a pointer to the record set
 5:      CRecordset* pSet = OnGetRecordset();
 6:      // Make sure that any changes to the current record
 7:      // have been saved
 8:      if (pSet->CanUpdate() && !pSet->IsDeleted())
 9:      {
10:          pSet->Edit();
11:          if (!UpdateData())
12:              return;
13:
14:          pSet->Update();
15:      }
16:      // Get the ID for the new record
17:      long m_lNewID = m_pSet->GetMaxID() + 1;
18:      // Add the new record
19:      m_pSet->AddNew();
20:      // Set the ID in the new record
21:      m_pSet->m_AddressID = m_lNewID;
22:      // Save the new record
23:      m_pSet->Update();
24:      // Refresh the record set
25:      m_pSet->Requery();
26:      // Move to the new record
27:      m_pSet->MoveLast();
28:      // Update the form
29:      UpdateData(FALSE);
30:  }
```

14

Add a new toolbar button for the New Record menu, and then compile and run your application. You should be able to add new records to the database, entering the data you want into the records.

Deleting Records

The only functionality remaining is the ability to delete the current record from the database. You'll need to add another menu entry to trigger this action. Once the action is triggered, you'll verify that the user really does want to delete the current record and then call the Delete function to remove the record. Once the record has been deleted, you'll call the MovePrev function to navigate to the previous record in the set.

To add this functionality to your application, you'll need a menu entry that the user can select to delete the current record from the database. Add a new menu entry to the Record menu. Configure the new menu entry with the properties in Table 14.9.

TABLE 14.9. MENU PROPERTY SETTINGS.

Object	Property	Setting
Menu Entry	ID	IDM_RECORD_DELETE
	Caption	&Delete Record
	Prompt	Delete the current record\nDelete Record

Using the Class Wizard, add an event-handler function for the COMMAND event message for this menu to the view class, CDbOdbcView. Edit this function, adding the code in Listing 14.6.

LISTING 14.6. THE CDbOdbcView OnRecordDelete FUNCTION.

```
 1: void CDbOdbcView::OnRecordDelete()
 2: {
 3:     // TODO: Add your command handler code here
 4:     // Make sure the user wants to delete this record
 5:     if (MessageBox("Are you sure you want to delete this record?",
 6:             "Delete this record?", MB_YESNO | MB_ICONQUESTION) ==
                ➥IDYES)
 7:     {
 8:         // Delete the record
 9:         m_pSet->Delete();
10:         // Move to the previous record
11:         m_pSet->MovePrev();
12:         // Update the form
13:         UpdateData(FALSE);
14:     }
15: }
```

Add another button to the toolbar and associate it with the IDM_RECORD_DELETE menu ID so that the user can delete the current record without having to go to the menu. If you compile and run your application at this point, you'll have a full-function database application in which you can add, edit, and delete records, as shown in Figure 14.10.

FIGURE 14.10.

The completed appli-cation.

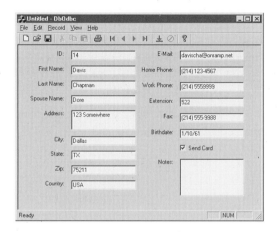

Summary

Today, you learned how you can use the ODBC interface to build database applications that can be easily run against any database you might need to use. You saw how the CRecordset class provides you with a substantial amount of functionality so that you can provide database functionality in your applications. You also saw how the AppWizard provides you with a large amount of database functionality without your typing a single line of code.

Tomorrow, you will learn about Microsoft's newest database access technology, ActiveX Data Objects, and how this can be combined with the ODBC interface to make your database access even easier.

Q&A

Q Why would I want to use the ODBC interface instead of the Data Access Objects?

A The Data Access Objects (DAO) use the Microsoft Jet database engine to perform all of the database access. This adds at least a megabyte of overhead to your application, and if you're using a SQL-based database, the database is already doing all of the work that the Jet engine is doing for you. What's more, the Jet database

14

engine uses the ODBC interface to access any SQL-based databases. As a result, unless you are using PC-based databases, such as Access, FoxPro, or Paradox, you get better performance from going directly to the ODBC interface yourself.

Q How can I add different record sets in an MDI application?

A You can add additional CRecordset-derived classes through the New Class Wizard in an MDI application project. You need to specify that the new class is an MFC class and that its base class is the CRecordset class. The New Class Wizard will have you specify the data source, just as the AppWizard had you do when creating the shell for today's application. Once you create the record set class, you can create a new view class the same way, specifying the base class as CRecordView. Once you click the OK button, the New Class Wizard asks you to specify which of the record set classes to use with the new record view class.

Workshop

The Workshop provides quiz questions to help you solidify your understanding of the material covered and exercises to provide you with experience in using what you've learned. The answers to the quiz questions and exercises are provided in Appendix B, "Answers."

Quiz

1. What does ODBC stand for?
2. What functions can you use to navigate the record set in a CRecordset object?
3. What view class should you use with an ODBC application?
4. What sequence of functions do you need to call to add a new record to a record set?
5. What function do you need to call before the fields in the CRecordset object can be updated with any changes?

Exercise

Add a menu entry and dialog to let the user indicate the record number to move to, and then move to that record.

WEEK 2

8

9

10

11

12

13

14

In Review

Now that you've finished the second week, you should be getting very comfortable working with Visual C++. You should be beginning to understand how you can use the MFC class hierarchy to provide a substantial amount of existing functionality in your applications. You should also be starting to understand how much supporting infrastructure your applications start with when you use the Visual C++ wizards to construct as much of your application as you can.

This is a good time to take a little break and try some of the things that you've learned on your own. Build an MDI application, using a custom document type that you've come up with yourself. See how you can save and restore the document, as well as maintain it. Practicing on your own is key to cementing your understanding of what you've learned in this book. This will help you identify any areas that you might need to go back and read again, as well as those areas where you feel comfortable enough to not review.

By this time, you should have a good understanding of the Document/View architecture and how it can be used to maintain the separation of the data from the representation of the data that is displayed for the user. You've used this model for both Single Document Interface (SDI) and Multiple Document Interface (MDI) style applications, and you've used it for reading and writing files to the disk drive. This model is one of the main building blocks of MFC applications built with Visual C++. You should know where to place any initialization information for a new set of data and where to clean up when closing a set of data.

You should also have a good understanding of how the SDI and MDI application styles are alike and how they differ from each other and from the dialog application style. You should have a good idea of when an application you are building should use one of these styles and when it should use a different style. You should be able to create your own SDI and MDI applications, as you need to, without any significant problems. If you've got any questions about either of these areas, you might want to take another look at Days 10 and 11 to review how the Document/View architecture works in both SDI and MDI style applications.

You should understand how, in SDI and MDI style applications, you can save and restore complex data structures in files on the system hard drive. You should be able to create mixed-type objects that you create and maintain in the document object in your applications, be able to use the Serialize function with the CArchive object to write the objects to a file, and then be able to restore the objects at a later time. If you are having any trouble understanding how this works or are running into any problems trying to implement this functionality in your own applications, review Day 13.

Along with reading and writing files, you also have learned how you can design and build toolbars for use in your SDI and MDI applications. At this point, you should be completely comfortable with designing and creating your own toolbars and using them in your applications. You should understand the importance of matching the toolbar button ID to the ID of the menu for which the toolbar will be used as a substitute. You should also have a basic understanding of creating and using your own customized status bar elements in SDI and MDI applications. You should understand how you can use the UPDATE_COMMAND_UI event message to evaluate and alter the status of menu, toolbar, and status bar elements, relieving you of all the work of setting each of these elements, and how to maintain their appearance and status yourself. If you aren't clear on how you can do any of these things, you might want to go back over Day 12 one more time.

You've seen how you can build a simple database application, pulling data from a database through the ODBC interface. You should have a basic understanding of how you can build database applications using this approach, how to maintain the data, how to add new records, and how to delete records. You should know how all the database interaction is directed through the record set class and how you can directly control the data through this object. If you're not sure of some of this, you might want to look back at Day 14 for a quick refresher.

You learned how easy it is to add ActiveX controls to your projects and how Visual C++ builds C++ classes around the control, enabling you to interact with the control as if it were just another C++ object. You should have a good grasp of how to add any ActiveX control (armed with the documentation for the control) to your application and interact with it in a seamless manner. You should be able to declare a variable for the control, set the control's properties, call its methods, and react to its events just as if it were a standard part of the Visual C++ development environment. If you aren't sure how you can do some of this, you might want to go back and reread Day 9.

Finally, you started this week by learning how to draw graphics on the windows of your applications. You learned how to draw lines, circles, and squares, using a variety of pens and brushes. You even learned how you can make a customized brush from a bitmap. You learned how you can load a bitmap image from a file and display it for the user to see. But most importantly, you learned about the device context and how it is used to draw all these features on the windows of your applications. You should be able to use these and other figure drawing device context methods to draw any image you might want to draw on the window for the user to see and interact with. If you are unsure about how you can do this, you probably want to look back at Day 8 once more.

By this time, you have built up quite a set of programming skills with Visual C++. You are probably ready to tackle most of the smaller programming tasks you might encounter—and maybe even a few not-so-small tasks. At this point, you are well on your way to becoming an accomplished Visual C++ programmer. That said—now is not the time to stop because there's still more to be learned. There's only one more week to go, so tallyho!

WEEK 3

At a Glance

For the third and final week, you'll be learning about several of the more advanced aspects of building applications with Visual C++. Some of these topics you'll use more than others, but if you do much work with Visual C++, odds are that you'll work with most, if not all, of these areas before long.

You'll begin the week by picking up where you left off the previous week with building database applications. On Day 15, you'll learn about Microsoft's latest database access technology, ActiveX Data Objects (ADO), and how you can incorporate it into your Visual C++ applications to provide database access to your application's users. You'll learn how using ADO is similar to and different from building database applications using ODBC.

On Day 16, you'll learn how to create your own custom classes and how to approach the design of these classes. You'll also learn how to build your functionality into library modules that you can give to other Visual C++ programmers for use in their applications.

On Day 17, you'll learn a different means of allowing other programmers to use your code by building DLLs. You'll learn how to build two different types of DLLs: those that can be used only by other Visual C++ applications and those that can be used by applications built with any other Windows development language or tool.

On Day 18, you'll learn how you can enable your applications to work on two or more separate tasks at the same time. You'll learn how to trigger some background processing whenever your application is sitting idle and how to spin off independent threads that continue to work even when your application is busy.

On Day 19, you'll learn how to build your own ActiveX controls that can be used in other applications or even in Web pages. You'll see how you can define the properties and methods for your control and how you can trigger events in the containing application from your control.

On Day 20, you'll learn how Internet applications communicate with each other using the Winsock interface. You'll learn how you can use this same interface to enable your applications to communicate over a network or even on the same machine.

Finally, on Day 21, you'll see how easy it is to incorporate the Microsoft Internet Explorer Web browser into your own Visual C++ application. You'll learn how you can control the Web browser, specifying what Web pages for it to display, and how you can provide the user with information about what the browser is doing.

When you finish this final week, you'll be knowledgeable about most areas of Visual C++ programming. Although there will still be areas and technologies that require more in-depth study for you to master, you'll know and understand what those areas are all about. You'll be prepared to dive head first into all areas of Visual C++ programming, and by then you might already have identified some areas that you want to learn more about than can be covered in this book.

You have only one week left to go, so go ahead and dive in and get going.

DAY 15

Updating and Adding Database Records Through ADO

Now that you've gotten your feet wet with an ODBC database application, one of the oldest Microsoft database access technologies, it's time to turn your attention to the newest Microsoft database access technology, ActiveX Data Objects (ADO). Designed for use with all of Microsoft's programming and scripting technologies, ADO presents the Visual C++ programmer with new challenges in database programming, while still keeping the functionality familiar. Today, you will learn

- How ADO works and how it uses the OLE DB technology for providing simple database access.
- How you can build a simple ADO application in a couple of minutes using ActiveX controls.

- How you can build a complete database application using regular forms controls.
- How you can use special ADO macros to build a custom record set class for use in your database applications.

Caution	This chapter works with some features that may not be included in all versions of Visual C++. Although ADO is an important new area of programming with Microsoft data access technologies, this chapter discusses some things that you may not have the ability to do with your version of Visual C++.

What Is ADO?

A couple years ago, Microsoft designed a new data access technology called OLE DB. This data access technology was intended to be much more than simply a way of getting data into and out of databases. This technology was intended to be the means of accessing data, regardless of where that data may be located. Through the OLE DB technology, you could access mail messages, spreadsheets, files, and so on. Anything that might have data could possibly be accessed through the OLE DB technology. This was one of the first technologies to be produced from the research and development of the object-oriented file system at the heart of what Microsoft has been calling "Cairo" for the past few years.

Note	Many of the technologies bundled under the product name of Cairo will be released some time next year in the Windows NT 5.0 operating system.

As you can imagine, with the range of functionality that OLE DB must have to access data in all of those different sources, it might be quite complex to work with this technology. Well, it is. This is where ActiveX Data Objects come into play. ADO was designed as another layer on top of OLE DB, specifically for providing database access.

One of the goals in designing ADO was to create a control that could be used to provide data access and control in Web pages, caching the data records on the client. Part of the reason for this goal was to allow a Web browser user to access an entire set of data records, without having to pull down each individual record, one at a time, to navigate and make changes to the records. Because of this capability with ADO, the ADO control is distributed with Microsoft's Internet Explorer Web browser (version 4.0 and above).

ADO Objects

To make ADO as easily usable in scripting languages such as VBScript as it is in programming environments such as Visual Basic, Microsoft tried to keep the number of objects to a minimum. As a result, you have a small number of basic objects:

- Connection
- Error
- Command
- Parameter
- Recordset
- Field

Along with these objects, you have collection objects for containing collections of Error, Parameter, and Field objects.

The Connection Object

The Connection object is used for establishing and maintaining a connection to a database. This object is configured with the connection information, including database location, user ID, and password, before opening the connection. Once all of this information is appropriately configured, the connection object should have its Open method called to open the connection. Once the Connection object goes out of scope, the connection is automatically closed. If you want more control over closing and opening the database connection, you can call the Connection object's Close method to close the connection.

The Connection object is also the object through which any high-level connection functionality is controlled. This includes all transaction control, through the Connection object's BeginTrans, CommitTrans, and RollbackTrans methods.

The Error Object

Whenever a database error occurs, the error information from the database is placed into an ADO Error object. The error information in the error object is the database error information, not ADO error information. Whenever you encounter an error and need to look up the error information to determine what went wrong, you'll need to examine the database error codes and descriptions, not the ADO error codes.

The Command Object

The Command object is used to execute commands in the database. You can use this object to run SQL statements or call stored procedures (SQL functions that are stored in the database). Any time that a command returns rows of data, you need to attach the Command object to a Recordset object for the returned data to be stored in.

When you call a stored procedure, as with functions in any other programming language, you'll often need to pass parameters to the stored procedure. To pass these parameters, you'll attach a series of Parameter objects to the Command object. Each of the Parameter objects will have the name of the parameter that it holds the value for, along with the value that should be passed to the database for that particular parameter.

The Parameter Object

The Parameter object is used for passing variables and for calling stored procedures or parameterized queries. These are attached to a Command object for use in calling the command that has been programmed into the Command object.

The Recordset Object

The Recordset object contains a set of records from the database. The set of records is the result of a command being sent to the database that results in a set of records being returned. You can navigate through the Recordset, much like you do with the Recordset objects for other database access technologies. You can also access the fields in each record in the Recordset through the Field objects that are associated with the Recordset. You can update the records in the Recordset, and then use the Recordset to update the database. You can also insert new records into the Recordset, or delete records and have those changes made in the database.

The Field Object

The Field object represents a single column in the Recordset. Each Field object contains the column name, data value, and how the data value should be represented. Because ADO was designed to be used in Microsoft's scripting languages, and the only data type available in these scripting languages is the Variant data type, the Field objects always contain a Variant data value. The data value is automatically converted to the correct data type when updating to the database. As the programmer working with the ADO objects, you will have to convert the value from a Variant to whatever data type you need it to be, as well as convert it back to a Variant when updating the value.

Using the ADO ActiveX Control

There are two different ways in which you can use the ADO control in your Visual C++ applications. The simple way to incorporate ADO into your application is through the use of ActiveX controls. You can add the ADO data control to your Visual C++ project, just like any other ActiveX control, as shown in Figure 15.1.

FIGURE 15.1.

Adding the ADO ActiveX control to a project.

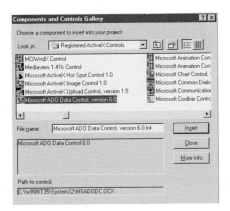

Once you add the ADO control to your project, and place it on a window, you'll need to specify the data connection in the control properties, as shown in Figure 15.2. You'll also need to specify the source for the records that will be retrieved by the control, as shown in Figure 15.3.

FIGURE 15.2.

Specifying the database connection.

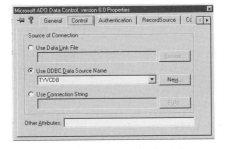

FIGURE 15.3.

Specifying the record source.

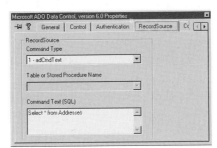

To use the ADO control efficiently, you'll also want to use data-bound controls that are ADO-enabled, such as the Microsoft DataGrid control. When you add these controls to the window with the ADO control, you'll specify the ADO control as the data source for the control, as shown in Figure 15.4. If the control is designed to only provide access to a single field in a record set, you'll also need to specify which field is to be used for the control.

FIGURE 15.4.

Specifying the data source.

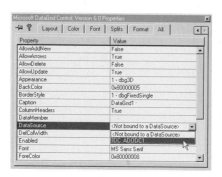

Once you add all these controls to the window and configure them, you can run your application and have full database access through ADO without having written a single line of code, as shown in Figure 15.5.

FIGURE 15.5.

A running ADO control database application.

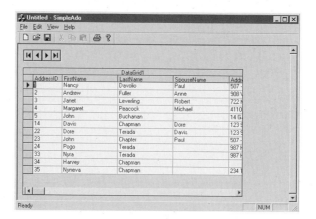

This is such a simple way to build database applications: Just place controls on a window and configure the properties to tell it where to get the data. What's the downside of building ADO applications this way? First, using this approach involves a lot of unnecessary overhead in building ADO applications. For each SQL query or table that you want to pull in a separate record set, you have to add a separate ADO control. Each of these ADO controls will establish a separate connection to the database, which could cause problems with databases that have a limited number of connections available (not to mention the additional overhead on the application). Finally, not all data-bound controls are ADO enabled. ADO is such a new technology that there are few controls that you can use with it at this time. You may find some controls that allow you to retrieve and display data for the user, but do not allow the user to change and edit the data. Others may not even provide you with that much functionality.

Importing the ADO DLL

If you look around in the MFC class hierarchy, you'll find that there are no classes for use with ADO. If you don't want to use the controls approach, then what are your options? Do you have to create the classes yourself? No, Microsoft has provided other means for you to create and use classes for each of the objects in ADO, through the use of a new C++ precompiler directive called #import.

The #import precompiler directive was first added to Visual C++ with the 5.0 release. You can use this directive to import an ActiveX DLL that has been built with the IDispatch interface description included in the DLL. This directive tells the Visual C++ compiler to import the DLL specified by the #import directive and to extract the object information from the DLL, creating a couple of header files that are automatically included in your project. These header files have the filename extensions .TLH and .TLI and are in the output directory for your project (the Debug or Release directory, the same directory where you'll find the executable application after you've compiled your project). These two files contain definitions of classes for each of the objects in the DLL that you can use in your code. The #import directive also tells the compiler to include the DLL as part of the project, eliminating the need to include the .LIB file for the DLL in your project.

You can import the ADO DLL by placing the following code at the beginning of the header file in which you are defining any database objects:

```
#define INITGUID
#import "C:\Program Files\Common Files\System\ADO\msado15.dll"
        ➥rename_namespace("ADOCG") rename("EOF", "EndOfFile")
using namespace ADOCG;
#include "icrsint.h"
```

In these four lines of directives, the first line defines a constant that needs to be defined for ADO. The second imports the ADO DLL, creating the two header files mentioned earlier. After the filename to be imported, this directive includes two attributes to the #import directive. The first, rename_namespace, renames the namespace into which the DLL has been imported. This is followed with the line following the #import, where the renamed namespace is specified as the one used. The second attribute, rename, renames an element in the header files that are created using the #import directive.

The reason you rename elements in these header files is to prevent conflicts with another element named elsewhere. If you examine the header file, the element specified is not renamed in the file, but when the compiler reads the file, the element is renamed. The final line includes the ADO header file, which contains the definition of some macros that you will use when writing your ADO applications.

Connecting to a Database

Before you can use any of the ADO objects, you need to initialize the COM environment for your application. You can do this by calling the `CoInitialize` API function, passing `NULL` as the only parameter, as follows:

```
::CoInitialize(NULL);
```

This enables you to make calls to ActiveX objects. If you leave out this one line of code from your application, or don't put it before you begin interacting with the objects, you get an COM error whenever you run your application.

When you are finished with all ADO activity, you also need to shut down the COM environment by calling the `CoUninitialize` function, as follows:

```
CoUninitialize();
```

This function cleans up the COM environment and prepares your application for shutting down.

Once you initialize the COM environment, you can create a connection to the database. The best way to do this is not to declare a `Connection` object variable, but to declare a `Connection` object pointer, `_ConnectionPtr`, and use it for all your interaction with the `Connection` object. Once you declare a `Connection` object pointer, you can initialize it by creating an instance of the `Connection` object, calling the `CreateInstance` function, passing it the UUID of the `Connection` object as its only parameter, as follows:

```
_ConnectionPtr pConn;
pConn.CreateInstance(__uuidof(Connection));
```

 Tip   When you work with these objects and functions, you need to use the correct number of underscore characters in front of the various object and function names. The `_ConnectionPtr` object has only a single underscore character, whereas the `__uuidof` function has two.

Once you create the object, you can call the `Open` function to establish the connection to the database. This function takes four parameters. The first parameter is the connection definition string. This string defines the OLE DB data source for the database. It may be an ODBC OLE DB driver, where OLE DB is sitting on top of an ODBC data source, as you'll use in your sample application. If you are using SQL Server or Oracle databases, it may be a direct connection to the OLE DB interface provided by the database itself. The second parameter is the user ID for connecting to the database. The third parameter is the password for connecting to the database. The fourth parameter is the cursor type to use with the database. These types are defined in the `msado15.tlh` header file that is created by the `#import` directive. A typical use of the `Open` function to connect to an ODBC data source that doesn't need a user ID or password is like the following:

```
pConn->Open(L"Provider=MSDASQL.1;Data Source=TYVCDB", L"", L"",
    ➥adOpenUnspecified);
```

Executing Commands and Retrieving Data

Once you have the connection open, you can use a `Command` object to pass SQL commands to the database. This is the normal method of executing SQL commands with ADO. To create a `Command` object, follow the same process that you used to create a `Connection` object. Declare a `Command` object pointer, `_CommandPtr`, and then create an instance of it using the `UUID` of the `Command` object, as follows:

```
_CommandPtr pCmd;
pCmd.CreateInstance(__uuidof(Command));
```

Once you create your `Command` object, assuming that you have already established the connection to the database, set the active connection property of the `Command` object to the open `Connection` object pointer, as follows:

```
pCmd->ActiveConnection = pConn;
```

Next, specify the SQL command to be executed by setting the `CommandText` property of the `Command` object, as follows:

```
pCmd->CommandText = "Select * from Addresses";
```

At this point, you have two options for how you execute this command and retrieve the records. The first is to call the `Command` object's `Execute` method, which will return a new `Recordset` object, which you'll want to set to a `Recordset` object pointer, as follows:

```
_RecordsetPtr pRs;
pRs = pCmd->Execute();
```

The other approach to running the command and retrieving the records is to specify that the `Command` object is the source for the records in the `Recordset`. This requires creating the `Recordset` object as follows:

```
_RecordsetPtr pRs;
pRs.CreateInstance(__uuidof(Recordset));
pRs->PutRefSource(pCmd);
```

Now, you'll need to create two `NULL` variant values to pass as the first two parameters to the `Recordset`'s `Open` method. The third parameter will be the cursor type to use, followed by the locking method to use. Finally, the fifth parameter to the `Recordset`'s `Open` method is an options flag that indicates how the database should evaluate the command being passed in. You do this with the following code:

```
// Create the variant NULL
_variant_t vNull;
vNull.vt = VT_ERROR;
vNull.scode = DISP_E_PARAMNOTFOUND;

// Open the recordset
pRs->Open(vNull, vNull, adOpenDynamic, adLockOptimistic, adCmdUnknown);
```

You could take another approach to accomplish all of the preceding tasks with only a few lines of code. Skip the use of the `Command` and `Connection` objects altogether, placing all the necessary connection information in the `Recordset`'s `Open` function. You can specify the SQL command as the first parameter and the connection information as the second parameter, instead of the two `NULL`s that you passed previously. This method reduces all of the preceding code to the following few lines:

```
_RecordsetPtr pRs;
pRs.CreateInstance(__uuidof(Recordset));
pRs->Open(_T("select * from Addresses")
          _T("Provider=MSDASQL.1;Data Source=TYVCDB"), adOpenDynamic,
          adLockOptimistic, adCmdUnknown);
```

Tip

> Although placing all of the command and connection information into the Recordset Open function is fine for a simple application, such as the one that you will build today, you are better off using the `Connection` object with any application that has more than a couple of database queries. This allows you to make a single connection to the database and use that one connection for all interaction with the database.

Navigating the `Recordset`

Once you've retrieved a set of records from the database, and you are holding them in a `Recordset` object, you'll need to navigate the set of records. This functionality is available, just as you would expect, through the `MoveFirst`, `MoveLast`, `MovePrevious`, and `MoveNext` functions. None of these functions take any parameters because they perform the functions that you would expect them to perform.

Along with these functions, the `Recordset` object also has two properties, `BOF` and `EOF` (which you should normally rename to prevent a collision with the default definition of `EOF`), which can be checked to determine if the current record in the set is beyond either end of the set of records.

Accessing Field Values

When you need to begin accessing the data values in each of the fields is where working with ADO in Visual C++ begins to get interesting. Because ADO is intended to be easy to use in Microsoft's scripting languages, VBScript and JScript, which only have `variant` data types, all data elements that you'll retrieve from fields in the ADO `Recordset` are `variant` values. They have to be converted into the data types that you need them to be. There are two ways of doing this. The first way is the straight-forward way of retrieving the values into a `variant` and then converting them, as in the following code:

```
_variant_t vFirstName;
CString strFirstName;

vFirstName = pRs->GetCollect(_variant_t("FirstName"));
vFirstName.ChangeType(VT_BSTR);
strFirstName = vFirstName.bstrVal;
```

The not-so-straight-forward way to do this is actually the better way, and in the long run, is a lot easier to work with. Microsoft has created a series of macros that perform the conversion for you and that maintain a set of variables of the records in the set. To do this, you'll define a new class to use as the interface for your record set. This class will be a descendent of the `CADORecordBinding` class, which is defined in the `icrsint.h` header file, which you included just after the `#import` directive. This class will not have any constructor or destructor but will have a series of macros, along with a number of variables. Each field in the set of records has two variables, an `unsigned long`, which is used to maintain the status of the variable, and the field variable itself. These variables must be regular C variables, and they cannot be C++ classes such as `CString`. A simple example of this class declaration is the following:

```
class CCustomRs :
    public CADORecordBinding
{
BEGIN_ADO_BINDING(CCustomRs)
    ADO_FIXED_LENGTH_ENTRY(1, adInteger, m_lAddressID, lAddressIDStatus,
    ➥FALSE)
    ADO_VARIABLE_LENGTH_ENTRY2(2, adVarChar, m_szFirstName,
        ➥sizeof(m_szFirstName), lFirstNameStatus, TRUE)
    ADO_FIXED_LENGTH_ENTRY(3, adDate, m_dtBirthdate, lBirthdateStatus,
    ➥TRUE)
    ADO_FIXED_LENGTH_ENTRY(4, adBoolean, m_bSendCard, lSendCardStatus,
    ➥TRUE)
```

```
END_ADO_BINDING()

public:
    LONG m_lAddressID;
    ULONG lAddressIDStatus;
    CHAR m_szFirstName[51];
    ULONG lFirstNameStatus;
    DATE m_dtBirthdate;
    ULONG lBirthdateStatus;
    VARIANT_BOOL m_bSendCard;
    ULONG lSendCardStatus;
};
```

Once you define this record layout class to match the record layout that will be returned by your database query, you can declare a variable of this class for use in your application, as follows:

```
CCustomRs m_rsRecSet;
```

Next, you need to create a pointer to an `IADORecordBinding` interface, as follows:

```
IADORecordBinding *picRs = NULL;
```

This is a pointer to a `COM` interface that is part of the ADO `Recordset` object. Once you retrieve the set of records, you need to retrieve the pointer to the `IADORecordBinding` interface and bind the custom record set class to the `Recordset` object, as in the following code:

```
if (FAILED(pRs->QueryInterface(__uuidof(IADORecordBinding), (LPVOID
➡*)&picRs)))
    _com_issue_error(E_NOINTERFACE);
picRs->BindToRecordset(&m_rsRecSet);
```

Now, as you navigate the records in the set, you just need to access the member variables of your custom record class to retrieve the current value for each field.

The BEGIN_ADO_BINDING and END_ADO_BINDING Macros

The key to the second method of accessing the data values in the record set is in the macros that are used in defining the record class. The set of macros start with the `BEGIN_ADO_BINDING` macro, which takes the class name as its only parameter. This macro sets up the structure definition that is created with the rest of the macros that follow.

The set of macros is closed by the `END_ADO_BINDING` macro. This macro doesn't take any parameters, and it wraps up the definition of the record binding structure that is created in the class. It is in the rest of the macros, which are used between these two, where the real work is done.

The ADO_FIXED_LENGTH_ENTRY Macros

The ADO_FIXED_LENGTH_ENTRY macro is used for any database fields that are fixed in size. It can be used with a date or boolean field, or even a text field that is a fixed size, with no option for any variation in the database. There are two versions of this macro; you add a 2 to the end of the name of the second version (ADO_FIXED_LENGTH_ENTRY2).

Both versions require the same first three and last parameters. The first version requires an additional parameter that is not required in the second version. The first parameter is the ordinal number of the field in the record set. This is the position in the field order as returned by the SQL query that is run to populate the record set. The second parameter is the data type of the field; the available data types are defined in the header file created by the #import directive. The third parameter is the variable into which the data value is to be copied. For the first version of the macro, the fourth parameter is the variable for the field status (the unsigned long that you defined with the variable for the actual value). The last variable is a boolean that specifies whether this field can be modified.

The ADO_NUMERIC_ENTRY Macros

You use the ADO_NUMERIC_ENTRY macros with numeric fields only. They are similar to the ADO_FIXED_LENGTH_ENTRY macros in that there are two different versions of the macro, named in the same way. In these macros, the first five parameters are the same in both versions, along with the final parameter. Like with the ADO_FIXED_LENGTH_ENTRY macros, the first version has an additional parameter that is not used in the second version.

The first three parameters for the ADO_NUMERIC_ENTRY macros are the same as those for the ADO_FIXED_LENGTH_ENTRY macros, as are the last parameter and the next to last parameter for the first version. It is the fourth and fifth parameters that are unique to these macros. The fourth parameter specifies the precision of the value in this field of the record set. The fifth parameter specifies the scale of the value. Both of these parameters are crucial in correctly converting the value to and from a variant data type.

The ADO_VARIABLE_LENGTH_ENTRY Macros

The final series of macros is the ADO_VARIABLE_LENGTH_ENTRY macros. You use this series of macros with database fields that are likely to vary in length. With a SQL-based database, you want to use this series of macros with any varchar (variable-length character string) columns. There are three versions of this macro. In all three versions, the first four parameters are the same, and the final parameter is the same. It is the parameters between them that vary.

The first parameter is the ordinal position of the column in the record set as returned by the SQL query. The second parameter is the data type. The third parameter is the variable in which the data value should be placed. The fourth parameter for all versions of the macro is the size of the variable into which the value is to be placed. This prevents the data from being written past the end of the variable that you defined for it to be placed in. As with the previous macros, the final parameter specifies whether the field is update-able.

In the first version of this macro, there are two parameters between the fourth and final parameters. The second version of this macro only has the first of these two parameters, and the third version only has the second of these two parameters. The first of these two parameters is the status variable for use with this field. The second of these two parameters is the length of the field in the database. The preceding example used the second version of this macro.

Updating Records

When you need to update values in a record in the recordset, how you handle it depends on which of the two methods you used to retrieve the data elements from the recordset. If you retrieved each field and converted it from a variant yourself, you need to update each individual field that has been changed. The update is done using the Recordset object's Update method, which takes two variables, the field being updated and the new value for the field. You could make this update using the following code:

```
_variant_t vName, vValue;
vName.SetString("FirstName");
vValue.SetString("John");
pRs->Update(vName, vValue);
```

If you created your record class and bound it to the recordset, updating the record is a little simpler. Once you have copied the new values into the variables in the record class, you can call the record-bound version of the Update function, as in the following:

```
picRs->Update(&m_rsRecSet);
```

This causes the record in the Recordset object to be updated with the values in the record class that you have bound to the set.

Adding and Deleting

Adding and deleting records from an ADO recordset is similar to how you accomplish it in other database access technologies. However, there are some slight subtleties to how you perform the addition of new records.

For deleting the current record, you can call the `Recordset` object's `Delete` method. This method requires a single parameter that specifies how the delete is supposed to be done. Most likely, you'll pass the `adAffectCurrent` value so that only the current record in the recordset is deleted, as in the following code:

```
pRs->Delete(adAffectCurrent);
pRs->MovePrevious();
```

As with any other database access technology, once you've deleted the current record, there is no current record, so you need to navigate to another record before allowing the user to do anything else.

When you are adding a new record, you can call the `Recordset` object's `AddNew` method. Once you have added a new record, the new record is the current record in the record set. If you check the variables in the record class that you created, you'll find that they are all empty. However, you cannot just begin entering data values into these fields. To allow the user to immediately enter the various data elements in the new record, you'll blank out the values in the record class and pass this variable as the only parameter to the Add New class. You need to call it through the record-binding interface pointer, as in the following example:

```
CString strBlank = " ";
COleDateTime dtBlank;

m_rsRecSet.m_lAddressID = 0;
strcpy(m_rsRecSet.m_szFirstName, (LPCTSTR)strBlank);
m_rsRecSet.m_dtBirthdate = (DATE)dtBlank;
m_rsRecSet.m_bSendCard = VARIANT_FALSE;
picRs->AddNew(&m_rsRecSet);
```

This allows you to provide the user with a blank record, ready for editing. Once the user has entered all the various values in the record, copy all these values back to the record variable. Then, call the `Update` method to save the record.

Closing the `Recordset` and `Connection` Objects

Once you finish working with a record set, you'll close the record set by calling the `Close` method, as follows:

```
pRs->Close();
```

Once you finish all database interaction for the entire application, you'll also close the connection to the database by calling the `Connection` object's `Close` method:

```
pConn->Close();
```

Building a Database Application Using ADO

The sample application that you will build today is another simple database application, basically the same as the one you built yesterday. You'll use ADO to retrieve a set of records from an Access database, providing functionality to navigate the record set. The user will be able to make changes to the data in the record set, and those changes will be reflected in the database as well. The user will also be able to add new records to the record set and delete records as desired. You will accomplish all of this using ADO as the means of accessing the database, which will go through the ODBC driver that was configured yesterday.

Creating the Application Shell

The application that you will build today will be an SDI-style application. As with several other sample applications that you build in the course of reading this book, everything that you do in today's application is just as applicable to an MDI or dialog-style application. To start the application, you'll use the MFC AppWizard to build the application shell, using most of the SDI-style application default settings.

To start your application, create a new AppWizard project, naming the project something appropriate, such as DbAdo. Specify on the first panel of the AppWizard that you are building an SDI-style application. Accept all the default settings for steps 2 through 5, being sure to leave the second step stating that you want no database support included in the application. On the final AppWizard step, specify that the view class should be inherited from the CFormView class.

Once you finish creating your application shell, design the main dialog form for use in your application. Add the standard controls for each of the fields in the Addresses table from the database you used yesterday (or if you used a different database yesterday, add controls for all the fields in the table that you used), as shown in Figure 15.6. Configure the controls using the properties listed in Table 15.1.

Tip

If you want to save a little time when building the example, you can leave out most of the controls and database fields from the application. The key fields that you'll need to include on the screen are ID, First and Last Names, Birthdate, and Send Card. If you want to leave out the other fields from the application, that's fine. You will need to include these fields in the CCustomRs class that you create in this chapter.

FIGURE 15.6.

The main form layout.

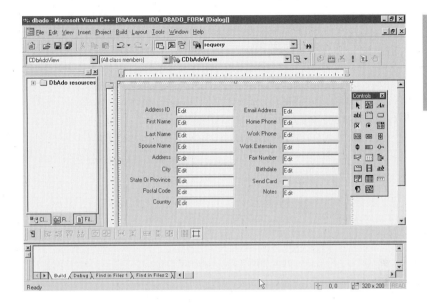

TABLE 15.1. CONTROL PROPERTY SETTINGS.

Object	Property	Setting
Static Text	ID	IDC_STATIC
	Caption	Address ID
Edit Box	ID	IDC_EDIT_ADDRESSID
Static Text	ID	IDC_STATIC
	Caption	First Name
Edit Box	ID	IDC_EDIT_FIRSTNAME
Static Text	ID	IDC_STATIC
	Caption	Last Name
Edit Box	ID	IDC_EDIT_LASTNAME
Static Text	ID	IDC_STATIC
	Caption	Spouse Name
Edit Box	ID	IDC_EDIT_SPOUSENAME
Static Text	ID	IDC_STATIC
	Caption	Address
Edit Box	ID	IDC_EDIT_ADDRESS

continues

TABLE 15.1. CONTINUED

Object	Property	Setting
Static Text	ID	IDC_STATIC
	Caption	City
Edit Box	ID	IDC_EDIT_CITY
Static Text	ID	IDC_STATIC
	Caption	State Or Province
Edit Box	ID	IDC_EDIT_STATEORPROVINCE
Static Text	ID	IDC_STATIC
	Caption	Postal Code
Edit Box	ID	IDC_EDIT_POSTALCODE
Static Text	ID	IDC_STATIC
	Caption	Country
Edit Box	ID	IDC_EDIT_COUNTRY
Static Text	ID	IDC_STATIC
	Caption	Email Address
Edit Box	ID	IDC_EDIT_EMAILADDRESS
Static Text	ID	IDC_STATIC
	Caption	Home Phone
Edit Box	ID	IDC_EDIT_HOMEPHONE
Static Text	ID	IDC_STATIC
	Caption	Work Phone
Edit Box	ID	IDC_EDIT_WORKPHONE
Static Text	ID	IDC_STATIC
	Caption	Work Extension
Edit Box	ID	IDC_EDIT_WORKEXTENSION
Static Text	ID	IDC_STATIC
	Caption	Fax Number
Edit Box	ID	IDC_EDIT_FAXNUMBER
Static Text	ID	IDC_STATIC
	Caption	Birthdate
Edit Box	ID	IDC_EDIT_BIRTHDATE
Static Text	ID	IDC_STATIC
	Caption	Send Card

Object	Property	Setting
Check Box	ID	IDC_CHECK_SENDCARD
Static Text	ID	IDC_STATIC
	Caption	Notes
Edit Box	ID	IDC_EDIT_NOTES

Once you add all of the controls to the form, use the Class Wizard to attach variables to each of these controls, as specified in Table 15.2. The variables should match the data types of the columns in the database that the control will be used to display.

TABLE 15.2. CONTROL VARIABLES.

Object	Name	Category	Type
IDC_CHECK_SENDCARD	m_bSendCard	Value	BOOL
IDC_EDIT_ADDRESS	m_strAddress	Value	CString
IDC_EDIT_ADDRESSID	m_lAddressID	Value	long
IDC_EDIT_BIRTHDATE	m_oledtBirthdate	Value	COleDateTime
IDC_EDIT_CITY	m_strCity	Value	CString
IDC_EDIT_COUNTRY	m_strCountry	Value	CString
IDC_EDIT_EMAILADDRESS	m_strEmailAddress	Value	CString
IDC_EDIT_FAXNUMBER	m_strFaxNumber	Value	CString
IDC_EDIT_FIRSTNAME	m_strFirstName	Value	CString
IDC_EDIT_HOMEPHONE	m_strHomePhone	Value	CString
IDC_EDIT_LASTNAME	m_strLastName	Value	CString
IDC_EDIT_NOTES	m_strNotes	Value	CString
IDC_EDIT_POSTALCODE	m_strPostalCode	Value	CString
IDC_EDIT_SPOUSENAME	m_strSpouseName	Value	CString
IDC_EDIT_STATEORPROVINCE	m_strStateOrProvince	Value	CString
IDC_EDIT_WORKEXTENSION	m_strWorkExtension	Value	CString
IDC_EDIT_WORKPHONE	m_strWorkPhone	Value	CString

Building a Custom Record Class

Before you go any further in building your application, you need to create your custom record class that you will bind to the record set. This class will need public variables for each of the columns in the database table that you are selecting, as well as status variables for each of these columns. You'll also build the set of macros to exchange the column values between the record set and the class variables. To create this class, create a new class using the same method you used in previous days, specifying a generic class. Specify a suitable class name, such as CCustomRs, and specify the base class as CADORecordBinding with public access.

Once you have created your new class, delete the constructor and destructor functions from both the header and source code files for the new class. Edit the header file for your new class, importing the ADO DLL and filling in the macros and variables, as in Listing 15.1.

LISTING 15.1. THE CUSTOM RECORD CLASS.

```
 1: #define INITGUID
 2: #import "C:\Program Files\Common Files\System\ADO\msado15.dll"
        ➥rename_namespace("ADOCG") rename("EOF", "EndOfFile")
 3: using namespace ADOCG;
 4: #include "icrsint.h"
 5:
 6: class CCustomRs :
 7:     public CADORecordBinding
 8: {
 9: BEGIN_ADO_BINDING(CCustomRs)
10:     ADO_FIXED_LENGTH_ENTRY(1, adInteger, m_lAddressID,
        ➥lAddressIDStatus,FALSE)
11:     ADO_VARIABLE_LENGTH_ENTRY2(2, adVarChar, m_szFirstName,
            ➥sizeof(m_szFirstName), lFirstNameStatus, TRUE)
12:     ADO_VARIABLE_LENGTH_ENTRY2(3, adVarChar, m_szLastName,
            ➥sizeof(m_szLastName), lLastNameStatus, TRUE)
13:     ADO_VARIABLE_LENGTH_ENTRY2(4, adVarChar, m_szSpouseName,
            ➥sizeof(m_szSpouseName), lSpouseNameStatus, TRUE)
14:     ADO_VARIABLE_LENGTH_ENTRY2(5, adVarChar, m_szAddress,
            ➥sizeof(m_szAddress), lAddressStatus, TRUE)
15:     ADO_VARIABLE_LENGTH_ENTRY2(6, adVarChar, m_szCity,
        ➥sizeof(m_szCity),lCityStatus, TRUE)
16:     ADO_VARIABLE_LENGTH_ENTRY2(7, adVarChar, m_szStateOrProvince,
            ➥sizeof(m_szStateOrProvince), lStateOrProvinceStatus, TRUE)
17:     ADO_VARIABLE_LENGTH_ENTRY2(8, adVarChar, m_szPostalCode,
            ➥sizeof(m_szPostalCode), lPostalCodeStatus, TRUE)
18:     ADO_VARIABLE_LENGTH_ENTRY2(9, adVarChar, m_szCountry,
            ➥sizeof(m_szCountry), lCountryStatus, TRUE)
19:     ADO_VARIABLE_LENGTH_ENTRY2(10, adVarChar, m_szEmailAddress,
            ➥sizeof(m_szEmailAddress), lEmailAddressStatus, TRUE)
20:     ADO_VARIABLE_LENGTH_ENTRY2(11, adVarChar, m_szHomePhone,
            ➥sizeof(m_szHomePhone), lHomePhoneStatus, TRUE)
21:     ADO_VARIABLE_LENGTH_ENTRY2(12, adVarChar, m_szWorkPhone,
            ➥sizeof(m_szWorkPhone), lWorkPhoneStatus, TRUE)
```

```
22:     ADO_VARIABLE_LENGTH_ENTRY2(13, adVarChar, m_szWorkExtension,
           ➥sizeof(m_szWorkExtension), lWorkExtensionStatus, TRUE)
23:     ADO_VARIABLE_LENGTH_ENTRY2(14, adVarChar, m_szFaxNumber,
           ➥sizeof(m_szFaxNumber), lFaxNumberStatus, TRUE)
24:     ADO_FIXED_LENGTH_ENTRY(15, adDate, m_dtBirthdate,
           ➥lBirthdateStatus,TRUE)
25:     ADO_FIXED_LENGTH_ENTRY(16, adBoolean, m_bSendCard,
           ➥lSendCardStatus,TRUE)
26:     ADO_VARIABLE_LENGTH_ENTRY2(17, adLongVarChar, m_szNotes,
           ➥sizeof(m_szNotes), lNotesStatus, TRUE)
27: END_ADO_BINDING()
28:
29: public:
30:     LONG m_lAddressID;
31:     ULONG lAddressIDStatus;
32:     CHAR m_szFirstName[51];
33:     ULONG lFirstNameStatus;
34:     CHAR m_szLastName[51];
35:     ULONG lLastNameStatus;
36:     CHAR m_szSpouseName[51];
37:     ULONG lSpouseNameStatus;
38:     CHAR m_szAddress[256];
39:     ULONG lAddressStatus;
40:     CHAR m_szCity[51];
41:     ULONG lCityStatus;
42:     CHAR m_szStateOrProvince[21];
43:     ULONG lStateOrProvinceStatus;
44:     CHAR m_szPostalCode[21];
45:     ULONG lPostalCodeStatus;
46:     CHAR m_szCountry[51];
47:     ULONG lCountryStatus;
48:     CHAR m_szEmailAddress[51];
49:     ULONG lEmailAddressStatus;
50:     CHAR m_szHomePhone[31];
51:     ULONG lHomePhoneStatus;
52:     CHAR m_szWorkPhone[31];
53:     ULONG lWorkPhoneStatus;
54:     CHAR m_szWorkExtension[21];
55:     ULONG lWorkExtensionStatus;
56:     CHAR m_szFaxNumber[31];
57:     ULONG lFaxNumberStatus;
58:     DATE m_dtBirthdate;
59:     ULONG lBirthdateStatus;
60:     VARIANT_BOOL m_bSendCard;
61:     ULONG lSendCardStatus;
62:     CHAR m_szNotes[65536];
63:     ULONG lNotesStatus;
64: };
```

Once you've created this class, you need to add a variable to the document class. Add a new member variable to the document class, specifying the variable type as CCustomRs, the name as m_rsRecSet, and the access as private. You'll also need to include the custom record class header file in the document source code file, as in Listing 15.2.

LISTING 15.2. THE DOCUMENT SOURCE CODE INCLUDES.

```
1: // dbadoDoc.cpp : implementation of the CDbAdoDoc class
2: //
3:
4: #include "stdafx.h"
5: #include "dbado.h"
6:
7: #include "CustomRs.h"
8: #include "dbadoDoc.h"
9: #include "dbadoView.h"
```

Another detail that you need to attend to before going any further is providing a way for the view to get a pointer to the record class from the document class. This function should return a pointer to the record class variable. To add this function to your application, add a new member function to the document class, specifying the function type as CCustomRs*, the function declaration as GetRecSet, and the function access as public. Edit this function, adding the code in Listing 15.3.

LISTING 15.3. THE CDbAdoDoc GetRecSet FUNCTION.

```
1: CCustomRs* CDbAdoDoc::GetRecSet()
2: {
3:     // Return a pointer to the record object
4:     return &m_rsRecSet;
5: }
```

One last piece of functionality that you'll add before getting to the real heart of ADO programming is the function for reporting ADO and database errors. This function will display a message to the user, reporting that an error occurred and displaying the error code and error message for the user. To add this function to your application, add a new member function to your document class. Specify the function type as void, the function declaration as GenerateError(HRESULT hr, PWSTR pwszDescription), and the access as public. Edit the function, entering the code in Listing 15.4.

LISTING **15.4.** THE CDbAdoDoc GenerateError FUNCTION.

```
 1: void CDbAdoDoc::GenerateError(HRESULT hr, PWSTR pwszDescription)
 2: {
 3:     CString strError;
 4:
 5:     // Format and display the error message
 6:     strError.Format("Run-time error '%d (%x)'", hr, hr);
 7:     strError += "\n\n";
 8:     strError += pwszDescription;
 9:
10:     AfxMessageBox(strError);
11: }
```

Connecting and Retrieving Data

You can perform all of the connecting to the database and retrieving the record set in the OnNewDocument function in the document class. Before you can add this functionality, you need to add a few more variables to the document class. You'll need a Recordset object pointer, an IADORecordBinding interface pointer, a couple of string variables for holding the database connection string, and the SQL command to execute to populate the record set. Add all of these variables to the document class as specified in Table 15.3.

TABLE 15.3. DOCUMENT CLASS MEMBER VARIABLES.

Name	Type	Access
m_pRs	_RecordsetPtr	Private
m_piAdoRecordBinding	IADORecordBinding*	Private
m_strConnection	CString	Private
m_strCmdText	CString	Private

In the OnNewDocument function, you'll perform a series of steps for connecting and retrieving the record set. First, you'll set the strings for the database connection and the SQL command to be run. Next, you'll initialize the COM environment and initialize the two pointers so that they are both NULL. You'll create the Recordset object using the CreateInstance function. Open the Recordset, connecting to the database and running the SQL command at the same time. Bind the record class to the record set using the IADORecordBinding interface pointer. Finally, tell the view class to refresh the bound data, displaying the initial record for the user using a view class function that you'll add in a little while. To add all this functionality, edit the OnNewDocument function in the document class, adding the code starting with line 8 in Listing 15.5.

LISTING 15.5. THE CDbAdoDoc OnNewDocument FUNCTION.

```
1: BOOL CDbAdoDoc::OnNewDocument()
2: {
3:     if (!CDocument::OnNewDocument())
4:         return FALSE;
5:
6:     // TODO: add reinitialization code here
7:     // (SDI documents will reuse this document)
8:     // Set the connection and SQL command strings
9:     m_strConnection = _T("Provider=MSDASQL.1;Data Source=TYVCDB");
10:    m_strCmdText = _T("select * from Addresses");
11:
12:    // Initialize the Recordset and binding pointers
13:    m_pRs = NULL;
14:    m_piAdoRecordBinding = NULL;
15:    // Initialize the COM environment
16:    ::CoInitialize(NULL);
17:    try
18:    {
19:        // Create the record set object
20:        m_pRs.CreateInstance(__uuidof(Recordset));
21:
22:        // Open the record set object
23:        m_pRs->Open((LPCTSTR)m_strCmdText, (LPCTSTR)m_strConnection,
24:            adOpenDynamic, adLockOptimistic, adCmdUnknown);
25:
26:        // Get a pointer to the record binding interface
27:        if (FAILED(m_pRs->QueryInterface(__uuidof(IADORecordBinding),
28:            (LPVOID *)&m_piAdoRecordBinding)))
29:          _com_issue_error(E_NOINTERFACE);
30:        // Bind the record class to the record set
31:        m_piAdoRecordBinding->BindToRecordset(&m_rsRecSet);
32:
33:        // Get a pointer to the view
34:        POSITION pos = GetFirstViewPosition();
35:        CDbAdoView* pView = (CDbAdoView*)GetNextView(pos);
36:        if (pView)
37:            // Sync the data set with the form
38:            pView->RefreshBoundData();
39:    }
40:    // Any errors?
41:    catch (_com_error &e)
42:    {
43:        // Display the error
44:        GenerateError(e.Error(), e.Description());
45:    }
46:
47:    return TRUE;
48: }
```

Before moving any further, it's a good idea to make sure that you add all the code necessary to clean up as your application is closing. You need to close the record set and release the pointer to the record binding interface. You'll also shut down the COM environment. To add all this functionality to your application, add a function to the `DeleteContents` event message in the document class. Edit this function, adding the code in Listing 15.6.

LISTING 15.6. THE CDbAdoDoc DeleteContents FUNCTION.

```
 1: void CDbAdoDoc::DeleteContents()
 2: {
 3:     // TODO: Add your specialized code here and/or call the base class
 4:     // Close the record set
 5:     if (m_pRs)
 6:         m_pRs->Close();
 7:     // Do we have a valid pointer to the record binding?
 8:     if (m_piAdoRecordBinding)
 9:         // Release it
10:         m_piAdoRecordBinding->Release();
11:     // Set the record set pointer to NULL
12:     m_pRs = NULL;
13:
14:     // Shut down the COM environment
15:     CoUninitialize();
16:
17:     CDocument::DeleteContents();
18: }
```

Populating the Form

To display the record column values for the user, you'll add a function for copying the values from the record class to the view variables. This function first needs to get a pointer to the record class from the document class. Next, it will check the status of each individual field in the record class to make sure that it's okay to copy, and then it will copy the value. Once all values have been copied, you can call `UpdateData` to display the values in the controls on the form. To add this functionality to your application, add a new member function to the view class. Specify the function type as `void`, the function declaration as `RefreshBoundData`, and the access as public. Edit this new function, adding the code in Listing 15.7.

LISTING 15.7. THE `CDbAdoView` `RefreshBoundData` FUNCTION.

```
 1: void CDbAdoView::RefreshBoundData()
 2: {
 3:     CCustomRs* pRs;
 4:
 5:     // Get a pointer to the document object
 6:     pRs = GetDocument()->GetRecSet();
 7:
 8:     // Is the field OK
 9:     if (adFldOK == pRs->lAddressIDStatus)
10:         // Copy the value
11:         m_lAddressID = pRs->m_lAddressID;
12:     else
13:         // Otherwise, set the value to 0
14:         m_lAddressID = 0;
15:     // Is the field OK
16:     if (adFldOK == pRs->lFirstNameStatus)
17:         // Copy the value
18:         m_strFirstName = pRs->m_szFirstName;
19:     else
20:         // Otherwise, set the value to 0
21:         m_strFirstName = _T("");
22:     if (adFldOK == pRs->lLastNameStatus)
23:         m_strLastName = pRs->m_szLastName;
24:     else
25:         m_strLastName = _T("");
26:     if (adFldOK == pRs->lSpouseNameStatus)
27:         m_strSpouseName = pRs->m_szSpouseName;
28:     else
29:         m_strSpouseName = _T("");
30:     if (adFldOK == pRs->lAddressStatus)
31:         m_strAddress = pRs->m_szAddress;
32:     else
33:         m_strAddress = _T("");
34:     if (adFldOK == pRs->lCityStatus)
35:         m_strCity = pRs->m_szCity;
36:     else
37:         m_strCity = _T("");
38:     if (adFldOK == pRs->lStateOrProvinceStatus)
39:         m_strStateOrProvince = pRs->m_szStateOrProvince;
40:     else
41:         m_strStateOrProvince = _T("");
42:     if (adFldOK == pRs->lPostalCodeStatus)
43:         m_strPostalCode = pRs->m_szPostalCode;
44:     else
45:         m_strPostalCode = _T("");
46:     if (adFldOK == pRs->lCountryStatus)
47:         m_strCountry = pRs->m_szCountry;
48:     else
```

```
49:      m_strCountry = _T("");
50:    if (adFldOK == pRs->lEmailAddressStatus)
51:        m_strEmailAddress = pRs->m_szEmailAddress;
52:    else
53:        m_strEmailAddress = _T("");
54:    if (adFldOK == pRs->lHomePhoneStatus)
55:        m_strHomePhone = pRs->m_szHomePhone;
56:    else
57:        m_strHomePhone = _T("");
58:    if (adFldOK == pRs->lWorkPhoneStatus)
59:        m_strWorkPhone = pRs->m_szWorkPhone;
60:    else
61:        m_strWorkPhone = _T("");
62:    if (adFldOK == pRs->lWorkExtensionStatus)
63:        m_strWorkExtension = pRs->m_szWorkExtension;
64:    else
65:        m_strWorkExtension = _T("");
66:    if (adFldOK == pRs->lFaxNumberStatus)
67:        m_strFaxNumber = pRs->m_szFaxNumber;
68:    else
69:        m_strFaxNumber = _T("");
70:    if (adFldOK == pRs->lBirthdateStatus)
71:        m_oledtBirthdate = pRs->m_dtBirthdate;
72:    else
73:        m_oledtBirthdate = 0L;
74:    if (adFldOK == pRs->lSendCardStatus)
75:        m_bSendCard = VARIANT_FALSE == pRs->m_bSendCard ? FALSE :
           ➥TRUE;
76:    else
77:        m_bSendCard = FALSE;
78:    if (adFldOK == pRs->lNotesStatus)
79:        m_strNotes = pRs->m_szNotes;
80:    else
81:        m_strNotes = _T("");
82:
83:    // Sync the data with the controls
84:    UpdateData(FALSE);
85: }
```

Note

Because you are working directly with the custom record class that you created in this function, you must include the header file for your custom record class in the view class source file, just as you did with the document class source file.

Saving Updates

When you need to copy changes back to the record set, reverse the process of copying data from the controls on the form to the variables in the record class. You could take the approach of copying all values, regardless of whether their values have changed, or you could compare the two values to determine which have changed and need to be copied back. Call the function that does this before navigating to any other records in the record set so that any changes that the user has made are saved to the database. To add this functionality to your application, add a new member function to the view class. Specify the function type as void, the function declaration as UpdateBoundData, and the access as private. Edit the function, adding the code in Listing 15.8.

LISTING 15.8. THE CDbAdoView UpdateBoundData FUNCTION.

```
 1: void CDbAdoView::UpdateBoundData()
 2: {
 3:     CCustomRs* pRs;
 4:
 5:     // Get a pointer to the document
 6:     pRs = GetDocument()->GetRecSet();
 7:
 8:     // Sync the controls with the variables
 9:     UpdateData(TRUE);
10:
11:     // Has the field changed? If so, copy the value back
12:     if (m_lAddressID != pRs->m_lAddressID)
13:         pRs->m_lAddressID = m_lAddressID;
14:     if (m_strFirstName != pRs->m_szFirstName)
15:         strcpy(pRs->m_szFirstName, (LPCTSTR)m_strFirstName);
16:     if (m_strLastName != pRs->m_szLastName)
17:         strcpy(pRs->m_szLastName, (LPCTSTR)m_strLastName);
18:     if (m_strSpouseName != pRs->m_szSpouseName)
19:         strcpy(pRs->m_szSpouseName, (LPCTSTR)m_strSpouseName);
20:     if (m_strAddress != pRs->m_szAddress)
21:         strcpy(pRs->m_szAddress, (LPCTSTR)m_strAddress);
22:     if (m_strCity != pRs->m_szCity)
23:         strcpy(pRs->m_szCity, (LPCTSTR)m_strCity);
24:     if (m_strStateOrProvince != pRs->m_szStateOrProvince)
25:         strcpy(pRs->m_szStateOrProvince,
                ➥(LPCTSTR)m_strStateOrProvince);
26:     if (m_strPostalCode != pRs->m_szPostalCode)
27:         strcpy(pRs->m_szPostalCode, (LPCTSTR)m_strPostalCode);
28:     if (m_strCountry != pRs->m_szCountry)
29:         strcpy(pRs->m_szCountry, (LPCTSTR)m_strCountry);
30:     if (m_strEmailAddress != pRs->m_szEmailAddress)
31:         strcpy(pRs->m_szEmailAddress, (LPCTSTR)m_strEmailAddress);
32:     if (m_strHomePhone != pRs->m_szHomePhone)
```

```
33:            strcpy(pRs->m_szHomePhone, (LPCTSTR)m_strHomePhone);
34:        if (m_strWorkPhone != pRs->m_szWorkPhone)
35:            strcpy(pRs->m_szWorkPhone, (LPCTSTR)m_strWorkPhone);
36:        if (m_strWorkExtension != pRs->m_szWorkExtension)
37:            strcpy(pRs->m_szWorkExtension, (LPCTSTR)m_strWorkExtension);
38:        if (m_strFaxNumber != pRs->m_szFaxNumber)
39:            strcpy(pRs->m_szFaxNumber, (LPCTSTR)m_strFaxNumber);
40:        if (((DATE)m_oledtBirthdate) != pRs->m_dtBirthdate)
41:            pRs->m_dtBirthdate = (DATE)m_oledtBirthdate;
42:        if (m_bSendCard == TRUE)
43:            pRs->m_bSendCard = VARIANT_TRUE;
44:        else
45:            pRs->m_bSendCard = VARIANT_FALSE;
46:        if (m_strNotes != pRs->m_szNotes)
47:            strcpy(pRs->m_szNotes, (LPCTSTR)m_strNotes);
48: }
```

Navigating the Record Set

For navigating the record set, add a series of menus for each of the four basic navigation choices: first, previous, next, and last. Because the Recordset object and the record-binding interface pointers are in the document object, the event messages for these menus must be passed to the document class to update the current record and then to navigate to the selected record. However, the view class needs to receive the event message first because it needs to copy back any changed values from the controls on the form before the update is performed. Once the navigation is complete, the view also needs to update the form with the new record's column values. Looking at the sequence of where the event message needs to be passed, it makes the most sense to add the event message handler to the view class, and from there, call the event message handler for the document class.

To add this functionality to your application, add the four menu entries and the corresponding toolbar buttons. Using the Class Wizard, add a event message handler function to the view class for the command event for all four of these menus. Edit the event function for the Move First menu, adding the code in Listing 15.9.

LISTING 15.9. THE CDbAdoView OnDataFirst FUNCTION.

```
1: void CDbAdoView::OnDataFirst()
2: {
3:     // TODO: Add your command handler code here
4:     // Update the current record
5:     UpdateBoundData();
```

continues

LISTING **15.9.** CONTINUED

```
 6:      // Navigate to the first record
 7:      GetDocument()->MoveFirst();
 8:      // Refresh the form with the new record's data
 9:      RefreshBoundData();
10: }
```

Now add the MoveFirst function to the document class and perform all the actual record set functionality for this function. To add this, add a member function to the document class in your application. Specify the function type as void, the declaration as MoveFirst, and the access as public. Edit this function, adding the code in Listing 15.10.

LISTING **15.10.** THE CDBADODOC MOVEFIRST FUNCTION.

```
 1: void CDbAdoDoc::MoveFirst()
 2: {
 3:     try
 4:     {
 5:         // Update the current record
 6:         m_piAdoRecordBinding->Update(&m_rsRecSet);
 7:         // Move to the first record
 8:         m_pRs->MoveFirst();
 9:     }
10:     // Any errors?
11:     catch (_com_error &e)
12:     {
13:         // Generate the error message
14:         GenerateError(e.Error(), e.Description());
15:     }
16: }
```

Edit and add the same set of functions to the view and document classes for the MovePrevious, MoveNext, and MoveLast ADO functions. Once you've added all these functions, you should be ready to compile and run your application. Your application will be capable of opening the Addresses database table and presenting you with each individual record, which you can edit and update, as in Figure 15.7.

FIGURE 15.7.

*The running
application.*

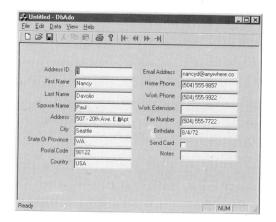

Adding New Records

Now that you are able to retrieve and navigate the set of records in the database table, it would be nice if you could add some new records to the table. You can add this functionality in exactly the same fashion that you added the navigation functionality. Add a menu, trigger an event function in the view class from the menu, update the current record values back to the record set, call a function in the document class, and refresh the current record from the record set. As far as the menu and the view class are concerned, the only difference between this functionality and any of the navigation menus and functions is the ID of the menu and the name of the functions that are called, just as with the different navigation functions. It's in the document function where things begin to diverge just a little.

In the document class function for adding a new record, once you've updated the current record, you'll make sure that adding a new record is an option. If it is, then you'll build an empty record and add it to the record set. Once you've added the empty record, navigate to the last record in the set because this will be the new record. At this point, you can exit this function and let the view class refresh the form with the data values from the new, empty record.

To add this functionality to your application, add a new menu entry for adding a new record. Add a command event-handler function to the view class for this new menu, adding the same code to the function as you did with the navigation functions, but call the AddNew function in the document class. Now, add the AddNew function to the document class. Add a new member function to the document class, specifying the type as void, the declaration as AddNew, and the access as public. Edit the function, adding the code in Listing 15.11.

LISTING 15.11. THE CDbAdoDoc AddNew FUNCTION.

```
 1: void CDbAdoDoc::AddNew()
 2: {
 3:     try
 4:     {
 5:         // Update the current record
 6:         m_piAdoRecordBinding->Update(&m_rsRecSet);
 7:         // Can we add a new record?
 8:         if (m_pRs->Supports(adAddNew))
 9:         {
10:             // Create a blank record
11:             CreateBlankRecord();
12:             // Add the blank record
13:             m_piAdoRecordBinding->AddNew(&m_rsRecSet);
14:             // Move to the last record
15:             m_pRs->MoveLast();
16:         }
17:     }
18:     // Any errors?
19:     catch (_com_error &e)
20:     {
21:         // Generate an error message
22:         GenerateError(e.Error(), e.Description());
23:     }
24: }
```

Now add the function that creates the blank record. In this function, you'll set each of the field variables in the record class to an almost empty string. To add this function to your class, add a new member function to the document class. Specify its type as void, its declaration as CreateBlankRecord, and its access as private. Edit this new function, adding the code in Listing 15.12.

LISTING 15.12. THE CDbAdoDoc CreateBlankRecord FUNCTION.

```
 1: void CDbAdoDoc::CreateBlankRecord()
 2: {
 3:     // Create the blank values to be used
 4:     CString strBlank = " ";
 5:     COleDateTime dtBlank;
 6:
 7:     // Set each of the values in the record object
 8:     m_rsRecSet.m_lAddressID = 0;
 9:     strcpy(m_rsRecSet.m_szFirstName, (LPCTSTR)strBlank);
10:     strcpy(m_rsRecSet.m_szLastName, (LPCTSTR)strBlank);
```

```
11:    strcpy(m_rsRecSet.m_szSpouseName, (LPCTSTR)strBlank);
12:    strcpy(m_rsRecSet.m_szAddress, (LPCTSTR)strBlank);
13:    strcpy(m_rsRecSet.m_szCity, (LPCTSTR)strBlank);
14:    strcpy(m_rsRecSet.m_szStateOrProvince, (LPCTSTR)strBlank);
15:    strcpy(m_rsRecSet.m_szPostalCode, (LPCTSTR)strBlank);
16:    strcpy(m_rsRecSet.m_szCountry, (LPCTSTR)strBlank);
17:    strcpy(m_rsRecSet.m_szEmailAddress, (LPCTSTR)strBlank);
18:    strcpy(m_rsRecSet.m_szHomePhone, (LPCTSTR)strBlank);
19:    strcpy(m_rsRecSet.m_szWorkPhone, (LPCTSTR)strBlank);
20:    strcpy(m_rsRecSet.m_szWorkExtension, (LPCTSTR)strBlank);
21:    strcpy(m_rsRecSet.m_szFaxNumber, (LPCTSTR)strBlank);
22:    m_rsRecSet.m_dtBirthdate = (DATE)dtBlank;
23:    m_rsRecSet.m_bSendCard = VARIANT_FALSE;
24:    strcpy(m_rsRecSet.m_szNotes, (LPCTSTR)strBlank);
25: }
```

If you compile and run your application, you should be able to insert and edit new records in the database table.

Deleting Records

The final piece of functionality that you'll add to your application is the ability to delete the current record from the set. This function can follow the same form as all the navigation and add functions with a menu entry calling an event-handler function in the view class. The function in the view class can even follow the same set of code that you used in these previous functions, updating the current record, calling the corresponding function in the document class, and then refreshing the current record to the form.

In the document class function, the record deletion should follow almost the same path that you took for adding a new record. Update the current record, check to see if it's possible to delete the current record, check with the user to verify that he wants to delete the current record, and then call the Delete function and navigate to another record in the set.

To add this functionality to your application, add a new menu entry for the delete function and then attach an event-handler function for the menu's command event in the view class. Edit this function, adding the same code as in the navigation and add record functions and calling the Delete function in the document class. Now, add a new member function to the document class. Specify the new function's type as void, the declaration as Delete, and the access as public. Edit this function, adding the code in Listing 15.13.

LISTING **15.13.** THE CDbAdoDoc Delete FUNCTION.

```
 1: void CDbAdoDoc::Delete()
 2: {
 3:      try
 4:      {
 5:          // Update the current record
 6:          m_piAdoRecordBinding->Update(&m_rsRecSet);
 7:          // Can we delete a record?
 8:          if (m_pRs->Supports(adDelete))
 9:          {
10:              // Make sure the user wants to delete this record
11:              if (AfxMessageBox("Are you sure you want to delete this
                 ➥record?",
12:                  MB_YESNO | MB_ICONQUESTION) == IDYES)
13:              {
14:                  // Delete the record
15:                  m_pRs->Delete(adAffectCurrent);
16:                  // Move to the previous record
17:                  m_pRs->MovePrevious();
18:              }
19:          }
20:      }
21:      // Any errors?
22:      catch (_com_error &e)
23:      {
24:          // Generate an error message
25:          GenerateError(e.Error(), e.Description());
26:      }
27: }
```

When you compile and run your application, you should be able to delete any records from the set that you want.

Summary

Today, you learned about Microsoft's newest database access technology, ActiveX Data Objects. You saw how you can use ADO as a simple ActiveX control to provide database access through data-bound controls without any additional programming. You also learned how to import the DLL, providing a rich set of data access functionality that you can use and control in your applications. You learned how to retrieve a set of data, manipulate the records in the set, and save your changes back in the database. You learned two different ways of accessing and updating the data values in a record in the record set and how you can do a little more work up front to save a large amount of work in the midst of the application coding.

Q&A

Q **Because Visual C++ doesn't support ADO with its wizards, why would I want to use it?**

A ADO is the database access technology direction for Microsoft. It's still in the early stages of this technology, but it will gradually become the data access technology for use with all programming languages and applications.

Q **If ADO uses ODBC to get to my database, why wouldn't I want to just go straight to the ODBC interface to access my database?**

A ADO can use ODBC to access those databases that don't have a native OLE DB interface. If you are using either Microsoft's SQL Server database or an Oracle database, there are OLE DB interfaces available, in which case ADO would not go through ODBC to get to the database. In these cases, using ADO gives your application better performance than using the ODBC interface. With the upcoming operating system releases from Microsoft, you'll find that using ADO is likely to provide you with access capabilities that extend far beyond conventional databases. ADO is a new technology that you'll start seeing in more use in the coming years. Because of its growing importance, it's a good thing to start working with ADO now so that you'll already be prepared to work with it when it's everywhere.

Workshop

The Workshop provides quiz questions to help you solidify your understanding of the material covered and exercises to provide you with experience in using what you've learned. The answers to the quiz questions and exercises are provided in Appendix B, "Answers."

Quiz

1. What does ADO stand for?
2. What does ADO use for database access?
3. What are the objects in ADO?
4. How do you initialize the COM environment?
5. How do you associate a `Connection` object with a `Command` object?
6. How do you associate a `Command` object with and populate a `Recordset` object?

Exercise

Enable and disable the navigation menus and toolbar buttons based on whether the recordset is at the beginning of file (BOF) or end of file (EOF, renamed to EndOfFile).

DAY 16

Creating Your Own Classes and Modules

Sometimes you need to build a set of application functionality that will be used in an application that another programmer is working on. Maybe the functionality will be used in a number of applications. Another possibility is that you want to separate some functionality from the rest of the application for organizational purposes. You might develop this separate set of functionality and then give a copy of the code to your friend to include in his application, but then every time you make any changes to your set of functionality, it has to be reincorporated into the other set of application code. It would be much more practical if you could give a compiled version of your functionality to the other programmer so that every time you updated your part, all you had to hand over was a new compiled file. The new file could just replace the previous version, without having to make any changes to the other programmer's code.

Well, it is possible to place your set of functionality into a self-contained compiled file, link it into another programmer's application, and avoid adding any new files to the finished application. Today, you will learn

- How to design your own classes.
- How to create compiled modules that can be linked into other applications.
- How to include these modules into an application.

Designing Classes

You've already designed and built your own classes over the past few days, so the basics of creating a new class is not a new topic. Why did you create these classes? Each of the new classes that you created encapsulated a set of functionality that acted as a self-contained unit. These units consisted of both data and functionality that worked together to define the object.

Encapsulation

Object-oriented software design is the practice of designing software in the same way that everything else in the world is designed. For instance, you can consider your car built from a collection of objects: the engine, the body, the suspension, and so on. Each of these objects consists of many other objects. For instance, the engine contains either the carburetor or the fuel injectors, the combustion chamber and pistons, the starter, the alternator, the drive chain, and so on. Once again, each of these objects consists of even more objects.

Each of these objects has a function that it performs. Each of these objects knows how to perform its own functions with little, if any, knowledge of how the other objects perform their functions. Each of the objects knows how it interacts with the other objects and how they are connected to the other objects, but that's about all they know about the other objects. How each of these objects work internally is hidden from the other objects. The brakes on your car don't know anything about how the transmission works, but if you've got an automatic transmission, the brakes do know how to tell the transmission that they are being applied; and the transmission decides how to react to this information.

You need to approach designing new classes for your applications in the same way. The rest of the application objects do not need to know how your objects work; they only need to know how to interact with your objects. This principle, called *encapsulation*, is one of the basic principles of object-oriented software.

Inheritance

Another key principle of object-oriented software design is the concept of *inheritance*. An object can be inherited from another object. The descendent object inherits all the existing functionality of the base object. This allows you to define the descendent object in terms of how it's different from the base object.

Let's look at how this could work with a thermostat. Suppose you had a basic thermostat that you could use in just about any setting. You could set the temperature for it to maintain, and it would turn on the heating or the air-conditioning as needed to maintain that temperature. Now let's say you needed to create a thermostat for use in a freezer. You could start from scratch and build a customized thermostat, or you could take your existing thermostat and specify how the freezer version differs from the original. These differences might include that it's limited to turning on the air conditioning and could never turn on the heater. You would probably also put a strict limit on the range of temperatures to which the thermostat could be set, such as around and below 32° Fahrenheit, or 0° Celsius. Likewise, if you needed a thermostat for an office building, you would probably want to limit the temperature range to what is normally comfortable for people and not allow the temperature to be set to an extremely cold or hot setting.

With inheritance in creating your own classes, this method just described represents the same principle that you want to apply. If possible, you should start with an existing C++ class that has the basic functionality that you need and then program how your class is different from the base class that you inherited from. You have the ability to add new data elements, extend existing functionality, or override existing functionality, as you see fit.

Visual C++ Class Types

In most application projects, when you are creating a new class, you have a few options on the type of class that you are creating. These options are

- Generic class
- MFC class
- Form class

Which of these types of classes you choose to create depends on your needs and what your class will be doing. It also depends on whether your class needs to descend from any of the MFC classes.

Generic Class

You use a generic class for creating a class that is inherited from a class you have already created. This class type is intended for creating classes that are not inherited from any MFC classes (although you have already seen where you need to use it to create classes that are based on MFC classes). If you want to create a more specialized version of the CLine class, for instance, a CRedLine class, that only drew in red, you create it as a generic class because it's inherited from another class that you created.

When you create a generic class, the New Class Wizard tries to locate the declaration of the base class (the header file with the class declared). If it cannot find the appropriate header file, it tells you that you might need to make sure that the header file with the base class definition is included in the project. If the base class happens to be an MFC class that is not accessible as an MFC class (such as CObject), then you can ignore this warning because the correct header file is already part of the project.

MFC Class

If you want to make a reusable class that is based on an existing MFC class, such as an edit box that automatically formats numbers as currency, you want to create an MFC class. The MFC class type is for creating new classes that are inherited from existing MFC classes.

Form Class

The form class is a specialized type of MFC class. You need to create this type of class if you are creating a new form style window. It can be a dialog, form view, or database view class. This new class will be associated with a document class for use with the view class. If you are building a database application, you will probably create a number of this style of classes.

Creating Library Modules

When you create new classes for your application, they might be usable in other applications as well. Often, with a little thought and effort, classes you create can be made flexible enough so that they could be used in other applications. When this is the case, you need some way of packaging the classes for other applications without having to hand over all your source code. This is the issue that library modules address. They allow you to compile your classes and modules into a compiled object code library that can be linked into any other Visual C++ application.

Library modules were one of the first means available to provide compiled code to other programmers for use in their applications. The code is combined with the rest of the application code by the linker as the final step in the compilation process. Library modules are still a viable means of sharing modules with other developers. All the developer needs is the library (.lib) file and the appropriate header files that show all the exposed classes, methods, functions, and variables, which the other programmer can access and use. The easiest way to do this is to provide the same header file that you used to create the library file, but you can also edit the header so that only the parts that other programmers need are included.

By using library files to share your modules with other programmers, you are arranging that your part of the application is included in the same executable file as the rest of the application. Your modules are not included in a separate file, such as a DLL or ActiveX control. This results in one less file to be distributed with the application. It also means that if you make any changes to the module, fix any bugs, or enhance any functionality, then the applications that use your module must be relinked. Using library files has a slight disadvantage to creating DLLs, where you may be able to just distribute the new DLL without having to make any changes to the application, but you'll learn all about that tomorrow.

Using Library Modules

To get a good idea of how to use library modules, it's helpful to create a library module, use it in another application, and then make some modifications to the library module. For today's sample application, you'll create a module that generates a random drawing on the window space specified. It'll be able to save and restore any of these drawings. You'll then use this module in an SDI application, where every time a new document is specified, a new drawing is generated. The initial module will only use eight colors and will generate only a limited number of line sequences. Later, you'll modify the module so that it will generate any number of colors and will generate a larger number of line sequences.

Creating the Library Module

To create a library module project, you need to specify in the New dialog that you want to create a Win32 Static Library, as shown in Figure 16.1. This tells Visual C++ that the output from the project compilation will be a library module instead of an executable application. From there, all you have to do is define the classes and add the code. You have the options of including support for MFC and using precompiled headers in your project, as in Figure 16.2, the only step in the Project Wizard.

The library that you will create for today's sample application will consist of two classes. The first class will be the CLine class that you first created on Day 10, "Creating Single Document Interface Applications." The second class will be the class that creates the random drawings on the drawing surface. This class will contain an object array of the CLine objects that it will create and populate with each of the drawing efforts. This second class will also need functionality to save and restore the drawing, as well as to delete the existing drawing so that a new drawing can be started. It will need to know the dimensions of the drawing area so that it can generate a drawing that will fit in the drawing area. Once you create this module, you'll take a look at how you can use this module in an application project.

FIGURE 16.1.

Specifying a library module project.

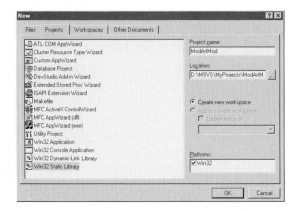

FIGURE 16.2.

Specifying project support options.

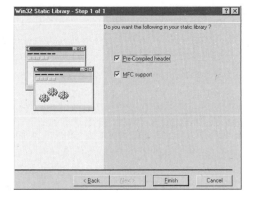

Creating a Library Project

To start the library project for today's example, you need to create a new project, specifying that the project is a Win32 Static Library project. Give the project a suitable name and click OK to create the project.

For today's sample project, specify on the one wizard step to include both MFC and precompiled header support. Although the precompiled header support is not necessary, it will speed up most compiles that you perform while building the module.

Once you create your module project, you'll find yourself working with a project that has no classes. You've got a blank slate from which you can create whatever type of module you need.

For your sample project, because you already have the CLine class built, copy it from the Day 10 project area into the project directory for today's project. Add both the header and source code file to today's project by choosing Project | Add To Project | Piles. Once you add both of these files to the project, you should see the CLine class appear in the Class View of your project.

Defining the Classes

Now that you've got a basic library module project ready to go, it's time to begin adding the meat of the module. Using the CLine class is an easy way of reusing some functionality that you created earlier in another setting. However, the real functionality of this module will be in its ability to generate random drawings, or squiggles. For this functionality, you'll need to create a new class.

To start this new class, add a new class to the project by selecting New Class from the pop-up menu in the Class View tab. The first thing that you'll notice in the New Class dialog is that you are limited to creating generic classes. Because you are creating a static library that will be linked into the application, Visual C++ is making some assumptions about the type of class that you want to create. Because this is not an MFC project, even though MFC support is included, you are prevented from creating a new MFC or form class. If you need to inherit a new class from an MFC class, you have to add it as if it were a generic class.

Use the New Class dialog to create your new class. Give the class a name that reflects its functionality, such as CModArt, and specify that it's derived from the CObject class as public. You'll receive the same warning that the base class header file cannot be found, but because you specified that MFC support should be included, you can ignore that message.

Once you create your class, you need to add a couple of variables to the class. First, you need somewhere to hold all the lines that will make up the drawing, so you'll add an object array. Second, you need to know the area of the drawing surface, so you'll want a CRect to hold the drawing area specification. You can add both of these variables to your new class using the types and names in Table 16.1.

TABLE 16.1. CModArt VARIABLES.

Type	Name	Access
static const COLORREF	m_crColors[8]	Public
CRect	m_rDrawArea	Private
CObArray	m_oaLines	Private

16

Setting the Drawing Area

Before you can draw anything, you need to know the area that you have to draw within. You can add a public function to your class that will copy the passed in CRect to the member CRect variable. To add this function to your project, add a new member function to your new class, specifying the type as void, the declaration as SetRect(CRect rDrawArea), and the access as public. Edit the function as in Listing 16.1.

LISTING **16.1.** THE CModArt SetRect FUNCTION.

```
1: void CModArt::SetRect(CRect rDrawArea)
2: {
3:     // Set the drawing area rectangle
4:     m_rDrawArea = rDrawArea;
5: }
```

Creating a New Drawing

One of the key pieces to this module is the ability to generate random squiggles that appear on the drawing area. By generating a whole series of these squiggles, your module will be able to create an entire drawing. Starting with the single squiggle, you can design a function that generates one squiggle and then calls this function a number of times to generate the entire drawing.

This first function, the squiggle generator, needs to determine how many lines will be in the squiggle. It needs to determine the color and width of the pen to be used when drawing the squiggle. It also needs to determine the starting point for the squiggle. From this point, it could loop through the appropriate number of lines, generating a new destination to continue the squiggle from the previous destination point.

To add this functionality to your project, add a new member function to the drawing class. Specify the function type as void, the definition as NewLine, and the access as private because this function will only be called by the master loop that is determining how many of these squiggles will be in the final drawing. Edit the new function with the code in Listing 16.2.

LISTING **16.2.** THE CModArt NewLine FUNCTION.

```
1:   void CModArt::NewLine()
2:   {
3:       int lNumLines;
4:       int lCurLine;
5:       int nCurColor;
6:       UINT nCurWidth;
```

```
 7:        CPoint pTo;
 8:        CPoint pFrom;
 9:
10:        // Normalize the rectangle before determining the width and height
11:        m_rDrawArea.NormalizeRect();
12:        // get the area width and height
13:        int lWidth = m_rDrawArea.Width();
14:        int lHeight = m_rDrawArea.Height();
15:
16:        // Determine the number of parts to this squiggle
17:        lNumLines = rand() % 100;
18:        // Are there any parts to this squiggle?
19:        if (lNumLines > 0)
20:        {
21:            // Determine the color
22:            nCurColor = rand() % 8;
23:            // Determine the pen width
24:            nCurWidth = (rand() % 8) + 1;
25:            // Determine the starting point for the squiggle
26:            pFrom.x = (rand() % lWidth) + m_rDrawArea.left;
27:            pFrom.y = (rand() % lHeight) + m_rDrawArea.top;
28:            // Loop through the number of segments
29:            for (lCurLine = 0; lCurLine < lNumLines; lCurLine++)
30:            {
31:                // Determine the end point of the segment
32:                pTo.x = ((rand() % 20) - 10) + pFrom.x;
33:                pTo.y = ((rand() % 20) - 10) + pFrom.y;
34:                // Create a new CLine object
35:                CLine *pLine = new CLine(pFrom, pTo, nCurWidth,
                        ➥m_crColors[nCurColor]);
36:                try
37:                {
38:                    // Add the new line to the object array
39:                    m_oaLines.Add(pLine);
40:                }
41:                // Did we run into a memory exception?
42:                catch (CMemoryException* perr)
43:                {
44:                    // Display a message for the user, giving him the
45:                    // bad news
46:                    AfxMessageBox("Out of memory", MB_ICONSTOP | MB_OK);
47:                    // Did we create a line object?
48:                    if (pLine)
49:                    {
50:                        // Delete it
51:                        delete pLine;
52:                        pLine = NULL;
53:                    }
54:                    // Delete the exception object
```

continues

16

LISTING 16.2. CONTINUED

```
55:                    perr->Delete();
56:            }
57:            // Set the starting point to the end point
58:            pFrom = pTo;
59:        }
60:    }
61: }
```

In this function, the first thing that you did was get the area that you had available for drawing with the following three lines:

```
m_rDrawArea.NormalizeRect();
int lWidth = m_rDrawArea.Width();
int lHeight = m_rDrawArea.Height();
```

In the first of these lines, you normalized the rectangle. This is necessary to guarantee that the width and height returned in the next two lines are both positive values. Because of the coordinate system used in Windows, getting the width by subtracting the left-side position from the right-side position can result in a negative number. The same can happen with the height. By normalizing the rectangle, you are guaranteeing that you'll get positive results for these two values.

Once you determined the drawing area, you determined the number of line segments you would use in this squiggle:

```
lNumLines = rand() % 100;
```

The rand function is capable of returning numbers in a wide range. By getting the modulus of 100, you are guaranteeing that the resulting number will be between 0 and 100. This is a common technique for generating random numbers within a certain range, using the modulus function with the upper limit of the value range (or the upper limit minus the lower limit, if the lower limit is not equal to 0, and then adding the lower limit to the resulting number). You use the same technique to determine the color, width, and starting position for the squiggle:

```
nCurColor = rand() % 8;
nCurWidth = (rand() % 8) + 1;
pFrom.x = (rand() % lWidth) + m_rDrawArea.left;
pFrom.y = (rand() % lHeight) + m_rDrawArea.top;
```

Notice how when you were determining the starting position, you added the left and top of the drawing area to the position that you generated. This guarantees that the starting position is within the drawing area. Once you enter the loop, generating all the line segments in the squiggle, you limit the available area for the next destination within 10 of the current position:

```
pTo.x = ((rand() % 20) - 10) + pFrom.x;
pTo.y = ((rand() % 20) - 10) + pFrom.y;
CLine *pLine = new CLine(pFrom, pTo, nCurWidth, m_crColors[nCurColor]);
m_oaLines.Add(pLine);
```

You can easily increase this distance to make the drawings more angular. Once you generate the next line segment, you create the line object and add it to the object array. Finally, you set the starting position to the ending position of the line segment you just generated:

```
pFrom = pTo;
```

Now you are ready to go through the loop again and generate the next line segment, until you have generated all line segments in this squiggle.

Now that you can generate a single squiggle, the rest of the process is easy. First, you determine how many squiggles will be in the drawing. Next, you loop for the number of squiggles that need to be generated and call the NewLine function once for each squiggle. To add this functionality to your project, add a new member function to the drawing class. Specify the type as void, the declaration as NewDrawing, and the access as public. Edit the function as in Listing 16.3.

LISTING 16.3. THE CModArt NewDrawing FUNCTION.

```
 1:  void CModArt::NewDrawing()
 2:  {
 3:      int lNumLines;
 4:      int lCurLine;
 5:
 6:      // Determine how many lines to create
 7:      lNumLines = rand() % 10;
 8:      // Are there any lines to create?
 9:      if (lNumLines > 0)
10:      {
11:          // Loop through the number of lines
12:          for (lCurLine = 0; lCurLine < lNumLines; lCurLine++)
13:          {
14:              // Create the new line
15:              NewLine();
16:          }
17:      }
18:  }
```

Displaying the Drawing

To draw the set of squiggles on the drawing area, you can add a function that will loop through the object array, calling the Draw function on each line segment in the array. This function needs to receive the device context as the only argument and must pass it along to each of the line segments. To add this function to your project, add a new member function to the drawing class. Specify the function type as void, the function declaration as Draw(CDC *pDC), and the access as public. Edit the function as in Listing 16.4.

LISTING 16.4. THE CModArt Draw FUNCTION.

```
1:  void CModArt::Draw(CDC *pDC)
2:  {
3:      // Get the number of lines in the object array
4:      int liCount = m_oaLines.GetSize();
5:      int liPos;
6:
7:      // Are there any objects in the array?
8:      if (liCount)
9:      {
10:         // Loop through the array, drawing each object
11:         for (liPos = 0; liPos < liCount; liPos++)
12:             ((CLine*)m_oaLines[liPos])->Draw(pDC);
13:     }
14: }
```

Serializing the Drawing

Because you are using the line segment class that you created earlier and have already made serializable, you do not need to add the serialization macros to the drawing class. What you do need to add is a Serialize function that passes the archive object on to the object array, letting the object array and line segment objects do all the serialization work. To add this function to your project, add a new member function to the drawing class. Specify the function type as void, the declaration as Serialize(CArchive &ar), and the access as public. Edit the function as in Listing 16.5.

LISTING 16.5. THE CModArt Serialize FUNCTION.

```
1:  void CModArt::Serialize(CArchive &ar)
2:  {
3:      // Pass the archive object on to the array
4:      m_oaLines.Serialize(ar);
5:  }
```

Clearing the Drawing

To provide full functionality, you need to be able to delete a drawing from the drawing class so that a new drawing can be created or an existing drawing can be loaded. This is a simple matter of looping through the object array and destroying every line segment object and then resetting the object array. To add this functionality to your project, add a new member function to the drawing class. Specify the type as void, the declaration as ClearDrawing, and the access as public. Edit the function as in Listing 16.6.

LISTING 16.6. THE CModArt ClearDrawing FUNCTION.

```
1:  void CModArt::ClearDrawing()
2:  {
3:      // Get the number of lines in the object array
4:      int liCount = m_oaLines.GetSize();
5:      int liPos;
6:
7:      // Are there any objects in the array?
8:      if (liCount)
9:      {
10:         // Loop through the array, deleting each object
11:         for (liPos = 0; liPos < liCount; liPos++)
12:             delete m_oaLines[liPos];
13:         // Reset the array
14:         m_oaLines.RemoveAll();
15:     }
16: }
```

Completing the Class

Finally, to wrap up your drawing class, you need to initialize the random number generator. The random number generator function, rand, generates a statistically random number sequence based on a series of mathematical calculations. If the number generator starts with the same number each time, then the sequence of numbers is the same each time. To get the random number generator to produce a different sequence of numbers each time your application runs, you need to seed it with a value that is different each time. The typical way to do this is to feed the current system time into the srand function, which seeds the random number generator with a different time each time that the application runs. This seeding of the number generator must be done only once each time the application is run, so you can add this functionality by editing the drawing class constructor with the code in Listing 16.7.

LISTING 16.7. THE CModArt CONSTRUCTOR.

```
1: CModArt::CModArt()
2: {
3:     // Initialize the random number generator
4:     srand((unsigned)time(NULL));
5: }
```

To complete the class, you need to include all of the necessary header files for the functionality that you've added to this class. The random number generator needs the stdlib.h and time.h header files, and the object array needs the header file for the CLine class. You also need to populate the color table for use when generating squiggles. You can add all of these finishing touches by scrolling to the top of the source code file for the drawing class and adding lines 5, 6, 9, and 12 through 21 in Listing 16.8.

LISTING 16.8. THE CModArt INCLUDES AND COLOR TABLE.

```
1:  // ModArt.cpp: implementation of the CModArt class.
2:  //
3:  //////////////////////////////////////////////////////////////////////
4:
5:  #include <stdlib.h>
6:  #include <time.h>
7:
8:  #include "stdafx.h"
9:  #include "Line.h"
10: #include "ModArt.h"
11:
12: const COLORREF CModArt::m_crColors[8] = {
13:     RGB(   0,   0,   0),    // Black
14:     RGB(   0,   0, 255),    // Blue
15:     RGB(   0, 255,   0),    // Green
16:     RGB(   0, 255, 255),    // Cyan
17:     RGB( 255,   0,   0),    // Red
18:     RGB( 255,   0, 255),    // Magenta
19:     RGB( 255, 255,   0),    // Yellow
20:     RGB( 255, 255, 255)     // White
21: };
```

You have now completed your library module. Before you go any further, you need to compile your project. Once you compile your project, you cannot run anything because you need to create an application that uses your library module in order to run and test your code. To get ready for creating this test application, close the entire workspace so that you will start with a clean workspace for the test application.

Creating a Test Application

To be able to test your module, you need to create a test application that uses the module. This plain application can contain just enough functionality to thoroughly test the module. All you want to do at this point is test all the functionality in the module; you don't have to create a full-blown application.

When you create your test application, you need to include the header file for the drawing class in the relevant classes in your application. In a typical SDI or MDI application, this means including the header file in the document class at a minimum and probably the view and application class source files also. You also have to add the library file that your module created in the application project so that it will be linked into your application.

Creating the Test App Shell

Creating a test application shell is a simple matter of creating a standard SDI or MDI application shell. For the purposes of keeping the test application as simple as possible, it's probably advisable to use an SDI application. However, if you've got some functionality in your module that is intended for use in an MDI application, then that application style might be a better selection as your test application.

For the test application for the sample module you created, create a standard SDI application shell using the AppWizard. Give the project a name such as TestApp or some other suitable name. Specify a file extension on the advanced button on the fourth AppWizard step. Otherwise, just go ahead and use the default settings for everything else.

Once you create the application shell, you need to add the library module to the project. You can do this by selecting Project | Add To Project | Files. Once in the Insert Files dialog, specify the file types as library files, as shown in Figure 16.3. Navigate to the debug directory of the module project to find the library module that you created with the previous project. This typically requires moving up one directory level, finding the project directory for the module, and then navigating through it to the debug directory. (If you are building the release version of the module and application, you want to navigate down to the release directory of the module project.) You should be able to find the library file for the module you created, as shown in Figure 16.4. Select this module and click OK to add it to the project.

FIGURE 16.3.

Specifying library files.

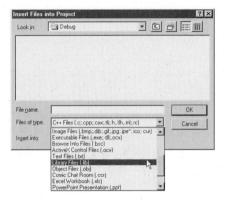

FIGURE 16.4.

Adding a library file to the project.

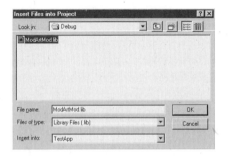

Once you add the library file to the project, you also need to add the header files for any of the classes in the module that will be used into the appropriate application source code files. For the test application that you are building, this entails adding line 7 in Listing 16.9. You want to add the same line in the include sections of the source code files for the view and application classes as well.

LISTING 16.9. THE CTestAppDoc INCLUDES.

```
1: // TestAppDoc.cpp : implementation of the CTestAppDoc class
2: //
3:
4: #include "stdafx.h"
5: #include "TestApp.h"
6:
7: #include "..\ModArtMod\ModArt.h"
8: #include "TestAppDoc.h"
```

The last thing that you need to do in preparing the application shell is add a variable for any classes from the library module that need to be included in any of the application classes. In the case of the test application that you are building, this is a variable in the document class of the drawing class that you created in the library module project. To add this variable to your application, add a new member variable to the document class. Specify the variable type as the drawing class from the library module (in this instance, CModArt) and specify the name as m_maDrawing and the access as private.

Creating a New Drawing

The first place where you want to put some of the functionality of your module is when you are creating a new document. This is the time to be generating a new drawing. As a result, you want to do two things. First, get the drawing area of the view class, passing it along to the drawing object. Second, tell the drawing object to generate a new drawing. This is all fairly straightforward. To add this functionality to your application, edit the OnNewDocument function in the document class, adding the lines 9–23 in Listing 16.10.

LISTING 16.10. THE CTestAppDoc OnNewDocument FUNCTION.

```
1:  BOOL CTestAppDoc::OnNewDocument()
2:  {
3:      if (!CDocument::OnNewDocument())
4:          return FALSE;
5:
6:      // TODO: add reinitialization code here
7:      // (SDI documents will reuse this document)
8:
9:      // Get the position of the view
10:     POSITION pos = GetFirstViewPosition();
11:     // Did we get a valid position?
12:     if (pos != NULL)
13:     {
14:         // Get a pointer to the view
15:         CView* pView = GetNextView(pos);
16:         RECT lWndRect;
17:         // Get the display area rectangle
18:         pView->GetClientRect(&lWndRect);
19:         // Set the drawing area
20:         m_maDrawing.SetRect(lWndRect);
21:         // Create a new drawing
22:         m_maDrawing.NewDrawing();
23:     }
24:
25:     return TRUE;
26: }
```

16

Saving and Deleting a Drawing

The other functionality that you want to add to the document class is to save and restore the drawing and to delete the current drawing. These tasks are the last of the document-related functionality of your library module.

To add the functionality to save and restore drawings to your application, edit the Serialize function in the document class. Delete all the current contents of the function, replacing it with a call to the drawing object's Serialize function, as in Listing 16.11.

LISTING **16.11**. THE CTestAppDoc Serialize FUNCTION.

```
1: void CTestAppDoc::Serialize(CArchive& ar)
2: {
3:      // Serialize the drawing
4:      m_maDrawing.Serialize(ar);
5: }
```

To add the functionality to delete the current drawing so that a new drawing can be generated or a saved drawing can be loaded, you need to add the event handler for the DeleteContents function to the document class. In this function, you call the drawing object's ClearDrawing function. To add this functionality to your application, use the Class Wizard to add the event handler for the DeleteContents event to the document class. Edit this function, adding line 5 in Listing 16.12.

LISTING **16.12**. THE CTestAppDoc DeleteContents FUNCTION.

```
1: void CTestAppDoc::DeleteContents()
2: {
3:      // TODO: Add your specialized code here and/or call the base class
4:      // Delete the drawing
5:      m_maDrawing.ClearDrawing();
6:
7:      CDocument::DeleteContents();
8: }
```

Viewing a Drawing

You need to add one final set of functionality to your test application before you can test your library module: the drawing functionality to the application. This functionality belongs in the view class because it is the object that knows when it needs to redraw itself. Before you can add this functionality to the view class, you need some way for the view class to get access to the drawing object. The easiest way to add this capability is to add another function to the document class that can be called to get a pointer to the drawing object. Once the view has this pointer, it can call the drawing object's own Draw function.

To add the capability to get a pointer to the drawing object to your document class, add a new member function to the document class. Specify the function type as a pointer to the drawing object, in this case, CModArt*, and specify the function declaration as GetDrawing and the access as public. Edit the function, adding the code in Listing 16.13.

LISTING 16.13. THE CTestAppDoc GetDrawing FUNCTION.

```
1: CModArt* CTestAppDoc::GetDrawing()
2: {
3:     // Return the drawing object
4:     return &m_maDrawing;
5: }
```

Adding the drawing functionality to the view class is a simple matter of editing the OnDraw function in the view class. In this function, you need to get a pointer to the drawing object and then call its Draw function, as in Listing 16.14.

LISTING 16.14. THE CTestAppView OnDraw FUNCTION.

```
1:  void CTestAppView::OnDraw(CDC* pDC)
2:  {
3:      CModTestAppDoc* pDoc = GetDocument();
4:      ASSERT_VALID(pDoc);
5:
6:      // TODO: add draw code for native data here
7:
8:      // Get the drawing object
9:      CModArt* m_maDrawing = pDoc->GetDrawing();
10:     // Draw the drawing
11:     m_maDrawing->Draw(pDC);
12: }
```

Once you add all this functionality, you can compile and run your application to test the functionality of your library module. Each time you select File | New from your application menu, a new drawing is created, as in Figure 16.5.

FIGURE 16.5.

Creating random squiggle drawings.

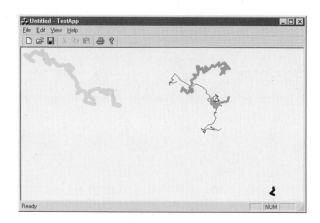

Updating the Library Module

Now that you have a working application, let's go back to the library module and make some changes. Whenever you make any changes to the library module code, no matter how minor, you need to relink all applications that use the module in order to get the updates into those applications. This is because the library module is linked into the EXE of the application. It does not remain in a separate file.

To see how this works, reopen the library module project. You will make three changes to this module. First, you'll increase the number of squiggles that may be included in a single drawing. Second, you'll increase the number of line segments that may make up a single squiggle. Third, you'll generate random colors, beyond just the eight colors included in the color table. Once you make these changes, you'll recompile your library module. Once you generate a new module, you'll relink your test application so that you can incorporate these changes into the application.

To make the first change in your module, increasing the number of squiggles that can be in a drawing, edit the NewDrawing function in the drawing class, increasing the modulus value in line 7 of the function, as in Listing 16.15. This will increase the number of possible squiggles in a single drawing from a maximum of 10 to a maximum of 50. There may still be an occasional drawing that doesn't have any squiggles, but you can ignore this possibility for now.

LISTING 16.15. THE MODIFIED CModArt NewDrawing FUNCTION.

```
1:   void CModArt::NewDrawing()
2:   {
3:       int lNumLines;
4:       int lCurLine;
```

```
 5:
 6:        // Determine how many lines to create
 7:        lNumLines = rand() % 50;
 8:        // Are there any lines to create?
 9:        if (lNumLines > 0)
10:        {
11:            // Loop through the number of lines
12:            for (lCurLine = 0; lCurLine < lNumLines; lCurLine++)
13:            {
14:                // Create the new line
15:                NewLine();
16:            }
17:        }
18: }
```

With the increased number of squiggles that can be included in a drawing, next you want to increase the number of line segments that may be in a squiggle. To do this, edit the NewLine function and increase the modulus number on line 20 in Listing 16.16 from 100 to 200. While you're in this function, you can also increase the number of colors that may be generated for use in each drawing. First, add three integer variable declarations, one for each of the three additive colors (red, green, and blue, as in lines 9 through 11 in Listing 16.16). Next, generate random values for each of these integers between the values of 0 and 255 (lines 26 through 28). Finally, when creating the CLine object, pass these colors through the RGB function to create the actual color that will be used in the drawing, as in line 41 of Listing 16.16.

LISTING 16.16. THE MODIFIED CModArt NewLine FUNCTION.

```
 1:  void CModArt::NewLine()
 2:  {
 3:        int lNumLines;
 4:        int lCurLine;
 5:  //    int nCurColor;
 6:        UINT nCurWidth;
 7:        CPoint pTo;
 8:        CPoint pFrom;
 9:        int cRed;
10:        int cBlue;
11:        int cGreen;
12:
13:        // Normalize the rectangle before determining the width and height
14:        m_rDrawArea.NormalizeRect();
15:        // get the area width and height
16:        int lWidth = m_rDrawArea.Width();
```

continues

LISTING 16.16. CONTINUED

```
17:      int lHeight = m_rDrawArea.Height();
18:
19:      // Determine the number of parts to this squiggle
20:      lNumLines = rand() % 200;
21:      // Are there any parts to this squiggle?
22:      if (lNumLines > 0)
23:      {
24:          // Determine the color
25: //       nCurColor = rand() % 8;
26:          cRed = rand() % 256;
27:          cBlue = rand() % 256;
28:          cGreen = rand() % 256;
29:          // Determine the pen width
30:          nCurWidth = (rand() % 8) + 1;
31:          // Determine the starting point for the squiggle
32:          pFrom.x = (rand() % lWidth) + m_rDrawArea.left;
33:          pFrom.y = (rand() % lHeight) + m_rDrawArea.top;
34:          // Loop through the number of segments
35:          for (lCurLine = 0; lCurLine < lNumLines; lCurLine++)
36:          {
37:              // Determine the end point of the segment
38:              pTo.x = ((rand() % 20) - 10) + pFrom.x;
39:              pTo.y = ((rand() % 20) - 10) + pFrom.y;
40:              // Create a new CLine object
41:              CLine *pLine = new CLine(pFrom, pTo, nCurWidth,
                        ➥RGB(cRed, cGreen, cBlue));
42:              try
43:              {
44:                  // Add the new line to the object array
45:                  m_oaLines.Add(pLine);
46:              }
47:              // Did we run into a memory exception?
48:              catch (CMemoryException* perr)
49:              {
50:                  // Display a message for the user, giving him the
51:                  // bad news
52:                  AfxMessageBox("Out of memory", MB_ICONSTOP ¦ MB_OK);
53:                  // Did we create a line object?
54:                  if (pLine)
55:                  {
56:                      // Delete it
57:                      delete pLine;
58:                      pLine = NULL;
59:                  }
60:                  // Delete the exception object
61:                  perr->Delete();
62:              }
63:              // Set the starting point to the end point
```

```
64:                    pFrom = pTo;
65:               }
66:          }
67: }
```

Now that you've made all the necessary changes to the library module, compile it so that it's ready for use in the test application. If you run your test application from the Start | Run Taskbar option, as in Figure 16.6, you'll notice that there is no noticeable difference in how your application behaves. This is because the application hasn't changed. The application is still using the old version of your library module. To get the test application to use the new version of the library module, reopen the test application project in Visual C++. Build the project, which should not do anything other than relink the project, and then run the application. You should see a significant difference in the drawings that your application is now generating, as shown in Figure 16.7.

FIGURE 16.6.

Run the test application from the Start menu.

FIGURE 16.7.

The updated test application.

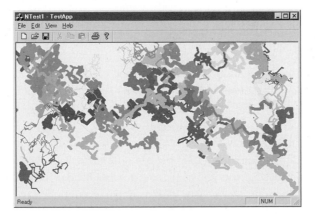

Summary

Today you learned about how to approach creating and designing new classes for your applications. You learned the differences between the different types of classes that are available to you through the New Class Wizard in Visual C++. You also learned how you can create a library module with a set of your functionality that you can hand to other programmers for including in their applications. You learned how this module will be linked into the actual applications, thus not requiring a separate file to be distributed along with the applications.

Tomorrow you will learn about a different approach to creating reusable packaged functionality that you can give to other programmers. You will learn how to create DLLs using Visual C++, what the differences are between creating library modules and DLL, and how you need to approach each task.

Q&A

Q Isn't most functionality packaged in DLLs now? Why would I want to create library modules instead of DLLs?

A Yes, the trend toward packaging functionality modules has been to create DLLs instead of library modules for a number of years now. However, there are still instances where library modules are preferable. If you are creating a module that contains proprietary functionality that you do not want to risk exposing to others, but that is needed for any applications that you or another programmer in your company is building, then you would probably want all that functionality packaged in a library module so that it is internal to the application. Using library modules makes it effectively inaccessible to your competition without significant disassembly and reverse engineering efforts.

Q Why does the header file need to be included in the application that is using my library file?

A The application needs to know about the objects that are in the library file. In the sample application, you didn't need to include the header file for the CLine class because the application didn't directly use or reference the CLine class. However, the application did use the drawing object that was in your library module, so it did need to know about that object, how it is defined, and what functions are available for it. If you don't want the other programmers to know all of the internal structure of your classes, then you can create another header file to be distributed with your library module. This header would contain definitions of all of the same classes that are in the library module but would only provide the public functions and variables that the other programmers can actually access.

Workshop

The Workshop provides quiz questions to help you solidify your understanding of the material covered and exercises to provide you with experience in using what you've learned. The answers to the quiz questions and exercises are provided in Appendix B, "Answers."

Quiz

1. When do you want to create a new MFC class?
2. When you make changes to a library file, what do you have to do to the applications that use the library file?
3. What are the different types of classes that you can create?
4. When you package some functionality in a library file, what do you need to give to other programmers who want to use your library module?
5. What are two of the basic principles in object-oriented software design?

Exercise

Separate the CLine class into a different library module from the drawing class so that you have two library modules instead of one. Link them into the test application.

DAY **17**

Sharing Your Functionality with Other Applications—Creating DLLs

Yesterday you learned how you could create a set of functionality that might be useful for multiple applications and how you could package it in a library file that could be linked into those applications. Today you will learn how to do this same thing, only with a much more dynamic package.

Often, a family of applications will have some functionality in common. When you place this shared functionality into DLLs instead of library modules, all the applications can use the same functionality with only a single copy of the functionality distributed in the form of DLLs, instead of duplicating the same functionality in each of the applications. This method saves disk space on any systems where the applications are installed.

Today, you will learn

- About the different types of DLLs that you can create with Visual C++ and how to determine which type best suits your needs.
- How to build two of these types of DLLs and the different approaches for the various DLL types.
- How to use the functionality for both of these types of DLLs in a Visual C++ application.
- How to determine when an application needs to be relinked when you make modifications to a DLL that is used by the application.

Why Create DLLs?

Dynamic link libraries (DLL) were introduced by Microsoft back in the early days of Windows. DLLs are similar to library modules in that they both contain sets of functionality that have been packaged for use by applications. The difference is when the applications link to the library. With a library module (LIB), the application is linked to the functionality in the library during the compile and build process. The functionality contained in the library file becomes part of the application executable file. With a DLL, the application links to the functionality in the library file when the application is run. The library file remains a separate file that is referenced and called by the application.

There are several reasons for creating DLLs instead of library module files. First, you can reduce the size of the application executable files by placing functionality that is used by multiple applications into DLLs that are shared by all of the applications. You can update and modify functionality in the DLLs without having to update the application executable (assuming that the exported interface for the DLL doesn't change). Finally, you can use DLLs with just about any other Windows programming language, which makes your functionality available to a wider number of programmers, not just fellow Visual C++ programmers.

Creating and Using DLLs

DLLs are library files with compiled code that can be used by other applications. The DLLs expose certain functions and classes to these applications by exporting the function. When a function is exported, it is added to a table that is included in the DLL. This table lists the location of all exported functions contained in the DLL, and it is used to locate and call each of these functions. Any functions that are not exported are not added to this table, and they cannot be seen or called by any outside application or DLL.

An application can call the functions in the DLL in two ways. The more involved method of calling these functions is to look up the location of the desired function in the DLL and get a pointer to this function. The pointer can then be used to call the function.

The other, much easier way (and the only way that you'll use in any of the examples in this book) is to link the application with the LIB file that is created with the DLL. This LIB file is treated by the linker as a standard library file, just like the one that you created yesterday. However, this LIB file contains stubs for each of the exported functions in the DLL. A stub is a pseudo-function that has the same name and argument list as the real function. In the interior of the function stub is a small amount of code that calls the real function in the DLL, passing all of the arguments that were passed to the stub. This allows you to treat the functions in the DLL as if they were part of the application code and not as a separate file.

17

Note

The LIB file for a DLL is automatically created for the DLL during the compiling of the DLL. There is nothing extra that you need to do to create it.

Tip

Not only is it easier to create your applications using the LIB files for any DLLs that you will be using, but also it can be safer when running the application. When you use the LIB files, any DLLs that are used by your application are loaded into memory the moment the application is started. If any of the DLLs are missing, the user is automatically informed of the problem by Windows, and your application does not run. If you don't use the LIB files, then you are responsible for loading the DLL into memory and handling any errors that occur if the DLL cannot be found.

There are two types of DLLs that you can easily create using Visual C++. These two types are MFC extension DLLs and regular DLLs.

Note

You can create other types of DLLs using Visual C++. All these other types of DLLs involve a significant amount of ActiveX functionality, so they are beyond the scope of this book. If you need to build ActiveX in-process server DLLs, or other types of ActiveX DLLs, I recommend that you find an advanced book on Visual C++ that provides significant coverage for these topics.

MFC Extension DLLs

MFC DLLs are the easiest to code and create because you can treat them just like any other collection of classes. For any classes that you want to export from the DLL, the only thing that you need to add is the AFX_EXT_CLASS macro in the class declaration, as follows:

```
class AFX_EXT_CLASS CMyClass
{
.
.
.
};
```

This macro exports the class, making it accessible to Visual C++ applications. You need to include this macro in the header file that is used by the applications that will use the DLL, where it will import the class from the DLL so that it can be used.

The one drawback to creating MFC extension DLLs is that they cannot be used by any other programming languages. They can be used with other C++ compilers as long as the compiler supports MFC (such as with Borland's and Symantec's C++ compilers).

Regular DLLs

The other type of DLL is a regular DLL. This type of DLL exports standard functions from the DLL, not C++ classes. As a result, this type of DLL can require a little more thought and planning than an MFC extension DLL. Once inside the DLL, you can use classes all you want, but you must provide straight function calls to the external applications.

To export a function, declare it as an export function by preceding the function name with

```
extern "C" <function type> PASCAL EXPORT <function declaration>
```

Include all this additional stuff in both the header file function prototype and the actual source code. The extern "C" portion declares that this is a standard C function call so that the C++ name mangler does not mangle the function name. PASCAL tells the compiler that all function arguments are to be passed in PASCAL order, which places the arguments on the stack in the reverse order from how they are normally placed. Finally, EXPORT tells the compiler that this function is to be exported from the DLL and can be called outside the DLL.

The other thing that you need to do to export the functions from your DLL is to add all the exported function names to the DEF file for the DLL project. This file is used to build the stub LIB file and the export table in the DLL. It contains the name of the DLL, or library, a brief description of the DLL, and the names of all functions that are to be exported. This file has to follow a specific format, so you should not modify the default DEF file that is automatically created by the DLL Wizard other than to add exported function names. A typical DEF file follows:

```
LIBRARY     "mydll"
DESCRIPTION 'mydll Windows Dynamic Link Library'

EXPORTS
    ; Explicit exports can go here
    MyFunc1
    MyFunc2
```

If you are using MFC classes in your regular DLLs, you need to call the AFX_MANAGE_STATE macro as the first line of code in all exported functions. This is necessary to make the exported functions threadsafe, which allows your class functions to be called simultaneously by two or more programs (or threads). The AFX_MANAGE_STATE macro takes a single argument, a pointer to a AFX_MODULE_STATE structure, which can be retrieved by calling the AfxGetStaticModuleState function. A typical exported function that uses MFC looks like the following:

```
extern "C" void PASCAL EXPORT MyFunc(...)
{
    AFX_MANAGE_STATE(AfxGetStaticModuleState());
    // normal function body here
    .
    .
    .
}
```

Designing DLLs

When you are designing your DLLs, you should be aware that any of the functions in your DLLs can be called simultaneously by multiple applications all running at the same time. As a result, all the functionality in any DLLs that you create must be threadsafe.

All variables that hold any values beyond each individual function call must be held and maintained by the application and not the DLL. Any application variables that must be manipulated by the DLL must be passed in to the DLL as one of the function arguments. Any global variables that are manipulated within the DLL may be swapped with variables from other application processes while the function is running, leading to unpredictable results.

Creating and Using an MFC Extension DLL

To see how easy it is to create and use an MFC extension DLL, you'll convert the library module that you created yesterday into an MFC extension DLL today. After you see how easy it is, and what types of changes you have to make to use the DLL, you'll then reimplement the same functionality as a regular DLL so that you can get an understanding of the different approaches that are necessary with the two DLL styles.

Creating the MFC Extension DLL

To convert the library module you created yesterday into an MFC extension DLL, you need to create a new MFC DLL Wizard project, specifying that the project is an MFC extension DLL. Copy the source code and header files for the line and drawing classes into the project directory. Load the files for the line and drawing classes into the current project. Add the AFX_EXT_CLASS macro to the drawing class. Finally, move the color table from a global static table to a local variable inside the function that creates the squiggles.

To create this DLL, start a new project. Give the project a suitable name, such as ModArtDll, and specify that the project is an MFC AppWizard (DLL) project, as in Figure 17.1. Once in the DLL Wizard, specify that the DLL is an MFC Extension DLL, as in Figure 17.2.

FIGURE 17.1.

Selecting the MFC DLL Wizard.

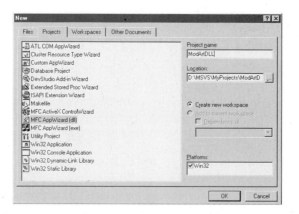

Once you create the DLL shell, open the file explorer and copy the source code and header files for the line and drawing classes (line.cpp, line.h, ModArt.cpp, and ModArt.h) from the library module project you created yesterday into the project directory that you just created. Add all four of these files to the project. Both classes should appear in the Class View of the workspace pane.

Figure 17.2.

Specifying the DLL type.

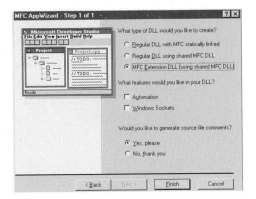

Open the header file containing the definition of the drawing class. Add the AFX_EXT_CLASS macro to the class declaration as shown in Listing 17.1. Remove the color table variable from the class declaration also.

Listing 17.1. The modified CModArt class declaration.

```
1:  class AFX_EXT_CLASS CModArt : public CObject
2:  {
3:  public:
4:      void NewDrawing();
5:      virtual void Serialize(CArchive &ar);
6:      void Draw(CDC *pDC);
7:      void ClearDrawing();
8:      void SetRect(CRect rDrawArea);
9:      CModArt();
10:     virtual ~CModArt();
11:
12: private:
13:     void NewLine();
14:     CRect m_rDrawArea;
15:     CObArray m_oaLines;
16: };
```

You cannot have public static tables in DLLs, so you cannot declare the color table as a public, static member of the drawing class, as it was yesterday. As a result, you'll move it to a local variable in the NewLine member function. Edit the NewLine function to add this local variable and to reset the function to behave as it did in its initial incarnation, as in Listing 17.2.

17

LISTING 17.2. THE CModArt NewLine FUNCTION.

```
1:   void CModArt::NewLine()
2:   {
3:       int lNumLines;
4:       int lCurLine;
5:       int nCurColor;
6:       UINT nCurWidth;
7:       CPoint pTo;
8:       CPoint pFrom;
9:
10:      // Normalize the rectangle before determining the width and height
11:      m_rDrawArea.NormalizeRect();
12:      // get the area width and height
13:      int lWidth = m_rDrawArea.Width();
14:      int lHeight = m_rDrawArea.Height();
15:
16:      COLORREF crColors[8] = {
17:      RGB(   0,   0,   0),    // Black
18:      RGB(   0,   0, 255),    // Blue
19:      RGB(   0, 255,   0),    // Green
20:      RGB(   0, 255, 255),    // Cyan
21:      RGB( 255,   0,   0),    // Red
22:      RGB( 255,   0, 255),    // Magenta
23:      RGB( 255, 255,   0),    // Yellow
24:      RGB( 255, 255, 255)     // White
25:      };
26:
27:      // Determine the number of parts to this squiggle
28:      lNumLines = rand() % 100;
29:      // Are there any parts to this squiggle?
30:      if (lNumLines > 0)
31:      {
32:          // Determine the color
33:          nCurColor = rand() % 8;
34:          // Determine the pen width
35:          nCurWidth = (rand() % 8) + 1;
36:          // Determine the starting point for the squiggle
37:          pFrom.x = (rand() % lWidth) + m_rDrawArea.left;
38:          pFrom.y = (rand() % lHeight) + m_rDrawArea.top;
39:          // Loop through the number of segments
40:          for (lCurLine = 0; lCurLine < lNumLines; lCurLine++)
41:          {
42:              // Determine the end point of the segment
43:              pTo.x = ((rand() % 20) - 10) + pFrom.x;
44:              pTo.y = ((rand() % 20) - 10) + pFrom.y;
45:              // Create a new CLine object
46:              CLine *pLine = new CLine(pFrom, pTo, nCurWidth,
                          ➥crColors[nCurColor]);
47:              try
```

```
48:                 {
49: // Add the new line to the object array
50:                 m_oaLines.Add(pLine);
51:             }
52:             // Did we run into a memory exception?
53:             catch (CMemoryException* perr)
54:             {
55:                 // Display a message for the user, giving him the
56:                 // bad news
57:                 AfxMessageBox("Out of memory", MB_ICONSTOP ¦ MB_OK);
58:                 // Did we create a line object?
59:                 if (pLine)
60:                 {
61:                     // Delete it
62:                     delete pLine;
63:                     pLine = NULL;
64:                 }
65:                 // Delete the exception object
66:                 perr->Delete();
67:             }
68:             // Set the starting point to the end point
69:             pFrom = pTo;
70:         }
71:     }
72: }
```

After making these changes to the drawing class, you are ready to compile your DLL. Once you compile the DLL, switch over to the file explorer, find the DLL in the debug subdirectory under the project directory, and copy the DLL to the debug directory in the test application project directory.

Adapting the Test Application

To adapt the test application to use the DLL, open the test application project that you created yesterday. You are going to delete the library module that you created yesterday and add the LIB file that was created with the DLL. You are also going to change the header file that is included for the drawing class. After making these two changes, your test application will be ready to use with the DLL.

To delete the library module from the project, open the File View in the workspace pane. Select the LIB file from the list of project files and press the Delete key. Once you delete the library file from the project, select Project | Add To Project | Files from the main menu. Specify the Library Files (.lib) file type, and then navigate to the debug directory of the DLL project. Select the LIB file that was created with your DLL, in this case, ModArtDll.lib. Click OK to add the file to the project.

Once you add the DLL's LIB file, edit the source-code files for the document, view, and application classes, changing the include of the drawing class to point to the project directory of the DLL, as in line 7 in Listing 17.3.

LISTING 17.3. THE CTestAppDoc INCLUDES.

```
1: // TestAppDoc.cpp : implementation of the CTestAppDoc class
2: //
3:
4: #include "stdafx.h"
5: #include "TestApp.h"
6:
7: #include "..\ModArtDll\ModArt.h"
8: #include "TestAppDoc.h"
```

After making this change to all three source-code files, you are ready to compile and run your test application. You should find your test application running just like it did yesterday, only generating shorter squiggles and using only the eight colors in the color table.

Changing the DLL

Now that you have the test application running with the DLL, you'll make the same changes to the DLL that you made to the library module yesterday. You'll increase the number of squiggles that can be included in a drawing, increase the possible length of each squiggle, and generate any number of colors for use in the squiggles.

To make these changes, switch back to the DLL project. Increase the number of lines that may be generated in the NewDrawing member function of the drawing class. Increase the possible length of the squiggles in the NewLine member function, and add the random colors back in, as in Listing 17.4.

LISTING 17.4. THE MODIFIED CModArt NewLine FUNCTION.

```
1:   void CModArt::NewLine()
2:   {
3:       int lNumLines;
4:       int lCurLine;
5:  //   int nCurColor;
6:       UINT nCurWidth;
7:       CPoint pTo;
8:       CPoint pFrom;
9:       int cRed;
10:      int cBlue;
11:      int cGreen;
12:
```

```
13:       // Normalize the rectangle before determining the width and height
14:       m_rDrawArea.NormalizeRect();
15:       // get the area width and height
16:       int lWidth = m_rDrawArea.Width();
17:       int lHeight = m_rDrawArea.Height();
18:
19: //    COLORREF crColors[8] = {
20: //    RGB(   0,   0,   0),    // Black
21: //    RGB(   0,   0, 255),    // Blue
22: //    RGB(   0, 255,   0),    // Green
23: //    RGB(   0, 255, 255),    // Cyan
24: //    RGB( 255,   0,   0),    // Red
25: //    RGB( 255,   0, 255),    // Magenta
26: //    RGB( 255, 255,   0),    // Yellow
27: //    RGB( 255, 255, 255)     // White
28: //    };
29:
30:       // Determine the number of parts to this squiggle
31:       lNumLines = rand() % 200;
32:       // Are there any parts to this squiggle?
33:       if (lNumLines > 0)
34:       {
35:           // Determine the color
36: //        nCurColor = rand() % 8;
37:           cRed = rand() % 256;
38:           cBlue = rand() % 256;
39:           cGreen = rand() % 256;
40:           // Determine the pen width
41:           nCurWidth = (rand() % 8) + 1;
42:           // Determine the starting point for the squiggle
43:           pFrom.x = (rand() % lWidth) + m_rDrawArea.left;
44:           pFrom.y = (rand() % lHeight) + m_rDrawArea.top;
45:           // Loop through the number of segments
46:           for (lCurLine = 0; lCurLine < lNumLines; lCurLine++)
47:           {
48:               // Determine the end point of the segment
49:               pTo.x = ((rand() % 20) - 10) + pFrom.x;
50:               pTo.y = ((rand() % 20) - 10) + pFrom.y;
51:               // Create a new CLine object
52:               CLine *pLine = new CLine(pFrom, pTo, nCurWidth,
                        ➥RGB(cRed, cGreen, cBlue));
53:               try
54:               {
55:                   // Add the new line to the object array
56:                   m_oaLines.Add(pLine);
57:               }
58:               // Did we run into a memory exception?
59:               catch (CMemoryException* perr)
60:               {
```

continues

LISTING 17.4. CONTINUED

```
61:                     // Display a message for the user, giving him the
62:                     // bad news
63:                     AfxMessageBox("Out of memory", MB_ICONSTOP | MB_OK);
64:                     // Did we create a line object?
65:                     if (pLine)
66:                     {
67:                         // Delete it
68:                         delete pLine;
69:                         pLine = NULL;
70:                     }
71:                     // Delete the exception object
72:                     perr->Delete();
73:                 }
74:                 // Set the starting point to the end point
75:                 pFrom = pTo;
76:             }
77:         }
78: }
```

After making these changes, compile the DLL again. Once you compile the DLL, switch
to the file explorer and copy the DLL into the debug directory of the test application
again. Once you copy the DLL, run the test application from the Start | Run Taskbar, as in
Figure 17.3. You should find that the application has been updated, and it is now including more squiggles and using many different colors.

FIGURE 17.3.

*Starting the sample
application.*

Creating and Using a Regular DLL

You might think that you broke the rules about using variables that are not owned by the
application in a DLL when you created and used the MFC extension DLL. Well, you
didn't. The instance of the drawing class was a member of the document class in the test
application. It was created and maintained by the application, not the DLL. Now that you
are turning your attention to implementing the same functionality as a regular DLL, this
will become clearer.

To convert the MFC extension DLL into a regular DLL, you'll have to convert the drawing class into a series of regular function calls. In the course of making this conversion,

the object array must become a member variable of the application document class and must be passed as an argument to every exported function in the DLL.

Creating the Regular DLL

To convert the MFC extension DLL into a regular DLL, you have to start a new project. Visual C++ has to build a project that tells the compiler what type of file it's creating. You can create this new project using the same steps you used to create the MFC extension DLL project, but specify on the DLL Wizard that you are creating a regular DLL. (You can leave the wizard at the default settings.) Once you create the project, you can copy the line and drawing class source code and header files into the project directory and add these files to the project. Once you add these files to the project, you need to begin the process of converting the drawing class into a series of straight function calls.

Altering the Header File

To start with, you need to radically alter the header file for the drawing class so that it will work for a regular DLL. You have to eliminate every trace of the actual class from the header file, leaving only the function calls. All of these functions must be passed in any objects that they need to work with. (Every function will need to be passed the object array as one of its arguments.) Next, you need to slightly modify all the function names so that the compiler does not get mixed up and call a member function of any class by mistake (such as the Serialize function). Finally, each of the public functions must be declared as an exportable function. Making these changes to the header file, you end up replacing the entire class declaration with the function prototypes in Listing 17.5.

17

LISTING **17.5.** THE MODIFIED ModArt HEADER FILE.

```
1: extern "C" void PASCAL EXPORT ModArtNewDrawing(CRect pRect,
        ➥CObArray *poaLines);
2: extern "C" void PASCAL EXPORT ModArtSerialize(CArchive &ar,
        ➥CObArray *poaLines);
3: extern "C" void PASCAL EXPORT ModArtDraw(CDC *pDC, CObArray *poaLines);
4: extern "C" void PASCAL EXPORT ModArtClearDrawing(CObArray *poaLines);
5: void NewLine(CRect pRect, CObArray *poaLines);
```

Note   Notice that the object array is always passed as a pointer to each of these functions. Because these functions are adding and removing objects from the array, they need to work with the actual array and not a copy of it.

Adapting the Drawing Generation Functions

Moving to the source-code file, you need to make numerous small yet significant changes to these functions. Starting with the NewDrawing function, you need to pass in the CRect object to get the drawing area. You dropped the function for setting the drawing area because you have no local variables in which you can hold this object. As a result, you are better off passing it to the drawing generation functions. The other change is where you pass in the object array as another argument to the function. You aren't doing anything with either of these arguments in this function, just passing them along to the squiggle generating function. The other alteration in this function is the addition of the AFX_MANAGE_STATE macro as the first line in the body of the function. After making these changes, the NewDrawing function will look like the one in Listing 17.6.

LISTING **17.6.** THE ModArtNewDrawing FUNCTION.

```
 1:   extern "C" void PASCAL EXPORT ModArtNewDrawing(CRect pRect,
         ➥CObArray *poaLines)
 2:   {
 3:       AFX_MANAGE_STATE(AfxGetStaticModuleState());
 4:       // normal function body here
 5:       int lNumLines;
 6:       int lCurLine;
 7:
 8:       // Initialize the random number generator
 9:       srand((unsigned)time(NULL));
10:       // Determine how many lines to create
11:       lNumLines = rand() % 50;
12:       // Are there any lines to create?
13:       if (lNumLines > 0)
14:       {
15:           // Loop through the number of lines
16:           for (lCurLine = 0; lCurLine < lNumLines; lCurLine++)
17:           {
18:               // Create the new line
19:               NewLine(pRect, poaLines);
20:           }
21:       }
22:   }
```

Another change that is required in the NewDrawing function is the addition of the random number generator seeding on line 9. Because there is no class constructor any more, you cannot seed the random number generator in it. Therefore, the next logical place to add this is in the NewDrawing function before any random numbers are generated.

On the NewLine function, the changes are more extensive. First, the CRect object and the object array are passed in as arguments. Second, because this is not an exported function, you do not need to add the AFX_MANAGE_STATE macro. Third, all the places where the CRect member variable is used must be changed to use the CRect that is passed as an argument to the function. Finally, when adding objects to the object array, you need to change this to use the object array pointer that was passed as an argument. Making these changes leaves you with the code in Listing 17.7.

LISTING 17.7. THE NewLine FUNCTION.

```
 1:    void NewLine(CRect pRect, CObArray *poaLines)
 2:    {
 3:          int lNumLines;
 4:          int lCurLine;
 5:    //    int nCurColor;
 6:          UINT nCurWidth;
 7:          CPoint pTo;
 8:          CPoint pFrom;
 9:          int cRed;
10:        int cBlue;
11:        int cGreen;
12:
13:          // Normalize the rectangle before determining the width and
              ➡height
14:          pRect.NormalizeRect();
15:          // get the area width and height
16:          int lWidth = pRect.Width();
17:          int lHeight = pRect.Height();
18:
19:    //      COLORREF crColors[8] = {
20:    //      RGB(   0,   0,   0),      // Black
21:    //      RGB(   0,   0, 255),      // Blue
22:    //      RGB(   0, 255,   0),      // Green
23:    //      RGB(   0, 255, 255),      // Cyan
24:    //      RGB( 255,   0,   0),      // Red
25:    //      RGB( 255,   0, 255),      // Magenta
26:    //      RGB( 255, 255,   0),      // Yellow
27:    //      RGB( 255, 255, 255)      // White
28:    //      };
29:
30:          // Determine the number of parts to this squiggle
31:          lNumLines = rand() % 200;
32:          // Are there any parts to this squiggle?
33:          if (lNumLines > 0)
34:          {
35:              // Determine the color
```

17

continues

LISTING 17.7. CONTINUED

```
36:   //        nCurColor = rand() % 8;
37:             cRed = rand() % 256;
38:             cBlue = rand() % 256;
39:             cGreen = rand() % 256;
40:             // Determine the pen width
41:             nCurWidth = (rand() % 8) + 1;
42:             // Determine the starting point for the squiggle
43:             pFrom.x = (rand() % lWidth) + pRect.left;
44:             pFrom.y = (rand() % lHeight) + pRect.top;
45:             // Loop through the number of segments
46:             for (lCurLine = 0; lCurLine < lNumLines; lCurLine++)
47:             {
48:                 // Determine the end point of the segment
49:                 pTo.x = ((rand() % 20) - 10) + pFrom.x;
50:                 pTo.y = ((rand() % 20) - 10) + pFrom.y;
51:                 // Create a new CLine object
52:                 CLine *pLine = new CLine(pFrom, pTo, nCurWidth,
                        ➥RGB(cRed, cGreen, cBlue));
53:                 try
54:                 {
55:                     // Add the new line to the object array
56:                     poaLines->Add(pLine);
57:                 }
58:                 // Did we run into a memory exception?
59:                 catch (CMemoryException* perr)
60:                 {
61:                     // Display a message for the user, giving him the
62:                     // bad news
63:                     AfxMessageBox("Out of memory", MB_ICONSTOP ¦ MB_OK);
64:                     // Did we create a line object?
65:                     if (pLine)
66:                     {
67:                         // Delete it
68:                         delete pLine;
69:                         pLine = NULL;
70:                     }
71:                     // Delete the exception object
72:                     perr->Delete();
73:                 }
74:                 // Set the starting point to the end point
75:                 pFrom = pTo;
76:             }
77:         }
78:  }
```

Adapting the Other Functions

Making the necessary changes to the other functions is less involved than the changes to
the drawing generation functions. With the rest of the functions, you must add a pointer

to the object array as a function argument and then alter the uses of the array to use the pointer instead of the no longer existing member variable. You also need to add the `AFX_MANAGE_STATE` macro as the first line in each of the remaining functions. This leaves you with the functions shown in Listings 17.8, 17.9, and 17.10.

LISTING 17.8. THE `ModArtDraw` FUNCTION.

```
 1:  extern "C" void PASCAL EXPORT ModArtDraw(CDC *pDC, CObArray *poaLines)
 2:  {
 3:      AFX_MANAGE_STATE(AfxGetStaticModuleState());
 4:      // normal function body here
 5:      // Get the number of lines in the object array
 6:      int liCount = poaLines->GetSize();
 7:      int liPos;
 8:
 9:      // Are there any objects in the array?
10:      if (liCount)
11:      {
12:          // Loop through the array, drawing each object
13:          for (liPos = 0; liPos < liCount; liPos++)
14:              ((CLine*)poaLines->GetAt(liPos))->Draw(pDC);
15:      }
16:  }
```

LISTING 17.9. THE `ModArtSerialize` FUNCTION.

```
 1: extern "C" void PASCAL EXPORT ModArtSerialize(CArchive &ar,
            ➡CObArray *poaLines)
 2: {
 3:      AFX_MANAGE_STATE(AfxGetStaticModuleState());
 4:      // normal function body here
 5:      // Pass the archive object on to the array
 6:      poaLines->Serialize(ar);
 7: }
```

LISTING 17.10. THE `ModArtClearDrawing` FUNCTION.

```
 1:  extern "C" void PASCAL EXPORT ModArtClearDrawing(CObArray *poaLines)
 2:  {
 3:      AFX_MANAGE_STATE(AfxGetStaticModuleState());
 4:      // Normal function body here
 5:      // Get the number of lines in the object array
 6:      int liCount = poaLines->GetSize();
 7:      int liPos;
```

continues

LISTING 17.10. CONTINUED

```
 8:
 9:      // Are there any objects in the array?
10:      if (liCount)
11:      {
12:          // Loop through the array, deleting each object
13:          for (liPos = 0; liPos < liCount; liPos++)
14:              delete (*poaLines)[liPos];
15:          // Reset the array
16:          poaLines->RemoveAll();
17:      }
18: }
```

Once you make the changes to these functions, the only thing remaining is to remove all code for the class constructor and destructor, along with the code for the SetRect function.

Building the Module Definition File

Before you compile the DLL, you need to add all the function names to the module definition file. You can find this file in the list of source-code files in the File View of the workspace pane. When you open this file, you'll find that it briefly describes the module that you are building in generic terms. You'll see a place at the bottom of the file where you can add the exports for the DLL. Edit this file, adding the exportable function names, as in Listing 17.11.

LISTING 17.11. THE DLL MODULE DEFINITION FILE.

```
 1:  ; ModArtRDll.def : Declares the module parameters for the DLL
 2:
 3:  LIBRARY        "ModArtRDll"
 4:  DESCRIPTION    'ModArtRDll Windows Dynamic Link Library'
 5:
 6:  EXPORTS
 7:      ; Explicit exports can go here
 8:      ModArtNewDrawing
 9:      ModArtSerialize
10:      ModArtDraw
11:      ModArtClearDrawing
```

You are now ready to compile your regular DLL. Once you compile the DLL, copy it into the debug directory of the test application.

Adapting the Test Application

To adapt the test application to use the new DLL that you have just created, you need to make a number of changes. First, you need to change the member variable of the document class from an instance of the drawing class to the object array. Next, you need to change the include in the document and view source code to include the header from the new DLL instead of the header from the old DLL. (You can completely remove the include in the application source-code file.) Drop the DLL LIB file and add the LIB file for the new DLL to the project. Change all of the drawing class function calls to call functions in the new DLL instead. Finally, change the GetDrawing function in the document class so that it returns a pointer to the object array, instead of the drawing object.

You can start making these changes by deleting the LIB file from the test application project. Once you delete the file, add the LIB file for the new DLL to the project by selecting Project | Add To Project | Files from the main menu.

Once you switch the LIB files in the project, edit the source code for the document and view classes to change the include statement, changing the project directory to the new DLL project directory. You can edit the application class source-code file and remove the include from this file. Because you are not creating any instances of the drawing class, the application file doesn't need to know about anything in the DLL.

Once you make all those changes, open the header file for the document class. Edit the document class declaration: Change the function type of the GetDrawing function to return a pointer to an object array, remove the drawing class variable, and add an object array variable, as in Listing 17.12. Make only these three changes; do not change anything else in the class declaration.

LISTING 17.12. THE CTestAppDoc CLASS DECLARATION.

```
1:  class CTestAppDoc : public CDocument
2:  {
3:  protected: // create from serialization only
4:      CTestAppDoc();
5:      DECLARE_DYNCREATE(CTestAppDoc)
6:  .
7:  .
8:  .
9:  // Implementation
10: public:
11:     CObArray* GetDrawing();
12:     virtual ~CTestAppDoc();
13: .
```

continues

LISTING **17.12.** CONTINUED

```
14: .
15: .
16: private:
17:     CObArray m_oaLines;
18: };
```

Modifying the Document Functions

Now that you've made the general changes to the test application, it's time to start making the functionality changes. All the calls to a class method of the drawing object must be changed to the appropriate function call in the new DLL.

The changes necessary in the OnNewDocument function consist of dropping the function call to pass the CRect to the drawing object and replacing the NewDocument function call with the new DLL function—in this instance, ModArtNewDrawing, as shown in line 19 in Listing 17.13.

LISTING 17.13. THE CTestAppDoc OnNewDocument FUNCTION.

```
1:  BOOL CTestAppDoc::OnNewDocument()
2:  {
3:      if (!CDocument::OnNewDocument())
4:          return FALSE;
5:
6:      // TODO: add reinitialization code here
7:      // (SDI documents will reuse this document)
8:
9:      // Get the position of the view
10:     POSITION pos = GetFirstViewPosition();
11:     // Did we get a valid position?
12:     if (pos != NULL)
13:     {
14:         // Get a pointer to the view
15:         CView* pView = GetNextView(pos);
16:         RECT lWndRect;
17:         // Get the display area rectangle
18:         pView->GetClientRect(&lWndRect);
19:         // Create a new drawing
20:         ModArtNewDrawing(lWndRect, &m_oaLines);
21:     }
22:
23:     return TRUE;
24: }
```

In the `Serialize` function, change the drawing object `Serialize` function call to the new DLL serialization function—in this case, `ModArtSerialize`, as in Listing 17.14.

LISTING 17.14. THE CTestAppDoc Serialize FUNCTION.

```
1: void CTestAppDoc::Serialize(CArchive& ar)
2: {
3:     // Serialize the drawing
4:     ModArtSerialize(ar, &m_oaLines);
5: }
```

For the `DeleteContents` function, you need to change the call to the `ClearDrawing` function to the new DLL function, `ModArtClearDrawing`, as in line 5 of Listing 17.15.

LISTING 17.15. THE CTestAppDoc DeleteContents FUNCTION.

```
1: void CTestAppDoc::DeleteContents()
2: {
3:     // TODO: Add your specialized code here and/or call the base class
4:     // Delete the drawing
5:     ModArtClearDrawing(&m_oaLines);
6:
7:     CDocument::DeleteContents();
8: }
```

Finally, for the `GetDrawing` function, you need to change the function declaration to designate that it's returning a pointer to an object array, just as you did in the header file. Next, you need to change the variable that is being returned to the object array variable that you added to the header file, as in Listing 17.16.

LISTING 17.16. THE CTestAppDoc GetDrawing FUNCTION.

```
1: CObArray* CTestAppDoc::GetDrawing()
2: {
3:     // Return the drawing object
4:     return &m_oaLines;
5: }
```

Modifying the View Functions

Switching to the view class, there's only one simple change to make to the `OnDraw` function. In this function, you need to change the type of pointer retrieved from the `GetDrawing` function from a drawing object to an object array object, as in line 9 of

Listing 17.17. Next, call the DLL function, ModArtDraw, to perform the drawing on the window, as shown in line 11.

LISTING 17.17. THE CTestAppView OnDraw FUNCTION.

```
1:   void CTestAppView::OnDraw(CDC* pDC)
2:   {
3:       CModTestAppDoc* pDoc = GetDocument();
4:       ASSERT_VALID(pDoc);
5:
6:       // TODO: add draw code for native data here
7:
8:       // Get the drawing object
9:       CObArray* m_oaLines = pDoc->GetDrawing();
10:      // Draw the drawing
11:      ModArtDraw(pDC, m_oaLines);
12:  }
```

After making all these changes to the test application, you are ready to compile and test it. You should find that the application is working just as it did with the previous DLL. You can also play around with it, going back and changing the DLL, copying the new DLL into the debug directory for the test application, and seeing how the changes are reflected in the behavior of the test application.

 Caution   The particular example of a regular DLL that you developed in this exercise is still not usable by other programming languages. The reason is that you are passing MFC classes as the arguments for each of the DLL's functions. This still limits the usage to other applications that are built using MFC. To make this DLL truly portable, you need to pass the bare-bones structures instead of the classes (such as the RECT structure instead of the CRect class) and then convert the structures to the classes inside the DLL.

Summary

Today you learned about two more ways that you can package your functionality for other programmers. You learned how you can easily package your classes as an MFC extension DLL and how easily it can be used by a Visual C++ application. You saw how you can make changes to the DLL without having to recompile the applications that use it. You also learned what's involved in creating a regular DLL that can be used with other, non-Visual C++ applications. You saw how you needed to convert the exported classes from the DLL into standard C-style functions and what's involved in adapting an application to use this style of DLL.

Q&A

Q **How can I convert the regular DLL so that it can be used by non-Visual C++ applications?**

A First, you have to make all the arguments to the functions use the bare-bones structures, instead of the MFC classes. For instance, to convert the `ModArtNewDrawing` function, change it to receive the `RECT` structure instead of the `CRect` class and also to receive a generic pointer instead of a pointer to an object array. You have to make the conversions to the appropriate classes in the DLL, as in lines 4 through 9 in Listing 17.18.

LISTING 17.18. THE `ModArtNewDrawing` FUNCTION.

```
 1:  extern "C" void PASCAL EXPORT ModArtNewDrawing(RECT spRect,
         ➥LPVOID lpoaLines)
 2:  {
 3:      AFX_MANAGE_STATE(AfxGetStaticModuleState());
 4:      CRect pRect;
 5:      pRect.top = spRect.top;
 6:      pRect.left = spRect.left;
 7:      pRect.right = spRect.right;
 8:      pRect.bottom = spRect.bottom;
 9:      CObArray* poaLines = (CObArray*)lpoaLines;
10:      // Normal function body here
11:      int m_lNumLines;
12:      int m_lCurLine;
13:
14:      // Initialize the random number generator
15:      srand((unsigned)time(NULL));
16:      // Determine how many lines to create
17:      m_lNumLines = rand() % 50;
18:      // Are there any lines to create?
19:      if (m_lNumLines > 0)
20:      {
21:          // Loop through the number of lines
22:          for (m_lCurLine = 0; m_lCurLine < m_lNumLines; m_lCurLine++)
23:          {
24:              // Create the new line
25:              NewLine(pRect, poaLines);
26:          }
27:      }
28:  }
```

17

You also have to add functions to create and destroy the object array, with the application storing the object array as a generic pointer as in Listing 17.19.

LISTING 17.19. THE ModArtInit FUNCTION.

```
1: extern "C" LPVOID PASCAL EXPORT ModArtInit()
2: {
3:     AFX_MANAGE_STATE(AfxGetStaticModuleState());
4:     // Create the object array
5:     return (LPVOID)new CObArray;
6: }
```

Q When do I need to recompile the applications that use my DLLs?

A Whenever you change any of the exported function calls. Changing, adding, or removing arguments to any of these functions would mean recompiling the applications that use the DLL. If you are working with an MFC extension DLL, the applications that use the DLL need to be recompiled if the public interface for the exported classes change or a new function or variable is added or removed. It doesn't matter if the application isn't using any of the functions that were changed; it's still good practice to recompile the applications, just to be sure.

Workshop

The Workshop provides quiz questions to help you solidify your understanding of the material covered and exercises to provide you with experience in using what you've learned. The answers to the quiz questions and exercises are provided in Appendix B, "Answers."

Quiz

1. What kind of DLL do you have to create to make classes in the DLL available to applications?
2. What do you have to add to the class to export it from a DLL?
3. What kind of DLL can be used with other programming languages?
4. If you make changes in a DLL, do you have to recompile the applications that use the DLL?
5. What function does the LIB file provide for a DLL?

Exercises

1. Separate the line class into its own MFC extension DLL and use it with the second (regular) DLL.
2. Alter the line class DLL so that it uses a consistent line width for all lines.

Doing Multiple Tasks at One Time—Multitasking

Sometimes it is convenient to let your applications do more than one thing at a time. Your application could write a backup file or print in the background while the user is working on the same document. Your application could perform calculations while the user enters new data or draws multiple images simultaneously. There are many different reasons why you might want to add this capability, called multitasking, to your applications. Windows provides several facilities specifically for building this into applications.

Today, you will learn

- How tasks can be performed while an application is idle.
- How tasks can run independently of the rest of the application.
- How to coordinate access to resources that are shared between multiple independent tasks.
- How to start and stop independently running tasks.

What Is Multitasking?

In the days of Windows 3.x, all Windows applications were single-threaded, with only one path of execution at any point in time. The version of multitasking that Windows 3.x offered is known as cooperative multitasking. The key to cooperative multitasking is that each individual application makes the decision about when to give up the processor for another application to perform any processing that it might be waiting to perform. As a result, Windows 3.x was susceptible to an ill-behaved application that would hold other applications prisoner while it performed some long, winding process or even got itself stuck in some sort of loop.

With Windows NT and Windows 95, the nature of the operating system changed. No more cooperative multitasking—the new method was preemptive multitasking. With preemptive multitasking, the operating system decides when to take the processor away from the current application and give the processor to another application that is waiting for it. It doesn't matter whether the application that has the processor is ready to give it up; the operating system takes the processor without the application's permission. This is how the operating system enables multiple applications to perform computation-intensive tasks and still let all the applications make the same amount of progress in each of their tasks. Giving this capability to the operating system prevents a single application from holding other applications prisoner while hogging the processor.

Note

With the 16/32 bit structure of Windows 95, it is still possible for an ill-behaved 16-bit application to lock up the system because a large amount of 16-bit code remains a core part of the operating system. The 16-bit code on Windows 95 is still a cooperative multitasking environment, so only one application can execute 16-bit code at a time. Because all the USER functions, and a good portion of the GDI functions, thunk down to the 16-bit version, it is still possible for a single 16-bit application to lock up the entire system.

On Windows NT, if all of the 16-bit applications run in a shared memory space, an ill-behaved application can lock up all of the 16-bit applications, but this has no effect on any 32-bit applications.

Performing Multiple Tasks at One Time

Along with the capability to allow multiple applications to run simultaneously comes the capability for a single application to execute multiple threads of execution at any time. A thread is to an application what an application is to the operating system. If an application has multiple threads running, it is basically running multiple applications within the whole application. This lets the application accomplish more things simultaneously, such as when Microsoft Word checks your spelling at the same time you are typing your document.

Idle Processing Threads

One of the easiest ways to let your application perform multiple tasks at one time is to add some idle processing tasks. An idle processing task is a task that is performed when an application is sitting idle. Literally, a function in the application class is called when there are no messages in the application message queue. The idea behind this function is that while the application is idle, it can perform work such as cleaning up memory (also known as garbage collection) or writing to a print spool.

The OnIdle function is a holdover from the Windows 3.x days. It is a member of the CWinApp class, from which your application class is inherited. By default, no processing in this function is added by the AppWizard, so if you want this function in your application, you must add it to your application class through the Class Wizard. (OnIdle is one of the available messages for the App class in your applications.)

The OnIdle function receives one argument, which is the number of times the OnIdle function has been called since the last message was processed by your application. You can use this to determine how long the application has been idle and when to trigger any functionality that you need to run if the application is idle for more than a certain amount of time.

One of the biggest concerns in adding OnIdle processing to your applications is that any functionality you add must be small and must quickly return control to the user. When an application performs any OnIdle processing, the user cannot interact with the application until the OnIdle processing finishes and returns control to the user. If you need to perform some long, drawn-out task in the OnIdle function, break it up into many small and quick tasks so that control can return to the user; then, you can continue your OnIdle task once the message queue is empty again. This means that you also have to track your application's progress in the OnIdle task so that the next time the OnIdle function is called, your application can pick up the task where it left off.

Spawning Independent Threads

If you really need to run a long background task that you don't want interfering with the user, you should spawn an independent thread. A thread is like another application running within your application. It does not have to wait until the application is idle to perform its tasks, and it does not cause the user to wait until it takes a break.

The two methods of creating an independent thread use the same function to create and start the thread. To create and start an independent thread, you call the AfxBeginThread function. You can choose to pass it a function to call for performing the thread's tasks, or you can pass it a pointer to the runtime class for an object derived from the CWinThread class. Both versions of the function return a pointer to a CWinThread object, which runs as an independent thread.

In the first version of the AfxBeginThread function, the first argument is a pointer to the main function for the thread to be started. This function is the equivalent of the main function in a C/C++ program. It controls the top-level execution for the thread. This function must be defined as a UINT function with a single LPVOID argument:

```
UINT MyThreadFunction( LPVOID pParam);
```

This version of the AfxBeginThread function also requires a second argument that is passed along to the main thread function as the only argument to that function. This argument can be a pointer to a structure containing any information that the thread needs to know to perform its job correctly.

The first argument to the second version of the AfxBeginThread function is a pointer to the runtime class of an object derived from the CWinThread class. You can get a pointer to the runtime class of your CWinThread class by using the RUNTIME_CLASS macro, passing your class as the only argument.

After these initial arguments, the rest of the arguments to the AfxBeginThread function are the same for both versions, and they are all optional. The first of these arguments is the priority to be assigned to the thread, with a default priority of THREAD_PRIORITY_NORMAL. Table 18.1 lists the available thread priorities.

TABLE 18.1. THREAD PRIORITIES.

Priority	Description
0	The thread will inherit the thread priority of the application creating the thread.
THREAD_PRIORITY_NORMAL	A normal (default) priority.
THREAD_PRIORITY_ABOVE_NORMAL	1 point above normal priority.
THREAD_PRIORITY_BELOW_NORMAL	1 point below normal priority.
THREAD_PRIORITY_HIGHEST	2 points above normal priority.
THREAD_PRIORITY_LOWEST	2 points below normal priority.
THREAD_PRIORITY_IDLE	Priority level of 1 for most threads (all non-real-time threads).
THREAD_PRIORITY_TIME_CRITICAL	Priority level of 15 for most threads (all non-real-time threads).

> **Note**
>
> Thread priority controls how much of the CPU's time the thread gets in relation to the other threads and processes running on the computer. If a thread will not be performing any tasks that need to be completed quickly, you should give the thread a lower priority when creating it. It is not advisable to give a thread a priority higher than normal unless it is vitally important that the thread perform its tasks faster than other processes running on the computer. The higher a thread's priority, the more CPU time that thread will receive, and the less CPU time all other processes and threads on the computer will receive.

The next argument to the AfxBeginThread function is the stack size to be provided for the new thread. The default value for this argument is 0, which provides the thread the same size stack as the main application.

The next argument to the AfxBeginThread function is the thread-creation flag. This flag can contain one of two values and controls how the thread is started. If CREATE_SUSPENDED is passed as this argument, the thread is created in suspended mode. The thread does not run until the ResumeThread function is called for the thread. If you supply 0 as this argument, which is the default value, the thread begins executing the moment it is created.

The final argument to the AfxBeginThread function is a pointer to the security attributes for the thread. The default value for this argument is NULL, which causes the thread to be created with the same security profile as the application. Unless you are building applications to run on Windows NT and you need to provide a thread with a specific security profile, you should always use the default value for this argument.

Building Structures

Imagine that you have an application running two threads, each parsing its own set of variables at the same time. Imagine also that the application is using a global object array to hold these variables. If the method of allocating and resizing the array consisted of checking the current size and adding one position onto the end of the array, your two threads might build an array populated something like the one in Figure 18.1, where array positions populated by the first thread are intermingled with those created by the second thread. This could easily confuse each thread as it retrieves values from the array for its processing needs because each thread is just as likely to pull a value that actually belongs to the other thread. This would cause each thread to operate on wrong data and return the wrong results.

18

Figure 18.1.

Two threads populating a common array.

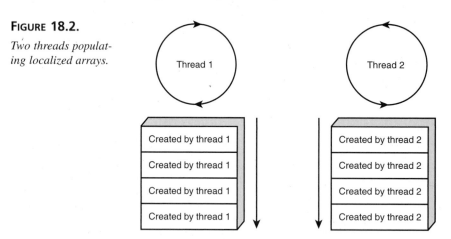

If the application built these arrays as localized arrays, instead of global arrays, it could keep access to each array limited to only the thread that builds the array. In Figure 18.2, for example, there is no intermingling of data from multiple threads. If you take this approach to using arrays and other memory structures, each thread can perform its processing and return the results to the client, confident that the results are correct because the calculations were performed on uncorrupted data.

Figure 18.2.

Two threads populating localized arrays.

Managing Access to Shared Resources

Not all variables can be localized, and you will often want to share some resources between all the threads running in your applications. Such sharing creates an issue with multithreaded applications. Suppose that three threads all share a single counter, which is generating unique numbers. Because you don't know when control of the processor is going to switch from one thread to the next, your application might generate duplicate "unique" numbers, as shown in Figure 18.3.

FIGURE 18.3.

Three threads sharing a single counter.

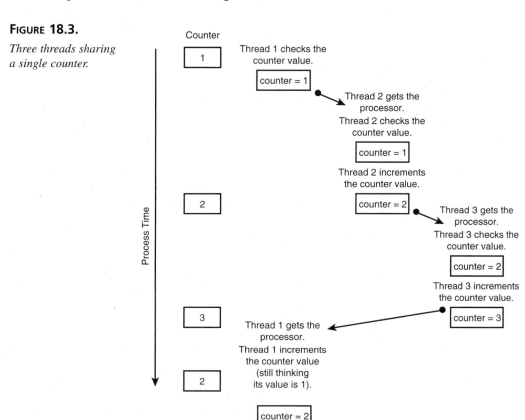

As you can see, this sharing doesn't work too well in a multithreaded application. You need a way to limit access to a common resource to only one thread at a time. In reality, there are four mechanisms for limiting access to common resources and synchronizing processing between threads, all of which work in different ways and whose suitability depends on the circumstances. The four mechanisms are

- Critical sections
- Mutexes
- Semaphores
- Events

Critical Sections

A critical section is a mechanism that limits access to a certain resource to a single thread within an application. A thread enters the critical section before it needs to work with the specific shared resource and then exits the critical section after it is finished accessing the resource. If another thread tries to enter the critical section before the first thread exits the critical section, the second thread is blocked and does not take any processor time until the first thread exits the critical section, allowing the second to enter. You use critical sections to mark sections of code that only one thread should execute at a time. This doesn't prevent the processor from switching from that thread to another; it just prevents two or more threads from entering the same section of code.

If you use a critical section with the counter shown in Figure 18.3, you can force each thread to enter a critical section before checking the current value of the counter. If each thread does not leave the critical section until after it has incremented and updated the counter, you can guarantee that—no matter how many threads are executing and regardless of their execution order—truly unique numbers are generated, as shown in Figure 18.4.

If you need to use a critical section object in your application, create an instance of the CCriticalSection class. This object contains two methods, Lock and Unlock, which you can use to gain and release control of the critical section.

Mutexes

Mutexes work in basically the same way as critical sections, but you use mutexes when you want to share the resource between multiple applications. By using a mutex, you can guarantee that no two threads running in any number of applications will access the same resource at the same time.

Because of their availability across the operating system, mutexes carry much more overhead than critical sections do. A mutex lifetime does not end when the application that created it shuts down. The mutex might still be in use by other applications, so the operating system must track which applications are using a mutex and then destroy the mutex once it is no longer needed. In contrast, critical sections have little overhead because they do not exist outside the application that creates and uses them. After the application ends, the critical section is gone.

If you need to use a mutex in your applications, you will create an instance of the CMutex class. The constructor of the CMutex class has three available arguments. The first argument is a boolean value that specifies whether the thread creating the CMutex object is the initial owner of the mutex. If so, then this thread must release the mutex before any other threads can access it.

FIGURE **18.4.**

Three threads using the same counter, which is protected by a critical section.

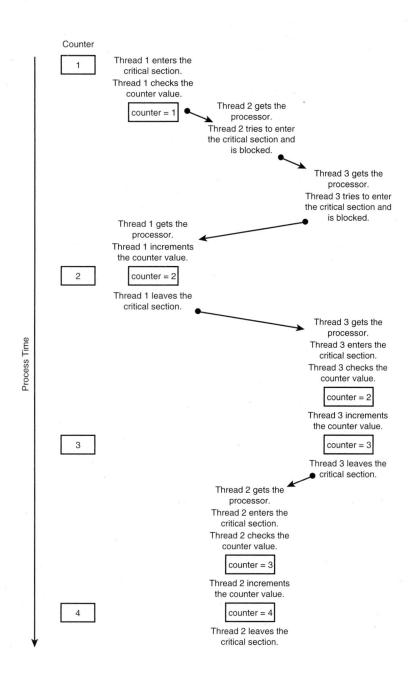

Counter

1

Thread 1 enters the critical section.
Thread 1 checks the counter value.

counter = 1

Thread 2 gets the processor.
Thread 2 tries to enter the critical section and is blocked.

Thread 3 gets the processor.
Thread 3 tries to enter the critical section and is blocked.

Thread 1 gets the processor.
Thread 1 increments the counter value.

2

counter = 2

Thread 1 leaves the critical section.

Thread 3 gets the processor.
Thread 3 enters the critical section.
Thread 3 checks the counter value.

counter = 2

Thread 3 increments the counter value.

3

counter = 3

Thread 3 leaves the critical section.

Thread 2 gets the processor.
Thread 2 enters the critical section.
Thread 2 checks the counter value.

counter = 3

Thread 2 increments the counter value.

4

counter = 4

Thread 2 leaves the critical section.

Process Time

18

The second argument is the name for the mutex. All the applications that need to share the mutex can identify it by this textual name. The third and final argument to the CMutex constructor is a pointer to the security attributes for the mutex object. If a NULL is passed for this pointer, the mutex object uses the security attributes of the thread that created it.

Once you create a CMutex object, you can lock and unlock it using the Lock and Unlock member functions. This allows you to build in the capabilities to control access to a shared resource between multiple threads in multiple applications.

Semaphores

Semaphores work very differently from critical sections and mutexes. You use semaphores with resources that are not limited to a single thread at a time— a resource that should be limited to a fixed number of threads. A semaphore is a form of counter, and threads can increment or decrement it. The trick to semaphores is that they cannot go any lower than zero. Therefore, if a thread is trying to decrement a semaphore that is at zero, that thread is blocked until another thread increments the semaphore.

Suppose you have a queue that is populated by multiple threads, and one thread removes the items from the queue and performs processing on each item. If the queue is empty, the thread that removes and processes items has nothing to do. This thread could go into an idle loop, checking the queue every so often to see whether something has been placed in it. The problem with this scenario is that the thread takes up processing cycles doing absolutely nothing. These processor cycles could go to another thread that does have something to do. If you use a semaphore to control the queue, each thread that places items into the queue can increment the semaphore for each item placed in the queue, and the thread that removes the items can decrement the semaphore just before removing each item from the queue. If the queue is empty, the semaphore is zero, and the thread removing items is blocked on the call to decrement the queue. This thread does not take any processor cycles until one of the other threads increments the semaphore to indicate that it has placed an item in the queue. Then, the thread removing items is immediately unblocked, and it can remove the item that was placed in the queue and begin processing it, as shown in Figure 18.5.

If you need to use a semaphore in your application, you can create an instance of the CSemaphore class. This class has four arguments that can be passed to the class constructor. The first argument is the starting usage count for the semaphore. The second argument is the maximum usage count for the semaphore. You can use these two arguments to control how many threads and processes can have access to a shared resource at any one time. The third argument is the name for the semaphore, which is used to identify the semaphore by all applications running on the system, just as with the CMutex class.

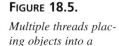

FIGURE 18.5.

Multiple threads plac-ing objects into a queue.

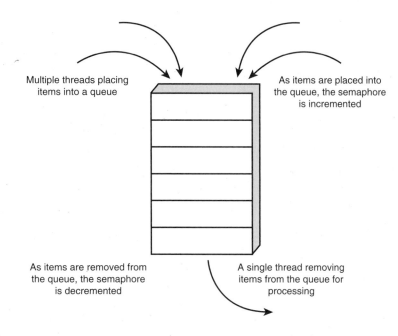

Multiple threads placing items into a queue

As items are placed into the queue, the semaphore is incremented

As items are removed from the queue, the semaphore is decremented

A single thread removing items from the queue for processing

18

The final argument is a pointer to the security attributes for the semaphore.

With the CSemaphore object, you can use the Lock and Unlock member functions to gain or release control of the semaphore. When you call the Lock function, if the semaphore usage count is greater than zero, the usage count is decremented and your program is allowed to continue. If the usage count is already zero, the Lock function waits until the usage count is incremented so that your process can gain access to the shared resource. When you call the Unlock function, the usage count of the semaphore is incremented.

Events

As much as thread synchronization mechanisms are designed to control access to limited resources, they are also intended to prevent threads from using unnecessary processor cycles. The more threads running at one time, the slower each of those threads performs its tasks. Therefore, if a thread does not have anything to do, block it and let it sit idle, allowing other threads to use more processor time and thus run faster until the conditions are met that provide the idle thread with something to do.

This is why you use events—to allow threads to be idle until the conditions are such that they have something to do. Events take their name from the events that drive most Windows applications, only with a twist. Thread synchronization events do not use the normal event queuing and handling mechanisms. Instead of being assigned a number and then waiting for that number to be passed through the Windows event handler, thread synchronization events are actual objects held in memory. Each thread that needs to wait for an event tells the event that it is waiting for it to be triggered and then goes to sleep. When the event is triggered, it sends wake-up calls to every thread that told it that it was waiting to be triggered. The threads pick up their processing at the exact point where they each told the event that they were waiting for it.

If you need to use an event in your application, you can create a CEvent object. You need to create the CEvent object when you need to access and wait for the event. Once the CEvent constructor has returned, the event has occurred and your thread can continue on its way.

The constructor for the CEvent class can take four arguments. The first argument is a boolean flag to indicate whether the thread creating the event will own it initially. This value should be set to TRUE if the thread creating the CEvent object is the thread that will determine when the event has occurred.

The second argument to the CEvent constructor specifies whether the event is an automatic or manual event. A manual event remains in the signaled or unsignaled state until it is specifically set to the other state by the thread that owns the event object. An automatic event remains in the unsignaled state most of the time. When the event is set to the signaled state, and at least one thread has been released and continued on its execution path, the event is returned to the unsignaled state.

The third argument to the event constructor is the name for the event. This name will be used to identify the event by all threads that need to access the event. The fourth and final argument is a pointer to the security attributes for the event object.

The CEvent class has several member functions that you can use to control the state of the event. Table 18.2 lists these functions.

TABLE 18.2. CEvent MEMBER FUNCTIONS.

Function	Description
SetEvent	Puts the event into the signaled state.
PulseEvent	Puts the event into the signaled state and then resets the event back to the unsignaled state.
ResetEvent	Puts the event into the unsignaled state.
Unlock	Releases the event object.

Building a Multitasking Application

To see how you can create your own multitasking applications, you'll create an application that has four spinning color wheels, each running on its own thread. Two of the spinners will use the `OnIdle` function, and the other two will run as independent threads. This setup will enable you to see the difference between the two types of threading, as well as learn how you can use each. Your application window will have four check boxes to start and stop each of the threads so that you can see how much load is put on the system as each runs alone or in combination with the others.

Creating a Framework

For the application that you will build today, you'll need an SDI application framework, with the view class inherited from the `CFormView` class, so that you can use the dialog editor to lay out the few controls on the window. It will use the document class to house the spinners and the independent threads, whereas the view will have the check boxes and variables that control whether each thread is running or idle.

To create the framework for your application, create a new project workspace using the MFC Application Wizard. Give your application a suitable project name, such as `Tasking`.

In the AppWizard, specify that you are creating a single document (SDI) application. You can accept the defaults through most of the rest of the AppWizard, although you won't need support for ActiveX controls, a docking toolbar, the initial status bar, or printing and print preview, so you can unselect these options if you so desire. Once you reach the final AppWizard step, specify that your view class is inherited from the `CFormView` class.

Once you create the application framework, remove the static text from the main application window, and add four check boxes at approximately the upper-left corner of each quarter of the window space, as in Figure 18.6. Set the properties of the check boxes as in Table 18.3.

TABLE 18.3. CONTROL PROPERTY SETTINGS.

Object	Property	Setting
Check Box	ID	IDC_CBONIDLE1
	Caption	On &Idle Thread 1
Check Box	ID	IDC_CBTHREAD1
	Caption	Thread &1

continues

18

TABLE 18.3. CONTINUED

Object	Property	Setting
Check Box	ID	IDC_CBONIDLE2
	Caption	On Idle &Thread 2
Check Box	ID	IDC_CBTHREAD2
	Caption	Thread &2

FIGURE 18.6.

The main window design.

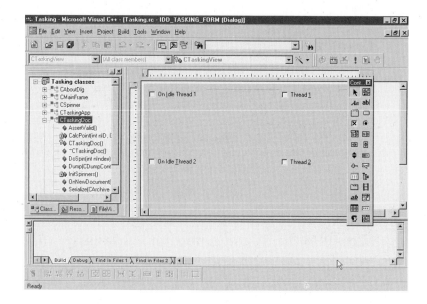

Once you add the check boxes to the window and configure their properties, use the Class Wizard to add a variable to each of them. Make all of the variables BOOL, and give them names like in Table 18.4.

TABLE 18.4. CONTROL VARIABLES.

Object	Name	Category	Type
IDC_CBONIDLE1	m_bOnIdle1	Value	BOOL
IDC_CBONIDLE2	m_bOnIdle2	Value	BOOL
IDC_CBTHREAD1	m_bThread1	Value	BOOL
IDC_CBTHREAD2	m_bThread2	Value	BOOL

Designing Spinners

Before you can start adding threads to your application, you'll create the spinning color wheel that the threads will operate. Because four of these color wheels will all spin independently of each other, it makes sense to encapsulate all of the functionality into a single class. This class will track what color is being drawn, where in the spinning it needs to draw the next line, the size of the color wheel, and the location of the color wheel on the application window. It will also need a pointer to the view class so that it can get the device context in which it is supposed to draw itself. For the independent spinners, the class will need a pointer to the flag that will control whether the spinner is supposed to be spinning.

To start the spinner class, create a new generic class, inherited from the `CObject` base class. Provide the new class with a name that is descriptive of what it will be doing, such as `CSpinner`.

Setting Spinner Variables

Once you create a new class for your spinner object, you'll add some variables to the class. To follow good object-oriented design principles, you need to make all these variables private and add methods to the class to set and retrieve the values of each.

The variables you'll add are

- The current color.
- The current position in the rotation of the color wheel.
- The size of the color wheel.
- The position on the application window for the color wheel.
- The color table from which the colors are picked for drawing in the color wheel.
- A pointer to the view object so that the spinner can get the device context that it will need for drawing on the window.
- A pointer to the check box variable that specifies whether the thread should be running.

You can add all these variables to the spinner class using the names and types specified in Table 18.5.

TABLE 18.5. `CSpinner` CLASS VARIABLES.

Name	Type	Description
m_crColor	int	The current color from the color table.
m_nMinute	int	The position in the rotation around the wheel.

continues

TABLE 18.5. CONTINUED

Name	Type	Description
m_iRadius	int	The radius (size) of the wheel.
m_pCenter	CPoint	The center point of the wheel.
m_crColors[8]	static COLORREF	The color table with all of the colors to be drawn in the color wheel.
m_pViewWnd	CWnd*	A pointer to the view object.
m_bContinue	BOOL*	A pointer to the check box variable that specifies whether this thread should be running.

Once you add all the necessary variables, you need to make sure that your class either initializes them or provides a suitable means of setting and retrieving the values of each. All the integer variables can be initialized as zero, and they'll work their way up from that point. The pointers should be initialized with NULL. You can do all of this initialization in the class constructor, as in Listing 18.1.

LISTING 18.1. THE CSpinner CONSTRUCTOR.

```
 1: CSpinner::CSpinner()
 2: {
 3:     // Initialize the position, size, and color
 4:     m_iRadius = 0;
 5:     m_nMinute = 0;
 6:     m_crColor = 0;
 7:     // Nullify the pointers
 8:     m_pViewWnd = NULL;
 9:     m_bContinue = NULL;
10: }
```

For those variables that you need to be able to set and retrieve, your spinner class is simple enough that you can write all the set and get functions as inline functions in the class declaration. The color and position will be automatically calculated by the spinner object, so you don't need to add set functions for those two variables, but you do need to add set functions for the rest of the variables (not counting the color table). The only variables that you need to retrieve from the spinner object are the pointers to the view class and the check box variable. You can add all these functions to the CSpinner class declaration by opening the Spinner header file and adding the inline functions in Listing 18.2.

LISTING 18.2. THE CSpinner CLASS DECLARATION.

```
 1: class CSpinner : public CObject
 2: {
 3: public:
 4:     BOOL* GetContinue() {return m_bContinue;}
 5:     void SetContinue(BOOL* bContinue) { m_bContinue = bContinue;}
 6:     CWnd* GetViewWnd() { return m_pViewWnd;}
 7:     void SetViewWnd(CWnd* pWnd) { m_pViewWnd = pWnd;}
 8:     void SetLength(int iLength) { m_iRadius = iLength;}
 9:     void SetPoint(CPoint pPoint) { m_pCenter = pPoint;}
10:     CSpinner();
11:     virtual ~CSpinner();
12:
13: private:
14:     BOOL* m_bContinue;
15:     CWnd* m_pViewWnd;
16:     static COLORREF m_crColors[8];
17:     int m_iRadius;
18:     CPoint m_pCenter;
19:     int m_nMinute;
20:     int m_crColor;
21: };
```

18

Now that you have added all the support functions for setting and retrieving the necessary variables, you need to declare and populate the color table. This will look just like the color table definition you added to the drawing application on Day 10, "Creating Single Document Interface Applications." The color table will consist of eight RGB values, with each value being either 0 or 255, with every combination of these two settings. The best place to add this table declaration is in the spinner source code file, just before the class constructor, as in Listing 18.3.

LISTING 18.3. THE CSpinner COLOR TABLE.

```
 1: static char THIS_FILE[]=__FILE__;
 2: #define new DEBUG_NEW
 3: #endif
 4:
 5: COLORREF CSpinner::m_crColors[8] = {
 6:     RGB(   0,   0,   0),    // Black
 7:     RGB(   0,   0, 255),    // Blue
 8:     RGB(   0, 255,   0),    // Green
 9:     RGB(   0, 255, 255),    // Cyan
10:     RGB( 255,   0,   0),    // Red
11:     RGB( 255,   0, 255),    // Magenta
12:     RGB( 255, 255,   0),    // Yellow
13:     RGB( 255, 255, 255)        // White
```

continues

LISTING 18.3. CONTINUED

```
14: };
15:
16: //////////////////////////////////////////////////////////////////
17: // Construction/Destruction
18: //////////////////////////////////////////////////////////////////
19:
20: CSpinner::CSpinner()
21: {
22:     // Initialize the position, size, and color
23:     m_iRadius = 0;
24: .
25: .
26: .
```

Drawing the Spinner

Now comes the fun part: getting the spinner object to actually spin. To accomplish this, you'll calculate the new position of the starting and ending points of each line, set the view port origination point, select the drawing color, and create a pen to draw in that color. Once you have all of this, you will be able to draw the line from the starting point to the ending point. Once the line is drawn, you can restore the pen to what it was before the line was drawn. Next, you'll calculate the position of the next line to draw before exiting the function.

To add this functionality to your spinner object, add a member function to the CSpinner class. Specify the type as void, the name as Draw, and the access as public. Edit the function, adding the code in Listing 18.4.

LISTING 18.4. THE CSpinner Draw FUNCTION.

```
1: void CSpinner::Draw()
2: {
3:     // Get a pointer to the device context
4:     CDC *pDC = m_pViewWnd->GetDC();
5:     // Set the mapping mode
6:     pDC->SetMapMode (MM_LOENGLISH);
7:     // Copy the spinner center
8:     CPoint org = m_pCenter;
9:     CPoint pStartPoint;
10:    // Set the starting point
11:    pStartPoint.x = (m_iRadius / 2);
12:    pStartPoint.y = (m_iRadius / 2);
13:    // Set the origination point
14:    org.x = m_pCenter.x + (m_iRadius / 2);
```

```
15:     org.y = m_pCenter.y + m_iRadius;
16:     // Set the viewport origination point
17:     pDC->SetViewportOrg(org.x, org.y);
18:
19:     CPoint pEndPoint;
20:     // Calculate the angle of the next line
21:     double nRadians = (double) (m_nMinute * 6) * 0.017453292;
22:     // Set the end point of the line
23:     pEndPoint.x = (int) (m_iRadius * sin(nRadians));
24:     pEndPoint.y = (int) (m_iRadius * cos(nRadians));
25:
26:
27:     // Create the pen to use
28:     CPen pen(PS_SOLID, 0, m_crColors[m_crColor]);
29:     // Select the pen for use
30:     CPen* pOldPen = pDC->SelectObject(&pen);
31:
32:     // Move to the starting point
33:     pDC->MoveTo (pEndPoint);
34:     // Draw the line to the end point
35:     pDC->LineTo (pStartPoint);
36:
37:     // Reselect the previous pen
38:     pDC->SelectObject(&pOldPen);
39:
40:     // Release the device context
41:     m_pViewWnd->ReleaseDC(pDC);
42:
43:     // Increment the minute
44:     if (++m_nMinute == 60)
45:     {
46:         // If the minutes have gone full circle, reset to 0
47:         m_nMinute = 0;
48:         // Increment the color
49:         if (++m_crColor == 8)
50:             // If we've gone through all colors, start again
51:             m_crColor = 0;
52:     }
53: }
```

That was quite a bit of code to type. What does it do? Well, to understand what this function is doing, and how it's going to make your spinner draw a color wheel on the window, let's take a closer look at the code.

To make efficient use of the spinner by the different threads, it'll only draw one line each time the function is called. This function will be called 60 times for each complete circle, once for each "minute" in the clockwise rotation. Each complete rotation will cause the spinner to switch to the next color in the color table.

One of the first things that you need to do in order to perform any drawing on the window is get the device context of the window. You do this by calling the GetDC function on the view object pointer:

```
CDC *pDC = m_pViewWnd->GetDC();
```

This function returns a CDC object pointer, which is an MFC class that encapsulates the device context.

Once you have a pointer to the device context, you can call its member function, SetMapMode, to set the mapping mode:

```
pDC->SetMapMode (MM_LOENGLISH);
```

The mapping mode determines how the x and y coordinates are translated into positions on the screen. The MM_LOENGLISH mode converts each logical unit to 0.01 inch on the screen. There are several different mapping modes, each converting logical units to different measurements on the screen.

At this point, you start preparing to draw the current line for the color wheel. You start by calculating the starting point for the line that will be drawn. This point will be consistent for all lines drawn by the spinner object. After you calculate the starting point for the line, you calculate the position of the viewport. The viewport is used as the starting point for the coordinates used for drawing.

Note   The starting point for the line to be drawn is calculated in an off-center position. If you want the starting point for the lines to be in the center of the color wheel, set both the x and y coordinates of the starting point to 0.

Once the viewport origination point is calculated, use the SetViewportOrg function to set the viewport:

```
pDC->SetViewportOrg(org.x, org.y);
```

Now that you've got the drawing area specified, and the starting point for the line that you are going to be drawing, you need to figure out where the other end of the line will be. You'll perform this calculation using the following three lines of code:

```
double nRadians = (double) (m_nMinute * 6) * 0.017453292;
pEndPoint.x = (int) (m_iRadius * sin(nRadians));
pEndPoint.y = (int) (m_iRadius * cos(nRadians));
```

In the first of these calculations, convert the minutes into degrees, which can then be fed into the sine and cosine functions to set the x and y coordinates to draw a circle. This sets the end point of the line that will be drawn.

Now that you've figured out the starting and ending points of the line, you'll create a pen to use in drawing the line:

```
CPen pen(PS_SOLID, 0, m_crColors[m_crColor]);
```

You've specified that the pen will be solid and thin, and you are picking the current color from the color table. Once you create the pen to use, select the pen for drawing, being sure to capture the current pen as the return value from the device context object:

```
CPen* pOldPen = pDC->SelectObject(&pen);
```

Now you are ready to draw the line, which is done using the `MoveTo` and `LineTo` functions that you're well familiar with by now. Once the line is drawn, release the device context so that you don't have a resource leak in your application:

```
m_pViewWnd->ReleaseDC(pDC);
```

At this point, you've drawn the line, so all that's left to do is increment the minute counter, resetting it if you've made it all the way around the circle. Each time you complete a circle, you increment the color counter until you've gone through all eight colors, at which time you reset the color counter.

In order to be able to use the trigonometric functions in this function, include the `math.h` header file in the `Spinner` class source file. To add this, scroll up to the top of the source code file and add another `#include` line, specifying the `math.h` header file as the file to be included, as in Listing 18.5.

LISTING 18.5. THE `CSpinner` SOURCE FILE.

```
1: // Spinner.cpp : implementation of the CSpinner class
2: //
3: /////////////////////////////////////////////////////////////////////
4:
5: #include "stdafx.h"
6: #include <math.h>
7: #include "Tasking.h"
8: #include "Spinner.h"
```

Supporting the Spinners

Now that you've created the spinner class for drawing the spinning color wheel on the window, add some support for the spinners. You can add an array to hold the four spinners in the document class, but you'll still need to calculate where each spinner should be placed on the application window and set all the variables in each of the spinners.

You can add all of this code to the document class, starting with the array of spinners. Add a member variable to the document class (in this instance, CTaskingDoc), specifying the type as CSpinner, the name as m_cSpin[4], and the access as private. Once you add the array, open the source code to the document class and include the spinner header file, as in Listing 18.6.

LISTING 18.6. THE CTaskingDoc SOURCE FILE.

```
 1: // TaskingDoc.cpp : implementation of the CTaskingDoc class
 2: //
 3:
 4: #include "stdafx.h"
 5: #include "Tasking.h"
 6:
 7: #include "Spinner.h"
 8: #include "TaskingDoc.h"
 9: #include "TaskingView.h"
10: .
11: .
12: .
```

Calculating the Spinner Positions

One of the preparatory things that needs to happen while initializing the application is determining the locations of all four spinners. The window is roughly broken up into four quarters by the check boxes that will turn the spinner threads on and off, so it makes sense to divide the window area into four quarter squares and place one spinner in each quarter.

To calculate the location of each spinner, it is easiest to create a function that calculates the location for one spinner, placing the spinner into the quarter square appropriate for the spinner number. If the function was passed a pointer to the spinner object, it could update the spinner object directly with the location.

To add this functionality to your application, add a new member function to the document class (for instance, in the CTaskingDoc class). Specify the function type as void, the declaration as CalcPoint(int nID, CSpinner *pSpin), and the access as private. Edit the function, adding the code in Listing 18.7.

LISTING 18.7. THE CTaskingDoc CalcPoint FUNCTION.

```
 1: void CTaskingDoc::CalcPoint(int nID, CSpinner *pSpin)
 2: {
 3:     RECT lWndRect;
 4:     CPoint pPos;
 5:     int iLength;
 6:     CTaskingView *pWnd;
 7:
 8:     // Get a pointer to the view window
 9:     pWnd = (CTaskingView*)pSpin->GetViewWnd();
10:     // Get the display area rectangle
11:     pWnd->GetClientRect(&lWndRect);
12:     // Calculate the size of the spinners
13:     iLength = lWndRect.right / 6;
14:     // Which spinner are we placing?
15:     switch (nID)
16:     {
17:     case 0:    // Position the first spinner
18:         pPos.x = (lWndRect.right / 4) - iLength;
19:         pPos.y = (lWndRect.bottom / 4) - iLength;
20:         break;
21:     case 1:    // Position the second spinner
22:         pPos.x = ((lWndRect.right / 4) * 3) - iLength;
23:         pPos.y = (lWndRect.bottom / 4) - iLength;
24:         break;
25:     case 2:    // Position the third spinner
26:         pPos.x = (lWndRect.right / 4) - iLength;
27:         pPos.y = ((lWndRect.bottom / 4) * 3) - (iLength * 1.25);
28:         break;
29:     case 3:    // Position the fourth spinner
30:         pPos.x = ((lWndRect.right / 4) * 3) - iLength;
31:         pPos.y = ((lWndRect.bottom / 4) * 3) - (iLength * 1.25);
32:         break;
33:     }
34:     // Set the size of the spinner
35:     pSpin->SetLength(iLength);
36:     // Set the location of the spinner
37:     pSpin->SetPoint(pPos);
38: }
```

18

In this function, the first thing that you do is move the pointer to the view window from the spinner object by calling the GetViewWnd function:

```
pWnd = (CTaskingView*)pSpin->GetViewWnd();
```

By moving the pointer directly from the spinner object, you save a few steps by taking a more direct route to get the information that you need.

Once you have a pointer to the view object, you can call the window's `GetClientRect` function to get the size of the available drawing area:

```
pWnd->GetClientRect(&lWndRect);
```

Once you have the size of the drawing area, you can calculate a reasonable color wheel size by dividing the length of the drawing area by 6:

```
iLength = lWndRect.right / 6;
```

Dividing the drawing area by 4 will position you at the middle of the upper-left square. Subtract the size of the circle from this point, and you have the upper-left corner of the drawing area for the first spinner:

```
pPos.x = (lWndRect.right / 4) - iLength;
pPos.y = (lWndRect.bottom / 4) - iLength;
```

You can then include variations on this position, mostly by multiplying the center of the quadrant by 3 to move it to the center of the right or lower quadrant, and you can calculate the positions of the other three spinners.

Once you calculate the length and position for the spinner, you call the `SetLength` and `SetPoint` functions to pass these values to the spinner that they have been calculated for:

```
pSpin->SetLength(iLength);
pSpin->SetPoint(pPos);
```

Initializing the Spinners

Because you wrote the previous function to calculate the location of each spinner on the window to work on only one spinner each time it is called, you need some routine that will initialize each spinner, calling the previous function once for each spinner. You need this function to get a pointer to the view object and pass that along to the spinner. You also need to get pointers to the check box variables for the spinners that will be used by the independently running threads. Your code can do all this by just looping through the array of spinners, setting both of these pointers for each spinner, and then passing the spinner to the function you just finished.

To create this function for your application, add a new member function to the document class (`CTaskingDoc` in this instance). Specify the type as void, and give the function a suitable name (for instance, `InitSpinners`), and then specify the access as private because you'll only need to call this function once when the application is starting. Edit the new function, adding the code in Listing 18.8.

LISTING 18.8. THE `CTaskingDoc InitSpinners` FUNCTION.

```
 1: void CTaskingDoc::InitSpinners()
 2: {
 3:     int i;
 4:
 5:     // Get the position of the view
 6:     POSITION pos = GetFirstViewPosition();
 7:     // Did we get a valid position?
 8:     if (pos != NULL)
 9:     {
10:         // Get a pointer to the view
11:         CView* pView = GetNextView(pos);
12:
13:         // Loop through the spinners
14:         for (i = 0; i < 4; i++)
15:         {
16:             // Set the pointer to the view
17:             m_cSpin[i].SetViewWnd(pView);
18:             // Initialize the pointer to the continuation indicator
19:             m_cSpin[i].SetContinue(NULL);
20:             switch (i)
21:             {
22:             case 1:    // Set the pointer to the first thread
23:                        // continuation indicator
24:                 m_cSpin[i].SetContinue(&((CTaskingView*)pView
                    ➥)->m_bThread1);
25:                 break;
26:             case 3:    // Set the pointer to the second thread
27:                        // continuation indicator
28:                 m_cSpin[i].SetContinue(&((CTaskingView*)pView
                    ➥)->m_bThread2);
29:                 break;
30:             }
31:             // Calculate the location of the spinner
32:             CalcPoint(i, &m_cSpin[i]);
33:         }
34:     }
35: }
```

In this function, you first went through the steps of getting a pointer to the view class from the document, as you did initially back on Day 10. Once you have a valid pointer to the view, start a loop to initialize each of the spinners in the array. You call the `SetViewWnd` spinner function to set the spinner's pointer to the view window and then initialize the spinner's pointer to the check box variable to `NULL` for all spinners. If the spinner is either of the two that will be used by independent threads, you pass a pointer to the appropriate check box variable. Once you set all of this, call the `CalcPoint` function that you created just a few minutes earlier to calculate the location of the spinner on the view window.

Note

> Although you've seen several examples of using pointers, the way that you are passing a pointer to the check box variable to the spinner deserves taking a closer look:
>
> `m_cSpin[i].SetContinue(&((CTaskingView*)pView)->m_bThread1);`
>
> In this statement, you take the pointer to the view object, pView, which is a pointer for a CView object, and cast it as a pointer to the specific view class that you have created in your application:
>
> `(CTaskingView*)pView`
>
> Now that you can treat the pointer to the view object as a CTaskingView object, you can get to the check box variable, m_bThread1, which is a public member of the CTaskingView class:
>
> `((CTaskingView*)pView)->m_bThread1`
>
> Once you access the m_bThread1 variable, get the address of this variable by placing an ampersand in front of this whole string:
>
> `&((CTaskingView*)pView)->m_bThread1`
>
> Passing this address for the m_bThread1 variable to the SetContinue function, you are, in effect, passing a pointer to the m_bThread1 variable, which can be used to set the pointer to this variable that the spinner object contains.

Now that you've created the routines to initialize all the spinners, make sure that this routine is called when the application is started. The best place to put this logic is the OnNewDocument function in the document class. This function will be called when the application is started, so it is a logical place to trigger the initialization of the spinner objects. To add this code to the OnNewDocument function, add the code in Listing 18.9 to the OnNewDocument function in the document class.

LISTING 18.9. THE CTaskingDoc OnNewDocument FUNCTION.

```
1: BOOL CTaskingDoc::OnNewDocument()
2: {
3:     if (!CDocument::OnNewDocument())
4:         return FALSE;
5:
6:     // TODO: add reinitialization code here
7:     // (SDI documents will reuse this document)
```

```
 8:
 9:      ////////////////////////
10:      // MY CODE STARTS HERE
11:      ////////////////////////
12:
13:      // Initialize the spinners
14:      InitSpinners();
15:
16:      ////////////////////////
17:      // MY CODE ENDS HERE
18:      ////////////////////////
19:
20:      return TRUE;
21: }
```

Spinning the Spinner

Once last thing that you'll add to the document class for now is a means of calling the Draw function for a specific spinner from outside the document class. Because the array of spinners was declared as a private variable, no outside objects can get access to the spinners, so you need to add access for the outside objects. You can add a function to provide this access by adding a new member function to your document class. Specify the function type as void, specify the function declaration with a name and a single integer argument for the spinner number, such as DoSpin(int nIndex), and then specify the function's access as public. Once you have added the function, you can add the code in Listing 18.10 to the function to perform the actual call to the specified spinner.

LISTING 18.10. THE CTaskingDoc DoSpin FUNCTION.

```
1: void CTaskingDoc::DoSpin(int nIndex)
2: {
3:      // Spin the Spinner
4:      m_cSpin[nIndex].Draw();
5: }
```

Adding the OnIdle Tasks

Now that you have the supporting functionality in place, it's time to turn your attention to adding the various threads that will turn the various spinners. The first threads to add are the ones executing while the application is idle. You'll add a clicked event handler for the two On Idle check boxes so that you can keep the variables for these two check boxes in sync with the window. You'll also add the code to the application's OnIdle function to run these two spinners when the application is idle and the check boxes for these two spinner threads are checked.

Note

> The use of the term *thread* in the preceding is slightly misleading. Any functionality that you place in the OnIdle function is running in the main application thread. All the OnIdle processing that you add to the sample application won't be running as an independent thread, but will be just functions that can be called from the main thread.

Starting and Stopping the OnIdle Tasks

The OnIdle function will check the values of the two check box variables that specify whether each should run, so all your application needs to do when either of these check boxes is clicked is make sure that the variables in the view object are synchronized with the controls on the window. All that you need to do to accomplish this is call the UpdateData function when either of these controls is clicked. You need to be able to start and stop the OnIdle tasks by adding a single event handler for both of the On Idle Thread check boxes and then calling the UpdateData function in this event function.

To add this to your application, open the Class Wizard and select the view class (in this case, CTaskingView). Select one of the On Idle check boxes and add a function for the BN_CLICKED event. Change the name of the suggested function to OnCbonidle and click OK. Do the same thing for the other On Idle check box. Once you specify that both of these events use the same code, click on the Edit Code button and add the code in Listing 18.11.

LISTING 18.11. THE CTaskingView OnCbonidle FUNCTION.

```
 1: void CTaskingView::OnCbonidle()
 2: {
 3:     // TODO: Add your control notification handler code here
 4:
 5:     /////////////////////////
 6:     // MY CODE STARTS HERE
 7:     /////////////////////////
 8:
 9:     // Sync the variables with the dialog
10:     UpdateData(TRUE);
11:
12:     /////////////////////////
13:     // MY CODE ENDS HERE
14:     /////////////////////////
15: }
```

Building the `OnIdle` Threads

If you examine the application class (`CTaskingApp`) source code, you'll find that the `OnIdle` function isn't there. All the functionality that the `OnIdle` function needs to perform by default is in the ancestor class of the application class that was created for your project. The only reason to have an `OnIdle` function in your application class is that your application needs some specific functionality to be performed during this event. As a result, you need to specifically add this event handler to your application using the Class Wizard.

Once you add the `OnIdle` function to your application class, what does it need to do? First, it needs to get a pointer to the view so that it can check the status of the check box variables. Next, it needs to get a pointer to the document class so that it can call the `DoSpin` function to trigger the appropriate spinner object. The key to both of these actions is getting pointers to each of these objects. When you begin looking at what is necessary to get these pointers, you'll find that you have to reverse the order in which you get the pointers. You need to get a pointer to the document object in order to get a pointer to the view. However, to get a pointer to the document, you have to go through the document template, getting a pointer to the template before you can get a pointer to the document. Each of these steps requires the same sequence of events, first getting the position of the first object and then getting a pointer to the object in that position. What you'll do is get the position of the first document template and then get a pointer to the document template in that position. Next, you'll use the document template to get the position of the first document and then use the document template to get a pointer to the document in that first position. Finally, you'll use the document to get the position of the first view and then use the document again to get a pointer to the view in the position specified. Once you've got a pointer to the view, you can check the value of the check boxes and call the appropriate spinner.

To add this functionality to your application, use the Class Wizard to add a function to the `OnIdle` event message for the application class (in this case, `CTaskingApp`). Once you add the function, click the Edit Code button and add the code in Listing 18.12.

LISTING 18.12. THE `CTaskingApp` `OnIdle` FUNCTION.

```
1: BOOL CTaskingApp::OnIdle(LONG lCount)
2: {
3:     // TODO: Add your specialized code here and/or call the base class
4:
5:     // Get the position of the first document template
6:     POSITION pos = GetFirstDocTemplatePosition();
7:     // Do we have a valid template position?
8:     if (pos)
```

continues

LISTING **18.12**. CONTINUED

```
 9:     {
10:         // Get a pointer to the document template
11:         CDocTemplate* pDocTemp = GetNextDocTemplate(pos);
12:         // Do we have a valid pointer?
13:         if (pDocTemp)
14:         {
15:             // Get the position of the first document
16:             POSITION dPos = pDocTemp->GetFirstDocPosition();
17:             // Do we have a valid document position?
18:             if (dPos)
19:             {
20:                 // Get a pointer to the document
21:                 CTaskingDoc* pDocWnd =
22:                     (CTaskingDoc*)pDocTemp->GetNextDoc(dPos);
23:                 // Do we have a valid pointer?
24:                 if (pDocWnd)
25:                 {
26:                     // Get the position of the view
27:                     POSITION vPos = pDocWnd->GetFirstViewPosition();
28:                     // Do we have a valid view position?
29:                     if (vPos)
30:                     {
31:                         // Get a pointer to the view
32:                         CTaskingView* pView =
➥(CTaskingView*)pDocWnd->GetNextView(vPos);
33:                         // Do we have a valid pointer?
34:                         if (pView)
35:                         {
36:                             // Should we spin the first idle thread?
37:                             if (pView->m_bOnIdle1)
38:                                 // Spin the first idle thread
39:                                 pDocWnd->DoSpin(0);
40:                             // Should we spin the second idle thread?
41:                             if (pView->m_bOnIdle2)
42:                                 // Spin the second idle thread
43:                                 pDocWnd->DoSpin(2);
44:                         }
45:                     }
46:                 }
47:             }
48:         }
49:     }
50:
51:     // Call the ancestor's idle processing
52:     return CWinApp::OnIdle(lCount);
53: }
```

If you compile and run your application now, you should be able to check either of the
On Idle Thread check boxes, and see the spinner drawing a color wheel, as shown in

Figure 18.7, as long as you are moving the mouse. However, the moment you let the application become totally idle—no mouse movement or anything else—the spinner will stop spinning.

FIGURE 18.7.

On Idle Thread draw-ing a color wheel.

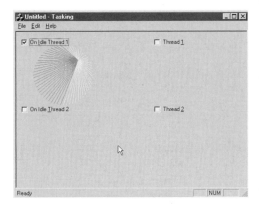

Making the `OnIdle` Tasks Continuous

It's not very practical to keep moving the mouse around to make your application contin-ue performing the tasks that it's supposed to do when the application is idle. There must be a way to get the application to continue to call the `OnIdle` function as long as the application is idle. Well, there is. If you look at the last line in the `OnIdle` function, you'll notice that the `OnIdle` function returns the result value from the ancestor `OnIdle` function. It just so happens that this function returns `FALSE` as soon as there is no `OnIdle` functionality to be performed.

You want the `OnIdle` function to always return `TRUE`. This will cause the `OnIdle` function to continue to be called, over and over, whenever the application is idle. If you move the call to the ancestor `OnIdle` function to the first part of the function and then return `TRUE`, as in Listing 18.13, you will get your spinner to continue turning, no matter how long the application sits idle.

LISTING 18.13. THE MODIFIED `CTaskingApp` `OnIdle` FUNCTION.

```
1: BOOL CTaskingApp::OnIdle(LONG lCount)
2: {
3:     // TODO: Add your specialized code here and/or call the base class
4:
5:     // Call the ancestor's idle processing
6:     CWinApp::OnIdle(lCount);
7:
```

continues

LISTING 18.13. CONTINUED

```
 8:        // Get the position of the first document template
 9:        POSITION pos = GetFirstDocTemplatePosition();
10:        // Do we have a valid template position?
11:        if (pos)
12:        {
  .
  .
  .
51:        }
52:        return TRUE;
53: }
```

If you compile and run your application, you can turn on the OnIdle tasks and see them continue to turn, even when you are not moving the mouse. However, if you activate any of the menus, or if you open the About window, both of these tasks come to a complete stop, as in Figure 18.8. The reason is that the open menus, and any open modal dialog windows, prevent the OnIdle function from being called. One of the limitations of OnIdle processing is that certain application functionality prevents it from being performed.

FIGURE 18.8.

On Idle Thread stopped by the menu.

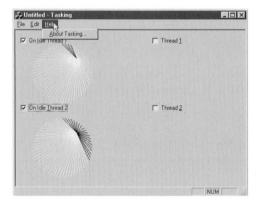

Adding Independent Threads

Now that you've seen what is involved in adding an OnIdle task, it's time to see what's involved in adding an independent thread to your application. To add a thread to your application, you'll add a main function for the threads. You'll also add the code to start and stop the threads. Finally, you'll add the code to the independent thread check boxes to start and stop each of these threads.

Creating the Main Thread Function

Before you can spin off any independent threads, the thread must know what to do. You will create a main thread function to be executed by the thread when it starts. This function will act as the main function for the thread, and the thread will end once the function ends. Therefore, this function must act as the primary control of the thread, keeping the thread running as long as there is work for the thread to do and then exiting once the thread's work is completed.

When you create a function to be used as the main function for a thread, you can pass a single parameter to this function. This parameter is a pointer to anything that contains all the information the thread needs to perform its tasks. For the application you've been building in this chapter, the parameter can be a pointer to the spinner that the thread will operate. Everything else that the thread needs can be extracted from the spinner object.

Once the thread has a pointer to its spinner, it can get a pointer to the check box variable that tells it whether to continue spinning or stop itself. As long as the variable is TRUE, the thread should continue spinning.

To add this function to your application, add a new member function to the document class in your application. Specify the function type as UINT, the function declaration as ThreadFunc(LPVOID pParam), and the access as private. You'll start the thread from within the document class, so there's no need for any other classes to see this function. Once you've added this function, edit it with the code in Listing 18.14.

18

LISTING **18.14**. THE CTaskingDoc ThreadFunc FUNCTION.

```
 1: UINT CTaskingDoc::ThreadFunc(LPVOID pParam)
 2: {
 3:     // Convert the argument to a pointer to the
 4:     // spinner for this thread
 5:     CSpinner* lpSpin = (CSpinner*)pParam;
 6:     // Get a pointer to the continuation flag
 7:     BOOL* pbContinue = lpSpin->GetContinue();
 8:
 9:     // Loop while the continue flag is true
10:     while (*pbContinue)
11:         // Spin the spinner
12:         lpSpin->Draw();
13:     return 0;
14: }
```

Starting and Stopping the Threads

Now that you have a function to call for the independent threads, you need some way of controlling the threads, starting and stopping them. You need to be able to hold onto a couple of pointers for CWinThread objects, which will encapsulate the threads. You'll add these pointers as variables to the document object and then use them to capture the return variable from the AfxBeginThread function that you will use to start both of the threads.

To add these variables to your application, add a new member variable to your document class. Specify the variable type as CWinThread*, the variable name as m_pSpinThread[2], and the variable access as private. This will provide you with a two slot array for holding these variables.

Now that you have a place to hold the pointers to each of the two threads, you'll add the functionality to start the threads. You can add a single function to start either thread, if it's not currently running, or to wait for the thread to stop itself, if it is running. This function will need to know which thread to act on and whether to start or stop the thread.

To add this functionality, add a new member function to the document class. Specify the function type as void, the function declaration as SuspendSpinner(int nIndex, BOOL bSuspend), and the function access as public, and check the Static check box. Edit the code for this function, adding the code in Listing 18.15.

LISTING **18.15**. THE CTaskingDoc SuspendSpinner FUNCTION.

```
 1: void CTaskingDoc::SuspendSpinner(int nIndex, BOOL bSuspend)
 2: {
 3:     // if suspending the thread
 4:     if (!bSuspend)
 5:     {
 6:         // Is the pointer for the thread valid?
 7:         if (m_pSpinThread[nIndex])
 8:         {
 9:             // Get the handle for the thread
10:             HANDLE hThread = m_pSpinThread[nIndex]->m_hThread;
11:             // Wait for the thread to die
12:             ::WaitForSingleObject (hThread, INFINITE);
13:         }
14:     }
15:     else    // We are running the thread
16:     {
17:         int iSpnr;
18:         // Which spinner to use?
19:         switch (nIndex)
20:         {
21:         case 0:
```

```
22:                    iSpnr = 1;
23:                    break;
24:                case 1:
25:                    iSpnr = 3;
26:                    break;
27:                }
28:                // Start the thread, passing a pointer to the spinner
29:                m_pSpinThread[nIndex] = AfxBeginThread(ThreadFunc,
30:                    (LPVOID)&m_cSpin[iSpnr]);
31:            }
32: }
```

The first thing that you do in this function is check to see if the thread is being stopped or started. If the thread is being stopped, check to see if the pointer to the thread is valid. If the pointer is valid, you retrieve the handle for the thread by reading the value of the handle property of the CWinThread class:

```
HANDLE hThread = m_pSpinThread[nIndex]->m_hThread;
```

Once you have the handle, you use the handle to wait for the thread to stop itself with the WaitForSingleObject function.

```
::WaitForSingleObject (hThread, INFINITE);
```

The WaitForSingleObject function is a Windows API function that tells the operating system you want to wait until the thread, whose handle you are passing, has stopped. The second argument to this function specifies how long you are willing to wait. By specifying INFINITE, you tell the operating system that you will wait forever, until this thread stops. If you specify a timeout value, and the thread does not stop by the time you specify, the function returns a value that indicates whether the thread has stopped. Because you specify INFINITE for the timeout period, you don't need to worry about capturing the return value because this function does not return until the thread stops.

If the thread is being started, you determine which spinner to use and then start that thread by calling the AfxBeginThread function.

```
m_pSpinThread[nIndex] = AfxBeginThread(ThreadFunc,
            (LPVOID)&m_cSpin[iSpnr]);
```

You passed the function to be called as the main function for the thread and the address of the spinner to be used by that thread.

Triggering the Threads from the View Object

Now that you have a means of starting and stopping each of the independent threads, you need to be able to trigger the starting and stopping from the check boxes on the window.

18

When each of the two check boxes is checked, you'll start each of the threads. When the check boxes are unchecked, each of the threads must be stopped. The second part of this is easy: As long as the variable tied to the check box is kept in sync with the control, once the check box is unchecked, the thread will stop itself. However, when the check box is checked, you'll need to call the document function that you just created to start the thread.

To add this functionality to the first of the two thread check boxes, use the Class Wizard to add a function to the BN_CLICKED event for the check box. Once you add the function, edit it with the code in Listing 18.16.

LISTING **18.16**. THE CTaskingView OnCbthread1 FUNCTION.

```
1: void CTaskingView::OnCbthread1()
2: {
3:     // TODO: Add your control notification handler code here
4:
5:     //////////////////////////
6:     // MY CODE STARTS HERE
7:     //////////////////////////
8:
9:     // Sync the variables with the dialog
10:     UpdateData(TRUE);
11:
12:     // Get a pointer to the document
13:     CTaskingDoc* pDocWnd = (CTaskingDoc*)GetDocument();
14:     // Did we get a valid pointer?
15:     ASSERT_VALID(pDocWnd);
16:
17:     // Suspend or start the spinner thread
18:     pDocWnd->SuspendSpinner(0, m_bThread1);
19:
20:     //////////////////////////
21:     // MY CODE ENDS HERE
22:     //////////////////////////
23: }
```

In this function, the first thing that you do is to call UpdateData to keep the variables in sync with the controls on the window. Next, you retrieve a pointer to the document. Once you have a valid pointer, you call the document's SuspendSpinner function, specifying the first thread and passing the current value of the variable tied to this check box to indicate whether the thread is to be started or stopped.

To add this same functionality to the other thread check box, perform the same steps, adding the code in Listing 18.17.

LISTING 18.17. THE `CTaskingView OnCbthread2` FUNCTION.

```
 1: void CTaskingView::OnCbthread2()
 2: {
 3:     // TODO: Add your control notification handler code here
 4:
 5:     ////////////////////////
 6:     // MY CODE STARTS HERE
 7:     ////////////////////////
 8:
 9:     // Sync the variables with the dialog
10:     UpdateData(TRUE);
11:
12:     // Get a pointer to the document
13:     CTaskingDoc* pDocWnd = (CTaskingDoc*)GetDocument();
14:     // Did we get a valid pointer?
15:     ASSERT_VALID(pDocWnd);
16:
17:     // Suspend or start the spinner thread
18:     pDocWnd->SuspendSpinner(1, m_bThread2);
19:
20:     ////////////////////////
21:     // MY CODE ENDS HERE
22:     ////////////////////////
23: }
```

18

Now that you've added the ability to start and stop the independent threads, compile and run your application. You'll see that you can start and stop the independent threads with their check boxes, as well as the `OnIdle` tasks.

At this point, if you play around with your application for a while, you'll notice a bit of a difference between the two types of threads. If you have all threads running and are actively moving the mouse, you might notice the `OnIdle` spinners slowing down in their spinning (unless you have a very fast machine). The independent threads are taking a good deal of the processor time away from the main application thread, leaving less processor time to be idle. As a result, it's easier to keep your application busy. The other thing that you might notice is that if you activate the menus or open the About window, although the `OnIdle` tasks come to a complete stop, the independent threads continue to run, as in Figure 18.9. These two threads are completely independent processes running within your application, so they are not affected by the rest of the application.

FIGURE 18.9.

The threads are not affected by the menu.

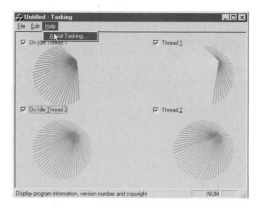

Shutting Down Cleanly

You might think that you are done with this application until you try to close the application while one or both of the independent threads are running. You'll see an unpleasant notification that you still have some work to do, as in Figure 18.10. It seems that leaving the threads running when you closed the application caused it to crash.

FIGURE 18.10.

Application error notification.

Even though the application was closing, the threads were continuing to run. When these threads checked the value of the variable indicating whether to continue running or spin their spinners, they were trying to access a memory object that no longer existed. This problem causes one of the most basic and most fatal application memory errors, which you should eliminate before allowing anyone else to use the application.

What you need to do to prevent this error is stop both of the threads before allowing the application to close. The logical place to take this action is the OnDestroy event message processing in the view class. This event message is sent to the view class to tell it to clean up anything that it needs to clean up before closing the application. You can add code to set both of the check box variables to FALSE so that the threads will stop themselves and then call the SuspendSpinner function for each thread to make sure that both threads have stopped before allowing the application to close. You do not need to call UpdateData to sync the variables with the controls because the user doesn't need to see when you've change the value of either check box.

To add this functionality to your application, add an event-handler function for the
OnDestroy event message to the view class. This function does not normally exist in the
view class that is created by the AppWizard, so you need to add it when it is needed in
the descendent view class. Edit the function, adding the code in Listing 18.18.

LISTING 18.18. THE CTaskingView OnDestroy FUNCTION.

```
 1: void CTaskingView::OnDestroy()
 2: {
 3:     CFormView::OnDestroy();
 4:
 5:     // TODO: Add your message handler code here
 6:
 7:     ///////////////////////
 8:     // MY CODE STARTS HERE
 9:     ///////////////////////
10:
11:     // Is the first thread running?
12:     if (m_bThread1)
13:     {
14:         // Specify to stop the first thread
15:         m_bThread1 = FALSE;
16:         // Get a pointer to the document
17:         CTaskingDoc* pDocWnd = (CTaskingDoc*)GetDocument();
18:         // Did we get a valid pointer?
19:         ASSERT_VALID(pDocWnd);
20:
21:         // Suspend the spinner thread
22:         pDocWnd->SuspendSpinner(0, m_bThread1);
23:     }
24:     // Is the second thread running?
25:     if (m_bThread2)
26:     {
27:         // Specify to stop the second thread
28:         m_bThread2 = FALSE;
29:         // Get a pointer to the document
30:         CTaskingDoc* pDocWnd = (CTaskingDoc*)GetDocument();
31:         // Did we get a valid pointer?
32:         ASSERT_VALID(pDocWnd);
33:
34:         // Suspend the spinner thread
35:         pDocWnd->SuspendSpinner(1, m_bThread2);
36:     }
37:
38:     ///////////////////////
39:     // MY CODE ENDS HERE
40:     ///////////////////////
41: }
```

18

In this function, you do exactly what you need to do. You check first one check box variable and then the other. If either is TRUE, you set the variable to FALSE, get a pointer to the document, and call the SuspendSpinner function for that thread. Now when you close your application while the independent threads are running, your application will close without crashing.

Summary

Today, you learned quite a bit. You learned about the different ways you can make your applications perform multiple tasks at one time. You also learned about some of the considerations to take into account when adding this capability to your applications. You learned how to make your application perform tasks when the application is sitting idle, along with some of the limitations and drawbacks associated with this approach. You also learned how to create independent threads in your application that will perform their tasks completely independently of the rest of the application. You implemented an application that uses both of these approaches so that you could experience how each approach works.

Tip

When you start adding multitasking capabilities to your applications to perform separate tasks, be aware that this is a very advanced aspect of programming for Windows. You need to understand a lot of factors and take into account far more than we can reasonably cover in a single day. If you want to build applications using this capability, get an advanced book on programming Windows applications with MFC or Visual C++. The book should include a substantial section devoted to multithreading with MFC and cover all the synchronization classes in much more detail than we did here. Remember that you need a book that focuses on MFC, not the Visual C++ development environment. (MFC is supported by most commercial C++ development tools for building Windows applications, including Borland and Symantec's C++ compilers, so coverage for this topic extends beyond the Visual C++ environment.)

Q&A

Q How can I use the other version of the AfxBeginThread to encapsulate a thread in a custom class?

A First, the other version of AfxBeginThread is primarily for creating user-interface threads. The version that you used in today's sample application is for creating what are called worker threads that immediately take off on a specific task. If you want to create a user-interface thread, you need to inherit your custom class from the CWinThread class. Next, override several ancestor functions in your custom class. Once the class is ready to use, you use the RUNTIME_CLASS macro to get a pointer to the runtime class of your class and pass this pointer to the AfxBeginThread function, as follows:

```
CWinThread* pMyThread =
            AfxBeginThread(RUNTIME_CLASS(CMyThreadClass));
```

Q Can I use SuspendThread and ResumeThread to start and stop my independent threads in my sample application?

A Yes, but you need to make a few key changes to your application. First, in the OnNewDocument function, initialize the two thread pointers to NULL, as shown in Listing 18.19.

LISTING 18.19. THE MODIFIED CTaskingDoc OnNewDocument FUNCTION.

```
 1: BOOL CTaskingDoc::OnNewDocument()
 2: {
 3:     if (!CDocument::OnNewDocument())
 4:         return FALSE;
 5:
 6:     // TODO: add reinitialization code here
 7:     // (SDI documents will reuse this document)
 8:
 9:     ///////////////////////
10:     // MY CODE STARTS HERE
11:     ///////////////////////
12:
13:     // Initialize the spinners
14:     InitSpinners();
15:
16:     // Initialize the thread pointers
17:     m_pSpinThread[0] = NULL;
18:     m_pSpinThread[1] = NULL;
19:
20:     ///////////////////////
21:     // MY CODE ENDS HERE
22:     ///////////////////////
23:
24:     return TRUE;
25: }
```

Next, modify the thread function so that the thread does not stop itself when the check box variable is FALSE but continues to loop, as shown in Listing 18.20.

LISTING 18.20. THE MODIFIED CTaskingDoc ThreadFunc FUNCTION.

```
 1: UINT CTaskingDoc::ThreadFunc(LPVOID pParam)
 2: {
 3:     // Convert the argument to a pointer to the
 4:     // spinner for this thread
 5:     CSpinner* lpSpin = (CSpinner*)pParam;
 6:     // Get a pointer to the continuation flag
 7:     BOOL* pbContinue = lpSpin->GetContinue();
 8:
 9:     // Loop while the continue flag is true
10:     while (TRUE)
11:         // Spin the spinner
12:         lpSpin->Draw();
13:     return 0;
14: }
```

Finally, modify the SuspendSpinner function so that if the thread pointer is valid, it calls the SuspendThread function on the thread pointer to stop the thread and the ResumeThread function to restart the thread, as shown in Listing 18.21.

LISTING 18.21. THE MODIFIED CTaskingDoc SuspendSpinner FUNCTION.

```
 1: void CTaskingDoc::SuspendSpinner(int nIndex, BOOL bSuspend)
 2: {
 3:     // if suspending the thread
 4:     if (!bSuspend)
 5:     {
 6:         // Is the pointer for the thread valid?
 7:         if (m_pSpinThread[nIndex])
 8:         {
 9:             // Suspend the thread
10:             m_pSpinThread[nIndex]->SuspendThread();
11:         }
12:     }
13:     else    // We are running the thread
14:     {
15:         // Is the pointer for the thread valid?
16:         if (m_pSpinThread[nIndex])
17:         {
18:             // Resume the thread
19:             m_pSpinThread[nIndex]->ResumeThread();
20:         }
21:         else
22:         {
23:             int iSpnr;
24:             // Which spinner to use?
25:             switch (nIndex)
```

```
26:                    {
27:                    case 0:
28:                        iSpnr = 1;
29:                        break;
30:                    case 1:
31:                        iSpnr = 3;
32:                        break;
33:                    }
34:                    // Start the thread, passing a pointer to the spinner
35:                    m_pSpinThread[nIndex] = AfxBeginThread(ThreadFunc,
36:                        (LPVOID)&m_cSpin[iSpnr]);
37:                }
38:            }
39: }
```

Workshop

The Workshop provides quiz questions to help you solidify your understanding of the material covered and exercises to provide you with experience in using what you've learned. The answers to the quiz questions and exercises are provided in Appendix B, "Answers."

Quiz

1. When is the OnIdle function called?

2. How can you cause the OnIdle function to be repeatedly called while the application is sitting idle?

3. What is the difference between an OnIdle task and a thread?

4. What are the four thread synchronization objects?

5. Why shouldn't you specify a higher than normal priority for the threads in your application?

Exercises

1. If you open a performance monitor on your system while the application that you built today is running, you'll find that even without any of the threads running, the processor usage remains 100 percent, as shown in Figure 18.11. The OnIdle function is continuously being called even when there is nothing to be done.

   Modify the OnIdle function so that if there's nothing to be done, neither of the OnIdle tasks are active. Then, the OnIdle function will not continue to be called until one of these threads is active, at which time it should be continuously called until both threads are once again turned off. This will allow the processor to drop to a minimal utilization, as shown in Figure 18.12.

FIGURE 18.11.

*Processor utilization at
100 percent.*

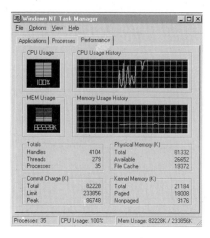

FIGURE 18.11.

*Processor utilization at
100 percent.*

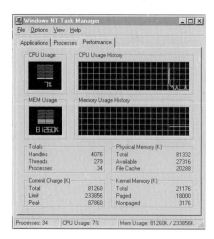

FIGURE 18.12.

*Processor utilization at
normal levels.*

2. When starting the independent threads, give one of the threads a priority of
   `THREAD_PRIORITY_NORMAL` and the other a priority of `THREAD_PRIORITY_LOWEST`.

DAY 19

Building Your Own Widgets—Creating ActiveX Controls

The software industry has seen a revolution over the past couple years. How software is built and packaged has moved from a model where all applications are large, monolithic pieces of executable code to a model where most applications consist of small building blocks. These small building blocks, often called components, can be created using any of several different languages and can take many different forms. One of the most popular components is the ActiveX control. If you know how to create your own ActiveX controls, you can build your own components and provide them to other programmers. Today, you will learn

- How to use the Visual C++ wizards to build ActiveX controls.
- How to add properties and methods to your controls using the Class Wizard.
- How to test your control using the tools provided with Visual C++.

What Is an ActiveX Control?

An ActiveX control is a set of functionality packaged in a COM (Component Object Model) object. This COM object is self-contained, although it does not have the ability to run by itself. An ActiveX control can only run within a ActiveX container, such as a Visual C++ or Visual Basic application.

As you learned on Day 9, "Adding ActiveX Controls to Your Application," ActiveX controls provide a series of interfaces used by the container application to trigger the various sets of functionality contained in the control. Many of these interfaces are used for triggering events in the control or in the containing application. Others are for specifying the property page of the control or for communicating whether the control has been activated. All in all, so many interfaces are built into most ActiveX controls that coding the functionality for each of these interfaces yourself would take quite some time. Luckily, the Visual C++ App and Class Wizards add much of this functionality for you, allowing you to focus on the specific functionality that the control is supposed to have.

Among the aspects of the control you create that you still must plan yourself are what properties, methods, and events you will expose for your control. You can add these elements to your control through the Class Wizard, but if any of the properties or events require special code on your part, then you must add it yourself. As should be expected with any methods that you add to your controls, you have to supply all of the code. The Class Wizard will add the surrounding structure and code to allow the containing application to see and call the method, just as it will add all the code necessary to call any event handlers for your applications.

Properties

Properties are attributes of controls that are visible to, and often modifiable by, the container application. The four basic types of properties are ambient, extended, stock, and custom. Ambient properties are provided by the container application to the control—such things as background color or the default font to be used—so that the control looks like part of the container application. Extended properties are not actually properties of the control but instead are provided and implemented by the container application, such as tab order. The control may extend these properties somewhat; for example, if the control contains two or more standard controls, it may control the tab order within the overall control, returning the tab order control to the application once the control has completed its internal tab order. Stock properties are implemented by the ActiveX control development kit, such as control font or control background color. The final type of properties, custom properties, are what you are most concerned with because these properties are specific to your control and are directly related to the functionality of your control.

You can specify any properties you need in your control using the Automation tab on the Class Wizard. When you add a new property to your control through the Class Wizard, you'll specify several aspects of the property.

The first aspect is the external property name, which is the name shown to the containing application for the property. Another aspect that you can specify is the internal variable name, which is used in your code, but only if the property is implemented as a member variable. You also specify the variable type for the property.

If you specify that the property is to be implemented as a member variable (the property is a member variable of the control class), then you can specify the name of the notification function, which is called when the property is changed by the containing application. If the property is not a member variable of the control class, you need to specify that it is altered and viewed through Get and Set methods, where the containing application calls a Get method to get the current value of the property and calls a Set method to change the value of the property. If the property is maintained through Get and Set methods, then you can specify the names of these two methods.

For all these aspects of a property, the Add Property dialog suggests appropriate names for everything once you enter the external name for the property. If you want to accept the default names, the only things you need to specify are the external name, the type, and whether the property is a member variable or uses Get and Set methods. If you choose a stock property from the list of available stock properties, the rest of the elements are automatically specified for you. Once you specify all of this information, the Class Wizard adds all of the necessary code and variables to your control project.

Methods

Methods are functions in the control that can be called by the container application. These functions are made available to other applications through the IDispatch interface, which we discussed on Day 9. Because of the way the IDispatch works in calling the methods in a control, the variables passed to the method have to be packaged in a structure that is passed to the control. This structure is machine independent so that it doesn't matter whether your control is running with Windows 95/98 on an Intel Pentium II or on a Windows NT with a MIPS or Alpha processor; the structure will look the same. It is the responsibility of each side of the function call to convert the parameters as necessary to fit them into the structure correctly or to extract them from the structure. This process of packaging the method parameters is called marshaling.

19

When you add a new method to your control through the Class Wizard on the Automation tab, the Class Wizard adds all of the necessary code to perform the marshaling of the parameters, as well as all other supporting functionality, including building the IDispatch interface and table.

When you add a new method to your control through the Class Wizard, you are asked to provide the external name for the method called by the container application. Your method will get a default internal name, which you can override by entering your own internal name. Other aspects of your control methods that you have to specify are the method's return type and the parameters for the method. Once you finish entering all this information, the Class Wizard adds all the necessary code to the control.

Events

Events are notification messages that are sent from the control to the container application. They are intended to notify the application that a certain event has happened, and the application can take action on that event if desirable. You can trigger two types of events from your control, stock or custom events. Stock events are implemented by the ActiveX control development kit and are available as function calls within the control. These stock events enable you to trigger events in the container application for mouse or keyboard events, errors, or state changes.

Along with the stock events, you can add your own custom events to be triggered in the container application. These events should be related to the specific functionality of your control. You can specify arguments to be passed with the event to the container application so that the application can have the data it needs for reacting to the event message.

When you need to trigger any of these events, all you do is call the internal event function that fires the event, passing all the necessary parameters to the function. The Class Wizard will have added all of the necessary code to trigger the event message from the internal function call.

Events are one of the three elements that you do not add to your controls through the Automation tab in the Class Wizard. Events are added through the ActiveX Events tab in the Class Wizard.

Creating an ActiveX Control

The ActiveX control that you will build as the example today is the squiggle drawing module that you packaged as a library module and then as DLLs on Day 16, "Creating Your Own Classes and Modules," and Day 17, "Sharing Your Functionality with Other Applications—Creating DLLs." In converting this module into an ActiveX control, you'll expose the maximum number of squiggles that the control will draw, as well as the maximum length of the squiggles, as properties that the container application can set. Every time the control is clicked, you'll program it to create a new squiggle drawing. You'll also add a method to load a squiggle drawing into the control that was created with the previous versions of the squiggle module. Finally, you'll have the control fire an event to let the container application know that the control has loaded the drawing.

Building the Control Shell

You've probably noticed by now that one of the options on the new project dialog is an MFC ActiveX Control Wizard. This is another project wizard just like the AppWizard for creating application and DLL projects. You can use it to build a shell for any ActiveX controls that you want to build. It will create all of the necessary files and configure the project so that the compiler will build an ActiveX control when you compile.

When you start the Control Wizard, you are asked some simple questions about your control project, such as how many controls will be in the project and whether the controls will have runtime licenses.

Note

> Runtime licenses are a means of making sure that the user of your control has purchased a license to use the control. Controls developed for selling to developers often have runtime licenses. The license prevents use of a control by users who haven't paid for it. When you use the control in an application, either the runtime license for the control is installed in the user's registry by the install routine or the runtime license is compiled into the application. These means prevent someone from using the control to build new applications.

19

In the second step of the Control Wizard, the questions get a little more involved but are still fairly easy to answer. In this step, you can click the Edit Names button to provide the control with descriptive names for the user. At the bottom of the Control Wizard, you'll find a combo box that lists a number of window classes that you can subclass in your control. If you want to create a special edit box that performs some special edits on anything the user types into the box, you choose EDIT from the list of window classes in the drop-down portion of this combo box. If you choose to click the Advanced button, the questions about your project require a fairly thorough understanding of ActiveX controls.

To begin the sample control project today, start a new project, selecting the MFC ActiveX Control Wizard and giving the project a suitable name, such as Squiggle, as shown in Figure 19.1.

FIGURE 19.1.

Starting an ActiveX control project.

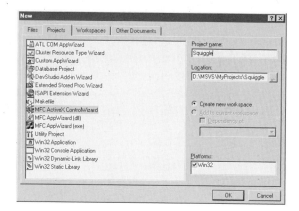

Leave all the options with their default settings in the first Control Wizard step because you'll create only a single control today, and you won't need to include any runtime licensing. On the second Control Wizard step, click the Edit Names button and make sure that the type name is sufficiently descriptive of the control. Click OK to approve the names, returning to the second Control Wizard step. If you had specified in the first step that you were creating multiple controls, then you would choose each control in the drop-down list beside the Edit Names button, specifying the names for each individual control in the project. You can leave the rest of the options in the Control Wizard at their default settings for this sample project.

Modifying the CModArt Class

Once you create the control shell, copy the Line and ModArt files from the library module project directory, the project you built on Day 16. Load all four of these files into the control project, adding the CLine and CModArt classes to the project.

The primary changes that you need to make to the CModArt class for your control is setting the maximum number of squiggles and length of squiggles variables that can be exposed as control properties. To be able to implement this, you'll add two member variables to the CModArt class, one to control the length of the squiggles and the other to control the number of squiggles. Add these two variables to the CModArt class as in Table 19.1.

TABLE 19.1. MEMBER VARIABLES FOR CModArt CLASS.

Name	Type	Access
m_iLength	int	Private
m_iSegments	int	Private

You need to provide a way for these variables to be retrieved and updated from the exposed properties. This means that you'll need functions for getting the current value, and for setting the new value, for each of these variables. To add these functions for the m_iLength variable, add a member function to the CModArt class, specifying the type as int, the declaration as GetLength, and the access as public. Edit the function with the code in Listing 19.1.

LISTING 19.1. THE CModArt GetLength FUNCTION.

```
1: int CModArt::GetLength()
2: {
3:     // Return the current value for the m_iLength variable
4:     return m_iLength;
5: }
```

Next, add another member function to the CModArt class, specifying the function type as void, the declaration as SetLength(int iLength), and the access as public. Edit this function, adding the code in Listing 19.2.

LISTING 19.2. THE CModArt SetLength FUNCTION.

```
1: void CModArt::SetLength(int iLength)
2: {
3:     // Set the current value for the m_iLength variable
4:     m_iLength = iLength;
5: }
```

Add the same two functions for the m_iSegments variable so that it can also be exposed as a property of the control.

Now that you have made these two properties available for the control, you'll make sure that they have been initialized to reasonable values before the control is used. To initialize these values, modify the CModArt constructor as in Listing 19.3.

LISTING 19.3. THE MODIFIED CModArt CONSTRUCTOR.

```
1: CModArt::CModArt()
2: {
3:     // Initialize the random number generator
4:     srand((unsigned)time(NULL));
5:     // Initialize the property variables
6:     m_iLength = 200;
7:     m_iSegments = 50;
8: }
```

19

Finally, you'll modify the two function that create the squiggle drawings so that they use these variables instead of the hard-coded values that they currently use. To modify the NewDrawing function, replace the maximum number of squiggles in line 7 with the variable m_iSegments, as in Listing 19.4.

LISTING 19.4. THE MODIFIED CModArt NewDrawing FUNCTION.

```
1: void CModArt::NewDrawing()
2: {
3:     int lNumLines;
4:     int lCurLine;
5:
6:     // Determine how many lines to create
7:     lNumLines = rand() % m_iSegments;
8:     // Are there any lines to create?
9:     if (lNumLines > 0)
10:     {
11:         // Loop through the number of lines
12:         for (lCurLine = 0; lCurLine < lNumLines; lCurLine++)
13:         {
14:             // Create the new line
15:             NewLine();
16:         }
17:     }
18: }
```

Finally, replace the maximum length of each squiggle with the m_iLength variable on line 20 in the NewLine function, as in Listing 19.5.

LISTING 19.5. THE MODIFIED CModArt NewLine FUNCTION.

```
1: void CModArt::NewLine()
2: {
3:     int lNumLines;
.
.
.
18:
19:     // Determine the number of parts to this squiggle
20:     lNumLines = rand() % m_iLength;
21:     // Are there any parts to this squiggle?
.
.
.
67: }
```

You have made all of the necessary modifications to the CModArt and CLine classes for your ActiveX control. Now you have to add an instance of the CModArt class to the control class as a member variable. Add a new member variable to the control class, CSquiggleCtrl, specifying its type as CModArt, its name as m_maDrawing, and its access as private. You also need to include the header file for the CModArt class in the control class source code file, so open this file, scroll to the top of the file, and add an include statement for the ModArt.h file, as in Listing 19.6.

LISTING **19.6.** THE `CSquiggleCtrl` INCLUDES.

```
1: // SquiggleCtl.cpp : Implementation of the CSquiggleCtrl ActiveX
Control class.
2:
3: #include "stdafx.h"
4: #include "Squiggle.h"
5: #include "SquiggleCtl.h"
6: #include "SquigglePpg.h"
7: #include "ModArt.h"
```

Adding Properties

Because the two variables that you added to the CModArt class are not variables of the control class (CSquiggleCtrl), you will probably want to add Get and Set methods to set and retrieve the property value. If these two variables were members of the control class, you could add them through the Class Wizard as member variables. You would still know when and if the variables had been changed because you would have a notification method in the control class that would be called when the property values are changed. However, because they are members of an internal class, you'll want to exercise a little more control over their values.

> **Tip**
>
> Even if the variables that you want to expose are member variables of the control class, you might still want to use the Get and Set methods for accessing the variables as control properties. Using the Get and Set methods allow you to add validation on the new value for the properties so that you can make certain that the container application is setting an appropriate value to the property.

To add these properties to your control, open the Class Wizard and select the Automation tab, as in Figure 19.2. Click on the Add Property button to add the first property. In the Add Property dialog, enter the external name that you want your property to have, such as `SquiggleLength`, and specify the type as `short` (the `int` type is not available, only `short` and `long`). Click the `Get/Set` methods radio button, and the dialog enters function names for these two methods, as in Figure 19.3. Click OK to add this property.

FIGURE 19.2.

The Class Wizard Automation tab.

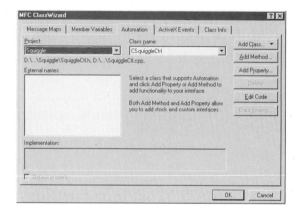

FIGURE 19.3.

The Add Property dialog.

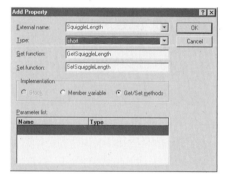

Click the Edit Code button to add the code for the `Get` and `Set` methods. In each method, you'll call the `Get` and `Set` functions that you added to the `CModArt` class to control access to the length variable. Edit these two methods as shown in Listing 19.7.

LISTING 19.7. THE `CSquiggleCtrl` Get/SetSquiggleLength FUNCTIONS.

```
1:   short CSquiggleCtrl::GetSquiggleLength()
2:   {
3:       // TODO: Add your property handler here
4:       // Return the result from the GetLength function
5:       return m_maDrawing.GetLength();
6:   }
7:
```

```
 8: void CSquiggleCtrl::SetSquiggleLength(short nNewValue)
 9: {
10:     // TODO: Add your property handler here
11:     // Set the new length value
12:     m_maDrawing.SetLength(nNewValue);
13:     SetModifiedFlag();
14: }
```

Add another property for the number of squiggles in a drawing by following the same steps, substituting an appropriate property name, such as NumberSquiggles.

One last property you might want to add to your control is a boolean property that the container application could use to keep the control from creating any new drawings and to keep the current drawing visible. Add a new property through the Class Wizard, giving it a suitable name such as KeepCurrentDrawing, and specify the type as BOOL. Leave this property set as a member variable and click OK. The Class Wizard automatically adds the variable to the control class, along with all of the necessary code to maintain the variable.

Designing and Building the Property Page

You need to provide a property page with your control that developers can use when they are working with your control. This property page will provide the users with a means of setting the properties of the control, even if their own development tools do not provide them with a facility to get to these properties in any way other than with code.

Adding a property page to your control is pretty easy. If you select the Resources view tab in the workspace and expand the dialog folder, you'll see a dialog for your control's property page already in the folder. Open this dialog, and you'll find that it's a standard dialog window that you can design using the standard controls available in the dialog designer. To design the property page for your sample control, lay out the property page dialog as shown in Figure 19.4, using the property settings in Table 19.2.

19

FIGURE 19.4.

The control property page layout.

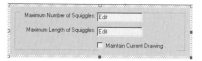

TABLE 19.2. CONTROL PROPERTY SETTINGS.

Object	Property	Setting
Static Text	ID	IDC_STATIC
	Caption	Maximum Number of Squiggles:
Edit Box	ID	IDC_ENBRSQUIG
Static Text	ID	IDC_STATIC
	Caption	Maximum Length of Squiggles:
Edit Box	ID	IDC_ELENSQUIG
Check Box	ID	IDC_CMAINTDRAW
	Caption	Maintain Current Drawing

Once you add all the controls and specify their properties, open the Class Wizard to add variables for these controls. When you add a variable to one of the controls on the property page dialog, you'll notice an additional combo box on the Add Member Variable dialog. This new combo box is for the external name of the property that the variable should be tied to in the control. The drop-down list on this combo box is a list of all of the standard properties that you might want to tie the property page control to, but if you are tying it to a custom property, you have to enter the property name yourself, as shown in Figure 19.5.

FIGURE 19.5.

The Add Member Variable dialog.

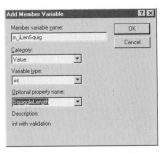

Add variables to the controls on the property page for your control, tying them to the control's properties, as specified in Table 19.3.

TABLE 19.3. CONTROL VARIABLES.

Object	Name	Category	Type	Property
IDC_CMAINTDRAW	m_bKeepDrawing	Value	BOOL	KeepCurrentDrawing
IDC_ELENSQUIG	m_iLenSquig	Value	int	SquiggleLength
IDC_ENBRSQUIG	m_iNbrSquiggles	Value	int	NumberSquiggles

Click the OK button to add all these variables to the control property page class.

Adding Basic Control Functionality

The basic functionality that your control needs is the ability to respond to mouse clicks by generating a new drawing. To control this behavior, you'll add a second boolean variable to the control class so that the OnDraw function knows that a mouse click has been triggered. The easiest place to get the drawing area of the control is the OnDraw function, so this is where the new drawing needs to be generated. Do you want the control to generate a new drawing every time the user moves the application using your control in front of another application? Probably not. You will most likely want a greater amount of control over the behavior of the control, so it makes sense to add this second boolean variable. Add a member variable to the control class (CSquiggleCtrl), specifying the variable type as BOOL, the variable name as m_bGenNewDrawing, and the variables access as private.

Before you start adding the code to perform all the various tasks, it's important that you initialize all the member variables in the control class. This consists of the member variable property, m_keepCurrentDrawing, and the member variable that you just added, m_bGenNewDrawing. You'll want your control to generate a new drawing right off the bat, and you probably don't want it to maintain any drawings, unless the container application explicitly specifies that a drawing is to be maintained. You'll set these two variables accordingly in the control class constructor, as shown in Listing 19.8.

LISTING 19.8. THE CSquiggleCtrl CONSTRUCTOR.

```
1: CSquiggleCtrl::CSquiggleCtrl()
2: {
3:     InitializeIIDs(&IID_DSquiggle, &IID_DSquiggleEvents);
4:
5:     // TODO: Initialize your control's instance data here.
6:     // Initialize the variables
7:     m_bGenNewDrawing = TRUE;
8:     m_keepCurrentDrawing = FALSE;
9: }
```

19

Next, you'll add the code to generate and display the squiggle drawings. The place to add this functionality is the OnDraw function in the control class. This function is called every time that the control needs to draw itself, whether it was hidden or something triggered the redrawing by calling the Invalidate function on the control. Once in the OnDraw function, you'll determine whether you need to generate a new drawing or just draw the existing drawing. Another thing to keep in mind is that you are responsible for drawing the entire area that the control occupies. This means that you need to draw the background of the squiggle drawing, or else the squiggles will be drawn on top of whatever was displayed in that same spot on the screen. (Who knows? That might be the effect you are looking for.) To add this functionality to your control, edit the OnDraw function in the control class, adding the code in Listing 19.9.

LISTING 19.9. THE CSquiggleCtrl OnDraw FUNCTION.

```
 1: void CSquiggleCtrl::OnDraw(
 2:               CDC* pdc, const CRect& rcBounds, const CRect& rcInvalid)
 3: {
 4: ·   // TODO: Replace the following code with your own drawing code.
 5:     //pdc->FillRect(rcBounds, CBrush::FromHandle((HBRUSH)
                  ➥GetStockObject(WHITE_BRUSH)));
 6:     //pdc->Ellipse(rcBounds);
 7:     // Do we need to generate a new drawing?
 8:     if (m_bGenNewDrawing)
 9:     {
10:         // Set the drawing area for the new drawing
11:         m_maDrawing.SetRect(rcBounds);
12:         // Clear out the old drawing
13:         m_maDrawing.ClearDrawing();
14:         // Generate the new drawing
15:         m_maDrawing.NewDrawing();
16:         // Reset the control flag
17:         m_bGenNewDrawing = FALSE;
18:     }
19:     // Fill in the background
20:     pdc->FillRect(rcBounds,
21:         CBrush::FromHandle((HBRUSH)GetStockObject(WHITE_BRUSH)));
22:     // Draw the squiggle drawing
23:     m_maDrawing.Draw(pdc);
24: }
```

Finally, you'll trigger the control to generate a new drawing whenever the control is clicked. This requires adding an event handler for the control's OnClick event. First, however, you'll add a stock method to the control to make sure that it receives the OnClick event message. To add this stock method, open the Class Wizard and select the Automation tab. Add a new method to the control class, selecting the DoClick method from the drop-down list of stock methods that can be added to your control, as shown in Figure 19.6. Click the OK button to add the method to your control, and then select the Message Maps tab in the Class Wizard. Select the OnClick event message from the list of available event messages, and add a function to handle this event message. Edit the code for the OnClick event handler, adding the code in Listing 19.10.

FIGURE 19.6.

The Add Method dialog.

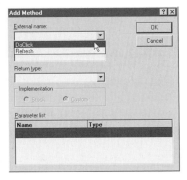

LISTING 19.10. THE `CSquiggleCtrl` OnClick FUNCTION.

```
 1: void CSquiggleCtrl::OnClick(USHORT iButton)
 2: {
 3:     // TODO: Add your specialized code here and/or call the base class
 4:     // Can we generate a new drawing?
 5:     if (!m_keepCurrentDrawing)
 6:     {
 7:         // Set the flag so a new drawing will be generated
 8:         m_bGenNewDrawing = TRUE;
 9:         // Invalidate the control to trigger the OnDraw function
10:         Invalidate();
11:     }
12:     COleControl::OnClick(iButton);
13: }
```

In the `OnClick` function, you check to see whether you could generate a new drawing or maintain the current drawing. If you could generate a new drawing, you set the `m_bGenNewDrawing` flag to `TRUE` and invalidated the control, which triggers the `OnDraw` function.

Adding Methods

Remember the functionality that you are going to give your control: One of the functions is loading a squiggle drawing created with the version of the Squiggle module that you created on Day 16. To add this functionality, you'll add a method to the control that the container application can call to pass a filename to be loaded. You've already added one method to your application, a stock method. Adding a custom method is similar, but you have to provide a little more information to the Add Method dialog.

In the method to load an existing drawing, you'll create a `CFile` object for the filename that was passed as a parameter. The `CFile` constructor will take the filename and the flag `CFile::modeRead` to let it know that you are opening the file for reading only. Once you

19

create the CFile object, you'll create a CArchive object to read the file. The CArchive constructor will take the CFile object that you just created and the CArchive::load flag to tell it that it needs to load the file. At this point, you can pass the CArchive object to the drawing object's Serialize function and let it read and load the drawing. Once the drawing is loaded, you need to display the drawing by invalidating the control. Before you invalidate the control, you probably want to make sure that the m_bGenNewDrawing flag is set to FALSE so that the drawing you just loaded won't be overwritten.

To add this functionality to your control, open the Class Wizard and select the Automation tab. Click the Add Method button to add a custom method. Enter the external method name in the first combo box; in this case, call it LoadDrawing. The internal name will automatically be generated based on the external name you entered. Next, specify the return type as BOOL so that you can let the container application know whether you were able to load the drawing. Finally, add a single parameter to the parameter list, giving it a name such as sFileName and specifying its type as LPCTSTR (the CString type is not available, but the LPCTSTR type is compatible), as shown in Figure 19.7. Click the OK button to add the method to your control. Once you add the method, click the Edit Code button to edit the method, adding the code in Listing 19.11.

FIGURE 19.7.

The Add custom Method dialog.

LISTING 19.11. THE CSquiggleCtrl LoadDrawing FUNCTION.

```
 1: BOOL CSquiggleCtrl::LoadDrawing(LPCTSTR sFileName)
 2: {
 3:     // TODO: Add your dispatch handler code here
 4:     try
 5:     {
 6:         // Create a CFile object
 7:         CFile lFile(sFileName, CFile::modeRead);
 8:         // Create a CArchive object to load the file
 9:         CArchive lArchive(&lFile, CArchive::load);
10:         // Load the file
```

```
11:            m_maDrawing.Serialize(lArchive);
12:            // Make sure that the loaded drawing won't be overwritten
13:            m_bGenNewDrawing = FALSE;
14:            // Draw the loaded drawing
15:            Invalidate();
16:        }
17:        catch (CFileException err)
18:        {
19:            return FALSE;
20:        }
21:        return TRUE;
22: }
```

Adding Events

The final part of building your control is adding the events that your control will trigger in the container application. When using your control, the user will be able to add code to be triggered on these events. Adding these events to your control is done through the ActiveX Events tab of the Class Wizard. If you want to add a stock event to be triggered by your control, then you just click the Add Event button and select a stock event from the drop-down list of stock events. If you need to add a custom event to your control, then in the Add Event dialog, instead of selecting a stock event, you enter the name of your custom event. At the bottom of the Add Event dialog is an area for adding parameters that you can pass from your control to the container application with the event.

For the sample control, you'll add one event, a custom event to let the application know that the drawing file specified has been loaded. To add this event, open the Class Wizard and select the ActiveX Events tab, as shown in Figure 19.8. Click the Add Event button to add the event. Enter the name for your custom event, FileLoaded. You'll notice that the Add Event dialog automatically builds an internal name for the event, in this case, FireFileLoaded, as shown in Figure 19.9. This internal name is the name for the function that you need to call in your code when you want to trigger this event. Click the OK button to add this event. To add a stock event, select the desired stock event from the drop-down list of stock events, and click the OK button to add this second event.

Now that you've added your event to your control, you need to make the necessary changes to the code to trigger this event at the appropriate places. You'll trigger your event at the end of your LoadDrawing function, assuming that you are able to load the drawing correctly. Add this additional functionality to the LoadDrawing function, as shown in line 17 of Listing 19.12.

19

FIGURE 19.8.

The ActiveX Events tab of the Class Wizard.

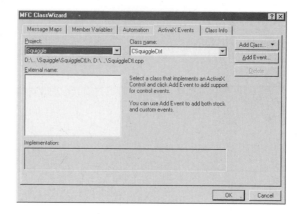

FIGURE 19.9.

The Add Event dialog.

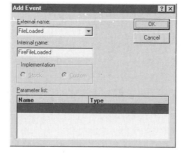

LISTING 19.12. THE MODIFIED `CSquiggleCtrl LoadDrawing` FUNCTION.

```
 1: BOOL CSquiggleCtrl::LoadDrawing(LPCTSTR sFileName)
 2: {
 3:     // TODO: Add your dispatch handler code here
 4:     try
 5:     {
 6:         // Create a CFile object
 7:         CFile lFile(sFileName, CFile::modeRead);
 8:         // Create a CArchive object to load the file
 9:         CArchive lArchive(&lFile, CArchive::load);
10:         // Load the file
11:         m_maDrawing.Serialize(lArchive);
12:         // Make sure that the loaded drawing won't be overwritten
13:         m_bGenNewDrawing = FALSE;
14:         // Draw the loaded drawing
15:         Invalidate();
16:         // Fire the FileLoaded event
17:         FireFileLoaded();
18:     }
19:     catch (CFileException err)
```

```
20:    {
21:        return FALSE;
22:    }
23:    return TRUE;
24: }
```

Testing the Control

Now you are ready to compile and begin testing your control. Before you run to the store to pick up a copy of Visual Basic, you already have a tool just for testing ActiveX controls. On the Tools menu is one entry labeled ActiveX Control Test Container. This is a utility that is designed specifically for testing ActiveX controls that you have built. Once you compile your control, run the ActiveX Control Test Container to test your control.

Tip

If Visual C++ is unable to register your control, but is able to compile it, you might need to register your control yourself. You can do this by selecting Tools | Register Control from the menu. This will register the compiled control in the Registry database.

When you first start the test container, you see a blank area where your control will appear. You need to insert your control into this container area by selecting Edit | Insert New Control. This will open the Insert Control dialog, as shown in Figure 19.10. Select your control from the list of available controls and click the OK button to add your control to the container area, as shown in Figure 19.11.

19

FIGURE 19.10.

The Insert Control dialog.

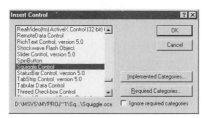

Now that you have your control loaded into the test container, you can play with it, resize it, click it, and check when it generates a new drawing and when it just redraws the existing drawing. If you trigger any events for your control, you'll see the event that your control fired in the bottom pane of the test container so that you can watch as each of the events you added to your control are triggered.

FIGURE **19.11.**

*The squiggle control in
the test container.*

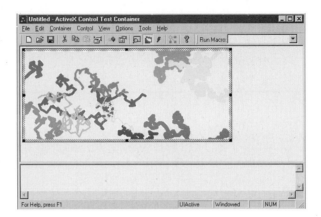

With your control selected, if you select Edit | Properties from the menu, you'll open the
property page that you designed for your control, allowing you to modify the various
properties of the control so that you can see whether they work correctly, as shown in
Figure 19.12.

FIGURE **19.12.**

*The Squiggle Control
Properties page.*

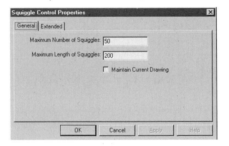

Finally, to test the methods that you added to your control, select Control | Invoke
Methods. This opens the Invoke Methods dialog, as shown in Figure 19.13. In here, you
can select from the list of available methods in your control, entering each of the parameters required for the methods, and then click the Invoke button to call that method.
You can watch as your methods are called and your control responds.

FIGURE 19.13.

The Invoke Methods dialog.

Summary

Today, you learned how you can use the tools and wizards in Visual C++ to build ActiveX controls with little effort on your part. You learned how you can create the shell of the control project using the Control Wizard. You also learned how you can use the Class Wizard to add properties, methods, and events to your control. You saw how you can design a property page for your control and how you can use the Class Wizard to attach the controls on this dialog to the properties you defined for your control without having to add any code. Finally, you learned how you can use the ActiveX Control Test Container to test your control, triggering all the functionality by using the tools of this utility.

Q&A

Q How do I change the icon that appears in the toolbox for my control?

A In the Resource View tab of the workspace pane, open the Bitmap folder. You should find a single bitmap in this folder. This image is displayed in the toolbox for your control when you add it to a Visual C++ or Visual Basic project. You should edit this bitmap so that it displays the image that you want to represent your control.

Q Why does my control have an About box?

A If you are building ActiveX controls that will be used by other developers, whether you sell the control or give it away, you probably want to include some way of indicating that you wrote the control, and that you, or your employer, owns the copyright on the control. This acts as a legal identification on the control so that whoever obtains your control cannot turn around and sell it as his creation.

19

Workshop

The Workshop provides quiz questions to help you solidify your understanding of the material covered and exercises to provide you with experience in using what you've learned. The answers to the quiz questions and exercises are provided in Appendix B, "Answers."

Quiz

1. What are the three aspects of a control that are visible to the container application?
2. Why do you need to design a property page for your control?
3. What are the four types of properties that a control might have?
4. What happens to the parameters that are passed to the methods of a control?
5. What tool can you use to test your controls?

Exercises

1. Add a method to your control to enable the container application to trigger the generation of a new squiggle drawing.
2. Add a method to your control to save a squiggle drawing. Use the `CFile::modeWrite` and `CArchive::store` flags when creating the `CFile` and `CArchive` objects.

DAY **20**

Internet Applications and Network Communications

Thanks in part to the explosion in popularity of the Internet, more applications have the ability to communicate with other applications over networks, including the Internet. With Microsoft building networking capabilities into its operating systems, starting with Windows NT and Windows 95, these capabilities are becoming commonplace in all sorts of applications.

Some applications perform simple networking tasks such as checking with a Web site to see whether there are any updates to the program and giving the user the option of updating her copy of the program. Some word processing applications will format documents as Web pages, giving the user the option of loading the pages onto the Web server. You've got computer games that allow the user to play against another person halfway around the world instead of just competing against the game itself.

Applications can have any number of networking functions, and they all are built around the Winsock interface. If you know and understand how to program using the Winsock interface and the MFC Winsock classes, this entire realm of application programming is open to you, expanding your programming options considerably. Today, you will learn

- How applications use the Winsock interface to perform network communications between two or more computers.
- The difference between a client and a server application and the role each plays in establishing a communications link.
- How the MFC Winsock classes simplify the process of writing Internet applications.
- How you can create your own Winsock class, descended from the MFC Winsock classes, to easily build an event-driven, networking application.

How Do Network Communications Work?

Most applications that communicate over a network, whether it's the Internet or a small office network, use the same principles and functionality to perform their communication. One application sits on a computer, waiting for another application to open a communication connection. This application is "listening" for this connection request, much like you listen for the phone to ring if you are expecting someone to call.

Meanwhile, another application, most likely on another computer (but not necessarily), tries to connect to the first application. This attempt to open a connection is similar to calling someone on the telephone. You dial the number and hope that the other person is listening for the phone on the other end. As the person making the call, you have to know the phone number of the person you are calling. If you don't know the phone number, you can look it up using the person's name. Likewise, the application trying to connect to the first application has to know the network location, or address, of the first application.

Once the connection is made between the two applications, messages can pass back and forth between the two applications, much like you can talk to the person on the other end of the phone. This connection is a two-way communications channel, with both sides sending information, as shown in Figure 20.1.

FIGURE 20.1.

*The basic socket con-
nection process.*

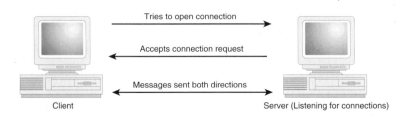

Client

Tries to open connection

Accepts connection request

Messages sent both directions

Server (Listening for connections)

Finally, once one or both sides have finished their sides of the conversation, the connection is closed, much like you hang up the phone after you have finished talking to the person you called. Once the connection is closed from either side, the other side can detect it and close its side, just like you can tell if the person on the other end of the phone has hung up on you or if you've been disconnected by some other means. This is a basic explanation of how network communications work between two or more applications.

Note This is a basic description of how network communications work with the TCP/IP network protocol, which is the primary network protocol over the Internet. Many other network protocols use a subtle variation on this description. Other protocols, such as the UDP protocol, are more like radio broadcasts, where there is no connection between the two applications; one sends messages, and the other is responsible for making sure that it receives all of the messages. These protocols are more involved than we have the luxury to discuss today. If you want to learn more about network protocols and how they work, many books cover this one topic and look at the various Internet applications and how they communicate over the connections they establish.

Sockets, Ports, and Addresses

The basic object used by applications to perform most network communications is called a socket. Sockets were first developed on UNIX at the University of California at Berkley. Sockets were designed so that most network communications between applications could be performed in the same way that these same applications would read and write files. Sockets have progressed quite a bit since then, but the basics of how they work are still the same.

During the days of Windows 3.x, before networking was built into the Windows operating system, you could buy the network protocols required for network communications from numerous different companies. Each of these companies had a slightly different way that an application performed network communications. As a result, any applications that performed network communications had a list of the different networking software that the application would work with. Many application developers were not happy with this situation. As a result, all the networking companies, including Microsoft, got together and developed the Winsock (Windows Sockets) API. This provided all application developers with a consistent API to perform all network communications, regardless of the networking software used.

20

When you want to read or write a file, you must use a file object to point to the file. Although this was hidden from you in most of the Visual C++ applications so far, with the ActiveX control you created yesterday, you had to work through the steps of creating the file object for reading and writing. A socket is similar; it is an object used to read and write messages that travel between applications.

Making a socket connection to another application does require a different set of information than opening a file. To open a file, you need to know the file's name and location. To open a socket connection, you need to know the computer on which the other application is running and the port on which it's listening. A port is like a phone extension, and the computer address is like the phone number. If you call someone at a large office building, you may dial the main office number, but then you need to specify the extension number. Likewise, ports are used to route network communications (see Figure 20.2). As with the phone number, there are means of looking up the port number, if you don't already know what it is, but this requires your computer to be configured with the information about which port the connecting application is listening on. If you specify the wrong computer address or port number, you may get a connection to a different application; with making the phone call, someone other than the person you called may answer the phone call. You also may not get an answer at all if there is no application listening at the other end.

Note

Only one application may be listening on any specific port on a single computer. Although numerous applications may listen for connection requests on a single computer at the same time, each of these applications must listen on a different port.

Creating a Socket

When you build applications with Visual C++, you can use the MFC Winsock classes to add network communications capabilities with relative ease. The base class, CAsyncSocket, provides complete, event-driven socket communications. You can create your own descendent socket class that captures and responds to each of these events.

Caution

This discussion of socket communications assumes that you check the AppWizard option for adding support for Windows Sockets. This adds supporting functionality to the application that is not discussed here.

FIGURE 20.2.

Ports are used to route network communications to the correct application.

The network interface in a computer uses socket ports to direct network messages to the correct application.

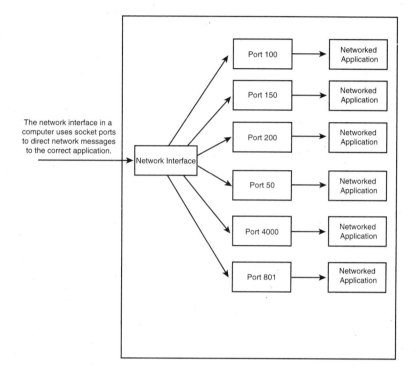

To create a socket that you can use in your application, the first thing you need to do is declare a variable of CAsyncSocket (or your descendent class) as a class member for one of the main application classes:

```
class CMyDlg : public CDialog
{
    .
    .
    .
private:
    CAsyncSocket m_sMySocket;
};
```

Before you can begin using the socket object, you must call its Create method. This actually creates the socket and prepares it for use. How you call the Create method depends on how you will be using the socket. If you will be using the socket to connect to another application, as the one placing the call (the client), then you do not need to pass any parameters to the Create method:

```
if (m_sMySocket.Create())
{
    // Continue on
```

20

```
}
else
    // Perform error handling here
```

However, if the socket is going to be listening for another application to connect to it, waiting for the call (the server), then you need to pass at least the port number on which the socket should be listening:

```
if (m_sMySocket.Create(4000))
{
    // Continue on
}
else
    // Perform error handling here
```

You can include other parameters in the `Create` method call, such as the type of socket to create, the events that the socket should respond to, and the address that the socket should listen on (in case the computer has more than one network card). All these options require a more thorough understanding of sockets than we'll be able to cover today.

Making a Connection

Once you create a socket, you are ready to open a connection with it. Three steps go along with opening a single connection. Two of these steps take place on the server, the application listing for the connection, and the third step takes place on the client, the one making the call.

For the client, opening the connection is a simple matter of calling the `Connect` method. The client has to pass two parameters to the `Connect` method: the computer name, or network address, and the port of the application to connect to. The `Connect` method could be used in the following two ways:

```
if (m_sMySocket.Connect("thatcomputer.com", 4000))
{
    // Continue on
}
else
    // Perform error handling here
```

The second form is

```
if (m_sMySocket.Connect("178.1.25.82", 4000))
{
    // Continue on
}
else
    // Perform error handling here
```

Once the connection is made, an event is triggered to let your application know that it is connected or that there were problems and the connection couldn't be made. (I'll cover how these events work in the section "Socket Events," later in this chapter.)

For the server, or listening, side of the connection, the application first must tell the socket to listen for incoming connections by calling the `Listen` method. The `Listen` method takes only a single argument, which you do not need to supply. This parameter specifies the number of pending connections that can be queued, waiting for the connection to be completed. By default this value is 5, which is the maximum. The `Listen` method can be called as follows:

```
if (m_sMySocket.Listen())
{
    // Continue on
}
else
    // Perform error handling here
```

Whenever another application is trying to connect to the listening application, an event is triggered to let the application know that the connection request is there. The listening application must accept the connection request by calling the `Accept` method. This method requires the use of a second `CAsyncSocket` variable, which is connected to the other application. Once a socket is placed into listen mode, it stays in listen mode. Whenever connection requests are received, the listening socket creates another socket, which is connected to the other application. This second socket should not have the `Create` method called for it because the `Accept` method creates the socket. You call the `Accept` method as follows:

```
if (m_sMySocket.Accept(m_sMySecondSocket))
{
    // Continue on
}
else
    // Perform error handling here
```

At this point, the connecting application is connected to the second socket on the listening application.

Sending and Receiving Messages

Sending and receiving message through a socket connection gets slightly involved. Because you can use sockets to send any kind of data, and they don't care what the data is, the functions to send and receive data expect to be passed a pointer to a generic buffer. For sending data, this buffer should contain the data to be sent. For receiving data, this buffer will have the received data copied into it. As long as you are sending and

20

receiving strings and text, you can use fairly simple conversions to and from CStrings with these buffers.

To send a message through a socket connection, you use the Send method. This method requires two parameters and has a third, optional parameter that can be used to control how the message is sent. The first parameter is a pointer to the buffer that contains the data to be sent. If your message is in a CString variable, you can use the LPCTSTR operator to pass the CString variable as the buffer. The second parameter is the length of the buffer. The method returns the amount of data that was sent to the other application. If an error occurs, the Send function returns SOCKET_ERROR. You can use the Send method as follows:

```
CString strMyMessage;
int iLen;
int iAmtSent;
.
.
.
iLen = strMyMessage.GetLength();
iAmtSent = m_sMySocket.Send(LPCTSTR(strMyMessage), iLen);
if (iAmtSent == SOCKET_ERROR)
{
    // Do some error handling here
}
else
{
    // Everything's fine
}
```

When data is available to be received from the other application, an event is triggered on the receiving application. This lets your application know that it can receive and process the message. To get the message, the Receive method must be called. This method takes the same parameters as the Send method with a slight difference. The first parameter is a pointer to a buffer into which the message may be copied. The second parameter is the size of the buffer. This tells the socket how much data to copy (in case more is received than will fit into the buffer). Like the Send method, the Receive method will return the amount that was copied into the buffer. If an error occurs, the Receive method also returns SOCKET_ERROR. If the message your application is receiving is a text message, it can be copied directly into a CString variable. This allows you to use the Receive method as follows:

```
char *pBuf = new char[1025];
int iBufSize = 1024;
int iRcvd;
CString strRecvd;

iRcvd = m_sMySocket.Receive(pBuf, iBufSize);
```

```
if (iRcvd == SOCKET_ERROR)
{
    // Do some error handling here
}
else
{
    pBuf[iRcvd] = NULL;
    strRecvd = pBuf;
    // Continue processing the message
}
```

> **Tip**
>
> When receiving text messages, it's always a good idea to place a NULL in the buffer position just after the last character received, as in the preceding example. There may be garbage characters in the buffer that your application might interpret as part of the message if you don't add the NULL to truncate the string.

Closing the Connection

Once your application has finished all of its communications with the other application, it can close the connection by calling the Close method. The Close method doesn't take any parameters, and you use it as follows:

```
m_sMySocket.Close();
```

> **Note**
>
> The Close function is one of the few CAsyncSocket methods that does not return any status code. For all the previous member functions that we have examined, you can capture the return value to determine if an error has occurred.

Socket Events

The primary reason that you create your own descendent class of CAsyncSocket is that you want to capture the events that are triggered when messages are received, connections are completed, and so on. The CAsyncSocket class has a series of functions that are called for each of these various events. These functions all use the same definition—the function name is the only difference—and they are intended to be overridden in descendent classes. All of these functions are declared as protected members of the CAsyncSocket class and probably should be declared as protected in your descendent classes. The functions all have a single integer parameter, which is an error code that

20

should be checked to make sure that no error has occurred. Table 20.1 lists these event functions and the events they signal.

TABLE 20.1. CAsyncSocket OVERRIDABLE EVENT-NOTIFICATION FUNCTIONS.

Function	Event Description
OnAccept	This function is called on a listening socket to signal that a connection request from another application is waiting to be accepted.
OnClose	This function is called on a socket to signal that the application on the other end of the connection has closed its socket or that the connection has been lost. This should be followed by closing the socket that received this notification.
OnConnect	This function is called on a socket to signal that the connection with another application has been completed and that the application can now send and receive messages through the socket.
OnReceive	This function is called to signal that data has been received through the socket connection and that the data is ready to be retrieved by calling the Receive function.
OnSend	This function is called to signal that the socket is ready and available for sending data. This function is called right after the connection has been completed. Usually, the other time that this function is called is when your application has passed the Send function more data than can be sent in a single packet. In this case, this is a signal that all of the data has been sent, and the application can send the next buffer-full of data.

Detecting Errors

Whenever any of the CAsyncSocket member functions return an error, either FALSE for most functions or SOCKET_ERROR on the Send and Receive functions, you can call the GetLastError method to get the error code. This function returns only error codes, and you have to look up the translation yourself. All the Winsock error codes are defined with constants, so you can use the constants in your code to determine the error message to display for the user, if any. You can use the GetLastError function as follows:

```
int iErrCode;

iErrCode = m_sMySocket.GetLastError();
switch (iErrCode)
{
case WSANOTINITIALIZED:
   .
   .
   .
}
```

Building a Networked Application

For the sample application that you will build today, you'll create a simple dialog application that can function as either the client or server in a Winsock connection. This will allow you to run two copies of the sample application, one for each end of the connection, on the same computer or to copy the application to another computer so that you can run the two copies on separate computers and see how you can pass messages across a network. Once the application has established a connection with another application, you will be able to enter text messages and send them to the other application. When the message has been sent, it will be added to a list of messages sent. Each message that is received will be copied into another list of all messages received. This will allow you to see the complete list of what is sent and received. It will also allow you to compare what one copy of the application has sent and what the other has received. (The two lists should be the same.)

Creating the Application Shell

For today's sample application, just to keep things simple, you'll create a dialog-style application. Everything that you are doing in today's application can be done in an SDI or MDI application just as easily as with a dialog-style application. By using a dialog-style application today, we are getting everything that might distract from the basic socket functionality (such as questions about whether the socket variable belongs in the document or view class, how much of the application functionality belongs in which of these two classes, and so on) away from the sample application.

To start today's sample application, create a new MFC AppWizard project, giving the project a suitable name, such as Sock. On the first step of the AppWizard, specify that the application will be a dialog-based application. On the second step of the AppWizard, specify that the application should include support for Windows Sockets, as in Figure 20.3. You can accept the default settings for the rest of the options in the AppWizard.

Window Layout and Startup Functionality

Once you create your application shell, you can lay out the main dialog for your application. On this dialog, you'll need a set of radio buttons to specify whether the application is running as the client or server. You'll also need a couple of edit boxes for the computer name and port that the server will be listening on. Next, you'll need a command button to start the application listening on the socket or opening the connection to the server, and a button to close the connection. You'll also need an edit box for entering the message to be sent to the other application and a button to send the message. Finally, you'll need a couple of list boxes into which you can add each of the messages sent and

20

received. Place all these controls on the dialog, as shown in Figure 20.4, setting all of the control properties as specified in Table 20.2.

FIGURE 20.3.

Including sockets support.

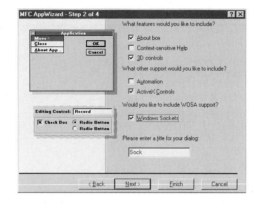

FIGURE 20.4.

The main dialog layout.

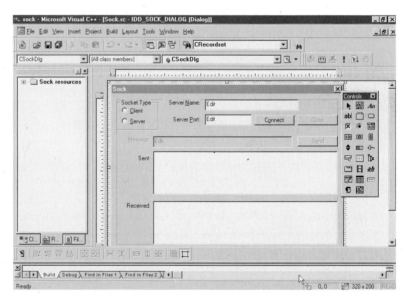

TABLE 20.2. CONTROL PROPERTY SETTINGS.

Object	Property	Setting
Group Box	ID	IDC_STATICTYPE
	Caption	Socket Type
Radio Button	ID	IDC_RCLIENT
	Caption	&Client
	Group	Checked

Object	Property	Setting
Radio Button	ID	IDC_RSERVER
	Caption	&Server
Static Text	ID	IDC_STATICNAME
	Caption	Server &Name:
Edit Box	ID	IDC_ESERVNAME
Static Text	ID	IDC_STATICPORT
	Caption	Server &Port:
Edit Box	ID	IDC_ESERVPORT
Command Button	ID	IDC_BCONNECT
	Caption	C&onnect
Command Button	ID	IDC_BCLOSE
	Caption	C&lose
	Disabled	Checked
Static Text	ID	IDC_STATICMSG
	Caption	&Message:
	Disabled	Checked
Edit Box	ID	IDC_EMSG
	Disabled	Checked
Command Button	ID	IDC_BSEND
	Caption	S&end
	Disabled	Checked
Static Text	ID	IDC_STATIC
	Caption	Sent:
List Box	ID	IDC_LSENT
	Tab Stop	Unchecked
	Sort	Unchecked
	Selection	None
Static Text	ID	IDC_STATIC
	Caption	Received:
List Box	ID	IDC_LRECVD
	Tab Stop	Unchecked
	Sort	Unchecked
	Selection	None

20

. Once you have the dialog designed, open the Class Wizard to attach variables to the controls on the dialog, as specified in Table 20.3.

TABLE 20.3. CONTROL VARIABLES.

Object	Name	Category	Type
IDC_BCONNECT	m_ctlConnect	Control	CButton
IDC_EMSG	m_strMessage	Value	CString
IDC_ESERVNAME	m_strName	Value	CString
IDC_ESERVPORT	m_iPort	Value	int
IDC_LRECVD	m_ctlRecvd	Control	CListBox
IDC_LSENT	m_ctlSent	Control	CListBox
IDC_RCLIENT	m_iType	Value	int

So that you can reuse the Connect button to place the server application into listen mode, you'll add a function to the clicked event message for both radio buttons, changing the text on the command button depending on which of the two is currently selected. To add this functionality to your application, add a function to the BN_CLICKED event message for the IDC_RCLIENT control ID, naming the function OnRType. Add the same function to the BN_CLICKED event message for the IDC_RSERVER control ID. Edit this function, adding the code in Listing 20.1.

LISTING 20.1. THE CSockDlg OnRType FUNCTION.

```
 1: void CSockDlg::OnRType()
 2: {
 3:     // TODO: Add your control notification handler code here
 4:     // Sync the controls with the variables
 5:     UpdateData(TRUE);
 6:     // Which mode are we in?
 7:     if (m_iType == 0)    // Set the appropriate text on the button
 8:         m_ctlConnect.SetWindowText("C&onnect");
 9:     else
10:         m_ctlConnect.SetWindowText("&Listen");
11: }
```

Now, if you compile and run your application, you should be able to select one and then the other of these two radio buttons, and the text on the command button should change to reflect the part the application will play, as in Figure 20.5.

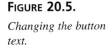

FIGURE 20.5.

Changing the button text.

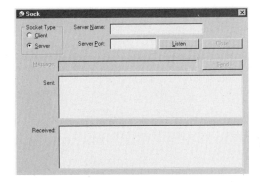

Inheriting from the CAsyncSocket Class

So that you will be able to capture and respond to the socket events, you'll create your own descendent class from CAsyncSocket. This class will need its own versions of the event functions, as well as a means of passing this event to the dialog that the object will be a member of. So that you can pass each of these events to the dialog-class level, you'll add a pointer to the parent dialog class as a member variable of your socket class. You'll use this pointer to call event functions for each of the socket events that are member functions of the dialog, after checking to make sure that no errors have occurred (of course).

To create this class in your application, select Insert | New Class from the menu. In the New Class dialog, leave the class type with the default value of MFC Class. Enter a name for your class, such as CMySocket, and select CAsyncSocket from the list of available base classes. This is all that you can specify on the New Class dialog, so click the OK button to add this new class to your application.

Once you have created the socket class, add a member variable to the class to serve as a pointer to the parent dialog window. Specify the variable type as CDialog*, the variable name as m_pWnd, and the access as private. You also need to add a method to the class to set the pointer, so add a member function to your new socket class. Specify the function type as void, the declaration as SetParent(CDialog* pWnd), and the access as public. Edit this new function, setting the pointer passed as a parameter to the member variable pointer, as in Listing 20.2.

20

LISTING 20.2. THE CMySocket SetParent FUNCTION.

```
1: void CMySocket::SetParent(CDialog *pWnd)
2: {
3:     // Set the member pointer
4:     m_pWnd = pWnd;
5: }
```

The only other thing that you need to do to your socket class is add the event functions, which you'll use to call similarly named functions on the dialog class. To add a function for the OnAccept event function, add a member function to your socket class. Specify the function type as void, the function declaration as OnAccept(int nErrorCode), and the access as protected and check the virtual check box. Edit this function, adding the code in Listing 20.3.

LISTING 20.3. The CMySocket OnAccept FUNCTION.

```
1: void CMySocket::OnAccept(int nErrorCode)
2: {
3:     // Were there any errors?
4:     if (nErrorCode == 0)
5:         // No, call the dialog's OnAccept function
6:         ((CSockDlg*)m_pWnd)->OnAccept();
7: }
```

Add similar functions to your socket class for the OnConnect, OnClose, OnReceive, and OnSend functions, calling same-named functions in the dialog class, which you'll add later. After you've added all these functions, you'll need to include the header file for your application dialog in your socket class, as in line 7 of Listing 20.4.

LISTING 20.4. THE CMySocket INCLUDES.

```
1: // MySocket.cpp: implementation file
2: //
3:
4: #include "stdafx.h"
5: #include "Sock.h"
6: #include "MySocket.h"
7: #include "SockDlg.h"
```

Once you've added all the necessary event functions to your socket class, you'll add a variable of your socket class to the dialog class. For the server functionality, you'll need two variables in the dialog class, one to listen for connection requests and the other to be connected to the other application. Because you will need two socket objects, add two member variables to the dialog class (CSockDlg). Specify the type of both variables as your socket class (CMySocket) and the access for both as private. Name one variable m_sListenSocket, to be used for listening for connection requests, and the other m_sConnectSocket, to be used for sending messages back and forth.

Once you've added the socket variables, you'll add the initialization code for all the variables. As a default, set the application type to client, the server name as `loopback`, and the port to 4000. Along with these variables, you'll set the parent dialog pointers in your two socket objects so that they point to the dialog class. You can do this by adding the code in Listing 20.5 to the `OnInitDialog` function in the dialog class.

Note

> The computer name `loopback` is a special name used in the TCP/IP network protocol to indicate the computer you are working on. It's an internal computer name that is resolved to the network address `127.0.0.1`. This is a computer name and address that is commonly used by applications that need to connect to other applications running on the same computer.

LISTING 20.5. THE CSockDlg `OnInitDialog` FUNCTION.

```
 1: BOOL CSockDlg::OnInitDialog()
 2: {
 3:      CDialog::OnInitDialog();
 4:
 5:      // Add "About..." menu item to system menu.
 6:
 .
 .
 .
26:      SetIcon(m_hIcon, FALSE);          // Set small icon
27:
28:      // TODO: Add extra initialization here
29:      // Initialize the control variables
30:      m_iType = 0;
31:      m_strName = "loopback";
32:      m_iPort = 4000;
33:      // Update the controls
34:      UpdateData(FALSE);
35:      // Set the socket dialog pointers
36:      m_sConnectSocket.SetParent(this);
37:      m_sListenSocket.SetParent(this);
38:
39:      return TRUE;  // return TRUE  unless you set the focus to a
         ➥control
40: }
```

20

Connecting the Application

When the user clicks the Connect button, you'll disable all the top controls on the dialog. At this point, you don't want the user to think that she is able to change the settings of the computer that she's connecting to or change how the application is listening. You'll call the `Create` function on the appropriate socket variable, depending on whether the application is running as the client or server. Finally, you'll call either the `Connect` or `Listen` function to initiate the application's side of the connection. To add this functionality to your application, open the Class Wizard and add a function to the `BN_CLICKED` event message for the Connect button (ID `IDC_BCONNECT`). Edit this function, adding the code in Listing 20.6.

LISTING 20.6. The `CSockDlg OnBconnect` FUNCTION.

```
 1: void CSockDlg::OnBconnect()
 2: {
 3:     // TODO: Add your control notification handler code here
 4:     // Sync the variables with the controls
 5:     UpdateData(TRUE);
 6:     // Disable the connection and type controls
 7:     GetDlgItem(IDC_BCONNECT)->EnableWindow(FALSE);
 8:     GetDlgItem(IDC_ESERVNAME)->EnableWindow(FALSE);
 9:     GetDlgItem(IDC_ESERVPORT)->EnableWindow(FALSE);
10:     GetDlgItem(IDC_STATICNAME)->EnableWindow(FALSE);
11:     GetDlgItem(IDC_STATICPORT)->EnableWindow(FALSE);
12:     GetDlgItem(IDC_RCLIENT)->EnableWindow(FALSE);
13:     GetDlgItem(IDC_RSERVER)->EnableWindow(FALSE);
14:     GetDlgItem(IDC_STATICTYPE)->EnableWindow(FALSE);
15:     // Are we running as client or server?
16:     if (m_iType == 0)
17:     {
18:         // Client, create a default socket
19:         m_sConnectSocket.Create();
20:         // Open the connection to the server
21:         m_sConnectSocket.Connect(m_strName, m_iPort);
22:     }
23:     else
24:     {
25:         // Server, create a socket bound to the port specified
26:         m_sListenSocket.Create(m_iPort);
27:         // Listen for connection requests
28:         m_sListenSocket.Listen();
29:     }
30: }
```

Next, to complete the connection, you'll add the socket event function to the dialog class for the `OnAccept` and `OnConnect` event functions. These are the functions that your socket class is calling. They don't require any parameters, and they don't need to return any result code. For the `OnAccept` function, which is called for the listening socket when another application is trying to connect to it, you'll call the socket object's `Accept` function, passing in the connection socket variable. Once you've accepted the connection, you can enable the prompt and edit box for entering and sending messages to the other application.

To add this function to your application, add a member function to the dialog class (`CSockDlg`). Specify the function type as void, the declaration as `OnAccept`, and the access as public. Edit the function, adding the code in Listing 20.7.

LISTING 20.7. THE `CSockDlg` `OnAccept` FUNCTION.

```
1: void CSockDlg::OnAccept()
2: {
3:     // Accept the connection request
4:     m_sListenSocket.Accept(m_sConnectSocket);
5:     // Enable the text and message controls
6:     GetDlgItem(IDC_EMSG)->EnableWindow(TRUE);
7:     GetDlgItem(IDC_BSEND)->EnableWindow(TRUE);
8:     GetDlgItem(IDC_STATICMSG)->EnableWindow(TRUE);
9: }
```

For the client side, there's nothing to do once the connection has been completed except enable the controls for entering and sending messages. You'll also enable the Close button so that the connection can be closed from the client side (but not the server side). To add this functionality to your application, add another member function to the dialog class (`CSockDlg`). Specify the function type as void, the function declaration as `OnConnect`, and the access as public. Edit the function, adding the code in Listing 20.8.

LISTING 20.8. THE `CSockDlg` `OnConnect` FUNCTION.

```
1: void CSockDlg::OnConnect()
2: {
3:     // Enable the text and message controls
4:     GetDlgItem(IDC_EMSG)->EnableWindow(TRUE);
5:     GetDlgItem(IDC_BSEND)->EnableWindow(TRUE);
6:     GetDlgItem(IDC_STATICMSG)->EnableWindow(TRUE);
7:     GetDlgItem(IDC_BCLOSE)->EnableWindow(TRUE);
8: }
```

20

If you could compile and run your application now, you could start two copies, put one into listen mode, and then connect to it with the other. Unfortunately, you probably can't even compile your application right now because your socket class is looking for several functions in your dialog class that you haven't added yet. Add three member functions to the dialog class (CSockDlg). Specify all of them as void functions with public access. Specify the first function's declaration as OnSend, the second as OnReceive, and the third as OnClose. You should now be able to compile your application.

Once you've compiled your application, start two copies of the application, side-by-side. Specify that one of these two should be the server, and click the Listen button to put it into listen mode. Leave the other as the client and click the Connect button. You should see the connection controls disable and the message sending controls enable as the connection is made, as in Figure 20.6.

FIGURE 20.6.

Connecting the two applications.

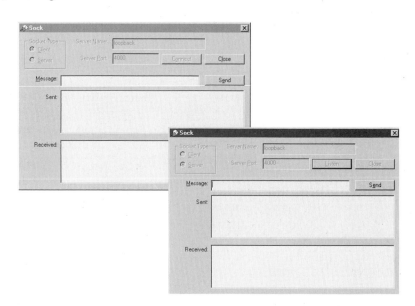

> | **Tip** | Be sure that you have the server application listening before you try to connect it to the client application. If you try to connect to it with the client application before the server is listening for the connection, the connection will be rejected. Your application will not detect that the connection was rejected because you haven't added any error handling to detect this event. |

> | **Tip** | To run these applications and get them to connect, you'll need TCP/IP running on your computer. If you have a network card in your computer, you may already have TCP/IP running. If you do not have a network card, and |

you use a modem to connect to the Internet, then you will probably need to be connected to the Internet when you run and test these applications. When you connect to the Internet through a modem, your computer usually starts running TCP/IP once the connection to the Internet is made. If you do not have a network card in your computer, and you do not have any means of connecting to the Internet, or any other outside network that would allow you to run networked applications, you may not be able to run and test today's applications on your computer.

Sending and Receiving

Now that you are able to connect the two running applications, you'll need to add functionality to send and receive messages. Once the connection is established between the two applications, the user can enter text messages in the edit box in the middle of the dialog window and then click the Send button to send the message to the other application. Once the message is sent, it will be added to the list box of sent messages. To provide this functionality, when the Send button is clicked, your application needs to check whether there is a message to be sent, get the length of the message, send the message, and then add the message to the list box. To add this functionality to your application, use the Class Wizard to add a function to the clicked event of the Send (IDC_BSEND) button. Edit this function, adding the code in Listing 20.9.

LISTING 20.9. The CSockDlg OnBsend FUNCTION.

```
 1: void CSockDlg::OnBsend()
 2: {
 3:     // TODO: Add your control notification handler code here
 4:     int iLen;
 5:     int iSent;
 6:
 7:     // Sync the controls with the variables
 8:     UpdateData(TRUE);
 9:     // Is there a message to be sent?
10:     if (m_strMessage != "")
11:     {
12:         // Get the length of the message
13:         iLen = m_strMessage.GetLength();
14:         // Send the message
15:         iSent = m_sConnectSocket.Send(LPCTSTR(m_strMessage), iLen);
16:         // Were we able to send it?
```

continues

20

LISTING 20.9. CONTINUED

```
17:            if (iSent == SOCKET_ERROR)
18:            {
19:            }
20:            else
21:            {
22:                // Add the message to the list box.
23:                m_ctlSent.AddString(m_strMessage);
24:                // Sync the variables with the controls
25:                UpdateData(FALSE);
26:            }
27:        }
28: }
```

When the OnReceive event function is triggered, indicating that a message has arrived, you'll retrieve the message from the socket using the Receive function. Once you've retrieved the message, you'll convert it into a CString and add it to the message-received list box. You can add this functionality by editing the OnReceive function of the dialog class, adding the code in Listing 20.10.

LISTING 20.10. THE CSockDlg OnReceive FUNCTION.

```
1: void CSockDlg::OnReceive()
2: {
3:      char *pBuf = new char[1025];
4:      int iBufSize = 1024;
5:      int iRcvd;
6:      CString strRecvd;
7:
8:      // Receive the message
9:      iRcvd = m_sConnectSocket.Receive(pBuf, iBufSize);
10:      // Did we receive anything?
11:      if (iRcvd == SOCKET_ERROR)
12:      {
13:      }
14:      else
15:      {
16:          // Truncate the end of the message
17:          pBuf[iRcvd] = NULL;
18:          // Copy the message to a CString
19:          strRecvd = pBuf;
20:          // Add the message to the received list box
21:          m_ctlRecvd.AddString(strRecvd);
22:          // Sync the variables with the controls
23:          UpdateData(FALSE);
24:      }
25: }
```

At this point, you should be able to compile and run two copies of your application, connecting them as you did earlier. Once you've got the connection established, you can enter a message in one application and send it to the other application, as shown in Figure 20.7.

FIGURE 20.7.

Sending messages between the applications.

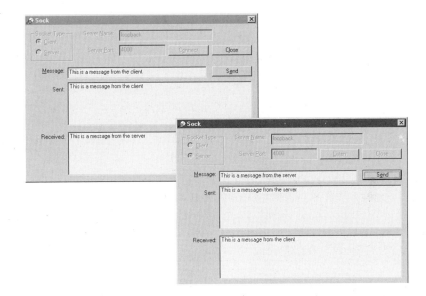

Ending the Connection

To close the connection between these two applications, the client application user can click the Close button to end the connection. The server application will then receive the OnClose socket event. The same thing needs to happen in both cases. The connected socket needs to be closed, and the message sending controls need to be disabled. On the client, the connection controls can be enabled because the client could change some of this information and open a connection to another server application. Meanwhile, the server application continues to listen on the port that it was configured to listen to. To add all this functionality to your application, edit the OnClose function, adding the code in Listing 20.11.

LISTING 20.11. THE CSockDlg OnClose FUNCTION.

```
1: void CSockDlg::OnClose()
2: {
```

20

continues

LISTING 20.11. CONTINUED

```
3:      // Close the connected socket
4:      m_sConnectSocket.Close();
5:      // Disable the message sending controls
6:      GetDlgItem(IDC_EMSG)->EnableWindow(FALSE);
7:      GetDlgItem(IDC_BSEND)->EnableWindow(FALSE);
8:      GetDlgItem(IDC_STATICMSG)->EnableWindow(FALSE);
9:      GetDlgItem(IDC_BCLOSE)->EnableWindow(FALSE);
10:     // Are we running in Client mode?
11:     if (m_iType == 0)
12:     {
13:         // Yes, so enable the connection configuration controls
14:         GetDlgItem(IDC_BCONNECT)->EnableWindow(TRUE);
15:         GetDlgItem(IDC_ESERVNAME)->EnableWindow(TRUE);
16:         GetDlgItem(IDC_ESERVPORT)->EnableWindow(TRUE);
17:         GetDlgItem(IDC_STATICNAME)->EnableWindow(TRUE);
18:         GetDlgItem(IDC_STATICPORT)->EnableWindow(TRUE);
19:         GetDlgItem(IDC_RCLIENT)->EnableWindow(TRUE);
20:         GetDlgItem(IDC_RSERVER)->EnableWindow(TRUE);
21:         GetDlgItem(IDC_STATICTYPE)->EnableWindow(TRUE);
22:     }
23: }
```

Finally, for the Close button, call the OnClose function. To add this functionality to your
application, use the Class Wizard to add a function to the clicked event for the Close button (IDC_BCLOSE). Edit the function to call the OnClose function, as in Listing 20.12.

LISTING 20.12. THE CSockDlg OnBclose FUNCTION.

```
1: void CSockDlg::OnBclose()
2: {
3:     // TODO: Add your control notification handler code here
4:     // Call the OnClose function
5:     OnClose();
6: }
```

If you compile and run your application, you can connect the client application to the
server, send some messages back and forth, and then disconnect the client by clicking the
Close button. You'll see the message-sending controls disable themselves in both applications, as in Figure 20.8. You can reconnect the client to the server by clicking the
Connect button again and then pass some more messages between the two, as if they had
never been connected in the first place. If you start a third copy of the application,
change its port number, designate it as a server, and put it into listening mode, you can
take your client back and forth between the two servers, connecting to one, closing the
connection, changing the port number, and then connecting to the other.

FIGURE 20.8.

Closing the connection between the applications.

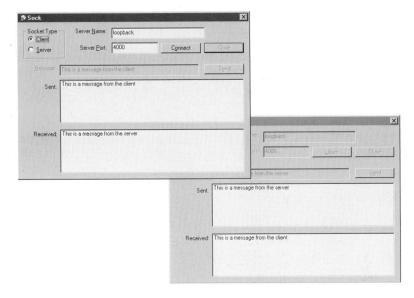

Summary

Today, you learned how you can enable your applications to communicate with others across a network or across the Internet by using the MFC Winsock classes. You took a good look at the CAsyncSocket class and learned how you could create your own descendent class from it that would provide your applications with event-driven network communications. You learned how to create a server application that can listen for and accept connections from other applications. You also learned how to build a client application that can connect to a server. You learned how to send and receive messages over a socket connection between two applications. Finally, you learned how to close the connection and how to detect that the connection has been closed.

Q&A

Q How do Internet applications work?

A Most Internet applications use the same functionality that you created today. The primary difference is that the applications have a script of messages that are passed back and forth. The messages consist of a command and the data that needs to accompany that command. The server reads the command and processes the data appropriately, sending back a status code to let the client know the success or failure of the command. If you want to learn more about how Internet applications do this, several books cover this subject area in detail.

20

Q **How does a server application handle a large number of simultaneous connections from clients?**

A With a full-strength server, the connection sockets are not declared as class variables. The server instead uses some sort of dynamic allocation of sockets, in an array or link-list, to create sockets for the clients as the connection requests come in. Another approach often taken by servers is to spin off a separate thread for each connection request. This allows the application to have a single socket connection per thread, and keeping track of the sockets is much easier. In any case, server applications don't normally have a single connection socket variable.

Workshop

The Workshop provides quiz questions to help you solidify your understanding of the material covered and exercises to provide you with experience in using what you've learned. The answers to the quiz questions and exercises are provided in Appendix B, "Answers."

Quiz

1. What are the two things that a client application must know to be able to connect to a server application?

2. What CAsyncSocket function is used to enable a server application to detect connection efforts by client applications?

3. What CAsyncSocket member function is called to signal that data has arrived through a socket connection?

4. What function is called to signal that a connection has been established?

5. What function do you use to send a message through a socket connection to the application on the other end?

Exercise

The server application that you wrote can handle only a single connection at a time. If a second application tries to open a connection to it while it's got an existing connection to an application, the server application will crash. The server tries to accept the second connection into the socket that is already connected to the first client application. Add a third socket object to the application that will be used to reject additional client connections until the first client closes the connection.

DAY **21**

Adding Web Browsing Functionality to Your Applications

When Microsoft made the decision a few years ago to make all its applications Internet-enabled, it wasn't just talking about making Word read and write HTML pages. It wanted to make the Internet an integrated part of every application, in some way or another. Well, when it comes to development tools, making the editor double as an email client isn't really a practical integration. However, making it easy for the users of development tools to build Internet-enabled applications is a very practical feature. And this is exactly what Microsoft did.

One of the capabilities that Microsoft made available to its application development tools is using Internet Explorer as an integrated part of any application. This means that you can include Internet Explorer, and all its associated components, in your own applications. The possibilities extend far beyond providing your users Web browsing capability; your applications can also house, and interact with, Java applets. You can provide your users with not one, but two macro languages, VBScript and JScript (Microsoft's version of JavaScript).

Today, you will learn

- How the Internet Explorer ActiveX Object Model enables you to integrate all the components into your applications.
- How the CHtmlView view class encapsulates most of the Internet Explorer functionality in a ready-made class.
- How to build a simple Web browser using the CHtmlView class and Internet Explorer.

The Internet Explorer ActiveX Model

When Microsoft came up with the idea of integrating ActiveX with its Web browser, Internet Explorer, it realized that it would need to reengineer Internet Explorer to support the use of ActiveX controls. Well, the developers looked at what they would need to do, and what was possible, and decided to make Internet Explorer a lot more than just a Web browser.

The first thing that Microsoft did was separate the Web browser from the ActiveX objects that perform all the work. As a result, it ended up with the Internet Explorer application, which is little more than an ActiveX document container, and the Internet Explorer HTML viewer control, which ran as an ActiveX document server inside the application. This meant that the Internet Explorer application could host more than just Web pages; it could also be used to host Word documents, Excel spreadsheets, PowerPoint presentations, and any other ActiveX document that had an ActiveX document server installed on the same computer, as shown in Figure 21.1.

Within the HTML viewer component, Microsoft added the capability to host other controls, including scripting engines and ActiveX controls, as shown in Figure 21.2. This gave Microsoft the flexibility to add more scripting languages to Internet Explorer as they were requested and created. This also enabled Internet Explorer to host any ActiveX controls that developers might want to create.

In designing Internet Explorer this way, Microsoft not only gave itself a lot of flexibility for future expansion of the functionality supported by Internet Explorer, but it also made the entire workings of Internet Explorer available to any developer that wants to take advantage of it and integrate Internet Explorer into his or her applications.

FIGURE 21.1.

The Internet Explorer ActiveX document model.

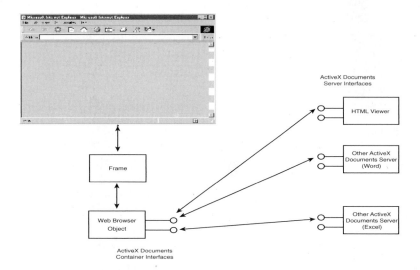

FIGURE 21.2.

The Internet Explorer HTML viewer ActiveX object model.

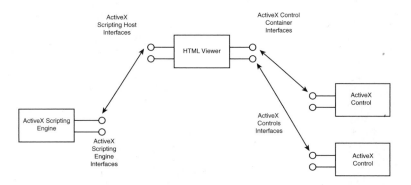

The `CHtmlView` Class

To make it easy to incorporate the Internet Explorer HTML viewer into Visual C++ applications, Microsoft wrapped it in the `CHtmlView` class. This class can be used as the base class for the view class in your Single Document Interface (SDI) or Multiple Document Interface (MDI) applications. You can easily create applications that have built-in Web browsing capabilities.

Navigating the Web

Several functions available in the `CHtmlView` class cover navigating the Web. There are functions for returning the browser to the starting page of the user or for taking the user

21

to an Internet search page. There are also functions for taking the user to the previous or next page or even to a remote Web page. All these functions are members of the CHtmlView class and thus are member functions of your application view class (when using the CHtmlView class as the base class for your view class).

The navigation functions for the CHtmlView class are listed in Table 21.1.

TABLE 21.1. CHtmlView NAVIGATION FUNCTIONS.

Function Definition	Description
GoBack()	Takes the user to the previous Web page.
GoForward()	Takes the user to the next Web page. (This assumes that the user has backed up from at least one Web page.)
GoHome()	Takes the user to the start page for Internet Explorer.
GoSearch()	Takes the user to an Internet search page.
Navigate(LPCTSTR URL)	Takes the user to the Web page specified in the URL variable.

The first four functions do not take any arguments and perform the exact same function as their toolbar equivalents in Internet Explorer. The last function does take arguments; the only required argument is the URL of the Web page to display.

Controlling the Browser

Along with the functions for navigating around the Web, you use some functions for controlling the browser. Two of these functions are Refresh(), which makes the HTML viewer control reload the current Web page, and Stop(), which halts a download in progress. As with most of the navigation functions, these functions do not take any arguments and work just like their equivalent toolbar buttons in Internet Explorer.

Getting the Browser Status

Another category of functions that are available in the CHtmlView class is informational in nature. You can use these functions to get information about the current state of the browser. For instance, if you want to get the current Web page in the browser, you can call GetLocationURL(), which returns a CString containing the URL. If you want to determine if the browser is busy with a download, you can call GetBusy(), which returns a boolean value specifying whether the browser is busy.

Many more functions are available in the CHtmlView class, and some of them only work on Internet Explorer itself, not on the browser control.

Building a Web-Browsing Application

For an example of how you can integrate the Internet Explorer Web browser component into your own applications, you will build a simple Web browser application. You will create an SDI application using the CHtmlView class as the base for your own view class. You'll add a menu with functions for the back and forward navigation options. You'll also add a dialog for getting from the user a URL that you will use to navigate the browser to the specified Web page.

Creating the Application Shell

To create a Web browser application, you can create a standard SDI or MDI application shell. The only other thing that you need to ensure is that Internet Explorer is installed on the computer where your application will run. For your development computer, this is not a problem because the Visual C++ installation probably required you to install the latest version of Internet Explorer. On any computers where you run your application, however, you might need to make sure that Internet Explorer is installed or install it yourself.

To create the shell of the application that you will build today, start a new project using the MFC AppWizard to create the application shell. Give the project a suitable name, such as WebBrowse, and click the OK button to start the AppWizard.

In the AppWizard, you can just as easily create an MDI Web browsing application as you can create an SDI application. For the purposes of the sample application that you are building today, go ahead and specify that the application is a Single document (SDI) application. You can accept the default settings for the rest of the AppWizard; for this example, however, choose the Internet Explorer ReBars for the toolbar appearance on the fourth AppWizard step.

Finally, on the sixth step, specify the CHtmlView class as the base class for your view class. This causes your application to be created using the Internet Explorer Web browser control as the main application view.

Once you finish generating the shell for your application, if you compile and run it while connected to the Internet, you'll find that you already have a working Web browser, as shown in Figure 21.3. However, you do not have the ability to specify where your browser will take you, other than clicking links in the Web pages displayed.

21

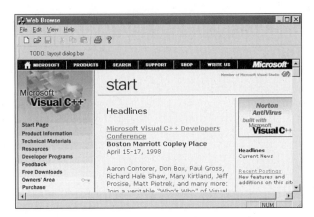

Adding Navigation Functionality

Now that you've got a working Web browser, it would be nice if you could control where it takes you. What you need to add is an edit control where the user can enter a URL. Looking at the toolbar of the running application, you notice there's a place to put this control.

Specifying a URL

You probably noticed when you ran your application that the second toolbar had some static text telling you to lay out the dialog bar. The dialog bar is different from what you have worked with before. It is a toolbar with dialog controls on it. You even design the bar in the dialog layout designer. When you look for this dialog bar in the resource tab, you won't find it in the toolbar folder; it's in the dialogs folder.

If you open the dialogs folder and double-click the IDR_MAINFRAME dialog to open it in the dialog designer, you'll see that it's the second toolbar in your application. You can place edit boxes, buttons, combo boxes, and check boxes on this toolbar. You can place any control that you can use on a dialog window on this toolbar.

For your Web browser, modify the static text control already on the dialog bar and add an edit box, as shown in Figure 21.4. Specify an ID for the edit box; for this example, use the ID IDC_EADDRESS.

Before you open the Class Wizard to begin adding variables and event functions to the dialog bar, be aware that the dialog bar will automatically send its events to the main frame class in your application. When you open the Class Wizard, it assumes that you need to associate the dialog bar with a class and prompts you to create a new class. This association is not necessary because you can map all its events through the frame and from there feed them to the view or document classes.

FIGURE 21.4.

The dialog bar layout.

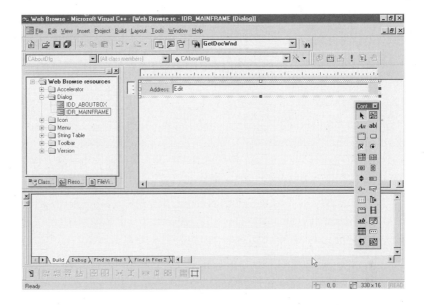

For this example, you don't even need to use the Class Wizard to add any event handlers to the dialog bar. You need to trigger an action when the user finishes entering a URL into the edit box. The closest event available to you through the Class Wizard is the EN_CHANGED event, which will trigger for each letter the user types. What you need is an event that will trigger when the user presses the Enter key. Fortunately, when the user types in the edit box on the dialog bar and presses the Enter key, the IDOK command ID is sent to the frame class. What you can do is add a command handler in the message map to call a function on the IDOK command.

In your command handler, you need to get the window text from the edit box on the dialog bar. You can pass this string to the Navigate function in the view class, making the browser go to the page specified by the user.

To add this functionality to your application, add a new member function to the CMainFrame class. Specify the function type as void, the function declaration as OnNewAddress, and the access as public. Edit the new function, adding the code in Listing 21.1.

LISTING 21.1. THE CMainFrame OnNewAddress FUNCTION.

```
1: void CMainFrame::OnNewAddress()
2: {
3:     CString sAddress;
4:
5:     // Get the new URL
```

21

continues

LISTING 21.1. CONTINUED

```
6:      m_wndDlgBar.GetDlgItem(IDC_EADDRESS)->GetWindowText(sAddress);
7:      // Navigate to the new URL
8:      ((CWebBrowseView*)GetActiveView())->Navigate(sAddress);
9: }
```

In this function, line 6 got the text in the edit box using the GetWindowText function, placing the text into the m_sAddress variable. The dialog bar was declared in the CMainFrame class as the m_wndDlgBar variable, so you were able to use the GetDlgItem function on the dialog bar variable to get a pointer to the edit box.

In line 8, you cast the return pointer from the GetActiveView function as a pointer to the CWebBrowseView class. This allowed you to call the Navigate function on the view class, passing it the URL that was entered into the edit box.

Now that you are able to take the URL that the user entered and tell the browser component to go to that Web page, how do you trigger this function? You have to add the message-map entry by hand because this is one that the Class Wizard isn't able to add. In the message map, after the closing marker of the AFX_MSG_MAP (the section maintained by the Class Wizard), add the ON_COMMAND macro, specifying the IDOK command and your new function as the handler to be called, as in Listing 21.2. You can also add this entry before the Class Wizard section as long as it's on either side and not inside the section maintained by the Class Wizard.

LISTING 21.2. THE CMainFrame MESSAGE MAP.

```
1: BEGIN_MESSAGE_MAP(CMainFrame, CFrameWnd)
2:      //{{AFX_MSG_MAP(CMainFrame)
3:          // NOTE - the ClassWizard will add and remove mapping macros
            ➥here.
4:          //    DO NOT EDIT what you see in these blocks of generated
            ➥code !
5:      ON_WM_CREATE()
6:      //}}AFX_MSG_MAP
7:      ON_COMMAND(IDOK, OnNewAddress)
8: END_MESSAGE_MAP()
```

If you compile and run your application, you can enter a URL into the edit box on the toolbar and press the Enter key, and your application should browse to the Web page you specified, as in Figure 21.5.

FIGURE 21.5.

Browsing to a specified URL.

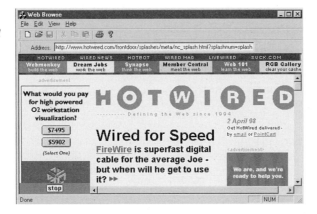

Displaying the Current URL

When surfing the Web, you often follow links on Web pages that take you to other Web sites. When you do this, you wouldn't know what Web site you accessed if your browser didn't place the URL into the address box, indicating the site where you are and providing the opportunity to copy or modify the URL to find another page on the same site.

Getting the current URL from the browser is a simple matter of calling the GetLocationURL function and passing the result to the dialog bar. The problem is when to get the URL. It turns out that some event functions in the CHtmlView class can be overridden in your class. These functions will be triggered on various events that are triggered by the browser control. There are event functions for starting the navigation, beginning a download, monitoring a download's progress, and, most important for our needs, indicating a download has finished. None of these event handler functions can be added to your view class through the Class Wizard. You have to add them all.

To add the download-complete event handler to your application, add a new member function to the view class of your application. Specify the function type as void, the function declaration as OnDocumentComplete(LPCTSTR lpszUrl), and the access as public. Edit the function, adding the code in Listing 21.3.

LISTING 21.3. THE CWebBrowseView OnDocumentComplete FUNCTION.

```
1: void CWebBrowseView::OnDocumentComplete(LPCTSTR lpszUrl)
2: {
3:     // Pass the new URL to the address bar
4:     ((CMainFrame*)GetParentFrame())->SetAddress(lpszUrl);
5: }
```

21

You'll notice in this function that you didn't need to call the `GetLocationURL` function after all. The URL that is downloaded is passed as an argument to this function. This allows you to pass the URL along to the frame, where you'll add another function to populate the edit box on the dialog bar with the URL.

To add the function to populate the dialog bar with the new URL, add a member function to the main frame class, `CMainFrame`. Specify the function type as `void`, the function declaration as `SetAddress(LPCTSTR lpszURL)`, and the access as public. Edit the function, adding the code in Listing 21.4.

LISTING 21.4. THE `CMainFrame` `SetAddress` FUNCTION.

```
1: void CMainFrame::SetAddress(LPCTSTR lpszURL)
2: {
3:     // Set the new URL in the address edit control
4:     m_wndDlgBar.GetDlgItem(IDC_EADDRESS)->SetWindowText(lpszURL);
5: }
```

In this function, you took the opposite path from the one you used to get the text from the edit box. You used the `SetWindowText` to change the text in the edit box to the URL that you are passing in. When you run your application, you should be able to see the URL address on the dialog bar change to reflect the Web page that you are viewing.

Back and Forth

Now that you can enter a URL into the dialog bar and have your application go to that Web site, and you can see the address of any Web sites that you view, it'd be nice if you could back up from where you might have gone. This is a simple matter of calling the `GoBack` and `GoForward` functions on the view class in your application. You can call these functions from menu entries, which also allows you to attach toolbar buttons to perform the same calls.

To add this functionality, open the main menu in the Menu Designer. You can delete the Edit menu from the bar, and all of the entries below it, because they are of no use in the application that you are building today. Grab the blank menu entry on the bar, and drag it to the left of the Help menu. Open the properties dialog for this menu entry and give it a caption of &Go. This is the menu where all navigation functions will be located.

To provide the back-and-forth functionality, you need to add two menu entries, one for the `GoBack` function and one for the `GoForward` function. Specify the properties for these two menu entries as shown in Table 21.2.

TABLE 21.2. MENU PROPERTY SETTINGS.

Object	Property	Setting
Menu Entry	ID	IDM_GO_BACK
	Caption	&Back\tCtrl + B
	Prompt	Back to the previous page\nBack
Menu Entry	ID	IDM_GO_NEXT
	Caption	&Next\tCtrl + N
	Prompt	Go forward to the next page\nNext

Once you add the menu entries, you can use the Class Wizard to add functions to the view class on both of these menu events. For the IDM_GO_BACK menu ID, add an event function on the COMMAND event message. Edit the function, adding the code in Listing 21.5.

LISTING 21.5. THE CWebBrowseView OnGoBack FUNCTION.

```
1: void CWebBrowseView::OnGoBack()
2: {
3:     // TODO: Add your command handler code here
4:
5:     // Go to the previous page
6:     GoBack();
7: }
```

Open the Class Wizard again, and add an event-handler function for the IDM_GO_NEXT object ID on the COMMAND event message. Edit this function with the code in Listing 21.6.

LISTING 21.6. THE CWebBrowseView OnGoNext FUNCTION.

```
1: void CWebBrowseView::OnGoNext()
2: {
3:     // TODO: Add your command handler code here
4:
5:     // Go to the next page
6:     GoForward();
7: }
```

Now you can run your application and use the menus to back up to the previous Web pages from wherever you surfed to and then trace your steps forward again. However, it's somewhat difficult using the menus, so what you need to do is add an accelerator for each of these menu entries.

21

If you open the accelerator table in the resources tree, you see a bunch of accelerators tied to menu IDs. Each of these accelerators consist of an ID and a key combination. If you right-click anywhere in the accelerator table, you see the option of adding a new accelerator to the table. Choosing this option presents you a dialog to enter the accelerator information. First, you need to specify the menu ID that the accelerator will be tied to. (As with toolbar buttons, accelerators are tied to menu entries.) Below that, you can enter the key that will trigger the accelerator, or you can select a key from the drop-down list.

On the right side of the dialog, you can select the modifiers for the key. Modifiers are the other keys that must be pressed in combination with the key that you've already specified for the accelerator to be triggered. Once you've entered all the necessary information for the accelerator, close the dialog and the information you specified is added to the table.

Tip

It's recommended that you use either the Ctrl or Alt key as one of the modifier keys on all accelerators using standard keys. If you don't use one of these two keys as part of the accelerator, your application might get confused about when the user is typing information into your application and when the user is triggering an accelerator.

To add accelerators to the back and forward menus in your application, delete the accelerator for the ID_FILE_OPEN menu ID because you won't use it in this application. Add a new accelerator and specify the ID as IDM_GO_BACK and the key as B and select the Ctrl modifier. Add a second accelerator, specifying the ID as IDM_GO_NEXT and the key as N and select the Ctrl modifier. When you run your application, you can use the Ctrl+B key combination to back up to the previous page and the Ctrl+N key combination to go forward.

To really make your application work like most available Web browsers, you would also add toolbar buttons for these two menu entries with arrows pointing to the left for back and to the right for forward.

Controlling the Browser

Often when browsing, you come across a Web page that you don't want to wait to download. You'll want to stop the transfer part-way through. Maybe you entered the wrong URL or maybe the download is taking too long. It doesn't matter why you want to stop the download; it's enough that you want to stop it. This is why the CHtmlView class has the Stop function. It cancels the download currently in progress. To add this functionality to your application, add a new menu entry to the View menu in the Menu Designer. Specify the menu entry properties in Table 21.3.

TABLE 21.3. MENU PROPERTY SETTINGS.

Object	Property	Setting
Menu Entry	ID	IDM_VIEW_STOP
	Caption	Sto&p
	Prompt	Stop the current transfer\nStop

Using the Class Wizard, add an event-handler function to the view class for this menu ID on the COMMAND event message. Edit the function with the code in Listing 21.7.

LISTING 21.7. THE CWebBrowseView OnViewStop FUNCTION.

```
1: void CWebBrowseView::OnViewStop()
2: {
3:     // TODO: Add your command handler code here
4:
5:     // Stop the current download
6:     Stop();
7: }
```

If you run your application, you can use this menu entry to stop any download of a Web page that you don't want to wait on. It would be more convenient if you added a toolbar button for this menu ID.

Another control function that most browsers have is the capability to reload the current Web page. This function is handy for Web pages that contain dynamic elements that change each time the page is downloaded. It's also helpful for Web pages that your browser may have in its cache so that it doesn't retrieve the newest version of the page. It's necessary to be able to force the browser to reload the page and not just display the cached version (especially if it's a Web page that you are in the process of creating). The browser component has the capability built in with the Refresh function. One call to this function means the current page is reloaded.

You can add this functionality to your application by adding another menu entry to the View menu. Specify the properties for the new menu entry using the settings in Table 21.4. You can add a separator bar between the two View menu entries that were originally there, and the two new entries, to make your menu look like the one in Figure 21.6.

21

TABLE 21.4. MENU PROPERTY SETTINGS.

Object	Property	Setting
Menu Entry	ID	IDM_VIEW_REFRESH
	Caption	&Refresh
	Prompt	Refresh the current page\nRefresh

FIGURE 21.6.

The modified View menu.

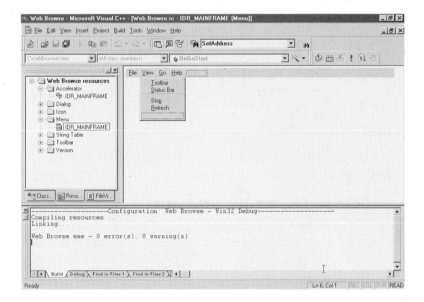

Once you add the menu entry, use the Class Wizard to add an event-handler function to the view class for the COMMAND event message for this menu entry. Edit the function, adding the code in Listing 21.8.

LISTING 21.8. THE CWebBrowseView OnViewRefresh FUNCTION.

```
1: void CWebBrowseView::OnViewRefresh()
2: {
3:     // TODO: Add your command handler code here
4:
5:     // Reload the current page
6:     Refresh();
7: }
```

Now you can test this functionality by finding a Web site that returns a different page each time that you refresh the browser, such as the Random Monty Python Skit Server in

Figure 21.7. As with the rest of the menu functions that you added to this application, this one should also be added to the toolbar.

FIGURE 21.7.

The Refresh function will perform a new download.

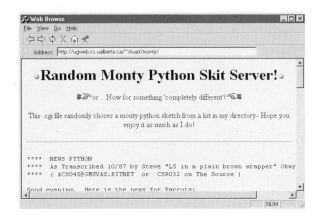

Summary

Today you learn how Microsoft designed its Internet Explorer Web browser as a series of ActiveX components that could be used in other applications. You saw how Microsoft encapsulated the browser into the CHtmlView class, which can be used in SDI and MDI applications to provide Web browsing functionality to almost any application. You learned how you can use this view class to build a Web browser. You saw how you could use the dialog bar to place controls on a toolbar and how the events for these controls can be handled in the frame class for the application. Finally, you learned how to add menus to your application to call the various functions of the Web browser to provide a complete surfing experience.

Q&A

Q Why is Print Preview not included on the default menus when I choose CHtmlView as the base class for my view class?

A The printing for the CHtmlView class is performed by the browser, not the view class. You don't have print preview because the browser doesn't support it.

Q How can I get the HTML source code from the browser so that I can see or edit it?

A The CHtmlView class has a member function, GetHtmlDocument, that returns a pointer to the IDispatch interface of the document object in the browser. You have to use the Invoke IDispatch function to call the functions in the document object

21

to retrieve the HTML source code. For documentation on how to do this, check out the Microsoft Developer Network CD that you received with your copy of Visual C++ 6.

Workshop

The Workshop provides quiz questions to help you solidify your understanding of the material covered and exercises to provide you with experience in using what you've learned. The answers to the quiz questions and exercises are provided in Appendix B, "Answers."

Quiz

1. What does the CHtmlView class encapsulate for use in Visual C++ applications?
2. How can you get the URL for the current Web page from the CHtmlView class?
3. What command is triggered for the frame class when the user presses the Enter key in the edit box on the dialog bar?
4. What functions can you call to navigate the browser to the previous and the next Web pages?
5. How can you stop a download in progress?

Exercises

1. Add the GoSearch function to the menu and toolbar.
2. Add the GoHome function to the menu and toolbar.
3. Disable the Stop toolbar button and menu entry when the application is not downloading a Web page.

WEEK 3

15

16

17

18

19

20

21

In Review

You made it! You now have the skills to tackle most of the Windows programming tasks in Visual C++, with the exception of those that require specialized knowledge and understanding. Although there's still plenty for you to learn, you have covered the vast majority of the topics in a very short amount of time. From here you will probably want to delve into one or two more specialized areas of Windows programming—the type that an entire book can be written on—because at this point, you've got just about all the generalized skills down.

Just in case you don't have them all down, it's not a bad idea to take some time once again to come up with some of your own applications where you can apply the things you've learned. This will help pinpoint any areas that you might need to go back and review before jumping into any more advanced topics. Let's take a quick look back at what you should have learned during the past week, just to make sure.

You started off the week by learning about Microsoft's latest database application development technology, ActiveX Data Objects (ADO). You learned how ADO sits on top of the OLE DB technology, simplifying database access considerably. You learned how you can easily build a database application by using ADO as an ActiveX control and connecting it to some ADO-compatible, data-bound ActiveX controls. You also learned how you can import the DLL and dive into the code, exerting complete control over how your application deals with the database. You learned how you can read and write each of the fields in a record in the record set by converting it from and to the variant data type. You also learned how you can design your own custom record class and can bind it to the record set object, providing you with a much more convenient way to access the individual field values in the database. If you are having problems with any of this, you might want to review Day 15 once more.

You learned three different ways of sharing the functionality modules that you develop with other programmers, without having to share your code. First you learned how to build your modules into library files that can be linked into applications by other Visual C++ developers. You saw how with this approach, if any change is made to the library module, then all the applications that it's used in have to be rebuilt. You learned how you can create these modules without making any special changes to the way you write your code. If you don't remember how you did all of this, you can go back to Day 16 to review it.

The second way that you learned to share your functionality with other programmers was to build DLLs. You learned how you can create two different types of DLLs: one that can be used only by other Visual C++ applications and one that can be used by any other application, regardless of what programming language was used to build it. You saw how you can create a DLL for use by other Visual C++ programmers without having to make any real changes to the way you design or code your modules. You also learned how you need to make dramatic changes to how your module is used and interacted with when creating DLLs that can be used by all programming languages. You learned how to provide straight function calls as an interface for use by other applications, with all necessary information to be passed in as parameters to the functions. You also learned how to build a definition file, with the names of all functions to be exported included in it. If you need any reminders of how you can do any of this, you'll want to look over Day 17 again.

The third and final way that you learned to share the functionality of your modules without sharing the code was to package it as an ActiveX control. You learned how to use the Control and Class Wizards to add in all the properties, methods, and events that you want to have in your control. You learned how to read and write the properties in your control. You saw how there are two different ways that the properties in your control can be implemented, and you learned how to determine which type is appropriate for each of your control's properties. You learned how you can raise events in the container application from your control by firing the event in your code. Along with all of this, you learned how you can use the ActiveX Control Test Container utility to test your control, calling all its methods and triggering all the events that it's capturing. You saw how you can monitor the events that your control is firing in the containing application to make sure that they are being fired as and when they should. If you need any reminders of how all this works, you can look back at Day 19 for a refresher.

An important thing that you learned was how you can enable your applications to per-form more than one task at a time. This is an important piece of functionality, and more applications are requiring this capability every day. Not only did you learn how to make your applications perform multiple tasks at once, but you also learned two different ways to do so. First, you learned about the OnIdle function and how you can hook into this function to trigger your own functionality to be run when the application is sitting idle. You also learned about the shortcomings of using this approach to adding a second task to your application and how it can prevent your application from responding to the user. You need to slice the background task into little pieces that can be done quickly, which requires you to develop some elaborate way of keeping track of where the task is and where it needs to pick back up when the application is idle again.

The second way that you learned to give your applications a second or third task to do is by spinning off separate threads, which run completely independent of the main user-interface thread. You learned how to create a callback function that controls the top level of execution for the threads and how you can start and stop the thread as necessary. You also saw how these independent threads are completely independent from the rest of the application and how they'll continue to run, even when the rest of the application is also busy. If you feel the need to look at all this a second time, you might want to read Day 18 again.

Another area of growing importance that you learned about was how to build Internet applications using the Winsock interface classes. You learned how you can build one application that connects to another over a network and sends messages back and forth. You learned that, just like with a telephone, for one application to connect to another, the second application has to be listening for the connection. You saw how easy it is to send messages and to be notified when a message has arrived after the connection between the two applications has been made. If you need to review some of this, you might want to look back at Day 20.

Finally, you learned how you can incorporate the Microsoft Internet Explorer Web browser into your application without any effort whatsoever. You learned how you can control the browser by specifying the URL that it should load and display for the user and how you can display informational messages to the user to show what the browser is doing and when it's busy. If you need to look back at this to refresh your memory, you can go back to Day 21.

That's it. You're done. You've covered a lot of ground and learned some advanced topics, especially over this last week. Now it's time to put this book down and get busy pro-gramming, building your own applications using what you've learned. Good luck. If you find that you need a little help or advice, a good place to turn is the Microsoft news-groups on the Internet. They are full of people who are both knowledgeable and helpful.

APPENDIX A

C++ Overview

The appendix is designed to provide you with a quick review of the fundamentals of the C++ programming language. After reading this appendix, you will have a thorough understanding of the various aspects of C++ and its syntax.

Creating Your First Application

Your first example is a simple program that displays "Hello World" on the screen. For this, you create a workspace and the C++ file required for the program. The procedure for writing a C++ program using Visual C++ is simple and easy. Follow these steps:

1. From the main menu, select Visual C++.

2. Select File | New from the Visual C++ toolbar.

   Make sure the Projects tab is selected (see Figure A.1).

3. Select Win32 Console Application from the options on the left.

Figure A.1.

*Setting up the Hello
workspace.*

FIGURE A.1.

*Setting up the Hello
workspace.*

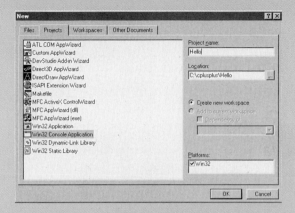

4. Type **Hello** on the right side under Project Name.

5. Select OK.

Visual C++ creates the workspace of your application. Visual C++ actually creates a
directory Hello, which enables you to store all files related to a particular project in one
area. You will begin adding the files you require for this project:

1. Once again, select File | New from the toolbar.

2. Select the Files tab if it is not already selected.

3. Highlight C++ Source File.

4. Check the Add to Project box on the right side.

5. In the File Name edit box, type **Helloworld** (see Figure A.2).

6. Click OK.

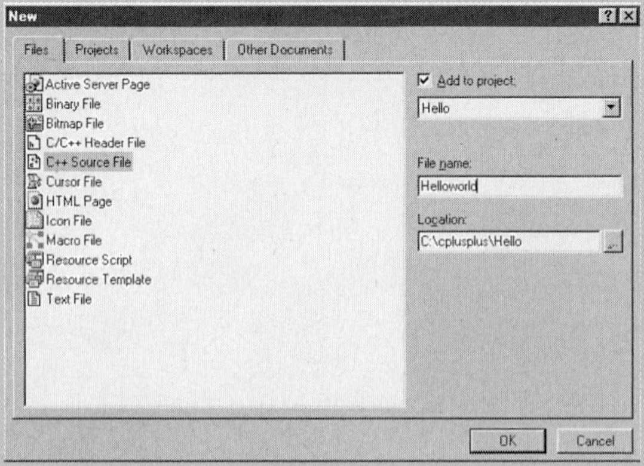

FIGURE A.2.

*Setting up the
Helloworld project.*

A

The `Helloworld.cpp` file is where you add the C++ source code. All C++ source code files have a `.cpp` extension. Later, I will cover other file types.

You create all the tutorial examples in this section in a similar way. The only difference is that the names of the workspaces and the files are different.

Helloworld.cpp

The Helloworld program displays HELLO WORLD on the screen. Listing A.1 contains the code. Type the code exactly as shown in the `Helloworld.cpp` window. Do not type the line numbers; they are for reference only. C++ is case sensitive, so `main` is not the same as MAIN, which is not the same as Main.

LISTING A.1. `Helloworld.cpp`.

```
1: // Workspace Name:   Hello
2: // Program Name:  Helloworld.cpp
3:
4: # include <iostream.h>
5:
6: int main()
7:
8: {
9: cout<< "HELLO WORLD \n";
10: return 0;
11: }
```

To run the program, follow these steps:

1. Select File|Save to save your work.
2. Select Build|Set Active Configuration (see Figure A.3).
3. Highlight Hello - Win32 Debug and click OK (see Figure A.4).
4. Select Build|Build `Hello.exe`.

Visual C++ compiles and links the program to create an executable file. The configuration window indicates the success or failure of the compilation. A successful compilation returns

```
Hello.exe - 0 error(s), 0 warning(s)
```

If you encounter any errors, verify that all the lines of the program were typed exactly as shown.

To execute the Helloworld program, select Build|Execute `Hello.exe`.

FIGURE A.3.

Setting the active con-figuration.

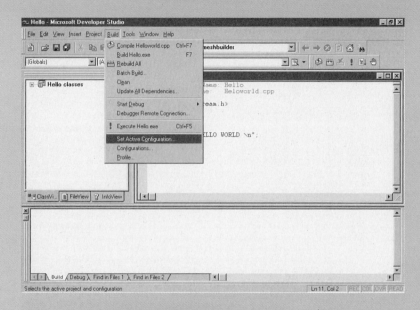

FIGURE A.4.

Selecting Win32 Debug.

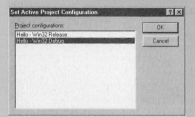

The program executes by opening an MS-DOS shell and displaying the text HELLO WORLD (see Figure A.5).

FIGURE A.5.

HELLO WORLD *display.*

A

Components of `Helloworld.cpp`

The first two lines of the program are comment lines:

```
// Workspace Name:  Hello
// Program Name:  Helloworld.cpp
```

The double slash command (//) tells the compiler to ignore everything after the slash. It is good programming practice to comment your work because it makes the program easier to read, especially for someone who did not write it. Comments become important when you are working on a complex program for months. When you want to make changes, comments assist you in recollecting your thoughts from more than a month ago.

The third line begins with the pound symbol (#):

```
# include <iostream.h>
```

This is a directive to the preprocessor to search for the filename that follows (iostream.h) and include it. The angled brackets (< >) cause the preprocessor to search for the file in the default directories. The iostream.h file contains definitions for the insertion (<<) and extraction (>>) operators. This directive is required to process the cout statement defined on line 9 in the program. The iostream.h file is a precompiled header provided with your compiler. You may experiment with the Helloworld program by commenting out the include line. To do this, insert the backslash (//) before the pound sign (#). When you compile and execute this program, you get an error:

```
Compiling...
Helloworld.cpp
C:\cplusplus\Hello\Helloworld.cpp(9) : error C2065:
➡ 'cout' : undeclared identifier
C:\cplusplus\Hello\Helloworld.cpp(9) : error C2297: '<<' : bad right
➡operand
Error executing cl.exe.

Hello.exe - 2 error(s), 0 warning(s)
```

Without the iostream.h file, the program does not recognize the cout command or the insertion operator (<<).

The next line of code, line 6, is actually where program execution begins. This is the entry point of your code:

```
int main()
```

This line tells the compiler to process a function named main. Every C++ program is a collection of functions. You will cover functions in greater detail later in this appendix. For now, you define a function as the entry point for a block of code with a given name. The empty parentheses indicate that the function does not pass any parameters. Passing parameters by functions is described in the section "Functions and Variables," later in this chapter.

Every C++ program must have the function `main()`. It is the entry point to begin program execution. If a function returns a value, its name must be preceded by the type of value it will return; in this case, `main()` returns a value of type `int`.

The block of code defined by any function should be enclosed in curly brackets ({ }):

```
{
cout<< "HELLO WORLD \n";
return 0;
}
```

All code within these brackets belongs to the named function—in this case, `main()`.

The next line executes the `cout` object. It is followed by the redirection operator `<<`, which passes the information to be displayed. The text to be displayed is enclosed in quotes. This is followed by the newline operator (`\n`). The redirection or insertion operator (`<<`) tells the code that whatever follows is to be inserted to `cout`.

Note   Line 9 ends with a semicolon. All statements in C++ must end with a semicolon.

Line 10 of the code has a `return` statement. Programmers often use `return` statements either to return certain values or to return errors. Also remember that on line 7 when you defined the `main()` function, you defined its return type to be an integer (`int`). You may rerun this code by deleting the return statement on line 10, in which case line 7 would have to be modified as follows:

```
void main()
```

It is good programming practice to include return codes for complex programs. They will help you identify and track down bugs in your program.

Functions and Variables

The Helloworld program consists of only one function, `main()`. A functional C++ program typically consists of more than a single function. To use a function, you must first declare it. A function declaration is also called its prototype. A prototype is a concise representation of the entire function. When you prototype a function, you are actually writing a statement, and as mentioned before, all statements in C++ should end with semicolons. A function prototype consists of a return type, name, and parameter list. The return type in the `main()` function is `int`, the name is `main`, and the parameter list is `()`, null.

A function must have a prototype and a definition. The prototype and the definition of a function must agree in terms of return type, name, and parameter list. The only difference is that the prototype is a statement and must end with a semicolon. Listing A.2 illustrates this point with a simple program to calculate the area of a triangle.

LISTING A.2. Area.cpp.

```
1: // Workspace:  Triangle
2: // Program name:  Area.cpp
3: // The area of a triangle is half its base times height
4: // Area of triangle = (Base length of triangle * Height of triangle)/2
5:
6: #include <iostream.h>          // Precompiled header
7:
8: double  base,height,area;      // Declaring the variables
9: double Area(double,double);    // Function Prototype/declaration
10:
11: int  main()
12: {
13: cout << "Enter Height of Triangle: ";  // Enter a number
14: cin >> height;                 // Store the input in variable
15: cout << "Enter Base of Triangle: ";    // Enter a number
16: cin >> base;                   // Store the input in variable
17:
18: area = Area(base,height);             // Store the result from the Area
    ➥function
19:                                       // in the variable area
20: cout << "The Area of the Triangle is: "<< area << endl ; // Output the
    ➥area
21:
22: return 0;
23: }
24:
25: double  Area (double base, double height)    // Function definition
26: {
27: area = (0.5*base*height);
28: return area;
29: }
```

This program declares three variables, `base`, `height`, and `area`, on line 8. Variables store values that are used by the program. The type of a variable specifies the values to be stored in the variable. Table A.1 shows the various types supported by C++.

TABLE A.1. VARIABLE DATA TYPES.

Variable Data Type	Values
unsigned short int	0 to 65,535
short int	−32,768 to 32,767
unsigned long int	0 to 4,294,967,925
long int	−2,147,483,648 to 2,147,483,647
int	−2,147,483,648 to 2,147,483,647 (32 bit)
unsigned int	0 to 4,294,967,295 (32 bit)
char	256 character values
float	1.2e–38 to 3.4e38
double	2.2e–308 to 1.8e308

To define a variable, you first define its type, followed by the name. You may also assign values to variables by using the assignment (=) operator, as in these two examples:

```
double base = 5;
```

```
unsigned long int base =5;
```

In C++, you may also define your own type definition. You do this by using the keyword typedef, followed by the existing type and name: .

```
typedef unsigned long int ULONG;
```

```
ULONG base =5;
```

Defining your own type does save you the trouble of typing the entire declaration.

The next line of the code, line 9, defines the prototype of your function:

```
double Area (double,double);
```

This function has a type double, a name Area, and a parameter list of two variables of type double. When you define the prototype, it is not necessary to define the parameters, but it is a good practice to do so. This program takes two inputs from the user, namely base and height of the triangle, and calculates the area of the triangle. The base, height, and area are all variables. The Helloworld.cpp example used the insertion (<<) operator. In this example, you use the extraction (>>) operator. The program queries the user to enter a value for the height of the triangle on line 13. When the user enters a value for height, the data from the screen is extracted and placed into the variable height. The process is repeated for the base of the triangle on lines 15 and 16. After accepting the input from the user, the function `main()` passes execution to the function `Area(base,height)` along with the parameter values for `base` and `height`. When `main()` passes the execution to the function `Area(base, height)`, it expects a value of type `double` in return from the function. The calculation of the area of the triangle is conducted on line 27:

```
area = (0.5*base*height);
```

 Note

Area is the name of a function, and area is a variable name. Because C++ is case sensitive, it clearly distinguishes these two names.

This statement uses the standard operators, the assignment operator (=), and the multiplication operator (*). The assignment operator assigns the result of (`0.5*base*height`) to the variable area. The multiplication operator (*) calculates the resulting values of (`0.5*base*height`). The assignment operator (=) has an evaluation order from right-to-left. Hence, the multiplication is carried out prior to assigning the values to `area`. The five basic mathematical operators are addition (+), subtraction (–), multiplication (*), division (/), and modulus (%).

Line 28 of the `Area` function returns the value of the variable `area` to the `main()` function. At this point, the control of the program is returned to line 18 of the `main()` function. The remainder of the program displays the result of `area` to the screen.

The `if` Statement, Operators, and Polymorphism

While programming large complex programs, it is often necessary to query the user and provide direction to the program based on his input. This is accomplished by using the `if` statement. The next example demonstrates the application of an `if` statement. The format of the `if` statement is

```
if (this expression)
    do this;
```

The `if` statement is often used in conjunction with relational operators. Another format of the `if` statement is

```
if (this expression)
    do this;
else
    do this;
```

Because `if` statements often use relational operators, let's review relational operators. Relational operators are used to determine if two expressions or numbers are equal. If the two expressions or numbers are not equal, the statement will evaluate to either 0 or false. Table A.2 lists the six relational operators defined in C++.

TABLE A.2. RELATIONAL OPERATORS.

Operator	Name
==	Comparative
!=	Not equal
>	Greater than
<	Less than
>=	Greater than or equal to
<=	Less than or equal to

C++ also has logical operators. The advantage of logical operators is the ability to compare two individual expressions and conclude whether they are true or false. Table A.3 lists the three logical operators.

TABLE A.3. LOGICAL OPERATORS.

Symbol	Operator
&&	AND
¦¦	OR
!	NOT

An important and powerful feature of C++ is function overloading, or polymorphism. *Polymorphism* is the ability to have more than one function with the same name that differ in their parameter lists. The next example is an extension of the previous triangle code. In this program, you will calculate the area of a triangle and a circle. You will be asked whether you want to calculate the area of a triangle or a circle. Depending upon your response, 1 for triangle and 2 for circle, the program collects your input and calculates the area. In Listing A.3, the Area function is overloaded. The same function name is used to calculate the area of the triangle or the circle. The functions differ only in their parameter lists.

LISTING A.3. Overload.ccp.

```
1: // Workspace Name:  Overload
2: // Program Name:  Overload.cpp
3:
4: # include <iostream.h>
5:
```

A

```
 6: double   base,height,radius;        // Global variables
 7: double   Area_of_triangle,Area_of_circle;  // Global variables
 8: int   choice;                  // Global variable
 9:
10: double   Area (double,double);        // Function prototype
11: double   Area (double);            // Function prototype
12:
13: const double   pi = 3.14;          // Constant variable
14:
15: void main()                // main function
16:
17: {
18:   cout << "To find the area of a Triangle, input 1 \n";
19:   cout << "To find the area of a Circle, input 2 \n";
20:   cin >> choice;
21:
22: if (choice == 1)
23:
24: {
25:   cout << "Enter the base of the triangle: ";
26:   cin >> base;
27:   cout << "Enter the height of the triangle: ";
28:   cin >> height;
29:
30: Area_of_triangle = Area(base,height);
31:
32:   cout << "The Area of the Triangle is: "<<Area_of_triangle<<endl;
33: }
34:
35: if (choice == 2)
36:
37: {
38:   cout << "Enter radius of the Circle: ";
39:   cin >> radius;
40:   Area_of_circle = Area(radius);
41:   cout << "The area of the Circle is: "<<Area_of_circle<<endl;
42: }
43:
44: if (choice != 1 && choice != 2)
45:
46: {
47:   cout << "Sorry! You must enter either 1 or 2 \n";
48: }
49: }
50:
51: double Area (double base, double height)
52: {
53:   return (0.5*base*height)
54: }
```

continues

```
55:
56: double Area(double radius)
57: {
58:    return (pi*radius*radius);
59: }
```

Global and Local Variables

In all of the preceding examples, the variables have been declared at the beginning of the program, prior to defining the main() function. Declaring variables in this fashion is more akin to C programs than C++. They are global variables and can be accessed by all the functions. However, you may also define local variables that have a scope only in a particular function. Local variables can have the same names as the global variables, but they do not change the global variables. Local variables refer only to the function in which they are defined. This difference can be confusing and lead to erratic results.

The program in Listing A.4 clearly shows the difference between global and local variables. You will calculate the area of a circle using global variables and local variables.

LISTING A.4. Global.cpp.

```
1: // Workspace:  Variable
2: // Program name:  Global.cpp
3:
4: #include <iostream.h>
5:
6: double  area;
7: double Area (double);
8: const double pi = 3.14;
9: double  radius = 5;
10:
11: int main()
12:
13: {
14: cout<<"This Program Calculates The Area Of A Circle \n";
15: area = Area (radius);
16: cout << "The Area of the Circle is: "<<area<<endl;
17: cout << "The Radius In the Main() Function is: "<<radius<<endl;
18: return 0;
19: }
20:
21: double  Area (double radius)
22: {
23: area = (pi*radius*radius);
24: cout<<"The Radius In the Area() Function is: "<<radius<<endl;
```

```
25: return area;
26: }
```

The variable radius is accessible in the main() function and also the Area() function, and it is the same. The result of executing this program is shown in Figure A.6.

FIGURE A.6.

Global.cpp—*using a global variable.*

As the program executes, it shows the value of the variable radius in the different functions. You will now modify the global variable to be a local variable. Add an additional line to the Area function defining a local variable:

```
double radius = 2;
```

Compile and execute this program. The results are shown in Figure A.7.

FIGURE A.7.

Global.cpp—*global and local variables.*

You will notice that the value of the variable radius remains unchanged in the main() function and changes locally in the Area() function. The area of the circle is calculated based on the value of the local variable, whereas at the same time, the value of the global variable is not changed but is hidden from the function Area().

Note It is always advisable to differentiate your global and local variables by pre-fixing them with a g for global and l for local.

Pointers

Pointers are one of the most important features of C++, and they are always confusing to new programmers of C++. Pointers work by providing access to the original data directly, which increases efficiency. Pointers primarily work with two operators, the indirection operator (*) and the address-of operator (&). It is common practice to add a p to the beginning of a pointer variable's name to distinguish it from other variables. A pointer is just another variable, but the difference is it holds a memory address. You declare a pointer by putting an asterisk (*) in front of the pointer name. To access the address of the variable, you put the & operator in front of the variable name.

To understand pointers, you need a brief overview of how variables are stored. You covered different variable types in Table A.1. Table A.4 shows the size of the variable types.

TABLE A.4. VARIABLE TYPE SIZES.

Variable Type	Size in Bytes
unsigned short int	2 bytes
short int	2 bytes
unsigned long int	4 bytes
long int	4 bytes
int	4 bytes (32 bit)
unsigned int	4 bytes(32 bit)
char	1 byte
float	4 bytes
double	8 bytes

In the program address.cpp in Listing A.5, the two variables base and radius each occupy 8 and 4 bytes. Assume that your computer memory has a certain space to store these variables, they are sequentially numbered from 1 through 12, and each space is 1 byte. When you declare the variable base of type double, it occupies 8 bytes. Assume these 8 bytes reside at locations beginning from 1 through 8. You also declared another variable radius of type int, which occupies 4 bytes and its location is byte 9 through byte 12. The location of each of these variables is termed as its address. Hence, the variable base has an address beginning at address 1 and ending at address 8. Similarly, the variable radius has an address beginning at address 9 and ending at address 12. When you use the address-of operator (&) on a variable, this is the address returned. The variable base has an address from 1 through 8, but the address-of operator returns its address as 1. Internally, the system already knows that the total addresses occupied are 8 because you defined its type as double.

Note

> The byte size shown in Table A.4 is not fixed. It can be different depending on your compiler and the hardware on which it runs. To determine the size of the variable for your individual compiler and hardware settings, use the sizeof() function as implemented in Listing A.5 on lines 13 and 16.

The program in Listing A.5 shows how to access the memory address of variables.

LISTING A.5. Address.cpp.

```
1: // Workspace:  Pointers
2: // Program name:  Address.cpp
3:
4: #include <iostream.h>
5:
6: double base = 5.0;
7: int radius = 2;
8:
9: void main()
10: {
11: cout<<"The VALUE of base is: "<<base<<endl;
12: cout<<"The ADDRESS of base is: "<<&base<<endl;
13: cout<<"The SIZE of double base is: "<<sizeof(double)<< "bytes \n";
14: cout<<"The VALUE of radius is: "<<radius<<endl;
15: cout<<"The ADDRESS of radius is: "<<&radius<<endl;
16: cout<<"The SIZE of integer radius is: "<<sizeof(int)<<" bytes \n";
17: }
```

The address of the variables is accessed directly on lines 12 and 15 by using the address-of operator (&). The addresses of the variables base and radius are shown in Figure A.8. The addresses of the variables depend on your system, so they might not be the same.

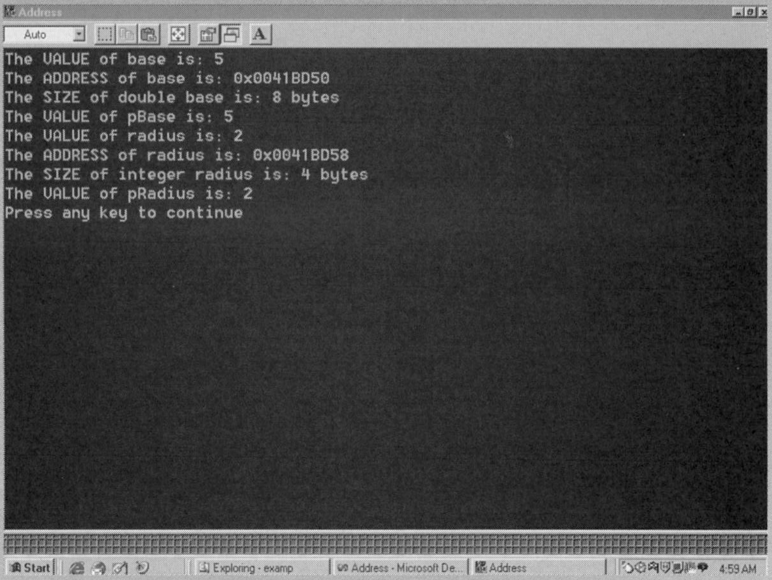

FIGURE A.8.

Using the address-of operator.

The indirection operator (*) operates by providing access to the value stored in the address of the variable. When a pointer is declared for a specific variable type (such as int), it should not be used with any other type unless it is recast to a new type. You should remember that a pointer is a variable, and like all other variables, it should be declared and initialized. A pointer that is not initialized could be dangerous. The program in Listing A.5 is modified to access the values of the variables radius and base. The modified program is provided in Listing A.6.

LISTING A.6. Address.cpp.

```
 1: // Workspace:  Pointers
 2: // Program name:  Address.cpp
 3:
 4: #include <iostream.h>
 5:
 6: double base =5.0;
 7: int radius =2;
 8:
 9: double *pBase =0;              // Initialize the pointer variable
10: int *pRadius =0;               // Initialize the pointer variable
11:
12: void main()
13: {
14: pBase = &base;                      // Assign the address of base
```

A

```
15: pRadius = &radius;                    // Assign the address of radius
16: cout<<"The VALUE of base is: "<<base<<endl;     // Output value of base
17: cout<<"The ADDRESS of base is: "<<&base<<endl;  // Output address of
         ➥base
18: cout<<"The SIZE of double base is: "<<sizeof(double)<< "bytes \n";
19: cout<<"The VALUE of pBase is: "<<*pBase<<endl;
         ➥ // Output redirected value of base
20:
21: cout<<"The VALUE of radius is: "<<radius<<endl;
         ➥// Output value of radius
22: cout<<"The ADDRESS of radius is: "<<&radius<<endl;
         ➥// Output address of radius
23: cout<<"The SIZE of integer radius is: "<<sizeof(int)<<" bytes \n";
24: cout<<"The VALUE of pRadius is: "<<*pRadius<<endl;
         ➥// Output redirected value of radius
25:
26: }
```

References

An important feature in C++ that is used often with function parameters is *references*. Reference is simply a synonym for variable. Until now, you have passed parameters in functions by value. You will learn how to pass parameters by reference. You create a reference variable by specifying its type and preceding the name with the reference operator (&). If you have a variable float radius, you create a reference with

```
void functionname (float &rfradius);
```

You can give the reference variable any name you want; in the following example, the reference variable names have an rf prefix. The advantage of a reference is that you can pass it as a parameter, like any other variable. However, unlike regular parameters, changes made to the reference's value while in a function are stored in the original variable. The example in Listing A.7 shows how the reference changes the value of the variable in the main() function.

LISTING A.7. Refer.cpp.

```
1: // Workspace:  Reference
2: // Program name:  Refer.cpp
3:
4: #include <iostream.h>
5:
6: void squareit (float &num);
7: int main()
8:
```

continues

```
 9: {
10: float num=5.0;
11:
12: cout<<"In Main: before squaring number: "<<num*num<<"\n";
13:
14: squareit (num);
15: cout<<"In Main: after squaring number: "<<num*num<<"\n";
16: return 0;
17:
18: }
19:
20: void  squareit (float &rfnum)
21: {
22:
23: cout<<"In Squareit: before squaring number: "<<rfnum*rfnum<<"\n";
24:
25: rfnum = rfnum+5;
26:
27: cout<<"In Squareit: after squaring number: "<<rfnum*rfnum<<"\n";
28:
29: }
```

You define a function squareit on line 6, and its parameters are references. This is the function prototype. On line 10, the variable num is given a value of 5. The square of the number is displayed to the screen on line 15. On line 14, you call the squareit function.

Note   You pass the variable num and not its address.

Only when execution jumps to line 20 from line 14 are the variables identified as references. On line 27, the references are squared and displayed. They should be the same as the variables because they are just like aliases for the variables. On line 25, you add 5 to the reference, which in turn changes the variable num. The incremented value is squared and displayed to the screen. Execution returns to main() on line 15, where the display confirms the variable was changed. The output for this program is shown in Figure A.9.

FIGURE A.9.

Passing parameters by reference.

A

Classes

In the previous sections, you used data types (int, float, and so on) that are inherently built into C++. In large complex programs, it is easier to define your own type, which could be a combination of the inherent types. Classes were added to C++ primarily for this purpose—to enable the programmer to be able to define custom data types and methods. The concept of classes in C++ evolved due to certain limitations of the concept of structures in C. To thoroughly understand classes, you have to step back into C and understand structures first.

A structure in C/C++ is a way of representing your own custom data. When you defined variables, you first defined their data types, followed by their names:

```
int radius;
```

To define your own data types, you use the keyword struct. The syntax for declaring a structure is

```
struct [structure_name]
  {
  data_members
  }
```

The *data_members* of a structure are variables and functions. When functions are associated with classes, they are more appropriately referred to as methods. From now on, you use the term function for program code that is not a part of a structure or class. A reference to methods indicates that the function is associated with a class structure. To understand how structures are used, review the example in Listing A.8.

LISTING A.8. Struct.cpp.

```
 1: // Workspace Name: Class1
 2: // Program Name:  Struct.cpp
 3: #include <iostream.h>
 4:
 5: struct farm_house
 6: {
 7: int pig_values;
 8: };
 9:
10: int main()
11: {
12: farm_house pig1, pig2, pig3;
13:
14: pig1.pig_values = 12;
15: pig2.pig_values = 13;
16: pig3.pig_values = 14;
17:
18: cout << "The value of pig1 is " << pig1.pig_values<< "\n";
19: cout << "The value of pig2 is " << pig2.pig_values << "\n";
20: cout << "The value of pig3 is " << pig3.pig_values << "\n";
21:
22: return 0;
23: }.
```

On line 5, the struct keyword is followed by the name of the structure. The actual definition of the structure is enclosed in the curly brackets. This particular structure defines a
data member of type int and name pig_values. If you remember, I mentioned earlier
that when you define a structure, you basically define a custom-made data type. All data
types end with a semicolon, so the structure should also end with a semicolon. On line
12, you define three instances of the same type of farm_house, each of which contains a
single int type variable.

Note

If you strictly use C, then to define instances on line 12, you must use the
keyword struct:

struct farm_house pig1, pig2, pig3;

This is no longer required in C++.

On lines 14 through 16, you assign values to the member variables of each structure. The structure member operator (.), also called the dot operator, is used to access member variables of the structure. On lines 18 through 20, the assigned values are output to the screen. Figure A.10 shows the output from this program.

FIGURE A.10.

Structure output.

The most important concept of object-oriented programming is encapsulation. Encapsulation can involve one or more classes. Encapsulation promotes safeguards and data hiding. The struct.cpp program had no encapsulation or classes. What do encapsulation and classes mean in object-oriented programming?

Let's start with describing the syntax and components of a class:

```
class class_name
{
public:
class_name_constructor;
~class_name_destructor;
class_method_prototypes();
class_member_variables;
private:
class_method_prototypes();
class_member_variables;
};
```

The words in bold are keywords. You declare a class by using the class keyword. This is followed by the name of the class. The data and methods of a class are enclosed in curly brackets ({ }). The methods of a class are function prototypes. They determine the behavior of the objects of your class. The member variables are the variables in your class. Classes have constructors and destructors. The methods and variables can be classified as either public or private.

You will now re-create the previous example of Struct.cpp in Listing A.8, employing the class and encapsulation methodology. The output from this program in Listing A.9 is identical to the previous example, Struct.cpp.

LISTING A.9. Clasfarm.cpp.

```
 1: // Workspace:  Class2
 2: // Program Name:  Clasfarm.cpp
 3: #include <iostream.h>
 4:
 5: class farm_house
 6: {
 7: int pig_values;
 8: public:
 9:  void set(int input);
10:  int get(void);
11: };
12:
13: void farm_house::set(int input)
14: {
15:    pig_values = input;
16: }
17:
18: int farm_house::get(void)
19: {
20:  return pig_values;
21: }
22:
23: int main()
24: {
25: farm_house pig1, pig2, pig3;
26:
27:
28:  pig1.set(12);
29:  pig2.set(13);
30:  pig3.set(14);
31:
32:  cout << "The value of pig1 is " << pig1.get() << "\n";
33:  cout << "The value of pig2 is " << pig2.get() << "\n";
34:  cout << "The value of pig3 is " << pig3.get() << "\n";
35:
36:  return 0;
37:
38: }
```

Compare the struct declaration of the Struct.cpp program in Listing A.8 (lines 5 through 7) to the class declaration of the Clasfarm.cpp program in Listing A.9 (lines 5 through 11). The difference is in the private and public portions of their declarations. In the struct declaration, everything is public, whereas in the class declaration, you begin with a private section. All data and methods at the beginning of a class are private. This means the member variable

```
int pig_values;
```

is private and hidden to methods outside the class. This means that the variable pig_values is not accessible inside main(). In other words, this member variable is hidden. This member variable is accessible to the methods of its class, mainly

```
void set (int input);
int get(void);
```

These methods are defined to be public. Because they are public, these methods can be accessed by any objects of this class. On line 25, you defined pig1, pig2, and pig3 to be instances or objects of the class. What? I am sure you are wondering why pig1 is an object.

You defined on line 5 a class farm_house. Remember when you declare a class, all you are doing is declaring a new type. When you declare a variable, you declare its type and then the variable name, as shown here:

```
long somevariable, anotherone, onemore;
```

Similarly, to define an object of a class, you declare the type, which in this case is farm_house, and the object name, which is pig1:

```
farm_house pig1,pig2,pig3;
```

On line 28, you set the value of pig1 to 12. This is done using the dot operator (.). The object pig1 has access to the method set(). The set() method is a method of the class farm_house, so it has access to its private data. The implementation of the set() method is shown on line 13. For the program to know that the set() method is within the scope of the class farm_house, you use the scope (::) operator. On line 15, the variable input is set to the variable pig_values.

The class farm_house declared two public methods. The other method is the get() method. The get() method is implemented on line 18. The get() method takes no parameters but only returns the pig_values because it also is within the scope of the class farm_house.

On line 32, the get() method is again called by the objects pig1, pig2, and pig3 to return the pig_values to the screen.

If you compare the two programs `struct.cpp` and `clasfarm.cpp`, you notice that one is about 23 lines, whereas the other is 38 lines. The code just got longer by implementing classes! This is true. The big benefits of using classes are really seen in more complex and larger programs. Also, because you hide critical data from the user, using classes is safer and less error prone. It enables the compiler to find mistakes before they become bugs.

Constructors and Destructors

Earlier, I defined the syntax of a class. In the syntax, I mentioned constructors and destructors. However, in the example `clasfarm.cpp`, you did not define any constructors or destructors. If a constructor or a destructor is not defined, the compiler creates one for you.

The Constructor Function

A *constructor* is a class initialization function that is executed automatically when a class instance is created. A constructor must abide by the following rules:

- The constructor must have the same name as its class name:

```
class farm_house
{
public:
farm_house();      //constructor
.....
.....
}
```

- The constructor cannot be defined with a return value.

- A constructor without any arguments is a default constructor.

- The constructor must be declared with the `public` keyword.

The Destructor Function

A destructor function is the opposite of a constructor function, which is executed automatically when the block in which the object is initialized is exited. A destructor releases the object and hence frees up the memory that was allocated. A destructor must abide by the following rules:

- The destructor must have the same name as the class.

- The destructor function must be preceded by ~.

- The destructor has neither arguments nor a return value.

- The destructor function must be declared with the keyword `public`.

```
class farm_house
{
```

```
public:
  farm_house ();          // Constructor function
  ~farm_house();          // Destructor function
  .....
  }
```

Friend Functions and Friend Classes

Methods and members that are declared private are accessible only to that part of the program that is part of the class. However, a function outside the class or another class may be defined as a friend class or function. You can declare an entire class or individual functions as friends. You must follow some critical rules when declaring friend functions:

- The use of friends should be kept to a minimum because it overrides the benefit of hiding the data.

- Declaring x as a friend of y does not necessarily mean that y has access to the methods and members of x.

Class Declarations and Definitions

Whenever you use classes, they have their own private and public member variables and methods. As you saw in the previous Clasfarm.cpp example, the program is getting lengthy. There are no hard rules, but there are some standard practices followed by almost all programmers. The procedure is to put all class declarations in the header files. A header file is a file with an .h or .hpp extension. All the class definitions are placed in the .cpp file. The beginning of the .cpp file has an include directive for the header file. For example, the clasfarm program would be separated into clasfarm.h and Clasfarm.cpp. The Clasfarm.h file would look like Listing A.10.

LISTING A.10. Clasfarm.h.

```
 1: // Workspace:  Class2
 2: // Program Name:  Clasfarm.h
 3: #include <iostream.h>
 4:
 5: class farm_house
 6: {
 7:  int pig_values;
 8: public:
 9:  void set(int input);
10:  int get(void);
11: };
```

The `Clasfarm.cpp` file is in Listing A.11.

LISTING A.11. `Clasfarm.cpp`.

```
 1: #include "clasfarm.h"
 2: void farm_house::set(int input)
 3: {
 4:  pig_values = input;
 5: }
 6:
 7: int farm_house::get(void)
 8: {
 9:  return pig_values;
10: }
11:
12: int main()
13: {
14: farm_house pig1, pig2, pig3;
15:
16:
17:  pig1.set(12);
18:  pig2.set(13);
19:  pig3.set(14);
20:
21:  cout << "The value of pig1 is " << pig1.get() << "\n";
22:  cout << "The value of pig2 is " << pig2.get() << "\n";
23:  cout << "The value of pig3 is " << pig3.get() << "\n";
24:
25:  return 0;
26:
27: };
```

Classes Within a Class

It is perfectly legal to have another class declaration within a given class. This is often referred to as nesting classes. The following example declares two classes, `Lot_size` and `Tax_assessment`. The `Tax_assessment` class object `taxes` is defined within the `Lot_size` class. The `main()` method has no objects of the `Tax_assessment` class, so the methods or members of the `Tax_assessment` class cannot be directly accessed from the `main()` function. Let's review the program in Listing A.12.

LISTING A.12. `Class3.cpp`.

```
 1: // Workspace Name: Class3
 2: // Program Name:   Class3.cpp
 3: #include <iostream.h>
```

A

```
 4:
 5: class Tax_assessment
 6: {
 7:   int city_tax;
 8:   int prop_tax;
 9: public:
10:   void set(int in_city, int in_prop)
11:       {city_tax = in_city; prop_tax = in_prop; }
12:   int get_prop_tax(void) {return prop_tax;}
13:   int get_city_tax(void) {return city_tax;}
14: };
15:
16:
17: class Lot_size {
18:   int length;
19:   int width;
20:   Tax_assessment taxes;
21: public:
22:   void set(int l, int w, int s, int p) {
23:       length = l;
24:       width = w;
25:       taxes.set(s, p); }
26:   int get_area(void) {return length * width;}
27:   int get_data(void) {return taxes.get_prop_tax() ;}
28:   int get_data2(void) {return taxes.get_city_tax() ;}
29: };
30:
31:
32: int main()
33: {
34: Lot_size small, medium, large;
35:
36:   small.set(5, 5, 5, 25);
37:   medium.set(10, 10, 10, 50);
38:   large.set(20, 20, 15, 75);
39:
40:
41:   cout << "For a small lot of area "<< small.get_area ()<< "\n";
42:   cout << "the city taxes are $ "<< small.get_data2 () << "\n";
43:   cout << "and property taxes are $ " << small.get_data ()<< "\n";
44:
45:   cout << "For a medium lot of area "<< medium.get_area ()<< "\n";
46:   cout << "the city taxes are $ "<< medium.get_data2 () << "\n";
47:   cout << "and property taxes are $ " << medium.get_data ()<< "\n";
48:
49:   cout << "For a Large lot of area "<< large.get_area ()<< "\n";
50:   cout << "the city taxes are $ "<< large.get_data2 () << "\n";
51:   cout << "and property taxes are $ " << large.get_data ()<< "\n";
52:   return 0;
53: }
```

When you execute this program, it outputs the area of an rectangle and also the hypothetical taxes on rectangular area. The output is shown in Figure A.11.

In lines 5 through 14, the class `Tax_assessment` is defined. It consists of two private data members, `int city_tax` and `int prop_tax`. The class has three public methods. It is important to note the declaration and definition of these methods. In the earlier examples, you only declared the methods in the class. The function definitions were accessed using the scope (`::`) operator. In this example, you declare the method and also write its definition. This technique is referred to as inline implementation of the function. If a function definition is small and concise, this is a good technique to employ. This technique is also used to increase program efficiency (speed of execution) because the program does not have to jump in and out of a function definition.

The data members `city_tax` and `prop_tax` are private so they can only be accessed via their member methods—namely, `set()`, `get_prop_tax()`, and `get_city_tax()`.

Lines 17 through 29 declare the class `Lot_size` with its data members and methods. On line 20, the class `Tax_assessment` is embedded in this class. The object `taxes` is also declared on this line, and it is under the privacy of the class `Lot_size`. The only methods that would be able to access this object are the ones belonging to the `Lot_size` class. The `Lot_size` class has four public methods declared and defined on line 22 and lines 26 through 28. Line 25 of the `set()` method has another `set()` method defined. This is not a recursive method but rather another example of function overloading. The `set()` method on line 10 and line 22 differ in the number of parameters. The `set()` method on line 25 can access the object `taxes` because it is defined under the class `Tax_assessment` on line 20.

The `main()` function begins on line 32 and has a return type `int`. On line 34, the objects of class `Lot_size` are declared. On lines 36 through line 38, the values of the objects are set using the `set()` method. An important point to note is that the class `Tax_assessment` has no objects in the `main()` method, so you cannot access any data member or method of this class from `main()`.

On line 41, the area of the `Lot_size` is output by operating the `get_area()` method on an object of class `Lot_size`. On line 42, the city taxes are output by operating the method `get_data2` on an object of `Lot_size`. This approach is required because the `city_tax` is a member data of class `Tax_assessment`, which cannot be operated on directly in the `main()` method. You use the method `get_data2`, which is a method of `Lot_size` and has access to the object taxes, which in turn can be accessed via `get_city_tax`.

Inheritance

One of the advantages of programming in C++ or any other object-oriented language is taking a global to local approach. Suppose you need to develop a program that comprehends all metals and their characteristics. If you take the class approach of the previous section, you would probably have one class named `metals`. The data members of `metals` would probably be `density` and `volume`. You could have another class named `gold` and one for `aluminum`. The data members describing `gold` and `aluminum` would need all the properties of `metals` in addition to their own data members such as `color` and `shine`. If you could devise a hierarchy of classes such that the classes for `gold` and `aluminum` would have only their individual data members but inherit the generic properties from the parent `metals` class—then you would be using inheritance.

Inheritance is also called derivation. The new class inherits the functionality of an existing class. The existing class is called the base class, and the new class is called the derived class. A similar inheritance can be derived for animals, mammals, and dogs.

To derive a new class from a base class, you use the colon (`:`) operator:

```
class human : public mammal
```

In this example, the new class `human` is derived from the base class `mammal`. The derived class `human` would have all the functionality of the base class `mammal`. In addition, the `human` class can have other functionality, such as the ability to drive a car and work for food. The example in Listing A.13 shows how to create the objects of type `human` and access its data and functions.

LISTING A.13. Inherit1.cpp.

```
 1: // Workspace Name:  Inherit
 2: // Program Name :   Inherit1.cpp
 3:
 4: #include <iostream.h>
 5: enum GENDER { MALE, FEMALE };
 6:
 7: class Mammal
 8: {
 9: public:
10:    // constructors
11:    Mammal():itsAge(35), itsWeight(180){}
12:    ~Mammal(){}
13:
14:    int GetAge()const { return itsAge; }
15:    void SetAge(int age) { itsAge = age; }
16:    int GetWeight() const { return itsWeight; }
17:    void SetWeight(int weight) { itsWeight = weight; }
18:
19:
20: protected:
21:    int itsAge;
22:    int itsWeight;
23:   };
24:
25: class Human : public Mammal
26: {
27: public:
28:
29:    // Constructors
30:    Human():itsGender(MALE){}
31:    ~Human(){}
32:
33:    GENDER GetGender() const { return itsGender; }
34:    void SetGender(GENDER gender) { itsGender = gender; }
35:
36:    void Drive() { cout << "Driving to work...\n"; }
37:    void Work() { cout << "working...\n"; }
38:
39: private:
40:    GENDER itsGender;
41: };
42:
43: void main()
44: {
45:    Human John_doe;
46:    John_doe.Drive();
47:    John_doe.Work();
48:    cout << "John_doe is " << John_doe.GetAge() << " years old\n";
```

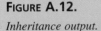

```
49: cout << "And weighs " <<John_doe.GetWeight() << " lbs \n";
50: }
```

The output from Listing A.13 is shown in Figure A.12.

FIGURE A.12.

Inheritance output.

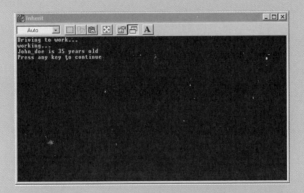

On line 5, a new keyword `enum` is defined. Enumerate defines a new data type with a list of identifiers. The identifiers are fixed values that increment automatically. In this example, the variable `MALE` has a value `0` and the variable `FEMALE` has a value `1` by default. You could also specify a value:

```
enum Alphabets ( A, B, C=5, D=1)
```

In this case, `A` has a value `0`, `B` is `1`, `C` is `5`, and `D` is `1`. If you did not specify any values, then

A is `0`

B is `1`

C is `2`

D is `3`

On line 20, another new keyword `protected` is defined in the class `Mammal`. You covered public and private in the section on classes where all the data members were defined under the `private` keyword. When the data member is defined as private, the derived class cannot access them. For the derived classes to be able to access the data members and methods of a class, they must be defined as protected. The `protected` keyword restricts the access only to the derived classes. Another alternative is to define these methods and members as public, in which case all classes have free access. Although this is a solution, it is not a desired solution because it moves you away from encapsulation.

Line 7 declares the base class `Mammal`. The constructor is on line 11, and the destructor is on line 12. In classes, whenever an object of the class is created, the class constructor is called. The constructor class performs an additional function of initializing its member data, `itsAge(35)` and `itsWeight(180)`. This could have been accomplished by initializing the member data in the body of the constructor, as shown in the following:

```
Mammal()
{
itsAge = 35;
itsWeight = 180;
};
```

The technique of initializing the data members in the constructor declaration (as shown on line 11 of Listing A.13) is far more efficient due to the internal initialization of classes in C++. Use this technique whenever possible because it increases code efficiency.

With derived classes, when an object is created in the derived class, the constructor of the base class is called first and then the constructor of the derived class is called. In this example, when the object `John_doe` is created for the first time, the constructor of the base class `Mammal` is called. The object `John_doe` is not created until both the base constructor and derived class constructor are called. With destructors, the reverse order is followed; when the object `John_doe` ceases to exist, the derived class destructor is called before the base class destructor. On line 25, you define the name of the derived class and its relevant base class.

Line 48 and line 49 are critical in terms of how the data is accessed and output. On lines 48 and 49, the `Human` object `John_doe` accesses information directly from the base class of `Mammal`. Remember from the example `class3.cpp`, to output data from a nested class, you had to use indirect access to the class `Tax_assessment`.

Inheritance is a significant tool in object-oriented programming, and if it's used effectively, it provides code reusability. The `inherit1.cpp` program gave you an overall flavor of inheritance and its properties. However, when programs are written in real life, they are structured more efficiently. The next program involves a more logical and formal process of writing a program.

Assume you are writing a program for the automobile market. The automobile market consists of cars, trucks, minivans, and SUVs (sport utility vehicles). `automobile` is the parent or base class, and the others are the derived classes. Let's start by defining the `automobile` class. Listing A.14 shows the code.

LISTING A.14. Auto.h.

```
1: // Workspace name: Inherit2
2: // Program name:  Auto.h
3:
4: #ifndef AUTO_H
5: #define AUTO_H
6:
7: class automobile
8: {
9: protected:
10:  int miles_per_gallon;
11:  float fuel_capacity;
12: public:
13:  void initialize(int in_mpg, float in_fuel);
14:  int get_mpg(void);
15:  float get_fuel(void);
16:  float travel_distance(void);
17: };
18:
19: #endif
```

Lines 4 and 5 include directives to the preprocessor. The directive on line 4 is covered in detail toward the end of this section. On line 7, the class automobile is defined. This class has two data members and four methods. The class is included in the header file only. The definition of the methods of this class are contained in the Auto.cpp file in Listing A.15.

LISTING A.15. Auto.cpp.

```
1: // Workspace name : Inherit2
2: // Program name :  Auto.cpp
3: #include "auto.h"
4:
5:
6: void automobile::initialize(int in_mpg, float in_fuel)
7: {
8:  miles_per_gallon = in_mpg;
9:  fuel_capacity = in_fuel;
10: }
11:
12:        // Get the rated fuel economy - miles per gallon
13: int automobile::get_mpg()
14: {
15:  return miles_per_gallon;
16: }
17:
```

continues

```
18:        // Get the fuel tank capacity
19: float automobile::get_fuel()
20: {
21:  return fuel_capacity;
22: }
23:
24:        // Return the travel distance possible
25: float automobile::travel_distance()
26: {
27:  return miles_per_gallon * fuel_capacity;
28: }
```

The method get_mpg provides the value for the miles per gallon for a particular vehicle. The get_fuel method provides the gas tank capacity. Next, you define the first derived class, a car, in Listing A.16.

LISTING A.16. Car.h.

```
1: // Workspace name: Inherit2
2: // Program name:  Car.h
3:
4: #ifndef CAR_H
5: #define CAR_H
6:
7: #include "auto.h"
8:
9: class car : public automobile
10: {
11:  int Total_doors;
12: public:
13:  void initialize(int in_mpg, float in_fuel, int door = 4);
14:  int doors(void);
15: };
16:
17: #endif
```

The class car is a derived class from the automobile class. Because it is a derived class, it has access to all of the methods of the base class automobile. In addition, this class has a data member for the number of doors in the car. The methods of this class are defined in Car.cpp in Listing A.17.

LISTING A.17. Car.cpp.

```
1: // Workspace name: Inherit2
2: // Program name:  Car.cpp
3:
4: #include "car.h"
5:
6: void car::initialize(int in_mpg, float in_fuel, int door)
7: {
8:  Total_doors = door;
9:  miles_per_gallon = in_mpg;
10:  fuel_capacity = in_fuel;
11: }
12:
13:
14: int car::doors(void)
15: {
16:  return Total_doors;
17: }
```

The initialization method is defined in lines 6 through 11. It is important to note that the base class of the automobile (auto.h) also had an initialization method. The initialization in the car class overrides the base class initialization. Last but not least is the main() definition. The main() method is defined in Allauto.cpp in Listing A.18.

LISTING A.18. Allauto.cpp.

```
1: // Workspace name: Inherit2
2: // Program name:  Allauto.cpp
3:
4: #include <iostream.h>
5: #include "auto.h"
6: #include "car.h"
7:
8: int main()
9: {
10:
11: car sedan;
12:
13:  sedan.initialize(24, 20.0, 4);
14:  cout << "The sedan can travel " << sedan.travel_distance() <<
15:                      " miles.\n";
16:  cout << "The sedan has " << sedan.doors() << " doors.\n";
17:
18:  return 0;
19: }
```

A

The main() definition has only one object defined. On line 11, an object of class car is declared. The initialization is on line 13. The initialization passes the fuel efficiency of the car (miles per gallon) and the tank capacity. This information is used to access the method travel_distance in the base class define in auto.cpp. The derived class has access to the methods of the base class. Additionally, the derived class passes information to its own data member about the number of doors in the vehicle. The result of executing this program is shown in Figure A.13.

FIGURE A.13.

Vehicle class results.

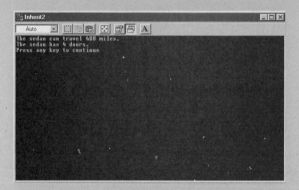

You can now add more classes for other vehicle types. You can make your own classes for a truck and minivan and derive them from the base class exactly like the car class.

If you add another class for trucks, it is important to include the preprocessor directives from Listing A.14's lines 4 and 19. These lines are listed again in the following:

```
4     #ifndef AUTO_H
5     #define AUTO_H
.
.
.
19    #endif
```

Because the truck class is derived from the parent class automobile, it must include the file Auto.h in Truck.h. The header of the car class, Car.h, already includes Auto.h for the same reason. Now, if you create a method that uses both the truck and car classes, you could potentially include Auto.h twice, which would generate in a compiler error. To prevent this, you add lines 4 and 5 of Listing A.14. Line 4 issues a command to the compiler to verify whether the class AUTO.H has been defined; if it hasn't been defined, the program jumps to line 5 and defines it, and if it has been defined, the program jumps to line 19 and ends.

Summary

Congratulations! You have covered almost all of the features and properties of C++. You should now have a solid footing to take full advantage of Visual C++ and object-oriented programming.

A

APPENDIX B

Answers

This appendix provides the answers to the quiz questions and exercises at the end of each chapter.

Day 1

Quiz

1. How do you change the caption on a button?

   In the window layout editor, select the button to be changed. Right-click the mouse and select Properties from the pop-up menu. Change the value in the Caption field.

2. What can you do with the Visual C++ AppWizard?

   You can use it to build a shell for your application, based on the type of application and the functionality needs of the application. The shell will have support for the desired functionality already built in.

3. How do you attach functionality to the click of a button?

   By using the Class Wizard, you can create a function and attach it to an object for handling a specific Windows message. The Class Wizard creates the function and can take you right to the spot in the function's code where you need to begin adding your own code.

Exercise

Add a second button to the About window in your application. Have the button display a different message from the one on the first window.

1. In the workspace pane, select the Resource View tab.

2. Expand the dialog tree branch and double-click the IDD_ABOUTBOX dialog, bringing it into the Developer Studio editor.

3. Click the button control on the toolbar.

4. Click and drag the mouse on the window where you want the button to be placed.

5. Open the properties dialog for the new button, changing the ID and caption to describe the message to be displayed by the button. Close the properties dialog.

6. Open the Class Wizard and add a new function for the clicked message for your new button.

7. Click the Edit Code button in the Class Wizard to take you to the spot in your code where your new function is.

8. Add the MessageBox function to display a message to the user.

9. Compile and run your application to test your new button.

Day 2

Quiz

1. Why do you need to specify the tab order of the controls on your application windows?

   By specifying the tab order of the controls on your application windows, you can control the order in which the user navigates the application window. If the user is using the keyboard to navigate around the application window, then the two primary means of navigating between controls are the tab key and mnemonics that jump directly to specific controls. The tab order helps provide the user with a consistent and predictable experience when using your application.

2. How can you include a mnemonic in a static text field that will take the user to the edit box or combo box beside the text control?

   If you place a mnemonic in a static text control and then make sure that the static text control is just before the edit control associated with the static text in the tab order, the user can select the mnemonic in the static text control to jump directly to the edit box control.

3. Why do you need to give unique object IDs to the static text fields in front of the edit box and combo boxes?

   The unique object IDs on the two static text controls were necessary because you need to manipulate those two controls with the check boxes that enable or disable and show or hide sets of controls.

4. Why do you need to call the UpdateData function before checking the value of one of the controls?

   If the user has changed the value of the control on the screen, the UpdateData function must be called, passing it TRUE as the function argument, to copy the values from the controls on the window to the variables that are associated with those controls. If UpdateData is not called, then the values of the variables may not correctly reflect what the user has changed on the screen.

Exercises

1. Add code to the Default Message button to reset the edit box to say Enter a message here.

   Using the Class Wizard, add a function to the Default Message button's clicked event. In this function, add the code in Listing B.1.

LISTING B.1. DAY2DLG.CPP—THE CODE TO PLACE A DEFAULT MESSAGE IN THE EDIT BOX.

```
 1: void CDay2Dlg::OnDfltmsg()
 2: {
 3:     // TODO: Add your control notification handler code here
 4:
 5:     /////////////////////////
 6:     // MY CODE STARTS HERE
 7:     /////////////////////////
 8:
 9:     // Set the message to a default message
10:     m_strMessage = "Enter a message here";
11:
12:     // Update the screen
13:     UpdateData(FALSE);
```

continues

B

LISTING B.1. CONTINUED

```
14:
15:        /////////////////////////
16:        // MY CODE ENDS HERE
17:        /////////////////////////
18: }
```

2. Add code to enable or disable and show or hide the controls used to select and run another application.

Add functions to the Enable and Show Program Action check boxes. In these functions, add the code in Listing B.2.

LISTING B.2. DAY2DLG.CPP—THE CODE TO ENABLE OR DISABLE AND SHOW OR HIDE THE RUN PROGRAM CONTROLS.

```
 1: void CDay2Dlg::OnCkenblpgm()
 2: {
 3:     // TODO: Add your control notification handler code here
 4:
 5:     /////////////////////////
 6:     // MY CODE STARTS HERE
 7:     /////////////////////////
 8:
 9:     // Get the current values from the screen
10:     UpdateData(TRUE);
11:
12:     // Is the Enable Program Action check box checked?
13:     if (m_bEnablePgm == TRUE)
14:     {
15:         // Yes, so enable all controls that have anything
16:         // to do with running a program
17:         GetDlgItem(IDC_PROGTORUN)->EnableWindow(TRUE);
18:         GetDlgItem(IDC_RUNPGM)->EnableWindow(TRUE);
19:         GetDlgItem(IDC_STATICPGM)->EnableWindow(TRUE);
20:     }
21:     else
22:     {
23:         // No, so disable all controls that have anything
24:         // to do with running a program
25:         GetDlgItem(IDC_PROGTORUN)->EnableWindow(FALSE);
26:         GetDlgItem(IDC_RUNPGM)->EnableWindow(FALSE);
27:         GetDlgItem(IDC_STATICPGM)->EnableWindow(FALSE);
28:     }
29:
30:     /////////////////////////
31:     // MY CODE ENDS HERE
32:     /////////////////////////
```

```
33: }
34:
35: void CDay2Dlg::OnCkshwpgm()
36: {
37:     // TODO: Add your control notification handler code here
38:
39:     /////////////////////////
40:     // MY CODE STARTS HERE
41:     /////////////////////////
42:
43:     // Get the current values from the screen
44:     UpdateData(TRUE);
45:
46:     // Is the Show Program Action check box checked?
47:     if (m_bShowPgm == TRUE)
48:     {
49:         // Yes, so show all controls that have anything
50:         // to do with running a program
51:         GetDlgItem(IDC_PROGTORUN)->ShowWindow(TRUE);
52:         GetDlgItem(IDC_RUNPGM)->ShowWindow(TRUE);
53:         GetDlgItem(IDC_STATICPGM)->ShowWindow(TRUE);
54:     }
55:     else
56:     {
57:         // No, so hide all controls that have anything
58:         // to do with running a program
59:         GetDlgItem(IDC_PROGTORUN)->ShowWindow(FALSE);
60:         GetDlgItem(IDC_RUNPGM)->ShowWindow(FALSE);
61:         GetDlgItem(IDC_STATICPGM)->ShowWindow(FALSE);
62:     }
63:
64:     /////////////////////////
65:     // MY CODE ENDS HERE
66:     /////////////////////////
67: }
```

3. Extend the code in the OnRunpgm function to allow the user to enter his own program name to be run.

   Modify the OnRunpgm function as in Listing B.3.

LISTING B.3. DAY2DLG.CPP—THE CODE TO RUN ANY PROGRAM NAME TYPED INTO THE RUN
PROGRAM COMBO BOX.

```
1: void CDay2Dlg::OnRunpgm()
2: {
3:     // TODO: Add your control notification handler code here
4:
```

continues

LISTING B.3. CONTINUED

```
 5:      ////////////////////////
 6:      // MY CODE STARTS HERE
 7:      ////////////////////////
 8:
 9:      // Get the current values from the screen
10:      UpdateData(TRUE);
11:
12:      // Declare a local variable for holding the program name
13:      CString strPgmName;
14:
15:      // Copy the program name to the local variable
16:      strPgmName = m_strProgToRun;
17:
18:      // Make the program name all uppercase
19:      strPgmName.MakeUpper();
20:
21:      // Did the user select to run the Paint program?
22:      if (strPgmName == "PAINT")
23:          // Yes, run the Paint program
24:          WinExec("pbrush.exe", SW_SHOW);
25:
26:      // Did the user select to run the Notepad program?
27:      if (strPgmName == "NOTEPAD")
28:          // Yes, run the Notepad program
29:          WinExec("notepad.exe", SW_SHOW);
30:
31:      // Did the user select to run the Solitaire program?
32:      if (strPgmName == "SOLITAIRE")
33:          // Yes, run the Solitaire program
34:          WinExec("sol.exe", SW_SHOW);
35:
36:          // Run any other program name typed into the combo box
37:          if ((strPgmName != "PAINT") && (strPgmName != "NOTEPAD") &&
38:              (strPgmName != "SOLITAIRE"))
39:              // Yes, run the program typed into the combo box
40:              WinExec(strPgmName, SW_SHOW);
41:
42:      ////////////////////////
43:      // MY CODE ENDS HERE
44:      ////////////////////////
45: }
```

Day 3

Quiz

1. What are the possible mouse messages that you can add functions for?

   WM_LBUTTONDOWN, WM_LBUTTONUP, WM_LBUTTONDBLCLK, WM_RBUTTONDOWN, WM_RBUTTONUP, WM_RBUTTONDBLCLK, WM_MOUSEMOVE, and WM_MOUSEWHEEL.

2. How can you tell if the left mouse button is down on the WM_MOUSEMOVE event message?

   You can mask the flags passed to the OnMouseMove function with the MK_LBUTTON flag, as follows:

   ((nFlags & MK_LBUTTON) == MK_LBUTTON)

3. How can you prevent the cursor from changing back to the default cursor after you set it to a different one?

   Return TRUE in the OnSetCursor event function, preventing the ancestor OnSetCursor function from being called.

Exercises

1. Modify your drawing program so that the left mouse button can draw in red and the right mouse button can draw in blue.

   Add a function for the WM_RBUTTONDOWN event message and write the code for it as in Listing B.4.

LISTING B.4. MOUSEDLG.CPP—THE OnRButtonDown FUNCTION.

```
 1: void CMouseDlg::OnRButtonDown(UINT nFlags, CPoint point)
 2: {
 3:     // TODO: Add your message handler code here and/or call default
 4:
 5:     /////////////////////////
 6:     // MY CODE STARTS HERE
 7:     /////////////////////////
 8:
 9:         // Set the current point as the starting point
10:     m_iPrevX = point.x;
11:     m_iPrevY = point.y;
12:
13:     /////////////////////////
14:     // MY CODE ENDS HERE
15:     /////////////////////////
16:
17:     CDialog::OnRButtonDown(nFlags, point);
18: }
```

Extend the OnMouseMove function as in Listing B.5.

LISTING B.5. MOUSEDLG.CPP—THE MODIFIED OnMouseMove FUNCTION.

```
 1: void CMouseDlg::OnMouseMove(UINT nFlags, CPoint point)
 2: {
 3:     // TODO: Add your message handler code here and/or call default
 4:
 5:     /////////////////////////
 6:     // MY CODE STARTS HERE
 7:     /////////////////////////
 8:
 9:         // Check to see if the left mouse button is down
10:     if ((nFlags & MK_LBUTTON) == MK_LBUTTON)
11:     {
12:         // Get the Device Context
13:         CClientDC dc(this);
14:
15:         // Create a new pen
16:         CPen lpen(PS_SOLID, 16, RGB(255, 0, 0));
17:
18:         // Use the new pen
19:         dc.SelectObject(&lpen);
20:
21:         // Draw a line from the previous point to the current point
22:         dc.MoveTo(m_iPrevX, m_iPrevY);
23:         dc.LineTo(point.x, point.y);
24:
25:         // Save the current point as the previous point
26:         m_iPrevX = point.x;
27:         m_iPrevY = point.y;
28:     }
29:
30:     // Check to see if the right mouse button is down
31:     if ((nFlags & MK_RBUTTON) == MK_RBUTTON)
32:     {
33:         // Get the Device Context
34:         CClientDC rdc(this);
35:
36:         // Create a new pen
37:         CPen rpen(PS_SOLID, 16, RGB(0, 0, 255));
38:
39:         // Use the new pen
40:         rdc.SelectObject(&rpen);
41:
42:         // Draw a line from the previous point to the current point
43:         rdc.MoveTo(m_iPrevX, m_iPrevY);
44:         rdc.LineTo(point.x, point.y);
45:
46:         // Save the current point as the previous point
```

```
47:        m_iPrevX = point.x;
48:        m_iPrevY = point.y;
49:    }
50:
51:    /////////////////////////
52:    // MY CODE ENDS HERE
53:    /////////////////////////
54:
55:    CDialog::OnMouseMove(nFlags, point);
56: }
```

2. Extend the OnKeyDown function to add some of the following standard cursors:

  - IDC_CROSS

  - IDC_UPARROW

  - IDC_SIZEALL

  - IDC_SIZENWSE

  - IDC_SIZENESW

  - IDC_SIZEWE

  - IDC_SIZENS

  - IDC_NO

  - IDC_APPSTARTING

  - IDC_HELP

Your modified OnKeyDown function can look something like the following:

```
void CMouseDlg::OnKeyDown(UINT nChar, UINT nRepCnt, UINT nFlags)
{
    // TODO: Add your message handler code here and/or call default

    /////////////////////////
    // MY CODE STARTS HERE
    /////////////////////////

    char lsChar;          // The current character being pressed
    HCURSOR lhCursor;     // The handle to the cursor to be displayed

    // Convert the key pressed to a character
    lsChar = char(nChar);

    // Is the character "A"
    if (lsChar == 'A')
    {
        // Load the arrow cursor
        lhCursor = AfxGetApp()->LoadStandardCursor(IDC_ARROW);
        // Set the cursor flag
```

B

```
        m_bCursor = TRUE;
        // Set the screen cursor
        SetCursor(lhCursor);
    }

    // Is the character "B"
    if (lsChar == 'B')
    {
        // Load the I beam cursor
        lhCursor = AfxGetApp()->LoadStandardCursor(IDC_IBEAM);
        // Set the cursor flag
        m_bCursor = TRUE;
        // Set the screen cursor
        SetCursor(lhCursor);
    }

    // Is the character "C"
    if (lsChar == 'C')
    {
        // Load the hourglass cursor
        lhCursor = AfxGetApp()->LoadStandardCursor(IDC_WAIT);
        // Set the cursor flag
        m_bCursor = TRUE;
        // Set the screen cursor
        SetCursor(lhCursor);
    }

    // Is the character "D"
    if (lsChar == 'D')
    {
        // Load the cross hair cursor
        lhCursor = AfxGetApp()->LoadStandardCursor(IDC_CROSS);
        // Set the cursor flag
        m_bCursor = TRUE;
        // Set the screen cursor
        SetCursor(lhCursor);
    }

    // Is the character "E"
    if (lsChar == 'E')
    {
        // Load the up arrow cursor
        lhCursor = AfxGetApp()->LoadStandardCursor(IDC_UPARROW);
        // Set the cursor flag
        m_bCursor = TRUE;
        // Set the screen cursor
        SetCursor(lhCursor);
    }

    // Is the character "F"
    if (lsChar == 'F')
```

```
{
    // Load the size cursor
    lhCursor = AfxGetApp()->LoadStandardCursor(IDC_SIZEALL);
    // Set the cursor flag
    m_bCursor = TRUE;
    // Set the screen cursor
    SetCursor(lhCursor);
}

// Is the character "G"
if (lsChar == 'G')
{
    // Load the up/right-down/left size cursor
    lhCursor = AfxGetApp()->LoadStandardCursor(IDC_SIZENWSE);
    // Set the cursor flag
    m_bCursor = TRUE;
    // Set the screen cursor
    SetCursor(lhCursor);
}

// Is the character "H"
if (lsChar == 'H')
{
    // Load the up/left-down/right size cursor
    lhCursor = AfxGetApp()->LoadStandardCursor(IDC_SIZENESW);
    // Set the cursor flag
    m_bCursor = TRUE;
    // Set the screen cursor
    SetCursor(lhCursor);
}

// Is the character "I"
if (lsChar == 'I')
{
    // Load the left-right size cursor
    lhCursor = AfxGetApp()->LoadStandardCursor(IDC_SIZEWE);
    // Set the cursor flag
    m_bCursor = TRUE;
    // Set the screen cursor
    SetCursor(lhCursor);
}

// Is the character "J"
if (lsChar == 'J')
{
    // Load the up-down size cursor
    lhCursor = AfxGetApp()->LoadStandardCursor(IDC_SIZENS);
    // Set the cursor flag
    m_bCursor = TRUE;
    // Set the screen cursor
    SetCursor(lhCursor);
}
```

B

```
            if (lsChar == 'K')
            {
                // Load the no cursor
                lhCursor = AfxGetApp()->LoadStandardCursor(IDC_NO);
                // Set the cursor flag
                m_bCursor = TRUE;
                // Set the screen cursor
                SetCursor(lhCursor);
            }

            if (lsChar == 'L')
            {
                // Load the app starting cursor
                lhCursor = AfxGetApp()->LoadStandardCursor(IDC_APPSTARTING);
                // Set the cursor flag
                m_bCursor = TRUE;
                // Set the screen cursor
                SetCursor(lhCursor);
            }

            if (lsChar == 'M')
            {
                // Load the help cursor
                lhCursor = AfxGetApp()->LoadStandardCursor(IDC_HELP);
                // Set the cursor flag
                m_bCursor = TRUE;
                // Set the screen cursor
                SetCursor(lhCursor);
            }

            // Is the character "X"
            if (lsChar == 'X')
            {
                // Load the arrow cursor
                lhCursor = AfxGetApp()->LoadStandardCursor(IDC_ARROW);
                // Set the cursor flag
                m_bCursor = TRUE;
                // Set the screen cursor
                SetCursor(lhCursor);
                // Exit the application
                OnOK();
            }

            ////////////////////////
            // MY CODE ENDS HERE
            ////////////////////////

            CDialog::OnKeyDown(nChar, nRepCnt, nFlags);
        }
```

Day 4

Quiz

1. What did you accomplish by adding the two timer IDs to the resource symbols?

   You defined the two IDs so that they were available as constants throughout the application.

2. What is another way to add these two IDs to the application?

   Add them as `#define` constants in the class header file (`TimerDlg.h`), as follows:

```
/////////////////////////////////////////////////////////////////////////
// CTimersDlg dialog

#define ID_CLOCK_TIMER 1
#define ID_COUNT_TIMER 2

class CTimersDlg : public CDialog
{
.
.
.
```

3. How can you tell two timers apart in the `OnTimer` function?

   You use the timer ID to determine which timer triggered the event.

4. How many timer events does your application receive if the timer is set for one second and your application has been busy for one minute, preventing it from receiving any timer event messages?

   One.

Exercise

Update your application so that when the counter timer is started, the clock timer is reset to run at the same interval as the counter timer. When the counter timer is stopped, return the clock timer to a one-second interval.

To change the interval at which a timer is running, you need to first stop the timer and then restart it, as in Listing B.6.

LISTING B.6. THE REVISED `OnStarttime` AND `OnStoptimer` FUNCTIONS.

```
 1: void CTimersDlg::OnStarttime()
 2: {
 3:     // TODO: Add your control notification handler code here
 4:
 5:     //////////////////////////
 6:     // MY CODE STARTS HERE
 7:     //////////////////////////
 8:
 9:     // Update the variables
10:     UpdateData(TRUE);
11:
12:     // Initialize the count
13:     m_iCount = 0;
14:     // Format the count for displaying
15:     m_sCount.Format("%d", m_iCount);
16:
17:     // Update the dialog
18:     UpdateData(FALSE);
19:     // Start the timer
20:     SetTimer(ID_COUNT_TIMER, m_iInterval, NULL);
21:
22:     // Stop the clock timer
23:     KillTimer(ID_CLOCK_TIMER);
24:     // Restart the clock timer with the counter interval
25:     SetTimer(ID_CLOCK_TIMER, m_iInterval, NULL);
26:
27:     // Enable the Stop Timer button
28:     m_cStopTime.EnableWindow(TRUE);
29:     // Disable the Start Timer button
30:     m_cStartTime.EnableWindow(FALSE);
31:
32:     //////////////////////////
33:     // MY CODE ENDS HERE
34:     //////////////////////////
35: }
36:
37: void CTimersDlg::OnStoptimer()
38: {
39:     // TODO: Add your control notification handler code here
40:
41:     //////////////////////////
42:     // MY CODE STARTS HERE
43:     //////////////////////////
44:
45:     // Stop the timer
46:     KillTimer(ID_COUNT_TIMER);
47:
48:     // Stop the clock timer
```

```
49:        KillTimer(ID_CLOCK_TIMER);
50:        // Restart the clock timer with 1 second interval
51:        SetTimer(ID_CLOCK_TIMER, 1000, NULL);
52:
53:        // Disable the Stop Timer button
54:        m_cStopTime.EnableWindow(FALSE);
55:        // Enable the Start Timer button
56:        m_cStartTime.EnableWindow(TRUE);
57:
58:        //////////////////////////
59:        // MY CODE ENDS HERE
60:        //////////////////////////
61: }
```

B

Day 5

Quiz

1. What are the possible return codes that your application might receive from the
   MessageBox function call when you specify the MB_RETRYCANCEL button combination?

   IDRETRY and IDCANCEL.

2. What are the common dialogs that are built into the Windows operating systems
   that are defined as MFC classes?

   The common Windows dialogs that are defined as MFC classes are

   - File selection
   - Font selection
   - Color selection
   - Page setup for printing
   - Printing
   - Find and replace

3. What is the difference between a modal dialog and a modeless dialog?

   A modal dialog stops all application processing until the user responds to the dialog. A modeless dialog allows the user to continue working with the rest of the
   application while the dialog is open for use.

4. How can you display a File Save dialog for the user instead of the File Open dialog that you did have in your application?

In the class instance variable declaration, pass FALSE instead of TRUE. This makes the variable declaration look like this:

```
CFileDialog m_ldFile(FALSE);
```

5. Why did you not need to create any functions and add any code to your custom dialog?

The only functionality that was needed on the custom dialog was calling UpdateData before closing the dialog. Because the OK and Cancel buttons were never deleted from the dialog, the OK button automatically performed this functionality.

Exercises

1. Modify your application so that it includes the directory with the filename in the application. (Hint: The GetPathName function returns the path and filename that was selected in the File Open dialog.)

Modify the OnFileopen function as follows:

```
void CDialogsDlg::OnFileopen()
{
    // TODO: Add your control notification handler code here

    ////////////////////////////
    // MY CODE STARTS HERE
    ////////////////////////////

    CFileDialog m_ldFile(TRUE);

    // Show the File open dialog and capture the result
    if (m_ldFile.DoModal() == IDOK)
    {
        // Get the filename selected
        m_sResults = m_ldFile.GetPathName();
        // Update the dialog
        UpdateData(FALSE);
    }

    ////////////////////////////
    // MY CODE ENDS HERE
    ////////////////////////////
}
```

The GetPathName function returns the path and filename, so changing the function call from GetFileName to GetPathName alters the display to include the path with the filename.

2. Add a button on the custom dialog that calls the MessageBox function with a Yes or No selection. Pass the result back to the main application dialog.

Follow these steps:

1. Using the Class View, add a member variable to the CMsgDlg class. Specify the variable type as int, the name as m_iYesNo, and the access as Public.

2. Using the Resource View, bring the custom dialog into the editor area. Add a command button to the window, named IDC_YESNO with a caption &Yes or No.

3. Using the Class Wizard, add a function to the new button you just added and edit the function. Include the following code:

```
void CMsgDlg::OnYesno()
{
    // TODO: Add your control notification handler code here

    /////////////////////////
    // MY CODE STARTS HERE
    /////////////////////////

    // Ask the user
    m_iYesNo = MessageBox("Choose Yes or No", "Yes or No",
➥MB_YESNO);

    /////////////////////////
    // MY CODE ENDS HERE
    /////////////////////////
}
```

4. Add a button to the main dialog window named IDC_YESNO with the caption Y&es or No.

5. Using the Class Wizard, add a function to the new button, including the following code:

```
void CDialogsDlg::OnYesno()
{
    // TODO: Add your control notification handler code here

    /////////////////////////
    // MY CODE STARTS HERE
    /////////////////////////

    // What did the user answer
    switch (m_dMsgDlg.m_iYesNo)
    {
    case IDYES:     // Did the user answer YES?
        m_sResults = "Yes!";
        break;
```

B

```
case IDNO:      // Did the user answer NO?
    m_sResults = "No!";
    break;
}

// Update the dialog
UpdateData(FALSE);

/////////////////////////
// MY CODE ENDS HERE
/////////////////////////
}
```

Day 6

Quiz

1. What event message does a menu selection send to the window message queue?

   COMMAND.

2. How do you attach a menu to a dialog window?

   In the dialog designer, open the properties dialog for the window, and choose the menu from the drop-down list of menus.

3. Which existing class do you specify for handling event messages for the menu?

   The dialog class for the window on which the menu appears.

4. What event message should a pop-up menu be triggered by?

   The WM_CONTEXTMENU event.

Exercises

1. Add a button to the main window and have it call the same function as the Hello menu entry.

   Follow these steps:

   1. Add a button to the dialog screen. Supply a button ID of IDC_HELLO and a caption of &Hello.

   2. Using the Class Wizard, add a function to the button. Name the function OnHello.

2. Add a pop-up menu to your application that uses the Help drop-down menu as the pop-up menu.

Follow these steps:

1. Using the Class Wizard, add a function for the WM_CONTEXTMENU event message in your dialog window.

2. Edit the function, adding the following code:

```
void CMenusDlg::OnContextMenu(CWnd* pWnd, CPoint point)
{
    // TODO: Add your message handler code here and/or call
➥default

    /////////////////////////
    // MY CODE STARTS HERE
    /////////////////////////

    // Declare local variables
    CMenu *m_lMenu;      // A pointer to the menu
    CPoint m_pPoint;     // A copy of the mouse position

    // Copy the mouse position to a local variable
    m_pPoint = point;
    // Convert the position to a screen position
    ClientToScreen(&m_pPoint);
    // Get a pointer to the window menu
    m_lMenu = GetMenu();
    // Get a pointer to the first submenu
    m_lMenu = m_lMenu->GetSubMenu(1);
    // Show the Pop-up Menu
    m_lMenu->TrackPopupMenu(TPM_CENTERALIGN + TPM_LEFTBUTTON,
        m_pPoint.x, m_pPoint.y, this, NULL);

    /////////////////////////
    // MY CODE ENDS HERE
    /////////////////////////

    CDialog::OnRButtonDown(nFlags, point);
}
```

Day 7

Quiz

1. How can you specify that the text is to be underlined?

   Pass 1 as the value for the bUnderline argument to the CreateFont function.

2. How can you print your text upside down?

   Pass 1800 as the nEscapement argument to the CreateFont function.

3. How many times is the `EnumFontFamProc` callback function called by the operating system?

The function is called once for each font that is available in the system, unless the callback function returns 0 and stops the listing of fonts.

Exercises

1. Add a check box to switch between using the entered text to display the font and using the font name to display the font, as in Figure 7.4.

Add the check box to the dialog. Set its properties as follows:

ID: IDC_CBUSETEXT

Caption: &Use Entered Text

Using the Class Wizard, attach a variable to this control. Specify the variable type as a boolean with the name m_bUseText.

Using the Class Wizard, add a function for the BN_CLICKED event message for the check box. Edit the function, adding the following code:

```
void CDay7Dlg::OnCbusetext()
{
    // TODO: Add your control notification handler code here

    /////////////////////////
    // MY CODE STARTS HERE
    /////////////////////////

    // Update the variables with the dialog controls
    UpdateData(TRUE);
    // Using the font name for the font sample?
    if (!m_bUseText)
        // Using the font name
        m_strDisplayText = m_strFontName;
    else
        // Using the entered text
        m_strDisplayText = m_strSampText;

    // Update the dialog
    UpdateData(FALSE);

    /////////////////////////
    // MY CODE ENDS HERE
    /////////////////////////
}
```

Modify the OnInitDialog function to initialize the check box as follows:

```
BOOL CDay7Dlg::OnInitDialog()
{
```

B

```
    CDialog::OnInitDialog();
    .
    .
    .

    // TODO: Add extra initialization here

    ////////////////////////
    // MY CODE STARTS HERE
    ////////////////////////

    // Fill the font list box
    FillFontList();

    // Initialize the text to be entered
    m_strSampText = "Testing";
    // Copy the text to the font sample area
    m_strDisplayText = m_strSampText;
    // Initialize the check box
    m_bUseText = TRUE;
    // Update the dialog
    UpdateData(FALSE);

    ////////////////////////
    // MY CODE ENDS HERE
    ////////////////////////

    return TRUE;  // return TRUE  unless you set the focus
                  // to a control
}
```

Modify the OnSelchangeLfonts function as follows:

```
void CDay7Dlg::OnSelchangeLfonts()
{
    // TODO: Add your control notification handler code here

    ////////////////////////
    // MY CODE STARTS HERE
    ////////////////////////

    // Update the variables with the dialog controls
    UpdateData(TRUE);
    // Using the font name for the font sample?
    if (!m_bUseText)
    {
        // Copy the font name to the font sample
        m_strDisplayText = m_strFontName;
        // Update the dialog with the variables
        UpdateData(FALSE);
    }
    // Set the font for the sample
    SetMyFont();
```

```
//////////////////////////
// MY CODE ENDS HERE
//////////////////////////
}
```

Finally, modify the OnChangeEsamptext function as follows:

```
void CDay7Dlg::OnChangeEsamptext()
{
    // TODO: If this is a RICHEDIT control, the control will not
    // send this notification unless you override the
    // CDialog::OnInitialUpdate()
    // function and call CRichEditCrtl().SetEventMask()
    // with the EN_CHANGE flag ORed into the mask.

    // TODO: Add your control notification handler code here

    //////////////////////////
    // MY CODE STARTS HERE
    //////////////////////////

    // Update the variables with the dialog controls
    UpdateData(TRUE);
    // Using the text for the font sample?
    if (m_bUseText)
    {
        // Copy the current text to the font sample
        m_strDisplayText = m_strSampText;
        // Update the dialog with the variables
        UpdateData(FALSE);
    }

    //////////////////////////
    // MY CODE ENDS HERE
    //////////////////////////
}
```

2. Add a check box to display the font sample in italics, as in Figure 7.5.

    Add the check box to the dialog. Set its properties as follows:

    ID: IDC_CBITALIC

    Caption: &Italic

    Using the Class Wizard, attach a variable to this control. Specify the variable type
    as a boolean with the name m_bItalic.

    Using the Class Wizard, add a function for the BN_CLICKED event message for the
    check box. Edit the function, adding the following code:

B

```
void CDay7Dlg::OnCbitalic()
{
    // TODO: Add your control notification handler code here

    ////////////////////////
    // MY CODE STARTS HERE
    ////////////////////////

    // Update the variables with the dialog controls
    UpdateData(TRUE);
    // Set the font for the sample
    SetMyFont();

    ////////////////////////
    // MY CODE ENDS HERE
    ////////////////////////
}
```

Modify the SetMyFont function as in the following code:

```
void CDay7Dlg::SetMyFont()
{
    CRect rRect;         // The rectangle of the display area
    int iHeight;         // The height of the display area
    int iItalic = 0;     // Italicize the font?

    // Has a font been selected?
    if (m_strFontName != "")
    {
        // Get the dimensions of the font sample display area
        m_ctlDisplayText.GetWindowRect(&rRect);
        // Calculate the area height
        iHeight = rRect.top - rRect.bottom;
        // Make sure the height is positive
        if (iHeight < 0)
            iHeight = 0 - iHeight;
        // Should the font be italicized?
        if (m_bItalic)
            iItalic = 1;
        // Create the font to be used
        m_fSampFont.CreateFont((iHeight - 5), 0, 0, 0,
                FW_NORMAL, iItalic, 0, 0, DEFAULT_CHARSET,
                OUT_CHARACTER_PRECIS, CLIP_CHARACTER_PRECIS,
                DEFAULT_QUALITY, DEFAULT_PITCH |
                FF_DONTCARE, m_strFontName);

        // Set the font for the sample display area
        m_ctlDisplayText.SetFont(&m_fSampFont);
    }
}
```

Day 8

Quiz

1. What are the three values that are combined to specify a color?

   Red, green, and blue.

2. What do you use to draw on windows without needing to know what graphics card the user has?

   The device context.

3. What size bitmap can you use to make a brush from it?

   8 pixels by 8 pixels.

4. What event message is sent to a window to tell it to redraw itself?

   The WM_PAINT message.

5. How can you cause a window to repaint itself?

   Use the Invalidate function on it.

Exercises

1. Make the second dialog window resizable, and make it adjust the figures drawn on it whenever it's resized.

   Open the second dialog in the dialog layout designer. Open the properties for the window. Select the Style tab. Change the border to Resizing. Open the Class Wizard and add an event-handler function for the WM_SIZE event message. Edit the function that you just created and call the Invalidate function, as in Listing B.7.

LISTING B.7. THE OnSize FUNCTION.

```
1: void CPaintDlg::OnSize(UINT nType, int cx, int cy)
2: {
3:     CDialog::OnSize(nType, cx, cy);
4:
5:     // TODO: Add your message handler code here
6:     // Redraw the window
7:     Invalidate();
8: }
```

2. Add a bitmap brush to the set of brushes used to create the rectangles and ellipses.

   Open the Resources View tab on the workspace pane. Right-click on the top folder of the resource tree. Select Insert from the pop-up menu. Select Bitmap from the list of available resources to add. Paint a pattern on the bitmap that you just created. Right-click on the bitmap ID in the workspace pane. Open the properties dialog and change the object ID to IDB_BITMAPBRUSH. Open the source code for the DrawRegion function. Add the code in Listing B.8, lines 22 through 24 and lines 105 through 112. Increase the number of loops in the for statement on line 39.

LISTING B.8. THE DrawRegion FUNCTION.

```
1:   void CPaintDlg::DrawRegion(CPaintDC *pdc, int iColor, int iTool, int
     ➥iShape)
2:   {
3:       // Declare and create the pens
  .
  .
  .
19:      CBrush lVertBrush(HS_VERTICAL, m_crColors[iColor]);
20:      CBrush lNullBrush(RGB(192, 192, 192));
21:
22:      CBitmap lBitmap;
23:      lBitmap.LoadBitmap(IDB_BITMAPBRUSH);
24:      CBrush lBitmapBrush(&lBitmap);
25:
26:      // Calculate the size of the drawing regions
27:      CRect lRect;
28:      GetClientRect(lRect);
  .
  .
  .
37:      int i;
38:      // Loop through all of the brushes and pens
39:      for (i = 0; i < 8; i++)
40:      {
41:          switch (i)
42:          {
  .
  .
  .
103:             pdc->SelectObject(&lVertBrush);
104:             break;
105:         case 7:    // Null - Bitmap
106:             // Determine the location for this figure.
107:             lDrawRect.left = lDrawRect.left + liHorz;
108:             lDrawRect.right = lDrawRect.left + liWidth;
109:             // Select the appropriate pen and brush
110:             pdc->SelectObject(&lNullPen);
111:             pdc->SelectObject(&lBitmapBrush);
112:             break;
113:         }
```

continues

LISTING B.8. CONTINUED

```
114:        // Which tool are we using?
  .

  .

  .
126:    pdc->SelectObject(lOldBrush);
127:    pdc->SelectObject(lOldPen);
128:}
```

Day 9

Quiz

1. How does an ActiveX container call methods in an ActiveX control?

   By using the `IDispatch` interface, the container can call the `Invoke` method, passing the DISPID of the control's method that the container wants to run.

2. How does an ActiveX control trigger events in the container application?

   The container application has its own `IDispatch` interface, through which the control can trigger events.

3. What AppWizard option must be selected for ActiveX controls to work properly in a Visual C++ application?

   You select the ActiveX Controls check box in the second step of the AppWizard.

4. How does Visual C++ make it easy to work with ActiveX controls?

   It generates C++ classes that encapsulate the control's functionality.

5. Why might it be difficult to work with older controls in Visual C++?

   Older controls might not contain the information necessary for Visual C++ to generate the C++ classes that are used to encapsulate the control's functionality.

Exercise

Modify the application so that the user can double-click a column header and make it the first column in the grid.

Using the Class Wizard, add a function to the `DblClick` event message for the grid control.

Edit the function in exercise 1 to add the following code:

```
void CActiveXDlg::OnDblClickMsfgrid()
{
    // TODO: Add your control notification handler code here
```

```
/////////////////////////
// MY CODE STARTS HERE
/////////////////////////

// Did the user click on a data row and not the
// header row?
if (m_ctlFGrid.GetMouseRow() != 0)
{
    // If so, then zero out the column variable
    // and exit
    m_iMouseCol = 0;
    return;
}
// Save the column clicked on
m_iMouseCol = m_ctlFGrid.GetMouseCol();
// If the selected column was the first column,
// there's nothing to do
if (m_iMouseCol == 0)
    return;
// Turn the control redraw off
m_ctlFGrid.SetRedraw(FALSE);
// Change the selected column position
m_ctlFGrid.SetColPosition(m_iMouseCol, 0);
// Resort the grid
DoSort();
// Turn redraw back on
m_ctlFGrid.SetRedraw(TRUE);

/////////////////////////
// MY CODE ENDS HERE
/////////////////////////
}
```

Day 10

Quiz

1. What does SDI stand for?

   Single Document Interface.

2. What functionality is in the view class?

   The view class is responsible for displaying the document for the user.

3. What function is called to redraw the document if the window has been hidden behind another window?

   The OnDraw function in the view class is called to redraw the document.

4. Where do you place code to clear out the current document before starting a new document?

   The DeleteContents function in the document class is where you place code to clear the current document.

5. What is the purpose of the document class?

   The document class is where the data is managed and manipulated. It maintains the abstract representation of the document being edited and processed.

Exercise

Add another pull-down menu to control the width of the pen used for drawing. Give it the following settings:

Menu Entry	Width Setting
Very Thin	1
Thin	8
Medium	16
Thick	24
Very Thick	32

Follow these steps:

1. Select the CLine class in the Class View tab of the workspace pane. Right-click the mouse and select Add Member Variable from the pop-up menu.

2. Specify the variable type as UINT, the name as m_nWidth, and the access as private. Click OK to add the variable.

3. Right-click the CLine constructor in the Class View tree. Select Go to Declaration from the pop-up menu.

4. Add UINT nWidth as a fourth argument to the constructor declaration.

5. Right-click the CLine constructor in the Class View tree. Select Go to Definition from the pop-up menu.

6. Modify the constructor to add the fourth argument and to set the m_nWidth member to the new argument, as in Listing B.9.

LISTING **B.9.** THE MODIFIED CLine CONSTRUCTOR.

```
1: CLine::CLine(CPoint ptFrom, CPoint ptTo, COLORREF crColor, UINT nWidth)
2: {
3:     //Initialize the from and to points
```

```
4:      m_ptFrom = ptFrom;
5:      m_ptTo = ptTo;
6:      m_crColor = crColor;
7:      m_nWidth = nWidth;
8: }
```

B

7. Scroll down to the Draw function and modify it as in Listing B.10.

LISTING B.10. THE MODIFIED Draw FUNCTION.

```
1: void CLine::Draw(CDC * pDC)
2: {
3:      // Create a pen
4:      CPen lpen (PS_SOLID, m_nWidth, m_crColor);
5:
6:      // Set the new pen as the drawing object
7:      CPen* pOldPen = pDC->SelectObject(&lpen);
8:      // Draw the line
9:      pDC->MoveTo(m_ptFrom);
10:     pDC->LineTo(m_ptTo);
11:     // Reset the previous pen
12:     pDC->SelectObject(pOldPen);
13: }
```

8. Scroll down to the Serialize function and modify it as in Listing B.11.

LISTING B.11. THE MODIFIED Serialize FUNCTION.

```
1: void CLine::Serialize(CArchive &ar)
2: {
3:      CObject::Serialize(ar);
4:
5:      if (ar.IsStoring())
6:          ar << m_ptFrom << m_ptTo << (DWORD) m_crColor << m_nWidth;
7:      else
8:          ar >> m_ptFrom >> m_ptTo >> (DWORD) m_crColor >> m_nWidth;
9: }
```

9. Select the CDay10Doc class in the Class View tab on the workspace pane. Right-click the mouse and choose Add Member Variable from the pop-up menu.

10. Specify the variable type as UINT, the name as m_nWidth, and the access as private. Click OK to add the variable.

11. Open the CDay10Doc source code (Day10Doc.cpp), scroll down to the OnNewDocument function, and edit it as in Listing B.12.

LISTING B.12. THE MODIFIED OnNewDocument FUNCTION.

```
 1: BOOL CDay10Doc::OnNewDocument()
 2: {
 3:     if (!CDocument::OnNewDocument())
 4:         return FALSE;
 5:
 6:     // TODO: add reinitialization code here
 7:     // (SDI documents will reuse this document)
 8:
 9:     /////////////////////////
10:     // MY CODE STARTS HERE
11:     /////////////////////////
12:
13:     // Initialize the color to black
14:     m_nColor = ID_COLOR_BLACK - ID_COLOR_BLACK;
15:     // Initialize the width to thin
16:     m_nWidth = ID_WIDTH_VTHIN - ID_WIDTH_VTHIN;
17:
18:     /////////////////////////
19:     // MY CODE ENDS HERE
20:     /////////////////////////
21:
22:     return TRUE;
23: }
```

12. Scroll down to the AddLine function, and modify it as in Listing B.13.

LISTING B.13. THE MODIFIED AddLine FUNCTION.

```
 1: CLine * CDay10Doc::AddLine(CPoint ptFrom, CPoint ptTo)
 2: {
 3:     static UINT nWidths[5] = { 1, 8, 16, 24, 32};
 4:
 5:     // Create a new CLine object
 6:     CLine *pLine = new CLine(ptFrom, ptTo,
        ➥m_crColors[m_nColor], nWidths[m_nWidth]);
 7:     try
 8:     {
 9:         // Add the new line to the object array
10:         m_oaLines.Add(pLine);
11:         // Mark the document as dirty
12:         SetModifiedFlag();
13:     }
14:     // Did we run into a memory exception?
15:     catch (CMemoryException* perr)
```

```
16:     {
17:         // Display a message for the user, giving him or her the
18:         // bad news
19:         AfxMessageBox("Out of memory", MB_ICONSTOP | MB_OK);
20:         // Did we create a line object?
21:         if (pLine)
22:         {
23:             // Delete it
24:             delete pLine;
25:             pLine = NULL;
26:         }
27:         // Delete the exception object
28:         perr->Delete();
29:     }
30:     return pLine;
31: }
```

13. Add a new member function to the CDay10Doc class. Specify the function type as UINT, the declaration as GetWidth, and the access as public.

14. Edit the GetWidth function, adding the code in Listing B.14.

LISTING B.14. THE GetWidth FUNCTION.

```
1: UINT CDay10Doc::GetWidth()
2: {
3:     // Return the current width
4:     return ID_WIDTH_VTHIN + m_nWidth;
5: }
```

15. Select the Resource View tab in the workspace pane. Expand the tree so that you can see the contents of the Menu folder. Double-click the menu resource.

16. Grab the blank top-level menu (at the right end of the menu bar) and drag it to the left, dropping it in front of the Color menu entry.

17. Open the properties for the blank menu entry. Specify the caption as &Width. Close the properties dialog.

18. Add submenu entries below the Width top-level menu. Specify the submenus in order, setting their properties as specified in Table B.1.

TABLE B.1. MENU PROPERTY SETTINGS.

Object	Property	Setting
Menu Entry	ID	ID_WIDTH_VTHIN
	Caption	&Very Thin
Menu Entry	ID	ID_WIDTH_THIN
	Caption	Thi&n
Menu Entry	ID	ID_WIDTH_MEDIUM
	Caption	&Medium
Menu Entry	ID	ID_WIDTH_THICK
	Caption	Thic&k
Menu Entry	ID	ID_WIDTH_VTHICK
	Caption	Very &Thick

19. Open the Class Wizard. Select the CDay10Doc in the Class Name combo box.

20. Add functions for both the COMMAND and UPDATE_COMMAND_UI event messages for all the width menu entries.

21. After you add the final menu entry function, click Edit Code.

22. Edit the Very Thin menu functions as in Listing B.15.

LISTING B.15. THE VERY THIN MENU FUNCTIONS.

```
 1: void CDay10Doc::OnWidthVthin()
 2: {
 3:     // TODO: Add your command handler code here
 4:
 5:     /////////////////////////
 6:     // MY CODE STARTS HERE
 7:     /////////////////////////
 8:
 9:     // Set the current width to Very Thin
10:     m_nwidth = ID_WIDTH_VTHIN - ID_WIDTH_VTHIN;
11:
12:     /////////////////////////
13:     // MY CODE ENDS HERE
14:     /////////////////////////
15: }
16:
17: void CDay10Doc::OnUpdateWidthVthin(CCmdUI* pCmdUI)
18: {
19:     // TODO: Add your command update UI handler code here
20:
```

B

```
21:     /////////////////////////
22:     // MY CODE STARTS HERE
23:     /////////////////////////
24:
25:     // Determine if the Very Thin menu entry should be checked
26:     pCmdUI->SetCheck(GetWidth() == ID_WIDTH_VTHIN ? 1 : 0);
27:
28:     /////////////////////////
29:     // MY CODE ENDS HERE
30:     /////////////////////////
31: }
```

23. Edit the Thin menu functions as in Listing B.16. Edit the remaining menu func-
    tions in the same way, substituting their menu IDs for ID_WIDTH_THIN.

LISTING B.16. THE THIN MENU FUNCTIONS.

```
 1: void CDay10Doc::OnWidthThin()
 2: {
 3:     // TODO: Add your command handler code here
 4:
 5:     /////////////////////////
 6:     // MY CODE STARTS HERE
 7:     /////////////////////////
 8:
 9:     // Set the current width to Thin
10:     m_nwidth = ID_WIDTH_THIN - ID_WIDTH_VTHIN;
11:
12:     /////////////////////////
13:     // MY CODE ENDS HERE
14:     /////////////////////////
15: }
16:
17: void CDay10Doc::OnUpdateWidthThin(CCmdUI* pCmdUI)
18: {
19:     // TODO: Add your command update UI handler code here
20:
21:     /////////////////////////
22:     // MY CODE STARTS HERE
23:     /////////////////////////
24:
25:     // Determine if the Thin menu entry should be checked
26:     pCmdUI->SetCheck(GetWidth() == ID_WIDTH_THIN ? 1 : 0);
27:
28:     /////////////////////////
29:     // MY CODE ENDS HERE
30:     /////////////////////////
31: }
```

Day 11

Quiz

1. What are the five base classes that are used in MDI applications?

   The CWinApp-derived class, the CMDIFrameWnd-derived class, the CMDIChildWnd-derived class, the CDocument-derived class, and the CView-derived class.

2. Why do you have to place the ON_COMMAND_RANGE message map entry outside the section maintained by the Class Wizard?

   The Class Wizard doesn't understand the ON_COMMAND_RANGE message map entry and thus would either remove or corrupt it.

3. What argument does ON_COMMAND_RANGE pass to the event function?

   The ID of the event message.

4. What event message should you use to display a pop-up menu?

   WM_CONTEXTMENU.

Exercise

Add the pull-down and context menus for the width, using the same pen widths as yesterday.

Follow these steps:

1. Add the Width handling code as in yesterday's exercise.

2. Add the Width menu entries using the same settings as yesterday.

3. Open the Day11Doc.h header file.

4. Scroll down toward the bottom of the header file until you find the protected section where the AFX_MSG message map is declared (search for //{{AFX_MSG(CDay11Doc)).

5. Add the function declarations in Listing B.17 before the line that you searched for. (The string that you searched for is the beginning marker for the Class Wizard maintained message map. Anything you place between it and the end marker, //}}AFX_MSG, is likely to be removed or corrupted by the Class Wizard.)

LISTING B.17. THE EVENT-HANDLER DECLARATIONS IN Day11Doc.H.

```
    .
    .
    .
1: #ifdef _DEBUG
2:     virtual void AssertValid() const;
3:     virtual void Dump(CDumpContext& dc) const;
```

```
 4: #endif
 5:
 6: protected:
 7:
 8: // Generated message map functions
 9: protected:
10:     afx_msg void OnColorCommand(UINT nID);
11:     afx_msg void OnWidthCommand(UINT nID);
12:     afx_msg void OnUpdateColorUI(CCmdUI* pCmdUI);
13:     afx_msg void OnUpdateWidthUI(CCmdUI* pCmdUI);
14:     //{{AFX_MSG(CDay11Doc)
15:         // NOTE - the ClassWizard will add and remove member functions
           //here.
16:         //     DO NOT EDIT what you see in these blocks of generated
           //code !
17:     //}}AFX_MSG
18:     DECLARE_MESSAGE_MAP()
19: private:
20:     UINT m_nColor;
21:     CObArray m_oaLines;
22: };
```

B

6. Open the Day11Doc.cpp source-code file.

7. Search for the line BEGIN_MESSAGE_MAP and add the lines in Listing B.18 just after it. It's important that this code be between the BEGIN_MESSAGE_MAP line and the //{{AFX_MSG_MAP line. If these commands are between the //{{AFX_MSG_MAP and //}}AFX_MSG_MAP lines, then the Class Wizard will remove or corrupt them.

LISTING B.18. THE EVENT-HANDLER MESSAGE MAP ENTRIES IN Day11Doc.cpp.

```
 1://////////////////////////////////////////////////////////////////
 2: // CDay11Doc
 3:
 4: IMPLEMENT_DYNCREATE(CDay11Doc, CDocument)
 5:
 6: BEGIN_MESSAGE_MAP(CDay11Doc, CDocument)
 7:     ON_COMMAND_RANGE(ID_COLOR_BLACK, ID_COLOR_WHITE, OnColorCommand)
 8:     ON_COMMAND_RANGE(ID_WIDTH_VTHIN, ID_WIDTH_VTHICK, OnWidthCommand)
 9:     ON_UPDATE_COMMAND_UI_RANGE(ID_COLOR_BLACK, ID_COLOR_WHITE,
        ➥OnUpdateColorUI)
10:     ON_UPDATE_COMMAND_UI_RANGE(ID_WIDTH_VTHIN, ID_WIDTH_VTHICK,
        ➥OnUpdateWidthUI)
11:     //{{AFX_MSG_MAP(CDay11Doc)
12:         // NOTE - the ClassWizard will add and remove mapping macros
           //here.
```

continues

LISTING B.18. CONTINUED

```
13:          //    DO NOT EDIT what you see in these blocks of generated
             //code!
14:      //}}AFX_MSG_MAP
15: END_MESSAGE_MAP()
16:
17: const COLORREF CDay11Doc::m_crColors[8] = {
18:     RGB(   0,   0,   0),    // Black
19:     RGB(   0,   0, 255),    // Blue
 .
 .
 .
```

8. Scroll to the bottom of the file and add the two event message handler functions in Listing B.19.

LISTING B.19. THE WIDTH MENU EVENT HANDLER FUNCTIONS.

```
 1: void CDay11Doc::OnWidthCommand(UINT nID)
 2: {
 3:     // Set the current width
 4:     m_nWidth = nID - ID_WIDTH_VTHIN;
 5: }
 6:
 7: void CDay11Doc::OnUpdateWidthUI(CCmdUI* pCmdUI)
 8: {
 9:     // Determine if the menu entry should be checked
10:     pCmdUI->SetCheck(GetWidth() == pCmdUI->m_nID ? 1 : 0);
11: }
```

9. Open the IDR_CONTEXTMENU in the Menu Designer.

10. In the Width cascading menu, add the width menu entries just like you did for the IDR_DAY11TYPE menu, using the same property settings. You can select the ID from the drop-down list of IDs if you would rather search for them instead of type.

Day 12

Quiz

1. How do you tie a toolbar button to a menu entry that triggers that same function?

   Give the toolbar button the same object ID as the menu entry.

2. How do you make sure that a toolbar can be docked with the frame window?

   Both must have docking enabled on the same sides (using the EnableDocking function) in the OnCreate function of the frame class.

3. How can you remove the Num Lock status indicator from the status bar?

   Remove the ID_INDICATOR_NUM from the indicators table near the top of the main frame source code file.

4. Why do you have to edit the resource file to add a combo box to a toolbar?

   You need to add a separator to the toolbar as a placeholder in the toolbar. The toolbar designer will do its best to prevent you from adding the separators, assuming that they are a mistake.

Exercises

1. Add another pane to the status bar to display the current width selected.

   Add an entry to the strings table with an ID of ID_INDICATOR_WIDTH and a caption of VERY THICK.

   Add another entry to the status bar indicators table at the beginning of CMainFrame.cpp:

```
static UINT indicators[] =
{
    ID_SEPARATOR,           // status line indicator
    ID_INDICATOR_WIDTH,
    ID_INDICATOR_COLOR,
    ID_INDICATOR_CAPS,
    ID_INDICATOR_NUM,
    ID_INDICATOR_SCRL,
};
```

   Add a new member function to the CToolbarDoc class. Specify the function type as afx_msg void, the function definition as OnUpdateIndicatorWidth (CCmdUI *pCmdUI), and the access as protected. Edit the function as follows:

```
void CToolbarDoc::OnUpdateIndicatorWidth(CCmdUI *pCmdUI)
{
    CString strWidth;

    // What is the current width?
    switch (m_nWidth)
    {
    case 0:    // Very Thin
        strWidth = "VERY THIN";
        break;
    case 1:    // Thin
        strWidth = "THIN";
        break;
    case 2:    // Medium
        strWidth = "MEDIUM";
        break;
    case 3:    // Thick
        strWidth = "THICK";
        break;
```

B

```
        case 4:    // Very Thick
            strWidth = "VERY THICK";
            break;
    }
    // Enable the status bar pane
    pCmdUI->Enable(TRUE);
    // Set the text of the status bar pane
    // to the current width
    pCmdUI->SetText(strWidth);
}
```

Edit the `CToolbarDoc` message map, adding the `ON_UPDATE_COMMAND_UI` message handler entry as follows:

```
/////////////////////////////////////////////////////////////////
// CToolbarDoc

IMPLEMENT_DYNCREATE(CToolbarDoc, CDocument)

BEGIN_MESSAGE_MAP(CToolbarDoc, CDocument)
    ON_UPDATE_COMMAND_UI(ID_INDICATOR_WIDTH,
➥OnUpdateIndicatorWidth)
    ON_UPDATE_COMMAND_UI(ID_INDICATOR_COLOR,
➥OnUpdateIndicatorColor)
    //{{AFX_MSG_MAP(CToolbarDoc)
    ON_UPDATE_COMMAND_UI(ID_WIDTH_VTHIN, OnUpdateWidthVthin)
    .
    .
    ON_COMMAND(ID_WIDTH_VTHIN, OnWidthVthin)
    //}}AFX_MSG_MAP
END_MESSAGE_MAP()
```

2. Add a button to the main toolbar that can be used to toggle the color toolbar on and off, as in Figure 12.7.

   Open the `IDR_MAINFRAME` toolbar in the toolbar designer. Paint an icon for the blank button at the end of the toolbar. Double-click the button to open its properties dialog. Specify the button ID as `ID_VIEW_COLORBAR` and enter an appropriate prompt for the button. Recompile and run your application, and the color toolbar toggle should be working on the main toolbar.

Day 13

Quiz

1. What two macros do you have to add to a class to make it serializable?

   `DECLARE_SERIAL` and `IMPLEMENT_SERIAL`.

2. How can you determine whether the `CArchive` object is reading from or writing to the archive file?

You call the IsStoring or IsLoading functions.

3. What arguments do you need to pass to the IMPLEMENT_SERIAL macro?

The class name, the base class name, and the version number.

4. What class do you need to inherit the view class from to be able to use the dialog designer to create a form for the main window in an SDI or MDI application?

CFormView.

5. What type of file does the CArchive write to by default?

CFile.

Exercise

Add a couple of radio buttons to the form to specify the person's sex, as in Figure 13.5. Incorporate this change into the CPerson class to make the field persistent.

In the window designer, add the two radio buttons and the static text prompt. Specify the control properties in Table B.2.

TABLE B.2. CONTROL PROPERTY SETTINGS.

Object	Property	Setting
Static Text	ID	IDC_STATIC
	Caption	Sex:
Radio Button	ID	IDC_RMALE
	Caption	Mal&e
	Group	Checked
Radio Button	ID	IDC_RFEMALE
	Caption	&Female

Move the mnemonic in the First button from &First to Fi&rst to prevent a conflict with the new radio buttons.

Attach a variable to the new radio buttons as in Table B.3.

TABLE B.3. CONTROL VARIABLES.

Object	Name	Category	Type
IDC_RMALE	m_iSex	Value	int

Increment the version number in the IMPLEMENT_SERIAL macro in the CPerson class. Add a new member variable to the CPerson class. Specify the type as int, the name as m_iSex, and the access as private. Update the CPerson constructor function, adding the m_iSex variable to the initializations as in line 8 of Listing B.20.

LISTING B.20. THE MODIFIED CPerson CONSTRUCTOR.

```
1: CPerson::CPerson()
2: {
3:     // Initialize the class variables
4:     m_iMaritalStatus = 0;
5:     m_iAge = 0;
6:     m_bEmployed = FALSE;
7:     m_sName = "";
8:     m_iSex = 0;
9: }
```

Add the inline functions to the CPerson class declaration to set and get the value of this new variable, as in lines 9 and 15 of Listing B.21.

LISTING B.21. THE MODIFIED CPerson CLASS DECLARATION.

```
1: class CPerson : public CObject
2: {
3:     DECLARE_SERIAL (CPerson)
4: public:
5:     // Functions for setting the variables
6:     void SetEmployed(BOOL bEmployed) { m_bEmployed = bEmployed;}
7:     void SetMaritalStat(int iStat) { m_iMaritalStatus = iStat;}
8:     void SetAge(int iAge) { m_iAge = iAge;}
9:     void SetSex(int iSex) { m_iSex = iSex;}
10:    void SetName(CString sName) { m_sName = sName;}
11:    // Functions for getting the current settings of the variables
12:    BOOL GetEmployed() { return m_bEmployed;}
13:    int GetMaritalStatus() { return m_iMaritalStatus;}
14:    int GetAge() {return m_iAge;}
15:    int GetSex() {return m_iSex;}
16:    CString GetName() {return m_sName;}
17:    CPerson();
18:    virtual ~CPerson();
19:
20: private:
21:    BOOL m_bEmployed;
22:    int m_iMaritalStatus;
23:    int m_iAge, m_iSex;
24:    CString m_sName;
25: };
```

Update the Serialize function in the CPerson class to include the m_iSex variable as in lines 9 and 12 of Listing B.22.

LISTING B.22. THE MODIFIED CPerson.Serialize FUNCTION.

```
 1: void CPerson::Serialize(CArchive &ar)
 2: {
 3:     // Call the ancestor function
 4:     CObject::Serialize(ar);
 5:
 6:     // Are we writing?
 7:     if (ar.IsStoring())
 8:         // Write all of the variables, in order
 9:         ar << m_sName << m_iAge << m_iMaritalStatus << m_bEmployed <<
        ➥m_iSex;
10:     else
11:         // Read all of the variables, in order
12:         ar >> m_sName >> m_iAge >> m_iMaritalStatus >> m_bEmployed >>
        ➥m_iSex;
13:
14: }
```

Modify the PopulateView function in the view object to include the Sex variable in the data exchange, as in line 19 of Listing B.23.

LISTING B.23. THE MODIFIED CSerializeView.PopulateView FUNCTION.

```
 1: void CSerializeView::PopulateView()
 2: {
 3:     // Get a pointer to the current document
 4:     CSerializeDoc* pDoc = GetDocument();
 5:     if (pDoc)
 6:     {
 7:         // Display the current record position in the set
 8:         m_sPosition.Format("Record %d of %d", pDoc->GetCurRecordNbr(),
 9:                 pDoc->GetTotalRecords());
10:     }
11:     // Do we have a valid record object?
12:     if (m_pCurPerson)
13:     {
14:         // Yes, get all of the record values
15:         m_bEmployed = m_pCurPerson->GetEmployed();
16:         m_iAge = m_pCurPerson->GetAge();
17:         m_sName = m_pCurPerson->GetName();
18:         m_iMaritalStatus = m_pCurPerson->GetMaritalStatus();
19:         m_iSex = m_pCurPerson->GetSex();
20:     }
21:     // Update the display
22:     UpdateData(FALSE);
23: }
```

Add an event handler for the clicked event of both new radio buttons, using the same function for both event handlers. Update the record object's field using the Set function, as in Listing B.24.

LISTING B.24. THE CSerializeView.OnSex FUNCTION.

```
 1: void CSerializeView::OnSex()
 2: {
 3:     // TODO: Add your control notification handler code here
 4:
 5:     // Sync the data in the form with the variables
 6:     UpdateData(TRUE);
 7:     // If we have a valid person object, pass the data changes to it
 8:     if (m_pCurPerson)
 9:         m_pCurPerson->SetSex(m_iSex);
10:     // Get a pointer to the document
11:     CSerializeDoc * pDoc = GetDocument();
12:     if (pDoc)
13:         // Set the modified flag in the document
14:         pDoc->SetModifiedFlag();
15: }
```

Day 14

Quiz

1. What does ODBC stand for?

   Open Database Connector.

2. What functions can you use to navigate the record set in a CRecordset object?

   Move, MoveNext, MovePrev, MoveFirst, MoveLast, and SetAbsolutePosition.

3. What view class should you use with an ODBC application?

   CRecordView.

4. What sequence of functions do you need to call to add a new record to a record set?

   AddNew, Update, and Requery.

5. What function do you need to call before the fields in the CRecordset object can be updated with any changes?

   Edit.

Exercise

Add a menu entry and dialog to let the user indicate the record number to move to, and then move to that record.

1. Create a new dialog, designing the dialog layout as in Figure B.1. Configure the controls as in Table B.4.

FIGURE B.1.

The Move To dialog layout.

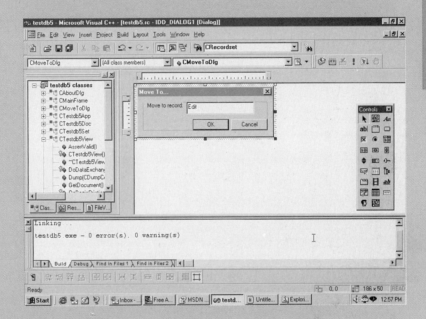

TABLE B.4. DIALOG PROPERTY SETTINGS.

Object	Property	Setting
Static Text	ID	IDC_STATIC
	Caption	Move to record:
Edit Box	ID	IDC_ERECNBR

2. Open the Class Wizard. Create a new class for the new dialog. Give the new class the name CMoveToDlg. After you create the new class, add a variable to the Edit Box control. Specify the variable type as long and the name as m_lRowNbr.

3. Add another menu entry to the main application menu. Specify the menu properties as in Table B.5.

TABLE B.5. MENU PROPERTY SETTINGS.

Object	Property	Setting
Menu Entry	ID	IDM_RECORD_MOVE
	Caption	&Move To...
	Prompt	Move to a specific record\nMove To

4. Open the Class Wizard and add an event-handler function for the COMMAND message for this new menu to the view class. Edit this function, adding the code in Listing B.25.

LISTING B.25. THE CDbOdbcView OnRecordMove FUNCTION.

```
 1:  void CTestdb5View::OnRecordMove()
 2:  {
 3:      // TODO: Add your command handler code here
 4:      // Create an instance of the Move To dialog
 5:      CMoveToDlg dlgMoveTo;
 6:      // Get the row number to move to
 7:      if (dlgMoveTo.DoModal() == IDOK)
 8:      {
 9:          // Get a pointer to the record set
10:          CRecordset* pSet = OnGetRecordset();
11:          // Make sure that there are no outstanding changes to be saved
12:          if (pSet->CanUpdate() && !pSet->IsDeleted())
13:          {
14:              pSet->Edit();
15:              if (!UpdateData())
16:                  return;
17:
18:              pSet->Update();
19:          }
20:          // Set the new position
21:          pSet->SetAbsolutePosition(dlgMoveTo.m_lRowNbr);
22:          // Update the form
23:          UpdateData(FALSE);
24:      }
25:  }
```

5. Include the header file for the new dialog in the view class source code, as in line 10 of Listing B.26.

LISTING B.26. THE CDbOdbcView INCLUDES.

```
 1: // DbOdbcView.cpp : implementation of the CDbOdbcView class
 2: //
 3:
 4: #include "stdafx.h"
 5: #include "DbOdbc.h"
 6:
 7: #include "DbOdbcSet.h"
 8: #include "DbOdbcDoc.h"
 9: #include "DbOdbcView.h"
10: #include "MoveToDlg.h"
```

---

6. Add a toolbar button for the new menu entry.

Day 15

Quiz

1. What does ADO stand for?

   ActiveX Data Objects.

2. What does ADO use for database access?

   OLE DB.

3. What are the objects in ADO?

   `Connection`, `Command`, `Parameter`, `Error`, `Recordset`, and `Field`.

4. How do you initialize the COM environment?

   `::CoInitialize(NULL);`

5. How do you associate a `Connection` object with a `Command` object?

   `pCmd->ActiveConnection = pConn;`

6. How do you associate a `Command` object with and populate a `Recordset` object?

   One of two ways:

   ```
   _RecordsetPtr pRs;
   pRs = pCmd->Execute();
   ```

   Or

   ```
   _RecordsetPtr pRs;
   pRs.CreateInstance(__uuidof(Recordset));
   pRs->PutRefSource(pCmd);
   ```

B

Exercise

Enable and disable the navigation menus and toolbar buttons based on whether the recordset is at the beginning of file (BOF) or end of file (EOF, renamed to EndOfFile).

Add event-handler functions to the document class for the navigation menu entries' UPDATE_COMMAND_UI event message. Edit these functions, adding the code in Listing B.27 to the functions for the First and Previous menus, and the code in Listing B.28 to the functions for the Last and Next menus.

LISTING B.27. THE CDbAdoDoc OnUpdateDataFirst FUNCTION.

```
 1: void CDbAdoDoc::OnUpdateDataFirst(CCmdUI* pCmdUI)
 2: {
 3:     // TODO: Add your command update UI handler code here
 4:     // Does the record set exist?
 5:     if (m_pRs)
 6:     {
 7:         // Are we at the BOF?
 8:         if (m_pRs->BOF)
 9:             pCmdUI->Enable(FALSE);
10:         else
11:             pCmdUI->Enable(TRUE);
12:     }
13: }
```

LISTING B.28. THE CDbAdoDoc OnUpdateDataLast FUNCTION.

```
 1: void CDbAdoDoc::OnUpdateDataLast(CCmdUI* pCmdUI)
 2: {
 3:     // TODO: Add your command update UI handler code here
 4:     // Does the record set exist?
 5:     if (m_pRs)
 6:     {
 7:         // Are we at the EOF?
 8:         if (m_pRs->EndOfFile)
 9:             pCmdUI->Enable(FALSE);
10:         else
11:             pCmdUI->Enable(TRUE);
12:     }
13: }
```

Day 16

Quiz

1. When do you want to create a new MFC class?

   When you need to create a new class that is inherited from an existing MFC class.

2. When you make changes to a library file, what do you have to do to the applications that use the library file?

   They all have to be relinked.

3. What are the different types of classes that you can create?

   MFC, generic, and form.

4. When you package some functionality in a library file, what do you need to give to other programmers who want to use your library module?

   The LIB library file and the header files for the objects in the module.

5. What are two of the basic principles in object-oriented software design?

   Encapsulation and inheritance. The third principle is polymorphism, which was not discussed today.

Exercises

Separate the CLine class into a different library module from the drawing class so that you have two library modules instead of one. Link them into the test application.

1. Create a new project. Specify that the project is a Win32 Static Library project. Give the project a suitable name, such as Line.

2. Specify that the project contain support for MFC and precompiled headers.

3. Copy the Line.cpp and Line.h files into the project directory. Add both of these files to the project. Compile the library module.

4. Open the original library module project. Delete the Line.cpp and Line.h files from the project. Edit the include statement at the top of the drawing object source-code file to include the Line.h file from the Line module project directory, as on line 9 of Listing B.29. Recompile the project.

LISTING B.29. THE CModArt INCLUDES AND COLOR TABLE.

```
1:  // ModArt.cpp: implementation of the CModArt class.
2:  //
3:  ////////////////////////////////////////////////////////////////////
4:
```

continues

LISTING B.29. CONTINUED

```
 5:  #include <stdlib.h>
 6:  #include <time.h>
 7:
 8:  #include "stdafx.h"
 9:  #include "..\Line\Line.h"
10: #include "ModArt.h"
```

5. Open the test application project. Add the Line library file to the project. Build the project.

Day 17

Quiz

1. What kind of DLL do you have to create to make classes in the DLL available to applications?

   An MFC extension DLL.

2. What do you have to add to the class to export it from a DLL?

   The AFX_EXT_CLASS macro in the class declaration.

3. What kind of DLL can be used with other programming languages?

   A regular DLL.

4. If you make changes in a DLL, do you have to recompile the applications that use the DLL?

   Normally, no. Only if changes were made in the exported interface for the DLL do you need to recompile the applications that use the DLL.

5. What function does the LIB file provide for a DLL?

   The LIB file contains stubs of the functions in the DLL, along with the code to locate and pass the function call along to the real function in the DLL.

Exercises

1. Separate the line class into its own MFC extension DLL and use it with the second (regular) DLL.

   Create a new project. Specify that the project is an AppWizard (DLL) project, and give the project a suitable name, such as LineDll.

   Specify that the DLL will be an MFC extension DLL.

After generating the project skeleton, copy the line source code and header files into the project directory. Add these files into the project.

Edit the CLine class declaration, adding the AFX_EXT_CLASS macro to the class declaration.

Compile the DLL. Copy the DLL into the debug directory for the test application.

Open the regular DLL project. Delete the line source code and header files from the project in the File View of the workspace pane. Add the line DLL LIB file to the project. Edit the drawing functionality source-code file, changing the line class header include to include the version in the CLine DLL project directory, as in Listing B.30.

LISTING B.30. THE CModArt INCLUDES.

```
 1: // ModArt.cpp: implementation of the CModArt class.
 2: //
 3: //////////////////////////////////////////////////////////////////////
 4:
 5: #include <stdlib.h>
 6: #include <time.h>
 7:
 8: #include "stdafx.h"
 9: #include "..\LineDll\Line.h"
10: #include "ModArt.h"
```

Compile the project. Copy the DLL into the test application project debug directory.

Run the test application.

2. Alter the line class DLL so that it uses a consistent line width for all lines.

Open the line class DLL project that you created in the previous exercise. Edit the class constructor, replacing the initialization of the m_nWidth variable with a constant value, as in Listing B.31.

LISTING B.31. THE CLine CONSTRUCTOR.

```
1: CLine::CLine(CPoint ptFrom, CPoint ptTo, UINT nWidth, COLORREF crColor)
2: {
3:     m_ptFrom = ptFrom;
4:     m_ptTo = ptTo;
5:     m_nWidth = 1;
6:     m_crColor = crColor;
7: }
```

Compile the DLL. Copy the DLL into the test application project debug directory. Run the test application.

Day 18

Quiz

1. When is the OnIdle function called?

   When the application is idle and there are no messages in the application message queue.

2. How can you cause the OnIdle function to be repeatedly called while the application is sitting idle?

   Returning a value of TRUE will cause the OnIdle function to continue to be called as long as the application remains idle.

3. What is the difference between an OnIdle task and a thread?

   An OnIdle task executes only when the application is idle and there are no messages in the message queue. A thread executes independently of the rest of the application.

4. What are the four thread synchronization objects?

   Critical sections, mutexes, semaphores, and events.

5. Why shouldn't you specify a higher than normal priority for the threads in your application?

   The rest of the threads and processes running on the computer will receive a greatly reduced amount of processor time.

Exercises

1. If you open a performance monitor on your system while the application that you built today is running, you'll find that even without any of the threads running, the processor usage remains 100 percent, as in Figure 18.11. The OnIdle function is continuously being called even when there is nothing to be done.

   Modify the OnIdle function so that if there's nothing to be done, neither of the OnIdle tasks are active. Then, the OnIdle function will not continue to be called until one of these threads is active, at which time it should be continuously called until both threads are once again turned off. This will allow the processor to drop to a minimal utilization, as in Figure 18.12.

   Edit the OnIdle function as in Listing B.32.

LISTING B.32. THE MODIFIED CTaskingApp OnIdle FUNCTION.

```
 1: BOOL CTaskingApp::OnIdle(LONG lCount)
 2: {
 3:     // TODO: Add your specialized code here and/or call the base class
 4:
 5:     // Call the ancestor's idle processing
 6:     BOOL bRtn = CWinApp::OnIdle(lCount);
 7:
 8:     // Get the position of the first document template
 9:     POSITION pos = GetFirstDocTemplatePosition();
10:     // Do we have a valid template position?
11:     if (pos)
12:     {
13:         // Get a pointer to the document template
14:         CDocTemplate* pDocTemp = GetNextDocTemplate(pos);
15:         // Do we have a valid pointer?
16:         if (pDocTemp)
17:         {
18:             // Get the position of the first document
19:             POSITION dPos = pDocTemp->GetFirstDocPosition();
20:             // Do we have a valid document position?
21:             if (dPos)
22:             {
23:                 // Get a pointer to the document
24:                 CTaskingDoc* pDocWnd =
25:                     (CTaskingDoc*)pDocTemp->GetNextDoc(dPos);
26:                 // Do we have a valid pointer?
27:                 if (pDocWnd)
28:                 {
29:                     // Get the position of the view
30:                     POSITION vPos = pDocWnd->GetFirstViewPosition();
31:                     // Do we have a valid view position?
32:                     if (vPos)
33:                     {
34:                         // Get a pointer to the view
35:                         CTaskingView* pView =
               ➡(CTaskingView*)pDocWnd->GetNextView(vPos);
36:                         // Do we have a valid pointer?
37:                         if (pView)
38:                         {
39:                             // Should we spin the first idle thread?
40:                             if (pView->m_bOnIdle1)
41:                             {
42:                                 // Spin the first idle thread
43:                                 pDocWnd->DoSpin(0);
44:                                 bRtn = TRUE;
45:                             }
46:                             // Should we spin the second idle thread?
47:                             if (pView->m_bOnIdle2)
```

continues

B

LISTING B.32. CONTINUED

```
48:                                      {
49:                                          // Spin the second idle thread
50:                                          pDocWnd->DoSpin(2);
51:                                          bRtn = TRUE;
52:                                      }
53:                                  }
54:                              }
55:                          }
56:                      }
57:                  }
58:              }
59:      return bRtn;
60: }
```

2. When starting the independent threads, give one of the threads a priority of
   THREAD_PRIORITY_NORMAL and the other a priority of THREAD_PRIORITY_LOWEST.

   Edit the SuspendSpinner function as in Listing B.33.

LISTING B.33. THE MODIFIED CTaskingDoc SuspendSpinner FUNCTION.

```
1: void CTaskingDoc::SuspendSpinner(int nIndex, BOOL bSuspend)
2: {
3:      // if suspending the thread
4:      if (!bSuspend)
5:      {
6:          // Is the pointer for the thread valid?
7:          if (m_pSpinThread[nIndex])
8:          {
9:              // Get the handle for the thread
10:             HANDLE hThread = m_pSpinThread[nIndex]->m_hThread;
11:             // Wait for the thread to die
12:             ::WaitForSingleObject (hThread, INFINITE);
13:         }
14:     }
15:     else    // We are running the thread
16:     {
17:         int iSpnr;
18:         int iPriority;
19:         // Which spinner to use?
20:         switch (nIndex)
21:         {
22:         case 0:
23:             iSpnr = 1;
24:             iPriority = THREAD_PRIORITY_NORMAL;
25:             break;
26:         case 1:
27:             iSpnr = 3;
28:             iPriority = THREAD_PRIORITY_LOWEST;
```

```
29:            break;
30:        }
31:        // Start the thread, passing a pointer to the spinner
32:        m_pSpinThread[nIndex] = AfxBeginThread(ThreadFunc,
33:            (LPVOID)&m_cSpin[iSpnr], iPriority);
34:    }
35: }
```

Day 19

Quiz

1. What are the three aspects of a control that are visible to the container application?

   Properties, methods, and events.

2. Why do you need to design a property page for your control?

   To provide the user with the ability to set the properties of the control.

3. What are the four types of properties that a control might have?

   Ambient, extended, stock, and custom.

4. What happens to the parameters that are passed to the methods of a control?

   They are marshaled into a standardized, machine-independent structure.

5. What tool can you use to test your controls?

   The ActiveX Control Test Container.

Exercises

1. Add a method to your control to enable the container application to trigger the generation of a new squiggle drawing.

   Open the Class Wizard to the Automation tab. Click the Add Method button. Enter a method name, such as GenNewDrawing, and specify the return type as void. Click OK to add the method. Edit the method, adding the code in Listing B.34.

LISTING B.34. THE `CSquiggleCtrl` GenNewDrawing FUNCTION.

```
1: void CSquiggleCtrl:: GenNewDrawing()
2: {
3:     // TODO: Add your specialized code here and/or call the base class
4:     // Set the flag so a new drawing will be generated
5:     m_bGenNewDrawing = TRUE;
6:     // Invalidate the control to trigger the OnDraw function
7:     Invalidate();
8: }
```

2. Add a method to your control to save a squiggle drawing. Use the `CFile::modeWrite` and `CArchive::store` flags when creating the `CFile` and `CArchive` objects.

Open the Class Wizard to the Automation tab. Click the Add Method button. Enter a method name, such as `SaveDrawing`, and specify the return type as `BOOL`. Add a single parameter, `sFileName`, with a type of `LPCTSTR`. Click OK to add the method. Edit the method, adding the code in Listing B.35.

LISTING B.35. THE `CSquiggleCtrl` SaveDrawing FUNCTION.

```
 1: BOOL CSquiggleCtrl::SaveDrawing(LPCTSTR sFileName)
 2: {
 3:     // TODO: Add your dispatch handler code here
 4:     try
 5:     {
 6:         // Create a CFile object
 7:         CFile lFile(sFileName, CFile::modeWrite);
 8:         // Create a CArchive object to store the file
 9:         CArchive lArchive(&lFile, CArchive::store);
10:         // Store the file
11:         m_maDrawing.Serialize(lArchive);
12:     }
13:     catch (CFileException err)
14:     {
15:         return FALSE;
16:     }
17:     return TRUE;
18: }
```

Day 20

Quiz

1. What are the two things that a client application must know to be able to connect to a server application?

The network address (or name) of the computer and the port on which the server is listening.

2. What `CAsyncSocket` function is used to enable a server application to detect connection efforts by client applications?

Listen.

3. What `CAsyncSocket` member function is called to signal that data has arrived through a socket connection?

   `OnReceive`.

4. What function is called to signal that a connection has been established?

   `OnConnect`.

5. What function do you use to send a message through a socket connection to the application on the other end?

   `Send`.

Exercises

The server application that you wrote can handle only a single connection at a time. If a second application tries to open a connection to it while it has an existing connection to an application, the server application will crash. The server tries to accept the second connection into the socket that is already connected to the first client application. Add a third socket object to the application that will be used to reject additional client connections until the first client closes the connection.

Follow these steps:

1. Add a member variable to the dialog class (`CSockDlg`). Specify the variable type as `BOOL`, the name as `m_bConnected`, and the access as private.

2. Initialize the variable as `FALSE` in the `OnInitDialog` function.

3. Set the variable to `TRUE` in the `OnAccept` dialog function once the connection has been accepted.

4. Set the variable to `FALSE` in the `OnClose` dialog function.

5. Modify the `OnAccept` dialog function as in Listing B.36.

LISTING B.36. THE MODIFIED `CSockDlg` `OnAccept` FUNCTION.

```
1: void CSockDlg::OnAccept()
2: {
3:     if (m_bConnected)
4:     {
5:         // Create a rejection socket
6:         CAsyncSocket sRjctSock;
7:         // Create a message to send
8:         CString strMsg = "Too many connections, try again later.";
9:         // Accept using the rejection socket
10:        m_sListenSocket.Accept(sRjctSock);
11:        // Send the rejection message
12:        sRjctSock.Send(LPCTSTR(strMsg), strMsg.GetLength());
```

continues

LISTING B.36. CONTINUED

```
13:          // Close the socket
14:          sRjctSock.Close();
15:      }
16:      else
17:      {
18:          // Accept the connection request
19:          m_sListenSocket.Accept(m_sConnectSocket);\
20:          // Mark the socket as connected
21:          m_bConnected = TRUE;
22:          // Enable the text and message controls
23:          GetDlgItem(IDC_EMSG)->EnableWindow(TRUE);
24:          GetDlgItem(IDC_BSEND)->EnableWindow(TRUE);
25:          GetDlgItem(IDC_STATICMSG)->EnableWindow(TRUE);
26:      }
27: }
```

Day 21

Quiz

1. What does the `CHtmlView` class encapsulate for use in Visual C++ applications?

   The Internet Explorer Web browser.

2. How can you get the URL for the current Web page from the `CHtmlView` class?

   `GetLocationURL()`.

3. What command is triggered for the frame class when the user presses the Enter key in the edit box on the dialog bar?

   `IDOK`.

4. What functions can you call to navigate the browser to the previous and the next Web pages?

   `GoBack()` and `GoForward()`.

5. How can you stop a download in progress?

   With the `Stop()` function.

Exercises

1. Add the `GoSearch` function to the menu and toolbar.

   Add a menu entry to the Go menu. Specify the menu entry properties in Table B.6.

TABLE B.6. MENU PROPERTY SETTINGS.

Object	Property	Setting
Menu Entry	ID	IDM_GO_SEARCH
	Caption	&Search
	Prompt	Search the Web\nSearch

Using the Class Wizard, add an event-handler function to the view class on the IDM_GO_SEARCH ID for the COMMAND event message. Edit the code as in Listing B.37.

LISTING B.37. THE CWebBrowseView OnGoSearch FUNCTION.

```
1: void CWebBrowseView::OnGoSearch()
2: {
3:     // TODO: Add your command handler code here
4:
5:     // Go to the search page
6:     GoSearch();
7: }
```

Add a toolbar button for the menu ID IDM_GO_SEARCH.

2. Add the GoHome function to the menu and toolbar.

Add a menu entry to the Go menu. Specify the menu entry properties in Table B.7.

TABLE B.7. MENU PROPERTY SETTINGS.

Object	Property	Setting
Menu Entry	ID	IDM_GO_START
	Caption	S&tart Page
	Prompt	Go to the start page\nHome

Using the Class Wizard, add an event-handler function to the view class on the IDM_GO_START ID for the COMMAND event message. Edit the code as in Listing B.38.

LISTING B.38. THE CWebBrowseView OnGoStart FUNCTION.

```
1: void CWebBrowseView::OnGoStart()
2: {
3:     // TODO: Add your command handler code here
```

continues

LISTING B.38. CONTINUED

```
4:
5:     // Go to the start page
6:     GoHome();
7: }
```

Add a toolbar button for the menu ID `IDM_GO_START`.

3. Disable the Stop toolbar button and menu entry when the application is not down-loading a Web page.

    Using the Class Wizard, add an event handler to the view class for the `IDM_VIEW_STOP` object ID on the `UPDATE_COMMAND_UI` event message. Edit the function, adding the code in Listing B.39.

LISTING B.39. THE `CWebBrowseView OnUpdateViewStop` FUNCTION.

```
1: void CWebBrowseView::OnUpdateViewStop(CCmdUI* pCmdUI)
2: {
3:     // TODO: Add your command update UI handler code here
4:
5:     // Enable the button if busy
6:     pCmdUI->Enable(GetBusy());
7: }
```

MFC Class Reference

Categorized MFC Classes

MFC is an application framework that allows the programmer to create complex applications. MFC does this by giving the programmer a rich set of objects to use. These objects focus on high-level application programming concepts. This approach shields the programmer from many operating system–level intricacies that would otherwise need to be considered. This reference section will present the most important of the MFC classes. These are the classes that are used to construct the user interface for an application. Few of these objects are of any use as a standalone object. MFC objects tend to fall into object groups.

The first part of the reference section presents an overview of each of these object groups, the classes that make up each group, and how they fit together. The second part of the reference section covers each of the classes individually. In this section, much more detail is given to describing each of the classes.

Programming Graphics

Graphics programming is a very important aspect of Windows programming. Because windows is a graphical user interface(GUI) most things are presented graphically. Several classes are used together to facilitate graphics programming.

The most important class for graphics programming is the device context class. This class, named CDC, represents a device context. A device context is any device, usually a window or the printer, that can receive graphic output. CDC provides a rich set of drawing commands and text commands.

Drawing frequently depends on creating lines and shapes. The CDC class has many line and shape drawing commands. These shapes are drawn using colored pen objects named CPen. Objects of type CPen must be created for any color needed by the device context. Once created, a pen is used by selecting it into the device context.

Drawing also frequently depends on large solid shapes. The CDC class also contains many solid shape methods. These enable shapes such as rectangles, circles, and polygons to be drawn. The interior color of these shares are determined by colored brushes. These brush objects, named CBrush, enable the color of solid shapes to be specified. One CBrush object must be created for each solid color that will be used by the application. Once created, a brush is used by selecting it into the device context.

Programming Databases

Database programming is an important part of most business applications. MFC provides classes to access the database's data programmatically using recordsets. MFC also provides high-level classes that assist in the display and editing of data.

MFC allows data to be accessed by several means. One of the most well known of these data access methods is open database connectivity (ODBC). ODBC has been around the longest of any MFC data access techniques and has the best driver support of any data access method. An ODBC database is represented by the CDatabase class. Records are returned from a database in CRecordset objects. ODBC data can be displayed to the user using the CRecordView class.

MFC also allows data to be accessed using the JET engine. This is the internal database behind Microsoft Access. This data access method, called DAO, allows a higher level access to data than does ODBC. The limitation of DAO, though, is that it only works with Microsoft Access(MDB) databases. A DAO database is represented by the CDAODatabase class. Records are returned from a database in CDAORecordset objects. DAO data can be displayed to the user using the CDAORecordView class.

DAO is not the only way to access a Microsoft Access database. ODBC can be used to access a Microsoft Access database. However, ODBC will not enable access to any specific MS Access features such as queries.

Programming User Interfaces

MFC provides three high-level user interfaces for applications. These three types meet the needs of differing types of applications. The three application interface types provided by MFC are dialog-based applications, multidocument applications, and single-document applications.

Dialog-based applications are usually just one or more dialog boxes. Applications of this type typically prompt the user for data and then perform some action based on that data. Simple utility programs are often implemented as dialog applications. An example of a dialog box application is the Windows 95 Find utility.

Single-document interface applications(SDI) display one document at a time. The user is allowed to work with this document and edit it. Additional top-level windows can be brought up as needed. An example of a single-document application is Notepad.

Multiple-document interface applications(MDI) can display several documents at a time. These documents are opened as child windows in the main MDI frame window. Many different types of windows can be opened within the frame window. MDI applications can also open more top-level windows. An example of an MDI application is Microsoft Word.

Programming Controls

Controls are objects that are placed on windows or dialog boxes. They often perform specialized tasks as they interact with the user. Examples of built-in controls to MFC include check boxes, edit boxes and radio buttons.

Most controls give application programs access to their display and properties through methods in their class file. These methods depend on which control is being used.

Visual C++ can automatically create an MFC compatible class for any OLE control. Once created, this class can be inserted into any MFC application and used normally.

Document/View Architecture

The Document/View architecture is a critical part of MFC. This architecture attempts to split common programming needs across the document, view, frame, and document template objects. Each of these objects has a specific responsibility to the application.

The document object, named `CDocument`, is where all document data should be stored. The document object is responsible for serialization of all document data. Serialization is the process of loading or saving document data to and from some storage device. This is usually a disk file, but it can be any stream-based device.

The document object should not display any of the data it contains. Data display and editing is handled by the view class. The view class, named `CView`, is responsible for interacting with the user to view and edit the data. The view works very closely with the document to store and retrieve data from the document.

The view and document objects are held together by a frame object. The frame object, named `CFrame`, is the actual window that is displayed. A frame can only have one document. Multiple views can be inserted into the same frame using a splitter.

Each document type should have a document template. The document template object, which is named `CDocTemplate`, determines what frame, document, and view objects should be used for each document type.

Dialog Boxes

Most Windows applications use dialog boxes. A dialog box is a window that is typically not on the screen during the entire run of the application. An exception to this is a dialog box–type application—in this case, the entire application is a dialog box. A dialog box collects data from the user and then returns it to the program. Dialog boxes can be either modal or modeless.

A modal dialog box will not enable the user to continue until the modal dialog box has been dismissed. A modal dialog box is created by creating a dialog box object and calling the `DoModal` method.

A modeless dialog box is very much like any other window on the screen. It allows the user to continue working with the application. A modeless dialog box is created by creating an instance of its class, and then calling the `Create` method.

C

File Access and Persistent Objects

File access and object persistence enable data to be stored after the application quits. MFC allows both high- and low-level file access. High-level file access allows objects to be written directly to a file stream. Low-level file access allows files to be read and written as binary streams of data.

The archive class, named `CArchive`, provides for high-level object persistence. This object can accept simple types or complex objects. Objects must be derived from `CObject` and support object serialization in order to be used with the archive object. The archive object is the primary way in which the document object saves its data to disk.

In addition to object-based file access, MFC also provides low-level access to files. `CFile` can be used to read/write files at a direct binary level. `CStdioFile` can be used to access text files.

Internet Programming

MFC provides both high- and low-level access to the Internet. At the highest level, a complete Web browser object is provided. At the low-level end, direct access to TCP/IP sockets is provided.

MFC provides a view that implements a Web browser. This view, named `CHTmlView`, allows the application to control and customize many features of the Web browser.

MFC also provides a very low-level interface into the socket level of TCP/IP. The `CSocket` class implements both server- and client-side sockets. Using these classes, MFC applications can directly communicate with each other, or nearly any application on the Internet.

CArchive   [CArchive]

The `CArchive` class allows an application to store, read, and write file data. This data can be a simple C++ datatype or a complex object. Any simple C++ type or `CObject`-derived class can easily be read or written to a `CArchive` object. These objects are usually stored to an underlying disk file, but this is not always the case. `CArchive` allows objects to be stored to any `CFile`-derived object stream.

`CArchive` objects are usually used in conjunction with `CDocument` objects. One single `CArchive` object is either reading or writing objects—both operations cannot be done at the same time.

Archive objects are most often used inside of a `Serialize` method of a `CDocument`-derived object. The following example demonstrates using a `CArchive` object to store document data.

For an example of `CArchive`, see the EditViewEx example found on the CD-ROM that accompanies this book.

Header Files

The following header files should be included when using this class:

`afx.h`

Properties

The `CArchive` class has the following properties:

m_pDocument	Pointer to the CDocument-derived object being archived

Methods

The CArchive class has the following methods:

CArchive	The constructor
Abort	Close after an error
Close	Close and write any buffered data
Flush	Write any buffered data
GetFile	Get a pointer to the underlying file
GetObjectScheme	Get version of object being stored
IsBufferEmpty	Is the write buffer empty?
IsLoading	Is this object for loading?
IsStoring	Is this object for storing?
MapObject	Map, but not store, an object
operator<<	Save an object
operator>>	Load an object
Read	Read binary data
ReadClass	Read class info
ReadObject	Read an object
ReadString	Read a string
SerializeClass	Read or writes class info
SetLoadParams	Sets properties for loading
SetObjectSchema	Set the version of the object
SetStoreParams	Sets properties for storing
Write	Write binary data
WriteClass	Write class info
WriteObject	Write an object
WriteString	Write a string

The CArchive Constructor

The CArchive constructor creates the CArchive object. The constructor must be passed a pointer to the file that the CArchive object will either read or store to. The CArchive constructor is used as follows:

```
CArchive( CFile* pFile, UINT nMode, int nBufSize = 512, void* lpBuf = NULL);
```

where

pFile	The CFile object being stored.
nMode	States what action should happen. Use CArchive::load if objects are being loaded, CArchive::store if objects are being saved. Normally CArchive will close the file pointed to by pFile when Close is called. If this file should be left open, use CArchive::bNoFlushOnDelete.
NBufSize	This parameter is rarely used. It allows the size of the buffer to be specified. The default size is 4,096 bytes. If a larger size is specified, file access may be faster.

LpBuf A user-supplied buffer. This is optional. If a NULL value is passed, CArchive will allocate a nBufSize-sized buffer. If a buffer is supplied, it must be the same size as nBufSize and must be freed by the user.

This constructor can throw the CMemoryException, CArchiveException, or CFileException.

The Abort Method

Void Abort();

 Note The Close() method may throw an exception if there is a problem with the underlying file.

The Abort() method will close the archive without throwing an exception. Call this method to clean up the archive after an error has occurred.

The Close Method

void Close();

The Close() method writes out any remaining buffered information and then closes the underlying CFile object. This method can throw the CArchiveException and CFileException exceptions.

The Flush Method

void Flush();

The Flush() method forces any buffered data to be written to the underlying CFile object. This method can throw the CFileException exception.

The GetFile() Method

CFile* GetFile( ) const;

A pointer to the underlying file is returned as a CFile.

The GetFile() method will return a pointer to the underlying CFile object. In order to ensure that data is written to the file in the proper order, it is necessary to call Flush() prior to using the CFile pointer returned by this method.

The GetObjectScheme Method

UINT GetObjectSchema();

The version of the object being stored is returned.

The GetObjectScheme method is called from Serialize to determine the version of the object being stored.

The IsBufferEmpty Method

The IsBufferEmpty method returns a BOOL value indicating if the buffer is empty.

BOOL IsBufferEmpty( ) const;

The `IsLoading` Method

The `IsLoading` method returns a `BOOL` value indicating if the `CArchive` object was created to load objects.

```
BOOL IsLoading( ) const;
```

The `IsStoring` Method

```
BOOL IsStoring( ) const;
```

The `IsStoring` method returns a `BOOL` value indicating if the `CArchive` object was created to store objects.

The `MapObject` Method

```
void MapObject( const CObject* pOb );
```

where

pOb	A pointer to the object to be read or stored to or from the underlying `CFile` object.

This method works the same as `ReadObject` and `WriteObject`, except that it does NOT read or write the object. This causes it to be mapped into the archive, but not actually stored.

The `Read` Method

```
UINT Read( void* lpBuf, UINT nMax );
```

where

lpBuf	Specifies the buffer to receive the bytes read.
nMax	Specifies how many bytes to read.

Returns the number of bytes actually read.

The `Read` method is used to directly read raw bytes directly from the underlying `CFile` object. This method can throw the CFileException exception.

The `ReadClass` Method

```
CRuntimeClass* ReadClass( const CRuntimeClass* pClassRefRequested = NULL,
➥UINT* pSchema = NULL, DWORD* obTag = NULL );
```

where

lpBuf	Specifies the buffer to receive the bytes read.
pClassRefRequested	Can be NULL. Specifies the type of `CRuntimeClass` requested. If the next object is not of that type, a CArchiveException is thrown.
pSchema	If not NULL, will contain the schema (version number) of the stored object.
obTag	Normally should be NULL. Allows access to a unique identifier for the object.

Returns a pointer to a `CRuntimeClass` object.

The `ReadClass` method is used to read a `CRuntimeClass` object previously stored with `WriteClass`. This method can throw the CArchiveException or the CNotSupportedException exceptions.

The `ReadObject` Method

`CObject* ReadObject( const CRuntimeClass* pClass );`

where

    lClass   The runtime class of the object type expected.

Returns a `CObject` pointer to the object just read. This pointer can be typecast to the actual type of the object.

The `ReadObject` is normally called by the `operator>>` method. It is used to read objects from the archive. This method can throw the CFileException, CArchiveException, or CMemoryException exceptions.

The `ReadString` Method

`Bool ReadString(CString& rString );`
`LPTSTR ReadString( LPTSTR lpsz, UINT nMax );`

where

    rString   A reference to a `CString` object to hold the string being read.

    lpsz   A pointer to a buffer in memory to hold the string being read.

    nMax   The maximum size of the buffer pointed to by `lpsz`.

Returns a `BOOL` that is `TRUE` if successful, `FALSE` otherwise.

The `ReadString` method reads a line of text from the archive. This method can throw the CArchiveException exception.

The `SerializeClass` Method

`void SerializeClass( const CRuntimeClass* pRuntimeClass );`

where

    pRuntimeClass   Pointer to the class that is either being stored or read.

Depending on how the `CArchive` object was constructed, the `SerializeClass` method will either store or read a class using the `ReadClass` or `WriteClass` methods.

The `SetLoadParams` Method

`void SetLoadParams( UINT nGrowBy = 1024 );`

where

    nGrowBy   The minimum number of element slots to allocate when the element array size is increased.

`CArchive` uses a load array when loading objects stored in the archive. If a large number of objects are to be loaded, setting this number larger will achieve greater performance.

The `SetObjectSchema` Method

`void SetObjectSchema( UINT nSchema );`

where

    nSchema   A object schema number.

The `SetObjectSchema` method will set the schema number for the current object.

The `SetStoreParams` Method

```
void SetStoreParams( UINT nHashSize = 2053, UINT nBlockSize = 128 );
```

where

nHashSize	The hash size used when storing objects.
nBlockSize	The block size used when storing objects.

If a large number of objects are to be stored, this method may increase performance by setting the hash size and block size to larger values.

The `Write` Method

```
void Write( const void* lpBuf, UINT nMax );
```

where

lpBuf	A pointer to a buffer containing bytes to be written.
nMax	How many bytes to write.

The `Write` Method will write `nMax` raw bytes stored at `lpBuf` to the archive. This method can throw the CFileException exception.

The `WriteClass` Method

```
void WriteClass( const CRuntimeClass* pClassRef );
```

where

pClassRef	The runtime class to be written.

The `WriteClass` will write a runtime class to the archive.

The `WriteObject` Method

```
void WriteObject( const CObject* pOb );
```

where

pOb	The object to be stored.

The `WriteObject` method will store an object to the archive. This method can throw the CFileException, and the CArchiveException exceptions.

This method will write a runtime class to the archive.

The `WriteString` Method

```
void WriteString( LPCTSTR lpsz );
```

where

lpsz	The string to be written.

The `WriteString` method will write a string to the archive. This method can throw the CFileException exception.

CAsyncSocket

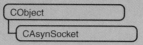

CAsyncSocket directly encapsulates a Windows socket. This class provides a very low-level interface to Windows sockets. This class leaves it to the programmer to handle blocking and Unicode conversions. For a more convenient interface that manages many of the low-level aspects of sockets, use the CSocket class.

Typically a socket maps to a TCP/IP connection. Other protocols are possible with the appropriate drivers.

For an example of CAsyncSocket, see the AtomClock example found on the CD-ROM that accompanies this book.

Header Files

The following header files should be included when using this class:

afxsock.h

Properties

The CAsyncSocket class has the following properties:

m_hSocket	The underlying SOCKET handle attached to this object.

Methods

The CAsyncSocket class has the following methods:

CAsyncSocket	The constructor
Accept	Accept a connection
AsyncSelect	Select event notification
Attach	Attach a SOCKET handle
Bind	Associate socket with local address
Close	Close the socket
Connect	Connect to a remote socket
Create	Create a socket
Detach	Disassociate a SOCKET handle
FromHandle	Create from a WinSock handle
GetLastError	Get the last error code
GetPeerName	Get the address of the remote (peer) socket
GetSockName	Get socket local name
GetSockOpt	Get status of a socket option
IOCtl	Control socket mode
Listen	Begin listening for connections

Receive	Receive data
ReceiveFrom	Receive from a specific source
Send	Send data
SendTo	Send to a specific destination
SetSockOpt	Set a socket option
ShutDown	Disable send/receive for this socket

The following methods are used to process messages sent to the class. These methods may be overridden if special handling is needed for these messages.

OnAccept	Notification that a client has connected
OnClose	Notification that a socket close has completed
OnConnect	Notification that a socket connect is complete
OnOutOfBandData	Notification of arrival of out-of-band data
OnReceive	Notification that there is data available from the socket
OnSend	Notification that a socket is ready to send data

The CAsyncSocket Constructor

The CAsyncSocket creates the CSocket. CAsyncSocket constructor is used as follows:

```
CAsyncSocket
```

The Accept Method

```
virtual BOOL Accept( CAsyncSocket& rConnectedSocket, SOCKADDR* lpSockAddr
➥= NULL, int* lpSockAddrLen = NULL );
```

where

rConnectedSocket	This will become the socket for the new connection.
lpSockAddr	Pointer to a SOCKADDR structure that will contain the address of the remotely connected socket.
lpSockAddrLen	Pointer to a long SOCKADDR structure that will hold the length of the address returned.

Call the Accept method to accept a connection for a server socket.

The AsyncSelect Method

```
BOOL AsyncSelect( long lEvent = FD_READ ¦ FD_WRITE ¦ FD_OOB ¦ FD_ACCEPT ¦
➥ FD_CONNECT ¦ FD_CLOSE );
```

where

lEvent	A bitmask that specifies what events notification is requested for.

Valid values for lEvent include

FD_READ	Notification of readiness for reading.
FD_WRITE	Notification when data is available to be read.
FD_OOB	Notification of the arrival of out-of-band data.

C

FD_ACCEPT	Notification of incoming connections.
FD_CONNECT	Notification of connection results.
FD_CLOSE	Notification when a socket has been closed by a peer.

Returns TRUE if successful.

The AsyncSelect method determines which notifications will be received.

The Attach Method

```
BOOL Attach( SOCKET hSocket, long lEvent = FD_READ ¦ FD_WRITE ¦ FD_OOB ¦
➡ FD_ACCEPT ¦ FD_CONNECT ¦ FD_CLOSE );
```

where

| hSocket | A socket handle. |
| lEvent | A bitmask that specifies what events notification is requested for. |

Valid values for lEvent include

FD_READ	Notification of readiness for reading.
FD_WRITE	Notification when data is available to be read.
FD_OOB	Notification of the arrival of out-of-band data.
FD_ACCEPT	Notification of incoming connections.
FD_CONNECT	Notification of connection results.
FD_CLOSE	Notification when a socket has been closed by a peer.

Returns TRUE if successful.

The Attach method takes an existing socket handle and attaches it to this CAsyncSocket object.

The Bind Method

```
BOOL Bind( UINT nSocketPort, LPCTSTR lpszSocketAddress = NULL );
BOOL Bind ( const SOCKADDR* lpSockAddr, int nSockAddrLen );
```

where

nSocketPort	The port identifying the application.
lpszSocketAddress	The network address.
lpSockAddr	The address to assign to the socket.
nSockAddrLen	The length of the address.

Returns TRUE if successful.

Call the Bind method to associate a local address to a socket.

The Close Method

```
void Close()
```

Call the Close method to close the socket. If there is a connection open, it will be broken.

The Connect Method

```
BOOL Connect( LPCTSTR lpszHostAddress, UINT nHostPort );
BOOL Connect( const SOCKADDR* lpSockAddr, int nSockAddrLen );
```

where

lpszHostAddress	The address to connect to.
nHostPort	The port to connect to.
lpSockAddr	The address and port to connect to.
nSockAddrLen	The length of the address.

Returns TRUE if successful.

Call the Connect method to connect to a remote server.

The Create Method

```
BOOL Create( UINT nSocketPort = 0, int nSocketType = SOCK_STREAM, long
➥lEvent = FD_READ ¦ FD_WRITE ¦ FD_OOB ¦ FD_ACCEPT ¦ FD_CONNECT ¦
➥FD_CLOSE, LPCTSTR lpszSocketAddress = NULL );
```

where

nSocketPort	The port that this socket will use.
nSocketType	The type of socket. Either SOCK_STREAM or SOCK_DGRAM.
lEvent	A bitmask that specifies what events notification is requested for.
lpszSocketAddress	The address of this socket.

Valid values for lEvent include

FD_READ	Notification of readiness for reading.
FD_WRITE	Notification when data is available to be read.
FD_OOB	Notification of the arrival of out-of-band data.
FD_ACCEPT	Notification of incoming connections.
FD_CONNECT	Notification of connection results.
FD_CLOSE	Notification when a socket has been closed by a peer.

Returns TRUE if successful.

The Create method creates a new socket and then calls Bind to bind the new socket to a local address.

The Detach Method

```
SOCKET Detach()
```

Returns the socket handle associated with this object.

Call the Detach method to detach the internal SOCKET handle from this object.

The FromHandle Method

```
static CAsyncSocket* PASCAL FromHandle( SOCKET hSocket );
```

where

hSocket	A SOCKET handle already created.

Returns a new CAsyncSocket object created from the handle.

Call the FromHandle method to create a new CAsyncSocket object from an already created SOCKET handle.

The GetLastError Method

```
DWORD GetLastError()
```

Returns the error code from the last socket operation.

The GetPeerName Method

```
BOOL GetPeerName( CString& rPeerAddress, UINT& rPeerPort );
BOOL GetPeerName( SOCKADDR* lpSockAddr, int* lpSockAddrLen );
```

where

rPeerAddress	Will contain the address of the other side of the socket connection.
rPeerPort	Will contain the port used by the other side of the socket connection.
lpSockAddr	Will contain the address and port used by the other side of the socket connection.
lpSockAddrLen	The length of the address.

Call the GetPeerName to get the address to the other side of a socket connection.

The GetSockName Method

```
BOOL GetSockName( CString& rSocketAddress, UINT& rSocketPort );
BOOL GetSockName( SOCKADDR* lpSockAddr, int* lpSockAddrLen );
```

where

rSocketAddress	CString that will receive the dotted number IP address.
rSocketPort	Reference to a unit that will receive the port.
lpSockAddr	Address that will get the port and address of the socket.
lpSockAddrLen	The length of the address.

Call the GetSocketName to get the address of the local side of a socket.

The GetSockOpt Method

```
BOOL GetSockOpt( int nOptionName, void* lpOptionValue, int* lpOptionLen,
➥int nLevel = SOL_SOCKET );
```

where

nOptionName	The desired socket option.
lpOptionValue	Pointer to a buffer that will get the value of the option requested.
lpOptionLen	A pointer to receive the size of the returned value.
nLevel	The level at which the option is defined. Must be either SOL_SOCKET, or IPPROTO_TCP.

The following are valid values for the nOptionName parameter.

SO_ACCEPTCONN(BOOL)	The socket is listening.
SO_BROADCAST(BOOL)	The socket is configured for transmission of broadcast messages.
SO_DEBUG(BOOL)	Debugging is enabled.
SO_DONTLINGER(BOOL)	If true, the SO_LINGER option is disabled.
SO_DONTROUTE(BOOL)	Routing is disabled.
SO_ERROR(int)	Retrieve error status and clear.
SO_KEEPALIVE(BOOL)	Keep-alives are being sent.
SO_LINGER(struct LINGER)	Returns the current linger options.
SO_OOBINLINE(BOOL)	Out-of-band data is being received.
SO_RCVBUF(int)	Buffer size for receives.
SO_REUSEADDR(BOOL)	The socket can be bound to an address which is already in use.
SO_SNDBUF(int)	Buffer size for sends.
SO_TYPE(int)	The type of the socket (for example, SOCK_STREAM).
TCP_NODELAY(BOOL)	Disables the Nagle algorithm for send coalescing.

Call the GetSocketOpt to get information about the socket.

The IOCtl Method

BOOL IOCtl(long lCommand, DWORD* lpArgument);

where

lCommand	The command to perform.
lpArgument	A parameter for the command.

Valid values for lpArgument include

FIONBIO	Enable or disable nonblocking mode. The argument is a DWORD. This should be 0 if blocking mode is disabled, otherwise it is enabled.
FIONREAD	Determines the maximum number of bytes that the Receive method can read at once. The argument is a DWORD.
SIOCATMARK	Returns non-zero if there is no out-of-band data to be read.

Call the IOCtl to perform various commands on the socket.

The Listen Method

BOOL Listen(int nConnectionBacklog = 5);

where

nConnectionBacklog	The maximum number of connections allowed to backlog.

Call the LISTEN socket in a server application to begin waiting for incoming connections. Before using LISTEN, Create should be called to create the socket.

The `Receive` Method

```
virtual int Receive( void* lpBuf, int nBufLen, int nFlags = 0 );
```

where

lpBuf	A buffer to hold the bytes read from the socket.
nBufLen	The number of bytes to receive.
nFlags	Must be either 0, MSG_PEEK, or MSG_OOB.

Returns the number of bytes actually read.

Call the `Receive` method to actually read data from the socket. If MSG_PEEK is specified, the data read will not be removed from the input buffer. If MSG_OOB is specified, out-of-band data will be read.

The `ReceiveFrom` Method

```
int ReceiveFrom( void* lpBuf, int nBufLen, CString& rSocketAddress, UINT&
➥rSocketPort, int nFlags = 0 );
int ReceiveFrom( void* lpBuf, int nBufLen, SOCKADDR* lpSockAddr, int*
➥lpSockAddrLen, int nFlags = 0 );
```

where

lpBuf	A buffer to hold the bytes read from the socket.
nBufLen	The number of bytes to receive.
nFlags	Must be either 0, MSG_PEEK, and MSG_OOB.
rSocketAddress	A CString that will receive a dotted number IP address.
nSocketPort	Holds the port that this message came from.
lpSockAddr	A pointer to a SOCKADDR that holds both the port and address of the sending socket.
lpSockAddrLen	A pointer to the length of the address in lpSockAddr.

Returns the number of bytes actually read.

Call the `ReceiveFrom` method to receive a datagram type packet. If MSG_PEEK is specified, the data read will not be removed from the input buffer. If MSG_OOB is specified, out-of-band data will be read.

The `Send` Method

```
virtual int Send( void* lpBuf, int nBufLen, int nFlags = 0 );
```

where

lpBuf	A buffer to hold the bytes read from the socket.
nBufLen	The number of bytes to receive.
nFlags	Must be either 0, MSG_DONTROUTE, or MSG_OOB.

Returns the number of bytes actually sent.

Call the `Send` method to actually send data over the socket connection. If MSG_DONTROUTE is specified, the data read will not be routed (Windows CAN ignore this). If MSG_OOB is specified, then out-of-band data will be sent.

The `SendTo` Method

```
int SendTo( const void* lpBuf, int nBufLen, UINT nHostPort, LPCTSTR
➥lpszHostAddress = NULL, int nFlags = 0 );
int SendTo( const void* lpBuf, int nBufLen, const SOCKADDR* lpSockAddr,
➥int nSockAddrLen, int nFlags = 0 );
```

where

lpBuf	A buffer to hold the bytes read from the socket.
nBufLen	The number of bytes to receive.
nFlags	Must be either `0`, `MSG_DONTROUTE`, or `MSG_OOB`.
nHostPort	The network port address to send this datagram is sent.
lpszHostAddress	The network address to send this datagram to.
lpSockAddr	A pointer to a `SOCKADDR` structure that contains the address of the target socket.
nSockAddrLen	The length of the target socket.

Returns the number of bytes actually sent.

Call the `Send` method to actually send a datagram over the socket connection. If `MSG_DONTROUTE` is specified, the data read will not be routed (Windows CAN ignore this). If `MSG_OOB` is specified, out-of-band data will be sent.

The `SetSockOpt` Method

```
BOOL SetSockOpt( int nOptionName, void* lpOptionValue, int* lpOptionLen,
➥int nLevel = SOL_SOCKET );
```

where

nOptionName	The desired socket option.
lpOptionValue	Pointer to a buffer that will get the value of the option requested.
lpOptionLen	A pointer to receive the size of the returned value.
nLevel	The level at which the option is defined. Must be either `SOL_SOCKET` or `IPPROTO_TCP`.

The following are valid values for the `nOptionName` parameter.

`SO_BROADCAST(BOOL)`	The socket is configured transmission of broadcast messages.
`SO_DEBUG(BOOL)`	Debugging is enabled.
`SO_DONTLINGER(BOOL)`	If true, the `SO_LINGER` option is disabled.
`SO_DONTROUTE(BOOL)`	Routing is disabled.
`SO_KEEPALIVE(BOOL)`	Keep-alives are being sent.
`SO_LINGER(struct LINGER)`	Returns the current linger options.
`SO_OOBINLINE(BOOL)`	Out-of-band data is being received.
`SO_RCVBUF(int)`	Buffer size for receives.
`SO_REUSEADDR(BOOL)`	The socket can be bound to an address that is already in use.
`SO_SNDBUF(int)`	Buffer size for sends.
`TCP_NODELAY(BOOL)`	Disables the Nagle algorithm for send coalescing.

Call the `GetSocketOpt` to set options about the socket.

C

The ShutDown Method

```
BOOL ShutDown( int nHow = sends );
```

where

    nHow   0 means no receives. 1 means no sends. 2 means neither sends nor receives.

Returns TRUE if successful.

Call the ShutDown method to disallow sends, receives, or both. This does NOT close the socket.

The OnAccept Method

```
virtual void OnAccept( int nErrorCode );
```

where

    nErrorCode   0 means the method executed successfully. WSAENETDOWN indicates an error occurred.

MFC calls OnAccept when a new connection has been received by a server. This method is usually overridden to provide specific processing for this event.

The OnClose Method

```
virtual void OnClose( int nErrorCode );
```

where

    nErrorCode   0 means the method executed successfully. Also returns WSAENETDOWN for a network failure, WSAECIBBRESET if the connection was reset, or WSAE-CONNABORTED if the connection timed out.

MFC calls OnClose when a socket has finished closing. This method is usually overridden to provide specific processing for this event.

The OnConnect Method

```
virtual void OnConnect( int nErrorCode );
```

where

    nErrorCode   0 if the method executed successfully; otherwise, an error code.

MFC calls OnConnect when a connection is complete. This method is usually overridden to provide specific processing for this event.

The OnOutOfBandData Method

```
virtual void OnOutOfBandData( int nErrorCode );
```

where

    nErrorCode   0 if the method executed successfully; otherwise, WSAENETDOWN if an error occurred.

MFC calls OnOutOfBandData when out-of-band data arrives. This method is usually overridden to provide specific processing for this event.

The OnReceive Method
virtual void OnReceive(int nErrorCode);

where

   nErrorCode   0 if the method executed successfully; WSAENETDOWN if an error occurred.

MFC calls OnReceive when data has been received. This method is usually overridden to provide specific processing for this event.

The OnSend Method
virtual void OnSend(int nErrorCode);

where

   nErrorCode   0 the method executed successfully; WSAENETDOWN if an error occurred.

MFC calls OnSend when a socket can send data. This method is usually overridden to provide specific processing for this event.

CBitmap

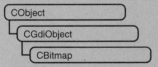

The CBitmap class is used to display and manipulate Windows standard bitmap files (BMP). CBitmap objects are usually loaded from .BMP files or resources.

For an example of CBitmap, see the BitmapEx example found on the CD-ROM that accompanies this book.

Header Files
The following header files should be included when using this class:

afxwin.h

Methods
The CBitmap class has the following methods:

CBitmap	Constructor
CreateBitmap	Create a bitmap
CreateBitmapIndirect	Create bitmap from a structure
CreateCompatibleBitmap	Create a bitmap that is compatible with a specific device
CreateDiscardableBitmap	Create a discardable bitmap that is compatible with a specific device
FromHandle	Create a bitmap from a HBITMAP handle
GetBitmap	Fill a BITMAP structure with information about this bitmap
GetBitmapBits	Get a pointer to the image data
GetBitmapDimension	Get the height and width of a bitmap

LoadBitmap	Load a bitmap from a resource
LoadMappedBitmap	Load a bitmap and map it to system colors
LoadOEMBitmap	Load a predefined Windows bitmap
operator HBITMAP	Get the bitmap as a HBITMAP handle
SetBitmapBits	Modify image data
SetBitmapDimension	Set the height and width of a bitmap

The CBitmap Constructor

The CBitmap creates the CBitmap object. The CBitmap constructor is used as follows:

CBitmap()

The CreateBitmap Method

BOOL CreateBitmap(int nWidth, int nHeight, UINT nPlanes, UINT nBitcount,
➥const void* lpBits);

where

nWidth	The width of the bitmap.
nHeigth	The height of the bitmap.
nPlanes	Number of color planes in the bitmap.
nBitcount	Specifies the color bits per pixel.
lpBits	An array of short ints used to initialize the bitmap. Set to NULL to leave the bitmap uninitiated.

Returns TRUE if successful.

The CreateBitmap method is used to create a new bitmap. Either nPlanes or nBitcount should be set to 1.

The CreateBitmapIndirect Method

BOOL CreateBitmapIndirect(LPBITMAP lpBitmap);

where

lpBitmap	Points to a BITMAP structure that contains info on how to setup the bitmap. This structure contains the same info as needed by the CreateBitmap method.

Returns TRUE if successful.

The CreateBitmapIndirect method is used to create a new bitmap.

The CreateCompatibleBitmap Method

HBITMAP CreateCompatibleBitmap(HDC hdc, int nWidth, int nHeight);

where

nWidth	The width of the bitmap.
nHeigth	The height of the bitmap.
pDC	A device context.

Returns TRUE if successful.

The `CreateCompatibleBitmap` method is used to create a new bitmap that is set up the same as a device context (CDC).

The `CreateDiscardableBitmap` Method

`BOOL CreateDiscardableBitmap( CDC *pDC,int nWidth, int nHeight );`

where

nWidth	The width of the bitmap.
nHeigth	The height of the bitmap.
pDC	A device context.

Returns TRUE if successful.

The `CreateDiscardableBitmap` method is used to create a new discardable bitmap that is set up the same as a device context (CDC). Windows can discard this bitmap when no applications have selected it into a device context.

The `FromHandle` Method

`static CBitmap* PASCAL FromHandle( HBITMAP hBitmap );`

where

hBitmap	A handle to a bitmap.

Returns a new CBitmap object if successful.

The `FromHandle` method is used to create a new CBitmap object from a bitmap handle (HBITMAP).

The `GetBitmap` Method

`int GetBitmap( BITMAP *pBitmap );`

where

pBitmap	Points to a BITMAP structure that will contain info about the bitmap. This structure contains the same info as needed by the CreateBitmap method.

Returns TRUE if successful.

The `CreateBitmap` method is used to get general information about a bitmap.

The `GetBitmapBits` Method

`DWORD GetBitmapBits( DWORD dwCount, LPVOID lpBits );`

where

dwCount	The number of bytes to be copied.
lpBits	Pointer to a buffer to receive the bytes.

Returns the number of bytes actually copied.

The `GetBitmapBits` method is used to access pixel-level data about the bitmap. The format of the data returned by this method will vary depending on the color depth of this image.

The `GetBitmapDimension` Method

`CSize GetBitmapDimension( ) const;`

Returns a `CSize` structure containing the dimensions of the bitmap. This size will be in 0.1mm units.

The `GetBitmapDimension` method will return a structure that contains the height and width of the bitmap expressed as a `CSize` structure.

The `LoadBitmap` Method

`BOOL LoadBitmap( LPCTSTR lpszResourceName );`
`BOOL LoadBitmap( UINT nIDResource );`

where

lpszResourceName	A bitmap resource with a text name.
nIDResource	A bitmap resource with a numeric name.

Returns TRUE if successful.

The `LoadBitmap` method will load a bitmap from the applications resource file.

The `LoadMappedBitmap` Method

`BOOL LoadMappedBitmap( UINT nIDBitmap, UINT nFlags = 0, LPCOLORMAP`
`➥lpColorMap = NULL, int nMapSize = 0 );`

where

nIDBitmap	The ID of a bitmap resource.
nFlags	Flags, must be either 0 or CMB_MASKED.
lpColorMap	A pointer to a color map. If NULL, the default color map is used.
nMapSize	The number of colors in the color map pointed to by lpColorMap.

Returns TRUE if successful.

The `LoadBitmap` method will load a bitmap from the applications resource file. This bitmap will be mapped to the color map specified when the method is called.

The `LoadOEMBitmap` Method

`BOOL LoadOEMBitmap( UINT nIDBitmap );`

where

nIDBitmap	The ID of a predefined bitmap.

Returns TRUE if successful.

The `LoadOEMBitmap` method will load a predefined bitmap. The following predefined bitmaps are included:

OBM_BTNCORNERS	OBM_BTSIZE
OBM_CHECK	OBM_CHECKBOXES
OBM_CLOSE	OBM_COMBO
OBM_DNARROW	OBM_DNARROWD
OBM_DNARROWI	OBM_LFARROW

OBM_LFARROWD	OBM_LFARROWI
OBM_MNARROW	OBM_OLD_CLOSE
OBM_OLD_DNARROW	OBM_OLD_LFARROW
OBM_OLD_REDUCE	OBM_OLD_RESTORE
OBM_OLD_RGARROW	OBM_OLD_UPARROW
OBM_OLD_ZOOM	OBM_REDUCE
OBM_REDUCED	OBM_RESTORE
OBM_RESTORED	OBM_RGARROW
OBM_RGARROWD	OBM_RGARROWI
OBM_SIZE	OBM_UPARROW
OBM_UPARROW	OBM_UPARROWD
OBM_ZOOM	OBM_ZOOMD

The **HBITMAP** Operator Method

`operator HBITMAP( ) const;`

Returns the bitmap handle(HBITMAP) for this bitmap.

The **SetBitmapBits** Method

`DWORD SetBitmapBits( DWORD dwCount, LPVOID lpBits );`

where

dwCount	The number of bytes to be copied.
lpBits	Pointer to a buffer to receive the bytes.

Returns the number of bytes actually copied.

The SetBitmapBits method is used to set pixel-level data about the bitmap. The format of the data needed by this method will vary, depending on the color depth of this image.

The **SetBitmapDimension** Method

`CSize SetBitmapDimension( int nWidth, int nHeight );`

where

nHeight	The height of the bitmap in 0.1 mm units.
lpBits	The width of the bitmap in 0.1 mm units.

Returns the previous bitmap dimensions.

The SetBitmapDimension method is used to set the height and width dimensions of the bitmap. This does not affect the actual bitmap, only the value returned by GetBitmapDimension.

CBrush

 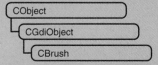

The CBrush class represents a brush object. A brush is used to fill in a region on the screen or some other device. A brush may be a solid color, a pattern, or image. The CBrush object is used with the CDC object for drawing operations.

Several hatch styles are available for hatch style brushes. The following constants can be used to specify hatch styles.

HS_BDIAGONAL	Downward hatch (left to right) at 45 degrees
HS_CROSS	Horizontal and vertical crosshatch
HS_DIAGCROSS	Crosshatch at 45 degrees
HS_FDIAGONAL	Upward hatch (left to right) at 45 degrees
HS_HORIZONTAL	Horizontal hatch
HS_VERTICAL	Vertical hatch

For an example of CBrush, see the BrushEx example found on the CD-ROM that accompanies this book.

Header Files

The following header files should be included when using this class:

afxwin.h

Methods

The CBrush class has the following methods:

CBrush	The constructor
CreateBrushIndirect	Create a brush from a structure
CreateDIBPatternBrush	Create a bitmap brush
CreateHatchBrush	Create a hatch brush
CreatePatternBrush	Create a pattern brush
CreateSolidBrush	Create a solid color brush
CreateSysColorBrush	Create a brush from a system color
FromHandle	Create a brush from a HBrush handle
GetLogBrush	Get a structure with info about the brush
operator HBRUSH	Get the HBrush handle for this brush

The CBrush Constructor

The CBrush creates the CBrush object. There are four constructors available. Each allows a different type of brush to be constructed. The CBrush constructor is used as follows:

```
CBrush( );
CBrush( COLORREF crColor );
CBrush( int nIndex, COLORREF crColor );
CBrush( CBitmap* pBitmap );
```

where

crColor	A color to create a solid brush from. If this is a hatched brush, the color of the hatching.
nIndex	Specified the hatch style of the brush.
pBitmap	Specified the bitmap used for the brush.

This constructor can throw the CResourceException exception.

The CreateBrushIndirect Method

```
BOOL CreateBrushIndirect( const LOGBRUSH* lpLogBrush );
```

where

lpLogBrush	A pointer to a logical brush structure (LOGBRUSH) that contains information on how the brush should be created.

Returns TRUE if successful.

The CreateBrush allows a brush to be created if the default constructor was used. The log contains the following properties.

lbStyle	A brush style.
lbColor	The color of the brush or hatch.
lbHatch	The hatch type (if any).

The following are valid styles for the lbStyle property.

BS_DIBPATTERN	A pattern brush defined by a device-independent bitmap. The lbHatch property contains a handle to a DIB.
	Under Windows 95, creating brushes from bitmaps or DIBs larger than 8×8 pixels is not supported. If a larger bitmap is given, only part the bitmap is used.
BS_DIBPATTERN8X8	Same as BS_DIBPATTERN.
BS_DIBPATTERNPT	A pattern brush defined by a device-independent bitmap (DIB) specification. The lbHatch property contains a pointer to a packed DIB.
BS_HATCHED	Hatched brush.
BS_HOLLOW	Hollow brush.
BS_NULL	Same as BS_HOLLOW.
BS_PATTERN	Pattern brush defined by a memory bitmap.
BS_PATTERN8X8	Same as BS_PATTERN.
BS_SOLID	Solid brush.

C

The `CreateDIBPatternBrush` Method

```
BOOL CreateDIBPatternBrush( HGLOBAL hPackedDIB, UINT nUsage );
BOOL CreateDIBPatternBrush( const void* lpPackedDIB, UINT nUsage );
```

where

hPackedDIB	A handle for a global memory object that contains a packed DIB.
nUsage	Specifies how the `bmiColors[]` property of the `BITMAPINFO` structure should be interpreted.
lpPackedDIB	Pointer to a packed DIB in memory.

Returns TRUE if successful.

The `CreateDIBPatternBrush` method is used to create a brush that is based on a bitmap. The bitmap must be a packed DIB. A packed DIB is a `BITMAPINFO` structure in memory that is immediately followed by pixel data.

The following values are valid for *nUsage*.

`DIB_PAL_COLORS`	The `bmiColors[]` property of the `BITMAPINFO` structure is an array of 16-bit indexes.
`DIB_RGB_COLORS`	The `bmiColors[]` property of the `BITMAPINFO` structure contains literal RGB values.

The following value is available only in the second version of this method:

`DIB_PAL_INDICES`	No color table is provided. The pixel data contains indices into the logical palette of the device context into which the brush will be selected.

The `CreateHatchBrush` Method

```
BOOL CreateHatchBrush( int nIndex, COLORREF crColor );
```

where

nIndex	Specifies the hatch type.
crColor	Specifies what color the hatch should be.

Returns TRUE if successful.

Use the `CreateHatchBrush` method to create a hatched brush. A list of valid values for the *nIndex* parameter can be found in the `CBrush` class definition.

The `CreatePatternBrush` Method

```
BOOL CreatePatternBrush( CBitmap* pBitmap );
```

where

pBitmap	Specifies a `CBitmap` object to use for this brush.

Returns TRUE if successful.

Use the `CreatePatternBrush` to create a brush that is based from a `CBitmap` object.

The **CreateSolidBrush** Method

```
BOOL CreateSolidBrush( COLORREF crColor );
```

where

    crColor   Specifies a color to create a brush for.

Returns TRUE if successful.

Use the CreateSolidBrush to create a brush of a solid color.

The **CreateSysColorBrush** Method

```
BOOL CreateSysColorBrush( int nIndex );
```

where

    nIndex   Specifies the hatch type.

Returns TRUE if successful.

Use the CreateSysColorBrush method to create a hatched brush of the system brush color. A list of valid values for the nIndex parameter can be found in the CBrush class definition.

The **FromHandle** Method

```
static CBrush* PASCAL FromHandle( HBRUSH hBrush );
```

where

    hBrush   A handle to a GDI brush object.

Returns a CBrush object.

Use the FromHandle method to create a brush from a brush handle.

The **GetLogBrush** Method

```
int GetLogBrush( LOGBRUSH* pLogBrush );
```

where

    pLogBrush   Specifies a pointer to a LOGBRUSH pointer.

Returns the number of bytes required to store the information.

Use the GetLogBrush method to get information about this brush. For the structure of LOGBRUSH see the CreateBrushIndirect method.

The **HBRUSH** Operator Method

```
operator HBRUSH( ) const;
```

Returns the handle(HBRUSH) for this brush.

CCmdTarget

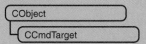

If a class is to receive messages, it must be derived from CCmdTarget. All of the MFC-based classes that receive messages are descended from CCmdTarget. These classes include CDocument, CFrameWnd, CView, CWinApp, and CWnd. CCmdTarget is also responsible for exposing OLE automation.

Header Files

The following header files should be included when using this class:

afxwin.h

Methods

The CCmdTarget class has the following methods:

BeginWaitCursor	Display hourglass cursor
EnableAutomation	Enable OLE-Automation for this object
EndWaitCursor	Return to a non-hourglass cursor
FromIDispatch	Create object based on an IDispatch pointer
GetIDispatch	Get an IDispatch pointer associated with this object
IsResultExpected	Determine if an automation function should return a value
RestoreWaitCursor	Restore hourglass cursor

The following methods are used to process messages sent to the class. These methods may be overridden if special handling is needed for these messages.

OnCmdMsg	Route command messages
OnFinalRelease	Called when last OLE reference has been released

The BeginWaitCursor Method

void BeginWaitCursor();

The BeginWaitCursor method will display a hourglass cursor. If a program is going to be processing for longer than a few seconds, an hourglass cursor should be displayed. Call BeginWaitCursor just before the block of code that will be processing. Call EndWaitCursor when processing is complete.

The EnableAutomation Method

void EnableAutomation();

The EnableAutomation method will enable OLE automation for the object. This method is usually called from the constructor of a descended class.

The EndWaitCursor Method

void EndWaitCursor();

The EndWaitCursor method will return the cursor to what it was before the BeginWaitCursor method was called. Every call to BeginWaitCursor should be matched with a call to EndWaitCursor.

The FromIDispatch Method

static CCmdTarget *FromIDispatch(LPDISPATCH lpDispatch);

where

lpDispatch	A pointer to an IDispatch object.

Returns a pointer to a CCmdTarget object created from the lpDispatch parameter. This method only works with MFC IDispatch objects.

The FromIDispatch is used to create a CCmdTarget for OLE automation objects.

The IsResultExpected Method

BOOL IsResultExpected( );

Returns TRUE if an automation function is expected to return a value; otherwise, it returns FALSE.

The GetIDispatch Method

static CCmdTarget *GetIDispatch(BOOL bAddRef);

where

> bAddRef   If TRUE, the reference count for this object will be incremented.

Returns an IDispatch pointer associated with this CCmdTarget object.

The RestoreWaitCursor Method

void RestoreWaitCursor();

The RestoreWaitCursor method will change the cursor back to an hourglass. This method should be called after a BeginWaitCursor method has been called and some other action has changed the cursor back to an arrow. This RestoreWaitCursor will restore the cursor to an hourglass without increasing the wait count as BeginWaitCursor would.

The OnCmdMsg Method

BOOL OnCmdMsg(UINT nID, int nCode, void* pExtra, AFX_CMDHANDLERINFO*
➡pHandlerInfo);

where

nID	The command ID.
pExtra	Use depends upon the value of nID.
pHandlerInfo	The NOT NULL OnCmdMsg should fill in pTarget and pmf members of pHandlerInfo rather than dispatching the command. This parameter is usually NULL.

Returns TRUE if the message was handled.

This method is the main component of MFC's message-handling structure. It is rarely directly used by application programs.

The OnFinalRelease Method

virtual void OnFinalRelease();

The OnFinalRelease method is called by MFC when the last OLE reference to or from this object is released. This object can be overridden to handle this situation. The standard OnFinalRelease method will delete the object.

CColorDialog

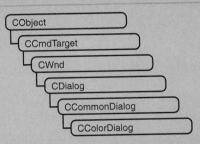

Windows provides several standard dialog boxes. One of these is a Color Selection dialog box. CColorDialog allows the Windows standard Color Selection dialog box to be used. The Color Selection dialog box allows the user to select an RGB-based color. This RGB value can be used with the drawing methods found in the CDC class.

For an example of CColorDialog, see the ColorDialogEx example found on the CD-ROM that accompanies this book.

Header Files

The following header files should be included when using this class:

afxdlgs.h

Properties

The CColorDialog class has the following properties:

m_cc	A CHOOSECOLOR structure that is used to customize the standard Color dialog box.

Methods

The CColorDialog class has the following methods:

CColorDialog	The constructor
DoModal	Display the dialog and wait for input
GetColor	Get the selected color
GetSavedCustomColors	Get custom colors
OnColorOK	Get custom colors
SetCurrentColor	Set the current color

The CColorDialog Constructor

The CColorDialog creates the CColorDialog object. The CColorDialog constructor is used as follows:

```
CColorDialog( COLORREF clrInit = 0, DWORD dwFlags = 0, CWnd* pParentWnd =
➡ NULL );
```

where

clrInit	The default color selection.
dwFlags	Flags used to customize behavior. For more information, see the CHOOSE-COLOR structure in the data structures section of the book.
pParentWnd	The parent window for this dialog box.

The DoModal Method

`virtual int DoModal();`

Returns IDOK if the user chose a color, or IDCANCEL if the user did not choose a color.

The DoModal method is called to display the color dialog box and wait for the user to select a color.

The GetColor Method

`COLORREF GetColor();`

Returns the color chosen by the user.

The GetSavedCustomColors Method

`static COLORREF *GetSavedCustomColors();`

Returns a pointer to an array of 16 custom colors that can be defined by the user.

The OnColorOK Method

`virtual BOOL OnColorOK();`

Returns TRUE if the dialog box should be canceled, or TRUE to accept the color.

The OnColorOK method will be called by the framework when the user clicks OK on the Color dialog box.

The SetCurrentColor Method

`void SetCurrentColor( COLORREF clr)`

where

| clr | A color value. |

Use the SetCurrentColor method after calling DoModal to force the user's color selection to clr.

CCommonDialog

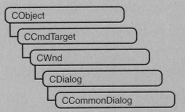

Windows provides several standard dialog boxes. These enable an application to query the user for information that is commonly needed. CCommonDialog is an abstract base class that is rarely used by application programmers. Application programmers commonly use the child classes of CCommonDialog box:

| CFileDialogBox | Used to ask for filenames |
| CFontDialogBox | Used to ask for font names |

CColorDialog	Used to ask for colors
CPageSetupDialog	Used to ask for page setup info
CPrintDialog	Used to prepare for a printout
CFindReplaceDialog	Used to find or replace text

Header Files

The following header files should be included when using this class:

afxdlgs.h

Methods

The CCommonDialog class has the following methods:

| CCommonDialog | The constructor |

The CCommonDialog Constructor

The CCommonDialog creates the CCommonDialog object. The CCommonDialog constructor is used as follows:

CCommonDialog(CWnd *pParentWnd)

where

| pParentWnd | The parent window for this dialog box. |

CControlBar

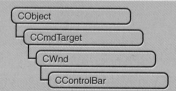

CControlBar is an abstract base class for the control bar classes found in MFC. A control bar is a window that is usually docked to one of the sides of a frame window. These windows can also float inside of the frame window. The control bars provided by MFC include CStatusBar, CToolBar, CDialogBar, CReBar, and COleResizeBar.

Header Files

The following header files should be included when using this class:

afxext.h

Properties

The CControlBar class has the following properties:

| m_bAutoDelete | Delete control bar when frame is deleted |

Methods

The CControlBar class has the following methods:

CalcDynamicLayout	Get the size of a dynamic control bar
CalcFixedLayout	Get the size of a fixed control bar
EnableDocking	Enable this control bar to dock or float
GetBarStyle	Get the control bar style
GetBorders	Get the border values for the control bar
GetCount	Get the number of elements in the control bar
GetDockingFrame	Get the frame to which the control bar is docked
IsFloating	Is the control bar floating?
SetBarStyle	Set the style of a control bar
SetBorders	Set the border values for a control bar

The following method is used to process messages sent to the CControlBar class.

OnUpdateCmdUI	Called to update the status of the control bar.

The CalcDynamicLayout Method

virtual CSize CalcDynamicLayout(int nLength, DWORD dwMode);

where

nLength	The requested length of the control bar.
dwMode	What mode the control bar is in.

Returns the size of the control bar in pixels.

The CalcDynamicLayout method is called by the framework to calculate the dimensions of a dynamic toolbar. In certain rare cases, an application may override this method to provide application-specific dynamic layout.

The following are valid values for the dwMode parameter.

LM_STRETCH	Tells if this control bar should be stretched to the size of the frame. Set only if the bar is not a docking bar; it should not be set when the bar is docked or floating. When set, LM_STRETCH ignores nLength and returns dimensions depending upon the LM_HORZ state.
LM_HORZ	Sets the bar to be either horizontally or vertically oriented.
LM_MRUWIDTH	Request the most recently used dynamic width.
LM_HORZDOCK	Request the horizontal docked dimensions.
LM_VERTDOCK	Request the vertical docked dimensions.
LM_LENGTHY	Set if nLength indicates height (Y-direction) instead of width.
LM_COMMIT	Resets LM_MRUWIDTH to current width of the floating control bar.

C

The `CalcFixedLayout` Method

`virtual CSize CalcFixedLayout( BOOL bStretch, BOOL bHorz );`

where

bStretch	TRUE if the bar should be stretched to the length of the frame.
bHorz	TRUE if the bar is horizontally oriented, FALSE if the bar is vertically oriented.

Returns the size of the control bar in pixels.

The `CalcFixedLayout` method is called by the framework to calculate the dimensions of a fixed toolbar. In certain rare cases, an application may override this method to provide application-specific layout.

The `EnableDocking` Method

`void EnableDocking( DWORD dwStyle );`

where

dwStyle	The sort of docking that this control bar allows.

The `EnableDocking` method is called to enable the control bar to be docked. The following are valid values for the `dwStyle` property:

CBRS_ALIGN_TOP	The bar may be docked at the top of the client area.
CBRS_ALIGN_BOTTOM	The bar may be docked at the bottom of the client area.
CBRS_ALIGN_LEFT	The bar may be docked at the left side of the client area.
CBRS_ALIGN_RIGHT	The bar may be docked at the right side of the client area.
CBRS_ALIGN_ANY	The bar may be docked at any side of the client area.
CBRS_FLOAT_MULTI	Multiple control bars may be floated in a single mini-frame window.

The `GetBarStyle` Method

`DWORD GetBarStyle();`

Returns the style of the control bar. See `SetBarStyle` for a complete list of styles.

The `GetBorders` Method

`CRect GetBorders();`

Returns a `CRect` that contains the current width and height of a control bar.

The `GetCount` Method

`int GetCount() const;`

Returns the number of nonwindow items on a control bar. Returns 0 for a `CDialogBar`.

The `GetDockingFrame` Method

`CFrameWnd *GetDockingFrame();`

Returns the frame that this control bar is associated with.

The `IsFloating` Method

`BOOL IsFloating();`

Returns TRUE if the control bar is floating.

The **SetBarStyle** Method

void SetBarStyle(DWORD dwStyle);

where

> *dwStyle*   The style to set the control bar to.

The SetBarStyle method allows the style of the control bar to be changed. See the EnableDocking method for a complete list of styles.

The **SetBorders** Method

void SetBorders(int cxLeft,int cxTop, int cxRight, int cxBottom);
void SetBorders(LPCRECT *lpRect*);

where

> *cxLeft*   The pixel width of the control bar's left border.
>
> *cxTop*   The pixel width of the control bar's top border.
>
> *cxRight*   The pixel width of the control bar's right border.
>
> *cxBottom*   The pixel width of the control bar's bottom border.
>
> *lpRect*   A rectangle that specifies the above four parameters.

The SetBorders method allows the border sizes for a control bar to be set.

CCriticalSection

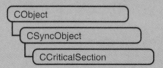

Windows supports multithreading. Multithreading enables your program to have several sections of itself running at the same time. Each of these sections is called a thread. If more than one thread is running, it may be desirable to define critical sections. When a thread enters a critical section, all other threads attempting to gain access to that critical section are blocked until the initial thread exits the critical section.

Header Files

The following header files should be included when using this class:

afxmt.h

Methods

The CCriticalSection class has the following methods:

> CCriticalSection   The constructor
>
> Lock   Lock and stop other threads
>
> Unlock   Unlock and continue other threads

The **CCriticalSection** Constructor

The CCriticalSection creates the CCriticalSection object. The CCriticalSection constructor is used as follows:

```
CCriticalSection()
```

The **Lock** Method

```
BOOL Lock( );
BOOL Lock( DWORD dwTimeout );
```

where

> *dwTimeout*   This parameter is ignored.

Returns TRUE if the object was successfully locked.

The Lock method waits for the critical section object to be unlocked. If the critical section object is not locked, this method returns immediately after locking the object. Unlock should then be called once processing is complete.

The **Unlock** Method

```
virtual BOOL Unlock( );
```

Returns TRUE if the object was successfully unlocked.

The Unlock method unlocks the critical section object after a Lock method has locked it.

CCtrlView

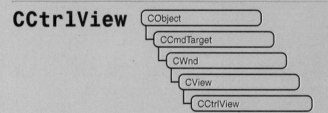

CCtrlView is an abstract base class that is not usually used by the application programmer. The MFC control views are all descended from this class. The MFC views descended from this class are CEditView, CListView, CTreeView, and CRichEditView.

Header Files

The following header files should be included when using this class:

```
afxwin.h
```

Properties

The CCtrlView class has the following properties:

> m_strClass   The window class name
>
> m_dwDefaultStype   The default style

Methods

The CCtrlView class has the following methods:

CCtrlView   The constructor

The CCtrlView Constructor

The CCtrlView creates the CCtrlView object. The CCtrlView constructor is used as follows:

CCtrlView(LPCTSTR lpszClass, DWORD dwStyle);

where

lpszClass   The Windows class name for the view.

dwStyle   Style of the view class.

The CCtrlView constructor creates a control view object. See the CView constructor for more information on creating a view.

CDaoDatabase

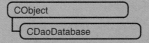

CDaoDatabase represents a database within a DAO workspace. DAO database objects access data through the Microsoft JET engine. All MFC database classes that use JET are prefixed with Dao.

For an example of CDaoDatabase, see the DAOEx example found on the CD-ROM that accompanies this book.

Header Files

The following header files should be included when using this class:

afxdao.h

Properties

The CDaoDatabase class has the following properties:

m_pWorkspace   A pointer to the workspace for this object

m_pDAODatabase   A pointer to the underlying DAO database

Methods

The CDaoDatabase class has the following methods:

CDaoDatabase   The constructor

CanTransact   Are transactions supported

CanUpdate   Are updates supported

Close   Close the database

Create   Create a connection to a   database

CreateRelation   Create a new relation

DeleteQueryDef   Delete a querydef

DeleteRelation	Delete a relation
DeleteTableDef	Delete a table
Execute	Execute a SQL command
GetConnect	Get the connect string
GetName	Get the database name
GetQueryDefCount	Get the number of querydefs
GetQueryDefInfo	Get information about a querydef
GetQueryTimeout	Get the timeout value for queries
GetRecordsAffected	Get the number of records affected by the last operation
GetRelationCount	Get a count of the relations in a database
GetRelationInfo	Get information about the specified relation
GetTableDefCount	Get a count of the tables in a database
GetTableDefInfo	Get information about the specified table
GetVersion	Get the database version
IsOpen	Is this database object open
Open	Open a connection to the database
SetQueryTimeout	Set the query timeout value

The CDaoDatabase Constructor

The CDaoDatabase creates the CDaoDatabase object. The CDaoDatabase constructor is used as follows:

CDaoDatabase(CDaoWorkspace *pWorkspace = NULL);

where

    pWorkspace   A pointer to the CDaoWorkspace to be associated with this database. If NULL is used, a temporary workspace is created.

The CanTransact Method

BOOL CanTransact();

Returns TRUE if this database supports transactions.

The CanUpdate Method

BOOL CanUpdate();

Returns TRUE if this database supports updates. If not, it is a read-only data source.

The Close Method

virtual void Close();

The Close method disconnects from the database. This method cancels any pending operations on the database. Any recordset, querydefs, and tabledefs created from this database should be closed prior to closing the database.

The Create Method

```
virtual void Create( LPCTSTR lpszName, LPCTSTR lpszLocale = dbLangGeneral,
➥int dwOptions = 0 );
```

where

lpszName	The filename for the database being created. This can be a local name such as `c:\mydb\data.mdb` or a UNC (universal naming convention) such as `\\myserver\c\mydb\data.mdb`.
lpszLocale	A string specifying the collating order to create the database.
dwOptions	Integer bitmap that specifies one or more options.

The `Create` method will create a new JET database. This method will only create JET databases.

Possible values for `lpszLocale` include

dbLangGeneral	English, German, French, Portuguese, Italian, and Modern Spanish
dbLangArabic	Arabic
dbLangCyrillic	Russian
dbLangCzech	Czech
dbLangDutch	Dutch
dbLangGreek	Greek
dbLangHebrew	Hebrew
dbLangHungarian	Hungarian
dbLangIcelandic	Icelandic
dbLangNordic	Nordic languages (Microsoft JET database engine version 1.0 only)
dbLangNorwdan	Norwegian and Danish
dbLangPolish	Polish
dbLangSpanish	Traditional Spanish
dbLangSwedfin	Swedish and Finnish
dbLangTurkish	Turkish

Possible values for `dwOptions` include

dbEncrypt	Create an encrypted database.
dbVersion10	Create a database with Microsoft JET database version 1.0.
dbVersion11	Create a database with Microsoft JET database version 1.1.
dbVersion20	Create a database with Microsoft JET database version 2.0.
dbVersion30	Create a database with Microsoft JET database version 3.0.

The `Create` method can throw the CMemoryException or the CDaoException.

The CreateRelation Method

```
void CreateRelation( LPCTSTR lpszName, LPCTSTR lpszTable, LPCTSTR
➥lpszForeignTable, long lAttributes, LPCTSTR lpszField, LPCTSTR
➥lpszForeignField );
void CreateRelation( CDaoRelationInfo& relinfo );
```

where

lpszName	The unique name for this relation. It may be up to 40 characters long. Punctuation and spaces are not allowed as part of the name.
lpszTable	The primary table for the relation.
lpszForeignTable	The foreign table in the relationship.
lAttributes	Integer specifying one or more attributes for this relationship.
lpszField	The primary field for this relationship. Must exist in `lpszTable`.
lpszForeignField	The foreign field in the relationship. Must exist in `lpszForeignTable`.
dwOptions	A `CDaoRelationInfo` object that contains the needed information.

The `CreateRelation` method will create a relation between two fields in one or more tables. The two fields must be from tables, and not querydefs. Relationships are used to automatically set up referential integrity between related tables.

Possible values for *lAttributes* include

`dbRelationUnique`	One-to-one relationship.
`dbRelationDontEnforce`	Relationship is not enforced.
`dbRelationInherited`	Relationship exists in a nonlocal table.
`dbRelationUpdateCascade`	Updates will cascade (affect related records).
`dbRelationDeleteCascade`	Deletions will cascade (affect related records).

The `CreateRelation` method can throw the CMemoryException or the CDAOException.

The `DeleteQueryDef` Method

`void DeleteQueryDef( LPCTSTR lpszName );`

where

    lpszName   Specifies the name of the querydef to delete.

The `DeleteQueryDef` method can throw the CMemoryException or the CDaoException.

The `DeleteRelation` Method

`void DeleteRelation( LPCTSTR lpszName );`

where

    lpszName   Specifies the name of the relation to delete.

The `DeleteQueryDef` method can throw the CMemoryException or the CDaoException.

The `DeleteTableDef` Method

`void DeleteTableDef( LPCTSTR lpszName );`

where

    lpszName   Specifies the name of the tabledef to delete.

The `DeleteTableDef` method can throw the CMemoryException or the CDaoException.

The **Execute** Method

`void Execute( LPCSTR lpszSQL,int nOptions );`

where

lpszSQL	A null-terminated or `CString` containing a valid SQL statement.
nOptions	A bitmask of options related to the integrity of the query.

The `Execute` method will directly execute the SQL command given. `Execute` does not return the results of the SQL command. Use a recordset to get back the results from a SQL command.

Possible values for *nOptions* include

dbDenyWrite	Deny write access to other users.
dbInconsistent	Inconsistent updates.
dbConsistent	Consistent updates.
dbSQLPassThrough	Pass the SQL statement directly through to ODBC.
dbFailOnError	Rollback if an error occurs.
dbSeeChanges	Generate a runtime error if another user changes the data being edited.

The `Execute` method can throw the CMemoryException or the CDaoException.

The **GetConnect** Method

`CString GetConnect();`

Returns the connect string if this `CDAODatabase` object was opened with a data source. For .MDB files this method will return an empty string.

The `GetConnect` method can throw the CMemoryException or the CDaoException.

The **GetQueryDefCount** Method

`short GetQueryDefCount( );`

Returns the number of querydefs defined in this database.

This method can throw the CDaoException or the CMemoryException exception.

The **GetQueryDefInfo** Method

`void GetQueryDefInfo( int nIndex, CDaoQueryDefInfo& querydefinfo, DWORD`
`➥dwInfoOptions = AFX_DAO_PRIMARY_INFO );`
`void GetQueryDefInfo( LPCTSTR lpszName, CDaoQueryDefInfo& querydefinfo,`
`➥DWORD dwInfoOptions = AFX_DAO_PRIMARY_INFO );`

where

nIndex	The index of the querydef in the querydef collection.
querydefinfo	A reference to a `CDaoQueryDefInfo` object that returns the requested information.
dwInfoOptions	Options that specify what information about the querydef to return.
lpszName	A string containing the name of the querydef.

The `GetQueryDefInfo` method will return information about the specified querydef.

C

Valid values for *dwInfoOptions* include

AFX_DAO_PRIMARY_INFO	Name and type.
AFX_DAO_SECONDARY_INFO	Name, type, date created, date of last update, returns records, updatable.
AFX_DAO_ALL_INFO	All available information.

The `GetQueryDefInfo` method can throw the CMemoryException or the CDaoException.

The `GetQueryTimeout` Method

```
short GetQueryTimeout( );
```

Returns the number of seconds before a query times out.

This method can throw the CDaoException or the CMemoryException exception.

The `GetRecordsAffected` Method

```
short GetRecordsAffected( );
```

Returns the number of records affected by the last call of `Execute`.

This method can throw the CDaoException or the CMemoryException exception.

The `GetRelationCount` Method

```
short GetRelationCount( );
```

Returns the number of relations defined in this database.

This method can throw the CDaoException or the CMemoryException exception.

The `GetRelationInfo` Method

```
void GetRelationInfo( int nIndex, CDaoRelationInfo& relinfo, DWORD
➥dwInfoOptions = AFX_DAO_PRIMARY_INFO );
void GetRelationInfo( LPCTSTR lpszName, CDaoRelationInfo& relinfo, DWORD
➥dwInfoOptions = AFX_DAO_PRIMARY_INFO );
```

where

nIndex	The index of the relation in the relation collection.
relinfo	A reference to a `CDaoRelationInfo` object that returns the requested information.
dwInfoOptions	Options that specify what information about the relation to return.
lpszName	A string containing the name of the relation.

The `GetRelationInfo` method will return information about the specified relation.

Valid values for *dwInfoOptions* include

AFX_DAO_PRIMARY_INFO	Name, table, foreign table.
AFX_DAO_SECONDARY_INFO	All available information.

The `GetRelationInfo` method can throw the CMemoryException or the CDaoException.

The `GetTableDefCount` Method

```
short GetTableDefCount( );
```

Returns the number of tabledefs defined in this database.

This method can throw the CDaoException or the CMemoryException exception.

The GetTableDefInfo Method

```
void GetTableDefInfo( int nIndex, CDaoTableDefInfo& tabledefinfo, DWORD
➡dwInfoOptions = AFX_DAO_PRIMARY_INFO );
void GetTableDefInfo( LPCTSTR lpszName, CDaoTableDefInfo& tabledefinfo,
➡DWORD dwInfoOptions = AFX_DAO_PRIMARY_INFO );
```

where

nIndex	The index of the tabledef in the tabledef collection.
tabledefinfo	A reference to a CDaoTableDefInfo object that returns the requested information.
dwInfoOptions	Options that specify what information about the tabledef to return.
lpszName	A string containing the name of the tabledef.

The GetTableDefInfo method will return information about the specified tabledef.

Valid values for dwInfoOptions include

AFX_DAO_PRIMARY_INFO	Name, updatable, attributes
AFX_DAO_SECONDARY_INFO	Name, updatable, attributes, date created, date last updated, source table name, connect
AFX_DAO_ALL_INFO	All available information

The GetTableDefInfo method can throw the CMemoryException or the CDaoException.

The GetVersion Method

```
BOOL GetVersion();
```

Returns the version of the Microsoft JET database file.

The GetVersion method can throw the CMemoryException or the CDaoException.

The IsOpen Method

```
BOOL IsOpen() const;
```

Returns TRUE if this CDaoDatabase object is currently open.

The Open Method

```
void Open( LPCTSTR lpszName, BOOL bExclusive = FALSE, BOOL bReadOnly =
➡FALSE, LPCTSTR lpszConnect = _T("") );
```

where

lpszName	The filename for the database being opened. This can be a local name such as c:\mydb\data.mdb or a UNC (universal naming convention) such as \\myserver\c\mydb\data.mdb.
lpszExclusive	If TRUE, this file is opened for exclusive access.
bReadOnly	If TRUE, this file will be opened read-only.
lpszConnect	The connect string.

The Open method is used to open a data connection to a JET file. If there is not enough information to properly open the database, a dialog box will be displayed to prompt the user for remaining information.

The Open method can throw the CMemoryException or the CDaoException.

C

The `SetQueryTimeout` Method

`void SetQueryTimeout( DWORD dwSeconds );`

where

> `dwSeconds`   Specifies the amount of time to wait for a query to complete.

The `SetQueryTimeout` method can throw the CMemoryException or the CDaoException.

CDaoQueryDef

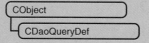

A DAO query definition encapsulates a database query. This query can be created in memory, or it can be saved in a database. This query object can then be used to create a CDaoRecordset that actually accesses the data.

For an example of `CDaoQueryDef`, see the DAOEx example found on the CD-ROM that accompanies this book.

Header Files

The following header files should be included when using this class:

`afxdao.h`

Properties

The `CDaoDatabase` class has the following properties:

`m_pWorkspace`	A pointer to the workspace for this object
`m_pDAODatabase`	A pointer to the underlying DAO database

Methods

The `CDaoQueryDef` class has the following methods:

`CDaoQueryDef`	The constructor
`Append`	Append this querydef
`CanUpdate`	Are updates supported
`Close`	Close the object
`Create`	Create a querydef object
`Execute`	Execute this querydef
`GetConnect`	Get the connect string
`GetDateCreated`	Get the date this query was created
`GetDateLastUpdated`	Get the last date this query was updated
`GetFieldCount`	Get the field count for this query
`GetFieldInfo`	Get info about the specified field
`GetName`	Get the name of the querydef
`GetODBCTimeout`	Get the timeout value for this querydef to execute

GetParameterCount	Get the count of the parameters used by this querydef
GetParameterInfo	Get information about the specified parameter
GetParamValue	Get the value of the specified parameter
GetRecordsAffected	Get the number of records affected by a query
GetReturnsRecords	Did this querydef return any records
GetSQL	Get the SQL form of this query
GetType	Get the query type
IsOpen	Is this object open?
Open	Open an existing querydef
SetConnect	Set the connect string
SetName	Set the name of the querydef
SetODBCTimeout	Get the timeout value for this querydef to execute
SetParamValue	Set the value of the specified parameter
SetReturnsRecords	Set whether the querydef returned any records
SetSQL	Set the querydef's SQL string

The CDaoQueryDef Constructor

The CDaoQueryDef creates the CDaoQueryDef object. The CDaoQueryDef constructor is used as follows:

CDaoQueryDef(CDaoDatabase *pDatabase);

where

    pDatabase   A pointer to an open CDaoDatabase object.

The Append Method

virtual void Append();

Append this querydef to the JET database file.

The Append method can throw the CMemoryException or the CDaoException.

The CanUpdate Method

BOOL CanUpdate();

Returns TRUE if this database supports updates. If not, it is a read-only database.

The CanUpdate method can throw the CMemoryException or the CDaoException.

The Close Method

virtual void Close();

The Close method should be called when the querydef is no longer needed in memory. This will not delete it from the database file.

The Close method can throw the CMemoryException or the CDaoException.

The Create Method

virtual void Create(LPCTSTR lpszName = NULL, LPCTSTR lpszSQL = NULL);

where

lpszName	A unique name for this querydef. If NULL, a temporary querydef is created. A temporary querydef will not be saved.
lpszSQL	A string specifying the query to run. If NULL, SetSQL must later be called.

The Create method will create a new querydef in a JET database.

The Create method can throw the CMemoryException or the CDAOException.

The Execute Method

```
virtual void Execute( int nOptions = dbFailOnError );
```

where

nOptions	A bitmask of options related to the integrity of the query.

The Execute method will run the query defined by the querydef object.

Possible values for *nOptions* include

dbDenyWrite	Deny write access to other users.
dbInconsistent	Inconsistent updates.
dbConsistent	Consistent updates.
dbSQLPassThrough	Pass the SQL statement directly through to ODBC.
dbFailOnError	Roll back if an error occurs.
dbSeeChanges	Generate a runtime error if another user changes the data being edited.

The Execute method can throw the CMemoryException or the CDaoException.

The GetConnect Method

```
CString GetConnect();
```

Returns the connect string associated with the CDAODatabase object for this querydef.

The GetConnect method can throw the CMemoryException or the CDaoException.

The GetDateCreated Method

```
COleDateTime GetDateCreated();
```

Returns the date that this querydef was created.

The GetDateCreated method can throw the CMemoryException or the CDaoException.

The GetDateLastUpdated Method

```
COleDateTime GetDateLastUpdated();
```

Returns the date that this querydef was last updated.

The GetDateLastUpdated method can throw the CMemoryException or the CDaoException.

The GetFieldCount Method

```
short GetFieldCount();
```

Returns the number of fields in this querydef.

The GetFieldCount method can throw the CMemoryException or the CDaoException.

The `GetFieldInfo` Method

```
void GetFieldInfo( int nIndex, CDaoFieldInfo& fieldinfo, DWORD
➥dwInfoOptions = AFX_DAO_PRIMARY_INFO );
void GetFieldInfo( LPCTSTR lpszName, CDaoFieldInfo& fieldinfo, DWORD
➥dwInfoOptions = AFX_DAO_PRIMARY_INFO );
```

where

nIndex	The index of the field in the field collection.
fieldinfo	A reference to a `CDaoFieldInfo` object that returns the requested information.
dwInfoOptions	Options that specify what information to return about the field.
lpszName	A string containing the name of the field.

The `GetFieldInfo` method will return information about the specified field.

Valid values for dwInfoOptions include

AFX_DAO_PRIMARY_INFO	Name, type, size, and attributes.
AFX_DAO_SECONDARY_INFO	Name, type, size, attributes, ordinal position, required, allow zero length string, source field, foreign name, source table, collating order.
AFX_DAO_ALL_INFO	All available information.

The `GetFieldInfo` method can throw the CMemoryException or the CDaoException.

The `GetName` Method

```
CString GetName();
```

Returns the name of the querydef.

The `GetName` method can throw the CMemoryException or the CDaoException.

The `GetODBCTimeout` Method

```
short GetODBCTimeout();
```

Returns the number of seconds to wait for the results of this querydef.

The `GetODBCTimeout` method can throw the CMemoryException or the CDaoException.

The `GetParameterCount` Method

```
short GetParameterCount();
```

Returns the number of parameters in this querydef.

The `GetParameterCount` method can throw the CMemoryException or the CDaoException.

The `GetParameterInfo` Method

```
void GetParameterInfo( int nIndex, CDaoParameterInfo& paraminfo, DWORD
➥dwInfoOptions = AFX_DAO_PRIMARY_INFO );
void GetParameterInfo( LPCTSTR lpszName, CDaoParameterInfo& paraminfo,
➥DWORD dwInfoOptions = AFX_DAO_PRIMARY_INFO );
```

where

C

nIndex	The index of the parameter in the parameter collection.
paraminfo	A reference to a `CDaoParameterInfo` object that returns the requested information.
dwInfoOptions	Options that specify what information about the parameter to return.
lpszName	A string containing the name of the parameter.

The `GetParameterInfo` method will return information about the specified parameter.

Valid values for `dwInfoOptions` include

AFX_DAO_PRIMARY_INFO   Name, type

The `GetParameterInfo` method can throw the CMemoryException or the CDaoException.

The `GetParamValue` Method

```
COleVariant GetParamValue( LPCTSTR lpszName );
COleVariant GetParamValue( int nIndex );
```

where

lpszName	The name of the specified parameter.
nIndex	The index of the specified parameter.

Returns the value of the specified parameter.

The `GetParamValue` method can throw the CMemoryException or the CDAOException.

The `GetRecordsAffected` Method

```
long GetRecordsAffected();
```

Returns the number of records affected by the last `Execute`.

The `GetRecordsAffected` method can throw the CMemoryException or the CDaoException.

The `GetReturnsRecords` Method

```
BOOL GetReturnsRecords();
```

Returns TRUE if this query will return records.

The `GetReturnsRecords` method can throw the CMemoryException or the CDaoException.

The `GetSQL` Method

```
CString GetSQL();
```

Returns the SQL statement that drives this querydef.

The `GetSQL` method can throw the CMemoryException or the CDaoException.

The `GetType` Method

```
short GetType();
```

Returns what type of query this is.

Valid return type numbers are

dbQSelect	Select
dbQAction	Action
dbQCrosstab	Crosstab

dbQDelete	Delete
dbQUpdate	Update
dbQAppend	Append
dbQMakeTable	Make-table
dbQDDL	Data-definition
dbQSQLPassThrough	Pass-through
dbQSetOperation	Union
dbQSPTBulk	Used with dbQSQLPassThrough to specify a query that does not return records

The GetType method can throw the CMemoryException or the CDaoException.

The IsOpen Method

`BOOL IsOpen() const;`

Returns TRUE if this querydef object is currently open.

The Open Method

`virtual void Open( LPCTSTR lpszName = NULL );`

where

> *lpszName*   The name of the querydef you wish to load.

The Open method will open a previously saved querydef.

The Open method can throw the CMemoryException or the CDaoException.

The SetConnect Method

`void SetConnect( LPCTSTR lpszConnect );`

where

> *lpszConnect*   The connect string.

The SetConnect method will set the connect string to the value specified.

The Create method can throw the CMemoryException or the CDAOException.

The SetName Method

`void SetName( LPCTSTR lpszConnect );`

where

> *lpszConnect*   The new name as a string.

The SetName method will set the querydef name to the value specified.

The SetName method can throw the CMemoryException or the CDAOException.

The SetODBCTimeout Method

`void SetODBCTimeout( short nODBCTimeout );`

where

> *nODBCTimeout*   The time in seconds that will be waited for an ODBC timeout.

The SetODBCTimeout method will set the ODBC timeout to the value specified.

The SetODBCTimeout method can throw the CMemoryException or the CDAOException.

The SetParamValue Method

```
void SetParamValue( LPCTSTR lpszName, const COleVariant& varValue );
void SetParamValue( int nOrdinal, const COleVariant& varValue );
```

where

lpszName	The name of the target parameter value to change.
nOrdinal	The index of the target parameter value to change.
varValue	The value to assign to this parameter.

The SetParamValue method will set the specified parameter to the value specified.

The SetParamValue method can throw the CMemoryException or the CDAOException.

The SetReturnsRecords Method

```
void SetReturnsRecords( BOOL bReturnsRecords );
```

where

bReturnsRecords	Sets whether this querydef returns records.

The SetReturnsRecords allows a pass-through SQL query to inform the program whether it is going to return records.

The SetReturnsRecords method can throw the CMemoryException or the CDAOException.

The SetSQL Method

```
void SetSQL( LPCTSTR lpszSQL );
```

where

lpszSQL	A valid SQL string to execute for this querydef.

The SetSQL method allows the SQL statement that drives the querydef to be specified.

The SetSQL method can throw the CMemoryException or the CDAOException.

CDaoRecordset

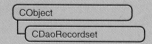

Any database query returns records. In MFC, these records are referred to as recordsets. CDaoRecordset allows access to this set of records.

For an example of CDaoRecordset, see the DAOEx example found on the CD-ROM that accompanies this book.

Header Files

The following header files should be included when using this class:

afxdao.h

Properties

The CDaoRecordset class has the following properties:

m_bCheckChacheForDirtyFields	Check cache for dirty fields
m_pDAORecordset	A pointer to the underlying DAO recordset
m_nFields	How many fields per row
m_nParams	The number of parameters
m_pDatabase	A pointer to the underlying DAO database
m_strFilter	String used to construct an SQL WHERE clause
m_strSort	String used to construct a ORDER BY clause

Methods

The CDaoRecordset class has the following methods:

CDaoRecordset	The constructor
AddNew	Prepare to add a new record
CanAppend	Are appends supported?
CanBookmark	Are bookmarks supported?
CancelUpdate	Stop a previously started update
CanRestart	Are restarts supported?
CanScroll	Is scrolling supported?
CanTransact	Are transactions supported?
CanUpdate	Are updates supported?
Close	Close this recordset
Delete	Delete the current record
Edit	Prepare to edit the current record
FillCache	Fill the local cache
Find	Find a record that matches a string
FindFirst	Find the first record that matches a string
FindLast	Find the last record that matches a string
FindNext	Find the next record that matches a string
FindPrev	Find the previous record that matches a string
GetAbsolutePosition	Get the current record number
GetBookmark	Get a bookmark to the current record
GetCacheSize	Get the size of the local cache
GetCacheStart	Get a bookmark of the first cached record
GetCurrentIndex	Get the name of the last index used on this recordset
GetDateCreated	Get the time the underlying table was created
GetDateLastUpdated	Get the time the underlying table was updated
GetEditMode	Get the editing state
GetFieldCount	Get the field count for this recordset

GetFieldInfo	Get information about the specified field
GetFieldValue	Get the value for the specified field
GetIndexCount	Get a count of how many indices were used for this recordset
GetIndexInfo	Get information about the specified index
GetLastModifiedBookmark	Get a bookmark to the last modified record
GetLockingMode	Get the locking mode
GetName	Get the name of this recordset
GetParamValue	Get the value of the specified parameter
GetPercentPosition	Get the percent position of a record
GetRecordCount	Get a count of how many records have been accessed
GetSQL	Get the SQL string for this recordset
GetType	Get the recordset type
GetValidationRule	Get the validation rule for the specified field
GetValidationText	Get the text displayed for validation failure
IsBOF	Is record before the beginning of the recordset?
IsDeleted	Is this record deleted?
IsEOF	Is this record after the end of the recordset?
IsFieldDirty	Is this field different than what is stored in the table?
IsFieldNull	Is this field NULL?
IsFieldNullable	Can this field be NULL?
IsOpen	Is this recordset open?
Move	Move a specified number of records
MoveFirst	Move to the first record
MoveLast	Move to the last record
MoveNext	Move to the next record
MovePrev	Move to the previous record
Open	Create a new recordset
Requery	Requery the recordset against the database
Seek	Locate a record using an index
SetAbsolutePosition	Set the position by absolute record number
SetBookmark	Move to the specified bookmark
SetCacheSize	Set the size of the local cache
SetCacheStart	Set the record to be first cached
SetCurrentIndex	Set an index on a table
SetFieldDirty	Set whether the specified field has a different value than the database
SetFieldNull	Set the specified field to have a NULL value
SetFieldValue	Set the value of the specified field
SetFieldValueNull	Set the specified field to have a NULL value

SetLockingMode	Set the record-locking mode
SetParamValue	Set the value of the specified parameter
SetParamValueNull	Set the value of the specified parameter to NULL
SetPercentPosition	Set the percent position of the record
Update	Complete an AddNew or Edit method

The following methods are usually overridden by the application program.

DoFieldExchange	Called to exchange data between field data members and the data source
GetDefaultDBName	Get the default data source
GetDefaultSQL	Get the default SQL string

The CDaoRecordset Constructor

The CDaoRecordset constructor creates the CDaoRecordset object. The CDaoRecordset constructor is used as follows:

```
CDaoRecordset( CDaoDatabase *pDatabase)
```

where

pDatabase	Contains a pointer to a CDaoDatabase object.

The AddNew Method

```
virtual void AddNew( );
```

The AddNew method begins the process for adding a new record to the recordset. If this is a dynaset recordset, the new record will be inserted at the end of the recordset. In a table recordset, if there is an index, records will be added in their proper order.

The recordset current record does not change when AddNew is called. To make the new record current, call SetBookmark to the bookmark identified by LastModified. Call Update to complete the process of adding a new record, or CancelUpdate to stop this process.

The AddNew method can throw the CMemoryException or the CDAOException.

The CanAppend Method

```
BOOL CanAppend();
```

Returns TRUE if records can be added using the AddNew method.

The CanBookmark Method

```
BOOL CanBookmark();
```

Returns TRUE the recordset supports bookmarks.

The CanBookmark method can throw the CMemoryException or the CDaoException.

The CanRestart Method

```
BOOL CanRestart();
```

Returns TRUE if Requery method can be called.

The CanRestart method can throw the CMemoryException or the CDaoException

C

The `CanScroll` Method

BOOL CanScroll();

Returns TRUE if recordset supports scrolling.

The `CanTransact` Method

BOOL CanTransact();

Returns TRUE if recordset supports transactions.

The CanTransact method can throw the CMemoryException or the CDaoException.

The `CanUpdate` Method

BOOL CanUpdate();

Returns TRUE if records can be updated from this recordset.

The CanAppend method can throw the CMemoryException or the CDaoException.

The `Close` Method

void Close();

The Close method should be called when the recordset is no longer needed in memory. This will not delete records from the database file.

The Close method can throw the CDaoException.

The `Delete` Method

virtual void Delete();

The Delete method deletes the current record. The deleted record will remain current until the recordset is scrolled to another record.

The Close method can throw the CMemoryException or the CDaoException.

The `Edit` Method

virtual void Edit( );

The Edit method begins the process for updating a record to the recordset. Any changes made to the fields after calling the Edit method will be stored to a buffer. This buffer will be copied to the disk when the Update method is called.

The Edit method can throw the CMemoryException or the CDAOException.

The `FillCache` Method

void FillCache(long* pSize = NULL, COleVariant* pBookmark = NULL);

where

pSize	A pointer to the number of rows to cache.
pBookmark	A pointer to a bookmark specifying where to start caching at.

The FillCache method will fill the recordset's cache with the specified records. If the pSize parameter is not provided, the CacheSize property value is used. If the pBookmark parameter is not provided, the CacheStart property is used.

The FillCache method can throw the CMemoryException or the CDAOException.

The Find Method

```
virtual BOOL Find( long lFindType, LPCTSTR lpszFilter );
```

where

lFindType	A value indicating the type of find desired.
lpszFilter	A pointer to a string that specifies what to search for (like the WHERE clause in an SQL statement without the word WHERE) used to locate the record.

Returns TRUE if a match was found.

The following are acceptable values for the lFindType parameter.

AFX_DAO_NEXT	Find the next matching string.
AFX_DAO_PREV	Find the previous matching string.
AFX_DAO_FIRST	Find the first matching string.
AFX_DAO_LAST	Find the last location matching string.

The Find method only works for dynaset and snapshot recordset types. Use the Seek method for table type recordsets.

The Find method can throw the CMemoryException or the CDAOException.

The FindFirst Method

```
BOOL FindFirst( LPCTSTR lpszFilter );
```

where

lpszFilter	A pointer to a string that specifies what to search for (like the WHERE clause in an SQL statement without the word WHERE) used to locate the record.

Returns TRUE if a match was found.

The FindFirst method finds the first record that matches the filter. The FindFirst method only works for dynaset and snapshot recordset types. Use the Seek method for table type recordsets.

The FindFirst method can throw the CMemoryException or the CDAOException.

The FindLast Method

```
BOOL FindLast( LPCTSTR lpszFilter );
```

where

lpszFilter	A pointer to a string that specifies what to search for (like the WHERE clause in an SQL statement without the word WHERE) used to locate the record.

Returns TRUE if a match was found.

The FindLast method finds the last record that matches the filter. The FindLast method only works for dynaset and snapshot recordset types. Use the Seek method for table type recordsets.

The FindLast method can throw the CMemoryException or the CDAOException.

The `FindNext` Method

BOOL FindNext(LPCTSTR lpszFilter);

where

    lpszFilter   A pointer to a string that specifies what to search for (like the WHERE clause in an SQL statement without the word WHERE) used to locate the record.

Returns TRUE if a match was found.

The FindNext method finds the next record that matches the filter. The FindNext method only works for dynaset and snapshot recordset types. Use the Seek method for table type recordsets.

The FindNext method can throw the CMemoryException or the CDAOException.

The `FindPrev` Method

BOOL FindPrev(LPCTSTR lpszFilter);

where

    lpszFilter   A pointer to a string that specifies what to search for (like the WHERE clause in an SQL statement without the word WHERE) used to locate the record.

Returns TRUE if a match was found.

The FindPrevious method finds the previous record that matches the filter. The FindPrevious method only works for dynaset and snapshot recordset types. Use the Seek method for table type recordsets.

The FindPrevious method can throw the CMemoryException or the CDAOException.

The `GetAbsolutePosition` Method

long GetAbsolutePosition( );

Returns TRUE if a match was found.

The GetAbsolutePosition method will return the physical record index for the current record in the recordset. Position 0 means the first record in the recordset.

The GetAbsolutePosition method can throw the CMemoryException or the CDAOException.

The `GetBookmark` Method

COleVariant GetBookmark( );

Returns a bookmark that uniquely identified this record.

The GetBookmark method will return a bookmark for the current record. This bookmark can be later used to return to this record.

The GetBookmark method can throw the CMemoryException or the CDAOException.

The `GetCacheSize` Method

long GetCacheSize( );

Returns the size of the cache.

The GetCacheStart method can throw the CMemoryException or the CDAOException.

The `GetCacheStart` Method

`COleVariant GetCacheStart( );`

Returns a bookmark to the first record that is cached.

The `GetCacheStart` method can throw the CMemoryException or the CDAOException.

The `GetCurrentIndex` Method

`CString GetCurrentIndex( );`

Returns a string specifying the last index used. Returns empty string if no index was used.

The `GetCurrentIndex` method can throw the CMemoryException or the CDAOException.

The `GetDateCreated` Method

`COleDateTime GetDateCreated();`

Returns the date that the base table was created.

The `GetDateCreated` method can throw the CMemoryException or the CDaoException.

The `GetDateLastUpdated` Method

`COleDateTime GetDateLastUpdated();`

Returns the date that the base was last updated.

The `GetDateLastUpdated` method can throw the CMemoryException or the CDaoException.

The `GetEditMode` Method

`short GetEditMode( );`

Returns the edit mode for the recordset.

This method will return one of the following values:

`dbEditNone`	No editing operation is in progress.
`dbEditInProgress`	`Edit` has been called.
`dbEditAdd`	`AddNew` has been called.

The `GetDateLastUpdated` method can throw the CMemoryException or the CDAOException.

The `GetFieldCount` Method

`short GetFieldCount();`

Returns the number of fields in this recordset.

The `GetFieldCount` method can throw the CMemoryException or the CDaoException.

The `GetFieldInfo` Method

```
void GetFieldInfo( int nIndex, CDaoFieldInfo& fieldinfo, DWORD
➡dwInfoOptions = AFX_DAO_PRIMARY_INFO );
void GetFieldInfo( LPCTSTR lpszName, CDaoFieldInfo& fieldinfo, DWORD
➡dwInfoOptions = AFX_DAO_PRIMARY_INFO );
```

where

`nIndex`	The index of the field in the field collection.
`fieldinfo`	A reference to a `CDaoFieldInfo` object that returns the requested information.

dwInfoOptions	Options that specify what information about the field to return.
lpszName	A string containing the name of the field.

The `GetFieldInfo` method will return information about the specified field.

Valid values for `dwInfoOptions` include

AFX_DAO_PRIMARY_INFO	Name, type, size, and attributes.
AFX_DAO_SECONDARY_INFO	Name, type, size, attributes, ordinal position, required, allow zero length string, source field, foreign name, source table, collating order.
AFX_DAO_ALL_INFO	All available information.

The `GetFieldInfo` method can throw the CMemoryException or the CDaoException.

The `GetFieldValue` Method

```
virtual void GetFieldValue( LPCTSTR lpszName, COleVariant& varValue );
virtual void GetFieldValue( int nIndex, COleVariant& varValue );
virtual COleVariant GetFieldValue( LPCTSTR lpszName );
virtual COleVariant GetFieldValue( int nIndex );
```

where

lpszName	The name of the field.
varValue	Will be changed to hold the value of the field.
nIndex	The index of the field.

Returns nothing if one of the two parameter calls is used. Returns a variant of the field's value if one of the parameter calls is used.

The `GetFieldValue` method is used to actually get data from fields in the recordset.

The `GetIndexCount` Method

```
short GetIndexCount( );
```

Returns the number of indexes available on a table type recordset.

The `GetIndexCount` method can throw the CMemoryException or the CDAOException.

The `GetIndexInfo` Method

```
void GetIndexInfo( int nIndex, CDaoIndexInfo& indexinfo, DWORD
➥dwInfoOptions = AFX_DAO_PRIMARY_INFO );
void GetIndexInfo( LPCTSTR lpszName, CDaoIndexInfo& indexinfo, DWORD
➥dwInfoOptions = AFX_DAO_PRIMARY_INFO );
```

where

nIndex	The index of the index in the index collection.
indexinfo	A reference to a CDaoIndexInfo object that returns the requested information.
dwInfoOptions	Options that specify what information about the index to return.
lpszName	A string containing the name of the index.

The `GetIndexInfo` method will return information about the specified index.

Valid values for dwInfoOptions include

AFX_DAO_PRIMARY_INFO	Name, field info, and fields.
AFX_DAO_SECONDARY_INFO	Name, field info, fields, primary, unique, clustered, ignore nulls, required and foreign.
AFX_DAO_ALL_INFO	All available information.

The GetIndexInfo method can throw the CMemoryException or the CDaoException.

The GetLastModifiedBookmark Method

COleVariant GetLastModifiedBookmark( );

Returns a bookmark for the record that was most recently updated or added.

The GetBookmark method will return a bookmark for the current record. This bookmark can be later used to return to this record.

The GetBookmark method can throw the CMemoryException or the CDAOException.

The GetLockingMode Method

BOOL GetLockingMode( );

Returns FALSE if locking is pessimistic or TRUE for optimistic locking.

Pessimistic locking locks a record the instant the Edit method is called. The record is released after the Update method is complete.

Optimistic locking locks a record only while the Update method is being called.

The GetLockingMode method can throw the CMemoryException or the CDAOException.

The GetName Method

CString GetName();

Returns the name of the recordset.

The GetName method can throw the CMemoryException or the CDaoException.

The GetParamValue Method

virtual COleVariant GetParamValue(int nIndex);
virtual COleVariant GetParamValue(LPCTSTR lpszName);

where

lpszName	The name of the parameter.
nIndex	The index of the field.

Returns a variant containing the value of the parameter.

The GetParamValue method can throw the CMemoryException or the CDaoException.

The GetPercentPosition Method

float GetPercentPosition();

Returns a float indicating the position of the current record base as a percent of the accessed records in the recordset. This percentage will be in the range of 0 to 100.

The GetPercentPosition method can throw the CMemoryException or the CDaoException.

C

The `GetRecordCount` Method

`long GetRecordCount();`

Returns the number of records accessed in the recordset.

The `GetRecordCount` method will only return the number of records accessed, not the total number of records. To get the total number of records actually in the recordset, you must call `MoveLast`, and then call `GetRecordCount`.

The `GetSQL` Method

`CString GetSQL();`

Returns the underlying SQL string for this the recordset.

The `GetSQL` method can throw the CMemoryException or the CDaoException.

The `GetType` Method

`short GetType();`

Returns the type of recordset that this object is. Can be any one of the following:

dbOpenTable	A table
dbOpenDynaset	A dynaset
dbOpenSnapshot	A snapshot

The `GetType` method can throw the CMemoryException or the CDaoException.

The `GetValidationRule` Method

`CString GetValidationRule();`

Returns the string value for the validation rule of this table.

The `GetValidationRule` method can throw the CMemoryException or the CDaoException.

The `GetValidationText` Method

`CString GetValidationText();`

Returns the string that is displayed if the validation rule is broken.

The `GetValidationText` method can throw the CMemoryException or the CDaoException.

The `IsBOF` Method

`BOOL IsBOF();`

Returns TRUE if the current record is before the beginning of the recordset.

The `IsBOF` method can throw the CMemoryException or the CDaoException.

The `IsDeleted` Method

`BOOL IsDeleted();`

Returns TRUE if the current record has been deleted.

The `IsDeleted` method can throw the CMemoryException or the CDaoException.

The `IsEOF` Method

`BOOL IsEOF();`

Returns TRUE if the current record is beyond the final record of the recordset.

The `IsEOF` method can throw the CMemoryException or the CDaoException.

The `IsFieldDirty` Method

BOOL IsFieldDirty(void *pv);

where

pv   A pointer to the field property to be checked.

Returns TRUE if the value of the indicated field has changed.

The `IsFieldDirty` method can throw the CMemoryException or the CDaoException.

The `IsFieldNull` Method

BOOL IsFieldNull(void *pv);

where

pv   A pointer to the field property to be checked.

Returns TRUE if the indicated field is NULL.

The `IsFieldNull` method can throw the CMemoryException or the CDaoException.

The `IsFieldNullable` Method

BOOL IsFieldNullable(void *pv);

where

pv   A pointer to the field property to be checked.

Returns TRUE if the indicated field can hold a NULL.

The `IsFieldNullable` method can throw the CMemoryException or the CDaoException.

The `IsOpen` Method

BOOL IsOpen() const;

Returns TRUE if this recordset is open.

 Caution Calling any of the Move methods when there are no records will throw an exception.

The `Move` Method

virtual void Move(long lRowsvoid *pv);

where

lRows   The number of rows to move.

The Move method will move the current record either forward or backward. Positive values for lRows will move forward. Negative values for lRows will move backward.

The Move method can throw the CMemoryException or the CDaoException.

The `MoveFirst` Method

`void MoveFirst();`

Move to the first record in the recordset.

The `MoveFirst` method can throw the CMemoryException or the CDaoException.

The `MoveLast` Method

`void MoveLast();`

Move to the last record in the recordset.

The `MoveLast` method can throw the CMemoryException or the CDaoException.

The `MoveNext` Method

`void MoveNext();`

Move to the next record in the recordset.

The `MoveNext` method can throw the CMemoryException or the CDaoException.

The `MovePrev` Method

`void MovePrev();`

Move to the previous record in the recordset.

The `MovePrev` method can throw the CMemoryException or the CDaoException.

The `Open` Method

```
virtual void Open( int nOpenType = AFX_DAO_USE_DEFAULT_TYPE, LPCTSTR
➥lpszSQL = NULL, int nOptions = 0 );
virtual void Open( CDaoTableDef* pTableDef, int nOpenType = dbOpenTable,
➥int nOptions = 0 );
virtual void Open( CDaoQueryDef* pQueryDef, int nOpenType = dbOpenDynaset,
➥int nOptions = 0 );
```

where

`nOpenType`	The type of recordset to open.
`lpszSQL`	SQL statement to build query from.
`nOptions`	Options for opening this recordset.
`pTableDef`	For table type recordset, this specifies the table to build recordset from.
`pQueryDef`	A querydef to build the recordset from.

Valid values for `nOpenType` include

`dbOpenDynaset`	For a dynaset-based recordset.
`dbOpenTable`	A table recordset.
`dbOpenSnapshot`	A snapshot-based recordset.

Valid values for lpszSQL include

A NULL pointer.	Open will call GetDefaultSQL to get the SQL string.
One or more tabledefs and/or querydefs.	Should be comma separated.
A SQL select.	
A pass-through query.	

One or more options may be ORed together to form the following list.

dbAppendOnly	New records can be appended (dynaset-type recordset only).
dbForwardOnly	The recordset is a forward-only scrolling snapshot.
dbSeeChanges	Generate an exception if another user changes this data.
dbDenyWrite	Do not allow other users to modify or add records.
dbDenyRead	Do not allow other users to view records (table-type recordset only).
dbReadOnly	Open in read-only mode.
dbInconsistent	Inconsistent updates are allowed (dynaset-type recordset only).
dbConsistent	Allow only consistent updates (dynaset-type recordset only).

The Open method opens a recordset and prepares it for use.

The Open method can throw the CMemoryException or the CDaoException.

The Requery Method
```
virtual void Requery();
```
Refresh the entire recordset from the database.

The Requery method can throw the CMemoryException or the CDaoException.

The Seek Method
```
BOOL Seek( LPCTSTR lpszComparison, COleVariant* pKey1, COleVariant* pKey2
= NULL, COleVariant* pKey3 = NULL );
BOOL Seek (LPCTSTR lpszComparison, COleVariant* pKeyArray, WORD nKeys );
```
where

lszComparison	One of the following string expressions: "<", "<=", "=", ">=", or ">".
pKey1	A pointer to a COleVariant value whose value is the first field in the index.
pKey2	A pointer to a COleVariant value whose value is the second field in the index.
pKey	A pointer to a COleVariant value whose value is the third field in the index.
pKeyArray	A pointer to an array of variants.
nKeys	The number of elements in the array.

The Seek method attempts to locate a record that matches the search criteria. Seek uses indexes set up on the tables to perform high-performance searches.

Returns NON-ZERO if matching records are found.

The Seek method can throw the CMemoryException or the CDaoException.

The `SetAbsolutePosition` Method

```
void SetAbsolutePosition(long lPosition);
```

where

    lPosition   The new current record based on ordinal position.

Call `SetAbsolutePosition` to move the current record by record number.

The `SetAbsolutePosition` method can throw the CMemoryException or the CDaoException.

The `SetBookmark` Method

```
void SetBookmark( COleVariant varBookmark );
```

where

    varBookmark   A bookmark to move the recordset to.

Call `SetBookmark` to move the current record to a bookmark.

The `SetBookmark` method can throw the CMemoryException or the CDaoException.

The `SetCacheSize` Method

```
void SetCacheSize( long lSize );
```

where

    lSize   The new size(in records) for the cache.

The `SetCacheSize` method can throw the CMemoryException or the CDaoException.

The `SetCacheStart` Method

```
void SetCacheStart( COleVariant varBookmark );
```

where

    varBookmark   The new starting location for the cache.

The `SetCacheStart` method can throw the CMemoryException or the CDaoException.

The `SetCurrentIndex` Method

```
void SetCurrentIndex( LPCTSTR lpszIndex );
```

where

    lpszIndex   The new index on this table.

The `SetCurrentIndex` method can throw the CMemoryException or the CDaoException.

The `SetFieldNull` Method

```
void SetFieldNull( void *pv, BOLL bNull = TRUE );
```

where

    pv   The data member to set to a NULL value.

    bNull   TRUE if this value should be set to NULL.

The `SetFieldNull` method can throw the CMemoryException or the CDaoException.

The `SetFieldValue` Method

```
void SetFieldValue( LPCTSTR lpszName, const COleVariant& varValue );
void SetFieldValue( int nOrdinal, const COleVariant& varValue );
void SetFieldValue( LPCTSTR lpszName, LPCTSTR lpszValue );
void SetFieldValue( int nOrdinal, LPCTSTR lpszValue );
```

where

lpszName	The field name to change.
varValue	The new value for the field.
nOrdinal	The field index to change.
lpszValue	The new value for the field as a string.

The `SetFieldValue` method sets the actual value of a field.

The `SetFieldValue` method can throw the CMemoryException or the CDaoException.

The `SetFieldValueNull` Method

```
void SetFieldValueNull( short nIndex );
void SetFieldValueNull( LPCTSTR lpszName );
```

where

lpszName	The field name to change.
nIndex	The field index to change.

The `SetFieldValueNull` method sets the value of a field to null.

The `SetFieldValueNull` method can throw the CMemoryException or the CDaoException.

The `SetLockingMode` Method

```
void SetLockingMode( BOOL bPessimistic );
```

where

pPessimistic	FALSE if locking is pessimistic, or TRUE for optimistic locking.

Pessimistic locking locks a record the instant that the `Edit` method is called. The record releases after the `Update` method is complete.

Optimistic locking locks a record only while the `Update` method is being called.

The `SetLockingMode` method can throw the CMemoryException or the CDaoException.

The `SetParamValue` Method

```
virtual void SetParamValue( int nIndex, const COleVariant& var );
virtual void SetParamValue( LPCTSTR lpszName, const COleVariant& var );
```

where

lpszName	The name of the parameter to set.
var	A variant with the new value of the parameter.
nIndex	The index of the parameter to change.

The `SetParamValue` method sets the actual value of a parameter.

The `SetParamValue` method can throw the CMemoryException or the CDaoException.

The `SetParamValueNull` Method

```
void SetParamValueNull( short nIndex );
void SetParamValueNull( LPCTSTR lpszName );
```

where

lpszName	The name of the parameter to set.
nIndex	The index of the parameter to change.

The `SetParamValueNull` method sets the value of a parameter to `NULL`.

The `SetParamValueNull` method can throw the CMemoryException or the CDaoException.

The `SetPercentPosition` Method

```
void SetPercentPosition( float fPosition );
```

where

fPosition	The new current record position by percent.

The `SetPercentPosition` method sets the current position to a percentage of the records accessed.

The `SetPercentPosition` method can throw the CMemoryException or the CDaoException.

The `Update` Method

```
virtual void Update();
```

Complete an add or update.

The `Update` method can throw the CMemoryException or the CDaoException.

CDaoRecordView

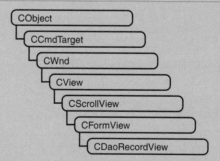

CDaoRecordView is a specialized view for accessing DAO recordsets. The view works from a dialog template resource. This template resource contains standard dialog box components that represent each field in the record. CDaoRecordView supplies a default implementation for basic record navigation and updating.

For an example of CDaoRecordView, see the DAOEx example found on the CD-ROM that accompanies this book.

Header Files

The following header files should be included when using this class:

```
afxdao.h
```

Methods

The CDaoRecordView class has the following methods:

CDaoRecordView	The constructor
OnGetRecordset	Created by Class Wizard, get a pointer to this object
IsOnLastRecord	Is the last record being displayed?
IsOnFirstRecord	Is the first record being displayed?
OnMove	Called when the user moves to a new record

The CDaoRecordView Constructor

The CDaoRecordView creates the CDaoRecordView object. The CDaoRecordView constructor is used as follows:

```
CDaoRecordView( LPCSTR lpszTemplateName );
CDaoRecordView( UINT nIDTemplate );
```

where

lpszTemplateName	The string value of a resource template that defines the look and feel of this form.
nIDTemplate	The int value of a resource template that defines the look and feel of this form.

The OnGetRecordset Method

```
virtual void CDaoRecordset *OnGetRecordset();
```

where

The OnGetRecordset method returns a pointer to this object. Child classes should override this method and return a pointer that matches the child class.

The IsOnLastRecord Method

```
BOOL IsOnLastRecord();
```

Returns TRUE if the user is on the last record.

The IsOnFirstRecord Method

```
BOOL IsOnFirstRecord();
```

Returns TRUE if the user is on the first record.

CDaoWorkspace

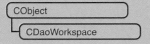

A workspace object manages all DAO database connections. Generally, only one CDaoWorkspace object is needed. One single user account can be used by a CDaoWorkspace object. If more than one user account is needed, then multiple CDaoWorkspace databases will be needed.

For an example of CDaoWorkspace, see the DAOEx example found on the CD-ROM that accompanies this book.

Header Files

The following header files should be included when using this class:

`afxdao.h`

Properties

The `CDaoWorkspace` class has the following properties:

`m_pDAOWorkspace`	Pointer to the underlying DAO workspace.

Methods

The `CDaoWorkspace` class has the following methods:

`CDaoWorkspace`	The constructor
`Append`	Append a workspace
`BeginTrans`	Begin a transaction
`Close`	Close the object
`CommitTrans`	Commit a transaction
`CompactDatabase`	Compact the underlying database
`Create`	Create a new DAO workspace
`GetDatabaseCount`	Get the number of databases in this workspace
`GetDatabaseInfo`	Get information about the specified database
`GetIniPath`	Get the JET database Registry settings location
`GetIsolateODBCTrans`	Are ODBC transactions isolated?
`GetLoginTimeout`	Get the timeout value for a login
`GetName`	Get the name of the workspace
`GetUserName`	Get the user's name
`GetVersion`	Get the version of the database engine
`GetWorkspaceCount`	Get the count of existing workspaces
`GetWorkspaceInfo`	Get information about the specified workspace
`Idle`	Enable the database to perform background tasks
`IsOpen`	Is the workspace open
`Open`	Open the workspace
`RepairDatabase`	Attempt to repair the database
`Rollback`	Roll back; discard all changes in this transaction
`SetDefaultPassword`	Set the default password
`SetDefaultUser`	Set the default user name
`SetIniPath`	Set the Registry location for JET
`SetIsolateODBCTrans`	Set whether ODCB transactions are isolated
`SetLoginTimeout`	Set the login timeout value

The `CDaoWorkspace` Constructor

The `CDaoWorkspace` creates the `CDaoWorkspace` object. The `CDaoWorkspace` constructor is used as follows:

```
CDaoWorkspace()
```

The `Append` Method

```
void Append();
```

The `Append` method should be called after the `Create` method is called. `Append` adds the newly created workspace to the database engine's workspace's collection.

Can throw CDaoException and CMemoryException.

The `BeginTrans` Method

```
BOOL BeginTrans();
```

Returns `TRUE` if successful.

A transaction is a group of SQL commands that can be canceled, or rolled back, if desired. When the `BeginTrans` method is called a transaction begins. All SQL commands issued will not become permanent until a `CommitTrans` method call is made. If `Rollback` is called, the changes will be discarded.

Can throw CDaoException and CMemoryException.

The `Close` Method

```
virtual void Close();
```

The `Close` method closes this workspace. This method also closes all objects contained in the workspace.

Can throw CDaoException and CMemoryException.

The `CommitTrans` Method

```
BOOL CommitTrans();
```

Returns `TRUE` if successful.

A transaction is a group of SQL commands that can be canceled, or rolled back, if desired. The `CommitTrans` method will commit all changes since the last `BeginTrans` call. To cancel the changes call the `Rollback` method.

Can throw CDaoException and CMemoryException.

The `CompactDatabase` Constructor

```
static void PASCAL CompactDatabase( LPCTSTR lpszSrcName, LPCTSTR
➥lpszDestName, LPCTSTR lpszLocale = dbLangGeneral, int nOptions = 0 );
static void PASCAL CompactDatabase( LPCTSTR lpszSrcName, LPCTSTR
➥lpszDestName, LPCTSTR lpszLocale, int nOptions, LPCTSTR lpszPassword );
```

where

`lpszSrcName`	The source database to compact.
`lpszDestName`	The destination database that will be created to hold the compacted version of the source database.
`lpszPassword`	The password if this is a password-protected database.
`lpszLocale`	Specifies the collating order for the new database.
`nOptions`	Specifies options for creating the new database.

Possible values for `lpszLocale` include

`dbLangGeneral`	English, German, French, Portuguese, Italian, and Modern Spanish
`dbLangArabic`	Arabic
`dbLangCyrillic`	Russian
`dbLangCzech`	Czech
`dbLangDutch`	Dutch
`dbLangGreek`	Greek
`dbLangHebrew`	Hebrew
`dbLangHungarian`	Hungarian
`dbLangIcelandic`	Icelandic
`dbLangNordic`	Nordic languages (Microsoft JET database engine version 1.0 only)
`dbLangNorwdan`	Norwegian and Danish
`dbLangPolish`	Polish
`dbLangSpanish`	Traditional Spanish
`dbLangSwedfin`	Swedish and Finnish
`dbLangTurkish`	Turkish

Possible values for `dwOptions` include

`dbEncrypt`	Encrypt the database while compacting.
`dbDecrypt`	Decrypt the database while compacting.
`dbVersion10`	Create a database with Microsoft JET database version 1.0.
`dbVersion11`	Create a database with Microsoft JET database version 1.1.
`dbVersion20`	Create a database with Microsoft JET database version 2.0.
`dbVersion30`	Create a database with Microsoft JET database version 3.0.

The `CompactDatabase` method will compact a database so it takes up less disk space. It does this by removing empty space that accumulates in a database after user activity.

The `Update` method can throw the CMemoryException or the CDaoException.

The `Create` Method

```
void Create( LPCTSTR lpszName, LPCTSTR lpszUserName, LPCTSTR lpszPassword );
```
where

lpszName	A name for the new workspace object.
lpszUserName	The name of the workspace owner.
lpszPassword	The password for the workspace owner.

The `Create` method will create a new workspace object.

The `Create` method can throw the CMemoryException or the CDAOException.

The `GetDatabaseCount` Method

```
short GetDatabaseCount();
```

Returns the number of databases in this workspace.

The GetDatabaseCount method can throw the CMemoryException or the CDaoException.

The GetIniPath Method

`static CString PASCAL GetIniPath();`

Returns a string that represents Registry location of the DAO information.

The GetIniPath method can throw the CMemoryException or the CDAOException.

The GetIsolateODBCTrans Method

`BOOL GetIsolateODBCTrans();`

Returns TRUE if ODBC transactions are isolated.

When more than one connection is open to an ODBC data source, these connections can either be isolated from each other, or virtualized into the same connection. Normally, these transactions do not need to be isolated. The GetIsolateODBCTrans method tells whether these transactions are being isolated.

The GetIsolateODBCTrans method can throw the CMemoryException or the CDAOException.

The GetLoginTimeout Method

`static short PASCAL GetLoginTimeout();`

Returns the number of seconds before a login attempt will timeout.

The GetLoginTimeout method can throw the CMemoryException or the CDaoException.

The GetName Method

`CString GetName();`

Returns the name of the workspace.

The GetName method can throw the CMemoryException or the CDaoException.

The GetUserName Method

`CString GetUserName();`

Returns the name of the user who is logged into the database.

The GetUserName method can throw the CMemoryException or the CDaoException.

The GetVersion Method

`static PASCAL CString GetVersion();`

Returns the version of the database engine.

The GetVersion method can throw the CMemoryException or the CDaoException.

The GetWorkspaceCount Method

`short GetWorkspaceCount();`

Returns the number of workspaces in the workspace collection.

The GetWorkspaceCount method can throw the CMemoryException or the CDaoException.

C

The `GetWorkspaceInfo` Method

```
void GetWorkspaceInfo( int nIndex, CDaoWorkspaceInfo& wkspcinfo, DWORD
➡dwInfoOptions = AFX_DAO_PRIMARY_INFO );
void GetWorkspaceInfo( LPCTSTR lpszName, CDaoWorkspaceInfo& wkspcinfo,
➡DWORD dwInfoOptions = AFX_DAO_PRIMARY_INFO );
```

where

nIndex	The index of the workspace in the workspace collection.
wkspcinfo	A reference to a CDaoWorkspaceInfo object that returns the requested information.
dwInfoOptions	Options that specify what information about the index to return.
lpszName	A string containing the name of the workspace.

The `GetWorkspaceInfo` method will return information about the specified database.

Valid values for `dwInfoOptions` include

AFX_DAO_PRIMARY_INFO	Name.
AFX_DAO_SECONDARY_INFO	Name, username.
AFX_DAO_ALL_INFO	All available information.

The `GetWorkspaceInfo` method can throw the CMemoryException or the CDaoException.

The `Idle` Method

```
static void PASCAL Idle(int nAction = dbFreeLocks);
```

Call `Idle` method to give the database engine a chance to process background tasks.

The `Idle` method can throw the CMemoryException or the CDaoException.

The `IsOpen` Method

```
BOOL IsOpen();
```

Returns TRUE if the workspace object is open.

The `IsOpen` method can throw the CMemoryException or the CDaoException.

The `Open` Method

```
virtual void Open( LPCTSTR lpszName = NULL );
```

where

lpszName	The name of the workspace to open, or NULL to open the default workspace.

The `Open` method will open a workspace.

The `Open` method can throw the CMemoryException or the CDaoException.

The `RepairDatabase` Method

```
static void PASCAL RepairDatabase(LPCTSTR lpszName );
```

where

lpszName	The full pathname of a database to repair.

The RepairDatabase method will attempt to repair a corrupted JET database.

The RepairDatabase method can throw the CMemoryException or the CDaoException.

The Rollback Method

BOOL Rollback();

Returns TRUE if successful.

A transaction is a group of SQL commands that can be canceled, or rolled back, if desired. All database actions since the last BeginTrans call will be discarded when the Rollback method is called.

The SetDefaultPassword Method

static void PASCAL SetDefaultPassword(LPCTSTR lpszName);

where

    lpszName   The default password.

The SetDefaultPassword method will set the default user password for a workspace.

The SetDefaultPassword method can throw the CMemoryException or the CDAOException.

The SetDefaultUser Method

void SetDefaultUser(LPCTSTR lpszDefaultUser);

where

    lpszName   The default username.

The SetDefaultUsername method will set the default username for a workspace.

The SetDefaultPassword method can throw the CMemoryException or the CDAOException.

The SetIniPath Method

static void PASCAL SetIniPath(LPCTSTR lpszRegistrySubkey);

where

    lpszRegistrySubkey   The Registry entry that holds all DAO settings.

The SetIniPath method will set a new Registry location to contain the DAO configuration information.

The SetIniPath method can throw the CMemoryException or the CDAOException.

The SetIsolateODBCTrans Method

void SetIsolateODBCTrans(BOOL bIsolateODBCTrans);

where

    bIsolateODBCTrans   TRUE if ODBC transactions are to be isolated, FALSE if not.

When more than one connection is open to an ODBC data source, these connections can either be isolated from each other, or virtualized into the same connection. Normally, these transactions do not need to be isolated. The SetIsolateODBCTrans method tells whether these transactions are to be isolated.

The SetIsolateODBCTrans method can throw the CMemoryException or the CDAOException.

C

The SetLoginTimeout Method

`static void PASCAL SetLoginTimeout( DWORD dwSeconds );`

where

dwSeconds   Specifies the amount of time to wait to login to a data source.

CDatabase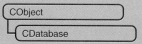

A CDatabase object represents a connection to an ODBC data source. ODBC data sources are usually referred to by data source names (DSNs), which are defined using the ODBC32 control panel in the Windows Control Panel. From this database connection recordsets are generated.

For an example of CDatabase, see the ODBCEx example found on the CD-ROM that accompanies this book.

Header Files

The following header files should be included when using this class:

`afxdb.h`

Properties

The CDatabase class has the following properties:

    m_hdbc   ODBC connection handle

Methods

The CDatabase class has the following methods:

BeginTrans	Begin a transaction
BindParameters	Bind parameters before an Execute
Cancel	Cancel an asynchronous database operation
CanTransact	Are transactions supported?
CanUpdate	Are updates supported?
Close	Close this data source connection
CommitTrans	Commit this transaction to the database
ExecuteSQL	Execute a SQL command
GetBookmarkPersistence	Identify which options will not cause bookmarks to lose their values
GetConnect	Get the connection string
GetCursorCommitBehavior	Identify the effect of a commit on a cursor
GetCursorRollbackBehavior	Identify the effect of a rollback on a cursor
GetDatabaseName	Get the database name
IsOpen	Is this object open?

Open	Open the database object
OpenEx	Open the database object with extended options
Rollback	Discard changes in this transaction
SetLoginTimeout	Set the login timeout value
SetQueryTimeout	Set the query timeout value

The following method is usually overridden by the application program:

| OnSetOptions | Called when the options change |

The CDatabase Constructor

```
CDatabase();
```

The CDatabase creates the CDatabase object. In order to use the CDatabase object, the Open or OpenEx method must be called to establish a connection to a data source.

The BeginTrans Method

```
BOOL BeginTrans();
```

Returns TRUE if successful.

A transaction is a group of SQL commands that can be canceled, or rolled back, if desired. When the BeginTrans method is called, a transaction begins. All SQL commands issued will not become permanent until a CommitTrans method call is made. If Rollback is called, then the changes will be discarded.

The BindParameters Method

```
virtual void BindParameters( HSTMT hstmt);
```

where

| hstmt | Specifies the ODBC statement handle to bind parameters. |

This method can be overridden when the program needs to bind parameters before ExecuteSQL is called.

The Cancel Method

```
void Cancel( );
```

This method will cancel an asynchronous query that might be running. MFC no longer supports asynchronous queries, and as a result, this method is of limited value.

The CanTransact Method

```
BOOL CanTransact();
```

Returns TRUE if this data source supports transactions.

The CanUpdate Method

```
BOOL CanUpdate();
```

Returns TRUE if this data source supports updates. If not, it is a read-only data source.

The Close Method

```
virtual void Close();
```

The Close method disconnects from the data source. After the Close method is called, the CDatabase object can be reopened later to any valid data source. This method cancels any pending operations on the database. Any recordsets created from this database should be closed prior to closing the database.

C

The `CommitTrans` Method

BOOL CommitTrans();

Returns TRUE if successful.

A transaction is a group of SQL commands that can be canceled, or rolled back, if desired. The CommitTrans method will commit all changes since the last BeginTrans call. To cancel the changes, call the Rollback method.

The `ExecuteSQL` Method

void ExecuteSQL(LPCSTR lpszSQL);

where

     lpszSQL   A NULL terminated or CString containing a valid SQL statement.

The ExecuteSQL method will directly execute the SQL command given. ExecuteSQL does not return the results of the SQL command. Use a recordset to get back the results from a SQL command.

The ExecuteSQL method can throw the CDBException.

The `GetBookmarkPersistence` Method

DWORD GetBookmarkPersistence();

Returns a DWORD value that contains a bitmask for which operations enable bookmarks to remain valid.

A bookmark is a way to return to a specific record. Certain operations on the database will make these bookmarks invalid. The following values are ORed together to create a value that indicates which of them will not cause bookmarks to become invalid.

SQL_BP_CLOSE	Bookmarks remain valid after a call to Requery.
SQL_BP_DELETE	Bookmarks are valid for a row after that row has been deleted using Delete.
SQL_BP_DROP	Bookmarks are valid after the Close method is called.
SQL_BP_SCROLL	Bookmarks are valid after the Move method is called. If this is not set, bookmarks are not supported.
SQL_BP_TRANSACTION	Bookmarks are valid after a CommitTrans or Rollback call.
SQL_BP_UPDATE	Bookmarks are valid after their rows have been updated.
SQL_BP_OTHER_HSTMT	Bookmarks for one recordset are valid for another recordset.

The `GetConnect` Method

const CString& GetConnect() const;

Returns the connect string if this CDatabase object was opened with Open or OpenEx. Otherwise, an empty string is returned.

The `GetCursorCommitBehavior` Method

int GetCursorCommitBehavior();

Returns an int that specifies how transactions affect cursors.

The following return values specify how transactions affect cursors.

SQL_CB_CLOSE	Requery must be called immediately following the commit for cursors to continue working.
SQL_CB_DELETE	The recordset must be closed and reopened for cursors to continue working.
SQL_CB_PRESERVE	No special precautions are needed.

The `GetCursorRollbackBehavior` Method

`int GetCursorRollbackBehavior();`

Returns an `int` that specifies how rollback transactions affect cursors.

The following return values specify how rollback transactions affect cursors.

SQL_CB_CLOSE	Requery must be called immediately following the commit for cursors to continue working.
SQL_CB_DELETE	The recordset must be closed and reopened for cursors to continue working.
SQL_CB_PRESERVE	No special precautions are needed.

The `GetDatabaseName` Method

`CString GetDatabaseName() const;`

Returns the database name if successful or an empty string if the method fails.

The `IsOpen` Method

`BOOL IsOpen() const;`

Returns TRUE if this CDatabase object is currently connected to a data source.

The `Open` Method

`virtual BOOL Open( LPCTSTR lpszDSN, BOOL bExclusive = FALSE, BOOL`
`➥bReadOnly = FALSE, LPCTSTR lpszConnect = "ODBC;", BOOL`
`➥bUseCursorLib = TRUE );`

where

lpszDSN	The data source name(DSN) to open a connection to.
bExclusive	Should this DSN be opened in exclusive mode? Not currently supported by MFC.
bReadOnly	Should this DSN be opened read-only?
lpszConnect	Specifies the connect string. This often includes the DSN, username, and password.
bUseCursorLib	Should the ODBC cursor library be used?

Returns TRUE if successful.

The Open method will open a connection to a data source. The information needed to connect to a data source is provided in the connect string. If not enough information is supplied, ODBC will present the user with a dialog that asks for the remaining information. The format of the connect string varies, depending on what sort of data source is being connected to.

The Open method can throw the CMemoryException or the CDBException.

The `OpenEx` Method

```
virtual BOOL OpenEx( LPCTSTR lpszConnectString, DWORD dwOptions = 0 );
```

where

    lpszConnectString   Specifies the connect string. This often includes the DSN, username, and password.

    dwOptions   A bitmask that specifies how to open this data source.

Returns TRUE if successful.

The `OpenEx` method will open a connection to a data source. The information needed to connect to a data source is provided in the connect string. If not enough information is supplied, ODBC will present the user with a dialog that asks for the remaining information. The format of the connect string varies, depending on what sort of data source is being connected to.

The following values may be ORed together to specify how to connect to the data source.

    `CDatabase::openExclusive`   Should this DSN be opened in exclusive mode. Not currently supported by MFC.

    `CDatabase::openReadOnly`   Open this DSN as read-only.

    `CDatabase::useCursorLib`   Use the ODBC cursor library.

    `CDatabase::noOdbcDialog`   Do not display the ODBC connection dialog box. Fail if not enough information in the connect string.

    `CDatabase::forceOdbcDialog`   Always display the ODBC connection dialog box.

The `OpenEx` method can throw the CMemoryException or the CDBException.

The `Rollback` Method

```
BOOL Rollback();
```

Returns TRUE if successful.

A transaction is a group of SQL commands that can be canceled, or rolled back, if desired. All database actions since the last `BeginTrans` call will be discarded when the `Rollback` method is called.

The `SetLoginTimeout` Method

```
void SetLoginTimeout( DWORD dwSeconds );
```

where

    dwSeconds   Specifies the amount of time to wait to login to a data source.

The `SetQueryTimeout` Method

```
void SetQueryTimeout( DWORD dwSeconds );
```

where

    dwSeconds   Specifies the amount of time to wait for a query to complete.

The `OnSetOptions` Method

```
virtual void OnSetOptions( HSTMT hstmt);
```

where

    hstmt   Specifies the ODBC statement handle that has options being set.

This method can be overridden when the program needs to set additional options before `ExecuteSQL` is called.

CDataExchange ⌐CDataExchange⌐

`CDataExchange` is rarely used directly by the application programmer. `CDataExchange` is used by MFC to move dialog box data between the dialog box controls and member variables of the dialog class.

Header Files

The following header file should be included when using this class:

`afxwin.h`

Properties

The `CDataExchange` class has the following properties:

m_bSaveAndValidate	TRUE if the DDX dialog box is saving.
m_pDlgWnd	Parent window.

Methods

The `CDataExchange` class has the following methods:

Fail	Called when validation fails
PrepareCtrl	Prepare the specified control
PrepareEditCtrl	Prepare the specified edit control

The `Fail` method

`void Fail();`

The `Fail` method is called by the framework when a control's value on the dialog box fails data validation. This method will set the focus to the control that contains bad data and then throw a `CUserException` exception.

The `PrepareCtrl` Method

`HWND PrepareCtrl( int nIDC );`

where

> *nIDC*   Specifies the ID of the control being prepared for DDX or DDV.

The `PrepareCtrl` method prepares a control for DDX or DDV. Do not use this method for edit controls. `PrepareEditCtrl` should be used for edit controls.

Throws a CNotSupportedException.

The `PrepareEditCtrl` Method

`HWND PrepareEditCtrl( int nIDC );`

where

> *nIDC*   Specifies the ID of the edit control being prepared for DDX or DDV.

The PrepareEditCtrl method prepares an edit control for DDX or DDV. Only use this method for edit controls. PrepareCtrl should be used for other control types.

Throws a CNotSupportedException.

CDC

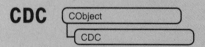

CDC is the class that allows output to any display device. The two display devices most commonly used are windows and printers. CDC allows complex drawing operations to be performed on windows and printers. Other than controls, CDC is the primary way in which an MFC program outputs data.

CDC is the largest of the MFC classes. Only the most commonly used methods have been included in this text. Advanced font handling, advanced printing (printer escape functions), metafile, and path methods have not been included.

For an example of CDC, see the CDCEx example found on the CD-ROM that accompanies this book.

Header Files

The following header file should be included when using this class:

afxwin.h

Properties

The CDC class has the following properties:

m_hDC	The underlying Windows HDC.
m_hAttribDC	The attribute device context used by this DC.

Methods

The CDC class has the following methods:

CDC	The constructor
AngleArc	Draw an arc using angles
Arc	Draw an arc
ArcTo	Draw an arc and update the current position
Attach	Attach a Windows device context
BitBlt	Display a bitmap
Chord	Draw a chord
CreateDC	Create a device context
CreateIC	Create an information context
CreateCompatibleDC	Create a compatible memory device context
DeleteDC	Delete the Windows device context
DeleteTempMap	Delete any temporary CDCs created by FromHandle
Detach	Detach the Windows device context from the CDC

DPtoLP	Device units to logical units
DPtoHIMETRIC	Device units to HIMETRIC units
Draw3dRect	Draw a 3D rectangle
DrawDragRect	Toggle display of a drag rectangle
DrawEdge	Draw the edge of a rectangle
DrawFocusRect	Draw a focus rectangle
DrawIcon	Draw an icon
DrawState	Draw an item with state information
DrawText	Draw text
Ellipse	Draw an ellipse
EnumObjects	Enumerate the objects available to this device context
ExcludeClipRect	Exclude this rectangle from the clipping region
ExcludeUpdateRgn	Exclude this region from the clipping region
ExtTextOut	Extended text out
ExtFloodFill	Extended flood fill
FillRect	Draw a rectangle with a specified brush
FillRgn	Fill the specified region
FillSolidRect	Draw a rectangle with a specified color
FloodFill	Flood fills at a point with a color
FrameRect	Draw a rectangle frame
FrameRgn	Draw a rectangle frame
FromHandle	Create object from an HDC handle
GetArcDirection	Get the direction of an arc
GetBkColor	Get the text background color
GetBkMode	Get the text background mode
GetBoundsRect	Get the bounding rectangle for the device context
GetBrushOrg	Get the current brush origin
GetClipBox	Get the clipping region's type
GetColorAdjustment	Get the color adjustment for the device context
GetCurrentBitmap	Get the currently selected bitmap
GetCurrentBrush	Get the currently selected brush
GetCurrentFont	Get the currently selected font
GetCurrentPalette	Get the current palette
GetCurrentPen	Get the currently selected pen
GetCurrentPosition	Get the current position
GetDeviceCaps	Get info about this device
GetHalftoneBrush	Get a dithered brush
GetMapMode	Get the current mapping mode
GetNearestColor	Get a nearest match color supported by this device

GetOutputTabbedTextExtent	Get the width and height for output tabbed text
GetOutputTextExtent	Get the width and height output text
GetOutputTextMetrics	Get the metrics for output text
GetPixel	Get the color value for a pixel
GetPolyFillMode	Get the fill mode for polygon display
GetROP2	Get the current drawing mode
GetStretchBltMode	Get the current drawing mode
GetSafeHdc	Get a Win32 HDC handle
GetTabbedTextExtent	Measure how large a selection of tabbed text is
GetTextAlign	Get the text alignment
GetTextColor	Get the current text color
GetTextExtent	Get the height and width of text
GetTextFace	Get the current typeface name
GetTextMetrics	Get metrics for the current font
GetViewportExt	Get the extents of a viewport
GetViewportOrg	Get the origin of a viewport
GetWindow	Get the window associated with this device context
GetWindowExt	Get the extents of the window
GetWindowOrg	Get the window origin
GrayString	Display a grayed string
HIMETRICtoDP	HIMETRIC units to device units
HIMETRICtoLP	HIMETRIC units to logical units
IntersectClipRect	Insert a rectangle into the clipping region
InvertRect	Invert the colors of a rectangle
InvertRgn	Invert the colors of a region
IsPrinting	TRUE if the device context is being used for printing
LineTo	Draw a line
LPtoDP	Convert logical points to device points
LPtoHIMETRIC	Logical units to HIMETRIC units
MaskBlt	Combine source and destination bitmaps
MoveTo	Move the current position
OffsetClipRgn	Move the clipping region
OffsetViewportOrg	Offset the viewport origin
PaintRgn	Fills a region with the current brush
PatBlt	Copy a pattern
PlgBlt	Copy a parallelogram
PolyBezier	Draw a series of Bézier curves
PolyBezierTo	Draw a series of Bézier curves and update the current position

PolyDraw	Draw a series of lines and Bézier curves
Polygon	Draw a polygon
Polyline	Draw a multisegment line
PolylineTo	Use current position to draw a multisegment line
PolyPolygon	Draw two or more polygons
PolyPolyline	Draw two or more multisegment lines
PtVisible	Is the specified point visible?
Rectangle	Draw a rectangle
RectVisible	Determine if a rectangle is visible
ReleaseAttribDC	Release the attribute device context but do not close it
ReleaseOutputDC	Release the output device context but do not close it
RealizePalette	Release the output device context but do not close it
ResetDC	Reset the device context to a DEVMODE structure
RestoreDC	Restore to specified state
RoundRect	Draw a rounded rectangle
SaveDC	Save the state of the device context
ScaleViewportExt	Scale the viewport
ScaleWindowExt	Scale the viewport
ScrollDC	Scroll an area on the device context
SelectClipRgn	Select a region as the current clip region
SelectObject	Select an object into the device context for use
SelectStockObject	Select a stock object into the device context
SelectPalette	Select a palette object into the device context
SetArcDirection	Set the direction for arcs
SetAttribDC	Set the attribute device context
SetBkColor	Set the background color for text
SetBkMode	Set the background mode for text
SetBoundsRect	Set the bounding rectangle for the device context
SetBrushOrg	Set the brush origin
SetMapMode	Set the mapping mode
SetOutputDC	Set the output device context
SetPixel	Set the color of a pixel, returns the actual color
SetPixelV	Set the color of a pixel
SetPolyFillMode	Set the fill mode for polygon display
SetROP2	Set the current drawing mode
SetStretchBltMode	Set the current drawing mode
SetTextAlign	Set the text alignment
SetViewportOrg	Set the viewport origin
SetViewportExt	Set the viewport extent

C

SetWindowOrg	Set the window origin
SetWindowExt	Set the window extent
SetTextColor	Set the color for text display
StretchBlt	Display and stretch a bitmap
TabbedTextOut	Display tabbed text
TextOut	Display text
UpdateColors	Update all colors in the device context to a new palette

The CDC Constructor

The CDC creates the CDC object. The CDC constructor is used as follows:

CDC();

The AngleArc Method

BOOL AngleArc(int x,int y, int nRadius,float fStartAngle, float fSweepAngle);

where

x	X coordinate of the center of the circle.
y	Y coordinate of the center of the circle.
nRadius	The radius of the circle.
fStartAngle	The starting angle of the arc.
fSweepAngle	The sweep angle relative to the starting angle.

Returns TRUE if successful.

The AngleArc method will draw an arc using the current pen.

The Arc Method

BOOL Arc(int x1,int y1, int x2,int y2,int x3,int y3, int x4,int y4);
BOOL Arc(LPCRECT lpRect, POINT ptStart, POINT ptEnd);

where

x1	X coordinate of upper-left corner of the bounding rectangle.
y1	Y coordinate of upper-left corner of the bounding rectangle.
x2	X coordinate of lower-right corner of the bounding rectangle.
y2	Y coordinate of lower-right corner of the bounding rectangle.
x3	X coordinate of the starting point of the arc.
y3	Y coordinate of the starting point of the arc.
x4	X coordinate of the ending point of the arc.
y4	Y coordinate of the ending point of the arc.
lpRect	The bounding rectangle.
ptStart	The starting point of the arc.
ptEnd	The ending point of the arc.

Returns TRUE if successful.

The Arc method will draw an arc using the current pen.

The ArcTo Method

```
BOOL ArcTo( int x1,int y1, int x2,int y2,int x3,int y3, int x4,int y4 );
BOOL ArcTo(LPCRECT lpRect, POINT ptStart, POINT ptEnd );
```

where

x1	X coordinate of upper-left corner of the bounding rectangle.
y1	Y coordinate of upper-left corner of the bounding rectangle.
x2	X coordinate of lower-right corner of the bounding rectangle.
y2	Y coordinate of lower-right corner of the bounding rectangle.
x3	X coordinate of the starting point of the arc.
y3	Y coordinate of the starting point of the arc.
x4	X coordinate of the ending point of the arc.
y4	Y coordinate of the ending point of the arc.
lpRect	The bounding rectangle.
ptStart	The starting point of the arc.
ptEnd	The ending point of the arc.

Returns TRUE if successful.

The ArcTo method will draw an arc using the current pen. The current position is updated to be the ending point of the arc.

The Attach Method

```
BOOL Attach( HDC hDC );
```

where

hDC	Specifies a Windows device context.

Returns TRUE if successful.

The Attach method attaches a Windows device context to this CDC object.

The BitBlt Method

```
BOOL BitBlt( int x, int y, int nWidth, int nHeight, CDC* pSrcDC, int
➥xSrc, int ySrc, DWORD dwRop );
```

where

x	X coordinate of the destination rectangle.
y	Y coordinate of the destination rectangle.
nWidth	Width of the destination rectangle.
nHeight	Height of the destination rectangle.
pSrcDC	The source device context.
xSrc	The X coordinate of the source rectangle.
ySrc	The Y coordinate of the source rectangle.
dwRop	Specifies how to copy the bits.

Returns TRUE if successful.

C

The `BitBlt` object is used to copy pixels from one device context to another. Usually the source device context is a memory-based device context with a bitmap selected into it.

The following are valid values for the `dwRop` parameter.

BLACKNESS	Outputs black. Source ignored.
DSTINVERT	Destination inverted. Source ignored.
MERGECOPY	Combines the destination and the source bitmap using the Boolean AND operator.
MERGEPAINT	Combines the inverted source bitmap with the destination bitmap using the Boolean OR operator.
NOTSRCCOPY	Copies the inverted source bitmap to the destination.
NOTSRCERASE	Inverts the result of combining the destination and source bitmaps using the Boolean OR operator.
PATCOPY	Copies the pattern to the destination bitmap.
PATINVERT	Combines the destination bitmap with the pattern using the Boolean XOR operator.
PATPAINT	Combines the inverted source bitmap with the pattern using the Boolean OR operator. Combines the result of this operation with the destination bitmap using the Boolean OR operator.
SRCAND	Combines pixels of the destination and source bitmaps using the Boolean AND operator.
SRCCOPY	Copies the source bitmap to the destination bitmap.
SRCERASE	Inverts the destination bitmap and combines the result with the source bitmap using the Boolean AND operator.
SRCINVERT	Combines pixels of the destination and source bitmaps using the Boolean XOR operator.
SRCPAINT	Combines pixels of the destination and source bitmaps using the Boolean OR operator.
WHITENESS	Output all white. Ignore source.

The `Chord` Method

```
BOOL Chord( int x1,int y1, int x2,int y2,int x3,int y3, int x4,int y4 );
BOOL Chord(LPCRECT lpRect, POINT ptStart, POINT ptEnd );
```

where

x1	X coordinate of upper-left corner of the bounding rectangle.
y1	Y coordinate of upper-left corner of the bounding rectangle.
x2	X coordinate of lower-right corner of the bounding rectangle.
y2	Y coordinate of lower-right corner of the bounding rectangle.
x3	X coordinate of the starting point of the arc.
y3	Y coordinate of the starting point of the arc.
x4	X coordinate of the ending point of the arc.

y4	Y coordinate of the ending point of the arc.
lpRect	The bounding rectangle.
ptStart	The starting point of the arc.
ptEnd	The ending point of the arc.

Returns TRUE if successful.

The Chord method will draw a line that would connect the end points of the arc specified by the parameters. This method uses the current pen.

The CreateDC Method

```
virtual BOOL CreateDC( LPCTSTR lpszDriverName, LPCTSTR lpszDeviceName,
➥LPCTSTR lpszOutput, const void *lpInitData);
```

where

lpszDriverName	The name of the driver(for example, Panasonic).
lpszDeviceName	The device to create a device context for. Should be something like Panasonic 1080.
lpszOutput	The output port, can be NULL to specify the default.
lpInitData	Optional device-specific initialization information. Can be NULL.

Returns TRUE if successful.

The CreateDC method is used to create a device context for a specific device.

The CreateIC Method

```
virtual BOOL CreateIC( LPCTSTR lpszDriverName, LPCTSTR lpszDeviceName,
➥LPCTSTR lpszOutput, const void *lpInitData);
```

where

lpszDriverName	The name of the driver(for example, Panasonic).
lpszDeviceName	The device to create a device context for. Should be something like Panasonic 1080.
lpszOutput	The output port, can be NULL to specify the default.
lpInitData	Optional device-specific initialization information. Can be NULL.

Returns TRUE if successful.

The CreateIC method is used to create a device context for a specific device. This device context can be used only to get information. This is much faster than a standard device context.

The CreateCompatibleDC Method

```
virtual BOOL CreateCompatibleDC( CDC *pDC );
```

where

pDC	Specifies a device context.

Returns TRUE if successful.

The CreateCompatibleDC method will create a CDC object that is of the same color depth as *pDC*.

The `DeleteDC` Method

```
BOOL DeleteDC( );
```

Returns TRUE if successful.

The `DeleteDC` method deletes the device context.

The `DeleteTempMap` Method

```
static void PASCAL DeleteTempMap();
```

The `DeleteTempMap` method is called automatically by MFC. `DeleteTempMap` deletes any unneeded temporary device context objects.

The `Detach` Method

```
HDC Detach();
```

Returns the device context formally used by this object.

The `Detach` method will disassociate the Windows device context with this object.

The `DPtoHIMETRIC` Method

```
void DPtoHIMETRIC( LPSIZE lpSize ) const;
```

where

      lpSize   Specifies the point to convert.

The `DPtoHIMETRIC` method will convert device units into HIMETRIC units.

The `DPtoLP` Method

```
void DPtoLP( LPPOINT lpPoints, int nCount = 1 ) const;
void DPtoLP( LPRECT lpRect ) const;
void DPtoLP( LPSIZE lpSize ) const;
```

where

lpRect	Specifies a Rect structure or a CRect object.
lpPoints	Pointer to an array of points.
lpCount	Specifies the number of points in the point array.
lpSize	Pointer to a SIZE or CSize object.

The `DPtoLP` method will convert device units into logical units.

The `Draw3dRect` Method

```
void Draw3dRect( LPCRECT lpRect, COLORREF clrTopLeft, COLORREF clrBottomRight );
void Draw3dRect( int x, int y, int cx, int cy, COLORREF clrTopLeft, COLORREF
➥clrBottomRight );
```

where

lpRect	Specifies a Rect structure or a CRect object.
clrTopLeft	The color for the top left region of the 3D rectangle.
clrBottomRight	The color for the bottom-right region of the 3D rectangle.
x	Upper-left X coordinate.

y	Upper-left Y coordinate.
cx	Width of the 3D rectangle.
cy	Height of the 3D rectangle.

The `Draw3dRect` method will draw a two-color 3D rectangle.

The `DrawDragRect` Method

```
void DrawDragRect( LPCRECT lpRect, SIZE size, LPCRECT lpRectLast, SIZE
➥sizeLast, CBrush* pBrush = NULL, CBrush* pBrushLast = NULL );
```

where

lpRect	Specifies a `Rect` structure or a `CRect` object for the ending position of the rectangle.
size	The displacement from the top-left corner of the outer border to the top-left corner of the inner border of the ending position of the rectangle.
lpRectLast	Specifies a `Rect` structure or a `CRect` object that is the original position of the rectangle.
sizeLast	The displacement from the top-left corner of the outer border to the top-left corner of the inner border of the original position of the rectangle.
pBrush	Pointer to a brush object.
pBrushLast	Pointer to the last brush object used.

The `DrawDragRect` method is used to draw a dragging rectangle. The first time it is called, the *lpRectLast* parameter should be `NULL`.

The `DrawEdge` Method

```
BOOL DrawEdge( LPRECT lpRect, UINT nEdge, UINT nFlags );
```

where

lpRect	Specifies a `Rect` structure or a `CRect` object.
nEdge	Specifies the type of inner and outer edge to draw. Should be a combination of one inner-boarder flag and one outer-boarder flag.
nFlags	The type of border to be drawn.

Returns `TRUE` if successful.

The following are valid values for the inner and outer border flags.

Inner-border flags:

`BDR_RAISEDINNER`	Raised inner edge.
`BDR_SUNKENINNER`	Sunken inner edge.

Outer-border flags:

`BDR_RAISEDOUTER`	Raised outer edge.
`BDR_SUNKENOUTER`	Sunken outer edge.

C

The *nEdge* parameter must be a combination of one inner and one outer border flag. The *nEdge* parameter can specify one of the following flags:

EDGE_BUMP	Combination of BDR_RAISEDOUTER and BDR_SUNKENINNER.
EDGE_ETCHED	Combination of BDR_SUNKENOUTER and BDR_RAISEDINNER.
EDGE_RAISED	Combination of BDR_RAISEDOUTER and BDR_RAISEDINNER.
EDGE_SUNKEN	Combination of BDR_SUNKENOUTER and BDR_SUNKENINNER.

The *nFlags* parameter types are as follows:

BF_RECT	Entire border rectangle.
BF_LEFT	Left side of border rectangle.
BF_BOTTOM	Bottom of border rectangle.
BF_RIGHT	Right side of border rectangle.
BF_TOP	Top of border rectangle.
BF_TOPLEFT	Top and left side of border rectangle.
BF_TOPRIGHT	Top and right side of border rectangle.
.BF_BOTTOMLEFT	Bottom and left side of border rectangle.
BF_BOTTOMRIGHT	Bottom and right side of border rectangle.

For diagonal lines, the BF_RECT flags specify the end point of the vector bounded by the rectangle parameter.

BF_DIAGONAL_ENDBOTTOMLEFT	Diagonal border. The end point is the bottom-left corner of the rectangle; the origin is top-right corner.
BF_DIAGONAL_ENDBOTTOMRIGHT	Diagonal border. The end point is the bottom-right corner of the rectangle; the origin is top-left corner.
BF_DIAGONAL_ENDTOPLEFT	Diagonal border. The end point is the top-left corner of the rectangle; the origin is bottom-right corner.
BF_DIAGONAL_ENDTOPRIGHT	Diagonal border. The end point is the top-right corner of the rectangle; the origin is bottom-left corner.

The DrawFocusRect Method

void DrawFocusRect(LPRECT lpRect);

where

lpRect	Specifies a rectangle.

The DrawFocusRect draws a dotted inverted rectangle around lpRect. Because this is an inverted rectangle, a second call to this method will erase the first if the rectangle remains constant.

The DrawFrameControl Method

BOOL DrawFrameControl(LPRECT lpRect, UINT nType, UINT state);

where

lpRect	Specifies a Rect structure or a CRect object.
nType	The type of control.
state	The state of the control frame to draw.

Returns TRUE if successful.

The DrawFrameControl method will draw the frame for the specified control in the specified state.

The **DrawIcon** Method

```
BOOL DrawIcon( int x, int y, HICON hIcon );
BOOL DrawIcon( POINT point, HICON hIcon );
```

where

x	X coordinate of where to draw the icon.
y	Y coordinate of where to draw the icon.
point	X,Y coordinates of where to draw the icon.
hIcon	The icon to draw.

Returns TRUE if successful.

The DrawIcon draws a icon.

The **DrawState** Method

```
BOOL DrawState( CPoint pt, CSize size, HBITMAP hBitmap, UINT nFlags,
➥HBRUSH hBrush = NULL );
BOOL DrawState( CPoint pt, CSize size, CBitmap* pBitmap, UINT nFlags,
➥CBrush* pBrush = NULL );
BOOL DrawState( CPoint pt, CSize size, HICON hIcon, UINT nFlags, HBRUSH
➥hBrush = NULL );
BOOL DrawState( CPoint pt, CSize size, HICON hIcon, UINT nFlags, CBrush*
➥pBrush = NULL );
BOOL DrawState( CPoint pt, CSize size, LPCTSTR lpszText, UINT nFlags, BOOL
➥bPrefixText = TRUE, int nTextLen = 0, HBRUSH hBrush = NULL );
BOOL DrawState( CPoint pt, CSize size, LPCTSTR lpszText, UINT nFlags, BOOL
➥ bPrefixText = TRUE, int nTextLen = 0, CBrush* pBrush = NULL );
BOOL DrawState( CPoint pt, CSize size, DRAWSTATEPROC lpDrawProc, LPARAM
➥lData, UINT nFlags, HBRUSH hBrush = NULL );
BOOL DrawState( CPoint pt, CSize size, DRAWSTATEPROC lpDrawProc, LPARAM
➥lData, UINT nFlags, CBrush* pBrush = NULL );
```

where

pt	The location of the image.
size	The size of the image.
hBitmap	A bitmap (HBITMAP).
flags	The image type and state.
hBrush	A brush (HBRUSH).
pBitmap	A bitmap (CBitmap).
pBrush	A brush (CBRUSH).
hIcon	A icon (HICON).
bPrefixText	Text to contain an accelerator mnemonic.
nTextLen	Length of the text string.
lpDrawProc	A pointer to a callback function to draw the image.
lData	The image data.

C

Returns TRUE if successful.

The DrawState method is used to draw an image in a specified state.

The DrawText Method

```
int DrawText( LPCTSTR lpszString, int nCount, LPRECT lpRect, UINT nFormat );
int DrawText( const CString& str, LPRECT lpRect, UINT nFormat );
```

where

lpszString	The string to be drawn.
nCount	The number of characters in this string.
lpRect	The destination rectangle for this string.
nFormat	Formatting flags.
str	A CString object.

The DrawText method will format text into the rectangle specified.

The following values are valid flags for *nFormat*.

DT_BOTTOM	Specifies bottom-justified text. This value must be combined with DT_SINGLELINE.
DT_CALCRECT	Determines the width and height of the rectangle.

If there are multiple lines of text, DrawText will use the width of the rectangle pointed to by *lpRect* and extend the base of the rectangle to bound the last line of text. If there is only one line of text, DrawText will modify the right side of the rectangle so it bounds the last character in the line. In either case, DrawText returns the height of the formatted text, but does not draw the text.

DT_CENTER	Centers text horizontally.
DT_EXPANDTABS	Expands tab characters. The default number of characters per tab is eight.
DT_EXTERNALLEADING	Includes the font's external leading in the line height. Normally, external leading is not included in the height of a line of text.
DT_LEFT	Aligns text flush-left.
DT_NOCLIP	Draws without clipping. DrawText is somewhat faster when DT_NOCLIP is used.
DT_NOPREFIX	Turns off processing of prefix characters.

Normally, DrawText interprets the ampersand (&) mnemonic-prefix character as a directive to underscore the character that follows, and the two-ampersand (&&) mnemonic-prefix characters as a directive to print a single ampersand. By specifying DT_NOPREFIX, this processing is turned off.

DT_RIGHT	Aligns text flush right.
DT_SINGLELINE	Specifies single-line only. Carriage returns and linefeeds do not break the line.
DT_TABSTOP	Sets tab stops. The high-order byte of *nFormat* is the number of characters for each tab. The default number of characters per tab is eight.
DT_TOP	Specifies top-justified text (single-line only).

| DT_VCENTER | Specifies vertically centered text (single-line only). |
| DT_WORDBREAK | Specifies word-breaking. Lines are automatically broken between words if a word would extend past the edge of the rectangle specified by *lpRect*. A carriage return/linefeed sequence will also break the line. |

The `Ellipse` Method

```
BOOL Ellipse( int x1, int y1, int x2, int y2 );
BOOL Ellipse( LPCRECT lpRect );
```

where

x1	X coordinate for the upper-left coordinate of a rectangle that bounds the ellipse.
y1	Y coordinate for the upper-left coordinate of a rectangle that bounds the ellipse.
x2	X coordinate for the lower-right coordinate of a rectangle that bounds the ellipse.
y2	Y coordinate for the lower-right coordinate of a rectangle that bounds the ellipse.
lpRect	Specifies a rectangle that bounds the ellipse.

Returns TRUE if successful.

The `DrawEllipse` method draws an ellipse with the current pen. The inside of the ellipse is filled with the current brush.

The `EnumObjects` Method

```
int EnumObjects(int nObjectType, int (CALLBACK EXPORT *lpfn)(LPVOID,LPARAM),
➥LPARAM lpData );
```

where

nObjectType	Specifies the type of objects to enumerate.
lpfn	Specifies a callback function that will receive the list of objects.
lpData	Application specific data to be passed to the callback function.

Returns the last value returned by the callback function.

The `EnumObjects` method is used to get a list of the available objects in a device context.

The `ExcludeClipRect` Method

```
int ExcludeClipRect( int x1, int y1, int x2, int y2 );
int ExcludeClipRect( LPCRECT lpRect );
```

where

x1	X coordinate for the upper-left coordinate of a rectangle.
y1	Y coordinate for the upper-left coordinate of a rectangle.
x2	X coordinate for the lower-right coordinate of a rectangle.
y2	Y coordinate for the lower-right coordinate of a rectangle.
lpRect	Specifies a rectangle.

Returns any of the following values:

COMPLEXREGION	The region has overlapping borders.
ERROR	No region was created.
NULLREGION	The region is empty.
SIMPLEREGION	The region has no overlapping borders.

The `ExcludeClipRect` method excludes the specified rectangle from the clipping region.

The `ExcludeUpdateRgn` Method

`int ExcludeUpdateRgn( CWnd* pWnd );`

where

pWnd	Pointer to a window being updated.

Returns any of the following values:

COMPLEXREGION	The region has overlapping borders.
ERROR	No region was created.
NULLREGION	The region is empty.
SIMPLEREGION	The region has no overlapping borders.

The `ExcludeUpdateRgn` method will exclude the areas outside of the update region of the specified window.

The `ExtFloodFill` Method

`BOOL ExtFloodFill( int x, int y, COLORREF crColor, UINT nFillType );`

where

x	The X coordinate of the pixel to fill at.
y	The Y coordinate of the pixel to fill at.
crColor	The desired color for the fill.
nFillType	The way in which to flood fill.

Returns TRUE if successful.

The `ExtFloodFill` method will perform a flood fill at the specified pixel.

The `ExtTextOut` Method

```
virtual BOOL ExtTextOut( int x, int y, UINT nOptions, LPCRECT lpRect,
➥LPCTSTR lpszString, UINT nCount, LPINT lpDxWidths );
BOOL ExtTextOut( int x, int y, UINT nOptions, LPCRECT lpRect,
➥const CString& str, LPINT lpDxWidths );
```

where

x	X coordinate for where the text is to be drawn.
y	Y coordinate for where the text is to be drawn.
nOptions	ETO_CLIPPED to clip the text to the rectangle, and ETO_OPAQUE fill the background of the rectangle with the current background color.

lpRect	Pointer to a rectangle to format to.
lpszString	The string being drawn.
str	The CString being drawn.
nCount	How many characters in the string.
lpDxWidths	An array of values that specify the distance between origins of adjacent character cells.

Returns TRUE if successful.

The ExtTextOut method will draw text to a rectangle.

The **FillRect** Method

void FillRect(LPCRECT lpRect, CBrush* pBrush);

where

| *pBrush* | The brush to use to draw the rectangle. |
| *lpRect* | Specifies a rectangle that bounds to be filled. |

The FillRect method will fill in a rectangle with the specified brush.

The **FillRgn** Method

void FillRgn(CRgn *pRgn, CBrush* pBrush);

where

| *pBrush* | The brush to use to draw the rectangle. |
| *pRgn* | Specifies a region to be filled. |

The FillRgn method will fill in a region with the specified brush.

The **FillSolidRect** Method

void FillSolidRect(LPCRECT lpRect, COLORREF clr);
void FillSolidRect(int x, int y, int cx, int cy, COLORREF clr);

where

x1	X coordinate for the upper-left coordinate of a rectangle to fill.
y1	Y coordinate for the upper-left coordinate of a rectangle to fill.
x2	X coordinate for the lower-right coordinate of a rectangle to fill.
y2	Y coordinate for the lower-right coordinate of a rectangle to fill.
lpRect	Specifies a rectangle to fill.
clr	The color to fill this rectangle with.

The FillSolidRect method fills in a solid rectangle.

The **FloodFill** Method

BOOL SetPixel(int x, int y, COLORREF crColor);

where

x	The X coordinate of the pixel to fill at.
y	The Y coordinate of the pixel to fill at.
crColor	The desired color for the fill.

Returns TRUE if successful.

The FloodFill method will perform a flood fill at the specified pixel.

The FloodFill Method

```
BOOL FloodFill( int x, int y, COLORREF crColor );
```

where

x	The X coordinate of the pixel to fill at.
y	The Y coordinate of the pixel to fill at.
crColor	The desired color for the fill.

Returns TRUE if successful.

The FloodFill method will perform a flood fill at the specified pixel.

The FrameRect Method

```
void FrameRect( LPCRECT lpRect, CBrush* pBrush );
```

where

lpRect	The rectangle to frame.
pBrush	Brush color to draw frame in.

The FrameRect method will draw a 1-pixel-wide rectangle frame using the specified brush.

The FrameRgn Method

```
void FrameRgn( CRgn *pRgn, CBrush *pBrush, int nWidth, int nHeight );
```

where

pRgn	The region to frame.
pBrush	Brush color to draw frame in.
nWidth	The width of the border.
nHeight	The height of the border.

The FrameRect method will draw a border around the specified region using the specified brush.

The FromHandle Method

```
static CDC* PASCAL FromHandle( HDC hDC );
```

where

hDC	A Windows HDC to create a CDC object form.

Returns a CDC pointer.

The FromHandle method will create a CDC object from a handle.

The GetArcDirection Method

```
int GetArcDirection() const;
```

Returns the direction that arcs will be drawn in. Will return either AD_COUNTERCLOCKWISE or AD_CLOCKWISE.

The **GetBkColor** Method

COLORREF GetBkColor( ) const;

Returns the current background color.

The **GetBkMode** Method

int GetBkMode( ) const;

Returns the current background mode. The background mode is OPAQUE, TRANSPARENT, or TRANSPARENT1.

The **GetBoundsRect** Method

UINT GetBoundsRect(LPRECT lpRectBounds, UINT flags);

where

lpRectBounds	The current bounding rectangle.
flags	Specifies if the bounding rectangle should be cleared.

Returns the state of the bounding rectangle.

The GetBoundsRect method will get the bounding rectangle.

The **GetBrushOrg** Method

CPoint GetBrushOrg() const;

Returns the current brush origin.

The **GetClipBox** Method

int GetClipBox(LPRECT lpRect) const;

where

lpRect	Pointer to a rectangle to receive the tightest bound rectangle for the clipping region.

Returns any of the following values:

COMPLEXREGION	The region has overlapping borders.
ERROR	Device context not valid.
NULLREGION	The region is empty.
SIMPLEREGION	The region has no overlapping borders.

The **GetColorAdjustment** Method

BOOL GetColorAdjustment(LPCOLORADJUSTMENT lpColorAdjust) const;

where

lpColorAdjust	Pointer to the color adjustment structure for this device context.

Returns TRUE if successful.

The GetColorAdjustment method will get the color adjustment for the device context.

The `GetCurrentBitmap` Method

`CBitmap* GetCurrentBitmap( ) const;`

Returns a pointer to the currently selected bitmap.

The `GetCurrentBrush` Method

`CBrush* GetCurrentBrush( ) const;`

Returns a pointer to the currently selected brush.

The `GetCurrentFont` Method

`CFont* GetCurrentFont( ) const;`

Returns a pointer to the currently selected font.

The `GetCurrentPalette` Method

`CPalette* GetCurrentPalette( ) const;`

Returns a pointer to the currently selected palette.

The `GetCurrentPen` Method

`CPen* GetCurrentPen( ) const;`

Returns a pointer to the currently selected pen.

The `GetCurrentPosition` Method

`CPoint GetCurrentPosition( ) const;`

Returns the current position. `MoveTo` is used to set this value.

The `GetDeviceCaps` Method

`int GetDeviceCaps( int nIndex ) const;`

where

> *nIndex*   Specifies the device capability being queried.

The `GetHalftoneBrush` Method

`static CBrush* PASCAL GetHalftoneBrush( );`

Returns a halftone brush. This brush has alternate pixels between the foreground and background colors.

The `GetMapMode` Method

`int GetMapMode() const;`

Returns the current mapping mode. See `SetMapMode` for more information.

The `GetNearestColor` Method

`COLORREF GetNearestColor( COLORREF crColor)`

where

> *crColor*   Specifies the desired color.

Returns the closest color to the desired color.

The GetOutputTextExtent Method

```
CSize GetOutputTextExtent( LPCTSTR lpszString, int nCount ) const;
CSize GetOutputTextExtent( const CString& str ) const;
```

where

lpszString	The string being measured.
nCount	How many characters are in the string.
str	A CString object to be measured.

Returns a CSize object specifying the width and height of the text.

The GetOutputTextMetrics Method

```
BOOL GetOutputTextMetrics( LPTEXTMETRIC lpMetrics ) const;
```

where

lpMetrics	Pointer to a TEXTMETRIC structure.

Returns TRUE if successful.

The GetOutputTextMetrics method will return information about the font in a TEXTMETRICS structure.

The GetPixel Method

```
COLORREF GetPixel( int x, int y ) const;
COLORREF GetPixel( POINT point ) const;
```

where

x	x coordinate of a pixel.
y	y coordinate of a pixel.
point	x,y coordinate of a pixel.

Returns the color value for the specified pixel.

The GetPolyFillMode Method

```
int GetPolyFillMode( ) const;
```

Returns the current polygon fill mode. Will be either ALTERNATE or WINDING.

The GetROP2 Method

```
int GetROP2( ) const;
```

Returns the current drawing mode.

The GetStretchBltMode Method

```
int GetStretchBltMode( ) const;
```

Returns the bitmap stretching mode.

The GetSafeHdc Method

```
HDC GetSafeHdc( ) const;
```

Returns the Windows HDC for this CDC object.

C

The `GetOutputTabbedTextExtent` Method

```
virtual CSize GetOutputTabbedTextExtent( int x,int y,LPCTSTR lpszString,
➡int nCount, int nTabPositions, LPINT lpnTabStopPositions );
CSize GetOutputTabbedTextExtent( int x,int y,CString &str, int nTabPositions,
➡LPINT lpnTabStopPositions );
```

where

x	The x coordinate to display the text at.
y	The y coordinate to display the text at.
lpszString	The string to display.
nCount	The number of characters to display.
str	The string to measure.
nTabPositions	The number of tab positions.
lpnTabStopPositions	An array of tab stop positions.

Returns the dimensions of the rectangle around the text to be measured.

The `GetTabbedTextExtent` Method

```
virtual CSize GetTabbedTextExtent( int x,int y,LPCTSTR lpszString, int
➡nCount, int nTabPositions, LPINT lpnTabStopPositions );
CSize GetTabbedTextExtent( int x,int y,CString &str, int nTabPositions,
➡LPINT lpnTabStopPositions );
```

where

x	The x coordinate to display the text at.
y	The y coordinate to display the text at.
lpszString	The string to display.
nCount	The number of characters to display.
str	The string to measure.
nTabPositions	The number of tab positions.
lpnTabStopPositions	An array of tab stop positions.

Returns the dimensions of the rectangle around the text to be measured.

The `GetTextColor` Method

```
COLORREF GetTextColor( ) const;
```

Returns the text color.

The `GetTextExtent` Method

```
CSize GetTextExtent( LPCTSTR lpszString, int nCount ) const;
CSize GetTextExtent( const CString& str ) const;
```

where

lpszString	The string being measured.
nCount	How many characters are in the string.
str	A `CString` object to be measured.

Returns a `CSize` object specifying the width and height of the text.

The **GetTextFace** Method

```
int GetTextFace( int nCount, LPTSTR lpszFacename ) const;
int GetTextFace( CString& rString ) const;
```

where

lpszFacename	The string to hold the face name.
nCount	How many characters are in the string.
rString	A CString object to take the face name.

Returns a string specifying the current face.

The **GetTextMetrics** Method

```
BOOL GetTextMetrics( LPTEXTMETRIC lpMetrics ) const;
```

where

lpMetrics	Pointer to a TEXTMETRIC structure.

Returns TRUE if successful.

The GetTextMetrics method will return information about the font in a TEXTMETRICS structure.

The **GetViewportExt** Method

```
CSize GetViewportExt( ) const;
```

Returns the x and y extents of the device context's viewport.

The **GetViewportOrg** Method

```
CPoint GetViewportOrg( ) const;
```

Returns the x and y origins of the device context's viewport.

The **GetWindow** Method

```
CWnd *GetWindow( ) const;
```

Returns the window associated with this device context.

The **GetWindowExt** Method

```
CPoint GetViewportExt( ) const;
```

Returns the x and y extents of the device context's window.

The **GetWindowOrg** Method

```
CSize GetViewportOrg( ) const;
```

Returns the x and y origins of the device context's window.

The **GrayString** Method

```
virtual BOOL GrayString( CBrush* pBrush, BOOL ( CALLBACK EXPORT*
➡lpfnOutput )( HDC, LPARAM, int ), LPARAM lpData, int nCount, int
➡x, int y, int nWidth, int nHeight );
```

where

pBrush	The brush to be used for dimming.
lpfnOutput	Callback function to draw the string. Can be NULL.
data	Data passed to the callback function.

nCount	The number of characters to display.
x	x coordinate to draw at.
y	y coordinate to draw at.
nWidth	The width of the rectangle that encloses the string.
nHeight	The height of the rectangle that encloses the string.

Returns TRUE if successful.

The GrayString method displays grayed text at the specified coordinate.

The **HIMETRICtoDP** Method

```
void HIMETRICtoDP( LPSIZE lpSize ) const;
```

where

| lpSize | Specifies the point to convert. |

The HIMETRICtoDP method will convert HIMETRIC units into device units.

The **HIMETRICtoLP** Method

```
void HIMETRICtoLP( LPSIZE lpSize ) const;
```

where

| lpSize | Specifies the point to convert. |

The HIMETRICtoLP method will convert HIMETRIC units into logical units.

The **IntersectClipRect** Method

```
int IntersectClipRect( int x1, int y1, int x2, int y2 );
int IntersectClipRect( LPCRECT lpRect );
```

where

x1	x coordinate for the upper-left coordinate of a rectangle.
y1	y coordinate for the upper-left coordinate of a rectangle.
x2	x coordinate for the lower-right coordinate of a rectangle.
y2	y coordinate for the lower-right coordinate of a rectangle.
lpRect	Specifies a rectangle.

Returns any of the following values:

COMPLEXREGION	The region has overlapping borders.
ERROR	No region was created.
NULLREGION	The region is empty.
SIMPLEREGION	The region has no overlapping borders.

The IntersectClipRect method adds the selected rectangle to the clipping region.

The **InvertRect** Method

```
void InvertRect( LPCRECT lpRect );
```

where

| lpRect | Specifies a rectangle that should be inverted. |

Returns TRUE if successful.

The InvertRect method inverts the specified rectangle.

The InvertRgn Method

```
void InvertRgn( CRgn *pRgn );
```

where

    pRgn   Specifies a region that should be inverted.

Returns TRUE if successful.

The InvertRgn method inverts the specified region.

The IsPrinting Method

```
BOOL IsPrinting() const;
```

Returns TRUE if the device context is being used for printer output.

The LineTo Method

```
BOOL LineTo( int x, int y );
BOOL LineTo( POINT point );
```

where

    x   x coordinate of where to draw the line to.

    y   y coordinate of where to draw the line to.

    point   x,y coordinate of where to draw the line to.

Returns TRUE if successful.

The LineTo draws a line using the current pen from the cursor position to the specified x,y coordinate.

The LPtoDP Method

```
void LPtoDP( LPPOINT lpPoints, int nCount = 1 ) const;
void LPtoDP( LPRECT lpRect ) const;
void LPtoDP( LPSIZE lpSize ) const;
```

where

    lpRect   Specifies a Rect structure or a CRect object.

    lpPoints   Pointer to an array of points.

    lpCount   Specifies the number of points in the point array.

    lpSize   Pointer to a SIZE or CSize object.

The LPtoDP method will convert logical units into device units.

The LPtoHIMETRIC Method

```
void LPtoHIMETRIC( LPSIZE lpSize ) const;
```

where

    lpSize   Specifies the point to convert.

The LPtoHIMETRIC method will convert HIMETRIC units into logical units.

C

The `MaskBlt` Method

```
BOOL MaskBlt( int x, int y, int nWidth, int nHeight, CDC* pSrcDC, int xSrc,
➡ int ySrc, CBitmap& maskBitmap, int xMask, int yMask, DWORD dwRop );
```

where

x	x coordinate of the destination rectangle.
y	y coordinate of the destination rectangle.
nWidth	Width of the destination rectangle.
nHeight	Height of the destination rectangle.
pSrcDC	The source device context.
xSrc	The x coordinate of the source rectangle.
ySrc	The y coordinate of the source rectangle.
maskBitmap	The monochrome bitmap used as a mask.
xMask	The x coordinate of the mask bitmap.
yMask	The y coordinate of the mask bitmap.
dwRop	Specifies how to copy the bits (see `BitBlt`).

Returns TRUE if successful.

The `MaskBlt` method is used to copy pixels from one device context to another. Usually the source device context is a memory-based device context with a bitmap selected into it. A mask is applied that allows only pixels with a 1 in the mask bitmap to be drawn. This method requires Windows NT.

The `MoveTo` Method

```
CPoint MoveTo( int x, int y );
CPoint MoveTo( POINT point );
```

where

x	X coordinate to move to.
y	Y coordinate to move to.
point	The X,Y coordinate for this command.

Returns old point that the current position was at.

The `OffsetClipRect` Method

```
int OffsetClipRgn( int x, int y );
int OffsetClipRgn( SIZE size );
```

where

x	The number of pixels to move the region to the right by.
y	The number of pixels to move the region to the left by.
size	The number of pixels to move down and to the right by.

Returns any of the following values:

COMPLEXREGION	The region has overlapping borders.
ERROR	No region was created.

| NULLREGION | The region is empty. |
| SIMPLEREGION | The region has no overlapping borders. |

The `OffestClipRect` method adds the selected rectangle to the clipping region.

The `OffsetViewportOrg` Method

`virtual CPoint OffsetViewportOrg( int nWidth, int nHeight);`

where

| nWidth | The number of device units to add to the origin's x coordinate. |
| y | The number of device units to add to the origin's y coordinate. |

Returns the previous viewport origin.

The `OffsetViewportOrg` method offsets the viewport origin for the device context.

The `PaintRgn` Method

`void PaintRgn( CRgn *pRgn);`

where

| pRgn | Specifies a region to be filled. |

The `PaintRgn` method will fill in a region with the current brush.

The `PatBlt` Method

`BOOL PatBlt( int x, int y, int nWidth, int nHeight, DWORD dwRop );`

where

x	X coordinate of the destination for the pattern.
y	Y coordinate of the destination for the pattern.
nWidth	The width of the destination rectangle.
nHeight	The height of the destination rectangle.
dwRop	Specifies how to copy the brush to the destination rectangle.

Returns TRUE if successful.

The `PatBlt` method creates a pattern on the device context by combining the current brush and the pattern already on the device.

The `PlgBlt` Method

`BOOL PlgBlt( POINT lpPoint, CDC *pSrcDC, int xSrc, int ySrc, int nWidth,`
`➥ int nHeight, CBitmap &maskBitmap, int xMask, int yMask );`

where

lpPoint	Array of three points that makes up a parallelogram.
pSrcDC	The source device context.
xSrc	x coordinate of the source rectangle.
ySrc	y coordinate of the source rectangle.
nWidth	Width of the source rectangle.
nHeight	Height of the source rectangle.

maskBitmap	A mask bitmap.
xMask	The X coordinate of the mask rectangle.
yMask	The Y coordinate of the mask rectangle.

Returns TRUE if successful.

The `PlgBlt` method is used to copy a parallelogram from one device context to another. This method is only supported by Windows NT.

The `PolyBezier` Method

```
BOOL PolyBezier( const POINT *lpPoints, int nCount );
```

where

| lpPoints | An array of points. |
| nCount | The number of points in the array. |

Returns TRUE if successful.

The `PolyBezier` method will draw a series of Bézier curves based on the array of points.

The `PolyBezierTo` Method

```
BOOL PolyBezierTo( const POINT *lpPoints, int nCount );
```

where

| lpPoints | An array of points. |
| nCount | The number of points in the array. |

Returns TRUE if successful.

The `PolyBezierTo` method will draw a series of Bézier curves based on the array of points. This method will update the current position.

The `PolyDraw` Method

```
BOOL PolyDraw( const POINT *lpPoints, const BYTE *lpTypes, int nCount );
```

where

lpPoints	An array of points.
lpTypes	Specifies how to use each of the points.
nCount	The number of points in the array.

Returns TRUE if successful.

The `PolyDraw` method will draw a series of lines and curves.

The `PolyLine` Method

```
BOOL PolyLine( LPPOINT lpPoints, int nCount );
```

where

| *lpPoints* | An array of points. |
| *nCount* | The number of points in the array. |

Returns TRUE if successful.

The PolyLine method will draw a series of line segments by connecting all of the points in the point array. The lines will be drawn with the current pen.

The PolylineTo Method

BOOL PolylineTo(const POINT* lpPoints, int nCount);

where

| *lpPoints* | An array of points. |
| *nCount* | The number of points in the array. |

Returns TRUE if successful.

The PolylineTo method will draw a series of line segments by connecting all of the points in the point array. The lines will be drawn with the current pen. PolylineTo will start with the current position and draw to the first point.

The PolyPolygon Method

BOOL PolyPolygon(LPPOINT lpPoints, LPINT lpPolyCounts, int nCount);

where

lpPoints	An array of points.
lpPolyCounts	An array of integers. Each specifies the number of points in one of the polygons in the *lpPoints* array.
nCount	The number of polygons to draw (must be at least 2).

Returns TRUE if successful.

The PolyPolygon method will draw a series of polygons. The lines will be drawn with the current pen. If these polygons are not closed, the last point will be connected to the first.

The PolyPolyline Method

BOOL PolyPolyline(const POINT* lpPoints, const DWORD* lpPolyPoints, int
➥nCount);

where

lpPoints	An array of points.
lpPolyCounts	An array of integers. Each specifies the number of points in one of the polygons in the *lpPoints* array.
nCount	The number of polygons to draw(must be at least 2).

Returns TRUE if successful.

The PolyPolyline method will draw a series of line segments. The lines will be drawn with the current pen.

The `PtVisible` Method

```
BOOL PtVisible( int x, int y );
BOOL PtVisible( POINT point );
```

where

x	X coordinate of a point.
y	Y coordinate of a point.
point	A point.

Returns TRUE if the specified point is visible.

The `Rectangle` Method

```
BOOL Rectangle( int x1, int y1, int x2, int y2 );
BOOL Rectangle( LPCRECT lpRect );
```

where

x1	X coordinate for the upper-left coordinate of a rectangle.
y1	Y coordinate for the upper-left coordinate of a rectangle.
x2	X coordinate for the lower-right coordinate of a rectangle.
y2	Y coordinate for the lower-right coordinate of a rectangle.
lpRect	Specifies a rectangle.

Returns TRUE if successful.

The Rectangle method draws a rectangle with the current pen. The rectangle is filled using the current brush.

The `RectVisible` Method

```
BOOL RectVisible( LPCRECT lpRect );
```

where

lpRect	A rectangle.

Returns TRUE if any part of the specified rectangle is visible.

The `ReleaseAttribDC` Method

```
void ReleaseAttribDC( );
```

The ReleaseAttribDC method will release the attribute device context. The device context will not be deleted, it will just no longer be associated with this object.

The `ReleaseOutputDC` Method

```
void ReleseOutputDC( );
```

The ReleaseOutputDC method will release the output device context. The device context will not be deleted, it will just no longer be associated with this object.

The `ResetDC` Method

```
BOOL ResetDC( const DEVMODE *lpDevMode );
```

where

lpDevMode	The DEVMODE structure to set the device context to.

Returns TRUE if successful.

The ResetDC method is used to reset the device context to what is specified by the DEVMODE structure.

The RealizePalette Method

```
UINT RealizePalette();
```

Returns the number of logical palette entries that mapped to physical colors.

The RealizePalette method is used to attempt to map the device context's logical palette into the physical palette.

The RestoreDC Method

```
virtual BOOL RestoreDC( int nSavedDC );
```

where

    nSavedDC   Which device context to restore. This value is returned from SaveDC.

Returns TRUE if successful.

The RestoreDC method restores the state information stored by SaveDC.

The RoundRect Method

```
BOOL RoundRect( int x1, int y1, int x2, int y2, int x3, int y3 );
BOOL RoundRect( int lpRect, POINT point);
```

where

x1	X coordinate for the upper-left coordinate of a rectangle.
y1	Y coordinate for the upper-left coordinate of a rectangle.
x2	X coordinate for the lower-right coordinate of a rectangle.
y2	Y coordinate for the lower-right coordinate of a rectangle.
x3	Width of the ellipse used to draw the rounded corner.
y3	Height of the ellipse used to draw the rounded corner.
lpRect	The rectangle to draw.
point	Height/width of the ellipse.

Returns TRUE if successful.

The RoundRect method draws a rounded rectangle with the current pen. The rectangle is filled using the current brush.

The SaveDC Method

```
virtual int SaveDC( );
```

Returns integer to identify the profile to which this device context was saved.

The SaveDC method will save the state information for the device context. Call RestoreDC with the value that this method returns to restore the state.

The ScaleViewportExt Method

```
virtual CSize ScaleViewportExt( int xNum, int xDenom, int yNum, int yDenom);
```

where

xNum	The amount to multiply the x extent of the viewport by.
xDenom	The amount to divide the extent of the viewport by.
yNum	The amount to multiply the y extent of the viewport by.
yDenom	The amount to divide the y extent of the viewport by.

Returns the previous size of the viewport.

The `ScaleViewportExt` method is used to scale the viewport extents.

The `ScaleWindowExt` Method

```
virtual CSize ScaleWindowExt( int xNum, int xDenom, int yNum, int yDenom);
```

where

xNum	The amount to multiply the x extent of the window by.
xDenom	The amount to divide the x extent of the window by.
yNum	The amount to multiply the y extent of the window by.
yDenom	The amount to divide the y extent of the window by.

Returns the previous size of the window.

The `ScaleWindowExt` method is used to scale the window extents.

The `ScrollDC` Method

```
BOOL ScrollDC( int dx, int dy, CONST RECT *lprcScroll, CONST RECT
*lprcClip,HRGN hrgnUpdate, LPRECT lprcUpdate );
```

where

dx	The number of horizontal scroll units.
dy	The number of vertical scroll units.
lpScrollRect	Pointer to a `Rect` structure that specifies the scroll rectangle.
lpRectClip	Pointer to a `Rect` structure that specifies the clip rectangle.
pRgnUpdate	Pointer to a region that is modified to hold the uncovered region.
lpRectUpdate	The rectangle that needs repainting.

Returns `TRUE` if successful.

The `ScrollDC` method is used to scroll data that has been already displayed to the screen.

The `SelectClipRgn` Method

```
virtual int SelectClipRgn( CRgn* pRgn );
int SelectClipRgn( CRgn* pRgn, int nMode );
```

where

| rgn | The region to be selected into the clipping area. |
| nMode | Specifies how the *rgn* should be moved into the existing clip region. |

Returns any of the following values:

| COMPLEXREGION | The region has overlapping borders. |
| ERROR | No region was created. |

NULLREGION	The region is empty.
SIMPLEREGION	The region has no overlapping borders.

The *nMode* parameter may be any of the following:

RGN_AND	The new clipping region combines the overlapping areas of the current clipping region and the region identified by *pRgn*.
RGN_COPY	The new clipping region is a copy of the region identified by *pRgn*. This functionality is identical to the first version of SelectClipRgn. If the region identified by *pRgn* is NULL, the new clipping region becomes the default clipping region (a NULL region).
RGN_DIFF	The new clipping region combines the areas of the current clipping region with those areas excluded from the region identified by *pRgn*.
RGN_OR	The new clipping region combines the current clipping region and the region identified by *pRgn*.
RGN_XOR	The new clipping region combines the current clipping region and the region identified by *pRgn* but excludes any overlapping areas.

The SelectObject Method

```
virtual CPen* SelectObject( CPen* pPen );
virtual CBrush* SelectObject( CBrush* pBrush );
virtual CFont* SelectObject( CFont* pFont );
CBitmap* SelectObject( CBitmap* pBitmap );
int SelectObject( CRgn* pRgn );
```

where

pPen	A CPen object.
pBrush	A CBrush object.
pFont	A CFont object.
pBitmap	A CBitmap object.
pRgn	A CRgn object.

Returns the old object that was selected. Returns one of the following if the CRegion version was used.

COMPLEXREGION	The region has overlapping borders.
ERROR	No region was created.
NULLREGION	The region is empty.
SIMPLEREGION	The region has no overlapping borders.

The SelectObject method is used to select an object into the device context.

The SelectStockObject Method

```
virtual CGdiObject* SelectStockObject( int nIndex );
```

where

nIndex	The index of the desired stock object.

Returns the old object that was selected.

The *nIndex* parameter can be any of the following stock objects.

BLACK_BRUSH	Black brush.
DKGRAY_BRUSH	Dark gray brush.
GRAY_BRUSH	Gray brush.
HOLLOW_BRUSH	Hollow brush.
LTGRAY_BRUSH	Light gray brush.
NULL_BRUSH	Null brush.
WHITE_BRUSH	White brush.
BLACK_PEN	Black pen.
NULL_PEN	Null pen.
WHITE_PEN	White pen.
ANSI_FIXED_FONT	ANSI fixed system font.
ANSI_VAR_FONT	ANSI variable system font.
DEVICE_DEFAULT_FONT	Device-dependent font.
OEM_FIXED_FONT	OEM-dependent fixed font.
SYSTEM_FONT	The system font. By default, Windows uses the system font to draw menus, dialog box controls, and other text. In Windows versions 3.0 and later, the system font is proportional width; earlier versions of Windows use a fixed-width system font.
SYSTEM_FIXED_FONT	The fixed-width system font used in Windows prior to version 3.0. This object is available for compatibility with earlier versions of Windows.
DEFAULT_PALETTE	Default color palette. This palette consists of the 20 static colors in the system palette.

The SelectPalette Method

```
CPalette* SelectPalette( CPalette* pPalette , BOOL bForceBackground );
```
where

pPalette	The palette to be selected.
pForceBackground	TRUE if the logical palette should be forced to the background palette.

Returns the old palette that was selected.

The SelectPalette method is used to select a palette into the device context.

The SetArcDirection Method

```
int SetArcDirection( int ArcDirection );
```
where

ArcDirection	The desired arc direction. Should be either AD_COUNTERCLOCKWISE or AD_CLOCKWISE.

Returns the previous arc direction.

The `SetAttribDC` Method

```
virtual void SetAttribDC( HDC hDC );
```

where

> *hDC*   The device context (*hdc*) to be used to get attributes.

The `SetAttributeDC` method sets the device context (*hdc*) that is used to get attributes.

The `SetBkColor` Method

```
COLORREF SetBkColor( COLORREF crColor );
```

where

> *crColor*   The desired background color.

Returns the previous background color.

The `SetBkMode` Method

```
int SetBkMode( int nBkMode );
```

where

> *nBkMode*   The desired background mode, can be either OPAQUE or TRANSPARENT.

Returns the previous background mode.

The `SetBoundsRect` Method

```
UINT SetBoundsRect( LPRECT lpRectBounds, UINT flags );
```

where

> *lpRectBounds*   The new bounding rectangle.
>
> *flags*   Specifies how to combine with the current bounding rectangle.

Returns the state of the bounding rectangle.

The `SetBoundsRect` method will set the bounding rectangle.

The `SetBrushOrg` Method

```
CPoint SetBrushOrg( int x, int y );
CPoint SetBrushOrg( POINT point );
```

where

> *x*   The X coordinate of the brush origin.
>
> *y*   The Y coordinate of the brush origin.
>
> *point*   The X,Y coordinates of the brush origin.

Returns the previous brush origin.

The `SetColorAdjustment` Method

```
BOOL SetColorAdjustment( LPCOLORADJUSTMENT lpColorAdjust ) const;
```

where

> *lpColorAdjust*   Pointer to the color adjustment structure for this device context.

Returns TRUE if successful.

C

The `SetColorAdjustment` method will set the color adjustment for the device context.

The `SetMapMode` Method

`int SetMapMode( int nMapMode ) const;`

where

    nMapMode   The mapping mode for the device context.

Returns the previous mapping mode.

The `SetMapMode` method will set the mapping mode for the device context.

The `SetOutputDC` Method

`void SetOutputDC( HDC hDC );`

where

    hDC   The device context for output.

The `SetOutputDC` method sets the device context to use for output.

The `SetPixel` Method

`COLORREF SetPixel( int x, int y, COLORREF crColor );`
`COLORREF SetPixel( POINT point, COLORREF crColor );`

where

    x   The X coordinate of the pixel.

    y   The Y coordinate of the pixel.

    crColor   The desired color for that pixel.

    point   The X,Y coordinate of the pixel.

Returns the actual color of the pixel.

The `SetPixel` method can set an individual pixel's color.

The `SetPixelV` Method

`BOOL SetPixelV( int x, int y, COLORREF crColor );`
`BOOL SetPixelV( POINT point, COLORREF crColor );`

where

    x   The X coordinate of the pixel.

    y   The Y coordinate of the pixel.

    crColor   The desired color for that pixel.

    point   The X,Y coordinate of the pixel.

Returns TRUE if successful.

The `SetPixelV` method can set an individual pixel's color, it does not need to return the actual color of the pixel.

The `SetPolyFillMode` Method

```
int SetPolyFillMode( int nMode );
```

where

nMode   The polygon filling mode. Should be either ALTERNATE or WINDING.

Returns the previous polygon filling mode.

The `SetPolyFillMode` method is called to set the fill mode for the polygon.

The `SetROP2` Method

```
int SetROP2( int nMode );
```

where

nMode   The drawing mode.

Returns the previous drawing mode.

The `SetROP2` method is called to set the drawing mode for the device context.

The `SetStretchBltMode` Method

```
int SetStretchBltMode( int nMode );
```

where

nMode   The bitmap stretching mode.

Returns the previous bitmap stretching mode.

The `SetStretchBltMode` method is called to set the bitmap stretching mode for the device context.

The `SetTextColor` Method

```
COLORREF SetTextColor( COLORREF crColor );
```

where

crColor   The desired color for text.

The `SetTextColor` method sets the color for text output.

The `SetViewportOrg` Method

```
virtual CPoint SetViewportOrg( int x, int y);
virtual CPoint SetViewportOrg( CPoint point);
```

where

x   The x coordinate of the viewport origin.

y   The y coordinate of the viewport origin.

point   The x and y coordinates of the viewport origin.

Returns the previous viewport origin.

The `SetViewportOrg` method sets the viewport origin for the device context.

C

The `SetViewportExt` Method

```
virtual CSize SetViewportExt( int x, int y);
virtual CSize SetViewportExt( CSize size);
```

where

x	The x extent of the viewport origin.
y	The y extent of the viewport origin.
size	The x and y extents of the viewport origin.

Returns the previous viewport extent.

The `SetViewportExt` method sets the viewport extent for the device context.

The `SetWindowOrg` Method

```
virtual CPoint SetWindowOrg( int x, int y);
virtual CPoint SetWindowOrg( CPoint point);
```

where

x	The x coordinate of the window origin.
y	The y coordinate of the window origin.
point	The x and y coordinates of the window origin.

Returns the previous window origin.

The `SetWindowOrg` method sets the window origin for the device context.

The `SetWindowExt` Method

```
virtual CSize SetWindowExt( int x, int y);
virtual CSize SetWindowExt( CSize size);
```

where

x	The x extent of the window origin.
y	The y extent of the window origin.
size	The x and y extents of the window origin.

Returns the previous window extent.

The `SetWindowExt` method sets the window extent for the device context.

The `StretchBlt` Method

```
BOOL StretchBlt( int x, int y, int nWidth, int nHeight, CDC* pSrcDC, int
➥xSrc, int ySrc, int nSrcWidth, int nSrcHeight, DWORD dwRop );
```

where

x	X coordinate of the destination rectangle.
y	Y coordinate of the destination rectangle.
nWidth	Width of the destination rectangle.
nHeight	Height of the destination rectangle.
pSrcDC	The source device context.
xSrc	The X coordinate of the source rectangle.

ySrc	The Y coordinate of the source rectangle.
nSrcWidth	The width of the source rectangle.
nSrcHeight	The height of the source rectangle.
dwRop	Specifies how to copy the bits(see `BitBlt`).

Returns TRUE if successful.

The `StrechBlt` object is used to copy pixels from one device context to another. Usually the source device context is a memory-based device context with a bitmap selected into it. If the source and destination rectangles are of different sizes, the bitmap will be stretched.

The `TabbedTextOut` Method

```
virtual CSize TabbedTextOut( int x,int y,LPCTSTR lpszString, int nCount,
➡int nTabPositions, LPINT lpnTabStopPositions, int nTabOrigin );
CSize TabbedTextOut( int x,int y,CString &str, int nTabPositions, LPINT
➡lpnTabStopPositions, int nTabOrigin );
```

where

x	The x coordinate to display the text at.
y	The y coordinate to display the text at.
lpszString	The string to display.
nCount	The number of characters to display.
str	The string to display.
nTabPositions	The number of tab positions.
lpnTabStopPositions	An array of tab stop positions.
nTabOrigin	The tab origin.

Returns the dimensions of the rectangle around the text displayed.

The `TabbedTextOut` method displays text at the specified coordinate in the current font and text color. This method interprets tabs as specified by the tab array.

The `TextOut` Method

```
virtual BOOL TextOut( int x,int y,LPCTSTR lpszString, int nCount );
BOOL TextOut( int x,int y,CString &str );
```

where

x	The x coordinate to display the text at.
y	The y coordinate to display the text at.
lpszString	The string to display.
nCount	The number of characters to display.
str	The string to display.

Returns TRUE if successful.

The `TextOut` method displays text at the specified coordinate in the current font and text color.

The **UpdateColors** Method

```
void UpdateColors();
```

The UpdateColors Method will update the colors displayed in a device context to the current physical palette.

CDialog

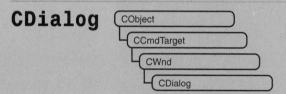

Dialog boxes are windows that consist primarily of controls. CDialog is the base class for windows of this type. A dialog box can be either modeless or modal. A modeless dialog box behaves much like a normal window, and stays on the screen until it is closed. A modal dialog will not allow the user to proceed until some action is taken that results in the closing of the dialog box.

A dialog template resource defines the look of a dialog box. This association is done automatically if the new dialog class was created using Class Wizard.

For an example of CDialog, see the DialogEx example found on the CD-ROM that accompanies this book.

Header Files

The following header files should be included when using this class:

```
afxwin.h
```

Methods

The CDialog class has the following methods:

CDialog	The constructor
Create	Create a dialog box
CreateIndirect	Create a dialog box
DoModal	Begin a modal dialog box
EndDialog	End a modal dialog box
GetDefID	Get the default pushbutton ID
GotoDlgCtrl	Move the focus to the specified control
InitModalIndirect	Create a non-resource based dialog
MapDialogRect	Convert dialog units to screen units
NextDlgCtrl	Move focus to the next dialog control
PrevDlgCtrl	Move focus to the previous dialog control
SetDefID	Set the default pushbutton ID
SetHelpID	Set the context-sensitive help ID for this dialog

The following methods are used to process messages sent to the CDialog class.

OnCancel	Called if Cancel is clicked
OnInitDialog	Called when dialog box starts
OnOK	Called if OK is clicked
OnSetFont	Called to set the font for the dialog box

The **CDialog** Constructor

The CDialog constructor creates the CDialog object. The CDialog constructor is used as follows:

```
CDialog( LPCTSTR lpszTemplateName, CWnd* pParentWnd = NULL );
CDialog( UINT nIDTemplate, CWnd* pParentWnd = NULL );
CDialog( );
```

where

lpszTemplateName	String that contains the name of the resource template.
pParentWnd	The parent window for this dialog box. If NULL, the parent window will be the main application window.
nIDTemplate	The ID of a resource template for the dialog box.

The CDialog constructor will create a dialog box based on a dialog template. If the default constructor is called, the Create method must be used to set up the dialog box.

The **Create** Method

```
BOOL Create( LPCTSTR lpszTemplateName, CWnd* pParentWnd = NULL );
BOOL Create( UINT nIDTemplate, CWnd* pParentWnd = NULL );
```

where

lpszTemplateName	String that contains the name of the resource template.
pParentWnd	The parent window for this dialog box. If NULL, the parent window will be the main application window.
nIDTemplate	The ID of a resource template for the dialog box.

Returns TRUE if successful.

The Create method will create a modeless dialog box based on a dialog template in a resource file.

The **CreateIndirect** Method

```
BOOL CreateIndirect( LPCDLGTEMPLATE lpDialogTemplate, CWnd* pParentWnd =
➥NULL );
BOOL CreateIndirect( HGLOBAL hDialogTemplate, CWnd* pParentWnd = NULL );
```

where

lpDlgTemplate	A pointer to a dialog template in memory.
pParentWnd	The parent window for this dialog box. If NULL, the parent window will be the main application window.
hDialogTemplate	A global handle to a dialog box template.

Returns TRUE if successful

The CreateIndirect method will create a modeless dialog box based on a dialog template in memory.

The `DoModal` Method

```
virtual int DoModal( );
```

>   *DoModal( )*   Returns the value passed to the `EndDialog` method that ended the modal dialog box.

The `DoModal` dialog box is called to display and process a modal dialog box. After it is called, this method will not return until the `EndDialog` method is called.

The `EndDialog` Method

```
void EndDialog( int nResult );
```

where

>   *nResult*   Value that `DoModal` should return.

The `EndDialog` method should be called sometime after `DoModal` has been called. The `EndDialog` method will cause the `DoModal` method to complete and return the *nResult* parameter. The `EndDialog` method should only be called for modal dialog boxes.

The `GetDefID` Method

```
DWORD GetDefID( ) const;
```

Returns a `DWORD`. If the default pushbutton has an ID value, the high-order word contains `DC_HASDEFID` and the low-order word contains the ID value. If the default pushbutton does not have an ID value, this method returns `0`.

The `GotoDlgCtrl` Method

```
void GotoDlgCtrl( CWnd *pWndCtrl);
```

where

>   *pWndCtrl*   A pointer to the control that is to receive focus.

The `GotoDlgCtrl` method changes focus. To get the pointer to any control on the dialog box, by ID number, use the `GetDlgItem` method of the `CWnd` class.

The `InitModalIndirect` Method

```
BOOL InitModalIndirect( LPCDLGTEMPLATE lpDialogTemplate, CWnd*
 pParentWnd = NULL );
BOOL InitModalIndirect( HGLOBAL hDialogTemplate, CWnd* pParentWnd
  = NULL );
```

where

>   *lpDialogTemplate*   A pointer to a dialog template in memory.
>
>   *pParentWnd*   The parent window for this dialog box. If `NULL`, the parent window will be the main application window.
>
>   *hDialogTemplate*   A global handle to a dialog box template.

Returns `TRUE` if successful

The `InitModalIndirect` method will create a modal dialog box based on a dialog template in memory.

The `MapDialogRect` Method

```
void MapDialogRect( LPRECT lpRect ) const;
```

where

    lpRect   A rectangle in dialog units.

The `MapDialogRect` method will convert dialog units to screen units (pixels).

The `NextDlgCtrl` Method

```
void NextDlgCtrl( ) const;
```

The `NextDlgCtrl` method will move focus to the next dialog control.

The `PrevDlgCtrl` Method

```
void PrevDlgCtrl( ) const;
```

The `PrevDlgCtrl` method will move focus to the previous dialog control.

The `SetDefID` Method

```
void SetDefID( UINT nID );
```

where

    nID   Specifies the dialog box button to become the default item.

The `SetDefID` method will set the default control for the dialog box.

The `SetHelpID` Method

```
void SetHelpID( UINT nIDR );
```

where

    nIDR   Specifies the context help ID for this dialog box.

The `SetHelpID` will set the help context ID for this dialog.

The `OnCancel` Method

```
virtual void OnCancel( );
```

This method is called when the user clicks the Cancel button or presses the Esc key. The default method calls `EndDialog` with `IDCANCEL`. Usually application programs override this method to provide processing for the Cancel button. Applications that override this method should not call the `CDialog` `OnCancel` method, as it will call `EndDialog`.

The `OnInitDialog` Method

```
BOOL OnInitDialog( );
```

Returns `TRUE` if Windows should set the input focus to the first control, `FALSE` if the application has set the input focus.

This method is called when the dialog box is setting up. Application programs generally override this method to perform any initialization.

The `OnOK` Method

```
virtual void OnOK( );
```

This method is called when the user clicks the OK button. The default method called `EndDialog` with `IDOK`. Usually application programs override this method to provide processing for the OK button. Applications that override this method should not call the `CDialog` `OnOK` method, as it will call `EndDialog`.

CDialogBar

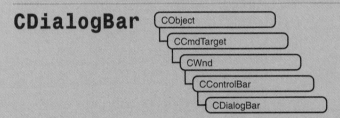

A `CDialogBar` object creates a specialized toolbar. A `CDialogBar` can contain any element that a dialog box can. Because this class is also a toolbar, it can be docked at the side of a frame window. `CDialogBar` objects are very similar to `CFormView` objects.

To create a `CDialogBar` object, a dialog resource template must be made. This dialog box item should have `WS_CHILD` and no other styles. The ID of this resource should be passed to the `Create` method.

Header Files

The following header file should be included when using this class:

`afxext.h`

Methods

The `CDialogBar` class has the following methods:

CDialogBar	The constructor
Create	Creates a dialog bar

The CDialogBar Constructor

The `CDialogBar` creates the `CDialogBar` object. The `CDialogBar` constructor is used as follows:

`CDialogBar( );`

The Create Method

```
BOOL Create( CWnd* pParentWnd, LPCTSTR lpszTemplateName, UINT nStyle, UINT
➥ nID );
BOOL Create( CWnd* pParentWnd, UINT nIDTemplate, UINT nStyle, UINT nID );
```

where

pParentWnd	The parent window.
lpszTemplateName	A dialog resource template name.
nStyle	How the bar should be dockable (see `EnableDocking` of `CControlBar` for more information).
nID	The control ID for this object.
nIDTemplate	A dialog resource template ID.

Returns TRUE if successful.

The Create method creates a dialog bar.

CDocTemplate

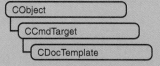

Document templates are an essential part of MFC's Document View architecture. Document templates enable MFC to coordinate document and view creation. CDocTemplate represents an abstract base class. CSingleDocTemplate and CMultiDocTemplate are the two classes that should be used by application programmers. If the application is based on a single document frame, CSingleDocTemplate should be used. If the application is based on a multiple document interface(MDI), CMultiDocTemplate should be used.

For an example of CDocTemplate, see the EditViewEx example found on the CD-ROM that accompanies this book.

Header Files

The following header file should be included when using this class:

afxwin.h

Methods

The CDocTemplate class has the following methods:

CDocTemplate	The constructor
AddDocument	Add a document
CloseAllDocuments	Close all documents
CreateNewDocument	Create a new document
CreateNewFrame	Create a new frame window containing a document/view pair
CreateOleFrame	Create an OLE-enabled frame window
GetDocString	Get a string associated with the associated document type
GetFirstDocPosition	Get the first known document type
GetNextDoc	Get the next known document type
InitialUpdateFrame	Initialize the frame window
LoadTemplate	Load the resource for this object
MatchDocType	Attempt to match a document type
OpenDocumentFile	Open a document file
RemoveDocument	Remove a document from this template
SaveAllModified	Save all modified documents
SetContainerInfo	Determine resources for OLE containers
SetDefaultTitle	Set the default title for a document
SetServerInfo	Determine needs for in-place editing

The `CDocTemplate` Constructor

The `CDocTemplate` creates the `CDocTemplate` object. The `CDocTemplate` constructor is used as follows:

```
CDocTemplate ( UINT nIDResource, CRuntimeClass* pDocClass, CRuntimeClass*
➡pFrameClass, CRuntimeClass* pViewClass );
```

where

nIDResource	The ID of the resources to be used with this document template.
pDocClass	The document class to be used with this document template.
pFrameClass	The frame class to be used with this document template.
pViewClass	The view class to be used with this document template.

The `CDocTemplate` constructor creates a document template that binds a view, frame, and document together. Call `AddDoc` from `CWinApp` to enable the application to begin using this document template.

The `AddDocument` Method

```
virtual void AddDocument( CDocument* pDoc );
```

where

pDoc	The document to be added.

The `AddDocument` method adds a document to a template. The derived classes `CMultiDocTemplate` and `CSingleDocTemplate` override this method.

The `CloseAllDocuments` Method

```
virtual void CloseAllDocuments( BOOL bEndSession );
```

where

bEndSession	TRUE if the session is ending.

The `CloseAllDocuments` method will close all documents (and their views and frames) of this type.

The `CreateNewDocument` Method

```
virtual CDocument* CreateNewDocument( );
```

Returns a pointer to the newly created document.

The `CreateNewDocument` method will create a new document of the type managed by this document template.

The `CreateNewFrame` Method

```
virtual CFrameWnd* CreateNewFrame( CDocument* pDoc, CFrameWnd* pOther );
```

where

pDoc	The document for the new frame, can be NULL.
pOther	The frame window upon which to base the new frame, can be NULL.

Returns a pointer to the newly created frame window.

The `CreateNewFrame` method creates a new frame window with a document.

The `CreateOleFrame` Method

```
CFrameWnd* CreateOleFrame( CWnd* pParentWnd, CDocument* pDoc, BOOL bCreateView );
```

where

pParentWnd	A pointer to the parent window for the frame.
pDoc	A pointer to the document to which the new OLE frame refers.
bCreateView	Determines whether a view is created.

Returns a pointer to the newly created frame window.

The `CreateOleFrame` method creates a new frame window that is OLE enabled.

The `GetDocString` Method

```
virtual BOOL GetDocString( CString& rString, enum DocStringIndex index ) const;
```

where

rString	A string reference that will contain the document string.
index	An index that specifies the document string desired.

Returns TRUE if the substring was found.

`GetDocString` returns an indexed string from the document template. Valid indexes are

CDocTemplate::windowTitle	The main window title (only SDI apps).
CDocTemplate::docName	Root name for all new untitled documents. For example, `"sheet"`.
CDocTemplate::fileNewName	Name of this document type.
CDocTemplate::filterName	Name of the filter for documents of this type (for example, `*.xls`).
CDocTemplate::filterExt	Extension for documents of this type (for example, `.xls`).
CDocTemplate::regFileTypeId	Identifier for the document type to be stored in the registration database maintained by Windows (for example, `ExcelWorksheet`).
CDocTemplate::regFileTypeName	Name of the document type to be stored in the registration database (for example, `"Microsoft Excel Worksheet"`).

The `GetFirstDocPosition` Method

```
virtual POSITION GetFirstDocPosition( ) const = 0;
```

Returns the position of the first document of this type.

The `GetNextDoc` Method

```
virtual CDocument* GetNextDoc( POSITION& rPos ) const = 0;
```

where

rPos	A position.

Returns a position to the next document after *rPos*.

The `InitialUpdateFrame` Method

```
virtual void InitialUpdateFrame( CFrameWnd* pFrame, CDocument* pDoc,
➡ BOOL bMakeVisible = TRUE );
```

where

pFrame	The frame window getting the initial update.
pDoc	The document to which the frame is associated. Can be NULL.
pMakeVisible	Should the frame be made visible?

The `InitialUpdateFrame` method should be called after a new frame is created with `CreateNewFrame`. This method allows these frames to receive their `OnInitialUpdate` calls.

The `LoadTemplate` Method

```
virtual void LoadTemplate( );
```

The `LoadTemplate` is called by the framework to load any resources needed by the document template.

The `MatchDocType` Method

```
virtual Confidence MatchDocType( LPCTSTR lpszPathName, CDocument*&
➡rpDocMatch );
virtual Confidence MatchDocType( LPCTSTR lpszPathName, DWORD dwFileType,
➡CDocument*& rpDocMatch );
```

where

lpszPathName	The file that the type is being determined for.
rpDocMatch	Pointer to a document that will be assigned the matching document if the file specified by *lpszPathName* is already open.
dwFileType	The type of the document (Macintosh only)

Returns the confidence level that the document type matches the document template.

The `OpenDocumentFile` Method

```
virtual CDocument* OpenDocumentFile( LPCTSTR lpszPathName, BOOL
➡bMakeVisible = TRUE ) = 0;
```

where

lpszPathName	The file being opened.
bMakeVisible	Should the new document be made visible?

Returns the CDocument object that is created from opening this file. Returns NULL on failure.

The `OpenDocumentFile` method is used to open saved documents.

The `RemoveDocument` Method

```
virtual void RemoveDocument( CDocument* pDoc );
```

where

pDoc	The document to remove.

Removes the document pointed to by *pDoc* from the list of documents associated with this template. The derived classes CMultiDocTemplate and CSingleDocTemplate override this method.

The `SaveAllModified` Method

```
virtual BOOL SaveAllModified( );
```

Saves all documents that have been modified.

The `SetContainerInfo` Method

```
void SetContainerInfo( UINT nIDOleInPlaceContainer );
```

where

> *nIDOleInPlaceContainer* The ID of the resources used when an embedded object is activated.

Sets the ID for the resources to use when an embedded object is activated.

The `SetDefaultTitle` Method

```
virtual void SetDefaultTitle( CDocument* pDocument ) = 0;
```

where

> *pDocument* Pointer to a document.

The `SetDefaultTitle` method will set the title from the specified document to the main title bar.

The `SetServerInfo` Method

```
void SetServerInfo( UINT nIDOleEmbedding, UINT nIDOleInPlaceServer = 0,
➡ CRuntimeClass* pOleFrameClass = NULL, CRuntimeClass* pOleViewClass = NULL );
```

where

> *nIDOleEmbedding* The ID of the resources used when an embedded object is opened in a separate window.
>
> *nIDOleInPlaceServer* The ID of the resources used when an embedded object is activated in-place.
>
> *nOleFrameClass* The frame window to be created for in-place editing.
>
> *pOleViewClass* The view to be created for in-place editing.

The `SetServerInfo` method is used to specify which resources are to be used with the application is used as an OLE server.

CDocument

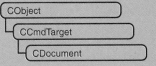

Every MFC application that supports the Document/View architecture should have at least one `CDocument` derived class. That class should hold all of the data related to a document that this application will process. Every `CDocument` derived class should have a `Serialize` method to read and write the data when needed.

For an example of `CDocument`, see the EditViewEx example found on the CD-ROM that accompanies this book.

Header Files

The following header files should be included when using this class:
afxwin.h

Methods

The CDocument class has the following methods:

CDocument	The constructor
AddView	Add a view to this document
CanCloseFrame	Can the frame window be closed?
DeleteContents	Delete the contents of this document
GetDocTemplate	Get the document template for this document
GetFile	Open a file
GetFirstViewPosition	Get the first view for this document
GetNextView	Get the next view for this document
GetPathName	Get path name for this document
GetTitle	Get the title for this document
IsModified	Has this document been modified
OnChangedViewList	Called when the view list changes
OnCloseDocument	Called when the document is going to close
OnFileSendMail	Called to send the document as an email attachment
OnNewDocument	Called when a new document is created
OnOpenDocument	Called when a document is first opened
OnSaveDocument	Called when the document is being saved
OnUpdateFileSendMail	Enables or disables send mail menu
PreCloseFrame	Called before the frame window closes
ReleaseFile	Release a file
RemoveView	Remove a view from this document
ReportSaveLoadException	Called if a load or save cannot complete
SaveModified	Called to ask the user if the document should be saved
SetModifiedFlag	Set the document's modified flag
SetPathName	Set the path name for the document
SetTitle	Set the title for this document
UpdateAllViews	Update all views

The CDocument Constructor

The CDocument creates the CDocument object. The CDocument constructor is used as follows:
CDocument( );

The `AddView` Method

```
void AddView( CView* pView );
```

where

    pView   Pointer to the view being added to this document.

The `AddView` method associates a view with this document.

The `CanCloseFrame` Method

```
virtual BOOL CanCloseFrame( CFrameWnd* pFrame );
```

where

    pFrame   Pointer to the frame window of a view attached to this document.

Returns TRUE if it is okay to close this frame.

The `CanCloseFrame` method is closed before a frame window is closed. If this is the only view on a document, the user is asked to save the document if that document has been modified.

The `DeleteContents` Method

```
virtual void DeleteContents( );
```

The `DeleteContents` method is used to delete the contents of a document from memory. Application programs should override this method to create a method that will delete application-specific data in the document.

The `GetDocTemplate` Method

```
CDocTemplate * GetDocTemplate() const;
```

Returns the document template associated with this document.

The `GetFile` Method

```
virtual CFile* GetFile( LPCTSTR lpszFileName, UINT nOpenFlags,
➥CFileException* pError );
```

where

    lpszFilename   The file to open.

    nOpenFlags   Open flags (see CFile for more info).

    pError   A file exception that will contain the completion status of the open.

Returns a CFile object for use with the specified file.

The `GetFile` method is used to get a pointer to a CFile object.

The `GetFirstViewPosition` Method

```
virtual POSITION GetFirstViewPosition( ) const;
```

Returns the position of the fist view associated with this dialog.

C

The `GetNextView` Method

```
virtual CView* GetNextView( POSITION& rPosition ) const;
```

where

    rPosition   A position.

Returns the next position after *rPosition*.

The `GetPathName` Method

```
const CString& GetPathName( ) const;
```

Returns the complete path for the underlying file.

The `GetTitle` Method

```
const CString& GetTitle( ) const;
```

Returns the title for this document.

The `IsModified` Method

```
BOOL IsModified( );
```

Returns TRUE if the document has been modified.

The `OnChangedViewList` Method

```
virtual void OnChangedViewList( );
```

The `OnChangedViewList` method is called by MFC when the view list changes for this document. Override this method if you need to do special processing when the view list changes.

The `OnCloseDocument` Method

```
virtual void OnCloseDocument( );
```

The `OnCloseDocument` method is called by MFC when the document is just about to close. Override this method if you need to do special processing when the document closes.

The `OnFileSendMail` Method

```
void OnFileSendMail( );
```

The `OnFileSendMail` method used to send the document as a mail message.

The `OnNewDocument` Method

```
virtual void OnNewDocument( );
```

The `OnNewDocument` method is called by MFC when a new document is created. Override this method if you need to do special processing when a new document is created.

The `OnOpenDocument` Method

```
virtual BOOL OnOpenDocument( LPCTSTR lpszPathName );
```

where

    lpszPathName   The path of the file being opened.

Returns TRUE if the file was opened successfully.

The `OnOpenDocument` method is called by MFC when the document is just about to open. Override this method if you need to do special processing when the document opens.

The `OnSaveDocument` Method

`virtual BOOL OnSaveDocument( LPCTSTR lpszPathName );`

where

> *lpszPathName*   The path of the file being saved.

Returns TRUE if the file was saved successfully.

The `OnSaveDocument` method is called by MFC when the document is just about to be saved. Override this method if you need to do special processing when the document saves.

The `OnUpdateFileSendMail` Method

`void OnUpdateFileSendMail( CCmdUI* pCmdUI );`

where

> *pCmdUI*   A pointer to the ID_FILE_SEND_MAIL CCmdUI object.

The `OnUpdateFileSendMail` method is called by MFC to determine whether the Send Mail menu item should be enabled or disabled. Overriding this method gives the application the capability to enable or disable mail sending based on conditions internal to the document.

The `PreCloseFrame` Method

`virtual void PreCloseFrame( CFrameWnd* pFrame );`

where

> *pFrame*   A frame window associated with this document.

The `PreCloseFrame` method is called before the frame window is destroyed. Override this method to provide custom processing.

The `ReleaseFile` Method

`virtual void ReleaseFile( CFile* pFile, BOOL bAbort );`

where

> *pFile*   A file object to be released.
>
> *bAbort*   If TRUE, the file is released with CFile::Abort. If FALSE, the file is released with CFile::Close.

The `ReleaseFile` method releases a file object created with the `GetFile` method.

The `RemoveView` Method

`void RemoveView( CView* pView );`

where

> *pView*   A view associated with this document.

The `RemoveView` method removes a view associated with this document. This method is rarely used as this method is generally done by the framework.

C

The `ReportSaveLoadException` Method

```
virtual void ReportSaveLoadException( LPCTSTR lpszPathName, CException*
➥e, BOOL bSaving, UINT nIDPDefault );
```

where

lpszPathName	The name of the document being loaded or saved.
e	A pointer to the exception that was thrown.
bSaving	TRUE if a save was in progress.
nIDPDefault	An identifier to a default error message.

The ReportLoadSaveException method is called if an exception occurs when loading or saving the document. The default implementation displays an error message based on what error occurred.

The `SaveModified` Method

```
virtual BOOL SaveModified( );
```

Returns TRUE if the document should be closed, FALSE if it should not be closed.

The SaveModified method is called to ask the user if a modified document should be saved.

The `SetModifiedFlag` Method

```
void SetModifiedFlag( BOOL bModified = TRUE );
```

where

bModified	Specifies whether the view has been modified.

The SetModifiedFlag method sets the modified flag for the document.

The `SetPathName` Method

```
virtual void SetPathName( LPCTSTR lpszPathName, BOOL bAddToMRU = TRUE );
```

where

lpszPathName	Specifies the new path name for the document.
bAddToMRU	Specifies if the name should be added to the most recently used list.

SetPathName sets the path name for the document.

The `SetTitle` Method

```
virtual void SetTitle( LPCTSTR lpszTitle );
```

where

lpszTitle	Specifies the new title for the document.

The SetTitle sets the title for the document.

The `UpdateAllViews` Method

```
void UpdateAllViews( CView* pSender, LPARAM lHint = 0L, CObject* pHint =
➥NULL );
```

where

pSender	Pointer to the view that modified the document. Can be NULL.
lHint	Contains information about the modification.
pHint	Points to an object that contains information about the modification.

The UpdateAllViews causes all views to be updated. A hint can be sent to tell the views what needs to be updated. The format of this hint can be anything the programmer decides. This method is usually called after the document data changes, so that each view can update itself.

CEditView

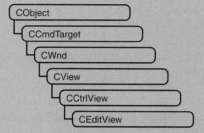

CEditView is a specialized view that creates a very simple word processor. A CEditView based window looks very similar to Notepad.

For an example of CEditView, see the EditViewEx example found on the CD-ROM that accompanies this book.

Header Files

The following header file should be included when using this class:

afxext.h

Properties

The CEditView class has the following properties:

| dwStyleDefault | The default style |

Methods

The CEditView class has the following methods:

CEditView	The constructor
FindText	Search for a string
GetBufferLength	Get the length of the text buffer
GetEditCtrl	Get the underlying edit control used for this view
GetPrinterFont	Get the printer font
GetSelectedText	Get the currently selected text
LockBuffer	Lock the text buffer
PrintInsideRect	Render text inside a rectangle
SerializeRaw	Called to load/save (serialize) this object

SetPrinterFont	Set the printer font
SetTabStops	Set tab stops
UnlockBuffer	Unlock the buffer

The following methods are usually over-ridden by the application program.

OnFindNext	Called when the user wants to find the next text
OnReplaceAll	Called when the user selects Replace All
OnReplaceSel	Called to replace the current selection
OnTextNotFound	Called if text is not found

The CEditView Constructor

The CEditView creates the CEditView object. The CEditView constructor is used as follows:

CEditView

The FindText Method

BOOL FindText(LPCTSTR lpszFind, BOOL bNext = TRUE, BOOL bCase = TRUE);

where

lpszFind	The text being searched for.
bNext	TRUE if search direction is toward the end. FALSE if search direction is toward the front.
bCase	TRUE if this is a case-sensitive search.

Returns TRUE if the text is located.

The FindText method searches for lpszFind in the document. If located, the selection is moved to that text.

The GetBufferLength Method

UINT GetBufferLength( ) const;

Returns the length of the text in the buffer.

The GetEditCtrl Method

CEdit& GetEditCtrl( ) const;

Returns a reference to the underlying edit control.

The GetPrinterFont Method

CFont* GetPrinterFont( ) const;

Returns a pointer to the printer font for this view.

The GetSelectedText Method

void GetSelectedText(CString& strResult) const;

where

strResult	The currently selected text is copied to this string.

The GetSelectedText method gets a copy of the currently selected text.

The `LockBuffer` Method

`LPCTSTR LockBuffer( ) const;`

Returns a string pointer to the start of the text buffer.

The `LockBuffer` method allows direct access to the text buffer of this view. Call `UnlockBuffer` when this pointer is no longer needed.

The `PrintInsideRect` Method

`UINT PrintInsideRect( CDC *pDC, RECT& rectLayout, UINT nIndexStart, UINT ➡nIndexStop );`

where

pDC	The device context to print to.
rectLayout	The rectangle to format outputted text to.
nIndexStart	The starting character for output.
nIndexStop	The ending character for output.

Returns the index of the character after the last character printed.

The `PrintInsideRect` method outputs the contents of the edit control to a rectangle. This output can be sent to any valid device context (CDC).

The SerializeRaw Method

`void SerializeRaw( CArchive& ar );`

where

ar	The archive to serialize to.

The `SerializeRaw` method is used to read or write the contents of the edit control. The file will be read and written as a standard Windows (CR/LF) text file.

The `SetPrinterFont` Method

`void SetPrinterFont( CFont* pFont );`

where

pFont	The font to be used for printer output.

The `SetPrinterFont` method allows the printer font to be specified for an edit view.

The `SetTabStops` Method

`void SetTabStops( int nTabStops );`

where

nTabStops	The width of each tab stop (in dialog units).

The `SetTabStops` method allows the size of tabs to be specified.

The `UnlockBuffer` Method

`void UnlockBuffer( ) const;`

The `UnlockBuffer` method unlocks the buffer after a call to the `LockBuffer` method.

The `OnFindNext` Method

```
virtual void OnFindNext( LPCTSRT lpszFind, BOOL bNext, BOOL bCase );
```

where

lpszFind	The text being searched for.
bNext	TRUE if search direction is toward the end. FALSE if search direction is towards the front.
bCase	TRUE if this is a case-sensitive search.

The `OnFindText` method is called by the framework to enable searching within the Edit View. To provide application-specific dialog boxes and searching, this method should be overridden.

The `OnReplaceAll` Method

```
virtual void OnReplaceAll( LPCTSTR lpszFind, LPCTSTR lpszReplace, BOOL
➥bCase );
```

where

lpszFind	The text being searched for.
lpszReplace	The text that should replace the text specified by *lpszFind*.
bCase	TRUE if this is a case-sensitive search.

The `OnReplaceAll` method is called by the standard find/replace dialog box in response to the user clicking Replace All.

The `OnReplaceSel` Method

```
virtual void OnReplaceSel( LPCTSTR lpszFind, BOOL bNext, BOOL bCase,
➥LPCTSTR lpszReplace );
```

where

lpszFind	The text being searched for.
lpszReplace	The text that should replace the text specified by *lpszFind*.
bNext	TRUE if this is a case-sensitive search.
bCase	TRUE if this is a case-sensitive search.

The `OnReplaceSel` method is called when the user selects Replace on the standard find/replace dialog box.

The `OnTextNotFound` Method

```
virtual void OnTextNotFound( LPCTSTR lpszFind );
```

where

lpszFind	The text being searched for.

The `OnTextNotFound` method is called when the text being searched for cannot be found.

CEvent

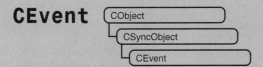

Allows multithreaded applications to synchronize threads. An event allows one thread to block (or wait) until a second thread releases an event.

Header Files

The following header file should be included when using this class:

afxmt.h

Methods

The CEvent class has the following methods:

CEvent	The constructor
PulseEvent	Release waiting threads
ResetEvent	Set the event to unavailable
SetEvent	Set the event to available
Unlock	Releases the event object

The CEvent Constructor

The CEvent constructor creates the CEvent object. The CEvent constructor is used as follows:

CEvent(BOOL bInitiallyOwn = FALSE, BOOL bManualReset = FALSE, LPCTSTR
➥lpszName = NULL, LPSECURITY_ATTRIBUTES lpsaAttribute = NULL);

where

bInitiallyOwn	TRUE if the thread owning the CMultiLock or CSingleLock object is enabled. Otherwise, all threads wanting access to the resource will wait.
bManualReset	TRUE if manual, FALSE if automatic.
lpszName	The name of this object.
lpsaAttribute	Security attributes.

The CEvent constructor creates a named or unnamed event object. To use this object, a CMultiLock or CSingleLock object must be used.

The PulseEvent Method

BOOL PulseEvent( );

Returns TRUE if successful.

The PulseEvent method sets the state to available, releases any waiting threads, and then resets the state to unavailable.

The ResetEvent Method

BOOL ResetEvent( );

Returns TRUE if successful.

The ResetEvent method sets the state to unavailable.

The SetEvent Method

```
BOOL SetEvent( );
```

Returns TRUE if successful.

The SetEvent method sets the state to available.

The Unlock Method

```
virtual BOOL Unlock( );
```

Returns TRUE if successful.

The Unlock method releases the event.

CException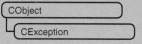

MFC uses exception-based error handling. Code inside try blocks can throw exceptions when an error occurs. CException is the base class for any type of exception MFC is going to throw.

Header Files

The following header files should be included when using this class:

```
afx.h
```

Methods

The CException class has the following methods:

CException	The constructor
Delete	Delete this exception object
GetErrorMessage	Get an error string to describe this error
ReportError	Display the error in a message box

The CException Constructor

The CException creates the CException object. The CException constructor is used as follows:

```
CException( BOOL b_AutoDelete );
```

where

bAutoDelete   Should be TRUE if the object was allocated on the heap. If this object was created on the stack (local variable) this parameter should be FALSE.

The Delete Method

```
void Delete( );
```

The Delete method will delete this exception. If this exception was constructed with *bAutoDelete* to TRUE, the memory associated with this exception is also deleted.

The GetErrorMessage Method

```
virtual BOOL GetErrorMessage( LPTSTR lpszError, UINT nMaxError, PUINT
➥pnHelpContext = NULL );
```

where

lpszError	A string that will have the error message text copied to it.
nMaxError	The maximum number of characters that can be stored to lpszError.
pnHelpContext	A unsigned int pointer that will receive the help context ID for this error.

The GetErrorMessage method is used to get a meaningful error message from an exception that has been thrown.

The ReportError Method

```
virtual int ReportError( UINT nType = MB_OK, UINT nMessageID = 0 );
```

where

nType	The type of message box to use to display the error.
nMessageID	A string resource ID for a default message to display if no message is available from the exception.

The ReportError method can be called to display a message box containing the error report generated by the exception.

CFile

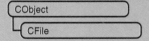

The CFile class is MFC's base file class. It provides unbuffered binary access to files. Indirectly, through its derived classes, it supports buffering and text files. Usually applications will use the CFile class through the CArchive class. For cases in which direct file access is needed, CFile should be used.

Header Files

The following header file should be included when using this class:

afx.h

Properties

The CFile class has the following properties:

m_hFile	The underlying file handle for this object.

Methods

The CFile class has the following methods:

CFile	The constructor
Abort	Close the file, disregard any errors
Close	Close the file and delete the object
Duplicate	Create a second object based on this file
Flush	Write any buffered data
GetFileName	Get the name of the file
GetFilePath	Get the complete path to the file
GetFileTitle	Get the title of the file
GetLength	Get the length of the file
GetPosition	Get the current position in the file
GetStatus	Get the current file status
LockRange	Lock a range in the file
Open	Open a file
Read	Read data from the file
ReadHuge	Read a huge amount of data from the file
Remove	Delete a file
Rename	Rename a file
Seek	Move to a specific position within a file
SeekToBegin	Move to the beginning of a file
SeekToEnd	Move to the end of a file
SetFilePath	Sets the full path for a file
SetLength	Change the length of a file
SetStatus	Set the status for a file
UnlockRange	Unlock a range of bytes
Write	Write to the file
WriteHuge	Write a huge amount of data to the file

The CFile Constructor

The CFile creates the CFile object. The default constructor can be used, or parameters can be provided to specify a file to open. The CFile constructor is used as follows:

```
CFile( );
CFile( int hFile );
CFile( LPCTSTR lpszFileName, UINT nOpenFlags );
```

where

hFile	A already opened file handle to create an object for.
lpszFileName	The file to open.
nOpenFlags	How to open the file.

For more information about how to open a file with the constructor, see the Open method.

This constructor can throw the CFileException exception.

The Abort Method

```
virtual void Abort( );
```

Closes the file after an error has occurred. Unlike Close, this method will not throw an exception.

The Close Method

```
void Close( );
```

Closes the file normally.

This method can throw the CFileException exception.

The Duplicate Method

```
virtual CFile * Duplicate( );
```

Returns a new file object that is identical to the current one.

This method can throw the CFileException exception.

The Flush Method

```
virtual void Flush( );
```

Write any unwritten data, but do not close the file.

This method can throw the CFileException exception.

The GetFileName Method

```
virtual CString GetFileName() const;
```

Returns the name of the file, not including the path.

The GetFilePath Method

```
virtual CString GetFilePath() const;
```

Returns the complete path to the file.

The GetFileTitle Method

```
virtual CString GetFileTitle() const;
```

Returns the title of the file, this does not include the path or extension.

The GetLength Method

```
virtual DWORD GetFileName() const;
```

Returns the length of the file.

This method can throw the CFileException exception.

The GetPosition Method

```
virtual DWORD GetPosition() const;
```

Returns the current position within the file.

This method can throw the CFileException.

The `GetFileName` Method

```
virtual CString GetFileName() const;
```

Returns the name of the file, not including the path.

The `GetStatus` Method

```
BOOL GetStatus( CFileStatus& rStatus ) const;
static BOOL PASCAL GetStatus( LPCTSTR lpszFileName, CFileStatus& rStatus );
```

where

rStatus	A structure to contain information about the specified file.
lpszFileName	The file to obtain status information.

Returns TRUE if successful.

The GetStatus method gets status information for either the current file or a specified file. The CFileStatus structure returned by the method has the following fields:

CTime m_ctime	The date and time the file was created.
CTime m_mtime	The date and time the file was last modified.
CTime m_atime	The date and time the file was last accessed for reading.
LONG m_size	The logical size of the file in bytes, as reported by the DIR command.
BYTE m_attribute	The attribute byte of the file.
char m_szFullName[_MAX_PATH]	The absolute filename in the Windows character set.

The `LockRange` Method

```
virtual void LockRange( DWORD dwPos, DWORD dwCount );
```

where

dwPos	The starting position(in bytes) for the range to be locked.
dwCount	The number of bytes to lock.

The LockRange method will lock a range of bytes so that other programs cannot access that section of the file.

This method can throw the CFileException.

The `Open` Method

```
virtual BOOL Open( LPCTSTR lpszFileName, UINT nOpenFlags, CFileException*
➥pError = NULL );
```

where

lpszFileName	The file to open.
nOpenFlags	How to open the file.
pError	A pointer to a CFileException that will receive error information.

Returns TRUE if successful. The *pError* parameter is only meaningful if FALSE is returned.

The Open method will open the specified file. The Open method will not throw an exception, but rather will return the exception that would have been thrown in the *pError* parameter.

The following flags are valid for the *nOpenFlags* parameter. Several can be specified by ORing them together.

CFile::modeCreate	Direct the constructor to create a new file. If the file exists already, it is truncated to zero length.
CFile::modeNoTruncate	Combine this value with modeCreate. If the file being created already exists, it is not truncated to zero length. Thus the file is guaranteed to open, either as a newly created file or as an existing file. This might be useful, for example, when opening a settings file that might or might not exist already. This option applies to CStdioFile as well.
CFile::modeRead	Open the file for reading only.
CFile::modeReadWrite	Open the file for reading and writing.
CFile::modeWrite	Open the file for writing only.
CFile::modeNoInherit	Prevent the file from being inherited by child processes.
CFile::shareDenyNone	Open the file without denying other processes read or write access to the file. Create fails if the file has been opened in compatibility mode by any other process.
CFile::shareDenyRead	Open the file and denies other processes read access to the file. Create fails if the file has been opened in compatibility mode or for read access by any other process.
CFile::shareDenyWrite	Open the file and denies other processes write access to the file. Create fails if the file has been opened in compatibility mode or for write access by any other process.
CFile::shareExclusive	Open the file with exclusive mode, denying other processes both read and write access to the file. Construction fails if the file has been opened in any other mode for read or write access, even by the current process.
CFile::shareCompat	This flag is not available in 32-bit MFC. This flag maps to CFile::shareExclusive when used in CFile::Open.
CFile::typeText	Sets text mode with special processing for carriage return–line-feed pairs (used in derived classes only).
CFile::typeBinary	Sets binary mode (used in derived classes only).

The Read Method

```
virtual UINT Read( void* lpBuf, UINT nCount );
```

where

lpBuf	A buffer to read data into.
nCount	The number of bytes to read.

Returns the number of bytes actually read.

The Read method will read the specified number of bytes from the file. This method can only read 64KB at once. To read a larger quantity of data, use the ReadHuge method.

This method can throw the CFileException exception.

The ReadHuge Method

```
DWORD ReadHuge( void* lpBuf, DWORD nCount );
```

where

lpBuf	A buffer to read data into.
nCount	The number of bytes to read.

Returns the number of bytes actually read.

The ReadHuge method will read the specified number of bytes from the file.

This method can throw the CFileException exception.

The Remove Method

```
static void PASCAL Remove( LPCTSTR lpszFileName );
```

where

lpszFileName	Specifies a file to delete.

The Remove method will delete a disk based file.

This method can throw the CFileException exception.

The Rename Method

```
static PASCAL void Rename( LPCTSTR lpszOldName, LPCTSTR lpszOldName );
```

where

lpszOldName	The original filename.
lpszNewName	The requested new filename.

The Rename method will change the name of a disk based file.

This method can throw the CFileException exception.

The Seek Method

```
virtual LONG Seek( LONG lOff, UINT nFrom )
```

where

lOff	The number of bytes to move within the file.
nFrom	Where to move from.

The Seek method will move the file pointer the specified number of bytes.

The following are valid values for the *nFrom* parameter:

CFile::begin	Move the file pointer from the beginning of the file.
CFile::current	Move the file pointer from its current position.
CFile::end	Move the file pointer from the end of the file.

This method can throw the CFileException exception.

The SeekToBegin Method

`void SeekToBegin( );`

The SeekToBegin method will move the file pointer the beginning of the file.

This method can throw the CFileException.

The SeekToEnd Method

`DWORD SeekToEnd( );`

The return value is the length of the file in bytes.

The SeekToEnd method will move the file pointer the end of the file.

This method can throw the CFileException.

The SetFilePath Method

`virtual void SetFilePath( LPCTSTR lpszNewName )`

where

    lpszNewName   The new path to associate this object with.

The SetFilePath method will associate the object with the specified path. The file is not opened, only the association is changed.

The SetLength Method

`virtual void SetLength( DWORD dwNewLen )`

where

    dwNewLen   The new length for the file.

The SetLength method is used to set the length of the file.

This method can throw the CFileException.

The SetStatus Method

`static void SetStatus( LPCTSTR lpszFileName, const CFileStatus& status );`

where

    status   A structure to contain information about the specified file.

    lpszFileName   The file to obtain status information.

The SetStatus method sets the status for a current file. The CFileStatus structure contains all this information. See the GetStatus method for more information on the structure of the status parameter.

The UnlockRange Method

`virtual void UnlockRange( DWORD dwPos, DWORD dwCount );`

where

    dwPos   The starting position(in bytes) for the range to be unlocked.

    dwCount   The number of bytes to unlock.

This method can throw a CFileException.

The `UnlockRange` method will unlock a range of bytes so that other programs can access that section of the file.

The `Write` Method

`virtual void Write( void* lpBuf, UINT nCount );`

where

lpBuf	A buffer to read data into.
nCount	The number of bytes to read.

The `Write` method will write the specified number of bytes to the file. This method can only write 64KB at a time. To write a larger quantity of data, use the `WriteHuge` method.

This method can throw the CFileException exception.

The `WriteHuge` Method

`void WriteHuge( void* lpBuf, UINT nCount );`

where

lpBuf	A buffer to read data into.
nCount	The number of bytes to read.

The `WriteHuge` method will write the specified number of bytes to the file.

This method can throw the CFileException exception.

`CFileDialog`

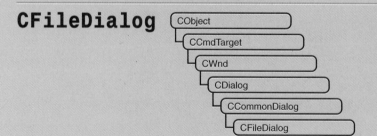

The `CFileDialog` method is used to display the standard file dialog box.

Header Files

The following header files should be included when using this class:
`afxdlgs.h`

Properties

The `CFileDialog` class has the following properties:

m_ofn	The `OPENFILENAME` structure that contains basic parameters for this object.

Methods

The CFileDialog class has the following methods:

CFileDialog	The constructor
DoModal	Process the dialog box
GetFileExt	Get the file extension
GetFileName	Get the filename
GetFileTitle	Get the file title
GetNextPathName	Get the next path name
GetPathName	Get the full path name
GetReadOnlyPref	Get the status of the read-only check box
GetStartPosition	Get the first element of the filename list

The following methods can be overridden to provide custom processing.

OnFileNameChange	Called when the filename changes
OnFileNameOK	Called to validate that the filename was entered correctly
OnFolderChange	Called when the folder changes
OnInitDone	Called when dialog box has finished initial setup
OnLBSelChangedNotify	Called when the list box data changes
OnShareViolation	Called when a share violation occurs

The CFileDialog Constructor

The CFileDialog creates the CFileDialog object. The CFileDialog constructor is used as follows:

```
CFileDialog( BOOL bOpenFileDialog, LPCTSTR lpszDefExt = NULL, LPCTSTR
➡lpszFileName = NULL, DWORD dwFlags = OFN_HIDEREADONLY ¦ OFN_
➡OVERWRITEPROMPT, LPCTSTR lpszFilter = NULL, CWnd* pParentWnd =
➡NULL );
```

where

bOpenFileDialog	TRUE if this is an open dialog box.
lpszDefExt	The default extension. If the user does not include an extension as part of the filename, this extension will be used. Can be NULL if no default extension is desired.
lpszFileName	The initial filename. Can be NULL for no initial filename.
dwFlags	One or more flags allowing the look of the dialog box to be changed.
lpszFilter	A series of string pairs that specify one or more filters.
pParentWnd	The parent window for this dialog box.

The filter string must contain string pairs as specified:

```
"Figrst Filter(*.txt)¦*.txt¦Second Filter(*.doc,*.asc)¦*.txt;*.asc¦"
```

The following flags are valid for the dwFlags structure:

OFN_ALLOWMULTISELECT	Specifies that the File Name list box allows multiple selections. If you also set the OFN_EXPLORER flag, the dialog box uses the Explorer-style user interface; otherwise, it uses the old-style user interface.
OFN_CREATEPROMPT	If the user specifies a file that does not exist, this flag causes the dialog box to prompt the user for permission to create the file. If the user chooses to create the file, the dialog box closes and the function returns the specified name; otherwise, the dialog box remains open.
OFN_ENABLETEMPLATE	Indicates that the lpTemplateName member points to the name of a dialog template resource in the module identified by the hInstance member.
OFN_ENABLETEMPLATEHANDLE	Indicates that the hInstance member identifies a data block that contains a preloaded dialog box template. The system ignores the lpTemplateName if this flag is specified.
OFN_EXPLORER	Indicates that any customizations made to the Open or Save As dialog box use the new Explorer-style customization methods. For more information, see the "Explorer-Style Hook Procedures" and "Explorer-Style Custom Templates" sections of the Common Dialog Box Library overview. If you want the old-style user interface, omit the OFN_EXPLORER flag and provide a replacement old-style template or hook procedure. If you want the old style but do not need a custom template or hook procedure, simply provide a hook procedure that always returns FALSE.
OFN_EXTENSIONDIFFERENT	Specifies that the user typed a filename extension that differs from the extension specified by lpstrDefExt. The function does not use this flag if lpstrDefExt is NULL.
OFN_FILEMUSTEXIST	Specifies that the user can type only names of existing files in the File Name entry field. If this flag is specified and the user enters an invalid name, the dialog box procedure displays a warning in a message box. If this flag is specified, the OFN_PATHMUSTEXIST flag should also be used.
OFN_HIDEREADONLY	Hides the Read Only check box.
OFN_LONGNAMES	For old-style dialog boxes, this flag causes the dialog box to use long filenames. If this flag is not specified, or if the OFN_ALLOWMULTISELECT flag is also set, old-style dialog boxes use short filenames (8.3 format) for filenames with spaces. Explorer-style dialog boxes ignore this flag and always display long filenames.

OFN_NOCHANGEDIR	Restores the current directory to its original value if the user changed the directory while searching for files.
OFN_NODEREFERENCELINKS	Directs the dialog box to return the path and filename of the selected shortcut (.LNK) file. If this value is not given, the dialog box returns the path and filename of the file referenced by the shortcut.
OFN_NOLONGNAMES	For old-style dialog boxes, this flag causes the dialog box to use short filenames (8.3 format). Explorer-style dialog boxes ignore this flag and always display long filenames.
OFN_NONETWORKBUTTON	Hides and disables the Network button.
OFN_NOREADONLYRETURN	Specifies that the returned file does not have the Read Only check box checked and is not in a write-protected directory.
OFN_NOTESTFILECREATE	Specifies that the file is not created before the dialog box is closed. This flag should be specified if the application saves the file on a create-nonmodify network sharepoint. When an application specifies this flag, the library does not check for write protection, a full disk, an open drive door, or network protection. Applications using this flag must perform file operations carefully, because a file cannot be reopened once it is closed.
OFN_NOVALIDATE	Specifies that the common dialog boxes allow invalid characters in the returned filename. Typically, the calling application uses a hook procedure that checks the filename by using the FILEOKSTRING message. If the text box in the edit control is empty or contains nothing but spaces, the lists of files and directories are updated. If the text box in the edit control contains anything else, nFileOffset and nFileExtension are set to values generated by parsing the text. No default extension is added to the text, nor is text copied to the buffer specified by lpstrFileTitle. If the value specified by nFileOffset is less than zero, the filename is invalid. Otherwise, the filename is valid, and nFileExtension and nFileOffset can be used as if the OFN_NOVALIDATE flag had not been specified.
OFN_OVERWRITEPROMPT	Causes the Save As dialog box to generate a message box if the selected file already exists. The user must confirm whether to overwrite the file.
OFN_PATHMUSTEXIST	Specifies that the user can type only valid paths and filenames. If this flag is used and the user types an invalid path and filename in the File Name entry field, the dialog box function displays a warning in a message box.
OFN_READONLY	Causes the Read Only check box to be checked initially when the dialog box is created. This flag indicates the state of the Read Only check box when the dialog box is closed.

C

| OFN_SHAREAWARE | Specifies that if a call to the OpenFile function fails because of a network sharing violation, the error is ignored and the dialog box returns the selected filename. If this flag is not set, the dialog box notifies your hook procedure when a network sharing violation occurs for the filename specified by the user. If you set the OFN_EXPLORER flag, the dialog box sends the CDN_SHAREVIOLATION message to the hook procedure. If you do not set OFN_EXPLORER, the dialog box sends the SHAREVISTRING registered message to the hook procedure. |
| OFN_SHOWHELP | Causes the dialog box to display the Help button. The hwndOwner member must specify the window to receive the HELPMSGSTRING registered messages that the dialog box sends when the user clicks the Help button. |

An Explorer-style dialog box sends a CDN_HELP notification message to your hook procedure when the user clicks the Help button.

The DoModal Method

virtual int DoModal()

Returns either IDOK or IDCANCEL.

The DoModal method will display the dialog box to the user and enable the user to select a file. If the user selects a file then IDOK is returned.

The GetFileExt Method

CString GetFileExt() const;

Returns the extension of the file selected. If the m_ofn.Flags property has the OFN_ALLOWMULTISELECT flag set, this string can contain several extensions separated by NULL values.

The GetFileName Method

CString GetFileName() const;

Returns the name of the file selected. If the m_ofn.Flags property has the OFN_ALLOWMULTISELECT flag set, this string can contain several names separated by NULL values.

The GetFileTitle Method

CString GetFileTitle() const;

Returns the title of the file selected. If the m_ofn.Flags property has the OFN_ALLOWMULTISELECT flag set, this string can contain several titles separated by NULL values.

The GetPathName Method

CString GetPathName() const;

Returns the full path of the file selected. If the m_ofn.Flags property has the OFN_ALLOWMULTISELECT flag set, this string can contain several paths separated by NULL values.

The `GetNextPathName` Method

`CString GetNextPathName( POSITION& pos ) const;`

where

      pos   A reference to a `POSITION` value returned by `GetNextPathName` or `GetStartPosition`.

Returns the path of the next file in the list.

The `GetNextPathName` method returns the next path in a multi-select file dialog box. See the constructor for more information on creating a multiselect file dialog box.

The `GetReadOnlyPref` Method

`BOOL GetReadOnlyPref( ) const;`

Returns `TRUE` if the user has checked the read-only check box.

The `GetStartPosition` Method

`POSITION GetStartPosition( ) const;`

Returns a position to the first file in the file list of a multiselect file dialog box. See the constructor for more information on creating a multiselect file dialog box.

The `OnFileNameChange` Method

`virtual void OnFileNameChange( );`

This method is called when the filename has been changed by the user. Applications can override this method and provide greater control over the processing of the standard file dialog box.

The `OnFileNameOK` Method

`virtual BOOL OnFileNameOK( );`

Returns `TRUE` if the filename is valid, `FALSE` otherwise.

This method is called by MFC to determine if the filename currently selected is valid. Applications can override this method and provide greater control over the processing of the standard file dialog box.

The `OnFolderChange` Method

`virtual void OnFolderChange( );`

This method is called by MFC whenever the folder is changed. Applications can override this method and provide greater control over the processing of the standard file dialog box.

The `OnInitDone` Method

`virtual void OnInitDone( );`

This method is called by MFC whenever the initialization of the dialog is complete. Applications can override this method and provide greater control over the processing of the standard file dialog box.

The `OnLBSelChangedNotify` Method

`virtual void OnLBSelChangedNotify( UINT nIDBox, UINT iCurSel, UINT nCode);`

where

      nIDBox   The ID of the box or combo box where this occurred.

      iCurSel   The index of the current selection.

      nCode   The control notification code.

This method is called by MFC whenever the selected item of a list or combo box changes. Applications can override this method and provide greater control over the processing of the standard file dialog box.

The following values are valid for the *nCode* parameter:

CD_LBSELCHANGE	*iCurSel* is the selected item in a single-selection list box.
CD_LBSELSUB	*iCurSel* has been deselected in a multi-selection list box.
CD_LBSELADD	*iCurSel* is selected in a multi-selection list box.
CD_LBSELNOITEMS	No selection exists in a multi-selection list box.

The `OnShareViolation` Method

```
virtual UINT OnShareViolation( LPCTSTR lpszPathName );
```

where

lpszPathName	The path of the file that caused a share violation.

Returns one of the following values:

OFN_SHAREFALLTHROUGH	The filename is returned from the dialog box.
OFN_SHARENOWARN	No further action needs to be taken.
OFN_SHAREWARN	The user receives the standard warning message for this error.

This method is called by MFC whenever a file share error occurs. Applications can override this method and provide greater control over the processing of the standard file dialog box.

The `OnTypeChange` Method

```
virtual void OnTypeChange( );
```

This method is called by MFC whenever the file type is changed. Applications can override this method and provide greater control over the processing of the standard file dialog box.

CFindReplaceDialog

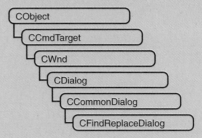

The `CFindReplaceDialog` class implements the find-replace dialog standard dialog box. This dialog box can be used for any sort of find replace operation.

Header Files

The following header file should be included when using this class:

```
afxdlgs.h
```

Property

The `CFindReplaceDialog` class has the following property:

m_fr	A structure used to customize this dialog.

Methods

The `CFindReplaceDialog` class has the following methods:

CFindReplaceDialog	The constructor
Create	Create the object
FindNext	Determine if the next occurrence should be found
GetFindString	Get the string being searched for
GetNotifier	Called from a message handler to get the FINDREPLACE structure
GetReplaceString	Get the string to be replaced
IsTerminating	Is the dialog box terminating?
MatchCase	Determine if case matters
MatchWholeWord	Determine if the user is only searching for whole words
ReplaceAll	Determine if the user wants to replace all words
ReplaceCurrent	Determine if the user wants the current word replaced
SearchDown	Determine if the user wants to search in a downward direction

The `CFindReplaceDialog` Constructor

The `CFindReplaceDialog` constructor creates the `CFindReplaceDialog` object. The default constructor can be used, or parameters can be provided to specify a file to open. The `CFindReplaceDialog` constructor is used as follows:

```
CFindReplaceDialog()
```

The `Create` Method

```
BOOL Create( BOOL bFindDialogOnly, LPCTSTR lpszFindWhat,
➡LPCTSTR lpszReplaceWith = NULL, DWORD dwFlags = FR_DOWN, CWnd*
➡pParentWnd = NULL );
```

where

bFindDialogOnly	TRUE if this is a find dialog box.
lpszFindWhat	The string to be searched for.
lpszReplaceWith	The default string to replace found strings with.
dwFlags	One or more flags specifying the look and operation of the dialog.
pParentWnd	A pointer to the parent window. Can be NULL.

Returns TRUE if successful.

The `Create` method is used to create the find replace dialog box. In order for the parent window to be notified of events from this dialog box, the `RegisterWindowMessage` function should be used to create a unique message number for these messages.

The `FindNext` Method

`BOOL FindNext( );`

Returns TRUE if the user has selected to find the next occurrence.

The `GetFindString` Method

`CString GetFindString( ) const;`

Returns the find string entered into the dialog box.

The `GetNotifier` Method

`static CFindReplaceDialog *PASCAL GetNotifier(LPARAM lParam);`

where

> *lParam*   The *lparam* value that was passed to the frame window's `OnFindReplace`
> method.

Returns the `CFindReplaceDialog` object associated with the *lParam* value.

The `GetNotifier` method should be called from the frame window's `OnFindReplace` method to determine the origin of the find replace message.

The `GetReplaceString` Method

`CString GetReplaceString( ) const;`

Returns the replace string that was entered into the dialog box.

The `IsTerminating` Method

`BOOL IsTerminating( );`

Returns TRUE if the dialog box is being terminated.

The `MatchCase` Method

`BOOL MatchCase( );`

Returns TRUE if the case match check box has been selected.

The `MatchWholeWord` Method

`BOOL MatchWholeWord( );`

Returns TRUE if the Match Whole Word check box has been selected.

The `ReplaceAll` Method

`BOOL ReplaceAll( );`

Returns TRUE if the Replace All check box has been selected.

The `ReplaceCurrent` Method

`BOOL ReplaceCurrent( );`

Returns TRUE if the user wishes to replace the current word.

The `SearchDown` Method

`BOOL SearchDown( );`

Returns TRUE if user is requesting a downward (default) search, FALSE if upward.

CFont

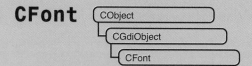

The CFont class represents a GDI font object. A font is a template for drawing text to the screen or printer. One of these objects must be created for each way fonts are to be displayed by the program.

For an example of CFont, see the CDCEx example found on the CD-ROM that accompanies this book.

Header Files

The following header file should be included when using this class:

afxwin.h

Methods

The CFont class has the following methods:

CFont	The constructor
CreateFont	Create a font
CreateFontIndirect	Create a font from a structure
CreatePointFont	Create a font based on point size
CreatePointFontIndirect	Create a font based on point size from a structure
FromHandle	Create a font from a handle to a font
GetLogFont	Get the font structure associated with this font
operator HFONT	Get the font handle associated with this object

The CFont Constructor

The CFont creates the CFont object. The CFont constructor is used as follows:

CFont();

The CreateFont Method

```
BOOL CreateFont( int nHeight, int nWidth, int nEscapement, int nOrientation,
➡int nWeight, BYTE bItalic, BYTE bUnderline, BYTE cStrikeOut, BYTE
➡nCharSet, BYTE nOutPrecision, BYTE nClipPrecision, BYTE nQuality,
➡BYTE nPitchAndFamily, LPCTSTR lpszFacename );
```

where

nHeight	The height in logical units for the font. If greater than zero, then the height is transformed into device units and matched against available fonts. If it is zero, a default size is used. If less than zero, the absolute value is matched against available character heights.
nWidth	Specifies the width in logical units for each character in the font. If zero, the default aspect ratio is applied to what was specified for *nHeight* to determine a reasonable width.
nEscapement	The angle (in 0.1 degree units) between the baseline of a character and the x axis.

nWeight	The darkness of the font. Should be between 0 and 1000.
nHeight	The height in pixels for the font.
bItalic	TRUE if this is an italic font.
bUnderline	TRUE if this is an underlined font.
cStrikeOut	TRUE if this is a strike out font.
nCharSet	The font's character set. Should be ANSI_CHARSET, DEFAULT_CHARSET, SYMBOL_CHARSET, SHIFTJIS_CHARSET, or OEM_CHARSET.
nOutPrecision	The output precision for this font. Should be OUT_CHARACTER_PRECIS, OUT_STRING_PRECIS, OUT_DEFAULT_PRECIS, OUT_STROKE_PRECIS, OUT_DEVICE_PRECIS, OUT_TT_PRECIS, or OUT_RASTER_PRECIS.
nClipPrecision	The clipping precision for this font. Should be CLIP_CHARACTER_PRECIS, CLIP_MASK, CLIP_DEFAULT_PRECIS, CLIP_STROKE_PRECIS, CLIP_ENCAPSULATE, CLIP_TT_ALWAYS, or CLIP_LH_ANGLES.
nQuality	The quality of the font. Should be DEFAULT_QUALITY, DRAFT_QUALITY, or PROOF_QUALITY.
nPatchAndFamily	The pitch and family of the font. These two values should be ORed together. The pitch should be DEFAULT_PITCH, VARIABLE_PITCH, or FIXED_PITCH. The family should be FF_DECORATIVE, FF_DONTCARE, FF_MODER, FF_ROMAN, FF_SCRIPT, or FF_SWISS.
lpszFaceName	The name of the typeface to base this font upon.

Returns TRUE if successful.

The Create method is used to actually create a font object. This font can be selected into a device context for use with the CDC object's text methods.

The **CreateFontIndirect** Method

BOOL CreateFontIndirect(const LOGFONT* lpLogFont);

where

lpLogFont	A pointer to a logical font structure.

Returns TRUE if successful.

The Create method is used to actually create a font object. This font can be selected into a device context for use with the CDC object's text methods. The LOGFONT structure contains the same information that the Create method needs. For more information on these fields see the Create method.

The **CreatePointFont** Method

BOOL CreatePointFont(int nPointSize, LPCTSTR lpszFaceName, CDC* pDC =
➥NULL);

where

nPointSize	The point size in tenths of a point (that is, 10 point = 100).
lpszFaceName	The requested typeface.
nDC	A device context to use to create this font. If NULL, the screen's device context is used.

Returns TRUE if successful.

The CreatePointFont method is used to actually create a font object. This font can be selected into a device context for use with the CDC object's text methods. This method differs from the Create method in that the font's size is specified in points.

The CreatePointFontIndirect Method

BOOL CreatePointFontIndirect(const LOGFONT* lpLogFont, CDC* pDC = NULL);

where

lpLogFont	A LOGFONT structure.
lpszFaceName	The requested typeface.
nDC	A device context to use to create this font. If NULL, the screen's device context is used.

Returns TRUE if successful.

The CreatePointFontIndirect method is used to create a font object. This font can be selected into a device context for use with the CDC object's text methods. This method differs from the Create method in that the font's size is specified in points. To specify the points, the lfHeight of the font structure must be set to tenths of a point rather than logical units.

The FromHandle Method

static CFont* PASCAL FromHandle(HFONT hFont);

where

hFont	A font handle

Returns TRUE if successful.

The FromHandle method is used to create a CFont object from a font handle.

The operator HFONT Method

operator HFONT( ) const;

The font handle associated with this object.

CFontDialog

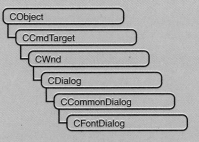

The CFontDialog class is used to display the standard font selection dialog box.

Header Files

The following header files should be included when using this class:

`afxext.h`

Properties

The `CFontDialog` class has the following properties:

m_cf	A structure used to customize the dialog box.

Methods

The `CFontDialog` class has the following methods:

`CFontDialog`	The constructor
`DoModal`	Called to process the dialog box
`GetColor`	The color selected
`GetCurrentFont`	Get the name of the current font
`GetFaceName`	Get the face name of the current font
`GetSize`	Get the size of the current font
`GetStyleName`	Get the style name of the current font
`GetWeight`	Get the font weight of the current font
`IsBold`	`TRUE` if the current font is bold
`IsItalic`	`TRUE` if the current font is italic
`IsStrikeOut`	`TRUE` if the current font is a strikeout font
`IsUnderline`	`TRUE` if the current font is underlined

The `CFontDialog` Constructor

The `CFontDialog` creates the `CFontDialog` object. The `CFontDialog` constructor is used as follows:

```
CFontDialog( LPLOGFONT lplfInitial = NULL, DWORD dwFlags = CF_EFFECTS |
➡CF_SCREENFONTS, CDC* pdcPrinter = NULL, CWnd* pParentWnd = NULL );
```

where

lplfInitial	Pointer to a `LOGFONT` structure that specifies the initial state of the dialog.
dwFlags	Specifies one or more flags that customize the look and usage of the dialog box.
pdcPrinter	Specifies a printer device context.
pParentWnd	Specifies the parent window for this dialog box.

The following are valid flags for the `dwFlags` parameter.

`CF_APPLY`	Causes the dialog box to display the Apply button. You should provide a hook procedure to process `WM_COMMAND` messages for the Apply button. The hook procedure can send the `WM_CHOOSEFONT_GETLOGFONT` message to the dialog box to retrieve the address of the `LOGFONT` structure that contains the current selections for the font.

CF_ANSIONLY	This flag is obsolete. To limit font selections to all scripts except those that use the OEM or Symbol character sets, use CF_SCRIPTSONLY. To get the Windows 3.1 CF_ANSIONLY behavior, use CF_SELECTSCRIPT and specify ANSI_CHARSET in the lfCharSet member of the LOGFONT structure pointed to by lpLogFont.
CF_BOTH	Causes the dialog box to list the available printer and screen fonts. The *hDC* member identifies the device context (or information context) associated with the printer. This flag is a combination of the CF_SCREENFONTS and CF_PRINTERFONTS flags.
CF_TTONLY	Specifies that ChooseFont should only enumerate and allow the selection of TrueType fonts.
CF_EFFECTS	Causes the dialog box to display the controls that allow the user to specify strikeout, underline, and text color options. If this flag is set, you can use the rgbColors member to specify the initial text color. You can use the lfStrikeOut and lfUnderline members of the LOGFONT structure pointed to by lpLogFont to specify the initial settings of the strikeout and underline check boxes. ChooseFont can use these members to return the user's selections.
CF_ENABLEHOOK	Enables the hook procedure specified in the lpfnHook member of this structure.
CF_ENABLETEMPLATE	Indicates that the hInstance and lpTemplateName members specify a dialog box template to use in place of the default template.
CF_ENABLETEMPLATEHANDLE	Indicates that the hInstance member identifies a data block that contains a preloaded dialog box template. The system ignores the lpTemplateName member if this flag is specified.
CF_FIXEDPITCHONLY	Specifies that ChooseFont should select only fixed-pitch fonts.
CF_FORCEFONTEXIST	Specifies that ChooseFont should indicate an error condition if the user attempts to select a font or style that does not exist.
CF_INITTOLOGFONTSTRUCT	Specifies that ChooseFont should use the LOGFONT structure pointed to by the lpLogFont member to initialize the dialog box controls.
CF_LIMITSIZE	Specifies that ChooseFont should select only font sizes within the range specified by the *nSizeMin* and *nSizeMax* members.
CF_NOOEMFONTS	Same as the CF_NOVECTORFONTS flag.
CF_NOFACESEL	When using a LOGFONT structure to initialize the dialog box controls, use this flag to selectively prevent the dialog box from displaying an initial selection for the font name combo box. This is useful when there is no single font name that applies to the text selection.

C

CF_NOSCRIPTSEL   Disables the Script combo box. When this flag is set, the lfCharSet member of the LOGFONT structure is set to DEFAULT_CHARSET when ChooseFont returns. This flag is used only to initialize the dialog box.

CF_NOSTYLESEL   When using a LOGFONT structure to initialize the dialog box controls, use this flag to selectively prevent the dialog box from displaying an initial selection for the font style combo box. This is useful when there is no single font style that applies to the text selection.

CF_NOSIZESEL   When using a LOGFONT structure to initialize the dialog box controls, use this flag to selectively prevent the dialog box from displaying an initial selection for the font size combo box. This is useful when there is no single font size that applies to the text selection.

CF_NOSIMULATIONS   Specifies that ChooseFont should not allow graphics device interface (GDI) font simulations.

CF_NOVECTORFONTS   Specifies that ChooseFont should not allow vector font selections.

CF_NOVERTFONTS   Causes the Font dialog box to list only horizontally oriented fonts.

CF_PRINTERFONTS   Causes the dialog box to list only the fonts supported by the printer associated with the device context (or information context) identified by the hDC member.

CF_SCALABLEONLY   Specifies that ChooseFont should allow only the selection of scalable fonts. (Scalable fonts include vector fonts, scalable printer fonts, TrueType fonts, and fonts scaled by other technologies.)

CF_SCREENFONTS   Causes the dialog box to list only the screen fonts supported by the system.

CF_SCRIPTSONLY   Specifies that ChooseFont should allow selection of fonts for all non-OEM and Symbol character sets, as well as the ANSI character set. This supersedes the CF_ANSIONLY value.

CF_SELECTSCRIPT   When specified on input, only fonts with the character set identified in the lfCharSet member of the LOGFONT structure are displayed. The user will not be allowed to change the character set specified in the Scripts combo box.

CF_SHOWHELP   Causes the dialog box to display the Help button. The hwndOwner member must specify the window to receive the HELPMSGSTRING registered messages that the dialog box sends when the user clicks the Help button.

| CF_USESTYLE | Specifies that the *lpszStyle* member points to a buffer that contains style data ChooseFont should use to initialize the Font Style combo box. When the user closes the dialog box, ChooseFont copies style data for the user's selection to this buffer. |
| CF_WYSIWYG | Specifies that ChooseFont should allow only the selection of fonts available on both the printer and the display. If this flag is specified, the CF_BOTH and CF_SCALABLEONLY flags should also be specified. |

The DoModal Method

virtual int DoModal()

Returns either IDOK or IDCANCEL.

The DoModal method will display the dialog box to the user and allow the user to select a font. If the user selects a font, IDOK is returned.

The GetColor Method

COLORREF GetColor():

Returns the color selected.

The GetCurrentFont Method

void GetCurrentFont(LPLOGFONT lplf);

where

| lplf | A pointer to a LOGFONT structure that specifies the currently selected font. |

The GetCurrentFont method gets a copy of the LOGFONT structure for the currently selected font.

The GetFaceName Method

CString GetFaceName() const:

Returns the face name of the currently selected font.

The GetSize Method

int GetSize() const:

Returns the size of the font in tenths of a point.

The GetStyleName Method

CString GetStyleName() const:

Returns the style of the currently selected font.

The GetWeight Method

int GetWeight() const:

Returns the currently selected font's weight.

The IsBold Method

BOOL IsBold() const:

Returns TRUE if the currently selected font is bold.

The IsItalic Method

BOOL IsItalic() const:

Returns TRUE if the currently selected font is italicized.

The IsStrikeOut Method

BOOL IsStrikeOut() const:

Returns TRUE if the currently selected font is strikeout.

The IsUnderline Method

BOOL IsUnderline() const:

Returns TRUE if the currently selected font is underlined.

CFormView

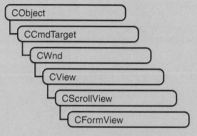

The CFormView class is used as the base class for all form views. A form view is one that is based on a dialog template. If scrolling is needed, the CScrollView functionality can be used.

For an example of CFormView, see the CFormViewEx example found on the CD-ROM that accompanies this book.

Header Files

The following header files should be included when using this class:

afxext.h

Methods

The CFormView class has the following methods:

    CFormView   The constructor

The CFormView Constructor

The CFormView creates the CFormView object. The CFormView constructor is used as follows:

```
CFormView( LPCTSTR lpszTemplateName );
CFormView( UINT nIDTemplate );
```

where

     lpszTemplateName   The string name of a dialog template resource.

     nIDTemplate   The ID of a dialog template resource.

The `CFormView` constructor creates a form view based on a dialog template resource.

CFrameWnd

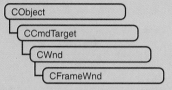

A frame window implements a single document interface (SDI) window. Frame windows usually have a view attached to them that handles the display of data within the client region.

For an example of `CFrameWnd`, see the FormViewEx example found on the CD-ROM that accompanies this book.

Header Files

The following header files should be included when using this class:

`afxwin.h`

Properties

The `CFrameWnd` class has the following properties:

`m_bAutoMenuEnable`	Controls automatic enabling and disabling of menu items.
`m_rectDefault`	This static `rect` object should be passed as a parameter when creating the frame window to allow Windows to choose the window's initial size and position.

Methods

The `CFrameWnd` class has the following methods:

`CFrameWnd`	The constructor
`ActivateFrame`	Called to make the frame visible and available to the user
`BeginModalState`	Set the window frame to be modal
`Create`	Create the frame window
`CreateView`	Create a within the frame
`DockControlBar`	Dock a control bar to this frame
`EnableDocking`	Allow docking inside of this frame
`EndModalState`	End a modal state
`FloatControlBar`	Float the control bar for this window
`GetActiveDocument`	Get the active document for this frame
`GetActiveFrame`	Get the active frame object

GetActiveView	Get the active view
GetControlBar	Get the control bar
GetDockState	Get the docking state
GetMessageString	Get the message string for an ID
InitialUpdateFrame	Called after a new frame is created
InModalState	TRUE if the frame is in a modal state
IsTracking	TRUE if the frame is tracking the mouse
LoadAccelTable	Load the accelerator table
LoadBarState	Load the state of the control bars
LoadFrame	Create a frame from resource information
RecalcLayout	Called to recalculate the layout of the form
SaveBarState	Save the state of the control bars
SetActiveView	Set the active view
SetDockState	Set the docking state
SetMessageText	Set the message text of a standard status bar
ShowControlBar	Show or hide a control bar
ShowOwnedWindows	Show all frame windows

The following methods can be overridden to allow for custom handling of messages and extended control.

GetMessageBar	Get a pointer to the message bar for this frame window
NegotiateBorderSpace	Called to define border space in the frame window
OnContextHelp	Handles Shift-F1 help
OnCreateClient	Creates the client window for the frame
OnSetPreviewMode	Sets the frame into and out of preview mode

The CFrameWnd Constructor

The CFrameWnd constructor creates the CFrameWnd object. The CFrameWnd constructor is used as follows:

CFrameWnd()

The ActivateFrame Method

virtual void ActivateFrame(int nCmdShow = -1);

where

    nCmdShow   How to display the frame window. See CWnd::ShowWindow for more information.

The ActivateFrame method is used to cause the frame window to become visible.

The BeginModalState Method

virtual void BeginModalState();

Call this method to make the frame window modal.

The Create Method

```
BOOL Create( LPCTSTR lpszClassName, LPCTSTR lpszWindowName, DWORD dwStyle =
➡ WS_OVERLAPPEDWINDOW, const RECT& rect = rectDefault, CWnd*
➡pParentWnd = NULL, LPCTSTR lpszMenuName = NULL, DWORD dwExStyle = 0,
➡CCreateContext* pContext = NULL );
```

where

lpszClassName	Specifies the class for this window. Should be a predefined class or one created using AfxRegisterClass.
lpszWindowName	The text to be placed in the window's title bar.
dwStyle	The style for the window. Include FWS_ADDTOTITLE to automatically display the name of the current document. See CWnd::Create for a complete list of styles.
rect	Specifies the size and location of the window.
pParentWnd	A pointer to the parent window.
lpszMenuName	The name of the menu resource to be used with this window. MAKEINTRESOURCE should be use if this is a numeric name. Can be NULL if there is no menu bar.
dwExStyle	The extended style. See CWnd::CreateEx for more information on extended styles.
pContext	A pointer to a CCreateContext structure. This parameter can be NULL.

Returns TRUE if successful.

The Create method is called to actually create a frame window.

The CreateView Method

```
CWnd* CreateView( CCreateContext* pContext, UINT nID = AFX_IDW_PANE_FIRST );
```

where

pContext	Specifies the type of view and document.
nID	The ID number of a view.

Returns a CWnd object.

The CreateView method is used to create a view within the frame. This method should be used to create views that are not CView derived.

The DockControlBar Method

```
void DockControlBar( CControlBar * pBar, UINT nDockBarID = 0, LPCRECT
➡lpRect = NULL );
```

where

pBar	Specifies the bar that is being docked.
nDockBarID	Which sides of the window to be considered for docking.
lpRect	Where, in screen coordinates, the control bar will be docked.

C

The `DockControlBar` method causes a control bar to be docked to this frame window. Valid values for `nDockBarID` are

AFX_IDW_DOCKBAR_TOP	Dock to the top.
AFX_IDW_DOCKBAR_BOTTOM	Dock to the bottom.
AFX_IDW_DOCKBAR_LEFT	Dock to the left.
AFX_IDW_DOCKBAR_RIGHT	Dock to the right.

The `EnableDocking` Method

```
void EnableDocking( DWORD dwStyle );
```
where

dwStyle	The sort of docking that this frame allows.

The `EnableDocking` method is called to allow the control bars to be docked to this frame. The following are valid values for the *dwStyle* property.

CBRS_ALIGN_TOP	The bars can be docked at the top of the client area.
CBRS_ALIGN_BOTTOM	The bars can be docked at the bottom of the client area.
CBRS_ALIGN_LEFT	The bars can be docked at the left side of the client area.
CBRS_ALIGN_RIGHT	The bars can be docked at the right side of the client area.
CBRS_ALIGN_ANY	The bars can be docked at any side of the client area.

The `EndModalState` Method

```
void EndModalState
```
Call this method to end a modal state started by the `BeginModalState` method.

The `FloatControlBar` Method

```
CFrameWnd* FloatControlBar( CControlBar * pBar, CPoint point, DWORD dwStyle =
➡ CBRS_ALIGN_TOP );
```
where

pBar	Specifies the bar that is being docked.
point	The point where the top-left corner of the bar will be placed.
dwStyle	Specifies whether to align the bar vertically or horizontally.

The `DockControlBar` method causes a control bar to be docked to this frame window. Valid values for `nDockBarID` are

CBRS_ALIGN_TOP	Align to the top.
CBRS_ALIGN_BOTTOM	Align to the bottom.
CBRS_ALIGN_LEFT	Align to the left.
CBRS_ALIGN_RIGHT	Align to the right.

The `GetActiveFrame` Method

```
virtual CFrameWnd* GetActiveFrame( );
```
Returns the active frame.

The `GetControlBar` Method

```
CControlBar* GetControlBar( UINT nID );
```

where

> *nID*   The ID of the control bar.

Returns the control bar that has the ID of *nID*.

The `GetDockState` Method

```
void GetDockState( CDockState &state) const;
```

where

> *state*   The docking state of the control bars.

The `GetDockState` method will get the docking state of the control bars.

The `GetMessageString` Method

```
virtual void GetMessageString( UINT nID, CString& rMessage ) const;
```

where

> *nID*   The ID of the desired string resource.
>
> *rMessage*   A `CString` to hold the message.

The `GetMessageString` method is called by the frame window to retrieve message strings. Override this method to provide application specific strings.

The `InitialUpdateFrame` Method

```
void InitialUpdateFrame( CDocument* pDoc, BOOL bMakeVisible );
```

where

> *pDoc*   The document that this frame window is associated with. Can be `NULL`.
>
> *rMessage*   `TRUE` if the frame should be made visible.

The `InitialUpdateFrame` method should be called just after the `Open` method. This causes all views in the frame to receive the `OnInitialUpdate` call.

The `InModalState` Method

```
BOOL InModalState( ) const;
```

Returns `TRUE` if the frame window is in a modal state.

The `IsTracking` Method

```
BOOL IsTracking( ) const;
```

Returns `TRUE` if the frame window is tracking the mouse. This is usually a result of the user dragging the splitter.

The `LoadBarState` Method

```
void LoadBarState( LPCTSTR lpszProfileName ) const;
```

where

> *lpszProfileName*   The `INI` or Registry location to load the state from.

The `LoadBarState` method will get the bar state of the frame from the Registry or an INI file.

The `LoadFrame` Method

```
virtual BOOL LoadFrame( UINT nIDResource, DWORD dwDefaultStyle = WS_
➥OVERLAPPEDWINDOW | FWS_ADDTOTITLE, CWnd* pParentWnd = NULL,
➥CCreateContext* pContext = NULL );
```

where

nIDResource	The ID for the resources associated with this frame.
dwDefaultStyle	The style for the window. Include FWS_ADDTOTITLE to automatically display the name of the current document. See `CWnd::Create` for a complete list of styles.
pParentWnd	A pointer to the parent window.
pContext	A pointer to a CCreateContext structure. This parameter can be NULL.

The `LoadFrame` method creates a frame window from resource information.

The `LoadAccelTable` Method

```
BOOL LoadAccelTable( LPCTSTR lpszResourceName );
```

where

lpszResourceName	The name of the accelerator table to load.

The `LoadAccelTable` method loads an accelerator table for use.

The `LoadBarState` Method

```
void LoadBarState( LPCTSTR lpszProfileName );
```

where

lpszProfileName	The name of the section in the INI file or Registry key that will store state information for the control bars.

The `LoadBarState` method is used to load the control bar state after a call to `SaveBarState`.

The `SaveBarState` Method

```
void SaveBarState( LPCTSTR lpszProfileName ) const;
```

where

lpszProfileName	The name of the section in the INI file or Registry key that will contain state information for the control bars.

The `SaveBarState` method is used to save the control bar state information.

The `ShowControlBar` Method

```
void ShowControlBar( CControlBar* pBar, BOOL bShow, BOOL bDelay );
```

where

pBar	Specifies a control bar to show or hide.
bShow	TRUE if the control bar is to be shown, FALSE if hidden.
bDelay	If TRUE, delay showing the control bar. If FALSE, show the control bar immediately.

The `ShowControlBar` method is used to show or hide a control bar.

The `GetDockState` Method

```
void GetDockState( const CDockState& state );
```

where

    state   Specifies the docking state.

The `GetDockState` method is used to get the state of the control bars using a state structure.

The `SetDockState` Method

```
void SetDockState( const CDockState& state );
```

where

    state   Specifies the docking state.

The `SetDockState` method is used to set the state of the control bars using a state structure.

The `RecalcLayout` Method

```
virtual void RecalcLayout( BOOL bNotify = TRUE );
```

where

    bNotify   Specifies whether the in-place item for the frame receives notification of the layout change.

The `RecalcLayout` method is used to lay out all control bars on the frame window when one of them moves.

The `SaveBarState` Method

```
void SoadBarState( LPCTSTR lpszProfileName ) const;
```

where

    lpszProfileName   The INI or Registry location to save the state to.

The `SaveBarState` method will set the bar state of the frame to the Registry or an INI file.

The `SetActiveView` Method

```
void SetActiveView( CView* pViewNew, BOOL bNotify = TRUE );
```

where

    pViewNew   The view to be made active, or NULL for no active view.

    bNotify   Specifies whether the view should be notified of its activation. If TRUE, the view's `OnActiveView` method will be called.

The `SetActiveView` method is used to set the active view for a frame window.

The `SetDockState` Method

```
void SetDockState( CDockState &state) const;
```

where

    state   The docking state of the control bars.

The `SetDockState` method will set the docking state of the control bars.

C

The `SetMessageText` Method

```
void SetMessageText( LPCTSTR lpszText );
void SetMessageText( UINT nID );
```

where

lpszText	The new message string.
nID	The resource ID for a string resource.

The `SetMessageText` method is used to set the text of the standard status bar for a frame window.

The `ShowOwnedWindows` Method

```
void ShowOwnedWindows( BOOL bShow );
```

where

bShow	Specifies to show or hide.

The `ShowOwnedWindows` method will show or hide all descendants of `CFrameWnd`.

The `GetMessageBar` Method

```
virtual CWnd* GetMessageBar( );
```

Returns a pointer to the status bar.

The `NegotiateBorderSpace` Method

```
virtual BOOL NegotiateBorderSpace( UINT nBorderCmd, LPRECT lpRectBorder );
```

where

nBorderCmd	Contains the type of border request. Should be either `borderGet`, `borderRequest`, or `borderSet`.
lpRectBorder	A rectangle structure containing the coordinates of the new border.

The `NegotiateBorderSpace` method is called to negotiate border space in a frame window during OLE in-place activation.

The `OnContextHelp` Method

```
afx_msg void OnContextHelp( );
```

The `OnContextHelp` method is called to handle Shift-F1 help requests. To enable this method to be called, the following line must be placed inside the application's message map:

```
ON_COMMAND( ID_CONTEXT_HELP, OnContextHelp )
```

The `OnCreateClient` Method

```
virtual BOOL OnCreateClient( LPCREATESTRUCT lpcs, CCreateContext* pContext );
```

where

lpcs	Pointer to a `CREATESTRUCT` structure.
pContext	A pointer to a `CCreateContext` structure.

The `OnCreateClient` method is called during the creation of the frame window.

The OnSetPreviewMode Method

virtual void OnSetPreviewMode(BOOL bPreview, CPrintPreviewState* pModeStuff);

where

bPreview	TRUE if the application is to be placed in print preview mode. FALSE will cancel preview mode.
pModeStuff	A pointer to a CPrintPreviewState structure.

The OnSetPreviewMode method is set the frame window in and out of preview mode.

CGdiObject

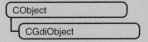

The CGdiObject is the base class for all the GDI objects. These include classes such as CPen and CBrush.

Header Files

The following header file should be included when using this class:

afxwin.h

Property

The CGdiObject class has the following property:

m_hObject	A handle to the GDI object.

Methods

The CGdiObject class has the following methods:

CGdiObject	The constructor
Attach	Attach a Windows GDI object
CreateStockObject	Creates an object based on a stock object
DeleteObject	Delete the object
DeleteTempMap	Delete any temporary objects
Detach	Detach a handle from this object
FromHandle	Create a CGdiObject from a GDI object handle
GetObject	Get information about the object
GetObjectType	Get the object type
GetSafeHandle	Get a handle to the object
UnrealizeObject	Reset the origin of an object

The CGdiObject Constructor

The CGdiObject creates the CGdiObject object. The CGdiObject constructor is used as follows:

CGdiObject()

The `Attach` Method

BOOL Attach(HGDIOBJ hObject);

where

   bObject   The GDI object to attach to this class.

Returns TRUE if successful.

The Attach method will attach an already existing GDI handle to the object.

The `CreateStockObject` Method

BOOL CreateStockObject(int nIndex);

where

   nIndex   The stock object to create an object for.

Returns TRUE if successful.

The CreateStockObject creates an object for one of the predefined stock objects.

The `DeleteObject` Method

BOOL DeleteObject( );

Returns TRUE if successful.

The DeleteObject method deletes the object.

The `DeleteTempMap` Method

static void PASCAL DeleteTempMap( );

Returns TRUE if successful.

The DeleteTempMap method deletes any temporary GDI objects.

The `Detach` Method

HGDIOBJ Detach( );

Returns the GDI object handle associated with the object.

The Detach method disassociates the underlying GDI object handle with this object.

The `FromHandle` Method

static CGdiObject* PASCAL FromHandle(HGDIOBJ hObject);

where

   hObject   A GDI object handle.

Returns a new CGDiObject that is associated with the *hObject*.

The `GetObject` Method

int GetObject(int nCount, LPVOID lpObject) const;

where

   nCount   The number of bytes to copy to the buffer.
   lpObject   Points to a buffer to hold information about the object.

Returns TRUE if successful.

The GetObject method gets information about the GDI object. What is returned by this method is dependent on the type of handle this object represents. The following table lists what is returned by each object type:

CPen	A LOGPEN structure
CBrush	A LOGBRUSH structure
CFont	A LOGFONT structure
CBitmap	A BITMAP structure
CPalette	A WORD
CRgn	Not supported

The GetObjectType Method

```
UINT GetObjectType();
```

Returns one of the following: OBJ_BITMAP, OBJ_BRUSH, OBJ_FONT, OBJ_PAL, OBJ_PEN, OBJ_EXTPEN, OBJ_REGION, OBJ_DC, OBJ_MEMDC, OBJ_METAFILE, OBJ_METADC, OBJ_ENG\HMETAFILE, or OBJ_ENHMETADC.

The GetSafeHandle Method

```
HGDIOBJ GetSafeHandle();
```

Returns a handle to the underlying GDI object.

The UnrealizeObject Method

```
BOOL UnrealizeObject();
```

Returns TRUE if successful.

The UnrealizeObject method will reset the origin of a brush or reset a logical palette.

CHtmlView

```
CObject
  CCmdTarget
    CWnd
      CView
        CScrollView
          CFormView
            CHtmlView
```

The CHtmlView class provides the functionality of the Web browser control in MFC Document/View architecture. This provides an application with graphical access to data on the World Wide Web.

Header Files

The following header file should be included when using this class:

```
afxhtml.h
```

Methods

The CHtmlView class has the following methods:

ExecWB	Execute a command
GetAddressBar	Determine if the address bar is visible
GetApplication	Get the application that currently contains the Internet Explorer application
GetBusy	Determine whether the browser is busy
GetContainer	Get the container of the Web browser control
GetFullName	Get the full name of the resource displayed in the browser window
GetFullScreen	Determine whether the browser is running in full-screen mode
GetHeight	Get the height of the browser control
GetHtmlDocument	Get the HTML document
GetLeft	Get the left location of the browser control
GetLocationName	Get the name of the current location
GetLocationURL	Get the URL the browser is currently showing
GetMenuBar	Determine whether the menu bar is visible
GetOffline	Determine whether the control is offline
GetParentBrowser	Get the browser's parent
GetProperty	Get a property associated with the control
GetReadyState	Get the ready state of the browser
GetRegisterAsBrowser	Get the registration state as the window to handle a target URL
GetRegisterAsDropTarget	Get the registration state as a target for drag and drop
GetSilent	Determine whether any dialog boxes can be shown
GetStatusBar	Determine whether the status bar is visible
GetTheaterMode	Determine whether the Web browser is in theater mode
GetToolBar	Determine whether the toolbar is visible
GetTop	Get the top coordinate for the control
GetTopLevelContainer	Get a value indicating whether the object is the top level container
GetType	Get the type name of the document
GetVisible	Determine whether the control is visible
GoBack	Go to the previously displayed HTML page
GoForward	Go to the last displayed HTML page
GoHome	Go to the home HTML page
GoSearch	Go to the search HTML page
LoadFromResource	Load a resource in the Web browser control
Navigate	Navigate to a resource identified by a URL
Navigate2	Navigate to a resource identified by a URL or full path
PutProperty	Set the value of the indicated property

QueryStatusWB	Query the status of the Web browser control
Refresh	Reload the current page
Refresh2	Reload the current page and prevent the `pragma:nocache` header from being sent
SetAddressBar	Shows or hides the address bar
SetFullScreen	Enter full-screen mode
SetHeight	Set the height of the control
SetLeft	Set the left location of the control
SetMenuBar	Show or hide the menu bar
SetOffline	Enter or exit offline mode
SetRegisterAsBrowser	Set the browser control as the target URL
SetRegisterAsDropTarget	Set the browser control as the drop target
SetSilent	Set the browser not to display dialog boxes
SetStatusBar	Show or hide the browser control
SetTheaterMode	Set the browser into theater mode
SetToolBar	Show or hide the toolbar
SetTop	Set the top of the browser control
SetVisible	Set the visibility of the browser
Stop	Stop the current browser action

The following methods can be overridden to provide special handling.

Create	Create the Web browser control
OnBeforeNavigate2	Called before a navigation occurs
OnCommandStateChange	Called to notify an application that the enabled state has changed
OnDocumentComplete	Called when a document finishes download
OnDownloadBegin	Called when a download begins
OnDownloadComplete	Called when a download completes
OnDraw	Called to redraw the browser control
OnFullScreen	Called when the browser control enters full screen
OnMenuBar	Called when the menu bar status has changed
OnNavigateComplete2	Called after a navigation
OnNewWindow2	Called when a new window is to be created
OnProgressChange	Called as a download progresses
OnPropertyChange	Called when a property changes
OnQuit	Called when the control is ready to quit
OnStatusBar	Called when the status bar property is changed
OnStatusTextChange	Called when the status text changes
OnTheaterMode	Called when the control enters theater mode
OnTitleChange	Called when the title of the control changes
OnToolBar	Called when the status of the toolbar property changes
OnVisible	Called when the Web browser becomes visible

The **ExecWB** Method

```
void ExecWB(OLECMDID cmdID, OLECMDEXECOPT cmdexecopt, VARIANT *pvaIn,
➡VARIANT *pvaOut );
```

where

cmdID	The command to execute.
cmdexecopt	The options set for executing the command.
pvaIn	A variant for input parameters.
pvaOut	A variant for output parameters.

The ExecWB method is used to execute a command in the browser control.

The **GetAddressBar** Method

```
BOOL GetAddressBar() const;
```

Returns TRUE if the address bar is visible.

The **GetApplication** Method

```
LPDISPATCH GetApplication() const;
```

Returns the application that currently holds the browser control.

The **GetBusy** Method

```
BOOL GetBusy( ) const;
```

Returns TRUE if the browser control is busy.

The **GetContainer** Method

```
LPDISPATCH GetContainer( ) const;
```

Returns the container that owns the browser control.

The **GetFullName** Method

```
CString GetFullName( ) const;
```

Returns the full pathname of the resource being displayed by the browser control.

The **GetFullScreen** Method

```
BOOL GetFullScreen( ) const;
```

Returns TRUE if the browser control is running in full-screen mode.

The **GetHeight** Method

```
long GetHeight( ) const;
```

Returns the height of the browser control.

The **GetHtmlDocument** Method

```
LPDISPATCH GetHtmlDocument( ) const;
```

Returns the active HTML document.

The **GetLeft** Method

```
long GetLeft( ) const;
```

Returns the left coordinate of the browser control.

The `GetLocationName` Method

`CString GetLocationName( ) const;`

Returns the name of the resource being viewed by the browser control.

The `GetLocationURL` Method

`CString GetLocationURL( ) const;`

Returns the URL of the resource being viewed by the browser control.

The `GetMenuBar` Method

`BOOL GetMenuBar GetLocationURL( ) const;`

Returns TRUE if the menu bar is visible.

The `GetOffline` Method

`BOOL GetOffline( ) const;`

Returns TRUE if the browser control is offline.

The `GetParentBrowser` Method

`LPDISPATCH GetParentBrowser( ) const;`

Returns the parent of the browser.

The `GetProperty` Method

`BOOL GetProperty( LPCTSTR lpszProperty, CString& strValue );`
`COleVariant GetProperty( LPCTSTR lpsz );`

where

lpszProperty	The desired property.
strValue	Returns the value of specified property.
lpsz	The desired property.

Returns TRUE on success, or a variant representation of the value.

The `GetRegisterAsBrowser` Method

`BOOL GetRegisterAsBrowser( ) const;`

Returns TRUE if this browser control is the current target.

The `GetRegisterAsDropTarget` Method

`BOOL GetRegisterAsDropTarget( ) const;`

Returns TRUE if this browser control is the current drag-and-drop target.

The `GetSilent` Method

`BOOL GetSilent( ) const;`

Returns TRUE if this browser control is in silent mode.

The `GetStatusBar` Method

`BOOL GetStatusBar( ) const;`

Returns TRUE if the status bar is visible.

C

The `GetTheaterMode` Method

`BOOL GetTheaterMode( ) const;`

Returns TRUE if this browser control is in theater mode.

The `GetToolBar` Method

`BOOL GetToolBar( ) const;`

Returns TRUE if the toolbar is visible.

The `GetTop` Method

`long GetTop( ) const;`

Returns the top of the browser control.

The `GetTopLevelContainer` Method

`BOOL GetTopLevelContainer( ) const;`

Returns TRUE if the browser control is the top-level browser container.

The `GetType` Method

`CString GetType( ) const;`

Returns a string indicating the type of resource currently being displayed.

The `GetVisible` Method

`BOOL GetVisible( ) const;`

Returns TRUE if the browser control is visible.

The `GoBack` Method

`void GoBack( );`

The GoBack method works the same as clicking the Back button on a browser toolbar. The browser control will go back to the previously displayed resource.

The `GoForward` Method

`void GoForward( );`

The GoForward method works the same as clicking the Forward button on a browser toolbar. The browser control will go forward one resource.

The `GoHome` Method

`void GoHome( );`

The GoHome method works the same as clicking the Home button on a browser toolbar. The browser control will go to the home page.

The `GoSearch` Method

`void GoSearch( );`

The GoSearch method works the same as clicking the Search button on a browser toolbar. The browser control will go to the search URL.

The `LoadFromResource` Method

```
BOOL LoadFromResource( LPCTSTR lpszResource );
BOOL LoadFromResource( UINT nRes );
```

where

lpszResource	The resource to load.
lpszResource	The numeric named resource to load.

The `LoadFromResource` method loads the specified resource into the browser control.

The `Navigate` Method

```
void Navigate( LPCTSTR URL, DWORD dwFlags = 0, LPCTSTR lpszTargetFrameName =
➥NULL, LPCTSTR lpszHeaders = NULL, LPVOID lpvPostData = NULL, DWORD
➥dwPostDataLen = 0 );
```

where

url	The URL to navigate to.
dwFlags	Flags specifying how to navigate to the new URL. Must be one of the members of the `BrowserNavConstants` enumeration.
lpszTargetFrameName	The name of the target frame.
lpszHeaders	Additional header information to send to the HTTP server.
lpvPostData	HTTP post data.
dwPostDataLen	HTTP post data length.

The `Navigate` method causes the browser control to navigate to the specified URL.

The `Navigate2` Method

```
void Navigate2( LPITEMIDLIST pIDL, DWORD dwFlags = 0, LPCTSTR
➥lpszTargetFrameName = NULL );
void Navigate2( LPCTSTR lpszURL, DWORD dwFlags = 0, LPCTSTR lpszTargetFrame
➥Name = NULL, LPCTSTR lpszHeaders = NULL, LPVOID lpvPostData = NULL,
➥DWORD dwPostDataLen = 0 );
void Navigate2( LPCTSTR lpszURL, DWORD dwFlags, CByteArray& baPostedData,
➥LPCTSTR lpszTargetFrameName = NULL, LPCTSTR lpszHeader = NULL );
```

where

pIDL	A pointer to an `ITEMIDLIST` structure.
lpszUrl	The URL to navigate to
dwFlags	Flags specifying how to navigate to the new URL. Must be one of the members of the `BrowserNavConstants` enumeration.
lpszTargetFrameName	The name of the target frame.
lpszHeaders	Additional header information to send to the HTTP server.
lpvPostData	HTTP post data.
dwPostDataLen	HTTP post data length.
baPostedData	A reference to a `CByteArray` object.

The `Navigate2` method causes the browser control to navigate to the specified URL or a full path.

C

The `PutProperty` Method

```
void PutProperty( LPCTSTR lpszPropertyName, const VARIANT& vtValue );
void PutProperty( LPCTSTR lpszPropertyName, double dValue );
void PutProperty( LPCTSTR lpszPropertyName, long lValue );
void PutProperty( LPCTSTR lpszPropertyName, LPCTSTR lpszValue );
void PutProperty( LPCTSTR lpszPropertyName, short nValue );
```

where

lpszPropertyName	The desired property
vtValue	New value of property as a variant
dValue	New value of property as a double
lValue	New value of property as a long
lpszValue	New value of property as a string
nValue	New value of property as a short

The `PutProperty` method changes the value of a property.

The `QueryStatusWB` Method

```
OLECMDF QueryStatusWB( OLECMDID cmdID ) const;
```

where

cmdID	The command that information is needed for.

Returns the address of the `OLECMDF` value that receives the status of the command.

The `Refresh` Method

```
void Refresh( );
```

The `Refresh` method causes the currently displayed resource to be reloaded.

The `Refresh2` Method

```
void Refresh2( int nLevel );
```

where

nLevel	Specifies the refresh level. The possible variables are defined in `RefreshConstants`.

The `Refresh2` method causes the currently displayed resource to be reloaded.

The `SetAddressBar` Method

```
void SetAddressBar( BOOL bNewValue );
```

where

bNewValue	TRUE to show the address bar.

The `SetAddressBar` method shows or hides the address bar.

The SetFullScreen Method

`void SetFullScreen( BOOL bNewValue );`

where

    bNewValue   TRUE to run in full screen.

The SetFullScreen method causes the browser control to run full screen.

The SetHeight Method

`void SetHeight( long nNewValue );`

where

    nNewValue   The new height of the control.

The SetHeight method is used to set the height of the browser control.

The SetLeft Method

`void SetLeft( long nNewValue );`

where

    nNewValue   The new left side of the control.

The SetLeft method is used to set the left side of the browser control.

The SetMenuBar Method

`void SetMenuBar( BOOL bNewValue );`

where

    bNewValue   TRUE to show the menu bar, FALSE to hide it.

The SetMenuBar method is used to display and hide the menu bar.

The SetMenuBar Method

`void SetMenuBar( BOOL bNewValue );`

where

    bNewValue   TRUE to show the menu bar, FALSE to hide it.

The SetMenuBar method is used to display and hide the menu bar.

The SetOffline Method

`void SetOffline( BOOL bNewValue );`

where

    bNewValue   TRUE to place the browser in offline mode.

The SetOffLineMode method is used to enable or disable offline mode. In offline mode, pages are only displayed from the cache.

C

The `SetRegisterAsBrowser` Method

void SetRegisterAsBrowser(BOOL bNewValue);

where

bNewValue   TRUE to set the browser as the default browser for name resolution.

The `SetRegisterAsBrowser` method is used to register the browser as the default browser to handle name resolution.

The `SetRegisterAsDropTarget` Method

void SetRegisterAsDropTarget(BOOL bNewValue);

where

bNewValue   TRUE to set the browser as the drag-and-drop target.

The `SetRegisterAsDropTarget` method is used to register the browser as the target for drag and drop.

The `SetSilent` Method

void SetSilent(BOOL bNewValue);

where

bNewValue   TRUE to enter silent mode.

The `SetSilent` method is used to enter or exit silent mode.

The `SetStatusBar` Method

void SetStatusBar(BOOL bNewValue);

where

bNewValue   TRUE to show the status bar.

The `SetStatusBar` method is used to show or hide the status bar.

The `SetTheaterMode` Method

void SetTheaterMode(BOOL bNewValue);

where

bNewValue   TRUE to enable theater mode.

The `SetTheaterMode` method is enter or exit theater mode. In theater mode, the browser is full-screen with a minimal set of navigation controls.

The `SetToolBar` Method

void SetToolBar(BOOL bNewValue);

where

bNewValue   TRUE to show the toolbar

The `SetToolBar` method is used to show or hide the toolbar.

The SetTop Method

void SetTop(long nNewValue);

where

     nNewValue   The new top of the control

The SetTop method is used to set the top of the browser control.

The SetVisible Method

void SetVisible(BOOL bNewValue);

where

     bNewValue   TRUE to show the browser control

The SetVisible method is used to show or hide the browser control.

The Stop Method

void Stop();

The Stop method has the same effect as clicking the stop control when a browser is running. The Stop method stops any pending navigation or downloads.

The Create Method

virtual BOOL Create(LPCTSTR lpszClassName, LPCTSTR lpszWindowName, DWORD
➥dwStyle, const RECT& rect, CWnd* pParentWnd, UINT nID,
➥CCreateContext* pContext = NULL);

where

lpszClassName	Specifies the class for this window. Should be a predefined class or one created using AfxRegisterClass.
lpszWindowName	The text to be placed in the window's title bar.
dwStyle	The style for the window. Include FWS_ADDTOTITLE to automatically display the name of the current document. See CWnd::Create for a complete list of styles.
rect	Specifies the size and location of the window.
pParentWnd	A pointer to the parent window.
lpszMenuName	The name of the menu resource to be used with this window. MAKEINTRESOURCE should be used if this is a numeric name. Can be NULL if there is no menu bar.
dwExStyle	The extended style. See CWnd::CreateEx for more information on extended styles.
pContext	A pointer to a CCreateContext structure. This parameter can be NULL.

Returns TRUE if successful.

The Create method is called to actually create a browser control window.

C

The `OnBeforeNavigate2` Method

```
virtual void OnBeforeNavigate2( LPCTSTR lpszURL, DWORD nFlags, LPCTSTR
➡lpszTargetFrameName, CByteArray& baPostedData, LPCTSTR lpszHeaders,
➡BOOL* pbCancel );
```

where

lpszUrl	The URL to navigate to.
dwFlags	Flags specifying how to navigate to the new URL. Must be one of the members of the `BrowserNavConstants` enumeration.
lpszTargetFrameName	The name of the target frame.
lpszHeaders	Additional header information to send to the HTTP server.
lpvPostData	HTTP post data.
dwPostDataLen	HTTP post data length.
baPostedData	A reference to a `CByteArray` object.
pbCancel	Set to `TRUE` if navigation is to be canceled.

The `OnBeforeNavigate2` method is called before the browser navigates to a specified URL. By overriding this function, applications can take specific action before the browser navigates somewhere.

The `OnCommandStateChange` Method

```
virtual void OnCommandStateChange( long nCommand, BOOL bEnable );
```

where

nCommand	ID of command whose enabled state has changed.
bEnable	`TRUE` if the command has been enabled.

The `OnCommandStateChange` method notifies the application that the enabled state of certain commands has changed.

The `OnDocumentComplete` Method

```
virtual void OnDocumentComplete( LPCTSTR lpszURL );
```

where

lpszURL	The document that this notification is for

The `OnDocumentComplete` is sent after a document has been transferred.

The `OnDownloadBegin` Method

```
void OnDownloadBegin( );
```

The `OnDownloadBegin` method is called just before a download begins.

The `OnDownloadComplete` Method

```
void OnDownloadComplete( );
```

The `OnDownloadComplete` method is called just after a download begins.

The **OnDraw** Method

void OnDraw(CDC* pDC);

where

    pDC   A device context to draw to.

The OnDraw method is called by MFC when the browser control needs to be redrawn or printed.

The **OnFullScreen** Method

void OnFullScreen(BOOL bFullScreen);

where

    bFullScreen   TRUE if the browser has become full screen.

The OnFullScreen method is called by MFC whenever the full-screen state of the browser control changes.

The **OnMenuBar** Method

void OnMenuBar(BOOL bMenuBar);

where

    bMenuBar   TRUE if the menu bar is visible.

The OnMenuBar method is called by MFC whenever the state of the menu bar changes.

The **OnNavigateComplete2** Method

void OnNavigateComplete2(LPCTSTR strURL);

where

    strURL   Where the control navigated to.

The OnNavigateComplete2 method is called by MFC whenever navigation completes.

The **OnNewWindow2** Method

virtual void OnNewWindow2(LPDISPATCH* ppDisp, BOOL* Cancel);

where

    ppDisp   Pointer to the newly created window.

    Cancel   Set to TRUE to cancel creation of the new window.

The OnNewWindow2 method is called before a new window is opened by the browser control.

The **OnProgressChange** Method

virtual void OnProgressChange(long nProgress, long nProgressMax);

where

    nProgress   How far along the download is.

    nProgressMax   How far *nProgress* must go before the download is complete.

The OnProgressChange method is used as a download progresses to allow the application to give visual feedback of the progress of the download.

The `OnPropertyChange` Method

```
void OnPropertyChange( LPCTSTR lpszProperty );
```

where

> *lpszProperty*   Specifies the property that has changed in value.

The `OnPropertyChange` method is called whenever the value of a property changes.

The `OnQuit` Method

```
void OnQuit( );
```

The `OnQuit` method is called just before the browser quits.

The `OnStatusBar` Method

```
void OnStatusBar( BOOL bStatusBar );
```

where

> *bStatusBar*   TRUE if the status bar is visible.

The `OnStatusBar` method is called whenever the visibility status of the status bar changes.

The `OnStatusTextChange` Method

```
void OnStatusTextChange( LPCTSTR lpszText );
```

where

> *lpszText*   Specifies the text that is to be displayed.

The `OnStatusTextChange` method is called whenever the status text changes.

The `OnTheaterMode` Method

```
void OnTheaterMode( BOOL bTheaterMode );
```

where

> *bTheaterMode*   TRUE if the browser is in theater mode.

The `OnTheaterMode` method is called when the browser switches in and out of theater mode.

The `OnTitleChange` Method

```
void OnTitleChange( LPCTSTR lpszText );
```

where

> *lpszText*   The new title.

The `OnTitleChange` method is called when the title of the browser window should change.

The `OnToolBar` Method

```
void OnToolBar( BOOL bToolBar );
```

where

> *bToolBar*   TRUE if the toolbar is visible.

The `OnToolBar` method is called when the display status of the toolbar changes.

The `OnVisible` Method

```
virtual void OnVisible( BOOL bVisible );
```

where

>   *bVisible*   TRUE if the browser control is visible.

The `OnVisible` method is called when ever the control becomes visible or invisible.

CListView

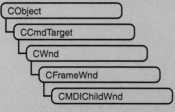

The `CListView` class is used to implement a view based on a list control.

Header Files

The following header file should be included when using this class:

```
afxcview.h
```

Methods

The `CListView` class has the following methods:

>   `CListView`   The constructor.
>
>   `GetListCtrl`   Get the underlying list control.

The `CListView` Constructor

The `CListView` creates the `CListView` object. The `CListView` constructor is used as follows:

```
CListView();
```

The `GetListCtrl` method

```
CListCtrl& GetListCtrl() const;
```

Returns the underlying list control.

CMDIChildWnd

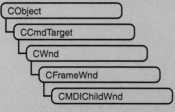

The `CMDIChildWnd` class forms the base class for any window that needs to be the child of the MDI frame window.

For an example of CMDIChildWnd, see the MDIEx example found on the CD-ROM that accompanies this book.

Header Files

The following header file should be included when using this class:

afxwin.h

Methods

The CMDIChildWnd class has the following methods:

CMDIChildWnd	The constructor
Create	Create an MDI child window
GetMDIFrame	Get the MDI frame for this child window
MDIActivate	Activate an MDI child window
MDIDestroy	Destroy an MDI child window
MDIMaximize	Maximize an MDI child window
MDIRestore	Restore an MDI child window

The CMDIChildWnd Constructor

The CMDIChildWnd constructor creates the CMdiChildWnd object. The CMDIChildWnd constructor is used as follows:

CMdiChildWnd()

The Create Method

BOOL Create(LPCTSTR lpszClassName, LPCTSTR lpszWindowName, DWORD dwStyle =
➥WS_CHILD¦WS_VISIBLE¦WS_OVERLAPPED, const RECT& rect = rectDefault,
➥CMDIFrameWnd* pParentWnd = NULL, CCreateContext* pContext = NULL);

where

lpszClassName	Specifies the class for this window. Should be a predefined class or one created using AfxRegisterClass.
lpszWindowName	The text to be placed in the window's title bar.
dwStyle	The style for the window. Include FWS_ADDTOTITLE to automatically display the name of the current document. See CWnd::Create for a complete list of styles.
rect	Specifies the size and location of the window.
pParentWnd	A pointer to the parent window.
pContext	A pointer to a CCreateContext structure. This parameter can be NULL.

Returns TRUE if successful.

The Create method is called to actually create an MDI child window.

The GetMDIFrame Method

CMDIFrameWnd *GetMDIFrame( );

The GetMDIFrame method gets the MDI frame that this window is associated with.

The `MDIActivate` Method

`void MDIActivate();`

The `MDIActivate` method is called to activate this child window.

The `MDIDestroy` Method

`void MDIDestroy();`

The `MDIDestroy` method is called to destroy this child window.

The `MDIMaximize` Method

`void MDIMaximize();`

The `MDIMaximize` method is called to maximize this child window.

The `MDIRestore` Method

`void MDIRestore();`

The `MDIRestore` method is called to restore the child window.

C

CMDIFrameWnd

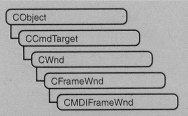

The `CMDIFrameWnd` window creates a specialized frame that implements a multiple-document interface frame window (MDI). This window can have many child windows inside it.

For an example of `CMDIFrameWnd`, see the MDIEx example found on the CD-ROM that accompanies this book.

Header Files

The following header files should be included when using this class:

`afxwin.h`

Methods

The `CMDIFrameWnd` class has the following methods:

CMDIFrameWnd	The constructor
CreateClient	Create an MDI client window
GetWindowMenuPopup	Get the pop-up window for the frame window
MDIActivate	Activate a child window
MDICascade	Cascades the child windows
MDIGetActive	Get the active child window

MDIIconArrange	Arrange the minimized icon windows
MDIMaximize	Maximize a child window
MDINext	Activate the next child window
MDIRestore	Restore a child window
MDISetMenu	Replace the menu of an MDI frame
MDITile	Tile the child windows

The CMDIFrameWnd Constructor

The CMDIFrameWnd creates the CMDIFrameWnd object. The CMDIFrameWnd constructor is used as follows:

```
CMDIFrameWnd();
```

The CreateClient Method

```
virtual BOOL CreateClient( LPCREATESTRUCT lpCreateStruct , CMenu *pWindowMenu );
```

where

    lpCreateStruct   A structure containing creation information for the client window.

Returns TRUE if successful.

The CreateClient method is called to create an MDI client window.

The GetWindowMenuPopup Method

```
virtual HMENU GetWindowMenuPopup( HMENU hMenuBar );
```

where

    hMenuBar   The current menu bar.

Returns the handle of the pop-up menu or NULL if none exists.

The MDIActivate Method

```
void MDIActivate( CWnd *pWndActivate );
```

where

    pWndActivate   The window to be activated.

The MDIActivate method activates the specified window.

The MDICascade Method

```
void MDICascade( );
void MDICascade(int nType );
```

where

    nType   Can only be MDITILE_SKIPDISABLED, which causes disabled windows to be skipped.

The MDICascade method will tile the MDI child windows in a cascaded pattern.

The **MDIGetActive** Method

```
CMDIChildWnd *MDIGetActive( BOOL *pbMaximized = NULL );
```

where

    pbMaximized   Set to TRUE if the active window is maximized. If NULL, this parameter is ignored.

Returns the active MDI child window.

The **MDIIconArrange** Method

```
void MDIIconArrange();
```

The MDIIconArrange method arranges all minimized child windows.

The **MDIMaximize** Method

```
void MDIMaximize( CWnd *pWnd );
```

where

    pWnd   The window to be maximized.

The MDIMaximize method activates the specified window.

The **MDINext** Method

```
void MDINext();
```

The MDINext method activates the next child window.

The **MDIRestore** Method

```
void MDIRestore( CWnd *pWndActivate );
```

where

    pWndActivate   The window to be restored.

The MDIRestore method activates the specified window.

The **MDISetMenu** Method

```
CMenu* MDISetMenu( CMenu* pFrameMenu, CMenu* pWindowMenu );
```

where

    pFrameMenu   The new frame menu. If NULL, the menu is not changed.

    pWindowMenu   The new window menu. If NULL, the menu is not changed.

The MDISetMenu replaces the menu of an MDI frame window. The application must call DrawMenuBar after calling this method to properly update the menu bar. This method should only be called if MFC is not being used to manage the MDI child windows.

The **MDITile** Method

```
void MDITile( );
void MDITile( int nType );
```

where

    nType   The type of tile requested.

The MDITile method will tile the child windows in a specific pattern, as specified by *nType*. Valid patterns are

MDITILE_HORIZONTAL	Tiles MDI child windows so that one window appears above another.
MDITILE_SKIPDISABLED	Prevents disabled MDI child windows from being tiled.
MDITILE_VERTICAL	Tiles MDI child windows so that windows appear beside each another.

CMenu

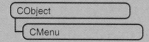

The CMenu class represents all menus based on the HMENU handle. Menus are usually loaded in from resource files. CMenu also provides functions for dynamically creating menus within the program.

Header Files

The following header file should be included when using this class:

afxwin.h

Properties

The CMenu class has the following properties:

m_hMenu	The underlying menu handle.

Methods

The CMenu class has the following methods:

CMenu	The constructor
AppendMenu	Append a new item to this menu
Attach	Attach a menu handle to this object
CheckMenuItem	Check a menu item
CheckMenuRadioItem	Place a radio button near a menu
CreateMenu	Create a menu object
CreatePopupMenu	Create a pop-up menu object
DeleteMenu	Delete a specific item
DeleteTempMap	Delete the temporary objects
DestroyMenu	Destroy the menu object
Detach	Detach a menu handle from this object
EnableMenuItem	Enable a menu item
FromHandle	Create a CMenu object from a menu handle
GetDefaultItem	Get the default item
GetMenuContextHelpId	Get the help context for the menu

GetMenuItemCount	Get the item count
GetMenuItemID	Get a menu item's ID
GetMenuItemInfo	Get information on a menu item
GetMenuState	Get the menu's state
GetMenuString	Get the menu string
GetSafeHmenu	Get a handle to the menu object
GetSubMenu	Get the pointer to a pop-up menu
InsertMenu	Insert a new item at a specific location
LoadMenu	Load a menu resource
LoadMenuIndirect	Load a menu from a template in memory
ModifyMenu	Change an existing menu item
RemoveMenu	Remove a menu item
SetDefaultItem	Set the default menu item
SetMenuContextHelpId	Set the menu context help
SetMenuItemBitmaps	Set the bitmaps for the menu items
TrackPopupMenu	Track a pop-up menu

The following methods can be overridden to provide special handling:

DrawItem	Called when the visual aspect of an owner-drawn menu changes
MeasureItem	Used to determine the dimensions of a menu

The CMenu Constructor

The CMenu constructor creates the CMenu object. The CMenu constructor is used as follows:

CMenu()

The AppendMenu Method

BOOL AppendMenu(UINT nFlags, UINT nIDNewItem = 0, LPCTSTR lpszNewItem =
➥NULL);
BOOL AppendMenu(UINT nFlags, UINT nIDNewItem, const CBitmap* pBmp);

where

nFlags	The state of the new menu item.
nIDNewItem	The ID for the new item.
lpszNewItem	The text for the new item.
pBmp	The bitmap for the new item.

The following values are valid for the nFlags parameter:

MF_OWNERDRAW	Menu item is drawn by application program
MF_STRING	Menu item is a string
MF_SEPARATOR	Menu item is a separator

The AppendMenu method will append a new menu item to the menu.

The `Attach` Method

```
BOOL Attach( HMENU hMenu );
```

where

      hMenu   A menu handle to attach to this object.

The `Attach` method will attach the specified menu handle to the menu object.

The `CheckMenuItem` Method

```
UINT CheckMenuItem( UINT nIDCheckItem, UINT nCheck );
```

where

      nIDCheckItem   A menu item to be checked.

      nCheck   Specifies how to check the menu item. Should be MF_CHECKED, or MF_UNCHECKED(with MF_BYPOSITION or MF_BYCOMMAND, which specifies whether nIDCheckItem is a position or command number).

Returns the previous state of the item or 0xffffffff if the menu item did not exist.

The `CheckMenuItem` method will check or uncheck the specified menu item.

The `CheckMenuRadioItem` Method

```
BOOL CheckMenuRadioItem( UINT nIDFirst, UINT nIDLast, UINT nIDItem,
➡UINT nFlags );
```

where

      nIDFist   The first menu item of the radio button group.

      nIDLast   The last menu item of the radio button group.

      nIDItem   The item to be checked.

      nFlags   Should be MF_BYCOMMAND if three menu item parameters are menu commands, or MF_BYPOSITION if they are indexes.

Returns TRUE if successful.

The `CheckMenuRadioItem` method will uncheck all items in the radio button group and then check the specified item.

The `CreateMenu` Method

```
BOOL CreateMenu();
```

Returns TRUE if successful.

The `CreateMenu` method creates a new empty menu.

The `CreatePopupMenu` Method

```
BOOL CreatePopupMenu();
```

Returns TRUE if successful.

The `CreatePopupMenu` method creates a new empty menu to be used as a pop-up menu.

The **DeleteMenu** Method

`BOOL DeleteMenu( UINT nPosition, UINT nFlags );`

where

nPosition	The menu item to delete.
nFlags	Should be `MF_BYCOMMAND` if the position parameter is a menu command, or `MF_BYPOSITION` if it is an index.

Returns `TRUE` if successful.

The `DeleteMenu` method will delete the specified menu item.

The **DeleteTempMap** Method

`static void PASCAL DeleteTempMap( );`

The `DeleteTempMap` method will delete any temporary `CMenu` objects created by the `FromHandle` method.

The **DestroyMenu** Method

`BOOL DestroyMenu( );`

Returns `TRUE` if successful.

The `DestroyMenu` method will destroy the menu and any resources it is using.

The **Detach** Method

`HMENU Detach( );`

Returns the menu handle associated with this object.

The `Detach` method will disassociate the underlying menu handle with this object.

The **EnableMenuItem** Method

`UINT EnableMenuItem( UINT nIDEnableItem, UINT nEnable );`

where

nIDEnableItem	A menu item to be checked.
nEnable	Specifies how to enable the menu item. Should be `MF_ENABLED`, `MF_DIS-ABLED`, or `MF_GRAYED` (with `MF_BYPOSITION` or `MF_BYCOMMAND`, which specifies is `nIDCheckItem` is a position or command number).

Returns the previous state of the item or `0xffffffff` if the menu item did not exist.

The `EnableMenuItem` method will enable or disable the specified menu item.

The **FromHandle** Method

`static CMenu* PASCAL FromHandle( HMENU hMenu );`

where

hMenu	A menu handle.

Returns a `CMenu` object associated with *hMenu*.

The **GetDefaultItem** Method

`UINT GetDefaultItem( UINT gmdiFlags, BOOL fByPos = FALSE );`

where

gmdiFlags	Specifies how the method searches for menu items.
fByPos	Specifies whether to retrieve the menu's ID or position.

Returns the position of the default menu item.

The following values are valid for the *gmdiFlags* parameter:

GMDI_GOINTOPOPUPS	Specifies that if the default item opens pop-up menus, they should be searched.
GMDI_USEDISABLED	Specifies that this method should return the default menu item, even if it's disabled.

The `GetMenuContextHelpId` Method

`DWORD GetMenuContextHelpId( ) const;`

Returns the help context for this menu.

The `GetMenuItemCount` Method

`UINT GetMenuItemCount( ) const;`

Returns the number of items in this menu.

The `GetMenuItemID` Method

`UINT GetMenuItemID( int nPos ) const;`

where

nPos	A menu item position.

Returns the menu item ID for the specified position.

The `GetMenuItemInfo` Method

`BOOL GetMenuItemInfo( UINT nIDItem, LPMENUITEMINFO lpMenuItemInfo, BOOL byPos = FALSE);`

where

nIDItem	The menu item to get information for.
lpMenuItemInfo	A structure to hold information about this menu.
byPos	TRUE if *nIDItem* is a position, FALSE if it's a menu ID.

Returns TRUE if successful.

The GetMenuItemInfo method will return a structure with information about the specified menu item.

The `GetMenuState` Method

`UINT GetMenuState( UINT nID, UINT nFlags ) const;`

where

nID	The menu item to get information for.
nFlags	Should be MF_BYPOSITION or MF_BYCOMMAND, which specify that nIDCheckItem is a position or command number.

Returns one or more of the following values, which indicates the state of the menu item:

MF_CHECKED	The menu item is checked.
MF_DISABLED	The menu item is disabled.
MF_ENABLED	The menu item is enabled.
MF_GRAYED	The menu item is grayed.
MF_MENUBARBREAK	The menu item is in a new line on a pop-up menu.
MF_MENUBREAK	The menu item will be on a new line in a static menu.
MF_SEPARATOR	The menu item is a separator.
MF_UNCHECKED	The menu item is not checked

The GetMenuString Method

```
int GetMenuString( UINT nIDItem, LPTSTR lpString, int nMaxCount, UINT
➥nFlags ) const;
int GetMenuString( UINT nIDItem, CString& rString, UINT nFlags ) const;
```

where

nIDItem	A menu item.
lpString	Will contain the text from the menu item.
nIDItem	The maximum characters that can be stored in lpString.
nFlags	Should be MF_BYPOSITION or MF_BYCOMMAND, which specifies that nIDCheckItem is a position or command number.
rString	Will contain the text from the menu item.

Returns the number of bytes copied.

The GetMenuString method will return the menu text for the specified item.

The GetSafeHmenu Method

```
HMENU GetSafeHmenu( );
```

Returns the menu handle that was associated with this object.

The GetSubMenu Method

```
CMenu* GetSubMenu( int nPos ) const;
```

where

nPos	The menu item (zero for the first menu item).

Returns the submenu associated with *nPos*, or NULL if there is no submenu.

The InsertMenu Method

```
BOOL InsertMenu( UINT nPosition, UINT nFlags, UINT nIDNewItem = 0, LPCTSTR
➥lpszNewItem = NULL );
BOOL InsertMenu( UINT nPosition, UINT nFlags, UINT nIDNewItem, const CBitmap*
➥pBmp );
```

where

nPosition	The menu item before which this menu will be inserted.
nFlags	Should be MF_BYPOSITION or MF_BYCOMMAND, which specifies that nIDCheckItem is a position or command number).

nIDNewItem	Specifies the command ID of the new menu item, or the HMENU of the pop-up menu if *nflags* has MF_POPUP.
lpszNewItem	Specifies the content of the new item.
pBmp	A bitmap.

Returns TRUE if successful.

The InsertMenu method is used to add a menu item or pop-up menu to the menu.

The LoadMenu Method

```
BOOL LoadMenu( LPCTSTR lpszResourceName );
BOOL LoadMenu( UINT nIDResource );
```

where

lpszResourceName	The resource name to load.
nIDResource	The ID of the resource to load.

Returns TRUE if successful.

The LoadMenu method is used to load a menu resource from the resource template.

The LoadMenuIndirect Method

```
BOOL LoadMenuIndirect( const void* lpMenuTemplate );
```

where

lpMenuTemplate	A memory-based menu template.

Returns TRUE if successful.

The LoadMenuIndirect method is used to load a menu direct from memory.

The ModifyMenu Method

```
BOOL ModifyMenu( UINT nPosition, UINT nFlags, UINT nIDNewItem = 0, LPCTSTR
➡lpszNewItem = NULL );
BOOL ModifyMenu( UINT nPosition, UINT nFlags, UINT nIDNewItem, const
➡CBitmap* pBmp );
```

where

nPosition	The menu item before which this menu will be inserted.
nFlags	Should be MF_BYPOSITION or MF_BYCOMMAND, which specifies that nIDCheckItem is a position or command number.
nIDNewItem	Specifies the command ID of the new menu item, or the HMENU of the pop-up menu if *nflags* has MF_POPUP.
lpszNewItem	Specifies the content of the new item.
pBmp	A bitmap.

Returns TRUE if successful.

The ModifyMenu method is used to modify a menu item.

The `RemoveMenu` Method

```
BOOL RemoveMenu( UINT nPosition, UINT nFlags );
```

where

nPosition	The menu item to get remove for.
nFlags	Should be MF_BYPOSITION or MF_BYCOMMAND, which specifies that nIDCheckItem is a position or command number.

Returns TRUE if successful.

The RemoveMenu method is called to remove an item.

The `SetDefaultItem` Method

```
BOOL SetDefaultItem( UINT nPosition, UINT nFlags );
```

where

nPosition	The menu item to get default for.
nFlags	Should be MF_BYPOSITION or MF_BYCOMMAND, which specifies that nIDCheckItem is a position or command number.

Returns TRUE if successful.

The SetDefaultMenuItem method is called to set the default menu item.

The `SetMenuContextHelpId` Method

```
BOOL SetMenuContextHelpId( DWORD dwContextHelpId );
```

where

dwContextHelpID	The help ID.

Returns TRUE if successful.

The SetMenuContextHelpId method is called to set the help context for this menu.

The `SetMenuItemBitmaps` Method

```
BOOL SetMenuItemBitmaps( UINT nPosition, UINT nFlags, const CBitmap*
➥pBmpUnchecked, const CBitmap* pBmpChecked );
```

where

nPosition	The menu item.
nFlags	Should be MF_BYPOSITION or MF_BYCOMMAND, which specifies that nIDCheckItem is a position or command number.
pBmpUnchecked	Pointer to a bitmap when the item is not checked.
pBmpChecked	Pointer to a bitmap when the item is checked.

Returns TRUE if successful.

The SetMenuItemBitmaps method is called to set the checked and unchecked bitmaps for a menu item.

The `TrackPopupMenu` Method

```
BOOL TrackPopupMenu( UINT nFlags, int x, int y, CWnd* pWnd, LPCRECT lpRect =
➥NULL );
```

where

nFlags	Screen-position and mouse-button flags.
x	X position, in screen coordinates, of where the pop-up is to be displayed.
y	Y position, in screen coordinates, of where the pop-up is to be displayed.
pWnd	Pointer to a window that owns the pop-up.
lpRect	Pointer to the rectangle that the user can click without dismissing the pop-up.

Returns TRUE if successful.

The TrackPopupMenu method displays and tracks a floating pop-up menu.

The DrawItem Method

```
virtual void DrawItem( LPDRAWITEMSTRUCT lpDrawItemStruct );
```

where

| *lpDrawItemStruct* | Information about the type of drawing required. |

The DrawItem method is called by MFC to draw an owner-drawn menu item.

The MeasureItem Method

```
virtual void MeasureItem( LPMEASUREITEMSTRUCT lpMeasureItemStruct );
```

where

| *lpMeasureItemStruct* | A MEASUREITEMSTRUCT structure. |

The MeasureItem method is called by MFC to determine the size of an item in an owner-drawn menu.

CMutex

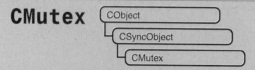

The CMutex class implements a mutex. A mutex is a synchronization object that allows one thread to have mutually exclusive access to a resource. Mutexes are used when only one thread can access something at a time. The mutex allows that thread to signal that it is busy with the resource, and all other threads must wait.

Header Files

The following header files should be included when using this class:

```
afxmt.h
```

Methods

The CMutex class has the following methods:

| CMutex | The constructor. |

The CMutex Constructor

The CMutex creates the CMutex object. The CMutex constructor is used as follows:

```
CMutex( BOOL bInitiallyOwn = FALSE, LPCTSTR lpszName = NULL, LPSECURITY_
➥ATTRIBUTES lpsaAttribute = NULL );
```

where

bInitiallyOwn	Specifies whether the thread creating the mutex initially has access to the resource controlled by the mutex.
lpszName	The name of the mutex. NULL if this is to be an unnamed mutex.
lpsaAttribute	The security attributes.

The constructor can create a named or unnamed mutex. To actually use the mutex object, use a CMultiLock or CSingle lock object's Lock and Unlock methods.

CObject [CObject]

C

The CObject is the base class for nearly every object in MFC. CObject provides base functionality that nearly every MFC class needs. Serialization support is the capability to store objects in some persistent form, usually a disk file. Runtime class information allows CObject derived classes to determine each other's type at runtime. Object diagnostic output allows the debugger to gain a better understanding of CObject-derived classes.

MFC also provides an extensive set of collection classes. The collection classes provide common data structures such as linked lists and hash tables. Any object to be used with these container classes must be derived from CObject.

Header Files

The following header file should be included when using this class:

afx.h

Methods

The CObject class has the following methods:

CObject	The constructor
CObject copy constructor	The copy constructor
AssertValid	Determine whether this object is valid
Dump	Diagnostic report of object
GetRuntimeClass	Get the runtime class
IsKindOf	Tests the object's relationship to another
IsSerializable	Is this object serializable?
operator =	Assignment operator
operator delete	Delete operator
operator new	New operator
Serialize	Serialize the object

The CObject Constructor

The CObject constructor creates the CObject object. The CObject constructor is used as follows:

```
CObject();
CObject( const CObject &objectSrc); // Copy constructor
```

where

> objectSrc   A reference to another CObject.

If the copy constructor is called, the new CObject will be a clone of the objectSrc object.

The AssertValid Method

```
void AssertValid() const;
```

The AssertValid method will assert if this object is not valid.

The Dump Method

```
virtual void Dump( CDumpContext& dc ) const;
```

where

> dc   A diagnostic dump context for dumping. Usually afxDump.

The Dump method will dump the contents of the object to the dump context.

The GetRuntimeClass Method

```
virtual CRuntimeClass* GetRuntimeClass( ) const;
```

The GetRuntimeClass method returns the CRuntimeClass associated with this class.

The IsKindOf Method

```
BOOL IsKindOf( const CRuntimeClass* pClass ) const;
```

where

> pClass   The object being compared to this object.

Returns TRUE if pClass is the same class or is derived from this class.

The IsSerializable Method

```
BOOL IsSerializable( ) const;
```

Returns TRUE if object is serializable.

The = Operator

```
void operator =( const CObject& src );
```

where

> src   An object to be copied to this object.

The = operator defined in CObject will produce an error. Derived classes must override this operator if they are to include support for it.

The delete Operator

```
void operator delete( void* p );
```

where

    p   The object to be deleted.

The release version of the delete operator simply frees the memory associated with this object. The debugging version attempts to detect memory leaks.

The new Operator

```
void* operator new( size_t nSize );
void* operator new( size_t nSize, LPCSTR lpszFileName, int nLine );
```

The release version of the new operator, similar to malloc, works to allocate the memory needed by the object. The debugging version attempts to detect memory leaks.

This operator will throw the CMemoryException exception if an error occurs.

The Serialize Method

```
void Serialize( CArchive &ar)
```

where

    ar   An archive object to serialize to.

The Serialize method will write the object to the archive. This method should be overridden for each new object type that is to support serialization.

This method can throw the CMemoryException, CArchiveException, or CFileException exceptions.

COleDBRecordView

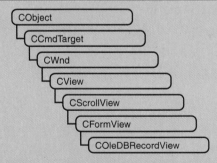

A COleDBRecordView class is a view that can display database information in controls. The form is directly connected to a CRowset object. The COleDBRecordView uses DDX and the navigation functionality built into CRowset to allow movement through the data. This class is used to access data sources through OLEDB data access.

Header Files

The following header files should be included when using this class:

```
afxoledb.h
```

Methods

The `COleDBRecordView` class has the following methods:

`COleDBRecordView`	The constructor
`OnGetRowset`	Returns a pointer to the `CRowset` object
`OnMove`	Updates the current record when a move action takes place

The `COleDBRecordView` Constructor

The `COleDBRecordView` creates the `COleDBRecordView` object. The `COleDBRecordView` constructor is used as follows:

```
COleDBRecordView( LPCTSTR lpszTemplateName );
COleDBRecordView( UINT nIDTemplate );
```

where

lpszTemplateName	The name of a dialog template resource.
nIDTemplate	The ID of a dialog template resource.

These constructors set up a form based on a dialog template.

The `OnGetRowset` Method

```
CRowset *OnGetRowset() = 0;
```

Returns a pointer to a `CRowset` object or `NULL`.

This method returns a pointer to the `CRowset` object associated with the view. This method must be overridden to provide a suitable rowset. If the class was created with Class Wizard, a default method has already been created.

The `OnMove` Method

```
BOOL OnMove( UINT nIDMoveCommand );
```

where

nIDMoveCommand	The type of move requested. Should be `ID_RECORD_FIRST`, `ID_RECORD_LAST`, `ID_RECORD_NEXT`, or `ID_RECORD_PREV`.

The `OnMove` method will move to a different record.

COleDocObjectItem

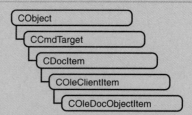

The `COleDocObjectItem` implements active document containment.

Header Files

The following header file should be included when using this class:

`afxole.h`

Methods

The `COleDocObjectItem` class has the following methods:

COleDocObjectItem	The constructor
GetActiveView	Get the document's active view
OnPreparePrinting	Prepare for printing
OnPrint	Print the container application's document
GetPageCount	Get the page count
ExecCommand	Execute a command

The `COleDocObjectItem` Constructor

The `COleDocObjectItem` creates the `COleDocObjectItem` object. The `COleDocObjectItem` constructor is used as follows:

`COleDocObjectItem( COleDocument *pContainerDoc = NULL );`

where

pContainerDoc	The container for this item.

The `GetActiveView` Method

`LPOLEDOCUMENTVIEW GetActiveView() const;`

Returns a pointer to the interface of the currently active view. If there is no view, the return value is NULL.

The `OnPreparePrinting` Method

`static BOOL OnPreparePrinting( CView *pCaller, CPrintInfo *pInfo, BOOL`
`➥bPrintAll = TRUE );`

where

pCaller	The CView that is sending the print command.
pInfo	The CPrintInfo object that describes the print job.
bPrintAll	Should the entire document be printed?

Returns TRUE if successful.

The `OnPreparePrinting` method is called by MFC to prepare a document to be printed.

The `OnPrint` Method

`static BOOL OnPrint( CView *pCaller, CPrintInfo *pInfo, BOOL bPrintAll =`
`➥TRUE );`

where

pCaller	The CView that is sending the print command.
pInfo	The CPrintInfo object that describes the print job.
bPrintAll	Should the entire document be printed?

Returns TRUE if successful.

The OnPrint method is called by MFC to print a document.

The GetPageCount Method

BOOL GetPageCount(LPLONG pnFirstPage, LPLONG pcPages);

where

pnFirstPage	A pointer to the number of the document's first page. Set to NULL if this value is not needed.
pcPages	A pointer to the page count for the document. Set to NULL if this value is not needed.

Returns TRUE if successful.

The GetPageCount method is called by MFC to determine the number of pages in the document.

The ExecCommand Method

BOOL ExecCommand(DWORD nCmdID, DWORD nCmdExecOpt=OLECMDEXECOPT_
➡DONTPROMPTUSER, const GUID *pguidCmdGroup = NULL);

where

nCmdID	The command to execute.
nCmdExecOpt	How to execute the command. By default, set to execute without asking the user.
pguidCmdGroup	Unique identifier of the command group. If the default value of NULL is used, the standard group is used.

Returns one of the following values:

E_UNEXPECTED	Unexpected error.
E_FAIL	Error occurred.
E_NOTIMPL	MFC should attempt to translate and dispatch the command.
OLECMDERR_E_UNKNOWNGROUP	*pguidCmdGroup* does not specify a recognized command group.
OLECMDERR_E_NOTSUPPORTED	*nCmdID* is not recognized as a valid command in the group *pGroup*.
OLE_CMDERR_DISABLED	The command identified by *nCmdID* is disabled.
OLECMDERR_NOHELP	No help information is available.
OLECMDERR_CANCELLED	The user canceled the operation.

This method will execute the command specified. The command is identified by *pguidCmdGroup* and *nCmdID*.

CPageSetupDialog

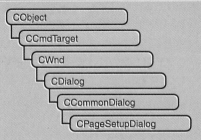

The CPageSetupDialog class represents the standard page setup dialog box. This dialog box allows the application to attain information about how the document should be printed out. After the information has been collected from the user, the CPageSetupDialog box object can create a printer device context.

Header Files

The following header file should be included when using this class:

afxdlgs.h

Properties

The CPageSetupDialog class has the following properties:

m_psd   A PAGESETUPDLG structure that is used to customize the dialog box.

Methods

The CPageSetupDialog class has the following methods:

CPageSetupDialog   The constructor
CreatePrinterDC   Create a printer device context
DoModal   Display the dialog and wait for user input
GetDeviceName   Get the name of the printer selected
GetDevMode   Get the DEVMODE of the printer
GetDriverName   Get the name of the device driver selected
GetMargins   Get the margin settings
GetPaperSize   Get the paper size
GetPortName   Get the port the printer is connected to

The following methods are used to process messages sent to the class. These methods may be overridden if special handling is needed for these messages.

OnDrawPage   Called by MFC to render a screen image of a printed page
PreDrawPage   Called by MFC before rendering a screen image of a printed page

The `CPageSetupDialog` Constructor

The `CPageSetupDialog` creates the `CPageSetup` object. The `CPageSetupDialog` constructor is used as follows:

```
CPageSetupDialog( DWORD dwFlags = PSD_MARGINS | PSD_INWININIINTLMEASURE,
➥CWnd* pParentWnd = NULL );
```

where

dwFlags	One or more flags to customize the dialog box.
pParentWnd	The parent window.

The following are valid flags for the `dwFlags` parameter:

PSD_DEFAULTMINMARGINS	Set the minimum allowable widths for the page margins to be the same as the printer's minimums. This flag is ignored if the `PSD_MARGINS` and `PSD_MINMARGINS` flags are also specified.
PSD_INWININIINTLMEASURE	Not implemented.
PSD_MINMARGINS	Causes the system to use the values specified in the `rtMinMargin` member as the minimum allowable widths for the left, top, right, and bottom margins. The dialog box will not allow the user to enter a width that is less than the minimum. If `PSD_MINMARGINS` is not specified, the margins will be set to the minimum allowable widths allowed by the printer.
PSD_MARGINS	Activates the margin control area.
PSD_INTHOUSANDTHSOFINCHES	Dialog units are 1/1000 of an inch.
PSD_INHUNDREDTHSOFMILLIMETERS	Dialog units are 1/100 of a millimeter.
PSD_DISABLEMARGINS	Disables the margin dialog box controls.
PSD_DISABLEPRINTER	Disables the Printer button.
PSD_NOWARNING	Do not warn if there is no default printer.
PSD_DISABLEORIENTATION	Disables the page orientation dialog control.
PSD_RETURNDEFAULT	Causes `CPageSetupDialog` to return `DEVMODE` and `DEVNAMES` structures initialized for the system default printer without displaying a dialog box. It is assumed that both `hDevNames` and `hDevMode` are `NULL`; otherwise, the function returns an error. If the system default printer is supported by an old printer driver (earlier than Windows version 3.0), only `hDevNames` is returned; `hDevMode` is `NULL`.
PSD_DISABLEPAPER	Disables the paper selection control.
PSD_SHOWHELP	Display the help button. The `hwndOwner` member must not be `NULL` if this flag is specified.

PSD_ENABLEPAGESETUPHOOK	Enables the hook function specified in lpfnSetupHook.
PSD_ENABLEPAGESETUPTEMPLATE	Causes the operating system to create the dialog box by using the dialog template box identified by hInstance and lpSetupTemplateName.
PSD_ENABLEPAGESETUPTEMPLATEHANDLE	Indicates that hInstance identifies a data block that contains a preloaded dialog box template. The system ignores lpSetupTemplateName if this flag is specified.
PSD_ENABLEPAGEPAINTHOOK	Enables the hook function specified in lpfnPagePaintHook.
PSD_DISABLEPAGEPAINTING	Disables the draw area of the dialog box.

The `CreatePrinterDC` Method

`HDC CreatePrinterDC( );`

Returns a device context handle created from the DEVMODE and DEVNAMES structures.

The `DoModal` Method

`int DoModal( );`

Returns an IDOK if the user pressed OK. Returns IDCANCEL if the user cancels the dialog.

The DoModal method is called to display the dialog box and wait for user input.

The `GetDeviceName` Method

`CString GetDeviceName( ) const;`

Returns the name of the selected printer.

The `GetDevMode` Method

`LPDEVMODE GetDevMode( ) const;`

Returns a pointer to the DEVMODE structure. This structure contains information about the print driver.

The `GetDriverName` Method

`CString GetDriverName( ) const;`

Returns the name of the selected device driver.

The `GetMargins` Method

`void GetMargins( LPRECT lpRectMargins, LPRECT lpRectMinMargins ) const;`

where

lpRectMargins	The rectangle pointed to by this parameter will contain the margins of the page. NULL should be passed if this value is not needed.
lpRectMinMargins	The rectangle pointed to by this parameter contains the minimum print margins of the page. NULL should be passed if this value is not needed.

The GetMargins method is used to determine the margins and minimum margins of the printer.

The `GetPaperSize` Method

`CSize GetPaperSize( ) const;`

Returns the size of the paper selected for printing.

The `GetPortName` Method

`CString GetPortName( ) const;`

Returns the port that the printer is on.

The `OnDrawPage` Method

`virtual UINT OnDrawPage( CDC* pDC, UINT nMessage, LPRECT lpRect );`

where

pDC	The printer device context.
nMessage	A message that specifies the area of the page being drawn.
lpRect	The coordinates of the drawing area.

Returns TRUE if this message was handled.

The following are valid messages that may be sent to the `OnDrawPage` method.

WM_PSD_FULLPAGERECT	The entire page area.
WM_PSD_MINMARGINRECT	Current minimum margins.
WM_PSD_MARGINRECT	Current margins.
WM_PSD_GREEKTEXTRECT	Contents of the page.
WM_PSD_ENVSTAMPRECT	Area reserved for a postage stamp representation.
WM_PSD_YAFULLPAGERECT	Area for a return address representation. This area extends to the edges of the sample page area.

The `OnDrawPage` method allows an application to print a page to a device context. This page is not printed to the printer, but rather is used to display a sample page in the dialog box. The default implementation draws a page of text.

The `PreDrawPage` Method

`virtual UINT PreDrawPage( WORD wPaper, WORD wFlags, LPPAGESETUPDLG pPSD );`

where

wPaper	Specifies the paper size.
wFlags	Indicates the orientation of the page.
pPSD	Pointer to a page setup dialog box.

Returns TRUE if the message was processed.

The following are valid values for the *wFlags* parameter.

0x001	Paper is in landscape mode and the printer is dot matrix
0x003	Paper is in landscape mode and the printer is laser
0x005	Paper is in portrait mode and the printer is dot matrix
0x007	Paper is in portrait mode and the printer is laser

0x00b	Envelope is in landscape mode and the printer is laser
0x00d	Envelope is in portrait mode and the printer is laser
0x019	Envelope is in landscape mode and the printer is dot matrix
0x01f	Envelope is in portrait mode and the printer is dot matrix

The PreDrawPage method is drawn just before the screen image is drawn.

CPaintDC

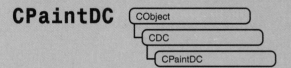

The CPaintDC class implements a repaint device context. This device context is used to repaint a window in response to a WM_PAINT message. The CPaintDC class is identical to CDC, except that it paints only to the regions of the window that need to be repainted.

For an example of CPaintDC, see the CDCEx example found on the CD-ROM that accompanies this book.

Header Files

The following header file should be included when using this class:

afxwin.h

Properties

The CPaintDC class has the following properties:

| m_ps | The PAINTSTRUCT used to paint the client area. |
| m_hwnd | The HWND to which this CPaintDC object is attached. |

Method

The CPaintDC class has the following method:

| CPaintDC | The constructor. |

The CPaintDC Constructor

The CPaintDC creates the CPaint object. The CPaintDC constructor is used as follows:

CPaintDC(CWnd* pWnd);

where

| pWnd | The window this object will be used to update. |

The CPaintDC method can throw the CResourceException exception.

CPalette

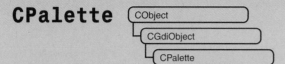

The CPalette class ivmplements a Windows palette. A palette is a color table that is used to specify which colors a device should currently be displaying. A palette object is usually selected into a device context (CDC).

Header Files

The following header file should be included when using this class:

afxwin.h

Methods

The CPalette class has the following methods:

CPalette	The constructor
AnimatePalette	Immediately replace colors in the physical palette
CreateHalftonePalette	Create a halftone palette
CreatePalette	Create a palette
FromHandle	Create a palette from a handle
GetEntryCount	Count the number of palette entries
GetNearestPaletteIndex	Get the palette index that most closely matches a real color
GetPaletteEntries	Get a range of palette entries
operator HPALETTE	Get a handle to this palette object
ResizePalette	Change the palette size
SetPaletteEntries	Change some of the palette entries

The CPalette Constructor

The CPalette constructor creates the CPalette object. The CPalette constructor is used as follows:

CPalette

The AnimatePalette Method

void AnimatePalette(UINT nStartIndex, UINT nNumEntries, LPPALETTEENTRY
➡lpPaletteColors);

where

nStartIndex	The starting index of where to replace color entries.
nNumEntries	The number of color entries to replace.
lpPaletteColors	A pointer to the new color entries to replace the old ones.

The AnimatePalette method is used to replace entries in the CPalette object. These colors are immediately changed, and as a result the client area of the screen does not need to be redrawn. This allows colors to be changed very quickly, and can be used for certain animated effects.

The CreateHalftonePalette Method

```
BOOL CreateHalftonePalette( CDC* pDC );
```

where

      pDC   A device context.

The CreateHalftonePalette method is called to create a half-tone palette for the specified device context.

The CreatePalette Method

```
BOOL CreatePalette( LPLOGPALETTE lpLogPalette );
```

where

      lpLogPalette   A logical palette structure that specifies the colors of the newly created palette.

Returns TRUE if successful.

The CreatePalette method is used to create a palette from a color table specified by lpLogPalette.

The FromHandle Method

```
static CPalette* PASCAL FromHandle( HPALETTE hPalette );
```

where

      hPalette   A palette handle.

Returns a CPalette object.

The FromHandle method is used to create a CPalette object from a palette handle.

The GetEntryCount Method

```
int GetEntryCount();
```

Returns the number of color entries in the palette.

The GetNearestPaletteIndex Method

```
UINT GetNearestPaletteIndex( COLORREF crColor ) const;
```

where

      crColor   A 24-bit color value.

Returns the index to the closest match to the color specified by *crColor*.

The GetPaletteEntries Method

```
UINT GetPaletteEntries( UINT nStartIndex, UINT nNumEntries, LPPALETTEENTRY
➡lpPaletteColors ) const;
```

where

      nStartIndex   The starting index of where to retrieve colors from.

      nNumEntries   The number of color entries to retrieve.

      lpPaletteColors   A pointer to a color table to receive the colors.

Returns 0 if the method fails; otherwise, returns the number of colors retrieved.

The GetPaletteEntries method is used to get the 24-bit color values for entries in the CPalette object.

The HPALETTE Operator

`operator HPALETTE( ) const;`

Returns the palette handle associated with this object.

The ResizePalette Method

`BOOL ResizePalette( UINT nNumEntries );`

where

    nNumEntries   The number of entries to realize.

Returns TRUE if successful.

The ResizePalette method resizes the palette.

The SetPaletteEntries Method

`UINT SetPaletteEntries( UINT nStartIndex, UINT nNumEntries, LPPALETTEENTRY`
➥`lpPaletteColors );`

where

    nStartIndex   The starting index of where to replace color entries.

    nNumEntries   The number of color entries to replace.

    lpPaletteColors   A pointer to the new color entries that are to replace the old ones.

The SetPaletteEntries method is used to replace entries in the CPalette object.

CPen

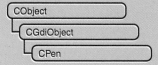

The CPen class implements a GDI pen object. A pen is used to specify how to draw lines.

Header Files

The following header files should be included when using this class:

`afxwin.h`

Methods

The CPen class has the following methods:

CPen	The constructor
CreatePen	Create a pen object
CreatePenIndirect	Create a pen object from a structure
FromHandle	Create a pen object from a pen handle
GetExtLogPen	Get a EXTLOGPEN structure for the pen
GetLogPen	Get a LOGPEN structure for the pen operator
HPEN	Get the handle to the pen

The CPen Constructor

The CPen constructor creates the CPen object. CPen constructor is used as follows:

```
CPen( );
CPen( int nPenStyle, int nWidth, COLORREF crColor );
CPen( int nPenStyle, int nWidth, const LOGBRUSH* pLogBrush, int nStyleCount =
➡ 0, const DWORD* lpStyle = NULL );
```

where

nPenStyle	Specifies the style of the pen.
nWidth	Specifies the width of the pen.
crColor	Specifies the color of the pen.
pLogBrush	Specifies a structure that contains the attributes of the pen.
nWidth	Specifies the length, in 32-bit units, of the size of the lpStyle array.
lpStyle	Specifies an array of 32-bit values that specifies a user-defined pen style.

The following values are valid for the nPenStyle parameter:

PS_SOLID	A solid pen.
PS_DASH	A dashed pen. Pen width must be one or less.
PS_DOT	A dotted pen. Pen width must be one or less.
PS_DASHDOT	A pen that alternates between dashes and dots. Pen width must be one or less.
PS_DASHDOTDOT	A pen that alternates between one dash and two dots. Pen width must be one or less.
PS_NULL	A NULL pen.
PS_INSIDEFRAME	Specifies that the pen should draw its line inside the GDI drawing methods.
PS_GEOMETRIC	A geometric pen.
PS_COSMETIC	A cosmetic pen.
PS_ALTERNATE	A pen that sets every other pixel.
PS_USERSTYLE	A pen that uses the style array.
PS_ENDCAP_ROUND	A pen with round endcaps.
PS_ENDCAP_SQUARE	A pen with square endcaps.
PS_ENDCAP_FLAT	A pen with flat endcaps.
PS_JOIN_BEVEL	Joins are beveled.
PS_JOIN_MITER	Joins are mitered when they are within the current limit set by the SetMiterLimit API function.
PS_JOIN_ROUND	Joins are rounded.

The CPen constructor can throw the CResourceException exception.

The CreatePen Method

```
BOOL CreatePen( int nPenStyle, int nWidth, COLORREF crColor );
BOOL CreatePen( int nPenStyle, int nWidth, const LOGBRUSH* pLogBrush, int
➡nStyleCount = 0, const DWORD* lpStyle = NULL );
```

where

nPenStyle	Specifies the style of the pen (see the constructor for a list of valid styles).
nWidth	Specifies the width of the pen.
crColor	Specifies the color of the pen.
pLogBrush	Specifies a structure that contains the attributes of the pen.
nWidth	Specifies the length, in 32-bit units, of the size of the lpStyle array.
lpStyle	Specifies an array of 32-bit values that specifies a user-defined pen style.

Returns TRUE if successful.

The CreatePen method is used to create a pen.

The CreatePenIndirect Method

BOOL CreatePenIndirect(LPLOGPEN lpLogPen);

where

lpLogPen	Specifies the LOGPEN structure used to create the pen.

Returns TRUE if successful.

The CreatePenIndirect method is used to create a pen from a LOGPEN structure.

The FromHandle Method

static CPen* PASCAL FromHandle(HPEN hPen);

where

hPen	A pen handle.

Returns a CPen object.

The FromHandle method is used to create a CPen object from a pen handle.

The GetExtLogPen Method

int GetExtLogPen(EXTLOGPEN* pLogPen);

where

pLogPen	A pointer to a EXTLOGPEN structure that will contain information about the pen.

Returns TRUE if successful.

The GetExtLogPen method is used to get extended information about the pen.

The GetLogPen Method

int GetLogPen(LOGPEN* pLogPen);

where

pLogPen	A pointer to a LOGPEN structure that will contain information about the pen.

Returns TRUE if successful.

The GetLogPen method is used to get information about the pen.

CPoint   [CPoint]

The CPoint class implements a Windows POINT structure as an object. A CPoint object can be used whenever a POINT structure is valid. A point is an x,y-based coordinate.

Header Files

The following header file should be included when using this class:

afxwin.h

Methods

The CPoint class has the following methods:

CPoint	The constructor
Offset	Add x,y values to the point
operator ==	Equal comparison
operator !=	Not equal comparison
operator +=	Add a size or point
operator -=	Subtract a size or point
operator +	Return the sum of a CPoint and a size or point
operator -	Return the difference of a CPoint and a size or point

The CPoint Constructor

The CPoint constructor creates the CPoint object. The CPoint constructor is used as follows:

```
CPoint( );
CPoint( int initX, int initY );
CPoint( POINT initPt );
CPoint( SIZE initSize );
CPoint( DWORD dwPoint );
```

where

initX	The initial x coordinate of the point.
initY	The initial y coordinate of the point.
initPt	The initial x,y coordinates of the point.
initSize	The initial x,y coordinates of the point from a size structure.
dwPoint	The initial x,y coordinates as a long. The low-order word contains x, and the high-order word contains y.

The Offset Method

```
void Offset( int xOffset, int yOffset );
void Offset( POINT point );
void Offset( SIZE size );
```

where

xOffset	The x offset.
yOffset	The y offset.
point	The x,y offsets as a point.
size	The x,y offsets as a size.

The Offset method will add the x and y offsets to the point.

The == Operator

```
BOOL operator ==( POINT point ) const;
```

where

> *point*   The point structure or CPoint object to compare to.

Returns TRUE if the two points are equal.

The != Operator

```
BOOL operator !=( POINT point ) const;
```

where

> *point*   The point structure or CPoint object to compare to.

Returns TRUE if the two points are not equal.

The += Operator

```
void operator +=( SIZE size );
void operator +=( POINT point );
```

where

> *point*   The x,y offsets as a point.
>
> *size*   The x,y offsets as a size.

The += operator will add the x and y offsets to the point.

The -= Operator

```
void operator -=( SIZE size );
void operator -=( POINT point );
```

where

> *point*   The x,y offsets as a point.
>
> *size*   The x,y offsets as a size.

The += operator will subtract the x and y offsets to the point.

The + Operator

```
CPoint operator +( SIZE size ) const;
CPoint operator +( POINT point ) const;
CRect operator +( const RECT* lpRect ) const;
```

where

> *point*   The x,y offsets as a point.
>
> *size*   The x,y offsets as a size.
>
> *rect*   A rectangle to add the point to.

The + operator will add the x and y offsets to the point. If the rectangle version is used, the x and y coordinates of the point will be added to both points in the rectangle.

The - Operator

```
CPoint operator -( SIZE size ) const;
CPoint operator -( POINT point ) const;
CRect operator -( const RECT* lpRect ) const;
```

where

point	The x,y offsets as a point.
size	The x,y offsets as a size.
rect	A rectangle to add the point to.

The - operator will subtract the x and y offsets from the point. If the rectangle version is used, the x and y coordinates of the point will be subtracted from both points in the rectangle.

CPropertySheet

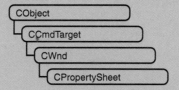

The CPropertySheet class creates a dialog box that has several property pages. These pages are selected using a tabbed control. To create a property sheet, one CPropertySheet class should be created. Then one or more CPropertyPages should be created and attached to the CPropertySheet object.

Header Files

The following header file should be included when using this class:

afxdlgs.h

Property

The CPropertySheet class has the following property:

m_psh	A PROPSHEETHEADER structure.

Methods

The CPropertySheet class has the following methods:

CPropertySheet	The constructor
AddPage	Add a page to the property sheet
Construct	Construct the object
Create	Create the object as a modeless dialog box
DoModal	Display the dialog box and wait for user input
EnableStackedTabs	Enable stacked tabs

EndDialog	Called to end the dialog
GetActiveIndex	Get the active index
GetActivePage	Get the active page
GetPage	Get a page
GetPageCount	Get the page count
GetPageIndex	Get the index of a specified page
GetTabControl	Get the underlying tab control
PressButton	Simulate pressing one of the buttons
RemovePage	Remove a page
SetActivePage	Set the active page
SetFinishText	Set the text for the finish button
SetTitle	Set the title for the dialog box
SetWizardButtons	Setup wizard buttons
SetWizardMode	Enter wizard mode

The CPropertySheet Constructor

The CPropertySheet creates the CPropertySheet object. The CPropertySheet constructor is used as follows:

```
CPropertySheet( );
CPropertySheet( UINT nIDCaption, CWnd *pParentWnd = NULL, UINT iSelectPage = 0 );
CPropertySheet( LPCTSTR pszCaption, CWnd *pParentWnd = NULL, UINT
➡iSelectPage = 0 );
```

where

nIDCaption	Resource ID of a caption for the dialog box.
pszCaption	The caption for the dialog box.
pParentWnd	The parent window for the dialog box.
iSelectPage	The initially selected page.

The constructor is called to actually construct the object. One or more AddPage methods should be called to add pages to the dialog box. Then DoModal should be called.

The AddPage Method

```
void AddPage( CPropertyPage *pPage );
```

where

| pPage | The page to be added. |

The AddPage method adds the specified CPropertyPage object to the dialog box.

The Construct Method

```
Construct( UINT nIDCaption, CWnd *pParentWnd = NULL, UINT iSelectPage = 0 );
Construct( LPCTSTR pszCaption, CWnd *pParentWnd = NULL, UINT
➡iSelectPage = 0 );
```

where

nIDCaption	Resource ID of a caption for the dialog box.
pszCaption	The caption for the dialog box.
pParentWnd	The parent window for the dialog box.
iSelectPage	The initially selected page.

The Construct method is called to actually construct the object. This method should be called only if the default constructor was used. One or more AddPage methods should be called to add pages to the dialog box. Then DoModal should be called.

The Create Method

```
BOOL Create( CWnd* pParentWnd = NULL, DWORD dwStyle = (DWORD)ñ1, DWORD
➥dwExStyle = 0 );
```

where

pParentWnd	The parent window.
dwStyle	The window style for the property sheet.
dwExStyle	The extended window style for a property sheet.

The Create method creates the property sheet dialog box as a modeless dialog box.

The DoModal Method

```
int DoModal( );
```

Returns IDOK if the user selected OK, IDCANCEL for Cancel. This method will return 0 or -1 for an error.

The EnableStackedTabs Method

```
void EnableStackedTabs( BOOL bStacked );
```

where

| bStacked | TRUE if stacked tabs are enabled. |

The EnableStackedTabs method allows or disallows stacked tabs. Tab stacking allows the tabs to form rows when they no longer completely fit on a single row.

The EndDialog Method

```
void EndDialog( int nEndID );
```

where

| nEndID | The value that should be returned by DoModal. |

The EndDialog method is called to end the dialog box after a call has been made to DoModal.

The GetActiveIndex Method

```
int GetActiveIndex( ) const;
```

This method returns the page index of the currently selected page.

The GetActivePage Method

```
CPropertyPage* GetActivePage( ) const;
```

This method returns the currently selected page.

The `GetPage` Method

`CPropertyPage* GetPage( int nPage ) const;`

where

    nPage   The page index to retrieve.

Returns the page specified by *nPage*.

The `GetPageCount` Method

`int GetPageCount( );`

Returns the page count.

The `GetPageIndex` Method

`int GetPageIndex( CPropertyPage* pPage ) const;`

where

    pPage   A page in this property sheet.

Returns the index of *pPage*.

The `GetTabControl` Method

`CTabCtrl* GetTabControl( );`

Returns a pointer to the underlying tab control.

The `PressButton` Method

`BOOL PressButton( int nButton );`

where

    nButton   The button to press.

Returns TRUE if successful.

The `PressButton` method simulates one of the buttons being pressed. The following values are valid for *nButton*:

PSBTN_BACK	Back button
PSBTN_NEXT	Next button
PSBTN_FINISH	Finish button
PSBTN_OK	OK button
PSBTN_APPLYNOW	Apply button
PSBTN_CANCEL	Cancel button
PSBTN_HELP	Help button

The `RemovePage` Method

`void RemovePage( CPropertyPage *pPage );`
`void RemovePage( int nPage );`

where

    pPage   The page to be removed.

    nPage   The page to be removed.

The RemovePage method removes the specified CPropertyPage object from the dialog box.

The SetActivePage Method

```
void SetActivePage( CPropertyPage *pPage );
void SetActivePage( int nPage );
```

where

    pPage   The page to be made active.

    nPage   The page to be made active.

The SetActivePage method causes the specified CPropertyPage object to be made active.

The SetFinishText Method

```
void SetFinishText( LPCTSTR lpszText );
```

where

    lpszText   The text for the finish button.

The SetFinishText sets the caption for the finish button.

The SetWizardButtons Method

```
void SetWizardButtons( DWORD dwFlags );
```

where

    dwFlags   Sets which wizard buttons should appear.

The following values are valid buttons to display:

PSWIZB_BACK	Back button
PSWIZB_NEXT	Next button
PSWIZB_FINISH	Finish button
PSWIZB_DISABLEDFINISH	Disabled finish button

The SetWizardMode Method

```
void SetWizardMode();
```

The SetWizardMode method should be called before DoModal if the property sheet is to be in wizard mode. In wizard mode, no tabs are shown and the user must move between the property sheets using forward and backward buttons.

CRecordset

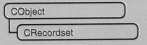

The CRecordset class is used to access an ODBC recordset. Any database query returns records. In MFC, these records are referred to as recordsets. CRecordset allows access to this set of records.

For an example of CRecordset, see the ODBCEx example found on the CD-ROM that accompanies this book.

Header Files

The following header files should be included when using this class:

`afxdb.h`

Properties

The `CRecordset` class has the following properties:

m_hstmt	Contains the ODBC statement handle for the recordset.
m_nFields	How many fields per row.
m_nParams	The number of parameters.
m_pDatabase	A pointer to the underlying ODBC database.
m_strFilter	String used to construct a SQL WHERE clause.
m_strSort	String used to construct an ORDER BY clause

Methods

The `CRecordSet` class has the following methods:

CRecordset	The constructor
AddNew	Prepare to add a new record
CanAppend	Are appends supported?
CanBookmark	Are bookmarks supported?
Cancel	Cancel asynchronous operation
CancelUpdate	Stop a previously started update
CanRestart	Are restarts supported?
CanScroll	Is scrolling supported?
CanTransact	Are transactions supported?
CanUpdate	Are updates supported?
Close	Close this recordset
Delete	Delete the current record
Edit	Prepare to edit the current record
FlushResultSet	Determine if another resultset is to be retrieved
GetBookmark	Get a bookmark to the current record
GetFieldValue	Get the value for the specified field
GetODBCFieldCount	Get the number of fields in this recordset
GetODBCFieldInfo	Get information about the specified field
GetRecordCount	Get a count of how many records have been accessed
GetRowsetSize	Get a count of how many records have been accessed
GetRowsFetched	Get the number of rows fetched
GetRowStatus	Get the status of a row
GetSQL	Get the SQL string for this recordset

GetStatus	Get the status of the recordset
GetTableName	Get the underlying table name
IsBOF	Is record before the beginning of the recordset?
IsDeleted	Is this record deleted?
IsEOF	Is this record after the end of the recordset?
IsFieldDirty	Is this field different than what is stored in the table?
IsFieldNull	Is this field NULL?
IsFieldNullable	Can this field be NULL?
IsOpen	Is this recordset open?
Move	Move a specified number of records
MoveFirst	Move to the first record
MoveLast	Move to the last record
MoveNext	Move to the next record
MovePrev	Move to the previous record
Open	Create a new recordset
RefreshRowset	Refresh the rowset
Requery	Requery the recordset against the database
SetAbsolutePosition	Set the position by absolute record number
SetBookmark	Move to the specified bookmark
SetFieldDirty	Set whether the specified field has a different value than the database
SetFieldNull	Set the specified field to have a NULL value
SetLockingMode	Set the record locking mode
SetParamValueNull	Set the value of the specified parameter to NULL
Update	Complete an AddNew or Edit method

The following methods are usually overridden by the application program.

Check	Examine the return code of an ODBC API function
CheckRowsetError	Handle errors during record fetching
DoBulkFieldExchange	Called to exchange bulk rows of data
DoFieldExchange	Called to exchange data between field data members and the data source
GetDefaultConnect	Get the default connection
GetDefaultSQL	Get the default SQL string
OnSetOptions	Called when options are set
SetRowsetSize	Called to set the rowset size

C

The `CRecordset` Constructor

The `CRecordset` constructor creates the `CRecordset` object. The `CRecordset` constructor is used as follows:

```
CRecordset( CDatabase *pDatabase)
```

where

      pDatabase   Contains a pointer to a `CDatabase` object.

The `AddNew` Method

```
virtual void AddNew( );
```

The `AddNew` method begins the process for adding a new record to the recordset. If this is a dynaset recordset, the new record will be inserted at the end of the recordset. If there is an index in a table recordset, records will be added in their proper order.

The current record does not change when `AddNew` is called. To make the new record current, call `SetBookmark` to the bookmark identified by the `LastModified`. Call `Update` to complete the process of adding a new record, or `CancelUpdate` to stop this process.

The `AddNew` method can throw the CDBException.

The `CanAppend` Method

```
BOOL CanAppend();
```

Returns TRUE if records can be added using the `AddNew` method.

The `CanBookmark` Method

```
BOOL CanBookmark();
```

Returns TRUE if the recordset supports bookmarks.

The `Cancel` Method

```
void Cancel();
```

The `Cancel` method is called to cancel an asynchronous database action.

The `CancelUpdate` Method

```
void CancelUpdate();
```

The `CancelUpdate` method is called to cancel a database update.

The `CanRestart` Method

```
BOOL CanRestart();
```

Returns TRUE if the `Requery` method can be called.

The `CanScroll` Method

```
BOOL CanScroll();
```

Returns TRUE if the recordset supports scrolling.

The `CanTransact` Method

```
BOOL CanTransact();
```

Returns TRUE if the recordset supports transactions.

The `CanUpdate` Method

`BOOL CanUpdate();`

Returns TRUE if records can be updated from this recordset.

The `Close` Method

`virtual void Close();`

The `Close` method should be called when the recordset is no longer needed in memory. This will not delete records from the database file.

The `Delete` Method

`virtual void Delete();`

The `Delete` method deletes the current record. The deleted record will remain current until the recordset is scrolled to another record.

The `Delete` method can throw the CDBException.

The `Edit` Method

`virtual void Edit( );`

The `Edit` method begins the process for updating a record to the recordset. Any changes made to the fields after calling the `Edit` method will be stored to a buffer. This buffer will be copied to the disk when the `Update` method is called.

The `Edit` method can throw the CDBException or CMemoryException.

The `FlushResultSet` Method

`BOOL FlushResultSet( ) const;`

The `FlushResultSet` will retrieve the next resultset of a stored procedure.

The `FlushResultSet` method can throw the CDBException.

The `GetBookmark` Method

`void GetBookmark( CDBVariant &varBookmark );`

where

> *varBookmark*   The bookmark.

The `GetBookmark` method will return a bookmark for the current record. This bookmark can be later used to return to this record.

The `GetBookmark` method can throw the CDBException or CMemoryException.

The `GetODBCFieldCount` Method

`short GetODBCFieldCount();`

Returns the number of fields in this recordset.

The `GetFieldInfo` Method

`void GetODBCFieldInfo( int nIndex, CODBCFieldInfo& fieldinfo );`
`void GetODBCFieldInfo( LPCTSTR lpszName, CODBCFieldInfo& fieldinfo );`

where

nIndex	The index of the field in the field collection.
fieldinfo	A reference to a CDaoFieldInfo object that returns the requested information.
lpszName	A string containing the name of the field.

The GetODBCFieldInfo method will return information about the specified field.

The GetODBCFieldInfo method can throw the CDBException.

The GetFieldValue Method

```
void GetFieldValue( LPCTSTR lpszName, CDBVariant& varValue,
➡short nFieldType = DEFAULT_FIELD_TYPE );
void GetFieldValue( short nIndex, COleVariant& varValue , short
➡nFieldType = DEFAULT_FIELD_TYPE );
void GetFieldValue( LPCTSTR lpszName, CString &strValue );
void GetFieldValue( int nIndex, CString &strValue );
```

where

lpszName	The name of the field.
varValue	Will be changed to hold the value of the field.
nIndex	The index of the field.
strValue	The field value as a string.

The GetFieldValue method is used to actually get data from fields in the recordset.

The GetRecordCount Method

```
long GetRecordCount() const;
```

Returns the number of records accessed in the recordset.

The GetRecordCount method will only return the number of records accessed, not the total number of records. To get the total number of records actually in the recordset, you must call MoveLast, and then call GetRecordCount.

The GetRowsetSize Method

```
DWORD GetRowsetSize() cibst;
```

Returns the number of records in the recordset.

The GetRowsFetched Method

```
DWORD GetRowsFetched() const;
```

Returns the number of records retrieved in a fetch.

The GetRowStatus Method

```
WORD GetRowStatus( WORD wRow ) const;
```

where

wRow	A row in the recordset, starting with one.

Returns status information about the row. Valid values are

SQL_ROW_SUCCESS	The row is unchanged
SQL_ROW_UPDATED	The row is updated
SQL_ROW_DELETED	The row is deleted
SQL_ROW_ADDED	The row has been added
SQL_ROW_ERROR	An error occurred while retrieving the row
SQL_ROW_NOROW	There is no row

The GetSQL Method

CString GetSQL();

Returns the underlying SQL string for the recordset.

The GetStatus Method

void GetStatus(CRecordsetStatus &rStatus) const;

where

    rStatus   The status of the current recordset.

The GetTableName Method

CString GetTableName();

Returns the underlying table for the recordset.

The IsBOF Method

BOOL IsBOF();

Returns TRUE if the current record is before the beginning of the recordset.

The IsDeleted Method

BOOL IsDeleted();

Returns TRUE if the current record has been deleted.

The IsEOF Method

BOOL IsEOF();

Returns TRUE if the current record is beyond the final record of the recordset.

The IsFieldDirty Method

BOOL IsFieldDirty(void *pv);

where

    pv   A pointer to the field property to be checked.

Returns TRUE if the value of the indicated field has changed.

The IsFieldDirty method can throw the CMemoryException.

The IsFieldNull Method

BOOL IsFieldNull(void *pv);

where

    pv   A pointer to the field property to be checked.

Returns TRUE if the indicated field is NULL.

The IsFieldNull method can throw the CMemoryException.

The `IsFieldNullable` Method

```
BOOL IsFieldNullable(void *pv);
```

where

pv	A pointer to the field property to be checked.

Returns TRUE if the indicated field can hold a NULL.

The IsFieldNullable method can throw the CMemoryException.

The `IsOpen` Method

```
BOOL IsOpen() const;
```

Returns TRUE if this recordset is open.

The `Move` Method

```
virtual void Move(long nRows, WORD wFetchType = SQL_FETCH_RELATIVE );
```

where

nRows	The number of rows to move.
wFetchType	The fetch type.

The Move method will move the current record either forward or backward. Positive values for *nRows* will move forward. Negative values for *nRows* will move backward.

The Move method can throw the CDBException or CDBMemoryException.

The `MoveFirst` Method

```
void MoveFirst();
```

Move to the first record in the recordset.

The MoveFirst method can throw the CDBException or CDBMemoryException.

The `MoveLast` Method

```
void MoveLast();
```

Move to the last record in the recordset.

The MoveLast method can throw the CDBException or CDBMemoryException.

The `MoveNext` Method

```
void MoveNext();
```

Move to the next record in the recordset.

The MoveNext method can throw the CDBException or CDBMemoryException.

The `MovePrev` Method

```
void MovePrev();
```

Move to the previous record in the recordset.

The MovePrev method can throw the CDBException or CDBMemoryException.

The Open Method
```
virtual void Open( int nOpenType = AFX_DB_USE_DEFAULT_TYPE, LPCTSTR
➥lpszSQL = NULL, int nOptions = 0 );
```
where

nOpenType	The type of recordset to open.
lpszSQL	SQL statement to build query from.
nOptions	Options for opening this recordset.

Valid values for nOpenType include

dbOpenDynaset	For a dynaset-based recordset.
dbOpenTable	A table-based recordset.
dbOpenSnapshot	A snapshot-based recordset.

Valid values for lpszSQL include

- A NULL pointer. Open will call GetDefaultSQL to get the SQL string.
- One or more tabledefs or querydefs. Should be comma separated.
- A SQL select.
- A pass-through query.

One or more options may be ORed together to form the following list:

dbAppendOnly	New records can be appended (dynaset-type recordset only).
dbForwardOnly	The recordset is a forward-only scrolling snapshot.
dbSeeChanges	Generate an exception if another user changes this data.
dbDenyWrite	Do not allow other users to modify or add records.
dbDenyRead	Do not allow other users to view records (table-type recordset only).
dbReadOnly	Open in read-only mode.
dbInconsistent	Inconsistent updates are allowed (dynaset-type recordset only).
dbConsistent	Allow only consistent updates (dynaset-type recordset only).

The Open method opens a recordset and prepares it for use.

The Open method can throw the CDBException.

The RefreshRowset Method
```
void RefreshRowset(WORD wRow, wLockType = SQL_LOCK_NO_CHANGE );
```
where

wRow	A row in the recordset.
wFetchType	How to lock the row after refresh. Should be SQL_LOCK_NO_CHANGE, SQL_LOCK_EXCLUSIVE, or SQL_LOCK_UNLOCK.

The RefreshRowset method will refresh and then optionally lock a row.

The RefreshRowset method can throw the CDBException or CDBMemoryException.

The `Requery` Method

`virtual BOOL Requery();`

Refresh the entire recordset from the database.

The `Requery` method can throw the CDBException or CMemoryException.

The `SetAbsolutePosition` Method

`void SetAbsolutePosition(long lPosition);`

where

    lPosition   The new current record based on ordinal position.

Call `SetAbsolutePosition` to move the current record by record number.

The `SetAbsolutePosition` method can throw the CDBException and the CMemoryException.

The `SetBookmark` Method

`void SetBookmark( CDBVariant &varBookmark );`

where

    varBookmark   A bookmark to move the recordset to.

Call `SetBookmark` to move the current record to a bookmark.

The `SetBookmark` method can throw the CDBException and the CMemoryException.

The `SetFieldDirty` Method

`void SetFieldDirty( void *pv, BOLL bDirty = TRUE );`

where

    pv   The data member to set to dirty.

    bDirty   TRUE if this value should be set to dirty.

The `SetFieldDirty` specifies that a field has a different value than the underlying database.

The `SetFieldNull` Method

`void SetFieldNull( void *pv, BOLL bNull = TRUE );`

where

    pv   The data member to set to a NULL value.

    bNull   TRUE if this value should be set to NULL.

The `SetLockingMode` Method

`void SetLockingMode( BOOL bPessimistic );`

where

    pPessimistic   FALSE if locking is pessimistic; TRUE for optimistic locking.

Pessimistic locking locks a record the instant the `Edit` method is called. The record is released after the `Update` method is complete.

Optimistic locking locks a record only while the Update method is being called.

The SetLockingMode method can throw the CDBException.

The SetParamNull Method

```
void SetParamNull( short nIndex, BOOL bNull = TRUE );
```

where

nIndex	The zero-based index of the parameter.
bNull	TRUE to flag this parameter as NULL.

The SetParamNull method sets the value of a parameter to NULL.

The Update Method

```
virtual void Update();
```

Complete an add or update.

The Update method can throw the CDBException.

The Check Method

```
virtual BOOL Check( RETCODE nRetCode ) const;
```

where

nRetCode	An ODBC API return code.

Returns nonzero if the value of nRetCode is SQL_SUCCESS, SQL_SUCCESS_WITH_INFO, SQL_NO_DATA_FOUND, or SQL_NEED_DATA; otherwise 0.

The Check method is called when an ODBC API error occurs.

The DoBulkFieldExchange Method

```
void DoBulkFieldExchange( CFieldExchange *pFX ) const;
```

where

pFX	A pointer to a CFieldExchange object.

The DoBulkFieldExchange method is called during bulk row fetching.

The DoBulkFieldExchange method can throw the CDBException.

The DoFieldExchange Method

```
virtual void DoFieldExchange( CFieldExchange *pFX ) const;
```

where

pFX	A pointer to a CFieldExchange object.

The DoFieldExchange method is called during row fetching.

The DoBulkFieldExchange method can throw the CDBException.

The GetDefaultConnect Method

```
virtual CString GetDefaultConnect();
```

Returns the default connect string.

The GetDefaultSQL Method

virtual CString GetDefaultSQL();

Returns the default SQL string.

The OnSetOptions Method

void OnSetOptions(HSTMT hstmt);

where

   hstmt   The ODBC statement that sets options.

The OnSetOptions method is called when the options for a recordset change.

The SetRowsetSize Method

virtual void SetRowsetSize(DWORD dwNewRoesetsize);

where

   dwNewRowsetSize   The new size of the rowset.

The SetRowsetSize method is called to change the size of the rowset.

CRecordView

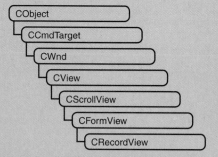

The CRecordView class is a view that displays recordset data. The view has the capability to map controls on a dialog template to individual fields from a recordset. Methods are provided for most common database actions, such as updates and cursor movement.

For an example of CRecordView, see the ODBCEx example on the CD-ROM that accompanies this book.

Header Files

The following header file should be included when using this class:

afxdb.h

Methods

The CRecordView class has the following methods:

   CRecordView   The constructor
   IsOnFirstRecord   Is the first record being displayed?
   IsOnLastRecord   Is the last record being displayed?

| OnGetRecordset | Gets the derived class |
| OnMove | Called to move between records |

The `CRecordView` Constructor

The `CRecordView` creates the `CRecordView` object. The `CRecordView` constructor is used as follows:

```
CRecordView( LPCSTR lpszTemplateName );
CRecordView( UINT nIDTemplate );
```

where

| *lpszTemplateName* | A string name for a dialog template resource. |
| *nIDTemplate* | A integer name for a dialog template resource. |

The `CRecordView` constructor creates a form based on the specified dialog template resource.

The `IsOnFirstRecord` Method

```
BOOL IsOnFirstRecord( );
```

Returns TRUE if the view is displaying the first record.

The `IsOnLastRecord` Method

```
BOOL IsOnLastRecord( );
```

Returns TRUE if the view is displaying the last record.

The `OnGetRecordset` Method

```
virtual CRecordset* OnGetRecordset( );
```

Returns a pointer to a derived type of recordset.

The `OnGetRecordset` method should be implemented for any derived class. This method should return a pointer to a new class of the same type as the derived class.

The `OnMove` Method

```
virtual BOOL OnMove( UINT nIDMoveCommand );
```

where

| *nIDMoveCommand* | The type of move requested. Should be ID_RECORD_FIRST, ID_RECORD_LAST, ID_RECORD_PREV, or ID_RECORD_NEXT. |

Returns TRUE if successful.

The `OnMove` method is called when the user wants to move to a different record.

CRect   `CRect`

The `CRect` class represents a rectangle. The rectangle is made up of an upper-left point and a lower-right point. Nearly all MFC methods that require rectangles as parameters use the `CRect` class.

For an example of `CRect`, see the CDCEx example on the CD-ROM that accompanies this book.

Header Files

The following header file should be included when using this class:

`afxwin.h`

Properties

The `CRect` class has the following properties:

bottom	The bottom y coordinate of the rectangle.
left	The left x coordinate of the rectangle.
right	The right x coordinate of the rectangle.
top	The top y coordinate.

Methods

The `CRect` class has the following methods:

CRect	The constructor
BottomRight	Get the bottom-right point
CenterPoint	Get the center point
CopyRect	Copy the rectangle
DeflateRect	Decrease the width and height
EqualRect	Determine whether two rectangles are equal
Height	Get the height of the rectangle
InflateRect	Increase the height and width of the rectangle
IntersectRect	Set to the intersection of two rectangles
IsRectEmpty	Determine whether the rectangle is empty
IsRectNull	Determine whether all coordinates are zero
NormalizeRect	Cause both height and width to be positive
OffsetRect	Move the rectangle by a specified number of points
operator -	Subtract the offsets from the rectangle
operator !=	Determine whether two rectangles are not equal
operator &	Calculate the intersection of two rectangles
operator &=	Set equal to the intersection of two rectangles
operator ¦	Create the union of two rectangles
operator ¦=	Set equal to the union of two rectangles
operator +	Inflate the rectangle
operator +=	Inflate and set equal to
operator =	Copy a rectangle
operator -=	Subtract the offsets and set equal to
operator ==	Compare two rectangles
operator LPCRECT	Get the rectangle as an `LPCRECT`
operator LPRECT	Get the rectangle as a `RECT`

PtInRect	Determine whether a point is inside the rectangle
SetRect	Set the dimensions of the rectangle
SetRectEmpty	Set the rectangle empty
Size	Calculate the size of the rectangle
SubtractRect	Subtract one rectangle from another
TopLeft	Get the top-left point of the rectangle
UnionRect	Set to the union of two rectangles
Width	Get the width of the rectangle

The CRect Constructor

The CRect creates the CRect object. The CRect constructor is used as follows:

```
CRect( );
CRect( int l, int t, int r, int b );
CRect( const RECT& srcRect );
CRect( LPCRECT lpSrcRect );
CRect( POINT point, SIZE size );
CRect( POINT topLeft, POINT bottomRight );
```

where

l	The left x coordinate.
t	The top y coordinate.
r	The right x coordinate.
b	The bottom y coordinate.
srcRect	A rectangle as a CRect.
lpSrcRect	A rectangle as a Rect.
point	The upper-left point.
size	The size of the rectangle.
bottomRight	The bottom-right point.
topLeft	The top-left point.

The BottomRight Method

```
CPoint& BottomRight( );
const CPoint& BottomRight( ) const;
```

Returns a reference to the bottom-right point that can be used to set or read this point.

The CenterPoint Method

```
CPoint CenterPoint( ) const;
```

Returns the calculated center point.

The CopyRect Method

```
void CopyRect( LPCRECT lpSrcRect );
```

where

| lpSrcRect | The source rectangle. |

The CopyRect method will copy the coordinates from the specified rectangle to this rectangle.

The `DeflateRect` Method

```
void DeflateRect( int x, int y );
void DeflateRect( SIZE size );
void DeflateRect( LPCRECT lpRect );
void DeflateRect( int l, int t, int r, int b );
```

where

x	The x coordinate.
y	The y coordinate.
size	x,y as a size.
lpRect	A rectangle.
l	The left x coordinate.
t	The top y coordinate.
r	The right x coordinate.
b	The bottom y coordinate.

The `DeflateRect` method will decrease the size of the rectangle by the coordinates specified.

The `EqualRect` Method

```
BOOL EqualRect( LPCRECT lpRect ) const;
```

where

lpRect	A rectangle.

Returns TRUE if the specified rectangle is identical to this rectangle.

The `Height` Method

```
int Height( ) const;
```

Returns height of the rectangle.

The `InflateRect` Method

```
void InflateRect( int x, int y );
void InflateRect( SIZE size );
void InflateRect( LPCRECT lpRect );
void InflateRect( int l, int t, int r, int b );
```

where

x	The x coordinate.
y	The y coordinate.
size	x,y as a size.
lpRect	A rectangle.
l	The left x coordinate.
t	The top y coordinate.
r	The right x coordinate.
b	The bottom y coordinate.

The `InflateRect` method will increase the size of the rectangle by the coordinates specified.

The IntersectRect Method

```
BOOL IntersectRect( LPCRECT lpRect1, LPCRECT lpRect2 );
```

where

lpRect1	A rectangle.
lpRect2	A rectangle.

Returns TRUE if the resulting rectangle is not empty.

The IntersectRect method creates a rectangle that is the intersection of the two specified rectangles.

The IsRectEmpty Method

```
BOOL IsRectEmpty() const;
```

Returns TRUE if the rectangle is empty.

The IsRectNull Method

```
BOOL IsRectNull() const;
```

Returns TRUE if the rectangle is null, that is, all coordinates are zero.

The NormalizeRect Method

```
void NormalizeRect();
```

The NormalizeRect method will adjust the points so that the height and width are both positive.

The OffsetRect Method

```
void OffsetRect( int x, int y );
void OffsetRect( POINT point );
void OffsetRect( SIZE size );
```

where

x	x coordinate.
y	y coordinate.
size	x,y as a size.
point	x,y as a point.

The OffsetRect method will move the rectangle by the specified x and y coordinates.

The - Operator

```
CRect operator -( POINT point ) const;
CRect operator -( SIZE size ) const;
CRect operator -( LPCRECT lpRect ) const;
```

where

size	x,y as a size.
point	x,y as a point.
lpRect	Two sets of x,y as a Rect.

The - operator will decrease the size of the rectangle if a rectangle is specified. If a point is specified, the rectangle will be moved by the coordinates specified.

The != Operator

```
BOOL operator !=( const RECT& rect ) const;
```

where

    rect   A rectangle.

Returns TRUE if the specified rectangle is not identical to this rectangle.

The & Operator

```
CRect operator &( const RECT& rect2 ) const;
```

where

    lpRect2   A rectangle.

Returns a rectangle that is the intersection of this rectangle and the specified rectangle.

The & Operator

```
CRect operator &( const RECT& rect2 ) const;
```

where

    lpRect2   A rectangle.

Returns a rectangle that is the intersection of this rectangle and the specified rectangle.

The + Operator

```
CRect operator +( POINT point ) const;
CRect operator +( LPCRECT lpRect ) const;
CRect operator +( SIZE size ) const;
```

where

    size   x,y as a size.

    point   x,y as a point.

    lpRect   Two sets of x,y as a Rect.

The + operator will increase the size of the rectangle by the coordinates specified.

The += Operator

```
void operator +=( POINT point );
void operator +=( SIZE size );
void operator +=( LPCRECT lpRect );
```

where

    size   x,y as a size.

    point   x,y as a point.

    lpRect   Two sets of x,y as a Rect.

The += operator will increase the size of the rectangle by the coordinates specified.

The = Operator

```
void operator =( const RECT& srcRect );
```

where

    srcRect   The rectangle being copied.

The = operator will copy the specified rectangle to the current one.

The -= Operator

```
void operator -=( POINT point );
void operator -=( SIZE size );
void operator -=( LPCRECT lpRect );
```

where

size	x,y as a size.
point	x,y as a point.
lpRect	Two sets of x,y as a Rect.

The - operator will decrease the size of the rectangle if a rectangle is specified. If a point is specified, the rectangle will be moved by the coordinates specified.

The == Operator

```
BOOL operator ==( const RECT& rect ) const;
```

where

    rect   A rectangle.

Returns TRUE if the specified rectangle is identical to this rectangle.

The PtInRect Method

```
BOOL PtInRect( POINT point ) const;
```

where

    point   A point.

Returns TRUE if the specified point is located inside of the rectangle.

The SetRect Method

```
void SetRect( int x1, int y1, int x2, int y2 );
```

where

x1	x coordinate for the upper-left corner of the rectangle.
y1	y coordinate for the upper-left corner of the rectangle.
x2	x coordinate for the lower-right corner of the rectangle.
y2	y coordinate for the lower-right corner of the rectangle.

The SetRect will set the rectangle's coordinates to those specified.

The `SetRectEmpty` Method

```
void SetRectEmpty( );
```

The `SetRectEmpty` method will set all rectangle coordinates to zero.

The `Size` Method

```
CSize Size( ) const;
```

Returns the size of the rectangle.

The `SubtractRect` Method

```
BOOL SubtractRect( LPCRECT lpRectSrc1, LPCRECT lpRectSrc2 );
```

where

lpRectSrc1	A rectangle to be subtracted.
lpRectSrc2	A rectangle to be subtracted.

Returns TRUE if successful.

The `Subtract` method will set the rectangle equal to the smallest rectangle that contains all of the points inside of *lpRectSrc1* and *lpRectSrc2*.

The `Size` Method

```
CSize Size( ) const;
```

Returns the size of the rectangle.

The `TopLeft` Method

```
CPoint& TopLeft( );
const CPoint& TopLeft( ) const;
```

Returns a reference to the top-left point that can be used to set or read this point.

The `UnionRect` Method

```
BOOL UnionRect( LPCRECT lpRect1, LPCRECT lpRect2 );
```

where

lpRect1	A rectangle.
lpRect2	A rectangle.

Returns TRUE if successful.

The `UnionRect` method will set the rectangle equal to the smallest rectangle that contains both *lpRect1* and *lpRect2*.

The `Width` Method

```
int Width( ) const;
```

Returns width of the rectangle.

CRichEditView

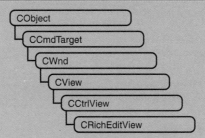

The CRichEditView method implements a view class that is based on a rich edit control. This view allows for the editing of RTF (rich text format) data. This allows text to contain formatting information such as bolding, fonts, and font sizes.

Header Files

The following header file should be included when using this class:

afxrich.h

Properties

The CRichEditView class has the following properties:

m_nBulletIndent	The amount to indent for bullet lists
m_nWordWrap	Word wrap constraints

Methods

The CRichEditView class has the following methods:

CRichEditView	The constructor
AdjustDialogPosition	Move a dialog box away from the selected text
CanPaste	Determine whether data can be pasted
DoPaste	Paste an OLE item
FindText	Locate text, display wait cursor
FindTextSimple	Locate text
GetCharFormatSelection	Get the format used for the selection
GetDocument	Get a pointer to the document
GetInPlaceActiveItem	Get the item that is currently in an active state
GetMargins	Get margins
GetPageRect	Get the page rectangle
GetPaperSize	Get the paper size
GetParaFormatSelection	Get the paragraph formatting attributes
GetPrintRect	Get the print rectangle
GetPrintWidth	Get the print width

GetRichEditCtrl	Get the underlying control
GetSelectedItem	Get the currently selected item
GetTextLength	Get the length of the text
InsertFileAsObject	Insert a file as an object
InsertItem	Insert an item
IsRichEditFormat	Determine whether the Clipboard contains rich text
OnCharEffect	Change the formatting for the current selection
OnParaAlign	Change the alignment for the current selection
OnUpdateCharEffect	Update the availability of character effects
OnUpdateParaAlign	Update the availability of paragraph alignments
PrintInsideRect	Format text within a given rectangle
PrintPage	Format the text within a given page
SetCharFormat	Set the character formatting for a given selection
SetMargins	Set the margins for the document
SetPaperSize	Set the paper size
SetParaFormat	Set the paragraph format for the current selection

The following methods are used to process messages sent to the class. These methods may be overridden if special handling is needed for these messages.

GetClipboardData	Get a Clipboard object for a range in this control
GetContextMenu	Get a context menu
IsSelected	Is a given OLE item selected?
OnFindNext	Find the next occurrence of a string
OnInitialUpdate	Refresh view when first attached to a document
OnPasteNativeObject	Paste native data from an old item
OnPrinterChanged	Called to change to another printer device
OnReplaceAll	Replace all occurrences of a string
OnReplaceSel	Replace the current selection
OnTextNotFound	Called when the text being searched for is not found
QueryAcceptData	See about an IDataObject
WrapChanged	Adjust output after word wrap changes

The CRichEditView Constructor

The CRichEditView creates the CRichView object. The CRichEditView constructor is used as follows:

CRichEditView( );

The AdjustDialogPosition Method

void AdjustDialogPosition(CDialog* pDlg);

where

    pDlg   A dialog.

The AdjustDialogPosition method will move the given dialog so it is not in front of the current selection.

The CanPaste Method

BOOL CanPaste( ) const;

Returns TRUE if the Clipboard contains data that can be pasted into this view.

The DoPaste Method

void DoPaste(COleDataObject& dataobj, CLIPFORMAT cf, HMETAFILEPICT
➡hMetaPict);

where

dataobj	The data to be pasted.
cf	The Clipboard format to be used.
hMetaPict	The metafile that represents the item being pasted.

The DoPaste method will paste an OLE item into this rich edit control.

The FindText Method

BOOL FindText(LPCTSTR lpszFind, BOOL bCase = TRUE, BOOL bWord = TRUE);

where

lpszFind	The string to search for.
bCase	TRUE if the search is case-sensitive.
bWord	TRUE if the search should match whole words only.

Returns TRUE if the text is found.

The FindText method will search for the given text and make it the current selection if found.

The FindTextSimple Method

BOOL FindTextSimple(LPCTSTR lpszFind, BOOL bCase = TRUE, BOOL bWord =
➡TRUE);

where

lpszFind	The string to search for.
bCase	TRUE if the search is case-sensitive.
bWord	TRUE if the search should match whole words only.

Returns TRUE if the text is found.

The FindTextSimple method will search for the given text and make it the current selection if found.

The GetCharFormatSelection Method

CHARFORMAT& GetCharFormatSelection( );

Returns the CHARFORMAT reference for the current selection.

The GetDocument Method

CRichEditDoc* GetDocument( ) const;

Returns a pointer to the document associated with this view.

The `GetInPlaceActiveItem` Method

`CRichEditCntrItem* GetInPlaceActiveItem( ) const;`

Returns a pointer to the OLE item currently in the in-place active state.

The `GetMargins` Method

`CRect GetMargins( ) const;`

Returns a rectangle that represents the margins of the document.

The `GetPageRect` Method

`CRect GetPageRect( ) const;`

Returns a rectangle that represents the page's rectangle for the document.

The `GetPaperSize` Method

`CSize GetPaperSize( ) const;`

Returns the size of the paper.

The `GetPrintRect` Method

`CRect GetPrintRect( ) const;`

Returns the printing rectangle. This value is measured in twips.

The `GetPrintWidth` Method

`int GetPrintWidth( ) const;`

Returns the width of the printing rectangle. This value is measured in twips.

The `GetRichEditCtrl` Method

`CRichEditCtrl& GetRichEditCtrl( ) const;`

Returns the underlying rich edit control.

The `GetSelectedItem` Method

`CRichEditCntrItem* GetSelectedItem( ) const;`

Returns the currently selected OLE item or NULL if none is selected.

The `GetTextLength` Method

`long GetTextLength( ) const;`

Returns the length of the text currently in the buffer.

The `InsertFileAsObject` Method

`void InsertFileAsObject( LPCTSTR lpszFileName );`

where

> *lpszFileName*   A file to be inserted.

The `InsertFileAsObject` will insert the specified filename as an object.

The `InsertItem` Method

HRESULT InsertItem(CRichEditCntrItem* pItem);

where

    pItem   A item to be inserted.

The `InsertItem` will insert the specified item into a the rich edit control.

The `IsRichEditFormat` Method

BOOL IsRichEditFormat(CLIPFORMAT cf);

where

    cf   A Clipboard format.

Returns TRUE if the specified Clipboard format is text, rich text, or rich text with OLE items.

The `OnCharEffect` Method

void OnCharEffect(DWORD dwMask, DWORD dwEffect);

where

    dwMask   The desired character formatting effects to modify.

    dwEffect   The desired character formatting effects.

The `OnCharEffect` method is called to change the formatting effects for the current selection.

The `OnParaAlign` Method

void OnParaAlign(WORD wAlign);

where

    wAlign   Desired paragraph alignment. Should be PFA_LEFT, PFA_RIGHT, or PFA_CENTER.

The `OnParaAlign` method is called by MFC to change the paragraph alignment for the selected text.

The `OnUpdateCharEffect` Method

void OnUpdateCharEffect(CCmdUI* pCmdUI, DWORD dwMask, DWORD dwEffect);

where

    pCmdUI   CCmdUI object for the character effects.

    dwMask   Character formatting mask.

    dwEffect   Character formatting effect.

The `OnUpdateCharEffect` method is called by MFC to determine which character effects should be available.

The `OnUpdateParaAlign` Method

void OnParaAlign(CCmdUI* pCmdUI, WORD wAlign);

where

    pCmdUI   CCmdUI object for the paragraph alignments.

    wAlign   Paragraph alignment. Should be PFA_LEFT, PFA_RIGHT, or PFA_CENTER.

C

The OnUpdateParaAlign method is called by MFC to determine which paragraph alignments should be available.

The PrintInsideRect Method

```
long PrintInsideRect( CDC* pDC, RECT& rectLayout, long nIndexStart, long
➦nIndexStop, BOOL bOutput );
```

where

pDC	The device context.
rectLayout	Rectangle that defines the output area.
nIndexStart	Zero-based index of starting character.
nIndexStop	Zero-based index of the final character.
bOutput	TRUE if the text should be rendered. FALSE if the text is just to be measured.

Returns the index of the last character that fits inside the rectangle.

The PrintInsideRect method will format a range of text to a device context.

The PrintPage Method

```
long PrintPage( CDC* pDC, long nIndexStart, long nIndexStop );
```

where

pDC	The device context.
nIndexStart	Zero-based index of the starting character.
nIndexStop	Zero-based index of the final character.

Returns the index of the last character that fits on the page, plus one.

The PrintPage method will output one page to the device context.

The SetCharFormat Method

```
void SetCharFormat( CHARFORMAT cf );
```

where

cf	A CHARFORMAT structure that contains the new default character attributes.

The SetCharFormat method will set the default character formatting attributes for new text entered or inserted into the edit view.

The SetMargins Method

```
void SetMargins( const CRect& rectMargin );
```

where

rectMargin	A rectangle that specifies the margins. This measurement is in twips.

The SetMargins method will set margins for the rich text view.

The **SetPaperSize** Method

```
void SetPaperSize( CSize sizePaper );
```

where

    sizePaper   A size that specifies the paper size. This measurement is in twips.

The SetPaperSize method will set the paper size.

The **SetParaFormat** Method

```
void SetParaFormat( PARAFORMAT& pf );
```

where

    pf   A PARAFORMAT structure that specifies the paragraph format.

The SetParaFormat method will set the paragraph format.

The **GetClipboardData** Method

```
virtual HRESULT GetClipboardData( CHARRANGE* lpchrg, DWORD dwReco,
➥LPDATAOBJECT lpRichDataObj, LPDATAOBJECT* lplpdataobj );
```

where

lpchrg	A CHARRANGE structure that specifies the range of characters.
dwReco	Clipboard operation flag.
lpRichDataObj	Pointer to an IDataObject that contains the Clipboard data.
lplpdataobj	Pointer to the pointer assigned to the address of the IDataObject representing this range.

Returns an HRESULT value representing the success or failure of this call.

The GetClipboardData method is called by the framework to get Clipboard data. This method is not generally directly called by applications.

The **GetContextMenu** Method

```
virtual HMENU GetContextMenu( WORD seltyp, LPOLEOBJECT lpoleobj, CHARRANGE*
➥lpchrg );
```

where

seltyp	The type of selection.
lpoleobj	Pointer to an OLEOBJECT structure that specifies the first selected OLE object. If no objects exist, lpoleobj is NULL.
lpRichDataObj	Pointer to an IDataObject that contains the Clipboard data.
lpchrg	Pointer to a CHARRANGE structure containing the current selection.

Returns a handle to the context menu.

The GetContextMenu method is called by MFC to get the context menu for an embedded OLE object.

The `IsSelected` Method

```
BOOL IsSelected( const CObject* pDocItem ) const;
```

where

     pDocItem   An OLE item.

Returns TRUE if the specified OLE item is selected.

The `OnFindNext` Method

```
virtual void OnFindNext( LPCTSTR lpszFind, BOOL bNext, BOOL bCase, BOOL
➥bWord );
```

where

lpszFind	The string to search for.
bNext	TRUE if the search is downward. FALSE if the search is upward.
bCase	TRUE if the search is case-sensitive.
bWord	TRUE if the search should match whole words only.

The OnFindNext method is called by MFC when processing the Find and Replace dialog box.

The `OnInitialUpdate` Method

```
virtual void OnInitialUpdate( );
```

The OnInitialUpdate method is called by MFC just before the first update of the view takes place.

The `OnPasteNativeObject` Method

```
virtual BOOL OnPasteNativeObject( LPSTORAGE lpStg );
```

where

     lpStg   Pointer to an IStorage object.

Returns TRUE if successful.

The OnPasteNativeObject method is called by MFC to load native data from an embedded item.

The `OnPrinterChanged` Method

```
virtual void OnPrinterChanged( const CDC& dcPrinter );
```

where

     dcPrinter   A device context for the new printer.

The OnPrinterChanged method is called to change the settings to a new printer.

The `OnReplaceAll` Method

```
virtual void OnReplaceAll( LPCTSTR lpszFind, LPCTSTR lpszReplace, BOOL
➥bCase, BOOL bWord );
```

where

lpszFind	The string to search for.
lpszReplace	The text to replace.

bCase	TRUE if the search is case-sensitive.
bWord	TRUE if the search should match whole words only.

The OnReplaceAll method is called by the Replace dialog to find and replace text in the view.

The **OnReplaceSel** Method

```
virtual void OnReplaceSel( LPCTSTR lpszFind, BOOL bNext, BOOL bCase, BOOL
➥bWord, LPCTSTR lpszReplace );
```

where

lpszFind	The string to search for.
bNext	TRUE if the search is downward. FALSE if the search is upward.
lpszReplace	The text to replace.
bCase	TRUE if the search is case-sensitive.
bWord	TRUE if the search should match whole words only.

The OnReplaceSel method is called by the Replace dialog to find and replace one occurrence of the specified text in the view.

The **OnTextNotFound** Method

```
virtual void OnTextNotFound( LPCTSTR lpszFind );
```

where

lpszFind	The text that was not found.

The OnTextNotFound method is called when the text being searched for is not found. This method can be overridden this method to display some sort of message.

The **QueryAcceptData** Method

```
virtual HRESULT QueryAcceptData( LPDATAOBJECT lpdataobj, CLIPFORMAT FAR *
➥lpcfFormat, DWORD dwReco, BOOL bReally, HGLOBAL hMetaFile );
```

where

lpdataobj	Pointer to the IDataObject to query.
lpcfFormat	Pointer to the acceptable data format.
dwReco	Not used.
bReally	Determines whether the paste operation should continue.
hMetaFile	A handle to a metafile used to draw the item's icon.

Returns an HRESULT value that indicates the success or failure of this call.

The QueryAcceptData method is called by MFC to paste an item into a rich edit view.

The **WrapChanged** Method

```
virtual void WrapChanged( );
```

where

pf	A PARAFORMAT structure that specifies the paragraph format.

The WrapChanged method is called by MFC when the printing characteristics change.

CRgn

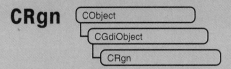

The CRgn class represents a region. A region specifies a shape that can be of nearly any form. A region is usually made by adding and removing rectangles or other regions. Regions are used as filters for drawing, allowing, or disallowing drawing in their areas.

For an example of CRgn, see the CDCEx example found on the CD-ROM that accompanies this book.

Header Files

The following header file should be included when using this class:

afxwin.h

Methods

The CRgn class has the following methods:

CRgn	The constructor
CombineRgn	Combine two regions
CopyRgn	Copy a region
CreateEllipticRgn	Create a region based on an ellipse
CreateEllipticRgnIndirect	Create a region based on an ellipse from a structure
CreateFromData	Create a region from region and transformation data
CreateFromPath	Create a region from a path
CreatePolygonRgn	Create a polygon region
CreatePolyPolygonRgn	Create a multi-polygon region
CreateRectRgn	Create a rectangular region
CreateRectRgnIndirect	Create a rectangular region from a structure
CreateRoundRectRgn	Create a rounded rectangle region
EqualRgn	Determine whether two regions are equal
FromHandle	Create a CRgn object from a handle
GetRegionData	Fills a structure with information about the region
GetRgnBox	Get the bounding rectangle for the region
OffsetRgn	Move a region
operator HRGN	Get the region handle
PtInRegion	Determine whether a point is in the region
RectInRegion	Determine whether a rectangle is in the region
SetRectRgn	Set the region equal to the specified rectangular region

The CRgn Constructor

The CRgn constructor creates the CRgn object. The CRgn constructor is used as follows:

CRgn( );

The CombineRgn Method

int CombineRgn(CRgn* pRgn1, CRgn* pRgn2, int nCombineMode);

where

pRgn1	The first region.
pRgn2	The second region.
nCombineMode	The combine mode. Should be RGN_AND, RGN_COPY, RGN_DIFF, RGN_OR, or RGN_XOR.

Returns any of the following values:

COMPLEXREGION	The region has overlapping borders.
ERROR	No region was created.
NULLREGION	The region is empty.
SIMPLEREGION	The region has no overlapping borders.

The CombineRgn method will combine the two regions as specified.

The CopyRgn Method

int CopyRgn(CRgn* pRgnSrc);

where

pRgnSrc	The first region.

Returns any of the following values:

COMPLEXREGION	The region has overlapping borders.
ERROR	No region was created.
NULLREGION	The region is empty.
SIMPLEREGION	The region has no overlapping borders.

The CopyRgn method will copy the specified region to this one.

The CreateEllipticRegion Method

BOOL CreateEllipticRgn(int x1, int y1, int x2, int y2);

where

x1	The x coordinate of the upper-left corner of the bounding rectangle for the ellipse.
y1	The y coordinate of the upper-left corner of the bounding rectangle for the ellipse.
x2	The x coordinate of the lower-right corner of the bounding rectangle for the ellipse.
y2	The y coordinate of the lower-right corner of the bounding rectangle for the ellipse.

Returns TRUE if successful.

The `CreateEllipticalRgn` method will create an elliptical region.

The `CreateEllipticalRgnIndirect` Method

`BOOL CreateEllipticRgnIndirect( LPCRECT lpRect );`

where

    lpRect   A rectangle that specifies the ellipse.

Returns TRUE if successful.

The `CreateEllipticalRgnIndirect` method will create an elliptical region.

The `CreateFromData` Method

`BOOL CreateFromData( const XFORM* lpXForm, int nCount, const RGNDATA*`
➡`pRgnData );`

where

    lpXForm   Pointer to an XFORM data structure. This structure defines the transformation to be performed on the structure. If NULL, the identity transformation is performed.

    nCount   Number of bytes specified by *pRgnData*.

    pRgnData   Pointer to a RGNDATA structure that contains region data.

Returns TRUE if successful.

The `CreateFromData` method will create a region from a region and transformation data.

The `CreateFromPath` Method

`BOOL CreateFromPath( CDC* pDC );`

where

    pDC   A device context that contains a closed path.

Returns TRUE if successful.

The `CreateFromPath` method will create region from a closed path that is selected into a device context.

The `CreatePolygonRgn` Method

`BOOL CreatePolygonRgn( LPPOINT lpPoints, int nCount, int nMode );`

where

    lpPoints   An array of points.

    nCount   The count of points.

    nMode   The filling mode should be either ALTERNATE or WINDING.

Returns TRUE if successful.

The `CreatePolygonRgn` method will create a region from a series of points.

The `CreatePolyPolygonRgn` Method

```
BOOL CreatePolyPolygonRgn( LPPOINT lpPoints, LPINT lpPolyCounts, int nCount,
➥int nPolyFillMode );
```

where

lpPoints	An array of points.
lpPolyCounts	An array of integers specifying how many points in each polygon.
nCount	How many polygons.
nMode	The filling mode should be either ALTERNATE or WINDING.

Returns TRUE if successful.

The `CreatePolyPolygonRgn` method will create a region from a series of closed polygons. These polygons might be overlapping or disjointed.

The `CreateRectRgn` Method

```
BOOL CreateRectRgn( int x1, int y1, int x2, int y2 );
```

where

x1	The x coordinate of the upper-left corner of the bounding rectangle.
y1	The y coordinate of the upper-left corner of the bounding rectangle.
x2	The x coordinate of the lower-right corner of the bounding rectangle.
y2	The y coordinate of the lower-right corner of the bounding rectangle.

Returns TRUE if successful.

The `CreateRectRgn` method will create a rectangular region.

The `CreateRectRgnIndirect` Method

```
BOOL CreateEllipticRgnIndirect( LPCRECT lpRect );
```

where

lpRect	A rectangle.

Returns TRUE if successful.

The `CreateRectRgnIndirect` method will create a rectangular region.

The `CreateRoundRectRgn` Method

```
BOOL CreateRoundRectRoundRgn( int x1, int y1, int x2, int y2, int x3, int
➥y3 );
```

where

x1	The x coordinate of the upper-left corner of the bounding rectangle.
y1	The y coordinate of the upper-left corner of the bounding rectangle.
x2	The x coordinate of the lower-right corner of the bounding rectangle.
y2	The y coordinate of the lower-right corner of the bounding rectangle.
x3	The width of the corner ellipse.
y3	The height of the corner ellipse.

Returns TRUE if successful.

C

The CreateRoundRectRgn method will create a rectangular region.

The EqualRgn Method

```
BOOL EqualRgn( CRgn* pRgn ) const;
```
where

    pRgn   A region.

Returns TRUE if this region is equal to the region specified.

The FromHandle Method

```
static CRgn* PASCAL FromHandle( HRGN hRgn );
```
where

    hRgn   A region handle.

Returns a temporary region created from the specified handle.

The GetRegionData Method

```
int GetRegionData( LPRGNDATA lpRgnData, int nCount ) const;
```
where

lpRgnData	A pointer to a RGNDATA structure array.
nCount	The size in bytes of the region data buffer.

Returns any of the following values:

COMPLEXREGION	The region has overlapping borders.
ERROR	No region was created.
NULLREGION	The region is empty.
SIMPLEREGION	The region has no overlapping borders.

The GetRegionData method will get the data associated with the region.

The GetRgnBox Method

```
int GetRgnBox( LPRECT lpRect ) const;
```
where

    lpRect   A rectangle.

Returns any of the following values:

COMPLEXREGION	The region has overlapping borders.
ERROR	No region was created.
NULLREGION	The region is empty.
SIMPLEREGION	The region has no overlapping borders.

The GetRgnBox method will get the bounding rectangle for this region.

The `OffsetRgn` Method

```
int OffsetRgn( int x, int y );
int OffsetRgn( POINT point );
```

where

x	The x coordinate.
y	The y coordinate.
point	The x and y coordinate.

Returns any of the following values:

COMPLEXREGION	The region has overlapping borders.
ERROR	No region was created.
NULLREGION	The region is empty.
SIMPLEREGION	The region has no overlapping borders.

The `OffsetRgn` method will move the region by the specified coordinates.

The `PtInRegion` Method

```
BOOL PtInRegion( int x, int y ) const;
BOOL PtInRegion( POINT point ) const;
```

where

x	The x coordinate.
y	The y coordinate.
point	The x and y coordinate.

Returns TRUE if the specified point is inside the region.

The `RectInRgn` Method

```
BOOL RectInRegion( LPCRECT lpRect ) const;
```

where

lpRect	A rectangle.

Returns TRUE if the specified rectangle is inside of the region.

The `SetRectRgn` Method

```
void SetRectRgn( int x1, int y1, int x2, int y2 );
void SetRectRgn( LPCRECT lpRect );
```

where

x1	The x coordinate of the upper-left corner of the bounding rectangle.
y1	The y coordinate of the upper-left corner of the bounding rectangle.
x2	The x coordinate of the lower-right corner of the bounding rectangle.
y2	The y coordinate of the lower-right corner of the bounding rectangle.
lpRect	The rectangle.

C

The SetRectRgn will create a rectangular region. No additional memory is allocated, so a region must already exist for this method to be called.

The HRGN Operator Method

```
operator HRGN( ) const;
```

Returns the region handle for this region.

CScrollView

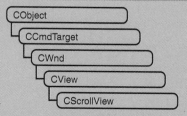

The CScrollView class implements a scrolling view. This allows the document to be much larger than the available window space.

Header Files

The following header file should be included when using this class:

```
afxwin.h
```

Methods

The CScrollView class has the following methods:

CScrollView	The constructor
FillOutsideRect	Fill the area outside the scrolling area
GetDeviceScrollPosition	Get the current scroll position in device units
GetDeviceScrollSizes	Get the scroll sizes in device units
GetScrollPosition	Get the scroll position
GetTotalSize	Get the total size of the scroll view
ResizeParentToFit	Resize the frame to fit the view
ScrollToPosition	Scroll to the given position
SetScaleToFitSize	Scale the view so the entire document fits
SetScrollSizes	Set the scrollbar sizes

The CScrollView Constructor

The CScrollView creates the CScrollView object. The CScrollView constructor is used as follows:

```
CScrollView( );
```

The FillOutsideRect Method

```
void FillOutsideRect( CDC* pDC, CBrush* pBrush );
```

where

| pDC | Device context in which filling is to be done. |
| pBrush | Brush to be used to fill this area. |

The FillOutsideRect method will erase the area outside of the scrolling area. It should be called as part of the view's OnEraseBkgnd method.

The GetDeviceScrollPosition Method

CPoint GetDeviceScrollPosition( ) const;

Returns the position of both the horizontal and vertical scrollbars in device units.

The GetDeviceScrollSizes Method

void GetDeviceScrollSizes(int& nMapMode, SIZE& sizeTotal, SIZE& sizePage,
➥SIZE& sizeLine) const;

where

nMapMode	Returns the mapping mode for this view.
sizeTotal	Returns the total size of the scroll view in device units.
sizePage	The amount to scroll for each click in the scroll shaft.
sizeLine	The amount to scroll for each click in the scroll arrow.

The GetDeviceScrollSizes method will get the current mapping mode and scroll information for the scrolling view.

The GetScrollPosition Method

CPoint GetScrollPosition( ) const;

Returns the position of both the horizontal and vertical scrollbars in logical units.

The GetTotalSize Method

CSize GetTotalSize( ) const;

Returns the total size of the entire document.

The ResizeParentToFit Method

void ResizeParentToFit(BOOL bShrinkOnly = TRUE);

where

| bShrinkOnly | TRUE will shrink the window if needed. FALSE will always resize the frame exactly. |

The ResizeParentToFit method will resize the frame window to fit the scrolling view.

The ScrollToPosition Method

void ScrollToPosition(POINT pt);

where

| pt | The point to scroll to. |

The ScrollToPosition method will scroll the view to include the specified point.

The `SetScaleToFitSize` Method

```
void SetScaleToFitSize( SIZE sizeTotal );
```

where

    sizeTotal   The horizontal and vertical sizes to fit the view to.

The `SetScaleToFitSize` method scales the view to the specified size.

The `SetScrollSizes` Method

```
void SetScrollSizes( int nMapMode, SIZE sizeTotal, const SIZE& sizePage =
➥sizeDefault, const SIZE& sizeLine = sizeDefault );
```

where

nMapMode	The mapping mode for this view.
sizeTotal	The total size of the scroll view in device units.
sizePage	The amount to scroll for each click in the scroll shaft.
sizeLine	The amount to scroll for each click in the scroll arrow.

The `SetScrollSizes` method scales the view to the specified size.

CSemaphore

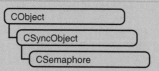

The `CSemaphore` class implements a semaphore object. A semaphore allows only a limited number of threads to access a single resource.

Header Files

The following header file should be included when using this class:

`afxmt.h`

Methods

The `CSemaphore` class has the following methods:

`CSemaphore`

The `CSemaphore` Constructor

The `CSemaphore` constructor creates the `CSemaphore` object. The `CSemaphore` constructor is used as follows:

```
CSemaphore( LONG lInitialCount = 1, LONG lMaxCount = 1, LPCTSTR pstrName =
➥NULL, LPSECURITY_ATTRIBUTES lpsaAttributes = NULL );
```

where

lInitialCount	The initial usage count for the semaphore. Must be greater than or equal to zero, but less than or equal to *lMaxCount*.
lMaxCount	The maximum usage count for the semaphore. Must be greater than 0.

pstrName	The name of the semaphore. Can be NULL.
lpsaAttributes	A pointer to security attributes.

CSize

The CSize class is similar to a Windows SIZE structure. The CSize class contains cx and cy, which specify a size.

Header Files

The following header file should be included when using this class:

afxwin.h

Properties

The CSize class has the following properties:

cx	An x coordinate.
yx	A y coordinate.

Methods

The CSize class has the following methods:

CSize	The constructor
operator -	Subtract two sizes
operator !=	Check to see that two sizes are not equal
operator +	Add to a size
operator +=	Add to a size
operator -=	Subtract from a size
operator ==	Check to see that two sizes are equal

The CSize Constructor

The CSize creates the CArchive object. The CSize constructor is used as follows:

```
CSize( );
CSize( int initCX, int initCY );
CSize( SIZE initSize );
CSize( POINT initPt );
CSize( DWORD dwSize );
```

where

initCX	Initial cx value
initXY	Initial cy value
initSizeXY	Initial x and y as a SIZE
initPt	Initial x and y as a POINT
dwSize	Initial x and y as a DWORD

The == Operator

```
BOOL operator ==( SIZE size ) const;
```

where

    size   A size.

Returns TRUE if the point is equal to the specified point.

The != Operator

```
BOOL operator !=( SIZE size ) const;
```

where

    size   A size.

Returns TRUE if the point is not equal to the specified point.

The += Operator

```
void operator +=( SIZE size );
```

where

    size   A size.

The += operator adds a size to this size.

The -= Operator

```
void operator -=( SIZE size );
```

where

    size   A size.

The -= operator subtracts a size from this size.

The + Operator

```
CSize operator +( SIZE size ) const;
CPoint operator +( POINT point ) const;
CRect operator +( const RECT* lpRect ) const;
```

where

    size   A size to be added.
    point   A point to be added.
    lpRect   A rectangle.

The + operator will move the size, point, or rectangle by the specified amount.

The - Operator

```
CSize operator -( SIZE size ) const;
CPoint operator -( POINT point ) const;
CRect operator -( const RECT* lpRect ) const;
CSize operator -( ) const;
```

where

size	A size to be added.
point	A point to be added.
lpRect	A rectangle.

The · operator will move the size, point, or rectangle by the specified amount.

CSocket

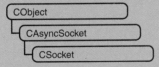

The CSocket class implements a Windows socket. A socket allows communication between processes on one or more computers. CSocket implements Windows sockets at a higher level than CAsyncSocket. CSocket allows data types to be directly communicated, when used with the CArchive object.

For an example of CSocket, see the AtomClock example on the CD-ROM that accompanies this book.

Header Files

The following header files should be included when using this class:

afxsock.h

Methods

The CSocket class has the following methods:

CSocket	The constructor
Attach	Attach a socket handle
CancelBlockingCall	Cancel a blocking call in progress
Create	Create a socket
FromHandle	Create a CSocket object from a handle
IsBlocking	Determine whether the socket is blocking

The following method is used to process messages sent to the class. This method can be overridden if special handling is needed for these messages.

| OnMessagePending | Process messages while blocking |

The CSocket Constructor

The CSocket creates the CSocket object. The CSocket constructor is used as follows:

CSocket( );

The Attach Method

BOOL Attach(SOCKET hSocket);

where

| hSocket | The socket to attach. |

Returns TRUE if successful

The Attach method will attach the specified socket handle to this object.

The `CancelBlockingCall` Method

```
void CancelBlockingCall( );
```

The `CancelBlockingCall` method will cancel any blocking call in progress.

The `Create` Method

```
BOOL Create( UINT nSocketPort = 0, int nSocketType = SOCK_STREAM, LPCTSTR
➥lpszSocketAddress = NULL );
```

where

nSocketPort	The port number for the socket. Specify 0 to have MFC select a port.
nSocketType	The socket type should be either SOCK_STREAM or SOCK_DGRAM.
lpszSocketAddress	An address, such as "128.0.0.1".

Returns TRUE if successful

The `Create` method will create the specified socket. Create automatically calls Bind to bind the socket to the specified address.

The `FromHandle` Method

```
static CSocket* PASCAL FromHandle( SOCKET hSocket );
```

where

hSocket	A socket handle.

Returns a temporary socket object created from the specified handle.

The `IsBlocking` Method

```
BOOL IsBlocking( );
```

Returns TRUE if the socket is blocking.

The `OnMessagePending` Method

```
BOOL OnMessagePending( );
```

Returns TRUE if the message was handled.

The `OnMessagePending` method is called when a message has been sent to the socket.

CSplitterWnd

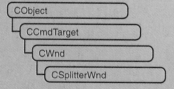

The `CSpliterWnd` allows a frame window to split itself into multiple panes. Each of these panes can contain its own view or CWnd-derived object. To create a splitter window, take the following steps:

1. Embed a CSplitterWnd member in the frame window.

2. Create an overridden OnCreateClient in the frame window.

3. Call the Create or CreateStatic method inside the embedded splitter window.

Header Files

The following header file should be included when using this class:

afxext.h

Methods

The CSplitterWnd class has the following methods:

CSplitterWnd	The constructor
ActivateNext	Move to the next or previous pane
CanActivateNext	Can the next pane be reached
Create	Create the splitter window
CreateScrollBarCtrl	Create scrollbar control
CreateStatic	Create the splitter window
CreateView	Create a view
DeleteColumn	Delete a column
DeleteRow	Delete a row
DeleteView	Delete a view
DoKeyboardSplit	Perform the keyboard split command
DoScroll	Perform synchronized scrolling of split windows
DoScrollBy	Scroll the window by the given number of pixels
GetActivePane	Get the active pane
GetColumnCount	Get the column count
GetColumnInfo	Get column info
GetPane	Get a pane
GetRowCount	Get a row count
GetRowInfo	Get row information
GetScrollStyle	Get the scroll style information
IdFromRowCol	Return the ID of a child window by row and column
IsChildPane	Determine whether this is a child window
OnDrawSplitter	Called to draw the splitter
OnInvertTracker	Called to draw the image of the splitter window to the same size as the frame window
RecalcLayout	Recalculate the split window layout
SetActivePane	Set the active pane
SetColumnInfo	Set the column information
SetRowInfo	Set the row information
SetScrollStyle	Set the scroll style
SplitColumn	Split a column
SplitRow	Split a row

The `CSplitterWnd` Constructor

The CSplitterWnd creates the CArchive object. The CSplitterWnd constructor is used as follows:
CSplitterWnd()

The `ActivateNext` Method

virtual void ActivateNext(BOOL bPrev = FALSE);

where

    bPrev   TRUE for previous frame, FALSE for next.

The ActivateNext method will move to the next or previous pane.

The `CanActivateNext` Method

virtual BOOL CanActivateNext(BOOL bPrev = FALSE);

where

    bPrev   TRUE for previous frame, FALSE for next.

Returns TRUE if the next or previous pane can be activated.

The `Create` Method

BOOL Create(CWnd* pParentWnd, int nMaxRows, int nMaxCols, SIZE sizeMin,
➡CCreateContext* pContext, DWORD dwStyle = WS_CHILD ¦ WS_VISIBLE
➡¦WS_HSCROLL ¦ WS_VSCROLL ¦ SPLS_DYNAMIC_SPLIT, UINT nID =
➡AFX_IDW_PANE_FIRST);

where

pParentWnd	The parent frame window for this splitter.
nMaxRows	The maximum number of rows. Must not exceed 2.
nMaxCols	The maximum number of columns. Must not exceed 2.
sizeMin	The minimum size to display a frame.
pCreateContext	The create context structure passed to OnCreateClient.
dwStyle	The style of the window.
nID	The child ID of the window.

Returns TRUE if successful.

The Create method will create a dynamic splitter window. This window will allow the user to change the size and number of splits automatically.

The `CreateScrollBarCtrl` Method

virtual BOOL CreateScrollBarCtrl(DWORD dwStyle, UINT nID);

where

dwStyle	The style for the scrollbar.
nID	The child ID of the window.

Returns TRUE if successful.

The `CreateScrollBarCtrl` method will create a shared scrollbar control. This method can be overridden to include additional controls by the scrollbar.

The `CreateStatic` Method

```
BOOL CreateStatic( CWnd* pParentWnd, int nRows, int nCols, DWORD dwStyle
➥= WS_CHILD | WS_VISIBLE, UINT nID = AFX_IDW_PANE_FIRST );
```

where

pParentWnd	The parent frame window for this splitter.
nRows	The number of rows. Must not exceed 16.
nCols	The number of columns. Must not exceed 16.
dwStyle	The style of the window.
nID	The child ID of the window.

Returns TRUE if successful.

The `CreateStatic` method will create a static splitter window. A static splitter has a fixed number of rows and columns.

The `CreateView` Method

```
virtual BOOL CreateView( int row, int col, CRuntimeClass* pViewClass, SIZE
➥sizeInit, CCreateContext* pContext );
```

where

row	The row to create the view at.
col	The column to create the view at.
pViewClass	Specifies the view to be created.
dwStyle	The style of the window.
sizeInit	Specifies the size of the new view.
pCreateContext	The create context structure passed to OnCreateClient.

Returns TRUE if successful.

The `CreateView` method will create a view within the splitter.

The `DeleteColumn` Method

```
virtual void DeleteColumn( int colDelete );
```

where

nID	The ID of the column to delete.

The `DeleteColumn` method will delete the specified column.

The `DeleteRow` Method

```
virtual void DeleteRow( int rowDelete );
```

where

nID	The ID of the row to delete.

The `DeleteColumn` method will delete the specified column.

The `DeleteView` Method

`virtual void DeleteView( int row, int col );`

where

row	The ID of the row to delete.
col	The ID of the column to delete.

The `DeleteView` method will delete the specified column.

The `DoKeyboardSplit` Method

`virtual BOOL DoKeyboardSplit( );`

Returns TRUE if successful.

The `DoKeyboardSplit` method is called by MFC to perform a keyboard split.

The `DoScroll` Method

`virtual BOOL DoScroll( CView* pViewFrom, UINT nScrollCode, BOOL bDoScroll =`
➥ `TRUE );`

where

pViewFrom	A pointer to the view from which the scrolling message originates.
nScrollCode	A scrollbar code that specifies how to scroll.
bDoScroll	Specifies whether the scrolling should happen.

Returns TRUE if the scrolling occurs.

The `DoScroll` method will scroll all views in the manner specified.

The `DoScrollBy` Method

`virtual BOOL DoScrollBy( CView* pViewFrom, CSize sizeScroll, BOOL bDoScroll =`
➥ `TRUE );`

where

pViewForm	A pointer to the view from which the scrolling message originates.
sizeScroll	The number of pixels to scroll.
bDoScroll	Specifies whether the scrolling should happen.

Returns TRUE if the scrolling occurs.

The `DoScrollBy` method is called by MFC in response to a user message to perform synchronized scrolling.

The `GetActivePane` Method

`CWnd* GetActivePane(int* pRow = NULL, int* pCol = NULL);`

where

pRow	A pointer to the variable that will receive the active row.
pCol	A pointer to the variable that will receive the active column.

Returns the window that is the active pane.

The `GetColumnCount` Method

```
int GetColumnCount( );
```

Returns the column count.

The `GetColumnInfo` Method

```
void GetColumnInfo( int col, int& cxCur, int& cxMin );
```

where

col	A column.
cxCur	A variable that will receive the current width of the column.
cxMin	A variable that will receive the minimum width of the column.

The `GetColumnInfo` method will retrieve information about the specified column.

The `GetPane` Method

```
CWnd* GetPane( int row, int col );
```

where

row	The ID of the row to delete.
col	The ID of the column to delete.

The `GetPane` method returns a pointer to the specified pane.

The `GetRowCount` Method

```
int GetRowCount( );
```

Returns the row count.

The `GetRowInfo` Method

```
void GetRowInfo( int row, int& cyCur, int& cyMin );
```

where

row	A row.
cyCur	A variable that will receive the current height of the row.
cyMin	A variable that will receive the minimum height of the column.

The `GetRowInfo` method will retrieve information about the specified row.

The `GetScrollStyle` Method

```
DWORD GetScrollStyle( ) const;
```

Returns the type of shared scrollbars managed by the splitter. Should be either or both WS_HSCROLL or WS_VSCROLL.

The `IdFromRowCol` Method

```
int IdFromRowCol( int row, int col );
```

where

row	The ID of the row to get.
col	The ID of the column to get.

The `IdFromRowCol` method returns the ID of the specified pane.

The `IsChildPane` Method

`BOOL IsChildPane( CWnd* pWnd, int& row, int& col );`

where

pWnd	A window to be tested.
row	A variable to hold the row of the specified window (if it's a child).
col	A variable to hold the column of the specified window (if it's a child).

Returns TRUE if the specified window is a child of this splitter. Also returns the coordinates of where it is located at through *row* and *col*.

The `OnDrawSplitter` Method

`virtual void OnDrawSplitter( CDC* pDC, ESplitType nType, const CRect& rect );`

where

pDC	A device context to draw to.
nType	The type of splitter to draw. Should be `splitBox`, `splitBar`, `splitBorder`, or `spliteIntersection`.
rect	Specifies where to draw the splitter.

The `OnDrawSplitter` method will draw the splitter to the specified device context.

The `OnInvertTracker` Method

`virtual void OnInvertTracker( const CRect& rect );`

where

rect	The tracking rectangle.

The `OnInvertTracker` method is called by MFC during resizing of the splitters.

The `RecalcLayout` Method

`void RecalcLayout( );`

The `RecalcLayout` method should be called after calls to `SetRowInfo` and `SetColumnInfo` to reposition the splitter correctly.

The `SetActivePane` Method

`virtual void SetActivePane( int row, int col, CWnd* pWnd = NULL );`

where

row	The row to be made active.
col	The column to be made active.
pWnd	A CWnd object to be made active. If NULL, the *row* and *col* values are used.

The `SetActivePane` method will set the specified pane active.

The `SetColumnInfo` Method

`void SetColumnInfo( int col, int cxIdeal, int cxMin );`

where

col	A column.
cxIdeal	The ideal width of the column.
cxMin	The minimum width of the column.

The `SetColumnInfo` method set the column as specified.

The `SetRowInfo` Method

`void SetRowInfo( int row, int cyIdeal, int cyMin );`

where

row	A row.
cyIdeal	The ideal height of the row.
cyMin	The minimum height of the column.

The `SetRowInfo` method will set information about the specified row.

The `SetScrollStyle` Method

`void SetScrollStyle( DWORD dwStyle );`

where

dwStyle	The style of the scrollbar can be `WS_HSCROLL` and `WS_VSCROLL`.

The `SetScrollStyle` method will set the shared scrollbars as specified.

The `SplitColumn` Method

`virtual BOOL SplitColumn( int cxBefore );`

where

cxBefore	The location, before which the split occurs.

The `SplitColumn` method is called to split the specified column.

The `SplitRow` Method

`virtual BOOL SplitRow( int cyBefore );`

where

cyBefore	The location, before which the split occurs.

The `SplitRow` method is called to split the specified row.

CStatusBar

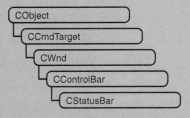

`CStatusBar` method implements the status bar. A status bar is placed at the bottom of a frame window, and conveys status information to the user.

For an example of `CStatusBar`, see the MDIEx example found on the CD-ROM that accompanies this book.

Header Files

The following header file should be included when using this class:

`afxext.h`

Methods

The `CStatusBar` class has the following methods:

`CStatusBar`	The constructor
`CommandToIndex`	Get the index for a given ID
`Create`	Create the status bar
`CreateEx`	Extended create the status bar
`GetItemID`	Get the ID for a given index
`GetItemRect`	Get the rectangle taken by an item
`GetPaneInfo`	Get the ID, style, and width for a given index
`GetPaneStyle`	Get the style for a given index
`GetPaneText`	Get the text for a given index
`GetStatusBarCtrl`	Get the underlying status bar control
`SetIndicators`	Set the indicator IDs
`SetPaneInfo`	Set the ID, style, and width for a given index
`SetPaneStyle`	Set the style for a given index
`SetPaneText`	Set the text for a given index

The following method is used to process messages sent to the class. This method can be overridden if special handling is needed for these messages.

`DrawItem`	Called when the bar needs to be redrawn

The `CStatusBar` Constructor

The `CStatusBar` constructor creates the `CStatusBar` object. The `CStatusBar` constructor is used as follows:

`CStatusBar( );`

The `CommandToIndex` Method

`int CommandToIndex( UINT nIDFind ) const;`

where

`nIDFind`	The string ID of the indicator whose index is being retrieved.

Returns the index of the specified indicator, or –1 if not successful.

The **Create** Method

```
BOOL Create( CWnd* pParentWnd, DWORD dwStyle = WS_CHILD | WS_VISIBLE |
➡CBRS_BOTTOM, UINT nID = AFX_IDW_STATUS_BAR );
```

where

pParentWnd	The parent window of the status bar.
dwStyle	The style of the status bar.
nID	The ID of the status bar.

Returns TRUE if successful.

The Create method is called to create a status bar.

The **DrawItem** Method

```
void DrawItem( LPDRAWITEMSTRUCT lpDrawItemStruct );
```

where

lpDrawItemStruct	Information about the type of drawing required.

The DrawItem method is called by MFC when some visual aspect of the status bar changed.

The **GetItemID** Method

```
UINT GetItemID( int nIndex ) const;
```

where

nIndex	The index of the identifier.

The GetItemID method is called to determine the ID of the specified index.

The **GetItemRect** Method

```
void GetItemRect( int nIndex, LPRECT lpRect ) const;
```

where

nIndex	The index of the indicator whose rectangle coordinates are to be retrieved.
lpRect	A rectangle that will be filled with the coordinates of the specified indicator.

The GetItemRect method is called to retrieve the coordinates of the specified indicator.

The **GetPaneInfo** Method

```
void GetPaneInfo( int nIndex, UINT& nID, UINT& nStyle, int& cxWidth ) const;
```

where

nIndex	The index of the pane whose information is to be retrieved.
nID	A variable that will receive the ID of the pane.
nStyle	A variable that will receive the style of the pane.
cxWidth	A variable that will receive the width of the pane.

The GetPaneInfo method is called to retrieve information about the specified pane.

The `GetPaneStyle` Method

```
UINT GetPaneStyle( int nIndex ) const;
```

where

    nIndex   The index of the pane whose style is to be retrieved.

Returns the style of the specified pane.

The `GetPaneText` Method

```
CString GetPaneText( int nIndex ) const;
void GetPaneText( int nIndex, CString& rString ) const;
```

where

    nIndex   The index of the pane whose text is to be retrieved.

    rString   A string to hold the text being retrieved.

Returns the text of the specified pane.

The `GetStatusBarCtrl` Method

```
CStatusBarCtrl& GetStatusBarCtrl( ) const;
```

Returns the underlying status bar control.

The `SetIndicators` Method

```
BOOL SetIndicators( const UINT* lpIDArray, int nIDCount );
```

where

    lpIDArray   Pointer to an array of IDs.

    nIDCount   Number of elements in the array.

Returns TRUE if successful.

The `SetIndicators` method will set the IDs of all the indicators.

The `SetPaneInfo` Method

```
void SetPaneInfo( int nIndex, UINT nID, UINT nStyle, int cxWidth );
```

where

    nIndex   Index of the pane whose information is to be set.

    nID   New ID for the pane.

    nStyle   New style for the pane.

    cxWidth   New width for the pane.

The `SetPaneInfo` method will set the information for the specified pane.

The `SetPaneStyle` Method

```
void SetPaneStyle( int nIndex, UINT nStyle );
```

where

| *nIndex* | Index of the pane whose style is to be set. |
| *nStyle* | New style for the pane. |

The SetPaneStyle method will set the style for the specified pane.

The **SetPaneText** Method

BOOL SetPaneText(int nIndex, LPCTSTR lpszNewText, BOOL bUpdate = TRUE);

where

| *nIndex* | Index of the pane whose text is to be set. |
| *bUpdate* | Set to TRUE if the pane is invalidated after the text is set. |

The SetPaneText method will set the text for the specified pane.

CString   [CString]

The CString class implements a string in MFC. This class allows the string to grow as needed. Several methods are provided for parsing the data contained by the string. The CString class is the type used for nearly any MFC string operation.

For an example of CString, see the DialogEx example found on the CD-ROM that accompanies this book.

Header Files

The following header file should be included when using this class:

afx.h

Methods

The CString class has the following methods:

CString	The constructor
AllocSysString	Create a BSTR
AnsiToOem	Convert ANSI characters to OEM characters
Collate	Compare two strings using locale-specific information
CollateNoCase	Compare two strings using locale-specific information, ignoring case
Compare	Compare a string
CompareNoCase	Compare a string, ignoring case
Delete	Delete part of the string
Empty	Empty the string
Find	Find a substring
FindOneOf	Find one of several characters
Format	Format the string using printf style output
FormatMessage	Format a message
FormatV	Format like vsprintf

FreeExtra	Free extra space
GetAt	Get the character at a specific index
GetBuffer	Get a pointer to the buffer
GetBufferSetLength	Get a pointer to the string of a specific length
GetLength	Get the length of the string
Insert	Insert a substring into the string
IsEmpty	Is the string empty
Left	Take the left substring
LoadString	Load a string from the resources
LockBuffer	Lock the buffer for direct access
MakeLower	Make the entire string lowercase
MakeReverse	Reverse the string
MakeUpper	Make the entire string uppercase
Mid	Get a middle substring
OemToAnsi	Convert OEM characters to ANSI characters
operator []	Access individual characters
operator +	Concatenate two string
operator +=	Concatenate two strings
operator <<	Insert the string into an archive or dump context
operator =	Assign one string to another
operator ==, <, and so on	Equality/greater/less comparison
operator >>	Extract the string from an archive
operator LPCTSTR	Get a pointer to the buffer
ReleaseBuffer	Release the buffer after use
Remove	Remove characters from the string
Replace	Replace characters from the string
ReverseFind	Search for a substring starting from the end
Right	Get the right substring
SetAt	Change an idividual character
SetSysString	Set an existing BSTR with data from this object
SpanExcluding	Extract a substring that does not include the specified characters
SpanIncluding	Extract a substring that includes the specified characters
TrimLeft	Trim leading whitespace characters from the string
TrimRight	Trim trailing whitespace characters from the string
UnlockBuffer	Unlock the buffer previously locked by LockBuffer

The CString Constructor

The CString creates the CString object. The CString constructor is used as follows:

```
CString( );
CString( const CString& stringSrc );
```

```
CString( TCHAR ch, int nRepeat = 1 );
CString( LPCTSTR lpch, int nLength );
CString( const unsigned char* psz );
CString( LPCWSTR lpsz );
CString( LPCSTR lpsz );
```

where

stringSrc	A string object to use to initialize this string.
ch	A character to initialize this string.
nRepeat	How many times to repeat *ch*.
lpch	Pointer to a buffer in memory to initialize this string.
nLength	How long the buffer pointed to by *lpch* is.
psz	A zero-terminated string.
lpsz	A zero-terminated string.

This constructor can throw the CMemoryException exception.

The **AllocSysString** Method

```
BSTR AllocSysString ( ) const;
```

Returns a BSTR object for the string.

This method can throw the CMemoryException exception.

The **AnsiToOem** Method

```
void AnsiToOem( );
```

The AnsiToOem method converts the string from ANSI characters to OEM characters.

The **Collate** Method

```
int Collate( LPCTSTR lpsz ) const;
```

where

lpsz	A string to compare against.

Returns 0 if the strings are identical. Returns <0 if this CString object is less than *lpsz*, or >0 if this CString is greater than *lpsz*.

The Collate method will perform a case-sensitive comparison using whatever the current code page is.

The **CollateNoCase** Method

```
int CollateNoCase( LPCTSTR lpsz ) const;
```

where

lpsz	A string to compare against.

Returns 0 if the strings are identical. Returns <0 if this CString object is less than *lpsz*, or >0 if this CString is greater than *lpsz*.

The CollateNoCase method will perform a comparison that is not case-sensitive using whatever the current code page is.

The `Compare` Method

```
int Compare( LPCTSTR lpsz ) const;
```

where

    lpsz   A string to compare against.

Returns 0 if the strings are identical. Returns <0 if this `CString` object is less than *lpsz*, or >0 if this `CString` is greater than *lpsz*.

The `Compare` method will perform a case-sensitive comparison.

The `CompareNoCase` Method

```
int CompareNoCase( LPCTSTR lpsz ) const;
```

where

    lpsz   A string to compare against.

Returns 0 if the strings are identical. Returns <0 if this `CString` object is less than *lpsz*, or >0 if this `CString` is greater than *lpsz*.

The `CompareNoCase` method will perform a case-sensitive comparison.

The `Delete` Method

```
int Delete( int nIndex, int nCount = 1 ) const;
```

where

    nIndex   Where to start deleting.
    nCount   How many characters to delete.

Returns the length of the new string.

The `Delete` method will delete the specified characters from the string.

The `Delete` method can throw the CMemoryException exception.

The `Empty` Method

```
void Empty( );
```

The `Empty` method will delete the contents of the string, giving it zero length.

The `Find` Method

```
int Find( TCHAR ch ) const;
int Find( LPCTSTR lpszSub ) const;
int Find( TCHAR ch , int nStart ) const;
int Find( LPCTSTR lpszSub , int nStart ) const;
```

where

    ch   A character to search for.
    lpszSub   A string to search for.
    nStart   An index to start searching at.

Returns the index at which the character or string was found. Returns -1 if not found.

The FindOneOf Method

```
int FindOneOf( LPCTSTR lpszCharSet ) const;
```

where

> *lpszCharSet*   A character set to search for.

Returns the index of the first occurrence of one of the characters of the specified character set. Returns –1 if not found.

The Format Method

```
void Format( LPCTSTR lpszFormat, ... );
void Format( UINT nFormatID, ... );
```

where

> *lpszFormat*   A format string.
>
> *nFormatID*   A resource ID for a format string.

The Format method works exactly like sprintf, allowing the string to be specified from a sprintf-style format string.

The FormatV Method

```
void FormatV( LPCTSTR lpszFormat, va_list argList );
void FormatV( UINT nFormatID, va_list argList );
```

where

> *lpszFormat*   A format string.

The FormatV method works exactly like vsprintf, allowing the string to be specified from a vsprintf-style format string.

The FormatMessage Method

```
void FormatMessage( LPCTSTR lpszFormat, ... );
void FormatMessage( UINT nFormatID, ... );
```

where

> *lpszFormat*   A format string.
>
> *nFormatID*   A resource ID for a format string

The FormatMessage method works exactly like ::FormatMessage, allowing the string to be specified from a ::FormatMessage-style format string.

The FreeExtra Method

```
void FreeExtra( );
```

The FreeExtra method is called to free any extra memory no longer used by the string.

The GetAt Method

```
TCHAR GetAt( int nIndex ) const;
```

where

> *nIndex*   A zero-based index into the string.

Returns the character at the position specified by *nIndex*.

The `GetBuffer` Method

```
LPTSTR GetBuffer( int nMinBufLength );
```
where

     nMinBufLength   The minimum size of the buffer.

Returns a pointer to the internal buffer.

The `GetBuffer` method can throw the CMemoryException exception.

The `GetBufferSetLength` Method

```
LPTSTR GetBufferSetLength( int nNewLength );
```
where

     nNewLength   The new size of the string. The string will be modified, if necessary, to fit into this length.

Returns a pointer to the internal buffer.

The `GetBuffer` method can throw the CMemoryException exception.

The `GetLength` Method

```
int GetLength( ) const;
```
Returns the length of the string.

The `Insert` Method

```
int Insert( int nIndex , TCHAR ch );
int Insert( int nIndex , LPCTSTR pstr );
```
where

     nIndex   The index to insert at.

     ch   The character to insert.

     pstr   The string to insert.

Returns the new length of the string.

The `Insert` method will insert the specified character or string into this string.

The `Insert` method can throw the CMemoryException exception.

The `IsEmpty` Method

```
BOOL IsEmpty( ) const;
```
Returns TRUE if the string is empty.

The `Left` Method

```
CString Left( int nCount ) const;
```
where

     nCount   The number of characters requested.

Returns the first *nCount* characters in the string.

The `Left` method can throw the CMemoryException exception.

The `LoadString` Method

`BOOL LoadString( UINT nID );`

where

    nID   The resource ID to load.

Returns TRUE if successful.

The `LoadString` method will load the specified string from the resources.

The `LoadString` method can throw the CMemoryException exception.

The `LockBuffer` Method

`LPTSTR LockBuffer( );`

Returns a pointer to a NULL-terminated string.

The `LockString` locks the buffer until the `UnlockString` method is called.

The `MakeLower` Method

`void MakeLower( );`

The `MakeLower` method will convert all characters in the string to their lowercase values.

The `MakeReverse` Method

`void MakeReverse( );`

The `MakeReverse` method will invert the order of the characters of the string.

The `MakeUpper` Method

`void MakeUpper( );`

The `MakeUpper` method will convert all characters in the string to their uppercase values.

The `Mid` Method

`CString Mid( int nFirst ) const;`
`CString Mid( int nFirst, int nCount ) const;`

where

    nFirst   The first character to extract.

    nCount   How many characters to extract. If this value is not specified, all remaining characters are extracted.

Returns the substring specified by the parameters. This can be an empty string.

The `Mid` method can throw the CMemoryException exception.

The `OemToAnsi` Method

`void OemToAnsi( );`

The `OemToAnsi` method will convert all characters in the string from Oem to ANSI characters.

The ReleaseBuffer Method

```
void ReleaseBuffer( int nNewLength = -1 );
```

where

    nNewLength   The number of characters in the string. Setting to –1 assumes a NULL-terminated string.

The ReleaseBuffer method should be called after a call to GetBuffer.

The Remove Method

```
int Remove( TCHAR ch );
```

where

    ch   A character to be removed from the string.

Returns the count of characters removed from the string.

The Remove method will remove every occurrence of *ch* from the string.

The Replace Method

```
int Replace( TCHAR chOld , TCHAR chNew );
int Replace( LPCTSTR lpszOld , lpszNew );
```

where

    chOld   A character to be replaced.

    lpszOld   A string to be replaced.

    chNew   The character that is replacing each occurrence of *chOld*.

    lpszNew   The string that is replacing each occurrence of *lpszOld*.

Returns the number of times the replacement was made.

The Replace method will replace each occurrence of the old string with the new one.

The ReverseFind Method

```
int ReverseFind( TCHAR ch ) const;
```

where

    ch   A character to search for.

Returns the index at which the character was found. Returns –1 if not found.

The Right Method

```
CString Right( int nCount ) const;
```

where

    nCount   The number of characters requested.

Returns the last *nCount* characters in the string.

The Right method can throw the CMemoryException exception.

The **SetAt** Method

```
void SetAt( int nIndex, TCHAR ch );
```

where

nIndex	The zero-based index of the character to be replaced.
ch	The character that is to be set at the specified index.

The SetAt method will set the specified character to value in *ch*.

The **SetSysString** Method

```
BSTR SetSysString( BSTR* pbstr ) const;
```

where

bstr	A BSTR to be reallocated.

Returns the new BSTR.

The SetSysString method will reallocate the specified BSTR to contain the string in this string object.

The **SpanExcluding** Method

```
CString SpanExcluding( LPCTSTR lpszCharSet ) const;
```

where

lpszCharSet	A set of characters to be excluded.

Returns a string that does not include any of the specified characters.

The **SpanIncluding** Method

```
CString SpanIncluding( LPCTSTR lpszCharSet ) const;
```

where

lpszCharSet	A set of characters to be included.

Returns a string that includes only the characters specified.

The **TrimLeft** Method

```
void TrimLeft( );
```

Removes all whitespace characters from the beginning of the string.

The **TrimRight** Method

```
void TrimRight( );
```

Removes all whitespace characters from the end of the string.

The = Operator

```
const CString& operator =( const CString& stringSrc );
const CString& operator =( TCHAR ch );
const CString& operator =( const unsigned char* psz );
const CString& operator =( LPCWSTR lpsz );
const CString& operator =( LPCSTR lpsz );
```

where

stringSrc	A string object to use to initialize this string.
ch	A character to initialize this string.
psz	A zero-terminated string.
lpsz	A zero-terminated string.

The = operator will assign the string to the string specified.

The LPCTSTR Operator

```
operator LPCTSTR ( ) const;
```

The LPCTSTR operator will return a pointer to the string's buffer.

The << and >> Operators

```
friend CArchive& operator <<( CArchive& ar, const CString& string );
friend CArchive& operator >>( CArchive& ar, CString& string );
```

where

| ar | An archive object. |
| string | A string. |

The << and >> operators will read and write the string to and from a CArchive object.

The + Operator

```
friend CString operator +( const CString& string1, const CString& string2 );
friend CString operator +( const CString& string, TCHAR ch );
friend CString operator +( TCHAR ch, const CString& string );
friend CString operator +( const CString& string, LPCTSTR lpsz );
friend CString operator +( LPCTSTR lpsz, const CString& string );
```

where

string1	A string object to concatenate.
string2	A string object to concatenate.
string3	A string object to concatenate.
ch	A character to concatenate or be concatenated to.
lpsz	A pointer to a NULL-terminated string.

Returns a concatenated string of the two values specified.

The += Operator

```
const CString& operator +=( const CString& string );
const CString& operator +=( TCHAR ch );
const CString& operator +=( LPCTSTR lpsz );
```

where

string	A string object to concatenate.
ch	A character to concatenate or be concatenated to.
lpsz	A pointer to a NULL-terminated string.

Returns the concatenated string.

The += operator will concatenate the specified item with this string.

The Comparison Operators

```
BOOL operator ==( const CString& s1, const CString& s2 );
BOOL operator ==( const CString& s1, LPCTSTR s2 );
BOOL operator ==( LPCTSTR s1, const CString& s2 );
BOOL operator !=( const CString& s1, const CString& s2 );
BOOL operator !=( const CString& s1, LPCTSTR s2 );
BOOL operator !=( LPCTSTR s1, const CString& s2 );
BOOL operator <( const CString& s1, const CString& s2 );
BOOL operator <( const CString& s1, LPCTSTR s2 );
BOOL operator <( LPCTSTR s1, const CString& s2 );
BOOL operator >( const CString& s1, const CString& s2 );
BOOL operator >( const CString& s1, LPCTSTR s2 );
BOOL operator >( LPCTSTR s1, const CString& s2 );
BOOL operator <=( const CString& s1, const CString& s2 );
BOOL operator <=( const CString& s1, LPCTSTR s2 );
BOOL operator <=( LPCTSTR s1, const CString& s2 );
BOOL operator >=( const CString& s1, const CString& s2 );
BOOL operator >=( const CString& s1, LPCTSTR s2 );
BOOL operator >=( LPCTSTR s1, const CString& s2 );
```

where

s1	A string to compare.
s2	Another string to compare.

Returns TRUE if the two parameters meet the comparison.

The [] Operator

```
TCHAR operator []( int nIndex ) const;
```

where

nIndex	A zero-based index into the string.

Returns the character at the position specified by *nIndex*.

CSyncObject

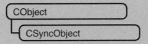

The CSyncObject class is pure virtual. It provides common functionality to all of the synchronization objects in Win32. These are CEvent, CMutex, CcriticalSection, and CSemaphore.

Header Files

The following header file should be included when using this class:

afxmt.h

Methods

The CSyncObject class has the following methods:

CSyncObject	The constructor
Lock	Gain access to this object

| operator HANDLE | Get the handle for this object |
| Unlock | Release access to this object |

The `CSyncObject` Constructor

The `CSyncObject` constructor creates the `CSyncObject` object. The `CSyncObject` constructor is used as follows:

```
CSyncObject( LPCTSTR pstrName );
```

where

> *pstrName*   The name of the object.

The `Lock` Method

```
BOOL Lock( DWORD dwTimeout = INFINITE );
```

where

> *dwTimeout*   The amount of time to wait for the resource. Specify `INFINITE` to specify no timeout.

Returns `TRUE` if successful.

The `Lock` method will wait for the resource to become available.

The `HANDLE` Operator

```
operator HANDLE( ) const;
```

Returns a `HANDLE` to this object.

The `Unlock` Method

```
virtual BOOL Unlock( ) = 0;
virtual BOOL Unlock( LONG lCount, LPLONG lpPrevCount = NULL );
```

where

> *lCount*   Not used by default implementation.
>
> *lPrevCount*   Not used by default implementation.

Returns `TRUE` if successful.

The `Unlock` method is called to release the resource.

CToolBar

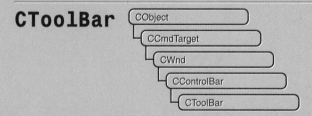

The `CToolBar` class implements a Windows toolbar. A toolbar is a collection of bitmapped buttons that is linked to a frame window.

For an example of CtoolBar, see the MDIEx example found on the CD-ROM that accompanies this book.

Header Files

The following header file should be included when using this class:

afxext.h

Methods

The CToolBar class has the following methods:

CToolBar	The constructor
CommandToIndex	Get the index of a given button
Create	Create a toolbar
CreateEx	Create a toolbar with extended styles
GetButtonInfo	Get info on a button
GetButtonStyle	Get a button's style
GetButtonText	Get a button's text
GetItemID	Get the command ID of a button
GetItemRect	Get an item's rectangle
GetToolBarCtrl	Get the underlying toolbar control
LoadBitmap	Load a bitmap that contains the buttons
LoadToolBar	Load a toolbar resource
SetBitmap	Set the bitmap
SetButtonInfo	Set button info
SetButtons	Set the button's styles and index
SetButtonStyle	Set the button's style
SetButtonText	Set the button's text
SetHeight	Set the height of the toolbar
SetSizes	Set the sizes of the buttons

The CToolBar Constructor

The CToolBar creates the CToolBar object. The CToolBar constructor is used as follows:

CToolBar( );

The CommandToIndex Method

int CommandToIndex(UINT nIDFind) const;

where

nIDFind   The command ID of the button whose index is being retrieved.

Returns the index of the specified button, or –1 if not successful.

The Create Method

```
BOOL Create( CWnd* pParentWnd, DWORD dwStyle = WS_CHILD | WS_VISIBLE |
➥CBRS_TOP, UINT nID = AFX_IDW_TOOLBAR );
```

where

pParentWnd	The parent window of the toolbar.
dwStyle	The style of the toolbar.
nID	The ID of the toolbar.

Returns TRUE if successful.

The Create method is called to create a toolbar.

The CreateEx Method

```
BOOL CreateEx( CWnd* pParentWnd, DWORD dwCtrlStyle = TBSTYLE_FLAT, DWORD
➥dwStyle = WS_CHILD | WS_VISIBLE | CBRS_TOP, CRect rcBorders =
➥CRect(0,0,0,0), UINT nID = AFX_IDW_TOOLBAR );
```

where

pParentWnd	The parent window of the status bar.
dwCtrlStyle	Additional creation styles.
dwStyle	The style of the toolbar.
nID	The ID of the toolbar.
rcBorders	The width of the toolbar borders.

Returns TRUE if successful.

The CreateEx method is called to create a toolbar.

The GetButtonInfo Method

```
void GetButtonInfo( int nIndex, UINT& nID, UINT& nStyle, int& iImage ) const;
```

where

nIndex	The index of the toolbar button to be retrieved.
nID	A variable to receive the command ID of the button.
nStyle	A variable to receive the style of the button.
iImage	A variable to receive the index of the button's bitmap.

The GetButtonInfo method will retrieve the ID, style, and image of the specified index.

The GetButtonStyle Method

```
UINT GetButtonStyle( int nIndex ) const;
```

where

nIndex	The index of the toolbar button to be retrieved.

Returns the style of the specified button.

The `GetButtonText` Method

```
CString GetButtonText( int nIndex ) const;
void GetButtonText( int nIndex, CString& rString ) const;
```

where

nIndex	The index of the button whose text is to be retrieved.
rString	A string to hold the text being retrieved.

Returns the text of the specified button.

The `GetItemID` Method

```
UINT GetItemID( int nIndex ) const;
```

where

nIndex	The index of the button.

The `GetItemID` method is called to determine the ID of the specified index.

The `GetItemRect` Method

```
virtual void GetItemRect( int nIndex, LPRECT lpRect ) const;
```

where

nIndex	The index of the button whose rectangle coordinates are to be retrieved.
lpRect	A rectangle that will be filled with the coordinates of the specified button.

The `GetItemRect` method is called to retrieve the coordinates of the specified button.

The `GetToolBarCtrl` Method

```
CToolBarCtrl& GetToolBarCtrl( ) const;
```

Returns the underlying control.

The `LoadBitmap` Method

```
BOOL LoadBitmap( LPCTSTR lpszResourceName );
BOOL LoadBitmap( UINT nIDResource );
```

where

lpszResourceName	The name of the resource to be loaded.
nIDResource	The ID of the resource to be loaded.

Returns TRUE if successful.

The `LoadBitmap` method will load the specified bitmap for use as the button backgrounds.

The `LoadToolBar` Method

```
BOOL LoadToolBar( LPCTSTR lpszResourceName );
BOOL LoadToolBar( UINT nIDResource );
```

where

lpszResourceName	The name of the resource to be loaded.
nIDResource	The ID of the resource to be loaded.

Returns TRUE if successful.

The `LoadToolBar` method will load the specified toolbar from the resources.

The `SetBitmap` Method

`BOOL SetBitmap( HBITMAP hbmImageWell );`

where

hbmImageWell	A handle to a bitmap.

Returns TRUE if successful.

The `SetBitmap` method will set the bitmap to be used as the background for the buttons.

The `SetButtonInfo` Method

`void SetButtonInfo( int nIndex, UINT nID, UINT nStyle, int iImage );`

where

nIndex	The index of the toolbar button to be set.
nID	The command ID of the button.
nStyle	The style of the button.
iImage	The index of the button's bitmap.

The `SetButtonInfo` method will set the ID, style, and image of the specified index.

The `SetButtons` Method

`BOOL SetButtons( const UINT* lpIDArray, int nIDCount );`

where

lpIDArray	Pointer to an array of command IDs.
nIDCount	How many IDs are in the array.

The `SetButtons` method will set the IDs for the toolbar buttons.

The `SetButtonStyle` Method

`void SetButtonStyle( int nIndex, UINT nStyle );`

where

nIndex	The index of the toolbar button to be set.
nStyle	The style of the button.

The `SetButtonStyle` method will set the style for the specified button.

The `SetButtonText` Method

`BOOL SetButtonText( int nIndex, LPCTSTR lpszText );`

where

nIndex	The index of the button whose text is to be set.
lpszText	A string that specifies the button text.

Returns TRUE if successful.

The `SetButtonText` method will set the text to the specified button.

The SetHeight Method

```
void SetHeight( int cyHeight );
```

where

    cyHeight   The height of the toolbar.

The SetHeight method will set the height of the toolbar.

The SetSizes Method

```
void SetSizes( SIZE sizeButton, SIZE sizeImage );
```

where

    sizeButton   The size of the buttons.

    sizeImage   The size of the images.

The SetSizes method will set the size of the buttons.

CTreeView

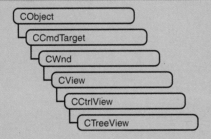

The CTreeView class creates a view based upon a tree control.

Header Files

The following header file should be included when using this class:

```
afxcview.h
```

Methods

The CTreeView class has the following methods:

    CTreeView   The constructor

    GetTreeCtrl   Get the underlying tree control

The CTreeView Constructor

The CTreeView constructor creates the CTreeView object. The CTreeView constructor is used as follows:

```
CTreeView();
```

The `GetTreeCtrl` Method

`CTreeCtrl& GetTreeCtrl( ) const;`

Returns the underlying tree control.

CView

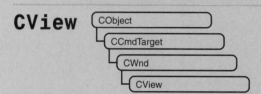

The `CView` class implements a view. A view handles the display and user interface for a document. Views cannot be displayed on their own; they are always displayed through frame windows.

Header Files

The following header file should be included when using this class:

`afxwin.h`

Methods

The `CView` class has the following methods:

`CView`	The constructor
`DoPreparePrinting`	Prepare to print
`GetDocument`	Get the document

The following methods are used to process messages sent to the class. These methods can be overridden if special handling is needed for these messages.

`OnDragEnter`	Called when an item is first dragged over the view
`OnDragLeave`	Called when an item is dragged out of the view
`OnDragOver`	Called when an item is again dragged into the view
`OnDrop`	Called when an item is dropped on the view, default handler
`OnDropEx`	Called when an item is dropped on the view, primary handler
`OnDragScroll`	Called to determine whether the cursor is dragging into a scroll region
`OnInitialUpdate`	Called before the first update
`OnScrollBy`	Called when a view that contains an in-place activated OLE item is scrolled
`OnScroll`	Called when OLE items are dragged from the view
`IsSelected`	Tests whether a document item is selected
`OnActivateView`	Called when the view is activated
`OnActivateFrame`	Called when the frame is activated
`OnBeginPrinting`	Called before printing begins
`OnDraw`	Called to render the view
`OnEndPrinting`	Called after printing

OnEndPrintPreview	Called after a print preview
OnPrepareDC	Called before the OnDraw method
OnPreparePrinting	Called before the OnDraw method for printing
OnPrint	Called to print
OnUpdate	Called to update

The CView Constructor

The CView creates the CView object. The CView constructor is used as follows:

CView();

The DoPreparePrinting Method

BOOL DoPreparePrinting(CPrintInfo* pInfo);

where

        pInfo   Information about the current print job.

The DoPreparePrinting method will invoke the standard print dialog box.

The IsSelected Method

virtual BOOL IsSelected(const CObject *pDocItem) const;

where

        pDocItem   A document item to be tested.

Returns TRUE if the specified item is selected.

The GetDocument Method

CDocument *GetDocument() const;

Returns a handle to the document associated with this view.

The OnActivateView Method

virtual void OnActivateView(BOOL bActivate, CView *pActivateView, CView *
➥pDeactivateView);

where

        bActivate   TRUE if the view is being activated.

        pActivateView   The view being activated.

        pDeactivateView   The view being deactivated.

The OnActivateView method is called when the active view changes.

The OnActivateFrame Method

virtual void OnActivateFrame(UINT nState, CFrame *pFrameWnd);

where

        nState   The state of the frame window. Should be WA_INACTIVE, WA_ACTIVE, or WA_CLICKACTIVE.

        pFrameWnd   Frame window being activated.

The OnActivateFrame method is called when the active frame changes.

The `OnDragEnter` Method

```
virtual DROPEFFECT OnDragEnter( COleDataObject* pDataObject, DWORD
➡dwKeyState, CPoint point );
```

where

pDataObject	A `COleDataObject` being dragged into the drop area of the view.
dwKeyState	The modifier key state. Can be any combination of `MK_CONTROL`, `MK_SHIFT`, `MK_ALT`, `MK_LBUTTON`, `MK_MBUTTON`,or `MK_RBUTTON`.
point	The current mouse position relative to the client area.

Returns one of the following:

`DROPEFFECT_NONE`	The data object cannot be dropped in this window.
`DROPEFFECT_LINK`	Creates a link between the object and its server.
`DROPEFFECT_COPY`	Creates a copy of the dragged object.
`DROPEFFECT_MOVE`	Creates a copy and deletes the original of the dragged object.

The `OnDragEnter` method is called when an OLE item is first dragged into the view.

The `OnDragLeave` Method

```
virtual void OnDragLeave( );
```

The `OnDragLeave` method is called during a drag operation when an OLE item is dragged from the view.

The `OnDragOver` Method

```
virtual DROPEFFECT OnDragOver( COleDataObject* pDataObject, DWORD
➡dwKeyState, CPoint point );
```

where

pDataObject	A `COleDataObject` being dragged into the drop area of the view.
dwKeyState	The modifier key state. Can be any combination of `MK_CONTROL`, `MK_SHIFT`, `MK_ALT`, `MK_LBUTTON`, `MK_MBUTTON`, or `MK_RBUTTON`.
point	The current mouse position relative to the client area.

Returns one of the following:

`DROPEFFECT_NONE`	The data object cannot be dropped in this window.
`DROPEFFECT_LINK`	Creates a link between the object and its server.
`DROPEFFECT_COPY`	Creates a copy of the dragged object.
`DROPEFFECT_MOVE`	Creates a copy of the dragged object and deletes the original.

The `OnDragOver` method is called when an OLE item is dragged into the view.

The `OnDragScroll` Method

```
virtual DROPEFFECT OnDragScroll( DWORD dwKeyState, CPoint point );
```

where

dwKeyState	The modifier key state. Can be any combination of `MK_CONTROL`, `MK_SHIFT`, `MK_ALT`, `MK_LBUTTON`, `MK_MBUTTON`, or `MK_RBUTTON`.
point	The current mouse position relative to the client area.

Returns one of the following:

DROPEFFECT_NONE	The data object cannot be dropped in this window.
DROPEFFECT_LINK	Creates a link between the object and its server.
DROPEFFECT_COPY	Creates a copy of the dragged object.
DROPEFFECT_MOVE	Creates a copy of the dragged object and deletes the original.

The OnDragScroll method is to determine whether an OLE item has been dragged into a scrolling region.

The **OnDraw** Method

```
virtual void OnDraw( CDC* pDC ) = 0;
```

where

pDC	A device context to draw to.

The OnDraw method is used to render the view. OnDraw is called both for screen and printer rendering. Every application must override this method to control the output of its applications.

The **OnDrop** Method

```
virtual BOOL OnDrop( COleDataObject* pDataObject, DROPEFFECT dropEffect,
➥CPoint point );
```

where

pDataObject	The COleDataObject being dragged into the drop area of the view.
dropEffect	The effect requested. See the following list.
point	The current mouse position relative to the client area.

Returns TRUE if successful.

The *dropEffect* parameter can be any of the following:

DROPEFFECT_NONE	The data object cannot be dropped in this window.
DROPEFFECT_LINK	Creates a link between the object and its server.
DROPEFFECT_COPY	Creates a copy of the dragged object.
DROPEFFECT_MOVE	Creates a copy of the dragged object and deletes the original.

The OnDrop method is called when an OLE item is dropped into the view.

The **OnDropEx** Method

```
virtual DROPEFFECT OnDropEx( COleDataObject* pDataObject, DROPEFFECT
➥dropDefault, DROPEFFECT dropList, CPoint point );
```

where

pDataObject	The COleDataObject being dragged into the drop area of the view.
dropDefault	The effect requested. See the following list.
dropList	The drop effects supported. See the following list.
point	The current mouse position relative to the client area.

Returns TRUE if successful.

The *dropDefault* and *dropList* parameters can be any of the following:

DROPEFFECT_NONE	The data object cannot be dropped in this window.
DROPEFFECT_LINK	Creates a link between the object and its server.
DROPEFFECT_COPY	Creates a copy of the dragged object
DROPEFFECT_MOVE	Creates a copy of the dragged object and deletes the original.

The OnDropEx method is called when an OLE item is dropped into the view.

The OnEndPrinting Method

```
virtual void OnEndPrinting( CDC* pDC, CPrintInfo* pInfo );
```

where

pDC	The device context used for printing.
pInfo	Information about the current print job.

The OnEndPrinting method is called when printing is complete. This method is usually overridden to free any resources that were needed during printing.

The OnEndPrintPreview Method

```
virtual void OnEndPrintPreview( CDC* pDC, CPrintInfo* pInfo, POINT point,
➡CPreviewView* pView );
```

where

pDC	A printer device context.
pInfo	Information about the current print job.
point	The point on the page that was last displayed.
pView	The view used for previewing.

The OnEndPrintPreview method is called when a print preview is complete. This method is usually overridden to free any resources that were needed during printing.

The OnInitialUpdate Method

```
void OnInitialUpdate( );
```

The OnInitialUpdate method is called before the first update.

The OnPrepareDC Method

```
virtual void OnPrepareDC( CDC* pDC, CPrintInfo* pInfo = NULL );
```

where

pDC	A printer device context.
pInfo	Information about the current print job.

The OnPrepareDC method is called before OnDraw. This method allows for any customization of the device context that might be needed.

The `OnPreparePrinting` Method

```
virtual BOOL OnPreparePrinting( CPrintInfo* pInfo );
```

where

    pInfo   Information about the current print job.

The `OnPreparePrinting` method is called before a print job.

The `OnPrint` Method

```
virtual void OnPrint( CDC* pDC, CPrintInfo* pInfo );
```

where

    pDC   A printer device context.

    pInfo   Information about the current print job.

The `OnPrint` method is called to print out the view.

The `OnUpdate` Method

```
virtual void OnUpdate( CView* pSender, LPARAM lHint, CObject* pHint );
```

where

    pSender   The view requesting the update.

    lHint   Information about the updates (application defined).

    pHint   Points to an object storing information about the modifications (application defined).

The `OnUpdate` method is called to redraw the view.

The `OnScrollBy` Method

```
BOOL OnScrollBy( CSize sizeScroll, BOOL bDoScroll = TRUE );
```

where

    sizeScroll   Number of pixels to scroll.

    bDoScroll   TRUE if this scrolling should actually happen.

Returns TRUE if successful.

The `OnScrollBy` method is called when an OLE item is dragged beyond the edge of the window.

The `OnScroll` Method

```
virtual BOOL OnScroll(UINT nScrollCode , UINT nPos, BOOL bDoScroll=TRUE);
```

where

    nScrollCode   The region of the scrollbar used. Should be SB_BOTTOM, SB_LINEDOWN, SB_LINEUP, SB_PAGEDOWN, SB_PAGEUP, SB_THUMBTRACK, or SB_TOP.

    nPos   The position of the thumb if *nScrollCode* is SB_THUMBTRACK.

    bDoScroll   TRUE if this scrolling should actually happen.

Returns TRUE if successful.

The `OnScroll` method is when the user interacts with the scrollbar.

CWaitCursor   `CWaitCursor`

The `CWaitCursor` class provides a quick way to display a wait cursor. Simply construct the object, and a wait cursor will appear. After the object is destroyed, the cursor returns to normal.

The `CWaitCursor` class can never be a global object or be allocated with the `new` keyword. It must always be a local variable.

Header Files

The following header file should be included when using this class:

`afxwin.h`

Methods

The `CWaitCursor` class has the following methods:

`CWaitCursor`	The constructor
`Restore`	Restores the cursor after it's been changed

The `CWaitCursor` Constructor

The `CWaitCursor` constructor creates the `CWaitCursor` object. After it is created, the cursor is changed to an hourglass. The `CWaitCursor` constructor is used as follows:

`CWaitCursor();`

The `Restore` Method

`void Restore();`

The `Restore` method will restore the cursor to an hourglass after it has been changed.

CWinApp

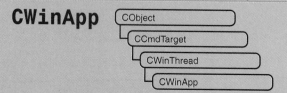

The `CWinApp` class is the base class from which an MFC application class is built. Only one `CWinApp` object can be created per Windows application.

Header Files

The following header file should be included when using this class:

`afxwin.h`

Properties

The CWinApp class has the following properties:

m_bHelpMode	Indicates whether the user is in help context mode
m_hInstance	The instance handle for the application
m_hPrevInstance	Holds a NULL value in 32-bit apps
m_lpCmdLine	The command line for this application
m_nCmdShow	How the main window is to be displayed
m_pActiveWnd	Pointer to the main window of the container application when an OLE server is in-place active
m_pszAppName	The application name
m_pszExeName	The name of the executable file
m_pszHelpFilePath	The path to the help file
m_pszProfileName	The .INI filename for this application
m_pszRegistryKey	The Registry key for this application

C

Methods

The CWinApp class has the following methods:

CWinApp	The constructor
AddDocTemplate	Add a document template
AddToRecentFileList	Add to recent file list
CreatePrinterDC	Create a printer device context
Enable3dControls	Enable 3D controls for DLL
Enable3dControlsStatic	Enable 3D controls for static lib
EnableShellOpen	Enable opening from the shell
GetFirstDocTemplatePosition	Get the position of the first document template
GetNextDocTemplate	Get the next document template
GetPrinterDeviceDefaults	Get printer driver defaults
GetProfileInt	Get a profile int
GetProfileString	Get a profile string
LoadCursor	Load a cursor
LoadIcon	Load an icon
LoadOEMCursor	Load an OEM cursor
LoadOEMIcon	Load an OEM icon
LoadStandardCursor	Load the standard cursor
LoadStandardIcon	Load the standard icon
LoadStdProfileSettings	Load the standard profile settings
OpenDocumentFile	Open a document file
ParseCommandLine	Parse the command line

`ProcessShellCommand`	Process any shell commands
`RegisterShellFileTypes`	Register the file types for this application
`RunAutomated`	Run for use with OLE automation
`RunEmbedded`	Run as an embedded object
`SelectPrinter`	Select a printer
`SetDialogBkColor`	Set the dialog background color
`SetRegistryKey`	Set the Registry key
`WriteProfileInt`	Write profile `int`
`WriteProfileString`	Write profile string

The following methods are used to process messages sent to the class. These methods can be overridden if special handling is needed for these messages.

`CloseAllDocuments`	Close all documents
`DoMessageBox`	Implements `AfxMessageBox`
`DoWaitCursor`	Display wait cursor
`ExitInstance`	Called when the application terminates
`HideApplication`	Called to hide the application
`InitInstance`	Called when a new instance of the application begins
`OnContextHelp`	Called when the user requests context help
`OnDDECommand`	Called for DDE commands
`OnFileNew`	Called for the file new command
`OnFileOpen`	Called for the file open command
`OnFilePrintSetup`	Called for the file print setup command
`OnHelp`	Called for the help command
`OnHelpFinder`	Called to process the help finder
`OnHelpIndex`	Called for the on help index command
`OnHelpUsing`	Called for the on help using command
`OnIdle`	Called when the application is idle
`PreTranslateMessage`	Called before messages are translated
`ProcessMessageFilter`	Intercept certain messages
`ProcessWndProcException`	Intercept all unhanded exceptions
`Run`	Run the default message loop
`SaveAllModified`	Save all modified documents
`WinHelp`	Called to process help requests

The `CWinApp` Constructor

The `CWinApp` creates the `CWinApp` object. The `CWinApp` constructor is used as follows:

`CWinApp( LPCTSTR lpszAppName = NULL );`

where

lpszAppName	The application name. If not specified, MFC uses the resource string `AFX_IDS_APP_TITLE`.

The AddDocTemplate Method

```
void AddDocTemplate( CDocTemplate* pTemplate );
```

where

    pTemplate   A document template.

The AddDocTemplate method is called to add a document template to the application.

The AddToRecentFileList Method

```
virtual void AddToRecentFileList( LPCTSTR lpszPathName );
```

where

    lpszPathName   A document file.

The AddToRecentFileList method is called to add a document to the recent file list.

The CloseAllDocuments Method

```
void CloseAllDocuments( BOOL bEndSession );
```

where

    bEndSession   TRUE if the windows session is ending.

The CloseAllDocuments method is called to close all document windows.

The CreatePrinterDC Method

```
BOOL CreatePrinterDC( CDC& dc );
```

where

    dc   The printer device context.

Returns TRUE if successful.

The CreatePrinterDC method will create a printer device context.

The DoMessageBox Method

```
virtual int DoMessageBox( LPCTSTR lpszPrompt, UINT nType, UINT nIDPrompt );
```

where

    lpszPrompt   The prompt for the message box.

    nType   The message box type.

    nIDPrompt   An ID to a help context string.

Returns the result from the message box.

The DoMessageBox method will display a Windows message box.

The DoWaitCursor Method

```
virtual void DoWaitCursor( int nCode );
```

where

    nCode   If 1, the wait cursor appears. If 0, the wait cursor is restored. If –1 ,the wait cursor ends.

The DoWaitCursor method will display a wait cursor.

The `Enable3dControls` Method

`BOOL Enable3dControls( );`

The `Enable3dControls` method for the DLL version of MFC.

Returns `TRUE` if successful.

The `Enable3dControlsStatic` Method

`BOOL Enable3dControlsStatic( );`

Returns `TRUE` if successful.

The `Enable3dControls` for the static linked version of MFC.

The `EnableShellOpen` Method

`void EnableShellOpen( );`

The `EnableShellOpen` method enables files to be opened by double-clicking them.

The `ExitInstance` Method

`virtual int ExitInstance( );`

Returns the exit code for the application.

The `ExitInstance` method is called when an MFC app is exiting.

The `GetFirstDocTemplatePosition` Method

`POSITION GetFirstDocTemplatePosition( ) const;`

Returns the position of the first document template.

The `GetNextDocTemplate` Method

`CDocTemplate* GetNextDocTemplate( POSITION& pos ) const;`

where

      pos   The previous position. Moved to the next position.

Returns the document template, or `NULL` if no more exist.

The `GetNextDocTemplate` method will move to the next document template.

The `GetPrinterDeviceDefaults` Method

`BOOL GetPrinterDeviceDefaults( PRINTDLG* pPrintDlg );`

where

      pPrintDlg   A `PRINTDLG` structure.

Returns `TRUE` if successful.

The `GetPrinterDeviceDefaults` method will get the printer default items.

The `GetProfileInt` Method

`UINT GetProfileInt( LPCTSTR lpszSection, LPCTSTR lpszEntry, int nDefault );`

where

lpszSection	The section containing the entry.
lpszEntry	The entry.
nDefault	The default value.

Returns the specified profile int, or the default if this entry does not exist.

The GetProfileString Method

```
CString GetProfileString( LPCTSTR lpszSection, LPCTSTR lpszEntry, LPCTSTR
➥lpszDefault = NULL );
```

where

lpszSection	The section containing the entry.
lpszEntry	The entry.
lpszDefault	The default value.

Returns the specified profile string, or the default if this entry does not exist.

The HideApplication Method

```
void HideApplication( );
```

The HideApplication method is called to hide an application.

The InitInstance Method

```
virtual BOOL InitInstance( );
```

The InitInstance method is called when an application starts up.

The LoadCursor Method

```
HCURSOR LoadCursor( LPCTSTR lpszResourceName ) const;
HCURSOR LoadCursor( UINT nIDResource ) const;
```

where

| *lpszResourceName* | Name of the resource to be loaded. |
| *nIDResource* | ID of the resource to be loaded. |

Returns a handle to the cursor loaded, or NULL if failure.

The LoadIcon Method

```
HICON LoadIcon( LPCTSTR lpszResourceName ) const;
HICON LoadIcon( UINT nIDResource ) const;
```

where

| *lpszResourceName* | Name of the resource to be loaded. |
| *nIDResource* | ID of the resource to be loaded. |

Returns a handle to the icon loaded, or NULL if failure.

C

The `LoadOEMCursor` Method

```
HCURSOR LoadOEMCursor( UINT nIDCursor ) const;
```

where

    nIDCursor   ID of the cursor to be loaded.

Returns a handle to the cursor loaded, or NULL if failure.

The `LoadOEMIcon` Method

```
HICON LoadOEMIcon( UINT nIDIcon ) const;
```

where

    nIDIcon   ID of the icon to be loaded.

Returns a handle to the icon loaded, or NULL if failure.

The `LoadStandardCursor` Method

```
HCURSOR LoadStandardCursor( LPCTSTR lpszCursorName ) const;
```

where

    lpszCursorName   Name of the cursor to be loaded.

Returns a handle to the cursor loaded, or NULL if failure.

The `LoadStandardIcon` Method

```
HCURSOR LoadStandardIcon( LPCTSTR lpszIconName ) const;
```

where

    lpszIconName   Name of the icon to be loaded.

Returns a handle to the icon loaded, or NULL if failure.

The `LoadStdProfileSettings` Method

```
void LoadStdProfileSettings( UINT nMaxMRU = _AFX_MRU_COUNT );
```

where

    nMaxMRU   Max number of items in the MRU list.

The LoadStrProfileSettings method loads the standard profile settings from the profile. This includes the MRU list.

The `OnContextHelp` Method

```
afx_msg void OnContextHelp( );
```

The OnContextHelp method is called to process context help requests.

The `OnDDECommand` Method

```
virtual BOOL OnDDECommand( LPTSTR lpszCommand );
```

where

    lpszCommand   A DDE command.

Returns TRUE if the command is handled.

The OnDDECommand method is called to process DDE commands to the application.

The `OnFileNew` Method

`afx_msg void OnFileNew( );`

The OnFileNew method is called to process a new file menu command.

The `OnFileOpen` Method

`afx_msg void OnFileOpen( );`

The OnFileOpen method is called to process a file open command.

The `OnFilePrintSetup` Method

`afx_msg void OnFilePrintSetup( );`

The OnFilePrintSetup method is called to process a print setup command.

The `OnHelp` Method

`afx_msg void OnHelp( );`

The OnHelp method is called to process the help menu item.

The `OnHelpFinder` Method

`afx_msg void OnHelpFinder( );`

The OnHelpFinder method is called to process the help finder menu item.

The `OnHelpIndex` Method

`afx_msg void OnHelpIndex( );`

The OnHelpIndex method is called to process the help index menu item.

The `OnHelpUsing` Method

`afx_msg void OnHelpUsing( );`

The OnHelpUsing method is called to process the help using menu item.

The `OnIdle` Method

`virtual BOOL OnIdle( LONG lCount );`

where

lCount	A counter that is increased each time idle is called. This count is reset with each new message in the queue.

Returns TRUE to request more idle time.

The OnIdle method is called when the application is in an idle state.

The `OpenDocumentFile` Method

`virtual CDocument* OpenDocumentFile( LPCTSTR lpszFileName );`

where

lpszFileName	The document to open.

Returns the document opened or NULL if failure.

The OpenDocumentFile method is called to open a document file.

The `ParseCommandLine` Method

```
void ParseCommandLine( CCommandLineInfo& rCmdInfo );
```

where

    rCmdInfo   Command line info.

The ParseCommandLine method is called to parse the command line passed to the application.

The `PreTranslateMessage` Method

```
virtual BOOL PreTranslateMessage( MSG* pMsg );
```

where

    pMsg   The message.

Returns TRUE if the message was processed.

The PreTranslateMessage method is called prior to the application translating the message.

The `ProcessMessageFilter` Method

```
virtual BOOL ProcessMessageFilter( int code, LPMSG lpMsg );
```

where

    code   The hook code.

    pMsg   The message.

Returns TRUE if the message was processed.

The ProcessMessageFilter method is called to filter certain Windows messages.

The `ProcessShellCommand` Method

```
BOOL ProcessShellCommand( CCommandLineInfo& rCmdInfo );
```

where

    rCmdInfo   Command line info.

Returns TRUE if successful.

The ProcessShellCommand method is called to process any shell commands sent.

The `ProcessWndProcException` Method

```
virtual LRESULT ProcessWndProcException( CException* e, const MSG* pMsg );
```

where

    e   An uncaught exception.

    msg   The Windows message that caused the exception.

Returns the value that should be returned to Windows.

The ProcessWndProcException method is called to handle any exceptions that are not caught.

The `RegisterShellFileTypes` Method

`void RegisterShellFileTypes( BOOL bCompat = FALSE );`

where

    bCompat   TRUE to add entries for print and print to.

The `RegisterShellFileTypes` method is called to register all shell file types.

The `Run` Method

`virtual int Run( );`

Returns the application exit code.

The `Run` method is called to process the main Windows message loop.

The `RunAutomated` Method

`BOOL RunAutomated( );`

Returns TRUE if the option was found.

The `RunAutomated` method is called to run the application as an OLE automation server.

The `RunEmbedded` Method

`BOOL RunEmbedded( );`

Returns TRUE if the option was found.

The `RunEmbedded` method is called to run the application as an embedded OLE item.

The `SaveAllModified` Method

`virtual BOOL SaveAllModified( );`

Returns TRUE if it is safe to terminate the application.

The `SaveAllModified` method is called to save all modified documents.

The `SelectPrinter` Method

`void SelectPrinter( HANDLE hDevNames, HANDLE hDevMode, BOOL bFreeOld = TRUE );`

where

    hDevNames   A handle to a device name structure that identifies the driver, device, and port of a printer.

    hDevMode   A handle to a device mode structure.

    bFreeOld   TRUE to free the previously selected printer.

The `SelectPrinter` method is called to select a specific printer.

The `SetDlgBkColor` Method

`void SetDialogBkColor( COLORREF clrCtlBk = RGB(192, 192, 192), COLORREF`
➡`clrCtlText = RGB(0, 0, 0) );`

where

    clrCtlBk   The dialog background color for the application.

    clrCtlText   The text color for a dialog box.

The `SetDialogBkColor` method should be called from `InitInstance` to set the dialog colors.

C

The `SetRegistryKey` Method

```
void SetRegistryKey( LPCTSTR lpszRegistryKey );
void SetRegistryKey( UINT nIDRegistryKey );
```

where

lpszRegistryKey	A string containing a Registry key.
nIDRegistryKey	The ID or index of the resource item that specified a Registry key.

The `SetRegistryKey` method causes all `.INI` file settings to be mapped to the specified Registry key.

The `WinHelp` Method

```
virtual void WinHelp( DWORD dwData, UINT nCmd = HELP_CONTEXT );
```

where

dwData	Specifies additional data.
nCmd	The help command requested.

The `WinHelp` method is used to interface to the Windows help system, and invoke the WinHelp application.

The `WriteProfileInt` Method

```
BOOL WriteProfileInt( LPCTSTR lpszSection, LPCTSTR lpszEntry, int nValue );
```

where

lpszSection	The section containing the entry.
lpszEntry	The entry.
nValue	The value to be written.

Returns TRUE if successful.

The `WriteProfileInt` method writes the specified value to the profile.

The `WriteProfileString` Method

```
BOOL WriteProfileString( LPCTSTR lpszSection, LPCTSTR lpszEntry, LPCTSTR
➡lpszValue );
```

where

lpszSection	The section containing the entry.
lpszEntry	The entry.
lpszValue	The string to be written.

Returns TRUE if successful.

The `WriteProfileString` method writes the specified value to the profile.

CWnd

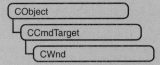

CWnd is the base class for all Windows classes in MFC. A CWnd object is very closely related to the WIN32 API window object. CWnd is used to create both parent and child windows.

Header Files

The following header file should be included when using this class:

afxwin.h

Methods

The CWnd class has the following methods:

CWnd	The constructor
ArrangeIconicWindows	Arrange any iconic child windows
Attach	Attach an HWND
BeginPaint	Begin an update
BindDefaultProperty	Bind the default property of a data-bound control
BindProperty	Bind a property of a data-bound control
BringWindowToTop	Bring this window to the top
CalcWindowRect	Called to calculate the client area of a window
CancelToolTips	Cancel tooltips help
CenterWindow	Center a window
ChangeClipboardChain	Change the Clipboard viewer change
CheckDlgButton	Check a dialog button
CheckRadioButton	Check a dialog radio button
ChildWindowFromPoint	Get the child window that contains a point
ClientToScreen	Convert client coordinates to screen coordinates
ContinueModal	Determine whether a dialog should continue in a modal state
Create	Create a window
CreateCaret	Create a caret
CreateControl	Create a control
CreateEx	Extended create
CreateGrayCaret	Create a grayed caret
CreateSolidCaret	Create a solid caret
Default	Call default window processing
DeleteTempMap	Delete any temporary windows
DestroyWindow	Destroy the window

C

Detach	Detach an HWND from the window
DlgDirList	Fill a list box with a file or directory listing
DlgDirListComboBox	Fill a combo box with a file or directory listing
DlgDirSelect	Get the current selection in a list box
DlgDirSelectComboBox	Get the current selection in a combo box
DragAcceptFiles	Call to tell this window to accept dropped files
DrawMenuBar	Draw the menu bar
EnableScrollBar	Enable scrollbars
EnableScrollBarCtrl	Enable the scrollbar control
EnableToolTips	Enable tooltips
EnableWindow	Enable the window
EndModalLoop	End a modal dialog loop
EndPaint	Stop updating a window
ExecuteDlgInit	Initiate a dialog resource
FilterToolTipMessage	Filter tooltip messages
FindWindow	Find a window
FlashWindow	Flash this window
FromHandle	Create a temporary CWnd from an HWND
FromHandlePermanent	Create a non-temporary CWnd from an HWND
GetActiveWindow	Get the active window
GetCapture	Get the capture state
GetCaretPos	Get the position of the caret
GetCheckedRadioButton	Get a checked radio button's status
GetClientRect	Get the client Rect of a window
GetClipboardOwner	Get the Clipboard owner
GetClipboardViewer	Get the Clipboard viewer
GetControlUnknown	Get the IUnknown interface to this window
GetCurrentMessage	Get the current message
GetDC	Get a device context for this window
GetDCEx	Get an extended device context for this window
GetDescendantWindow	Get a pointer to the descendant window
GetDesktopWindow	Get the desktop window
GetDlgCtrlID	Get a dialog control's ID
GetDlgItem	Get a dialog item
GetDlgItemInt	Get a dialog item as an integer
GetDlgItemText	Get the text associated with a dialog item
GetDSCCursor	Get the underlying data set cursor for a window
GetExStyle	Get the extended style info for the window
GetFocus	Get the current focus

GetFont	Get the current font
GetForegroundWindow	Get the foreground window
GetIcon	Get the icon for this window
GetLastActivePopup	Get the last active pop-up window
GetMenu	Get the menu for this window
GetNextDlgGroupItem	Get the next dialog group item
GetNextDlgTabItem	Get the next dialog tab item
GetNextWindow	Get the next window
GetOpenClipboardWindow	Get the window that has the Clipboard open
GetOwner	Get the window's owner
GetParent	Get the window's parent
GetParentFrame	Get the parent frame
GetParentOwner	Get the parent's owner
GetProperty	Get an OLE control property
GetSafeHwnd	Get the HWND associated with this window
GetSafeOwner	Get the owner window
GetScrollBarCtrl	Get the scrollbar associated with this window
GetScrollInfo	Get information about the scrollbar
GetScrollLimit	Get the scrollbar limit information
GetScrollPos	Get the scrollbar position
GetScrollRange	Get the scrollbar range
GetStyle	Get the scrollbar style
GetSystemMenu	Get the system menu
GetTopLevelFrame	Get the top-level frame
GetTopLevelOwner	Get the top-level owner
GetTopLevelParent	Get the top-level parent
GetTopWindow	Get the top-level window
GetUpdateRect	Get a rectangle that bounds the update region
GetUpdateRgn	Get the update region
GetWindow	Get a specific child or top-level window
GetWindowContextHelpId	Get the window's help context ID
GetWindowDC	Get a window DC
GetWindowPlacement	Get the window placement
GetWindowRect	Get the window's rectangle
GetWindowRgn	Get the window's region
GetWindowText	Get the window's text
GetWindowTextLength	Get the length of the window's text
HideCaret	Hide the caret
HiliteMenuItem	Highlight a menu item

C

Invalidate	Invalidate an entire client region
InvalidateRect	Invalidate a rectangle in the client region
InvalidateRgn	Invalidate a region in the client region
InvokeHelper	Invoke an OLE method
IsChild	Is this window a child window?
IsDialogMessage	Is this a dialog message?
IsDlgButtonChecked	Is a dialog button checked?
IsIconic	Is the window iconic?
IsWindowEnabled	Is this window enabled?
IsWindowVisible	Is the window visible?
IsZoomed	Is the window zoomed?
KillTimer	Kill a window timer
LockWindowUpdate	Disable or enable drawing in a window
MapWindowPoints	Map points from one window to another
MessageBox	Display a message box
ModifyStyle	Modify the window's style
ModifyStyleEx	Modify the window's extended style
MoveWindow	Move the window
OnAmbientProperty	Obtain an ambient property from an OLE control
OnToolHitTest	Is a point inside the rectangle of a tool
OpenClipboard	Open the Clipboard
PostMessage	Post a message to this window
PreCreateWindow	Called before the window is created
PreSubclassWindow	Called before the window is subclassed
PreTranslateMessage	Called before messages are translated
Print	Called to print
PrintClient	Print the client region
RedrawWindow	Redraw the window
ReleaseDC	Release a device context
RepositionBars	Reposition the scrollbars
RunModalLoop	Run a modal dialog box loop
ScreenToClient	Convert screen coodinates to client coordinates
ScrollWindow	Scroll the window
ScrollWindowEx	Extended scrolling
SendDlgItemMessage	Send a dialog item a message
SendMessage	Send a message
SendMessageToDescendants	Send a message to all descendants
SendNotifyMessage	Send a notification message
SetActiveWindow	Set the active window

SetCapture	Set the capture state
SetCaretPos	Set the caret position
SetClipboardViewer	Set the Clipboard viewer
SetDlgCtrlID	Set the control ID
SetDlgItemInt	Set a dialog item's text as an integer
SetDlgItemText	Set a dialog item's text
SetFocus	Set the current focus
SetFont	Set the current font
SetForegroundWindow	Set the foreground window
SetIcon	Set the window's icon
SetMenu	Set the window's menu
SetOwner	Set the window's owner
SetParent	Set the window's parent
SetProperty	Set an OLE property
SetRedraw	Allow/disallow redraws
SetScrollInfo	Set scrollbar information
SetScrollPos	Set the scrollbar position
SetScrollRange	Set the scrollbar range
SetTimer	Set a Windows timer
SetWindowContextHelpId	Set the window help context ID
SetWindowPlacement	Set the window placement
SetWindowPos	Set the window position
SetWindowRgn	Set the window region
SetWindowText	Set the window text
ShowCaret	Show the caret
ShowOwnedPopups	Show any owned pop-ups
ShowScrollBar	Show the scrollbars
ShowWindow	Show a window
SubclassDlgItem	Dynamically subclass a dialog item
SubclassWindow	Dynamically subclass a window
UnlockWindowUpdate	Unlock the window update
UnsubclassWindow	Unsubclass a window
UpdateData	Update a window's data
UpdateDialogControls	Update dialog controls
UpdateWindow	Update a window
ValidateRect	Validate a rectangle
ValidateRgn	Validate a region
WindowFromPoint	Return a handle to a window that contains a point

C

The following methods are used to process messages sent to the class. These methods can be overridden if special handling is needed for these messages.

DefWindowProc	The default window proc
DoDataExchange	Called to exchange data
OnActivate	Called when a window becomes active
OnActivateApp	Called when an application becomes active
OnAskCbFormatName	Called when a Clipboard name is needed
OnCancelMode	Called to cancel any internal mode
OnCaptureChanged	Called when the status of a capture changes
OnChangeCbChain	Called when the Clipboard viewer changes
OnChar	Called when a character is received from the keyboard
OnCharToItem	Called when a list box sends a WM_CHARTOITEM message
OnChildActivate	Called when a child window activates
OnChildNotify	Called when a child window notifies
OnClose	Called when the window is closing
OnCommand	Called when a command is sent
OnCompacting	Called when the memory is low
OnCompareItem	Called to determine the location of a child window
OnCopyData	Called to copy data from one application to another
OnCreate	Called when the window is initially created
OnCtlColor	Called when a child control is about to be drawn
OnDeadChar	Called after keystrokes
OnDeleteItem	Called when an item in a combo box is deleted
OnDestroy	Called when the window is destroyed
OnDestroyClipboard	Called when the contents of the Clipboard are destroyed
OnDeviceChange	Called when a device driver changes
OnDevModeChange	Called when a device driver changes modes
OnDrawClipboard	Called the Clipboard should be redrawn
OnDrawItem	Called when an owner-drawn item must be redrawn
OnDropFiles	Called when files are dropped on this window
OnDSCNotify	Called to notify the window when a recordset sends a notification
OnEnable	Called when the window is enabled
OnEndSession	Called when the Windows session is ending
OnEnterIdle	Called upon entering a idle state
OnEnterMenuLoop	Called when a menu modal loop is entered
OnEraseBkgnd	Called when the background of a window should be erased
OnExitMenuLoop	Called when a menu modal loop is exited
OnFontChange	Called when the window font has changed
OnGetDlgCode	Called to handle arrow and tab key input

OnGetMinMaxInfo	Called to get information about a window's maximized size
OnHScroll	Called for horizontal scrollbar messages
OnHScrollClipboard	Called for horizontal scrollbar message to the Clipboard viewer
OnIconEraseBkgnd	Called when an iconic window should erase its background
OnInitMenu	Called when the menu is set up
OnInitMenuPopup	Called when a pop-up menu is set up
OnKeyDown	Called when a key is pressed
OnKeyUp	Called when a key is released
OnKillFocus	Called when a window loses focus
OnLButtonDblClk	Called when the left mouse button is double-clicked
OnLButtonDown	Called when the left mouse button is pressed
OnLButtonUp	Called when the left mouse button is released
OnMButtonDblClk	Called when the middle mouse button is double-clicked
OnMButtonDown	Called when the middle mouse button is pressed
OnMButtonUp	Called when the middle mouse button is released
OnMDIActivate	Called when an MDI child window is activated
OnMeasureItem	Called to measure an item for an owner-drawn control
OnMenuChar	Called when a key is pressed in a menu
OnMenuSelect	Called when a menu item is selected
OnMouseActivate	Called when a window is activated by a mouse click
OnMouseMove	Called when the mouse moves
OnMouseWheel	Called as the mouse wheel moves
OnMove	Called when the window moves
OnMoving	Called as the window moves
OnNcActivate of activation	Called when the non-client area needs to be redrawn as the result
OnNcCalcSize	Called to calculate the size of the non-client area
OnNcCreate	Called to create the non-client area
OnNcDestroy	Called to destroy the non-client area
OnNcHitTest	Called to determine whether a click is in the non-client area
OnNcLButtonDblClk	Called when the left mouse button is double-clicked in the non-client area
OnNcLButtonDown	Called when the left mouse button is pressed in the non-client area
OnNcLButtonUp	Called when the left mouse button is released in the non-client area
OnNcMButtonDblClk	Called when the middle mouse button is double-clicked in the non-client area
OnNcMButtonDown	Called when the middle mouse button is pressed in the non-client area

C

OnNcMButtonUp	Called when the middle mouse button is released in the non-client area
OnNcMouseMove	Called when the mouse is moved in the non-client area
OnNcPaint	Called when the non-client area needs to be painted
OnNcRButtonDblClk	Called when the right mouse button is double clicked in the non-client area
OnNcRButtonDown	Called when the right mouse button is pressed in the non-client area
OnNcRButtonUp	Called when the right mouse button is released in the non-client area
OnNotify	Called to notify the window of a notification message
OnPaint	Called to repaint the window
OnPaintClipboard	Called to repaint the Clipboard in a Clipboard viewer
OnPaletteChanged	Called when the palette changes
OnPaletteIsChanging	Called before the palette is changed
OnParentNotify	Called when a child is created or destroyed
OnQueryDragIcon	Called to determine the minimized icon to use for a window
OnQueryEndSession	Called to determine whether it is okay to end the Windows session
OnQueryNewPalette	Called to see if it is okay to change to a new palette
OnQueryOpen	Called to see if it is okay to open a window from a minimized state
OnRButtonDblClk	Called when the right mouse button is double-clicked
OnRButtonDown	Called when the right mouse button is pressed
OnRButtonUp	Called when the right mouse button is released
OnRegisteredMouseWheel	Called as the mouse wheel moves
OnRenderAllFormats	Called when the window should render all formats to the Clipboard
OnRenderFormat	Called when the window should render a specific format to the Clipboard
OnSetCursor	Called to change the cursor
OnSetFocus	Called when the focus is set
OnShowWindow	Called when the window is shown or hidden
OnSize	Called when the window is resized
OnSizeClipboard	Called when the size of the Clipboard viewer changes
OnSizing	Called as the window is resized
OnSpoolerStatus	Called when a job is added or removed from the print queue
OnStyleChanged	Called when the window style has changed
OnStyleChanging	Called when the window style is about to change
OnSysChar	Called when a system character is received

OnSysColorChange	Called when a system color changes
OnSysCommand	Called when a system command is received
OnSysDeadChar	Called with each system character
OnSysKeyDown	Called when a system key is pressed
OnSysKeyUp	Called when a system key is released
OnTimeChange	Called when the time is changed
OnTimer	Called when a timer message is received
OnVKeyToItem	Called when a list box receives a virtual key
OnVScroll	Called for messages to the vertical scrollbar messages
OnVScrollClipboard	Called when the vertical scrollbar is used on a Clipboard
OnWindowPosChanged	Called for a vertical scrollbar message to the Clipboard viewer
OnWindowPosChanging	Called when the window position is changed
OnWinIniChange	Called when the windows.ini file changes
OnWndMsg	Called for a window message
PostNcDestroy	Called after a window has been destroyed
ReflectChildNotify	Called to reflect a message back at its source
ReflectLastMsg	Reflect the last message
SendChildNotifyLastMsg	Called to provide a notification message to a child window
WindowProc	The window proc

The CWnd Constructor

The CWnd constructor creates the CWnd object. The CWnd constructor is used as follows:

CWnd()

The ArrangeIconicWindows Method

UINT ArrangeIconicWindows();

Returns the height of one row of icons if successful, or 0 if unsuccessful.

The ArrangeIconicWindows method will arrange all minimized child windows. This method can also be called for the desktop window by using the GetDesktopWindow method.

The Attach Method

BOOL Attach(HWND hWndNew);

where

    hWndNew   A handle to an existing window.

Returns TRUE if successful.

The Attach method will attach a window handle (HWND) to this CWnd object.

The BeginPaint Method

CDC* BeginPaint(LPPAINTSTRUCT lpPaint);

where

    lpPaint   A pointer to a paint structure.

Returns a pointer to a paint device context if successful, or NULL if unsuccessful.

The BeginPaint method will create a device context that will only draw to the update region. This device context should be used only inside a Paint method. For drawing outside the Paint method, use the GetDC method. After painting is complete, the EndPaint method should be called.

The `BindDefaultProperty` Method

```
void BindDefaultProperty( DISPID dwDispID, VARTYPE vtProp, LPCTSTR
➥szFieldName, CWnd * pDSCWnd );
```

where

dwDispID	The DISPID of the property in a data-bound control that is to be bound to a data source control.
vtProp	The type of property to be bound. Should be a VT_ constant such as VT_BSTR or VT_VARIANT.
szFieldName	The name of the column in the data source control that the property should be bound to.
pDSCWnd	The window that hosts the data source control that this property will be bound to. Call GetDlgItem to get this value.

The BindDefaultProperty method will bind the calling object's default simple bound property to the underlying cursor defined by the data source.

The `BindProperty` Method

```
void BindProperty( DISPID dwDispID, CWnd * pWndDSC );
```

where

dwDispID	The DISPID of the property in a data-bound control that is to be bound to a data source control.
pDSCWnd	The window that hosts the data source control that this property will be bound to. Call GetDlgItem to get this value.

The BindProperty method will bind a data-bound object, such as a grid, to a data source property.

The `BringWindowToTop` Method

```
void BringWindowToTop();
```

The BringWindowToTop method will bring this CWnd object to the top of any overlapping windows.

The `CalcWindowRect` Method

```
virtual void CalcWindowRect( LPRECT lpClientRect, UINT nAdjustType =
➥adjustBorder );
```

where

lpClientRect	Will contain the window rectangle. Initially should contain the desired client rectangle size.
pDSCWnd	Determines how to calculate this value. If CWnd::adjustBorder, scrollbar sizes are ignored. If CWnd::adjustOutside is specified, then scrollbar sizes are considered.

The `CalcWindowRect` method will calculate how big a window's rectangle should be to accommodate a given client rectangle size.

The `CancelToolTips` Method

```
static void CancelToolTips( BOOL bKeys = FALSE );
```

where

    bKeys   TRUE if tooltips are canceled when a key is pressed, FALSE otherwise.

The `CancelToolTips` method is called to cancel a tooltip if one is currently being displayed.

The `CenterWindow` Method

```
void CenterWindow( CWnd* pAlternateOwner = NULL );
```

where

    pAlternateOwner   Pointer to a window (other than the parent) that this window should be centered to.

The `CenterWindow` method will center the window relative to the parent window, or to another window if specified.

The `ChangeClipboardChain` Method

```
BOOL ChangeClipboardChain( HWND hWndNext );
```

where

    hWndNext   The window that follows this one in the Clipboard viewer chain.

The `ChangeClipboardChain` method will remove this window from the Clipboard viewer chain, and make the window specified the descendant of this object's ancestor in the chain.

The `CheckDlgButton` Method

```
void CheckDlgButton( int nIDButton, UINT nCheck );
```

where

    nIDButton   The button to be modified.

    nCheck   0 to uncheck the button, non-zero to check the button. For a three-state button, 2 specifies the indeterminate state.

The `CheckDlgButton` method is used to check dialog buttons that support being checked. These include buttons such as radio buttons or check boxes.

The `CheckRadioButton` Method

```
void CheckRadioButton( int nIDFirstButton, int nIDLastButton, int
➡nIDCheckButton );
```

where

    nIDFirstButton   The first button in a group of radio buttons.

    nIDLastButton   The last button in a group of radio buttons.

    nIDCheckButton   The button that should be checked.

The CheckRadioButton method will first clear the check from each button in the group. Then the button specified by *nIDCheckButton* will be checked.

The ChildWindowFromPoint Method

```
CWnd* ChildWindowFromPoint( POINT point ) const;
CWnd* ChildWindowFromPoint( POINT point, UINT nFlags ) const;
```

where

point	The point being checked.
nFlags	Specifies which windows are to be checked.

Returns a pointer to the child window that this point falls in. Returns NULL if the call was not successful.

Valid values for *nFlags* include

CWP_ALL	Do not skip any child windows
CWP_SKIPINVISIBLE	Skip invisible child windows
CWP_SKIPDISABLED	Skip disabled windows
CWP_SKIPTRANSPARENT	Skip transparent windows

The ChildWindowFromPoint method will determine which child window the specified point falls within.

The ClientToScreen Method

```
void ClientToScreen( LPPOINT lpPoint ) const;
void ClientToScreen( LPRECT lpRect ) const;
```

where

lpPoint	A point to convert to screen coordinates.
lpRect	A rectangle to convert to screen coordinates.

The ClientToScreen method will convert client-relative coordinates to screen coordinates.

The ContinueModal Method

```
virtual BOOL ContinueModal();
```

Returns TRUE if the modal state should continue.

The ContinueModal method determines whether the modal loop should continue. By default, this method returns zero until EndModalLoop is called.

The Create Method

```
virtual BOOL Create( LPCTSTR lpszClassName, LPCTSTR lpszWindowName, DWORD
➥dwStyle, const RECT& rect, CWnd* pParentWnd, UINT nID,
➥CCreateContext* pContext = NULL);
```

where

lpszClassName	The window class. Should be any name registered with the AfxRegisterWndClass global method. If NULL, will use the default Windows class.
lpszWindowName	The window name.

dwStyle	The window style.
rect	The size and position of the window.
pParentWnd	The parent window.
nID	The ID of the child window.
pContext	The create context.

Returns TRUE if successful.

The Create method will create a window with the given specifications.

The CreateCaret Method

```
void CreateCaret( CBitmap* pBitmap );
```

where

| pBitmap | A bitmap that defines the caret shape. |

The CreateCaret method changes the shape of the system caret.

The CreateControl Method

```
BOOL CWnd::CreateControl( LPCTSTR lpszClass, LPCTSTR lpszWindowName, DWORD
➥dwStyle, const RECT& rect, CWnd* pParentWnd, UINT nID, CFile*
➥pPersist = NULL, BOOL bStorage = FALSE, BSTR bstrLicKey = NULL );
BOOL CWnd::CreateControl( REFCLSID clsid, LPCTSTR lpszWindowName, DWORD
➥dwStyle, const RECT& rect, CWnd* pParentWnd, UINT nID, CFile*
➥pPersist = NULL, BOOL bStorage = FALSE, BSTR bstrLicKey = NULL );
```

where

lpszClassName	An OLE "short name" (ProgID) for the class. The name must match the Registry entry for the control. This parameter may also be a CLSID in braces form {C7DDB9B1-4658-11d2-8176-644A03000000}.
lpszWindowName	The window name.
dwStyle	The window style.
rect	The size and position of the window.
pParentWnd	The parent window.
nID	The ID of the child window.
pPersist	A pointer to a CFile object. If specified, this file should contain persistent state information about the control.
bStorage	If TRUE, the data in the file is stored as IStorage; otherwise, it is IStream data.
bstrLicKey	License information.
clsid	The class ID of this control.

The CreateControl method creates a CWnd object that represents a control.

The `CreateEx` Method

```
BOOL CreateEx( DWORD dwExStyle, LPCTSTR lpszClassName, LPCTSTR
➥lpszWindowName, DWORD dwStyle, int x, int y, int nWidth, int
➥nHeight, HWND hwndParent, HMENU nIDorHMenu, LPVOID lpParam = NULL );
BOOL CreateEx(DWORD dwExStyle, LPCTSTR lpszClassName, LPCTSTR lpszWindowName,
➥DWORD dwStyle, const RECT& rect, CWnd* pParentWnd, UINT nID, LPVOID
➥lpParam = NULL);
```

where

dwExStyle	The extended window style.
lpszClassName	The window class. Should be any name registered with the `AfxRegisterWndClass` global method. If NULL, will use the default Windows class.
lpszWindowName	The window name.
dwStyle	The window style.
rect	The size and position of the window.
x	The x coordinate of the window.
y	The y coordinate of the window.
nWidth	The width of the window.
nHeight	The height of the window.
hwndParent	The parent window.
nIDorHMenu	The menu ID.
lpParam	Pointer to the data referenced by the *lpCreateParams* field of CREATESTRUCT.
pParentWnd	The parent window.
nID	The ID of the child window.
pContext	The create context.

Returns TRUE if successful.

The `CreateEx` method will create a window with the given specifications.

The `CreateGrayCaret` Method

```
void CreateGrayCaret( int nWidth, int nHeight );
```

where

nWidth	The width of the caret in logical units. If 0, the width is set to a system-defined border width.
nHeight	The height of the caret in logical units. If 0, the width is set to a system-defined border height.

The `CreateGrayCaret` method changes the system caret to a gray caret.

The `CreateSolidCaret` Method

`void CreateSolidCaret( int nWidth, int nHeight );`

where

nWidth	The width of the caret in logical units. If 0, the width is set to a system-defined border width.
nHeight	The height of the caret in logical units. If 0, the width is set to a system-defined border height.

The `CreateSolidCaret` method changes the system caret to a solid caret.

The `Default` Method

`LRESULT Default( );`

Return value is dependent on the message sent.

The `Default` method calls the Windows default procedure for any message. This method ensures that every message is processed.

The `DeleteTempMap` Method

`static void PASCAL DeleteTempMap();`

The `DeleteTempMap` method deletes any temporary `CWnd` objects created by the `FromHandle` method.

The `DestroyWindow` Method

`virtual BOOL DestroyWindow();`

Returns `TRUE` if successful.

The `DestroyWindow` method is called to destroy the window.

The `Detach` Method

`virtual HWND Destach();`

Returns the `HWND` associated with this window.

The `Detach` method disassociates the underlying `HWND` from this object.

The `DlgDirList` Method

`int DlgDirList( LPTSTR lpPathSpec, int nIDListBox, int nIDStaticPath,`
`➥UINT nFileType );`

where

lpPathSpec	Pointer to a `NULL`-terminated filename or path.
nIDListBox	The list box to fill. Specify 0 to not fill a list box.
nIDStaticPath	Specifies the static text control to display the current drive and directory. If 0, no static text control is updated.
nFileType	Specifies the attributes of the files to be displayed. Can be any of the following: `DDL_READWRITE`, `DDL_READONLY`, `DDL_HIDDEN`, `DDL_SYSTEM`, `DDL_DIRECTORY`, `DDL_ARCHIVE`, `DDL_DRIVES`, `DDL_EXCLUSIVE`, or `DDL_POSTMSGS`.

Returns `TRUE` if successful.

The `DlgDirList` method will fill a list box with a file or directory listing.

C

The `DlgDirListComboBox` Method

```
int DlgDirListComboBox( LPTSTR lpPathSpec, int nIDComboBox, int
➥nIDStaticPath, UINT nFileType );
```

where

lpPathSpec	Pointer to a NULL-terminated filename or path.
nIDComboBox	The combo box to fill. Specify 0 to not fill a list box.
nIDStaticPath	Specifies the static text control to display the current drive and directory. If 0, no static text control is updated.
nFileType	Specifies the attributes of the files to be displayed. Can be any of the following: DDL_READWRITE, DDL_READONLY, DDL_HIDDEN, DDL_SYSTEM, DDL_DIRECTORY, DDL_ARCHIVE, DDL_DRIVES, DDL_EXCLUSIVE, or DDL_POSTMSGS.

Returns TRUE if successful.

The `DlgDirListComboBox` method will fill a combo box with a file or directory listing.

The `DlgDirSelect` Method

```
BOOL DlgDirSelect( LPTSTR lpString, int nIDListBox );
```

where

lpString	String that will receive the current selection.
nIDListBox	The list box to query.

Returns TRUE if successful.

The `DlgDirSelect` method will return what is selected in a directory list box.

The `DlgDirSelectComboBox` Method

```
BOOL DlgDirSelectComboBox( LPTSTR lpString, int nIDListBox );
```

where

lpString	String that will receive the current selection.
nIDComboBox	The combo box to query.

Returns TRUE if successful.

The `DlgDirSelectComboBox` method will return what is selected in a directory combo box.

The `DragAcceptFiles` Method

```
void DragAcceptFiles( BOOL bAccept = TRUE );
```

where

bAccept	Flag that indicates whether to accept dragged files.

The `DragAcceptFiles` method determines whether this window will accept dragged files.

The `DrawMenuBar` Method

```
BOOL DrawMenuBar( HWND hWnd );
```

where

    hWnd   The window whose menu bar should be redrawn.

The `DrawMenuBar` method draws the menu bar for the specified window.

The `EnableScrollBar` Method

```
BOOL EnableScrollBar( int nSBFlags, UINT nArrowFlags = ESB_ENABLE_BOTH );
```

where

    nSBFlags   Specifies the sort of scrollbars desired. Should be SB_BOTH, SB_HORZ, or SB_VERT.

    nArrowFlags   Specifies whether the scrollbar arrows are enabled or disabled. Should be ESB_ENABLE_BOTH, ESB_DISABLE_LTUP, ESB_DISABLE_RTDN, or ESB_DISABLE_BOTH.

Returns TRUE if successful.

The `EnableScrollBar` method enables the default scrollbars for the window.

The `EnableScrollBarCtrl` Method

```
void EnableScrollBarCtrl( int nBar, BOOL bEnable = TRUE );
```

where

    nBar   Specifies the scrollbar to be modified.

    bEnable   Specifies whether the scrollbar is enabled or disabled.

The `EnableScrollBarCtrl` method enables or disables the specified scrollbar.

The `EnableToolTips` Method

```
BOOL EnableToolTips( BOOL bEnable );
```

where

    bEnable   TRUE if tooltips are to be enabled.

Returns TRUE if successful.

The `EnableToolTips` method is called to enable or disable tool tips.

The `EnableWindow` Method

```
BOOL EnableWindow( BOOL bEnable = TRUE);
```

where

    bEnable   TRUE if window should be enabled.

Returns TRUE if successful.

The `EnableWindow` method is called to enable or disable the window.

C

The `EndModalLoop` Method

```
void EndModalLoop( int nResult );
```

where

> nResult   The value that should be returned to the caller of `RunModalLoop`.

The `EndModalLoop` method will terminate a call to `RunModalLoop`.

The `EndPaint` Method

```
void EndPaint( LPPAINTSTRUCT lpPaint );
```

where

> lpPaint   Pointer to a paint structure that was obtained from a call to `BeginPaint`.

The `EndPaint` method is called after a window update is complete. `EndPaint` should only be called with a paint structure returned from a `BeginPaint` call.

The `ExecuteDlgInit` Method

```
BOOL ExecuteDlgInit( LPCTSTR lpszResourceName );
BOOL ExecuteDlgInit( LPVOID lpResource );
```

where

> lpszResourceName   A resource item's name.
>
> lpResource   A resource pointer.

Returns TRUE if successful.

The `ExecuteDlgInit` method will prepare a dialog resource for use.

The `FilterToolTipMessage` Method

```
void FilterToolTipMessage( MSG *pMsg );
```

where

> pMsg   A pointer to a tooltip message.
>
> lpResource   A resource pointer.

The `FilterToolTipMessage` method will display the proper tooltip in response to a message. Usually called by the `PreTranslateMessage` method.

The `FindWindow` Method

```
static CWnd* PASCAL FindWindow( LPCTSTR lpszClassName, LPCTSTR
➥lpszWindowName );
```

where

> lpszClassName   The class name being searched for. NULL if the class name does not
>   matter.
>
> lpszWindowName   The window name of the window being searched for. NULL if the win-
>   dow name does not matter.

Returns a temporary pointer to the window object.

The `FindWindowMethod` can be used to search through all child windows for a specific window.

The `FlashWindow` Method

`BOOL FlashWindow( BOOL bInvert );`

where

    bInvert   Specifies if the window is to be flashed or returned to its original state.

Returns TRUE if the window was active before the call.

The `FlashWindow` method will flash the window once.

The `FromHandle` Method

`static CWnd* PASCAL FromHandle( HWND hWnd );`

where

    hWnd   A window handle to be expressed as a CWnd object.

Returns a CWnd object that represents the *hWnd* object.

The `FromHandle` method creates a temporary CWnd object for the *hWnd* parameter.

The `FromHandlePermanent` Method

`static CWnd* PASCAL FromHandlePermanent( HWND hWnd );`

where

    hWnd   A window handle to be expressed as a CWnd object.

Returns a CWnd object that represents the *hWnd* object.

The `FromHandlePermanent` method creates a CWnd object for the *hWnd* parameter.

The `GetActiveWindow` Method

`static CWnd* PASCAL GetActiveWindow( );`

Returns a temporary pointer to the current window.

The `GetCapture` Method

`static CWnd* PASCAL GetCapture( );`

Returns a temporary pointer to the window that has captured the mouse.

The `GetCaretPos` Method

`static CPoint PASCAL GetCaretPos( );`

Returns the coordinates of the caret.

The `GetCheckedRadioButton` Method

`int GetCheckedRadioButton( int nIDFirstButton, int nIDLastButton );`

where

    nIDFirstButton   The first button in a radio button group.

    nIDLastButton   The last button in a radio button group.

Returns the selected radio button of the group.

The `GetClientRect` Method

`void GetClientRect(LPRECT lpRect);`

where

    lpRect   A rectangle structure to contain the client area.

The `GetClientRect` method will get the rectangle occupied by the client region, in client coordinates.

The `GetClipboardOwner` Method

`static CWnd* PASCAL GetClipboardOwner( );`

Returns a temporary pointer to the window that owns the Clipboard.

The `GetClipboardViewer` Method

`static CWnd* PASCAL GetClipboardViewer( );`

Returns a temporary pointer to the window that is the Clipboard viewer.

The `GetControlUnknown` Method

`LPUNKNOWN GetControlUnknown();`

Returns a pointer to IUnknown interface for the OLE control.

The `GetCurrentMessage` Method

`static const MSG* PASCAL GetCurrentMessage( );`

Returns a pointer to current message.

The `GetDC` Method

`CDC *GetDC();`

Returns a newly created device context for this window.

The `GetDCEx` Method

`CDC* GetDCEx( CRgn* prgnClip, DWORD flags );`

where

    prgnClip   A region to be combined with the visible region of the window.

    flags   Specifies the type of DC being sought.

Returns a newly created device context for this window.

Valid values for flags include

`DCX_CACHE`	Returns a device context from the cache.
`DCX_CLIPCHILDREN`	Excludes the visible regions of all children.
`DCX_CLIPSIBLINGS`	Excludes the visible regions of all siblings.
`DCX_EXCLUDERGN`	Excludes the clipping region identified by `prgnClip`.
`DCX_INTERSECTRGN`	Intersects the region specified by `prgnClip` with the visible region.
`DCX_LOCKWINDOWUPDATE`	Allows drawing even if there is a `LockWindowUpdate` call in effect.

| DCX_PARENTCLIP | Uses the visible region of the parent. |
| DCX_WINDOW | Returns a device context for the window rather than the client area. |

The `CreateDCEx` method will create a specialized device context for the window.

The `GetDescendantWindow` Method

`CWnd* GetDescendantWindow( int nID, BOOL bOnlyPerm = FALSE ) const;`

where

| *nID* | Specifies the identifier of the control or child window. |
| *bOnlyPerm* | Specifies whether the returned CWnd should be a permanent object. |

Returns a CWnd object for one of the descendants of this window.

The `GetDesktopWindow` Method

`static CWnd* PASCAL GetDesktopWindow( );`

Returns a temporary pointer to the desktop window.

The `GetDlgCtrlID` Method

`int GetDlgCtrlID( ) const;`

Returns the control ID for this window.

The `GetDlgItem` Method

`CWnd* GetDlgItem( int nID ) const;`
`void GetDlgItem( int nID, HWND* phWnd ) const;`

where

| *nID* | Specifies the dialog item. |
| *phWnd* | A pointer to a handle that will receive the HWND for that dialog item. |

Returns a temporary CWnd for the specified dialog box item.

The `GetDlgItemInt` Method

`UINT GetDlgItemInt( int nID, BOOL* lpTrans = NULL, BOOL bSigned = TRUE )`
`➡const;`

where

nID	Specifies the dialog item.
lpTrans	A pointer to a BOOL that receives a TRUE if successful, or a FALSE if failure.
bSigned	TRUE if the value may have a + or – sign.

Returns an integer representing the value of the specified dialog item.

The `GetDlgItemText` Method

`int GetDlgItemText( int nID, LPTSTR lpStr, int nMaxCount ) const;`
`int GetDlgItemText( int nID, CString& rString ) const;`

where

nID	Specifies the dialog item.
lpStr	Pointer to a string to receive the control's title or text.
nMaxCount	The maximum number of characters that can be copied to *lpStr*.
string	A string object to receive the control's title or text.

Returns the number of bytes copied.

The GetDlgItemText method will retrieve a dialog box control item's title or text.

The GetDSCCursor Method

IUnknown *GetDSCCursor();

Returns the data source control for this window.

The GetExStyle Method

DWORD GetExStyle() const;

Returns the window's extended style.

The GetFocus Method

static CWnd* PASCAL GetFocus( );

Returns a temporary pointer to the window that has focus.

The GetFont Method

CFont* GetFont( );

Returns a temporary pointer to the font for this window.

The GetForegroundWindow Method

static CWnd* PASCAL GetForegroundWindow( );

Returns a temporary pointer to the foreground window.

The GetIcon Method

HICON GetIcon(BOOL bBigIcon) const;

where

     bBigIcon   If TRUE, a 32×32 icon is returned; otherwise, a 16×16 icon is returned.

Returns the icon associated with this window.

The GetLastActivePopup Method

CWnd* GetLastActivePopup( ) const;

Returns the window for the last active pop-up window.

The GetMenu Method

CMenu* GetMenu( ) const;

Returns a temporary CMenu object for this window's menu bar.

The `GetNextDlgGroupItem` Method

`CWnd* GetNextDlgGroupItem( CWnd* pWndCtl, BOOL bPrevious = FALSE ) const;`

where

pWndCtl	The control to be used as a starting point.
bPrevious	If TRUE, the previous button is sought. If FALSE, the next button is sought.

Returns a temporary pointer to the next or previous item in a group of controls.

The `GetNextDlgTabItem` Method

`CWnd* GetNextDlgTabItem( CWnd* pWndCtl, BOOL bPrevious = FALSE ) const;`

where

pWndCtl	The control to be used as a starting point.
bPrevious	If TRUE, the previous button is sought. If FALSE, the next button is sought.

Returns a temporary pointer to the next or previous item in tab order.

The `GetNextWindow` Method

`CWnd* GetNextWindow( UINT nFlag = GW_HWNDNEXT ) const;`

where

nFlag	GW_HWNDNEXT if the next window is sought, or GW_HWNDPREV if the previous window is sought.

Returns a temporary pointer to the next or previous window.

The `GetNextWindow` Method

`CWnd* GetNextWindow( UINT nFlag = GW_HWNDNEXT ) const;`

where

nFlag	GW_HWNDNEXT if the next window is sought, or GW_HWNDPREV if the previous window is sought.

Returns a temporary pointer to the next or previous window.

The `GetOpenClipboardWindow` Method

`static CWnd* PASCAL GetOpenClipboardWindow( );`

Returns a temporary pointer to the window that has the clipboard open.

The `GetOwner` Method

`CWnd* GetOwner( ) const;`

Returns a temporary pointer to the window that owns this one.

The `GetParent` Method

`CWnd* GetParent( ) const;`

Returns a temporary pointer to the window that is the parent of this one.

The `GetParentFrame` Method

`CFrameWnd* GetParentFrame( ) const;`

Returns a temporary pointer to the frame window for this child window.

The `GetParentOwner` Method

`CWnd* GetParentOwner( ) const;`

Returns a temporary pointer to the owner of this window's parent.

The `GetProperty` Method

`void GetProperty( DISPID dwDispID, VARTYPE vtProp, void* pvProp )const;`

where

dwDispID	The property to be retrieved. Usually filled in by component gallery.
vtProp	The type of property to be retrieved. Should be a `VT_` constant such as `VT_BSTR` or `VT_VARIANT`.
pvProp	Address of the variable to receive the property.

The `GetProperty` method is used to read a property from a control.

The `GetSafeHwnd` Method

`HWND GetSafeHwnd( ) const;`

Returns the window handle for this window.

The `GetSafeOwner` Method

`CWnd* PASCAL GetSafeOwner( CWnd* pParent, HWND* pWndTop );`

where

pParent	A pointer to a parent window.
pWndTop	A pointer to a window that is currently on top.

Returns the owner window that should be used as the parent window for dialog boxes.

The `GetScrollBarCtrl` Method

`virtual CScrollBar* GetScrollBarCtrl( int nBar ) const;`

where

nBar	The bar to be retrieved; should be either `SB_HORZ` or `SB_VERT`.

Returns a pointer to either one of the standard scrollbars for a window.

The `GetScrollInfo` Method

`BOOL GetScrollInfo( int nBar, LPSCROLLINFO lpScrollInfo );`

where

nBar	The bar to be retrieved; should be either SB_HORZ or SB_VERT.
lpScrollInfo	A structure to hold information about the specified scrollbar.

Returns TRUE if successful.

The `GetScrollLimit` Method

```
int GetScrollLimit( int nBar );
```

where

> *nBar*   The bar to be retrieved; should be either SB_HORZ or SB_VERT.

Returns the maximum scrolling limit of the specified scrollbar.

The `GetScrollPos` Method

```
int GetScrollPos( int nBar );
```

where

> *nBar*   The bar to be retrieved, should be either SB_HORZ or SB_VERT.

Returns the current position of the specified scrollbar.

The `GetScrollRange` Method

```
void GetScrollRange( int nBar, LPINT lpMinPos, LPINT lpMaxPos ) const;
```

where

nBar	The bar to be retrieved; should be either SB_HORZ or SB_VERT.
lpMinPos	The integer variable that is to receive the minimum position.
lpMaxPos	The integer variable that is to receive the maximum position.

The GetScrollRange method is called to retrieve the allowable range of values for a scrollbar.

The `GetStyle` Method

```
DWORD GetStyle( ) const;
```

Returns the window's style.

The `GetSystemMenu` Method

```
CMenu* GetSystemMenu( BOOL bRevert ) const;
```

where

> *bRevert*   TRUE if the system menu should be reverted back to its initial state.

Returns a temporary pointer to the system menu.

The `GetStyle` Method

```
DWORD GetStyle() const;
```

Returns the window style.

The `GetTopLevelFrame` Method

```
CFrameWnd* GetTopLevelFrame( ) const;
```

Returns a temporary pointer to the top-level window frame.

The `GetTopLevelOwner` Method

`CWnd* GetTopLevelOwner( ) const;`

Returns a temporary pointer to the owner of the top-level window frame.

The `GetTopLevelParent` Method

`CWnd* GetTopLevelParent( ) const;`

Returns a temporary pointer to the parent of the top-level window frame.

The `GetTopWindow` Method

`CWnd* GetTopWindow( ) const;`

Returns a temporary pointer to the top-level window frame.

The `GetUpdateRect` Method

`BOOL GetUpdateRect( LPRECT lpRect, BOOL bErase = FALSE );`

where

lpRect	Pointer to a rectangle to receive the bounding rectangle for the update region.
bErase	TRUE if the update region should be erased.

Returns TRUE if successful.

The GetUpdateRect method is called to retrieve the bounding rectangle for the update region.

The `GetUpdateRgn` Method

`BOOL GetUpdateRect( CRgn *pRgn, BOOL bErase = FALSE );`

where

pRgn	Pointer to a region to receive the update region for this window.
bErase	TRUE if the update region should be erased.

Returns TRUE if successful.

The GetUpdateRgn method is called to retrieve the update region for this window.

The `GetWindow` Method

`CWnd* GetWindow( UINT nCmd ) const;`

where

nCmd	Specifies the type of window being sought.

Returns a pointer to the window being sought or NULL if it cannot be found.

Valid values for nCmd include

GW_CHILD	Finds the first child window of this window.
GW_HWNDFIRST	Finds the first sibling window of this window.
GW_HWNDLAST	Finds the last sibling window of this window.
GW_HWNDNEXT	Returns the next window.
GW_HWNDPREV	Returns the previous window.
GW_OWNER	Returns the owner.

The `GetWindowContextHelpId` Method

DWORD GetWindowContextHelpId( ) const;

Returns the help context ID for this window.

The `GetWindowDC` Method

CDC* GetWindowDC( );

Returns a device context for the entire window, not just the client area.

The `GetWindowPlacement` Method

BOOL GetWindowPlacement(WINDOWPLACEMENT* lpwndpl) const;

where

    lpwndpl   Pointer to a window placement structure.

Returns TRUE if successful.

The GetWindowPlacement method gets the window's placement.

The `GetWindowRect` Method

void GetWindowRect(LPRECT lpRect) const;

where

    lpRect   A rectangle structure to contain the window area.

The GetWindowRect method will get the rectangle occupied by the window, in screen coordinates.

The `GetWindowRgn` Method

int GetWindowRgn(HRGN hRgn)const;

where

    hRgn   A region to be set to the region occupied by the window.

Returns NULLREGION if the region is empty, SIMPLEREGION if the region is a rectangle, COMPLEXREGION if the region is more than a rectangle, or ERROR if an error occurs.

The GetWindowRgn method will get the region occupied by the window, in screen coordinates.

The `GetWindowText` Method

int GetWindowText(LPTSTR lpszStringBuf, int nMaxCount) const;
void GetWindowText(CString& rString) const;

where

    lpszStringBuf   Pointer to a string to receive the window's title or text.

    nMaxCount   The maximum number of characters that can be copied to *lpszStringBuf*.

    rString   A string object to receive the control's title or text.

Returns the number of bytes copied.

The GetWindowText method will copy the window's title or text to a specified string.

The `GetWindowTextLength` Method

```
int GetWindowTextLength( ) const;
```

Returns the number of bytes in the window's title or text.

The `HideCaret` Method

```
void HideCaret( );
```

The `HideCaret` method will hide the caret.

The `HiliteMenuItem` Method

```
BOOL HiliteMenuItem( CMenu* pMenu, UINT nIDHiliteItem, UINT nHilite );
```

where

pMenu	The top-level menu that contains the item to be highlighted.
nIDHiliteItem	The ID of the item to be highlighted.
nHilite	Specifies whether the menu item is highlighted or removed. Also specifies whether *nIDHiliteItem* is a position or command ID. The flags `MF_HILITE` and `MF_UNHILITE` specify the highlight status. The flags `MF_BYCOMMAND` and `MF_BYPOSITION` specify the meaning of *nIDHiliteItem*.

Returns `TRUE` if the item was highlighted.

The `HiliteMenuItem` method will highlight a menu item.

The `Invalidate` Method

```
void Invalidate( BOOL bErase = TRUE );
```

where

bErase	Specifies whether the backround should be erased.

The `Invalidate` method will invalidate the entire window.

The `InvalidateRect` Method

```
void InvalidateRect( LPRECT lpRect, BOOL bErase = TRUE );
```

where

lpRect	Specifies rectangle to invalidate. Can be `NULL` to invalidate the entire window.
bErase	Specifies whether the background should be erased.

The `InvalidateRect` method will invalidate part of the window.

The `InvalidateRgn` Method

```
void InvalidateRgn( CRgn* pRgn, BOOL bErase = TRUE );
```

where

pRgn	Specifies region to invalidate.
bErase	Specifies whether the background should be erased.

The `InvalidateRgn` method will invalidate the specified region.

The **InvokeHelper** Method

```
void InvokeHelper( DISPID dwDispID, WORD wFlags, VARTYPE vtRet, void*
➥pvRet, const BYTE* pbParamInfo, ... );
```

where

dwDispID	Specifies the dispatch ID of the method to be invoked.
bFlags	Specifies the context of the call.
vtRet	Specifies the type return value.
pvRet	Specifies the return value.

The InvokeHelper method will call an OLE method.

The InvokeHelper method can throw the COleException or the COleDispatchException exceptions.

The **IsChild** Method

```
BOOL IsChild( const CWnd* pWnd ) const;
```

where

pWnd	Specifies the window to test.

Returns TRUE if *pWnd* is a child of this window.

The **IsDialogMessage** Method

```
BOOL IsDialogMessage( LPMSG lpMsg );
```

where

lpMsg	Specifies the message to test.

Returns TRUE if message is a dialog message.

The **IsDlgButtonChecked** Method

```
UINT IsDlgButtonChecked( int nIDButton ) const;
```

where

nIDButton	The dialog button to check.

Returns TRUE if specified dialog button is checked.

The **IsIconic** Method

```
BOOL IsIconic( ) const;
```

Returns TRUE if the window is minimized.

The **IsWindowEnabled** Method

```
BOOL IsWindowEnabled( ) const;
```

Returns TRUE if the window is enabled.

The **IsWindowVisible** Method

```
BOOL IsWindowVisible( ) const;
```

Returns TRUE if the window is visible.

The `IsZoomed` Method

```
BOOL IsZoomed( ) const;
```

Returns TRUE if the window is zoomed.

The `KillTimer` Method

```
BOOL KillTimer( int nIDEvent );
```

where

    nIDEvent   The timer to kill.

Returns TRUE if successful.

The KillTimer method will kill the specified timer.

The `LockWindowUpdate` Method

```
BOOL LockWindowUpdate( );
```

Returns TRUE if successful.

The LockWindowUpdate method will prevent drawing from occurring on the menu until it is unlocked.

The `MapWindowPoints` Method

```
void MapWindowPoints( CWnd* pwndTo, LPRECT lpRect ) const;
void MapWindowPoints( CWnd* pwndTo, LPPOINT lpPoint, UINT nCount ) const;
```

where

pwndTo	The window to map to.
lpRect	The rectangle to map.
lpPoint	The array of points to map.
nCount	How many points in the array.

The MapWindowPoints method will map the specified points from the current window's coordinates to the specified window's coordinates.

The `MessageBox` Method

```
int MessageBox( LPCTSTR lpszText, LPCTSTR lpszCaption = NULL, UINT nType =
➡ MB_OK );
```

where

lpszText	The text for the message box.
lpszCaption	The caption for the message box. If NULL, the message box's parent's title will be used.
nType	The type of message box to display.

Return value is dependent on the type of message box used.

The MessageBox method displays a simple message box to convey information to the user.

The `ModifyStyle` Method

```
BOOL ModifyStyle( DWORD dwRemove, DWORD dwAdd, UINT nFlags = 0 );
```

where

dwRemove	Specifies the window styles to be removed.
dwAdd	Specifies the window styles to be added.
nFlags	Specifies the flags to be passed to SetWindowPos.

Returns TRUE if successful.

The ModifyStyle method allows the window style to be modified.

The ModifyStyleEx Method

```
BOOL ModifyStyleEx( DWORD dwRemove, DWORD dwAdd, UINT nFlags = 0 );
```

where

dwRemove	Specifies the window styles to be removed.
dwAdd	Specifies the window styles to be added.
nFlags	Specifies the flags to be passed to SetWindowPos.

Returns TRUE if successful.

The ModifyStyleEx method allows the window's extended style to be modified.

The MoveWindow Method

```
void MoveWindow( int x, int y, int nWidth, int nHeight, BOOL bRepaint =
➡ TRUE );
void MoveWindow( LPCRECT lpRect, BOOL bRepaint = TRUE );
```

where

x	The new x coordinate for the window.
y	The new y coordinate for the window.
nWidth	The new width for the window.
nHeight	The new height for the window.
bRepaint	TRUE if the window should be repainted.
lpRect	The new rectangle to be occupied by the window. Specifies both location and size.

The MoveWindow method both moves and resizes the window.

The OnAmbientProperty Method

```
BOOL OnAmbientProperty( COleControlSite* pSite, DISPID dispid, VARIANT* pvar )
```

where

pSite	The site of the control that requested the property.
dispid	The dispatch ID of the requested ambient property.
pvar	The caller-allocated variant structure that the ambient property will return.

The OnAmbientProperty method is called by the framework to obtain ambient property values from a window that contains OLE controls.

The `OnToolHitTest` Method

```
virtual int OnToolHitTest( CPoint point, TOOLINFO* pTI ) const;
```

where

point	The coordinates of the cursor.
pTI	A `TOOLINFO` structure.

The `OnToolHitTest` is called by the framework to determine whether the cursor is in a position that requires a tooltip help message to be displayed.

The `OpenClipboard` Method

```
BOOL OpenClipboard( );
```

Returns `TRUE` if the Clipboard was successfully opened.

The `PostMessage` Method

```
BOOL PostMessage( UINT message, WPARAM wParam = 0, LPARAM lParam = 0 );
```

where

message	The message ID to be posted.
wParam	The wparam value for this message.
lparam	The lparam value for this message.

Return value is dependent on which message is sent.

The `PostMessage` method will post the specified message to this window's message queue.

The `PreCreateWindow` Method

```
virtual BOOL PreCreateWindow( CREATESTRUCT& cs );
```

where

cs	The `CREATESTRUCT` structure for this window.

Returns `TRUE` if the window creation should continue.

The `PreCreateWindow` method is called by the framework just before a window is created.

The `PreSubclassWindow` Method

```
virtual void PreSubclassWindow( );
```

The `PreSubclassWindow` is called just before the window is subclassed. Overriding this method allows processing to be done before the window is subclassed.

The `PreTranslateMessage` Method

```
virtual BOOL PreTranslateMessage( MSG* pMsg );
```

where

pMsg	The message about to be translated.

Returns `TRUE` if the translation should continue.

The `PreTranslate` method is called by MFC just before the specified message is translated.

The Print Method

```
void Print( CDC* pDC, DWORD dwFlags ) const;
```

where

pDC	The device context to output to. Usually a printer device context.
dwFlags	Specifies drawing options.

The following values are valid for the *dwFlags* parameter:

PRF_CHECKVISIBLE	Draw only if the window is visible.
PRF_CHILDREN	Draw all visible children.
PRF_CLIENT	Draw the client area of the window.
PRF_ERASEBKGND	Erase the background before drawing the window.
PRF_NONCLIENT	Draw the non-client area of the window.
PRF_OWNED	Draw all owned windows.

The Print method is called to print the window.

The PrintClient Method

```
void PrintClient( CDC* pDC, DWORD dwFlags ) const;
```

where

pDC	The device context to output to. Usually a printer device context.
dwFlags	Specifies drawing options.

The following values are valid for the dwFlags parameter:

PRF_CHECKVISIBLE	Draw only if the window is visible.
PRF_CHILDREN	Draw all visible children.
PRF_CLIENT	Draw the client area of the window.
PRF_ERASEBKGND	Erase the background before drawing the window.
PRF_NONCLIENT	Draw the non-client area of the window.
PRF_OWNED	Draw all owned windows.

The PrintClient method is called to print the client region.

The RedrawWindow Method

```
BOOL RedrawWindow( LPCRECT lpRectUpdate = NULL, CRgn* prgnUpdate = NULL,
►UINT flags = RDW_INVALIDATE ¦ RDW_UPDATENOW ¦ RDW_ERASE );
```

where

lpRectUpdate	The update rectangle for the window.
prgnUpdate	The update region for the window.
flags	Specifies how the redraw should be done.

Returns TRUE if successful.

The following values are valid for the *flags* parameter:

C

RDW_ERASE	Causes the window to receive a WM_ERASEBKGND message when the window is repainted. The RDW_INVALIDATE flag must also be specified; otherwise, RDW_ERASE has no effect.
RDW_FRAME	Causes any part of the nonclient area of the window that intersects the update region to receive a WM_NCPAINT message. The RDW_INVALIDATE flag must also be specified; otherwise, RDW_FRAME has no effect.
RDW_INTERNALPAINT	Causes a WM_PAINT message to be posted to the window regardless of whether the window contains an invalid region.
RDW_INVALIDATE	Invalidate lpRectUpdate or prgnUpdate (only one may be not NULL). If both are NULL, the entire window is invalidated.

The following flags are used to validate the window:

RDW_NOERASE	Does not process any WM_ERASEBKGND messages.
RDW_NOFRAME	Does not process any WM_NCPAINT messages.
RDW_NOINTERNALPAINT	Does not process any internal WM_PAINT messages. This flag does not affect WM_PAINT messages resulting from invalid areas.
RDW_VALIDATE	Validates lpRectUpdate or prgnUpdate (only one may be not NULL). If both are NULL, the entire window is validated. This flag does not affect internal WM_PAINT messages.
RDW_ERASENOW	Causes the affected windows (as specified by the RDW_ALLCHILDREN and RDW_NOCHILDREN flags) to receive WM_NCPAINT and WM_ERASEBKGND messages, if necessary, before the function returns. WM_PAINT messages are deferred.
RDW_UPDATENOW	Causes the affected windows (as specified by the RDW_ALLCHILDREN and RDW_NOCHILDREN flags) to receive WM_NCPAINT, WM_ERASEBKGND, and WM_PAINT messages, if necessary, before the function returns.
RDW_ALLCHILDREN	Includes child windows, if any, in the repainting operation.
RDW_NOCHILDREN	Excludes child windows, if any, from the repainting operation.

The RedrawWindow method is used to redraw the window.

The **ReleaseDC** Method

```
int ReleaseDC( CDC* pDC );
```

where

| pDC | The device context to be released. |

Returns TRUE if successful.

The ReleaseDC method will release a device context that was obtained with the GetDC method.

The **RepositionBars** Method

```
void RepositionBars( UINT nIDFirst, UINT nIDLast, UINT nIDLeftOver, UINT
➥nFlag = CWnd::reposDefault, LPRECT lpRectParam = NULL, LPCRECT
➥lpRectClient = NULL );
```

where

nIDFirst	The first ID in a range of control bars to reposition and resize.
nIDLast	The last ID in a range of control bars to reposition and resize.
nIDLeftOver	The ID of the pane that fills the rest of the client area.
nFlag	Can have one of the following values: CWnd::reposDefault, CWnd::reposQuery, or CWnd::reposExtra.
lpRectParam	A rect structure parameter.
lpRectClient	The available client area.
bStretch	TRUE if the bar should be stretched to the frame.

The RepositionBars method will reposition the control bars on a window after the window is resized.

The RunModalLoop Method

```
int RunModalLoop( DWORD dwFlags );
```
where

| dwFlags | Specifies the window messages to be sent. |

Returns the value specified by the EndModalLopp method.

The following values are valid for the dwFlags parameter:

MLF_NOIDLEMSG	Don't send WM_ENTERIDLE messages to the parent.
MLF_NOKICKIDLE	Don't send WM_KICKIDLE messages to the window.
MLF_SHOWONIDLE	Show the window when the message queue goes idle.

The RunModalLoop method is called to process messages when a window is in a modal state.

The ScreenToClient Method

```
void ScreenToClient( LPPOINT lpPoint ) const;
void ScreenToClient( LPRECT lpRect ) const;
```
where

| lpPoint | A point to convert to client coordinates. |
| lpRect | A rectangle to convert to client coordinates. |

The ClientToScreen method will convert screen relative coordinates to client coordinates.

The ScrollWindow Method

```
void ScrollWindow( int xAmount, int yAmount, LPCRECT lpRect = NULL, LPCRECT
➥lpClipRect = NULL );
```
where

xAmount	The amount to scroll in the x direction. Can be a negative number.
yAmount	The amount to scroll in the y direction. Can be a negative number.
lpRect	The region to scroll.
yAmount	The region to clip to.

The ScrollWindow method will scroll the client region of a window.

The `ScrollWindowEx` Method

```
int ScrollWindowEx( int dx, int dy, LPCRECT lpRectScroll, LPCRECT
➡lpRectClip, CRgn* prgnUpdate, LPRECT lpRectUpdate, UINT flags );
```

where

dx	The amount to scroll in the x direction. Can be a negative number.
dy	The amount to scroll in the y direction. Can be a negative number.
lpRectScroll	The region to scroll.
lpRectClip	The region to clip to.
prgnUpdate	The region that needs to be updated.
lpRectUpdate	The rectangle that needs to be updated.
flags	Flags that specify how to scroll. Should be SW_ERASE, SW_INVALIDATE, or SW_SCROLLCHILDREN.

The `ScrollWindow` method will scroll the client region of a window.

The `SendDlgItemMessage` Method

```
LRESULT SendDlgItemMessage( int nID, UINT message, WPARAM wParam = 0,
➡LPARAM lParam = 0 );
```

where

nID	The dialog item to receive the message.
message	The message ID to be posted.
wParam	The wparam value for this message.
lparam	The lparam value for this message.

The `SendDlgItemMessage` method will send the specified message to one of the dialog item controls.

The `SendMessage` Method

```
LRESULT SendMessage( UINT message, WPARAM wParam = 0, LPARAM lParam = 0 );
```

where

message	The message ID to be posted.
wParam	The wparam value for this message.
lparam	The lparam value for this message.

Return value is dependent on which message is sent.

The `SendMessage` method will directly post the specified message to this window message procedure and not return until it is processed.

The `SendMessageToDescendants` Method

```
void SendMessageToDescendants( UINT message, WPARAM wParam = 0, LPARAM
➡lParam = 0, BOOL bDeep = TRUE, BOOL bOnlyPerm = FALSE );
```

where

message	The message ID to be posted.
wParam	The wparam value for this message.
lparam	The lparam value for this message.

| *bDeep* | If TRUE, the message will be sent to all sub-children. |
| *bOnlyPerm* | If TRUE, the message will be sent to only permanent windows. |

The SendMessageToDescendants method will directly post the specified message to this window message procedure and not return until it is processed.

The `SendNotifyMessage` Method

```
BOOL SendNotifyMessage( UINT message, WPARAM wParam, LPARAM lParam );
```

where

message	The message ID to be posted.
wParam	The wparam value for this message.
lparam	The lparam value for this message.

The SendNotifyMessage method will directly post the specified notification message to this window message procedure and not return until it is processed.

The `SetActiveWindow` Method

```
CWnd* SetActiveWindow( );
```

Returns the window that was last active.

The SetActiveWindow method will set this window to be the active window.

The `SetCapture` Method

```
CWnd* SetCapture( );
```

Returns the window that last captured the mouse.

The SetCapture method will capture the mouse for this window.

The `SetCaretPos` Method

```
static void PASCAL SetCaretPos( POINT point );
```

where

| *point* | The coordinates to move the caret to. |

The SetCaretPos method will move the caret to the specified location.

The `SetCapture` Method

```
HWND SetClipboardViewer( );
```

Returns the next window in the Clipboard viewer chain.

The SetClipboardViewer method adds this window into the Clipboard viewer chain.

The `SetDlgCtrlID` Method

```
int SetDlgCtrlID( int nID );
```

where

| *nID* | The new control ID. |

Returns the previous control ID for this window.

The SetDlgCtrlID method will set the dialog control ID for this window.

The `SetDlgItemInt` Method

```
void SetDlgItemInt( int nID, UINT nValue, BOOL bSigned = TRUE );
```

where

nID	The control ID.
nValue	The control value.
nSigned	TRUE if this is a signed number.

The `SetDlgItemInt` method will set the value of the dialog item as an integer.

The `SetDlgItemText` Method

```
void SetDlgItemText( int nID, LPCTSTR lpszString );
```

where

nID	The control ID.
lpszString	The string value to set the control to.

The `SetDlgItemText` method will set the value of the dialog item as a string.

The `SetFocus` Method

```
CWnd* SetFocus( );
```

Returns the window that was last the focus.

The `SetFocus` method will set this window to be the focus window.

The `SetFont` Method

```
void SetFont( CFont* pFont, BOOL bRedraw = TRUE );
```

where

pFont	The new font.
bRedraw	TRUE if the window should be redrawn.

The `SetFont` method will set the default font for the window.

The `SetForegroundWindow` Method

```
BOOL SetForegroundWindow( );
```

Returns TRUE if successful.

The `SetForegroundWindow` method will set this window to be the foreground window.

The `SetIcon` Method

```
HICON SetIcon( HICON hIcon, BOOL bBigIcon );
```

where

hIcon	The new icon.
bBigIcon	TRUE if the icon is 32×32, FALSE if 16×16.

Returns a handle to the previous icon.

The `SetIcon` method will set the icon for the window.

The `SetIcon` Method

```
BOOL SetMenu( CMenu* pMenu );
```

where

pMenu   The new icon.

Returns TRUE if successful.

The SetMenu method will set the menu for the window to the menu specified.

The `SetOwner` Method

```
void SetOwner( CWnd* pOwnerWnd );
```

where

pOwnerWnd   The new owner window.

The SetOwner method will set the owner for this window.

The `SetParent` Method

```
CWnd* SetParent( CWnd* pWndNewParent );
```

where

pWndNewParent   The new parent window for this window.

Returns the previous parent window.

The SetParent method will set the parent for this window.

The `SetProperty` Method

```
void SetProperty( DISPID dwDispID, VARTYPE vtProp, ... );
```

where

dwDispID   Identifies the property to be set.

vtProp   Identifies the type of the property.

...   A single parameter of the type vtProp.

The SetProperty method will set the specified property in a control window.

The `SetRedraw` Method

```
void SetRedraw( BOOL bRedraw = TRUE );
```

where

bRedraw   Allows or disallows updates.

The SetRedraw method will allow or disallow updates.

The `SetScrollInfo` Method

```
BOOL SetScrollInfo( int nBar, LPSCROLLINFO lpScrollInfo, BOOL bRedraw =
➥TRUE );
```

where

C

nBar	Specifies the scrollbar. Should be SB_HORZ or SB_VERT. Can also be SB_CTL if the m_hwnd member holds the scrollbar handle.
lpScrollInfo	A structure containing information about the scrollbar.
bRedraw	TRUE if the scrollbar should be redrawn.

Returns TRUE if successful.

The SetScrollInfo method will set scrollbar information for the specified scrollbar.

The **SetScrollPos** Method

```
int SetScrollPos( int nBar, int nPos, BOOL bRedraw = TRUE );
```

where

nBar	Specifies the scrollbar. Should be SB_HORZ or SB_VERT. Can also be SB_CTL if the m_hWnd member holds the scrollbar handle.
nPos	The new position for the scrollbar.
bRedraw	TRUE if the scrollbar should be redrawn.

Returns the previous position of the scrollbar.

The SetScrollPos method is used to set the position of the thumb for the scrollbar.

The **SetScrollRange** Method

```
void SetScrollRange( int nBar, int nMinPos, int nMaxPos, BOOL bRedraw =
➡TRUE );
```

where

nBar	Specifies the scrollbar. Should be SB_HORZ or SB_VERT.
nMinPos	The new minimum position for the scrollbar.
nMaxPos	The new maximum position for the scrollbar.
bRedraw	TRUE if the scrollbar should be redrawn.

The SetScrollRange method is used to set the allowable range of values for the scrollbar.

The **SetTimer** Method

```
UINT SetTimer( UINT nIDEvent, UINT nElapse, void (CALLBACK EXPORT*
➡lpfnTimer)(HWND, UINT, UINT, DWORD) );
```

where

nIDEvent	The ID for this timer.
nElapse	The amount of time in milliseconds that should elapse between ticks.
lpfnTimer	A callback function. Optional; if not specified, WM_TIMER messages will be sent.

Returns the identifier of the new timer.

The SetTimer method is used to set up a window's timer.

The `SetWindowContextHelpID` Method

```
BOOL SetWindowContextHelpId( DWORD dwContextHelpId );
```

where

    dwContextHelpID   The new context help ID for this window.

Returns TRUE if successful.

The `SetWindowContextHelpID` method is the window's help context ID.

The `SetWindowPlacement` Method

```
BOOL SetWindowPlacement( const WINDOWPLACEMENT*lpwndpl );
```

where

    lpwndpl   The new window placement structure.

Returns TRUE if successful.

The `SetWindowPlacement` method is the window's placement.

The `SetWindowPos` Method

```
BOOL SetWindowPos( const CWnd* pWndInsertAfter, int x, int y, int cx, int
➥cy, UINT nFlags );
```

where

pWndInsertAfter	The window that will appear before this window in z-order. Can also be wndBotton, wndTop, wndTopMost, or wndNoTopMost.
x	The new x position.
y	The new y position.
cx	The new x position for the left side of the window.
cy	The new y position for the bottom side of the window.
y	The new y position.
flags	Several position flags.

Returns TRUE if successful.

Valid values for *flags* include

SWP_DRAWFRAME	Draws a frame around the window.
SWP_FRAMECHANGED	Sends a WM_NCCALCSIZE message to the window, even if the window's size is not being changed. If this flag is not specified, WM_NCCALCSIZE is sent only when the window's size is being changed.
SWP_HIDEWINDOW	Hides the window.
SWP_NOACTIVATE	Does not activate the window. If this flag is not set, the window is activated and moved to the top of either the topmost or another group (depending on the setting of the *pWndInsertAfter* parameter).
SWP_NOCOPYBITS	Discards the entire contents of the client area. If this flag is not specified, the valid contents of the client area are saved and copied back into the client area after the window is sized or repositioned.

C

SWP_NOMOVE	Retains current position (ignores the x and y parameters).
SWP_NOOWNERZORDER	Does not change the owner window's position in the Z-order.
SWP_NOREDRAW	Does not redraw changes. If this flag is set, no repainting of any kind occurs. This applies to the client area, the nonclient area (including the title and scrollbars), and any part of the parent window uncovered as a result of the moved window. When this flag is set, the application must explicitly invalidate or redraw any parts of the window and parent window that must be redrawn.
SWP_NOREPOSITION	Same as SWP_NOOWNERZORDER.
SWP_NOSENDCHANGING	Prevents the window from receiving the WM_WINDOWPOSCHANGING message.
SWP_NOSIZE	Retains current size (ignores the cx and cy parameters).
SWP_NOZORDER	Retains current ordering (ignores pWndInsertAfter).
SWP_SHOWWINDOW	Displays the window.

The SetWindowPos method is used to set the window's position.

The SetWindowRgn Method

int SetWindowRgn(HRGN hRgn, BOOL bRedraw);

where

| hRgn | The new region for the window. |
| bRedraw | TRUE if the window should be redrawn. |

Returns TRUE if successful.

The SetWindowRgn method is used to set the window's region.

The SetWindowText Method

void SetWindowText(LPCTSTR lpszString);

where

| lpszString | The new caption or text. |

The SetWindowText method is used to set the window's caption or text.

The ShowCaret Method

void ShowCaret( );

The ShowCaret method will show the caret.

The ShowOwnedPopups Method

void ShowOwnedPopups(BOOL bShow = TRUE);

where

| bShow | TRUE if the pop-ups should be displayed. |

The ShowOwnedPopus method is used hide or display any pop-ups owned by the window.

The `ShowScrollBar` Method

```
void ShowScrollBar( UINT nBar, BOOL bShow = TRUE );
```

where

nBar	Specifies the scrollbar. Should be SB_BOTH, SB_HORZ, or SB_VERT.
bShow	TRUE if the scrollbar should be shown.

The `ShowScrollBar` method is to show or hide the scrollbars.

The `ShowWindow` Method

```
BOOL ShowWindow( int nCmdShow );
```

where

nCmdShow	Specifies the hide and show status of the window.

Returns TRUE if successful.

The following values are valid for *nCmdShow*.

SW_HIDE	Hide the window.
SW_MINIMIZE	Minimize the window.
SW_RESTORE	Restore the window.
SW_SHOW	Show the window.
SW_SHOWMAXIMIZED	Show and then maximize the window.
SW_SHOWMINIMIZED	Show and then minimize the window.
SW_SHOWMINNOACTIVE	Display as an icon.
SW_SHOWNA	Show window in the current state.
SW_SHOWNOACTIVATE	Show but do not activate.
SW_SHOWNORMAL	Show; if minimized, activate.

The `ShowWindow` method is used to show and hide the window.

The `SubclassDlgItem` Method

```
BOOL SubclassDlgItem( UINT nID, CWnd* pParent );
```

where

nID	The control's ID.
pParent	The controls parent.

Returns TRUE if successful.

The `SubclassDlgItem` method is used to dynamically subclass controls on a dialog template.

The `SubclassWindow` Method

```
BOOL SubclassWindow( HWND hWnd );
```

where

hWnd	The parent window.

Returns TRUE if successful.

The `SubclassWindow` method is used to dynamically subclass a window.

C

The `UnlockWindowUpdate` Method

```
void UnlockWindowUpdate();
```

The `UnlockWindowUpdate` method is used to allow updates after a call to `LockWindowUpdate`.

The `UnsubclassWindow` Method

```
HWND UnsubclassWindow( );
```

Returns TRUE if the window was successfully unsubclassed.

The `UpdateData` Method

```
BOOL UpdateData( BOOL bSaveAndValidate = TRUE );
```

where

  bSaveAndValidate   TRUE if data is being saved from the dialog box control.

Returns TRUE if successful.

The `UpdateData` method is responsible for moving data to and from the dialog controls.

The `UpdateDialogControls` Method

```
void UpdateDialogControls( CCmdTarget* pTarget, BOOL bDisableIfNoHndler );
```

where

  pTarget   Pointer to the main frame window for the application.
  bDisableIfNoHndler   TRUE if controls that have no update handler should be disabled.

The `UpdateDialogControls` method is called to update the state of dialog controls.

The `UpdateWindow` Method

```
void UpdateWindow( );
```

The `UpdateWindow` method is called to send a WM_PAINT message to the window to update it.

The `ValidateRect` Method

```
void ValidateRect( LPCRECT lpRect );
```

where

  lpRect   Pointer to rectangle to be validated.

The `ValidateRect` method is called to validate (remove from the update region) a rectangle.

The `ValidateRgn` Method

```
void ValidateRgn( CRgn* pRgn );
```

where

  pRgn   Pointer to region to be validated.

The `ValidateRgn` method is called to validate (remove from the update region) a region.

The **WindowFromPoint** Method

`static CWnd* PASCAL WindowFromPoint( POINT point );`

where

point	A point.

Returns the window that the specified point is contained by.

The **DefWindowProc** Method

`LRESULT DefWindowProc( UINT message, WPARAM wParam, LPARAM lParam );`

where

message	The message ID.
wParam	The wparam value for this message.
lparam	The lparam value for this message.

Return value is dependent on which message is sent.

The `DefWindowProc` method will pass messages sent to it to the default window's message handler.

The **OnActivate** Method

`afx_msg void OnActivate( UINT nState, CWnd* pWndOther, BOOL bMinimized );`

where

nState	Specifies the state of the window. Should be either WA_INACTIVE, WA_ACTIVE, or WA_CLICKACTIVE.
pWndOther	Pointer to the CWnd being activated or deactivated.
bMinimized	Specifies the minimized state of the window.

The `OnActivate` method is called by MFC whenever a window is activated or deactivated.

The **OnActivateApp** Method

`afx_msg void OnActivateApp( BOOL bActive, HTASK hTask );`

where

bActive	TRUE if the app is being activated, FALSE if the app is being deactivated.
hTask	Specifies the task.

The `OnActivateApp` method is called by MFC whenever an application is activated or deactivated.

The **OnAskCbFormatName** Method

`afx_msg void OnAskCbFormatName( UINT nMaxCount, LPTSTR lpszString );`

where

nMaxCount	Specifies the maximum number of bytes to copy.
lpszString	Specifies the string to copy the format name into.

The `OnAskCbFormatName` method is called by MFC to generate a clipboard format name string.

C

The OnCancelMode Method

`afx_msg void OnCancelMode( );`

The `OnCancelMode` method is called by MFC to cancel any internal modes.

The OnCaptureChanged Method

`afx_msg void OnCaptureChanged( CWnd* pWnd );`

where

> *pWnd*   The window that captured the mouse.

The `OnCaptureChanged` method is called by MFC when a window captures the mouse.

The OnChangeCbChain Method

`afx_msg void OnChangeCbChain( HWND hWndRemove, HWND hWndAfter );`

where

> *hWndRemove*   The window being removed from the clipboard chain.
>
> *hWndAfter*   Specifies the window that follows the window being removed.

The `OnChangeCbChain` method is called by MFC when a clipboard viewer is removed from the chain.

The OnChar Method

`afx_msg void OnChar( UINT nChar, UINT nRepCnt, UINT nFlags );`

where

> *nChar*   The character code of the key.
>
> *nRepCnt*   The repeat count for the key.
>
> *nFlags*   The scan code for the key. Bits 0–15 are the repeat count. Bits 16–23 are the scan code. Bit 24 specifies an extended key. Bit 29 specifies the Alt key. Bit 30 is set if the key was down before the message was sent. Bit 31 specifies the transition state, 1 if the key is being released.

The `OnChar` method is called by MFC when a keystroke translates into a non-system character.

The OnCharToItem Method

`afx_msg int OnCharToItem( UINT nChar, CListBox* pListBox, UINT nIndex );`

where

> *nChar*   The character code of the key.
>
> *pListBox*   A pointer to the list box.
>
> *nIndex*   The current caret position.

Returns -2 if the application handled all aspects of selecting the item and needs no further action by the list box. Returns -1 if the list box should perform the default action in response to the keystroke. A return value of 0 or greater specifies the zero-based index of an item in the list box.

The `OnCharToItem` method is called by MFC when a keystroke is processed by a list box.

The **OnChildActivate** Method

`afx_msg void OnChildActivate( );`

The `OnChildActivate` method is called when an MDI child window is activated.

The **OnChildNotify** Method

`virtual BOOL OnChildNotify( UINT message, WPARAM wParam, LPARAM lParam,`
`➥LRESULT* pLResult );`

where

message	The message ID.
wParam	The wparam value for this message.
lParam	The lparam value for this message.
lpResult	A pointer to a value to be returned to the parent.

Returns TRUE if the window is responsible for handling the message.

The `OnChildNotify` method is called by the parent window to notify the child.

The **OnChildActivate** Method

`afx_msg void OnClose( );`

The `OnClose` method is called when a window is to be closed. The default implementation calls `DestroyWindow`.

The **OnCommand** Method

`virtual BOOL OnCommand( WPARAM wParam, LPARAM lParam );`

where

wParam	The wparam value for this message.
lParam	The lparam value for this message.

Returns TRUE if the application processed the message.

The `OnCommand` method is called when a WM_COMMAND message is received.

The **OnCompacting** Method

`afx_msg void OnCompacting( UINT nCpuTime );`

where

nCpuTime	The ratio of how much time the CPU is spending compacting memory.

The `OnCompacting` method is called when the system is nearly out of memory.

The **OnCompareItem** Method

`afx_msg int OnCompareItem( int nIDCtl, LPCOMPAREITEMSTRUCT lpCompareItemStruct );`

where

nIDCtrl	The identifier of the control that sent the WM_COMPAREITEM.
lpCompareItemStruct	A pointer to a COMPAREITEMSTRUCT that identifies two items in a combo or list box.

Returns -1 if item 1 is before item 2. Returns 0 if item 1 and 2 are the same. Returns 1 if item 1 is after item 2.

The OnCompareItem method is called to compare two items in a combo or list box that has sorting enabled.

The OnCopyData Method

```
afx_msg BOOL OnCopyData( CWnd *pWnd, COPYDATASTRUCT *pCopyDataStruct );
```

where

pWnd	The window sending data.
pCopyDataStruct	A pointer to a COPYDATASTRUCT that contains the data being sent.

Returns TRUE if the receiving application accepts the data.

The OnCopyData method is to copy data from one application to another.

The OnCreate Method

```
afx_msg int OnCreate( LPCREATESTRUCT lpCreateStruct );
```

where

lpCreateStruct	A pointer to a CREATESTRUCT.

Returns 0 to continue creation, or -1 to destroy the window.

The OnCreate method is called when a window is created.

The OnCtlColor Method

```
afx_msg HBRUSH OnCtlColor( CDC* pDC, CWnd* pWnd, UINT nCtlColor );
```

where

pDC	A pointer a device context for the child window.
pWnd	A pointer the control asking for the color.
nCtlColor	Contains one of the following values: CTLCOLOR_BTN, CTLCOLOR_DLG, CTLCOLOR_EDIT, CTLCOLOR_LISTBOX, CTLCOLOR_MSGBOX, CTLCOLOR_SCROLLBAR, or CTLCOLOR_STATIC.

Returns a handle to the brush that is used to paint the control background.

The OnCtlColor method is called determine the correct background color for the specified type of control.

The OnDeadChar Method

```
afx_msg void OnDeadChar( UINT nChar, UINT nRepCnt, UINT nFlags );
```

where

nChar	The character code of the key.
nRepCnt	The repeat count for the key.
nFlags	The scan code for the key. Bits 0–15 are the repeat count. Bits 16–23 are the scan code. Bit 24 specifies an extended key. Bit 29 specifies the Alt key. Bit 30 is set if the key was down before the message was sent. Bit 31 specifies the transition state, 1 if the key is being released.

The OnDeadChar method is called by MFC when a keystroke translates into a non-system character. OnDeadChar is usually called to process after each keystroke.

The OnDeleteItem Method

`afx_msg void OnDeleteItem( int nIDCtl, LPDELETEITEMSTRUCT lpDeleteItemStruct );`

where

nIDCtl	The list or combo box that is deleting an item.
lpDeleteItemStruct	A DELETEITEMSTRUCT data structure that contains information about the item deleted from the box.

The OnDeleteItem method is called by MFC when a combo box or list box deletes an item.

The OnDestroy Method

`afx_msg void OnDestroy( );`

The OnDestroy method is called by MFC when a window is about to be destroyed.

The OnDestroyClipboard Method

`afx_msg void OnDestroyClipboard( );`

The OnDestroyClipboard method is called by MFC when the contents of the Clipboard are destroyed.

The OnDeviceChange Method

`afx_msg BOOL OnDeviceChange( UINT nEventType, DWORD dwData );`

where

nEventType	An event type.
dwData	A structure that contains event-specific information.

The OnDeviceChange method is called by MFC when a device driver is changed.

The OnDeviceChange Method

`afx_msg void OnDevModeChange( LPTSTR lpDeviceName );`

where

lpDeviceName	A device specified in win.ini.

The OnDevModeChange method is called by MFC when a device driver's mode is changed.

The OnDrawClipboard Method

`afx_msg void OnDrawClipboard( );`

The OnDrawClipboard method is called by MFC when a Clipboard viewer needs to be redrawn.

The OnDrawItem Method

`afx_msg void OnDrawItem( int nIDCtl, LPDRAWITEMSTRUCT lpDrawItemStruct );`

where

nIDCtrl	An owner-drawn item that should be redrawn.
lpDrawItemStruct	A DRAWITEMSTRUCT data structure that contains information about the item to be drawn.

The OnDrawItem method is called by MFC when an owner-drawn item is about to be redrawn.

C

The `OnDropFiles` Method

afx_msg void OnDropFiles(HDROP hDropInfo);

where

    hDropInfo   A handle to information about the files that were dropped on this window.

The `OnDropFiles` method is called by MFC when files are dropped on the window.

The `OnDSCNotify` Method

afx_msg BOOL OnDSCNotify(DSCSTATE nState, DSCREASON nReason, BOOL pBool);

where

    nState   The state of the recordset.

    nReason   The reason for the notification.

    pBool   A Boolean answer indicating whether the operation should continue.

The `OnDSCNotify` method is called by MFC when a data source notification occurs.

The `OnEnable` Method

afx_msg void OnEnable(BOOL bEnable);

where

    bEnable   TRUE if the window is being enabled.

The `OnEnable` method is called by MFC when the window is enabled or disabled.

The `OnEndSession` Method

afx_msg void OnEndSession(BOOL bEnding);

where

    bEnding   TRUE if session is ending.

The `OnEndSession` method is called by MFC when the Windows session is shutting down.

The `OnEnterIdle` Method

afx_msg void OnEnterIdle(UINT nWhy, CWnd* pWho);

where

    pWhy   Why the application entered idle mode. Should be MSGF_DIALOGBOX if a dialog box put the system into an idle mode. Should be MSGF_MENU if a menu put the system into an idle mode.

    pWho   The dialog or window that caused the application to become idle.

The `OnEnterIdle` method is called by MFC when the window enters an idle mode.

The **OnEnterMenuLoop** Method

`afx_msg void OnEnterMenuLoop( BOOL bIsTrackPopupMenu );`

where

    bIsTrackPopupMenu   Specifies whether the menu involved is a pop-up menu.

The `OnEnterMenuLoop` method is called by MFC when the window enters a menu loop.

The **OnEraseBkgnd** Method

`afx_msg BOOL OnEraseBkgnd( CDC* pDC );`

where

    pDC   A device context to erase.

The `OnEraseBkgnd` method is called by MFC when the window's background should be erased.

The **OnExitMenuLoop** Method

`afx_msg void OnExitMenuLoop( BOOL bIsTrackPopupMenu );`

where

    bIsTrackPopupMenu   Specifies if the menu involved is a pop-up menu.

The `OnExitMenuLoop` method is called by MFC when the window exits a menu loop.

The **OnFontChange** Method

`afx_msg void OnFontChange( );`

The `OnFontChange` method is called by MFC when the window font changes.

The **OnGetDlgCode** Method

`afx_msg UINT OnGetDlgCode( );`

Returns a value indicating what type of input the application processes. Should be any of the following:

`DLGC_BUTTON`	Button
`DLGC_DEFPUSHBUTTON`	Default pushbutton
`DLGC_HASSETSEL`	EM_SETSEL messages
`DLGC_UNDEFPUSHBUTTON`	No default pushbutton processing
`DLGC_RADIOBUTTON`	Radio button
`DLGC_STATIC`	Static control
`DLGC_WANTALLKEYS`	All keyboard input
`DLGC_WANTARROWS`	Arrow keys
`DLGC_WANTCHARS`	WM_CHAR messages
`DLGC_WANTMESSAGE`	All keyboard input
`DLGC_WANTTAB`	Tab key

The `OnGetDlgCode` method is called by MFC when to determine what sort of messages the application wants.

C

The `OnGetMinMaxInfo` Method

afx_msg void OnGetMinMaxInfo(MINMAXINFO FAR* lpMMI);

where

    lpMMI   Points to a MINMAXINFO structure that contains information about the window's minimized and maximized state.

The OnGetMinMaxInfo method is called by MFC to get minimize and maximize information about the window.

The `OnHScroll` Method

afx_msg void OnHScroll(UINT nSBCode, UINT nPos, CScrollBar* pScrollBar);

where

nSBCode	Contains the scrollbar code.
nPos	Contains the new scrollbar position.
pScrollBar	Pointer to the scrollbar that generated the message.

Valid values for the nSBCode parameter include

SB_LEFT	Scroll to far left.
SB_ENDSCROLL	End scroll.
SB_LINELEFT	Scroll left.
SB_LINERIGHT	Scroll right.
SB_PAGELEFT	Scroll one page left.
SB_PAGERIGHT	Scroll one page right.
SB_RIGHT	Scroll to far right.
SB_THUMBPOSITION	Scroll to absolute position. The current position is specified by the *nPos* parameter.
SB_THUMBTRACK	Drag scroll box to specified position. The current position is specified by the *nPos* parameter.

The OnHScroll method is called by MFC when the horizontal scrollbar generates a message.

The `OnHScrollClipboard` Method

afx_msg void OnHScrollClipboard(CWnd* pClipAppWnd, UINT nSBCode, UINT nPos);

where

pClipAppWnd	The Clipboard viewer window.
nSBCode	Contains the scrollbar code.
nPos	Contains the new scrollbar position.

Valid values for the nSBCode parameter include

SB_LEFT	Scroll to far left.
SB_ENDSCROLL	End scroll.
SB_LINELEFT	Scroll left.

`SB_LINERIGHT`	Scroll right.
`SB_PAGELEFT`	Scroll one page left.
`SB_PAGERIGHT`	Scroll one page right.
`SB_RIGHT`	Scroll to far right.
`SB_THUMBPOSITION`	Scroll to absolute position. The current position is specified by the *nPos* parameter.
`SB_THUMBTRACK`	Drag scroll box to specified position. The current position is specified by the *nPos* parameter.

The `OnHScrollClipboard` method is called by MFC when the horizontal scrollbar in a Clipboard viewer generates a message.

The `OnEraseBkgnd` Method

`afx_msg BOOL OnIconEraseBkgnd( CDC* pDC );`

where

    pDC   A device context to erase.

The `OnIconEraseBkgnd` method is called by MFC when the window's background should be erased and the window is in an iconic state.

The `OnInitMenu` Method

`afx_msg void OnInitMenu( CMenu* pMenu );`

where

    pMenu   The menu to be initialized.

The `OnInitMenu` method is called by MFC when the window's menu bar is about to be initialized.

The `OnInitMenuPopup` Method

`afx_msg void OnInitMenuPopup( CMenu* pPopupMenu, UINT nIndex, BOOL bSysMenu );`

where

pPopupMenu	The menu object of the pop-up menu.
nIndex	Specifies the index of the pop-up menu in the main menu.
bSysMenu	TRUE if the pop-up menu is the control menu.

The `OnInitMenuPopup` method is called by MFC when a pop-up menu is first initialized.

The `OnKeyDown` Method

`afx_msg void OnKeyDown( UINT nChar, UINT nRepCnt, UINT nFlags );`

where

nChar	The character code of the key.
nRepCnt	The repeat count for the key.
nFlags	The scan code for the key. Bits 0–15 are the repeat count. Bits 16–23 are the scan code. Bit 24 specifies an extended key. Bit 29 specifies the Alt key. Bit 30 is set if the key was down before the message was sent. Bit 31 specifies the transition state, 1 if the key is being released.

The OnKeyDown method is called by MFC when a key is pressed.

The **OnKeyUp** Method

`afx_msg void OnKeyUp( UINT nChar, UINT nRepCnt, UINT nFlags );`

where

nChar	The character code of the key.
nRepCnt	The repeat count for the key.
nFlags	The scan code for the key. Bits 0–15 are the repeat count. Bits 16–23 are the scan code. Bit 24 specifies an extended key. Bit 29 specifies the Alt key. Bit 30 is set if the key was down before the message was sent. Bit 31 specifies the transition state, 1 if the key is being released.

The OnKeyDown method is called by MFC when a key is released.

The **OnKillFocus** Method

`afx_msg void OnKillFocus( CWnd* pNewWnd );`

where

pNewWnd	The new window to receive focus.

The OnKillFocus method is called by MFC when a window loses focus.

The **OnLButtonDblClick** Method

`afx_msg void OnLButtonDblClk( UINT nFlags, CPoint point );`

where

nFlags	Flags that specify any keys that were held down while the click occurred. Should be one or more of the following: MK_CONTROL, MK_LBUTTON, MK_MBUTTON, MK_RBUTTON, or MK_SHIFT.
point	The point at which the mouse click occurred.

The OnLButtonDblClick method is called by MFC when the left mouse button is double-clicked.

The **OnLButtonDown** Method

`afx_msg void OnLButtonDown( UINT nFlags, CPoint point );`

where

nFlags	Flags that specify any keys that were held down while the click occurred. Should be one or more of the following: MK_CONTROL, MK_LBUTTON, MK_MBUTTON, MK_RBUTTON, or MK_SHIFT.
point	The point at which the mouse click occurred.

The OnLButtonDown method is called by MFC when the left mouse button is pressed.

The **OnLButtonUp** Method

`afx_msg void OnLButtonUp( UINT nFlags, CPoint point );`

where

nFlags	Flags that specify any keys that were held down while the click occurred. Should be one or more of the following: MK_CONTROL, MK_LBUTTON, MK_MBUTTON, MK_RBUTTON, or MK_SHIFT.
point	The point at which the mouse click occurred.

The OnLButtonUp method is called by MFC when the left mouse button is released.

The `OnMButtonDblClick` Method

`afx_msg void OnMButtonDblClk( UINT nFlags, CPoint point );`

where

nFlags	Flags that specify any keys that were held down while the click occurred. Should be one or more of the following: MK_CONTROL, MK_LBUTTON, MK_MBUTTON, MK_RBUTTON, or MK_SHIFT.
point	The point at which the mouse click occurred.

The OnMButtonDblClick method is called by MFC when the middle mouse button is double-clicked.

The `OnMButtonDown` Method

`afx_msg void OnMButtonDown( UINT nFlags, CPoint point );`

where

nFlags	Flags that specify any keys that were held down while the click occurred. Should be one or more of the following: MK_CONTROL, MK_LBUTTON, MK_MBUTTON, MK_RBUTTON, or MK_SHIFT.
point	The point at which the mouse click occurred.

The OnMButtonDown method is called by MFC when the middle mouse button is pressed.

The `OnMButtonUp` Method

`afx_msg void OnMButtonUp( UINT nFlags, CPoint point );`

where

nFlags	Flags that specify any keys that were held down while the click occurred. Should be one or more of the following: MK_CONTROL, MK_LBUTTON, MK_MBUTTON, MK_RBUTTON, or MK_SHIFT.
point	The point at which the mouse click occurred.

The OnMButtonUp method is called by MFC when the middle mouse button is released.

The `OnMDIActivate` Method

`afx_msg void OnMDIActivate( BOOL bActivate, CWnd* pActivateWnd, CWnd*`
`➥pDeactivateWnd );`

where

bActivate	TRUE if the window is being activated.
pActivateWnd	Contains a pointer to an MDI child window to be activated.
pDeactivated	Contains a pointer to an MDI child window to be deactivated.

The OnMDIActivate method is called by MFC when an MDI child window is activated or deactivated.

The `OnMeasureItem` Method

```
afx_msg void OnMeasureItem( int nIDCtl, LPMEASUREITEMSTRUCT
➡lpMeasureItemStruct );
```

where

nIDCtrl	The ID of the control.
lpMeasureItemStruct	Pointer to a structure used to measure the item.

The `OnMeasureItem` method is called by MFC when an owner-drawn item must be measured.

The `OnMenuChar` Method

```
afx_msg LRESULT OnMenuChar( UINT nChar, UINT nFlags, CMenu* pMenu );
```

where

nChar	The character that was pressed.
nFlags	Contains `MF_POPUP` if the menu is a pop-up menu. Contains `MF_SYSMENU` if the menu is a system menu.
pMenu	Contains a pointer to the selected `CMenu`.

The `OnMenuChar` method is called by MFC when the user presses a key while a menu is opened.

The `OnMenuSelect` Method

```
afx_msg void OnMenuSelect( UINT nItemID, UINT nFlags HMENU hSysMenu );
```

where

nItemID	The menu item selected.
nFlags	Contains any combination of the following flags: `MF_BITMAP`, `MF_CHECKED`, `MF_DISABLED`, `MF_GRAYED`, `MF_MOUSESELECT`, `MF_OWNERDRAW`, `MF_POPUP`, `MF_SEPARATOR`, and `MF_SYSMENU`.
hSysMenu	Contains a handle to the system menu if `MF_SYSMENU` is enabled.

The `OnMenuSelect` method is called by MFC when the user selects a menu item.

The `OnMouseActive` Method

```
afx_msg int OnMouseActivate( CWnd* pDesktopWnd, UINT nHitTest, UINT message );
```

where

pDesktopWnd	Pointer to the top-level parent window of the window being activated.
nHitTest	Specifies the hit test area code. Used to determine the location of the cursor.
message	The mouse message number.

The `OnMouseActive` method is called by MFC when a window becomes active by a mouse click.

The `OnMouseMove` Method

```
afx_msg void OnMouseMove( UINT nFlags, CPoint point );
```

where

| *nFlags* | Flags that specify any keys that were held down while the move occurred. Should be one or more of the following: MK_CONTROL, MK_LBUTTON, MK_MBUTTON, MK_RBUTTON, and MK_SHIFT. |
| *point* | The point at which the mouse move occurred. |

The OnMouseMove method is called by MFC as the mouse moves over the window.

The OnMouseWheel Method

`afx_msg BOOL OnMouseWheel( UINT nFlags, short zDelta, CPoint pt );`

where

nFlags	Flags that specify any keys that were held down while the move occurred. Should be one or more of the following: MK_CONTROL, MK_LBUTTON, MK_MBUTTON, MK_RBUTTON, and MK_SHIFT.
zDelta	The amount the mouse wheel moved. Can be negative to indicate backward movement.
pt	The point at which the mouse move occurred.

The OnMouseMove method is called by MFC as the mouse moves over the window. Note: This method only works for Windows NT 4.0 and higher. For Windows 95 and Windows NT 3.51, use OnRegisteredMouseWheel.

The OnMove Method

`afx_msg void OnMove( int x, int y );`

where

| *x* | The new x coordinate of the window. |
| *y* | The new y coordinate of the window. |

The OnMove method is called by MFC when the window is moved.

The OnMoving Method

`afx_msg void OnMoving( UINT nSide, LPRECT lpRect );`

where

| *nSide* | The edge of the window to be moved. |
| *lpRect* | The item's coordinates. |

The OnMoving method is called by MFC as the user moves a window.

The OnNcActivate Method

`afx_msg BOOL OnActivate( BOOL bActive );`

where

| *bActive* | TRUE if the window is being activated. |

Returns TRUE if Windows should proceed with default processing for this message.

The OnNcActivate method is called by MFC whenever the non-client region of a window is activated or deactivated.

C

The OnNcCalcSize Method

`afx_msg void OnNcCalcSize( BOOL bCalcValidRects, NCCALCSIZE_PARAMS* lpncsp );`

where

bCalcValidRects	TRUE if the application should specify which part of the client area contains valid information.
lpncsp	Pointer to a NCCALCSIZE_PARAMS data structure that contains information about the non-client area.

The OnNcCalcSize method is called by MFC whenever the size of the non-client region of a window needs to be calculated.

The OnNcCreate Method

`afx_msg BOOL OnNcCreate( LPCREATESTRUCT lpCreateStruct );`

where

lpCreateStruct	A pointer to a CREATESTRUCT.

Returns TRUE if the non-client region is created.

The OnNcCreate method is called when a window is created to create the non-client region of the window.

The OnNcDestroy Method

`afx_msg void OnNcDestroy( );`

The OnNcDestroy method is called by MFC when a window's non-client region is about to be destroyed.

The OnNcHitTest Method

`afx_msg UINT OnNcHitTest( CPoint point );`

where

point	The point at which the mouse was clicked.

Returns the hit-test code for where the mouse was clicked.

The OnNcHitTest determines which part of the non-client region has been hit.

The OnNcLButtonDblClk Method

`afx_msg void OnNcLButtonDblClk( UINT nHitTest, CPoint point );`

where

nHitTest	A pointer to the hit-test code for where the cursor was clicked.
point	The point (in screen coordinates) at which the cursor was clicked.

The OnNcLButtonDblClk method is called when the user double clicks the left mouse button in the non-client region of the window.

The OnNcLButtonDown Method

`afx_msg void OnNcLButtonDown( UINT nHitTest, CPoint point );`

where

nHitTest	A pointer to the hit-test code for where the cursor was clicked.
point	The point (in screen coordinates) at which the cursor was clicked.

The OnNcLButtonDown method is called when the user presses the left mouse button in the non-client region of the window.

The **OnNcLButtonUp** Method

afx_msg void OnNcLButtonUp(UINT nHitTest, CPoint point);

where

nHitTest	A pointer to the hit-test code for where the cursor was clicked.
point	The point (in screen coordinates) at which the cursor was clicked.

The OnNcLButtonUp method is called when the user releases the left mouse button in the non-client region of the window.

The **OnNcMButtonDblClk** Method

afx_msg void OnNcMButtonDblClk(UINT nHitTest, CPoint point);

where

nHitTest	A pointer to the hit-test code for where the cursor was clicked.
point	The point (in screen coordinates) at which the cursor was clicked.

The OnNcMButtonDblClk method is called when the user double-clicks the middle mouse button in the non-client region of the window.

The **OnNcMButtonDown** Method

afx_msg void OnNcMButtonDown(UINT nHitTest, CPoint point);

where

nHitTest	A pointer to the hit-test code for where the cursor was clicked.
point	The point (in screen coordinates) at which the cursor was clicked.

The OnNcMButtonDown method is called when the user presses the middle mouse button in the non-client region of the window.

The **OnNcMButtonUp** Method

afx_msg void OnNcMButtonUp(UINT nHitTest, CPoint point);

where

nHitTest	A pointer to the hit-test code for where the cursor was clicked.
point	The point (in screen coordinates) at which the cursor was clicked.

The OnNcMButtonUp method is called when the user releases the middle mouse button in the non-client region of the window.

The **OnNcMouseMove** Method

afx_msg void OnNcMouseMove(UINT nHitTest, CPoint point);

where

| *nHitTest* | A pointer to the hit-test code for where the cursor was moved. |
| *point* | The point (in screen coordinates) at which the cursor was moved. |

The OnNcMouseMove method is called when the user moves the mouse over the non-client region of the window.

The **OnNcPaint** Method

`afx_msg void OnNcPaint( );`

The OnNcPaint method is called by MFC when the non-client region needs to be repainted.

The **OnNcRButtonDblClk** Method

`afx_msg void OnNcRButtonDblClk( UINT nHitTest, CPoint point );`

where

| *nHitTest* | A pointer to the hit-test code for where the cursor was clicked. |
| *point* | The point (in screen coordinates) at which the cursor was clicked. |

The OnNcRButtonDblClk method is called when the user double-clicks the right mouse button in the non-client region of the window.

The **OnNcRButtonDown** Method

`afx_msg void OnNcRButtonDown( UINT nHitTest, CPoint point );`

where

| *nHitTest* | A pointer to the hit-test code for where the cursor was clicked. |
| *point* | The point (in screen coordinates) at which the cursor was clicked. |

The OnNcRButtonDown method is called when the user presses the right mouse button in the non-client region of the window.

The **OnNcRButtonUp** Method

`afx_msg void OnNcRButtonUp( UINT nHitTest, CPoint point );`

where

| *nHitTest* | A pointer to the hit-test code for where the cursor was clicked. |
| *point* | The point(in screen coordinates) at which the cursor was clicked. |

The OnNcRButtonUp method is called when the user releases the right mouse button in the non-client region of the window.

The **OnNotify** Method

`virtual BOOL OnNotify( WPARAM wParam, LPARAM lParam, LRESULT* pLResult );`

where

wParam	The wparam value for this message.
lparam	The lparam value for this message.
lpResult	A pointer to a value to be returned to the parent.

Returns TRUE if method processes the message.

The OnNotify method is called by MFC when the window receives child window notification messages.

The `OnPaint` Method

`afx_msg void OnPaint( );`

The `OnPaint` method is called by MFC when the window is ready to repaint itself.

The `OnPaintClipboard` Method

`afx_msg void OnPaintClipboard( CWnd* pClipAppWnd, HGLOBAL hPaintStruct );`

where

pClipAppWnd	Pointer to the Clipboard application window.
hPaintStruct	A `PAINTSTRUCT` data structure that identifies which part of the client area to paint.

The `OnPaintClipboard` method is called by MFC when the Clipboard owner has placed `CF_OWNERDISPLAY` format data on the Clipboard.

The `OnPaletteChanged` Method

`afx_msg void OnPaletteChanged( CWnd* pFocusWnd );`

where

pFocusWnd	The window that caused the palette change.

The `OnPaletteChanged` method is called by MFC when the system palette changes.

The `OnPaletteIsChanging` Method

`afx_msg void OnPaletteIsChanging( CWnd* pFocusWnd );`

where

pFocusWnd	Specifies a pointer to the window that is causing the palette to change.

The `OnPaletteChanged` method is called by MFC just before the system palette changes.

The `OnParentNotify` Method

`afx_msg void OnParentNotify( UINT message, LPARAM lParam );`

where

message	The wparam value for this message.
lparam	The lparam value for this message.

The `OnParentNotify` method is called by MFC when a child window is created or destroyed.

The `OnQueryDragIcon` Method

`afx_msg HCURSOR OnQueryDragIcon( );`

Returns a cursor to be used when dragging.

The `OnQueryEndSession` Method

`afx_msg BOOL OnQueryEndSession( );`

Returns 0 if the Windows session is not to be ended.

The `OnQueryEndSession` is called to make sure it is okay to close down Windows.

The `OnQueryNewPalette` Method

`afx_msg BOOL OnQueryNewPalette( );`

Returns zero if the window's palette is not realized.

The `OnQueryNewPalette` is called to give the window a chance to realize the new palette.

The `OnQueryOpen` Method

`afx_msg BOOL OnQueryOpen( );`

Returns 0 if the icon can be opened.

The `OnQueryOpen` method is called before a window is restored.

The `OnRButtonDblClick` Method

`afx_msg void OnRButtonDblClk( UINT nFlags, CPoint point );`

where

nFlags	Flags that specify any keys that were held down while the click occurred. Should be one or more of the following: `MK_CONTROL`, `MK_LBUTTON`, `MK_MBUTTON`, `MK_RBUTTON`, and `MK_SHIFT`.
point	The point at which the mouse click occurred.

The `OnRButtonDblClick` method is called by MFC when the right mouse button is double-clicked.

The `OnRButtonDown` Method

`afx_msg void OnRButtonDown( UINT nFlags, CPoint point );`

where

nFlags	Flags that specify any keys that were held down while the click occurred. Should be one or more of the following: `MK_CONTROL`, `MK_LBUTTON`, `MK_MBUTTON`, `MK_RBUTTON`, and `MK_SHIFT`.
point	The point at which the mouse click occurred.

The `OnRButtonDown` method is called by MFC when the right mouse button is pressed.

The `OnRButtonUp` Method

`afx_msg void OnRButtonUp( UINT nFlags, CPoint point );`

where

nFlags	Flags that specify any keys that were held down while the click occurred. Should be one or more of the following: `MK_CONTROL`, `MK_LBUTTON`, `MK_MBUTTON`, `MK_RBUTTON`, and `MK_SHIFT`.
point	The point at which the mouse click occurred.

The `OnRButtonUp` method is called by MFC when the right mouse button is released.

The `OnRegisteredMouseWheel` Method

`afx_msg LRESULT OnRegisteredMouseWheel( WPARAM wParam, LPARAM lParam );`

where

wParam	Horizontal position of the pointer.
lParam	Vertical position of the pointer.

Returns 0 always.

The `OnRegisteredMouseWheel` method is called by MFC as the mouse wheel turns. Note: This method only works under Windows 95. Use `OnMouseWheel` for Windows NT 4.0 and higher.

The `OnRenderAllFormats` Method

`afx_msg void OnRenderAllFormats( );`

The `OnRenderAllFormats` method is called by MFC to cause the window to render to the Clipboard in all supported formats.

The `OnRenderFormat` Method

`afx_msg void OnRenderFormat( UINT nFormat );`

where

>   *nFormat*   The desired format.

The `OnRenderFormat` method is called by MFC to render a specific format to the Clipboard.

The `OnSetCursor` Method

`afx_msg BOOL OnSetCursor( CWnd* pWnd, UINT nHitTest, UINT message );`

where

>   *pWnd*   A pointer to the window that contains the cursor.
>   *nHitTest*   Specifies the hit-test area.
>   *message*   The mouse message number.

Return TRUE for further processing.

The `OnSetCursor` method is called by MFC to set the cursor to the desired shape depending on what region of the window it is over.

The `OnSetFocus` Method

`afx_msg void OnSetFocus( CWnd* pOldWnd );`

where

>   *pOldWnd*   A pointer to the old window that previously had focus.

The `OnSetFocus` method is called by MFC when the focus is shifted to this window.

The `OnShowWindow` Method

`afx_msg void OnShowWindow( BOOL bShow, UINT nStatus );`

where

>   *bShow*   TRUE if the window is being shown. FALSE if the window is being
>   hidden.
>   *nStatus*   Should be SW_PARENTCLOSING or SW_PARENTOPENING.

The `OnShowWindow` method is called by MFC when the window is being shown or hidden.

The **OnSize** Method

`afx_msg void OnSize( UINT nType, int cx, int cy );`

where

nType	The type of resize. Should be one of the following: SIZE_MAXIMIZED, SIZE_MINIMIZED, SIZE_RESTORED, SIZE_MAXHIDE, or SIZE_MAXSHOW.
cx	The new width of the client area.
cy	The new height of the client area.

The OnSize method is called by MFC when the window is resized.

The **OnSizeClipboard** Method

`afx_msg void OnSizeClipboard( CWnd* pClipAppWnd, HGLOBAL hRect );`

where

pClipAppWnd	The Clipboard application window.
hRect	A global memory object to a RECT structure that specifies the area for the Clipboard owner to paint.

The OnSizeClipboard method is called by MFC when the Clipboard contains data of the format CF_OWN-ERDISPLAY.

The **OnSizing** Method

`afx_msg void OnSizing( UINT nSide, LPRECT lpRect );`

where

nType	The type of resize. Should be one of the following: SIZE_MAXIMIZED, SIZE_MINIMIZED, SIZE_RESTORED, SIZE_MAXHIDE, or SIZE_MAXSHOW.
cx	The new width of the client area.
cy	The new height of the client area.

The OnSizing method is called by MFC as the window is resized.

The **OnSpoolerStatus** Method

`afx_msg void OnSpoolerStatus( UINT nStatus, UINT nJobs );`

where

nStatus	Specifies the SP_JOBSTATUS flag.
nJobs	The number of jobs waiting in the Print Manager queue.

The OnSpoolerStatus method is called by MFC whenever a job is added or removed from the print queue.

The **OnStyleChanged** Method

`afx_msg void OnStyleChanged( int nStyleType, LPSTYLESTRUCT lpStyleStruct );`

where

nStyleType	Specifies the style type. Should be one or both of `GWL_EXZSTYLE` and `GWL_STYLE`.
lpStyleStruct	Contains the window's new style.

The `OnStyleChanged` method is called by MFC whenever the style of a window changes.

The `OnStyleChanging` Method

`afx_msg void OnStyleChanging( int nStyleType, LPSTYLESTRUCT lpStyleStruct );`

where

nStyleType	Specifies the style type. Should be one or both of `GWL_EXZSTYLE` and `GWL_STYLE`.
lpStyleStruct	Contains the window's new style.

The `OnStyleChanging` method is called by MFC whenever the style of a window is about to change.

The `OnSysChar` Method

`afx_msg void OnSysChar( UINT nChar, UINT nRepCnt, UINT nFlags );`

where

nChar	The character code of the key.
nRepCnt	The repeat count for the key.
nFlags	The scan code for the key. Bits 0–15 are the repeat count. Bits 16–23 are the scan code. Bit 24 specifies an extended key. Bit 29 specifies the Alt key. Bit 30 is set if the key was down before the message was sent. Bit 31 specifies the transition state, 1 if the key is being released.

The `OnSysChar` method is called by MFC when a system character is detected.

The `OnSysColorChange` Method

`afx_msg void OnSysColorChange( );`

The `OnSysColorChange` method is called by MFC when a system color changes.

The `OnSysCommand` Method

`afx_msg void OnSysCommand( UINT nID, LPARAM lParam );`

where

nID	The system menu item. Should be `SC_CLOSE`, `SC_HOTKEY`, `SC_HSCROLL`, `SC_KEYMENU`, `SC_MAXIMIZE`, `SC_MINIMIZE`, `SC_MOUSEMENU`, `SC_MOVE`, `SC_NEXTWINDOW`, `SC_PREVWINDOW`, `SC_RESTORE`, `SC_SCREENSAV`, `SC_SIZE`, `SC_TASKLIST`, or `SC_VSCROLL`.
lparam	Contains the cursor coordinates for the mouse.

The `OnSysColorChange` method is called by MFC when a system color changes.

The `OnSysDeadChar` Method

`afx_msg void OnSysDeadChar( UINT nChar, UINT nRepCnt, UINT nFlags );`

where

nChar	The character code of the key.
nRepCnt	The repeat count for the key.
nFlags	The scan code for the key. Bits 0–15 are the repeat count. Bits 16–23 are the scan code. Bit 24 specifies an extended key. Bit 29 specifies the Alt key. Bit 30 is set if the key was down before the message was sent. Bit 31 specifies the transition state, 1 if the key is being released.

The OnSysDeadChar method is called by MFC when a system character is detected. This method is overridden to provide processing on each system keystroke.

The **OnSysKeyDown** Method

afx_msg void OnSysKeyDown(UINT nChar, UINT nRepCnt, UINT nFlags);

where

nChar	The character code of the key.
nRepCnt	The repeat count for the key.
nFlags	The scan code for the key. Bits 0–15 are the repeat count. Bits 16–23 are the scan code. Bit 24 specifies an extended key. Bit 29 specifies the Alt key. Bit 30 is set if the key was down before the message was sent. Bit 31 specifies the transition state, 1 if the key is being released.

The OnSysKeyDown method is called by MFC when a system key is pressed.

The **OnSysKeyUp** Method

afx_msg void OnSysKeyUp(UINT nChar, UINT nRepCnt, UINT nFlags);

where

nChar	The character code of the key.
nRepCnt	The repeat count for the key.
nFlags	The scan code for the key. Bits 0–15 are the repeat count. Bits 16–23 are the scan code. Bit 24 specifies an extended key. Bit 29 specifies the Alt key. Bit 30 is set if the key was down before the message was sent. Bit 31 specifies the transition state, 1 if the key is being released.

The OnSysKeyUp method is called by MFC when a system key is released.

The **OnTimeChange** Method

afx_msg void OnTimeChange( );

The OnTimeChange method is called with the system time changes.

The **OnTimer** Method

afx_msg void OnTimer(UINT nIDEvent);

where

nIDEvent	The event code for the timer.

The OnTimer method is called by MFC when a timer event occurs.

The OnVKeyToItem Method

protafx_msg int OnVKeyToItem(UINT nKey, CListBox* pListBox, UINT nIndex);

where

nKey	The virtual keycode pressed by the user.
pListBox	Specifies a pointer to the list box.
nIndex	The current caret position.

Returns -2 if the application handled all aspects of selecting the item and requires no further action by the list box. Returns -1 if the list box should perform the default action in response to the keystroke. A return value of 0 or greater specifies the zero-based index of an item in the list box.

The OnVKeyToItem method is called by MFC to map a virtual key to an owner-drawn combo or list box.

The OnVScroll Method

afx_msg void OnVScroll(UINT nSBCode; UINT nPos, CScrollBar* pScrollBar);

where

nSBCode	Contains the scrollbar code.
nPos	Contains the new scrollbar position.
pScrollBar	Pointer to the scrollbar that generated the message.

Valid values for the nSBCode parameter include

SB_LEFT	Scroll to far left.
SB_ENDSCROLL	End scroll.
SB_LINELEFT	Scroll left.
SB_LINERIGHT	Scroll right.
SB_PAGELEFT	Scroll one page left.
SB_PAGERIGHT	Scroll one page right.
SB_RIGHT	Scroll to far right.
SB_THUMBPOSITION	Scroll to absolute position. The current position is specified by the *nPos* parameter.
SB_THUMBTRACK	Drag scroll box to specified position. The current position is specified by the *nPos* parameter.

The OnVScroll method is called by MFC when the vertical scroll bar generates a message.

The OnVScrollClipboard Method

afx_msg void OnVScrollClipboard(CWnd* pClipAppWnd, UINT nSBCode, UINT
➥nPos);

where

pClipAppWnd	The Clipboard viewer window.
nSBCode	Contains the scrollbar code.
nPos	Contains the new scrollbar position.

Valid values for the nSBCode parameter include

SB_LEFT	Scroll to far left.
SB_ENDSCROLL	End scroll.
SB_LINELEFT	Scroll left.
SB_LINERIGHT	Scroll right.
SB_PAGELEFT	Scroll one page left.
SB_PAGERIGHT	Scroll one page right.
SB_RIGHT	Scroll to far right.
SB_THUMBPOSITION	Scroll to absolute position. The current position is specified by the *nPos* parameter.
SB_THUMBTRACK	Drag scroll box to specified position. The current position is specified by the *nPos* parameter.

The OnVScrollClipboard method is called by MFC when the vertical scrollbar in a Clipboard viewer generates a message.

The OnWindowPosChanged Method

afx_msg void OnWindowPosChanged(WINDOWPOS* lpwndpos);

where

lpwndpos   A pointer to a WINDOWPOS structure that contains information about the window.

The OnWindowPosChanged method is called by MFC when the window position or size changes.

The OnWindowPosChanging Method

afx_msg void OnWindowPosChanging(WINDOWPOS* lpwndpos);

where

lpwndpos   A pointer to a WINDOWPOS structure that contains information about the window.

The OnWindowPosChanging method is called by MFC as the window position changes.

The OnWinIniChange Method

afx_msg void OnWinIniChange(LPCTSTR lpszSection);

where

lpszSection   The section that has changed.

The OnWinIniChange method is called by MFC when the win.ini file changes.

The OnWndMsg Method

virtual BOOL OnWndMsg(UINT message, WPARAM wParam, LPARAM lParam, LRESULT*
➡pResult);

where

message	The message ID to be posted.
wParam	The wparam value for this message.
lparam	The lparam value for this message.

Return value is dependent on which message is sent.

The OnWndMsg method is called by WindowProc or during message reflection.

The PostNcDestroy Method

```
virtual void PostNcDestroy( );
```

The PostNcDestroy method is called to post a destroy message to the non-client region of the window.

The ReflectChildNotify Method

```
BOOL ReflectChildNotify( UINT message, WPARAM wParam, LPARAM lParam,
➥LRESULT* pResult );
```

where

message	The message ID to be posted.
wParam	The wparam value for this message.
lparam	The lparam value for this message.
pResult	The result of this message.

Return value is TRUE if the message was reflected.

The ReflectChildNotify method is called by OnChildNotify to reflect notifications back at their source.

The ReflectLastMsg Method

```
static BOOL PASCAL ReflectLastMsg( HWND hWndChild, LRESULT* pResult =
➥NULL );
```

where

| hWndChild | The child window. |
| pResult | The result. |

Return value is TRUE if the message was handled.

The ReflectLastMsg method is called to reflect a notification message back at its source.

The WindowProc Method

```
virtual LRESULT WindowProc( UINT message, WPARAM wParam, LPARAM lParam );
```

where

message	The message ID to be posted.
wParam	The wparam value for this message.
lparam	The lparam value for this message.

Return value is dependent on which message is sent.

The WindowProc method provides a window proc for the window that dispatches messages throughout the window.

APPENDIX D

Standard and Common Control Reference

CStatic

The CStatic control is used to place static text, a bitmap, or an icon on a window. This control is static because the user does not directly interact with it. The application program can change visual features of the static control as needed.

Header Files

The following header file should be included when using this class:

```
afxwin.h
```

Methods

The CStatic class has the following methods:

CStatic	The constructor
Create	Create a static control
GetBitmap	Get the bitmap associated with the control
GetCursor	Get the cursor associated with the control
GetEnhMetaFile	Get the enhanced metafile associated with the control
GetIcon	Get the icon associated with the control
SetBitmap	Set the bitmap associated with the control
SetCursor	Set the cursor associated with the control
SetEnhMetaFile	Set the enhanced metafile associated with the control
SetIcon	Set the icon associated with the control

The CStatic Constructor

The CStatic constructor creates the CStatic object. The CStatic constructor is used as follows:

CStatic( );

The Create Method

BOOL Create(LPCTSTR lpszText, DWORD dwStyle, const RECT& rect, CWnd*
➡pParentWnd, UINT nID = 0xffff);

where

lpszText	The button name
rect	The rectangle the button should occupy
pParentWnd	The window into which this button is to be inserted
nID	The child window ID for this control

Returns TRUE if successful.

The Create method will create a CStatic control.

The GetBitmap Method

HBITMAP GetBitmap( ) const;

Returns a handle to the current bitmap, or NULL if there is no bitmap.

The `GetCursor` Method

```
HCURSOR GetCursor( );
```

Returns a handle to the current bitmap, or NULL if there is no cursor.

The `GetEnhMetaFile` Method

```
HENHMETAFILE GetEnhMetaFile( ) const;
```

Returns a handle to the current enhanced metafile, or NULL if there is no metafile.

The `GetIcon` Method

```
HICON GetIcon( ) const;
```

Returns a handle to the current icon, or NULL if there is no icon.

The `SetBitmap` Method

```
HBITMAP SetBitmap( HBITMAP hBitmap );
```

where

> *hBitmap*   The bitmap to make current

Returns the old bitmap handle.

The SetBitmap method will set the current bitmap to the bitmap handle specified.

The `SetCursor` Method

```
HCURSOR SetCursor( HCURSOR hCursor );
```

where

> *hCursor*   The cursor to make current

Returns the old cursor handle.

The SetCursor method will set the current cursor to the cursor handle specified.

The `SetEnhMetaFile` Method

```
HENHMETAFILE SetEnhMetaFile( HENHMETAFILE hMetaFile );
```

where

> *hMetaFile*   The cursor to make current

Returns a handle to the old metafile.

The SetEnhMetaFile method will set the current metafile to the metafile handle specified.

D

The `SetIcon` Method

```
HICON SetIcon( HICON hIcon );
```

where

> *hIcon*   The icon to make current

Returns a handle to the old icon.

The `SetIcon` method will set the current icon to the icon handle specified.

CEdit

The CEdit control handles most text editing done by a Windows application. The edit control allows for single or multiline editing. The edit control can be a small control in a dialog box, or a large multiline text editor.

Header Files

The following header file should be included when using this class:

```
afxwin.h
```

Methods

The `CEdit` class has the following methods:

CEdit	The constructor
CanUndo	Determine whether the control is in a state where the Undo method can be used
CharFromPos	Get the line and character indices for the character closest to a position
Clear	Clear the contents of the edit control
Copy	Copy the current selection to the clipboard
Create	Create the edit control
Cut	Cut the current selection
EmptyUndoBuffer	Empty the undo buffer
FmtLines	Set whether to include soft line breaks
GetFirstVisibleLine	Determine the topmost visible line
GetHandle	Get a handle to the edit control

GetLimitText	Get the maximum amount of text the control allows
GetLine	Get one line of text from the edit control
GetLineCount	Get the total line count
GetMargins	Get the page margins
GetModify	Determine whether the document was modified
GetPasswordChar	Get the character used as the password character
GetRect	Get the control's bounding rectangle
GetSel	Get the current selection
LimitText	Set the amount of text the control allows
LineFromChar	Get the line number that contains the specified character
LineIndex	Get the index of the first character in the specified index
LineLength	Get the length of the specified line
LineScroll	Scroll by the specified number of lines
Paste	Insert text from the clipboard
PosFromChar	Get the coordinates for the specified character
ReplaceSel	Replace the current selection
SetHandle	Set the handle used by this edit control
SetLimitText	Set the limit as to how much text this control will take
SetMargins	Set the margins for this control
SetModify	Set whether this control was modified
SetPasswordChar	Set the password character
SetReadOnly	Set this control as read only
SetRect	Set the rectangle for this control
SetRectNP	Set the rectangle for this control, but do not repaint
SetSel	Set the current selection
SetTabStops	Set the tab stops
Undo	Undo the last operation

D

The CEdit Constructor

The CEdit constructor creates the CEdit object. The CEdit constructor is used as follows:

```
CEdit
```

The CanUndo Method

```
BOOL CanUndo( ) const;
```

Returns TRUE if the previous action can be undone.

The CharFromPos Method

```
int CharFromPos( CPoint pt ) const;
```

where

    pt   An x,y coordinate that specifies a position inside of the edit control

Returns the character index in the low-order word. The line index is returned in the high-order word.

The CharFromPos method will retrieve the line and character index for the specified pixel in the edit control.

The Clear Method

```
void Clear( );
```

The Clear method will clear all text from the edit control.

The Copy Method

```
void Copy( );
```

The Copy method will copy the selected text to the clipboard.

The Create Method

```
BOOL Create( DWORD dwStyle, const RECT& rect, CWnd* pParentWnd,
➥UINT nID );
```

where

dwStyle	The style of this edit control
rect	The coordinates this control should occupy
pParentWnd	The window to insert this edit control into
nID	The child window ID

Returns TRUE if successful.

The Create method will create a new edit control and place it into a parent window.

The Cut Method

```
void Cut( );
```

The Cut method will copy the selected text to the clipboard. The selected region will then be deleted.

The EmptyUndoBuffer Method

void EmptyUndoBuffer( );

The EmptyUndoBuffer method will empty the undo buffer.

The FmtLines Method

BOOL FmtLines(BOOL bAddEOL);

where

      bAddEOL   TRUE if end-of-line characters should be inserted

Returns TRUE if successful.

The FmtLines method will format the edit control so that soft line breaks are inserted or not inserted. This only affects the data returned by the GetHandle method.

The GetFirstVisibleLine Method

int GetFirstVisibleLine( ) const;

Returns the first visible line number. Single-line controls always return 0.

The GetHandle Method

HLOCAL GetHandle( ) const;

Returns the first visible line number. Single-line controls always return 0.

The GetLimitText Method

UINT GetLimitText( ) const;

Returns the maximum number of characters that this edit allows.

The GetLine Method

int GetLine(int nIndex, LPTSTR lpszBuffer) const;
int GetLine(int nIndex, LPTSTR lpszBuffer, int nMaxLength) const;

where

      nIndex   The zero-based index of the line to retrieve

      lpszBuffer   The string buffer to receive the line

      nMaxLength   The maximum length of the line buffer

Returns the number of bytes copied.

The GetLine method will retrieve the specified line from the edit control.

D

The `GetLineCount` Method

```
int GetLineCount( ) const;
```

Returns the number of lines in the edit control.

The `GetMargins` Method

```
DWORD GetMargins( ) const;
```

Returns the margins for the edit control. The left margin is in the low-order word. The right margin is in the high-order word.

The `GetModify` Method

```
BOOL GetModify( ) const;
```

Returns TRUE if the edit control's text has been modified.

The `GetPasswordChar` Method

```
TCHAR GetPasswordChar( ) const;
```

Returns the password character for the edit control.

The `GetRect` Method

```
void GetRect( LPRECT lpRect ) const;
```

where

lpRect	Will receive the bounding rectangle for the control

The GetRect method will return the bounding rectangle for the control.

The `GetSel` Method

```
DWORD GetSel( ) const;
void GetSel( int& nStartChar, int& nEndChar ) const;
```

where

nStartChar	Variable to receive the starting character of the current selection
nEndChar	Variable to receive the ending character of the current selection

Returns the current selection. The low-order word contains the starting position. The high-order word contains the ending position.

The `LimitText` Method

```
void LimitText( int nChars = 0 );
```

where

nChars   The maximum allowable characters for this control

The `LimitText` method sets the maximum allowable characters for this control.

The `LineFromChar` Method

```
int LineFromChar( int nIndex = -1 ) const;
```

where

nIndex   The zero-based index of a character, or -1 for the current line

Returns the zero-based index of the line containing the specified character.

The `LineIndex` Method

```
int LineIndex( int nLine = -1 ) const;
```

where

nLine   A zero-based line index

Returns zero-based character index of the specified line, or -1 if *nLine* does not exist.

The `LineLength` Method

```
int LineLength( int nLine = -1 ) const;
```

where

nLine   A zero-based character index to a character in the line whose length is to be determined. Can be -1 for the current line.

Returns the length of the specified line, or -1 if failure.

The `LineScroll` Method

```
void LineScroll( int nLines, int nChars = 0 );
```

where

nLines   The number of lines to scroll vertically

nChars   The number of characters to scroll horizontally

The `LineScroll` method will scroll the contents of the edit control horizontally and/or vertically.

D

The `Paste` Method

```
void Paste( );
```

The `Paste` method will insert the text contents of the clipboard into the edit control.

The `PosFromChar` Method

```
CPoint PosFromChar( UINT nChar ) const;
```

where

    nChar   A zero-based character index

Returns the coordinates for the top-left corner of the character specified.

The `ReplaceSel` Method

```
void ReplaceSel( LPCTSTR lpszNewText, BOOL bCanUndo = FALSE );
```

where

    lpszNewText   Pointer to a string that contains new text to replace the currently selected text

    bCanUndo   TRUE if this action can be undone

The `ReplaceSel` method will replace the selected text with the text specified.

The `SetHandle` Method

```
void SetHandle( HLOCAL hBuffer );
```

where

    hBuffer   A handle to a buffer in local memory

The `SetHandle` method will set the edit control's buffer to the specified handle.

The `SetLimitText` Method

```
void SetLimitText( UINT nMax );
```

where

    nMax   The maximum number of bytes this control can hold

The `SetLimitText` method will set the maximum allowable length of the text inside of an edit control.

The `SetMargins` Method

```
void SetMargins( UINT nLeft, UINT nRight );
```

where

nLeft	The width of the left margin
nRight	The width of the right margin

The SetMargins method will set the margins for the edit control.

The **SetModify** Method

```
void SetModify( BOOL bModified = TRUE );
```

where

bModified	TRUE if the control should be marked as modified

The SetModify method will set the modify flag for the control.

The **SetPasswordChar** Method

```
void SetPasswordChar( TCHAR ch );
```

where

ch	The character that should be displayed if this control is a password control

The SetPasswordChar method will set the character that is used to block out passwords.

The **SetReadOnly** Method

```
BOOL SetReadOnly( BOOL bReadOnly = TRUE );
```

where

bReadOnly	TRUE if the edit control is read only

The SetReadOnly method will set the control to be read only.

The **SetRect** Method

```
void SetRect( LPCRECT lpRect );
```

where

lpRect	The rectangle for the control

The SetRect method will set the bounding rectangle for the edit control. The control will be repainted.

The `SetRectNP` Method

```
void SetRectNP( LPCRECT lpRect );
```

where

    lpRect   The rectangle for the control

The `SetRectNP` method will set the bounding rectangle for the control, without causing the control to be repainted.

The `SetSel` Method

```
void SetSel( DWORD dwSelection, BOOL bNoScroll = FALSE );
void SetSel( int nStartChar, int nEndChar, BOOL bNoScroll = FALSE );
```

where

dwSelection	The starting position is in the low-order word, and the ending position is in the high-order word. To select all text, specify `0xffff0000`. If the low-order word is `-1`, any selection is removed.
bNoScroll	`TRUE` if the caret should not be scrolled into view.
nStartChar	The starting character for the selection.
nEndChar	The ending character for the selection.

The `SetSel` method will set the selected region for an edit control. If *nStarChar* is `0` and *nEndChar* is `-1`, all text is selected.

The `SetTabStops` Method

```
void SetTabStops( );
BOOL SetTabStops( const int& cxEachStop );
BOOL SetTabStops( int nTabStops, LPINT rgTabStops );
```

where

cxEachStop	The tabs should be placed at every *cxEachStop* dialog units
nTabStops	The number of tab stops
rgTabStops	A pointer to an array of tab stops

Returns `TRUE` if successful.

The `SetTabStops` method will set the tab stops to either a fixed width for each tab, or an array of values that specifies the tab stops individually.

The Undo Method

BOOL Undo( );

Returns TRUE if successful.

The Undo method will undo the last action.

CButton

The CButton class provides the functionality for all Windows buttons. This includes push buttons, radio buttons, and check boxes.

Header Files

The following header file should be included when using this class:

afxwin.h

Methods

The CButton class has the following methods:

CButton The constructor

Create Create a button

GetBitmap	Get the bitmap associated with this button
GetButtonStyle	Get the button style
GetCheck	Get the checked status of this button
GetCursor	Get the cursor associated with this button
GetIcon	Get the icon associated with this button
GetState	Get the state of this button
SetBitmap	Set the bitmap associated with this button
SetButtonStyle	Set the style of this button
SetCheck	Set the checked status of this button
SetCursor	Set the cursor associated with this button
SetIcon	Set the icon associated with this button
SetState	Set the state of this button

The following method is used to process messages sent to the class. This method can be overridden if special handling is needed for these messages.

DrawItem	Called when the button should be updated

D

The `CButton` Constructor

The `CButton` creates the CButton object. The `CButton` constructor is used as follows:

```
CButton();
```

The `Create` Method

```
BOOL Create( LPCTSTR lpszCaption, DWORD dwStyle, const RECT& rect, CWnd*
➥pParentWnd, UINT nID );
```

where

lpszCaption	The caption for the button
dwStyle	The style of this button
rect	The coordinates this control should occupy
pParentWnd	The window to insert this button into
nID	The child window ID

Returns `TRUE` if successful.

The `Create` method will create a new button and place it into a parent window.

The `DrawItem` Method

```
void DrawItem( LPDRAWITEMSTRUCT lpDrawItemStruct );
```

where

lpDrawItemStruct	Specifies how to draw the control

.The `DrawItem` method is called by MFC when a owner-drawn button control should be redrawn.

The `GetBitmap` Method

```
HBITMAP GetBitmap( ) const;
```

Returns a handle to the current bitmap, or `NULL` if there is no bitmap.

The `GetButtonStyle` Method

```
UINT GetButtonStyle( ) const;
```

Returns a handle to the current bitmap, or `NULL` if there is no bitmap.

The `GetCheck` Method

```
int GetCheck( ) const;
```

Returns the checked state of the button. Returns 0 for unchecked, 1 for checked, or 2 for indeterminate.

The GetCursor Method

```
HCURSOR GetCursor( );
```

Returns a handle to the current bitmap, or NULL if there is no cursor.

The GetIcon Method

```
HICON GetIcon( ) const;
```

Returns a handle to the current icon, or NULL if there is no icon.

The GetState Method

```
UINT GetState( ) const;
```

Returns the state of the control. Returns 3 for the check state, 4 for the highlight state, or 8 for the focus state.

The SetBitmap Method

```
HBITMAP SetBitmap( HBITMAP hBitmap );
```

where

> hBitmap   The bitmap to make current

Returns the old bitmap handle.

The SetBitmap method will set the current bitmap to the bitmap handle specified.

The SetButtonStyle Method

```
void SetButtonStyle( UINT nStyle, BOOL bRedraw = TRUE );
```

where

> nStyle   The button style
>
> bRedraw   TRUE if the button is to be redrawn

The SetButtonStyle method sets the button style and optionally redraws the button.

The SetCheck Method

```
void SetCheck( int nCheck );
```

where

> nCheck   The check state of the button. Should be 0 for unchecked,
>   1 for checked, or 2 for indeterminate.

The SetCheck method sets the check state of the button.

D

The `SetCursor` Method

```
HCURSOR SetCursor( HCURSOR hCursor );
```

where

    hCursor   The cursor to make current

Returns the old cursor handle.

The `SetCursor` method will set the current cursor to the cursor handle specified.

The `SetIcon` Method

```
HICON SetIcon( HICON hIcon );
```

where

    hIcon   The icon to make current

Returns a handle to the old icon.

The `SetIcon` method will set the current icon to the icon handle specified.

The `SetState` Method

```
void SetState( BOOL bHighlight );
```

where

    bHighlight   The highlight state of the button

Should be 3 for the check state, 4 for the highlight state, or 8 for the focus state.

The `SetState` method will set the state for the button.

CComboBox

The `CComboBox` implements a combo box control. A combo box is a cross between a list box and an edit control.

Header Files

The following header file should be included when using this class:

```
afxwin.h
```

Methods

The CComboBox class has the following methods:

CComboBox	The constructor
AddString	Add a string
Clear	Clear the contents of the edit control
CompareItem	Called to compare two items
Copy	Copy the contents of the edit control to the clipboard
Create	Create a combo box
Cut	Cut the text in the edit control to the clipboard
DeleteItem	Delete an item from the list box
DeleteString	Delete a string from the list box
Dir	Add a list of filenames
DrawItem	Redraw an item
FindString	Find a string in the list box
FindStringExact	Find an exact string in the list box
GetCount	Get a count of items in the list box
GetCurSel	Get the current selection in the list box
GetDroppedControlRect	Get the rectangle for the drop list
GetDroppedState	Determine whether the list is dropped
GetDroppedWidth	Get the width of the drop list
GetEditSel	Get the selection in the edit control
GetExtendedUI	Determine whether the combo box has an extended user interface
GetHorizontalExtent	Set the width in pixels that the list box occupies
GetItemData	Get the 32-bit value associated with each item
GetItemDataPtr	Get the 32-bit value associated with each item as a void pointer
GetItemHeight	Get the height of the list box items
GetLBText	Get string from the list box
GetLBTextLen	Get the length of a string in the list box
GetLocale	Get the locale identifier of a combo box
GetTopIndex	Get the index of the top item in list box

D

InitStorage	Preallocate space to store item list
InsertString	Insert a string into the list box
LimitText	Limit the amount of text in the edit box
MeasureItem	Measure a item

The following methods are used to process messages sent to the class. These methods can be overridden if special handling is needed for these messages.

Paste	Paste data from the clipboard into the edit control
ResetContent	Clear the list box
SelectString	Search for a string in the list box
SetCurSel	Set the current selection in the list box
SetDroppedWidth	Set the width for the dropped list
SetEditSel	Set the selection in the edit control
SetExtendedUI	Set the extended user interface aspects of this control
SetHorizontalExtent	Set the width in pixels for the drop list control
SetItemData	Set the item data associated with an item in the list box
SetItemDataPtr	Set the item data associated with an item as a void pointer
SetItemHeight	Set the item height
SetLocale	Set the locale
SetTopIndex	Set the item that should be the top of the list box
ShowDropDown	Show or hide the drop down list

The **CComboBox** Constructor

The CComboBox creates the CComboBox object. The CComboBox constructor is used as follows:

```
CComboBox();
```

The **AddString** Method

```
int AddString( LPCTSTR lpszString );
```

where

> *lpszString*   A string to add to the end of the list box

Returns CB_ERROR on error.

The AddString method will add the specified string to the bottom of the list portion of the combo box.

The Clear Method

```
void Clear( );
```

The Clear method will clear the contents of the edit control portion of the combo box.

The CompareItem Method

```
int CompareItem( LPCOMPAREITEMSTRUCT lpCompareItemStruct );
```

where

     lpCompareItemStruct   A structure that specifies a compare structure

Returns -1 if item 1 is before item 2. Returns 0 if item 1 and 2 are the same. Returns 1 if item 1 is after item 2.

The CompareItem method will compare the two specified items.

The Copy Method

```
void Copy( );
```

The Copy method will copy the contents of the edit portion of the combo box to the clipboard.

The Create Method

```
BOOL Create(  DWORD dwStyle, const RECT& rect, CWnd* pParentWnd, UINT nID
➥= 0xffff );
```

where

rect	The rectangle the combo box is to occupy
pParentWnd	The window into which this combo box is to be inserted
nID	The child window ID for this control

Returns TRUE if successful.

The Create method will create the CComboBox control.

The Cut Method

```
void Cut( );
```

The Cut method will copy the selected region of the edit portion of the combo box to the clipboard. The selected region of the edit text portion will be deleted by this method.

D

The `DeleteItem` Method

```
void DeleteItem( LPDELETEITEMSTRUCT lpDeleteItemStruct );
```

where

> *lpDeleteItemStruct*   A structure that specifies the item to delete

The `DeleteItem` method will delete the specified item from the list box portion of the combo box control.

The `DeleteString` Method

```
int DeleteString( UINT nIndex );
```

where

> *nIndex*   The zero-based index of the item to delete

Returns `CB_ERR` on error.

The `DeleteString` method will delete the specified item from the list box portion of the combo box.

The `Dir` Method

```
int Dir( UINT attr, LPCTSTR lpszWildCard );
```

where

> *attr*   The attribute that specifies which sort of files the `dir` command is looking for
>
> *lpszWildCard*   A wildcard string that specifies which files to include

Returns `CB_ERR` on error.

The `Dir` method will fill the list box with a list of filenames.

The `DrawItem` Method

```
void DrawItem( LPDRAWITEMSTRUCT lpDrawItemStruct );
```

where

> *lpDrawItemStruct*   A structure that specifies how to draw an item

The `DrawItem` method is called by MFC when an owner-drawn combo box item should be redrawn.

The FindString Method

```
int FindString( int nStartAfter, LPCTSTR lpszString ) const;
```

where

nStartAfter	The zero-based index of the item before the first item to be searched. If -1, the entire list box is searched.
lpszString	The string being searched for.

Returns CB_ERROR on failure, or the zero-based index of the list box item that matched the search.

The FindString method is called by MFC to search for the first occurrence of the specified prefix string in the list box.

The FindStringExact Method

```
int FindStringExact( int nStartAfter, LPCTSTR lpszString ) const;
```

where

nStartAfter	The zero-based index of the item before the first item to be searched. If -1, the entire list box is searched.
lpszString	The string being searched for.

The FindStringExact method is called by MFC to search for the first occurrence of the specified string in the list box.

The GetCount Method

```
int GetCount( ) const;
```

Returns the total number of items in the list box.

The GetCurSel Method

```
int GetCurSel( ) const;
```

Returns the zero-based currently selected list box item. Returns CB_ERR if there is none.

The GetDroppedControlRect Method

```
void GetDroppedControlRect( LPRECT lpRect ) const;
```

where

lpRect	A rectangle to contain the rectangle occupied by the drop list

The GetDroppedControlRect method retrieves the screen coordinates of the dropped list.

D

The `GetDroppedState` Method

```
BOOL GetDroppedState( ) const;
```

Returns TRUE if the dropped list box is visible.

The `GetDroppedWidth` Method

```
int GetDroppedWidth( ) const;
```

Returns the width of the dropped list.

The `GetEditSel` Method

```
DWORD GetEditSel( ) const;
```

Returns the current selection in the edit control. The low-order word contains the starting position. The high-order word contains the ending position.

The `GetExtendedUI` Method

```
BOOL GetExtendedUI( ) const;
```

Returns TRUE if the combo box has an extended user interface.

The `GetHorizontalExtent` Method

```
UINT GetHorizontalExtent( ) const;
```

Returns the amount that the list box can be scrolled horizontally.

The `GetItemData` Method

```
DWORD GetItemData( int nIndex ) const;
```

where

     nIndex   The zero-based index of the item for which data is being sought

Returns the 32-bit data value associated with the specified item.

The GetItemData method will return the user-defined 32-bit data item that can be associated with any item in the list box.

The `GetItemDataPtr` Method

```
void* GetItemDataPtr( int nIndex ) const;
```

where

     nIndex   The zero-based index of the item for which data is being sought

Returns the 32-bit data value associated with the specified item as a pointer.

The GetItemDataPtr method will return the user-defined 32-bit data item that can be associated with any item in the list box as a pointer.

The GetItemHeight Method

```
int GetItemHeight( int nIndex ) const;
```

where

nIndex   The zero-based index of the item for which the height
                        is being sought

Returns the height of the specified list box item.

The GetLBText Method

```
int GetLBText( int nIndex, LPTSTR lpszText ) const;
void GetLBText( int nIndex, CString& rString ) const;
```

where

nIndex   The zero-based index of the list box item to retrieve

lpszText   A buffer to receive the value of the specified list box item

rString   A string to receive the value of the specified list box item

Returns the length of the string.

The GetLBText method will get the text from one of the list box controls.

The GetLBTextLen Method

```
int GetLBTextLen( int nIndex ) const;
```

where

nIndex   The zero-based index of the item for which the length
                        is being sought

Returns the length of the specified list box item.

The GetLocale Method

```
LCID GetLocale( ) const;
```

Returns the locale (LCID) value of the control.

The GetTopIndex Method

```
int GetTopIndex( ) const;
```

Returns the index of the topmost visible list box item.

D

The `InitStorage` Method

```
int InitStorage( int nItems, UINT nBytes );
```

where

nItems	The number of items
nBytes	The number of bytes per item

Returns the number of items the list box can store without an error. Returns `CB_ERR` on error.

The `InsertString` Method

```
int InsertString( int nIndex, LPCTSTR lpszString );
```

where

nIndex	The zero-based index to the position that will receive the string; specify -1 to add the string at the end of the list
lpszString	The string to insert

Returns the zero-based index of where the string was inserted. Returns `CB_ERR` on error.

The `InsertString` method is used to add the specified string to the list box.

The `LimitText` Method

```
void LimitText( int nChars = 0 );
```

where

nChars	The maximum allowable characters for the edit control

The `LimitText` method sets the maximum allowable characters for the edit control.

The `MeasureItem` Method

```
virtual void MeasureItem( LPMEASUREITEMSTRUCT lpMeasureItemStruct );
```

where

lpMeasureItemStruct	A measure item structure

The `MeasureItem` method sets a measure item structure that contains display information about a list box item.

The `Paste` Method

```
void Paste( );
```

The `Paste` method will insert the text contents of the clipboard into the edit control.

The ResetContent Method

void ResetContent( );

The ResetContent method will clear all items from the list box.

The SelectString Method

int SelectString(int nStartAfter, LPCTSTR lpszString);

where

    nStartAfter   The index to start searching for

Returns the zero-based index of the selected string. Returns CB_ERR on error.

The SelectString method searches for the first string that starts with the specified string. When found it is selected.

The SetCurSel Method

int SetCurSel(int nSelect);

where

    nSelect   The index to select

Returns the zero-based index of the selected string. Returns CB_ERR on error.

The SetCurSel method will select the specified item in the list box.

The SetDroppedWidth Method

int SetDroppedWidth(UINT nWidth);

where

    nWidth   The width of the list box

Returns width of the list box. Returns CB_ERR on error.

The SetDroppedWidth method will set the width for the list box.

The SetEditSel Method

BOOL SetEditSel(int nStartChar, int nEndChar);

where

    nStartChar   The zero-based index to start selection at
    nEndChar   The zero-based index to end selection at

Returns TRUE if successful.

D

The SetEditSel method will set selection in the edit control.

The **SetExtendedUI** Method

```
int SetExtendedUI( BOOL bExtended = TRUE );
```

where

    bExtended   TRUE if this combo box supports an extended user interface

Returns CB_OKAY if successful, or CB_ERR on error.

The SetExtendedUI method will set the combo box to either have or not have an extended user interface.

The **SetHorizontalExtent** Method

```
void SetHorizontalExtent( UINT nExtent );
```

where

    nExtent   The horizontal width that the list box scrolls to

The SetHorizontalExtent method will set the horizontal extent of the list box. This is the true width of the list box that the horizontal scrollbar scrolls.

The **SetItemData** Method

```
int SetItemData( int nIndex, DWORD dwItemData );
```

where

    nIndex   The index of the item to set data for

The SetItemData method will set the item data for the specified item.

The **SetItemDataPtr** Method

```
int SetItemDataPtr( int nIndex, void* pData );
```

where

    nIndex   The index of the item to set data for

The SetItemData method will set the item data for the specified item as a pointer.

The **SetItemHeight** Method

```
int SetItemHeight( int nIndex, UINT cyItemHeight );
```

where

    nIndex   The index of the item to set the height for

    cyItemHeight   The desired height

Returns CB_ERR on error.

The SetItemHeight method will set the height of the specified item.

The SetLocale Method

LCID SetLocale(LCID nNewLocale);

where

    nNewLocale   The new locale ID (LCID) for the combo box

Returns the previous locale ID (LCID) for the combo box.

The SetLocale method will set the locale ID for the combo box.

The SetTopIndex Method

int SetTopIndex(int nIndex);

where

    nIndex   The index to be made topmost

Returns LB_ERR on error.

The SetTopIndex method will set the top index for the list box. This is the first item that is in view.

The ShowDropDown Method

void ShowDropDown(BOOL bShowIt = TRUE);

where

    bShowIt   TRUE if the drop list should be shown

The ShowDropDown method will show or hide the drop down list box.

CComboBoxEx

The CComboBoxEx implements an extended combo box. An extended combo box is a combo box that can contain images.

Header Files

The following header file should be included when using this class:

afxcmn.h

Methods

The CComboBoxEx class has the following methods:

Create	Create the extended combo box
DeleteItem	Delete an item from the extended combo box
GetComboBoxCtrl	Get the underlying combo control
GetEditCtrl	Get the underlying edit control
GetExtendedStyle	Get the extended style
GetImageList	Get the image list
GetItem	Get an item
HasEditChanged	Determine if the edit control has changed
InsertItem	Insert an item
SetExtendedStyle	Set the extended style
SetImageList	Set the image list
SetItem	Set the specified item

The CComboBoxEx Constructor

The CComboBoxEx constructor creates the CComboBoxEx object. The CComboBoxEx constructor is used as follows:

CComboBoxEx();

The Create Method

BOOL Create(DWORD dwStyle, const RECT& rect, CWnd* pParentWnd,
➡UINT nID);

where

dwStyle	The style of the combo box
rect	The rectangle the combo box is to occupy
pParentWnd	The window into which this combo box is to be inserted
nID	The child window ID for this control

Returns TRUE if successful.

The Create method will create the CComboBoxEx control.

The `DeleteItem` Method

```
int DeleteItem( int iIndex );
```

where

   iIndex   The item to delete

The `DeleteItem` method will delete the specified item from the list box portion of the combo box control.

The `GetComboBoxCtrl` Method

```
CComboBox* GetComboBoxCtrl( );
```

Returns a pointer to the underlying combo box control.

The `GetEditCtrl` Method

```
CEdit* GetEditCtrl( );
```

Returns a pointer to the underlying edit control.

The `GetExtendedStyle` Method

```
DWORD GetExtendedStyle( ) const;
```

Returns the extended style of the combo box.

The `GetImageList` Method

```
CImageList* GetImageList( ) const;
```

Returns a pointer to the image list.

The `GetItem` Method

```
BOOL GetItem( COMBOBOXEXITEM* pCBItem );
```

where

   pCBItem   The item to get the information to, and a structure to hold the data

Returns TRUE if successful.

The `GetItem` method will get information about the specified item.

The `HasEditChanged` Method

```
BOOL HasEditChanged( );
```

Returns TRUE if the user has typed in the edit box.

D

The `InsertItem` Method

```
int InsertItem( const COMBOBOXEXITEM* pCBItem );
```

where

   pCBItem   The item to be inserted

Returns the index at which the item was inserted.

The `InsertItem` method will insert the specified item into the list box.

The `SetExtendedStyle` Method

```
DWORD SetExtendedStyle( DWORD dwExMask, DWORD dwExStyles );
```

where

   dwExMask   The extended styles to mask out
   dwExStyles   The extended styles to set

Returns the styles previously used.

The `SetExtendedStyle` method will set the extended styles for the combo box.

The `SetImageList` Method

```
CImageList* SetImageList( CImageList* pImageList );
```

where

   pImageList   The new image list

Returns the previous image list.

The `SetImageList` method will set the image list.

The `SetItem` Method

```
BOOL SetItem( const COMBOBOXEXITEM* pCBItem );
```

where

   pCBItem   The item to set the information to, and a structure that the data

Returns `TRUE` if successful.

The `SetItem` method will set information about the specified item.

CListBox

The CListBox class implements a Windows list box. A list box is a control that displays a list of items for the user to choose from.

Header Files

The following header file should be included when using this class:

afxwin.h

Methods

The CListBox class has the following methods:

CListBox	The constructor
AddString	Add a string
Create	Create the control
DeleteString	Delete a string from the list box
Dir	Add a list of filenames
FindString	Find a string in the list box
FindStringExact	Find an exact string in the list box
GetAnchorIndex	Get the index of the anchor item
GetCaretIndex	Get the index of the item that has focus
GetCount	Get a count of the items in the list box
GetCurSel	Get the currently selected item in the list box
GetHorizontalExtent	Get the width in pixels that the list box scrolls to
GetItemData	Get the 32-bit value associated with each item
GetItemDataPtr	Get the 32-bit value associated with each item as a pointer
GetItemHeight	Get the item's height
GetItemRect	Get the item's rectangle
GetLocale	Get the locale
GetSel	Get the current selection
GetSelCount	Get a count of how many selected items
GetSelItems	Get the selected items

D

`GetText`	Get the text from a list box item
`GetTextLen`	Get the length of a list box item
`GetTopIndex`	Get the index of the top item in the list box
`InitStorage`	Preallocate space to store the item list
`InsertString`	Insert a string into the list box
`ItemFromPoint`	Determine an item from a point
`ResetContent`	Clear the list box content
`SelectString`	Search for a string
`SelItemRange`	Select a range of items
`SetAnchorIndex`	Set the index of the anchor item
`SetCaretIndex`	Set the current focus
`SetColumnWidth`	Set the column width
`SetCurSel`	Set the current selection
`SetHorizontalExtent`	Set the width in pixels for the scrolling area of the list box
`SetItemData`	Set the item data for one item
`SetItemDataPtr`	Set the item data as a pointer for one item
`SetItemHeight`	Set the height of an item
`SetLocale`	Set the locale
`SetSel`	Set the current selection
`SetTabStops`	Set the tab stops
`SetTopIndex`	Set the top index

The following methods are used to process messages sent to the class. These methods can be overridden if special handling is needed for these messages.

`CharToItem`	Determine an index from a character
`CompareItem`	Compare two items
`DeleteItem`	Delete an item
`DrawItem`	Draw an item
`MeasureItem`	Measure an item
`VKeyToItem`	Change a virtual key to an item

The `CListBox` Constructor

The `CListBox` constructor creates the CListBox object. The `CListBox` constructor is used as follows:

```
CListBox();
```

The `AddString` Method

```
int AddString( LPCTSTR lpszString );
```

where

> *lpszString*   A string to add to the end of the list box

Returns `CB_ERROR` on error.

The `AddString` method will add the specified string to the bottom of the list box.

The `CharToItem` Method

```
int CharToItem( UINT nKey, UINT nIndex );
```

where

> *pKey*   A key
>
> *nIndex*   The index to search forward from

Returns the item index that matches the specified character key.

The `CompareItem` Method

```
int CompareItem( LPCOMPAREITEMSTRUCT lpCompareItemStruct );
```

where

> *lpCompareItemStruct*   A structure that specifies a compare structure

Returns -1 if item 1 is before item 2. Returns 0 if items 1 and 2 are the same. Returns 1 if item 1 is after item 2.

The `CompareItem` method will compare the two specified items.

The `Create` Method

```
BOOL Create( DWORD dwStyle, const RECT& rect, CWnd* pParentWnd, UINT nID );
```

where

> *dwStyle*   The style of the list box
>
> *rect*   The rectangle the list box is to occupy

D

> *pParentWnd*   The window into which this list box is to be inserted
>
> *nID* ·   The child window ID for this control

Returns TRUE if successful.

The Create method will create the CListBox control.

The DeleteItem Method

```
void DeleteItem( LPDELETEITEMSTRUCT lpDeleteItemStruct );
```

where

> *lpDeleteItemStruct*   A structure that specifies the item to delete

The DeleteItem method will delete the specified item from the list box portion of the list box control.

The DeleteString Method

```
int DeleteString( UINT nIndex );
```

where

> *nIndex*   The zero-based index of the item to delete.

Returns CB_ERR on error.

The DeleteString method will delete the specified item from the list box.

The Dir Method

```
int Dir( UINT attr, LPCTSTR lpszWildCard );
```

where

> *attr*   The attribute that specifies what sort of files the dir command is looking for
>
> *lpszWildCard*   A wildcard string that specifies which files to include

Returns CB_ERR on error.

The Dir method will fill the list box with a list of filenames.

The DrawItem Method

```
void DrawItem( LPDRAWITEMSTRUCT lpDrawItemStruct );
```

where

> *lpDrawItemStruct*   A structure that specifies how to draw an item

The `DrawItem` method is called by MFC when an owner-drawn list box item should be redrawn.

The `FindString` Method

```
int FindString( int nStartAfter, LPCTSTR lpszString ) const;
```

where

nStartAfter	The zero-based index of the item before the first item to be searched. If -1, the entire list box is searched.
lpszString	The string being searched for.

Returns `CB_ERROR` on failure, or the zero-based index of the list box item that matched the search.

The `FindString` method is called by MFC to search for the first occurrence of the specified prefix string in the list box.

The `FindStringExact` Method

```
int FindStringExact( int nStartAfter, LPCTSTR lpszString ) const;
```

where

nStartAfter	The zero-based index of the item before the first item to be searched. If -1, the entire list box is searched.
lpszString	The string being searched for.

The `FindStringExact` method is called by MFC to search for the first occurrence of the specified string in the list box.

The `GetAnchorIndex` Method

```
int GetAnchorIndex( ) const;
```

Returns the index of the anchor item. The anchor is the first item in a list of contiguously selected items.

The `GetCaretIndex` Method

```
int GetCaretIndex( ) const;
```

Returns the index of the currently selected item.

The `GetCount` Method

```
int GetCount( ) const;
```

Returns the total number of items in the list box.

D

The GetCurSel Method

```
int GetCurSel( ) const;
```

Returns the zero-based currently selected list box item. Returns LB_ERR if there is none.

The GetHorizontalExtent Method

```
UINT GetHorizontalExtent( ) const;
```

Returns the amount that the list box can be scrolled horizontally.

The GetItemData Method

```
DWORD GetItemData( int nIndex ) const;
```

where

> *nIndex*   The zero-based index of the item for which data is being sought

Returns the 32-bit data value associated with the specified item.

The GetItemData method will return the user-defined 32-bit data item that can be associated with any item in the list box.

The GetItemDataPtr Method

```
void* GetItemDataPtr( int nIndex ) const;
```

where

> *nIndex*   The zero-based index of the item for which data is being sought

Returns the 32-bit data value associated with the specified item as a pointer.

The GetItemDataPtr method will return the user-defined 32-bit data item that can be associated with any item in the list box as a pointer.

The GetItemHeight Method

```
int GetItemHeight( int nIndex ) const;
```

where

> *nIndex*   The zero-based index of the item for which the height is
>   being sought

Returns the height of the specified list box item.

The `GetItemRect` Method

`BOOL GetItemRect( HTREEITEM hItem, LPRECT lpRect, BOOL bTextOnly );`

where

hItem	The item to get the rectangle for.
lpRect	Will contain the rectangle of the item.
bTextOnly	TRUE if the rectangle should only include text.

Returns TRUE if successful.

The `GetItemRect` method will retrieve the bounding rectangle for the image.

The `GetLocale` Method

`LCID GetLocale( ) const;`

Returns the locale ID (LCID) value of the control.

The `GetSel` Method

`int GetSel( int nIndex ) const;`

where

nIndex	The zero-based index of the item

Returns the selected status of the specified item.

The `GetSelCount` Method

`int GetSelCount( ) const;`

Returns number of items selected.

The `GetSelItems` Method

`int GetSelItems( int nMaxItems, LPINT rgIndex ) const;`

where

nMaxItems	The maximum number of items the array can hold
rgIndex	A pointer to an index to hold the selection values

Returns the number of items placed in the array.

The `GetSelItems` method will copy the selection status of each item into the specified array.

D

The `GetText` Method

```
int GetText( int nIndex, LPTSTR lpszText ) const;
void GetText( int nIndex, CString& rString ) const;
```

where

nIndex	The zero-based index of the list box item to retrieve
lpszText	A buffer to receive the value of the specified list box item
rString	A string to receive the value of the specified list box item

Returns the length of the string.

The `GetText` method will get the text from one of the list box controls.

The `GetTextLen` Method

```
int GetTextLen( int nIndex ) const;
```

where

nIndex	The zero-based index of the item for which the length is being sought

Returns the length of the specified list box item.

The `GetTopIndex` Method

```
int GetTopIndex( ) const;
```

Returns the index of the topmost visible list box item.

The `InitStorage` Method

```
int InitStorage( int nItems, UINT nBytes );
```

where

nItems	The number of items
nBytes	The number of bytes per item

Returns the number of items the list box can store without an error. Returns `CB_ERR` on error.

The `InsertString` Method

```
int InsertString( int nIndex, LPCTSTR lpszString );
```

where

nIndex	The zero-based index to the position that will receive the string; specify -1 to add the string at the end of the list
lpszString	The string to insert

Returns the zero-based index of where the string was inserted. Returns `LB_ERR` on error.

The `InsertString` method is used to add the specified string to the list box.

The `ItemFromPoint` Method

```
UINT ItemFromPoint( CPoint pt, BOOL& bOutside ) const;
```

where

pt	The point relative to the client area of the list box
bOutside	A Boolean that specifies whether the point was outside the list box

Returns the zero-based index of what item was selected. Returns `LB_ERR` on error.

The `InsertString` method is used to track a point to a item.

The `MeasureItem` Method

```
virtual void MeasureItem( LPMEASUREITEMSTRUCT lpMeasureItemStruct );
```

where

lpMeasureItemStruct	A measure item structure

The `MeasureItem` method sets a measure item structure that contains display information about a list box item.

The `ResetContent` Method

```
void ResetContent( );
```

The `ResetContent` method will clear all items from the list box.

The `SelectString` Method

```
int SelectString( int nStartAfter, LPCTSTR lpszString );
```

where

nStartAfter	The index to start searching for

Returns the zero-based index of the selected string. Returns `CB_ERR` on error.

The SelectString method searches for the first string that starts with the specified string. When found, it is selected.

The SelItemRange Method

```
int SelItemRange( BOOL bSelect, int nFirstItem, int nLastItem );
```

where

bSelect	TRUE to select items, FALSE to deselect items
nFirstItem	The first item to select
nLastItem	The last item to select

Returns LB_ERR on error.

The SelItemRange method will select or deselect a range of items.

The SetAnchorIndex Method

```
void SetAnchorIndex( int nIndex );
```

where

nIndex	Index of the anchor item to set

The SetAnchorIndex method will set the anchor index to that specified.

The SetCaretIndex Method

```
int SetCaretIndex( int nIndex, BOOL bScroll = TRUE );
```

where

nIndex	Index of the item that is to receive the focus
bScroll	TRUE if the list box should be scrolled to include this item

Returns LB_ERR on error.

The SetCaretIndex method will set the focus rectangle to the specified index. If this item is not visible to the user, it will be scrolled into view.

The SetColumnWidth Method

```
void SetColumnWidth( int cxWidth );
```

where

cxWidth	The width of a column

Returns LB_ERR on error.

The `SetColumnWidth` method will set the width of a column. This applies only to a multicolumn list box.

The `SetCurSel` Method

```
int SetCurSel( int nSelect );
```

where

> *nSelect*   The index to select

Returns the zero-based index of the selected string. Returns `CB_ERR` on error.

The `SetCurSel` method will select the specified item in the list box.

The `SetHorizontalExtent` Method

```
void SetHorizontalExtent( UINT nExtent );
```

where

> *nExtent*   The horizontal width that the list box scrolls to

The `SetHorizontalExtent` method will set the horizontal extent of the list box. This is the true width of the list box that the horizontal scrollbar scrolls.

The `SetItemData` Method

```
int SetItemData( int nIndex, DWORD dwItemData );
```

where

> *nIndex*   The index of the item to set data for

The `SetItemData` method will set the item data for the specified item.

The `SetItemDataPtr` Method

```
int SetItemDataPtr( int nIndex, void* pData );
```

where

> *nIndex*   The index of the item to set data for

The `SetItemDataPtr` method will set the item data for the specified item as a pointer.

The `SetItemHeight` Method

```
int SetItemHeight( int nIndex, UINT cyItemHeight );
```

D

where

    nIndex   The index of the item to set the height for

    cyItemHeight   The desired height

Returns `CB_ERR` or error.

The `SetItemHeight` method will set the height of the specified item.

The `SetLocale` Method

```
LCID SetLocale( LCID nNewLocale );
```

where

    nNewLocale   The new locale ID (LCID) for the list box

Returns the previous locale ID (LCID) for the list box.

The `SetLocale` method will set the locale ID for the list box.

The `SetTabStops` Method

```
void SetTabStops( );
BOOL SetTabStops( const int& cxEachStop );
BOOL SetTabStops( int nTabStops, LPINT rgTabStops );
```

where

    cxEachStop   Tabs are set to each *cxEachStop* dialog units

    nTabStops   The number of tab stops

    rgTabStops   A pointer to an array of tab stops

Returns `LB_ERR` on error.

The `SetTabStops` method will set the tab stops for the list box.

The `SetTopIndex` Method

```
int SetTopIndex( int nIndex );
```

where

    nIndex   The index to be made topmost

Returns `LB_ERR` on error.

The `SetTopIndex` method will set the top index for the list box. This is the first item that is in view.

The ShowDropDown Method

`void ShowDropDown( BOOL bShowIt = TRUE );`

where

bShowIt	TRUE if the drop list should be shown

The ShowDropDown method will show or hide the drop-down list box.

The VKeyToItem Method

`int VKeyToItem( UINT nKey, UINT nIndex );`

where

pKey	A virtual key
nIndex	The index to search forward from

Returns the item index that matches the specified character virtual key.

CScrollBar

The CScrollBar class implements a Windows scrollbar. A scrollbar is a horizontal or vertical control that enables the user to select a point in a range. This point is usually some location inside of a document that is visually displayed on the window or view.

Header Files

The following header file should be included when using this class:

`afxwin.h`

Methods

The CScrollBar class has the following methods:

CScrollBar	The constructor
Create	Create the scrollbar
EnableScrollBar	Enable or disable the scrollbar
GetScrollInfo	Set the scrollbar information
GetScrollLimit	Set the scrollbar limit
GetScrollPos	Set the scrollbar position
GetScrollRange	Set the allowable range for the scrollbar
SetScrollInfo	Set the scrollbar information

D

SetScrollPos	Set the scrollbar position
SetScrollRange	Set the allowable range for the scrollbar
ShowScrollBar	Show the scrollbar

The CScrollBar Constructor

The CScrollBar constructor creates the CScrollBar object. The CScrollBar constructor is used as follows:

```
CScrollBar();
```

The Create Method

```
BOOL Create( DWORD dwStyle, const RECT& rect, CWnd* pParentWnd,
➥UINT nID );
```

where

dwStyle	The style of the scrollbar
rect	The rectangle the scrollbar is to occupy
pParentWnd	The window into which this scrollbar is to be inserted
nID	The child window ID for this control

Returns TRUE if successful.

The Create method will create the CScrollBar control.

The EnableScrollBar Method

```
BOOL EnableScrollBar( UINT nArrowFlags = ESB_ENABLE_BOTH );
```

where

| nArrowFlags | Specifies which of the two arrows to enable |

Returns TRUE if successful.

The EnableScrollBar method will enable the specified scroll directions.

The GetScrollInfo Method

```
BOOL GetScrollInfo( LPSCROLLINFO lpScrollInfo, UINT nMask );
```

where

| lpScrollInfo | A structure to receive information about the scrollbar |
| nMask | Specifies which information to retrieve |

Returns TRUE if successful.

The GetScrollInfo method will get information about the specified scrollbar.

The GetScrollLimit Method

```
int GetScrollLimit( );
```

Returns the maximum value of a scrollbar.

The GetScrollPos Method

```
int GetScrollPos( ) const;
```

Returns the current position of the scrollbar.

The GetScrollRange Method

```
void GetScrollRange( LPINT lpMinPos, LPINT lpMaxPos ) const;
```

where

lpMinPos	A pointer to an int to receive the minimum scroll position
lpMaxPos	A pointer to an int to receive the maximum scroll position

Returns TRUE if successful.

The GetScrollRange method will get the scroll range for the scrollbar.

The SetScrollInfo Method

```
BOOL SetScrollInfo( LPSCROLLINFO lpScrollInfo, BOOL bRedraw = TRUE );
```

where

lpScrollInfo	A structure to set information about the scrollbar
bRedraw	TRUE if the scrollbar should be redrawn

Returns TRUE if successful.

The SetScrollInfo method will set information about the specified scrollbar.

The SetScrollPos Method

```
int SetScrollPos( int nPos, BOOL bRedraw = TRUE );
```

where

nPos	The position to set the scrollbar to
bRedraw	TRUE if the scrollbar should be redrawn

D

Returns the old position.

The SetScrollPos method will set the scrollbar position.

The SetScrollRange Method

```
void SetScrollRange( int nMinPos, int nMaxPos, BOOL bRedraw = TRUE );
```

where

nMinPos	A pointer to an int to set the minimum scroll position
nMaxPos	A pointer to an int to set the maximum scroll position
bRedraw	TRUE if the scrollbar should be redrawn

The SetScrollRange method will set the allowable scroll range for a scrollbar.

The ShowScrollBar Method

```
void ShowScrollBar( BOOL bShow = TRUE );
```

where

bShow	TRUE if the scrollbar should be shown

The ShowScrollBar method will show or hide the scrollbar.

CSpinButtonCtrl

The CSpinButtonCtrl class implements a spin control. A spin control consists of two arrows that enable the user to increase or decrease the control's value.

Header Files

The following header file should be included when using this class:

afxcmn.h

Methods

The CSpinButtonCtrl class has the following methods:

CSpinButtonCtrl	The constructor
Create	Create a spin control
GetAccel	Get the acceleration for the spin control
GetBase	Get the base for the spin control
GetBuddy	Get the buddy for the spin control

GetPos	Get the position of the spin control
GetRange	Get the spin control's range
GetRange32	Get the 32-bit range for the spin control
SetAccel	Set the acceleration for the spin control
SetBase	Set the base for the spin control
SetBuddy	Set the buddy for the spin control
SetPos	Set the position of the spin control
SetRange	Set the range for the spin control
SetRange32	Set the 32-bit range for the spin control

The CSpinButtonCtrl Constructor

The CSpinButtonCtrl constructor creates the CSpinButtonCtrl object. The CSpinButtonCtrl constructor is used as follows:

```
CSpinButtonCtrl();
```

The Create Method

```
BOOL Create( DWORD dwStyle, const RECT& rect, CWnd* pParentWnd,
➥UINT nID );
```

where

dwStyle	The style of the control
rect	The rectangle the control is to occupy
pParentWnd	The window into which this control is to be inserted
nID	The child window ID for this control

Returns TRUE if successful.

The Create method will create a CSpinButtonCtrl control.

The GetAccel Method

```
UINT GetAccel( int nAccel, UDACCEL* pAccel ) const;
```

where

| nAccel | The number elements in the accelerator array |
| pAccel | An array of acceleration values |

Returns TRUE if successful.

D

The GetAccel method will get the accelerator values.

The GetBase Method

```
UINT GetBase( ) const;
```

Returns the base value for the spin control.

The GetBuddy Method

```
CWnd* GetBuddy( ) const;
```

Returns the buddy window.

The GetPos Method

```
int GetPos( ) const;
```

Returns the position of the spin control.

The GetRange/GetRange32 Methods

```
DWORD GetRange( ) const;
void GetRange( int &lower, int& upper ) const;
void GetRange32( int &lower, int &upper ) const;
```

where

upper	Will contain the upper value for the spin control
lower	Will contain the lower value for the spin control

Returns a DWORD containing both the upper and lower values for the spin control. The low-order word is for the upper limit, and the high-order word is for the lower limit.

The GetRange/GetRange32 methods will get the range of the spin control as either a 32- or 16-bit value.

The SetAccel Method

```
BOOL SetAccel( int nAccel, UDACCEL* pAccel );
```

where

nAccel	The number elements in the accelerator array
pAccel	An array of acceleration values

Returns TRUE if successful.

The SetAccel method will set the accelerator values.

The `SetBase` Method

```
int SetBase( int nBase );
```

where

>   *nBase*   The new base for the spin control

Returns the old base.

The `SetBase` method will set the accelerator values.

The `SetBuddy` Method

```
CWnd* SetBuddy( CWnd* pWndBuddy );
```

where

>   *pWndBuddy*   The new buddy window

Returns the old buddy window.

The `SetBuddy` method will set the buddy window.

The `SetPos` Method

```
int SetPos( int nPos );
```

where

>   *nPos*   The new position for the spin control

Returns the old position.

The `SetPos` method will set the position of the spin control.

The `SetRange/SetRange32` Methods

```
void SetRange( int nLower, int nUpper );
void SetRange32( int nLower, int nUpper );
```

where

>   *nUpper*   Contains the upper value for the spin control
>
>   *nLower*   Contains the lower value for the spin control

The `SetRange/SetRange32` methods will set the range of the spin control as either a 32- or 16-bit value.

D

CProgressCtrl

The CProgressCtrl class implements a Windows progress control. A progress control is a control that graphically indicates the progress of some action.

Header Files

The following header file should be included when using this class:

afxcmn.h

Methods

The CProgressCtrl class has the following methods:

CProgressCtrl	The constructor
Create	Create the control
GetPos	Get the position
GetRange	Get the range
OffsetPos	Advances the control
SetPos	Sets the position
SetRange	Sets the range
SetRange32	Sets the range as a 32-bit value
SetStep	Set the step value
StepIt	Step by the step value

The CProgressCtrl Constructor

The CProgressCtrl constructor creates the CProgressCtrl object. The CProgressCtrl constructor is used as follows:

CProgressCtrl();

The Create Method

BOOL Create(DWORD dwStyle, const RECT& rect, CWnd* pParentWnd,
➥UINT nID);

where

dwStyle	The style of the control
rect	The rectangle the control is to occupy
pParentWnd	The window into which this control is to be inserted
nID	The child window ID for this control

Returns TRUE if successful.

The Create method will create the CProgressCtrl control.

The GetPos Method

```
int GetPos( ) const;
```

Returns the position of the progress control.

The GetRange Method

```
void GetRange( int& nLower, int& nUpper );
```

where

upper	Will contain the upper value for the progress control
lower	Will contain the lower value for the progress control

The GetRange methods will get the range of the progress control.

The OffsetPos Method

```
int OffsetPos( int nPos );
```

where

nPos	Amount to advance the progress control by

The OffsetPos method will move the control forward by the specified amount.

The SetPos Method

```
int SetPos( int nPos );
```

where

nPos	The new position for the progress control

Returns the old position.

The SetPosition method will set the position of the progress control.

The SetRange/SetRange32 Methods

```
void SetRange( short nLower, short nUpper );
void SetRange32( int nLower, int nUpper );
```

where

nUpper	Contains the upper value for the progress control
nLower	Contains the lower value for the progress control

D

The SetRange/SetRange32 methods will set the range of the progress control as either a 32- or 16-bit value.

The SetStep Method

```
int SetStep( int nStep );
```

where

    nStep   The amount to step

Returns the old amount to step.

The SetStep method will set the amount to advance the control by the next time that StepIt is called.

The StepIt Method

```
int StepIt( );
```

Returns the old position of the progress control.

The StepIt method will advance the control by the amount specified in the SetStep method.

CSliderCtrl

The CSliderCtrl class implements a Windows slider. A slider is a control that is dragged by the mouse to indicate values.

Header Files

The following header file should be included when using this class:

afxcmn.h

Methods

The CSliderCtrl class has the following methods:

CSliderCtrl	The constructor
ClearSel	Clear the selection
ClearTics	Clear any ticks
Create	Create a slider control
GetBuddy	Get the buddy window

GetChannelRect	Get the rectangle for the channels
GetLineSize	Get the line size
GetNumTics	Get the number of ticks
GetPageSize	Get the page size
GetPos	Get the position of the slider
GetRange	Get the range of the slider
GetRangeMax	Get the max range of the slider
GetRangeMin	Get the min range of the slider
GetSelection	Get the selection of the slider
GetThumbRect	Get the thumb rectangle of the slider
GetTic	Get the tick
GetTicArray	Get the tick array
GetTicPos	Get the tick position
GetToolTips	Get the tool tip control associated with this control
SetBuddy	Set the buddy of this control
SetLineSize	Set the line size
SetPageSize	Set the page size
SetPos	Set the position of the slider control
SetRange	Set the range of the slider control
SetRangeMax	Set the max range of the slider control
SetRangeMin	Set the min range of the slider control
SetSelection	Set the selection of the slider control
SetTic	Set the tick for the slider control
SetTicFreq	Set the tick frequency for the slider control
SetTipSide	Set the tip control
SetToolTips	Set the tool tips control
VerifyPos	Verify the position

D

The CSliderCtrl Constructor

The CSliderCtrl constructor creates the CSliderCtrl object. The CSliderCtrl constructor is used as follows:

```
CSliderCtrl();
```

The `ClearSel` Method

```
void ClearSel( BOOL bRedraw = FALSE );
```

where

    bRedraw   TRUE if the control should be redrawn

The `ClearSel` method will clear the selection.

The `ClearTics` Method

```
void ClearTics( BOOL bRedraw = FALSE );
```

where

    bRedraw   TRUE if the control should be redrawn

The `ClearTics` method will clear the ticks from the control.

The `Create` Method

```
BOOL Create( DWORD dwStyle, const RECT& rect, CWnd* pParentWnd,
➥UINT nID );
```

where

    dwStyle   The style of the control

    rect   The rectangle the control is to occupy

    pParentWnd   The window into which this control is to be inserted

    nID   The child window ID for this control

Returns TRUE if successful.

The `Create` method will create the CSliderCtrl control.

The `GetBuddy` Method

```
CWnd* GetBuddy( BOOL fLocation = TRUE ) const;
```

where

    fLocation   TRUE to get the left buddy, FALSE to get the right buddy

Returns the left or right buddy window.

The `GetChannelRect` Method

```
void GetChannelRect( LPRECT lprc ) const;
```

where

> *lprc*   The rectangle of the channel

The `GetChannelRect` will get the channel rectangle for the control. The channel is the area that the slider is slid over.

The `GetLineSize` Method

```
int GetLineSize( ) const;
```

Returns the line size for the control.

The `GetNumTics` Method

```
UINT GetNumTics( ) const;
```

Returns the number of ticks in the control.

The `GetPageSize` Method

```
int GetPageSize( ) const;
```

Returns the page size.

The `GetPos` Method

```
int GetPos( ) const;
```

Returns the position of the control.

The `GetRange` Methods

```
void GetRange( int &lower, int& upper ) const;
```

where

> *upper*   Will contain the upper value for the slider control
>
> *lower*   Will contain the lower value for the slider control

The `GetRange` method will get the range of the slider control.

The `GetRangeMax` Method

```
int GetRangeMax( ) const;
```

Returns the max range of the control.

The `GetRangeMin` Method

```
int GetRangeMin( ) const;
```

Returns the minimum range of the control.

D

The `GetSelection` Method

```
void GetSelection( int& nMin, int& nMax ) const;
```

where

nMin	Will contain the minimum value in the selection
nMax	Will contain the maximum value in the selection

The `GetSelection` method will get the selection range of the slider control.

The `GetThumbRect` Method

```
void GetThumbRect( LPRECT lprc ) const;
```

where

lprc	The rectangle of the thumb

The `GetThumbRect` method will get the thumb rectangle for the control.

The `GetTic` Method

```
int GetTic( int nTic ) const;
```

where

nTic	The zero-based index of the tick to get

The `GetTic` method will get position of the specified tick.

The `GetTicArray` Method

```
DWORD* GetTicArray( ) const;
```

The `GetTicArray` method will get the tick array.

The `GetTicPos` Method

```
int GetTicPos( int nTic ) const;
```

where

nTic	The zero-based index of the tick to get

The `GetTicPos` method will get position of the specified tick.

The `GetToolTips` Method

```
CToolTipCtrl* GetToolTips( ) const;
```

Returns the tool tips control.

The **SetBuddy** Method

CWnd* SetBuddy(CWnd* pWndBuddy, BOOL fLocation = TRUE);

where

    pWndBuddy   The new buddy window

    fLocation   TRUE to get the left buddy, FALSE to get the right buddy

The SetBuddy method will get position of the specified tick.

The **SetLineSize** Method

int SetLineSize(int nSize);

where

    nSize   The size of the line

Returns the old line size.

The SetLineSize method will set the line size.

The **SetPageSize** Method

int SetPageSize(int nSize);

where

    nSize   The size of the page

Returns the old page size.

The SetPageSize method will set the page size.

The **SetPos** Method

void SetPos(int nPos);

where

    nSize   The position of the thumb

Returns the old position.

The SetPos method will set the position.

The **SetRange** Method

void SetRange(int nMin, int nMax, BOOL bRedraw = FALSE);

D

where

nMin	The minimum value of the range
nMax	The maximum value of the range
bRedraw	TRUE if the control should be redrawn

The SetRange method will set the range of the slider control.

The SetRangeMax Method

```
void SetRangeMax( int nMax, BOOL bRedraw = FALSE );
```

where

nMax	The maximum value of the range
bRedraw	TRUE if the control should be redrawn

The SetRangeMax method will set the maximum range of the slider control.

The SetRangeMin Method

```
void SetRangeMin( int nMin, BOOL bRedraw = FALSE );
```

where

nMin	The minimum value of the range
bRedraw	TRUE if the control should be redrawn

The SetRangeMin method will set the minimum range of the slider control.

The SetSelection Method

```
void SetSelection( int nMin, int nMax );
```

where

nMin	The minimum value of the selection
nMax	The maximum value of the selection

The SetSelection method will set the selection of the slider control.

The SetTic Method

```
BOOL SetTic( int nTic );
```

where

nTic	The value of the tick

Returns TRUE if the tick was able to be set.

The SetTic method will set the tick value.

The SetTicFreq Method

```
void SetTicFreq( int nFreq );
```

where

    nFreq   The frequency of the tick

The SetTicFreq method will set the tick frequency.

The SetTipSide Method

```
int SetTipSide( int nLocation );
```

where

    nLocation   The location to display tips

Returns the old location to display tips.

The SetTipSide method sets the location to display tips.

The SetToolTips Method

```
void SetToolTips( CToolTipCtrl* pWndTip );
```

where

    pWndTip   The location to display tips

The SetToolTips method sets the tool tip control.

The VerifyPos Method

```
void VerifyPos();
```

The VerifyPos method will verify that the thumb is within the max and min values.

CHotKeyCtrl

The CHotKeyCtrl method implements a hot key control. A hot key is a keyboard combination that enables a user to perform an action quickly.

Header Files

The following header file should be included when using this class:

```
afxcmn.h
```

Methods

The CHotKeyCtrl class has the following methods:

CHotKeyCtrl	The constructor
Create	Create the hot key
GetHotKey	Get the hot key
SetHotKey	Set the hot key
SetRules	Set the rules

The CHotKeyCtrl Constructor

The CHotKeyCtrl constructor creates the CHotKeyCtrl object. The CHotKeyCtrl constructor is used as follows:

```
CHotKeyCtrl();
```

The Create Method

```
BOOL Create( DWORD dwStyle, const RECT& rect, CWnd* pParentWnd,
➥UINT nID );
```

where

dwStyle	The style of the control
rect	The rectangle the control is to occupy
pParentWnd	The window into which this control is to be inserted
nID	The child window ID for this control

Returns TRUE if successful.

The Create method will create the CHotKeyCtrl control.

The GetHotKey Method

```
DWORD GetHotKey( ) const;
void GetHotKey( WORD &wVirtualKeyCode, WORD &wModifiers ) const;
```

where

wVirtualKeyCode	The key code
wModifiers	The modifiers

Returns a DWORD containing the virtual-key code and modifier flags. The low-order word is the virtual-key code, and the high-order word is the modifier flags.

The GetHotKey method will get the hot key.

The `SetHotKey` Method

`void SetHotKey( WORD wVirtualKeyCode, WORD wModifiers );`

where

wVirtualKeyCode	The key code
wModifiers	The modifiers

The `SetHotKey` method will set the hot key.

The `SetRules` Method

`void SetRules( WORD wInvalidComb, WORD wModifiers );`

where

wInvalidComb	Invalid key codes
wModifiers	The modifiers

The `SetRules` method specifies certain keycodes that are invalid.

CIPAddressCtrl

D

The `CIPAddressCtrl` method implements an IP address control. This enables the user to enter an IP address.

Header Files

The following header file should be included when using this class:

`afxcmn.h`

Methods

The `CIPAddressCtrl` class has the following methods:

CIPAddressCtrl	The constructor
ClearAddress	Called to clear the address
Create	Called to create the control
GetAddress	Called to get the address
IsBlank	Is the control blank
SetAddress	Set the address
SetFieldFocus	Set the focus
SetFieldRange	Set the range

The `CIPAddressCtrl` Constructor

The CIPAddressCtrl constructor creates the CIPAddressCtrl object. The CIPAddressCtrl constructor is used as follows:

```
CIPAddressCtrl();
```

The `ClearAddress` Method

```
void ClearAddress( );
```

The ClearAddress method will clear the IP address from the control.

The `Create` Method

```
BOOL Create( DWORD dwStyle, const RECT& rect, CWnd* pParentWnd, UINT nID
);
```

where

dwStyle	The style of the control
rect	The rectangle the control is to occupy
pParentWnd	The window into which this control is to be inserted
nID	The child window ID for this control

Returns TRUE if successful.

The Create method will create the CIPAddressCtrl control.

The `GetAddress` Method

```
int GetAddress( BYTE& nField0, BYTE& nField1, BYTE& nField2,
➥BYTE& nField3 );
int GetAddress( DWORD& dwAddress );
```

where

nField0	Will contain the first byte of the IP address
nField1	Will contain the second byte of the IP address
nField2	Will contain the third byte of the IP address
nField3	Will contain the fourth byte of the IP address
dwAddress	Will contain the double word value for the address

Returns the number of bytes returned.

The GetAddress method will get an IP address from the control.

The `IsBlank` Method

```
BOOL IsBlank( ) const;
```

Returns TRUE if the IP address control is blank.

The `SetAddress` Method

```
void SetAddress( BYTE nField0, BYTE nField1, BYTE nField2, BYTE nField3 );
void SetAddress( DWORD dwAddress );
```

where

nField0	Contains the first byte of the IP address
nField1	Contains the second byte of the IP address
nField2	Contains the third byte of the IP address
nField3	Contains the fourth byte of the IP address
dwAddress	Contains the double word value for the address

The `SetAddress` method will get the IP address for the control.

The `SetFieldFocus` Method

```
void SetFieldFocus( WORD nField );
```

where

nField	The zero-based index of the field to make current

The `SetFieldFocus` method will get the IP address for the control.

The `SetFieldRange` Method

```
void SetFieldRange( int nField, BYTE nLower, BYTE nUpper );
```

where

nField	The zero-based index of the field to set the range for
nLower	The zero-based index of the lower character to begin the range
nUpper	The zero-based index of the upper character to end the range

The `SetFieldRange` method will set the range for one of the bytes.

CReBar

The `CReBar` class implements a rebar control. A rebar control is a toolbar that can contain child windows and controls.

Header Files

The following header file should be included when using this class:

`afxext.h`

Methods

The `CReBar` class has the following methods:

Create	Create the rebar control
AddBar	Add a band to the rebar
GetReBarCtrl	Get the underlying rebar control

The Create Method

```
BOOL Create( CWnd* pParentWnd, DWORD dwCtrlStyle = RBS_BANDBORDERS, DWORD
➥dwStyle = WS_CHILD ¦ WS_VISIBLE ¦ WS_CLIPSIBLINGS ¦ WS_CLIPCHILDREN
➥¦ CBRS_TOP, UINT nID = AFX_IDW_REBAR );
```

where

dwStyle	The style of the control
dwCtrlStyle	The rebar style of the control
pParentWnd	The window into which this control is to be inserted
nID	The child window ID for this control

Returns TRUE if successful.

The Create method will create the CReBar control.

The AddBar Method

```
BOOL AddBar( CWnd* pBar, LPCTSTR lpszText = NULL, CBitmap* pbmp = NULL,
➥DWORD dwStyle = RBBS_GRIPPERALWAYS ¦ RBBS_FIXEDBMP );
BOOL AddBar( CWnd* pBar, COLORREF clrFore, COLORREF clrBack, LPCTSTR
pszText
➥= NULL, DWORD dwStyle = RBBS_GRIPPERALWAYS );
```

where

pBar	A child window to insert into the bar
lpszText	Text to appear on the rebar; can be NULL
pBmp	A background bitmap
dwStyle	The style
clrFore	The foreground color
clrBack	The background color

Returns TRUE if successful.

The AddBar method will the specified child window as a bar.

The GetReBarCtrl Method

```
CReBarCtrl& GetReBarCtrl( ) const;
```

Returns the underlying rebar control.

CTreeCtrl

The CTreeCtrl class implements a tree control. A tree control is a control that displays data in an outline form. The most common example of a tree control is the Windows Explorer.

Header Files

The following header file should be included when using this class:

afxcmn.h

Methods

The CTreeCtrl class has the following methods:

CTreeCtrl	The constructor
Create	Create a tree control
CreateDragImage	Create a bitmap for dragging
DeleteAllItems	Delete all items from the tree
DeleteItem	Delete one item from the tree
EditLabel	Enable the user to edit in-place
EnsureVisible	Ensure that a tree item is visible
Expand	Expand the child items
GetBkColor	Get the background color for the control
GetCheck	Get the check status for an item
GetChildItem	Get a child item
GetCount	Get a count of the number of items
GetDropHilightItem	Get the target of a drag and drop
GetEditControl	Get the edit control used for in-place editing
GetFirstVisibleItem	Get the first visible item

D

`GetImageList`	Get the image list
`GetIndent`	Get the indent between a child and parent
`GetInsertMarkColor`	Get the color used to draw the insertion mark
`GetItem`	Get an item
`GetItemData`	Get the data associated with an item
`GetItemHeight`	Get the item height
`GetItemImage`	Get an item's image
`GetItemRect`	Get an item's rectangle
`GetItemState`	Get an item's state
`GetItemText`	Get an item's text
`GetNextItem`	Get the next item
`GetNextSiblingItem`	Get the next sibling item
`GetNextVisibleItem`	Get the next visible item
`GetParentItem`	Get the next parent item
`GetPrevSiblingItem`	Get the previous sibling item
`GetPrevVisibleItem`	Get the previous visible item
`GetRootItem`	Get the root item
`GetSelectedItem`	Get the selected item
`GetTextColor`	Get the text color
`GetToolTips`	Get the tool tip control
`GetVisibleCount`	Get a count of visible items
`HitTest`	Get the position of the cursor
`InsertItem`	Insert an item
`ItemHasChildren`	Determine whether an item has children
`Select`	Scrolls an item into view
`SelectDropTarget`	Select a drop target
`SelectItem`	Select an item
`SelectSetFirstVisible`	Select and set the first visible item
`SetBkColor`	Set the background color
`SetCheck`	Set a check item
`SetImageList`	Set the image list
`SetIndent`	Set the indent

SetInsertMark	Set the insert mark
SetInsertMarkColor	Set the insert mark color
SetItem	Set an item
SetItemData	Set item data
SetItemHeight	Set item height
SetItemImage	Set an item's image
SetItemState	Set an item's state
SetItemText	Set an item's text
SetTextColor	Set the text color
SetToolTips	Set the tool tips control
SortChildren	Sort the children
SortChildrenCB	Sort the children using an application defined short

The `CTreeCtrl` Constructor

The CTreeCtrl constructor creates the CTreeCtrl object. The CTreeCtrl constructor is used as follows:

```
CTreeCtrl();
```

The `Create` Method

```
BOOL Create( DWORD dwStyle, const RECT& rect, CWnd* pParentWnd,
➥UINT nID );
```

where

dwStyle	The style of the control
rect	The rectangle the control is to occupy
pParentWnd	The window into which this control is to be inserted
nID	The child window ID for this control

Returns TRUE if successful.

The Create method will create the CTreeCtrl control.

The `CreateDragImage` Method

```
CImageList* CreateDragImage( HTREEITEM hItem );
```

where

| hItem | A tree item |

D

Returns a drag image for the specified item.

The `CreateDragImage` method will create a drag image for the specified item.

The `DeleteAllItems` Method

```
BOOL DeleteAllItems( );
```

Returns TRUE if successful.

The `DeleteAllItems` method will delete all items in the tree control.

The `DeleteItem` Method

```
BOOL DeleteItem( HTREEITEM hItem );
```

where

   hItem   A tree item

Returns TRUE if successful.

The `DeleteItem` method will delete the specified tree item.

The `EditLabel` Method

```
CEdit* EditLabel( HTREEITEM hItem );
```

where

   hItem   A tree item

Returns a pointer to the edit control for the specified item.

The `EnsureVisible` Method

```
BOOL EnsureVisible( HTREEITEM hItem );
```

where

   hItem   A tree item

Returns TRUE if successful.

The `EnsureVisible` method will scroll the tree control so that the specified item is visible.

The `Expand` Method

```
BOOL Expand( HTREEITEM hItem, UINT nCode );
```

where

hItem	A tree item.
nCode	How to expand. Should be TVE_COLLAPSE, TVE_COLLAPSERESET, TVE_EXPAND, or TVE_TOGGLE.

Returns TRUE if successful.

The Expand method will expand the specified item.

The `GetBkColor` Method

```
COLORREF GetBkColor( ) const;
```

Returns the background color.

The `GetCheck` Method

```
BOOL GetCheck( HTREEITEM hItem ) const;
```

where

hItem	A tree item

Returns TRUE if successful.

The GetCheck method will determine the checked status of the specified item.

The `GetChildItem` Method

```
HTREEITEM GetChildItem( HTREEITEM hItem );
```

where

hItem	A tree item

Returns the child item of the specified item.

The `GetCount` Method

```
UINT GetCount( );
```

Returns the total number of items in the tree control.

The `GetDropHilightItem` Method

```
HTREEITEM GetDropHilightItem( );
```

Returns the drop target for drag and drop. Returns NULL on error.

D

The `GetEditControl` Method

`CEdit* GetEditControl( );`

Returns the underlying edit control, used for in-place editing.

The `GetFirstVisibleItem` Method

`HTREEITEM GetFirstVisibleItem( );`

Returns the first visible item. This is the topmost item that is not scrolled from view.

The `GetImageList` Method

`CImageList* GetImageList( UINT nImage );`

where

> *nImage*   The image list to be retrieved. Should be `TVSIL_NORMAL` or `TVSIL_STATE`.

Returns the specified image list.

The `GetIndent` Method

`UINT GetIndent( );`

Returns the indent value for the control. This is the amount of space a child is indented under a parent.

The `GetInsertMarkColor` Method

`COLORREF GetInsertMarkColor( ) const;`

Returns the color used for the insert mark.

The `GetItem` Method

`BOOL GetItem( TVITEM* pItem );`

where

> *pItem*   The item to get

Returns `TRUE` if successful.

The `GetItemData` Method

`DWORD GetItemData( HTREEITEM hItem ) const;`

where

> *hItem*   The item to get

Returns the `DWORD` value associated with the specified item.

The `GetItemHeight` Method

```
SHORT GetItemHeight( ) const;
```

Returns the height of an item.

The `GetItemImage` Method

```
BOOL GetItemImage( HTREEITEM hItem, int& nImage, int& nSelectedImage )
➡const;
```

where

hItem	The item to get the image to
nImage	Will contain the index of the image
hItem	Will contain the index of the selected version of the image

Returns TRUE if successful.

The `GetItemImage` method will retrieve the index of both the normal and selected version of the image.

The `GetItemRect` Method

```
BOOL GetItemRect( HTREEITEM hItem, LPRECT lpRect, BOOL bTextOnly );
```

where

hItem	The item to get the rectangle for
lpRect	Will contain the rectangle of the item
bTextOnly	TRUE if the rectangle should only include text

Returns TRUE if successful.

The `GetItemRect` method will retrieve the bounding rectangle for the image.

The `GetItemState` Method

```
UINT GetItemState( HTREEITEM hItem, UINT nStateMask ) const;
```

where

hItem	The item to get the state for
nStateMask	Specifies the states to return

Returns the state of the specified item.

The `GetItemState` method will return the state of the specified item.

D

The `GetItemText` Method

```
CString GetItemText( HTREEITEM hItem ) const;
```

where

    hItem   The item to get the text for

Returns the string associated with the specified item.

The `GetNextItem` Method

```
HTREEITEM GetNextItem( HTREEITEM hItem, UINT nCode );
```

where

    hItem   A tree item
    nCode   The type of relation to return

Returns the next item.

The `GetNextSiblingItem` Method

```
HTREEITEM GetNextSiblingItem( HTREEITEM hItem );
```

where

    hItem   A tree item

Returns the next sibling item.

The `GetNextVisibleItem` Method

```
HTREEITEM GetNextVisibleItem( HTREEITEM hItem );
```

where

    hItem   A tree item

Returns the next visible item.

The `GetParentItem` Method

```
HTREEITEM GetParentItem( HTREEITEM hItem );
```

where

    hItem   A tree item

Returns the parent item.

The GetPrevSiblingItem Method

```
HTREEITEM GetPrevSiblingItem( HTREEITEM hItem );
```

where

    hItem   A tree item

Returns the previous sibling item.

The GetPrevVisibleItem Method

```
HTREEITEM GetPrevVisibleItem( HTREEITEM hItem );
```

where

    hItem   A tree item

Returns the previous visible item.

The GetRootItem Method

```
HTREEITEM GetRootItem( );
```

Returns the root item.

The GetSelectedItem Method

```
HTREEITEM GetSelectedItem( );
```

Returns the selected item.

The GetTextColor Method

```
COLORREF GetTextColor( ) const;
```

Returns the text color.

The GetToolTips Method

```
CToolTipCtrl* GetToolTips( );
```

Returns the tool tips control.

The GetVisibleCount Method

```
UINT GetVisibleCount( );
```

Returns the visible item count.

The HitTest Method

```
HTREEITEM HitTest( CPoint pt, UINT* pFlags );
HTREEITEM HitTest( TVHITTESTINFO* pHitTestInfo );
```

D

where

pt	A point in client coordinates to test
pFlags	Will contain information about where the point "hit"
pHitTestInfo	Contains both the point and will be modified to indicate where the point "hit"

Returns the item the point is over or NULL if none.

The HitTest method can be used to determine where a point is in relation to the items of the tree control.

The InsertItem Method

```
HTREEITEM InsertItem( LPTVINSERTSTRUCT lpInsertStruct );
HTREEITEM InsertItem(UINT nMask, LPCTSTR lpszItem, int nImage, int
➥nSelectedImage, UINT nState, UINT nStateMask, LPARAM lParam,
➥HTREEITEM hParent, HTREEITEM hInsertAfter );
HTREEITEM InsertItem( LPCTSTR lpszItem, HTREEITEM hParent = TVI_ROOT,
➥HTREEITEM hInsertAfter = TVI_LAST );
HTREEITEM InsertItem( LPCTSTR lpszItem, int nImage, int nSelectedImage,
➥HTREEITEM hParent = TVI_ROOT, HTREEITEM hInsertAfter = TVI_LAST);
```

where

lpInsertStruct	A structure that specifies the item to insert
nMask	Specifies which attributes to set
lpszItem	The text for this item
nImage	Index of this item's image
nSelectedImage	The index of this item's selected image
nState	The item's state
nStateMask	Specifies which states to set
lParam	A 32-bit application specific value to associate with the item
hParent	The item's parent
hInsertAfter	The item that this one should be inserted after

Returns the newly created item, or NULL if error.

The InsertItem method is used to insert new items into the tree control.

The ItemHasChildren Method

```
BOOL ItemHasChildren( HTREEITEM hItem );
```

where

    hItem   A tree item

Returns TRUE if the specified item has child items.

The `Select` Method

```
BOOL Select( HTREEITEM hItem, UINT nCode );
```

where

    hItem   A tree item

    nCode   Specifies how to select the item

Returns TRUE if successful.

The `Select` method will select the specified item.

The `SelectDropTarget` Method

```
BOOL SelectDropTarget( HTREEITEM hItem );
```

where

    hItem   A tree item

Returns TRUE if successful.

The `SelectDropTarget` method will select the specified item as the drop target.

The `SelectItem` Method

```
BOOL SelectItem( HTREEITEM hItem );
```

where

    hItem   A tree item

Returns TRUE if successful.

The `SelectItem` method will select the specified item.

The `SelectSetFirstVisible` Method

```
BOOL SelectSetFirstVisible( HTREEITEM hItem );
```

where

    hItem   A tree item

Returns TRUE if successful.

D

The `SelectSetFirstVisible` method will select the specified item and cause it to be the first visible item.

The `SetBkColor` Method

```
COLORREF SetBkColor( COLORREF clr );
```

where

      clr   Specifies a color to set to the background color

Returns the previous background color.

The `SetBkColor` method will set a new background color.

The `SetCheck` Method

```
BOOL SetCheck( HTREEITEM hItem, BOOL fCheck = TRUE );
```

where

hItem	Specifies an item to set the check status for
fCheck	`TRUE` to check the item, `FALSE` to uncheck the item

Returns the previous checked value.

The `SetCheck` method will set the check status for the item.

The `SetImageList` Method

```
CImageList* SetImageList( CImageList * pImageList, int nImageListType );
```

where

pImageList	Specifies the image list.
nImageListType	Specifies the type of image list. Should be `TVSIL_STATE` or `TVSIL_NORMAL`.

Returns the previous image list.

The `SetImageList` method will set the image list to that specified.

The `SetIndent` Method

```
void SetIndent( UINT nIndent );
```

where

      nIndent   Specifies the indent value

The `SetIndent` method will set the indent value to that specified.

The `SetInsertMark` Method

```
BOOL SetInsertMark( HTREEITEM hItem, BOOL fAfter = TRUE );
```

where

hItem	A tree item
fAfter	TRUE if the insert mark should be placed after the item

Returns TRUE if successful.

The SetInsertMark method will set the insert mark before or after the item specified.

The `SetInsertMarkColor` Method

```
COLORREF SetInsertMarkColor( COLORREF clrNew );
```

where

clrNew	The color of the insert mark

Returns the old color of the insert mark.

The SetInsertMarkColor method will set the insert mark to the color specified.

The `SetItem` Method

```
BOOL SetItem( TVITEM* pItem );
BOOL SetItem( HTREEITEM hItem, UINT nMask, LPCTSTR lpszItem, int nImage,
➡int nSelectedImage, UINT nState, UINT nStateMask, LPARAM lParam );
```

where

pItem	A structure that specifies the item attributes
hItem	The item to set the attributes for
nMask	Specifies which attributes to set
lpszItem	The text for this item
nImage	Index of this item's image
nSelectedImage	The index of this item's selected image
nState	The item's state
nStateMask	Specifies which states to set
lParam	A 32-bit application specific value to associate with the item

Returns TRUE if successful.

The SetItem method will set the attributes for the specified item.

D

The `SetItemData` Method

```
BOOL SetItemData( HTREEITEM hItem, DWORD dwData );
```

where

hItem	A tree item
dwData	A 32-bit data value to associate with the item

Returns TRUE if successful.

The `SetItemData` method will set the 32-bit value for the item specified.

The `SetItemHeight` Method

```
SHORT SetItemHeight( SHORT cyHeight );
```

where

cyHeight	The item height

Returns the previous item height.

The `SetItemHeight` method will set the item height.

The `SetItemImage` Method

```
BOOL SetItemImage( HTREEITEM hItem, int nImage, int nSelectedImage );
```

where

hItem	The item to set
nImage	Index of this item's image
nSelectedImage	The index of this item's selected image

Returns TRUE if successful.

The `SetItemImage` method will set the selected and unselected images for the specified item.

The `SetItemState` Method

```
BOOL SetItemState( HTREEITEM hItem, UINT nState, UINT nStateMask );
```

where

hItem	The item to set
nState	The item's state
nStateMask	The state mask

Returns TRUE if successful.

The `SetItemState` method will set the state for the specified item.

The `SetItemText` Method

```
BOOL SetItemText( HTREEITEM hItem, LPCTSTR lpszItem );
```

where

hItem	The item to set
lpszItem	The string to set the item to

Returns TRUE if successful.

The `SetItemText` method will set the text for the specified item.

The `SetTextColor` Method

```
COLORREF SetTextColor( COLORREF clr );
```

where

clr	The new text color

Returns the old text color.

The `SetTextColor` method will set the color of the text.

The `SetToolTips` Method

```
void SetToolTips( CToolTipCtrl* pWndTip );
CToolTipCtrl* SetToolTips( CToolTipCtrl* pWndTip );
```

where

pWndTip	The tool tip control to use

Returns a pointer to the old tool tip control.

The `SetToolTips` method will set the tool tip control to be used.

The `SortChildren` Method

```
BOOL SortChildren( HTREEITEM hItem );
```

where

hItem	The item whose children are to be sorted

Returns TRUE if successful.

The `SortChildren` method will sort the children of the specified item.

D

The `SortChildrenCB` Method

BOOL SortChildrenCB(LPTVSORTCB pSort);

where

pSort   A structure that specifies how to sort the children

Returns TRUE if successful.

The `SortChildrenCB` method will sort the children of the specified item in an application-defined way.

CTabCtrl

The `CTabCtrl` class implements a Windows tab control. A tab control item displays a series of tabs that are selectable by the user.

Header Files

The following header file should be included when using this class:

afxcmn.h

Methods

The `CTabCtrl` class has the following methods:

CTabCtrl	The constructor
AdjustRect	Calculate the display area
Create	Create a tab control
DeleteAllItems	Delete all items from the tab control
DeleteItem	Delete an item from the tab control
DeselectAll	Deselect all items from the tab control
GetCurFocus	Get the current focus
GetCurSel	Get the current selection
GetExtendedStyle	Get the extended style
GetImageList	Get the image list
GetItem	Get an item
GetItemCount	Get the item count

GetItemRect	Get an item's rectangle
GetItemState	Get an item's state
GetRowCount	Get the row count
GetToolTips	Get the tool tips control
HighlightItem	Highlight an item
HitTest	Test to see where a point is at
InsertItem	Insert an item
RemoveImage	Remove an image
SetCurFocus	Set the current focus
SetCurSel	Set the current selection
SetExtendedStyle	Set the extended style
SetImageList	Set the image list
SetItem	Set the attributes for an item
SetItemExtra	Set extra attributes for an item
SetItemSize	Set an item's size
SetItemState	Set an item's state
SetMinTabWidth	Set the minimum tab width
SetPadding	Set the padding
SetToolTips	Set the tool tips control

D

The CTabCtrl Constructor

The CTabCtrl constructor creates the CTabCtrl object. The CTabCtrl constructor is used as follows:

```
CTabCtrl();
```

The AdjustRect Method

```
void AdjustRect( BOOL bLarger, LPRECT lpRect );
```

where

bLarger	TRUE if *lpRect* specifies a display rectangle, FALSE for a window rectangle
lpRect	Will receive the rectangle requested

The AdjustRect method calculates the proper display rectangle for a tab control.

The Create Method

```
BOOL Create( DWORD dwStyle, const RECT& rect, CWnd* pParentWnd,
➥UINT nID );
```

where

dwStyle	The style of the control
rect	The rectangle the control is to occupy
pParentWnd	The window into which this control is to be inserted
nID	The child window ID for this control

Returns TRUE if successful.

The Create method will create the CTabCtrl control.

The DeleteAllItems Method

```
BOOL DeleteAllItems( );
```

Returns TRUE if successful.

The DeleteAllItems method will delete all items from the tab control.

The DeleteItem Method

```
BOOL DeleteItem( int nItem );
```

where

nItem	The item to delete

Returns TRUE if successful.

The DeleteItem method will delete the specified item.

The DeselectAll Method

```
void DeselectAll( BOOL fExcludeFocus );
```

where

fExcludeFocus	TRUE if the focus should remain selected

The DeselectAll method will deselect all items.

The DrawItem Method

void DrawItem(LPDRAWITEMSTRUCT lpDrawItemStruct);

where

> *lpDrawItemStruct*   Specifies how to draw the control

The DrawItem method is called by MFC when an owner-drawn tab control should be redrawn.

The GetCurFocus Method

int GetCurFocus( ) const;

Returns the zero-based index of the tab that has focus.

The GetCurSel Method

int GetCurSel( ) const;

Returns the zero-based index of the tab that is selected.

The GetExtendedStyle Method

DWORD GetExtendedStyle( );

Returns extended style of the tab control.

The GetImageList Method

HIMAGELIST GetImageList( ) const;

Returns the image list associated with this control.

The GetItem Method

BOOL GetItem(int nItem, TCITEM* pTabCtrlItem) const;

where

> *nItem*   The item to get
>
> *pTabCtrlItem*   A structure that will receive information about the item

Returns TRUE if successful.

The GetItem method is called to get information about the specified item.

The GetItemCount Method

int GetItemCount( ) const;

Returns the item count for the control.

D

The `GetItemRect` Method

```
BOOL GetItemRect( int nItem, LPRECT lpRect ) const;
```

where

nItem	The item to get
lpRect	Will hold the rectangle for the specified item

Returns TRUE if successful.

The GetItemRect method is called to get the rectangle for the specified item.

The `GetItemState` Method

```
BOOL GetItemState( int nItem, DWORD dwMask, DWORD& dwState ) const;
```

where

nItem	The item to get
dwMask	The state attributes to get
dwState	Will hold the state attributes

Returns TRUE if successful.

The GetItemState method is called to get the state of the specified item.

The `GetRowCount` Method

```
int GetRowCount( ) const;
```

Returns the row count.

The `GetToolTips` Method

```
CToolTipCtrl* GetToolTips( ) const;
```

Returns the tool tips control.

The `HighlightItem` Method

```
BOOL HighlightItem( int idItem, BOOL fHighlight = TRUE );
```

where

nItem	The item to highlight
fHighlight	TRUE if the tab should be highlighted

Returns TRUE if successful.

The HighlightItem method will highlight the specified item.

The `HitTest` Method

```
int HitTest( TCHITTESTINFO* pHitTestInfo ) const;
```

where

> *pHitTestInfo*   Contains the point and will be modified to indicate
> where the point "hit"

Returns the item the point is over or NULL if none.

The HitTest method can be used to determine where a point is in relation to the items of
the tab control.

The `InsertItem` Method

```
BOOL InsertItem( int nItem, TCITEM* pTabCtrlItem );
BOOL InsertItem( int nItem, LPCTSTR lpszItem );
BOOL InsertItem( int nItem, LPCTSTR lpszItem, int nImage );
BOOL InsertItem( UINT nMask, int nItem, LPCTSTR lpszItem, int nImage,
➡LPARAM lParam );
```

where

> *nItem*   The zero-based index of the item to add
>
> *lpszItem*   The filename
>
> *nImage*   The image to be associated with this item

Returns the item the new item number, or -1 on error.

The InsertItem method will insert a tab item into the tab control.

The `RemoveImage` Method

```
void RemoveImage( int nImage );
```

where

> *nItem*   The item to remove

The RemoveImage method will remove the specified image.

The `SetCurFocus` Method

```
void SetCurFocus( int nItem );
```

where

> *nItem*   The item to get the focus

The SetCurFocus method will set the focus to the specified item.

D

The `SetCurSel` Method

```
int SetCurSel( int nItem );
```

where

    nItem   The item to select

The `SetCurSel` method will set the selection to the specified item.

The `SetExtendedStyle` Method

```
DWORD SetExtendedStyle( DWORD dwExMask, DWORD dwExStyles );
```

where

    dwExMask   The extended styles to mask out.

    dwExStyles   The extended styles to set.

Returns the styles previously used.

The `SetExtendedStyle` method will set the extended styles for the combo box.

The `SetImageList` Method

```
CImageList* SetImageList( CImageList * pImageList, int nImageListType );
```

where

    pImageList   Specifies the image list.

    nImageListType Specifies the type of image list. Should be `TVSIL_STATE` or `TVSIL_NORMAL`.

Returns the previous image list.

The `SetImageList` method will set the image list to that specified.

The `SetItem` Method

```
BOOL SetItem( int nItem, TCITEM* pTabCtrlItem );
```

where

    nItem   The item to set

    pTabCtrlItem   A structure that specified information about the item

Returns `TRUE` if successful.

The `SetItem` method will set the specified item to the values contained in *pTabCtrlItem*.

The `SetItemExtra` Method

BOOL SetItemExtra(int nBytes);

where

> *nBytes*   The number of extra bytes to hold for each item

Returns TRUE if successful.

The SetItemExtra method will set the number of extra bytes held for each item.

The `SetItemSize` Method

CSize SetItemSize(CSize size);

where

> *size*   The new item size

Returns the old item size.

The SetItemSize method will set the item size.

The `SetItemState` Method

BOOL SetItemState(int nItem, DWORD dwMask, DWORD dwState);

where

> *nItem*   The item to set
>
> *dwMask*   The state attributes to remove
>
> *dwState*   The state attributes to set

Returns TRUE if successful.

The SetItemState method will set the item's state.

The `SetMinTabWidth` Method

int SetMinTabWidth(int cx);

where

> *cx*   The new minimum tab width

Returns the previous minimum tab width.

The SetMinTabWidth method will set the minimum tab width.

D

The `SetPadding` Method

```
void SetPadding( CSize size );
```

where

    size   The new amount of padding

The `SetPadding` method will set the amount of padding for the control.

The `SetToolTips` Method

```
void SetToolTips( CToolTipCtrl* pWndTip );
```

where

    pWndTip   The new tool tips control

The `SetToolTips` method will set the tool tips control to be used with the tab control.

CAnimateCtrl

The `CAnimateCtrl` class implements an animated control. An animated control is based from an AVI file or resource. The control simply displays the animation. No audio data is used.

Header Files

The following header file should be included when using this class:

```
afxcmn.h
```

Methods

The `CAnimateCtrl` class has the following methods:

CAnimateCtrl	The constructor
Close	Close an AVI file or resource
Create	Create the animated control
Open	Open an AVI file
Play	Play an AVI file
Seek	Seek to a position in an AVI file
Stop	Stop playing an AVI file

The `CAnimateCtrl` Constructor

The `CAnimateCtrl` constructor creates the CAnimateCtrl object. The `CAnimateCtrl` constructor is used as follows:

```
CAnimateCtrl();
```

The `Close` Method

```
BOOL Close( );
```

Returns TRUE if successful.

The `Close` method will close an AVI file that was opened by `Open`.

The `Create` Method

```
BOOL Create( DWORD dwStyle, const RECT& rect, CWnd* pParentWnd, UINT nID
= 0xffff );
```

where

dwStyle	The style of the control
rect	The rectangle the control is to occupy
pParentWnd	The window into which this control is to be inserted
nID	The child window ID for this control

Returns TRUE if successful.

The `Create` method will create the CAnimateCtrl control.

The `Open` Method

```
BOOL Open( LPCTSTR lpszFileName );
BOOL Open( UINT nID );
```

where

lpszFileName	The style of the control
nID	The rectangle the control is to occupy

Returns TRUE if successful.

The `Open` method will open an AVI file or resource. When opened, the AVI file or resource can be played in the control.

D

The Play Method

BOOL Play(UINT nFrom, UINT nTo, UINT nRep);

where

nFrom	The zero-based index of the starting frame.
nTo	The zero-based index of the ending frame. To play to the ending frame, specify -1.
nRep	The number of times to repeat, or -1 to repeat infinitely.

Returns TRUE if successful.

The Play method will begin playing the animation. This method will return, while the animation plays in the background.

The Seek Method

BOOL Seek(UINT nTo);

where

nTo	The zero-based index to move to; specify -1 for the final frame

Returns TRUE if successful.

The Seek method will begin move to the specified frame.

The Stop Method

BOOL Stop( );

Returns TRUE if successful.

The Stop method will stop playing the AVI file.

CRichEditCtrl

The CRichEditCtrl class implements a rich text control. A rich text control is a text editing control that enables formatting.

Header Files

The following header file should be included when using this class:

afxcmn.h

Methods

The CRichEditCtrl class has the following methods:

CRichEditCtrl	The constructor
CanPaste	Can a paste be done
CanUndo	Can an undo be done
Clear	Clear the contents
Copy	Perform a copy
Create	Create the rich text control
Cut	Perform a cut
DisplayBand	Display output from the control
EmptyUndoBuffer	Empty the undo buffer
FindText	Find text
FormatRange	Format a range
GetCharPos	Get a character range
GetDefaultCharFormat	Get the default character format
GetEventMask	Get the event mask
GetFirstVisibleLine	Get the first visible line
GetIRichEditOle	Get a pointer to the IRichEditOle for this control
GetLimitText	Get the text limit
GetLine	Get a line of text
GetLineCount	Get a line count for the total control
GetModify	Determine whether the text has been modified
GetParaFormat	Get the paragraph format
GetRect	Get the rectangle for the control
GetSel	Get the selection range
GetSelectionCharFormat	Get the selection character format
GetSelectionType	Get the selection type
GetSelText	Get the selected text
GetTextLength	Get the length of the text
HideSelection	Hide the selection
LimitText	Set the text limit

D

LineFromChar	Determine a line from a character
LineIndex	Determine a line from a index
LineLength	Get a line length
LineScroll	Scroll the text
Paste	Perform a paste
PasteSpecial	Perform a special paste
ReplaceSel	Replace a selection
RequestResize	Force the control to send resize notifications
SetBackgroundColor	Set the background color
SetDefaultCharFormat	Set the default character format
SetEventMask	Set the event mask
SetModify	Set the modification flag
SetOLECallback	Set the IRichEditOleCallback for the control
SetOptions	Set the control options
SetParaFormat	Set the paragraph format
SetReadOnly	Set the read-only status
SetRect	Set the rectangle for the control
SetSel	Set the selection for the control
SetSelectionCharFormat	Set the selection character format
SetTargetDevice	Set the target device
SetWordCharFormat	Set the word character format
StreamIn	Store text from an input stream into this control
StreamOut	Store text from this control to an output stream
Undo	Perform an undo

The CRichEditCtrl Constructor

The CRichEditCtrl constructor creates the CRichEditCtrl object. The CRichEditCtrl constructor is used as follows:

```
CRichEditCtrl();
```

The CanPaste Method

```
BOOL CanPaste( UINT nFormat = 0 ) const;
```

where

> *nFormat*   A clipboard format

Returns TRUE if the specified clipboard format can be pasted to this control.

The CanUndo Method

```
BOOL CanUndo( ) const;
```

Returns TRUE if last action can be undone.

The Clear Method

```
void Clear( );
```

The Clear method will clear the text from the control.

The Copy Method

```
void Copy( );
```

The Copy method will copy the selection to the clipboard.

The Create Method

```
BOOL Create( DWORD dwStyle, const RECT& rect, CWnd* pParentWnd,
➥UINT nID );
```

where

> *dwStyle*   The style of the control
>
> *rect*   The rectangle the control is to occupy
>
> *pParentWnd*   The window into which this control is to be inserted
>
> *nID*   The child window ID for this control

Returns TRUE if successful.

The Create method will create the CRichEditCtrl control.

The Cut Method

```
void Cut( );
```

The Cut method will copy the selection to the clipboard, and then delete the current selection.

D

The `DisplayBand` Method

```
BOOL DisplayBand( LPRECT pDisplayRect );
```

where

      pDisplayRect   The display rectangle

Returns TRUE if successful.

The `DisplayBand` method will display the specified band. This allows only a portion of the text to be displayed.

The `EmptyUndoBuffer` Method

```
void EmptyUndoBuffer( );
```

The `EmptyUndoBuffer` method will clear the undo buffer.

The `FindText` Method

```
long FindText( DWORD dwFlags, FINDTEXTEX* pFindText ) const;
```

where

      dwFlags   Specifies how to search. Should be FR_MATCHCASE or FR_WHOLEWORD.

      pFindText   A structure that specifies what to search for.

Returns the zero-based character position if found, or -1 if not found.

The `FormatRange` Method

```
long FormatRange( FORMATRANGE* pfr, BOOL bDisplay = TRUE );
```

where

      pfr   Pointer to a structure that contains information about the output device

      bDisplay   TRUE if the text should be rendered

Returns the last character that fits in the range, plus one.

The `FormatRange` method enables the program to determine how much text will fit in a display range.

The **GetCharPos** Method

```
CPoint GetCharPos( long lChar ) const;
```

where

     lChar   A zero-based character index

Returns the coordinates for the top-left corner of the specified character.

The **GetDefaultCharFormat** Method

```
DWORD GetDefaultCharFormat( CHARFORMAT& cf ) const;
```

where

     cf   Will receive the default character format

Returns the dwMask data member of *cf*.

The GetDefaultCharFormat member will get the default character format. This is the format that any new text will take.

The **GetEventMask** Method

```
long GetEventMask( ) const;
```

Returns the event mask.

The GetEventMask member will get the event mask for the control. The event mask specifies which notification messages are sent to the parent.

The **GetFirstVisibleLine** Method

```
int GetFirstVisibleLine( ) const;
```

Returns the zero-based index of the first visible line.

The **GetIRichEditOle** Method

```
IRichEditOle* GetIRichEditOle( ) const;
```

Returns a pointer to the IRichEditOle interface for the control. Returns NULL if the interface is not accessible.

The **GetLimitText** Method

```
long GetLimitText( ) const;
```

Returns the maximum number of characters the control can accept.

D

The `GetLine` Method

```
int GetLine( int nIndex, LPTSTR lpszBuffer ) const;
int GetLine( int nIndex, LPTSTR lpszBuffer, int nMaxLength ) const;
```

where

nIndex	Zero-based index of the line to get
lpszBuffer	Buffer to receive the line
nMaxLength	Maximum size of the buffer

Returns the number of characters copied to the buffer.

The `GetLine` method will get the specified line from the edit control.

The `GetLineCount` Method

```
int GetLineCount( ) const;
```

Returns number of text lines in the control.

The `GetModify` Method

```
BOOL GetModify( ) const;
```

Returns `TRUE` if the text has been modified.

The `GetParaFormat` Method

```
DWORD GetParaFormat( PARAFORMAT& pf ) const;
```

where

pf	Will receive the paragraph format

Returns the `dwMask` data member of *pf*.

The `GetParaFormat` method will get the paragraph format for the current selection.

The `GetRect` Method

```
void GetRect( LPRECT lpRect ) const;
```

where

lpRect	Will receive bounding rectangle for the control

The `GetRect` method will get the bounding rectangle for the control.

The `GetSel` Method

```
void GetSel( CHARRANGE& cr ) const;
void GetSel( long& nStartChar, long& nEndChar ) const;
```

where

cr	Will hold the selection range as a structure
nStartChar	Will hold the starting character of the selection range
nEndChar	Will hold the ending character of the selection range

The `GetSel` method will get the selection range.

The `GetSelectionCharFormat` Method

```
DWORD GetSelectionCharFormat( CHARFORMAT& cf ) const;
```

where

cf	Will hold the character format of the selection

The `GetSelectionCharFormat` method will get the selection character format.

The `GetSelectionType` Method

```
WORD GetSelectionType( ) const;
```

Returns the selection type. Will be one of SEL_EMPTY, SEL_TEXT, SEL_OBJECT, SEL_MUL-TICHAR, or SEL_MULTIOBJECT.

The `GetSelText` Method

```
long GetSelText( LPTSTR lpBuf ) const;
CString GetSelText( ) const;
```

where

lpBuf	Buffer to receive the selected text

Returns the number of characters copied to the buffer. Can also return a CString that represents the selected text.

The `GetSelText` method will get the currently selected text.

The `GetTextLength` Method

```
long GetTextLength( );
```

Returns the length of the text in the control.

The `HideSelection` Method

```
void HideSelection( BOOL bHide, BOOL bPerm );
```

where

bHide	TRUE to hide the selection
bPerm	TRUE if this is a permanent change

The `HideSelection` method will show or hide the current selection.

The `LimitText` Method

```
void LimitText( long nChars = 0 );
```

where

nChars	The number of characters to limit the text to; pass a zero to allow the maximum number of characters

The `LimitText` method will limit the amount of text that can be entered into the control.

The `LineFromChar` Method

```
long LineFromChar( long nIndex ) const;
```

where

nIndex	A zero-based character index

Returns the zero-based line number that contains the specified character index.

The `LineIndex` Method

```
int LineIndex( int nLine = -1 ) const;
```

where

nLine	A zero-based line number index. Specify -1 for the current line.

Returns the zero-based character index for the specified line.

The `LineLength` Method

```
int LineLength( int nLine = -1 ) const;
```

where

nLine	A zero-based line number index. Specify -1 for the current line.

Returns the length of the specified line.

The `LineScroll` Method

```
void LineScroll( int nLines, int nChars = 0 );
```

where

nLines	The number of lines to scroll
nChars	The number of characters to scroll

The `LineScroll` method scrolls the display of the rich edit control.

The `Paste` Method

```
void Paste( );
```

The `Paste` method will insert the clipboard text or object in place of the current selection (if any).

The `PasteSpecial` Method

```
void PasteSpecial( UINT nClipFormat, DWORD dvAspect = 0,
➡HMETAFILE hMF = 0 );
```

where

nClipFormat	Clipboard format to place
dwAspect	Aspect ratio of data
hMF	Metafile that contains the iconic version of the data to be pasted

The `PasteSpecial` method will paste clipboard data of a specific format into the control.

The `ReplaceSel` Method

```
void ReplaceSel( LPCTSTR lpszNewText, BOOL bCanUndo = FALSE );
```

where

lpszNewText	New text to replace the selection
bCanUndo	TRUE if this action can be undone

The `ReplaceSel` method will replace the current selection with new text.

The `RequestResize` Method

```
void RequestResize( );
```

The `RequestResize` method will force the rich edit control to send out resize notifications.

D

The `SetBackgroundColor` Method

```
COLORREF SetBackgroundColor( BOOL bSysColor, COLORREF cr );
```

where

bSysColor	TRUE to set the background color to the system color; if FALSE, use the specified color
cr	The background color

Returns the previously selected background color.

The SetBackgroundColor method will set the background color for the rich edit control.

The `SetDefaultCharFormat` Method

```
BOOL SetDefaultCharFormat( CHARFORMAT& cf );
```

where

cf	Will receive the default character format

Returns TRUE if successful.

The SetDefaultCharFormat member will set the default character format. This is the format that any new text will take.

The `SetEventMask` Method

```
DWORD SetEventMask( DWORD dwEventMask );
```

where

dwEventMask	The event mask

Returns the previous event mask.

The SetEventMask method will set what notification messages are sent by the rich edit control.

The `SetModify` Method

```
void SetModify( BOOL bModified = TRUE );
```

where

bModified	TRUE to set the control to a modified state

The SetModify method will set the modify flag for this control.

The **SetOLECallback** Method

BOOL SetOLECallback(IRichEditOleCallback* pCallback);

where

      pCallback   A pointer to the IRichEditOleCallback object for this control

Returns TRUE if successful.

The SetOLECallback method will set the IRichEditOleCallback pointer for this control.

The **SetOptions** Method

void SetOptions(WORD wOp, DWORD dwFlags);

where

      wOp   The type of operation

      dwFlags   The options to be set or reset

The SetOptions method is used to set the options for this control.

The **SetParaFormat** Method

BOOL SetParaFormat(PARAFORMAT& pf);

where

      pf   The paragraph format

Returns TRUE if successful.

The SetParaFormat method will set the paragraph format for the current selection.

The **SetReadOnly** Method

BOOL SetReadOnly(BOOL bReadOnly = TRUE);

where

      bReadOnly   TRUE if the control is read only

Returns the previous read-only value.

The SetReadOnly method sets the read-only status of the control.

The **SetRect** Method

void SetRect(LPCRECT lpRect);

D

where

    lpRect   The bounding rectangle for the control

The `SetRect` method will set the bounding rectangle for the control.

The `SetSel` Method

```
void SetSel( long nStartChar, long nEndChar );
void SetSel( CHARRANGE& cr );
```

where

    cr   The selection range as a structure

    nStartChar   The starting character of the selection range

    nEndChar   The ending character of the selection range

The `SetSel` method will set the selection range.

The `SetSelectionCharFormat` Method

```
BOOL SetSelectionCharFormat( CHARFORMAT& cf );
```

where

    cf   The character format

Returns `TRUE` if successful.

The `SetSelectionCharFormat` method will set the character format for the current selection.

The `SetTargetDevice` Method

```
BOOL SetTargetDevice( HDC hDC, long lLineWidth );
BOOL SetTargetDevice( CDC& dc, long lLineWidth );
```

where

    hDC   A handle to a device context

    dc   A device context object (CDC)

Returns `TRUE` if successful.

The `SetTargetDevice` method will set the target output device.

The `SetWordCharFormat` Method

```
BOOL SetWordCharFormat( CHARFORMAT& cf );
```

where

   cf   A character format

Returns TRUE if successful.

The SetWordCharFormat method will set character formatting for the currently selected word.

The StreamIn Method

```
long StreamIn( int nFormat, EDITSTREAM& es );
```

where

   nFormat   The format of the input stream. Should be SF_TEXT or SF_RTF.

   es   A stream.

Returns the number of characters read from the stream.

The StreamIn method will read data into the control from a stream.

The StreamOut Method

```
long StreamOut( int nFormat, EDITSTREAM& es );
```

where

   nFormat   The format of the output stream. Should be SF_TEXT or SF_RTF.

   es   A stream.

Returns the number of characters written to the stream.

The StreamOut method will write data from the control into a stream.

The Undo Method

```
BOOL Undo( );
```

Returns TRUE if successful.

The Undo method will undo the last operation.

CDateTimeCtrl

The CDateTimeCtrl method implements a date and time picker control.

D

Header Files

The following header file should be included when using this class:

afxdtctl.h

Methods

The CDateTimeCtrl class has the following methods:

CDateTimeCtrl	The constructor
Create	Create the control
GetMonthCalColor	Get the color for a range in the month control
GetMonthCalCtrl	Get the month control
GetMonthCalFont	Get the month control's font
GetRange	Get the min and max allowed dates
GetTime	Get the time entered
SetFormat	Set the format
SetMonthCalColor	Set the color for a range in the month control
SetMonthCalFont	Set the font for the month control
SetRange	Set min and max allowed dates
SetTime	Set the time

The CDateTimeCtrl Constructor

The CDateTimeCtrl constructor creates the CDateTimeCtrl object. The CDateTimeCtrl constructor is used as follows:

CDateTimeCtrl();

The Create Method

BOOL Create(DWORD dwStyle, const RECT& rect, CWnd* pParentWnd,
➡UINT nID);

where

dwStyle	The style of the control
rect	The rectangle the control is to occupy
pParentWnd	The window into which this control is to be inserted
nID	The child window ID for this control

Returns TRUE if successful.

The Create method will create the CDateTimeCtrl control.

The `GetMonthCalColor` Method

```
COLORREF GetMonthCalColor( int iColor );
```

where

    iColor   Which area of the month control to retrieve

Returns the color for the specified area of the month control.

The `GetMonthCalColor` method will get the color associated with the specified area of the month control.

The `GetMonthCalCtrl` Method

```
CMonthCalCtrl* GetMonthCalCtrl( ) const;
```

Returns the month control.

The `GetMonthCalFont` Method

```
CFont *GetMonthCalFont() const;
```

Returns the font used by the date and time picker.

The `GetRange` Method

```
DWORD GetRange( COleDateTime* pMinRange, COleDateTime* pMaxRange ) const;
DWORD GetRange( CTime* pMinRange, CTime* pMaxRange ) const;
```

where

    pMinRange   The minimum date/time that the control will accept as a COleDateTime or a CTime

    pMaxRange   The maximum date/time that the control will accept as a COleDateTime or a CTime

Returns flags that indicate which of the ranges are set.

The `GetRange` method will get the range accepted by the control.

The `GetTime` Method

```
BOOL GetTime( COleDateTime& timeDest ) const;
DWORD GetTime( CTime& timeDest ) const;
DWORD GetTime( LPSYSTEMTIME pTimeDest ) const;
```

where

    timeDest   Will get the time as either a COleDateTime, CTime, or a SYSTEMTIME

Returns TRUE if successful, or the value of the dwFlag member.

D

The GetTime method will get the time of the control.

The SetFormat Method

```
BOOL SetFormat( LPCTSTR pstrFormat );
```

where

    pstrFormat   The format specifier

Returns TRUE if successful.

The SetFormat method will set the format for time/date display.

The SetMonthCalColor Method

```
COLORREF SetMonthCalColor( int iColor, COLORREF ref );
```

where

    iColor   Which area of the month control to set

    ref   The new color to set

Returns the previous color.

The SetMonthCalColor method will set the color of the specified month area.

The SetMonthCalFont Method

```
void SetMonthCalFont( HFONT hFont, BOOL bRedraw = TRUE );
```

where

    hFont   The font to set

    bRedraw   TRUE to redraw the control

The SetMonthCalFont method will set the font of the month control.

The SetRange Method

```
BOOL SetRange( const COleDateTime* pMinRange, const COleDateTime*
pMaxRange );
BOOL SetRange( const CTime* pMinRange, const CTime* pMaxRange );
```

where

    pMinRange   The minimum date/time that the control will accept as a COleDateTime or a CTime

    pMaxRange   The maximum date/time that the control will accept as a COleDateTime or a CTime

Returns TRUE if successful.

The SetRange method will set the range accepted by the control.

The SetTime Method

```
BOOL SetTime( const COleDateTime& timeNew );
BOOL SetTime( const CTime* pTimeNew );
BOOL SetTime( LPSYSTEMTIME pTimeNew = NULL );
```

where

> *timeNew*   The time as either a COleDateTime, CTime, or a SYSTEMTIME

Returns TRUE if successful.

The SetTime method will set the time of the control.

CMonthCalCtrl

The CMonthCalCtrl class implements a calendar control. This enables the user to view a month at a time and select a date.

Header Files

The following header file should be included when using this class:

afxdtctl.h

Methods

The CMonthCalCtrl class has the following methods:

CMonthCalCtrl	The constructor
Create	Create the calendar control
GetColor	Get the color of an area of the calendar
GetCurSel	Get the current selection
GetFirstDayOfWeek	Get the first day of the week
GetMaxSelCount	Get the maximum selection count
GetMinReqRect	Get the minimum required rectangle
GetMonthDelta	Set the scroll speed for months
GetMonthRange	Get the range of allowed months
GetRange	Get the date range

GetSelRange	Get the selection range
GetToday	Get the date specified as today
HitTest	Determine where a point is on the calendar control
SetColor	Set the color for a section of the calendar control
SetCurSel	Set the current selection
SetDayState	Set display to days
SetFirstDayOfWeek	Set the first day of the week
SetMaxSelCount	Set the maximum selection count
SetMonthDelta	Set the month scroll speed
SetRange	Set a range
SetSelRange	Set the selection range
SetToday	Set the date specified as today
SizeMinReq	Repaint to minimum one-month type

The CMonthCalCtrl Constructor

The CMonthCalCtrl constructor creates the CMonthCalCtrl object. The CMonthCalCtrl constructor is used as follows:

```
CMonthCalCtrl();
```

The Create Method

```
BOOL Create( DWORD dwStyle, const RECT& rect, CWnd* pParentWnd,
➡UINT nID );
BOOL Create( DWORD dwStyle, const POINT& pt, CWnd* pParentWnd, UINT nID );
```

where

dwStyle	The style of the control
rect	The rectangle the control is to occupy
pt	The point at which to locate the control
pParentWnd	The window into which this control is to be inserted
nID	The child window ID for this control

Returns TRUE if successful.

The Create method will create the CMonthCalCtrl control.

The `GetColor` Method

```
COLORREF GetColor( int nRegion ) const;
```

where

> `nRegion`   A region of the month control

Returns the color of the specified region.

The `GetCurSel` Method

```
BOOL GetCurSel( COleDateTime& refDateTime ) const;
BOOL GetCurSel( CTime& refDateTime ) const;
BOOL GetCurSel( LPSYSTEMTIME pDateTime ) const;
```

where

> `refDateTime`   Will get the time as either a COleDateTime, CTime, or
> a SYSTEMTIME

Returns TRUE if successful.

The GetCurSel method will get the selected date in the control.

The `GetFirstDayOfWeek` Method

```
int GetFirstDayOfWeek( BOOL* pbLocal = NULL ) const;
```

where

> `pbLocal`   TRUE if the control's setting does not match the control panel

Returns the first day of the week. The values 0 through 6 represent Monday through
Sunday.

The `GetMaxSelCount` Method

```
int GetMaxSelCount( ) const;
```

Returns the maximum selection count.

The `GetMinReqRect` Method

```
BOOL GetMinReqRect( RECT* pRect ) const;
```

where

> `pRect`   Will hold the minimum required rectangle

Returns TRUE if successful.

Returns the minimum required rectangle for the control.

D

The `GetMonthDelta` Method

```
int GetMonthDelta( ) const;
```

Returns the scroll rate for the month control.

The `GetMonthRange` Method

```
int GetMonthRange( COleDateTime& refMinRange, COleDateTime& refMaxRange,
➥DWORD dwFlags ) const;
int GetMonthRange( CTime& refMinRange, CTime& refMaxRange, DWORD dwFlags
➥) const;
int GetMonthRange( LPSYSTEMTIME pMinRange, LPSYSTEMTIME pMaxRange, DWORD
➥dwFlags ) const;
```

where

pMinRange	The minimum date/time that the control will accept as a COleDateTime, SYSTEMTIME, or a CTime.
pMaxRange	The maximum date/time that the control will accept as a COleDateTime, SYSTEMTIME, or a CTime.
dwFlags	Specifies the scope. Should be GMR_DAYSTATE or GMR_VISIBLE.

Returns the range in months spanned by minimum and maximum.

The GetMonthRange method will get the month range for the control.

The GetRange Method

```
DWORD GetRange( COleDateTime* pMinRange, COleDateTime* pMaxRange ) const;
DWORD GetRange( CTime* pMinRange, CTime* pMaxRange ) const;
DWORD GetRange( LPSYSTEMTIME pMinRange, LPSYSTEMTIME pMaxRange ) const;
```

where

pMinRange	The minimum date/time that the control will accept as a COleDateTime, SYSTEMTIME, or a CTime
pMaxRange	The maximum date/time that the control will accept as a COleDateTime, SYSTEMTIME, or a CTime

Returns flags that indicate which of the ranges are set.

The GetRange method will get the range accepted by the control.

The `GetSelRange` Method

```
BOOL GetSelRange( COleDateTime& refMinRange, COleDateTime& refMaxRange )
➥const;
BOOL GetSelRange( CTime& refMinRange, CTime& refMaxRange ) const;
BOOL GetSelRange( LPSYSTEMTIME pMinRange, LPSYSTEMTIME pMaxRange ) const;
```

where

pMinRange	The minimum date/time that is selected as a COleDateTime, SYSTEMTIME, or a CTime
pMaxRange	The maximum date/time that is selected as a COleDateTime, SYSTEMTIME, or a CTime

Returns flags that indicate which of the ranges are set.

The GetSelRange method will get the range selected on the control.

The **GetToday** Method

```
BOOL GetToday( COleDateTime& refDateTime ) const;
BOOL GetToday( CTime& refDateTime ) const;
BOOL GetToday( LPSYSTEMTIME pDateTime ) const;
```

where

refDateTime, pDateTime	Will get the time marked as "today" as either a COleDateTime, CTime, or a SYSTEMTIME

Returns TRUE if successful.

The GetToday method will get the date that is marked as today.

The **HitTest** Method

```
DWORD HitTest( PMCHITTESTINFO pMCHitTest );
```

where

pMCHitTest	A structure containing hit testing points for the calendar

Returns the *uHit* member of *pMCHitTest*.

The HitTest method will determine which part of the calendar control a point is over.

The **SetColor** Method

```
COLORREF SetColor( int nRegion, COLORREF ref );
```

where

nRegion	A region of the calendar control. Should be MCSC_BACK-GROUND, MCSC_MONTHBK, MCSC_TEXT, MCSC_TITLEBK, MCSC_TITLETEXT, or MCSC_TRAILINGTEXT.
ref	A color value.

Returns the old color value.

The SetColor method will set the color of the specified area.

The `SetCurSel` Method

```
BOOL SetCurSel( const COleDateTime& refDateTime );
BOOL SetCurSel( const CTime& refDateTime );
BOOL SetCurSel( const LPSYSTEMTIME pDateTime );
```

where

    refDateTime   Will set the current selection as either a COleDateTime, CTime, or a SYSTEMTIME.

Returns TRUE if successful.

The SetCurSel method will set the selected date in the control.

The `SetDayState` Method

```
BOOL SetDayState( int nMonths, LPMONTHDAYSTATE pStates );
```

where

    nMonths   How many items are in the states array.

    pStates   An array of structures that specifies how each date is to be drawn.

Returns TRUE if successful.

The SetDayState method will set the state of the days on the control.

The `SetFirstDayOfWeek` Method

```
BOOL SetFirstDayOfWeek( int iDay, int* lpnOld = NULL );
```

where

    iDay   The first day of the week. The values 0 through 6 represent Monday through Sunday.

    lpnOld   The old first day of the week.

Returns TRUE if successful.

The `SetMaxSelCount` Method

```
BOOL SetMaxSelCount( int nMax );
```

where

    nMax   The maximum selection count

Returns TRUE if successful.

The SetMaxSelCount method will set the maximum selection count for the control.

The `SetMonthDelta` Method

```
int SetMonthDelta( int iDelta );
```

where

    iDelta   The scroll rate for the month

Returns the old month delta.

The `SetMonthDelta` method will set the scroll rate for the month.

The `SetRange` Method

```
BOOL SetRange( const COleDateTime* pMinRange, const COleDateTime*
➥pMaxRange );
BOOL SetRange( const CTime* pMinRange, const CTime* pMaxRange );
BOOL SetRange( const LPSYSTEMTIME pMinRange, const LPSYSTEMTIME pMaxRange
);
```

where

    pMinRange   The minimum date/time that the control will accept as a
                      COleDateTime, SYSTEMTIME, or a CTime.

    pMaxRange   The maximum date/time that the control will accept as a
                      COleDateTime, SYSTEMTIME, or a CTime.

Returns TRUE if successful.

The `SetRange` method will set the range accepted by the control.

The `SetSelRange` Method

```
BOOL SetSelRange( const COleDateTime& pMinRange, const COleDateTime&
➥pMaxRange );
BOOL SetSelRange( const CTime& pMinRange, const CTime& pMaxRange );
BOOL SetSelRange( const LPSYSTEMTIME pMinRange, const LPSYSTEMTIME
➥pMaxRange );
```

where

    pMinRange   The minimum date/time that is selected as a
                      COleDateTime, SYSTEMTIME, or a CTime

    pMaxRange   The maximum date/time that is selected as a
                      COleDateTime, SYSTEMTIME, or a CTime

Returns TRUE if successful.

The `SetSelRange` method will set the range selected on the control.

The `SetToday` Method

```
void SetToday( const COleDateTime& refDateTime );
void SetToday( const CTime* pDateTime );
void SetToday( const LPSYSTEMTIME pDateTime );
```

where

       refDateTime, pDateTime   The time marked as "today" as either a
                                     COleDateTime, CTime, or a SYSTEMTIME

The `SetToday` method will set the date that is marked as today.

The `SizeMinReq` Method

```
BOOL SizeMinReq( BOOL bRepaint = TRUE );
```

where

       bRepaint   TRUE to repaint the control

Returns TRUE if successful.

The `SizeMinReq` method will size the control to the minimum allowable size.

APPENDIX E

Microsoft Developer Studio for Visual C++

Getting Started—Program Layout

Developer Studio integrates program editing, compilation, and debugging with a similar look and feel. Microsoft Developer Studio is shown in Figure E.1.

The Microsoft Developer Studio window can be divided into three major areas. The first area is the editing area. The second area is an editing area with a workspace area that lists the documents edited within that area. The third area, the output pane, displays any output from the compiler.

Editing Area

The editing area is the largest region of the Microsoft Developer Studio screen. This is where the documents listed in the work space are viewed and edited. These documents can either be textual source code documents or graphical representations of resources.

FIGURE E.1

Microsoft Developer Studio for Visual C++ 6.0

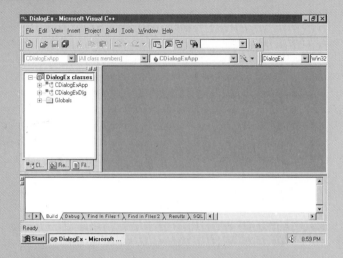

Workspace Panel

The workspace panel enables the project to be displayed in a tree control format. This pane presents several tabs that enable different aspects of the program to be viewed.

The Class View shows all program classes. These classes can be clicked to reveal their methods and properties. From here the corresponding source code can easily be opened to modify these properties or methods.

The Resource View shows all the program resources. This enables new resources to be added, or existing resources to be edited.

The File View shows the files that make up the application. Files are grouped by type, with the CPP files first. Other dependent files are also shown.

Output Panel

The output panel contains nearly all textual output from Developer Studio. The status is generated here when a program is compiled. This includes any errors or warnings, and other general information about the build. The output window also holds the results from finds in files.

Compiling

The Build menu contains many options related to both compiling and debugging. With these menu items all or part of the program can be compiled. Several debugging commands are also included.

The first section deals with building the application. The first menu item gives the option of compiling the current source file. The Build menu item will rebuild the entire project. Only those files that have changes that would affect the logic of the program will be recompiled. The Rebuild All menu item will rebuild the entire project, regardless of whether each file is up to date or not. Batch Build enables only certain subprojects to be compiled. The Clean menu item will remove any unnecessary compiler-generated files.

The second section deals with debugging. The Start Debug menu item will start debugging the application. The debugger remote connection enables a program on a remote computer to be debugged. The third section enables a program to be executed without debugging.

AppWizard

AppWizard generates code for an MFC application. This code is a generic template that must be modified to suit your application's needs. AppWizard enables a code to be generated for an MFC application. This code gives most applications a good starting point for further development. The first thing that must be decided in AppWizard is what sort of an application is to be created. AppWizard can create single-document, multidocument, or dialog-based applications, as seen in Figure E.2.

FIGURE E.2

MFC AppWizard Step 1: Select application type.

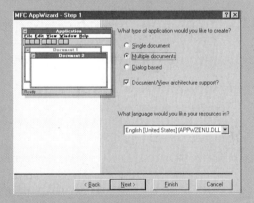

E

Single/Multidocument Application

Step two (see Figure E.3) enables you to select what type of database support the application will have. Header Files Only will include just the header files needed for low-level database access. Database View With/Without File Support presents a high-level view of the data to the user. The with or without file support options enable the application to include the standard New, Open, Close, and so on, File menu commands.

FIGURE E.3

AppWizard Step 2: Database support options.

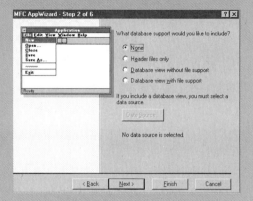

Step three enables OLE support to be added (see Figure E.4). The application can be a server, a container, or both. A container is an application that can hold OLE items. A mini-server is an application that is embedded into other programs, but cannot run on its own. A full-server can be embedded into other programs, and can be run on its own. Compound files are special document files that can contain OLE items. The application can also choose to support OLE automation or ActiveX controls.

FIGURE E.4

AppWizard Step 3: OLE/COM options.

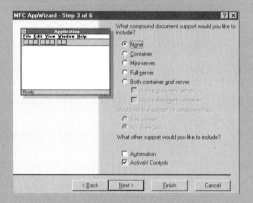

Step four enables many features to be turned on or off (see Figure E.5). MFC applications can have a docking tool bar to enable quick access to menu items. A status bar is displayed near the bottom of the application to give status information. The application can have support for Print and Print Preview. Context-sensitive Help can be activated to link the Help file to certain areas of the program. 3D controls can give the program the current Windows look and feel. MAPI enables messaging-based applications to be written. Windows sockets can be added to allow the program to communicate over the Internet.

Step four also enables the number of recent files to be selected, as well as the format of the toolbars.

FIGURE E.5

AppWizard Step 4: User interface elements.

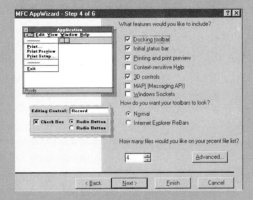

Step five enables several general application settings to be specified. The style of the application can be set to look like Windows Explorer, or like a normal Windows application. An Explorer application has a tree view at the side and a document at the right. Source file comments can be optionally generated. MFC itself can be linked to the application, or used from an external DLL file, as in Figure E.6.

FIGURE E.6

AppWizard Step 5: Miscellaneous options.

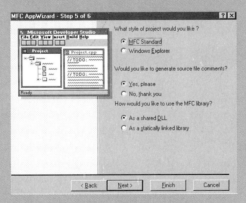

E

In Figure E.7, a general summary of the classes about to be created is displayed. The names of any of these classes can be changed. The type of view the application will use can also be specified here.

FIGURE E.7

AppWizard Step 6:
Final options.

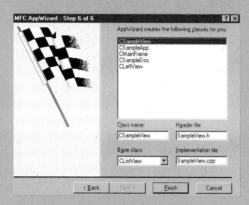

Dialog-Based Applications

Figure E.8, showing step two, enables general information about the dialog to be specified. The dialog box can have an About dialog box. Context-sensitive Help can be provided for each control. 3D controls will give the dialog the current Windows look and feel. The dialog box can support OLE automation and OLE controls. Windows sockets support can be added for Internet connectivity. The title of the dialog box can also be specified.

FIGURE E.8

AppWizard Step 2 for
Dialog Version: User
interface options.

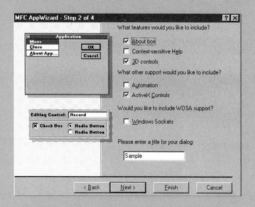

Step three enables several general application settings to be specified. Source file comments can be optionally generated. MFC itself can be linked to the application, or used from an external DLL file. (Refer to Figure E.6.)

Step six displays a general summary of the classes about to be created. The names of any of these classes can be changed. The type of view the application will use can also be specified here. (Refer to Figure E.7.)

Class Wizard

AppWizard can only be used once per application. After the application is generated, Class Wizard is used to add new classes. Class Wizard enables new classes to be created and existing classes to be modified (see Figure E.9).

FIGURE E.9

MFC Class Wizard.

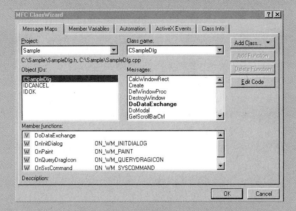

The Message Maps tab of Class Wizard enables message handler functions to be created. The Class Name combo box enables the desired class to be selected.

The list box on the left displays all elements of the object that can generate messages. The list box at the right specifies all messages available for the selected item. By choosing Add Function and selecting one item from each of the two list boxes, a message handler is created. Code can then be entered into that handler to handle that event.

If the class being edited is a dialog box, the Member Variables tab can be used to add member variables for each control. Each of the dialog controls can be mapped to a member variable. This enables the contents of that control to be changed by modifying the member variable.

Resource Editor

Developer Studio provides an integrated resource editor. This resource editor can edit any of the standard Windows resource types.

Accelerator Editor

Windows accelerators are shortcut keys that can perform menu items. The accelerator editor can set up these relationships.

E

Bitmap Editor

Bitmaps are the graphic format of choice for a Windows application. The bitmap editor provides a basic editing environment for bitmaps. This editor is good for viewing and making quick changes to bitmaps. For more advanced bitmap editing, a third-party graphics package should be considered.

Cursor Editor

The cursor editor enables cursors to be edited. These are custom mouse cursors that can be selected to replace the standard arrow cursor in the application. The cursor editor is similar to the bitmap editor in functionality.

Dialog Editor

The dialog editor is used to create and edit dialog boxes. This editor provides a toolbar that enables the user to insert both standard and ActiveX controls to the dialog box. Other tools are also provided to help lay out the dialog box.

HTML Editor

A simple HTML editor is also included. It enables HTML files to be created and edited.

Icon Editor

The icon editor can be used to create Windows icons. Icons are used by the operating system to display application icons. Icons can also be displayed internally by the program. The icon editor can create compound icons that consist of several resolutions. A compound icon will use the best-fit resolution to the screen when displayed.

Menu Editor

The menu editor enables menus to be edited. These menus can either pop up or be attached to a menu bar. The menu editor visually displays the menu or menu bar as it is being created.

String Table Editor

The string table editor enables string tables to be edited. An application should place all internal string data in a string table. This enables the application to be easily translated into another language.

Toolbar Editor

The toolbar editor enables toolbars to be created or edited. These toolbars are shortcuts for menu items.

Version Editor

The version editor enables the version resource to be edited or created. This resource contains version information about the application that can be displayed by the Explorer.

E

APPENDIX F

Structures and Global Functions

Structures

The CHOOSECOLOR Structure

```
typedef struct {
DWORD          lStructSize;
HWND           hwndOwner;
HWND           hInstance;
COLORREF       rgbResult;
COLORREF*      lpCustColors;
DWORD          Flags;
LPARAM         lCustData;
LPCCHOOKPROC   lpfnHook;
LPCTSTR        lpTemplateName;
} CHOOSECOLOR;
```

The CHOOSECOLOR structure is used by the Choose Color common dialog box. It specifies information about the look and feel of the dialog, and also serves to return the selected color.

lStructSize	The structure size. Should be set to sizeof(CHOOSECOLOR).
hwndOwner	The owner window. Can be NULL if the dialog is to be owned by the desktop.
hInstance	The instance handle for the program.
rgbResult	The color selected by the user.
lpCustColors	Custom colors the user can choose from.
Flags	A set of flags that defines the look and feel of the dialog.
lCustData	Additional custom data.
lpfnHook;	The hook procedure.
lpTemplateName	A dialog template name.

The following flags are valid for the Flags property:

CC_ANYCOLOR	Displays all basic colors.
CC_ENABLEHOOK	Enables the hook procedure. This is specified by lpfnHook.
CC_ENABLETEMPLATE	Enables the dialog template.
CC_ENABLETEMPLATEHANDLE	Enables the dialog template using a handle.
CC_FULLOPEN	Enables the user to create custom colors.
CC_PREVENTFULLOPEN	Disables custom colors.
CC_RGBINIT	Uses the value in rgbResult as the initially selected color.
CC_SHOWHELP	Shows the Help button.
CC_SOLIDCOLOR	Displays only solid colors.

The CHOOSEFONT Structure

```
typedef struct {
DWORD        lStructSize;
HWND         hwndOwner;
HDC          hDC;
LPLOGFONT    lpLogFont;
INT          iPointSize;
DWORD        Flags;
DWORD        rgbColors;
LPARAM       lCustData;
LPCFHOOKPROC lpfnHook;
```

```
LPCTSTR       lpTemplateName;
HINSTANCE     hInstance;
LPTSTR        lpszStyle;
WORD          nFontType;
WORD          ___MISSING_ALIGNMENT__;
INT           nSizeMin;
INT           nSizeMax;
} CHOOSEFONT;
```

The CHOOSEFONT structure is used by the Choose Font common dialog box. It specifies information about the look and feel of the dialog, and also serves to return the selected font.

lStructSize	The structure size. Should be set to sizeof(CHOOSEFONT).
hwndOwner	The owner window. Can be NULL if the dialog is to be owned by the desktop.
hDC	A device context to base the font on.
lpLogFont	A logical font structure.
iPointSize	The point size of the font.
Flags	A set of flags that defines the look and feel of the dialog.
rgbColors	The text color.
lCustData	Additional custom data.
lpfnHook	The hook procedure.
lpTemplateName	A dialog template name.
hInstance	The instance handle for the program.
lpszStyle	The font style.
nFontType	The font type.
nSizeMin	The minimum point size for the font.
nSizeMax	The maximum point size for the font.

The following flags are valid for the Flags property:

CF_APPLY	Display the Apply button. A hook procedure must be provided to process this button.
CF_ANSIONLY	No longer used.
CF_BOTH	Display both screen and printer fonts.
CF_TTONLY	Display only TrueType fonts.

F

CF_EFFECTS	Enable effects to be specified for the font.
CF_ENABLEHOOK	Enable the hook procedure.
CF_ENABLETEMPLATE	Use a dialog template.
CF_ENABLETEMPLATEHANDLE	Use a dialog template handle.
CF_FIXEDPITCHONLY	Only allow fixed-pitch fonts.
CF_FORCEFONTEXIST	Only allow fonts that exist.
CF_INITTOLOGFONTSTRUCT	Use the LOGFONT structure to initialize.
CF_LIMITSIZE	Limit the size by the nSizeMin and nSizeMax members.
CF_NOOEMFONTS	Same as the CF_NOVECTORFONTS flag.
CF_NOFACESEL	Do not display a name for a LOGFONT font.
CF_NOSCRIPTSEL	Disable the script combo box.
CF_NOSTYLESEL	Do not use the style control.
CF_NOSIZESEL	Do not use the size control.
CF_NOSIMULATIONS	Do not simulate fonts.
CF_NOVECTORFONTS	Do not allow vector fonts.
CF_NOVERTFONTS	Do not allow horizontal fonts.
CF_PRINTERFONTS	Only list printer fonts.
CF_SCALABLEONLY	Only allow scalable fonts.
CF_SCREENFONTS	List only screen fonts.
CF_SCRIPTSONLY	Allow non-OEM and symbol fonts.
CF_SELECTSCRIPT	Allow only fonts with the character set in lfCharSet.
CF_SHOWHELP	Show the Help button.
CF_USESTYLE	The lpszStyle member specifies the style.
CF_WYSIWYG	Only fonts that are both printer and screen.

The DEVNAMES Structure

```
typedef struct tagDEVNAMES {
WORD    wDriverOffset;
WORD    wDeviceOffset;
WORD    wOutputOffset;
WORD    wDefault;
} DEVNAMES;
```

The DEVNAMES structure specifies a printer.

wDriverOffset	Offset to the print driver.
wDeviceOffset	Offset to the device.
wOutputOffset	Offset to the DOS device name.
wDefault	Used to verify whether this is the default printer.

FINDREPLACE

```
lStructSize;
HWND            hwndOwner;
HINSTANCE       hInstance;
DWORD           Flags;
LPTSTR          lpstrFindWhat;
LPTSTR          lpstrReplaceWith;
WORD            wFindWhatLen;
WORD            wReplaceWithLen;
LPARAM          lCustData;
LPFRHOOKPROC    lpfnHook;
LPCTSTR         lpTemplateName;
} FINDREPLACE;
```

The FINDREPLACE structure is used to communicate with the standard Find Replace dialog box.

lStructSize	The structure size. Should be set to sizeof(FINDREPLACE).
hwndOwner	The owner window. Can be NULL if the dialog is to be owned by the desktop.
hInstance	The instance handle.
Flags	Flags that specify the look and feel.
lpstrFindWhat	The text to find.
lpstrReplaceWith	What to replace the text with.
wFindWhatLen	The length of lpstrFindWhat.
wReplaceWithLen	The length of lpstrRepaceWith.
lCustData	Custom data.
lpfnHook	A procedure hook.
lpTemplateName	A template name.

F

LOGBRUSH

```
typedef struct tag LOGBRUSH {
UINT      lbStyle;
COLORREF lbColor;
LONG      lbHatch;
} LOGBRUSH;
```

The LOGBRUSH structure specifies a logical brush. This structure is often used to create a brush.

lbStyle	The brush style.
lbColor	The brush color.
lbHatch	The hatching value.

LOGFONT

```
typedef struct tagLOGFONT {
LONG lfHeight;
LONG lfWidth;
LONG lfEscapement;
LONG lfOrientation;
LONG lfWeight;
BYTE lfItalic;
BYTE lfUnderline;
BYTE lfStrikeOut;
BYTE lfCharSet;
BYTE lfOutPrecision;
BYTE lfClipPrecision;
BYTE lfQuality;
BYTE lfPitchAndFamily;
CHAR lfFaceName[LF_FACESIZE];
} LOGFONT;
```

The LOGFONT structure is used to specify a logical font. This structure is often used when creating a font.

lfHeight	The height of the font.
lfWidth	The width of the font. Specify zero to calculate w width.
lfEscapement	The font's escapement value.
lfOrientation	The font's orientation.
lfWeight	The font's weight.
lfItalic	TRUE if the font is italic.
lfUnderline	TRUE if the font is underlined.

lfStrikeOut	TRUE if the font is stricken out.
lfCharSet	The character set.
lfOutPrecision	The output precision.
lfClipPrecision	The clipping precision.
lfQuality	The quality of the font.
lfPitchAndFamily	The pitch and family of the font.
lfFaceName[LF_FACESIZE]	The face name.

LOGPEN

```
typedef struct tagLOGPEN {
UINT     lopnStyle;
POINT    lopnWidth;
COLORREF lopnColor;
} LOGPEN;
```

The LOGPEN structure is used to specify a logical pen. This structure is often used to create a pen.

lopnStyle	The pen style.
lopnWidth	The pen width.
lopnColor	The pen color.

OFNOTIFY

```
typedef struct _OFNOTIFY {
NMHDR          hdr;
LPOPENFILENAME lpOFN;
LPTSTR         pszFile;
} OFNOTIFY, FAR *LPOFNOTIFY;
```

The OFNOTIFY structure contains a notification from an Explorer-style Open or Save As.

hdr	Identifies the type of message being sent.
lpOFN	A OPENFILENAME structure.
pszFile	Filename for which a network violation occurred.

F

OPENFILENAME

```
typedef struct tagOFN {
DWORD          lStructSize;
HWND           hwndOwner;
HINSTANCE      hInstance;
LPCTSTR        lpstrFilter;
```

```
LPTSTR           lpstrCustomFilter;
DWORD            nMaxCustFilter;
DWORD            nFilterIndex;
LPTSTR           lpstrFile;
DWORD            nMaxFile;
LPTSTR           lpstrFileTitle;
DWORD            nMaxFileTitle;
LPCTSTR          lpstrInitialDir;
LPCTSTR          lpstrTitle;
DWORD            Flags;
WORD             nFileOffset;
WORD             nFileExtension;
LPCTSTR          lpstrDefExt;
DWORD            lCustData;
LPOFNHOOKPROC    lpfnHook;
LPCTSTR          lpTemplateName;
} OPENFILENAME;
```

The OPENFILENAME structure is used to communicate with a standard File Open or Save dialog box.

lStructSize	The structure size. Should be set to sizeof(FIND-REPLACE).
hwndOwner	The owner window. Can be NULL if the dialog is to be owned by the desktop.
hInstance	The instance handle.
lpstrFilter	The standard filter to use.
lpstrCustomFilter	A custom filter to use.
nMaxCustFilter	The size of the custom filter buffer.
nFilterIndex	A index into the filter array.
lpstrFile	The file or files selected. If multiple files are selected, they are separated by NULLs.
nMaxFile	The maximum number of files to select.
lpstrFileTitle	The file's title.
nMaxFileTitle	The maximum title size.
lpstrInitialDir	The initial directory.
lpstrTitle	Title of the dialog box.
Flags	Flags that define the look and feel of the dialog box.
nFileOffset	Offset to the filename.
nFileExtension	Offset to the extension.

lpstrDefExt	The default extension.
lCustData	Custom data.
lpfnHook	Hook procedure.
lpTemplateName	Resource template to use.

PAGESETUPDLG

```
typedef struct tagPSD {
DWORD           lStructSize;
HWND            hwndOwner;
HGLOBAL         hDevMode;
HGLOBAL         hDevNames;
DWORD           Flags;
POINT           ptPaperSize;
RECT            rtMinMargin;
RECT            rtMargin;
HINSTANCE       hInstance;
LPARAM          lCustData;
LPPAGESETUPHOOK lpfnPageSetupHook;
LPPAGEPAINTHOOK lpfnPagePaintHook;
LPCTSTR         lpPageSetupTemplateName;
HGLOBAL         hPageSetupTemplate;
} PAGESETUPDLG, * LPPAGESETUPDLG;
```

The PAGESETUPDIALOG structure is used to set up for a printout.

lStructSize	The structure size. Should be set to sizeof(FIND-REPLACE).
hwndOwner	The owner window. Can be NULL if the dialog is to be owned by the desktop.
hInstance	The instance handle.
hDevMode	Pointer to a global DEVMODE structure.
hDevNames	Pointer to a global DEVNAMES structure.
Flags	Flags that specify the look and feel of the dialog.
ptPaperSize	The paper size.
rtMinMargin	The minimum margin.
rtMargin	The margin.
lCustData	Custom data.
lpfnPageSetupHook	Page setup hook procedure.
lpfnPagePaintHook	Page paint hook.
lpPageSetupTemplateName	Template name.
hPageSetupTemplate	Template handle.

F

PRINTDLG

```
typedef struct tagPD {
DWORD       lStructSize;
HWND        hwndOwner;
HANDLE      hDevMode;
HANDLE      hDevNames;
HDC         hDC;
DWORD       Flags;
WORD        nFromPage;
WORD        nToPage;
WORD        nMinPage;
WORD        nMaxPage;
WORD        nCopies;
HINSTANCE   hInstance;
DWORD       lCustData;
LPPRINTHOOKPROC lpfnPrintHook;
LPSETUPHOOKPROC lpfnSetupHook;
LPCTSTR     lpPrintTemplateName;
LPCTSTR      lpSetupTemplateName;
HANDLE      hPrintTemplate;
HANDLE      hSetupTemplate;
} PRINTDLG;
```

The PRINTDLG structure is used communicate with a standard Print dialog box.

lStructSize	The structure size. Should be set to sizeof(FIND-REPLACE).
hwndOwner	The owner window. Can be NULL if the dialog is to be owned by the desktop.
hInstance	The instance handle.
hDevMode	Pointer to a global DEVMODE structure.
hDevNames	Pointer to a global DEVNAMES structure.
Flags	Flags that specify the look and feel of the dialog.
hDC	The device context to print to.
nFromPage	The from page.
nToPage	The to page.
nMinPage	The minimum value for the page range.
nMaxPage	The maximum value for the page range.
nCopies	The number of copies.
lCustData	Custom data.
lpfnPrintHook	The print hook procedure.

lpfnSetupHook	The setup hook procedure.
lpPrintTemplateName	The print template name.
lpSetupTemplateName	The setup template name.
hPrintTemplate	The print template handle.
hSetupTemplate	The setup template handle.

Methods

The AfxBeginThread Method

```
CWinThread* AfxBeginThread( AFX_THREADPROC pfnThreadProc, LPVOID pParam,
➥int nPriority = THREAD_PRIORITY_NORMAL, UINT nStackSize = 0,
➥DWORD dwCreateFlags = 0, LPSECURITY_ATTRIBUTES lpSecurityAttrs =
➥NULL );
CWinThread* AfxBeginThread( CRuntimeClass* pThreadClass, int nPriority =
➥THREAD_PRIORITY_NORMAL, UINT nStackSize = 0, DWORD dwCreateFlags
➥= 0, LPSECURITY_ATTRIBUTES lpSecurityAttrs = NULL );
```

where

pfnThreadProc	The thread procedure.
pfnThreadClass	The thread class.
pParam	A parameter to pass to the thread.
nPriority	The thread priority.
nStackSize	The thread's stack size.
dwCreateFlags	The thread's creation flags.
lpSecurityAttrs	The thread's security attributes.

returns the newly created thread class.

The AfxBeginThread method will start a thread under MFC.

The AfxEndThread Method

```
void AfxEndThread( UINT nExitCode );
```

where

| nExitCode | The thread's exit code. |

The AfxEndThread method will end a thread under MFC.

F

The `AfxGetApp` Method

```
CWinApp* AfxGetApp( );
```

returns the application object.

The `AfxGetAppName` Method

```
LPCTSTR AfxGetAppName( );
```

returns the application name.

The `AfxGetInstanceHandle` Method

```
HINSTANCE AfxGetInstanceHandle( );
```

returns the application instance handle.

The `AfxGetMainWnd` Method

```
CWnd* AfxGetMainWnd( );
```

returns the main application window.

The `AfxGetResourceHandle` Method

```
HINSTANCE AfxGetResourceHandle( );
```

returns the resource handle.

The `AfxGetThread` Method

```
CWinThread* AfxGetThread( );
```

returns the current thread.

The `AfxMessageBox` Method

```
int AfxMessageBox( LPCTSTR lpszText, UINT nType = MB_OK,
➡UINT nIDHelp = 0 );
int AFXAPI AfxMessageBox( UINT nIDPrompt, UINT nType = MB_OK, UINT nIDHelp
➡= (UINT) -1 );
```

where

lpszText	The message box text.
nIDPrompt	The message box text, as a resource.
nType	The message box type.
nIDHelp	The Help context ID.

The return value is dependent on what type is used.

The `Afx MessageBox` method will display a message box.

The `AfxRegisterClass` and `AfxRegisterWndClass` Methods

```
BOOL AFXAPI AfxRegisterClass( WNDCLASS* lpWndClass );
LPCTSTR AFXAPI AfxRegisterWndClass( UINT nClassStyle, HCURSOR hCursor = 0,
➥HBRUSH hbrBackground = 0, HICON hIcon = 0 );
```

where

lpWndClass	A window class structure.
nClassStyle	The class style.
hCursor	The cursor type.
hbrBackground	The background brush.

Returns TRUE if successful. Second function returns the name of the new class.

The `AfxRegisterClass`/`AfxRegisterWndClass` methods will register the specified window class.

F

APPENDIX G

ANSI/ASCII/UNICODE Charts

TABLE G.1   ANSI CHARACTER COUNTS

Dec	Hex	Char	Dec	Hex	Char	Dec	Hex	Char
†000	00		032	20		064	40	@
†001	01		033	21	!	065	41	A
†002	02		034	22	"	066	42	B
†003	03		035	23	#	067	43	C
†004	04		036	24	$	068	44	D
†005	05		037	25	%	069	45	E
†006	06		038	26	&	070	46	F
†007	07		039	27	'	071	47	G
†008	08		040	28	(	072	48	H
†009	09		041	29	)	073	49	I
†010	0A		042	2A	*	074	4A	J
†011	0B		043	2B	+	075	4B	K
†012	0C		044	2C	'	076	4C	L
†013	0D		045	2D	-	077	4D	M
†014	0E		046	2E	.	078	4E	N
†015	0F		047	2F	/	079	4F	O
†016	10		048	30	0	080	50	P
†017	11		049	31	1	081	51	Q
†018	12		050	32	2	082	52	R
†019	13		051	33	3	083	53	S
†020	14		052	34	4	084	54	T
†021	15		053	35	5	085	55	U
†022	16		054	36	6	086	56	V
†023	17		055	37	7	087	57	W
†024	18		056	38	8	088	58	X
†025	19		057	39	9	089	59	Y
†026	1A		058	3A	:	090	5A	Z
†027	1B		059	3B	;	091	5B	[
†028	1C		060	3C	<	092	5C	\
†029	1D		061	3D	=	093	5D	]
†030	1E		062	3E	>	094	5E	^
†031	1F		063	3F	?	095	5F	_

Dec	Hex	Char	Dec	Hex	Char	Dec	Hex	Char
096	60	`	†129	81		162	A2	¢
097	61	a	130	82	‚	163	A3	£
098	62	b	131	83	ƒ	164	A4	¤
099	63	c	132	84	„	165	A5	¥
100	64	d	133	85	…	166	A6	¦
101	65	e	134	86	†	167	A7	§
102	66	f	135	87	‡	168	A8	¨
103	67	g	136	88	ˆ	169	A9	©
104	68	h	137	89	‰	170	AA	ª
105	69	i	138	8A	Š	171	AB	«
106	6A	j	139	8B	‹	172	AC	¬
107	6B	k	140	8C	Œ	173	AD	-
108	6C	l	†141	8D		174	AE	®
109	6D	m	†142	8E		175	AF	¯
110	6E	n	†143	8F		176	B0	°
111	6F	o	†144	90		177	B1	±
112	70	p	145	91	'	178	B2	²
113	71	q	146	92	'	179	B3	³
114	72	r	147	93	"	180	B4	´
115	73	s	148	94	"	181	B5	µ
116	74	t	149	95	•	182	B6	¶
117	75	u	150	96	–	183	B7	·
118	76	v	151	97	—	184	B8	¸
119	77	w	152	98	˜	185	B9	¹
120	78	x	153	99	™	186	BA	º
121	79	y	154	9A	š	187	BB	»
122	7A	z	155	9B	›	188	BC	¼
123	7B	{	156	9C	œ	189	BD	½
124	7C	|	†157	9D		190	BE	¾
125	7D	}	†158	9E		191	BF	¿
126	7E	~	159	9F	Ÿ	192	C0	À
†127	7F		160	A0		193	C1	Á
†128	80		161	A1	¡	194	C2	Â

G

continues

TABLE G.1 CONTINUED

Dec	Hex	Char	Dec	Hex	Char	Dec	Hex	Char
195	C3	Ã	216	D8	Ø	237	ED	í
196	C4	Ä	217	D9	Ù	238	EE	î
197	C5	Å	218	DA	Ú	239	EF	ï
198	C6	Æ	219	DB	Û	240	F0	ð
199	C7	Ç	220	DC	Ü	241	F1	ñ
200	C8	È	221	DD	Ý	242	F2	ò
201	C9	É	222	DE	Þ	243	F3	ó
202	CA	Ê	223	DF	β	244	F4	ô
203	CB	Ë	224	E0	à	245	F5	õ
204	CC	Ì	225	E1	á	246	F6	ö
205	CD	Í	226	E2	â	247	F7	÷
206	CE	Î	227	E3	ã	248	F8	ø
207	CF	Ï	228	E4	ä	249	F9	ù
208	D0	Ð	229	E5	å	250	FA	ú
209	D1	Ñ	230	E6	æ	251	FB	û
210	D2	Ò	231	E7	ç	252	FC	ü
211	D3	Ó	232	E8	è	253	FD	ý
212	D4	Ô	233	E9	é	254	FE	þ
213	D5	Õ	234	EA	ê	255	FF	ÿ
214	D6	Ö	235	EB	ë			
215	D7	×	236	EC	ì			

¹ *denotes nonprinting character*

TABLE G.2 ASCII CHARACTER CHART

Dec	Hex	Char	Dec	Hex	Char	Dec	Hex	Char
000	00	null	007	07	•	014	0E	♪
001	01	☺	008	08	◘	015	0F	☼
002	02	☻	009	09	○	016	10	►
003	03	♥	010	0A	◙	017	11	◄
004	04	♦	011	0B	♂	018	12	↕
005	05	♣	012	0C	♀	019	13	‼
006	06	♠	013	0D	♪	020	14	¶

Dec	Hex	Char	Dec	Hex	Char	Dec	Hex	Char
021	15	§	054	36	6	087	57	W
022	16	–	055	37	7	088	58	X
023	17	↕	056	38	8	089	59	Y
024	18	↑	057	39	9	090	5A	Z
025	19	↓	058	3A	:	091	5B	[
026	1A	→	059	3B	;	092	5C	\
027	1B	←	060	3C	<	093	5D	]
028	1C	∟	061	3D	=	094	5E	^
029	1D	↔	062	3E	>	095	5F	_
030	1E	▲	063	3F	?	096	60	`
031	1F	▼	064	40	@	097	61	a
032	20	space	065	41	A	098	62	b
033	21	!	066	42	B	099	63	c
034	22	"	067	43	C	100	64	d
035	23	#	068	44	D	101	65	e
036	24	$	069	45	E	102	66	f
037	25	%	070	46	F	103	67	g
038	26	&	071	47	G	104	68	h
039	27	'	072	48	H	105	69	i
040	28	(	073	49	I	106	6A	j
041	29	)	074	4A	J	107	6B	k
042	2A	*	075	4B	K	108	6C	l
043	2B	+	076	4C	L	109	6D	m
044	2C	,	077	4D	M	110	6E	n
045	2D	-	078	4E	N	111	6F	o
046	2E	.	079	4F	O	112	70	p
047	2F	/	080	50	P	113	71	q
048	30	0	081	51	Q	114	72	r
049	31	1	082	52	R	115	73	s
050	32	2	083	53	S	116	74	t
051	33	3	084	54	T	117	75	u
052	34	4	085	55	U	118	76	v
053	35	5	086	56	V	119	77	w

continues

G

TABLE G.2 CONTINUED

Dec	Hex	Char	Dec	Hex	Char	Dec	Hex	Char
120	78	x	153	99	Ö	186	BA	‖
121	79	y	154	9A	Ü	187	BB	╗
122	7A	z	155	9B	¢	188	BC	╝
123	7B	{	156	9C	£	189	BD	╜
124	7C	¦	157	9D	¥	190	BE	╛
125	7D	}	158	9E	₧	191	BF	┐
126	7E	~	159	9F	ƒ	192	C0	└
127	7F	Δ	160	A0	á	193	C1	┴
128	80	Ç	161	A1	í	194	C2	┬
129	81	ü	162	A2	ó	195	C3	├
130	82	é	163	A3	ú	196	C4	─
131	83	â	164	A4	ñ	197	C5	+
132	84	ä	165	A5	Ñ	198	C6	╞
133	85	à	166	A6	ª	199	C7	╟
134	86	å	167	A7	º	200	C8	╚
135	87	ç	168	A8	¿	201	C9	╔
136	88	ê	169	A9	⌐	202	CA	╩
137	89	ë	170	AA	¬	203	CB	╦
138	8A	è	171	AB	½	204	CC	╠
139	8B	ï	172	AC	¼	205	CD	=
140	8C	î	173	AD	¡	206	CE	╬
141	8D	ì	174	AE	«	207	CF	╧
142	8E	Ä	175	AF	»	208	D0	╨
143	8F	Å	176	B0	▓	209	D1	╤
144	90	É	177	B1	▒	210	D2	╥
145	91	æ	178	B2	▓	211	D3	╙
146	92	Æ	179	B3	│	212	D4	╘
147	93	ô	180	B4	┤	213	D5	╒
148	94	ö	181	B5	╡	214	D6	╓
149	95	ò	182	B6	╢	215	D7	╫
150	96	û	183	B7	╖	216	D8	╪
151	97	ù	184	B8	╕	217	D9	┘
152	98	ÿ	185	B9	╣	218	DA	┌

Dec	Hex	Char	Dec	Hex	Char	Dec	Hex	Char
219	DB	■	232	E8	Φ	245	F5	⌡
220	DC	■	233	E9	θ	246	F6	÷
221	DD	▌	234	EA	Ω	247	F7	≈
222	DE	▐	235	EB	δ	248	F8	°
223	DF	▪	236	EC	∞	249	F9	•
224	E0	α	237	ED	ø	250	FA	·
225	E1	β	238	EE	∈	251	FB	√
226	E2	Γ	239	EF	∩	252	FC	ⁿ
227	E3	π	240	F0	≡	253	FD	²
228	E4	Σ	241	F1	±	254	FE	■
229	E5	σ	242	F2	≥	255	FF	
230	E6	μ	243	F3	≤			
231	E7	γ	244	F4	⌠			

Unicode 2.1

The Unicode Standard divides its code-space into a number of blocks.

This chart provides a handy reference to the character codes and their ranges.

TABLE G.3   UNICODE CHARACTER CHART

Range	Code Type
U+0000 to U+007F	C0 Controls and Basic Latin
U+0000 to U+007F	**C0 Controls and Basic Latin**
U+0080 to U+00FF	C1 Controls and Latin-1 Supplement
U+0100 to U+017F	Latin Extended-A
U+0180 to U+024F	Latin Extended-B
U+0250 to U+02AF	IPA Extensions
U+02B0 to U+02FF	Spacing Modifier Letters
U+0300 to U+036F	Combining Diacritical Marks
U+0370 to U+03FF	Greek
U+0400 to U+04FF	Cyrillic
U+0530 to U+058F	Armenian
U+0590 to U+05FF	Hebrew

G

continues

TABLE G.3   CONTINUED

Range	Code Type
U+0600 to U+06FF	Arabic
U+0900 to U+097F	Devanagari
U+0980 to U+09FF	Bengali
U+0A00 to U+0A7F	Gurmukhi
U+0A80 to U+0AFF	Gujarati
U+0B00 to U+0B7F	Oriya
U+0B80 to U+0BFF	Tamil
U+0C00 to U+0C7F	Telugu
U+0C80 to U+0CFF	Kannada
U+0D00 to U+0D7F	Malayalam
U+0E00 to U+0E7F	Thai
U+0E80 to U+0EFF	Lao
U+0F00 to U+0FBF	Tibetan
U+10A0 to U+10FF	Georgian
U+1100 to U+11FF	Hangul Jamo
U+1E00 to U+1EFF	Latin Extended Additional
U+1F00 to U+1FFF	Greek Extended
U+2000 to U+206F	**General Punctuation**
U+2070 to U+209F	Superscripts and Subscripts
U+20A0 to U+20CF	Currency Symbols
U+20D0 to U+20FF	Combining Diacritical Marks for Symbols
U+2100 to U+214F	Letter-like Symbols
U+2150 to U+218F	**Number Forms**
U+2190 to U+21FF	**Arrows**
U+2200 to U+22FF	**Mathematical Operators**
U+2300 to U+23FF	**Miscellaneous Technical**
U+2400 to U+243F	Control Pictures
U+2440 to U+245F	Optical Character Recognition
U+2460 to U+24FF	Enclosed Alpha-numerics
U+2500 to U+257F	**Box Drawing**

Range	Code Type
U+2580 to U+259F	Block Elements
U+25A0 to U+25FF	Geometric Shapes
U+2600 to U+26FF	**Miscellaneous Symbols**
U+2700 to U+27BF	**Dingbats**
U+3000 to U+303F	CJK Symbols and Punctuation
U+3040 to U+309F	Hiragana
U+30A0 to U+30FF	Katakana
U+30A0 to U+30FF	Bopomofo
U+3130 to U+318F	Hangul Compatibility Jamo
U+3190 to U+319F	Kanbun
U+3200 to U+32FF	Enclosed CJK Letters and Months
U+3300 to U+33FF	CJK Compatibility
U+4E00 to U+9FA5	CJK Unified Ideographs
U+AC00 to U+D7A3	Hangul Syllables
U+D800 to U+DB7F	High Surrogates
U+DB80 to U+DBFF	High Private Use Surrogates
U+DC00 to U+DFFF	Low Surrogates
U+E000 to U+F8FF	Private Use Area
U+F900 to U+FAFF	CJK Compatibility Ideographs
U+FB00 to U+FB4F	Alphabetic Presentation Forms
U+FB50 to U+FDFF	Arabic Presentation Forms-A
U+FE20 to U+FE2F	Combining Half Marks
U+FE30 to U+FE4F	CJK Compatibility Forms
U+FE50 to U+FE6F	Small Form Variants
U+FE70 to U+FEFF	Arabic Presentation Forms-B
U+FF00 to U+FFEF	Halfwidth and Fullwidth Forms
U+FFF0 to U+FFFF	Specials

The following are some of the more important and fun UNICODE Charts and are those in **BOLD** above. For more information regarding these and other UNICODE Charts, see http://charts.unicode.org/Unicode.charts/normal/Unicode.html.

Reader, please note that empty cells are for future development.

G

	000	001	002	003	004	005	006	007
0	NUL	DLE	SP	0	@	P	`	p
1	STX	DC1	!	1	A	Q	a	q
2	SOT	DC2	"	2	B	R	b	r
3	ETX	DC3	#	3	C	S	c	s
4	EOT	DC4	$	4	D	T	d	t
5	ENQ	NAK	%	5	E	U	e	u
6	ACK	SYN	&	6	F	V	f	v
7	BEL	ETB	'	7	G	W	g	w
8	BS	CAN	(	8	H	X	h	x
9	HT	EM	)	9	I	Y	i	y
A	LF	SUB	*	:	J	Z	j	z
B	VT	ESC	+	;	K	[	k	{
C	FF	FS	,	<	L	\	l	|
D	CR	GS	-	=	M	]	m	}
E	SO	RS	.	>	N	^	n	~
F	SI	US	/	?	O	_	o	DEL

FIGURE G.1 *C0 Controls and Basic Latin—Range: U+0000 to U+007F.*

	200	201	202	203	204	205	206
0	NQ SP	-	†	‰	⌢		
1	MQ SP	-	‡	‱	⸌		
2	EN SP	—	•	′	*∗		
3	EM SP	—	▶	″	▪		
4	3/M SP	—	·	‴	⁄		
5	4/M SP	—	··	‵	⎡		
6	6/M SP	‖	···	‶	⎤		
7	F SP	=	·	‷			
8	P SP	'	L SEP	‸			
9	TH SP	'	P SEP	‹			
A	H SP	'	LRE	›			SS
B	ZW SP	'	RLE	※			A SS
C	ZW NJ	"	PDF	‼			I AFS
D	ZW J	"	LRO	⁇			A AFS
E	LRM	"	RLO	‾			NA DS
F	RLM	"		⌣			NO DS

FIGURE G.2 *General Punctuation—Range: U+2000 to U+206F.*

G

	215	216	217	218
0		I	i	ⅭⅮ
1		II	ii	Ⅾ
2		III	iii	ⅭⅮ
3	⅓	IV	iv	
4	⅔	V	v	
5	⅕	VI	vi	
6	⅖	VII	vii	
7	⅗	VIII	viii	
8	⅘	IX	ix	
9	⅙	X	x	
A	⅚	XI	xi	
B	⅛	XII	xii	
C	⅜	L	l	
D	⅝	C	c	
E	⅞	D	d	
F	⅟	M	m	

FIGURE G.3 *Number Forms—Range: U+2150 to U+218F.*

	219	21A	21B	21C	21D	21E	21F
0	←	→⟩	⇃	→	⇐	⇠	
1	↑	↓	↱	⇁	⇑	⇡	
2	→	↤	↲	⇂	⇒	⇢	
3	↓	↣	↳	⇃	⇓	⇣	
4	↔	↤	↴	⇄	⇔	⇤	
5	↕	↥	↵	⇅	⇕	⇥	
6	↖	↦	↶	⇆	⇖	⇦	
7	↗	↧	↷	⇇	⇗	⇧	
8	↘	↨	↸	⇈	⇘	⇨	
9	↙	↩	↹	⇉	⇙	⇩	
A	↚	↪	↺	⇊	⇚	⇪	
B	↛	↫	↻	⇋	⇛		
C	↜	↬	↼	⇌	⇜		
D	↝	↭	↽	⇍	⇝		
E	↞	↮	↾	⇎	⇞		
F	↟	↯	↿	⇏	⇟		

FIGURE G.4 *Arrows—Range: U+2190 to U+21FF.*

G

	220	221	222	223	224	225	226	227	228	229	22A	22B	22C	22D	22E	22F
0	∀	∐	∠	∰	≀	≐	≠	≰	⊀	⊐	⊠	⋋	⋀	⋐	⋠	⋰
1	∁	∑	∡	∱	≁	÷	≡	≱	⊁	⊑	⊡	⋌	⋁	⋑	⋡	⋱
2	∂	−	∢	∲	≂	≒	≢	≲	⊂	⊒	⊢	⋍	⋂	⋒	⋢	
3	∃	∓	∣	∳	≃	≓	≣	≳	⊃	⊓	⊣	⋎	⋃	⋓	⋣	
4	∄	∔	∤	∴	≄	≔	≤	≴	⊄	⊔	⊤	⋏	⋄	⋔	⋤	
5	∅	∕	∥	∵	≅	≕	≥	≵	⊅	⊕	⊥	⋐	⋅	⋕	⋥	
6	∆	∖	∦	∶	≆	≖	≦	≶	⊆	⊖	⊦	⋚	⋆	⋖	⋦	
7	∇	∗	∧	∷	≇	≗	≧	≷	⊇	⊗	⊧	⋛	⋇	⋗	⋧	
8	∈	∘	∨	∸	≈	≘	≨	≸	⊈	⊘	⊨	⊸	⋈	⋘	⋨	
9	∉	∙	∩	∹	≉	≙	≩	≹	⊉	⊙	⊩	⋒	⋉	⋙	⋩	
A	∊	√	∪	∺	≊	≚	≪	≺	⊊	⊚	⊪	⊤	⋊	⋚	⋪	
B	∋	∛	∫	∻	≋	≛	≫	≻	⊋	⊛	⊫	⊻	⋋	⋛	⋫	
C	∌	∜	∬	∼	≌	≜	≬	≼	⊌	⊜	⊬	⊼	⋌	⋜	⋬	
D	∍	∝	∭	∽	≍	≝	≭	≽	⊍	⊝	⊭	⊽	⋍	⋝	⋭	
E	∎	∞	∮	∾	≎	≞	≮	≾	⊎	⊞	⊮	⊾	⋎	⋞	⋮	
F	∏	∟	∯	∿	≏	≟	≯	≿	⊏	⊟	⊯	⊿	⋏	⋟	⋯	

FIGURE G.5 *Mathematical Operators—Range: U+2200 to U+22FF.*

	230	231	232	233	234	235	236	237	238	239	23A	23B	23C	23D	23E	23F
0	⌀	⌐	⌠	⌨	⍀	⍐	⍘	⍠								
1		⌑	⌡	⌱	⍁	⍑	⍙	⍡								
2	⌂	⌒	⌢	⌲	⍂	⍒	⍚	⍢								
3	⌃	⌓	⌣	⌳	⍃	⍓	⍛	⍣								
4	⌄	⌔	⌤	⌴	⍄	⍔	⍜	⍤								
5	⌅	⌕	⌥	⌵	⍅	⍕	⍝	⍥								
6	⌆	⌖	⌦	⌶	⍆	⍖	⍞	⍦								
7	⌇	⌗	⌧	⌷	⍇	⍗	⍟	⍧								
8	⌈	⌘	⌨	⌸	⍈	⍘	⍠	⍨								
9	⌉	⌙	〈	⌹	⍉	⍙	⍡	⍩								
A	⌊	⌚	〉	⌺	⍊	⍚	⍢	⍪								
B	⌋	⌛	⌫	⌻	⍋	⍛	⍣									
C	⌌	⌜	⌬	⌼	⍌	⍜	⍤									
D	⌍	⌝	⌭	⌽	⍍	⍝	⍥									
E	⌎	⌞	⌮	⌾	⍎	⍞	⍦									
F	⌏	⌟	⌯	⌿	⍏	⍟	⍧									

FIGURE G.6 *Miscellaneous Technical—Range: U+2300 to U+23FF.*

G

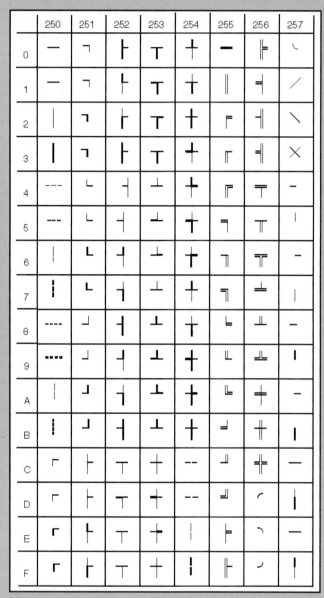

FIGURE G.7 *Box Drawing—Range: U+2500 to U+257F.*

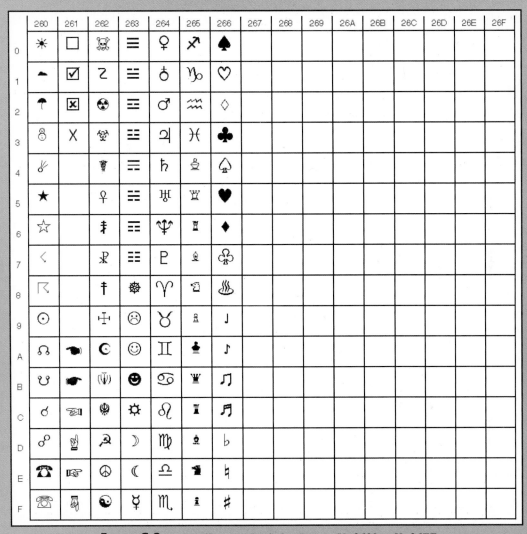

FIGURE G.8   *Miscellaneous Symbols—Range: U+2600 to U+26FF*

G

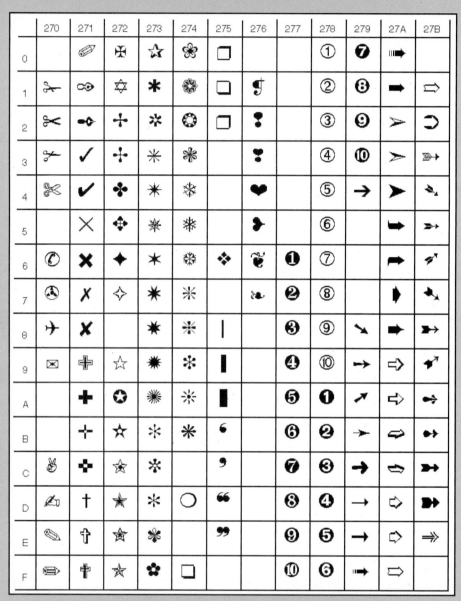

FIGURE G.9 *Dingbats—Range: U+2700 to U+27B.F*

APPENDIX H

Windows Types

The following table lists the C++ and MFC-based types. All of the MFC-based types were originally declared from the primitive C++ types. The size and declaration are given for each of these types. MFC abstracts many of the base types with new names. The declaration listed shows the type that was used to create the new MFC-based type. All the MFC types were created with the C `typedef` command.

TABLE H.1 C++ AND MFC-BASED TYPES

Type	Size	Declaration	Description
ATOM	16	WORD	Global atom, used for DDE
bool	8	bool	C++ boolean value, can only be TRUE or FALSE
BOOL	32	int	Boolean, should be either TRUE or FALSE
BYTE	8	unsigned char	Represents a byte of memory
char	8	char	C++ type, single character
COLORREF	32	DWORD	24-bit color value (stored in RGB)

continues

TABLE H.1 CONTINUED

Type	Size	Declaration	Description
double	64	double	C++ type, floating-point number
DWORD	32	unsigned long	Double word
FARPROC	32	typedef int (FAR WINAPI *)()	Pointer to a procedure
float	32	float	C++ type, floating-point number
FLOAT	32	float	Floating-point number
GLOBALHANDLE	32	HANDLE	Global handle
HACCEL	32	HANDLE	Handle to an accelerator resource
HBITMAP	32	HANDLE	Handle to a bitmap resource
HBRUSH	32	HANDLE	Handle to a brush
HCOLORSPACE	32	HANDLE	Handle to a color space
HCURSOR	32	HICON	Handle to a cursor
HDC	32	HANDLE	Handle to a device context
HDESK	32	HANDLE	Handle to a desktop
HENHMETAFILE	32	HANDLE	Handle to a meta file
HFILE	32	int	Handle to a file
HFONT	32	HANDLE	Handle to a font
HGLOBAL	32	HANDLE	Handle to memory
HICON	32	HANDLE	Handle to an icon
HINSTANCE	32	HANDLE	Handle to an instance of a program
HKL	32	HANDLE	Handle to a keyboard layout
HLOCAL	32	HANDLE	Handle to local memory
HMENU	32	HANDLE	Handle to a menu
HMETAFILE	32	HANDLE	Handle to a meta file
HOMDULE	32	HINSTANCE	Handle to a module in memory
HPALETTE	32	HANDLE	Handle to a palette
HPEN	32	HANDLE	Handle to a pen
HRGN	32	HANDLE	Handle to a region
HRSRC	32	HANDLE	Handle to a resource
HSTR	32	HANDLE	Handle to a string resource
HTASK	32	HANDLE	Handle to a task
HWINSTA	32	HANDLE	Handle to a workstation

H

int	n/a	int	C++ type, integer
INT	32	int	Integer
LOCALHANDLE	32	HANDLE	Local handle
long	32	long	C++ type, long integer
LPARAM	32	LONG	Long parameter
LPBOOL	32	BOOL far *	Long pointer to a boolean
LPBYTE	32	BYTE far *	Long pointer to a byte
LPCOLORREF	32	DWORD	Long pointer to a color reference
LPCVOID	32	CONST void far *	Long pointer to an undefined type
LPDWORD	32	DWORD far *	Long pointer to a double word
LPHANDLE	32	HANDLE FAR *	Long pointer to a handle
LPINT	32	int far *	Long pointer to a integer
LPLONG	32	long far *	Long pointer to a long
LPVOID	32	void far *	Long pointer to a undefined type
LPWORD	32	WORD far *	Long pointer to a word
LRESULT	32	LONG	A result
NEARPROC	32	int (NEAR WINAPI *)()	A near procedure
PBOOL	32	BOOL near *	Pointer to a boolean
PBYTE	32	BYTE near *	Pointer to a byte
PDWORD	32	DWORD near *	Pointer to a double word
PFLOAT	32	FLOAT *	Pointer to a float
PINT	32	int near *	Pointer to an integer
PROC	32	int (WINAPI *)()	A procedure
PSZ	32	char *	Pointer to a zero-terminated string
PUCHAR	32	UCHAR *	Pointer to an unsigned character
PUINT	32	unsigned int *	Pointer to an unsigned integer
PULONG	32	ULONG *	Pointer to an unsigned long
PUSHORT	32	USHORT *	Pointer to an unsigned short
PWORD	32	WORD near *	Pointer to a word
SPHANDLE	32	HANDLE NEAR *	Pointer to a near handle
UCHAR	8	unsigned char	Unsigned character
UINT	32	unsigned int	Unsigned integer

continues

TABLE H.1 CONTINUED

Type	Size	Declaration	Description
ULONG	32	unsigned long	Unsigned long
USHORT	16	unsigned short	Unsigned short
WORD	16	unsigned short	Word
WPARAM	32	UINT	Word parameter

APPENDIX I

MFC Messages

Window messages inform an application when certain events occurred. These events originate from the user, the system, and other applications. Any MFC class derived from CCmdTarget can receive messages. Table I.1 lists the most common window messages, and which MFC function will handle them.

TABLE I.1   COMMON WINDOW MESSAGES

Message	MFC Function	Comment
WM_ACTIVATE	OnActivate	The Activate message is sent when a window is either activated or deactivated.
WM_ACTIVATEAPP	OnActivateApp	The Activate App message is sent when the entire application is either activated or deactivated.
WM_CAPTURECHANGED	OnCaptureChanged	The Capture Changed message is sent when the capture status of the mouse changes.
WM_CHAR	OnChar	The Char message is sent to the focus window when a keyboard event occurs.
WM_CHILDACTIVATE	OnChildActivate	The Child Activate message is sent to an MDI child window when it becomes active.
WM_CLOSE	OnClose	The Close message is sent to a window to request it to close.
WM_CONTEXTMENU	OnContextMenu	The Context Menu message is sent to a window when the user right-clicks that window.
WM_CREATE	OnCreate	The Create message is sent to a window just after the window is created.
WM_DESTROY	OnDestroy	The Destroy message is sent to a window just before the window is destroyed.
WM_DROPFILES	OnDropFiles	The Drop Files message is sent to a window when a file is dropped in the window.
WM_ENABLE	OnEnable	The Enable message is sent to enable or disable a window.
WM_ENDSESSION	OnEndSession	The End Session message is sent when the window's session is ending.
WM_ERASEBKGND	OnEraseBkgnd	The Erase Background message is sent to a window when the window's background should be redrawn.

Message	MFC Function	Comment
WM_GETMINMAXINFO	OnGetMinMaxInfo	The Get MinMax Info message is sent to a window to retrieve the minimum and maximum size of a window.
WM_HELPINFO	OnHelpInfo	The Help Info message is sent to a window when the user presses the F1 key.
WM_HSCROLL	OnHScroll	The Horizontal Scroll message is sent to a window to report activity with the window's standard horizontal scroll bar.
WM_ICONERASEBKGND	OnIconEraseBkgnd	The Icon Erase Background message is sent to a minimized window when the background of its icon should be redrawn.
WM_INITMENU	OnInitMenu	The Init Menu message is sent to a window just before a menu becomes active.
WM_INITMENUPOPUP	OnInitMenuPopup	The Init Menu Popup message is sent to a popup menu just before it becomes active.
WM_KEYDOWN	OnKeyDown	The Key Down message is sent to the focus window when the user presses down a nonsystem keyboard key.
WM_KEYUP	OnKeyUp	The Key Up message is sent to the focus window when the user releases a nonsystem key.
WM_KILLFOCUS	OnKillFocus	The Kill Focus message is sent to the focus window when it is about to lose focus.
WM_LBUTTONDBLCLK	OnLButtonDblClk	The Left Button Double Click message is sent when the user double-clicks the left mouse button in the window.
WM_LBUTTONDOWN	OnLButtonDown	The Left Button Down Click message is sent when the user presses down the left mouse button in the window.

continues

TABLE I.1 CONTINUED

Message	MFC Function	Comment
WM_LBUTTONUP	OnLButtonUp	The Left Button Up message is sent when the user releases the left mouse button in the window.
WM_MBUTTONDBLCLK	OnMButtonDblClk	The Middle Button Double Click message is sent when the user double-clicks the middle mouse button in the window.
WM_MBUTTONDOWN	OnMButtonDown	The Middle Button Down Click message is sent when the user presses down the middle mouse button in the window.
WM_MBUTTONUP	OnMButtonUp	The Middle Button Up message is sent when the user releases the middle mouse button in the window.
WM_MDIACTIVATE	OnMDIActivate	The MDI Activate message is sent to activate a new MDI child window.
WM_MENUSELECT	OnMenuSelect	The Menu Select message is sent to a window when a menu item is selected.
WM_MOUSEACTIVATE	OnMouseActivate	The Mouse Activate message is sent to an inactive window when the mouse is clicked in it.
WM_MOUSEMOVE	OnMouseMove	The Mouse Move message is sent to windows as the mouse moves over them.
WM_MOUSEWHEEL	OnMouseWheel	The Mouse Wheel message is sent as the mouse wheels move.
WM_MOVE	OnMove	The Move message is sent to a window when the window is moved.
WM_MOVING	OnMoving	The Moving message is sent to a window when the window is moving.
WM_PAINT	OnPaint	The Paint message is sent to a window when its client area should be repainted.
WM_QUERYENDSESSION	OnQueryEndSession	The Query End Session message is sent to see if an application does not object to a window's shutdown.

Message	MFC Function	Comment
WM_RBUTTONDBLCLK	OnRButtonDblClk	The Right Button Double Click message is sent when the user double-clicks the middle mouse button in the window.
WM_RBUTTONDOWN	OnRButtonDown	The Right Button Down Click message is sent when the user presses down the middle mouse button in the window.
WM_RBUTTONUP	OnRButtonUp	The Right Button Up message is sent when the user releases the middle mouse button in the window.
WM_SETCURSOR	OnSetCursor	The Set Cursor message is sent when the window should change the mouse cursor to the appropriate shape.
WM_SETFOCUS	OnSetFocus	The Set Focus message is sent when the window receives focus.
WM_SHOWWINDOW	OnShowWindow	The Show Window Message is sent when the window is shown or hidden.
WM_SIZE	OnSize	The Size message is sent when the window's size is changed.
WM_SIZING	OnSizing	The Sizing message is sent when the window is being resized.
WM_SYSCHAR	OnSysChar	The System Character message is sent when a system character is pressed.
WM_SYSKEYDOWN	OnSysKeyDown	The Sys Key Down message is sent to the focus window when the user presses down a system keyboard key.
WM_SYSKEYUP	OnSysKeyUp	The Sys Key Up message is sent to the focus window when the user releases a system key.
WM_TIMER	OnTimer	The Timer message is sent when a timer event occurs.
WM_VSCROLL	OnVScroll	The Vertical Scroll message is sent to a window to report activity with the window's standard vertical scroll bar.

APPENDIX J

What's on the CD-ROM

The *Sams Teach Yourself Visual C++ 6 in 21 Days, Professional Reference Edition* CD-ROM includes sample files that have been presented in this book, as well as a wealth of other applications and utilities.

 Note | Please refer to the readme.wri file on the CD-ROM (Windows) for the latest listing of software.

Source Code

The source code found in the book is also available on the accompanying CD-ROM.

Software

- **Data Dynamics ActiveBar and DynamiCube**

  ActiveBar is an ActiveX control that lets you effortlessly create dockable toolbars, detachable menus, tabbed toolboxes, and more.

DynamiCube is an open, interactive OLAP desktop solution, implemented as an Internet-enabled lightweight ActiveX control. DynamiCube makes it possible for you to build Internet and client/server applications that allow end users live interaction with massive databases, enabling them to explore and summarize staggering quantities of data instantaneously.

- **ESRI's MapObjects and MapObjects LT**

  MapObjects is a collection of powerful mapping and GIS components including an ActiveX control (OCX) and more than 30 ActiveX automation objects. Pan and zoom through multiple map layers. Display data using classifications, graduated symbols, and dot density. Use ESRI shapefiles, ARC/INFO coverages, and Spatial Database Engine (SDE) layers. Use a wide variety of image formats. Perform spatial analysis and query. Use relational databases and SQL queries. Perform address matching and geocoding. Track real-time events with global positioning systems (GPSs). MapObjects LT uses a simpler interface.

- **FarPoint Technologies ButtonMaker, Calendar ObjX, Daily PlanIt, Input Pro, List Pro, Spread, and Tab Pro Button Objx (previously ButtonMaker)**

  FarPoint Technologies ButtonMaker, Calendar ObjX, Daily PlanIt, Input Pro, List Pro, Spread, and Tab Pro Button Objx (previously ButtonMaker) is the most comprehensive button-like control available. Not only can you replace the Windows button control to create visually enhanced buttons, you can create fully customized active buttons and toolbars, as well as custom-shaped containers.

  Calendar ObjX provides three controls: a Calendar control that you can customize to support different calendar formats and appearances, a Clock control that lets you create customized analog and digital clocks, and a Poster control that lets you display pictures in your application.

  Daily PlanIt is a customizable daily planner. Daily PlanIt's flexibility lets you provide hourly and daily schedule planners or minute-by-minute time tracking tools.

  Input Pro is a suite of 8 data-aware formatted edit custom controls designed for database applications or use as a standalone control. The data-entry controls include Boolean, Currency, DateTime, DoubleSingle, LongInteger, Mask, Memo and Text.

  If you use a combo box or list box control, make sure you download this trial. List Pro supports two billion list items and breaks the 64KB limit using its Virtual Data Manager. It supports multicolumn, grouping of headers, merging of cells, multiline rows, searching and sorting, plus many more features.

  Spread 2.5 has become the most popular spreadsheet/data-entry grid control. It includes 250 properties, a WYSIWYG Spread Designer that allows you to set runtime properties at design-time, printing, sorting, calc.engine, twelve different cell types, plus many more features.

See why Tab Pro was recently named "Tab Control of Choice" by a national programming magazine! Tab Pro includes seven different appearance styles to customize the look of the control, 150 properties, 15 events, and 9 functions.

- **Global Majic Software ActiveX Libraries**

  Instrumentation ActiveX Library: AlphaNumeric LED, Angular Gauge, Knob, LED, Linear Gauge, Odometer, Percent, Selector, Slider, Strip Chart, and Toggle

  Aircraft ActiveX Library: Aircraft Instruments and Joystick

  Automobile Instruments ActiveX: Car

- **HexaTech's AceToolbar and XRosyGUI**

  AceToolbar is an award-winning active toolbar OCX/ActiveX control for creating a variety of active toolbars (and menus), including but not limited to, Internet Explorer toolbar, Office 97 toolbars, and other innovative toolbars.

  XRosyGUI is 16- and 32-bit OCX/ActiveX controls for developing versatile, intuitive, and great-looking GUIs.

- **ProtoView's ActiveX Component Suite and InterAct**

  ActiveX Component Suite includes

  Data Explorer v3.0—The intuitive "Windows Explorer UI" in an easy-to-program component. The Data Explorer integrates a TreeView, splitter bar, and right-hand data viewer pane into one control that fully supports visually binding and displaying OLE DB/ADO hierarchical recordsets.

  DataTable v5.0—The next generation of grid components. DataTable lets developers visually bind and display hierarchical rowsets in minutes. Child recordsets and their column headers are easily viewed in a grid format. DataTable features printing support (including inside Internet Explorer), OLE drag-and-drop, virtual memory, multiple headers, saving and loading configuration files (templates), multibyte support, and integration with WinX components for data validation (for example, use a drop-down calendar for date fields).

  TreeViewX v3.0—The advanced TreeView included with the WinX Component Library is now available as a separate product. Using its property pages, visually create tree hierarchies and bind to OLE DB/ADO recordsets. The TreeViewX also includes MDAC support, advanced searching, sorting, multiple selection, tool tips, and multiple columns.

  WinX Component Library v3.0—The WinX Component Library offers a wide range of editing and display capabilities. Its 17 ActiveX controls feature data input,

J

formatting, database binding, graphical, and three-dimensional display options. This new version focuses on the latest in Internet/intranet features to provide developers with seamless integration into browser-based applications. Included are data-bound advanced TreeView, Date Edit with drop-down calendar, Mask Edit, Currency, Numeric, and many more.

Interact is a reusable ActiveX component. Developers can easily harness all the power needed to create Visio-like applications without the unnecessary overhead of megabytes worth of support files.

- **Supernova's Visual Concepts**

  Supernova's Visual Concepts is the world's first complete platform-, data source-, and language-independent environment for the management, assembly, and deployment of component-based applications.

About the Software

Please read all documentation associated with a third-party product (usually contained with files named readme.txt or license.txt) and follow all guidelines.

INDEX

G

Other Related Titles

Sams Teach Yourself Visual C++ 6 in 24 Hours
Mickey Williams
ISBN: 0-672-31303-0
$24.99 USA/$35.95 CAN

Windows NT Win32 API SuperBible
Richard J. Simon
ISBN: 0-57169-089-1
$64.99 USA/$91.95 CAN

Building Enterprise Solutions with Visual Studio 6
G. A. Sullivan
ISBN: 0-672-31489-4
$49.99 USA/$71.95 CAN

Sams Teach Yourself Active Server Pages 2.0 in 21 Days
Sanjaya Hettihewa
ISBN: 0-672-31333-2
$34.99 USA/$49.95 CAN

Special Edition Using Visual C++ 6
Kate Gregory
ISBN: 0-7897-1539-2
$39.99 USA/$57.95 CAN

Using Visual C++ 6
Jon Bates & Timothy Tompkins
ISBN: 0-7897-1635-6
$29.99 USA/$42.95 CAN

Sams Teach Yourself Visual C++ 6 Complete Compiler Edition
Davis Chapman
ISBN: 0-672-31403-7
$49.99 USA/$71.95 CAN

Sams Teach Yourself C++ in 21 Days
Jesse Liberty
ISBN: 0-672-31070-8
$29.99 USA/$42.95 CAN

ActiveX Programming with Visual C++ 5
Jerry Anderson
ISBN: 0-7897-1030-7
$49.99 USA/$71.95 CAN

Sams Teach Yourself Database Programming with Visual C++ 6 in 21 Days
Lyn Robison
ISBN: 0-672-31350-2
$34.99 USA/$49.95 CAN

Programming Windows 98/NT Unleashed
Viktor Toth
ISBN: 0-672-31353-7
$49.99 USA/$71.95 CAN

SAMS

www.samspublishing.com

All prices are subject to change.

Microsoft Foundation Class Hierarchy - Version 6.0

(Shaded boxes are new to version 6.0)

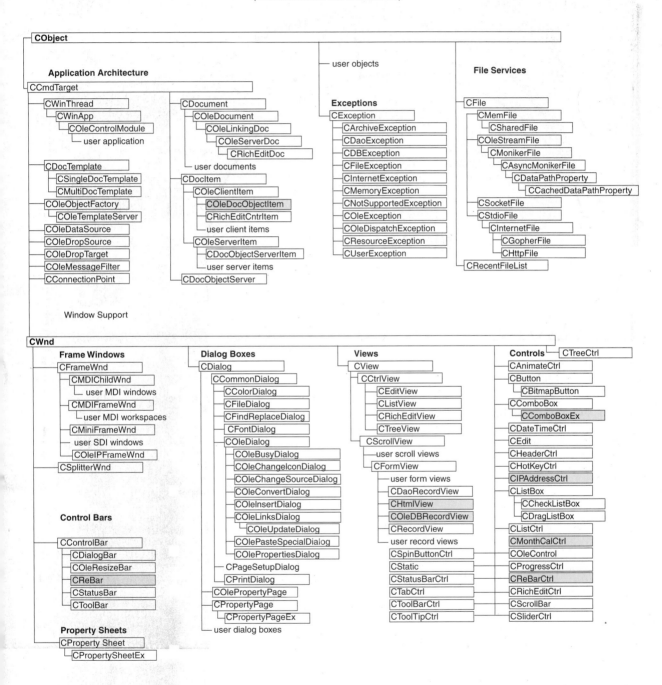

Microsoft Foundation Class Hierarchy - Version 6.0

CObject

Graphical Drawing

CDC
- CClientDC
- CMetaFileDC
- CPaintDC
- CWindowDC

Control Support

CDockState
CImageList

Graphical Drawing Objects

CGdiObject
- CBitmap
- CBrush
- CFont
- CPalette
- CPen
- CRgn

Menus

CMenu

Command Line

CCommandLineInfo

ODBC Database Support

CDatabase
CRecordset

user recordsets

CLongBinary

DAO Database Support

CDaoDatabase
CDaoQueryDef
CDaoRecordset
CDaoTableDef
CDaoWorkspace

Synchronization

CSyncObject
- CCriticalSection
- CEvent
- CMutex
- CSemaphore

Arrays

CArray(Template)
CByteArray
CDWordArray
CObArray
CPtrArray
CStringArray
CUIntArray
CWordArray

— arrays of user types

Lists

CList (Template)
CPtrList
CObList
CStringList

— lists of user types

Maps

CMap (Template)
CMapWordToPtr
CMapPtrToWord
CMapPtrToPtr
CMapWordToOb
CMapStringToPtr
CMapStringToOb
CMapStringToString

— maps of user types

Internet Services

CInternetSession
CInternetConnection
- CFtpConnection
- CGopherConnection
- CHttpConnection
CFileFind
- CFtpFileFind
- CGopherFileFind
CGopherLocator

Windows Sockets

CAsyncSocket
- CSocket

Internet Server API

CHtmlStream
CHttpFilter
CHttpFilterContext
CHttpServer
CHttpServerContext

Runtime Object Model Support

CArchive
CDumpContext
CRuntimeClass

Simple Value Types

CPoint
CRect
CSize
CString
CTime
CTimeSpan

Structures

CCreateContext
CMemoryState
COleSafeArray
CPrintInfo

Classes Not Derived from CObject

Support Classes

CCmdUI
- COleCmdUI
CDaoFieldExchange
CDataExchange
CDBVariant
CFieldExchange
COleDataObject
COleDispatchDriver
CPropExchange
CRectTracker
CWaitCursor

Typed Template Collections

CTypedPtrArray
CTypedPtrList
CTypedPtrMap

OLE Type Wrappers

CFontHolder
CPictureHolder

OLE Automation Types

COleCurrency
COleDateTime
COleDateTimeSpan
COleVariant

Synchronization

CMultiLock
CSingleLock